THE THIRD REICH

Also by Michael Burleigh

Germany Turns Eastwards:
A Study of *Ostforschung* in the Third Reich

The Racial State:
Germany 1933–1945

Death and Deliverance:
'Euthanasia' in Germany 1900–1945

Confronting the Nazi Past:
New Debates on Modern German History (ed.)

Ethics and Extermination:
Reflections on Nazi Genocide

THE THIRD REICH

A New History

MICHAEL BURLEIGH

HILL AND WANG
A DIVISION OF FARRAR, STRAUS AND GIROUX
NEW YORK

Hill and Wang
A division of Farrar, Straus and Giroux
19 Union Square West, New York 10003

Copyright © 2000 by Michael Burleigh
Distributed in Canada by Douglas & McIntyre Ltd.
Printed in the United States of America
First published in 2000 by Macmillan, Great Britain
First published in the United States by Hill and Wang
First American edition, 2000
Third printing, 2001

Library of Congress Cataloging-in-Publication Data
Burleigh, Michael, 1955–
    The Third Reich: a new history / Michael Burleigh.— 1st ed.
    p. cm.
    Includes bibliographical references and index.
    ISBN 0-8090-9325-1 (alk. paper)
    1. Germany—History—1933–1945. I. Title.
DD256.5 .B94 2000
943.086—dc21   00-031838

For A.P.; S.F.; and A.W.

wise friends

and L.M.B. with love

FAUST: The mob streams up to Satan's throne;
  I'd learn things there I've never known . . .
MEPHISTOPHELES: The whole mob streams and strives uphill:
  One thinks one's pushing and one's pushed against one's will

J. W. von Goethe, *Faust*

Men never do evil so completely and cheerfully as when they do it from religious conviction

Blaise Pascal, *Pensées*

However modern their terminology, however realistic their tactics, in their basic attitudes Communism and Nazism follow an ancient tradition – and are baffling to the rest of us because of those very features that would have seemed so familiar to a chiliastic *propheta* of the Middle Ages.

Norman Cohn, *The Pursuit of the Millennium*

CONTENTS

LIST OF ILLUSTRATIONS

Page 26. Freidrich Ebert. *(Copyright © Bilderdienst Süddeutscher Verlag)*

148. Leading policemen and SS figures in 1934. *(Copyright © AKG London)*

218. The commemoration of the Nazis 'martyred' during the 1923 putsch. *(Copyright © Bilderdienst Süddeutscher Verlag)*

280. The annexation of Austria triggered innumerable antisemitic outrages. *(Copyright © AKG London)*

344. 'The gardening state'. *(Copyright © Bildarchiv Preußischer Kulturbesitz, Berlin)*

406. The first Vichy government. *(Copyright © AKG London)*

484. The multinational invasion of the Soviet empire commenced in the searing heat of the summer of 1941. *(Copyright © AKG London)*

570. Felix Nussbaum's *Death Triumphant*. *(Copyright © Kulturgeschichtliches Museum, Osnabruck)*

664. Ulrich von Hassell. *(Copyright © Bildarchiv Preußischer Kulturbesitz, Berlin)*

730. American aircrew returning from a mission in June 1944. *(Copyright © Hulton Getty)*

ACKNOWLEDGEMENTS

Anthony Harwood and Sally Riley of Gillon Aitken Associates have been the best literary agents one could hope for, as was David Godwin at an earlier stage in the proceedings.

Georgina Morley, Elisabeth Sifton and Walter H. Pehle brought a wealth of experience, insight and knowledge to a scrappy typescript, which Peter James then ironed out in detail with courtesy and patience. That we are all still talking is an unexpected bonus.

The archivists and librarians of the United States Holocaust Museum, Washington DC, the Zentrale Stelle des Landesjustizverwaltungen, Ludwigsburg, and the Wiener Library, London, facilitated the research for this book, although it is a work of interpretation rather than an archival monograph. I would especially like to thank Aaron Kornblum, Rosemarie Neif and, earlier, Christa Laqueur, née Wichmann, for helping locate materials, a task which also befell my doughty research assistant, Joseph Whelan, one of several outstanding people it has been my good luck to teach, from whose insights I have benefited.

The time and space to embark on such a book was generously made available by Sir Brian Smith, the Vice-Chancellor of Cardiff University, while the British Academy and Wellcome Trust helped out with a small grant or two. A congenial intellectual environment to test out ideas was provided by Rutgers University's excellent Center for Historical Analysis. It is invidious to discriminate among my generous and sophisticated colleagues at Rutgers, but Omer Bartov and Matt Matsuda deserve my thanks for making such a refreshing year possible, while Jeremy, Frank, Max, Richard, Robert, Scott and Yosef kept me company on the doorstep. Agnes and Lynn provided exceptionally professional support services.

Those friends to whom I owe most of all come last. I would like to thank Amos, Desmond, Harvey, Jonathan, Adolf, John, Ian, Fritz, Niall, Steve and above all Richard (J. Overy) and Saul, for their constructive criticism of all or parts of the manuscript, or for supporting the author less directly, a debt which I would like to repay by dedicating the book to three of them. Thanking my wife seems superfluous, but she gets a separate dedication anyway.

Michael Burleigh
Lexington, Virginia
September 2000

MAPS

PRE-WAR GERMAN TERRITORIES

300 miles
500 kilometres

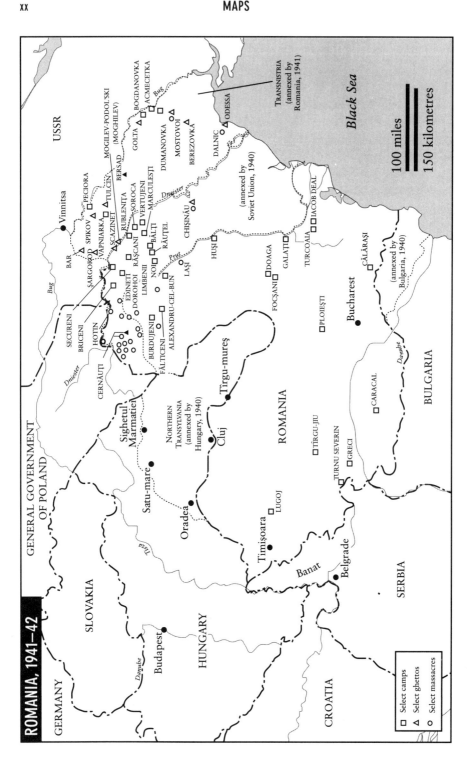

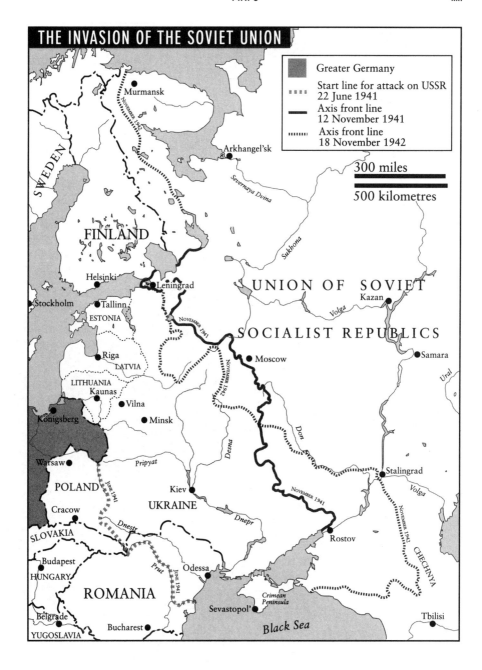

THE INVASION OF THE SOVIET UNION

GERMAN-OCCUPIED EUROPE, NOVEMBER 1942

300 miles

500 kilometres

NORWAY

SWEDEN

Oslo

Stockholm

Göteborg

REICH

DENMARK

Copenhagen

LITHUANIA

Königsberg

IRELAND

Dublin

UNITED
KINGDOM

Hamburg

Berlin

Warsaw

London

NETHERLANDS

The Hague

BELGIUM

Brussels

GERMANY

Frankfurt

Dresden

Prague

Atlantic
Ocean

Paris

Loire

Rennes

FRANCE

Danube

Munich

Vienna

Bratislava

SLOVAKIA

Bern

SWITZ.

AUSTRIA

Budapest

HUNGARY

Vichy

Bilbao

VICHY
FRANCE

Rhône

Po

Zagreb

Belgrade

Duero

PORTUGAL

Tajo

Madrid

YUGOSLAVIA

Sarajevo

Lisbon

Barcelona

Corsica

ITALY

Rome

SPAIN

Tirane

Naples

ALBANIA

Sevilla

Balearic Is.

Sardinia

Gibraltar

Mediterranean Sea

Palermo

Sicily

Rabat

Casablanca

Algiers

Tunis

MALTA

MOROCCO

ALGERIA

TUNISIA

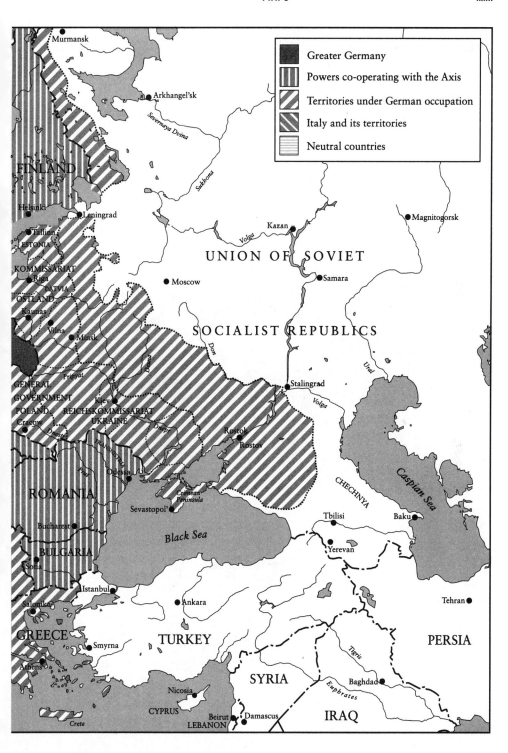

POST-WAR GERMAN TERRITORIES

300 miles

500 kilometres

INTRODUCTION – 'AN EXTRAORDINARY RAPE OF THE SOUL':
NATIONAL SOCIALISM, POLITICAL RELIGIONS AND TOTALITARIANISM

This book is about what happened when sections of the German elites and masses of ordinary people chose to abdicate their individual critical faculties in favour of a politics based on faith, hope, hatred and sentimental collective self-regard for their own race and nation. It is therefore a very twentieth-century story.[1]

The book deals with the progressive, and almost total, moral collapse of an advanced industrial society at the heart of Europe, many of whose citizens abandoned the burden of thinking for themselves, in favour of what George Orwell described as the tom-tom beat of a latterday tribalism. They put their faith in evil men promising a great leap into a heroic future, with violent solutions to Germany's local, and modern society's general, problems. The consequences, for Germany, Europe and the wider world, were catastrophic, but no more so than for European Jews, who were subjected to a deliberate campaign to excise and expunge each and every one of them, which we rightly recognise as a uniquely terrible event in modern history.

In a local sense, Germany suffered its second massive and total defeat in the twentieth century. This was the price of mass stupidity and overweening ambition, paid with the lives of its citizens, whether directly compromised by dreadful crimes, or characterised by moral indifference or innocence. In a wider sense, other peoples were subjected to the compromises, indignities and terrors of occupation, forced and slave labour, or mass murder in the case of Europe's Jews, while for over four years the human, cultural and productive resources of the Allied nations were skewed into repulsing and destroying a regime antipathetical to the civilised, free, humane and tolerant values that we cherish. A dystopian 'quick fix' to Germany's manifold problems ultimately resulted in the deaths of some fifty million people in a conflict whose legacy Europe has fully recovered from only after half a century, for the process of healing and reconciliation has been a long one. That the Second World War also briefly lent fresh, but spurious, moral and political legitimacy to a no less ruthless and sanguinary Soviet tyranny is one of the multiple ironies of this story. For what we in the West (and many Russians) regard as a straightforward contest of good and evil seems less categorical from the perspective of, say, the Balts, Chechens, Crimean Tatars, Croats, Poles or Ukrainians, for whom 1944–5 did not bring deliverance from tyranny, but rather several decades of imperialist oppression from which at least one of these nations is still struggling to liberate itself after the turn of the millennium.[2] In this sense, this book is about the wider international context of Nazi Germany (and its ideological confederates), something otherwise European-minded German scholars, and many of those who traipse in their footsteps, have neglected in their understandable preoccupation with their own local legacy. There is no respectable reason why the intellectual agendas of histories of this period should be exclusively fabricated in Germany, however much scholars there have contributed to knowledge and understanding of this dismal period of their contemporary history, which, in a profound sense, is not their 'own' story.

Although this book has some thoughts about the ultimate horrors which Hitler and his subordinates were responsible for, it is not solely focused on mass killing, about which there is perhaps less mystery than is sometimes suggested, quite apart from the ways in which such a preoccupation is itself indicative of a decadent appetite for the lurid, which regrettably is part of contemporary interest in this subject. The author claims no special insights into the motives for individual participation in murder and mayhem, beyond those that have characterised such conduct since the beginnings of human history, and to which classical literature, the Bible, Shakespeare or Dostoevsky are as serviceable guides as the works of any contemporary historian. In this sense, this book divests itself of any over-large claims before it has even started.[3]

Rather, *The Third Reich: A New History* is an account of the longer-term, and more subtle, moral breakdown and transformation of an advanced industrial society, whose consequences astute observers, with an instinct for these things, could predict someways before they happened. But encouraged by irresponsible and self-interested sections of the elite, whom the philosopher of history Eric Voegelin once memorably described as 'an evil rabble', the mass propelled itself against charity, reason and scepticism, investing its faith in the otherwise farcical figure of Hitler, whose own miserable existence gained meaning as he discovered that his rage against the world was capable of indefinite generalisation. Ground down by defeat and endemic crisis, many Germans looked at his carefully selected range of poses, and saw their own desired self-image reflected. As Konrad Heiden, Hitler's first and greatest biographer, wrote in 1944: 'The people dream and a soothsayer tells them what they are dreaming.'[4] I say 'many Germans' because there were others, such as Heiden or Voegelin, whose instincts, humanity or intelligence prohibited such a suspension of disbelief, or whose core political or religious values checked their descent into moral neo-barbarism. These two men ended their days in exile, in respectively Maryland and Louisiana, but they symbolise countless others, who washed up in Brooklyn, Florida or, for that matter, Turkey. The demonstrable existence of such people makes the irresponsible stupidity of those who placed their faith in Hitler all the more remarkable, even as it surely militates against an indiscriminate condemnation of the German people in general.

Although this book is subtitled *A New History*, its general approach has a lengthy intellectual pedigree, for this is emphatically not the first time that Nazism has been studied as a form either of political religion or of totalitarianism, though it is only since the early 1990s that these approaches have once again become fashionable. Its guiding ideas are more indebted to a number of philosophers, political scientists and historians of culture and ideas than to the general run of historians of this subject. In that sense, this book reasserts an important intellectual tradition, which sought to identify the essence of the Nazi phenomenon beneath the surface scratchings about whether Hitler slept with his niece, loved his dog or had plans for the Duke and Duchess of Windsor, relatively trivial matters which Heiden or Voegelin would have regarded with Olympian indifference. For, however unfashionable it may be, there are serious intellectual issues almost buried beneath the avalanche of morbid kitsch and populistic trivia which this subject generates, and from which no end or relief is in sight even sixty years later, a theme which in itself causes increasing unease among sophisticated contemporary observers. But let's turn now from these musings about our own time and culture to the ideas which have guided this book's content, core concerns and structure.

Classical antiquity shaped most of our political vocabulary, leaving us such terms as democracy, despotism, dictatorship and tyranny.

Occasionally, these words seemed insufficient to describe certain challenging developments, prompting commentators to seek new terms,
sometimes in vain. Alexis de Tocqueville expressed this problem when
he wrestled to describe North American democracy:

> I think, then, that the species of oppression by which democratic
> nations are menaced is unlike anything that ever before existed in the
> world; our contemporaries will find no prototype of it in their memor-
> ies. I seek in vain for an expression that will accurately convey the
> whole of the idea I have formed of it; the old words despotism and
> tyranny are inappropriate: the thing itself is new, and since I cannot
> name it, I must attempt to define it.[5]

The advent of Bolshevik, Fascist and National Socialist regimes in
Russia and Europe successively between 1917 and 1933 led some
contemporary intellectuals to wonder whether their own terminology
adequately conveyed the scope of these regimes' pretensions or the
horrors they were responsible for. Of course, many intellectuals did
not view them as horrors at all, but rather as the collateral costs of
supposedly bright futures.[6] In the summer of 1920, the British philosopher Bertrand Russell travelled in the Soviet Union on the coat-tails
of a visiting Labour Party delegation. After a visit of about a month
Russell wrote:

> I cannot share the hopes of the Bolsheviks any more than those of the
> Egyptian anchorites; I regard both as tragic delusions, destined to bring
> upon the world centuries of darkness and futile violence. . . . The
> principles of the Sermon on the Mount are admirable, but their effect
> upon average human nature was very different from what was
> intended. Those who followed Christ did not learn to love their
> enemies or to turn the other cheek. . . . The hopes which inspire
> Communism are, in the main, as admirable as those instilled by the
> Sermon on the Mount, but they are held as fanatically, and are likely
> to do as much harm. Cruelty lurks in our instincts, and fanaticism is a
> camouflage for cruelty. Fanatics are seldom genuinely humane, and
> those who sincerely dread cruelty will be slow to adopt a fanatical
> creed. . . . The war has left throughout Europe a mood of disillusion-
> ment and despair which calls aloud for a new religion, as the only
> force capable of giving men the energy to live vigorously. Bolshevism
> has supplied the new religion.[7]

Just over a decade later similar thoughts would occur to people
living in National Socialist Germany. For example, on 14 July 1934,

Victor Klemperer, the Dresden philologist whose diary has recently become famous, discussed with his wife Eva a speech by Hitler booming from an outdoor loudspeaker. Klemperer noted: 'The voice of a fanatical preacher. Eva says: Jan van Leyden. I say: Rienzi,' as he opted for one of Wagner's earliest operatic heroes.[8]

Eva Klemperer was not alone in drawing comparisons between Hitler and Anabaptist sectarians of the sixteenth century. The same comparison occurred to another diarist, Friedrich Reck-Malleczewen, a misanthropic aristocrat later to die in Dachau, who in 1937 penned a portrait of Hitler only thinly disguised as the Anabaptist leader Jan Böckelson, responsible for a reign of terror in sixteenth-century Münster. The book was subtitled *History of a Mass Lunacy*.[9] These contemporary voices, and many more besides, will recur throughout this book, for sometimes their insights and sensibility are of a higher order than those of historians and other contemporary commentators whose investment is often in some methodological dogma or theory rather than in the spirit of those times. The analogy with religion also struck those with a more serenely secular view of the world than the dyspeptic Reck-Malleczewen. In April 1937, an anonymous writer produced a remarkable report for the exiled Social Democratic Party leadership in Prague on the 'struggle' between the Nazis and the Christian Churches. Following earlier writers on both Italian Fascism and National Socialism, the reporter explicitly compared Nazism to a secularised religion. He called the result a 'church-state' or a state 'counter-church', with its own intolerant dogma, preachers, sacred rites and lofty idioms that offered total explanations of the past, present and future, while demanding unwavering dedication from its adherents. Acquiescence was not enough; such regimes demanded constant affirmation and enthusiasm from their own populations.[10] Some of these insights will be explored both in this Introduction and throughout this book, but there was something else which this reporter drew attention to which will concern us as we follow the story of Nazi Germany from the First World War to the beginnings of post-war West German democratic reconstruction.

The reporter coined an exceptionally striking metaphor for the moral transformations Nazism was effecting, a concern almost absent from modern historical writing, with its social science notions of freedom from value judgements, as if morality is related to moralising, rather than intrinsic to the human condition and philosophical reflection about it. This reporter compared the process of Nazism's attempted moral transformation of German society to rebuilding a railway bridge. Engineers could not simply demolish an existing structure, because of the impact on rail traffic. Instead, they slowly renewed each bolt, girder and rail, work which hardly caused passengers to glance up from their newspapers. However, one day, they would realise that the old bridge had gone and a gleaming new structure stood in its stead.[11] Nothing so coherent as Nazi 'ethics' ever emerged, to rival say Judaeo-Christian or utilitarian ethics, and by definition extreme racism lacked universal applicability. But the intimations were nonetheless highly disturbing. Unlike the Soviet experiment in engineering souls, the Nazis went a stage further in seeking to engineer bodies as well as minds, although the inhuman characteristics both regimes sought to inculcate, especially in the young, were often hard to distinguish. This assault on decency will figure large in this book.[12]

Viewing political movements as pseudo- or substitute religions, with eclectic liturgies, ersatz theologies, vices and virtues, has a history that is worth recounting. Much earlier, Tocqueville, with whom we began, explicitly compared the French Revolution to 'a religious revival', calling it 'a species of religion', which 'like Islam [has] overrun the whole world with its apostles, militants, and martyrs'. For opposed reasons, Robespierre agreed. When seeking to insulate the Revolution from both sceptics and the mortality of its own apostles, he wrote: 'What silences or replaces this pernicious instinct [of scepticism], and what makes good the insufficiency of human authority, is the religious instinct which imprints upon our souls the idea of a sanction given to the moral precepts by a power that is higher than man.'[13] This was not a cynical ploy to mobilise emotions and enthusiasms that politics could not reach, still less the usurpation of sacred language and rites to heighten feeling.[14] For these devices and tricks would be unremarkable, given that preachiness and sententiousness are common to some advanced democracies as well as dictatorships. Rather, it reflected the belief that Providence had sanctified a specific social order through which alone happiness would reign on earth. Anyone who opposed this belief was not only in error, but part of a demonic conspiracy, a conviction whose own origins go back to the earliest conflicts within, and between, Judaism and Christianity, when Satan himself was transformed from an angel who tested mankind by throwing obstacles in their path into the embodiment of evil, lurking behind any manifestation of religious heterodoxy. Opponents were not simply misguided, and hence amenable to persuasion, but fit only for extinction, regardless of whether they had done anything other than to exist.[15]

To the chagrin of those messianic nationalists, from Naples to Poland, whose vision of the modern nation was one of daily quasi-religious affirmation, the external forms of religion were adopted by empires and states whose democratic credentials were either non-existent or dubious. Civic religions, focused on the nation and state, or certain values, were commonplace throughout nineteenth-century Europe and North America, which often saw itself as a latterday Israel. Their bombastic physical presence punctuates the centres of many European cities, as anyone who has clambered up the vast wedding-cake-like monument to King Vittorio Emanuele II in central Rome will acknowledge. At the time, there were also days of national self-celebration, such as Unification Day in Italy or Sedan Day in Germany. By their very nature, these monuments and fixtures in the annual calendar seemed empty and soulless to the advocates of a more messianic nationalism, who wanted their people to be in a permanent state of emotional fervour. They also thought the modern nation states were flawed, in terms either of whom they included or excluded or of whose interest they represented. The largest excluded group, labour, or at least that part of it which was organised in unions and political parties, itself developed alternative cults and rituals, even when the ideology they espoused was militantly anti-religious. Those who were on the margins of official civic religions dominated by the great and good, but who were also antagonistic towards organised labour, often constituted fascism's and Nazism's social potential.

This book begins with the First World War, the seminal catastrophe for most of the horrors in the twentieth century. It created the emotional effervescence which Emil Durkheim regarded as integral to religious experience. The Great War and its disturbed aftermath led to an intensified revival of this pseudo-religious strain in politics, which exerted its maximum appeal in times of extreme crisis, just as medieval millenarianism, or the belief that the thousand-year interval before the Day of Judgement was at hand, had thrived in times of sudden change and social dislocation.[16] Grief-stricken relatives of the dead sought consolation in the often poignant monuments, erected in every town or village, which depicted stoical heroism in bronze or stone. The seriously unconsoled sought answers in the spirit world, with ghostly images of marching soldiers 'caught' on film by photographic hucksters. These

illusions and temptations had their political analogues. The abyss of
the Great War dragged down the liberal civilisation which appeared to
have caused it, leading some to take flight from the chaos and horror
of war in the universal creed of Communism, which resumed where
the unfulfilled promise of 1789 had broken off. Although the European
far right antedated the First World War, the combination of war,
chaos and revolution lent it a renewed lease of life, amid mass death,
as did a new generation of demagogic messiahs, brutal, manipulative,
self-aware and determined to avoid the mistakes of their exemplars
and progenitors.

These false messiahs' initial disciples were little more than marginal
sects of desperadoes cum believers, but under the impact of ontological
crises (that is, crises which struck at people's very sense of being), they
rapidly burgeoned into masses of people, who were moved by an
intensity of emotional engagement not seen since the French Revolution or periodic upsurges of national fervour during war or crisis.
Italian Fascists and German National Socialists, and many of their
lesser imitators across Europe, espoused the politics of faith, and
placed their idols, the lictorial symbols and the swastika, on nationalistic altars that were already part built, and appropriated much of the
language of patriotism for their own strange purposes. There was
enough familiar here to attract traditionalists, and enough also for
those seeking the frisson of the radically different. And enough too
for those for whom violence had become a way of life, an object of
nostalgia or a pseudo-philosophy with purgative properties.

The mournful cemetery culture of the war dead was transformed
into cults of the militant undead, in which victims of the Great War
were seamlessly elided with the casualties of the extreme right's own
terroristic rampages, who then marched together into eternal glory in
plangent ceremonies. A warm bathetic glow left glaring contradictions
unremarked and unexplored. Mournfulness was replaced by adolescent
morbidity. A dreadful mass sentimentality, compounded of anger, fear,
resentment and self-pity, replaced the customary politics of decency,
pragmatism, property and reason, as well as the idea that national
destiny should be determined by the sovereign judgement of separate
individuals. Belief, faith, feeling and obedience to instinct routed
debate, scepticism and compromise. People voluntarily surrendered to
group or herd emotions, some of a notoriously nasty kind. Among
committed believers, a mythic world of eternal spring, heroes, demons,
fire and sword – in a word, the fantasy world of the nursery – displaced

reality. Or rather invaded it, with crude images of Jews, Slavs, capitalists and kulaks populating the imagination. This was children's politics for grown-ups, bored and frustrated with the prosaic tenor of post-war liberal democracy, and hence receptive to heroic gestures and politics as a form of theatrical stunt, even at the expense of their personal freedom. In a more restricted sense, this form of politics was very modern, with its potent emphasis on images and ethnic sentimentality – indeed 'post-modern', in that Europe's demagogues were archly aware of the manipulative techniques they needed to generate mass faith, knowing about the impact of masses, flags, song, symbols and colours. These men were artist-politicians.[17]

The advent of the Italian Fascist and Nazi regimes in 1922 and 1933 marked the beginnings of serious reflections on these political religions, as distinct from anecdotal intuitions of their existence. The thinkers concerned were often those most dissatisfied with materialist explanations of political phenomena, or who treated ideas seriously, rather than as something secondary to 'facts' or to allegedly 'deeper' socio-economic structures, which on closer scrutiny explained rather little. As Russell wrote, 'To understand Bolshevism it is not sufficient to know facts; it is necessary also to enter with sympathy or imagination into a new spirit.'

The leading twentieth-century exponents of viewing political movements as religions were the German Catholic intellectuals Waldemar Gurian (1902–54) and Eric Voegelin (1901–85), who fled Nazi Germany successively in 1937 and 1938 to teach at respectively Notre Dame and the State University of Louisiana; the great French liberal conservative thinker Raymond Aron (1905–83); and Jacob Talmon (1916–80), a Polish Jew working in England and Israel who produced a major, but flawed, trilogy on these problems.[18] Voegelin and Aron are both the subjects of enormous contemporary interest in France, Germany and America; outside Israel Talmon is known to academics of a certain age, while Gurian is largely forgotten, despite his rather fine books on Bolshevism.

Some of these thinkers, who severally were more or less resistant to being categorised in a Zhadanovite way as 'conservatives', had direct experience of the realities of totalitarianism. In Voegelin's case, two books which he published in 1937, *The Race Idea in Intellectual History* and *Race and the State*, were soon rendered 'unavailable', for they not only highlighted the scientific inadequacies of Nazi racial theories, but also bracketed together Nazism with liberalism and

Marxism, as symptoms of a broader spiritual malaise. His next book, *The Political Religions* (1938), which depicted Nazism as a latterday immanentist heresy, that is, one which promised salvation in the here and now, was confiscated by the Gestapo as it came off the printing presses. The Gestapo began to harass Voegelin and his wife in their own home, confiscating *The Communist Manifesto* and other proscribed texts from his library, but declining his suggestion that they remove Hitler's *Mein Kampf* too, if only, as he ironically put it, to reflect the catholicity of his intellectual interests. When the Gestapo next tried to confiscate Voegelin's passport, and placed a guard outside his house, Voegelin decided to flee to Switzerland and on to the United States.[19] These men were not arguing that fascism, National Socialism or Communism were the exact counterparts of a religion, for each lacked the depth of Buddhism, Christianity, Islam or Judaism, and was not primarily focused on the transcendent. A puddle contains water, but it is not an ocean. Voegelin regarded all these political movements as by-products of an absence of religion in a world he regarded as decadent, where ideologies akin to Christian heresies of redemption in the here and now had fused with post-Enlightenment doctrines of social transformation. Neither Hitler nor Mussolini dispensed entirely with God as a source of ultimate validation for his political mission. However, political religions were emphatically 'this-worldly', partly to distinguish them from a supposedly obsolescent Christianity, whose values they sought to replace, whatever their tactical accommodations with the Churches. Nor did they function like religions, unless one equates the enthusiasm they encouraged with 'worshipping' a football team. Rather, they caricatured fundamental patterns of religious belief, in modern societies where sacralised collectivities, such as class, nation or race, had already partly supplanted God as objects of mass enthusiasm or veneration. The united nation, purged of all racial or political contaminants, and bereft of any external moral reference points, became a congregation of the faithful, with new 'leaders', who spoke with an emotional power best described by one willing Italian participant as 'an extraordinary rape of the soul'.[20]

This way of thinking about fascism and National Socialism has never fallen into disuse. On the contrary, it shows signs of growing stronger. During the 1960s and 1970s it informed important studies by Norman Cohn, George Mosse, James Billington, James Rhodes, Hans-Joachim Gamm, Uriel Tal and Klaus Vondung, while the general nature of the 'politics of faith' concerned the philosopher Michael

Oakeshott.[21] Both Tal, who died while relatively young, and Mosse, who lived to a ripe old age, produced work that has had a major impact on this book. Interest in political religions is currently undergoing a renaissance in several countries, with powerful contributions from historians as diverse as Saul Friedländer, Philippe Burrin, Emilio Gentile, Michael Ley, Claus-Ekkehard Bärsch, Hans Maier, Julius Schoeps and Jean-Pierre Sironneau.[22] In a general way, political religions also interest anthropologists, although as often as not their global perspective flattens meaningful comparisons. Unfortunately, the study of political irrationalism has itself become severely rationalist, or beguiled by the most rational-sounding explanations for matters which may have far deeper antecedents.[23]

Like most large historical literatures, that on political religions has sub-contracted its labours. One line of inquiry has been to ask how various regimes utilised sacred language and rites, even when they aggressively rejected religion, until as in the Soviet Union under Stalin its despised virtues became temporarily expedient to their war effort. This is the level at which this way of regarding Nazism is easiest to grasp, namely its pseudo-liturgical rites or deliberate evocations of the Bible for rhetorical purposes. A more recent interest has been in the effects of political religions upon ethics, although the results of abandoning values which have served humanity well for a couple of thousand years were uniformly disastrous, in so far as those who could not be remade anew, because of some ineradicable class or racial taint, were cast out and murdered. Here historians dispense with conventional historical chronologies, for moral climates have fuzzy boundaries, even though anyone who has lived through the 1960s or 1980s will no more dispute their reality than their forefathers did in 1914–18 or the 1930s.[24] Scholars also have a growing interest in the choices made by individuals of the time, with compelling new biographies of Heidegger, Heisenberg or Speer, among the major figures.[25] There has also been much interest in the effects of faith in eugenics on medical ethics under Nazism, in the conversion of ordinary men into demi-human predators on the Eastern Front, and in the exploitation of charity, the work ethic and the quest for social justice, variously to distract, galvanise and reward the German population. Partly because of a tradition of Catholic moral theology, especially in Poland, studies of the daily corruptions of life under Communist regimes are in advance of anything written about Nazi Germany, with the exception of a highly sophisticated literature on opposition and resistance.[26] But in a wider sense it can also be argued that totalitarian ideologies themselves shadowed the belief patterns of conventional religions, in that once power had been invested in elite groups, based on either alleged natural superiority or the claim that they alone represented the true interests of the toiling masses, salvation would not be long in coming.

Nazi ideology offered redemption from a national ontological crisis, to which it was attracted like a predatory shark to blood. The opening chapter of this book tries to convey something of this climate of despair and hopelessness, and to show why the National Socialist movement, rather than more traditional political parties, tempted such significant numbers of people. Nazism offered intense inclusivity in a society that had been scarred by deep divisions, dynamism where there was stagnation, and a sense of lofty purpose, almost a national mission, in a society where material interests seemed all-pervasive. Moreover, what Hannah Arendt called totalitarianism's ideological 'sixth sense' offered a simple diagnosis of what was *really* afoot beneath the surface, which appealed to a widespread desire to believe that hidden forces were responsible for Germany's post-war tribulations. All people had to do was to make the quantum leap of faith; unified national self-belief was the solution to every mundane problem. As both Mussolini and Hitler remarked, faith could indeed move mountains or make mountains seem to move.[27]

But Nazism was distinct from other political creeds which regarded present sacrifices as the price worth paying for deferred bliss, or which claimed that all virtue resided in one group of people, whose enemies were vessels of demonic iniquity. It lacked Communism's deferred, but dialectically assured, 'happy ending', and was haunted by and suffused with apocalyptic imaginings and beliefs which were self-consciously pagan and primitive.[28] Although it paradoxically claimed to speak the language of applied reason, and was capable of sophisticated calculation, Nazism had one foot in the dark irrationalist world of Teutonic myth, where heroic doom was regarded positively, and where the stakes were all or nothing – national and racial redemption or perdition.

At first sight, the claim that Nazi ideology had religious content seems to be contradicted by the evidence. In September 1938 Hitler censured Heinrich Himmler and Alfred Rosenberg, respectively the SS chief and the Party's would-be ideological supremo, for trying to construe Nazism as a religious cult. He reminded them:

National Socialism is a cool and highly reasoned approach to reality based on the greatest of scientific knowledge and its spiritual expression. . . . The National Socialist movement is not a cult movement; rather, it is a *völkisch* and political philosophy which grew out of considerations of an exclusively racist nature. This philosophy does not advocate mystic cults, but rather aims to cultivate and lead a nation determined by its blood.[29]

Hitler was concerned that a full-blown religion might function independently of him, the sole source of all doctrinal authority, and that it might provoke the Christian churches to abandon support for a regime which, incredibly enough, they often believed was restoring authority and morality after the drift of the Weimar Republic. In fact, Nazism's long-term triumph would have spelled the end of everything they stood for. But Hitler was also acknowledging that Nazism was not simply applied biology, but the expression of eternal scientific laws, revealed by God and in turn invested with sacred properties. Science and nature were re-enchanted. Clarity was compatible with mystery, religion with science, and adolescent morbidity with vitalism.[30] Nazi racism was not just an aberrant product of pseudo-science, let alone something which should indict 'science' in general, for we would surely be much the poorer without it. There were advantages in giving racism a scientific gloss, whether to latch on to the allegedly ascendant intellectual force of the day, or to justify radical, rather than piecemeal, solutions to racial 'problems'. As has often been remarked, resort to the language of parasitology entailed an implacable logic and radicality, while hygienic zeal was evident among those who, in 'iron times', took it upon themselves to use 'iron brooms' to purify the world of racial contagions. This was politics as a biological mission, but conceived in a religious way.

But just as Hitler eschewed the far from cosy antisemitic folk prejudices of peasants, so as a self-proclaimed 'artist' he needed something more vaulting than the abstruse ideas of musty academics. According to the historian Saul Friedländer, whose insights here are unrivalled, Hitler assimilated biological notions of degeneration and purification to religious narratives of perdition and redemption. In the Wagnerian Bayreuth circle he found a suitably arty and elite coterie to deliver this specific mixture, namely an Aryan–Germanic mission to redeem Graeco-Roman civilisation, to affirm a non-Jewish or de-orientalised Christianity and to lead the peoples into a 'new, splendid and light-filled future', which only the Jews issuing from darkness could thwart. A mutant, racialised Christianity, divested of unGerman 'Jewish' elements, and purged of humanitarian sentimentality, that is sin, guilt and pity, was a very potent ideal indeed. In this sense, Nazism was neither simply science run riot, however much this definition suits critics of modern genetics, nor bastardised Christianity, however much this suits those who see Nazism simply as the outgrowth of Christian antisemitism. It was a creative synthesis of both. Armed with his religious science, Hitler was not only a latterday Robert Koch or Louis Pasteur, zealously battling lethal pathogens who happened to be fellow human beings, but God's partner in ordering and perfecting that part of mankind which concerned him. While one can point to the moment when Nazism became hubristic – the December 1941 decision to take on America as well as Soviet Russia still seems the most plausible choice – it is important to understand that, in this profounder sense, Hitler's politics were hubristic all along.[31]

Another powerful tradition in writing about these phenomena has been to analyse them in terms of totalitarianism. To many commentators and scholars, this still seems the best way of describing Nazism's horrid aspiration to determine both social being and ultimate meanings through ideology, propaganda and terror. This is a view I share. While the 'ism' part of the word is unappealing, the 'total' part captures most strikingly the insatiable, invasive character of this form of politics, which regarded the individual, freedom, autonomous civil society and the rule of law with uncomprehending hatred. Unlike conventional dictatorships, which took a single step from democracy, by for example banning trade unions, totalitarian regimes took two steps, in so far as they created pseudo-unions, against which workers would have to fight, before they could contemplate asserting their rights against their employer, which in the Soviet case was impossible, since the employer was supposed to be the sum total of themselves.[32] Though over the last three decades attempts have been made to banish the term 'totalitarianism' from polite academic society, it is still a useful concept, for anyone who does not baulk at mentioning National Socialism in the same breath as Soviet Communism, and for anyone interested in the fundamental psychology rather than the surface of things.

A brief history of the concept goes something like this. It first gained currency in Italian Fascist and right-wing German intellectual circles whose members advocated a new, highly focused and permanently mobilised state, which would counteract all the allegedly divisive and weak attributes of modern 'societies' that threatened to engulf it. The term was much more popular in Fascist Italy than in Nazi Germany, where there was greater emphasis on both race and a dynamic 'movement' than upon the state. The advent of regimes appearing to reflect such principles in turn concerned commentators in the democracies. *The Times* of London used the term 'totalitarianism' in 1929 to describe a growing rejection of liberal democracy; the first symposium on the subject was held in the United States exactly ten years later, shortly after the Molotov–Ribbentrop Pact seemed to confirm the amoral affinities of Nazi Germany and the Soviet Union, and the West was forced to ally itself with a power which Churchill mentioned in the same breath as the Devil. George Orwell captured this cynicism perfectly in *Nineteen Eighty-Four* when the Outer Party propagandists simply switch without missing a beat from Oceania's war against Eurasia to the war against Eastasia which the Inner Party had decreed, ensuring that the former war was erased from memory. In the totalitarian press across Europe, there was a similarly effortless switching of the points, as the trains of ideology trundled forward in a new direction.[33]

What a minority regard as the most dubious features of theories of totalitarianism – their apparent exculpation of authoritarian or merely dictatorial governments – originally derived from left-wing thinkers. Leon Trotsky, the founder of the Red Army, was one of the first to distinguish between limited absolutist regimes and modern totalitarianism, when he contrasted Louis XIV's comparatively modest dictum 'L'état, c'est moi' with Stalin's limitless 'I am society'.[34] For totalitarianism did not confine itself to the usual realms allotted to the state, but sought to control the family and private morality, and to direct the arts and sciences in ways which exceeded the mere exertion of influence. Had Trotsky cared about law, he might have added that totalitarian regimes abandoned bureaucratic predictability and the rule of law as 'bourgeois' impediments, preferring the convenience of arbitrary government.

Although the impression is sometimes given that the term 'totalitarian' is exclusive to people often stereotyped as 'Cold War warriors', keen to damn Soviet Communism by association with Nazism, in fact mainstream democratic socialists, not to speak of Trotskyite sectarians, had an honourable record in exposing the nightmare that was the Soviet Union, and frequently used the term 'totalitarian' to do so. After all, many of these people had first-hand experience of dealing with Stalinists in their local political contexts. As the British post-war

Labour Foreign Secretary Ernest Bevin remarked after his first meeting with Molotov, 'But they are just like the bloody Communists!' whom he had already encountered in local British politics.

Possibly the most compelling vision of a developed totalitarian society was George Orwell's great minatory novel *Nineteen Eighty-Four*. There were important prototypes, such as Yevgeny Zamyatin's futuristic novel *We* and Arthur Koestler's *Darkness at Noon*, but Orwell's book excelled them both. The achievement was all the more remarkable given that Orwell's experience of the subject was confined to Spanish Communists in Civil War Catalonia and what he had observed in British left-wing circles, whose 'doublethink' towards the Soviet Motherland was notorious. He began what he originally entitled *The Last Man in Europe* during the final years of the Second World War. The distilled characteristics of Nazism and Stalinism were blended with Orwell's experiences of British bureaucracies such as that of the BBC; the zones Eastasia, Eurasia and Oceania invented in the novel, with London the capital of Oceania's Airstrip One, echoed the division of the spoils of war agreed at the 1943 Teheran Conference. Zamyatin's 'The Benefactor' is transformed into 'Big Brother', whose omnipresent features owe much to Stalin, while a Rumpelstiltskin figure preaching hate with an outstretched fist is derived from the Nazi propagandist Joseph Goebbels.[35] Of course this does not exhaust the hundreds of sources which Orwell drew upon, including his own instincts, expressed in the novel in a phrase about 'horses being able to smell bad hay'. Orwell's book was especially effective because it was composed in an English language deliberately pared down to suit its subject; as under real existing totalitarianism, the place described by Orwell resembles a photograph drained of local colour, both somewhere and everywhere, although it is unmistakably a portrait of Stalin's Russia, where delation and repression combined with food that tasted of nothing, blunt razor-blades, oily gin and weak beer, lies and real chronic shortages amid theoretical statistical abundance.

Designed as a warning to middle-class intellectuals who flirted with totalitarianism, as epitomised by the story's amoral interrogator O'Brien, for whom power has become a religion, the book was also a defence of the almost vanished decencies of middle-class life – of a world of books, objets d'art and fine wines – even though on the novel's surface the socialist Orwell had faith in the unreconstructed proletariat. The destruction of this world of decency is symbolised by the smashing of a glass paperweight in which a delicate strand of coral is suspended. O'Brien explains the essence of the new philosophy: 'Always, at every moment, there will be the thrill of victory, the sensation of trampling on an enemy who is helpless. If you want a picture of the future, imagine a boot stamping on a human face – for ever.' Both Communism, the systemisation of bourgeois guilt or self-loathing and working-class resentment cloaked in universal benignity, and fascism or Nazism, the solipsistic, quasi-tribal veneration of one race or nation, shared this antipathy towards the world of civility, decency, prudence, law and order, and explicitly glorified violence.[36]

In the late 1940s, the political philosopher Hannah Arendt (1906–75) turned to these themes, although her inspissated tome hardly compares with Orwell's clarity of mind and prose. This was partly because she gathered together a range of discrete topics which had interested her for over a decade, and decided to mix in the Soviet Union at a relatively advanced stage. Much of her approach in *The Origins of Totalitarianism* seems flawed, whether the undifferentiated critique of European imperialism or the conservative indictment of atomisation, the mob and the masses, since Arendt liked to offend all constituencies simultaneously and, by many accounts, was herself an advancing cloud of difficulty.[37]

Arendt moved boldly from one big theme to the next: from the South African Boers, insulating themselves with racial doctrines against the shock encounter with the savage Other, to Lawrence of Arabia and the British imperial bureaucracy, although in neither case was the link with either German or Soviet totalitarianism made explicit. Arendt was also keen not to derive totalitarianism from European high culture, hence the attraction for her of Joseph Conrad's *Heart of Darkness*, with its deracinated Europeans released from law, responsibility and conventional restraint. If this was an extreme rendition of European imperialism, which had less sanguinary and even positive features amid its rich diversity, her descriptions contained a kernel of truth, in that conditions in wartime occupied eastern Europe and Russia had resembled a lawless no-man's land in which civilised beings degenerated into demi-human predators. But, again, the connection was not obvious. Arendt also vehemently rejected notions of a separate German histori-cal path to modernity, and favoured a radical rupture with the course of European civilisation, almost as if Hitler and Stalin were temporary visitors from Mars. How could she think otherwise, when she herself was a product of that nation which saw itself as the apogee of civilisation? A literature that many regard as narcissistic and precious has been built on that well-worn paradox about Germany as the quintessential *Kulturnation*, a view many of her neighbours find difficult to accept.

Yet these criticisms should not detract from her book's flashes of insight. Arendt understood the centrality of the rule of law to free societies, expressing this through the paradox that under totalitarianism people were safer if they had been convicted of a crime than as natives, refugees or concentration-camp inmates, when they were put beyond the law in a murderous limbo where everything was possible. She also captured the nightmarish quality of totalitarianism. People were killed under totalitarian rule by dint of absolute historical or racial laws, without anger or utilitarian calculation. Suffering was determined by categories, divorced from anything done by the individual victims, whose ranks could be redefined or replenished almost *ad infinitum*. The need for constant alarums and enemies virtually guaranteed inflation within the economy of terror. Reality was violently adjusted to suit a theoretical ought-world. The esoteric views of an inner militant core were hidden from the ordinary sympathisers, from whom a ladder of enlightenment rose upwards to the leading *Gott-Mensch*, their support giving the inner core the illusion that they were rooted in normality.[38] Where this sort of mentality led is discussed here in chapters devoted to eugenics, antisemitism and the wartime Holocaust.

Theories of totalitarianism have rarely been incompatible with theories of political religions, and such leading exponents of the former as Raymond Aron, Karl-Dietrich Bracher, Carl Friedrich and Zbigniew Brzezinski have employed these terms almost interchangeably.[39] Political religions deal with profound layers of human experience, and theories about them try to explain how religious forms and sentiments have been replicated for political purposes, while theories of totalitarianism address more contemporary phenomena, for which the creation of the modern state was an indispensable precondition. The technological reach of the modern state made the fantasies of earlier dystopians and utopians feasible.[40]

Political religions and totalitarianism were most systematically fused by Jacob Talmon, although there are those who say that Talmon's own monumental constructions themselves resembled totalitarian edifices in their lack of byways and loose ends. Like many historians inspired by the urgent events of their own time, rather than by olympian imperatives to tell it as it was, Talmon sought the origins of the murderous turn taken by the Russian Revolution in the Jacobin phase of the French Revolution, which he dubbed 'totalitarian democracy'. In other words he was partly inspired by Tocqueville's quest for the origins of democratic despotism. Talmon applied a psychoanalytical method to the revolutionary-salvationist mentality which he believed underpinned several radical causes, and which he regarded as the imposition of an ought-world on reality. His trilogy began, controversially, with Rousseau, and the argument about the general will of the people, which could not be opposed; and it ended, more straightforwardly, with Robespierre, Saint-Just and Babeuf, and their ever madder totalitarian stratagems to make recalcitrant reality conform to what he called their 'pencil sketch' of the ought-world. According to Talmon, a clairvoyant revolutionary elite divined the general will and the direction of history, guillotining into existence their universal view of happiness until the 'happiness' they had created consumed them. He contrasted this first totalitarian democracy with liberal pragmatism, regarding both as products of the Enlightenment. Apart from his lack of interest in the Dutch, English, German, Scottish or Virginian enlightenments, he considerably underrated the extent to which parliamentary democracy drew on institutions, ideas and intuitions much older than the eighteenth century, as when it provided consensus for taxation or defence against novel monarchical assaults on anterior rights and privileges. But then Talmon was an ideas rather than a privilege or tax man.[41] He was also perplexed by nationalism. He said little about its cosmopolitan 'Springtime of Nations' varieties, preferring instead – doubtless with the experience of Nazism in mind – to highlight its racially exclusionary and messianic forms, which he then merged with the more internationalist strain of totalitarian democracy that had interested him all along.[42]

From these examples it should be apparent that theories of totalitarianism have not always involved static models of totalitarian states, a sort of checklist of identifying features, against which scholars indicate whether a given regime qualifies as totalitarian. Some have tried such approaches, often with some cogency, but even when they do draw up lists of common symptoms, they accomplish more than mere classification.[43] Academic political science may favour such typologies, but the literature on totalitarian regimes also includes Arthur Koestler, George Orwell, Czesław Miłosz and Vladimir Bukovsky, whose approaches are more imaginative. Nor do any of these approaches reflect lack of awareness of important differences among ideologies, movements and regimes, even when it is argued that there are underlying affinities despite nominal ideological antipathies. Raymond Aron, to take an obvious example, sharply differentiated between Nazism and Communism, but he did not abandon totalitarianism as a means of describing their similarity in terms of 'the extent of ambition, the radicalism of attitude and the extremism of the methods used'. Nonetheless, he was careful to add: 'for the Soviet undertaking, I would recall the well-worn formula: he who would create an angel creates a beast; for that of the Nazi undertaking: man should not try to resemble a beast of prey because, when he does so, he is only too successful'.[44] The same point has been made less analogically by Carl Friedrich and Zbigniew Brzezinski when they argued that totalitarian regimes were 'basically alike' but not 'wholly alike'. This is the view maintained throughout this book, which periodically compares and contrasts Nazi Germany, Fascist Italy and the Soviet Union, whenever this seems appropriate.[45]

Nor should it be assumed that use of the term totalitarianism to describe an all-encompassing political aspiration has somehow been superseded by the discoveries of modern scholarship on Nazi Germany or the Soviet Union, about the inevitable discrepancies between ideal and reality; the dualistic frictions between party and state; or rivalries between overlapping bureaucratic competences, which acted, as Leonard Schapiro wrote as long ago as 1972, 'progressively, like some evil cancer, which ate their way into the fabric of *both* the state *and* society'. After all, most writers on totalitarianism had read the patron saints of contemporary structuralist history without feeling the need, evidently, to modify substantially their own conclusions.[46]

Finally, theories about totalitarianism were not merely the products of the West's Cold War ideology, as if historians were merely the academic arm of the CIA or MI6. Are those who insinuate such connections defending regimes which murdered tens of millions of people? These theories have pre-Cold War antecedents, and writing which uses the term totalitarian, either as an organising principle or just instinctively, which may be the best thing of all, thrived even in the 1990s, a decade after the end of the Cold War. The term is employed by a politically heterogeneous range of commentators and academics, including Omer Bartov, Alain Besançon, Karl-Dietrich Bracher, Stéphane Courtois, Richard Crampton, Robert Conquest, Norman Davies, István Deák, François Furet, Timothy Garton Ash, Emilio Gentile, Ulrich Herbert, Michael Ignatieff, Claude Lefort, Martin

Malia, Barrington Moore Jr, Jeremy Noakes, Fritz Stern, Tzvetan Todorov, Andrzej Walicki and Amir Weiner, to take a few distinguished names at random; and indeed by those who presided over totalitarian systems, such as former General Secretary Mikhail Gorbachev, who clearly finds 'totalitarianism' more compelling than such deadly academic coinage as 'authoritarian pluralism' or 'welfare state authoritarianism'. Presumably he knows what he is talking about. To claim that eastern Europeans or Russians (not to speak of the Western thinkers listed above) are somehow less sophisticated in these matters than Western academics is patronising, since they, of all people, had respectively forty and seventy years' direct personal experience of what in the West are ostensibly academic questions. Western academics can afford to celebrate the most advanced crèches known to human history; eastern Europeans and Russians know about the KGB and the Stasi in their bones. So do the Afghans, Chechens and Cubans.[47]

The literature in which Nazism is studied as a political religion or as a form of totalitarianism is dwarfed by the industrial scale of literature on Nazi Germany as a whole. The subject of one chapter in this book is the object of over 55,000 titles, and many of the other chapters concern issues covered with something approaching this density. Such a body of work requires its own historiographical guides, although these are not substitutes for the classics of the literature. This book seeks neither to reinvent the wheel nor to discover some novel overarching explanation, but to see where the accumulated insights of political religions and the concept of totalitarianism lead us, in making sense of an era of European history which continues to inform, and sometimes misinform, the post-Cold War world.[48]

One feature of this book is that it ranges beyond the immediate confines of *German* history between 1933 and 1945, not least because during six of those years German history became the history of Europe and the wider world, although the impact of Nazism was evident before the war, whether as streams of refugees fleeing Germany and Austria for the free world or as ever more unprincipled and violent disruptions of the post-First World War international system on the part of Germany's and Italy's new rulers. Courageous German historians who wrote about these subjects when a dignified silence was preferred were sometimes accused of fouling their own nest, so it is not appropriate to disparage them, but sometimes one wishes for a supra-German perspective. As successive chapters, on occupied Europe, the invasion of Russia, the wartime Holocaust and, last but not least, the Allied war effort, make plain, this story does not exclusively concern Germans (or Austrians), nor is there an orthodox way of telling it. Hence some issues which have figured very prominently within the German historiography, or non-German work which shadows its concerns, for example the allegedly 'modernising' impact of the dictatorship or the relative roles of ideological intention and structures in the origins of the 'Final Solution', are hardly mentioned here at all.

Moreover, without this wider optic, the history of Germany sometimes seems more exceptional than it was, bringing in its wake clichés about national character that would not occur to anyone reading Orwell's *Nineteen Eighty-Four*, which, while set in England, is curiously not of it, as those who lived through Nazi Germany or Stalin's Russia have recognised from their own experience. Much the same could be said of another great classic of the literature on totalitarianism, Czesław Miłosz's *The Captive Mind*, which few would regard as being uniquely pertinent to the behaviour of intellectuals in Communist Poland during the late 1940s and 1950s. This is why there are discussions of non-German (or Austrian) perpetrators of the Holocaust, or of the dirty communal wars which were waged in the Balkans or Poland and Ukraine, beneath the more familiar global conflict.[49] The Nazi transEuropean rampage may have been the catalyst which unleashed these unholy forces, but this hardly absolves these countries from some responsibility for what happened next in terms of 'ethnic cleansing' and racial mass murder.

This book would have been impossible to write without the major advances in our understanding of Nazism made by an international community of diplomatic, economic, intellectual, military, political and social historians, whose detailed or synthetic labours command enormous respect. If it encourages others to explore some of its themes in greater detail, then it will have achieved one of its aims. Without the quality and quantity of detailed research produced in Europe, Israel and North America, this book would not have been conceivable, even if it deliberately revisits perspectives which have been around for some while, rather than 'discovering' some half-cock theory regarding why human beings are beastly to each other when given the opportunity. A Select Bibliography highlights the outstanding titles for anyone who wishes to pursue individual subjects further, many of them having far greater scope than the subject of Nazi Germany, which is hardly an object of infinite fascination. I have not tried to treat each subject comprehensively; nor is the form adopted a straightforward narrative of events, with everything resolved by Hitler's suicide in a Berlin bunker. Neither antisemitism nor 'eugenics' would be comprehensible without reaching back beyond the years 1933–45 or ranging beyond the borders of Germany into countries with otherwise impeccable democratic credentials. Unlike the collapse of Communism in eastern Europe and the former Soviet Union in 1989–91, in which popular revolutions, notably by the Roman Catholic workers of Poland, often played a major part in reversing the consequences of the original *coup d'état*, the destruction of Nazi Germany was solely due to the herculean efforts of her opponents, which are also part of this story. Editorial choices have also been made about, for example, which aspects of wartime occupation or the Holocaust to discuss, for to write fully about either would require at least one huge book and there are many excellent alternatives already available, including Raul Hilberg's and Saul Friedländer's studies of the Holocaust. If the Holocaust is the central revealed truth about a regime that was unparalleled in its destructive nihilism, it does not exhaust everything there is to say about the time of National Socialism. But this is to anticipate the end, rather than to find a serviceable beginning. Let us return to where the history of Nazi Germany may have started. The year 1918 is as arbitrary as any other point of entry. We may even have to go as far back as 1914, or for that matter 1870.

1

THE WEIMAR REPUBLIC
AND THE NATIONAL SOCIALIST
GERMAN WORKERS' PARTY,
1918–1933

Friedrich Ebert, the first President of the Weimar Republic,
managed to restore some semblance of normality to a
defeated Germany.

THE GREAT WAR AND ITS AFTERMATH

When war broke out in the summer of 1914, most European capitals briefly heaved with crowds of chauvinistic clerks. Less excitable observers realised that an era had ended – that they were witnesses to something both dreadful and unprecedented. On 4 August 1914, the American novelist Henry James wrote from his home in England – 'under the blackness of the most appalling huge and sudden state of general war' – to his friend and fellow writer Edward Waldo Emerson. Five nations were already at war, and Britain was about to join them. James commented:

> It has all come as by the leap of some awful monster out of his lair –
> he is upon us, he is upon all of us here, before we have had time to
> turn round. It fills me with anguish & dismay & makes me ask myself
> if this then is what I have grown old for, if this is what all the
> ostensibly or comparatively serene, all the supposedly bettering past,
> of our century, has meant & led up to. It gives away everything one
> has believed in & lived for – & I envy those of our generation who
> haven't lived on for it. It's as if the dreadful nations couldn't not
> suddenly pull up in a convulsion of horror & shame. One said that
> yesterday, alas – but it's clearly too late to say it today. . . . It brings to
> me the outbreak of the Wartime of our youth – but the whole thing
> here is nearer, closer upon us, huger, & all in a denser & finer world.[1]

In 1914 millions of men across Europe rallied to the colours. They were maimed or killed in unimaginable numbers, the quick commingled with the dead in muddy hellholes, in the service of either furthering or frustrating Germany's first bid for domination in the twentieth century. Since the 1860s Europe's statesmen had learned to live with the consequences of the brief but limited wars of German unification, which many welcomed as a positive international development in a part of Europe about which outsiders had few negative preconceptions. But by the mid-summer of 1914 more than a decade of belligerent erraticism by German leaders, who lacked the diplomatic skill and self-restraint of Chancellor Otto von Bismarck, contributed to the feeling among Germany's neighbours that there were bounds which she should not be permitted to cross. Hence, a regional Balkan conflict involving Germany's ally Austria–Hungary and a Serbia supported by her Russian patron rapidly escalated first into a continental and then a general world war.

Imperial Germany's bid for continental domination by force of arms was stymied almost from the start. The German High Command had planned a war of movement that would be crowned by a stunning opening victory, but after the Battle of the Marne the conflict in the west degenerated into a war of attrition amid lines of trenches extending from Belgium to the Swiss border. Conscious of the deep fissures in German society, which some historians have claimed influenced the initial decision to go to war, Germany's Kaiser Wilhelm II proclaimed a 'civil truce' (or *Burgfrieden*). Domestic confessional, social and political conflicts were to be put in suspended animation, to be miraculously resolved through a German victory, which would preserve the authoritarian domestic social and political status quo from widespread demands for liberalisation. The enormous strains of over four years of total war left this civic truce in tatters.

Contrary to the expectations of Germany's rulers, the privations of total war between major industrial economies exacerbated pre-existing social tensions and generated new grievances and resentments. Industrialised warfare massively distorted the German economy, blasting vast amounts of human and material resources up in smoke, to no ascertainable strategic advantage, save endlessly to crater battlefields in Flanders which had long since been blasted bare already. The financial costs were as impossible as the death toll. An increasingly effective Allied naval blockade diminished government revenues from customs duties, while the well-to-do thwarted the introduction of more equitable franchises in local state parliaments, together with the fairer tax regimes that would have accompanied them. Taxation only covered some 14 per cent of German government expenditures throughout nearly five years of war. Instead, the imperial government financed the war through borrowing, in the form of war bonds purchased by patriotic citizens which would be redeemed through huge reparations to be exacted from Germany's defeated opponents. Since even this pecuniary patriotism failed to match the spiralling costs of war, the German government simply printed more money, which sent the annual average rate of inflation sky-rocketing from 1 per cent in 1890–1914 to 32 per cent, a figure which did not include the effects of a flourishing black market. By 1918 the German Mark had lost three-quarters of its pre-war value.[2]

Prolonged industrialised warfare also had severe social effects, although the classes most distressed by war were often its most diehard supporters. By 1917, one-third of the country's artisan workshops had disappeared, their proprietors either conscripted or starved of raw materials voraciously consumed by massive plants which were accorded priority because of efficiencies of scale. Shopkeepers were undercut by factories which sold cheaply and directly to their own workforces. Civil service and white-collar salaries stagnated in contrast to the inflated wages of skilled workers in war-related industries and often failed to match rising prices. An influx of women into these occupations depressed salaries further. People in jobs regarded as superfluous to the war effort sank into poverty; people regarded as burdensomely unproductive, such as psychiatric patients, died of disease and neglect as they were assigned low priority by wartime triage. An ever growing percentage of the population became dependent on local or state support, their meagre entitlements being hopelessly out of kilter with the spiralling cost of living. In a workforce that was becoming radical, rootless, young and increasingly female, strikes proliferated, despite the government's habit of conscripting or imprisoning their ring-leaders, a policy pursued too, of course, in wartime Britain, where the number of strikers was significantly greater than in Germany.

Wartime upheavals had their less tangible consequences. Moralists discerned increases in crime, divorce, incivility, unbridled sexuality, venereal diseases and the numbers of fatherless young people with too much time and money on their hands. Housing shortages resulting from an abatement of inessential construction work made for cramped living conditions and an absence of either privacy or shame. The war contributed to what one observer called a 'moratorium on morality' in personal conduct, it being both necessary and legitimate to get along by any means, no matter how underhand.[3]

The burgeoning black market undermined conventional notions of honesty, of due rewards for a hard day's labour, and of who had the most right to certain goods. The corollary was a re-emergence of quasi-medieval notions of a 'just' price, with profiteers standing in for medieval usurers in wartime folklore.[4] Farmers sought to circumvent state controls through illicit slaughtering and the black market; starving urban consumers descended on the fields to forage for food and sometimes ransacked food-supply trains. Farmers who had taken in millions of evacuated urban children gratis unsurprisingly resented these further incursions. What amounted to governmental affirmative action for urban consumers led to stringent bureaucratic controls and a regime of inspection for producers, not to mention such base practices as denunciation of those trying to turn a dishonest penny.[5]

Since these town–country cleavages showed the inadequacies of the German state's own distribution mechanisms, the government lost credibility in the eyes of people accustomed to a legendarily efficient administration. Artisans, farmers and shopkeepers saw themselves as powerless victims of corporatist collusion between labour and major vested interests, the plight of the little fellow being a constant refrain in the years to come. The question of who was fighting and who malingering took on racial overtones, leading to a notorious 1916 'Jew count' by the War Ministry, designed to investigate claims that cowardice was ethnically specific. When the survey proved the opposite, it was suppressed. The presence of Jewish businessmen in agencies purchasing raw materials abroad, and of the philosophising industrialist Walter Rathenau as war materials supremo in 1914–15, were used to give the impression that Jews were prospering while others were dying – this being a variant of an older habit of ascribing unattractive traits to Jews in order to heighten one's own virtuousness, a practice not confined to modern Germany. As a Leipzig rabbi commented: 'It is called patriotism if one profits from cannons or armoured plate, but treason sets in with eggs or stockings.'[6] In fact, these allegations that Jews were malingering would be controverted by the stony testimony to twelve thousand Jewish war dead in Germany's Jewish cemeteries, where families proclaimed their pride in those who had fallen for Kaiser and Fatherland.[7]

But the Jewish minority were not most Germans' principal concern. Across Europe 'ancient' hatreds were fomented. At first, educated Englishmen were horrified to be aligned with backward Tsarist Russia against the land of the much admired PhD. Within a few years, they would be baying for the blood of the 'barbaric' Hun, seeking to extirpate a Prussian militarism easily caricatured with its hair cut *en brosse*, duelling scars and monocles.[8] In Germany itself, enmities gradually focused upon similarly stereotypical notions, of England as the home of rapacious 'Manchester' capitalism, or of France as the embodiment of the ideas represented by the date 1789, or as the home of a 'can-can' civilisation that seemed irredeemably frivolous to devotees of high *Kultur*. Among German intellectuals of an already illiberal cast of mind, such writers as the Russian novelist Fedor Dostoevsky, who were rabidly anti-Western, became modish.[9] As the war dragged on, these hatreds began to refocus on targets within Germany itself. Relatively liberal and unmilitaristic southern Germans began to blame the presiding military caste in Prussia for the prolongation of senseless slaughter.

The detailed course of the war need not concern us. Only how it ended is relevant to this story. The peace of Brest-Litovsk, imposed by Germany on the Russian Bolshevik regime in March 1918, which surrendered huge territories in the west for the chance to consolidate its contested grip on Russian society, enabled Germany to mass troops for an onslaught against the Western Allies, which since 1917 had included the United States of America. But this final spring offensive was checked when the Allies, refreshed by a million American troops, counter-attacked in the summer. The presence of such forces, and the enormous industrial resources supporting them, may have exerted a demoralising effect on German troops, especially given the views of President Woodrow Wilson, who was wedded to realising a juster new world, in which the prospect of such devastating conflicts would be considerably diminished. Germany's allies, first Austria–Hungary, then Bulgaria, began to abandon ship, seeking their own separate peace terms.[10]

The imperial German army rapidly imploded, although precisely why remains unclear. Rifts opened up between officers and ranks, or between front-line and rear-area troops. Restive soldiers, no longer prepared to be killed to no obvious purpose, spread demoralisation to civilians, who had reason enough to be depressed themselves. According to monitors of military mail, soldiers thought the war was a murderous 'swindle', a view that was, of course, shared by large numbers of 'muzhiki', 'poilous' and 'tommies' in the enemy trenches. Images of the once celebrated German commanders Hindenburg and Ludendorff screened in military cinemas evoked whistling and shouts of 'knives out and a couple of pots to catch the blood'. Civilians meeting soldiers on trains were shocked to hear their casual talk of desertion and self-mutilation, or of arms being smuggled home for an impending revolution.[11]

A once formidable fighting force began to surrender in ever greater numbers. Sailors mutinied in Kiel, baulking at the prospect of a final showdown with the British fleet which was designed to sabotage concurrent ceasefire negotiations. Disaffection spread through the German provinces before signs of it began to appear in the Berlin capital. Soldiers, sailors and industrial workers – as well as peasants and middle-class people – formed 'Councils' or 'Soviets' in towns across Germany. These Councils adopted the idioms current among Russian oppositional circles since 1905, not the narrowly sectarian social-revolutionary goals of the later Bolsheviks. The young Heinrich Brüning, a future chancellor of the Weimar Republic, but in 1918 a company commander on the Western Front, was elected chairman of a soldiers' Soviet. He recalled that, while these metalworkers in civilian life may have sung the Communist hymn, the 'Internationale', his news that Lenin's Bolsheviks had banned strikes in Russia made a keen impression on them.[12]

These signs of disaffection were symptoms, rather than the cause, of Germany's collapse. The rot started at the apex of the army, with the dawning realisation that the last roll of the strategic dice in the spring of 1918 had failed. During that final offensive the German army advanced about forty miles on the Western Front, but this bold move overstretched its supply lines, and resulted in horrendous casualties. Having inflicted defeat on himself, their commander, Erich Ludendorff, recommended an armistice and the formation of a government responsible to parliament. He hoped to deflect blame for the failings of the High Command itself on to democratic politicians. The more intelligent generals realised that a democratic government would check the prospect of a Bolshevik revolution, and be more likely to secure less draconian peace terms from the Allies.

Germany's defeat was closely followed by a peaceful republican revolution, there being no time between the two to mourn, or reflect upon more than two and a half million war dead and four million wounded. This was part of the terrible gap torn out of the lives of generations of Europeans (and their imperial allies), which even the most sensitive war memorials – such as the Cenotaph in London's Whitehall – could convey only through the architectural invocation of nothingness. Across Europe and the wider world, there were more than nine million war dead, killed at an average rate of more than six thousand per day for more than four and a quarter years. A way of life had vanished too, along with vast numbers of young men, in a catastrophe which, for many contemporary Europeans, is more present in their emotions and imaginations than the supervening Second World War and Holocaust. Ten years after the event, Dick Diver, the hero of Scott Fitzgerald's *Tender is the Night*, caught the mood: 'All my beautiful lovely safe world blew itself up here [on the Somme] with a great gust of high-explosive love.'[13]

War and revolution destroyed three great empires. In Germany, the summit of the old order collapsed swiftly. In Munich, the rule of the venerable Wittelsbach dynasty was terminated when the Independent Social Democrat, the former Berlin journalist Kurt Eisner, led a left-wing coup in 1918 establishing a Bavarian Republic. In Berlin, the Majority Social Democrats took advantage of a unique opportunity. The absence from Berlin of crucial leaders of their Independent Socialist rivals left them with the initiative, while units of the army hitherto noted for their loyalty to the old order decided to support the Majority Social Democrats. The last Kaiser of the Hohenzollern dynasty, Wilhelm II, was prevailed upon to abdicate on 9 November; fleeing military headquarters at Spa in Belgium for what became a life in exile in Holland until his death in 1941. Although many Social Democrat leaders were indifferent to the matter of whether to retain the monarchy, provided it was not called Hohenzollern, Germany was proclaimed a republic. An interim chancellor resigned in favour of Friedrich Ebert, who formed a provisional government consisting of three members of his Majority SPD and three men from the more radical Independent Socialists. Briefly mulling over the offer, Ebert remarked, 'It is a difficult office, but I will assume it.'[14]

On 10 November, Quarter-Master General Wilhelm Groener offered Ebert military support, provided he upheld the authority of the traditional officer corps, whose insignia were already being torn off by insubordinate soldiers, and agreed to combat vigorously the threat of Bolshevism. These arrangements, which perpetuated the close wartime relationship between organised labour and the armed forces, ensured a remarkably smooth demobilisation of Germany's field armies. But there was no positive declaration of support for the new state by the army, nor would there be. More generally, Germany's traditional elites were stunned by the speed of defeat and change, regarding the onset of a democratic republic with scarcely concealed hostility and incomprehension. Their world had collapsed.[15]

The revolution that commenced in the autumn of 1918 as a bloodless popular push for peace and democracy assumed that winter the character of a sectarian class conflict involving ferocious violence. Whereas the initial push for a more democratic polity had enjoyed widespread support among the liberal bourgeoisie as well as moderate workers, a subsequent push for social revolution enjoyed the support only of a minority within the working class and of the intellectuals who claimed to represent their interests. The Majority Social Democrats had achieved their goals and wanted to get on with the non-utopian business of demobilisation, peacemaking and restoration of economic normality. As good committee men they were uncomfortable with spontaneous manifestations on the streets, and suspected the Councils even when their own rank and file dominated them. These men were pragmatic realists. Regardless of their Marxist rhetoric, they realised that incremental reform had paid off, and recoiled from the prospect of risking everything they had achieved already with a roll of the revolutionary dice. The Social Democrat leaders were also conscious of being responsible for Germans of all classes, and spoke themselves of the 'national community', and to them this meant calls for early elections for a National Assembly and a rejection of violent escapades on the part of revolutionary sectarians. Ebert demonstrated a commendable degree of patriotic responsibility, and of disinclination to submit to dictation by irresponsible and unrepresentative minorities. Whatever choices he and his colleagues made should also be understood in terms of Allied insistence that there be some sort of central German government with which they could negotiate to make an eventual peace settlement stick.[16]

Conservatism with a small 'c' was also apparent in the industrial wing of the labour movement. The socialist Free Trades Unions had long been loath to let their members be used as industrial cannon fodder by excitable radical intellectuals, against some of whom the union leaders had rather old-fashioned prejudices. An Auxiliary Service Law in 1916 had advanced their interests by guaranteeing the right to organise, and giving them a degree of co-determination of wages and working conditions. One pragmatic bird in hand was worth ten passionately advocated utopias in the bush. Indeed, the unions believed that, through their own co-optation into running the war effort, they had already advanced a form of state socialism. More concessions had been secured through the November 1918 Central Working Association Agreements between the unions and the temporarily paralysed major employers' associations. The employers abandoned their support for their own emasculated trades unions, introduced a shorter working day without reducing wages, and recognised works' committees in larger concerns. In return, the unions renounced deep 'socialisation' of the means of production.[17] What appeared to union functionaries as gains within an emergent corporatist framework did not always play that way on the factory floors or in the mines, where the consequences of wartime trade union co-optation seemed to be the abrogation of industrial safety measures, longer hours and inadequate representation by union leaders who spent too much time in the bosses' offices. The early years of Weimar would be plagued by localised outbreaks of worker militancy, sometimes triggered by anarcho-syndicalist elements, which the unions themselves were sometimes powerless to control. German trades union leaders thought that 'syndicalist actions will lead to anarchic excesses of the most anti-social nature', while the Majority Social Democrats claimed that 'there can be said to be only one truly dangerous enemy of the German revolution at the present time, and that is the German working class'.[18]

The Independent Social Democrats, who had broken with the main Party in 1917, included a democratic majority who wished to incorporate the workers' and soldiers' Councils into a parliamentary form of government, using the Councils to diminish permanently the might of generals and industrialists. Like the Majority SPD they desired a National Assembly, but wanted to delay elections, exploiting the interim period to carry out thoroughgoing socialisation of Germany's economy and society. In other words, they were not confident that an elected assembly would go down this route, and so wished to make the decision for it. The three Independent government ministers resigned from the cabinet in December 1918, after the government bungled an attempt to use military force to rescue Social Democrats who were being held hostage in a barracks by striking sailors. The Independents' extreme left wing rejected parliamentary democracy, but was in an ideological quandary about whether disciplined factory workers or amorphous crowds were the optimum vehicles of revolution. During the winter of 1918/19, these Spartacists coalesced with other far-left sects based in Bremen and Hamburg to form the Communist Party of Germany (KPD), an unstable union of intellectuals and angry young workers who opposed parliamentary democracy and favoured putschist violence. The Comintern agent Karl Radek formed the link with Lenin's Bolsheviks.[19] Fired by 'a spirit of utopian fanaticism', the radical left made a bid for power in early January 1919, the pretext being the Prussian government's dismissal of Emil Eichhorn,

Berlin's extreme left-wing police chief, who had afforded help to the mutinous sailors who had held hostage leading Social Democrats during the Christmas disturbances in the capital. Armed demonstrators occupied the offices of leading newspapers including the Social Democrat organ *Vorwärts*, in an attempt to destroy freedom of the press and to prevent the summoning of a constituent assembly. To restore order, Gustav Noske, the Defence Minister, decided to deploy volunteer Free Corps, as well as the regular army and troops avowedly loyal to the Republic. He told Ebert, 'You can relax now. Everything will be all right!'

The Social Democrats' allies of convenience included nihilistic counter-revolutionaries, whose view of Germany's new Republic was that it was, as one of them put it, 'an attempt of the slime to govern. Church slime, bourgeois slime, military slime.'[20] The Free Corps were latterday *condottieri*, consisting of former shock troops, junior and temporary officers, university students who had missed the war 'experience' and anyone still spoiling for blood or incapable of psychological demobilisation. Intense masculine camaraderie and a sense of isolation and serial betrayal characterised these bands, whose actions were supported by the regular army and the republican government. They began fighting Poles and Soviets on Germany's eastern frontiers of Silesia and the Baltic, in the last instance with the toleration of the Allies, who wished to check the spread of Bolshevism, but they quickly adapted to fighting fellow Germans.

These roughly four hundred thousand men were atypical of the millions of German war veterans who wanted normality and quiet, rather than an apocalypse on the nation's streets. Although many of them were middle class, they had absorbed an anti-bourgeois ideology in the pre-war youth movement, which had been hyper-radicalised during the war when intellectual propagandists had called the conflict one between 'German' and Western liberal democratic values, and when warrior–writers like Ernst Jünger and Ernst von Salomon had aestheticised carnage. Nietzschean vitalist individualism was transmuted into the amoral celebration of sheer brutality on the part of warriors more like machines than human beings.[21] Here is Salomon describing his own kind:

> When we probe into the make-up of the Free Corps fighter we can find all the elements which ever played a role in German history except one: the bourgeois. And that is only natural because the peculiar experience of these men . . . had forged them into one single force of consuming destructiveness. . . . The task required [of the warrior is] . . . that all

ballast, all sentimentalism, all other values must be ruthlessly cast aside so that his whole strength could be set free.[22]

These gaunt survivors of the trenches brought the wartime polarities of friend and foe on to Germany's streets. In a clear departure from the anti-socialist repression experienced in the years before the war, but in line with their 'White' or Fascist equivalents in Hungary and Italy, these men had no scruples about killing political opponents. Among those to meet a bloody end at their hands were the left-wing activists Karl Liebknecht and Rosa Luxemburg, who were murdered by Free Corps officers on 15 January 1919. In other parts of Germany, Free Corps units stormed centres of working-class militancy.

International events raised Germany's domestic temperature in complex ways. On the right, an egregious elision of ethnic and political issues gained ground. Wartime aspersions about Jews and cowardice were superseded by the vicious game of identifying, or as with Lenin misidentifying, Jews and revolutionaries as one and the same. Originating as a Tsarist survival mechanism, this response became commonplace beyond Germany, with British officials convinced that 'the Bolsheviks are all organised and directed by Jews', and an American general fighting in Russia certain that Latvian Chekists (the Bolshevik's political police force) were predominantly Jews.[23]

It was true that some radicalised Jews were prominent in Bolshevik Russia and Hungary, and in attempts to install such regimes in Germany. The Hungarian revolutionary Béla Kun; Tibor Szamuely the head of the Red Guards; and Hungary's War Minister Vilmos Böhm were Jews, as were many political commissars and the personnel of revolutionary tribunals.[24] And that some of these characters were quite ghastly can be gauged from the fact that in his Soviet exile, after the failure of the Hungarian Revolution, Béla Kun acted as chief of the Cheka in the Crimea, when some sixty thousand indigenous Tatars were murdered as the Bolsheviks eradicated their autonomy.[25] Trotsky (born Bronstein), Luxemburg and Eisner were Jews, but their Jewishness was nominal, their cosmopolitan universalism antipathetic to Jewish patriotic and religious particularism, and their utopian extremism was unrepresentative of the Jewish populations of their respective countries. Indeed, in the nineteenth century, many Russian Jewish families declared a week of mourning when a child decided to join the anti-Tsarist revolutionaries.[26] But these nuances counted for nothing in the vicious climate of post-war Europe, the quintessential time of the *grands simplificateurs.* As the Chief Rabbi of Moscow famously had it: 'The Trotskys made the revolutions, but the Bronsteins paid the bill.' They were irrelevant to the antisemitic right, wherever it hailed from. Rightist White Russian and Baltic German émigrés, notably Erwin Scheubner-Richter, Alfred Rosenberg and Count Ernst zu Reventlow, were prominent in propagating an antisemitic interpretation of the human disaster that had befallen Russia, and they influenced Adolf Hitler, who came from a background where the forging of simple connections between Jews and revolutionaries was already commonplace.[27] The antisemitic *völkisch* right admitted exploiting political chaos and 'using the situation for fanfares against Jewry, and the Jews as lightning conductors for all grievances'.[28]

There is one further point about the international impact of the Bolshevik Revolution which needs to be made emphatically. It is totally misleading to imagine that horror of Bolshevik dictatorship was confined to the political right. Indeed some German conservatives hated the Poles and France, which was Poland's main protector, so implacably that they would ally with the Devil to undo them, and they welcomed business or military opportunities in the new Russia, where Trotsky provided the German army with facilities for the covert manufacture of aircraft, toxic gas and tanks in violation of Allied restrictions on German armaments.[29] In Germany, the most consistent opponents of the Bolshevik tyranny were the Majority Social Democrats, who after welcoming the overthrow of the Tsar quickly turned to exposing the nightmarish quality of life in the Soviet Union. The Roman Catholic Centre Party did much the same. Agency wire services, delegations, travellers and, last but not least, the Menshevik opposition to the Bolsheviks, which even managed to smuggle out accounts of life in Lenin's concentration camps, supplied the factual basis for the SPD newspaper *Vorwärts*' coverage of events in Russia:

> Mass terror against the bourgeoisie had gone much further than the fighting methods of the French Revolution, which condemned individuals for individual actions. Holding a class responsible for the actions of individual persons is a judicial novum, which in another type of social system could well serve as a justification for those seeking to make the working class responsible for the actions of a fanatic, as has already happened so frequently in milder form.

The SPD rejected what *Vorwärts* dubbed Bolshevik 'Socialismus asiaticus', proclaiming, 'We don't want Russian conditions, because we know that under Bolshevik rule the Russian people are dying of hunger, even though Russia is a predominantly agrarian country.' The Prussian Social Democrat leader Otto Braun spoke of the 'Russian madhouse', while Ebert warned: 'Socialism excludes every form of arbitrariness. . . . Disorder, personal wilfulness, acts of violence are the deadly enemies of socialism.'[30] Moreover, luridly accurate reports of Bolshevik atrocities were not confined to the rabid right – with the implication that these reports were unreliable. Thanks to the remarkable American historian Vladimir Brovkin, anyone who wishes to know, and some apparently don't, can easily sample the information sent out to western Europe by persecuted *socialists* within Russia, which another talented scholar, Uwe-Kai Merz, has followed in relation to the Social Democrat press of the Weimar Republic. The Social Democrat press exposed Bolshevik-induced mass starvation, or the violence meted out to recalcitrant workers and peasants, or to dissenting socialists, by what they called 'Chinese and Korean' troops (for the Social Democrats shared a number of prejudices with their fellow Germans) and the crimes of the murderers and torturers deployed by the Bolsheviks' Polish secret police chief Felix Dzerzhinsky. To ascribe these things to the malevolent right is a denial of the enormous courage of socialists of several countries who tried to make the facts of the Bolshevik despotism known at the time.[31]

The vicious international scene affected Germany, where both anti-socialism and antisemitism had home-grown roots, as they did in many other European countries. In Bavaria, events centred on Munich, an island of anarchic bohemianism and political radicalism in an otherwise predominantly Roman Catholic rural sea of small towns and timber houses scattered across the foothills of the Alps. These were the sort of places where grudges and hatreds of Scandinavian-epic proportions could germinate and linger. After a hundred days in power, during which Bavaria was plunged into chaos, Premier Kurt Eisner was assassinated by Count Anton Arco-Valley, while *en route* to the state parliament, to offer his resignation more than a month after his party had lost an election. His publication of official documents regarding German diplomacy in the period before the outbreak of war did not increase his popularity in nationalist circles. A member of the Revolutionary Workers' Council retaliated by shooting the Majority SPD leader Erhard Auer and a delegate from the Bavarian wing of the Centre Party, which indicated that the extreme right enjoyed no monopoly on terroristic violence. Unable to master the ongoing turbulence, another Majority SPD figure, Johannes Hoffmann, withdrew the legitimate government to Bamberg, thus allowing an array of anarchists and bohemian oddities, based in the arty quarter Schwabing, to assume power in Munich for six days. Of these men, only the new Foreign Minister was clinically insane, cabling Lenin and the Pope about the whereabouts of the key to the lavatory door. A Red Army managed to fight off Republican troops dispatched by the legitimate Bavarian government.[32]

Following this eccentric interlude, power was briefly seized by the Communists, who proclaimed a Bavarian Soviet Republic. Their leader, Eugen Levine, received the blessing of Lenin, who characteristically wished to know how many bourgeois hostages had been taken. A 'classist' tone was soon apparent. Milk shortages were rationalised with the argument: 'What does it matter? . . . Most of it goes to the children of the bourgeoisie anyway. We are not interested in keeping them alive. No harm if they die – they'd only grow into enemies of the proletariat.'[33] The exiled Bavarian government received help from Noske in Berlin, in the form of thirty-five thousand Free Corps soldiers, who bore down on the radical Red Army. On 30 April, the Red Army commander Egelhofer ordered the murder of ten hostages held in the Luitpoldgymnasium, including members of the rabidly antisemitic Thule Society and one woman hostage. Entering Munich in early May, the Free Corps embarked on a reign of terror, with summary shootings and perfunctory tribunals. Battlefield niceties went by the board in conditions of a largely one-sided civil war in which 606 people were killed. Officers encouraged their men to set conscience aside, it being better to kill a few innocent people than let the guilty escape. The innocent included twenty members of the Catholic St Joseph Society, dragged from a meeting and shot as 'Communist terrorists'. Levine was tried and executed for high treason; many of his associates were summarily shot. The revolutionaries' dream of a chain of Bolshevik republics, linking Bavaria, Austria and Hungary to the Soviet Union, effectively collapsed. As for the workers' and soldiers' Councils, these disappeared as local governments refused to fund them, or as the Kaiser's army was demobilised.[34]

The threat from the extreme left had been neutralised, albeit in a fashion that soured relations between Social Democrats and Communists up to and beyond the eventual advent of a Nazi government, although a united labour movement was no obstacle to either authoritarianism or fascism elsewhere. Intimate hatreds are often said to be the worst, and that was certainly the case here, at least at the highest rather than at local level, where the 'comrades' sometimes co-operated with each other in the fight against 'fascism'. The Communists accused the Social Democrats of betraying the revolution and enabling capitalism to survive through reforms; the Social Democrats hated the Communists for being the cat's-paws of sinister Muscovite forces, and for their apparent faith in salvation through absolute immiseration. These mutual dislikes were compounded by the differences in age, background and temperament between their respective constituencies. There were also appreciable differences in mentality and tone, of the sort that led to Foreign Secretary Ernest Bevin's remark after his first meeting with Molotov, 'But they are just like the bloody Communists!'

It is sometimes assumed that the Majority Social Democratic government of Germany in those momentous months immediately after the Great War could, or should, have acted otherwise, although none of the alternatives seems especially cogent.[35] The sentimental belief that the working class was a homogeneous repository of untapped virtue, whose revolutionary spontaneity was predestined to betrayal, is an example of wishful thinking, an emotional investment in the allegedly unique value of a largely imagined social class. The Social Democrats might have tried harder to raise their own republican militias, lessening their dependence on the Free Corps, middle-class Home Guard units or the regular army, whose loyalties were tenuous. But the working class, indoctrinated for decades with a pacificism made militant by time in the trenches, did not flock to such formations or were discouraged from doing so. Forces such as the Red Army in the Ruhr were as unstable as the Free Corps, and just as bent on overthrowing the democratic order. Besides, Bolshevik activity in the Baltic and Polish nationalist insurgency in Silesia, not to speak of the real Red Army of the Soviet Union threatening Poland, made this an inauspicious moment for radical experiments in military reorganisation.

Yet at the same time, with remarkable speed, Germany's new government demobilised six million soldiers and returned them to productive life, albeit in a manner which accelerated the inflation inherited from wartime and deferred stabilisation of the German economy. Rather than raising taxes and pursuing rigorous deflationary policies, which resulted in high levels of unemployment in other countries, post-war German governments concentrated on welfare, creation of jobs and fulfilment of obligations they had undertaken to the war wounded, widows and orphans. A fairer social policy became a substitute for deeper 'socialisation'. Deflation and unemployment were not options that the unions were prepared to countenance.[36]

The SPD might have expropriated large landowners or nationalised heavy industry, although neither strategy recommended itself then, any more than it does nowadays, as a panacea for society's ills. Wherever this strategy has been tried, notably in the Soviet Union, it has resulted in backwardness and decay, not to speak of appalling environmental and health costs, mainly inflicted upon the working class in whose name these policies were pursued. Expropriation of land would not have stabilised the food supply, which was critical because of a prolonged Allied blockade designed to force Germany to comply with the peace terms, while nationalisation of industry might have facilitated Allied reparations exactions by simplifying complex lines of ownership of private property, which as good capitalists the Allies respected. Since the extended state controls over the economy during wartime had been inefficient and unpopular, it is unlikely that their peacetime extension would have been widely welcomed. Indeed, the continuance of some of these measures into the 1920s partly accounts for the widespread alienation of the farming community from the major political parties and hence from the Weimar Republic. And it is hard to imagine how a government based on a political version of dual-control driving involving the Soviet Councils would have functioned in practice, even assuming that they would not be fatally prone to subversion by totalitarian parties, as they had been in Russia, where democratic control was the preferred route to despotism.

The Majority SPD might also have edged out the tenured bureaucratic holdovers from the imperial regime, but neither they nor the *ad hoc* Councils possessed the requisite technical expertise to run a complex modern country or its armed forces. Wholesale purges of bureaucrats, judges or university professors can set ugly precedents. Would they have stopped short of the anti-republican Protestant clergy or Bavaria's Michael Cardinal Faulhaber, who in 1922 memorably declared: 'The Revolution was perjury and high treason, and will remain tainted and branded with the mark of Cain'?[37] The nub of the matter was that, for all her flaws, imperial Germany was an advanced industrial country, with a political system which combined a parliamentary franchise that was more democratic than Britain's with an otherwise autocratic form of government. If government ground to a halt in Russia, a nation of peasant farmers would not starve, as we can see today when the former industrial proletariat have reverted to subsistence farming in the absence of wages. This was not true of Germany, where two-thirds of the population lived by industry and trade. The Majority Social Democrats reasoned that most people had more to forfeit than gain through radical social experimentation, which, it should be noted, included political arrangements that would have represented a regression from a system in which all men and women over twenty now had the vote. They were not going to jeopardise the advances they had made before, during and after the war by going in search of utopia. Germany's new leaders looked backwards as well as forward, and decided not to follow the Russian road to chaos and repression.[38]

Temporarily relieved of the threat of extreme socialist dictatorship, Germany's National Assembly, consisting of delegates elected in mid-January 1919, convened in the small Thuringian town of Weimar to draft and approve a republican constitution, while the government scrutinised Allied peace terms. The two things were connected, in that the choice of meeting place was designed to show the Allies that a new Germany, informed by the town of Goethe, had come into being.

The fundaments of the constitution were established before the Assembly met: there was to be a democratic, federal republic based on the dualism of presidency and parliament. Earlier agreements among political, industrial and military leaders set the limits on what was thought possible, and the constitution effectively enshrined the compromises of the first non-violent phase of Germany's revolution. On 11 February the Assembly elected Ebert president, who in turn called on Philipp Scheidemann to form a government based on a coalition of Majority Social Democrats, the Catholic Centre Party and the liberal German Democratic Party, parties which had a wartime track-record of co-operation and which, in January, had obtained a mandate consisting of over 76 per cent of votes cast. Left-liberal lawyers assumed the main burden of drafting the constitution, although the influence of representatives of the Churches and the federal states made themselves felt for better or for worse. There were sticking points over the national flag, the status of religious education and the rights of the constituent regional states, but these constitutional deliberations were concluded remarkably swiftly between February and August 1919.

Since the liberal drafters of the constitution were historically wary of overweening parliamentary powers, the constitution combined an elected presidency, which was granted emergency powers, with an elected parliament for which all persons over twenty could vote. The electoral cycle for parliament was four years, and seven years for the presidency. The presidency was designed to be a largely honorary figurehead position, filling the vacuum left by Germany's exiled monarch, although the occupants (only the second of whom, Hindenburg, was popularly elected) showed few signs of charismatic appeal. Apart from the obligation to perform tasks which normally befall heads of state, the president had the power to dissolve parliament, to nominate as chancellors persons either enjoying or likely to enjoy the support of a parliamentary majority (which was by no means a foregone conclusion), and, under Article 48, to issue emergency legislation and to deploy the armed forces to restore order. This last stipulation was ominously vague. Ebert availed himself 136 times of emergency decrees, many of a very technical nature and mostly during the crises that arose in 1923, while Hindenburg, his successor, issued none between 1925 and 1930, and rescinded eight of Ebert's.[39] At the time few thought of the potential misuse of this last power; and Weimar's constitution can hardly be held responsible alone for the advent of a racist, totalitarian dictatorship.

The adoption of proportional representation (without a qualifying 5 per cent threshhold, along the lines adopted in 1952 by the Federal Republic) meant that many fringe parties had deputies in parliament. However, detailed computations using alternative electoral models suggest that a National Socialist victory might just have well have been accelerated rather than delayed by voting according to a British-style 'first past the post' system, given the effect upon voters of factors unrelated to the electoral system. In other words, the Nazis might have come to power in 1930 rather than three years later. At most, the new system of voting for pre-selected party lists may have somewhat diminished the personal bonds between a deputy and electors. On the positive side, proportional representation gave a voice to, for example, Catholic or Protestant diasporas in areas otherwise dominated by the rival creed. Similarly, the baleful influence on Weimar democracy of initiatives and plebiscites, originally designed to provide a democratic outlet between electoral cycles, may have been exaggerated by commentators, not least because none of Weimar's seven plebiscitary initiatives succeeded. The new state favoured neither Protestant nor Catholic Churches, a stance pleasing Catholics rather more than Protestants, who had been part of the previous 'throne and altar' dispensation. And the single concession to the Councils movement, Article 165, which concerned the creation of a Reich Economic Council, had little enduring significance. There was an impressive catalogue of basic individual rights, including Article 163, guaranteeing every German the right to work.[40]

Significantly, sixty-seven delegates from parties represented in the governing coalition – including a quarter of the SPD, a quarter of the right-liberal DVP and a fifth of the left-liberal DDP caucuses – declined to vote for the constitutional settlement, and subsequent attempts to mobilise popular enthusiasm with lectures on Constitution Day on 11 August proved no crowd puller.[41] The Republic's opening ceremony, the inauguration of Ebert as president, was a maladroit affair, and it was not helped by the Ullstein group newspaper which published photographs of Ebert and Noske, the Defence Minister, in bathing trunks. Harry Count Kessler wrote of the ceremony: 'All very decorous but lacking go, like a confirmation in a decent middle class home. The republic should avoid ceremonies; they are not suited to this type of government. It is like a governess dancing a ballet.'[42] Other contemporaries, such as the publishing magnate Hermann Ullstein, deplored the ways in which the Republic hid its virtues under a bushel. The Republic eschewed military parades, partly because of socialist anti-militarism, but also because the loyalties of the new Reichswehr were too tenuous to march its units safely through the streets. But if the President of France could ride in a horse-drawn coach to Longchamps, flanked by glittering cuirassiers, why couldn't Ebert make the same showing at the German races in Hamburg? Ullstein commented that a failure of propaganda was to 'make one's enemy's bed'.[43] Later, General Schleicher would make a similar point to Heinrich Brüning, Germany's Chancellor in 1930–2, suggesting he ride up and down Unter den Linden, Berlin's main governmental thoroughfare, once a day in a coach with a cavalry escort. President Ebert was a decent patriotic man, but as the distinguished Impressionist artist Max Liebermann put it, 'one couldn't paint him'. Even the Republic's eagle was found wanting, soon acquiring the epithet 'bankrupt vulture' because of its drooping wings. Other symbolic failures, largely attributable to the dogmatism of the left about trivial issues, included a refusal to strike a commemorative medal for survivors of one of the greatest armed conflicts in global history.[44]

The new republican red, black and gold flag also failed to rouse the enthusiasm of those wedded to the imperial black, white and red. A feeble compromise was adopted whereby the old flag was used by merchant ships, because the republican gold was allegedly indistinct at sea. A deranged minority thought the gold was a 'yellow Jewish blemish' on the new flag.[45] On the extreme right, where the newly founded German Racial Defence and Combat League was the main racist umbrella organisation, encompassing a couple of hundred thousand members, the liberal Jew Hugo Preuss's role in drafting the constitution was another link in an alleged chain of nefarious Jewish activities. This commenced with Social Democratic Party success in the 'Jewish elections' of 1912, then the 'Jewish war' and 'Jewish revolution', and on to the 'Jewish victory' and 'Jewish Republic'. The Versailles peace conference brought further refinement to this self-reinforcing paranoid fiction, with the German bankers Melchior and Warburg allegedly conniving with their New York relatives.[46]

At Versailles in May 1919, the German delegation to the peace negotiations was shocked to discover that President Wilson's principles of self-determination excluded their country. Under the first terms offered, which were bolstered with Allied ultimata, Germany lost all her overseas colonies and the territories claimed by her neighbours; union between Germany and Austria was forbidden; limitations were imposed on the size and nature of her armed forces, and officer cadet academies, the General Staff, tanks and the incipient air force were abolished. There were to be reparations, as yet unspecified, by way of atonement for allegedly causing the war, as reflected in Article 231 ascribing sole 'war guilt' to Germany. Military manpower shrank from 800,000 in April 1919 to 100,000 in January 1921, while 30,000 of the 34,000 officers corps were discharged.[47] If the military restrictions struck at a primary symbol of national prowess, and at the caste personifying it, the 'war guilt' clause and demands that Germany surrender her alleged war criminals seemed unjust and vindictive. The Allied commissions that would monitor both disarmament and reparations payments seemed like a semi-permanent impairment of sovereignty. The latter is a touchy issue now wherever similar arrangements are imposed, and it was a sensitive issue then, especially since Germany had been defeated without a single Allied soldier entering her own territory. German attempts to divide the Allies with counter-proposals and threats of non-compliance only reinforced Allied unity and raised the prospect of further military incursions beyond the bridgeheads and demilitarised zones called for in the treaty. The only minor Allied concession to German sensibilities was the decision to grant a plebiscite to determine the future of Upper Silesia, a vote whose result the Poles tried to overturn by force.[48]

Virtually all sectors of German opinion angrily denounced the Allied peace terms, which differed so radically from expectations built on Wilsonian idealism. German socialists, such as Eduard Bernstein or Kurt Eisner, who tried to spill the beans on the empire's pre-war diplomatic machinations were a tiny minority. Interned in his bugged hotel room, the German Versailles conference delegation leader Foreign Minister Brockdorff-Rantzau played to the domestic gallery, laying his black gloves on his copy of the treaty, and treating his Allied interlocutors to a speech, by turns plangent and strident, while maladroitly remaining seated. His audience was not impressed. The German government's response to the treaty was equally emotive, with Chancellor Scheidemann remarking, 'What hand would not wither that binds itself and us in these fetters?' A nation in chains became the convenient metaphor, and Germany's losses were dramatically illustrated in countless maps and graphics, with once historic regions brutally wrenched away by foreign powers. The Versailles treaty appeared to be the triumph of an Allied conspiracy to enmesh Germany in a network of restrictions and obligations in perpetuity, for the reparations burden was left ominously open-ended. This perception discredited the international institutions and idealistic values of the post-war era, as did the United States Senate's refusal to ratify the treaties or to endorse the League of Nations. Rightist German intellectuals pooh-poohed international law, morality and talk of universal peace, preferring instead doctrines based on the inevitability of conflict among different peoples and races.[49]

Nationality issues were especially likely to be coloured by a sense of historic grievance, even when the peacemakers endeavoured to protect minority rights. In an ethnically complicated post-imperial eastern Europe, efforts to impose a framework of nation states on formerly multi-national empires were bound to lead to injustices for various minorities, including the Germans themselves, yet these problems were ultimately regarded as secondary to France's search for stable allies to replace Tsarist Russia and Poland's two-hundred-year-old quest for independent statehood. Minority ethnic German exclaves in various newly founded eastern European countries were subjected to acts of local chauvinism; Germany made corresponding cultural and economic efforts to keep ethnic Germans where they were.

No German minority in a given territory meant no German territorial claim on it, a strategy realised far more radically in the same region after 1945.[50] As the Balkan joke had it, 'why should I be a national minority in your state, when you can be one in mine?' Thus around 13 per cent of the German population was now marooned beyond the borders of the former German Reich, and they were sometimes treated in a discriminatory and offensive manner. Ethnic Germans under the thumb of French authorities in Alsace-Lorraine and the Rhineland or Polish troops in West Prussia and Silesia contributed to the emotional intensification of *völkisch* thinking, providing examples of persecution and suffering, and fuelling the belief that all Germans would be better off within an ethnically exclusive 'national community'.

However reasonable the Allied case for Germany's obligation to provide restitution for material damage and loss of shipping, and to pay pensions for veterans, widows and orphans, the political message seemed to be that the Versailles treaty was prolonging the war by economic means. For, beyond a desire to neutralise Germany's military might, there seemed to be an intention to disable permanently the economic power underpinning it, regardless of transformed domestic political circumstances, and despite the deleterious economic and psychological consequences for the stability of the Weimar Republic. All these fears, some of them justified, coupled with the Allies' latent threat of armed intervention to enforce the treaty's terms, contributed to the view that Germany after 1918 was engaged in a sort of cold war.[51]

Superficially speaking, Versailles created unanimity among Germans. But this overworked paradox was more apparent than real. Moderate opponents of the treaty opted for negotiation to obtain revised terms, the line pursued ineptly or shrewdly by successive Weimar chancellors and their foreign ministers from Joseph Wirth via Gustav Stresemann to Heinrich Brüning, but diehard opponents of the Republic convinced themselves that the 'November criminals', as they dubbed the republicans who had toppled the Kaiser and surrendered to the Allies, were responsible for Germany's defeat and this shamefully onerous peace treaty. Once people had worked themselves into a lather, reality counted for nothing. No matter how ingeniously a great statesman such as Stresemann employed reconciliation and an ideology of Europeanism to dismantle the Versailles framework, he could never satisfy appetites whetted since the 1880s by visions of Germany's obtaining both a continental and an overseas empire at one fell swoop, which would redress the grievance Germany felt towards more established colonial powers. The Republic's foreign policy inevitably fell short of such insatiable expectations, as had also happened during the Wilhelmine empire, whose foreign policy had never been quite strident enough for sections of nationalist opinion.

The German cabinet divided over whether to accept or reject the Allied terms, but it eventually complied. Parliament reluctantly authorised compliance with the treaty, and it was signed on 28 June at Versailles. Germany's Protestant Churches declared a day of national mourning.[52] The treaty was the complex product of such Allied considerations as human and material losses; mutual war debts; minority and nationalist lobbying; and public opinion in Allied countries, and legitimate national security concerns of the 'once bitten, twice shy' variety. Again, as with the Weimar constitution, we should not make automatic connections between the peace settlement and the rise of Nazism over a decade later. Versailles did not irrevocably diminish Germany's long-term existence as a great power, and its terms bore scant resemblance to the sort of vindictive ones imposed by imperial Germany herself in 1918 on Russia's new Bolshevik government in the Treaty of Brest-Litovsk. As the Belgian Foreign Minister commented, after an intemperate performance by the right-wing liberal German industrialist Hugo Stinnes at the Spa reparations deliberations: 'What would have become of us if such a man had had the chance to emerge as the victor?'[53] If one was to go by the terms of Brest-Litovsk, Germany's defeated opponents would have had to forfeit 90 per cent of their coal capacity and 50 per cent of their industry. Nor did the Versailles terms concerning Germany compare unfavourably with those imposed under separate treaties on Austria, Hungary or Turkey, with Hungary losing 70, as opposed to Germany's forfeiture of 13 per cent, of her pre-war territory. But the comparative perspective was closed to a people focused on their own misery, and so was any rational cost-benefit appraisal of Germany's forfeiting of economically backward eastern agricultural areas, however beguiling (for some) the heavily subsidised aristocratic lifestyle that once thrived there.

Rejection of the Versailles treaty was common across the Weimar political spectrum, including the Communists, who regarded it as part of a wider intra-imperialist plot. There was no distinctive political advantage in opposing it. Many of the most transparently coercive features of the settlement – such as military inspectorates, occupied zones and reparations – had largely unravelled before Nazism became a mass political movement, in a Europe which was by no means universally unsympathetic to Germany's legitimate grievances.

However, the widely acknowledged iniquities of the Versailles treaty were elided by many right-wing Germans with a broader charge of treason against the alleged 'November criminals', which was both inaccurate and preposterous. *Ad hominem* libels and political terrorism which supported and furthered these false accusations were avowedly intended to undermine the newly democratic order. This order was also traduced by the intellectual right as an alien, mechanical, Westernised import, an aberration from Germany's allegedly authoritarian national tradition which had recently transformed myriad sleepy principalities into a great European power. This line simply ignored the vibrant party political culture that had marked the Wilhelmine empire. The fictive 'civic truce', which some Germans claimed had characterised German society during the war, mutated into an imagined 'national community' transcending class conflict, where obligation and order superseded Western liberal notions of individual rights. Of course, in other parts of German life, among Catholics and socialists, there were alternative versions of 'national community' – based on Christian principles, loyalty to the Republic and a desire for social justice – which deserve not to be overlooked. But the unreconciled right was more interested in going forward boldly into the future in search of an imaginary past. Accuracy, fair play and respect for either persons or institutions were not high priorities in its enraged milieu, and their chorus was joined, from the far left, by venomous assaults against the alleged betrayers of the socialist revolution and snide demi-mondiste attacks on putative German national characteristics which irritated plain provincial people. The so-called intelligentsia which took this line scorned the dull and worthy politicians of the day, and they mocked the armed forces and their fellow countrymen in general, whose stolid values and virtues they despised, just as their right-wing counterparts fulminated against 'the masses' and Germany's new inorganic Weimar political 'system', a word well chosen for insinuating something inauthentically alien and mechanical.[54]

Republican leaders had to resort to the courts to defend themselves against defamatory allegations. In 1920, Matthias Erzberger sued the conservative Karl Helfferich, who had made serious allegations against him. As a signatory to the armistice, and author of major tax reforms which disfavoured the rich, Erzberger was especially hated on the right. The legal action turned out badly for him: though awarded derisory damages of 300 Marks, he was revealed in court to have practised tax avoidance himself, and to have made money from knowledge gained while in government. Similarly, President Ebert had to bring some 170 libel actions against right-wing journalists who impugned his conduct during a wartime strike by munitions workers. Although a Magdeburg court acknowledged that Ebert had joined the strike leadership with the intention of drawing off its radicalism, it nonetheless implicitly endorsed the charges of treason. By delaying an urgent appendectomy, the trial contributed to the death of the fifty-four-year-old President.[55]

By contrast, considerable latitude was afforded Field Marshal Hindenburg when he condescended to appear before a parliamentary committee investigating the causes of Germany's military collapse in 1918. This was the first time that the new republican democratic Germany confronted a senior representative of the old imperial order. The results were like trying to get answers from a stone wall. Hindenburg read from a prepared statement whose final flourish was a reference to the opinion of 'an English general' to the effect that 'the German army was stabbed in the back'. This was a subtle reworking of the incredulous response of a British officer to claims made by Ludendorff: 'You mean you were stabbed in the back?'[56] But high-level denial of responsibility for Germany's military defeat went far beyond her wartime generals. Ebert himself had joined in the denials when he ostentatiously greeted Germany's returning 'undefeated' demobilised soldiery. Apart from this 'stab in the back' legend, whose reality had been a 'stab in the front', a further explanation for imperial Germany's defeat was the alleged superiority of the British press, notably those newspapers owned by Lord Northcliffe, whose 'horror propaganda' had demonised the 'Huns'. The guileless German Siegfried, a favourite personification of the German nation, had not gone down in a fair fight, but rather to the black arts of the *Daily Mail*.[57]

Allied restrictions on the size of Germany's post-war armed forces had consequences for the Free Corps, whose operations in the Baltic and Poland were abruptly terminated. While a few units were incorporated within the new army, the Reichswehr, or into state police forces, others dissolved into a host of 'athletic societies', 'circuses', 'detective agencies', 'haulage companies' and 'labour gangs' on large estates, taking their 'machine tools' with them to use against aggrieved agricultural labourers or distinguished Weimar politicians. An anti-Weimar assault took the form of political exploitation of mass distress, a putsch and a campaign of assassination.[58]

Disgruntled Free Corps leaders provided the force behind a putsch in March 1920. Their backers included regular army officers, often noblemen, and the conservative bourgeoisie from the countryside east of the Elbe. Their leaders included Ludendorff and Wolfgang Kapp, both formerly involved in the Fatherland Party, founded in 1917 to mobilise support for extravagant war aims. The putschists' brief occupation of Berlin's government quarter was facilitated by malevolent neutrality within the regular army. Guardianship of the abstract state which the Reichswehr thought it embodied did not extend to defence of its legitimate republican government. The various elements of the so-called Kapp–Luttwitz putsch did not gel. Kapp was yesterday's man, reluctant to follow the Free Corps creed that 'Everything would still have been all right if we had shot more people'. The local Home Guards, though hostile to the Republic, were impressed neither by Kapp's desire to restore the old order nor by Free Corps nihilism. Several leading industrialists, such as Carl Duisberg, were distinctly cool towards the impetuosity of what they dubbed the 'military party'.

The putsch collapsed amid a massive general strike called by the government before it fled to Dresden, but which was masterminded by the socialist trade unions. Since there was full employment, the strike had its optimum effect. Moreover, Social Democrats, Catholics and Communists co-operated, though the latter initially opposed the strike, refusing as they put it 'to lift a finger for the democratic republic'. Ironically, although the putsch was an ignominious failure, forces were unleashed to oppose it which were hard to contain. The unions began to dictate their own terms to the government, including the composition of the cabinet, while a fifty-thousand-strong Red Army roamed the Ruhr. Government attempts to disarm this force through negotiation came to nothing, and in the resulting clashes with the army about a thousand of the rebels were killed.[59] It was indicative of the times that when twenty students from Marburg University escorted fifteen 'Spartacist' captives from a village to Gotha, they shot them all somewhere along a railway line.[60]

Although the Republic survived the Kapp putsch, at elections in June 1920 the electorate decisively rejected the parties of the original Weimar coalition. The Majority Social Democrats and left-liberal DDP lost respectively half and three-fifths of their previous support, while support for liberal conservatives and conservative nationalists and for the radical Independent Socialists swelled. In other words, the middle classes moved more to the right, while some of the working class moved further left.

After the failure of the 1920 putsch, the right adopted other tactics and mutated in complex ways. Bavaria became the 'cell of order', the term the right used to describe local indulgence towards anti-democratic subversion. In March, a conservative regime led by Gustav Ritter von Kahr took over in Bavaria, whose combined particularist sensitivities and right-wing sympathies enabled the extreme right to flourish there. Bavarian rightists took the lead in forming the Escherich Organisation, or 'Orgesch', which combined the vociferous pursuit of middle-class interests with preparations for a military takeover. Its leaders envisaged apocalyptic scenarios, in which strikes by producers and professionals would provoke a predictable 'Red' response that the counter-revolutionary right and the Reichswehr could use to crush the left in general. As it happened some on the left thought along similar lines, for sometimes the extremes were involved in a *pas de deux* in which each depended on the provocations and responses of the other. In 1920, the Independent Social Democrats split, with about 350,000 of their members joining the Communists, who became a mass party for the first time. The old Communist leadership was purged, in favour of those whose task was to take the heat off the Soviet Union by fomenting trouble in Germany. In other words, the Communists were a tool of an alien power. Specifically they sought to provoke the Escherich Organisation into action, although the latter needed little encouragement. In March 1921, Communist agents, including Béla Kun, and domestic desperadoes were responsible for wildcat strikes, bank robberies and acts of terrorism. Government forces had little difficulty in suppressing these externally directed activities.

Shadowy right-wing groups, such as the Organisation Consul, waged a campaign of assassination and terror. Terrorists masquerading as patriots killed Erzberger and threw prussic acid into former Chancellor Philipp Scheidemann's face in 1921; and the following year shot Foreign Minister Walter Rathenau while he was *en route* to his office. This last murder was probably designed to provoke a left-wing uprising, which conservative forces could then crush with impunity. The right-wing press crowed that these men had got their just deserts. Those who had coined such rhymes as 'Kill off Walter Rathenau, The goddamned Jewish sow' had their hopes realised.[61] These were the most notorious examples of more than 350 political murders committed by rightist terrorists during the Weimar years.[62] Although the assassins routinely fled, sometimes aided by the police, or were treated with understanding by anti-republican judges, the government passed a law in July 1922 for the Protection of the Republic, in order to placate public outrage, which was taking the form of mass demonstrations, in which millions of people participated to reach out, in death at least, to the dead Foreign Minister, the first German Jew to hold such an office. Bavarian particularism stymied republican attempts to counter right-wing extremism in a state which was especially prone to it.

Allied reparations demands occasioned Weimar Germany's next bout of crises. In April 1921 an Allied commission presented the bill. It totalled 132 billion gold Marks or about US$30 billion. This was the scaled-down figure, for only British and American pressure had stymied France's demands for 269 billion Marks. Chancellor Joseph Wirth opted for tactical compliance, if only to demonstrate Germany's incapacity to pay. For the Allies, having imposed reparations on Germany, unhelpfully passed the business of deciding how to raise the money on to the Germans themselves to avoid the costs of military occupation. France threatened to extend the occupation, but this was a bluff waiting to be called, especially since such influential Englishmen as the economist John Maynard Keynes were by no means unsympathetic to equally weighty German descriptions of Germany's alleged plight.[63]

The payment arrangements meant that reparations to the Allies had to compete with the German government's desire to purchase social peace by postponing the stabilisation of the economy, at a time when the Allies were experiencing deflation and high unemployment. The Allies suspected that Germany was exploiting her currency depreciation to minimise her obligations, and to dump export goods, and these suspicions were compounded by the erratic impression left by the 1922 Rapallo agreement between Germany and the Soviet pariah, which in Western eyes threatened to squeeze Poland, France's 'gendarme on the Vistula', between an East–West vice.

When over Christmas and New Year 1922–3 Germany twice defaulted on her reparations obligations, seventy thousand French and Belgian troops occupied the Ruhr, ostensibly to protect engineers seizing telegraph poles and timber, but really to secure the economic edge that France and Belgium had failed to acquire under the Versailles treaty. The new centre-right cabinet of the Hamburg businessman Wilhelm Cuno, whom Ebert had appointed to make an impression of seriousness on the Allies, ironically endorsed a campaign of passive resistance among the Ruhr's inhabitants, having undertaken no advanced planning or stockpiling for this eventuality. Passive resistance in the Ruhr led to the French authorities expelling or imprisoning recalcitrants. To be precise, about 46,200 civil servants, railwaymen and police were directly affected, together with a hundred thousand of their relatives. Sporadic sabotage and low-level acts of terrorism, which according to some exponents were explicitly modelled on the corrosive acts of Irish Republican terrorism against the British, were countered robustly with shootings, hostage-taking and collective fines. Having already blotted their copybooks by knocking German civilians off the pavements, the occupying forces compounded their errors by aggressive house searches, and identity checks, and summary executions. Courts martial created nationalist martyrs, notoriously Albert Leo Schlageter, who was shot in 1923 by the French occupation authorities.

Exhibiting their usual amoral opportunism, the Communists adopted Schlageter as a hero, with Karl Radek of the Moscow Comintern eulogising the fallen 'fascist' as a martyr. Ruth Fischer, who was half Jewish, dabbled in antisemitism – 'Whoever cries out against Jewish capitalists is already a class warrior, even when he does not know it. . . . Kick down the Jewish capitalists, hang them from the lampposts, and stamp upon them' – in a cynical attempt to woo nationalist and *völkisch* support.[64] Other solidarities were as surprising. Social Democrat workers rallied around their 'national comrade', the industrialist Fritz Thyssen, when he and various mine owners were tried by a French military court for refusing reparation deliveries of coal. Joint employer–union committees distributed payments to the strikers, and Heinrich Brüning, by now a leading light of the Christian trades union movement, was one of those who brought them suitcases filled with illicit cash. Ironically, the one party not to partake in this national mood of resistance was the ultra-patriotic Nazis, who enjoined Germans not to let themselves be distracted by France, but to concentrate on toppling their own 'November criminals'.

The economic consequences of the Allies' occupation of the Ruhr in 1923 were catastrophic. The German government used deficit spending to subsidise workers summarily dismissed from their posts while purchasing coal from Britain. The cessation of deliveries of raw materials from the Ruhr resulted in waves of cutbacks in production and layoffs elsewhere. Unemployment rose from 2 to 23 per cent. Tax revenue declined to the point where by October 1923 it covered a mere 1 per cent of total government expenditure. The volume of money circulating in Germany grew astronomically, by the autumn flowing in improbable denominations from nearly two thousand presses operating around the clock. A banknote-printers' bill appeared as 32776899763734490417 Marks and 5 pfennige in Reichsbank accounts. Banks had to hire more clerical workers to calculate these lengthening digits. Production slowed as workers trundled carts laden with a day's pay to the banks, and shops shut as the owners ceased to be able to purchase new stock with yesterday's takings. In a chapter entitled 'The Death of Money', Konrad Heiden tells the following story:

> A man who thought he had a small fortune in the bank might receive a letter from the directors: 'The bank deeply regrets that it can no longer administer your deposit of sixty-eight thousand marks, since the costs are out of all proportion to the capital. We are therefore taking the liberty of returning your capital. Since we have no bank-notes in small enough denominations at our disposal, we have rounded out the sum to one million marks. Enclosure: one 1,000,000-mark bill'. A cancelled stamp for five million marks adorned the envelope.

A barter economy developed and the prudent middle classes began selling their most cherished possessions, although there were only so many Steinway pianos a peasant house could accommodate. Books were devoted to the moral inversions inflation caused.[65]

The perception grew that, as in wartime, the scum rose to the top. Decent hardworking people thought they were being exploited by amoral spivs, flashing their ill-gotten gains in nightclubs and restaurants, while doctors, lawyers and students had to resort to manual labour or soup kitchens. There was an unappetising type abroad in the land:

> Connoisseurs of the time should wander one evening through the parlours and fancy eating establishments – everywhere, in every lousy corner you will smack up against the same plump face of the pot-bellied profiteers of war and peace.

According to the author of this essay, entitled 'Berlin is becoming a whore', the hundred thousand prostitutes who allegedly serviced Berlin were no longer servants who had been dismissed after an upstairs–downstairs liaison, but nice middle-class girls:

> A university professor earns less than a streetcar conductor, but the scholar's daughter was used to wearing silk stockings. It is no accident

that the nude dancer Celly de Rheidt is the wife of a former Prussian officer. Thousands of bourgeois families are now being forced, if they want to live uprightly on their budget, to leave their six room apartments and adopt a vegetarian diet. This impoverishment of the bourgeoisie is necessarily bound up with women accustomed to luxury turning into whores. . . . The impoverished noblewoman becomes a bar maid; the discharged naval officer makes films; the daughter of the provincial judge cannot expect her father to make her a present of her winter clothes.[66]

Differentials between earnings were erased, leading to an acute sense of social declassification, which was soon epitomised by a middle-class Militant League of Beggars. People suffering from clinical malnutrition, and unable to afford adequate food or medicine, were susceptible to tuberculosis or rickets. Although the 'Mark is a Mark' policy was endorsed by the courts and enabled farmers and mortgagees to pay off their creditors, pensioners, savers and elderly people living off modest rental incomes were plunged into poverty and insecurity. Sometimes their only escape from indignity was through suicide.[67]

The German government's policy of resistance to French authority in the Ruhr, which prevented France from gaining a permanent foothold there, was abandoned in late September 1923. Gustav Stresemann, the right-liberal German People's Party leader, became the new Chancellor of a 'Grand Coalition' that included his own party as well as the SPD. These arrangements were facilitated by the desire of both left and right to blame each other for having to call off the policy of passive resistance to French occupation. On the extreme right, this abandonment of the Ruhr struggle compounded the republicans' founding treason of November 1918.[68] Stresemann was only chancellor for a hundred days, but he acted as Foreign Minister down to his death in October 1929. He was an extraordinary statesman who transcended his youthful belligerent reputation as 'Ludendorff's young man', and whose statements of 'prudential loyalty' to the Republic and desire for an international fresh start were wholly sincere.

During October and November 1923 Stresemann overcame both extremist and separatist threats to the government. However, some extremists were within the forces of law and order themselves. Since the autumn the Reichswehr commander General Seeckt, the Pan-German leader Heinrich Class and right-wing industrialists within Stresemann's own party had calculated that a Communist uprising

would enable them to mobilise the entire right behind a dictatorial
'Directory', which after being legally installed in power by the President would crush the Communists, suspend parliamentary democracy
and abolish the earlier concessions to organised labour.

By way of preparation, the army intensified its links with frontier
protection units and with the illegal or 'Black' Reichswehr, which
comprised clandestine paramilitaries that had been established with its
connivance to circumvent Allied restrictions on German military might.
Some of these units stationed near Berlin were not prepared to wait on
Seeckt, and they precipitately launched a putsch he disfavoured, for he
was notorious as a man who would advance to the Rubicon to fish in
rather than cross. They were disarmed by regular army troops acting
under Seeckt's orders. Meanwhile, the Communists essayed their next
attempted overthrow of the 'bourgeois' Republic.[69]

In October 1923, Communists entered coalition governments with
the Social Democrats in Saxony and Thuringia. Various provocative
policies ensued, as well as the formation of armed Proletarian Hundreds to carry out a 'German October', a development actively solicited
and supported by the Comintern in Moscow, as part of its strategy
of stabilising the Bolshevik regime at the expense of stability in
Germany.[70] Vicious mobs extracted food from recalcitrant farmers, or
assaulted employers and draped red flags and placards around their
necks in public degradation sessions reminiscent of what Nazis would
later do to Jewish people, although this similarity is seldom remarked
on.[71] The government proclaimed an emergency and used regular army
troops to disarm the Communists; the only sign of a 'German October'
occurred in Hamburg, where thirteen hundred Communists besieged
the police stations. Although this rising was crushed, the activities of
the former pugilist Ernst Thälmann, in the Barmbeck district, only
helped his ascendancy within the Party later in the 1920s, when
veterans of this rising, who fled to the Soviet Union, returned to
Germany to organise Communist subversion. Whereas the Reichswehr
acted swiftly to crush the Communists in central Germany, they were
conspicuously indulgent to right-wing plots afoot in Bavaria, so much
so that on 3 November 1923 the Social Democrats left the national
government, remaining aloof for the next four and a half years. Of
course, they shared some of the responsibility too for the coalition
arrangements with the Communists in Saxony and Thuringia, which
had acted as a red rag to an already enraged extreme-right bull. It was
also an unrealistic strategy, since it was commonly known that deals

with Communists were akin to the relationship of a rope to a hanged man.[72]

Communist conspiracies provided a welcome pretext for Bavarian paramilitaries to mass on the state's northern borders, the goal being an Italian-style 'March on Berlin'. The idea of using Bavaria as a launch pad for a strike against the Berlin government was common to both Kahr and the *völkisch* right wing under Ludendorff – for the general had become a politician – and his younger sidekick, a former Bavarian army corporal, Adolf Hitler, an odyssey we will discuss presently. But, once the army had crushed the left in Saxony and Thuringia, the mainstream Bavarian right hesitated. Kahr, despite having offended Seeckt by protecting General Lossow, the Reichswehr commander in Bavaria, when Lossow refused to close down the Munich newspaper the *Völkischer Beobachter* after it attacked the Reichswehr leader, was unwilling to move on Berlin without Seeckt's own involvement, and his involvement was conditional upon Kahr's distancing himself from the putschism of Ludendorff and Hitler. Seeckt explained the army's dilemma to Kahr without concealing his antagonism to the Republic:

> The Reichswehr must not be brought into a position in which it has to fight, for a government which is alien to it, against people who have the same convictions as the army. On the other hand, it cannot permit irresponsible and unauthorized circles to try and bring about a change by force. If the army has to defend the authority of the state on two fronts it will break up. Then we have played the game of France and have offered the last chance of success to Muscovite Communism.[73]

Kahr, Lossow and Bavaria's state police chief, Seisser, awaited events in the north. Hitler, sensing a conservative sell-out and fearful of losing the support he had garnered from an uneasy coalition of *völkisch* paramilitaries, hijacked a Kahr–Lossow meeting in the Bürgerbräukeller, and proclaimed a 'national *völkisch* revolution'. The whole performance reminded one eyewitness of 'Mexico' or 'Latin America'. Having been railroaded into supporting Hitler's precipitate bid for power, Kahr, Lossow and Seisser abandoned ship at the first opportunity. On 9 November 1923, Hitler and Ludendorff led a march of about two thousand extremists through Munich, which was dispersed near the Feldherrnhalle by a few salvoes from the Bavarian state police. A lightly wounded Hitler slunk away, although the events of that day would become part of Nazi mythology, for the confrontation provided the Party's earliest, and hence most holy, martyrs.

This tawdry episode spelled the end of paramilitary putsches against the Weimar Republic. When the extreme right made its next bid for power, it would use much more insidious methods, namely a combination of the ballot box and street violence. But, for the time being, rampant inflation was checked by issuance of a new Reichsmark, backed with gold to a minimum of 40 per cent, which was exchanged for bundles of worthless paper. Under the 1924 Dawes Plan, the emotive reparations issue was transformed into a technical problem involving international experts concerned with the wider stabilisation of European capitalism. Elections in Britain and France in 1923–4 brought to power governments which were not so overtly ill-disposed towards Germany as their predecessors. The United States of America's positive involvement on the continent of Europe was also crucial. A loan of 800 million gold Marks promoted confidence in the new currency, and acted as a priming aid for a regularised schedule of payments on the reparations. Since these stretched into the infinity of the late 1980s, and involved foreign control of Germany's railways and central bank, they did not allay nationalist resentments, any more than currency stabilisation placated the struggling middle classes, or the industrial working class, which had also suffered grievously through inflation. But the Republic appeared to have weathered its greatest hour of crisis.

There was even a lucky break to the East, although that was soon not so evident to the Russian people: Stalin's ascendancy within the troika which dominated the Soviet Communist Party after the death of Lenin. One consequence of Stalin's hatred of Trotsky was that the latter's insistence on endemic world revolution was replaced by the doctrine of building 'socialism in one country' and coexistence with the 'imperialist' states. Since the German Communists were little more than tools of the Comintern and Soviet foreign policy, this meant that there were to be no more 'German Octobers'.[74]

THE POLITICAL PARTIES AND WEIMAR SOCIETY

It takes an effort of the imagination, in a contemporary developed world where liberal democracy and free- or social-market capitalism appear to have seen off most alternatives, to envisage a time when liberalism was regarded as a waning force, rapidly being superseded by authoritarianism, Communism, fascism and Nazism – the alleged forces of the future. Liberal democracy was in danger of becoming an extinct species in inter-war Europe, where by 1939 undemocratic regimes already outnumbered constitutional democracies by sixteen to twelve. Before turning to the rise of the Nazis, it may be helpful to say a little about politics in the Weimar Republic in general.[75]

By pre-1914 or post-1945 German standards, Weimar politics were highly unstable, although some nations have experienced comparable political instability without degenerating into totalitarian dictatorship. But instability combined with chronic economic problems was liable to engender a sense of despair and hopelessness, though there was no simple correlation between acute economic distress and extremist politics. Some background factors were beyond human agency. Although the war and a massive influenza epidemic in 1918 – which killed more Europeans than had died in the war – meant that the German population had contracted, a pre-war population increase still surged on to the labour market in the 1920s, so that by 1925 there were five million more workers than jobs available. This trend decelerated only in 1931–2.[76] The surplus of workers was matched by the loss of jobs, for competition with the United States, and an obsession with technology and scale, encouraged machine-driven rationalisation in certain industries such as coalmining and automobile production. Assembly lines and coal-cutting machines may have resulted in dramatic productivity gains, but they also entailed structural unemployment and the latent threat of over-production. Because of simultaneous inflation, there was an understandable disinclination to save, and the corollary was an inordinate reliance on foreign sources of investment capital. Foreign loans and reparations arrangements also reduced government's room for manoeuvre, as did the political decision to subsidise such constituencies as the civil service, the industrial working class and the farmers through social policies, wage rises and protective agricultural tariffs. Two of these policies were incompatible.[77]

Between 1919 and 1933 there were twenty governments in Germany, the most durable of which, Hermann Müller's 'Great Coalition' (1928–30), lasted only twenty-one months, an improvement on the twelve-week lifespan of his 1920 cabinet. Only two parliaments survived the full five-year cycle, with two years being a good stretch and many lasting a few months. This chronic political instability, in economically good times and bad, diminished respect for parliament and politicians, in a society where neither was axiomatic. What was true of national politics was not always true of politics in the federal states, where contentious foreign policy issues did not poison politics. The largest state, Prussia, had a coalition government led by Social Democrats throughout almost the entire Weimar period. The difficulty with the federal arrangement included certain duplications of functions, and institutionalised wrangling about respective state and national competences. Criticism of professional politicians who had largely replaced gentlemen amateurs took several forms.[78]

The periods of horse-trading that preceded the formation of Weimar's many coalition cabinets were inherently unedifying, leaving outsiders in the dark regarding what deals had been struck and what principles sacrificed. Sometimes no deals were struck at all, often because of the ideological obtuseness of the participants. On two occasions, the President turned to prominent businessmen, who formed governments of 'apolitical' experts. Even when a coalition had been formed it was not guaranteed support from the parliamentary caucuses of its partner parties, some of which behaved like anarchist collectives, although a few called this democracy. For example, forty-five Social Democrats in the Assembly refused to approve Stresemann's first cabinet, including four of their own cabinet representatives, while their presence in turn led twenty-two of Stresemann's right liberals to join them in the 'no' lobby. Several coalitions ran aground over difficult policy decisions concerning, for example, the distribution of the domestic burden of external obligations or military versus social expenditures, decisions that touched neuralgic points of basic principle. In 1927 thirty-eight members of the conservative German Nationalist People's Party or DNVP mutinied when their cabinet representatives approved renewal of the 1922 Law for the Protection of the Republic, because it included prolongation of their beloved Kaiser's exile.[79]

Similarly, in 1928 the rump SPD voted against naval appropriations that the Müller cabinet had reluctantly approved, forcing the Chancellor and other SPD cabinet members to veto their own policy. Ideological rigidity, and hence the non-viability of certain coalition permutations, was also partly dictated by the imperative of party cohesion. Since the political parties all contained centrifugal forces, they risked losing supporters to other parties if they made too many compromises. Apart from the toing and froing on the left, with the Independent socialists either joining the Communists in 1920 or returning to the Social Democratic Party fold two years later, the conservative and particularist Bavarian wing of the Catholic Centre Party became completely autonomous; while some left-wing Catholics broke away in 1920 to form a Christian-Social Reich Party. There were successive secessions from the conservative nationalist DNVP. In 1922, three antisemitic deputies left to join a splinter group of the Nazi Party.[80] Two sets of moderates left the Party too: Siegfried von Kardorff defected to the liberal DVP, and later Walter Lambach formed a People's Conservative Association. The disturbing influence of the media mogul Alfred Hugenberg upon conservative politics in the late 1920s led to an exodus of moderates, including the Party chairman Westarp.[81] A belated bid by the left liberals to become a broad-based 'bourgeois' party also proved catastrophic. In 1930 the DDP leader Erich Koch-Weser announced the formation of a new German State Party, which was closely linked to the right-wing Young German Order. Apart from the latter's explicit antisemitism, which was hardly likely to reassure Jewish voters, it was ominous that these revamped moderate liberals decided to drop the term 'democratic' from their new name. The liberal left of the Democratic Party promptly defected to the Social Democrats. Politics was not quite so dismal as this suggests, for there were countervailing tendencies for socially minded Catholic politicians to co-operate with both moderate socialists and conservatives, or at least to practise passive toleration.

Germany's politicians were perceived as a distinctive class, with group characteristics which transcended their ostensible party allegiances. In truth, parliamentary delegates worked very long hours, mostly in committees, and apparently had a craze for liquid yoghurt rather than cognac. However, the public perception was that they were *bons vivants*, returning to the Reichstag from Berlin's bars and restaurants only to wheel and deal or conduct intemperate exchanges involving Communists tooting the 'Internationale' on toy trumpets while conservative nationalists sang the national anthemn. In state parliaments, Communist deputies donned red gloves for the obligatory handshakes with their opponents after the swearing-in ceremonies, or, worse, brought along tin bowls so that they could literally wash off any ideological contamination. Of course, this sort of ostentatious silliness has its counterparts in some contemporary democracies. Contempt for politicians as a class was compounded by the widespread view that political parties divided Germany into artificial confessional, ideological or socio-economic camps, within the context of a republic that many Germans regarded as akin to a foreign occupying power. This made the attractions of an imagined pre-political yesteryear – of which the wartime 'civic truce' became the idealised template – all the greater, and increased the temptations of any political party that promised both consensual transcendence and national deliverance, especially when that party denied being a conventional political party at all. The Nazi 'movement' mastered that particular sleight of hand to perfection.

Much of the foregoing is unexceptional in many modern democracies, and hardly unique to the Weimar Republic. Many historians try to explain Weimar's endemic political instability by pointing to the legacy of Germany's imperial past, when relatively powerless political parties struck largely negative ideological postures, a habit they found hard to overcome when they were given real political responsibility. More cogently, one might argue that, once the smoke-and-mirrors illusions of the empire had vanished, Germans were left with nothing but the spectacle of competing special interests, which the Republic's threadbare symbolism poorly concealed. This view was current at the time, among such right-wing constitutional theorists as Carl Schmitt, who wished to reassert the primacy of the state over mere society. Other scholars focus on the demagogic populism of such extra-parliamentary nationalist associations as the Navy League or the Pan-German League of the Wilhelmine period as a harbinger of extreme fascist potential, although these seem fuddy-duddy affairs compared with the more plebeian, intemperate and violent National Socialists. Members of the Navy League did not physically attack socialists or Jews.

Some vital moral threshold was crossed during the war, transforming the conduct of German politics; this was certainly the case in other

European countries where political violence also became endemic. Support for terrorist violence did not magically abate before the august portals of Weimar's parliament. Apart from the Communists and Nazis, whose belief in violence as a form of purification was explicit, the conservative nationalists were accused by a leading Social Democrat of involvement in the murder of Foreign Minister Walter Rathenau, to which a senior Centre Party politician added: 'The enemy stands on the right, trickling his poison into the nation's wounds.'[82] Leaving aside the question of the extent of their involvement in terrorism, it is undeniable that many conservative nationalists were unreconciled to Weimar's democratic polity, with only a minority practising 'prudential republicanism', itself hardly a ringing endorsement of Germany's fledgling democracy. It was also worrying that in addition to the Nazi SA (Sturmabteilung) and the Communist Red Front Fighters League, the conservative nationalists and Social Democrats had paramilitary formations – respectively the Stahlhelm, named after the coalscuttle-shaped helmets worn in the First World War, and the Reich Banner Black-Red-Gold, all of whom were involved in violence against their opponents. In the mid-1920s some German states had to ban glass ashtrays from political meeting places and the carrying of walking sticks in public, for too many of these objects were being used as offensive weapons.[83]

The deficiencies and limitations of existing parties must partly explain the extraordinary success of the National Socialists, who from 1928 went from a vote of just over 2 per cent of the electorate, which would not entitle them to one seat in the present German parliament, to more than 37 per cent four years later.[84]

The Social Democrats in Weimar suffered from the perennial affliction of left-wing parties, namely the question whether to subordinate reality to theory, or to revise old dogmas so as to correspond with changing social circumstances. Those who set the Party's ideological sails were faced with the unenviable choice between sounding radical, to keep the once Independent leftists on board, and abandoning the rhetoric of 'class struggle' in order to broaden the Party's appeal to other constituencies, such as farmers, petit-bourgeois intellectuals and salaried white-collar employees. This latter, revisionist course enjoyed a brief triumph at the Party's 1921 Gorlitz congress, but then an influx from the left redogmatised the official line at Heidelberg in 1925 as the price for their continued support. Although this was not the last attempt to woo supporters beyond the working class, such voters were unlikely to be attracted to a party that routinely put proletarian interests first, and against all the evidence preached that farmers and small businessmen were doomed to disappear as the collateral casualties of the onward march of history.[85] In fact, in advanced societies it was the classical industrial proletariat that had been reduced to a minority by the end of the twentieth century. However comprehensible tactically it was to insist on this ideological purity, it put paid to any chances of the SPD's becoming a broadly based 'people's party'. In social policy and welfare reform the Social Democrats enjoyed greater unanimity, for it was easier for left and right to agree about ameliorating the lot of the workers. Their progressive social policies included compulsory wage bargaining, factory councils and, from 1927, an impressive system of unemployment benefits, measures supported equally by the Catholic Centre Party. But wage rises and the enhanced costs of these social policies antagonised and radicalised many employers, to the point where they looked to some authoritarian alternative to what they dubbed the 'trade union state'.

The costly purchase of social tranquillity was evident elsewhere too. Ambitious city bosses of various political hues built airports, bridges, exhibition halls, libraries, parks, planetaria, stadia, swimming pools, trams and utilities works, mostly with the aid of foreign credit.[86] While these measures improved the quality of life for many people, they bore a price-tag. International bankers regarded with dismay what New York's Federal Reserve Bank described as the politics of Tammany Hall. Respectable Wall Street houses such as J. P. Morgan stayed away, leaving investment in Germany to less risk-averse operators. So much money flowing along the municipal corridors of power brought instances of corruption with it. Moreover, some politicians who advocated class war for others preferred nice homes and expensive restaurants for themselves, and their hypocrisy angered moralists of all persuasions.[87]

The Social Democrats also irritated their bourgeois opponents. In state governments, where they often controlled cultural and educational portfolios, they tried to make education comprehensive and secular, and to subsidise various artistic and theatrical experiments thought provocative at the time, though they seem tame and tedious in retrospect. Interference with religious schools in Prussia had immediately brought sixty thousand Catholics out on to the streets. The Social Democrats' uncouth tone also sometimes gave offence in more genteel circles. Local studies, such as William Sheridan Allen's classic account of Northeim, a predominantly civil service town on a major railway junction, show that middle-class citizens resented having to deal with 'oilers' and 'track-walkers' in council chambers, who were often 'touchy, aggressive [and] demanding'. A strident socialist rhetoric of 'rights' confronted pompous talk of 'duty' in a dialogue of the deaf.[88]

Although the SPD seemed impressive on paper, with a million members and five million sympathetic trade-unionist supporters, secular social trends reinforced the Party's ideological self-isolation. Classical proletarians working in big smoke stack plants in the cities were a stagnating minority of the German working class: about 30 per cent of the labour force, though about 60 per cent of the Social Democrats' membership, most of them craftsmen.[89] Sixty per cent of Germany's workers did not belong to trades unions. And while unions had close connections at the top with the Social Democrats, this did not mean that their members automatically voted for that party. Between a third and a half of workers did not vote for either 'Marxist' (that is, Social Democrat or Communist) party.

Most workers, like most people, probably had complex, divided loyalties. It seems plausible, for example, that they might identify with the well-being of the business or industry that gave them work. Not all German bosses were union-bashers like the mine owner Emil Kirdorf, a Dickensian or Lawrentian parody of a hardfaced employer; firms such as the Zeiss optics firm in Jena promoted worker loyalty through socially responsible capitalism. Workers might also identify with their immediate colleagues and, sometimes, management, rather than with an abstract class, despite the efforts of Marxists to claim otherwise.[90]

The homogeneity of the working class was an ideological hope rather than an ascertainable socio-economic fact. Just as terms such as 'businessmen' or 'farmers' covered diverse lifestyles, so the term 'workers' covered significant differences in age, gender, skill, pay and working conditions. What united domestic servants, postmen, railwaymen, rural labourers and highly skilled craftsmen and foremen? Moreover, some of these 'workers' lived in milieux where socialism was culturally dominant, others where socialist organisation and tradition were weak. Some lived close by their workplace, while others like Hessian building craftsmen who laboured in Frankfurt am Main tramped miles to work from smaller towns. Some were Catholics, others Protestant, a further difference that militated against uniform political behaviour.

And since there was no homogeneous working class, one should not expect that workers acted or thought in a unified way. Moreover, many so-called petit-bourgeois intellectuals and salaried employees, who earned modest incomes in non-manual occupations at night, returned to working-class neighbourhoods and to parents, husbands and siblings who regarded themselves as workers. By contrast, many workers did not work in factories and did not regard themselves as proletarians, wore uniforms to work rather than overalls, or worked in workshops where the patron had a human face and was a good chap who wore overalls too, and was not too proud to get his hands dirty. Through enough enterprise and hard work, a skilled craftsman might become a boss too.

The SPD was well entrenched in the industrial heartlands of Germany, but in Rhineland-Westphalia and Upper Silesia, where confessional allegiances had greater importance than socio-economic solidarities, it faced stiff competition from the Catholic Centre Party. While the Centre Party, in whose counsels Catholic trades unionists such as Adam Stegerwald were increasingly important, co-operated with the Social Democrats on social policy issues, the co-operation was limited on questions affecting religion, and it alienated conservative Catholics in any case. Although the Social Democrats enjoyed some initial popularity in the countryside, this broke down once their insistence on cheap food for urban workers clashed with the farmers' desire for protective tariffs, which raised prices.

Nor did the SPD and the Communist Party noticeably appeal to women, especially when the patriarchal practice prevailed over sententious talk or pseudo-scientific sociological opium challenged other forms of faith. Female membership of the SPD never rose above 20 per cent, while that of the Communists was even lower.[91] According to contemporary opinion polls, most Social Democrats wanted women to work in the home, and had what were then conventional views about beating their own children. Since disaffected young people perennially concern middle-aged academics, scholars have routinely noted that the Social Democrats failed to excite young people. Whereas three-quarters of Communists were under forty, and one-third under thirty, just over 17 per cent of Social Democrats were in the latter age group (most were between forty and sixty). Impetuous youth was alienated from a party which believed in its comrades working their passage up its hierarchy of committees. The natural inclination of young people towards miners' choirs or discussions of Marx and Kautsky was also lessened by a Weimar environment with its dance halls, glittering shops and Hollywood movies which converted hypothetical class warriors into weekend hedonists and mass consumers.[92] A minority of workers were dedicated members of the Social Democrats sub-culture of bicycle clubs, choirs and cremation societies; but the majority were not. Along with younger members of the bourgeoisie, who also sometimes broke with their traditional cultural moorings, younger workers were participants in what has since become a universal mass culture. Weimar Germany may have been a 'class society', but this was showing appreciable signs of fraying.

The Social Democrats preferred the luxury of opposition rather than the difficulties or responsibilities of national government. From 1923 to 1928, the SPD avoided coalition governments, which would have entailed compromising its ideology of class struggle and losing support to the extreme left. The Party that had created the Republic was intimidated by a vociferous minority of dogmatic fundamentalists who claimed: 'This republic has the same economic fabric as did the old authoritarian state ... and this determines the fundamental position of the Social Democratic movement. It is oppositional.'[93] Partly because of the dogmatic intransigence of business interests within the right-wing liberal DVP, the ideological rigidity of the SPD condemned it to wander in the wilderness of opposition during years when it was both possible and vital to stabilise the Republic. The Party returned to share power only on the eve of the Great Depression, which was rather like offering to captain a ship during a hurricane.

Nor were the non-Marxist parties happy ships, as they steamed past each other in the night, and their non-Catholic voters jumped aboard a powerful vessel looming on the starboard side. Geography and religion diminished the nationwide scope of both the Catholic Centre and conservative nationalist parties, although there were Catholic diasporas within otherwise solidly Protestant areas. The conservative nationalists extended their electorate westwards, but 40 per cent of their support still came from east of the Elbe river, even though both proportional representation and the advent of populist rural parties rendered the tied-cottage vote far from automatic.

The Centre Party spanned a socially varied constituency, and its Reichstag delegation included a number of Protestants. It had to reconcile several interests, including a clergy increasingly taken with the non-political Catholic Action movement, left-leaning trade unionists, and a right wing represented by such arch anti-democratic figures as the future Chancellor Franz von Papen. Intimately connected to business, landowning and military elites, Papen enjoyed considerable influence, not least by acting as a frontman for the businessmen who owned *Germania*, the Centre Party's main newspaper.[94] The Centre Party increasingly lined up with the moderate right in national politics, but its composition made it a natural party of compromise, except when confessional issues were at stake, which explains why it was able to ally with the Social Democrats in the largest state of Prussia, while in Bavaria its offshoot worked closely with the conservative nationalists.

The Centre Party vote was strongest in small rural communities, where the Catholic Church and a traditional religious milieu made support for it predictable; but that support grew patchier in larger cities, where Catholics were exposed to pluralist influences, or to the Social Democrats' entrenched political culture. This was also true of rural areas that attracted tourists. Some country Catholics, such as those in the Black Forest, were hostile to the SPD but also deeply anti-clerical, a stance which left them without a political home.[95] In areas where Catholics were surrounded by Protestant majorities, support for the Centre Party tended to be stronger. The Centre Party's relations with its Catholic voters were complicated by the fact that the Catholic Church across Europe was beginning to turn its back on political parties in favour of a narrower focus on moral and spiritual issues through Catholic Action.[96] The Catholic response to the challenge of National Socialism was also ambivalent. The hierarchy was prepared to instruct the faithful on how to vote, and it was hostile to Nazi anti-clericalism and neo-paganism. Roman Catholic priests in Germany were enjoined to shun National Socialism, and the Nazis did not get from them the clerical endorsement they often enjoyed in Protestant areas. Only a handful of priests supported Nazism, mostly malcontents or naifs, like Abbot Schachleiter, who argued that 'if the Catholics do not co-operate with the NSDAP, there is a danger that National Socialism will become a purely Protestant movement'. The country priests who conjured up links between one's vote and the likelihood of damnation were probably more typical; a Bavarian priest who told his women parishioners that the Nazis were planning to execute all women over sixty was more eccentric.[97]

However, it is important not to depict German Catholicism in too rosy a light. Often coming from backward, ill-educated, rural sections of the population, Catholics had prejudices against Jews, whom they regarded as identical with anti-clerical liberals, atheistical Marxists, sharp businessmen and indeed Protestantism, for Jews and Protestants sometimes shared theological faculties. This prejudice was partly counterbalanced by the distinguished efforts of Catholic politicians such as Konstantin Fehrenbach and Heinrich Krone in the Association to Resist Antisemitism.[98] But, as Italy and Spain demonstrated, the Church's institutional authoritarianism gave it a latent affinity with political authoritarianism; in Germany this was shown in the rightwards turn of the Centre Party after 1928, when it was headed by the first cleric to lead the party, Monsignor Ludwig Kaas.[99]

Germans were predominantly Protestant, with a Lutheran majority and a Reformed minority, and Protestants had not required a confessional political party. They were victors, not victims. For the imputation of being internationally connected 'enemies of the Reich' had been one of the main stimuli towards the formation of a Catholic political party in the first place. However, Protestantism's rather feeble grip on the urban working class led some clerics to embrace such secular ideologies as antisemitism. Thus equipped, former court preacher Adolf Stoecker had vainly endeavoured to lure the workers of Berlin into his Christian Social Workers Party in the late 1870s.[100] The Protestant clergy formally subscribed to political neutrality, if only to avoid alienating parishioners whose politics were stronger than their faith. However, various factors inclined the clergy to the right, especially in rural areas. In eastern Germany, 60 per cent of the Protestant clergy were beneficiaries of the large landowners, whose families had built the churches. Seated below the salt, they tended to agree with the hand that fed them. Country clergy also shared in the pervasive mood of agrarian crisis, which they coupled with a moralising defence of the countryside against the urban asphalt 'cesspools'. They blessed the conservative nationalists and the Stahlhelm veterans association. They felt that Weimar favoured political Catholicism, regarded the Social Democrats with loathing and quaked at the thought of the abortions and free love practised in the Soviet Union. Some of them espoused an antisemitism that would have been crude enough for Martin Luther, sometimes using this line to attack Catholics too. They may have had reservations about 'German Christian' elements in the Nazi Party, but when their landlord patrons and their parishioners inclined that way, they followed, especially when the Nazis assured them that 'Religion is the foundation of ethics and morality.'[101]

Most political liberals in Germany were Protestants, but the liberal parties also attracted the support of three-quarters of Germany's Jews. Like the Social Democrats, who sometimes refrained from putting up Jewish candidates, the left-liberal Democratic Party were embarrassed by this allegiance, and claimed that Jewish candidates lost more votes than there were Jewish voters.[102] Most liberal Jews were Germans first, liberals second and Jews third. Many of them agreed with Willy Helpach, the Democratic Party's presidential candidate in the 1925 elections, that assimilation was guaranteed to frustrate antisemitic prejudice. Practice emulated prescription. By 1927, there was one mixed marriage of German Jews and German Christians for every two marriages of German Jews. Attendance at synagogues slumped, and liberal Jews ignored separate Jewish schools, believing they fostered a ghetto mentality prejudicial to a German–Jewish cultural symbiosis in which they took great pride. Liberal community leaders blocked funding for these schools. A partial revival of Jewish spirituality, for which there was some evidence, was not incompatible with this trend.[103]

Assimilated Jews were also wary of the influx of 'eastern Jews', that is Polish and Russian Jews, and they called for enhanced immigration controls and for the enlightenment of these immigrants in the mores of Germany. Predominantly middle class, and devotees of German high culture, German Jews had next to nothing in common with Jews from the backward 'East', who seemed like the incarnation of some earlier embarrassing self. They believed that people should cease to behave like peasants, or in this case to cease acting like the inhabitants of small-town shtetls, a view shared with the bourgeoisie elsewhere in an age without contemporary inhibitions about instructing people in decorous behaviour. German Jews may also have felt that their own carefully constructed self-image of refined restraint was somehow undermined by these unreconstructed immigrants. Attempts to deny eastern Jews communal voting rights and representation were also driven by fears that orthodoxy or Zionism would steal a march on Germany's established Jewish liberal oligarchy. When the Prussian authorities in Recklinghausen attempted to ensure voting rights for eastern Jews, Jewish liberals talked darkly of 'black hordes' and the 'sons of the steppes of Asia'.[104]

But the 'Jewish Question' was not the most animated issue of the day, least of all in liberal circles, Gentile or Jewish, which had other preoccupations. Beyond bigots, who exist in all times and places, most

Germans did not spend their waking hours thinking about Jews, although the impression is inadvertently conveyed by a vast scholarly literature focused exclusively on relations between Germans and Jews. People had to be encouraged to think about Jews at all. Most Germans were probably much more exercised by issues of class and religion than by less than 1 per cent of their population. Sections of the working class clearly hated those above them; many of the lower-middle class feared sinking into the proletariat; and some, but not all, sections of big business were antipathetical towards organised labour. Of course, this does not exhaust the range of animosities in Weimar Germany, as elsewhere at the time, but it does suggest that a Judaeo-centric view of the period may be exaggerated. Religious issues also played a crucial role at certain times. An example of this was the failure of the Catholic Wilhelm Marx's bid for the Presidency in 1925, when sporadic Protestant anti-Catholicism and Social Democrat irre-ligion combined with an unhelpful Communist candidacy to deny Marx victory.[105]

Both liberal parties, the German Democratic Party (DDP) and the German People's Party (DVP), lacked confessional bonds or regional roots, and their social basis was as fragmented as the middle classes they mainly represented. Some liberals on the left regarded themselves as a bourgeois bridge to the Social Democrats, others on the right combined nationalism with assertive free enterprise. Various attempts to merge the two parties were compared to the union of two brothers who had both failed to find brides, in an era which did not know of same-sex marriages. Both parties underwent bouts of severe internal tensions, among the right-wing liberals between industrialists and white-collar supporters, among the left-liberals between businessmen on the one hand and intellectuals and pacifists on the other. The strata they sought to mobilise, ranging from civil servants and industrialists to peasants, lacked apparent cohesion, while the interest groups upon which they depended were often mutually antagonistic. Farmers who had to sell a proportion of their harvest to the state did not warm to the 'asphalt Democrats' who were partly responsible for initiating this policy. Civil service supporters of the German People's Party did not view kindly leaders who thought the economy could dispense with surplus pen-pushers. While neither party developed nationwide party machines, the individualist character of liberal voters – whether academics, professionals, peasants or shopkeepers – did not mean that politics was always uppermost in their thoughts. Both parties created youth organisations, but these lost members as the 1920s progressed.[106]

The conservative right merits close attention, for had it been a more effective vehicle for nationalist opinion it might not have been so brutally outflanked by an extremist competitor: wherever conservatism is confident and strong, extremist fringes generally do not flourish. Since one in three Nazi voters were defectors from the conservative camp, it is important to comprehend it. The German National People's Party or DNVP was an unstable coalition of three pre-war parties, with an admixture from the *völkisch* fringe that sought to make it monomaniacally antisemitic. It encompassed reactionary elitists, some still wedded to a narrow Prussianism unadulterated by union with the rest of Germany; elitists masquerading as populists and revolutionaries; and a Christian Social wing, closely tied to conservative trade unions, which was influenced by Disraelian 'Tory democracy'. Some conservatives wished to collaborate in government to protect landed, industrial and union interests; others rejected any involvement with the detested Weimar 'system'.

Conservative nationalists were also divided along generational lines as well as by style and radicality of temperament. Older reactionaries were misty-eyed for the old empire; others, including younger intellectuals, were rather desperately excited by the possibilities that the war and revolution had brought about. Some of these bright young chaps, such as Edgar Julius Jung, combined intelligence with murderousness: Jung was one of the main movers in the assassination of the Rhenish separatist Josef Heinz. He himself was subsequently murdered by the Nazis. Other young conservative nationalists were less contemptuous of the common folk than Jung, seeing the disciplined, patriotic working classes of 1914 and the soldier–machines of the trenches as the instruments of the future. Renationalised, they thought, the modern mass might have its limited uses. It might be helpful to sample what passed for quality thought in these circles, although much of it seems banal and pretentious, even when it was not bonkers.[107]

Arthur Moeller van den Bruck was one of the most influential 'young' conservatives of Weimar, although by the 1920s he was well into middle age. Having left pre-war Germany to avoid military service, this grammar-school drop-out had drifted around Europe on a sizeable private income, idealising Germany the more the further away he was from it. He returned home during the war, a nervous illness preventing his service in the army. In his prolific writings, Moeller argued that the world consisted of young and old nations, a notion of stunning banality, and that the young German nation had been defeated by old Britain and France in 1918 because the latter had co-opted a gullible, young United States on to their side. Germany's destiny now lay with the other young power to the east, or, rather, Germany should occupy a halfway house between Western liberal individualism and Slavic collectivism.

Moeller was the leading light of the Juni-Klub, a forum for mainly right-wing people (the name deriving from the month of the ratification of the Treaty of Versailles). Occasionally figures from the far left flirted with these people, notably Karl Radek of the Comintern, when the Communists were bent on their 'Schlageter line'. Moeller ran an influential journal called *Conscience* and a seminar series, which Hitler addressed like a beer-hall audience in 1922. In that year, Moeller published his most influential book. He originally wished to call it 'The Third Party', but since this smacked of the very politics he sought to transcend, he opted for the more mystical-sounding *The Third Reich*, with its echo of the thousand-year empire before the Last Judgement described by the medieval mystic Joachim of Fiore. Moeller rejected old-fashioned conservatism and excoriated liberalism: 'every man who no longer feels part of a community is somehow a liberal man'. He believed in a conservative revolution that would reconcile the classes and restore authority. He offered the vision of a nationalist socialism, under an authoritarian leader, which would lead Germany into a new age where all its contradictions would be reconciled for ever more. This future end-state was the Third Reich. Although Moeller had a nervous breakdown, committing suicide in 1924, and was subsequently disowned by the Nazis, a concept had been born.[108]

One of the reasons why the Nazis were not interested in Moeller was that he was not an antisemite. Other conservatives were less reliable than him on this issue. Although the incorporation of antisemitism into the pre-war conservative Tivoli programme had not halted the decline of the conservative vote, post-war conservative nationalists duly ventured down this road. Assistance came from the German National Defensive and Combat League, which infiltrated local conservative party branches to force them formally to adopt antisemitism in the Party's programme. From 1920 the Party programme included the clause: 'Therefore we fight against every subversive, unGerman spirit, whether it emanates from Jewish or other circles. We are expressly opposed to the ever more ominous dominance of Jewry in government and public life since the Revolution. The flow of foreign races over our borders must cease.' Like the liberals and the SPD, the conservative nationalists avoided having Jewish candidates, and welcomed the votes that an antisemitic candidate brought in the big cities, but there were limits beyond which the Party refused to stray. It drew a line at prohibiting Jews from belonging to the Party, which led to the exodus of the *völkisch* right.[109]

Conservatives already not zealous enough on the 'Jewish Question' suffered another handicap from the Nazi point of view. However rhetorically populist, and despite their significant working-class following, they never overcame the image of being a party that only admitted ordinary folk by the servants' door, and this impression was not dispelled when they held their meetings in the best hotels in town. (The Nazis too were not averse to Munich's splendid hotel, the Vier Jahreszeiten.)[110] A few young conservative admirers of soldier–workers could not counteract these tendencies, and, besides, men like Jung or Moeller were intellectual elitists, bright sparks flitting around the most exclusive gentlemen's clubs in Berlin. Even when they spoke to a sympathetic interest group, such as the civil service, they managed to talk to 'the intellectual and cultural aristocracy' in its upper echelons, excluding the mass of humdrum pen-pushers, of railway and public-utility workers.[111] This impression became indelible in late 1926, when the DNVP took the lead in opposing Communist and Social Democratic moves to expropriate the holdings of Germany's former royalty. Ruined middle-class people were not overly impressed by the DNVP party line: 'the Hohenzollern once possessed assets of 88.5 million marks in mortgages, cash and securities. But don't you know that, just like you, they lost their assets in the inflation? Only one million in cash remains. Is that too much for a big family of forty-nine?' Clearly, many thought it was.[112] By the early 1930s conservatism seemed to consist of little more than elitist conspiracies to disfranchise the masses and emasculate the Reichstag, neither likely to be great vote-winners.

It was this air of hypocrisy, privilege and snobbish ineffectuality that enabled Hitler to outflank not only the 'new' and 'old' right, but rival *völkisch* organisations such as the Pan-Germans that otherwise espoused an ideology similar to his, by depicting their leaders as well-meaning academic cranks. As he wrote in January 1922,

The racialists were not capable of drawing the practical conclusions from correct theoretical judgements, especially in the Jewish question.

In this way the German racialist movement developed a pattern similar to that of the 1880s and 1890s. As in those days, its leadership gradually fell into the hands of highly honourable but fantastically naive men of learning, professors, district councillors, schoolmasters, and lawyers – in short a bourgeois, idealistic and refined class. It lacked the warm breath of the nation's youthful vigour.

Just as the two liberal parties' rhetoric did not keep their voters from leaving in droves to join parties more responsive to their mundane problems, so conservative-nationalist monarchist, racist and revanchist rhetoric did not stem the outflow of supporters leaving for a party that spoke more closely to their interests in tones they could easily comprehend.[113] Indeed, since some conservative leaders were plotting to find ways of excluding the masses once again from politics, the Nazis could temporarily pose as the defenders of democratic rights won since 1918, if only better to abolish them entirely.

The electoral profile of the National Socialist Party has been described as an integrative people's party with an accentuated middle-class character, or, less pretentiously, as having the profile of a man with a pot belly. Leaving aside for the moment the sizeable working-class support for the Nazis, let us take a closer look at this *Mittelstand*, a word which does not translate as 'middle class'. American historians such as Thomas Childers and Larry Eugene Jones have expertly charted the collapse of support for the 'bourgeois' parties in the aftermath of Weimar's inflation and currency stabilisation. The party rhetoric blew past an electorate whose concerns were both material and moral: what use was Stresemann's insistence on linking foreign reconciliation and domestic economic recovery when he refused to protect wine growers in his own Hesse-Nassau constituency?

Millions of prudent people had been ruined by the hyperinflation; others were affected by austerities during the ensuing currency stabilisation (although there were major anomalies within broad patterns of winners and losers). These shockwaves echoed beneath the surface of the Republic even during its ostensibly most stable period between 1924 and 1928. Civil servants and white-collar workers were dismissed in record numbers because of government cuts and because new office technology eradicated many clerical jobs. Perhaps as many as 750,000 government and state employees were laid off between 1923 and 1924, a massive blow to people who thought they belonged to a caste with life tenure. One hundred and fifty thousand jobs vanished in banking, then the most secure form of white-collar employment. And there was more to come.[114]

Apart from losing the symbolic rewards that the empire had bestowed upon them – important in a society where people listed occupation and titles in the telephone directory – civil servants in Germany were no longer paid quarterly in advance, and joined other employees receiving a monthly pay cheque. The earnings gap between civil servants and workers, which had been huge under the empire, significantly closed. Rumours of reforms designed to restrict permanent tenure to the administrative-grade elite opened up internal rifts between the core of professional civil servants and other state employees, and heightened resentments towards outsiders with political appointments. Inflation promoted the spread of multi-purpose department stores providing jobs for a small army of clerical and sales staff (which partly explains the relative coolness of commercial employees towards National Socialism), but these stores also undermined small uncompetitive service-sector businesses. Inflation and austerity measures also diminished private and co-operative sources of credit, so that artisans and small traders had to turn to the industrial capital market, despite falling consumer demand and rising taxes. There were more bankruptcies, the middle-class analogue of unemployment, in 1924 than in the previous five years together.[115]

Rural Germany had long been anxious about a long-term flight from the land and the competition of cheaper foreign foodstuffs, and the anxiety had already occasioned romantic and resentful rhetoric even before the war. During the war the government introduced ineffective controls which heightened tensions between town and country dwellers. Farmers began to emulate Social Democratic workers by forming union-like associations. The Versailles treaty then entailed a loss of more than 14 per cent of Germany's agricultural acreage. Reforms initiated by Germany's post-war governments defeudalised relations between agricultural labourers and their masters in favour of contractual arrangements, and the Weimar constitution required landowners to employ the land in the collective interest, if necessary creating plots for landless peasants.[116] Inflation enabled German farmers to liquidate thirteen billion Reichsmarks of debt, but they were retroactively penalised by exceptional levies and taxes on landed property, which, they thought, were being used to subsidise the unemployed and a burgeoning army of bureaucrats. Nature also handed them a raw deal. There were floods, hail and outbreaks of foot-and-mouth disease, even a plague of mice, while a return of phylloxera decimated the hybridised American vines that had been planted after the first outbreak of the disease. All of this meant that farmers were soon back in debt, either to pay their ten separate taxes (not including employee insurance) or to purchase fertiliser, machines, seed and stock. Because of the collapse of cheap long-range credit, they had to resort to expensive short-term loans. Chronic rural indebtedness upset inheritance customs, and old farmers clung on to their farms like grim death, while younger sons no longer got cash settlements to speed them from the family nest. Since job opportunities in rural towns were limited, these young men tended to be available for trouble.[117]

Some farmers were more blighted than others. To take the most elementary difference, there were vast disparities between the three million farms of under five acres, and the three thousand estates of more than five hundred acres. And size translated into political influence. Large cereal-producing estates were protected by high grain tariffs and, in the Prussian east, by a politically driven package of emergency subsidies with an obvious geo-political agenda. By contrast, small dairy and meat farmers, who had no direct channels to the estate-owning President Hindenburg, were exposed to cheap imports from Denmark, Holland, France and Poland. Wine growers were adversely affected by trade agreements with France and Spain that flooded the country with cheap alcohol. In 1924 and 1925 there were demonstrations by farmers in Pomerania, Saxony and Schleswig-Holstein, while in the Mosel fifteen hundred wine growers assembled in Bernkastel and, accompanied by the shades of peasant protests past, marched under a black flag to sack the customs and tax offices.[118]

Property owners, pensioners and modest rentiers were also hit by the currency stabilisation. Householders who had eradicated their mortgages during the inflation found themselves subjected to controls on rents. Individuals, including the elderly, whose hard-earned money went into bonds, gilt-edged securities or savings accounts saw them evaporate. Distressed gentlefolk were at the mercy of insensitive welfare bureaucracies, which appeared to be obsessed with the problems of young people. The elderly were well on the way to becoming a burden on younger people.[119] Creditors seeking a revaluation of debts in gold rather than in devalued paper money were appalled when the government bypassed parliament and used the Third Emergency Tax Decree of 24 February 1924 to revalue paper debts at 15 per cent of their gold-mark value, exempting government debt from the process *sine die*. The conservative nationalists tried to exploit the discontent by calling for a 25 per cent revaluation, but this was a transparent betrayal of the original demands for 100 per cent by a party forced by big business interests to support revaluation legislation.

Many middle-class victims of inflation and stabilisation were angry enough to threaten to go Communist, but they actually migrated to interest parties representing their small voices amid the cacophony of big business and big labour.[120] The absurdly rhetorical threat of turning Communist was worrying, though, since it betokened acute middle-class desperation. Many of these middle-class voters began to oscillate between liberal, conservative and special-interest parties before disillusionment took them to a much more radical alternative.[121] Local and special-interest parties were nothing new on the German political scene. Some twenty-nine parties had had candidates for the National Assembly in 1919, which together won some 2 per cent of the vote. By 1924 they took 8 per cent, passing the left liberals and almost catching up with Stresemann's DVP. Angry members of the middle classes found new political homes in the mid-1920s, including at the national level the Economics Party of the Middle Class (WP); the Reich Party for People's Right and Revaluation (VRP), better known as the People's Justice Party; the German Peasants' Party (DB), and the Christian National Peasants' and Farmers' Party (CNBLP). There were various regional parties, such as the Hanoverian Guelphs, but loyalty to a dynasty was less in evidence than hatred of Prussia, and especially 'Red' Berlin.[122] In a state election in Saxony in 1926, two of these smaller parties did strikingly well, while the liberals and conservatives lost about 40 per cent of their vote. In national elections in May 1928, the splinter parties scored a total of 14 per cent, exceeding the combined strength of the liberals and equalling the conservatives. The increase since the early 1920s could not be more glaring. Before the onset of the Depression, about a third of middle-class voters had abandoned the mainstream middle-class parties, for these no longer used the right rhetoric on the issues that mattered to them.[123]

These splinter parties reflected the militancy of the German middle classes. They were disillusioned with the mainstream 'bourgeois' parties, which seemed too preoccupied with big business's struggle with organised labour, a clash of titans in which farmers and small businessmen were of negligible importance. As the Economics Party had it: 'Big business and Marxism are both striving for the annihilation of the

Mittelstand.'[124] Self-interest wore the mantles of morality and patriotism, for these people genuinely regarded themselves as uniquely virtuous – decent, honest, loyal, prudent, responsible, and so forth – and as the 'state-supporting' bedrock of society. They considered themselves an estate rather than a class. Pensioners and war veterans could also make tears flow. They wanted 'justice'; a drastic curtailment of government, taxes and welfare; a strong state; and an occupational or corporatist alternative to parliament. Above all else, they wanted to be insulated against changes which were often beyond the powers of government.

Farmers were the most militant segment of this stratum, and they sometimes resorted to direct action, including murder and throwing bombs, against the people they considered foes. Farmers regarded themselves as vital to the economy and society, a view that prevailing government trade policies appeared to disregard in the interests of feeding urban workers cheaply. They wanted the state to protect a romanticised version of rural life, yet their own practice was thoroughly modern: land changed hands like any other commodity; farmers borrowed money and employed labour and labour-saving machinery. But they also sought to preserve a traditional way of life that these practices often undermined. They wanted the benefits of capitalism, with the state insulating them from its consequences and risks. This was as unacceptable to most people then as it is now.[125]

Grassroots rural militancy was partly an expression of people habituated to co-operation – whether through extended families or rural co-operatives – who had no framework to advance their goals collectively. The National Rural League was ineffectual and lacked the political clout of the defunct pre-war Agrarian League, at least as far as small pig farmers rather than large cereal producers were concerned. Debt and taxes as well as natural disasters massively radicalised the farming community. Although the debt problem affected large farmers most, it soon spread to more modest landholders. Compulsory auctions and foreclosures became commonplace: there were more than ten thousand auctions of farms smaller than fifty acres in 1931–2 alone.[126] These auctions became targets for incensed farmers, as were the government customs and tax offices that housed proof of their liabilities (just as insurgent medieval peasants had once made bonfires of manorial records). Militancy spread to Bavaria, the Rhineland, Hesse, Pomerania, Schleswig-Holstein and Württemberg. In early 1928, thirty thousand farmers demonstrated in Oldenburg; forty thousand in

Stuttgart; one hundred and forty thousand in the towns of Schleswig-Holstein.

Each regional epicentre of rural protest was subtly different. In Schleswig-Holstein, direct action took semi-terrorist form, with a bombing campaign against government agencies. A sanitised view of the farmers' actions was presented in Hans Fallada's novel *Bauern, Bonzen und Bomben*. Schleswig-Holstein was a frontier region, whose inhabitants thought they had been annexed by Prussia in 1866. Paramilitary and *völkisch* organisations, including Nazis, were thick on the ground there during the Weimar period. Since agrarian interest groups were relatively weak there, there was nothing to act as a buffer between the peasantry and malign political agitators.[127]

By contrast, agrarian interest groups steered peasant radicalism in Brandenburg, Pomerania and Thuringia, although eventually these groups became nazified. In southern and western Germany, priests as well as the Catholic Centre Party and its Bavarian equivalent led many rural protests, while simultaneously reminding the farmers that theirs was not the only distressed sector of society.[128] It was symptomatic of agrarian micro-politics that they were endlessly fissiparous. The Mosel wine-growers, for example, split between those cultivating high-quality native vintages and those growing hybridised American vines which yielded wine for the cheaper end of the market. Such conflicts often undermined the homogeneity of their own peasant associations.[129]

These are but some indications of the fractures within German society. These were partly structural determinants in an enormous country that straddled diverse worlds and that was riven by confessional differences. But much the same could be said about many other countries that were also divided along confessional lines and had large differences between metropolitan and peripheral regions. 'Red' Berlin had its analogues in 'Red' Madrid and 'Red' Vienna. Economic problems and political tensions were tearing the Weimar Republic apart, and the political parties were unable to transcend their respective milieux. People whose post-war experience was of chaos and dislocation understandably wanted predictability and security in their lives. Virtually every party, including the right-wing Social Democrats, conjured with the rhetoric of a 'national community', with some form of authoritarian collectivism as the ideal solution to Germany's divisions.

Yet one can overstate the significance of these divisions. It was noted earlier that the Weimar Republic suffered from a form of symbolic deficit. In one respect this proved to be untrue. In 1925

President Ebert died. He was one of the most decent figures of the period, and the first Social Democrat leader to exhibit qualities of statesmanship. In his stead, the reactionary and very elderly military figure Field Marshal Paul von Hindenburg was elected president, pushing the liberal Catholic Wilhelm Marx, behind whom the Social Democrat voters, if not all Social Democrat Party, had rallied, into second place. Although the Communist Ernst Thälmann won only 6.4 per cent, this denied Marx a majority. As a liberal newspaper headline put it: 'Hindenburg by the grace of Thälmann'. The right exhibited an unnatural coherence on this occasion. Victory celebrations were loud and sometimes violent, as members of the Stahlhelm took to beating up socialists and throwing rocks through SPD office windows. Popular in ways that the Social Democrat Ebert had not been, even within such constituencies as the dockers of Kiel, Hindenburg's birthday on 3 October became the occasion for yearly reminders of a 'real Germany' beneath the transient Weimar Republic.

Four points about the election of Hindenburg are worth stressing. First, there was a close correlation between the electorate which voted for Hindenburg in 1925 and those which supported the National Socialists in September 1930 and July 1932. Second, both the election and Hindenburg Day took on counter-symbolic importance, underlining the fact that the 'Reds' were no longer masters of the streets, but could be challenged and defeated, not least by the Stahlhelm, with its sizeable following of workers. Third, rightist activism had no consolidated political home, since the conservative nationalists and right liberals could not co-operate with each other, their leaders – Stresemann and Hindenburg – being personally antagonistic. And finally, although Hindenburg promised to uphold the constitution, his election meant a return to influence, often exercised through backstairs channels, of the armed forces and major landowners, for the new President was very much one of their own. Germany's anti-democratic elites were back in business.[130]

The Hindenburg election in 1925 presaged certain political possibilities. Yet only one party hit upon a formula that combined nationalism with a form of 'moral economic' socialism, based on 'justice', and with the vague promise to put 'common' over 'individual' interests. In other words, its appeal went far beyond the constituencies that voted for Hindenburg in 1925. Consciously emulating the rhetoric of war, this party spoke of duty and sacrifice rather than of individual or group rights, let alone class warfare or the redistribution of wealth.

Instead it talked of race. Paradoxically, it denied being a party at all. It claimed to be an unstoppable movement, a sort of surging human tide, whose leader spoke in apocalyptic and messianic terms. It promised to restore authority and order, yet its leaders used a radical rhetoric in which attacks on Marxists and Jews were accompanied by sneering at the ineffectual bourgeoisie. Its leader recognised, as early as 1923, that 'one cannot take away from the people the false idols of Marxism without giving them a better God'. This leader was Adolf Hitler; the novel phenomenon National Socialism.[131]

THE ODDITY'S ODYSSEY

Hitler's rake's progress from Braunau am Inn to the Bürgerbräukeller has been so frequently rehearsed that only the briefest outline need be given here. Born in 1889, little in Hitler's Austrian provincial family background gave much inkling of the world-historical monster he would become. Changes of name among families recently released from illiteracy, itinerancy bordering on vagrancy and the incidence of slightly too close relations between blood relatives were hardly confined to the Austrian countryside of the late nineteenth century. These things probably do not bear the weight sometimes put upon them. Much about Hitler's childhood and youth would evoke sympathy were anyone else involved. Following the death of his stern customs-officer father in 1903, Hitler, his mother, an aunt and younger sister, moved to Linz, where he lived a carefree and cosseted existence. Nothing much happened there, save for the thrice-weekly passage of the Orient Express bearing the wealthy to Constantinople or Paris, though the young Hitler took an interest in the Boer and Russo-Japanese Wars, always electing to play the part of an Afrikaner or Japanese combatant when these faraway conflicts were translated into children's games. After increasingly lengthy visits to Vienna, Linz began to seem constrained and provincial to a teenager with delusions of artistic greatness. In the autumn of 1907 Hitler moved to the imperial capital, only returning to Linz for a few months that winter to be with his dying mother. Thanks to the scholarship of Brigitte Hamann, we know much about Hitler's years in Vienna between 1907 and 1913, an account often strikingly at variance with that he gave later in *Mein Kampf*. What a kaleidoscope this city must have been, with huge discrepancies between rich and poor, about thirty thousand new migrants each year, the artistic experimentation of Gustav Klimt, Egon Schiele, Arthur Schnitzler and Gustav Mahler, and an aged Emperor Franz Joseph still going daily in his coach to and from the Schonbrunn Palace.

Hitler's aim in going to Vienna was to study at the Academy of

Fine Arts. After failing the entrance tests he remained in Vienna, where due to subventions from his family he subsisted as one of the idle poor. He developed an obsessive interest in the operas of Richard Wagner, visiting the opera house with all the train-spotting compulsiveness of a certain type of Briton at the annual promenade concerts in London's Albert Hall. This supplied an heroic fantasy world markedly different from the life Hitler was leading, which makes understanding his career in conventional political categories exceptionally difficult. There was a fantastical aspect to him which would distinguish him from common or garden authoritarian rulers merely bent upon keeping an iron grip on the status quo. Consuming rather than seeking to increase his meagre resources, Hitler gradually bankrupted himself, chiefly it seems on visits to the opera. He spiralled downwards through ever shabbier lodgings until, shortly before Christmas 1909, unable to pay even modest rent, he found himself alongside society's bottom feeders in a municipal flop-house. He possessed nothing other than the blue suit he wore, which had run to purple from over-exposure to the elements. These months may have soured his view of humanity as a whole, or at the very least led to the freezing-over of whatever human feelings he possessed. He began the slow ascent from this nadir when he moved into a well-appointed Men's Home, itself the product of the charitable largesse of such families as the Rothschilds. The habituées were down at heel rather than down and out. This establishment, in which Hitler lived for three years, provided a base for hawking his paintings and postcards, all copied from prints rather than executed in the open air. By all accounts, he had amiably exploitative relationships with a number of Jews who sold his pictures to their mainly Jewish clientele. Of course, this tells us little about when he became an antisemite.

A writing saloon in the Men's Home provided reading materials and a seminar for the many in-house autodidacts. At night Hitler read in his cubicle, rather than mixing with *hoi polloi* of soldiers, working men and Czech serving girls in Vienna's louche Prater district with its funfair and ferris wheel. He did not drink or smoke and was not the type to dance. Despite his ability to switch on a courtly charm, women frightened him as a potential source of venereal disease. Although he later claimed to have been a construction worker, his background and his lack of physical robustness make this unlikely. What he read is difficult to establish. Since newspapers and pamphlets frequently published the 'representative' thoughts of any number of writers and thinkers, it was easy to give the appearance of wide erudition, without having read much at all, in the same way that people who read newspaper supplements entitled 'one hundred great twentieth-century scientists' do not know very much about Einstein. As a self-conscious outsider, Hitler sympathised with authors whose fantasies had consigned them to the fringes of Vienna's academic and intellectual community. Like them, he regarded this ostracism as a sure indication of higher insight and originality. There were several learned lunatics to choose from, obsessed with Aryans, Jews and swastikas, or pseudo-scientific doctrines such as 'world ice teaching', whose details need not detain us. Many of these barmy thinkers dispensed with human scale, preferring grandiose visions of the cosmos, or a view of mankind which reached back to the prehistoric mists of time or into the mysteries of our biological makeup. Ironically, modern analogues of such books often involve fictions about Hitler and Nazism of the 'I Discovered Martin Bormann in the Woodshed' variety.

Hitler was also affected by many of the passionately argued causes and hatreds of that polyglot city in those times, where violence among students from different national backgrounds was commonplace and chairs or inkwells were hurled around in the fractious parliament. One of these hatred-provoking beliefs was that ethnic Germans were being swamped by the Slavic majority of the multi-national Austro-Hungarian empire; another was that assimilated Jews were too conspicuously predominant, while unassimilated eastern Jews, fleeing successive pogroms in the Tsarist empire, were part of the Slavic inundation. A sense of German beleaguerment was exploited by Pan-German nationalist politicians, who wanted the ethnic German Austrians to break out of what they regarded as the multinational 'zoo' of the Habsburg empire, to join up with their mighty Teutonic northern neighbour, leaving the South Slavs in the Balkans to kill each other. Very few Germans shared this first enthusiasm, not least because it would mean that German Protestants would be outnumbered by Roman Catholics.

The most voluble representative of this Pan-German tendency was Georg Ritter von Schönerer, a belligerent drunk and landed philanthropist whose increasing resort to violence against opponents eventually ensured that he ended up in prison. His star waned when his strident attacks on Roman Catholicism and advocacy of conversion to Protestantism to expedite Austria's merger with Germany began to irk the Catholic majority in the German-speaking regions of the Habsburg empire. However, much of Schönerer's hyper-teutomania – vetting of marriage partners to exclude Jews or Slavs; christening children with ostentatiously German names rather than those derived from the Bible; and adopting a calendar wherein a victory of the ancient Teutons over the Romans in 113 BC supplanted Christ's birth as the beginning of the modern era and January became 'Hartung' or April 'Ostermond' – clearly anticipated many later Nazi obsessions, as did Schönerer's pathological racial antisemitism. Among Schönerer's supporters, teutomania was explicitly held up as a surrogate religion.

Hitler was also mightily impressed by Karl Lueger, the Christian Social mayor of Vienna between 1897 and 1910. He was first elected mayor in 1895, but the Emperor Franz Joseph, sensing trouble, twice declined to accept the will of the voters. Lueger subscribed to many of the same hatreds as Schönerer, with the key difference that his party wished to maintain the Empire as a Roman Catholic German-dominated monarchy. Antisemitism was central to this platform, given its manifest appeal among the Austrian intermediate classes. Although Lueger liked to go about the city accompanied by incense-swinging clerics (even taking along the archbishop to consecrate a new gasworks), this air of piety was rapidly displaced by the sardonic vituperation of the gutter and streams of sweat whenever he set to work on an audience. The quondam lawyer to the little folk, for, like Schönerer, Lueger had a powerful vocation to do good, quickly shed his learning and became a ranting demagogue, railing against Czechs and Jews. When leading Social Democrats, some of whom were Jews, welcomed the failed liberal Revolution in Russia in 1905, Lueger's tirades against wealthy Jews began to be overlayered with anxieties about the Jew as menacing revolutionary. It seems likely that Hitler was influenced by these concerns and impressed by the mode of delivery, but it is doubtful whether they amounted to anything more than a series of impressions and prejudices rather than a developed ideological system.[132]

In 1913 Hitler, now possessed of a modest legacy, left Vienna for Munich, partly to avoid service in the Habsburg army. A year later the Austrian authorities caught up with him and he had to undergo an embarrassing magistrate's hearing, although military service proved academic since he was discharged as being physically unfit. This prolonged period of drift, combining heady idealism with purposelessness, not untypical of young central Europeans of his time, was resolved by the outbreak of the First World War. The twenty-five-year-old Hitler volunteered for the Bavarian Army, serving with some distinction as a dispatch runner on the Western Front. A personality already prone to transforming personal resentments into ideological categories was brutalised and coarsened by his experiences in the war, which included being temporarily blinded during an Allied poisoned-gas attack. The depths of the doss-house were overlain with the experience of mass death; there were no countervailing experiences of human decency. This alienated and intolerant young man now encountered a climate that entirely suited him.[133]

The climate of post-war Munich into which Hitler debouched upon demobilisation was suitably agitated, extreme and paranoid for him to thrive in. After he had been adopted on to an army political indoctrination course, his superiors were impressed by his as yet hardly honed oratorical skills, and decided to use him to monitor the fringes of Munich's political life. Specifically, he was assigned to keep tabs on the German Workers' Party, which had been founded in January 1919. Making short work of one of its professorial adherents, Hitler joined the Party, which consisted of a few likeminded souls gathered in a Munich pub. The Party's treasury, all of five or fifteen Marks, was kept in a cigar box. Although the Party issued a turgid programme in February 1920, the essence of its appeal was to claim that the conservative nationalists lacked a social conscience, while the left was utterly without patriotic zeal. This last proposition was false. In that month, the Party changed its name to National Socialist German Workers' Party (or NSDAP). Its membership increased from about two hundred to two thousand by the end of 1920, and Party branches began to proliferate outside Munich and even Bavaria. It acquired a newspaper, the *Völkischer Beobachter*, which initially appeared twice a week. 'Comrade Hitler', as he was styled within the Party, took advantage of his winning powers as an orator to force through abandonment of a committee-style leadership in favour of himself as authoritarian 'chairman'. In mid-1921, the Party announced the formation of its own strong-arm squad, the 'Storm Detachments', or SA, which welcomed into its ranks former members of the banned Free Corps. By the eve of the November 1923 Munich putsch, the Nazi Party had developed a reputation for its rough ways with opponents and the spectacular intensity of its public meetings. At that point its membership stood at about fifty-five thousand.[134]

Hitler and the other leaders of the putsch stood trial for high treason in February 1924. Hitler exploited the hearings to present himself as an ultra-patriotic martyr let down by lesser figures, such as Kahr and Lossow, who testified as witnesses for the prosecution. He skilfully incriminated these witnesses in his own machinations, and directed his exculpatory rhetoric to the 'Eternal Court of History'. Put into a quandary by the highly dubious activities of the former government of Bavaria, the court decided to acquit Ludendorff and to imprison Hitler for five years. Conditions were hardly onerous within the Landsberg prison, as Hitler effectively held court there. To abate his constant and voluble expression of opinions, his companions asked him to write a book. Unfortunately for them, he dictated the first part of *Mein Kampf*, his mythopoeia cum political philosophy, although that term affords this poisonous and turgid concoction a coherence it lacks. He constructed a new narrative of his political 'awakening', pushing back to his time in pre-war Vienna stances which he adopted only when he returned to Munich after the war. It is unclear what Hitler read by way of sources. He had dabbled in the literatures of antisemitism, eugenics and geo-politics, although it is unknown whether this was directly or in the form of degenerated copies. Despite considerable editorial input, the book was execrably written and punctuated with mad outbursts. A discussion of the passing youth fashions led on to the following:

> The girl should get to know her beau. If physical beauty were today not forced entirely into the background by our foppish fashions, the seduction of hundreds of thousands of girls by bow-legged, repulsive Jewish bastards would not be possible.[135]

The reader is inside the head of a hardcore antisemite, where the ideological mishmash he cobbled together became a substitute for the personal alienations of a man whom few would have described as clinically insane. Autodidactic indiscipline and experience, real or imagined, created a totally inflexible worldview, in which new facts were slotted into a rigid framework. Hitler claimed that his worldview was the result of blinding revelations, of 'real' or 'higher' truths, all increasingly impervious to counter-argument or reason. As Hannah Arendt remarked: 'Ideological thinking becomes emancipated from the reality that we perceive with our five senses, and insists on a "truer" reality concealed behind all perceptible things, dominating them from this place of concealment and requiring a sixth sense that enables us to become aware of it.'[136]

In Hitler's case, notions of biological determinism fused with an apocalyptic, conspiratorial and paranoid view of the world. He combined being the worst sort of reductionist scientific bore, forever citing cats and rats, with being a saloon-bar conspiracy theorist, forever banging on about Jews. Normally such people go quietly crazy amid genteel delapidation, like hippies gone to seed in seaside towns. Unfortunately for humanity as a whole, this one did not. According to Hitler, there were higher and lower races, whose interbreeding allegedly engendered cultural, political and racial decline, a notion derived from such reactionary thinkers as Joseph Count de Gobineau in the previous century. This process, whose accompaniment was humanitarian sentimentality towards the eugenically unfit, was being promoted by the Jews, who Hitler believed were engaged in conspiracy to achieve global domination. Deranged tracts emanating from the pre-revolutionary Russian Tsarist right appeared to show the Jews plotting in dark rooms somewhere near the Eiffel Tower. Since such an ideology could accommodate the most convoluted somersaults, Marxism was construed as the political instrument of what he regarded as an ethnically specific Jewish will to power. According to Hitler, this lay at the heart of the Bolshevik Revolution, where the 'blood Jew' had 'killed or starved about thirty million people with positively fanatical savagery, in part amid inhuman tortures, in order to give a gang of Jewish journalists and stock exchange bandits domination over a great people', a description hard to reconcile with the reality of life under Lenin.[137] For, since at least 1920, Hitler's antisemitic obsessions had coalesced with virulent anti-Marxism to produce the image of the Jewish Bolshevik, a nightmare figure who sat alongside other hostile renditions of 'the Jew', as malingerer, rapacious capitalist or seducer of fair maidens, in Hitler's demonology.

Hitler's refashioned and selective account of his own life consisted of a series of dramatic awakenings like Paul on the road to Damascus:

> Vienna appeared to me in a different light than before. Wherever I went, I began to see Jews, and the more I saw, the more sharply they became distinguished in my eyes from the rest of humanity. . . . In a short time I was made more thoughtful than ever by my slowly rising insight into the type of activity carried on by the Jews in certain fields. Was there any form of filth or profligacy, particularly in cultural life, without at least one Jew involved in it? If you cut even cautiously into such an abscess, you found, like a maggot in a rotting body, often dazzled by the sudden light – a little Jew.

In reality, Hitler's relations with Jewish acquaintances and associates in pre-war Vienna seem to have been, on his part, quite unremarkable, although that tells us rather less than the weight it is sometimes being asked to bear. But there were also passages where his preoccupation with disease and death – with maggots, vermin and vampires – assumed apocalyptic proportions, with a corresponding increase in his own messianic delusions. The following passage, with its pseudo-scholarly mannerisms – 'thus', 'the application of such a law', 'the premise' – and its 'greatest of all recognisable organisms' warrants longer citation:

> The Jewish doctrine of Marxism rejects the aristocratic principle of Nature and replaces the eternal privilege of power and strength by the mass of numbers and their dead weight. Thus it denies the value of personality in man, contests the significance of nationality and race, and thereby withdraws from humanity the premise of its existence and its culture. As a foundation of the universe, this doctrine would bring about the end of any order intellectually conceivable to man. And as, in this greatest of all recognisable organisms, the result of an application of such a law could only be chaos, on earth it could only be destruction for the inhabitants of this planet.
>
> If, with the help of his Marxist creed, the Jew is victorious over the other peoples of the world, his crown will be the funeral wreath of humanity and this planet will, as it did thousands of years ago, move through the ether devoid of men. Eternal nature inexorably avenges the infringement of her commands. Hence today I believe that I am acting in accordance with the will of the Almighty Creator: by defending myself against the Jew, I am fighting for the work of the Lord.[138]

Hitler was obsessed with an eternal struggle between two hostile forces, the 'Aryan' and the 'Jew', the stakes of which were the survival of mankind and the planet. The Aryan was poorly described as a wandering creative force whose destiny was to dominate lesser humans. He was a sort of 'God-man'. There were not many of them, but their strength lay in collective power and preservation of racial purity. For the Aryan was not a lonely Nietzschean 'superman', overcoming his own nature on the side of a mountain, but a collective being: 'The Aryan is not greatest in his mental qualities as such, but in the extent of his willingness to put all of his abilities in the service of the community. In him the instinct of self-preservation has reached the noblest form, since he willingly subordinates his own ego to the life of the community and, if the hour demands, even sacrifices it.' In other words, a bombastic rendition of Nietzscheanism combined with crude biological determinism and the solidarity of the wartime front.[139]

In so far as this Aryan hero could be envisaged, Hitler, an avid fan of Karl May's westerns, did so in terms of cowboys and Indians. Fired by May's stories of hunters and trappers in the Wild West, he compared North America, whose 'population consists in by far the largest part of Germanic elements who mixed but little with the lower coloured peoples', with Latin America, 'where the predominantly Latin immigrants often mixed with the aborigines on a large scale'.[140] It was a story of racial perdition, with the fall involving 'race suicide' through breeding with lesser races: 'the fall of man in paradise has always been followed by his expulsion'. The source of subversion was an eternal opponent who constantly metamorphosed: a Jewish Satan in contrast to the Aryan Archangel. Here, the hazy description of the heroic Aryan was counterposed with a thickly described evil. Hitler regarded 'the Jew' as an awesome opponent, for only a being equal in power to a weapon of mass destruction could conceivably result in a deserted planet progressing 'through the ether'. This ascription of power to the enemy distinguished antisemitism from other forms of racism, for power is rarely ascribed to the hated object in mere bigotry and prejudice.

Hitler's antisemitism was both genuine and instrumental, in the sense that a secondary cast of villains, such as Social Democrats and the effete bourgeoisie, were seen as dupes, puppets and tools of the Jewish foe. The fact that he understood the manipulative worth of his beliefs does not detract from their intense and unwavering sincerity. Hitler's beliefs were more than a demagogic pose or a trick; their clarity was a substitute for the turmoil within, as well as a way of making sense of the apparent chaos of the world without.

The faintest origins of antisemitism are to be sought in the complex relations of Christians and Jews, although some commentators detect a legacy of immutable hatred from classical antiquity onwards, a view that many would reject out of hand as crassly unnuanced.[141] Christian anti-Judaism doubtless spawned ugly folkloric beliefs about Jews, as both pariahs and agents of diabolic forces. Such beliefs endured, beneath the increasingly rational, secular surface, as archetypes lurking in the subconscious. As this century has shown, it took little to reactivate these dormant sentiments, even in circumstances, such as post-Holocaust eastern Europe, where there are hardly any Jews at all.[142]

Prejudices towards Jews did not divide neatly along lines of political affiliation.[143] As we have seen, liberalism harboured an antipathy to all forms of religious recalcitrance in the face of 'progress', and espoused the view that emancipation of the Jews was a reward by the state which was conditional upon their assimilation. Assimilation was potentially insatiable. Where was it supposed to cease? With dress, hairstyles, language? Dietary laws and holy days? Did they have to abandon their faith or adopt a range of occupations conforming with those of the dominant society?[144] Marxist socialism also had dark nooks and crannies where Jews were regarded as money-mad capitalists or as an 'obsolete' people who refused to join the onward march of secular progress towards a moneyless society.[145] Anarchists also suffered from this contagion, with the Russian Mikhail Bakunin raving: 'Now the whole Jewish world – which constitutes one race of leeches, one single devouring parasite, intimately bound together not only across national boundaries, but also across all divergence of political opinion – now this Jewish world today stands in large part at the disposal of Marx on the one hand and of Rothschild on the other.'[146] Conservatives resented Jews as agents of democratic modernisation, as beneficiaries of unbridled capitalism, and as champions of liberalism and Marxism. Obviously, since none of these ideologies was peculiarly German, such views were common across Europe and beyond, sometimes being more virulent in other countries than they were in Germany. Moreover, these ideas were held everywhere in concentric circles of virulence, ranging outwards from an obsessive core – of whom Hitler was the leading example – to those for whom expressions of prejudice towards Jews were more casual, rather than being part of an obsessive ideological system. There were correspondingly different solutions to what was perceived as the 'Jewish problem', there being a considerable gap between wanting Jews to become more English, French or German and regarding them as parasites who should be exterminated.[147]

Since Hitler's obsessions concerned an abstraction dubbed 'the Jew', rather than actual Jews who were conservative, liberal, socialist, Zionist or unpolitical; observant, non-observant, Christian, agnostic or atheist; rich, middling or poor; German or foreign, it is idle to seek a cause.[148] The contours of Germany's Jewish community have been well outlined; it is a story of group excellence, with few signs of mediocrity, among people whom prejudice may have sometimes encouraged to excel. A minority of less than 1 per cent of the German population, the Jewish population of Germany was largely urbanised.[149] In 1905, some 95 per cent of German towns and villages had no Jewish inhabitants at all, although that has never been an impediment to antisemitism. Twenty per cent of German Jews lived in Berlin and Frankfurt am Main. Some Jews enjoyed distinguished political careers; it is hard to construe German Jewish history as solely one of exclusion. By 1871 the majority were middle class, denizens of academia and the arts, banking and commerce, medicine, science, journalism and the professions, although by no means all Jews were comfortably off or middle class. The Jewish merchant-banking princes were already vaguely anachronistic and were being superseded by gentile corporate conglomerates. Professions such as law or medicine spanned enormous divides of prestige and wealth, while academia was often a passport to genteel poverty and journalism a notoriously rackety occupation for all but the most successful. And then below the not inconsiderable Jewish petit bourgeoisie were the *Luftmenschen* who appeared to live on fresh air. But the perceived group identity may explain much of the resentment others apparently harboured towards them. In a 1932 essay on antisemites, Carl von Ossietzky made the telling point that in other countries 'competition among people of different origins is considered stimulating, and certainly not troublesome. In the English press and letters, for instance, the flexible Celtic mind is dominant. And we were taught in school to admire the wisdom of the great Elector because he admitted French refugees into Prussia.'[150] But this comparative and historical perspective on the dynamism of newcomers, which was far from correct in the English case, was depressingly absent in Germany. Of course, even prejudice occasionally had its silver lining, for anyone dedicated, persistent and talented enough to overcome it. One minor irony of an atmosphere often marred by prejudice towards Jews was that a number of Jewish scientists, excluded from university teaching careers, were able to devote themselves to pure research, becoming highly regarded and well-paid members of the prestige research institutes which were established by leading industrialists under the patronage of the antisemitic Kaiser Wilhelm II. This is not a simple story.[151]

Although many Jews were ultra-patriotic and permeated with German *Bildung* (cultural and moral education) and *Kultur*, they were not part of an abstract or mystical *Volk*, a concept with greater potential purchase than universal Enlightenment values. The *Volk* concept was doubly effective in a new nation state in which belonging was considered to be derived through blood as well as culture, rather than through subscription to shared civic values or venerable institutions. Faith in rationality and universal civilised values made it literally inconceivable that someone as primitive and uncouth as Hitler could ever achieve prominence in the land of Beethoven, Goethe, Planck and Einstein. But this is an over-familiar trope. One can also argue that a narcissistic and precious identification with German high culture, coupled with an insecure, snobbish disdain for uncultured people, resulted in a failure to comprehend deeper undercurrents or the extent to which educated Germans were abandoning universal for narrower values. There was also a misplaced belief that Germany's elites would ensure that a marginal demagogue such as Hitler did not come to power, a belief which grew out of the dependence of pre-Emancipation Jewry upon rulers for protection against the baser instincts of the many.[152]

The enhanced social and economic mobility of the Jews – their acceptance and integration rather than exclusion from German society – became for antisemites a nightmare of Jewish elusivity, shapelessness and subversion.[153] They wanted to turn the clock back, to put these unwelcome 'interlopers' back in a well-defined space somewhere on society's margins, to eradicate the need to deal with this ambiguous and ascendant other. Historians routinely emphasise the rise of 'scientific' antisemitism in nineteenth-century Germany, with Hitler as the teleological outcome of ideas hatched by a succession of malign thinkers and maniacs. This Teutonic brand of the history of ideas, or *Geistesgeschichte*, meticulously traces alleged intellectual influences, almost as if it were supplying Hitler with a retrospective reading list. Its limitations indicate a lack of awareness.

Science was the language of authority in the nineteenth century, so antisemitism followed where economics, history or psychology ventured too. The renegade socialist journalist Wilhelm Marr's coining of the term 'antisemitism' in 1879 was a clever double stroke. It parodied more comprehensive ideologies such as conservatism, liberalism or socialism, and its aggressive secularism suggested that more was afoot than mere Christian folk prejudice against Jews.[154] Indeed, some antisemites combined antipathy towards Jews with strident sub-Nietzschean attacks against Christianity and its core values, and construed Christianity itself as a Jewish trick. Scientific absolutisation of the 'Jewish Question' in the form of racial laws and truths closed the escape routes of assimilation or baptism, for biological inheritance was inescapable. Science supplied certainty and a dehumanising vocabulary, and people borrowed its terms when they construed Jewish people as deadly pathogens. This was part of an emerging bio-political vision based on ideas of racial fitness and purity which was not without religious undertones. For there was one further element to antisemitism and teutomania which deserves mention, namely what in German is called *Glaubensneid* or envy of another's belief, for what was at work here was a strong desire to build up national self-belief to the extent that the Jews, in all their complexity, would be irrelevant to the Germans' refashioned and simple moral universe.

Hitler's antisemitism was not the sum total of Christian fantasies regarding Jews, nor simply prejudice masquerading as racial science. The former was fit for peasants, the latter for the racialist professors he despised as cranks, who, he said, 'forgot they were not living in the year 600 or 700 but in 1920'.[155] He needed something altogether more vaulting, a prejudice worthy of a Führer. Hitler was not a man of science, but a (failed) artist with messianic delusions. The historian Saul Friedländer has cogently argued that Hitler assimilated visions of racial degeneration and cleansing to religious narratives of perdition and redemption. Christianity would have to be refashioned, for it was too Jewish and unGerman in its received form, but, equipped with this new instrument, Hitler could indeed see himself as the agent of the Almighty. The source of this distinctive fusion seems to have been Richard Wagner's Bayreuth circle, the suitably arty and elite coterie of antisemites, and their Jewish acolytes, who massively impressed Hitler. These were not dry-as-dust *völkisch* professors, with abstruse theories and maladroit manners, but socially polished intimates of a creative genius, with whom an obsequious Führer would take tea. The 'maestro' spoke to another 'artist' through the medium of the guardians of his spirit.[156]

This is not to pursue the fallacy that Wagner's own hateful views on Jews were simply replicated in his operas. That Wagner conceived epic hatreds against individual Jews, notably the composer Giacomo Meyerbeer, and unattractively exploited Jewish acolytes and associates he despised, is not in doubt, though he is surely not the only creative genius who practised deceit and hypocrisy in his personal relations. He was also not the only great artist to have peculiar views on Jews, as anyone even fleetingly acquainted with Edgar Degas, Fedor Dostoevsky, T. S. Eliot or George Orwell can confirm.[157] But Wagner the early revolutionary admirer of Bakunin and Proudhon became a non-political composer, impressed more by Schopenhauerism and Buddhist affinities with animals than by Bernhard Förster's 1881 Antisemitic Petition, which he refused to sign. To identify such characters in his operas as Beckmesser, Alberich, Mime, Klingsor and Kundry with Jews is either too literal-minded or entirely speculative, while the themes of his operas admit of interpretations which Hitler would have found unsatisfactory. Hitler's understanding of those operas, which included allegories of doomed bourgeois civilisation and explorations of the power of love and compassion in settings that oscillated between pagan myth and a reworking of medieval Christianity, was as unsophisticated as his grip on Charles Darwin, himself a key influence on Wagner.[158]

The fact that the Nazis went to great lengths to appropriate Wagner should put one on one's guard in making too literal connection. They alighted on Nietzsche too, as refashioned by his sister Elizabeth and her barmy husband, Bernhard Förster, but few serious readers of Nietzsche would take this manufactured connection seriously. Much of Nietzsche's thought has to be suppressed to construe him as a proto-Nazi, principally his view of antisemites as part of the nihilistic 'herd' or 'mob' whom he despised: 'worm-eaten physiological casualties [are] all men of *Ressentiment*, a whole vibrating realm of subterranean revenge, inexhaustible and insatiable in its eruptions against the happy, and likewise in masquerades of revenge and pretexts for revenge'.[159] Nietzsche welcomed the creative involvement of Jews in what he hoped would be 'the strongest possible European mixed race', a notion hard to square with Hitler's obsession with racial purity. Wagner's coterie and family were another matter. They did indeed help to transform Wagnerism into a surrogate nationalist religion, a trend Nietzsche also despised, along with nationalism itself. Ruthless in his capacity for mocking self-analysis, Nietzsche was too intelligent to fall for their mock-profundities, plangency and mystical racism.

The English bore some responsibility for creating a distinctively German brand of racist Christianity. Wagner's Francophone and Germanophile ultra-cosmopolitan English son-in-law, Houston Stewart Chamberlain, was a writer who tried to reconcile scientific absolutism with religious mysticism. The disciple outdid the original: Chamberlain claimed that Germans were the heroic saviours of Graeco-Roman civilisation and a non-Jewish Christianity, who having harnessed modern industry would lead the peoples into a 'new, splendid, and light-filled' future. Jews, who had also retained their racial purity and strength, would correspondingly seek to thwart this 'Aryan-Germanic' mission to redeem humanity.[160] Wagner's English daughter-in-law Winifred was responsible for inviting Hitler to Wahnfried in 1923, where he inspected Wagner's rooms and grave, tears welling in his eyes. Having been awestruck by the heroics of Lohengrin and Rienzi as a youth, Hitler found Winifred to be a devoted follower – she joined the Party in 1926 – who not only attempted to politicise the Bayreuth festival, but gave Hitler emotional succour and the illusion of belonging to a distinguished family.[161]

Mein Kampf was not solely an account of Hitler's antisemitism, although that was its most salient feature. It dealt with other subjects, including foreign policy, Esperanto, pets and public speaking. Hitler's earlier antipathy towards Britain was replaced in it by the idea of a division of labour whereby the British would tend their colonial empire while the Germans expanded at the expense of Bolshevik Russia. Hitler departed from the russophile tendency which had survived the Bolshevik Revolution, but he retained a conventional animosity towards France. Not being a Prussian, he had next to nothing to say about Poland.

What does *Mein Kampf* tell us about Hitler's wider values?[162] The racial egotism meant boundless contempt for other societies and cultures; he viewed attempts to civilise or educate other peoples such as 'the Hottentots and Zulu Kaffirs' as tantamount to racial treason.[163] Social Darwinism fused with a pseudo-Nietzschean contempt for humanitarian succour of the weak. In line with many advocates of eugenic sterilisation and euthanasia at the time, Hitler believed that anyone not fit for life should perish, and that the state could give nature a helping hand. Since this was a bitter pill for the general public to swallow, it was coated in the language of duty and of sacrifice, which individuals must render the community: 'there is only one disgrace: despite one's own sickness and deficiencies, to bring children into the world, and one highest honour: to renounce doing so'.[164] As we shall see, this was unexceptional in international eugenic circles at the time. War was considered a positive force for racial regeneration: 'the bloodiest civil wars have often given rise to a steeled and healthy people, while artificially cultivated states of peace have more than once produced a rottenness that stank to high Heaven'. Hitler was hardly alone in believing that.[165]

What Hitler rather grandly called 'a new philosophy of life' had contempt for bourgeois values: 'our present bourgeoisie has become worthless for every exalted task of mankind, simply because it is without quality and no good'.[166] It was anti-intellectual, believing that the educational system was training bureaucrats and technical specialists rather than men: 'our whole intellectual leadership had received only "intellectual" education and hence could not help but be defence-less the moment not intellectual weapons but the crowbar went into action on the opposing side'.[167] Characteristics many would regard as demerits – notably 'blind obedience', dogmatism and fanaticism, all of which he admired in the Roman Catholic Church – were held up as exemplary virtues.[168] As he remarked in 1927: 'Be assured, we too put faith in the first place and not cognition. One has to be able to believe in a cause. Only faith creates a state. What motivates people to go and do battle and die for religious ideas? Not cognition, but blind faith.'[169] Hitler advertised, rather than concealed, his desire to inflict violence on his enemies. He lamented that in 1914–18 the government had not 'exterminated mercilessly the agitators who were leading the nation. If the best men were dying at the front, the least we could do was to wipe out the vermin.'[170] There was also his notorious observation that

> if at the beginning of the War and during the War twelve or fifteen thousand of these Hebrew corrupters of the people had been held under poison gas, as happened to hundreds of thousands of our very best German workers in the field, the sacrifice of millions at the front would not have been in vain. On the contrary: twelve thousand scoundrels eliminated in time might have saved the lives of a million real Germans, valuable for the future.[171]

This, and many less notorious statements, might be thought to have been sufficient to disqualify Hitler permanently from consideration as a politician. But it did not. Although some who observed him thought Hitler unremarkable, with hyperthyroid eyes staring from a bleached face, some smart circles were impressed by his radical and rough demeanour, which made intervals of charm seem all the more beguil-ing, while before large audiences this otherwise unremarkable man learned to transform himself into a, by turns, beseeching, plangent or raging force, let loose upon audiences who soon could not distinguish whether they were 'pushing or being pushed against their will'. The journalist Konrad Heiden, who before his exile in 1933 had closely studied Hitler for about ten years, has left us a remarkable study of Hitler the man on his way to becoming Hitler the Führer:

> With unerring sureness, Hitler expressed the speechless panic of the masses faced by an invisible enemy and gave the nameless spectre a name. He was a pure fragment of the modern mass soul, unclouded by any personal qualities. Once scarcely need ask with what arts he conquered the masses; he did not conquer them, he portrayed and

represented them. His speeches are day-dreams of this mass soul; they are chaotic, full of contradictions, if their words are taken literally, often senseless as dreams are, and yet charged with deeper meaning. Vulgar vilification, flat jokes alternate with ringing, sometimes exalted, phrases. The speeches always begin with deep pessimism and end in overjoyed redemption, a triumphant, happy ending; often they can be refuted by reason, but they follow the far mightier logic of the subconscious, which no refutation can touch. Hitler has given speech to the speechless terror of the modern mass, and to the nameless fear he has given a name. That makes him the greatest mass orator of the mass age.

Without this audience, Hitler reminded Heiden of a windless flag hanging slackly on a pole, a human 'nullity' waiting once more for the next occasion to seem a somebody.[172]

AMONG THE BELIEVERS

Hitler was released from prison on 23 December 1924. Bavaria's Minister President Heinrich Held reluctantly accepted Hitler's fake protestations of future adherence to legality, and decided not to deport the Austrian felon (who would not adopt German citizenship until 1932). Partly due to the adverse effect of political disturbances on tourism, Bavaria's authorities were as keen to be shot of Hitler as Austria's Christian Social Chancellor, Ignaz Seipel, was loath to readmit a notorious agitator who, he felt, had forfeited Austrian citizenship by serving in the German army during the war. Hitler was prohibited from speaking in most German states until 1927–8, the exception being Thuringia, where a handful of Nazi deputies ruled the roost in conditions of political stalemate. The Thuringian anomaly suggested that parliamentarism had its uses.[173]

Because of the speaking ban, Hitler concentrated upon consolidating his grip on a party which, in his enforced absence, had disintegrated into regionally based warring factions. The National Socialists forbade multiple membership in racist organisations, and entry to the Party was given only to individuals rather than to leaders with phalanxes of followers. One by one, the rival organisations fell into line. Hitler also embarked on a new course in which denigration of democracy involved its exploitation, 'pursuing parliamentarism with Parliament itself *ad absurdum*'. With Ludendorff discredited, Hitler was rapidly becoming the uncontested leader of a 'movement', the word used to distinguish Nazism from a conventional political party, a paramilitary army or a *völkisch* sect, for while National Socialism contained elements of all of these, it also transcended them. The emergent totalitarian style of leadership – notwithstanding Hitler's equivocating indolence – was not universally popular in the Party. One leading Nazi remarked, 'even leaders are only servants of the people's soul, from which the movement stems . . . absolute obedience is impossible, otherwise one breeds dependent creatures. The misuse of the leader in the end went so far that at the mention of certain names our stargazers broke out into hysterical shrieks of Heil! Those who did not shriek with us will be shot was the main precept of these screaming monkeys.'[174]

Having seen off *völkisch* challengers, Hitler was confronted by north–south tensions within the Party. In northern and western Germany, dynamic leaders such as Gregor Strasser and the Elberfeld journalist Joseph Goebbels wanted to concentrate on breaking into the urban socialist vote. They were both sceptical of Hitler's strategic talents, and antagonistic to the clique surrounding him in Munich. These men espoused a Prussian socialism. Whereas Hitler had recently vented his animosity towards Russia, they regarded it 'as the socialist nationalist state for which consciously or unconsciously the younger generation in all countries long'. Their socialism may have brought them into the same orbit as Othmar Spann or Oswald Spengler, but it does not mean that they forfeited every commonality with socialist parties, whose own heterogeneous historical roots included artisanal–utopian and statist tendencies.[175]

At a hastily convened conference in Bamberg in early 1926, Hitler quashed plans to support SPD and KPD initiatives to expropriate the holdings of Germany's former ruling dynasties, and forbade any further discussion of first principles. Having reasserted his grip, Hitler appointed Gregor Strasser to the Party leadership with responsibility for propaganda, with Heinrich Himmler as his factotum, and promoted his new admirer Goebbels as Gauleiter of 'Red' Berlin. Having created something which was more than a *völkisch* sect or a conventional political party, Hitler also checked the independence of the movement's paramilitary wing. In mid-1926, he replaced Ernst Röhm as SA chief by Franz Felix Pfeffer von Salomon, whose brief was to check its aspirations to quasi-military status by firmly subordinating it to the Party's political and propaganda goals. The SA was to perform two functions: to rough up opponents during elections, a practice Hitler seems to have admired across the Atlantic, and to assert the Nazi presence on the streets. As Hitler wrote to Pfeffer: 'We have to teach Marxism that the future master of the streets is National Socialism, just as one day it will be master of the state.'[176] The SA continued to have attitudinal problems. These would eventually be corrected, with their blood on cell walls, by a smaller force that multiplied under their aegis but grew apart from them in terms of their focused fanaticism: Hitler's SS (Schutzstaffeln) praetorian guard consisted of men who were better educated, leaner, taller and older than the eighteen-year-olds, if not the pot-bellied middle-aged bullies, who comprised the SA. The SS included bullies too, but they were superior, academically educated examples of the type.

The Nazis' enthusiastic resort to political violence distinguished them from the 'bourgeois' parties, but Nazism's primary focus on 'Reds' and secondary focus on Jews or Poles did not diminish its appeal to respectable citizens. Unlike Communist violence, which challenged the state head on, Nazi violence was rarely directed against the police.[177] Many Nazi sympathisers were also members of church committees, of business, dining or sporting clubs, and they indirectly domesticated an extremist party more effectively than any propaganda could, particularly when they did not advertise their ideological commitment with a buttonhole badge or a copy of the *Völkischer Beobachter*. In Marburg, for example, a university and service-sector town of just below thirty thousand people, the 194 mainly student Nazi Party members before January 1933 had cross-affiliations with 375 non-political voluntary associations, as Rudy Koshar has shown.[178] It is often said that word of mouth is the best form of advertising; here were people well placed to speak about Nazism favourably. Their conventional social involvements neutralised any negative impressions given by their membership in a party that combined extremist agendas with the promise of anti-political transcendence. An insurgent movement was likely to appeal to people whose outlook had long included an 'apolitical' antipathy towards divisive political parties. In Ingolstadt in Upper Bavaria, a distinguished physician and Liberal Party councillor, Dr Ludwig Liebl, became the organisational tyro of the local National Socialist Party branch, financing the local Nazi newspaper from his own pocket.[179] In Northeim in Hanover, a gentle bookshop owner from an old patrician family became the town's first Nazi, leading fellow citizens to remark: 'If he is in it, it must be all right.' Neither man was a ranter or thug, in fact quite the opposite, although many of their associates were. Studies of early Nazis in Hessen reveal a high proportion of miserable drunken misfits.[180]

A similar naturalisation of National Socialism took place in the countryside, where village elites – local landowners, larger farmers, pastors and schoolmasters – lent authority and respectability to the National Socialist penetration of disgruntled rural communities.[181] However, the reverse also occurred, when the village poor were repelled by Nazis who were among the village rich. In the case of the pastors who favoured Nazism, they may also have been following their flocks in a pathetic bid for popularity, like trendy vicars of the 'happy-clappy' persuasion playing electric guitars in their churches. If such people claimed to espouse Nazism, for what often seemed to be idealistic motives – preserving a declining way of life, the integrity of the family or religious values – then what could be wrong with it? Pastors and schoolteachers were also professionally articulate, well versed in putting over their views to their captive audiences. In Pomerania, estate owners either were benevolently neutral towards Nazism or led entire districts from the conservative nationalists over to the extreme right. Exceptions such as Ewald von Kleist-Schmenzin proved the rule.[182] The Nazis also appropriated patriotism, choosing army officers and ace U-boat captains as guest speakers. No one minded when these patriotic heroes included Free Corps veterans with backgrounds in political murder and intimidation of Poles, or renegade Communists (of whose political conversions the Nazi propaganda machine made much).[183] Sometimes the speakers were deranged, but this only contributed to the spectacle. A defrocked pastor, Ludwig Münchmeyer, who talked on such Biblical texts as 'He who knoweth the truth and says it not, verily he is a miserable wretch', was a bracing change from rational forms of political discourse.

It is important to emphasise that Nazi egalitarianism and emphasis upon character, initiative and willpower signified recognition that 'a farmer's boy who has got complete control of his village is of more value to the movement than so-called "leading personalities" whose activity is practically worthless'.[184] Strikingly, whenever the Nazis rolled out blue-blooded speakers, such as Prince August Wilhelm of Prussia, they were careful to pair each one with a farmer.[185] As Hitler told a meeting in Upper Bavaria, the NSDAP was 'not a party of men with the doctor's title'. Since peasants in remote regions such as East Friesland or the Lüneburg Heath were mistrustful of outsiders, Nazi agitators there included men like Jan Blankenmeyer, who spoke the local Low German patois. Nazi word of mouth was accompanied by Nazi infiltration of interest groups and also the creation of parallel organisations, which gave the impression of a party listening attentively to particular grievances. It also reflected a totalitarian aspiration, in the sense that Nazis believed that no area of life was to remain unpolitical, and a very modern view that an aggregation of interests would facilitate an eventual political takeover. Sectoral associations also created an informal Nazi nexus, whereby the Party could call upon the voluntary expertise of different professionals. Nazism developed its own self-help network, a society in miniature.

There were separate Nazi organisations for grammar school pupils and university students, as well as the broader Hitler Youth and League of German Maidens, which combined discipline with swastika-daubing delinquency. Students were often attracted by the Party's action-focused, anti-intellectual cynicism, a mood that was encouraged by their professors, given the latter's own propensity for chauvinism, mean-minded grudges and feuds. Having been psychologically mobilised during the First World War, Germany's academic mandarins failed to make the transition to peacetime, a manoeuvre not assisted by widespread boycotts of German scholars in foreign academic and scientific circles. But the old did not have to work too hard at encouraging the resentments of the young. *Völkisch* ideology was already rife among students, especially those organised since the summer of 1919 in the Hochschulring Deutscher Art. By 1922, this organisation had forced the publicly subsidised national student association, representing 110,000 students, to accept the affiliation of Austrian and Sudetenland student unions that explicitly excluded non-Aryan members.[186] From the mid-1920s, a separate, less elitist Nazi student organisation made the running. By 1930, Nazi students had a majority in the unions of nine universities; by 1931 they had seized control of the national Deutsche Studentenschaft.[187]

Despite their dire economic plight, for the inflation had wiped out the savings which their parents used to pay fees, students had time to spend on politics; they transferred between institutions; and they were regarded indulgently as the future elite rather than as idlers and layabouts. The semi-autonomous world of gown often protected them against town. The wider culture was attuned to smile indulgently at inane student japes. In Marburg, such pranksters included a student who donned a cardboard tube covered in antisemitic slogans, and went about as a 'wandering kiosk'.[188] For students were one of the hardcore constituencies of antisemitism. Jews had been banned from certain student societies before the First World War, and between 1919 and 1921. Duelling fraternities introduced exclusionary 'Aryan paragraphs'. Inflation meant there was no money for fees and maintenance, and impoverished Weimar governments had no funds for stipends: students alighted upon Jewish classmates as the cause of their woes, as people who did not belong to the *Volk*, which was a grandiose way of saying that there were too many of them in the lecture halls or the careers that these led on to.[189] This attitude went hand in hand with a rejection of 'alien' Western ideas, whether the laissez-faire economics of the British or the values of the French Revolution. Taught to value objectivity, or how to subtract humane values from their studies, many students rejected folk antisemitism as too emotively primitive, preferring instead a more 'scientific' variety that appealed to the intellectual pretensions of the semi-educated. They were encouraged in their spiritual provincialism by prejudiced academics for whom the competition of ideas and the wider world were often closed books, although they knew much about accidie and micro-politics.[190] When that impeccably liberal historian Friedrich Meinecke could remark *after* the Second World War of pre-war Germany, 'Among those who drank too hastily and greedily of the cup of power which had come to them were many Jews,' we must wonder what his less temperate colleagues might have been saying at the time, for in no sense of the word did Jews enjoy anything resembling 'power' in either imperial or Weimar Germany.[191]

Nazi students' entrance into the professions partly explains the proliferation in the late 1920s of separate Nazi organisations for architects, lawyers, doctors and teachers. However, the initiative came from within the professions rather than from aspirant malcontents seeking a first rung on the career ladder. Established physicians included many veterans of the Free Corps and ferocious antisemites whose hatred of Jews was not assuaged by the fact that Jews comprised 10 per cent of Germany's medical practitioners and between 30 and 40 per cent in cities such as Berlin and Frankfurt. Many antisemitic doctors were also much taken with the fashionable faiths of eugenics and racial science, which promised to promote physicians as guardians of the national gene pool. This promise of vocational grandeur contrasted with their widespread dissatisfaction with an allegedly ineffectual professional body, the Hartmannbund, which they thought was failing to check the spread of socialised medicine, a deleterious drift from general practice to either mass insurance 'voucher' medicine or excessive specialisation, all of which diminished the independence of physicians by downgrading them to subordinate technicians. If the medical contingent lent Nazism respectability, so too did representatives of the arts. A League of Struggle for German Culture united artists and writers ill disposed to Weimar modernism or pernicious foreign influences, although by no means all 'modernists' were liberals or leftists.[192]

Nazi penetration of entire socio-economic classes took the form of parallel sectoral organisations, or entryism into existing bodies with a view to carrying out internal *coups d'état* against the established leaderships. The initiative to form Nazi factory cells began in 1925 with Nazi workers in Berlin, Hamburg, Saxony and Thuringia, in major plants such as those of the electrical firm Siemens, as well as in smaller enterprises and among miners and railwaymen. Municipal power workers were well to the fore and, indeed, occasioned some controversy in the Party. Hitler was not antipathetic to non-political trades unions, but he also did not want to alienate business by sponsoring working-class militants. He recognised a contradiction between claims to be uniting the 'national community' above politics and class, and sponsorship of the interests of one socio-economic grouping. Since the Nazi factory cells sometimes participated in strikes, occasionally teaming up with the Communists against the Social Democrats, they deserve to be called militant. Other Nazi leaders favoured the infiltration of existing unions, chiefly because the National Socialist Factory Cell Organisation (NSBO) had no funds for strike and welfare payments. By 1931–2 the NSBO was affiliated to the Party and, with a quarter of a million members, was larger than the Communist Revolutionary Trade Union Opposition.[193]

More success was registered among Germany's already aggrieved and militant farmers. The National Socialists began as an urban party and had initially neglected agriculture in its original programme, but the surprising success the Party enjoyed in rural areas in the 1928 election meant that it paid more attention to agriculture: organisation, like propaganda, sometimes follows prior commitment. Earlier plans 'to expropriate land for collective purposes' were rewritten as 'being particularly intended for Judaic companies engaged in property speculation'. Hitler's Argentine–German admirer Richard Walther Darré was given the go-ahead to form an Agrarian-Political Apparatus, consisting of Nazi farmers who would advise and agitate from within the heart of their rural communities.[194] New publications, both academic and demotic, focused on the farmers, who were prized as the fount of biological health and future national greatness. Whether they found much solace in runic inscriptions seems doubtful. Nazi flattery was probably of secondary importance compared to widespread peasant alienation from democracy and democratic parties – the paradoxical effect of the obvious democratisation of peasant politics since the war. A predisposition to militancy, peasant disenchantment with interest groups often dominated by the local gentry, and the ephemerality or failure of rural parties and such umbrella organisations as the 'green front' all facilitated Nazi incursions into the farming constituency.[195] Nazi activists among the farming community challenged Rural League representatives for election to local Agricultural Chambers, from which platform they engineered their own representatives on to the League's national steering body. The extent of subsequent Nazi infiltration of that organisation can be gauged from its support of Hitler rather than Hindenburg in the March 1932 presidential elections, even though the latter was a major landowner.[196]

Nazi electoral success was not simply a product of superior organisation. Propaganda played a vital part, too, and it was propaganda that encompassed activities mercifully alien to the contemporary democratic process. The success of Nazi propaganda was not due to its being ahead of its time, for the left-liberal DDP had a sophisticated, 'Americanised' propaganda machine, using films and doling out ties and pencils emblazoned with the word 'Democrat', none of which proved of much use.[197] Most modern television documentaries about the Nazis' rise to power that emphasise Nazi propaganda are misleading, since they routinely show Nazi films made after the Party was in a position to shape cinematic reality, and neglecting the arguments and forms the Nazis used earlier to win votes in Weimar Germany during what they liked to call 'the time of struggle'.

The Nazis differed from other parties by holding meetings before, during and between elections, often selecting particular regions for saturation coverage. These meetings were a means of reinforcing solidarity among isolated activists. Their electoral machinery was permanently mobilised. They disposed of printers ready to rebut opponents instantly, and judges ready to issue libel writs. There was no such thing as passive membership. Pamphlets were even issued in braille to attract blind Nazi voters.

Hitler wrote of socialist demonstrations that they converted 'paltry worms' into 'part of a great dragon'.[198] People whose ideological commitment was potentially damaging to their careers and physically dangerous discovered others who were ready to make the same level of sacrifice. For it is not automatic that hard times led people to Nazism. Many Nazi activists lost their jobs because they were incapable of separating their political commitments from their workplace. These included such figures as the physician Kurt Blöme, fired from a hospital in 'Red' Rostock; Franz Schwede, dismissed from an engineering post in Coburg's electricity station; the defrocked Lutheran pastor Münchmeyer; or the sacked Bavarian schoolmaster Hans Schemm, all of whom went on to major positions after 1933.[199] Once in power, former 'old fighters' were sometimes asked about their backgrounds. One respondent was by then an SS-Obergruppenführer and head of the Düsseldorf police. His criminal record for the period 1927–32 contained thirteen entries for insulting officials, illegal possession of weapons, malicious wounding and brawling with the police or opponents.[200]

Meetings were a vital source of income, too, with entry charges and collections.[201] This put a premium on stirring public orators who were paid seven Reichsmarks per speech and were housed and fed by Party sympathisers. It became a kind of work-creation scheme. Promising speakers were sponsored for Party training courses run by Fritz Reinhardt in Herrsching. About six thousand people enrolled in these correspondence courses before 1933, correcting specimen examples of what not to say, learning how to field tricky questions, practising in front of mirrors. Whether these men were effective public speakers seems doubtful: they were risible imitations of Hitler at best. Increased Nazi membership in the Reichstag facilitated speaking engagements, since deputies enjoyed free first-class railway travel as well as parliamentary immunity. Goebbels noted, after his own election in 1928, 'I am an immune Member of the Reichstag and that is the main thing.'[202] After a month's experience of this 'ape's theatre' he pronounced: 'Parliamentarism is over-ripe for destruction. We will ring its funerary bell. I've already had enough of this theatre. One won't get to see much of me in this high and mighty house.' The leader of the burgeoning Nazi Reichstag caucus, Wilhelm Frick, described himself as 'the pike in the carp pond'.[203]

Meetings were too static for a movement that revelled in activist violence and militarism, the characteristic that distinguished National Socialism from other parties or *völkisch* sects, whose meetings had all the longueurs of a dull afternoon at a scientific conference. Ready resort to violence was a means of demonstrating a revolutionary contempt for 'bourgeois law', as one party of stormtroopers in Eutin put it, before pursuing Communist opponents into a house and beating them up with broken furniture.[204] Since Nazi violence often relied on passive aggression – provoking their opponents to attack them – and rarely involved acts against representatives of the state, it did not directly collide with society's desire for law and order. This was why Nazi leaders such as Goebbels actively incited their left-wing opponents to use violence against them, because violence itself was a form of propaganda. When opponents attacked the Nazis, they were playing their game, for people think it takes two to tango. Since Communists were prone to attack the police, the Nazis benefited from a gradual drift of police sympathies towards them. As with most forms of political violence, Nazi violence was accompanied by moral self-righteousness, a most repellent human characteristic.

If heated Nazi meetings where something was always afoot brought excitement to somnolent rural backwaters, the SA provided an opportunity for young men to display their anti-social proclivities in the service of an ideology and in uniform. In rural areas, what might have been gangs of under- or unemployed young men – say the sons of farmers, apprentices and labourers – loafing menacingly outside bars and dance halls, regrouped in uniform under the control of older, more experienced agitators with lengthy records of paramilitary violence.[205] The SA scene was superficially akin to any delinquent sub-culture. Gang members daubed slogans and swastikas on walls, then graduated via drunken brawling to semi-terrorism. Pranks and stunts added their own frissons – scaling tall chimneys to unfurl banners, tying opponents' chairs together to deny them weapons. In Hessen, a thirty-three-strong gang based in the Café Treusch in Langen screamed around the countryside on motorcycles with crash helmets and pistols.[206] The SA were often drunk: for Nazi politics exuded stale beer, cigar smoke and sweat, a nightmare of a certain kind of masculinity, which in the Munich beerhalls routinely resulted in what Patrick Leigh Fermor, the British travel writer, called 'hoggish catalepsy'.

There was more going on here than first meets the eye. Take the uniform. From 1928 onwards, these were issued by a quarter-master, from a job lot of brown shirts once used by colonial forces. Sales of the full kit with such accessories as armbands, and belts with buckles that could be used as knuckle-dusters, swelled Party coffers. If SA members were too poor to purchase their kits, wealthy sponsors occasionally did so for them.[207] Many clearly were too poor, since photographs show SA men barefoot in winter. The uniform transformed young men, otherwise utterly unremarkable in their daily workclothes, into aggressive authority figures. *En masse*, the SA lent the Nazis a visible and voluble presence that was difficult to ignore.

Marching men created noise and spectacle, with bands, cheery or mournful songs, and shouts of 'Judah perish!' The songs fused nationalism, racism and socialism:

> Arise Hitler folk, close the ranks
> we're ready for the final racial struggle
>
> we want to consecrate the flag with blood
> as a sign of a new age
> our black swastika shimmers on a red ground in a white field
>
> the victory trumpets are already sounding
> soon the dawn will brightly break
> Germany's future will be National Socialism!
>
> We are the true socialists
> we don't want reactionaries
> We hate the Jews and Marxists
> a cheer for the German Revolution
> We are workers good and true
> we want a free fatherland.
>
> Out, brothers, to the barricades
> when Hitler calls, we immediately follow
> the reactionaries have betrayed us
> but despite that the Third Reich is coming
> Our freedom column pours forth from offices and workshops.

Some songs were transparently adapted from their Communist opponents:

> Brothers in mines and pits, brothers behind the plough
> follow our banner's path from factories and offices
>
> Stock exchange crooks and rascals enslave the fatherland
> we want to earn honestly, busy with our creative hands.
>
> Hitler is our Führer, he doesn't take the golden fee
> which rolls before his feet from the Jew's throne.
>
> The day of revenge is coming, one day we will be free
> productive Germany arises, break your chains in two.
>
> So let the banner fly, so that our foes can see it
> we will always win if we stand together
>
> Devoted loyal to Hitler, loyal unto death.
> Hitler will one day lead us from this dire need.[208]

Torchlight processions added a touch of the sacred, a whiff of fire and brimstone. For the SA were an integral element in the sacralisation of politics; the National Socialists' mobilisation of sentiments went beyond brawling, despair and hatred into a heroic and quasi-religious dimension. They were necessary sacrificial victims, martyrs indeed, strewn strategically along their leader's march to power.

The Nazis mobilised other ranges of human sentiment beyond material interest. Nazism out-emoted and out-shouted not only republican politicians who preferred reason, but also their confessional opponents, by taking the emotions and forms of religion and effectively synthesising them into a political religion. Their doing so should not be confused with attempts to revive pagan alternatives to Christianity, although some people clearly liked whooping around camp fires in the blackness of the forests, or stripping off to chuck medicine balls around in the bright sunlight. Hitler himself was deeply averse to anything that might alienate the Churches or demean the movement and make it seem a merely cranky sect. It might also be argued that paganism was rather too harmless and tolerant, at least in its stream- and tree-worshipping manifestations, to be of much use to him. A party prone to attacking politicised clerics nonetheless systematically drew upon religious emotions for political purposes. This was part of its self-understanding: 'We lack a ritual. National Socialism must become the Germans' state religion. My party is my church.'

If run-of-the-mill Nazi meetings were characterised by debate and chaos, the Party's major manifestations began to have ritualised overtones: a messianic Hitler was central to that process. Hitler was fully aware of the one gift which life had granted him, talent as a demagogue. As he wrote: 'the power which has always started the greatest religious and political avalanches in history has been, from time immemorial, none but the magic power of the word'. He compared the spoken word to a torch tossed on to dry brushwood, contrasting his incendiarism with the 'soda-sweet outpourings of aestheticizing litterateurs and drawing room heroes'. Words were hammer blows 'opening the gates to a people's heart'. By his own account, the models for Hitler's oratory were the demagogues of the French and Bolshevik revolutions, the Austrian and German Social Democrats, and the fiery Welsh windbag Lloyd George, subsequently something of a Führer-admirer himself. Hitler wrote:

> the speeches of this Englishman [sic] were the most wonderful performances, for they testified to a positively amazing knowledge of the soul of the broad masses of the people. . . . in his speeches he found that

form and expression which opened to him the heart of his people and in the end made this people serve his will completely. Precisely in the primitiveness of his language, the primordiality of his expression, and the use of easily intelligible examples of the simplest sort lies the proof of the towering political ability of this Englishman [sic].[209]

Equipped with models of how to, or how not to, address audiences, the latter derived from visits he paid to meetings of bourgeois parties, Hitler honed his oratorical skills on ever larger audiences. These included such meetings as the October 1922 'German Day' in Coburg, organised by the German Racial Defensive and Combat League, where Hitler was a guest speaker because of his income-generating power.[210] He became 'practised in the pathos and the gestures which a great hall, with its thousands of people, demands'. He learned that time and place were as important as what was said. After a hostile reception in a Munich beerhall on a Sunday morning – 'the mood was ice cold' – he chose locations more carefully, often speaking at night, when dark thoughts could take wing. As Hitler wrote: 'At night . . . they succumb more easily to the dominating force of a stronger will. . . . The same purpose, after all, is served by the artificially made and yet mysterious twilight in Catholic churches, the burning lamps, incense, censers etc.'[211] He admired Roman Catholicism's alleged dogmatic inflexibility, and the egalitarian way it selected priests from the common folk. When he spoke in 1930 to an audience of Nazi press officers, one of those present reported Hitler's making comparisons between bishops and Gauleiter or between preachers and activists, with himself in the role of Führer–Pope, 'just as he unhesitatingly carried over the notions of authority, obedience and belief from the spiritual into the worldly field without intimating the change of notions'. There were acid whispers about 'His Eminence and Holiness Dr Josef Goebbels'.[212]

Major engagements involving Hitler began to assume a separate style. Care was taken with the venue, which was bedecked with flowers and Nazi symbols. SA men were forbidden to drink alcohol or smoke, and stood ready to pounce on any hecklers, since argument was fast being subordinated to acclamation and the instant silencing of dissent. Anticipation was heightened by long preliminaries and the delayed appearance of the main speaker. Anthems, hymns and stage lighting were used to generate mass pathos and sentimentality. Hitler swept in accompanied by drums, fanfares and salutes, and then embarked on speeches that could last for hours. The overall effect was like being whirled around inside a warm wave of unfathomable emotions. Contemporaries noted that after low, meandering beginnings, 'after about fifteen minutes something occurs which can only be described by the ancient primitive metaphor: the spirit enters into him'. For Hitler had something of the revivalist huckster transplanted to central Europe. In the act of speaking, he was transformed into a man with absolute convictions, expressed with total sincerity, that less remarkable late-twentieth-century political currency, at least in the Anglo-Saxon world, where politicians of all parties advertise their religious faith.

Hitler's voice has been described as being from 'South German social no-man's land . . . the voice of no one and all'.[213] His speeches had a predictable schematic form. He routinely began with his own mysterious odyssey from Braunau to national notoriety – mysterious because, despite his habitual extreme self-preoccupation, which was designed to suggest authenticity, he projected the illusion of being a prophet emerging from nowhere. His vague origins were part of his appeal in a society where politicians were identifiable with tangible interests. His audiences conspired in this illusion and increasingly referred to him as 'the Führer' rather than 'Hitler'. 'Providence' had chosen a humble unknown soldier as a great leader whose vocation was to restore the vanished honour of two million war dead. A dedicated band of brothers – he sometimes spoke exclusively of 'Herr Drexler and me', referring to an early Nazi leader whom he edged sideways – was becoming a mass movement. The awkward business of his flight from Munich's Odeonplatz in 1923 while his followers were shot became a Party legend whereby their heroic self-sacrifice was necessary to speed Hitler on his mission to revive a great nation.[214] Germany had been betrayed and ruined by her post-war leaders, every one of them puppets of sinister forces. And at this point Hitler introduced the anti-type to the altruistic, idealistic Aryan hero, namely the egotistical and sinister Jew. The parties ostensibly responsible for the shambles of modern Germany had had a decade to sort it out but had failed to do so. Plain people had been ruined, but now deliverance and vengeance were at hand. Those laughing now would soon be weeping. Faith, sacrifice and (always) 'iron' willpower would win the day.

The future was as contourless as heaven. Harmony would replace division, not least by making the two most powerful ideologies of the age – socialism and nationalism – work in concert rather than against each other. There was to be a renewed 'peace of the fortress', in which

the extremes of ideological politics were synthesised rather than suspended, in the interests of a dynamic national whole. There would be
bread and work in abundance.

Drained and bathed in sweat, Hitler at the end of his speech was
like a man reposing after coition, for that was precisely how he
regarded having conquered a mass audience. Mussolini felt rather the
same way.[215] And conquered many certainly were. A Hamburg school-
teacher wrote of a meeting she attended in 1932: 'How many look up
to him with touching faith! As their helper, their saviour, their deliverer
from unbearable distress – to him who rescues the Prussian prince, the
scholar, the clergyman, the farmer, the worker, the unemployed, who
rescues them from the parties back into the nation.'[216] In 1933 an SA
sergeant set out his reasons for becoming a National Socialist. He
wrote:

> Our opponents therefore committed a fundamental error when equat-
> ing us as a party with the Economic Party, the Democrats or the
> Marxist parties. All these parties were only interest groups, they lacked
> soul, spiritual ties. Adolf Hitler emerged as bearer of a new political
> religion. This religion was born out of the German national awakening
> of 1 August 1914 and our people's great struggle between 1914 and
> 1918.[217]

In 1934, Wilhelm Abel, an American sociologist, was permitted to
organise an essay competition in which adherents of National Socialism explained their backgrounds and political choices. Among the
seven hundred responses, a worker wrote: 'Faith was the one thing
that always led us on, faith in Germany, faith in the purity of our
nation and faith in our leader. Holy was our battle and holy our
victory. . . . Some day the world will recognize that the Reich we
established with blood and sacrifice is destined to bring peace and
blessing to the world.'[218]

What seem to an observer, rather than participant, to have been
parodies of religious forms proliferated. The Gauleiter of Franconia
Julius Streicher was characteristically least inhibited, enjoining pilgrims
to his annual rallies in Hesselberg to kneel to hear his pornographic
profanities about Jews. The first Party rally was held in Weimar
because Hitler was not prohibited from speaking in Thuringia; after
1927 they migrated to Nuremberg. Discussion was confined to closed
sessions, whose chairmen were not inclined to democratic decision-
making nor were the plenary sessions democratic. But discussion was

beside the point. The rallies were a combination of open-air festival, military display and solemn occasion. The bathetic low point was the consecration of SA banners, a matter of touching the bloodstained banner of 9 November 1923 to the flags of new formations.[219]

For the events of 9 November 1918 and 1923 became central to the evolving liturgy of National Socialism. The first date signified the 'blackest day in German history', the second the moment of rebirth, for from death springs life eternal. By 1926, the Party had declared 9 November the Reich Day of Mourning. Although the dead of the Munich putsch were central to this occasion, the mourned included the dead of the Great War, Free Corps casualties of battles in the Baltic and Silesia, and an increasing number of Nazis who, it was claimed, had been killed in the line of duty. The Nazis usurped the memories of millions of people, eliding the war dead with victims of their own political fanaticism. By 1932 they had a printed liturgy to co-ordinate local acts of commemoration: flags were lowered and wreaths laid; steel helmets were rested on altars covered in black, watched over by honour guards; artificial light was eschewed in favour of candles and torches; children were banned. At larger gatherings, orchestras played the funeral march of the 'Eroica'; there was mournful singing of 'I once had a comrade'. In Munich, where these ceremonies reached their emotional apogee, there was much conjuration with the 'blood flag' of the putschists, whose names were read from a book of martyrs, accompanied by much earnest clutching of standards and manly contact of eyes.[220]

The ranks of potential martyrs swelled, for politics of this kind had inherent liabilities. Five Nazis were killed in 1928, seventeen in 1930, forty-three in 1931 and eighty-four in 1932. Of course, neither their lives nor the circumstances of their deaths qualified most of these people for 'martyrdom' and care was taken in selecting official martyrs. The arrival of Goebbels in 1926 as pint-sized generalissimo in the 'battle for Berlin' had brought an immediate change of pace, as symbolised by his new paper *Der Angriff* ('The Attack'), which appeared the following year. His diaries are testimony to the avidity with which he sought a local martyr. In late November 1928 he thought he had found one, when a 'Party comrade', Hans Kütemeyer, was apparently beaten up by 'the Marxists' and thrown into the Landwehrkanal, where he drowned.[221] Things began to go awry when the police pursued other lines of inquiry, and the press implied suicide. In his newspaper Goebbels did his best to imagine the details of the affair: a taxi containing a 'Red and bloodthirsty gang' became part of the story, its occupants pummelling Kütemeyer's 'pale features into a bloody Ecce-homo' with iron bars. Various kitschy details were introduced involving Kütemeyer's wife, for unfortunately there were no grief-stricken children. Kitsch continued at the graveside. Where a pastor spoke forcefully against cowardice, Frau Kütemeyer 'wept heartbreakingly'. Wreaths were laid by Kütemeyer's silent comrades, one of whom, 'a worker, white as chalk', stepped forward, 'the Storm flag in his fist': 'his hands began to shake, and then he said: "I was one of those who marched side by side in the same formation with our dead comrade. I vow here that I will hasten after him, and will fight until his death is avenged". Then he stood there shaking and wept like a child.'[222]

In 1929, Goebbels again alighted upon a potential martyr, a nineteen-year-old called Walter Fischer who had died in a Communist raid on an SA base. But he proved unsuitable, because he had left the SA and Party under duress from his Social Democrat father, and had merely taken a stray Communist bullet when in an SA bar. Then early in the New Year, Goebbels found what he wanted, ironically someone who had stood at Walter Fischer's grave a month earlier. Horst Wessel was the twenty-three-year-old son of the pastor of Berlin's Nicolai-Kirche. He had a grammar school and university education, but had become a building worker and SA activist. He wrote SA songs, and copied the Communists by organising an SA band playing schawms. He was prominent in SA incursions into the Fischerkiez, a district near the Alexanderplatz notorious for the fluid relations there between Communists and its criminal underworld; Wessel called it a 'Bolshevik robbers' den' to provoke its inhabitants. He became a marked man, with KPD flyers reading, 'Note that face! Horst Wessel Storm Leader–Murderer of Workers', and supplying his address.

In 1929, Wessel began a liaison with Erna Jaenicke, with whom he moved into a room in an apartment of the widow Salm. Tensions between tenants and landlady arose, which Frau Salm sought to resolve by turning to Communist comrades of her late husband. At first they were unhelpful, since Salm's husband had received a religious funeral, but the name Wessel soon overcame this doctrinaire fastidiousness. Two members of the Communist RFB (the Red Front Fighters' League), including a tattooed pimp named Albrecht 'Ali' Höhler, set off to evict Wessel. Höhler shot him when he answered the door. Since Höhler had known Erna Jaenicke, probably in his professional capacity, the murder was as much motivated by the jealousy of a jilted pimp as by an eviction or ideology. Communists at their headquarters in the Liebknecht-House organised the assassin's flight, and instructed Frau Salm to convert a political murder into a tale about two men fighting over a retired tart.[223]

As Wessel lay dying in hospital, Goebbels set about converting this improbable figure into a latterday Jesus. For there was a literary imagination at work here, like that of a director of television commercials pillaging classic films. Even before Wessel was cold, Goebbels got the lowdown from his grieving mother: 'Like a Dostoevsky novel: the idiot, the worker, the tart, the bourgeois family, eternal torment of conscience, eternal agony'.[224] On 23 February 1930 Wessel expired; Goebbels commented, 'A new martyr for the Third Reich.'

Considerable effort went into turning Wessel's funeral into an act of anti-Communist provocation, starting with an extraordinary obituary in *Der Angriff*:

He went forth as a preacher in the wilderness . . . harvesting hate rather than gratitude, and only persecution instead of recognition. . . . They laughed at him, mocked him, spat at him, wherever he came among them, and turned their backs on him with abhorrence. . . . In the end he was prepared . . . to forsake his mother and the parental home, going among those who mocked and spat at him. . . . Beyond, in a proletarian quarter, high above in a mansard room of a block of flats he created an austere young man's existence. A Christian socialist! One who through his deeds cries: 'Come to me, I will redeem you'. . . . Five weeks long he lay in agony close to death. . . . He did not complain. . . . And in the end, tired and wracked with pain, he gave up the ghost. They bore him to the grave . . . those he sought to save threw stones at the dead. . . . He drank the pain-filled chalice down to the dregs. . . . The deceased who is with us, raises his weary hand and points into the dim distance: Advance over the graves! At the end lies Germany!

A song Wessel had composed in 1929 became the battle hymn of the National Socialist movement:

> Oh, raise the flag and close your ranks up tight!
> SA men march with bold, determined tread.
> Comrades felled by Reds and Ultras in fight
> March at our side, in spirit never dead.

'Ali' Höhler was not overlooked either. In early 1933, SA men dragged him from prison and murdered him.

Meetings, marches and quasi-religious events were one facet of the Nazis' attempt to monopolise the public forum. Marching or striking Austrian or German Social Democrats were the model for their physical domination of the streets. They also shamelessly plundered the literary and visual repertory of their 'Marxist' opponents in order to sow confusion and exploit similar aspirations and resentments. The primary aim was to discredit terminally the parties most closely identified with the hated Weimar 'system' with a view to winning the workers back from 'Marxist' socialism. Broadly speaking, Nazi propaganda was a matter of saying 'Anything you can do, we can hijack and do better,' pretty much par for the course nowadays.

As Hitler recounted in *Mein Kampf*, much trouble was taken in establishing a powerful symbol. The Nazis recolonised the red flag, setting within it the swastika symbol, which in turn they hijacked from earlier *völkisch* sects and the Free Corps, cunningly incorporating the imperial black and white into the overall scheme. Red also dominated their banners and posters. Since Nazi propaganda was both professional and reactive, when red became inopportune, to a party casting its net wider, they duly opted for a plurality of colours. In their respect for imagery and flexibility these people were very modern.[225]

Propaganda involved content as well as form. The Nazis were heavily indebted to their Marxist opponents for the dramatisation and sentimentalisation of labour's uncomplicated virtues. Hitler may have despised the gullible malleability of the masses, but he became positively emotional whenever talking of the horny-handed sons of toil. A sponge-like capacity was evident in other areas. If the Social Democrats had their satirical magazine *Simplicissimus*, the Nazis responded with the *Brennessel*; if the Communists had a picture paper, the *Arbeiter-Illustrierte*, the Nazis produced an *Illustrierte-Beobachter*. Since the Nazis believed that the working class were biologically sound, honest dupes of Marxist 'false consciousness', posters were overwhelmingly 'workerist'. A brawny 'Prolet-Arier' Prometheus rent his chains asunder, smashed his betrayers with a hammer or crushed the Reichstag with a pneumatic compressor. Further borrowings from the left included images of capitalist 'money-bags' and 'wire-pullers' that would not have embarrassed any Soviet propagandist. Another tactic was to raid the left-Social Democrat and Communist store of venom towards the Party 'bosses' of the SPD. In addition to depicting them as the authors of the 1919 'betrayal', the Nazis caricatured them as hypocrites who, squeezing their capacious bulk into dinner jackets, were tripping the light fantastic on caviar, champagne and oysters while their followers were unemployed and hungry. From 1929 the Nazis deployed the sleazy details of the three Sklarek brothers' relationship with the Berlin SPD city government, some of whose members had been caught red-handed, so to speak, taking fur coats from the shady siblings, who as Jewish Social Democrats were made in heaven for the Nazis.

Nazi posters used similar techniques to drive a wedge between the leadership of the Catholic Centre Party and the faithful. Attacks were made on the political activities of priests, not on religion in general, a line also pursued in the Party's non-religious assaults on the Jewish population. When the Nazis stooped to attack liberals or conservative nationalists, it was either to focus on Streseman or to ridicule the top hats and tailcoats of a vanishing era, particularly in their campaigns against Papen. Whenever Communists figured in their propaganda, it was as 'Asiatic' incendiaries and murderers, a view of them that was not confined to the right of the political spectrum but was shared by many SPD leaders, who in this respect were thoroughly conventional.

It seems generally established that the primary thrust of Nazi propaganda at all times and in most places was virulently anti-Marxist, with the Social Democrats first in the line of fire. Many Germans feared a Communist takeover, and not without good reason, even if the Communists turned out to be a paper tiger. Antisemitism was confined to publications for the existing pool of Nazi bigots. Oded Heilbronner has carried out a careful comparison of a welter of local and regional histories in search of manifestations of antisemitism in Nazi propaganda. Even allowing for biases among the historians – such as whether they were liberal or Marxist, German or foreign, local or alien to the area – his conclusions are striking: antisemitism was expressed only in places such as Franconia or Hessen where it had a pre-history or special purchase, or where the local Nazi boss was a committed antisemite. By contrast, it hardly figured in Baden, Danzig, the Rhineland, Schleswig-Holstein or Württemberg, where the local potentate was indifferent to it or there were alternative hate objects, such as Danes or Poles.[226]

MASS UNEMPLOYMENT

The onset of the 1929 world economic Depression immeasurably radicalised the political climate in Germany. The collapse in the share prices of such US firms as General Electric and Goldman Sachs led to a wider investors' panic and an urgent need to repatriate American capital invested abroad. In Germany, short-term loans had been invested in long-term projects, making it impossible to go liquid overnight. The Depression created an atmosphere of despair and led to a corresponding resort to desperate solutions. Germany literally became unsafe as paramilitary armies (although that term dignifies squalid thuggery) contested each other on the nation's streets. In December, Interior Minister Carl Severing gloomily noted the decline in public safety, the unbridled rhetoric – 'black-red-shit', 'hang them from a tree' – and the increased incidence of politically motivated brawls, muggings and stabbings.[227] Violence bred further violence, with the leader of the largest paramilitary army of all posing as a defender of law and order, even as he exculpated the murders committed by his own followers. The Nazis' dual-track strategy of the ballot box and the gun, boot or fist immeasurably complicated the responses of the authorities to them.

Connections between economic distress and political extremism were not straightforward. Chronic unemployment was as likely to lead to a day in bed as to seeking to overthrow the Weimar constitution. And the unemployed had minds of their own, when others – notably Communists and Nazis – cynically tried to exploit their plight for political purposes.

The number of registered unemployed rose from 1.6 million in October 1929 to 6.12 million in February 1932. Since these figures did not include the 'invisible' unregistered unemployed, the 1932 figure can be increased to a minimum of 7.6 million, perhaps a million or so more. Thirty-three per cent of the workforce were without jobs. Taking into account dependants, perhaps twenty-three million people were affected by unemployment. Unemployment of this magnitude over-stretched an insurance system designed to cope with only eight hundred thousand jobless people. By early 1933, only nine hundred thousand among in more than six million unemployed received national insurance assistance. Certain categories of worker – in farming, fishing and forestry – were excluded altogether, as were most workers under twenty-one years of age. This iniquity was justified by the inevitable modesty of their insurance contributions and by claims that they should be supported in the family home. In reality, it was a way of fiddling the unemployment statistics. Similar arguments were used to cut local payments to pensioners. Apart from compelling them to sell their assets and possessions, government admonished their families with moralising homilies about their duty to support them; family rhetoric had a cost-benefit side.

The unemployed received national insurance assistance for twenty-six weeks, according to complicated formulas at the rate of between 35 and 75 per cent of their previous incomes, with small supplements for dependent family. After this period, which the government repeatedly reduced, they received crisis aid, provided they had worked for at least thirteen weeks in the year prior to unemployment. When all this emergency aid was exhausted, they depended upon locally administered assistance, consisting of subsistence payments sometimes coupled with compulsory work. Climbing unemployment quickly overtaxed this system and occasioned a political crisis.[228] Already by December 1929, the federal agency responsible for these payments was 342 million Marks in debt to the Reich government. Municipal tax revenues also failed to keep pace with welfare spending. The city of Bochum, for example, had tax revenues of 18.6 million Marks and welfare expenses of 22.5 million Marks. The Müller cabinet's emergency budget scraped through parliament, but fundamental conflicts between the right-wing liberal DVP, representing employers who wished to see benefits cut and taxes shifted from business to consumption, and the Social Democrats, representing unions that wanted unemployment benefits increased and emergency taxation imposed, led to the collective resignation of the coalition cabinet in March 1930.[229]

A precipitating factor was President Hindenburg's refusal to allow Chancellor Müller to govern by emergency decree, the *modus operandi* that had been used effectively when Ebert was president to check hyperinflation. By this time, Hindenburg had found an alternative 'anti-Marxist' cabinet, to be led by the Centre Party politician Heinrich

Brüning and to include representatives of the liberals and smaller parties held over from the previous cabinet. Parliament voted down a package of financial austerity measures, but it was imposed by presidential emergency decree. When parliament protested, it was dissolved.

Elections in July 1930 increased Nazi representation to 107 deputies, the Communists' to 77. Defying a ban on the SA, the Nazi delegates turned up to the first session of the Reichstag in brown uniforms while their colleagues outside smashed the windows of Jewish-owned businesses until the Prussian police restored order. Since the composition of the Reichstag rendered a government majority impossible, Brüning depended upon the toleration of the Social Democrats. The deal was that Brüning could have his austerity measures, but the Social Democrats would whittle them down when, as the constitution required, they were discussed in parliament. In this and other respects, Brüning was scrupulous in his observance of the constitution. He also trusted and respected the Social Democrats. But what did the latter hope to get from this deal? First, they hoped to prevent Brüning from entering into corresponding arrangements with the Nazis – with whose leader he held secret talks that got nowhere – and secondly, they wished to preserve their powerful coalition with the Catholic Centre Party in Prussia, which was unlikely to survive if they did not support Brüning at the national level. The price of these arrangements was that the Social Democrats could not function as an effective opposition, a role which now fell by default to the Communists and above all the National Socialists, neither of whom were tainted by association with highly unpopular government measures.[230]

Brüning's two years in power witnessed the steady atrophy of parliamentary government. Each year parliament sat for fewer days: ninety-four in 1930; forty-two in 1931; thirteen in 1932. The increasing resort to presidential emergency decrees marginalised the legislature, and unelected senior civil servants who drafted these often highly technical instruments gained in importance. Over time, this exceptional form of government, suspended between parliamentary democracy and authoritarianism, came to seem normal. But Brüning grew dangerously dependent on Hindenburg and the unelected coterie of powerbrokers surrounding him. Relations between Brüning and Hindenburg became literally distant, since the octogenarian President spent increasing time on his estate at Neudeck, with access to him guarded by his son Oskar and State Secretary Otto Meissner. Whatever protestations of loyalty Hindenburg made to Brüning in 1930, he was a weak man who felt truly comfortable only with army officers and the landed aristocracy. Brüning was chancellor on sufferance.[231]

There were other worrying developments at the state level. In 1930–2 the Nazis entered state governments in Anhalt, Brunswick, Mecklenburg, Oldenburg and Thuringia. They and the Communists lowered the tone in state parliaments, predictably calling for increased public seating areas to maximise their audience, for to them democratic politics was theatre. In the Brunswick diets, twenty-eight sessions in 1930–1 were interrupted in total more than eight thousand times. More than half of these episodes were attributable to Nazi deputies; their average being that of 406 interruptions each. This was twice that for deputies from other parties, but it was eclipsed by the Communist average of 475.[232] In government, the Nazis adopted such populist tactics as refusing full salaries. They also purged socialists from the police, schools and educational inspectorates and, in Thuringia, introduced an enabling law used to make cuts in the state bureaucracy. They were most active in the cultural field. Daily prayers were reimposed on schools, 'Germany arise! Lord set us free!' being typical. Allegedly seditious books and plays such as Erich Maria Remarque's novel *All Quiet on the Western Front* were banned, and 'degenerate art' disappeared from Weimar's Schlossmuseum. By contrast, H. K. F. 'Rassen' Günther was appointed to a new chair of social anthropology at Jena in the face of strong opposition from the faculty, and Hitler came to his inaugural lecture. In Brunswick, much effort was expended preventing a Black Lutheran pastor from Togoland from preaching. Here was a foretaste of some features of the national scene after January 1933. This formed the depressing political background to Germany's most catastrophic economic crisis. Entire communities and generations of people were scarred by unemployment.[233]

It is perhaps salutary to remind ourselves what unemployment involved: in places where it was chronic and virtually total, people suffered a gradual loss of self-worth, a shrinking of mental horizons, a diminution of skills and often a collapse of the will to work. This last became one justification for imposing compulsory labour, such as dredging canals and ditches or mowing verges. Local governments also used compulsory labour to offload the burden of unemployment back on federal government, claiming that the work requalified the unemployed for national insurance.

The unemployed spent their days reading newspapers, smoking, standing in meal queues, squabbling at benefit offices or loitering aimlessly in parks and on street corners. Men tried to keep warm in waiting rooms and fed themselves by scavenging in dustbins. Their clothing became frayed and threadbare, the soles of their shoes worn, making it harder to find jobs since appearances counted. Others held signs or carried placards advertising their desire to work. Many became apathetic and resigned to being unemployed. Others grew desperate. By 1932, the German suicide rate stood at 260 per million (as against 85 in Britain and 133 in the United States). Since women were paid less than men, they found it easier to get jobs and worked while their husbands and sons brooded at home, an inversion of the gender roles normal at the time that made for domestic fractiousness. Hopelessness spread to children, who absorbed their parents' despair. Malnourished and fatigued – there was a new fashion for cheap child labour – they could not concentrate at school. In big cities, some teenagers went around in anti-social packs – the 'Wild cliques', numbering fourteen thousand in Berlin alone, led by 'clique bulls' surrounded by simpering 'clique cows'. There was a rise in juvenile crime, prostitution, vagrancy and vandalism, and also in the population in remand homes and the juvenile wings of prisons.[234]

Since unemployment was concentrated in certain regions – at its highest in the fifty industrial cities and lowest in Germany's less industrialised south – some four hundred thousand people took to the roads in search of work, which stimulated further anxieties about tramps and vagrants. Those dependent on meagre local benefits lived on bread and potatoes or whatever they could beg or steal, with heating fuel scratched off the slagheaps. People stood in line for the unappetising fare of soup kitchens. There was a shocking increase in cases of impetigo, rickets and pulmonary illnesses. As the proportion of income spent on housing rose from 10 to 50 per cent, the number of evictions mounted, and many unemployed workers moved to squatter settlements in the suburbs. Former industrial workers went back to being subsistence gatherers and farmers, stealing or scratching food from allotments. An enterprising few tried to make a go of it by selling beer, fruit or razor blades on street corners. This vicious circle of self-help by the unemployed undercut small businesses, already suffering from a drop in demand. And the poverty of urban workers affected the countryside. Livestock farmers in Schleswig-Holstein borrowed money to purchase calves in spring, which after being fattened throughout the summer were slaughtered and sold in Altona, Hamburg, Kiel and Lübeck in the autumn to liquidate their debts. Since the unemployed could barely afford bread and potatoes, this spelled ruin for many livestock farmers.

Germans who did have jobs faced wage cuts – some introduced through direct appeals to the workforce over the heads of the union representatives – shortened work hours, or compulsory alternation with the unemployed. In some plants, for example at I. G. Farben, chemists and engineers over fifty-five years of age were let go and younger men kept a form of industrial triage. The workers' trust in their union representatives declined, as the latter clung to unrealistic wage levels even if this meant a factory would close down. Depression both reinforced and undermined solidarities. In some plants, management received anonymous denunciations of idling union officials: 'Out with the trades union bosses, the party is over here.' War veterans wanted the 'red cowards' who 'had never seen trenches, dirt, lice and hardship or heard the fire of three thousand cannon' first out of the factory doors.[235]

Mass unemployment contributed to political extremism in complex ways. That many unemployed people were extremely bitter is unsurprising, but their bitterness was expressed in forms often only tangentially related to what those seeking to exploit their distress envisaged. Bailiffs who planned evictions were sometimes scared off by organised mobs, while municipal benefits offices became extremely charged environments, where the staff exasperated the unemployed by insensitive probing into their affairs, the result being flying chairs and inkwells and the arrival of the police, who were sometimes more sympathetic to the unemployed.[236] Extremist parties cynically attempted to exploit people's misery. In Berlin, Goebbels' *Der Angriff* published lists of suicides, along with digs at the initial promises of the Republic: 'He was no longer able to bear the good fortune of this life in beauty and dignity.'[237] The SA opened up hostels where its unemployed members were sure of a bed and a square meal, arrangements that gave the Nazis a pool of toughs and, when this access to free soup was extended to the unemployed, advertised their brand of real, existing socialism.[238] But the Nazis were only indirect political beneficiaries of unemployment. Middle-class reactions to unemployment alternated between compassion and fear. The former took the form of free food and cheap fuel. The latter was a compound in most of the responses to the crisis discussed here, such as rising juvenile crime, but also in the middle-class accusations that the unemployed were workshy and the visceral anxiety that unemployment might trigger bankruptcies. Finally, since about 30 per cent of the unemployed showed a clear sympathy for the Communists, the increase in their vote and the heightening of their anti-capitalist rhetoric helped to propel other anxious voters towards the Nazis.[239]

The gulf between those in and out of work translated eventually into political affiliation. Since the Social Democrats were most intimately associated with the creation and operation of Weimar's welfare system, they bore the blame for its manifest failings and injustices, even when they were locally implementing cuts decreed by Brüning's government. The Communists encouraged the idea that the Social Democrats and socialist unions were primarily concerned with protecting the interests of those still in work, and less concerned about the unemployed trailing. And Communists and Nazis tried to outdo each other with denunciations of Social Democrat 'bosses'. Uninvolved in government, the Communists could deny any responsibility for implementing welfare cuts or for the Weimar Republic in general. They constantly pointed to the allegedly heavenly conditions prevailing in the Soviet Union as evidenced by the flow of contracts from Russia still reaching German manufacturing firms.[240] A depressing number of Western dupes and stooges, spearheaded by George Bernard Shaw, traipsed around showcase housing and factories in the Soviet Union, while elsewhere in that country people starved to death or were incarcerated in Arctic and Siberian concentration camps. Stalin's Russia figured prominently in the KPD organ *Rote Fahne*, frequently in the form of here-and-there contrasts between alleged living conditions of German and Russian workers. The Nazi press replied with articles by purported returning eyewitnesses of Soviet corruption, denunciations, mass starvation and shootings, secret police terror and deplorable living and working conditions.[241]

Those unemployed Germans who retained any interest in politics turned in large numbers to the Communist Party, eagerly portraying itself as the tribune of the most distressed sections of the population. Party membership trebled between 1928 and 1932, while its share of the vote rose from just over 10 to nearly 17 per cent.[242] While the Communists registered disproportionate gains in precisely those areas with high unemployment – such as inner-city Berlin, Saxony and Thuringia – and began to pick up rural support too, the Nazis did correspondingly badly.[243] But the growth in Communist support was in several respects illusory. The new members were evidently very fickle, liable to leave after brief involvement: the Party was a means of registering their anger, an emotional rather than an ideological option. Self-evidently the unemployed were not in factories – although a few strikes were called by people employed by municipalities, which, relieved of an unwanted burden, promptly sacked them – so that the Communists were denied their preferred choice of battlefield. By default, they opted for demonstrations on the streets and extended their grip over entire working-class neighbourhoods through advocacy and political violence. This was agit-prop in action. Shops were robbed during cashless 'proletarian shopping trips'. Shopkeepers who refused to pay political protection money were closed down by boycotts.[244]

The Nazis' and Communists' respective paramilitary organisations were set on a collision course. They lived cheek by jowl and were both hell-bent on appealing to similar constituencies in imagery and rhetoric that became progressively harder to distinguish. In Berlin, the atmosphere was heated by Goebbels' talk of the Communists' 'assaults' against 'Red' Berlin's working-class quarters (Neukölln, Wedding or the Fischerkiez, where Wessel had been murdered). These were inner-city ghettos, from which skilled Social Democratic Party supporters had long since fled for more salubrious suburbs. There were brawls at meetings, organised assaults on rival hang-outs and headquarters, and parallel tit-for-tat provocations and assassinations; in some of these cases politics were probably used as a cover for settling personal scores. Although they had no inhibitions about murderous violence, the Communists suffered one disadvantage: since unemployed Communists could not afford beer, the Nazis easily persuaded pub landlords to cater exclusively to their beer-swilling clientele, especially when there were agreed monthly sales.[245] In this way, SA Sturm 21 ensconced itself in a street-front pub on Richardstrasse, where its members' anti-social behaviour included threatening children, shooting at windows, carousing and urinating in hallways. The Communists organised a rent strike to eject the publican and, when this appeared to be failing, staged a decoy demonstration to lure the police away, then blocked the police-station exit with a heavy chain and formed a crowd in front of the pub. Four or five gunmen fired about twenty rounds into the building, wounding four people as well as the publican, who died three hours later from a bullet in the head. The assassins were spirited away to the Soviet Union.

Although the events in Richardstrasse, Neukölln, can be depicted as a picaresque vignette of violence between SA toughs and Communist street-fighters, several aspects of the story require further elaboration.

As experts on the Comintern have remarked, 'the "view from below" is inherently flawed if it neglects or attenuates the powerful role of the Comintern Executive in Moscow'.[246] The Communists had several paramilitary organisations in Germany, such as the Red Front Fighters' League, which the government banned in 1929, but which continued as an underground group, and the Fighting League Against Fascism, its successor formed in 1930, when the Communists also created a Proletarian Self-Defence Force with a secret cell-based inner cadre. In 1928 a former commander of the 1923 Hamburg putschists returned from Moscow and established an Anti-Military Apparatus, with head-quarters accessible only by a hidden staircase in the Liebknecht-House, the Communist HQ in Berlin; the team was responsible for monitoring opponents, spying and terrorism. German Stalinists were unsurprisingly in thrall to their true Fatherland, the Soviet Union. These organisations, many of which had considerable quantities of guns and explosives, were closely linked both to the Moscow-based German section of the Comintern and to GPU agents in a 'special tasks' section of the Soviet Union's Berlin embassy; they were also planted in numerous trade groups and worked on the loose as freelance agitators all over Germany. The Soviets provided the KPD with large amounts of money, some of it taxed from Russian workers in the form of forced contributions to International Red Aid. They also instructed German Communists at the Moscow Military Academy and GPU headquarters in the forgery of documents, and in the conduct of espionage, sabotage, terrorism and military operations. More impressive on paper than in reality, the existence of such agencies further terrified the bourgeoisie.

By the late 1920s, Stalin had decided on the basis of increased electoral support for the KPD, that Germany was on the brink of revolution. The real agenda was his need to tack 'left' in order to strike at the Bukharinite 'right' within the Soviet Communist Party. The preliminaries to this 'German Revolution', designed purely to serve domestic Stalinist ends, would be mass demonstrations and strikes, followed by armed insurrection.[247] While some Communist groups were being solicitous of the unemployed, their clandestine wings were preparing maps of army bases and police stations, learning how to use guns and explosives in woods and quarries, and carrying out sabotage in factories. Since politicised strikes were infrequent during the Depression, mass demonstrations were the preferred tactic, not least because the actions of the police, many of whom were Social Democrats, gave Communist terrorist organisations opportunities to shoot them down. Police attempts to impose order in Communist-dominated areas met rooftop snipers; ordinary policemen were frequently assassinated. In August 1931 in Berlin three policemen were murdered outside the Babylon cinema near the Bülowplatz. The murders had been planned by the KPD politburo, including Walter Ulbricht, and involved teams brought in from Saxony as well as from north Berlin. The assassins included Erich Mielke, post-war head of the East German Ministry of State Security (the Stasi); he was smuggled out of Germany to the Soviet Union.

Although the Nazis waged vicious, personalised campaigns against individual police chiefs – notably Goebbels' vendetta against Bernhard 'Isidor' Weiss in Berlin – they deliberately avoided confrontations with the police and appeared to sympathise with their predicament as victims of Communist aggression. Of course, SA violence went beyond encroaching on territory the Communists regarded as their own. The brownshirts showed an alarming capacity to terrorise entire towns or whole provinces, which gave a foretaste of what they would unleash legally after January 1933, once the organs of state power were on their side rather than in their way. In August 1932, comparatively disappointing election results for the Nazis and the Communist stabbing of a Nazi agitator resulted in a reign of SA terror in the East Prussian capital of Königsberg. Arson and bombings were directed at liberal and Social Democratic offices and newspapers, while several prominent Communists were either killed or wounded. Violence spread to East Prussian towns such as Allenstein, Elbing and Marienburg. A parallel campaign in Silesia lasting ten days was launched by the rabid Silesian SA there with carefully planned shooting and grenade attacks on dozens of separate Centre Party, Social Democrat and Communist targets. They had the cunning to stage a few attacks on their own offices, to create the illusion that they were responding to Communist provocation.[248]

What political terrorism meant in practice was graphically illustrated in the Silesian village of Potempa near the border with Poland: the incident sheds light on the man then striving to become Germany's chancellor. A team of drunken SA men arrived to settle a grudge with one Konrad Pietzuch, an unemployed Polish Communist labourer. Breaking into his cottage, they shot and strangled him, treading on his windpipe for good measure. Nine men were arraigned for murder in a special anti-terrorist court sitting in Beuthen. Five of the accused were sentenced to death. Hitler telegraphed his 'unbounded loyalty' to them and promises of help. The sentences were commuted to life imprison-ment, and the murderers were freed by Chancellor Hitler within seven months.[249]

Communist–National Socialist relations were not simply heroic street battles or incidents that camouflaged the settling of old scores. Political meetings in the Weimar period sometimes featured opponents who had been invited so they could be used as stooges by the main speaker. In early 1931, Berlin's Friedrichshain assembly hall was the scene of an epic verbal duel, a sort of King Kong versus Godzilla, between Goebbels and the KPD's Walter Ulbricht, which about four thousand people attended. A lone Social Democrat's attempts to speak were drowned out by both sides of the audience, which after the meeting set upon each other with table- and chair-legs.[250] Debate sometimes led to apostasy and conversion among those whose political loyalties met at the extremes. The young British traveller Patrick Leigh Fermor encountered such men in a Rhineland workers' pub, a few months after Hitler had come to power. His new acquaintances were factory workers in overalls who had just left the night shift. Invited to stay the night by one of his new friends, Fermor climbed up to an attic room that 'turned out to be a shrine of Hitleriana'. What he learned there is worth citing at some length:

> The walls were covered with flags, photographs, posters, slogans and emblems. His SA uniform hung neatly ironed on a hanger. He explained these cult objects with fetishist zest, saving up till the last the centrepiece of his collection. It was an automatic pistol, a Luger parabellum, I think, carefully oiled and wrapped in a mackintosh, accompanied by a pile of green cardboard boxes packed with bullets. He stripped and reassembled the pistol, loaded the magazine and smacked it home and ejected it again, put on a belt and crossbrace with a holster, whipped the gun in and out like a cowboy, tossed it in the air and caught it, spun it round by the trigger-guard and danced about with one eye shut, going through the motions of aiming and firing with loud clicks of the tongue. . . . When I said that it must be rather claustrophobic with all that stuff on the walls, he laughed and sat down on the bed, and said: 'Mensch! You should have seen it last year! You would have laughed! Then it was all red flags, stars, hammers and sickles, pictures of Lenin and Stalin and Workers of the World, Unite! I used to punch the heads of anyone singing the Horst Wessel Lied! It was all the Red Flag and the Internationale then! I wasn't only a Sozi, but a Kommi, ein echter Bolschewik!' He gave a clenched fist salute. 'You should have seen me! Street fights! We used

to beat hell out of the Nazis, and they beat hell out of us. We laughed ourselves silly – Man hat so tot gelacht. Then suddenly, when Hitler came to power, I understood it was all nonsense and lies. I realized Adolf was the man for me. All of a sudden!' He snapped his fingers in the air. 'And here I am!' What about all his old pals, I asked. 'They changed too! – all those chaps in the bar. Every single one! They're all in the SA now.' Had a lot of people done the same, then? 'Millions! I tell you, I was astonished how easily they all changed sides!'[251]

Ever since Helmuth Gerlach, writing in 1930, commentators have tried to pinpoint the sources of Nazi support. One matter Gerlach got right was that Nazi support was a mile wide but, beyond a hardcore of fanatics, only an inch deep. As he wrote, 'If the sun shines once more on the German economy, Hitler's voters will melt away like snow.'[252] The Depression, with the sensational boost it gave to the Communist vote, not only decided the political choices of many middle-class Germans, many of whom had by then forsaken their traditional allegiances, but also extended Nazi support to a sizeable proportion of the working classes, so successfully that some historians doubt the value of social class as an analytical tool for examining the electorate. We probably need to distinguish carefully here between defections from Social Democracy (about every tenth Nazi voter hailed from this camp) and the voting habits of the working class as a whole. If this is less than impressive when set against the one in three Nazis who were former conservative voters or the one in four who were ex-liberals, the electoral behaviour of the working classes in general is far less reassuring, and more in line with what one sees in Israel or South Africa. According to Jürgen Falter's sophisticated computer studies of electoral data, 40 per cent of Nazi voters were workers and 40 per cent of Party members were, too; these figures rise to 60 per cent in the SA, and there was significant workers' representation within the classless racial elite of the SS.[253]

If in the past it was customary to minimise Nazi working-class support, there is nowadays a corresponding danger of exaggerating it, although the reasons for doing so seem obscure. Nazi workers were found in the industrial heartlands of the Ruhr and Saxony, and up to three million Nazi voters throughout Germany between 1928 and 1932 were former Social Democrats, not people who had never voted before, or disillusioned supporters of former 'bourgeois' parties.[254] Several reasons explain why many workers, as distinct from Social Democrats, voted for the Nazis. The Social Democrats had become

tainted by their involvement in government – whether directly or
through their tacit support of Brüning – and by the manifest ineffec-
tiveness of the system they had created to help workers in hard times.
Years of impressive advances – with higher wages, material improvements and enhanced security – were followed by years of crushing
circumstances: a pattern guaranteed to radicalise opinion. In areas
where Social Democracy was entrenched, disaffection from it was
expressed in the privacy of the polling booths; elsewhere it did not
bother to disguise itself. For worker support of the Nazis was more
than the sum total of the failure of Social Democracy to organise
certain groups of workers and the atrophy of its apparatus.[255]

The National Socialists not only joined the Communists in
denouncing Social Democratic bosses, but also practised egalitarianism, unlike the bourgeois parties. One should not underestimate the
extent to which working-class people bitterly resented being treated as
infantile inferiors by the middle and upper classes. One of Wilhelm
Abel's essay-writers was a rabidly antisemitic driver–handyman – he
may have been especially chippy and sensitive to social slights – who
in 1926 went to work on a landed estate where the casual harvest
hands included seven brownshirts. Drawn to them, he wrote:

'The carriers were of even lower rank than the laborers, and it was
considered impossible to associate with them constantly. . . . I myself
had class arrogance, no matter how strange that may sound; I considered myself higher than these fellow-countrymen who were only
carriers.' He lost his job in 1928, and went to Berlin as a housekeeper.
In 1931 he joined the Nazi Party and began to attend weekly meetings
in a restaurant: 'I was received there with extraordinary warmth. The
spirit was one of pure comradeship, and from the very first moment I
felt at home. As I learned then, these evenings were mainly for officers,
but I was allowed to participate. . . . Class arrogance had been completely eliminated among us in the Party.'[256]

These workers had a keen desire to be treated with respect and wanted
factors such as 'character' to count more than birth or privilege. Those
who had fought in the war, in which 'what a person was, not what he
seemed to be, counted', chafed under the reimposition of traditional
hierarchies. Many of them also had little time for Marxist internationalism, since they were not just workers but products of homes and an
educational system that valued patriotism.

The Nazis offered what seemed to be bold prescriptions for pulling

Germany out of the Depression, together with rhetoric which celebrated the German common man. More to the point, while they stressed both egalitarianism and entrepreneurialism, they avoided any talk of redistribution of wealth, so as not to scare off the middle classes. If the Communists offered a general strike (absurd in conditions of mass unemployment) and revolution whose bleak consequence would be the socialist slavery then being imposed in the Soviet Union, the Nazis offered a combination of economic nationalism with unorthodox anti-cyclical measures to stimulate employment. Quasi-leftist crudities derived from Gottfried Feder about 'interest slavery' were superseded from 1931 by concrete policies hatched by the Munich-based Economic Political Office of the Party, which drew upon both in-house and outside academic and business expertise.[257] The economy would be reorganised to serve the interests of the nation, whose international involvements would be secondary to those of a German-dominated economic union in central and south-eastern Europe: both a market for German industry and a source for agricultural goods that did not compete with those produced by German farmers. Successive Nazi economic programmes had a no-nonsense chauvinism and apparently benign toughness: autarchy was combined with calls for work-creation programmes such as housing and road building or land reclamation. The Nazis called for the repatriation of foreign labour, notably Polish seasonal workers, or for compulsory labour service, which would rediscipline a youth gone wayward because of unemployment. Autarchy appealed to workers in industries that were not primarily export-oriented and that had been ravaged by 'rationalisation', one effect of which was to diminish the skilled labour force in favour of the unskilled. But it was not designed to appeal to workers in dynamic, export-driven sectors, who were correspondingly under-represented in the Nazis' working-class following.[258]

The Nazis were offering a powerful bargain: work in return for political support. They were also apparently keen to restore the dignity of German labour, their classless national community, and they deflected worker resentments on to Social Democratic 'bosses' and on to a small, and hence identifiable, cast of international Jewish capitalists (as opposed to faceless capitalism in general). Ironically, Social Democratic economists and unionists devised their own programme for stimulating employment through deficit spending – the 1931 Woytinsky–Tarnow–Baade, or WTB, plan – but this attempt to intervene vigorously in the economy came to naught. It was not radical enough for those who sought nationalisation, or for Marxists who saw themselves as the heirs of a dying capitalism. It was too radical for the majority of people who had nightmare memories of the inflation. Compared with the Nazis' daring fusion of deficit spending with economic nationalism, it was pathetic.[259]

Finally, the energies of the two 'Marxist' parties were increasingly turned against themselves, whatever local arrangements they made at the grassroots. The Social Democrats were adamant that they did not want 'a deformed socialism that creates a mass prison': 'we want to liberate, not oppress'. The Stalinised Communists, since 1929 committed to their 'social fascist' line, were convinced that the 'Nazis and Social Democrats stand on the foundation of capitalist private property and were slaves of capital and enemies of the workers'.[260]

This ideological contortion was achieved by imagining that, in conditions of extreme crisis, capitalism would either co-opt an increasingly 'bourgeois', reformist Social Democracy or combine the bourgeoisie with marginal 'lumpen' elements to create the mass base for a terroristic form of dictatorship. According to the Stalinist view that the most insidious enemies were immediately to the left – which had Stalin's NKVD imposing discipline on Trotskyites with a bullet in the head – leftist Social Democrats were the most dangerous of the 'social fascists'.[261] Whether or not the accuracy of this interpretation was confirmed by the anti-Communist policies of socialist parties in many European countries, or whether its radicalism served to unite the comrades, it was subversive of any united response by the left to Nazism. The specific threat of National Socialism was obscured amid generalised talk of the perils of 'fascists', a term egregiously applied to Brüning, Social Democrats and all and sundry. Dogmatic catastrophist theorising led the Communists actively to underplay the Nazis: Ernst Thalmann warned the KPD Central Committee in February 1932 'that nothing would be more disastrous than an opportunistic overestimation of Hitler-fascism'. Actually there would be, namely, dogmatically induced underestimation of National Socialism's unique ideological potency.[262]

Brüning was a profoundly austere individual from a Catholic trades union background whose entrance into a room was said to spread an inhibiting chill. He was demanding of himself, and he never married so as to devote himself more fully to his country. He expected the whole nation to practise Prussian virtues of diligence and self-sacrifice. His super-patriotism may have been a form of over-compensation for the fact that he was a Catholic. As a holder of the Iron Cross from the Great War, he loathed the Nazis' usurpation of patriotism, and told their Reichstag caucus:

> You are always talking about the 'system', sometimes you call it the Brüning system, sometimes the system of 9th November. . . . Gentlemen, don't you dare to connect me in any way with 9th November! . . . Where was I on 9th November?. . . . Gentlemen, on 9th November I belonged to the army unit formed from the spearhead of the Winterfelde Group for the suppression of the revolution.[263]

Brüning's deflationary economic strategy was in line with orthodox economic opinion, including that of John Maynard Keynes himself in the particular case of Germany, and reflected the overwhelming dread of inflation that extended into the SPD and the trades unions, which tacitly supported policies whose effects they publicly criticised. Lower prices and wages would enhance the competitiveness of German exports, it was believed, and indirectly force the Allied powers to revise the Young Plan's revised schedule of reparations, since meeting reparations payments was the ostensible purpose of Germany's having an export surplus. Brüning did not deliberately engineer mass unemployment – on the contrary, he periodically pushed public-works programmes. Still less was he endeavouring to restore the monarchy, since he knew that the Hohenzollerns were a divided and hopeless house, though he showed a general preference for constitutional monarchy. He hoped that his apparently even-handed attacks on inefficient and selfish capitalist cartels, against which he had a genuine social Catholic animus, and on profligate municipal government of various political hues would compensate for inevitable hardships, and keep the unions and Social Democrats on his side. This was a high-risk strategy, its success dependent on when the Depression would bottom out, and it was almost guaranteed to irritate the right, for whom Social Democrats were traitors.[264]

To compensate for falling revenue, Brüning increased taxes, reduced civil service salaries, froze wages at 1927 levels and made unemployment insurance harder to come by. Care for the unemployed was shunted on to the shoulders of local government, whom Brüning hoped to force into making grown-up budgetary choices. Inevitably, the rhetoric of Prussian stoicism began to pall among those with nothing to eat and no shoes on their feet. Stoicism sounded specious when there were no cuts in expenditure on the armed forces and large-scale eastern agrarians were protected through the ramping of grain prices by protective tariffs and cheap credit that sustained a lifestyle rather than a way of life. The notional justification for this insulation of an influential minority against market mechanisms was that it would stem the decline of 'Germandom' in the east. Brüning was among those who realised that this was rhetoric disguising naked self-interest.

These deflationary policies were so unpopular that Brüning took to going about Germany in a train with the blinds permanently down, for crowds tended to throw rocks if they caught sight of him. Letters to President Hindenburg demanding the Chancellor's head and the formation of a more right-wing cabinet apparently filled baskets and trays. Against this backdrop of worsening economic crisis, Brüning's government attempted a more upbeat foreign policy. Brüning and his Foreign Ministry were disinclined to continue Stresemann's policy of close relations with France. They dismissed a French plan for economic co-operation, and eagerly took up requests from Austria's Foreign Minister Schöber to explore a customs union, arguing that this was not legally prohibited under the terms of the Versailles treaty. France regarded this as a German attempt to undercut Austrian independence (all Austrian political parties except the Christian Socialists favoured union), and as a sinister extension of German influence into south-eastern Europe. If Czechoslovakia were to join the customs union, France's chief ally Poland would be so weakened that she would have to trade frontier adjustments for German economic aid. France had investments of seven billion francs in that region and wider security concerns about her Polish ally. The customs-union project coincided with the collapse of Austria's banking system, which, since only France possessed the gold reserves to bail the banks out, meant this was not the most auspicious moment to alienate her. The banking collapse spread to Germany, not least because Brüning coupled a new round of cuts with the news that Germany had reached the limits of what she could endure under the reparations regimen, thus panicking foreign creditors who withdrew their short-term loans. Unsurprisingly, Pierre Laval's government in Paris attached stringent political conditions to France making any loans to Germany. Since the absolute collapse of the German economy was inimical to American interests and the international economy, in the summer of 1931 President Herbert Hoover pushed through a moratorium on German reparations and the servicing of inter-Allied debt. Brüning derived no credit for this significant development.

In October 1931, President Hindenburg forced Brüning to refashion his cabinet, and the retreat from democratic government continued. Brüning's dependence upon Hindenburg rather than parliament became fateful. In early 1932, he further offended Hindenburg by refusing to have him re-elected by plebiscite with no other candidates, failing to get Hindenburg's reconfirmation for an extended term on the nod from a hostile Reichstag. Brüning, loyally throwing himself into Hindenburg's re-election campaign, revealed hidden talents as an orator and an uncharacteristic willingness to allow illegal use of state funds to finance the campaign. In April, Hindenburg secured 53 per cent of the vote in a second ballot. His closest rival was Hitler, who had secured almost 37 per cent (after Nazis in the state government of Brunswick had first conferred German citizenship on him). Hindenburg scored badly in what should have been his core constituencies of Pomerania, Thuringia and Schleswig-Holstein, but better in the west, where he received the grudging support of Catholics and the SPD. But this was not support Hindenburg welcomed.

Brüning's fate was increasingly being decided by rightist lobby groups and the army's General Kurt von Schleicher, who had served in the Third Foot Guards with Hindenburg's son. Such casual connections began to have political moment, which was a depressing indication of the atrophy of democratic politics and the disproportionate weight exerted by utterly unrepresentative elites. The rising tide of public violence, and the discovery that the SA in Hesse had plans for a coup in the event of a Communist rising, led Brüning to ban the wearing of political uniforms, and then prohibit the SA itself. Defence Minister General Groener implemented the SA ban on 13 April 1932. The police closed SA hostels and confiscated banners, tents and trucks. Even Goebbels' chauffeur-driven car was confiscated. However, the ban played havoc with General Schleicher's plans to use the SA for pre-military training prior to expansion of the army and for the rightward reconstruction of the government, without Brüning, whom Schleicher regarded as too dependent upon the left. This government was to include Nazi ministers – the first ominous appearance of the strategy of 'taming' them by giving them governmental responsibility, a strategy Brüning rejected. Schleicher undermined Groener by giving Hindenburg allegedly shocking material about the behaviour of the Social Democrat paramilitary Reichsbanner, which the right wished proscribed too, but most of this material consisted of partial clippings from right-wing newspapers. No serious comparison could be made between the Reichsbanner and the SA at all. However, Hindenburg withdrew his confidence from the Defence Minister; he was a stickler for propriety in the officer corps, and he had never cared for Groener, whose wife was a former housekeeper and whose child had been born too soon after their marriage. Following Groener's poor defence in the Reichstag of the SA ban, Schleicher told Hindenburg that the Defence Minister had forfeited the confidence of the senior officer corps. Since Brüning supported the doomed Groener almost to the bitter end, Groener's resignation weakened him too.[265]

Brüning's own demise ensued when he was erroneously identified with plans put forward by the Minister of Labour, Adam Stegerwald, his Christian trades unionist mentor, both to nationalise sections of heavy industry and to expropriate bankrupt East Elbian estates. The intention was to compensate for the government's rejection of trades union calls for limited reflationary economic policies, and Brüning proposed an alternative policy of scrapping grain subsidies. But his enemies chose to confuse this with the policy of expropriation he had rejected, and claimed he advocated 'agrarian Bolshevism'. He was done for. After a curt interview, Hindenburg asked for Brüning's resignation. Brüning belatedly grasped that the President who, with tears in his eyes, had once asked him to form a government cared nothing for him and everything about his own aristocratic clique. Some weeks before, Schleicher had conferred with Hitler and had struck a bargain whereby the ban on the SA would be lifted and fresh elections would be called, in return for which Hitler would not oppose a more rightist presidential cabinet. The Social Democrats' tolerance of Brüning was to be replaced by the Nazis' tolerance of his successor. Schleicher had already decided on the new Chancellor and on who else would be in the cabinet. Things were deteriorating quickly. Apparently both Brüning and other members of his government literally took to their beds in despair.

Franz von Papen was a Westphalian Catholic petty aristocrat with markedly anti-democratic views, and he was much beholden to agrarian and industrial interests. Born in 1879, Papen had been a royal page, before joining the General Staff as a candidate from the First Uhlan Guards Regiment. He married into substantial Saarland money, which paid for his military career and financed his love of riding. Posted as a military attaché to Washington in 1914, he was caught red-handed trying to sabotage the Canadian Pacific Railway, along which American arms flowed to the Entente, the First World War Allies, while fostering connections with the Irish Republican terrorist Sir Roger Casement. He was declared *persona non grata*. After the war, Papen became a Centre Party deputy in the Prussian state parliament, although in most respects he was more suited to the DNVP. A founder member of the gentlemen's Lords Club, Papen was hostile to parliamentary democracy on both ideological and religious grounds. Only his francophilia and hatred of Russian Bolshevism distinguished him from anti-Western East Elbian conservatives, who sought a Russian orientation to undermine France's ally Poland. He was hostile to the continuation of the dualism of Prussia (Germany's largest federal state) and the Reich, for the conservative hegemony of pre-war Prussia had been supplanted by a Centre Party Social Democratic coalition under the Weimar Republic. In 1925, Papen played a part in helping the Protestant Hindenburg, who was politically obligated to him, defeat the Catholic Marx in the presidential elections, a favour which in 1928 led Hindenburg to consider Papen as Defence Minister.[266]

Schleicher's choice of Papen now, in 1932, was influenced by the view that as a Centre Party politician he would console a party angered by the dismissal of Brüning, who indeed became more popular in opposition than he had ever been in government. As a prominent ideological conservative, Papen was also acceptable to the DNVP and he had never come into conflict with the Nazis. Schleicher's choice of other ministers (he added the Defence portfolio to his own responsibilities) included so many aristocrats that the regime was known as the 'cabinet of barons', though there were three bourgeois: Franz Gürtner at Justice, and two IG Farben and Krupp board members holding the Economics and Labour portfolios.[267] The new government had no constructive policies to offer the nation, only airy talk of monarchy being Germany's natural form of government and calls for a Christian polity. This was hopeless during a massive economic crisis. The cabinet pursued cavalier policies with aristocratic insouciance. This commenced when Papen decided to use the radio, rather than parliament, to announce his policies, and for an unseemly diatribe against 'cultural Bolshevism' and parliamentary democracy. Unemployment assistance was cut by nearly a quarter and subjected to almost immediate means testing, employer contributions were reduced, and increased subventions flowed to East Elbian agrarians. If many employers and industrialists thought they had at last got their kind of government, its iniquitous policies and biased social composition meant that the Nazis could not tolerate it so long as they sought the workers' votes.

Schleicher still had to keep his bargain with Hitler by calling new elections. Increased levels of violence after the lifting of the earlier ban on the SA gave Papen and Schleicher a pretext to strike at the independence of Prussia, which they perceived as the main obstacle to the authoritarian reconstruction of the Reich. Although the Nazis were principally responsible for public disorder, Papen claimed that the Prussian government was incapable of maintaining public order. This belied the past conduct of Carl Severing, Prussia's Interior Minister, and the Prussian police force, which had been active and even-handed in combating both totalitarian parties in a large state which had the misfortune to include virtually every centre of acute political disorder in Germany. The events of 'Bloody Sunday' in Altona on 17 July 1932, in which eighteen civilians were killed in the crossfire between KPD and SA, gave Papen the excuse he sought for a *coup d'état* against Prussia's government. On 20 July, ten days before the election, he deposed Prussia's legitimate caretaker government of the Social Democrat Otto Braun, merging the office of German chancellor and Prussian minister-president, and appointed a Reich commissioner as Prussian interior minister. The new Interior Minister Heinrich Bracht inaugurated purges of socialist, Roman Catholic and Jewish civil servants, and the Prussian government's prohibition against Nazis becoming civil servants was lifted.[268] The dismissed officials were mainly replaced by noblemen, thereby undoing twelve years of republican democratisation of the administration. Given the record levels of unemployment, there was no prospect of a repeat of the general strike which had thwarted the Kapp putsch in 1920. Berlin Gauleiter Goebbels' anxiety that Papen's government 'is doing too much and is not leaving us much more to do' was both unduly modest regarding the future and an indictment of Papen's destruction of one of the few remaining bastions of resistance to a prospective dictatorship. The Nazis achieved their best result in the elections on 30 July, with just over 37 per cent of the vote and 230 seats in parliament. Conservatives, liberals and splinter parties were decimated. The conservatives polled 5.9 per cent; the two liberal parties respectively 1.2 and 1 per cent. Twelve people were killed in terrorist incidents on the day of the polls. But the Nazis began to detect signs of voter boredom at meetings, so they relied more on the mindless razzamatazz of entertainment, parades and marches. By contrast, their rivals on the left developed a belated appreciation of the emotional potency of symbols and the irrational.

Emboldened by the election result, Hitler reneged on his agreement to tolerate Papen's government and insisted upon its refashioning, with himself as chancellor. On 13 August he met Hindenburg, to whom he repeated these demands. Hindenburg offered him and his supporters positions in a government headed by Papen, but he added that neither his conscience nor his sense of duty could permit him 'to transfer the whole authority of government to a single party, especially to a party that was biased against people who had different views from their own'. This was German understatement, since Hindenburg was talking about a party which used bombs, guns and knives to kill its opponents, as had been demonstrated three nights before in the Silesian village of Potempa. Hitler resolved to go into opposition. The interview concluded with Hindenburg remarking, 'We are both old comrades and we want to remain so, since the course of events may bring us together once again later on.' The door to power was left ajar.

Before it had even presented its policies, Papen's cabinet was humiliated by a Communist-inspired vote of no confidence, 512 to 42, on 12 September 1932. In so far as Papen had any policies, these were to replace parliamentary democracy, a plebiscitary presidency and an Upper House representing economic 'estates' with a franchise restricted to mature family people, the intention being to disfranchise Germany's many young radicals. The Reichstag was dissolved and, after a brief period in which the cabinet discussed indefinitely postponing fresh elections, new ones were called for November. In the interim, General Schleicher decided to dispense with Papen. The Defence Minister had become tantalised by the political permutations represented in the Günther Gereke circle, an informal discussion group, which included Nazis, Social Democrats, trade unionists and the nationalist Stahlhelm. Schleicher began to envisage what is known as a diagonal formula: a government led by himself that rested on support from the army, the unions and the Strasser wing of the NSDAP, which was restive with Hitler's accommodating stance towards big business and his uncompromising desire to gain the chancellorship. Schleicher was taken with the ideas of the Tat circle, which advocated a 'third way' between Western laissez-faire liberalism and Marxist totalitarianism. A little socialism would make a large dose of military authoritarianism palatable to the workers, for by now political options were being shaped by the ideas of the right alone.

STARING FAILURE IN THE FACE

In the 6 November 1932 elections, the Nazi vote fell by two million, or about 4 per cent, with their Reichstag seats reduced from 230 to 196.[269] The chief beneficiaries of the election were the conservative nationalists, who gained eight hundred thousand votes, and the Communists, whose share of the vote rose from 14.5 to 16.9 per cent. Collusion between the Nazi NSBO and the Communist Revolutionary Trades Unions in a strike that paralysed the Berlin transport network during the first week of November propelled many conservatives back to their traditional allegiance. Remarkably, people who formerly called each other 'Brown plague' or 'Red sub-humans' had developed considerable solidarities on the barricades which went up as the Berlin strike turned vicious.[270] Goebbels calculated that, while middle-class alienation from the NSDAP would be temporary, Nazi failure to support the strikers would forfeit worker support for good.[271] The Party's line became tortuously hard to follow: attacks on conservatives, too, were necessary, because their policies were driving people to the Communists. Voter sympathy for the Nazis was not enhanced by the SA's autumnal rampage through Silesia, including the gruesome Potempa murder.

In his diaries, Goebbels acknowledged that activism was abating, for the activists were wearying of giving their all for a party that baulked at opportunities to share power. There was a chronic shortage of funds since supporters were often unemployed and the party was thought to have overdrawn on people's goodwill. (This comment of Goebbels suggests that the Party depended on members' contributions rather than on the alleged generosity of big business, which in fact spread its bets across several right-wing parties.) For the first time, what had seemed since 1930 to be an unstoppable movement showed signs of fatigue and internal strain.[272] While the Nazi vote appeared to be in the doldrums, the increase in support for the Communists had one noticeable effect: some influential industrialists now began to switch their support from the ineffectual conservatives and right-wing liberals to the NSDAP as the only way of halting the growth of the KPD.

In December 1932 the socially conscious General Streicher succeeded Papen as chancellor, without the slightest assurance from any of the parties involved that they would support his policy of the diagonal, on to which he tacked work-creation schemes and 'winter aid' for the unemployed. He offered Gregor Strasser the post of vice-chancellor, but the latter then tried to argue Hitler into giving his assent, and resigned all his Nazi Party offices when this was not forthcoming. Although Hitler was plunged into a suicidal depression, he soon rallied, reimposing his authority on the Gauleiter while Strasser took a holiday in the South Tyrol. By loyally declining to seize the moment, Strasser had effectively signed his own death warrant, as he would discover during the 1934 'Night of the Long Knives'. These conspiracies apart, there was no disguising the fact that the Nazi Party was in trouble and that the longer it remained out of power the worse it would become. On 4 December, the Nazi vote dropped again in communal elections in Thuringia, losing up to 35 per cent of its previous support in towns such as Weimar.[273]

Analysing the November and December 1932 election results, the liberal *Vössische Zeitung* saw grounds for hope: 'the nimbus of constant success has vanished, mass propaganda has lost its sensational appeal, the most superlative promises fall on deaf ears. The recovery of health can commence.' Optimism returned abroad, too. Harold Laski, the left-wing British scholar–seer of the London School of Economics, thought that Nazism was a spent force. Exhibiting an unerring capacity to get the major issues hopelessly wrong, Laski predicted that Hitler was destined to spend the evening of his life in a Bavarian village, reminiscing in a beer garden about how he had nearly ruled the Reich.[274]

2

'MISS BECKER, YOUR HEAD IS AT STAKE, YOUR HEAD IS WOBBLING': THE DEMISE OF THE RULE OF LAW

Leading policemen and SS figures in 1934, including several figures
who would later achieve notoriety. Front row, left to right: Kurt Daluege
(Head of the Order Police), Reichsfuhrer-SS Heinrich Himmler, Erhard
Milch, Friedrich-Wilhelm Kruger (who would become Higher SS and Police
Leader in the Polish General Government), SS-Truppfuhrer von Schutz.
Back row, left to right: SS-Oberfuhrer Wolf, Police Captain Bonin,
Reinhard Heydrich (later head of the Reich Main Security Office
who would mastermind the Holocaust of European Jews).

SMART COMPANY

Hitler's final ascent to the German chancellorship was due to his own political skills, the sins of commission and omission of his immediate predecessors, and President Hindenburg's decision to pursue this fateful option. It was fateful because the Nazis had frequently announced their contempt for the rule of law, and by 1932 were vowing to intern Communist and Social Democrat opponents in concentration camps.[1]

The Nazis used the melodramatic term 'seizure of power' to describe what was actually a complex process of bargaining and intrigue in which they were not always the main actors. The outcome was never certain, for at least once during this high-stakes poker game a despondent Hitler spoke of suicide, if his party should disintegrate under the weight of frustrated expectations.[2] His depression was the source of others' elation. Papen was determined to return to power – whether as front- or back-seat driver was a secondary consideration – but for this he needed to demonstrate that he had the support of a major party, which his recent administration had lacked. A Nazi Party which had suffered an electoral setback became correspondingly amenable to deals its leader had ostentatiously rejected. Papen met Hitler on 4 January 1933 in the home of the Cologne banker Baron Kurt von Schroeder, who indicated that the business world – for which he did not speak – would welcome a Papen–Hitler combination. In the course of their discussions, Hitler explained that he was bent on 'the removal of all Social Democrats, Communists and Jews from leading positions in Germany and the restoration of order in public life'. Papen did not demur.[3]

As Brüning had done before him, Schleicher learned that the price of popular policies was the alienation of elites with access to the President. Schleicher's attempts to mollify organised labour antagonised heavy industry, while his enthusiasm for the export sector alienated large landowners. When Schleicher revived Brüning's schemes to settle agricultural labourers on bankrupt estate, the sand in his hourglass began to flow. Papen's other weapon against Schleicher was sheer proximity to the President, who had never forgiven the General for forcing him to dismiss Papen. While his official residence was being refurbished, Hindenburg moved into the Chancellery complex. Schleicher and Hindenburg may have shared office space, but Schleicher went home elsewhere at night, leaving Papen free to pay the President informal visits from his apartment, which was separated from the Chancellery only by a garden behind the building.[4] Papen turned Hindenburg's dislike of Schleicher into disaffection. The Nazi-influenced Agrarian League simultaneously stoked Hindenburg's anger over Schleicher's refusal to countenance protective agrarian tariffs or to extend periods of grace to bankrupt farmers facing foreclosure. To add insult to injury, at the prompting of the Social Democrats a budgetary committee of the Reichstag began investigating evidence of fraud involving Hindenburg's Junker friends, who appeared to be using eastern agricultural subsidies for motoring holidays on the Riviera. Papen probably ensured that Hindenburg made a false connection between exposure of this scandal and Schleicher's lack of indulgence towards impoverished farmers.[5]

Schleicher's schemes to divide and rule the Nazis ran into the sands, and succeeded only in massively antagonising Hitler. Without Nazi support, the Chancellor's entire political strategy collapsed. He became superfluous in circles which talked much about Prussian loyalty but had no compunction in stabbing their friends in the back. The first sign of this was Hindenburg's refusal to grant Schleicher unlimited emergency powers and a dissolution of the Reichstag. While Hindenburg was administering that rebuff, Papen secretly met Hitler, accompanied by Hindenburg's son Oskar and Otto Meissner, the chief of the presidential staff. The setting for this 18 January meeting was Joachim Ribbentrop's home; the other important guest was Hermann Göring, one of the few senior Nazis who could make a passing stab at being a roguish sort of gentleman. While Hitler treated Oskar von Hindenburg to a rambling monologue, Papen signalled his readiness to settle for the office of vice-chancellor, leaving him well positioned if, as widely expected, a Chancellor Hitler cracked under the strains of government. Göring outlined to Meissner the Nazis' apparently modest ambition of one further cabinet post. In the course of further negotiations with Papen, Hitler introduced some deft modifications to their earlier bargain. He insisted on Nazi occupancy of both the Reich and Prussian Interior Ministries, which would bring control of the police, and on fresh elections. An anticipated Nazi majority would facilitate an enabling law with which Hitler could rule, without either emergency decrees or the Reichstag. Once Papen had patched together an apparently representative conservative cabinet, in which the Nazis seemed hopelessly outnumbered, and with an apparently reliable General Blomberg as Defence Minister, Hindenburg was prevailed upon to swear in Hitler as German chancellor. Papen hastened this outcome by portraying loose military talk about the army's capacity to carry out a putsch as an alleged plot by Schleicher to depose the aged President. Arguably, this imaginary outcome would have been a lesser evil than what in fact happened, but since Schleicher was opposed to such a solution, and wanted to scuttle back to the defence portfolio, an authoritarian military interim alternative to Nazism remained hypothetical.[6]

Those who had engineered Hitler into the chancellorship imagined that they had finally achieved a viable conservative coalition, with the National Socialists alongside the German National People's Party and the Stahlhelm, together with a scattering of expert ministers. Papen exuded confidence that Hitler could be contained, marginalised and dropped, before government reverted to those who thought they had an entitlement to it.[7] His effete drawing-room Machiavellianism underestimated Hitler's rat-like cunning. Across town, Hitler was receiving manly handshakes from his comrades, who, Goebbels recorded in his diary, all had tears of joy in their eyes.[8]

The Nazi dictatorship profited from the atrophy of democratic institutions during the three years of presidential chancellorships. After 30 January 1933, the Nazis and their conservative nationalist partners accelerated creeping authoritarianism to the point where it became categorically distinct from what had gone before, in terms of its illegality, violence and limitless ambition. Many call this distinct phenomenon totalitarianism, which in the absence of more cogent terms will be the word used here to describe the aspirations of the Nazi regime. Emergency decrees and terror shaped the outcome of elections called for 5 March 1933, although the result was short of overwhelming. On 17 February, Göring incited the Prussian police to use firearms against political opponents. On the 22nd, he augmented the police with 50,000 'auxiliaries' co-opted from the SA, SS and Stahlhelm. The Reichstag Fire six days later, which the Nazis reinterpreted to their own advantages, provided the pretext for the Decree of the President for the Protection of People and State of 28 February, which abolished rights guaranteed by the Weimar constitution. Hitler informed the cabinet that the 'struggle against the [KPD] must not be dependent upon legal considerations'. The decree suspended freedom of assembly and expression, authorised wiretaps and opening of mail, and sanctioned search and indefinite detention without warrants. This formed the basis of police power, until the police became so powerful that they eventually required no written authorisation at all. The police and SA or SS auxiliaries embarked on waves of arbitrary arrests, often settling scores with political opponents. Revenge was especially evident wherever the Nazis had been numerically inferior to their opponents. Since police cells and prisons began to burst at the seams, places of detention included SA barracks and bars, as well as ships, water towers and the cold cellar of the Oranienburg brewery north of Berlin. Those kidnapped in this fashion, the majority being Communists, were subjected to appalling brutality.[9]

The Reichstag Fire Decree rested on a fiction, since the Leipzig Supreme Court established no connection between the Dutch arsonist Marinus van Lubbe and the Comintern delegates tried for conspiracy, a decision which confirmed Hitler's animus against the judiciary. One fiction led to another. By employing the concept of 'mediate danger', the police and courts used the decree to repress anti-Communists, such as youthful Catholic hikers or Jehovah's Witnesses, on the ground that their 'divisiveness' allegedly furthered the goals of Communism, 'notwithstanding', as a court ruling had it, 'the fact that the associations affected by police regulations are themselves opposed to atheistic Communism'.[10]

Repression was accompanied by an electoral campaign in which Hitler made a virtue of having no concrete policy proposals at all. In his first speech as chancellor, on 10 February 1933, relayed live from Berlin's Sportspalast, he turned his opponents' demands to reveal his policies against them, by chronicling fourteen years of failure and asking, 'What was *your* programmne?' His own programme consisted of not making 'cheap promises'. Recovery would come about through willpower and hard work, without foreign aid. Having outlined points one to three, Hitler averred that 'we [will] rebuild our *Volk* not according to theories hatched by some alien brain, but according to the eternal laws valid for all time. Not according to theories of class, not according to concepts of class.' And so on to the verities of blood and soil, and the need to reconcile the classes: 'Never, never will I stray from the task of stamping out Marxism and its side-effects in Germany, and never will I be willing to make any compromises on this point.' The peasant responsible for racial renewal received due praise, but so did the worker, who would be reintegrated from his alienated condition into the German 'national community'. In other words, the main emphasis was on what we nowadays call inclusivity. Decency, self-respect and a 'genuinely German culture' were to prevail. In sum, 'this programme will be a programme of national resurrection in all areas of life, intolerant of anyone who sins against the nation, but a brother and friend to anyone who has the will to fight with us for the resurrection of his *Volk*, of our nation'. Anyone who opposed the Nazis was a traitor. Hitler's final peroration is worth citing in full:

> I cannot divest myself of my faith in my *Volk*, cannot disassociate myself from the conviction that this nation will one day rise again, cannot divorce myself from my love for this, my *Volk*, and I cherish the firm conviction that the hour will come at last in which the millions who despise us today will stand by us and with us hail the new, hard-won and painfully acquired German Reich we have created together, the new German kingdom of greatness and power and glory and justice. Amen.[11]

There was no programme, just a mood, consisting of millenarian hopes and the certainty of revenge, in which the Lord's Prayer was invoked to stimulate a quasi-religious sentimentality. Goebbels summed up this 'fantastic speech': 'At the end great pathos: "Amen"!' Soon the Christian doxology would be replaced by affirmative cries of 'Sieg Heil!'[12]

In the March elections, the Nazis and their allies reaped 52 per cent of the vote, which translated into 340 of 647 Reichstag seats. This fell short of the two-thirds majority needed to alter the constitution, and indicates that support for the 'national uprising' was less than total. The votes of eighty-one Communist deputies, most of whom were in detention, were discounted. The Reichstag's rules were amended so that deputies absent without adequate excuse were counted as present. The Catholic Centre Party was fatally undermined by the circumstance that the Vatican's interest in securing an inter-state concordat with Germany along the lines of the 1929 Lateran treaties with Mussolini was greater than its interest in the survival of a once great political party. Impressed by Hitler's considerate emollience towards the institutional Church, the German hierarchy discovered his hitherto hidden virtues. In a statement issued by the Fulda Conference of Bishops on 28 March, the tone was surprisingly Lutheran: 'Catholic Christians, for whom the opinion of their Church is sacred, need no particular admonition to be loyal to the legally constituted authorities, to fulfil their civic duties conscientiously, and to reject absolutely any illegal or revolutionary activity.'[13] Centre Party politicians weighed up the advantages of heroic gesture against loss of hypothetical influence, and opted for tactical collaboration. Fourteen of the seventy-four Reichstag delegates wished to join Brüning in opposing the Law for the Alleviation of the People's and the Reich's Misery, otherwise known as the Enabling Law, but they were warned that their safety might be in jeopardy and were finally won over by Papen's assurances that he and the cabinet would still vet every government decree.[14]

The terror on the streets temporarily gravitated to the Kroll-Opera House, where the Reichstag had found a temporary home. SA mobs were audible outside, greeting deputies with calls of 'Centre pig' or 'Marxist sow', while SA and SS men lined the walls, looming over the shoulders of Social Democrat deputies, of whom 94, rather than 120, were present.[15] The young Nazi historian Walter Frank, a prince of nastiness in a field with myriad pretenders, approvingly compared these arrangements with the French Revolutionary Convention.[16] In the ensuing debate, the Social Democrat Otto Wels bravely defended democratic ideals, including a 'real national community' based on 'equality of rights'. The Nazi caucus laughed. Hitler's impromptu reply rehearsed the preceding fourteen years of alleged failure: 'You say you are the only pillar of Socialism. You were the pillar of that mysterious Socialism of which, in reality, the German *Volk* never had a glimpse. . . . By your fruits shall ye, too, be known! The fruits testify against you!' And so to repeated cries of 'Bravo!' and 'Hear, hear!', the Enabling Law passed by a majority of 444 to 94. The Nazi's academic claque made comparisons with the English 'Glorious Revolution'.[17] Two former chancellors, Joseph Wirth and Heinrich Brüning, fled the country, the latter by now under surveillance and changing his lodgings every couple of weeks, appearing to friends as 'a hunted animal, constantly startled and already exhausted, just waiting the final bullet'. Fear and illegality were palpable. Another recent Chancellor, General Schleicher, could not break with a lifetime of conspiracy and began to have dealings with both the French ambassador and the SA leader Röhm. This would cost him his life.

The Enabling Law permitted the government to pass budgets and promulgate laws, including those altering the constitution, for four years without parliamentary approval. In democracies, constitutional amendments are especially solemn moments; here they were easier than changing the traffic regulations. None of the guarantees Hitler extended to the Churches or the judiciary in his address to the Reichstag amounted to a hill of beans. The remnants of the Weimar constitution were retained for reasons of convenience, and to foster an impression of continuity and legality. There was no need to promulgate a new Nazi constitution – which might have been self-constraining – for the substantive parts of the Weimar constitution had been nullified. Thenceforth, draft laws circulated among relevant ministers until consensus emerged. Perfunctory generalities were elaborated in detailed administrative decrees, which routinely flouted those parts of the constitution still technically in operation. Cabinet government lapsed entirely by 1938. The Enabling Law was renewed in 1937 without much fanfare, until in 1943 Hitler declared it perpetual.[18]

Hitler was never the nation's representative, but the self-styled embodiment of its unified will. Only a country in the depths of economic disaster, and with a historical and philosophical culture prone to salvationist rhetoric and mystification, could take this at all seriously. Poetry had more pitfalls than prose. The nation was occasionally encouraged to express a childlike faith in the Führer's decisions, largely for external consumption. A parliament which voted to emasculate itself became a redundant prop on the dictatorial *mise-en-scène*. In elections on 12 November 1933, the 'Führer's list' of the Nazi Party and its 'guests' received 92 per cent of votes cast, rising to 99 per cent in two subsequent elections. The Reichstag met infrequently whenever Hitler determined, passing some seven laws before the outbreak of war, notoriously the 1935 Nuremberg Laws. The Reichstag no longer debated anything, since the only speaker was Hitler; the uniformed delegates were there to assent with enthusiasm. Since sessions concluded with the national anthem or the Horst Wessel Song, wits called the 876 deputies 'the world's best-paid male-voice choir'. Around eighty former members of the Weimar Reichstag died as a result of Nazi persecution; over 160 experienced exile.[19]

Representative democracy was replaced by referenda. These reaffirmed unanimity between a leader guided by his own destiny and a people who were invited to endorse this mysterious communion rather than express personal choices. Plebiscites registered yes votes of 90 per cent or more for departure from the League of Nations or supporting the 1938 Anschluss with Austria. They were a purely propagandistic exercise, since Hitler felt bound not by majorities his regime could rig, but by such nebulous entities as 'destiny', 'history' or 'Providence' which guided his steps. By 1936 he used the metaphor of a 'sleep-walker', unerringly going forth, oblivious to danger, conscience or doubt. By definition, only he knew where Providence was leading him; the people were simply expected to follow.[20]

Opposition parties were eliminated or dissolved themselves. The Communists were proscribed on 7 March 1933; the Social Democrats on 22 June, on the ground that the attentiste rump SPD remaining in Germany had not expelled the dissident exiled SPD leadership in Prague, an ominous sign of how sins of omission became those of commission. After unfortunate attempts to reach an accommodation with the regime, by paddling away from the SPD, labour unions were 'co-ordinated'. Their leaders were arrested, assets seized and members compulsorily enrolled in the new German Labour Front. In succession, confessional, conservative and liberal parties dissolved themselves. On 14 July the NSDAP became the sole legal party, the corollary being that opposition was illegal. The rich party culture of Wilhelmine and Weimar Germany had been extinguished with both bangs and whimpers.[21]

After an initial stab at routine, Hitler reverted to his indolent habits, although we should not expect a leader who saw himself as an artist–politician genius to behave with the legendary assiduity of academic committee men. He was not in power to deal with coal prices in Silesia, any more than Stalin was concerned with the educational arrangements of Uzbekistan. As orthodox historical opinion tells us, government was characterised by multi-centred incoherence, with a war of all against all, bordering on chaos.[22] But the exceptional nature of Nazi governmental chaos can be pushed too far. Democratic governments are riven with factional intrigues and personal rivalries; suffer duplication of functions; rely on outsiders to galvanise sluggish bureaucracies; and are constrained by innumerable external factors. Moreover, many modern corporations and institutions, even including universities, thrive on managerial Darwinism, based on divide and rule, to no obvious loss of profitability, or productivity in the case of universities. In other words, what has been increasingly elevated into the explanatory master-key of Nazi rule, namely the mutually radical-ising effects of competing agencies, may be both insufficient, and less remarkable, as an explanation for the single-mindedness with which the Nazis went about realising their ideological goals. If what is said to be uniquely characteristic of Nazism also typifies many other modern governments and organisations, then this alone can hardly explain a regime of rare destructiveness. The massive documentary evidence of endless squabbles within the regime proves little, since consensus, like happiness in love, requires no written expression.

One aspect of dictatorship seems in need of more emphasis than it nowadays tends to receive – the supercession of the rule of law by arbitrary police terror. This was not some prosaic B-movie, before the lurid A-movie of the regime's wartime racial rampage, but the crucial breach with the most fundamental characteristic of free societies. It was not a side-issue, which once unaccountably preoccupied an older generation of historians and is now best left to legal historians, but *the* most important departure from civilised values engineered by the Nazi government.

HEALTHY POPULAR INSTINCT

The Nazis followed many authoritarian Weimar constitutional theorists in claiming that existing law was abstract, unGermanic and over-concerned with individual rights and material interests. A desiccated law had ceased to reflect 'racial' morality and pulsating popular instinct.[23] Revolutionist contempt for 'bourgeois' justice combined with righteous indignation about the Nazis' own persecution during the time of the 'system'. They claimed that the judicial system was biased against them, while police officers were dupes of politicised senior officers. Both the pro-Nazi biases of the Weimar judiciary and Papen's dismissal in July 1932 of Prussian police presidents with Social Democrat sympathies were omitted from this mythologisation of the recent past. A general animus towards law and lawyers persisted.[24]

Indignation against those identified with the previous democratic legal order took the form of moblike expulsions of Social Democrats and Jews from courts in Breslau, Cologne and Kaiserslautern, followed by a legalised purge under the Law for the Restoration of the Professional Civil Service. The law's title insinuated that the Weimar civil service and judiciary had been permeated by political appointments, which was totally untrue. It included an 'Aryan' clause, with the result that 128 Jewish judges and state prosecutors were dismissed in Prussia alone. Since non-state sector professionals and trades followed suit, often of their own volition, this amounted to a general licence to decide who could or could not work.

Although only one judge was directly assaulted by a mob thereafter, threats of violence against judges by senior Party figures were not uncommon. For example, a judge who convicted several people in 1935 for outrages against a Jewish livestock dealer was informed that his regional Gauleiter was of the view that 'Judges cannot be removed from office, but they are not immune from physical attack.' By withdrawing guarantees of protection from aggression perpetrated by Nazi circles, the Gauleiter ensured that the judge sought a transfer elsewhere. More outrageously, Benno Köhler, a Berlin state prosecutor who in 1930 had indicted Goebbels for infringing a ban on Nazi symbols and a Nazi editor for libelling the Republic in print, was sent to a concentration camp. But such direct intimidation was exceptional.[25]

Partisan disdain for the law was evident, too, in the release of the Potempa murderers, and the amnestying of men sought in connection with the assassination of armistice signatory and leading Catholic politician Matthias Erzberger. Commemoration of Rathenau's killer became a state occasion. A general pardon for crimes committed during the 'seizure of power' was issued on 21 March 1933, with further indulgence shown towards 'over-zealous' Nazis on 7 August 1934.[26] By contrast, that same August two Dortmund Communists were executed for fatally stabbing an SA man in June 1932, notwithstanding an interim Weimar amnesty and the fact that their offences did not incur the death penalty at the time of commission. Those who had inadvertently created the movement's martyrs, such as Ali Höhler, who had been jailed for killing Horst Wessel, were extracted from prison and murdered.[27]

The most spectacular legitimisation of the gravest of crimes was the retroactive Law Concerning Measures for the Defence of the State of 3 July 1934, whereby Hitler legalised dozens of murders he had ordered days or hours earlier during the 'Night of the Long Knives'. The lurid details need not detain us. Suffice it to say that this was a multipurpose strike against several foes, principally the SA leadership, whose aggressive conduct and paramilitary pretensions were undermining Hitler's relations with the armed forces, but also dissident young conservatives in the entourage of Vice-Chancellor Papen, whom we will re-encounter in a later discussion of resistance. Since Hitler needed the army by his side, it was only a question of time before Röhm and his fellow advocates of a 'second revolution' had to go, in the interests of concord with the generals, and in line with an evolutionary, rather than revolutionary, approach to government, which did not grate with respectable opinion. General Reichenau, Blomberg's Chief of Staff, helped determine who was to die, while the army loaned the SS trucks and weapons to carry out the deed. In late June 1934, the opportunity was seized to clear the decks of all actual or potential opponents in a nationwide bloodbath. This was what the Law was intended retroactively to excuse.[28]

The conservative Minister of Justice, Franz Gürtner, in the cabinet as a token nod to Catholic opinion, signed up to the Law, expecting that a one-off measure would limit future illegalities, but also because the murder of senior SA figures eliminated a source of constant arbitrary interference in the legal system.[29] But Gürtner was a minor player in this drama. Ten days after the Law was promulgated, Hitler used an aggressive confession to the Reichstag to demonstrate his total disdain for the rule of law. He outlined dark conspiracies as a prelude to his resonant theme that a mutiny had been pre-empted – a claim that was wholly irrelevant to the killing of civilians or of such innocent parties as a misidentified music critic, a publican and the wife of General Schleicher:

> Mutinies are crushed only by the everlasting laws of iron. If anyone reproaches me and asks why we did not call upon the regular courts for sentencing, my only answer is this: in that hour, I was responsible for the fate of the German nation and was thus the Supreme Judge of the German *Volk*! Mutinous divisions have always been recalled to order by decimation. Only one State did not make use of its wartime legislation, and the result was the collapse of this State: Germany. I did not want to abandon the young Reich to the fate of the old. . . .
>
> . . . When people confront me with the view that only a trial in court would have been capable of accurately weighing the measure of guilt and expiation, I must lodge a solemn protest. He who rises up against Germany commits treason. He who commits treason is to be punished not according to the scope and proportions of his deed, but rather according to his cast of mind as revealed therein. . . . It is not my responsibility to ascertain whether and, if so, which of these conspirators, agitators, nihilists, and well-poisoners of German public-opinion and, in a wider sense, of world opinion too, has been dealt too hard a lot; rather, my duty is to make certain that Germany's lot is bearable.[30]

Nazi Germany ventured nothing so radical as Lenin's replacement of the existing legal personnel with 'our people', regardless of their incompetence, but both dictatorships shared a revolutionist contempt for the law *per se*. Law was an incidental means to utopian ends, rather than an absolute value in itself. It masked the extra-judicial activities of the police. Moreover, since courts in both Germany and Soviet Russia remained public, they could be used to publicise what was or was not tolerated by their governments.[31] If in Russia social-revolutionary ideals and resentments led to deeper changes in the legal personnel, in Germany a need to retain an impression of legality combined with an absence of qualified Nazi personnel to produce a hybrid system. Special tribunals were grafted on to the existing system, albeit often staffed by the old personnel, together with lay Party appointments. For, despite its egalitarian rhetoric, Nazi Germany eschewed the doctrine of aggressive class war, whatever revolutionist animosities lingered, against the limp bourgeoisie in general. This revamped legal apparatus co-operated and competed with, but was increasingly marginalised by, the Gestapo and SS – that is, the state political police and the Nazi Party's own elite paramilitary formation. The erstwhile executive servants of the judicial apparatus became not just its rivals but its masters, eventually contemplating such novel arrangements as replacing prosecutors with policemen, and removing entire groups of people from the law's limited protection.

The Ministry of Justice under Gürtner endeavoured to move the law in a highly authoritarian direction, while maintaining legal predictability, procedure and propriety vis-à-vis the SS and Gestapo. However, the latter simply subtracted entire groups of people from the aegis of the law, the intention being to act as prosecution and judge in their own affairs, save when they needed the courts to hand down exemplary sentences.[32] Gürtner acquiesced in what he imagined to be a temporary state of emergency, in which arbitrary police powers were overwhelmingly directed against the left, but tried to salvage something from the ensuing police terror. This forlorn attempt was akin to striking damp matches on a windy night. Much the same dilemma was faced by the officials of the Soviet Commissariat, and later Ministry of Justice, as they fell foul of Stalin's attempt to combine an external impression of restored legality with arbitrary police terror. But, before exploring these arrangements in detail, a few animating principles are indispensable, for it was the new 'spirit' informing the law which counted, rather than formal enactments. This should not be confused with the theories of those who sought to cloak Nazi tyranny in quasi-philosophical garb. The new dispensation suffered no dearth of amorally clever people, notably Ernst Hüber, Otto Koellreuter and Carl Schmitt, keen to elaborate a bespoke Nazi jurisprudence, but their function was ornamental, however enthusiastic their attempts at ingratiation.[33] For the Nazi view was that: 'Just as the old state will not return, the old constitutional theory will cease to have any meaning. It is equally useless, however, to write learned treatises about the nature of the new state – here, too, the pens are scribbling in vain. Today, only one person knows what the new structure of the state will look

like after ten years, the Führer, and he won't allow himself to be
influenced in this knowledge by any writers, no matter how learned.'[34]

The notions informing law in the Third Reich are not difficult to
grasp. Some features were common to other totalitarian regimes,
notwithstanding contextual differences, such as the Wild West conditions prevailing among the populations slammed together in anomic
Soviet cities, with their high incidences of drunkenness or 'hooliganism'. There was a Bolshevik contempt for, and subordination of law
to, blatant ideological ends, for procedural quiddities were obstruc-
tions on the road to utopia. There was a similar emphasis upon judicial
'elasticity', for which read 'revolutionary consciousness'; resort to
analogy; retroactive penalties; objective guilt and subjective intent; and
the danger a person represented to the 'national community', which in
Russia meant enemies of the proletariat. A class bias reflected in harsh
sentences for the enemies of the toilers, including many toilers themselves, was paralleled by Nazi discrimination on grounds of race. This
comparison between two evil systems only seems to surprise those who
evidently have difficulty in including kulaks or Kazakhs in the human
race, or who insist, too much for many tastes, that human suffering is
ethically divisible. In both systems, law was overshadowed by the
extra-judicial powers of the police, excepting whenever the Cheka,
NKVD or Gestapo thought that a show trial was more desirable than
disappearance. Both systems erased distinctions between ordinary and
political crime, while criminalising harmless utterances.[35]

Of course, differences are part and parcel of any meaningful
comparison. Nazi Germany experienced nothing akin to the 'campaign
justice' which denuded Soviet cities of law in order to enforce rural
collectivisation by charging peasants with sabotage if their tractor
broke down, or with theft if they slaughtered livestock to prevent it
being stolen by the state. Since the Nazis did not engage in reckless
industrialisation, they also had no need of regular show trials of
'wreckers' to cover up accidents, production breakdowns and shoddy
workmanship of the kind which ensued from the Soviet leadership's
own policies. Canteen cooks in Nazi Germany could also sleep safely
abed in the knowledge that the discovery of a cockroach or a nail in
the food would not entail charges of Trotskyite intent to kill the
workforce.[36]

Widespread recognition before 1933 that the Prussian and then
imperial criminal codes of 1851 and 1871 required reform, which
had resulted in piecemeal progressive measures, paradoxically enhanced

acceptance of retrogressive innovations, without anyone much noticing the difference. Plans to reform the whole criminal code were shelved after reaching an advanced stage, because unlike traditional despots, with their concern for predictability and security, Hitler regarded written rules as potentially restrictive of his capricious will. Instead of a new Nazi code, the rule of law was curtailed by a swift series of cuts which gradually bled the notion of content. Typically, Stalin appeared to restore vestiges of legality for external consumption, just as he was gearing up to purge imaginary opponents, including many of the judiciary.

In the course of promising judges security of tenure, which was immediately violated by the Law for the Restoration of the Professional Civil Service, Hitler indicated that he expected judges to evince 'flexibility'. Empty talk from Hans Frank, leader of the Nazi League of Jurists, about restoring the judiciary's quasi-regal autonomy, alluring in a system without the British division of elite judges and lay magistrates, came with the expectation that judges would abandon impartial objectivity, a quality normally synonymous with their profession. They were to grasp the essence of a case, approaching it with 'healthy prejudice' and in line with 'the main principles of the Führer's government'. This was an invitation to cut every procedural corner: a general mandate for courtroom tyrants, of whom there were many.

Flexibility was required elsewhere. Lawyers and state prosecutors had to practise 'unanimity of aim', whereby defence and prosecution recognised the same objectives. Procedural technicalities ceased to be loopholes. Superficially speaking, state prosecutors enjoyed an increase of power, as procurators enjoyed in Vyshinsky's Soviet Union. They were the primary transmission belts for ensuring that directives from the Ministry of Justice were followed by the courts.[37] They decided which courts tried what cases, effectively guaranteeing outcomes, while their rights of appeal against unsatisfactory sentences were massively enhanced as those of defendants diminished. But, since the Gestapo bypassed the courts with arbitrary detention, enhanced powers were an illusion within a wider context of contraction.[38] Defence lawyers were in a delicate position within this as in other dictatorships, where relations between judges, prosecutors and police were indulgently close. While they sometimes excelled the prosecution in denouncing their own clients, limp legal representation was more usual. Rather than risk challenging the facts or their clients' presumed guilt, defence lawyers routinely relied upon extenuating circumstances. Since

acquittals were potentially dangerous, for the Gestapo could correct
them with 'protective custody', lawyers sometimes contrived to have
innocent clients sentenced to terms of regular imprisonment, whose
rigours were less lethal than concentration camps.[39]

Violations of Western norms included the use of analogy and
retroactive penalties. Analogy was sanctioned in 1935, to replace
'formal wrongdoing' with the idea that 'every violation against the
goals towards which the community is striving is wrong *per se*'. In
Gürtner's formulation:

> What is right may be learned not only from the law but also from the
> concept of justice which lies behind the law and may not have found
> perfect expression in the law. The law certainly continues to be the
> most important source for the determination of right and wrong
> because the leaders of the nation express their will in the law. But the
> legislator is aware of the fact that he cannot give exhaustive regulations
> covering all the situations which may occur in life; he therefore entrusts
> the judge with filling in the gaps.[40]

Although much of this is commonplace in every Western legal system,
there was no 'concept of justice' informing German law at all. Ostensibly
justified with offences arising from new technologies, such as
defrauding public call boxes or illegally tapping the electricity supply,
the analogy principle had indefinite potential, even if its use was
relatively sparing. Thus the illegitimate son of a Jewish woman who
had named his 'Aryan' adoptive parents on an application to join the
Nazi Party was charged with falsifying official documents, even though
the Nazi Party was not a state authority: 'there can be no doubt that,
according to the healthy instincts of the people, actions such as these,
which can do serious damage to the image of the NSDAP, deserve
punishment'.[41]

The retroactive imposition of the death penalty for crimes Hitler
deemed especially heinous commenced with the Lex Lubbe, whose
purpose was to hang, demeaningly, the Dutch arsonist, although he
was nobly beheaded. Similar interventions followed, in the case of
extortionate child kidnapping, or those who used roadblocks to rob
motorists on the new *Autobahnen*. This breached one of the central
principles of Western jurisprudence, namely no punishment without
prior legal sanction, and, as officials remarked at the time, admitted
Germany to the exclusive club of the Soviet Union and China. Between
1933 and 1939 the number of capital offences rose from three to

twenty-five and then to over forty.[42] But the increase in capital offences was merely the most sensational aspect of a system which erased distinctions between degrees of culpability, lowered the age of criminal responsibility, judged people according to their race or 'type', and subordinated individual rights to the interests of the collective.

Law was to protect and serve the collective interests of the national community, rather than to defend the rights of the individual against an arbitrary executive. This fundamental characteristic of democracies was nullified in a system which fused executive and judiciary into one arbitrary identity. As the slogan had it, 'the common good precedes individual good'. In other words, the rights of the individual were subordinate to those of the 'community', that common excuse for collectivist oppression, usually by the community's self-appointed spokesmen. Law was not subject to such quaint ideas as conformity with the constitution, whose extant guarantees of, for example, freedom of religious association were routinely violated. According to Hans Frank: 'We start from the law of the community, and this communal law is the real reversal of our legal point of view and our legal system.' The interests and values of the 'national community', as expressed through the 'Führer principle' – what the leader said became law – became paramount. Hitler's instincts grasped the 'national community's' instincts, in ways which were inherently opaque and resistant to reasoned expression. Judges were expected to be rooted in the *Volk*, which meant being emotionally liberated from desiccated legal procedures, and open to demotic suasion as refracted through Nazi propaganda. What did mere procedures matter, against the unfolding bio-political mission? For, as elsewhere, the urgent desire to achieve utopia at any cost served to cut through the delicate restraining threads which characterise civilised societies.

Since the 'national community' was effectively defined by race, it was progressively exclusionary. Only one or two aspects of this warrant discussion here. Notions of equality before the law were replaced by a system of legal apartheid. Racial aliens did not belong, and nor did those whose criminal 'parasitism' on the body of the nation resulted in temporary or permanent outlawry, one of several revivals of barbaric custom. For crime was construed as an act of betrayal of the 'national community', hence all crime and all deviant attitudes and behaviour were potentially political. A burglar in the blackout became a 'plunderer'; a Jew or Pole who had sexual congress with an 'Aryan' woman was guilty of 'racial defilement'. In further departure from civilised norms, words became crimes. Public suspicions about the causes of the Reichstag Fire resulted in the 1933 Decree against Malicious Attacks, which criminalised hostile remarks about the leadership, Party and state. The courts and police assumed responsibility for enforcing a mood of Panglossian optimism, by punishing even the most inadvertent or innocent of remarks which impugned the 'new times' in the 'new state' in general. Contentment and happiness were enforced.[43]

The paramountcy of collective interests was apparent too in new criminal legislation. As in many other societies, German criminologists, that is doctors, lawyers and psychiatrists, debated the respective influences of nature and nurture. By the 1930s, those who stressed hereditary factors had gained the upper hand. They sought to discern habitual criminal types, supposedly differently constituted from opportunist offenders or ordinary people. The idea that such people were lesser beings combined with the necessity to protect the 'national community' from future harm through reproduction of their genetic matter. This assumed a racially specific character, so that Blacks, Gypsies and Jews were regarded as especially prone to certain forms of criminality, a view already anchored in folk belief, in Germany and elsewhere, whether it was well-poisoning Jews or Gypsy kidnappers of children.[44]

The November 1933 Law against Dangerous Habitual Criminals and Measures for their Detention and Improvement fused retribution for actual crime with the prior right of the 'national community' to be protected from potential offenders. This meant that, in addition to the sentence incurred for an offence, judges or the police could subjectively determine that a person was a permanent danger to the community, requiring castration in the case of sexual offenders, or a further period of detention, in asylums, prisons or workhouses, after they had served their sentence. Sentimental pandering to the parents of child victims was used to justify detention of people whose record involved unrelated forms of crime, or whose lifestyle was regarded as unacceptable.[45]

Nazi politics was both tantalised by the preventive potentialities of biological science and suffused with wonderment at a barbaric past, in this last respect standing on the firm ground of demotic opinion in many countries. The term 'healthy instincts of the *Volk*' encapsulated this barbaric, biological populism. Law and policing became branches of epidemiology, a means of excluding racial aliens or redefining crime as illness, which was frequently regarded as untreatable. Both had their analogues in other totalitarian dictatorships, where resort to the language of parasitology was common, although the later Soviet practice of categorising dissidents as schizophrenics set in once it was no longer routine to shoot them.[46]

While Nazi justice and policing became a form of crude biological engineering, it also reflected retributive sentiments, and accorded with atavistic lessons from the very remote past. Biological politics could accommodate this quite easily. Demands for revenge and retribution were reconstrued as expressions of racial self-preservation, and ugly sentiments assumed an air of scientific inevitability. Those who implemented these policies were privileged to be involved in a progressive project designed to promote the general well-being.[47] Those more taken with the emotionally liberated past than with microscopes and mug-shots could rejoice in a regression to barbarity. This seems to have included the regime's leaders. Hence admiring references to such alleged tribal customs as drowning strangled homosexuals in peatbogs or the annihilation of the 'clans' of those accused of high treason proved thoroughly compatible with an otherwise modernist culture of card-sorting machines and advanced forensic or racial science, just as medieval legal principles operate alongside such technologies in modern democracies.[48]

General principles were one thing, implementation another. No matter how conformist or zealous, the inherited legal machinery and personnel had their own vested interests and *modus operandi*, which conflicted with the activist desire of the SS and Gestapo for swift surgical solutions. The latter were invariably supported by Hitler, with whose will they were most keenly identified. The composition and outlook of the judiciary were unsatisfactory from a Nazi viewpoint. Partly this was a matter of age, for it was more difficult to exert leverage on people near retirement than on middle-aged judges and lawyers whose future careers were at stake. Opposition probably frequently took the form of early retirement, as those tired of this mockery of their values decided to tend their gardens or play with their grandchildren, rather than work in a progressively mad system. An exodus of the weary was accompanied by at least one judicial suicide. Younger men did not have the option of early retirement. Their intimidation was sometimes crude and unpleasant. A trainee judge who fined an SA-Standartenführer 1000 Reichsmarks for calling a leading cleric a traitor was told by his Party Gauleiter, 'It is good that I have seen you. . . . I will make provision for your future professional advancement.'[49]

Once a minority of liberals, Social Democrats and Jews had been subtracted from the judiciary, the Nazis were left with a group among whom committed National Socialists were the exception and whose collective identity was reactionary rather than revolutionary. Belated membership of the Party did not alter this impression, since judges and state prosecutors were routinely criticised for passive involvement. They were expected to perform humdrum tasks not congruent with their self-esteem, while their professional subordinates often enjoyed higher Party rank than they did. Other issues rankled. Whereas senior Party leaders and members of Nazi formations enjoyed the use of motorcars, senior judges and state prosecutors did not. Moreover, the absence of a standardised judicial uniform counted in situations where social prominence was determined by uniforms and insignia.[50]

Party membership meant that judges and lawyers were subject to Party jurisdiction, for in 1933 former courts of honour became local, regional and national Party courts. Designed to settle disputes between Party members and to facilitate purges, the source of law was the cryptic Party programme and copies of *Mein Kampf*. The only substantial penalty was exclusion from the Party. Party courts were also responsible for the Party's image, a remit covering the professional conduct and private behaviour of 'national comrades'. Thus a judge who quashed a case against a woman who had called local SS leaders alcoholics, homosexuals and 'arseholes', for she might have been right, was brought before a Party court. Since judges and lawyers could deploy legal technicalities to justify their unsatisfactory conduct in court, the preferred line of attack concerned their wider role within society. A judge who since 1918 had regularly lunched with eight friends, including a Jew, endeavoured to help the latter emigrate in the mid-1930s. In 1938, the judge was expelled from the Party for 'unprecedented indifference . . . towards such a burning question for the German nation', and invited to retire prematurely from the judiciary.[51]

Indoctrination of the aspirant judiciary commenced with a legal education which included compulsory classes in Nazi ideology, physical training and involvement with the lives of ordinary people. Ideology was also communicated through informal association, although the judge who took a 'working community' of trainee lawyers on a visit to a lunatic asylum on Hitler's birthday was clearly making a different point. Informal conferences of judges and lawyers degenerated into convivial occasions, while six weeks' pre-final-examinations exertions at the Hanns Kerrl camp in Jüterbog were resented by men of a sedentary disposition, who wished to brush up on the law rather than puff along on twenty-mile marches. Character assessments by camp staff who were permanently drunk or frequently involved in brawls with the locals or each other were often resented.[52]

Subversion of the rule of law occurred through formal and informal channels. The new spirit was spread by criticism and example, or through the creative tension generated by institutionalised competition. The former commenced long before the introduction of 'judicial letters' in 1942–4 providing ten thousand jurists with examples of judgements deemed 'good, and significant for the national community'.[53] Presiding judges and state prosecutors were routinely invited to conferences in the Ministry of Justice, and expected to relay the required line through conferences for their own subordinates. Both the Ministry and local prosecutors liaised with the Gestapo, either through formalised channels or over the telephone. This included routine notification of the acquittal or release of prisoners, which facilitated their rearrest. While much information flowed from the judicial system to the Gestapo, an organisation swathed in secrecy offered nothing in return. Internal praise or blame of judicial decisions was paralleled by wider monitoring. From August 1933, regional Gestapo offices recorded verdicts in political cases, a practice Reinhard Heydrich, the deputy SS chief, centralised from 1935 onwards.

From 1935, the SS weekly *Schwarze Korps* routinely criticised or ridiculed instances of judicial leniency, sparking angry exchanges with the official *Deutsche Justiz*. Formal channels of intra-administrative communication were replaced by gutter journalism. This was mirrored in the Soviet Union, where attacks on judicial 'right deviationists' drove up sentences for 'terrorism', that is such crimes as punching a Stakhanovite. In 1937 *Schwarze Korps* explained the primary obligation of lawyers to the 'national community'. It began with apparent appreciation of the contemporary lawyer's dilemma:

> What was 'law' yesterday is often unlawful today, what was unlawful yesterday can be lawful today. The lawyer can no longer uphold the law of yesterday without breaking the law, and what he upholds as law today, he could not have upheld yesterday, because it would have been considered 'unlawful'.

Instead of using an actor's eloquence or legal technicalities know-ingly to help the guilty, lawyers were to understand that 'the "interests" of their clients are only to be upheld as long as they do not harm the real interests of the national community'. Streicher's nox-ious illustrated magazine *Stürmer* also ran attacks on a senior judge whose wife shopped in stores owned by Jews. The woman was too frightened to venture on to Düsseldorf's streets, while her husband was ejected from his rented Bavarian holiday home, and interviewed by the Party district leadership about his wife's shopping habits. But external pressures were only part of a story involving widespread self-coordination by men whose existing prejudices often required slight synchronisation, even when they were otherwise lukewarm towards National Socialism.[54]

Various forms of jiggery-pokery were used to suit horses to courses. Prosecutors decided which courts to use to guarantee the worst out-come from the defendant's point of view. After 1935, trials of clerics were confined to one court per district, to ensure standardised practice in this especially treacherous area. From 1937 onwards, collegial allocation of judges to types of cases was replaced by more autocratic arrangements, whereby the presiding judge could send softies to the land registry and iron men to criminal tribunals.[55] Those who came before the courts on political charges often emerged after months of confinement, during which confessions were extracted with threats and violence. They caught belated sight of the charges, and received a public defender, for many of the accused were penniless. Since treason cases routinely involved batches of accused, courts were swollen with defendants and guards, which conspired to de-individualise the accused, while making them seem dangerous – presentational tactics not unknown to police forces in democratic countries. Trials were swift and unpleasant, with some judges contributing to this atmos-phere. Not all the toughies were card-carrying Nazis.

Take Ernst Hermsen, a presiding judge of the court at Hamm in Rhineland-Westphalia. A practising Catholic, and member of the Centre Party between 1924 and 1933, Hermsen privately refused to use the salutation 'Heil Hitler!' while permitting his wife to protest the closure of confessional schools. He also pathologically hated the left. Defence claims that indictments included errors encountered the response that this was to be expected, while defendants were routinely treated to such outbursts as 'Shut your dirty mouth, you pathetic spectacle [*Jammergestalt*]'. An elderly defendant who broke down was told to 'Stop your mewling, you'll have plenty of time for that in your cell,' while the suicide of another called Selig ('blessed' in German) prompted the witticism that 'Herr Selig is now blessedly asleep.' Defendants who claimed to have been tortured were told, 'If one didn't beat you Communists like rabid dogs, one would never get anything out of you,' while a woman Communist defendant was constantly reminded, 'Miss Becker, your head is at stake, your head is wobbling.'[56]

Specific types of crime were hived off to special tribunals, not including the new Hereditary Health Courts dealing with eugenic issues, which will be discussed in a later chapter. 'Extraordinary courts' and a 'People's Court' had been pioneered by the Eisner regime in Munich in November 1918, and were reintroduced in 1922 and 1932 to combat political violence. Their peremptory procedures and restrictions on the rights of the accused were therefore familiar.[57] Under the Nazis the emergency became perpetual. In March 1933, twenty-seven Special Courts were created, rising to over seventy by 1938. Since the judges often included non-Party members, and indeed some classified as politically unreliable, these tribunals were not a Nazified excrescence, staffed solely by ideological fanatics. Some judges with histories of active Party membership before 1933 were regarded as 'soft', while the most zealous included multi-decorated war veterans with backgrounds in the Catholic Centre Party.[58]

Once political opponents had been subtracted into concentration camps and prisons, the Special Courts focused upon offences under the revamped 1933/4 Law against Malicious Attacks on State and Party and for the Protection of Party Uniforms. Since the last part of this was a dead letter, stemming from a period when Hitler believed Communists were masquerading as National Socialists to discredit them, most cases involved malicious remarks or rumour-mongering. Since anything which could be remotely construed as propagandising the Communist cause was prosecuted under the 1934 revised laws of treason, whether or not this involved a drunk weaving through the streets of Bochum shouting 'Heil Moscow' at moon and stars, malicious attacks involved more diffuse forms of disaffection. Just to be clear on this, the political authorities themselves determined which remarks were political.

Churches, pubs, barbers and railway waiting rooms were treacherous places in which to venture unguarded opinions to strangers, although even such private settings as Catholic confessionals were no guarantee of confidences. A high proportion of the accused had offended while intoxicated, like the man who, waiting in a barbers for a shave, opined to the customers in the adjacent ladies' salon that their 'bob cuts' would be wasted on a Führer who preferred fourteen-year-olds with long tresses. Offences where no leeway was accorded the accused included anything undermining the mystique or moral probity of the leadership and sole Party, that is, calling Hitler a 'poof', or the Party self-serving crooks. For example, a Düsseldorf docker who referred to Hitler as 'a prole' and 'sack of shit' received an eighteen-month prison sentence. Remarks which undercut propaganda stressing a radical break with the past, or comments about the hypocrisy of those who preached egalitarianism while enjoying a sybaritic lifestyle were routinely punished.[59] Any discussion of concentration camps was particularly liable to result in deterrent sentencing. In 1933, a naturalised Pole wrote to his sister-in-law in Łódź about the unbearable conditions in the new Germany, which included people being sent to camps or disappearing in lakes, their corpses weighted down with stones. His letter was opened and read by officials responsible for monitoring currency violations, and he received a two-year prison sentence for encouraging the spreading of false rumours.[60]

Special Courts also assumed responsibility for cases involving clerics, Jehovah's Witnesses and the more sensational felonies. This extension of jurisdiction partly reflected the self-justifying interest of the Gestapo and SD (the SS Security Service) in these areas, once political opposition had been discernibly broken. For enhanced police budgets, and newly won institutional niches, had to be justified by fresh armies of opponents, rather as intelligence agencies in the post-Cold War era have developed an interest in international drug trafficking or mafias, whose Ian Fleming baroque villainy apparently justifies cutting corners to apprehend them. But there were also anti-clerical and ideological agendas beyond these commonplaces of organisational *raison d'être*.

Trials of clerics were designed to restrict the clergy to sacerdotal functions, even though many of the alleged offences arose in reaction to provocative Nazi attacks on the clergy and religion. They were also intended to drive a wedge between clergy and laity. Critical remarks from the pulpit were prosecuted under amendment 130a to the Criminal Code, in deliberate evocation of the nineteenth-century *Kulturkampf*. Remarks outside the churches came under the Law against Malicious Attacks. Sentences of six to eight months' jail were passed on priests who questioned the official version of the Reichstag Fire, or how and why Röhm had met his maker.[61]

As the clergy became more circumspect, prosecutions shifted to currency and sexual offences. Show trials in Munich and Koblenz were designed to subvert the moral authority of the Catholic Church, at a time when it was challenging the ethical basis of eugenic sterilisation and defending its confessional schools and youth organisations against Nazi incursions.[62] That the trials were politically orchestrated can be seen from Hitler's insistence that they cease for the duration of the 1936 Olympic Games, as if the law functioned like a valve or tap. They intensified after Pius XI's March 1937 encyclical 'With burning concern', wherein the Holy Father condemned those who worshipped the idols of race, people or state. Goebbels dispatched muckraking reporters to the monastery at Ménage in Belgium to cover a murder by a servant of a boy, which was then generalised into claims that all ten thousand Brothers of Charity were homosexuals. In a speech broadcast on 28 May 1937, Goebbels spoke of 'a general corruption of morals such as the history of civilisation has scarcely ever known'. At the time, he was chasing the starlet Lida Baarova, while the Gestapo was using bribes and threats to secure charges of sexual molestation from children in Catholic homes and schools. Nazi newspaper coverage of these trials was so salacious that in some areas the number of subscriptions fell, while there was increased participation in religious processions.[63]

If some judges were inhibited vis-à-vis the clergy by their own confessional allegiances, or by the clergy's sometimes very able Catholic defence lawyers, they were unrestrained in their repression of sects such as the Jehovah's Witnesses. The latter were banned under the anti-Communist Reichstag Fire decree, notwithstanding constitutional guarantees of religious freedom. This did not inconvenience Special Courts, which passed stiff sentences against Jehovah's Witnesses, whom they regarded as lower-class madmen. Persecution of the Jehovah's Witnesses resulted from twofold pressures. In order to restock the depleted supply of enemies of the state, the Gestapo accused the sect of abusing religion for political ends, namely 'the destruction of all existing forms of state and governments and the establishment of the kingdom of Jehovah, in which the Jews as the chosen people shall be the rulers'. The anti-Communist content of *Watchtower* was ignored in the interests of depicting the sect as Communist stooges.

Gestapo detention of the Witnesses triggered a judicial reaction, for the Ministry of Justice sensed a challenge to the autonomy of the courts, and hence instructed them to avail themselves of maximum sentences against the sect. Special Courts were the optimal tribunal for heinous criminal cases, such as the two brothers who murdered four people in the course of stick-ups on the *Autobahnen*, where the crime, and the draconian response, required the full glare of publicity.[64]

Political interference in the law was as apparent in the cases which did not come to court as in those which did. Prosecutors had to negotiate a course between the exemplary stifling of disaffection and the weeding out of cases reeking of malice or which raised more awkward questions than they were worth. In 1938, state prosecutors dropped proceedings against a shoeshop girl who had torn up a copy of *SA-Mann*, remarking that it was 'not good enough for the lavatory'. News of this heinous offence reached the Gestapo from a young man in the shop next door, whose lunchtime sexual advances had been repulsed. He had then made remarks about her religion, provoking actions not aimed at the SA in general.[65] Other cases were dropped because of Party complaints about the demoralising effect upon otherwise loyal Party comrades. The courts also received instructions not to proceed with cases where the factuality of comments might be embarrassing in open court, so that those who described Horst Wessel as a pimp, or who suggested that National Socialism and religion were inimicable, were not given a chance to air these views in court.

A case which did come before a Special Court, and resulted in an acquittal, was symptomatic of the state of law in Nazi Germany. The scene of the crime was a cowshed. In 1935 a vet remarked to his peasant client apropos a cow: 'See, isn't the fellow as fat and well fed as Göring?' A labourer who overheard this became a hostile witness. The presiding judge of the Hanover Special Court threw out the case on the ground that the remarks were not public, since the two men did not know that the labourer had been listening. In a stinging rebuke, Göring claimed that, while he was reconciled to comments about his girth, he totally rejected Judge Brandmüller's view of what constituted the public. Since Brandmüller was manifestly indifferent to the honour of the leadership, 'your behaviour strikes me as being more dangerous to the state than that of the accused. The simple fact of not wanting publicly to disgrace the judicial authorities in general has deterred me from placing you in protective custody, as you undoubtedly deserve according to the healthy instincts of the nation.' The judge's candidacy for a senior appointment was blocked and he was no longer allowed to preside over a Special Court.[66]

The autonomy of the judicial system was subject to dual processes of exclusion and invasion by the SS and Gestapo, provoking rearguard action and proactive zealotry by the judicial authorities and the courts. A similar process occurred in Russia, where legal authorities speeded up court proceedings to prevent political cases being hijacked by the OGPU.[67] Attempts to stem the tide of illegality met apparent accommodation, although an early instance of this was hardly reassuring for those who wished to uphold the law. In his 13 July 1934 speech to the Reichstag, Hitler mentioned that a Gestapo officer and two SS guards had been shot during the 'Night of the Long Knives', having already been jailed for torturing and robbing inmates of a concentration camp at Bredow near Stettin.[68] In fact, they were replaced by SS men from a Berlin camp who had allegedly been 'disciplined' for torturing a Czech journalist, including subjecting him to mock execution, actions which had caused an international scandal.[69]

For, in reality, Hitler sanctioned SS chief Himmler's desire to deny camp inmates access to lawyers to question their detention, or its conditions, thus smoothing the way for greater enormities.[70] The only lawyers inmates could see were chosen from lists of those 'who are in full agreement with the political objectives of the state and the ideological aims of the movement'.[71] Camp extra-territoriality was guaranteed in other respects too. The obligation of state prosecutors to investigate unlawful punishments or suspicious deaths in custody was terminated. For example, prosecutors lost the right to conduct autopsies. These had uncovered such mysteries as prisoners hanging themselves after they had died; people shackled to bunks who had viciously attacked guards; or who had been shot from ranges of under a metre 'while trying to escape'. Thus in 1935 two suspected homosexuals were murdered within days of each other in Berlin's Columbia House detention centre. In the one case which prosecutors pursued, the victim had allegedly tried to seize a gun from guards resecuring him to a bunk, which resulted in his being shot in the shoulder. Four hours later, and despite his wounded shoulder, the prisoner allegedly attacked an SS medical orderly in the sickbay, who drew a pistol from beneath his white garb and shot the convalescent through the heart. This story strained credulity. Gürtner tried to combine this case with others to show a pattern of police brutality and illegality. Himmler rebuffed him with the news that he had reported these events to Hitler, and that no further measures were necessary. In February 1936 Hitler quashed the prosecution of the guards concerned.[72] Prosecutors who tried to investigate such crimes deserve respect. They found it advisable not to rely on their own secretaries, or to work up papers outside office hours. Their theoretical subordinates in the uniformed police were too frightened to assist, while the political police openly scorned their endeavours. Case documents vanished into bureaucratic black-holes, while SS malefactors were transferred to unknown locations. The only crimes in camps which prosecutors could still investigate involved prisoner on prisoner offences. Few bothered.[73]

Unlike Stalin's Russia, where the purges decimated the judiciary, the Gestapo stopped short of arresting and shooting judges, but had no inhibitions about detaining lawyers. This terminated politically tricky cases, or corrected suspect pathologies evident in the choice of client. Lawyers representing the widow of the Catholic Action leader slain in the 'Night of the Long Knives', in an action for damages, were arrested shortly before it came to court. Four weeks in the cells dampened their keenness to continue. Other lawyers were arrested for repeatedly representing certain categories of client; for their probing courtroom style; or for their hidden 'reactionary' agendas.[74] Since the Gestapo understood its remit as including the correction of acquittals or lenient sentences, it was normal for it to rearrest those acquitted, whether the aquittal was granted on the grounds of a prosecution being unproven or in the face of overwhelming evidence of innocence. Saving judicial face brought the minor concession of rearresting suspects outside the courts or after they had returned home.

A further area of friction was the manner in which confessions had been obtained, or the status of evidence provided by anonymous agents and voluntary informers. In November 1934, twenty-four Socialist Workers' Party activists, who had been deported from exile in Holland, were tried by the People's Court in a blaze of international publicity. This encouraged the defendants to expose the interrogation methods of the Gestapo, whose representative witness decided to take the fifth amendment. The court discounted confessions secured under duress, although preliminary indictment of the police and SA offenders was subsequently dropped by the state prosecutor on the grounds that the accused had merely suffered an excess of zeal.[75] Use of brutal interrogation methods received Hitler's sanction when he ordered dropping charges against Gestapo or policemen who used jiu-jitsu and lengths of cable to secure confessions from suspects. He personally ordered torture of a notorious child murderer after reading about the case in the newspapers. Judicial officials were reduced to negotiating with the Gestapo in June 1937 to regularise torture, a phenomenon not unknown in modern states which use violent methods.

Here the SS put forward its smooth face, in the shape of the former judge Werner Best, while his main interlocutor from the Ministry of Justice was himself the recipient of honorary SS rank. The Gestapo agreed to restrict violent interrogation methods to those accused of treason, arguing that it helped even the odds against silent cadres. Of course no such limitation occurred, for parallels were drawn between Communist cells and clandestine networks of homosexuals to legit-imise torturing the latter. A doctor was to be present after more than ten blows with a 'standardised stick', there being no mention of how often these methods were to be used. Once a week? Once a day? Or every morning and evening? Permission to do this had to be obtained in advance from Gestapo headquarters. Since the latter could retroac-tively authorise the spontaneous violence of their local operatives, judicial resort to what was now an internal Gestapo disciplinary affair was limited. The meeting overlooked such techniques as deprivation of food, light or sleep, which also belonged (and, in some countries, still belong) to the torturer's armoury.[76]

POLICEMAN'S BALL

The extra-judicial competences of the police increased by fits and bounds as Himmler outgrew the loose constraints of his nominal subordination to the Interior Ministry. For the police's political mission meant that they were instruments of the Führer's will, rather than executive auxiliaries of the judicial apparatus. This invested them with enormous power. Emergency powers of protective custody under the Reichstag Fire Decree of 28 February 1933 became permanent, for the enemies of the Reich apparently never slumbered. Protective custody (*Schutzhaft*) was a state of indeterminacy, somewhere between remand in police cells before judicial arraignment and a determinate prison sentence. This 'betweenness' was of its essence. Its application was extended from left-wing opponents to such groups as the priesthood or Jehovah's Witnesses, and was employed as a form of correction whenever courts acquitted the accused or imposed mild sentences. It both subverted the courts by challenging their sentencing monopoly and undermined them whenever it was used to correct their decisions. Objections from the judicial authorities were deflected with compromise measures, which appeared to restrict and regularise its application, but whose practical effects were minimal.[77] A measure aimed at political suspects underwent infinite expansion. Although there are no overall statistics for the numbers of persons held in 'protective custody', Heydrich's staff used a rubber stamp bearing his signature to authorise them. From 1934 onwards, the Gestapo recorded custody orders using the first initial of prisoners' surnames, followed by escalating digits. One of the last surviving orders, for prisoners whose names began with 'M', was 'M 34 591' issued in 1945.[78]

Protective custody was augmented by police preventive custody (*Vorbeugungshaft*), which reflected endemic conflation of criminal and political offences. The desire to combat chronic or professional criminality was widespread, and was amply catered for already by the November 1933 Law against Dangerous Habitual Criminals. But however much latitude this ceded courts, it depended upon commission of or intent to commit a crime, including being caught with the tools of the trade, rather than upon a suspect's general character defects. Arbitrary round-ups of pre-set quotas of known criminals commenced in Göring's Prussia. The rationale was that court proceedings were too costly or too slow, and that the primary victims of such offenders were poor people. Massive illegalities came with a social conscience. Himmler hugely extended these practices. In early 1937, he authorised the arrest of two thousand habitual and professional criminals and sexual offenders on the basis of information compiled by the criminal police. They were sent to concentration camps. In the following year, the police received fresh arrest quotas, but now for the 'anti-social' – that is, individuals who may not have committed any specific offence but whose behaviour was deemed unacceptable by the leaders of the 'national community'. By November 1938, only a third of inmates at Buchenwald, a concentration camp near Weimar, were political prisoners: the majority consisted of the 'anti-social'. Their detention solved labour shortages in the concentration camps' profit-making facilities, such as brick kilns and quarries, which in turn satisfied the architect Albert Speer's quest for building materials.[79]

Enough has been said about relations between the judicial apparatus and the police to show how normal relations between the police and judiciary had been inverted. But what of the police themselves? The majority of policemen in Nazi Germany were inherited from the Weimar Republic. Begrudging tribute to the past impartiality of the police was paid in a 1937 Party vetting report on the Gestapo chief Heinrich Müller: 'His sphere of activity was to supervise and deal with the left-wing movement. It must be admitted that he fought against it hard. . . . But it is equally clear that, if it had been his task to do so, Müller would have acted against the Right in just the same way.'[80] However, police attitudes towards extremists during the Republic were affected by the Communist view that the police were instruments of class rule, and by a campaign of terroristic violence. By contrast, excepting such targets as Berlin's vice-commissioner Bernhard Weiss, the Nazis under the Republic opted for a passive-aggressive stance towards the police, and were rhetorically strong on law and order. Police sympathies probably shifted rightwards, although this is difficult to determine with any exactitude, since they were forbidden to join the Nazi Party, as distinct from covertly sympathising with it.

Since venturing deeply into this world of bureaucratic acronyms would be tedious, only the barest of organisational facts are necessary, with discussion of leading police figures postponed to where this most mattered, namely in moulding the police in their own image. The Weimar Republic had no national police force. Each federal state had modest numbers of political police, drawn from a larger pool of detectives, plus barracks-based riot police and officers on patrol. Initially, the SS leader Heinrich Himmler was President of the Munich police and political police commander of Bavaria. He appointed Reinhard Heydrich head of the Munich police political department.[81] Since 1931, this cashiered naval officer had been responsible for creating an SS counter-intelligence service, a remit he and Himmler redefined the following year as an ideological research-intelligence agency called the Security Service or SD.[82] Its earliest recruits included the former fruit importer and tobacconist Carl Oberg – the future terror of occupied France – and a religious studies teacher who was Himmler's cousin.[83] The embryonic SD was reliant on unpaid volunteers, whose enthusiasms mutated into fixed branches of ideological surveillance. One early recruit brought an archive on Rhineland separatism, while a Russian émigré had a collection on Freemasonry.[84] Amateurism and lack of resources were evident from the use of garden furniture and sheds as desks and offices, while Heydrich's home cum office telephone was cut off in 1932 for non-payment. He and his colleagues compensated by living in a fantasy world of secret agents, in which Heydrich imagined himself as the counterpart of 'C' in the legendary British secret service.

While the SD was little more than an idea in Heydrich's mind, he and Himmler simultaneously gained control of all state political police forces, excepting the major prize of Prussia. The police in Germany's largest state were controlled by Göring. Berlin's small political branch was run by a civil servant called Rudolf Diels, who had already distinguished himself by transforming this force into an exclusively anti-Communist instrument during Papen's non-violent Prussian coup.[85] Diels created a centrally controlled network of regional Secret State Police posts. Göring's police force faced two separate challenges, from self-appointed SA auxiliary police, and from Wilhelm Frick's Interior Ministry, which sought to create a centralised Reich force integrated into the regular administration. To combat these challenges, in 1934 Göring detached the political police from Berlin police headquarters, and appointed Himmler head of what was now called the Gestapo, this last step being part of the powerplay with Frick. Executive control passed to Heydrich, while Diels was put out to grass in Cologne.

Over the following years, Himmler freed himself from administrative subordination to both Göring and Frick, while centralising control of federal political police forces under his Berlin headquarters. His ascendancy stemmed from the leading role the SS played in the June 1934 murders, after which Hitler and Himmler were literally bound by blood. Shortly afterwards, the SS was formally separated from the SA. The SD became the Party's sole intelligence agency. Various armed formations – the *Verfügungstruppe* – became the incipient Waffen-SS. Since these units were to free up regular army troops by themselves focusing on suppressing civil disorder in wartime, there was no repetition of the Party–military rivalry which had doomed the SA. Theodor Eicke of the SS Death's Head guard units became Inspector of the SS concentration camps, based in headquarters at Sachsenhausen. Murder paid institutional dividends.[86]

The residual struggle with Frick was resolved by the February 1936 Gestapo Law, which transformed the Gestapo into an independent national agency. Four months later, Hitler appointed Himmler Chief of the German Police. The withdrawal of the police from the state administration was symbolised by the fact that Himmler continued to work in Gestapo headquarters, with a pair of adjutants to liaise with Germany's police force. The political power of the police was reflected in his presence at cabinet meetings, although he was not a government minister. Organisational rearrangements ceded Heydrich control of the new combined Security Police, or Sipo and SD, including the Gestapo and Criminal Police, while the uniformed Order Police or Orpo were directed by SS-General Kurt Daluege, a vast thug of a man nicknamed 'Dummi-Dummi' by his detractors. The Gestapo was clearly the dominant partner vis-à-vis the police in general, while the twelve thousand or so criminal investigators, under Arthur Nebe, began to be indistinguishable from their political colleagues.[87] The eventual logic of these arrangements became explicit in 1940. In that year, the Gestapo announced its liberation from the 1933 Reichstag Fire Decree, hitherto the slender basis for its ramified activities. Henceforth, its powers stemmed from 'an overall commission', independent of all laws, decrees and ordinances. The police had become an autonomous source of political power, with mere state power trailing after them.[88]

Although the police were subject to secular processes of 'modern-isation', with enhanced data technology, fingerprinting, or more patrol cars to cope with rising traffic offences, these were perhaps not the most salient aspects of policing in the Third Reich. The political police and SD underwent rapid expansion. From around thirteen hundred personnel in 1933, the Gestapo grew to about seven thousand three years later. Its budget climbed from 1 million to 40 million Reichs-marks over this period. The SD mushroomed from two hundred and fifty to about five thousand over the period 1933–7, its budget being defrayed by the Party, partly from rerouted donations.[89]

These organisations may have been relatively small, and thinly distributed outside the capital, but it is important to remember that the intelligence agents of the SD could rely on the Gestapo, while the latter could deploy larger numbers of police or paramilitary auxiliaries whenever it needed to cordon off an area searching for weapons or Communist literature. In Berlin, in 1935, Gestapo raids on allotments in the north of the city involved two hundred regular policemen, a hundred auxiliaries and three mobile units consisting of armed motor-cycle police. The noise of their engines was sometimes broadcast live on the radio to maximise the impression of a drastic crackdown on crime. Total omniscience may have been in the eye of the beholder, but localised dominance was not illusory.[90] Terror both neutralised political opponents and repressed the wider population through a more pervasive insecurity. Whether their actual operational capacities were modest or dependent upon collusion from sections of the population is irrelevant, this last point never having been denied by those who described Nazi Germany as a totalitarian 'police state'.

As a consequence of expansion, the Gestapo included men from varied institutional backgrounds, characterised by distinctive tra-ditions, ethos, and training. The SS were represented at highest and lowest levels, but were not typical of those between. Gestapo regional leaders were mostly young, middle-class lawyers. Fanatical Nazis were uncommon. Some Gestapo chiefs had left-wing backgrounds, such as Heinz Graefe in Tilsit, or were Roman Catholics, with records of hostility towards National Socialism. A surfeit of lawyers over civil service posts, and the competitive salaries offered by the Gestapo, together with Werner Best's preference for men cast in his own image, may explain why such men joined the organisation.[91] By contrast, Heinrich Müller was keener on recruiting professional detectives like himself. The scion of a Catholic family and Bavarian Catholic People's

Party (BVP) sympathiser, Müller was a career policeman, having joined the Bavarian police in 1919 after war service as a much decorated airman. Transferred to Berlin in 1934, he joined the SS, with nominal membership of the SD. He finally joined the Party in 1939. For Müller had a proven expertise in suppressing the left, albeit with a professional regard for the interrogation techniques of the Soviet NKVD, never a handicap in these circles.[92]

Much of the modern literature on the Gestapo has conveyed the impression of desk-bound policemen, almost buried under the avalanche of denunciations from ordinary citizens, particularly regarding violations of racial legislation. This may be so. But this approach has its own limitations. In their desire to normalise Gestapo practice, some historians have claimed that there was no difference between Gestapo 'excesses' and those of policemen in America or Britain, although no comparative evidence is cited in support of this opinion, which derives from a remark made by Himmler and is of course completely ridiculous.[93]

The Gestapo's primary task was to destroy political and clerical opposition. It was clearly highly effective, for the Communist underground was smashed in waves of arrests, before sinking without trace between 1939 and 1941 as an inconvenience to Soviet foreign policy. The Gestapo did not simply stumble upon Communist networks. Apart from opening mail or tapping telephones (an engineer offering to replace a malfunctioning apparatus was the usual method), the most effective resource were contact agents, or *V-Leute*, as distinct from casual denouncers, informants and *agents provocateurs*. Opponents facing coercion or incarceration sometimes agreed to become Gestapo agents within underground organisations, with a boldly devious minority then operating as double agents, and ending up confused. Known Communists were summoned for an interview, shown an arrest order, a twenty-Reichsmark note and a contract of engagement as an agent, and told to choose. But fear was not the sole motivation. Some agents had grudges against erstwhile comrades, such as a Communist who in 1931 had been jailed for distributing leaflets while his salaried Party secretary, who refused to pay his fine, went on an expenses-paid holiday to the Soviet Union. For it is misleading to imagine that only the marginal or disgruntled small fry worked for the Gestapo. The best agents had lengthy backgrounds in Communist (or Social Democrat) politics, and the most effective of all, those in senior positions, could help the Gestapo roll up underground networks. Functionaries exiled abroad struck deals to return home, their part of the bargain being betrayal of everyone associated with them. Success also had its own dynamics. A Danzig district leader decided that 'it is hard to die, especially for a lost cause', and hence betrayed 170 people, whom he visited in their cells, telling them that 'further struggle was pointless'. Some were opportunists first, patriots second, and Communists last: 'I am a German. . . . I prefer to march with the army which wins.'[94] After 1945, many former Nazis marched in the opposite direction into the East German security police, which was not especially fastidious about recruiting ex-Nazis.

Coercion was a primary means of breaking organised political opposition. If democratic police forces contain individuals inclined to assault people in dark alleys, in no sense can this be said to be either general or sanctioned by forces which at an early stage communicate the rule of law down to their most humble members. On the other hand, the use of violence, or the threat of it, was endemic to the Gestapo, before and after the *modus operandi* was theoretically regulated with the judicial authorities. The Hamburg Gestapo chief Bruno Streckenbach came to a local arrangement in 1934 with the courts, whereby those who 'committed suicide' after he had smashed their kidneys with a knuckleduster were cremated to prevent autopsy.[95] Although Streckenbach may have been reliant on such methods, having no training in questioning suspects, his professionalised colleagues were just as vicious, either beating people up themselves or calling in rotating teams of SS employees to do it for them.[96] This was also why the Gestapo preferred to detain suspects in the Columbia House army detention centre on Berlin's Tempelhof, rather than in regular prisons such as Spandau, once the thirty-eight holding cells in its own headquarters cellars proved inadequate for requirements. Whereas the Prussian prison service could not be relied upon to give people more than a hard time, the SS in the Columbia House routinely beat people senseless in between torture sessions on the Gestapo's own premises.

An anonymous Social Democrat who experienced detention left a detailed account. The Gestapo arrived at his home at seven one morning, and conducted an amateurish search 'somewhat in the style of an older crime novel'. Each time the telephone rang, the callers rapidly hung up when the Gestapo agent answered, and he at once dialled 007 to discover their identities: in other words, the telephone was tapped. Transferred to Gestapo headquarters, the suspect was held in a communal cell before being taken upstairs for interrogation. There was a lot of shouting about signing a confession. At five in the evening, he was removed to the Columbia House. Stripsearched by young SS men, who were especially interested in circumcision, he went off to the showers. There, at his most vulnerable, he was beaten up by SS men who repeated the Gestapo's questions. After a meal, it was back to the Gestapo headquarters for more. After three or four days, mostly spent in holding cells, he returned to the Columbia House for further violence. Eventually, he was remanded to the Moabit prison, where conditions were tolerable. Since there was insufficient evidence against him, he was taken back to the Gestapo headquarters, and then to the Columbia House, where he was seriously assaulted and locked in a dark cell with no bed. It was cold in November.[97]

Functional separation of the Gestapo and SD arose in the wake of a number of incidents, as when it transpired that agents were monitoring passengers on a Nazi leisure organisation 'Strength through Joy' cruise liner without being aware of one another.[98] According to Heydrich's July 1937 dispositions, the Gestapo was responsible for executive action against 'Marxists, traitors and émigrés', while the SD dealt with monitoring academia, the arts, the Churches, education and youth, pacifism and Jewry.[99] Himmler explained what this meant at a briefing session for army officers. The SD would take an interest in, say, an academic keen to establish a distinctive Austrian identity, because this might eventuate in another Switzerland. Which German professors supported this theory, and what were their foreign connections? 'These are the areas which interest us.' By contrast:

> As the Security Service we are not interested in, shall we say, whether or not the KPD cell apparatus in Berlin-Wedding has been neutralised. That is a matter for the executive. One day it will be neutralised, or it has been already. That doesn't interest us; Germany won't be ruined because of this.[100]

The ensuing division of labour included an exchange of records, with the SD taking over the Gestapo's records on assimilated, orthodox and Zionist organisations. The Gestapo also agreed it would function as a front whenever the SD needed to correspond with the Foreign Ministry, so that SD external intelligence operations would remain concealed from the rival military Abwehr. Relations between the two agencies were close, with the Gestapo gradually acknowledging the SD's intellectual ascendancy in key areas.[101]

Unlike the Gestapo, with its inherited nucleus of lawyers and trained policemen, committed to bureaucratic procedure, the SD was recruited more randomly and rapidly, with its ethos and interests partly shaped by its intake. Judging from Himmler's admonitions, the Gestapo was stuck in the old mentality, with files lying idle, because higher civil servants had lower employees to transfer them from desk to desk, and had their eyes on the clock as it edged towards the hour which triggered a rush to the exits.[102] SD members were altogether more willing to take work home with them, or to do improving homework such as learning Hebrew. For the SD began to assume the air of a think-tank. Many of the more notorious SD figures, such as Helmut Knochen, Otto Ohlendorf and Franz Alfred Six, were recruited by the SD's professorial talent spotters, either from Nazi student activists or from academics on the lower rungs of the career ladder, whose ambition and lack of decency suited them to this line of work. Others joined because they thought Security Service connoted the leadership's bodyguard, a mistake made by the young Austrian SS man Adolf Eichmann, who after six months sorting index cards on Free-masons moved to section II/112, the SD's Jewish desk.[103]

Some 41 per cent of the SD had higher education, at a time when the national average was 2 or 3 per cent. Whether this warrants describing the SD as intellectuals is doubtful, unless one uses the term in the Marxist sense, rather than to distinguish people of independent mind, capable of disinterested reflection and imaginative sympathy with others, such as Arthur Koestler, Czesław Miłosz or George Orwell. SD 'intellectuals' combined mindless assiduity of a familiar kind with what is better described as fertility rather than creativity. Whatever their love of chess or pretensions to scientific objectivity, these men were driven by nihilism, paranoia and resentment. They are vaguely reminiscent of the highly logical people who, it is said, are drawn to the ideas of Scientology. While they clearly did not all have sad childhoods, and shared authoritarian fathers with most of mankind in that era, they were collectively marked by the experiences of their generation, by a lost war, revolution, foreign occupation and economic turbulence, which inclined them to elite forms of extreme right-wing politics.[104]

A further fact about the SD intellectuals is informative: they were not from social backgrounds traditionally associated with higher edu-cation. Take Franz Alfred Six. The son of an upholsterer and paper-hanger, Six studied journalism at Heidelberg. Ensconced in his humble lodgings, he developed a beam-sized chip against the university's quaint combination of academic bitchery and liberal high-mindedness.

Alienation propelled him into the camaraderie of Nazi student politics, giving him a taste for conspiracy, demagoguery and manipulation, which served him pretty well thereafter. He campaigned for alienated students and academics to integrate themselves into the 'real' world of work, and against a minority of politically active academics, such as Emil Gumbel, who was sacked after a demonstration of student patriotic self-righteousness against his statistical demonstration of bias in the judiciary's sentencing practices. Merely by substituting Nazism for Maoism or Marxist–Leninism, Six becomes a 1968er *avant la lettre*, with his faux radicalism providing an apprenticeship for the harm he would do in his career as a secret policeman. In 1934 he joined the SD, courtesy of one of his professors. This helped professionally, for at the age of thirty Six progressed from a chair in journalism at Königsberg to being professorial dean of Berlin University's new Foreign Affairs Institute, although the faculty could find no record of academic publications.[105]

As a press expert, Six's principal concern was building up the SD's records on the intellectual product of ideological opponents. This entailed combing through vast quantities of published materials, which were then categorised according to a bewildering array of hostile groups (Catholic Church, Freemasons, Monarchists, Reactionaries, Separatists and so forth) or deviant and opportunistic tendencies (Strasserites or the Spann Circle) before the sinister linkages between them were established, often with the aid of diagrams and wall-charts. Metaphors of convenience included hydras, octopuses and spiders, for the irrational lurked beneath the presentational surface. Wholly unconnected groups and individuals were transformed into a ramified paranoid conspiracy, behind which lurked an enemy so malign that it was not necessary, in these circles, to mention 'him' separately. This was 'the Jew'. In other words, these men inhabited a world in which what lay outside was populated with the equivalent of medieval demons.

The SD's distinctive approach to police work served multiple functions both psychological and political. For a start, the SD routinely disavowed anything so uncomplicated as hatred, prejudice or resentment, as well it might, for 'hot' emotion is not as indefinitely sustainable as 'cold' science. This approach enabled it to distance itself from ochlocratic passions, while simultaneously making use of the mob to justify its own rational solutions. Mob-like violence was not structurally divorced from the SD, as it sometimes pretended, but a factor it deliberately fed into their own calculations. It also realised that popular antisemitism was as evanescent as a wood fire, requiring constant tending, rather than universal or unique among the German people. Here it knew that rational-seeming presentation, using charts, diagrams, graphics and statistics, had greater potency than the quasi-pornography of *Der Stürmer*, with its images of 'Aryan' maidens and 'Jewish' seducers, which clashed with traditional proprieties.[106]

The SD's emphasis on in-depth research implied that Gestapo-style repression had merely skimmed off the oppositional political surface, leaving a more insidious range of enemies burrowing into the nation's vitals, another metaphor of convenience. Gestapo police work and exclusionary laws, which these men anticipated, were provisional stages in a more comprehensive and fundamental resolution of problems, a role the SD began assuming as it moved from a research-intelligence to more activist tasks, especially relating to the 'Jewish Question'. A change of purpose was virtually guaranteed by two further aspects of this agency, whose leader was constantly seeking out new areas to usurp. First, members of the SD were encouraged to exhibit initiative, while the task of regular reporting of activities to the centre gave mental fertility a built-in fillip. Secondly, the 'intellectuals' of the SD were constantly reminded that they were not airy-fairy theoreticians, but were engaged in the search for practical solutions, a point the thoroughly anti-intellectual Heydrich reinforced by having his more donnish subordinates carry out what is uncharmingly called 'wet-work'. Thus as the SD expanded into covert external operations, so Professor Dr Six led teams which carried out kidnappings and assassinations in Austria or Czechoslovakia, his targets including conservatives who had eluded the 'Night of the Long Knives', or who espoused aberrant brands of 'clerical fascism'. Future career highlights included designation as Higher SS- and Police Leader for Britain, and command of the SS task force intended for Moscow.

It is misleading to reduce the role of the SD to its activities in solving the 'Jewish Question', although, given its importance to Hitler and Himmler, that turned out to be the area with most potential. The SD also shaped opinion. From 1935 onwards, Heydrich's SD mission statements began appearing in the SS weekly *Schwarze Korps*, edited by the twenty-five-year-old journalist Günther d'Alquen.[107] This organ reveals much about SD thinking, for it was reliant on information from the agency for content and direction. The combination of eccentricity, human-interest stories and prurient attacks on groups and individuals is vaguely familiar. Gossip columns and horoscopes were missing, but there was much on naughty nuns, runes and sport to compensate, as well as athletic girls as surrogate pin-ups. The tone was scurrilous and self-righteous.

The weekly mounted personalised attacks, for example, against the 'white Jew' Werner Heisenberg, evidently still too indebted to 'Jewish' quantum physics for the tastes of his 'Aryan' experimentalist Nobel-prize-winning colleagues.[108] For the attack on Heisenberg was written by Johannes Stark, although Stark hid behind a 'commentary' on an article which reached the SD through an ex-pupil and professor of physics at Heidelberg, who belonged to the agency.[109] Similarly, despite his recent advocacy of racially identificatory footnotes in legal texts, the legal theorist Carl Schmitt was cut down to size by a journal which regarded him as an opportunist with too many pre-1933 Jewish acquaintances.

Buried amid pieces entitled 'Airports on the High Seas', 'What Is the Stone Age?', 'The Samurai' or 'Storks in Concentration Camps' was the line the SD wished to purvey on more contemporary subjects. The central obsession was not the Jews, but rather political Catholicism, to which *Schwarze Korps* devoted interminable analyses, together with attacks on senior clergy and a stream of anti-clerical smut, severally designed to demolish the moral authority of the Catholic Church. In a related sense, this was also where the SD dipped a toe to test public responses to advanced opinions, by anticipating such policies as 'euthanasia' through apparently innocuous human interest stories and readers' letters, or recommending a more radical approach to the unresolved 'Jewish Question' with such headlines as 'The Jews. What Now?'[110]

The SD also assumed responsibility for sociological monitoring of opinion, as a surrogate for free expression of public opinion. Reporting on opposition groups was extended to monitoring entire swathes of life, designed to gauge the extent to which the Nazi 'worldview' had made progress among the population. From early December 1939, the digests of these reports were called 'Reports from the Reich'. A 1938 report included what became routine surveys of Freemasonry, whose essentially benign activities have always been a bugbear to the paranoid left and right. It began with a disarming flourish of erudition, outlining the various lodges and national traditions. Organised Freemasonry had been smashed because of its Enlightenment legacy of 'humanity, tolerance and liberalism', and because it was a vehicle for promoting 'Jewish ideas and objectives'. But the remnants were recoalescing, like globules of oil spilled on the floor. There was a Dr Horneffer, giving dangerous lectures on 'Greek philosophy', not to speak of Anthrosophists, Rotarians, Rosicrucians and Theosophists with 'foreign' connections. The report duly recommended that Gestapo colleagues needed to pulverise what had been smashed once already.

Freemasons were allegedly active in the Party, the Reichsbank and the German railways. Worse, low-level masons, granted an amnesty by the Führer, were abusing his magnanimity to reorganise. Although some appeared to conform with the new dispensation, their 'almost total rejection' of the measures taken against the Jews, attributed to their 'philanthropic training and outlook', was sinister. So were the wider connections. Former Freemasons had many 'social relations' with Jews, 'oppositional Church circles' and 'reactionary associations', so that 'cross connections of a personal nature exist, which have been consolidated by the ideological affinity of both enemy groups'. A museum in Nuremberg was helping to counteract the view that the apron and trowel crowd were pretty innocuous. The SD also had its eyes on international Freemasonry, learnedly unravelling obscure doctrinal rows between the English and French masons, the progress of masonry in Brazil or Uruguay, and its repression in Hungary, Ireland and Poland. It was worrying that most of the French cabinet were masons, not to speak of Roosevelt or the Earl of Harewood. The anti-Nazi activities of the American masons warranted detailed attention.[111]

Differences in background and institutional rivalries between policemen were counterbalanced by the creeping influence of the SS. Himmler's intention was to create a consolidated, ideologically saturated, police force, as the domestic analogue of an army fighting on the external front. His plan to elevate the SD into the 'General Staff' of a police force of executants was abandoned, because the SD lacked trained policemen to plant in the Gestapo, and because of the way in which his dual control had been achieved. Instead, Himmler eased police access to both the SD and SS, while, as we have seen, the police bolstered their numbers with recruits from these backgrounds. Uniformed Order Police were encouraged to join the General SS, entitling them to wear runic flashes on their collars, while many Security Police joined the SD at equivalent rank, as we saw in the case of Heinrich Müller. Membership of the SS remained voluntary, although apparently it brought enhanced 'respect' in dealings with the administration or Party.[112]

Although they co-operated, there were stylistic tensions between the two agencies, which were perpetuated by their leaderships' habit of recruiting in their own individual images. While the lean and mean ideologues of the SD were contemptuous of 'pot-bellied old police commissars running around in SS uniforms', Gestapo officials, such as Müller, responded with the thought that 'one should herd the entire intelligentsia into a mine, and then blow it sky-high'. However, this clash of types had positive rather than negative dynamics. Both groups competed in evincing hardness, implacability and ruthlessness. Whether one follows current orthodoxy by dubbing this 'cumulative radicalisation', rather than creative tension, is a matter of taste rather than incontrovertible fact, a sociological versus a management theory.

Membership of the SS meant joining an elite organisation explicitly modelled on an ahistorical version of religious orders, such as the Teutonic Knights or the Jesuits, whose dedication to a higher idea was admired in these otherwise anti-clerical circles.[113] As SS membership became a mass affair, including every physically prepossessing farm-boy, the SD regarded itself as 'an elite within the elite', with unrevealed truths requiring incremental induction. Here it is impossible to post-pone consideration of the SS leadership, for the ethos was Himmler's mind projected on an institutional canvas, while the operational style largely derived from Heydrich. The Nazi leadership have become overly familiar, albeit as a *galère* of grotesques rather than as gods in ancient or pagan pantheons. Since the 'schoolmasterly' Himmler and the 'blond beast' Heydrich have acquired their own character attributes and mythologies, we need to divest them of respectively bizarre beliefs and putative Jewish ancestry, the stuff of cliché, to grasp how they created one of the most awesome and efficient concentrations of police power mankind has known.

Himmler's more *outré* obsessions should not distract from his manifestly astute grasp of how this highly chaotic and protean political system worked. Routinely out-manoeuvring his foes, his empire spread between the interstices of state, Party and army, throughout Germany, and then across the whole of occupied Europe. His manner may have been distracted and unassuming, but the coldness, moralising, prying and suspicion kept him in absolute control of subordinates, whose own utter ruthlessness was accompanied by human frailties which Himmler lacked. Here some of the obsessions cited to illustrate this moralising little creep's weirdness make sense within his own dim

terms of reference – except he did not confine his prurient sententiousness to how much his men drank or smoked, although that was surely
bad enough.

Moralising interventions in the marital affairs of his subordinates
were an example of how the watchers were watched, not to speak of
the information assembled on each SS man (up to and including
Heydrich) by eugenic and racial vetting stretching back to 1750 or
1800. This was leverage, for somewhere or other there was bound to
be a weak link, whether racial or eugenic, in the 'clan' pedigree. How
could there not be, when one filled tooth was enough to prohibit
admission? Even those of unimpeachable ancestry and impressive
physique were not yet home and dry. Himmler insisted that the SS
equivalent of livestock breeders cast an instinctive eye over the candidate, in search of subjective character defects. Suspicious watchfulness
was also part of a personal and institutional desire to create fear.
While the SD attempted to cultivate a friendly face, to facilitate delation, the SS deliberately sought to make others shudder. As Himmler
said in 1935: 'I know there are many people who fall ill when they see
this black uniform; we understand that and don't expect that we will
be loved by many people.'[114] He also set the tone in terms of absolute
contempt for legality. Speaking at the foundation of the Academy of
German Law in 1936, he told an audience of jurists:

> I am totally indifferent as to whether a legal clause opposes our
> actions. . . . during the months when it was about the life or death of
> the German nation, it was entirely irrelevant whether other people
> whined about breaking the law. Foreigners . . . naturally talked about
> lawless conditions in the police and therefore in the state. They called
> it lawless because it did not conform with their notions of law. In
> truth, through our labours we laid the foundations of a new law, the
> right to live of the German nation.[115]

The elite character of the SS derived from the proximity to Hitler
of its most presentable formations, and from stringent eugenic and
racial vetting, which was repeated whenever SS men married. A
changing membership bolstered this image. In 1937 Himmler reminded
his SS leaders of their social obligations. He recommended they venture
where plebeian Party revolutionaries refused to tread, attending balls
and other occasions where the 'reactionary' upper classes were omnipresent. There was 'damned good blood' among them, and an innate
capacity for leadership, notwithstanding a large number of chinless

wonders.[116] Recruitment of aristocrats was facilitated by the SS's praetorian image and the incorporation of equestrian activities, which attracted men from a horsey set who might otherwise have joined regular army cavalry or guards regiments. The result was an SS membership reeking of the *Almanach de Gotha*, not to speak of SS riders winning all prizes at the 1937 equestrian championships. Bankers, industrialists and senior civil servants were co-opted into the 'Friends of the Reichsführer-SS', an informal network of business cronies. As the son of a former tutor to Bavarian monarchs, Himmler was not immune to the snobbery of all servants, for he sought to license duelling as a means of settling questions of SS honour. Some duels were fought, until Hitler effectively stopped this class-bound and outmoded method of resolving conflict, adding that it should be permitted only for priests and lawyers. While the SS permitted suicide as an option for those facing honourable disgrace, dishonourably discharged SS homosexuals were routinely 'shot while fleeing' concentration camps.[117]

Aristocrats were submerged into a new synthetic elite within an organisation which espoused egalitarian meritocracy along with racial rather than social elitism.[118] Achievement and performance mattered more than accident of birth. Or rather aristocratic birth ceased to count within a racially selected elite, which also included a large quotient of expert professionals and quasi-piratical tough-guys. Farmboys could attend the Brunswick or Bad Tolz SS officer cadet schools, in marked contrast to the army officer corps, where class counted. These SS cadet academies were staffed by former regular army officers. Individual identities were submerged in well-tailored uniforms, whose badges, bands, collar studs, daggers, insignia, initials and signet rings could be read at a glance. From modest beginnings, with Heydrich running an office from a corner of a rented flat, the various SS, police and SD formations moved into discreet Dahlem villas, or imposing buildings in Berlin's government quarter, with the leaders acquiring squads of adjutants, butlers, cooks, drivers, secretaries and so forth, not to speak of coats of arms in Himmler's Wewelsburg castle. In other words, the SS developed its own hierarchies and vocabularies of power, not to speak of compulsory savings schemes designed to help those who fell on hard times.

But the interior new man mattered more than mere externals. An SS *esprit de corps* grew from rigorous training experiences, in which military hierarchies were relaxed in favour of camaraderie and *per Du* familiarity among volunteer 'fighters'. The armed formations of the SS developed a different dynamic, undergoing a process of remilitarisation. Like monks and priests, or Communist Party members, there was a lengthy novitiate or candidate-membership, involving ideological instruction, labour and military service, and the acquisition of sporting prowess.[119] Traditionally noble sports like boxing, climbing, fencing, riding and rowing were the most valued. Arcane initiation rites heightened the solemnity of being admitted to a privileged caste, a sort of secular priesthood. The midnight oath-swearing ceremony was apparently evocative, according to one eyewitness: 'Tears came to my eyes, when, by the light of torches, thousands of voices repeated the oath in chorus. It was like a prayer.' There was a bastardised catechism, in which the questions and responses included: 'Why do we believe in Germany and the Führer?' 'Because we believe in God, we believe in Germany which He created in His world and in the Führer, Adolf Hitler, whom He has sent us.' Like all sects and totalitarian organisations, the SS recognised no departures and no separate private sphere. The individual was in for life. Church marriages were prohibited for SS members, whose vows were solemnified in the SS's own ceremonies. Since spouses were subjected to exhaustive racial vetting, they were being co-opted into the emergent elite, with their fecundity being monitored through the unlikely medium of gifts of SS kitsch for the birth of each child.[120] Children of SS men underwent an alternative form of baptism, with the seventh child being eligible for having Himmler as godfather. The centrepiece of the ceremony was a portrait of Hitler; instead of clergy there were SS men bearing standards with the swastika and the legend 'Germany arise'. A more pragmatic reason for tracking the SS birthrate, which was below national averages, was that in future two-thirds of recruits were to come from SS families. All of this is entirely in keeping with the well-documented habits of sects and other totalitarian organisations in shaping the individual member's whole environment.

SS values were a synthetic mixture of the novel and traditional, overlain with death-fixated kitsch. Why, one might reasonably ask, should anyone want to go about wearing skulls and crossbones and runic symbols, unless they suffered from the morbid obsessions which animate juvenile motorbike gangs? The SS fused deracinated versions of traditional military virtues; attitudes derived from the war and its aftermath; and a new/old anti-Christian morality, which by conflating pseudo-Nietzscheanism and neo-paganism was too advanced for the conservative-minded Christian generality, clinging on to a God with a human countenance. Loyalty was a primary virtue, as reflected in the 'My honour is loyalty' motto impressed on SS belts. Normally, loyalty is an admirable quality, as in loyalty to friends, one's comrades, the constitution and so forth. Here it was divorced from any considerations based on conscience, and focused exclusively on the person of Hitler. Virtues intrinsic to soldiers, athletes and sportsmen were similarly detached from their limited objectives, freed of conditionality and elevated into an all-embracing outlook. One was no longer determined to win a game or race, subject to the rules of fair play, but determined *per se*, above all to destroy opponents by any available means, with no moderating rules at all.

Other generic SS characteristics were a legacy of war and its aftermath. Heroic realism was an intellectual by-product of the First World War, a fancy way of describing soldiers who fought to the bitter end, regardless of the imminence of defeat. It was one of the ways in which intellectuals tried to assert control of a situation in which hapless conscripts were slaughtered on chaotic battlefields or according to the whimsical *deus ex machina* of grand strategy. The fight itself was its own justification, a notion which chimed with a Darwinist view of life as struggle, engendering its own higher values. Of course, the intellectuals themselves were far too individualist to be drawn into Himmler's legions.[121]

The carapace of glacial, taciturn objectivity said to have characterised a wartime generation subjected to multiple shocks figured among SS virtues, which was reflected in a turning away from civilised, humanitarian 'sentimentalism' towards an unfeeling form of neo-barbarism.[122] If these were legacies of the war and its denouement, a managerialist emphasis upon competition and performance, in which ends justified means and nothing was to be deemed impossible, has an enduringly modern ring to it. One inadvertent result was men so wired up by their own activism that the SS suffered from high rates of suicide among age groups already prone to it.

SS men were volunteers. As Himmler once remarked, there was no room here for anyone seeking monetary gain, although, as he ruefully acknowledged, the Secret Service *Typ des Gentleman* was 'not going to be created in a generation; for that a nation must have a more fortunate 300–400-year history as a master race behind it, as is the case with England', a telling insight into an inferiority complex. They were de-individualised ideological 'fighters', voluntarily submitting their wills to the objectives of superiors, whose own reasoning lay beyond question. Absolution from individual responsibility, and a sense of embarkation on an urgent historic mission, was fostered by superficially pretentious talk about racial continuums and the Reichsführer's interest in astronomy. Mere links in big biological time or cosmic space, the SS had been granted a one-off opportunity to save future generations of their nation and race from chaos, subversion and oblivion, for the concept of race meant that one day the SS would be generalised beyond national borders. The murderers had a mission, whose accomplishment would justify any human cost. Since proximity to Hitler was intrinsic to the SS, it followed that the aura of a man sent by Providence to fulfil a redemptive mission literally rubbed off on his closest supporters. This assumed blasphemous proportions: 'When you see our Führer, it is like being in a dream; you forget everything around you, it is as if God has come to you.'[123]

It also followed that countervailing moral codes, vying for an individual's allegiance, had to be extinguished, or transformed beyond recognition. The main threat came from Christianity. SS antipathy towards Christianity exceeded traditional anti-clericalism, although there was evidence of this in abundance. The Church was a club for befrocked homosexuals, with bishops who looked like ageing actors, while Christianity itself was a Trojan horse for the 'related' designs and values of Jews and Bolsheviks.[124] Throughout history, the Church had tried to stamp out heretics, while the witch-craze was a form of 'gynocide' against 'half a million' German women and children, a view difficult to reconcile with attempts to elide Nazism with earlier examples of persecution, or racism with anti-feminism.

Nazism represented a sustained assault on fundamental Christian values, regardless of any tactical obeisance to the purchase it had on most Germans. Compassion, humility or love of one's neighbour were dismissed as humanitarian weakness by an organisation which regarded hardness, sacrifice and self-overcoming as positive virtues. The fact that this list included some secondary Christian virtues is no contradiction, but merely indicative of how the SS usurped Christian forms and values, stripping them down for anti-Christian ends. For, having discredited the 'immoral' or 'politicised' clergy, a more diffuse religiosity still had its uses. Himmler's prohibition of atheism as a declared option for SS men left them with the alternatives of Catholic, Protestant or 'believer in God' (*Gottgläubig*). This was deliberate. Atheism signified an egoistic belief that man was the measure of all things, and hence a refusal to acknowledge higher powers. In a word, it constituted a potential source of indiscipline.[125] A twofold process was at work here. Generalised recognition of transcendental forces counteracted the arrogant individualism stemming from membership of a racial elite. By contrast, consciousness of being a member of a racial elite was psychologically useful in making inadequate or insecure individuals act as a 'master race'. The mission here and now, for utopian ends on earth, became a substitute for the futility of earthly existence and the majesty of God.

It follows from this that the SS were not collectively 'amoral', although many of them undoubtedly were, for every corrupt or sadistic impulse was unleashed within an organisation which otherwise espoused puritanism about, say, alcoholism, childlessness or smoking, thus confusing the trivial with the dreadful. Excessive drinking or pilfering were significant moral failures; throwing a concentration-camp inmate off a cliff was unremarkable. This absence of a sense of proportion is a fundamental clue to the workings of the fanatical or zealous mind. It was precisely this combination of moralising about trivia, absolute self-righteousness, and the utopian doctrine of the perfectibility of mankind through a radical 'quick fix', which made the twin totalitarianisms of this century and the moralising zealots who sought to realise them so lethal. For the new tidings in Germany were ultimately designed to facilitate one purpose: to destroy enemies of National Socialism, who were literally placed outside the law.

DARK SIDE OF THE MOON

The end station for those designated as hostile or undesirable was imprisonment of temporary or permanent duration. This took several forms, with a judicial custodial system operating alongside extra-judicial forms of detention, and prisoners moving between them. The overwhelming majority of those imprisoned in either prisons or camps before the war were not Jews, but politically oppositional Gentile Germans, including those who fell foul of latitudinarian definitions of crime, often through who they were rather than what they did. The number of political prisoners in 'protective custody' reached one hundred thousand in 1933, before falling off to a few thousand that winter as the regime consolidated its power. Prisoner numbers rose in the wake of arrests of the 'anti-social', climbed to sixty thousand for a few months in 1938, although most Jewish detainees after the Reichs-kristallnacht pogrom that November were released in weeks, and then dropped to just over twenty thousand in August 1939, before war and occupation pushed the camp and prison population into hundreds of thousands.[126]

Generally speaking, members of the opposition regarded custody in regular prisons, as distinct from squalid police cells or pristine concentration camps, as the better option, provided the guards had not been exchanged for SA or SS men. This was not universally true, since those who visited inmates of a prison in Flensburg noted that their faces were bruised, allegedly from banging into doors.[127] Prisons were hopelessly overcrowded, one at Cottbus in Lusatia being 60 per cent over capacity in 1936, and the diet inadequate, but guards were often time-serving realists, who regarded political prisoners as less of a management problem than convicted criminals. If inmates obeyed the rules, their passage would not be too onerous. Attempts to import more violent regimes were sometimes deflected with the promise of a murderous prisoner response.[128]

The earliest camps were *ad hoc* affairs, set up by local Party bosses, the police and the SA, whose object was to concentrate prisoners too numerous for the regular penal system, which was too rule-bound to be an effective form of terror. It is misleading to call these 'wild' camps, for many were within existing penal institutions, while most were connected into the police and justice system. They were not maverick operations beyond the law, but integral parts of it.[129] Many early camps had a limited lifespan. For example, part of the former workhouse at Breitenau was used to house nearly five hundred mostly Communist detainees from the Kassel area between June 1933 and March 1934. The SA guards were replaced by the SS, whose final task was to sieve out inmates to be retained in their own major concentration camps, after a partial amnesty returned the recanting majority to the 'national community'.[130] These camps were not hidden in out-of-the-way places, but located in heavily populated areas. They were visible to the inhabitants, who could also read misleading accounts of what took place in them in their local newspapers, including the arrival of prominent prisoners, such as the son of former President Ebert. There were regular guided tours for both German and foreign dignitaries, as well as for trainee civil servants. Faced with adverse publicity about 'his' camp, after an escapee published an account of atrocious conditions, the commandant of Oranienburg published his own version of how he was re-educating 'brothers who have only forgotten that they are Germans', and brought in newsreel cameramen, whose short film about the camp was shown in all five thousand German cinemas.[131]

Prison overcrowding in the Bremerhaven–Bremen area led to the opening of regional concentration camps. Political prisoners from these relatively radical port cities were isolated on a German Alcatraz, a tiny island called Langlütjen, which the navy had used as a gun emplacement guarding the entrance to the Weser. Locked in subterranean casemates, they had nothing to do, except await the ebb and flow of tides, which left their cells inundated with cold seawater. Local anglers were able to discriminate human screams from cries of seagulls, before their boats were warned off with gunfire. Other internees were held on what soon became known as the 'ghost ship', a prison barge moored at Ochtumsand on the Weser opposite Bremen. Prisoners, who were dressed in firemen's uniforms with a white stripe on the trouser legs, were held in two holds, with barbed-wire fencing around the decks and along the wooden walkway which connected them with the shore, where they performed earth-moving labour. Prisoners were also subjected to chicanery or routinely beaten up.[132]

SS main concentration camps began with the opening in March
1933 of a camp with a capacity of five thousand in a disused powder
works in a Dachau suburb. Bavarian state police trained SS units, who
then replaced them. Excesses under the first commandant, and complications with the judicial authorities, led to his replacement that summer by Theodor Eicke. A former military paymaster, Eicke came from
a psychiatric clinic, where Professor Werner Heyde, a future organiser
of the 'euthanasia' programme, was the psychiatrist who gave him a
clean bill of mental health. Eicke built up a special guard formation
called the Death's Head units, after the aluminium skull and crossbones on their right collars. By December 1937, these units numbered
4,800 men. Strictly separated from the camp internal administration, which handled prisoners on a daily basis, these units were
dual-purpose: to guard the perimeters, and to act as a heavily armed
auxiliary police force in the event of civil disturbances during wartime.
To that end, from 1936 onwards, Heydrich began assembling a card
index on forty-six thousand people who would have to be immediately
detained. In the same year, Himmler started consolidating regional SS
and police powers in the form of the new Higher SS- and Police
Leaders, whose territories conformed with military corps areas.[133]

Under rules paradigmatic for the emerging SS camp empire, Eicke
sought to maximise brutality by appearing to regulate it. Random
excesses were theoretically replaced by organised brutality. The watch-
word for guards was 'Tolerance means weakness'; prisoners received
hortatory slogans emblazoned on gates, roofs and walls. Minor infractions resulted in solitary confinement or corporal punishment; anything
of a political nature or involving disobedience resulted in being hanged
or shot on the spot, which was wholly illegal. Execution orders derived
from perfunctory kangaroo courts, over which the commandant presided, with SS guards as the only other members. Guards were encouraged not to fire warning shots, and to shoot escapers or prisoners who
attacked them. Guards could also avail themselves of 'incidental
punishments' such as beating, repeated drills or hanging people by
their arms from a post.[134] Alongside the Columbia House detention
centre, Dachau became an academy of terror, for virtually all future
camp commandants graduated from these two institutions. Dachau, in
a Munich suburb, was followed by other camps, Sachsenhausen
(1936), Buchenwald (1937) and Flossenbürg and Mauthausen (1938),
which absorbed inmates of disbanded institutions, sometimes with
spare capacity for those to be detained upon the outbreak of war.

Unlike earlier camps, which were set up in existing places of confinement, or buildings which could be easily adapted, these new SS camps were purpose-built facilities, positioned near sources of building materials or factories.[135] They were anything but improvised affairs, one irony being that inmates of the Columbia House camp were used to work up the technical drawings for Sachsenhausen.[136] The result, in this case, was shaped like an inverted triangle, a panopticon affair, where a well-placed machine gun could sweep the entire camp with bursts of lead.

Hostile accounts of these camps in foreign or underground publications were countered by SS propaganda which employed photographs of heavily tatooed bruisers designed to insinuate that all inmates were criminals. The captions read 'A gallery of Jewish race-defilers. Don't these countenances say enough already?'[137] Typically, Himmler insisted on a moral, re-educative purpose in these licensed centres of brutality and terror. Speaking in 1939, he might have been describing an American reformatory or British borstal in the 1950s:

> Like every deprivation of liberty, the concentration camp is certainly a harsh and tough measure. Hard productive labour, a regular way of life, exceptional cleanliness in living conditions and personal hygiene, a faultless diet, firm but fair treatment, instruction in learning how to work again, and opportunities to acquire a trade, are the training methods. The motto which stands above these camps reads: There is only one road to freedom. Its milestones are called: Obedience, Diligence, Honesty, Orderliness, Cleanliness, Sobriety, Truthfulness, Self-Sacrifice and Love of the Fatherland.[138]

Little conformed with this mendacious description. These camps were designed to isolate potential opponents and to break their spirits. The pre-war concentration camps were beastly and ugly, although not comparable with the murderous conditions of wartime or the dedicated extermination centres in the occupied East, where most people were killed on arrival. In the former, prisoners received visits and gifts of food or money, which had to be exchanged into camp currency at an extortionate rate. But it would be misleading to imagine them as anything other than places of licensed brutality. How could it be otherwise, given the views of their commanders? In the wake of the Columbia House murders discussed above, the then commandant, a notorious drunk, explained to Himmler his view of the inmates, which survives in a third-person record of the Ministry of Justice:

In no way is one life to be regarded as akin to another life, rather the more worthwhile life must be protected against, to put it delicately, the worthless, in the interests of the nation, by necessity of state. . . . He was not a judge and would never take it upon himself, to act without orders from his superiors or to do anything which might harm the state and Führer, but one could hardly expect of him that these sorts of person, who are totally valueless and drag others into the swamp, are to be accorded the slightest consideration. This characterisation applies absolutely to the two men who were shot.[139]

Prisoners who served in SS messes recorded conversations in which the guards joked about maltreatment of inmates, or said that they 'were all swine who must be killed, because Mutschmann or some other higher leader of the NSDAP wanted it'.[140]

The existence of rules for concentration camps did not have the usual consequences. Rules are designed to foster predictability, even if this is disagreeable for those affected, who forfeit choice over every activity, being effectively reduced to childlike tutelage. In the camps logic and predictability stopped short of the wall or wire, while many unwritten rules governing daily conduct were *ad hoc* expressions of individual whim. As Primo Levi discovered much later in wartime Monowitz, 'there is no why here'.[141] Actually, there was: to grind people like him into dust. Rules, whether formal or informal, were designed not to make the running of the camps smoother, but to create opportunities to stage a cruel theatre, so that camp existence never relapsed into tedium, but consisted of endless alarums and drama. Analogies between camps and modern disciplined environments, with their mind-numbing routine, are beside the point. All prudential bets were off in other respects, for any sign of educational or social superiority, not to speak of racial difference, would solicit rather than inhibit assault by guards, whose resentments now found free expression.[142] The Oranienburg commandant's account of existence in his domain repeatedly made snide comments about 'noblemen', 'large income earners' or the academic degrees or dress sense of his detainees.

Since many 'rules' were invented by individual guards, obeying them was hopeless. The guards were not nature's jobsworths and turnkeys, working an easy passage in tense circumstances, for mutiny or riot were impossible when machine guns could mow down the inmates. Paradoxically, an anti-corruption drive in 1936, may have substantially worsened conditions. Guards were fertile in brutality, rather in the way that psychopathic adolescent gangs torture animals or each other for the thrill of it. If prisoners could never afford boredom, the guards, many of whom were indeed young, found novel ways of overcoming it. They tossed prisoners' caps over a trip wire, challenging the marksmanship of their colleagues in the watchtowers as they ordered the prisoner to retrieve it.[143] Since the guards received three days' leave for preventing escapes, this practice had incentives, the game being rendered easier by painting target markings on prisoners who were a known escape risk. Bored guards in Mauthausen's quarries periodically chucked 'parachutists' off the rim by way of entertainment.[144] Judging from earlier accounts of the camps, some guards were motivated by sadistic urges, which took the form of frenzied assaults, transcending both a casual kick or punch and the means-to-ends relationship theoretically involved in torture, where pain abates once information has been rendered. Prisoners were subjected to ferocious physical attacks for no purpose whatsoever. Judging from earliest prisoner accounts, notably by Benedikt Kautsky, a minority of guards also derived sexual gratification from corporal punishment, or raped both male and female inmates. There is no conceivable point in rehearsing the details.[145]

Camps were a totally controlled environment, whatever the countervailing power of political conviction or prayer. On entering the camps, prisoners forfeited all possessions, standing around in the open while endless bureaucratic formalities were completed by sluggish SS clerks. Prisoners underwent an Orwellian process of dehumanisation, with heads shorn and possessions stolen. It took about two hours to reduce a person to a number.[146] The new non-self was then photographed in the political department. The answer to the inquiry 'What are you?' was not 'A bricklayer' but 'A Marxist swine', for camp vocabulary was restricted. Instructions on how to make a bed, for military spartanism prevailed, were duly followed by hours of not getting it to SS satisfaction. Just for the hell of it, the SS might then throw the entire barracks into turmoil. Camp time for prisoners bereft of watches was marked by preternatural starts, at 4.15 in summer and an hour later in winter. Only at 9 p.m. could prisoners cease moving at the regulation double time, after which they had an hour's rest before lights out at ten. Nighttime was raked by searchlights and punctuated by barking dogs. Random rollcalls, regardless of weather conditions, were solely designed to harass people further who had to rise again before dawn.

Anonymity became a survival mechanism, in so far as conspicuousness sometimes killed. Better to hide amid the mass than stand at the front or on the edge of a line where the SS came within striking distance. Better not be Jewish either, judging by Osthofen, where Jews were forced to run round in circles in a special enclosure.[147] But we should not exaggerate the Jewish dimension at this stage. Crude camp uniforms bore the universal taxonomy of the camps, with colour-coded markings daubed on in waterproof paint becoming the primary identity. One was no longer a person, but an anti-social, criminal, Gypsy, homosexual, Jehovah's Witness, Jew or political, in involuntary anticipation of modern identity politics, with their replacement of persons by categories. The camp inmates had rather less value, even when their labour was exploited, than one of the Alsatians, Boxers or Dobermanns used to patrol the perimeters. When an SS dog-handler discovered his hound nestling in a prisoner's lap – for obvious reasons inmates were never permitted to tend these animals – he shot the dog, remarking, 'If you ruin another one of my dogs, I'll finish you off, understood?'[148]

Each day consisted of gruelling work, breaking stones, cutting peat, making bricks or carrying rocks, or deliberately pointless physical 'sports', for people whose constitution was run down by poor diet or maltreatment and who could be twenty or sixty. A gamesome chicanery was always liable to intervene. Any prisoner could be arbitrarily picked on for casual assault, or for formal public punishment sessions, at which any cry of pain that interrupted the sequence of numbered blows resulted in repetition of the sequence from the start. Further time was passed compulsorily singing Nazi songs to reinforce humiliation.[149]

Apart from their own informal clients and entertainers, an increasingly diverse camp population enabled SS guards to practise divide and rule, playing off criminal 'greens' against political 'reds', until the latter gained some ascendancy through greater self-discipline and organisation. Control was facilitated by co-opting prisoner hierarchies, or encouraging animosity towards homosexuals and others, who were usually bereft of group solidarities. Political detainees were keen to distinguish themselves from the anti-social and criminals, and not immune to their own brand of tyranny, with Communists colluding to exile Trotskyites to more lethal conditions. During the war, these antagonisms were compounded by national or political hatreds, with Catholic Poles who had fervently supported Franco failing to josh along with Spanish Republicans in Austrian Mauthausen.[150] For camp experience was not a form of automatic ennoblement, judging by grim Stalinists who after 1945 went on to destroy people with similar methods, up to and including using defunct camps to murder conservative, liberal and Social Democrat opponents along with former Nazis. Victimhood did not always confer secular sanctity, and extreme experiences often reveal less than ultimate truths about the human condition, although the contrary is a common assumption, especially among those who vicariously assume the mantle of moral authority on the basis of this fallacy.[151]

Detainees released from these camps signed a document forbidding them to discuss their experiences, on pain of being returned to 'protective custody'. In other words, release was conditional, a state of perpetual uncertainty. Many were so shaken by their experiences that they refrained from talking about it, in itself a powerful deterrent to others, although some people did. This raises the wider issue of controlling opinion, beyond prosecuting people for gossip, jokes and stray remarks. For this was not simply some slightly out-of-kilter version of life in free societies, although that view is often conveyed, but a travesty of what citizens of modern democratic countries take for granted every day of their lives, namely freedom under the rule of law.

GRACELANDS

State control of the radio had been introduced by Papen in 1932. Goebbels gained control of content and personnel by March 1933, with a proportion of the licence fee being siphoned off to his Ministry of Propaganda, one of whose departments now provided the news bulletins directly to regional stations. He confidently predicted that this 'most modern instrument for influencing the masses' would replace newspapers, thus anticipating the day when television would either marginalise or dominate the content of the press.[152] One of those most responsible for modernising radio broadcasting during Weimar, Hans Flesch, who had pioneered live reporting and audience participation, was sent to a concentration camp.

Cheap sets drove radio ownership from four to sixteen millions between 1933 and 1941. The sets themselves were minor propaganda items, since VE 301 (People's Receiver 301) commemorated the most important day in German history, 30 January 1933. For those who could not afford payment by instalments, or who did not wish to miss broadcasts when going about, there were six thousand loudspeakers in public places. Collective listening was encouraged, as a means of encouraging participation in the mass events being broadcast. A leading radio propagandist compared communal listening with the total experience of worship in a church.[153] 'Radio wardens' monitored compliance; it being forbidden to move from one's desk in an office until the broadcast had finished. Commentaries, fanfares and martial music set the emotional tone. Since people can have too much of a good thing, the overtly ideological content was rapidly relaxed, in favour of broadcasts of Beethoven or Wagner cycles, suggestive of spurious continuities, and compensating for the official muse's failure to inspire contemporary composers. There was a mounting diet of light entertainment. By the end of the 1930s, two-thirds of the radio programme consisted solely of music.[154]

As a former journalist, Goebbels took a keen interest in print journalism too. Germany's press culture was rich and varied, with nearly three and a half thousand newspapers and ten thousand periodicals in 1933. However, global statistics concealed an industry in trouble, while the circulation of many parish-pump papers was derisory. Of Bavaria's 479 newspapers, three-quarters had a readership below three thousand; a third reached under a thousand people. Only 5 per cent printed more than fifteen thousand copies. Many papers were one-man bands, printed on plates rather than rollers, and reliant on agencies for news, bulked out with advertisements, announcements and items written by keen amateurs. The main national dailies were also affected by declining circulation, partly a consequence of competition from radio, but also because of managerial incompetence in an adverse economic climate. There was also a full range of illustrated and women's magazines. Some of the biggest publishing magnates, such as Mosse or Ullstein, were Jews, who were about to discover that their influence, such as it was, was brittle in a dictatorship.[155]

Loss-making newspapers were plum targets for industrialists who thought they could do better, or who needed outlets for their views. Concentration of ownership had begun before 1933. Apart from Alfred Hugenberg's multi-media empire, Paul Reusch of the Gutehöffnungshütte had a controlling interest in Munich's main daily; Carl Bosch of IG Farben in the *Frankfurter Zeitung*, Hugo Stinnes in the Berlin *Deutsche Allgemeine Zeitung*, and so on. Although the Nazis' own press had a modest circulation, after 1933 they closed two hundred SPD and thirty-five Communist papers, either appropriating editorial offices and plant or liquidating the assets into the Eher Verlag, Max Amann's Nazi publishing empire.

Since this could also access confiscated trades union funds, it became the main player in the newspaper industry, especially since advertising revenue drifted to Nazi papers, weakening the already ailing competition. Publishing houses owned by Jews were expropriated under 'aryanisation' measures, with Goebbels delighting in ousting the Mosses, who had once rejected him for a job as a journalist. Capitalised at sixty million Marks, the Ullstein empire was knocked down to an Amann holding company at a tenth of this price, with the Ullstein family remaining unpaid, and unable to leave Germany with more than the obligatory ten Marks.[156] In the mid-1930s, the Eher Verlag's Phoenix holding company purchased most of the regional Catholic press, which lingered on as a licensed confessional media ghetto. The same fate awaited the haut-bourgeois *Frankfurter Zeitung*, which was cut some slack in the interests of foreign government readers, but which the Eher Verlag bought in April 1939 by way of an ironic gift to Hitler on his fiftieth birthday. Typefaces and journalistic style were not overtly Nazified, so as to give an impression of continuity. The Eher Verlag's ramified holding companies ended up controlling 82.5 per cent of the German press. Three hundred and fifty papers were controlled by the Party, and 625 were still privately owned, albeit with a combined market share of 17.5 per cent.[157] Beneficiaries of the Eher Verlag's enormous profits included Goebbels himself, who in 1936 received an advance of a quarter of a million Marks, to be followed by annual payments of one hundred thousand Marks, for the honour of publishing his diaries twenty-five years after his death. The advance paid for a sprawling 'summer house' on Berlin's exclusive Schwanenwerder island, with such touches as automatic windows – the venue for the most swanky parties during the 1930s.

If ownership was one means of getting a purchase on the press, other controls exercised a a grip on editors and journalists. As the biggest owner–publisher, Amann became chairman of the publishers association, while the journalist and Nazi press chief Otto Dietrich became head of the new Reich Association of the German Press, into which all journalists were subsumed. Not quite all, however, for by 1935 thirteen hundred Jewish and 'Marxist' journalists had been sacked or had fled the country. Sometimes Goebbels sacked journalists in person, summoning a music critic who was prevailed on by Wilhelm Furtwängler to run a favourable review of a new piece by Hindemith, in order to dismiss him from his profession. Although journalists received the trappings of professional status, with a code and courts, to wash off the air of trade, only those who passed racial or political screening could work as journalists at all. Under the October 1933 Editors Law, the powers of owners vis-à-vis editors were curtailed, but the responsibilities of editors to the government became absolute. Clause 20 read: 'Editors of a newspaper bear the professional responsibility and the responsibility before the criminal and civil law for its intellectual content in so far as they have composed it themselves or have accepted it for publication.' Newspaper publishers, such as Hermann Ullstein, also discovered that office telephones were tapped, that a high proportion of their staff were closet Nazis, and that they needed to take on a new species of adviser and fixer to help them in their dealing with the new authorities. A once obliging doorman now led the cries of 'Jews out!'[158]

The replacement of agency wire services with the state-owned DNB, which fed the provincial press, helped control news content. At his first press conference in power, Goebbels explained that the goal of the press was that people should 'think uniformly, react uniformly, and place themselves body and soul at the disposal of the government'. These daily midday press conferences at his Ministry of Propaganda were where the government insisted that it was fine to report positively on Greta Garbo, while Thomas Mann 'had to be erased from the memory of every German'. Instructions extended to the space to be given an article or the size of headline, or photographs that should not appear. These included any showing government members behind serried bottles at official receptions, or pictures of burning synagogues in November 1938.[159]

By contrast, illustrated or women's magazines extended coverage of filmstars to a laughing Führer on the telephone or admiring the exhibits at the Automobile Show, and to the wives and children of other Nazi leaders. Women's magazines included photographs of the coffee breaks enjoyed by the grateful inmates of concentration camps, amid the racially vetted models and tips on household management. Since slush knows no national boundaries, it is unsurprising that in 1938 Ignatius Phayre of the British *Homes and Gardens* profiled Hitler amid his cacti in majolica pots at Berchtesgaden, reassuring British readers that the Führer was 'a droll raconteur' and that the *caneton à la presse* and the *truite saumone à la Monseigneur* were passable.[160]

When a constant diet of propaganda proved counter-productive, Goebbels adopted the formula of 'uniformity of principles' but 'polyformity in the nuances'.[161] The political message was to be camouflaged with an apparent continuity, or hidden within the usual quotient of harmless trivia. Obviously, journalists had more scope on the arts or sports pages to express ambiguous attitudes between the lines than were open to political commentators or reporters.

The Nazis' own Party press found it difficult to make the transition from attacking to defending the government. If the scurrility and viciousness of the 'time of struggle' came naturally to them, the Party's hacks did not adjust easily to a regime of obligatory superlatives. Only items on the Jews and Catholics were a more restricted outlet for the earlier generalised spleen. The main Party newspaper, the *Völkischer Beobachter*, was printed in ever larger editions, and distributed to all civil servants. It appeared in separate regional editions, at each point of the compass, and employed two-colour printing and a broadsheet format at a time neither was common in Germany. If this matters at all, it was a very modern product. It was joined by large-circulation organisational newspapers, the SS *Schwarze Korps*, *Die Deutsche Arbeitsfront* and so forth. Other existing newspapers became court bulletins for particular leaders, with Göring dictating to the Essen *National-Zeitung*. The semi-pornographic *Stürmer* was effectively the private vehicle of the Franconian Gauleiter Julius Streicher, who had been dismissed from schoolteaching in 1928 for insisting that his classes greet him with 'Heil Hitler'. A sort of news of the sewers, it specialised in anything of a salacious nature, printing the names and addresses of anyone over-friendly with Jews, as well as discerning a Jewish conspiracy behind the 1937 *Hindenburg* airship disaster at Lakeside, New Jersey. Sometimes Goebbels and Hitler rebuked Streicher for the content of the paper, but this was more in the way of restraining a comrade who was a known 'character' than a reflection of any fundamental disagreement with the sentiments *Stürmer* expressed. Streicher claimed it was the only paper Hitler read from cover to cover.

The content of newspapers was increasingly dominated by the exciting events with which the regime sought to replace the inherited calendar and passage of the seasons. As we are often told, politics was reduced to mass theatrical spectacle, in which the perpetual star put lesser thespian egoists in the shade. Debate and reason were replaced by acclamation, presentation, regimentation and above all sentiment. But post-modern talk of theatres only reaches so far. For no matter how much one rehashes this history with rationalistic categories and concepts, there is a missing element which only reference to unfulfilled religious needs can reconstitute. For what else was the Führer than a messiah? What else were chosen races, leading classes and vanguard parties than privileged vehicles of destiny? What else underlay the spuriously scientific belief that, once demonic class or race enemies had been overcome, mankind would enter into a state of perfection? What else was the 'national community' than a reversion to times which knew no categorical separation of Church and state, and in which the one flowed effortlessly into the other?[162] The whole, moreover, was suffused with sentimentality, without an arch post-modern knowingness, and subtly different from the Nazis' use of psychological techniques to manipulate crowds, while eschewing the self-application of psychology. Sentimentality was arguably the most modern feature of National Socialism, in that turn-of-the-millennium politics are permeated, if not by presentiments of apocalypse, then by a cloying sentimentality from politicians hard to distinguish from preachers, and a wider culture of self-absorption, sincerity and victimhood. In this respect, Nazism was truly ahead of its time, beyond its unremarkable fascination with mere technology. This was politics as feeling.

Mass rallies, such as those at Nuremberg from 1933 to 1938, had multiple purposes, not least to distract from the grim underside of a police dictatorship by means of a spectacular surface. Each rally was themed, although the 1939 'rally of peace' had to be cancelled. This was how the regime wished to see itself, the apogee being Leni Riefenstahl's *Triumph of the Will*, a propagandistic exercise so definitive that it never needed to be repeated. Rallies combined popular festival, military parade, political meeting and sacred occasion, in which the highest value – the national community – was at its most tangible, and whose focus was on the individual embodiment of the national will. Here the nation became reality; countless petty existences acquired meaning. Hitler explained this in September 1937:

> How can the peasant in his village, the laborer in his workshop or factory, the employee in his office – how can they all grasp the extent of the total result of their innumerable personal sacrifices and their struggle? ·
>
> But once a year, on the occasion of the general display of the Party, they will stride forth as one from the modesty of their narrow existence to gaze upon and acknowledge the glory of the fight and the triumph! ... And when, during these few days, hundreds of thousands march once again to Nuremberg, and hence from all of Germany's Gaus an endless stream of warm life flows into this city, all of them ... will be able to come to the same conclusion: we are truly the witnesses of a transformation more tremendous than any the German nation has ever experienced.[163]

The venue had rich medieval and Wagnerian associations. However, this was but a quaint backdrop to events otherwise enacted in a modern purpose-built setting, designed to enhance the caesarian solitude of the Leader on his tribune. The formational tribes gathered slowly, in keen anticipation of the Führer's aircraft glinting as it dropped through a louring sky over the roofs of the venerable city. Following a very venerable tradition, the leader literally rode upon the rays of the sun. Or at least that was how Riefenstahl edited it. Daytime events involved the young, military march-pasts and workers assembled from across Germany, who responded lustily to calls of 'Comrade, where do you come from?' with 'from Friesland – from Bavaria – from the Danube, from the Rhine, from Silesia' and so on. Class struggle had been replaced by worker bonding, whose quasi-military aspect prompted one British observer to remark: 'somehow it does not seem absurd to be saluted with a spade'. If the sceptical British suspended belief, the *New York Times* man was carried away with enthusiasm.[164] Other messages were conveyed by huge military parades, in which the army was seamlessly elided with the white-gloved giants of the SS, negotiating Nuremberg's winding streets behind colour sergeants and with the crash of bands reverberating off the buildings. The days were followed by nighttime events, whose emotional register was enhanced by the world's largest electric organ, and Speer's cathedrals of light sending icy streams kilometres into the darkness, in a conscious evocation of substance-less cathedrals. Elsewhere, amid Hitler's favourite fiery element, the Party's old fighters, winkled out of the bar of the Hotel Deutscher Hof, could be safely presented to the public, although Speer found it impossible to get their beer-paunches into a pleasing line. Hitler's affectionate references to 'my hunchbacked ancients' conveyed the difficulty of refashioning this gnarled, piratical crew as supermen.[165]

The Führer himself milked these rallies for every last ounce of pathos.[166] Alone he strode through the ranks, to commune with the Party's martyrs, before consecrating new standards with a touching of the 'blood banner', a firm handshake and exchanges of prolonged manly stares.[167] Homoerotic comradeship alternated with lonely communing with the dead, as the Führer travelled from mortal to demidivinity. The old fighters took on the air of the earliest disciples of a leader who regarded himself as a messiah. On 10 September 1937 Hitler echoed the Gospel of St John when he told his Political Leaders:

> I am so pleased to have my Old Fighters before me again once a year. I always have the feeling that, as long as the human being has the gift of life, he should yearn for those with whom he has shaped his life. What would my life be without you! The fact that you once found your way to me and believed in me gave your life new meaning and a new goal! The fact that I found you was the prerequisite for my own life and my struggle.[168]

He could not quite control the weather, for the 1937 Party rally occurred in torrential rain, but he could turn the absence of 'Hitler weather' into a political allegory for an audience of Hitler Youth:

This morning I learned from our weather forecasters that, at present, we have the meteorological condition 'V.b.' That is supposed to be a mixture of very bad and bad. Now, my boys and girls, Germany has had this meteorological condition for fifteen years! And the Party had this meteorological condition too! For the space of a decade, the sun did not shine upon this Movement. It was a battle in which only hope could be victorious, the hope that in the end the sun would rise over Germany after all. And risen it has! And as you are standing here today, it is also good that the sun is not smiling down on you. For we want to raise a race not only for sunny, but also for stormy days![169]

For as Germany benefited from economic recovery and the negation of demeaning external constraints, so the credit for this was attributed to and claimed by this quasi-miraculous figure dispatched by Providence. Best of all, he was not some remote ancient Egyptian god–king, whose religion was for an elite, while mortals had to make do with Osiris, but a self-proclaimed ordinary man, miraculously returned from the holocaust of the Flanders trenches for whose dead he spoke.[170] Germany became 'Gracelands'. Hopes and longings were projected on to one man, whose propagandists busily converted his human demerits – the bohemian working habits or troubled relations with women – into attributes of genius or self-denying heroism.

Like other heads of state the world over, Hitler was the last refuge of the deranged, the desperate, the opportunistic and the pompous. People imagined his feelings from cinematic contact, rather in the way adolescent girls convince themselves that the latest moody boy-singer seems lonely or sad, a role the brooding Hitler was well suited to, albeit with a greasy forelock rather than a tussle of boyish hair. Cake makers, rose growers and shoe cream manufacturers vied to put Hitler's name on their products, requests which were routinely denied for reasons of *lèse majesté*, to the chagrin of Bruno, the Marienwerder baker of an 'Adolf-Hitler-Torte', for even then cooks had large pretensions. Churches wished to emblazon new bells with Hitler's name, while virtually every second village wanted to dedicate a tree or change its own historic name to Hitlerhöhe. Bridges and roads followed. Proud fathers requested permission to christen daughters 'Hitlerine', with 'Adolfine' being the recommended compromise. And in flowed the hand-crafted violins or a barber's swastika carefully woven from strands of human hair. Typically, the offer of a fine carpet from a professor in an ethnic German corner of Romania had to await consular inquiries into the surname 'Kornfeld'. Hopeful spinsters offered Hitler companionship on his rare visits to foreign parts, although the man who offered Mussolini his retinas, so that the Führer's only friend would not go blind, was probably taking the mood of enthusiastic sacrifice too far. Speaking of eyes, when Hitler's dog died, an Austrian couple offered Mitgard, whose 'loyal eye' would watch over 'the great gentleman', ever ready to 'fight for your Excellency down to the final breath'. There was occasionally room for clemency amid this stream of slush, whose full saccharine quality only comes across in a language which lends itself to it. Thus on his 1937 birthday Hitler acceded to the request of a small girl (they were never dumpy, gawky with spots and bottle-lensed spectacles) presenting him with flowers to release her father from jail, by staying his transfer to a concentration camp.

For children were a crucial component of the Führer-cult, pint-sized extras used to promote a warm glow of benignity coupled with vague hopes for the future. Although we have filtered them out of memory, they were as omnipresent as the statuesque SS men. On 20 April 1936, Hitler received a delegation of children representing the Reich Food Estate. It was his birthday. The programme read:

> The children, youth farmers and farm maidens all appear in peasant costume. The maidens have small posies of flowers in their hands. The little spokesgirl has a larger bouquet of flowers, which she presents to the Führer after her speech.

Text of Speech:

Dear Führer!

We lads and lasses from German peasant farms have come to you today. Father and Mother and all the neighbours in the village greet you warmly through us. They all love you heartily and wish you a very, very happy birthday.

Father has told us that you have a large farm. It is as big as the farms of all of the farmers put together. And Father says that the farm that Father has is only a small part of your big farm. Father says that the big farm is our Germany, and that you are the farmer of the big farm. And this great farm, says Father, has been very sick. Once upon a time, foreign neighbours invaded the farm and took away the horses, cattle and corn. But you have made everything good once again.

Father and Mother and all the neighbours are proud of you. They told us that we must really love you a lot, just as we really love Mother and Father. And one day, when we are as big as you, we will run our farms just as you lead the great farm – our Germany. And now you must have a little fun with us. Come, we wish to sing a little song for our Führer.

Length of Speech: 2 Minutes.

Then the children all sing the little song:

> Dear good Führer
> We love you much,
> We wish to present you with flowers
> with our tiny little hands
> Then you will love us too.
> Dear good Führer
> We love you very much
> You have the best spot
> in our little heartlets
> We love you very much.

Length of song: 1,5 minutes.[171]

Father clearly neglected history while tending his herds, for the 'neighbours' in his parable had been victims of invasion. The totalitarian aspiration behind this sentimental guff was expressed in a speech which Hitler delivered in 1938, in which he outlined the cradle-to-grave progression awaiting Germany's youth:

> these boys join our organisation at the age of ten and get a breath of fresh air for the first time, then, four years later, they move from the Jungvolk to the Hitler Youth and there we keep them for another four years. And then we are even less prepared to give them back into the hands of those who create class and status barriers, rather we take them immediately into the SA or into the SS, into the NSKK [Nazi Motorised Transport Corps] and so on. And if they are there for eighteen months or two years and have still not become real National Socialists, then they go into the Labour Service and are polished there for six or seven months, and all of this under a single symbol, the German spade. And if, after six or seven months, there are still remnants of class consciousness or pride in status, then the Wehrmacht will take over the further treatment for two years and when they return after two or four years then, to prevent them from slipping back into old habits once again we take them immmediately into the SA, SS etc. and they will not be free again for the rest of their lives. This was a compact with unfreedom many young Germans were only too willing to enter into, as a way of finding meaning and purpose which they lacked.[172]

3

REPLACING THE BRIDGE: NEW TIMES, NEW MAN

The commemoration in Munich each 9 November of the
Nazis 'martyred' during the 1923 putsch was the bathetic low-point
of the Party's calendar. This 1937 photograph shows Hitler and Göring
marching in the wake of the 'blood banner' of the 'Movement' with
Julius Streicher in pole position. Lining the route, pylons bearing
smouldering urns bore the names of those killed in the putsch.

FAITH, HOPE AND EVEN A LITTLE CHARITY TOO

If faith and hope were integral to National Socialism, so too, surprisingly enough, was charity. This ceased to be an uncomplicated reflection of human altruism, still less something individuals do discreetly for the good of their souls, or to reap tax exemptions and titles. Instead, it became a favoured means of mobilising communal sentimentality, that most underrated, but quintessential, characteristic of Nazi Germany.

During the Weimar Republic, embryonic Nazi welfare services consisted of localised initiatives, focused on indigent or injured Party or SA comrades.[1] They were housed and fed, and young women bandaged their broken heads. In 1931, the Berlin Gauleiter, Goebbels, alighted upon the propaganda potentialities of a small Nazi People's Welfare Association (NSV), founded by one of the capital's local Party branches. With Goebbels' support, this was taken over by Erich Hilgenfeldt, a wartime pilot and peacetime businessman, who proved his mettle with a collection campaign to mark Hitler's 20 April birthday. In May 1933, Hitler recognised People's Welfare as the Party's sole welfare agency throughout the Reich; Magda Goebbels became its patron.[2]

Hitler's favour enabled People's Welfare to establish its institutional autonomy vis-à-vis other Nazi organisations with claims in the welfare field, such as Ley's German Labour Front (DAF), Schirach's Hitler Youth (HJ), and Scholz-Klink's NS-Women's Association (NSF), whose respective clienteles overlapped with that of the NSV. Relations were often strained, but a succession of agreements during the 1930s resolved the most serious demarcation disputes. But there were existing non-Nazi players in the field of charity who had to be absorbed or pushed aside. Brief organisational orientation is indispensable to a fuller understanding of the 'co-ordination' of this sector.

At the outset, there were seven charitable peaks, or 'sisters', in the parlance of the oil industry. People's Welfare expropriated the assets of socialist welfare organisations, while dividing those of a now defunct Christian workers' welfare association with the confessional charities. The national Jewish charitable agency was disbarred from charitable counsels, and confined to an ethnic exclave. With three competitor organisations down from the outset, People's Welfare proceeded more circumspectly with the remaining charitable organisations, namely the Protestant Inner Mission (founded in 1848), the Roman Catholic Caritas Association (founded 1896) and the German branch of the International Red Cross. Together with a fifth charity, these belonged to a national umbrella association called the German League for Voluntary Welfare. The confessional welfare societies were elaborate organisations, with over 15,500 asylums, hospitals and homes, providing about 1,300,000 beds, or about half those available for the old, the sick and difficult children. They trained and employed tens of thousands of nurses and carers, who then staffed state hospitals.[3] Finally, the German Red Cross shed its reactionary Wilhelmine image as the upper crust's charity of choice, and negotiated the transition to the Republic by acquiring a series of civilian welfare responsibilities to replace its largely defunct military paramedical vocation.[4]

The black arts of 'co-ordination' are worth chronicling. First, Hilgenfeldt beefed up People's Welfare by absorbing smaller self-help groups, for the blind, deaf, dumb and distressed gentlefolk, rather like a tycoon ramping his assets before a takeover. Next, he inserted himself on to the national steering body of the remaining charities, forcing the 'fifth' charity into amalgamation with People's Welfare. At first, the latter's relations with the confessional charities were amicable enough. The Protestants of the Inner Mission thought confessional balance had been restored, in so far as the Roman Catholic Centre Party had been close to the heart of affairs during the Republic, putting Protestants without a dedicated political party at a disadvantage. Protestants discovered much patriotic common ground with the Nazis, while being receptive to eugenic solutions to the biological equivalent of original sin. A leading figure in the Inner Mission moved to a senior position within People's Welfare. The Catholic Caritas Association was as embarrassingly fulsome in its welcoming of an end to 'filth and smut', the restoration of family values, self-reliance and order. Roman Catholics may have baulked at sterilisation, but initially they deluded themselves that the 1933 Concordat concluded with the Vatican would afford them a protected niche within an authoritarian political system, a reflection of a more pervasive underestimation of Nazism's totalitarian ambitions.[5] The German Red Cross continued its process of adjustment by appointing Nazis to prominent positions, starting with the new President, HRH Carl Eduard Duke of Saxe-Coburg and Gotha, and introducing the 'Hitler greeting' and Nazi songs for public occasions.

Having corralled the confessional charities and Red Cross within a new national steering body, Hilgenfeldt replaced collegial deliberation with the Führer principle, employing various sleights of hand to marginalise his rivals. In 1934, legislation was introduced to restrict the confessional charities' ability to solicit funds outside the Churches. Mailshot campaigns were prohibited, and state permission had to be sought for charitable campaigns in general. The confessional charities were obliged to collect on behalf of the Nazis' own 'Winter Aid' programme, in return for a proportional share of the proceeds. Various Nazi organisations took the lion's share, leaving the combined religious charities and the Red Cross with a diminishing remnant as each year passed. Since the 1923 hyperinflation, they had received top-up subsidies from the state. Now disbursement was subject to the agreement of People's Welfare. In 1938, the Inner Mission requested 2.84 million Reichsmarks and the Caritas Association 1.2 million Reichsmarks; they received 15 and 12 per cent of what they needed. Their turnover was also subject to sales tax. In 1939, these payments were terminated, on the ground that People's Welfare itself had assumed enhanced reponsibilities in Austria and the Sudetenland. Hilgenfeldt argued that the Churches were secretly collecting funds for a confessional sector whose days were numbered. He also struck at the already self-coordinated Red Cross. Civilian welfare responsibilities it had developed in peacetime were relinquished to People's Welfare, while it was 'encouraged' to revert to its original paramedical military remit.[6] In 1937, the deputy presidency of the Red Cross went to the SS Reich Doctors Leader, Robert Grawitz. Three years later, the total co-ordination of the voluntary charitable sector was symbolised by the abolition of the steering committee on which they were notionally represented.[7]

The confessional charities accepted these arrangements as the lesser evil, in so far as Hilgenfeldt posed as their protector against regional and local Nazi bosses seeking to filch their assets. By 1939, People's Welfare had become the second largest Nazi mass organisation, after the German Labour Front, with twelve and a half million members, or 15 per cent of the population, covering over half the households in the land. It directly employed over eighty thousand people, with a further million or so unpaid volunteers. By 1938 these included nearly eight thousand 'brown sisters', that is People's Welfare community nurses, whose brief was to maintain the nation's biological strength, rather than to practise a form of secular or religious vocation expressed through caring for sick individuals. Through its membership dues and mass collection drives, People's Welfare disposed of vast sums of money. But these statistical details are almost worthy of the Nazis themselves in their suggestive banality.

Welfare assumes many forms across the globe, often with a complementary rather than antagonistic relationship to the voluntary sector. During the Weimar Republic, welfare had become a controversial subject across the entire confessional and political spectrum, with intense philosophical competition to determine the limits, purposes and thrust of what since 1919 had become an increased sphere of public welfare activity. Criticism of the Weimar system has a familiar ring to it, although we should resist making suggestive contemporary analogies. In the eyes of its critics, state welfare had resulted in bureaucratic insensitivity; a dependency and rights culture; failure to discriminate between the improvident and the prudent poor; and the vitiation of Christian and civic voluntarism. Many Christians felt that welfare had become an end in itself, divorced from spiritual goals; many welfare claimants felt bitter and disappointed at their meagre entitlements; doctors grumbled about the loss of professional autonomy entailed by socialised medicine. An over-ambitious system duly collapsed under the related strains of unfulfilled expectations and massive economic crisis.

The Nazis sought to rectify these failings by replacing faceless and obtuse bureaucracy with remorseless activism, and by fusing charity and welfare. Calling the resulting arrangements an aberrant apotheosis of the welfare state, or a 'racial welfare state', does not quite do justice to the subtlety of Nazi arrangements. Mass voluntarism demonstrated the national community in action, while enabling the government to divert public resources to ends other than welfare. The budget cuts of the Depression could be continued, because the financial burdens of welfare were increasingly assumed by the population itself. Charity also absorbed surplus cash, which by suppressing consumer demand indirectly benefited rearmament. The Nazis could demolish the welfare state, and its legal entitlements, while appearing to fill the gap with voluntarism and Party organisations against which the needy had no legal recourse. This was symptomatic of a broader process whereby ideology and organisations with no definable locus ate into the state and society in a corrosive fashion.[8] Finally, as Hitler explicitly acknowledged, charity had a didactic function which could never be achieved by taxation: 'Certainly [a welfare tax] would be much easier and much less burdensome for countless people, but this would precisely lack what we want to achieve with Winter Aid, namely education towards German national community.'[9] Much depended upon the maintenance of an activist climate. Here the talk was of duty and sacrifice for the well-being of the collective. People's Welfare members and supporters distributed charitable kitsch, thus encouraging light industry, and received certificates, badges and other awards, rather like adult boy scouts. Those who felt ambivalent or hostile towards other Nazi formations could join People's Welfare, if only because its coercive and exclusionary agendas were relatively well concealed beneath the benign surface. The major Nazi charitable enterprise was Winter Aid, designed to alleviate poverty during the most inclement months of the year, although here, as in many other areas, it was a scheme inherited from the Republic. Rather like late-Weimar work-creation schemes, its experiments in alleviating distress were engulfed in the final crisis.

Winter Aid had been pioneered by Brüning's government in 1931, but an amnesiac Hitler claimed sole credit when he inaugurated collection drives each October.[10] Although Winter Aid was organised by People's Welfare, Hilgenfeldt was subordinate to the Propaganda Minister Goebbels. The aim was to portray the 'national community' in action, displacing Marxist internationalism and marginalising religious charity with the Nazis' 'socialism of the deed'. Charity might even be extended to former Communists, provided they recanted their earlier views. Opening the October 1935 aid campaign, Hitler said: 'We hold that, by such visible demonstrations, we are continually stirring the conscience of our *Volk* and making each of you once more aware that you should perceive yourself as a national comrade, and that you should make sacrifices! . . . We want to show the whole world and our *Volk* that we Germans regard the word "community" not as a hollow phrase, but as something that for us really does entail an inner obligation.'[11] Two years later he contrasted his view of charity with that of the socialists and Christians:

Sometimes, when I see shabbily dressed girls, shivering with cold themselves, collecting with infinite patience for others who are cold, then I have the feeling that they are all apostles of a certain Christianity! This is a Christianity which can claim for itself as no other can: this is the Christianity of a sincere profession of faith, because behind it stands not the word, but the deed!

With the aid of this tremendous society, countless people are being relieved of the feeling of social abandonment and isolation. Many are thus regaining the firm belief that they are not completely lost and alone in this world, but sheltered in their national community; that they, too, are being cared for, that they, too, are being thought of and remembered. And beyond that: there is a difference between the theoretical knowledge of socialism and the practical life of socialism. People are not born socialists, but must first be taught how to become them.[12]

Unremarkably, Nazi charity exploited guilt towards the disadvantaged, and shame towards those who resisted its emotional blandishments. One-pot Sundays were held every second Sunday in the winter months, with the saving on more elaborate food being donated to Winter Aid. Nazi leaders, including Hitler himself, were photographed enjoying a vat of steaming stew. Using arguments which many found irresistible, Hitler said:

Don't tell me, 'All right, but it's still a bother to do all the collecting.' You have never known hunger, otherwise you would know what a bother it is to be hungry. . . . And if the other then says: 'But you know, all these stew Sundays – I would like to give something, but it's my stomach. I have stomach problems all the time anyway, I don't understand it. I'd give ten pfennigs just the same.' No, dear friend, there is a reason behind everything we do. It is particularly useful for you, someone who does not understand, if in this way at least we can guide you back to your *Volk*, to the millions of your national comrades who would be happy if they only had that stew all winter long that you perhaps eat once a month.[13]

The first Nazi Winter Aid drive netted a 400 per cent increase over sums collected during the winter of 1931/2. Under Winter Aid, prodigious quantities of material goods were shipped to and fro, including clothing, coal, firewood and potatoes. By purchasing 35 per cent of the nation's deep-sea catch, Winter Aid brought fresh fish to inhabitants of landlocked regions. At Christmas, efforts were made to provide children with presents their parents could not afford. That material goods were preferred to donations of money was suggestive, for the volumes involved could be better exploited for propaganda purposes. The age of the telethon and credit card pledges had not yet dawned, but by 1938 donors were invited to guess the regional totals collected, with the winner receiving a camera, a portrait of the Führer or a vacuum cleaner.[14] Goebbels could enumerate the millions of quintals of potatoes or the '3,734,752' theatre and film tickets given gratis to the underfed and under-entertained poor. Graphics showed the nine-metres-high wall of coal which could be hypothetically built around Germany with Winter Aid's aggregate gift over four years of 99.25 million hundredweight of coal. This may have impressed the gullible.[15]

But charity was also redefined, not only progressively to exclude 'racial aliens' – for whom People's Welfare encouraged other arrangements – but by focusing exclusively on needy national comrades who could produce and reproduce, leaving religious organisations to tend the chronically sick, old and otherwise hopeless. These people were no longer the preferred objects of human concern. Most obviously, concentration-camp inmates drifted out of view, or rather German welfare organisations sought to block the view of concerned foreign colleagues. In late 1933, the head of the German Red Cross explained to his Swedish colleagues that 'for the mass of [camp inmates] hailing from proletarian milieux, their material standard of living is higher than they knew in civilian life'. A Swiss International Committee inspection team concurred with this view after a sanitised tour of Dachau.[16]

The exclusionary character of Nazi charity differed from Christian tenets, in which everyone was equal in the sight of God, and no one written off as hopeless. Indeed, the greater the degree of disability, need or suffering, the greater the mystery of God's handiwork. Nazi charity and welfare also deviated from both traditional conservative and progressive liberal outlooks, not least because the emphasis was on the collective well-being and the practice racially exclusionary. No Weimar conservative or liberal welfare reformers contemplated excluding people on grounds of race or killing the mentally and physically handicapped. Since Nazi welfare was highly dirigiste, it should not be misconstrued as a harbinger of the minimalist, anti-dependency ideology of contemporary left- or right-wing libertarians. The nonconformist left regard welfare as a means of stabilising and perpetuating capitalism; the supply-side right see it as a self-interested plot by welfare professionals which inhibits those best suited to create generalisable prosperity. Nazism tackled the problem from a different direction.[17]

Rival calls on human kindness were eradicated, commencing with a Munich amputee and mother of four, bold or desperate enough to seek a handout from Himmler on the Marienplatz. Beggars were routinely rounded up and imprisoned in workhouses and concentration camps, which became indistinct.[18] This focused public generosity on Winter Aid, while removing those who most tangibly contradicted the image of well-being restored.[19] More generally, the Nazis practised displacement, by concentrating other people's generosity solely on the eugenically or racially unimpeachable.[20] Welfare ceased to be a general entitlement to state compensation for the misfortunes of life, but rather became state marshalling of privately funded assistance for the prospective contribution the family 'cell' would make to the 'national community'. Past wrangling about how to assess entitlement was swept aside, as Nazi charity went to any 'national comrade' in need, although no one had any legal claim on it. In other words, the distributive issues – if not the distributive problems – which had bedevilled welfare in an overloaded pluralist system were swept aside.[21]

While they marginalised the confessional welfare agencies, the Nazis reinforced voluntarism with compulsion. Posters reading 'I am a member of the NSV – and you?' appeared on buses and trams. Novel collection methods, such as co-opting zoo elephants to draw crowds, or horsemen holding tins aloft on sticks to reach upper-storey windows, soon palled. Contributions to Winter Aid were deducted at source from wages – anticipating levies for Nicaraguan or Vietnamese comrades in the later German Democratic Republic – with worker consent to this extortion negated by enrolling everyone into the People's Welfare at works assemblies, and asking anyone who dissented to make this publicly known.[22] Workers were then surprised to find People's Welfare pamphlets in their wage packets, for which further deductions had already been made.[23] Schoolteachers handed out large quantities of Winter Aid badges to children, in the knowledge that they would never be able to dispose of them, indirectly pressurising parents to make up the deficit to spare their offspring shame at school. Some schools introduced display boards showing which pupils had or had not succeeded in offloading their People's Welfare badges. Passengers on buses and trains morosely suffered conductors who withheld their change for charitable purposes. Winter Aid became a form of licensed extortion.

The ratchet of charitable coercion went beyond having a box or tin aggressively rattled under one's nose, a minor nuisance in the bigger scheme of things. The issuance of badges and flags enabled collectors to hone in on those not evincing the appropriate commitment. So did special forms which householders were obliged to complete, detailing what they had donated. Further forms involved a 'moral' assessment of the donor. Next came empty Winter Aid bags, suggestively deposited outside the front door. The use of Hitler Youth, SA and SS men as collectors only enhanced the impression of being mugged on behalf of charity.[24] Overt threats followed, for not fulfilling one's sacrificial duty implied a hostile attitude towards the collective educational goals of the National Socialist state. A choice had become a potential political crime. Not playing the game had dire consequences, which were often couched in terms of 'protecting' erring individuals from the righteous anger of the people, an insight into the perversions to which the far from inherently benign concept of 'community' was subject.

In 1935 a well-to-do hereditary farmer in Franconian Geislöhe received a minatory letter from his local Party branch in which he was admonished for failing to contribute to Winter Aid. If he did not comply within eight days, it would be necessary to take measures to pre-empt popular outrage. Where this was leading was made explicit in the worrying conclusion that: 'I believe that, as a farmer, you still possess sufficient pride not to allow things to go so far that you will end up where normally only enemies of the state and parasites upon the nation are detained.'[25] In Flensburg, a local Party boss coerced a businessman who had failed to contribute to Winter Aid by organising a public meeting which resulted in an angry mob appearing outside his home. The businessman was taken into 'protective custody', as a result of which he promised to integrate himself 'fully and wholly' into the 'national community' through significant contributions to Winter Aid.[26] In Chemnitz, another mob besieged the house of a judge whose wife had donated a sack of rotting pears, crying: 'She knew that these pears were rotten, the old pig, the old sow, sow, sow, sow!' This harnessing of Jacobin moral outrage was common to other totalitarian regimes at the time.[27]

For national comrades were irritated by the constant and increasingly coercive demands for donations for the poor, especially when these demands continued against a backdrop of economic recovery. They suspected that state resources saved were being hived off for military purposes, and resented the secondary corruption which collections entailed. Beneath the sea-green façade, corruption ran riot. Exile Social Democrat reports on conditions in Germany noted Nazi housing block leaders who had fled across the Dutch border with the proceeds of Winter Aid collections.[28] The poor were not happy either, converting Winter Aid's German acronym WHW into 'we are still starving'.[29] Increasing expectations were disappointed, with children glumly pondering such Winter Aid Christmas gifts as seven nuts, six biscuits and a packet of soiled male collars 'size 39 and 40', not intended as their present for Father.[30] One consequence of the Nazis' attempt to monopolise the charitable instinct was that people began to make ostentatious donations to religious charities such as the Caritas Association to register their dissatisfaction.[31]

Winter Aid was one aspect of the broader offensive of People's Welfare across the welfare sector. People's Welfare assumed responsibility for looking after discharged adult and juvenile offenders, aid services within major railway stations, and a Four Year Plan campaign to feed the nation's swine with kitchen waste. But these were minor affairs compared with its invasion of the intimate world of the family. The Weimar Republic had made significant advances in the fields of child allowances, maternity benefits, employment leave and the provision of midwives and social workers. However, many of these advances were undone by the Depression, while moralists of several political persuasions discerned a 'crisis' in the family.[32] Weimar is justly celebrated for its artistic exuberance and sexual experimentation, but there were over sixty organisations dedicated to the restoration of traditional artistic and moral values.

THE POLITICS OF SELF-RIGHTEOUSNESS

Anxieties about a declining birthrate and the need for pro-natalist state policies were commonplace in inter-war Europe. Much of what Nazism sought to do in this area would not have seemed bizarre in Britain or France, which shared a similar catastrophic experience. Obviously, the emphases were slightly different.[33] People's Welfare hijacked an earlier Protestant charitable campaign to assist mothers and small children, for an area so crucial to the future eugenic well-being of the German race could hardly be surrendered to the Churches. Anti-individualism was apparent in references to mothers as 'the eternal source of life' or to children as 'the bearers of our national future'.[34] Their bodies were the sole medium for transmitting the nation's collective 'blood' – mystically conceived – rather than individual DNA through human sperm. Apart from collections of bedding and food to alleviate the poverty of new mothers, People's Welfare provided home help, usually in the form of the League of German Maidens, postnatal recuperation homes or kindergartens and nurseries for the under-sixes. Mothers were selected for the recuperation homes, which were often situated in mountains or near the sea or springs. The care staff attended special training courses. The emphasis in these homes was upon community, with morning flag raising and a strong dose of Nazi ideology, as well as practical instruction in child care. Under-sixes took their first fateful steps along an institutional path which was to last all their lives. Rural kindergartens were primarily designed to relieve mothers for work at harvest times. The theme of integrating the nation by dissolving regional or town and country cleavages underlay the policy of sending older urban children to the countryside. Again, the Weimar Republic had pioneered recuperation rests for mothers, and between 1925 and 1932 had sent about two and half million urban children to the countryside, but this seems to have been forgotten.[35]

The Nazis' coldly instrumental view of women as bearers of the racially fit was enveloped in kitsch and sentiment. For a few days each year, the nation was transformed into the greetings card section of Woolworth's. One objective of the mother cult was to boost the flagging birthrate, to which end the Nazis introduced loans for newly married 'Aryan' couples, which were amortised with births of children. Single people and childless couples received enhanced tax bills to subsidise child allowances and one-off payments for other people's children. Although there was an appreciable shortlived increase in the birth of third or fourth children, the absence of a commensurate public housing policy did little to affect the secular drift towards modest nuclear families, with SS members especially distinguished by their failure to go forth and multiply.

Everything about the Nazis' manipulation of motherhood was fake, beginning with the cult's allegedly venerable origins. The Nazi calendar found room on 10 May for the Day of the German Mother, in line with ancient Teutonic custom, whereby the 'brave sons and brave daughters wove a coronet of flowers for their beloved, good mothers'. Actually, Mother's Day was the brainchild of the American Ann Jarvis, and had first become a US public holiday in 1914. Due to intense lobbying by moral conservatives and the German florist industry, it had become an unofficial day of celebration in Germany during the 1920s; tie manufacturers tried hard with Father's Day, but without the same success. The Nazis formalised and magnified the occasion, investing the Day of the German Mother with eugenic and quasi-religious overtones. An army of collectors, from the NSV, Hitler Youth, SA and SS, sprang into operation, often demanding contributions with menaces. Special poems and plays were broadcast and performed on the theme of motherhood.[36]

In 1938, the Nazis instituted Mothers' Crosses in bronze, silver and gold for women 'rich in children'. The French Superior Council for Natality had been doing this since 1920. Nominations for these awards by Nazi housing block or cell leaders – charged with developing a 'trusting' relationship with occupants – were subjected to multiple scrutiny by the health and welfare authorities, the Party and the police. Scrutiny was bad enough, but it was doubly hurtful when nominees were rejected for an award they had not solicited. There were no appeals or explanations of rejection. The selection criteria were designed to distinguish laudable, independent and orderly families 'rich in children' from unworthy, dependent and dysfunctional 'large families'. Quality counted more than quantity. Women who produced children serially with different partners were ineligible. So too were Jews and Gypsies, who were disqualified for awards which were designed to enhance respect for mothers in society, and from which preferential treatment ensued.

The ideal candidate was a conscientious, well-presented housewife with orderly domestic arrangements, whose husband worked and who had borne legitimate children. Avant-garde SS destigmatisation of illegitimacy was not widely shared. The ideal mother always took pregnancies to term, and did not smoke or drink. She had no lovers. Her husband could smoke like a chimney, but if he drank excessively the Mother's Cross would prove elusive. Neither husband nor wife had any criminal convictions, paid their rent and settled their debts, but if they were reliant upon welfare they expended it upon the children rather than inessentials. Here, childless couples were routinely censured for alleged egoism, tantamount to a dereliction of duty. Hence in 1938 the divorce laws were amended to include childlessness as grounds for separation, so that childless couples were subject to more than the usual pressures to surrender to mundanity.

Since the Mother's Cross candidates were often elderly, inquiries covered the lifestyles of their children, and every family member, one of whom in an asylum or eugenically sterilised would count as grounds for disqualification and much familial recrimination. These things had real human consequences. Thus an SS candidate for promotion was deeply disturbed when his mother-in-law failed to receive a Mother's Cross thanks to a past spell in an asylum due to depression, because of the implications of this for his wife and daughter, and hence for his promotion chances. Frustrated nominees indignantly claimed that they had borne ten or eleven children, 'there being no instances in the family of imprisonment, hard labour, subversive activities, alcohol abuse', which indicates the extent to which the selection criteria were known in the general population.

Women who received these Crosses could derive comfort from the claim that their bodies were the medium for the transmission of Nordic 'blood', even as they were being demeaned to the level of cows ruminating in the fields. But these over-familiar, racially driven pro-natalist policies do not quite exhaust what can be said about this aspect of Nazism, whose kitschy sentimentality was more indicative of the whole than appears at first sight. For the illusion of harmony, in this case the idyll of the cradle, brood and home hearth, was intimately related to the capacity to run amok through chaotic depredations, murdering the children of other mothers, burning down their homes, villages and cities in a frenzy of apocalyptic abandon. Motherhood joined the rest of the Nazi idyll in supplying restorative comfort – the equivalent of a warm bath in cheap, lurid, viscous substances – for people whose personalities were often not up to the messy realities of the racial mission they had set themselves. Although he was up for anything, Hitler himself epitomised this schizophrenic quality. On the one hand the desperately conventional figure doting on little boys and girls, scoffing cream cakes, in an atmosphere of forced gaiety; on the other a brooding warlord, more taken with smouldering cities under blue-grey, blood-flecked skies. His emotional range only covered the former.[37] Bearers of Mothers' Crosses were incorporated into this paradigm, for they soon discovered that the most acceptable child of all was he who fell for Motherland, for which double sacrifice they received these analogues of military decorations. This conflation of birth and violent death, so symptomatic of the adololescent, death-fixated, kitschy sensibility informing Nazi politics, was explicit in poetry:

> Mothers, your cradles,
> are like a slumbering army
> Ever ready for victory
> they will be empty never more.[38]

Weimar Germany's many moralists discerned a libertine miasma in the major cities, including visible homosexuality, prostitution and a libidinous 'new woman'. The latter meant clerks, sales assistants and typists who bobbed their hair and daydreamed about filmstars, but whose ambitions and desires were prosaic by the standards of the late twentieth century. Again, concern about 'her' was common to many European countries. Left and right may have differed in their analyses of alleged moral crises and how to solve them, but there was unanimity on the importance of the family. The Nazis latched on to the mood of panic among moralists. Typically, what may or may not have been grounds for legitimate concern, depending on one's point of view, was not seen as a temporary aberration generated by exceptionally disturbed circumstances, or as signs of greater tolerance. The alleged visibility of homosexuality and prostitution in Weimar cities was assimilated into a vision of imminent racial annihilation, or hope-lessly dramatised as an 'historically unprecedented overturning of all values'.[39]

The Nazis were strong on family values, attaching especial importance to youth. Some Nazi leaders may have wished to translate *de
facto* masculine hegemony into a formal ideology of 'male bonding',
but familial traditionalists prevailed over notions reeking of homosexuality. Although they employed a superficially conservative-sounding
familial rhetoric, abounding with terms such as duty or obedience, the
aims were collectivist and biological. The family was regarded as the
'core cell' of the biological totality. Out went Weimar tolerance of a
plurality of lifestyles, in which no official stigmas attached to being
single, childless or homosexual, and in came state-driven pro-natalist
policies designed to produce 'child rich' and qualitatively unimpeachable families, together with absolute intolerance of heterodox forms of
human sexuality or non-conformist lifestyles. It was not a good time
to be gay.[40]

The major exception to this rule was Hitler himself, whose view of
these issues was 'I am a completely non-family man with no sense of
the clan spirit,' and whose own emotional life consisted of a menacing
cloud of deviancy and difficulty bearing down on a succession of
gauche young women. Since Hitler's own arrangements could be
publicly rationalised as the sacrificial and spartan cost of duty, Joseph
and Magda Goebbels, with their handsome brood, stood in as first
family, even though Goebbels was a serial adulterer, whose wife joined
him in suicide after he had poisoned their children. But the sexual
hypocrisy of politicians is unremarkable, of interest merely to the
prurient.

A series of laws made marriage subject to intense eugenic vetting,
with marriages between healthy 'Aryans' and racial 'aliens' prohibited.
The most private sphere which law was designed to protect was now
invaded by law itself. Ideology rather than human affection ultimately
determined who could marry whom, or who had the right to reproduce, a novum in human history. All benefits for married couples and
their children, including marriage loans for furniture or child allowances, were subject to racial criteria. Biologistic objectives, rather than
moral objections, underpinned the banning of abortion and contraception for 'Aryans', since these facilities were left as options, together
with involuntary sterilisation, for the eugenically unfit, Arab or African
Germans, Gypsies and Jews. This explains why the Gestapo agency
responsible for their repression coupled homosexuality and abortion,
since both had deleterious effects on the birthrate. In 1938, divorce
laws were relaxed, to accelerate the number of new marriages and

hence the flow of births. Extreme anti-clericalism contributed to the destigmatisation of illegitimacy, with Himmler in the avant garde of condemning 'marriage laws as in themselves immoral', a product of Catholicism's 'satanic achievement' and 'middle-class morality'.[41] For these ideological artistes scorned the old ways that used shame to restrain human sexuality. To this end, Himmler established a network of 'Well of Life' homes, where unmarried pregnant girls and SS wives could have their babies, in optimum conditions, away from the moralising attentions of families and priests.[42] Not that the Nazis respected the moral authority of the latter, for, according to their leading pursuer of homosexuals, male homosexuality was an Asiatic vice, inflicted upon the innocent 'Nordic' races by the Catholic Church.[43]

Nazism may have paid lip service to family values, but its totalitarian regimentation of society weakened family ties and subverted traditional hierarchies, both in the home and at school. There was some point in the joke that with the father in the SA, the mother a member of the NSF, a son in the HJ and a daughter in the BDM (the League of German Maidens), the National Socialist family only crossed paths at the Nuremberg Rally.[44] The relentless activism which the regime encouraged, and which many enthusiastically engaged in, apparently took its toll on marriages, with periodic divorce applications from 'political widows'. The absence of a dedicated agency dealing with the family per se stood in marked contrast to a host of agencies concerned with mothers, youth, population and racial policy suggesting that the superficial conservatism of Nazi family policy was secondary to racial imperatives.

Capitalising on the anti-political idealism which had informed much of the Wilhelmine and Weimar youth movements, Nazism portrayed itself as the politics of future generations, a radical posture enabling it to dismiss liberal democracy as the gerontocratic politics of the past. Again, this emphasis upon 'newness' and youth was common to most of the inter-war European extreme right, as well as to Soviet Bolshevism. Liberalism's emphasis upon debate and the classical freedoms was seen as increasingly quaint. Nazism's permanently aggrieved tone appealed to aged cohorts inclined to moralising indignation, a further sign of Nazism's essentially adolescent sensibility.[45] Since, as we have seen, Nazi leaders were conspicuously younger than their democratic rivals, there was literal substance to the identification with young people. If politics go in cycles of youth versus experience, then here immaturity's overrated virtues had the upper hand. Hitler was prepared to write off the older generation, remarking in November 1933 that 'when an opponent says, "I will not come over to your side", I calmly say, "Your child belongs to us already. . . . You will pass on. Your descendants, however, now stand in the new camp. In a short time they will know nothing but this new community."'[46] A by-product of a politically driven obsession with newness, radicalism and youth was that the old and frail began to feel superfluous, before the regime's wartime policies gave them cause to feel very vulnerable.

A pluralistic youth culture – which had nothing in common with the fashion- and media-driven juvenile ('non'-)conformity of today – was replaced by the monolithic Hitler Youth and League of German Maidens for fourteen- to eighteen-year olds, and the German Young People and League of Young Girls for the ten to fourteens. The Hitler Youth was essentially the product of a similar process of 'co-ordination' of rivals and compulsion that we have seen in the case of People's Welfare.[47] Hence we do not need to go into the details. What quickly became the largest youth organisation in the world subscribed to the philosophy of 'youth leading youth', even though its leaders were part of an enormous bureaucratised enterprise, rather than representative of an autonomous youth culture.

Due to the fascination deviant sub-cultures exert on some historians, modern writing on youth under Nazism routinely revolves around a false juxtaposition of the prim conformists of the Hitler Youth and the delinquent juvenile gangs of the Rhineland.[48] Grudging respect is also paid to young middle-class Hamburg devotees of Western 'swing' music, on the dubious ground that taste in music is an index of wider non-conformity, a conclusion easily dispelled by the fifty-something, street-fighting merchant bankers at contemporary Rolling Stones concerts sponsored by Budweiser or Volkswagen. Since the Nazis' classic cinematic depiction of Hitler Youth and Young Communists, the film *Hitler Junge Quex*, contrasts the former's solid virtues with the smoking and smooching boy and girl comrades, we should probably treat these presumed polarities with scepticism.[49]

Viewed superficially, the Hitler Youth and their female analogue seem akin to a militarised version of the prohibited Boy Scouts, with a similar emphasis upon clean living, competition, drill, team work, sport and so forth. Specialist formations, the Hitler Youth air, motorised, and naval sections, had an overt military agenda, as did the generalised training in marksmanship and other weaponry. A Hitler Youth patrol service catered for would-be policemen.

While much of this sounds as if it might have been fun – particularly the opportunity to fire guns or fly gliders – the wider consequences were mixed. Some things would have been the same if all the Hitler Youth had been Boy Scouts. There was a diminution of parental control, as children began to visit their homes between school and youth activities, with parents reduced to a bed and breakfast service. They complained: 'We no longer have rights over our children.'[50] Further drawbacks included a succession of children with broken arms and legs sustained during riskier exercises, not to speak of the financial strain on households with disposable incomes of 5 Reichsmarks per week of an elaborate kit which could cost up to 135.40 Reichsmarks.[51] Whether parents minded children so clapped out by fifty-kilometre weekend hikes that they were inert for the rest of the week is uncertain. However, many dreaded their children's exposure to a not inconsiderable number of paedophiles and perverts among older Hitler Youth leaders, for whom politics were a cover for flushed and furtive pursuits. Employers discerned a decline in academic performance resulting from an over-emphasis upon physical activities. Hitler's insistence on the general relegalisation of boxing in schools, and his contempt for weedy intellectuals, was partly responsible.[52]

Other aspects of the Hitler Youth were *sui generis*. Parents, and others, were alarmed by the gradual brutalisation of manners, impoverishment of vocabulary and rejection of traditional values. According to the exiled SPD, the changed characters of their children prompted well-heeled families to reflect on the value of personal and political freedom.[53] Their children became strangers, contemptuous of monarchy or religion, and perpetually barking and shouting like pint-sized Prussian sergeant-majors. In sum, children appeared to have become more brutal, fitter and stupider than they were.[54]

Since many fourteen-year-olds worked a forty-eight-hour week, Hitler Youth membership compounded economic with political independence, albeit in a society in which they were too young to vote or see an adult film, though old enough to be killed by Allied soldiers. Exposure to the new ideological tidings, at meetings extending late into the night, exacerbated conflict within the home, as Hitler Youth members espoused values often at variance with those of their more traditionally minded parents, and from the vantage point of membership of a uniformed political formation. Denunciations of parents by children was encouraged, not least by schoolteachers who set essays entitled 'What does your family talk about at home?'[55] Parents also had to weigh up the comparabilities of a slap in the self-righteous youthful face.[56] The boorish Communist father shown hitting Hitler Youth Quex to the theme of the 'Internationale' in the famous Nazi film would have been ill advised to do so after 1933. Indeed, a heavily pregnant woman who slapped a Hitler Youth member was in turn knocked unconscious for violating the maxim that no one was allowed to strike a member of the formation.[57] Parents and teachers shared with Hitler Youth leaders the right to chastise children, although the retinue leader who walked into a garden to floor a boy for being too tired to attend a meeting was probably overdoing things when he informed the aghast parent: 'This is purely an official matter between the two of us, it doesn't concern the mother.' The Hitler Youth who stabbed his stepmother to death on the doorstep, on the ground that he was practising the ancient Teutonic rite of 'blood vengeance', was an extreme example of a general problem.[58] Those with children began to envy the childless.

If confidence-building measures and hierarchies of command produced boys and girls capable of intimidating their parents and teachers, the Hitler Youth was less successful in inducing conformity in its own members. How could it when alternative moral codes were excoriated and aggression or racial vitality celebrated? A licence to persecute entailed a licence to run wild. Priests were greeted on the streets with such impertinences as 'We'll kick your cardinal in the arse.' Confirmation classes became an ordeal, especially if the local schoolmaster was indoctrinating children with Nazi views. Thus the lessons of a priest in Stade were constantly interrupted with antisemitic taunts: 'The Jews are all fraudsters, cowards etc. Herr Holste [the teacher] said that the Bible is only half true. We don't need to learn the Bible. . . . The Jews hated Jesus Christ, so we must also hate the Jews.'[59] Priests who spoke sympathetically of the Jews were publicly vilified as 'friends of the Jews' in *Stürmer* or similar publications.[60]

Membership of the Hitler Youth was a bullies' charter. At least one boy seeking to join the SS had the honesty to say: 'It's really nice being able to lash out, without being hit back.'[61] The formation became a cover for common or garden delinquency, with farmers dreading urban tykes filching fruit and vegetables, or clergy terrorised by rowdy anti-clerical invasions of their services. The anti-clerical 'Pfaffenfresserei' of even the most radical free thinkers was eclipsed by Hitler Youth members.[62] Members of the Hitler Youth were as capable as anyone in their age group of misusing weapons to take pot-shots at illicit targets, like the seventeen-year-old, 'armed to the teeth', who shot a worker and an eleven-year-old from a rooftop vantage point.[63] They got horribly drunk, told smutty stories and impregnated underage BDM girls, who in turn argued that they were merely fulfilling the wishes of the Führer.[64]

WORKERS' PAYTIME OR PLAYTIME?

One late-September morning in 1933, over seven hundred unemployed men congregated before a Frankfurt labour exchange. Dressed in uniform, they marched to the Frankfurt bourse, which was bedecked with huge swastikas and a banner proclaiming 'Work and Peace!' The Hessian Gauleiter Jakob Sprenger promised that they would no longer have to register, but would join the 'three hundred thousand' men to be employed on the new *Autobahnen*. They swore an oath to the Führer, and were presented with shovels for the march to their new workplaces. Hitler had flown into Frankfurt that morning and was driven to the motorway building site in his favoured Daimler-Benz Cabriolet. Two cubic metres of earth were dumped before his feet, whereupon the Führer shovelled – 'not with a symbolic cut of the spade, but real earth-moving work' – until the first beads of sweat dripped to the ground. The spade touched by the hand of history disappeared, but by 1938 a replica was proudly displayed in Munich's German Museum. The spot Hitler had belaboured had to be fenced off, to deter workers taking handfuls of soil as relics. Thus was born one of the most potent propaganda images of the Third Reich.

In his speech to the road builders, Hitler was concerned to establish his horny-handed credentials. His heavily honed autobiography included a period minding a cement mixer:

> Workers, I myself was often attacked for my origins during the period of my struggle for power in Germany by those who pretended to represent the interests of the workers. At that time people were fond of saying: what does that ex-construction worker and painter want? I am happy and proud that Fate forced me to tread this path. In this way perhaps I have gained a greater understanding for the German worker, for his character, for his suffering, but also for that which makes up the vital necessities of his life.

There can be no doubt about the centrality of work within Hitler's scheme of values:

I ask you to bear in mind that we are living in an age which perceives its very essence in work itself; that we wish to build up a State which values work for its own sake and holds the worker in high regard because he is fulfilling a duty to the nation; a State which aims, by means of its labour service, to educate everyone – even the tender sons of highborn parents – to hold work in high regard and to respect physical labour in the service of the national community. . . . We want to educate the *Volk* so that it moves away from the insanity of class superiority, of arrogance of rank, and of the delusion that only mental work is of any value; we want the *Volk* to comprehend that every labour which is necessary ennobles its doer, and that there is only one disgrace, and that is to contribute nothing to the maintenance of the *Volk* itself. It is a necessary transposition which we will effect not with theories, not with declarations or with wishes and hopes, but which we will effect only by life itself, in that today we are setting millions of people the task of restoring health to the German economy.[65]

It is worth pursuing the limited theme of motorways a way further, since these were part of a more comprehensive vision. A typically Nazi *ad hoc* agency, under the Swabian civil engineer Fritz Todt, assumed responsibility for the annual target of one thousand kilometres of motorway, with the start-up capital and much of the skilled workforce initially derived from the national railways, an interesting sidelight on how a dictatorship could neutralise vested interests.[66] The Nazis hijacked earlier plans for a motorway network, while marginalising pioneer enthusiasts, such as Frankfurt's Jewish Oberbürgermeister Ludwig Landsmann and the racing-driver Willy Hof, in favour of the Führer's unique visionary genius.[67] The motorways were a national prestige project, which would literally bind the nation closer together, returning a purely notional figure of 'six hundred thousand' men to work. This most tangible and modernistic form of National Socialism at work had many propaganda advantages over less visible work-creation schemes, beginning with the stream of credulous foreigners who came to marvel at this asphalt and granite wonder of the world.[68]

The 'Adolf Hitler Highways' promised a society in which goods would move by lorry or soldiers conveyed to foreign frontiers, and every family would own a car for picnics in scenic laybys, a tantalising prospect for people whose radius rarely extended beyond their own villages or cities. Actually, the military preferred trains and thought that tracked vehicles would rip up the road surface and fracture bridges, whose load-bearing tolerances were only ascertained in spring

1939. They also worried that the motorways would provide route-maps for bombers targeting German cities. But the motorways were a social rather than a military vision. The new German would henceforth speed along, savouring the variety of passing landscapes, a primary cause of an increased number of fatal traffic accidents. All was cunningly integrated into the landscape, with bridges and viaducts in vernacular materials, and attention to how these latterday pyramids would appear ruined in a millennium. The modern motorway culture of Little Chefs and McDonalds was frustrated by a folksy-heritage kind of layby architecture, drawing upon the alpine chalet style at Bavarian Chiemsee. For this was the Nazi social vision in essence, a sanitised version of the fate of everyman in the late twentieth century. Huddles of motorists *en famille* with their Thermos flasks and bratwurst, next to roads mysteriously devoid of traffic jams, fumes, multiple pile-ups and signposts, but punctuated with the sculptor Josef Thorak's musclebound colossi heaving rocks skywards.[69]

Nothing approximating 'six hundred thousand' unemployed was absorbed by motorway construction, despite refusal to use heavy labour-saving machinery. In 1936, an all-time maximum of one hundred and twenty thousand workers were employed constructing the *Autobahnen*. Put differently, between 4 and 5 per cent of the six million registered unemployed in 1933 were subsequently employed building motorways. Even if ancillary industries employed double this number, the effect on unemployment was minimal.[70] There was not much joy in work among the motorway workforce. Road workers were housed in desolate shacks in the middle of nowhere. Apart from separation from their families, they were poorly paid, and not paid at all during foul weather. Conditions were lethal, with an estimated worker fatality for every six kilometres constructed. Visits from the comedian Jupp Hüssels failed to lift the sullen mood. As Todt tried to push the programme forward, against a background of full employment, road builders found themselves working between twelve and sixteen hours a day, discounting the time it took to reach remote sites.

Coercion soon reared its ugly head. The unemployed who refused to work on the motorways had their benefits terminated, or were threatened with being sent to concentration camps. Workers who downed tools in protest at these conditions were handed over to the Gestapo, while reliable members of the SA were brought in to monitor more disaffected colleagues. This sometimes meant beating them up. From 1939 onwards, delinquent road builders were dispatched to the

SS special camp at Hinzert in the Hunsrück for re-education. Although it was deemed inappropriate to employ Jews on the 'Adolf Hitler Highways', Jews were substituted for 'Aryans' in quarries, whose workforces were then redirected on to the motorways. By 1941, almost four thousand kilometres of motorway had been built, from a projected total of over twenty thousand kilometres, for megalomaniac vistas had intervened, with super-highways from Calais to Cologne or Trondheim to Oslo. The roads which were built were deserted and silent. In 1938, only 3 per cent of goods were transported by road rather than via canal or rail. Only a few hundred 'People's Cars' were ever built, before Volkswagen production was turned over to military uses, while existing car use was severely restricted.[71]

Work was central to the Nazi scheme of values. It was 'the measure of man . . . and of the personality itself'. The Nazis were beneficiaries of at least a century of serious reflection about both work and workers by an impressive range of commentators, experts and moralists.[72] Much of this discussion of work was inspired by alleged worker alienation and the susceptibility of the alienated to Marxian sociologising of envy, hatred and resentment. It was accompanied by company welfare strategies among progressive employers – such as Siemens – who pioneered leisure and sports programmes and in-house vocational training, and sought to engage the workforce through company newsletters and magazines. Instruction of female workers in the use of electric cookers suggests that this was related to marketing strategies.[73]

The Nazis immediately changed the basic terms of reference in the debate about work by demolishing the left-wing parties and the trades unions. An estimated one hundred thousand people, the overwhelming majority being from the left, passed through concentration camps and prisons in the first year. There, work had another meaning, namely as a means of breaking bodies and souls, under the mocking slogan 'Work sets free'. As in the Soviet Union, the Nazis determined who could work or not, although there were fewer instances of professors become forestry workers or janitors, chiefly because there was no commensurate emphasis on apostasy and recantation in a system with only one prophet and an ideology more like a collage than a canonical text. Thousands of socialists and Communists were arbitrarily dismissed from their jobs, including two thousand miners in the Ruhr, and replaced by Nazi sympathisers who received preferential consideration in employment.[74]

The Nazis did not rely upon repression alone. Belief in racial hierarchy, character and achievement was bound to impact in a subversive way on traditional notions of social class, and especially inherited privilege. Their assault on the shibboleth of social class resonated with people for whom 'national community' was a recent memory, men for whom the 'storm of steel' had been a great leveller. Those otherwise familiar with the ideology of class struggle were themselves not entirely immune, to the extent of believing in the desirability or feasibility of a classless society. Whether this was to be achieved by radical redistribution of wealth or by parity of social esteem became a secondary issue. The Nazis used exclusionary nationalism as an antidote to the influence of Marxist internationalism on sections of the industrial working class. Marxism was depicted as an alien import, notwithstanding the German origins of its two founding fathers, although it is doubtful whether attacks on Marx's Jewish origins made much of an impression on socialist workers. Nazism hijacked the idioms and sentiments of socialism, identifying aspects of the credo with which it could run, without being in any meaningful sense socialist. Borrowings included veneration of work and workers; the desire to democratise high culture and exclusive recreations; and the moral justification of ends through the constant invocation of social justice. There was a similar rhetoric of struggle, although under National Socialism this was to be perpetual, rather than preparatory to an afternoon's reading or fishing. In the national community, struggle would no longer be between social classes, but take the form of 'battles' for production, in which the worker was a sort of soldier, or struggles between nations and races for survival.

A subtle form of political positioning, astride a number of hitherto rigid postures, made the Nazis elusive opponents. This shapeless slipperiness ensured that the left would never defeat them, so long as they tried to depict Nazism merely as a bosses' plot, for the alleged marionettes of the men in pinstripe suits displayed a surprising wilfulness. It is worth trying to pin down what amounted to a series of calculated postures. Hitler declined to confuse the workers' self-styled representatives with the workers themselves, vehemently dismissing these 'international evangelists' as 'littérateurs, alien to the *Volk*, an alien mob'.[75] Marxism was excoriated as a front for 'Jewish' plans for world domination. Former socialist politicians and trades unionists were not only arrested, but routinely defamed as a corrupt bossocracy long after they had been neutralised. The Nazis also occupied the moral highground by deprecating the unions' narrow economistic concern with wages. In other words, a wedge was driven between the workers and their former leaders and representatives, while the ground was cut from under their claim to moral authority. But, had this been a straightforward example of anti-socialist repression, the 'Reports from Germany' of the exiled Social Democratic Party would not have regularly noted the popularity of Hitler, as distinct from his Party, among their own erstwhile constituency.

For, at least in psychological terms, other parts of the Nazi agenda were as important as the first. Several salient features of Nazism have to be ignored if the intention is to caricature it as an exclusively anti-Marxist movement. It certainly was anti-Marxist, but it was also much more. Being anti-Marxist was not the same as alignment with liberalism and the bourgeoisie. Hitler was deeply illiberal, while nothing in his background as a failed artist become war veteran inclined him to benevolence towards a class which had cold-shouldered him. After all, anti-bourgeois unconventionality was part of his self-dramatising artistic pose. His claim to being an artist–revolutionary depended upon a contrast with the complacent, hypocritical and satiated bourgeoisie, a clichéd conceit of the alienated, which spares them the effort of understanding decency, dignity, propriety, self-restraint and the non-apocalyptic virtues of a contented life. Since Hitler could hardly claim to be a paragon of Nordic physical perfection himself, he subscribed to the view that a touch of divinity inhered in the artist, in contrast to uninspired bourgeois philistines.[76]

Subtle repositioning was evident in Nazi thought on macro-economic questions. Rapacious 'Jewish' finance capitalism was distinguished from the creative 'Aryan' industrial variety, a sleight of hand which avoided criticism of capitalism *per se*. Criticism was confined to the deleterious human consequences of capitalism, namely its contribution to the creation of alienated 'grey' proletarians.[77] Henceforth, the 'leaders' of the 'works community' were temporary usufructuaries of enterprises on behalf of the national community, whose general well-being overrode any particular interests. A narrow emphasis on profit, or an arrogant and exploitative attitude towards the workforce, would amount to character failing, which in theory could result in disciplinary measures by new industrial Courts of Honour. If heavy industry put pursuit of profit before national goals, it would pay the consequences. Just enough employers were brought to book in this fashion for the claim not to seem entirely spurious.

But this is not a discussion of the organisation of the German economy.[78] The Nazis were not bent on destroying Marxism *on behalf* of the 'bourgeoisie', for in their vitalist scheme of things the German 'bourgeoisie' were cowardly, effete, hypocritical materialists. They were almost the last people they would wish to preserve under any circumstances. Their greed, snobbery and sham patriotism had been largely responsible for propelling the working class into the clutches of the Marxists; in fact they had been primarily responsible for class conflict.[79] This was a view Hitler shared with many of his lesser followers. One respondent to a survey of Nazi Party supporters wrote: 'My own view of life and my own observations of life led me to see that the class struggle was not a condition brought about by the working group. The middle class created the prerequisites for it.'[80] Hitler was nobody's 'agent', least of all of the despised bourgeoisie, a stance which led him to detect hidden virtue even in the Communists. Thus on 14 September 1936 he said:

> We did not defend Germany against Bolshevism back then because we were intending to do anything like conserve a bourgeois world or go so far as to freshen it up. Had Communism really intended nothing more than a certain purification by eliminating isolated rotten elements from among the ranks of our so-called 'upper ten thousand' or our equally worthless Philistines, one could have sat back quietly and looked on for a while.[81]

In early 1942 he reminisced about a pre-war visit to Rome. The reception committee had not impressed the German Führer: 'I was greeted at the station by the Duke of Pistoia, a real degenerate. Beside him there was another duke, no less degenerate. There was an admiral there, who looked like a court toad, a bogus coin, a liar.' This company prompted the following thought: 'Perhaps the Duce came on the scene a year or two too early with his revolution. He probably should have let the Reds have their own way for a bit first – they'd have exterminated the aristocracy. The Duce would have become Head of a Republic. Thus the abscess would have been lanced.'[82] Like the conservative nationalists, Marxists had their uses, if only to destroy residual obstacles to the racist meritocracy Hitler envisaged.

Hitler had an aversion towards the existing aristocracy and bourgeoisie, whose inherited privileges were at variance with his desire for a new meritocratic and racial elite. Were it not for hatred being too effortful, it was reciprocated, at least among the German branches of the European higher nobility, whose cosmopolitan backgrounds and lifestyles, Ascot, Cowes, Gstaad, Oxford and so forth, tended to immunise them against extreme chauvinism, and whose sensibilities were offended by the regime's parvenu and provincial leaders.[83] In one of his characteristic formulations, Hitler spoke of 'the upper class . . . in reality no more than the scum produced by a societal mutation gone haywire from having had its blood and thinking infected by cosmopolitanism'. The language may have been baroquely virulent, but the sentiments appealed to the resentful.[84]

Whereas Hitler had surprisingly little to say about the middling classes, merely regarding them as representative symbols of social mobility, and pandered to peasant virtues only when obliged to, he was eloquent on workers of 'brain or fist'. His comments on social class, whether private or public, had a consistency which suggests that they were not merely designed for propaganda consumption. This was only partly because in his self-referential scheme of things Hitler regarded himself as a worker, a pose which endeared him to many workers, even as they recoiled from his Party. In Hitler's view, the workers had proven themselves 'good comrades' at Verdun and Flanders. They had 'animal strength', biological vitality, a capacity for brutality, and an absence of guile. True, the working class may have been boorish and stupid, but 'it does have one thing: it has faith, it has persistence, it has stability'. These were good fellows who had been led astray.[85] For their part, the workers were confused by the signals Hitler emitted, for here was a politician of an unfamiliar kind. They saw a man who could not be accused of pursuing any obvious self-interest, an advantage in a society where political parties had become synonymous with them. Speaking in that characteristic tone of personal sincerity, in March 1936 Hitler told an audience of Krupp locomotive workers:

> Whatever I have undertaken I have always done with the conviction: it must be done for our *Volk*. Whenever I stand up for the German peasant, it is for the sake of the *Volk*. I have neither ancestral estate nor manor. . . . I do not stand up for arming the German *Volk* because I am a shareholder. I believe I am the only statesman in the world who does not have a bank account. I hold no stock, I have no shares in any companies. I do not draw any dividends.[86]

Moreover, here was an ostensibly plain man – a uniformed Charlie Chaplin – who through street cunning was showing not just the top people but the leaders of Europe a thing or two, a political cheeky-chappie, whose diplomatic adventures took on the character of a daring high-wire act or a dance around the rim of a gaping manhole. Hitler's capacity to court and elude nemesis at the eleventh hour was part of his fascination, just as the Nazis themselves claimed to have intervened at that hour to save Germany. The fascination progressively diminished whenever the stakes became too high.

While he was not a classical socialist egalitarian, bent on achieving utopia through redistributive taxation, Hitler subscribed to the meritocratic notion of equality of opportunity, albeit within the context of eugenic and racial policies which denied some people any meaningful life at all. Everyone was to be allotted an equal position on the starting blocks. In an interview with the American correspondent Louis Lochner, Hitler chose a revealing metaphor:

> We do not want to become a primitive *Volk*, but one with the highest possible standard of living. In my opinion, the Americans are right in not wanting to make everyone the same but rather in upholding the principle of the ladder. However, every single person must be granted the opportunity to climb up the ladder.[87]

Hitler held up the Party as a model of social mobility:

> Next to me stand German people from every class of life who today are part of the nation's leadership: former agricultural workers who are now Reichstatthalters; former metalworkers who are today Gauleiters, etc. Though, mind you, former members of the bourgeoisie and former aristocrats also have their place in this Movement. To us it makes no difference where they come from; what counts is that they are able to work for the benefit of our *Volk*.[88]

A self-styled 'honest broker' between antagonistic classes, Hitler wished to destigmatise manual labour, thereby fusing workers of 'brain and fist'. The latter would be transformed from alienated proletarians into upright 'national comrades' or German workers. This involved encouraging upward mobility, with the more enterprising and younger workers being able to better themselves through enhanced vocational training in preparation for flight from the urban ghetto. More unusually, Hitler spoke of encouraging the less academic scions of rich families to work in factories or to learn a trade. If this was pie in the sky, compulsory labour service would at least familiarise those whose background destined them for command or management with the circumstances of their future subordinates. Apart from fiddling the unemployment statistics, this was one of the principal objectives of compulsory labour service. According to British observers, the fruits of egalitarian bonding were meagre:

> To me the bringing together of individuals from classes has never seemed more than the symbol of a solution. I find the idea of working boys and public schoolboys occupying the same camp a distasteful one. If it is not ingenuous, then it is cynical. The boys play together in apparent equality – and then one goes back to the workshop and the other to his public school. All the cheers and community singing and linked arms do not alter that fact. And the organisers and distinguished patrons are left with the smug feeling that something has been done, whereas nothing has been done.[89]

Workers were encouraged to overcome a trades union mentality – Ley's German Labour Front (DAF) rapidly ceased to describe itself as such – and to think in terms of a 'socialism' transcending mere bread and butter issues.[90] In a departure from labourist economism, the Nazis recognised the workers' need for respect, and the pride they took in their work, their skill, their tools and the products of their labour, attitudes already evident in modern technological sectors, such as aircraft or optical manufacturing. This lends plausibility to the idea that they were embarked on a revolution in consciousness, changing the way people perceived the world, rather than its material circumstances. In other words, it was a revolution in esteem and status rather than economic realities. On a symbolic level, Nazi politicians were more than prepared to glad-hand and talk to workers without the faintest trace of unease.

Hitler did not emulate his Italian colleague, who regularly bared his barrelled torso at harvest time, but he was frequently to be seen manfully wielding a spade. The First of May became a paid national holiday, absorbing many features of the socialist May Day, while transforming it into a 'national festival'. There were some clever egalitarian touches. Representative workers were flown to Berlin to meet Hindenburg and Hitler. Radio interviews eked out the crucial propaganda response that this was their first experience of flight. Unskilled workers circled the million or so gathered on Berlin's Tempelhofer Feld in the Zeppelin airship, sharing the observation platform with diplomats and generals.[91] The Nazis reached out to the workers, involving them in the mood of revival, apparently transforming passive objects into participating subjects of decisions hitherto taken behind closed doors in boardrooms and ministries, even if this did not correspond with the reality of 'works communities' where employer powers were enhanced vis-à-vis the 'retinue'. Demeaning practices in the workplace were abrogated or universalised. Out went divisive clock punching, but in came obligatory morning assembly.[92] So too did Labour Front 'shock troops', who were to be the advanced brigade of a militarised workforce.

Nazism built on existing belief in the German workers' assiduity and the quality of their craftsmanship, in contrast to the shoddy mass production of the Anglo-Saxons and Soviets, ironically one of the factors contributing to the latter's victory on the wartime economic front.[93] Apparently inspired by the tidy coalmines of the Netherlands, the 'Beauty of Labour' section of the Labour Front tackled physical surroundings, providing improved air, light and space; decent canteens and washing facilities, and exteriors designed to make factories less forbidding. Employers with scruffy premises were warned and then stigmatised by inspectors. Each campaign was conducted under a slogan such as 'Clean people in a clean plant' or 'Struggle against noise'.[94] Holistic talk of factory communities and of the whole man replaced over-emphasis upon the more limited question of enhancing worker productivity.[95] Apart from situating physical improvements near the factory gates, the industrial-age equivalent of Potemkin villages, some rearrangements were far from benign, such as the deliberate introduction of physical divisions within a workplace to diminish worker communication and solidarity. For, as with the replacement of collective, trans-industrial wage bargaining with individualised performance-related piecework rates, the intention was to atomise the labour force, whose average wages were suppressed, whatever exceptions occurred in arms-related industries.

In line with more progressive employment practices both in Weimar Germany and elsewhere, the Nazis addressed themselves to worker recreation. The Labour Front's leisure arm, 'Strength through Joy' (KdF), was heavily influenced by the ideas of the apostate Belgian socialist Hendrik de Man, who sought to fuse Marx and Freud, and the practice of such firms as Siemens in Berlin. There was also the example of the Italian Fascist Opera Nazionale Dopolavoro. Surveys of the Siemens workforce discovered that few of them had travelled, been to a theatre or read books. Resources were abundant, since the Labour Front's Bank of German Labour disposed of confiscated trades union funds, money siphoned off from Winter Aid, membership dues and the fruits of worker insurance and savings schemes for Volkswagen cars or holidays.

'Strength through Joy' had multiple objectives. It was literally an attempt to banish boredom, for as Ley explained: 'From boredom spring stupid, heretical, yes, in the end, criminal ideas and trains of thought. Gloomy dullness makes people complain; gives them a feeling of homelessness; in a word, the feeling of absolute superfluity. Nothing is more dangerous to the State than that.'[96] Leisure had to be collective and organised, up to and including the People's Educational Enterprise arm of the Labour Front taking over private clubs devoted to such hobbies as chess or stamp collecting. Regimentation coalesced with rationalisation. Subsidised vacations, the majority consisting of bathing or hiking holidays, would maintain minds and bodies drained by the relentless tempo of routinised work, and afford workers a sense of Germany as a whole. A monstrous Nazified Butlin's emerged on the island of Rügen.[97] There was also an egalitarian impulse, appealing to those sensitive to exclusion. Activities hitherto confined to the rich, such as golf, sailing, skiing and tennis, were opened up to those on modest incomes, for the DAF could use its enormous resources to secure price discounting.[98] Beginning with a voyage to the Isle of Wight, the KdF ran cheap cruises, to the Azores and Canaries, Madeira or Norwegian fjords. Conditions on chartered ships were commensurate with the extremely low cost (under 60 Reichsmarks all inclusive from Würzburg to Norway), and not much better on purpose-built ships such as the *Wilhelm Gustloff* or *Robert Ley* itself. In the latter case, sixteen hundred passengers competed for forty lavatories and one hundred showers, although they were well catered for with 156 loudspeakers relaying on-board propaganda. Since most photographs of the passengers show people dressed in summer clothes, it is unlikely that many of them were workers.[99] Under the slogan 'Kultur für alle', high culture was popularised. Concerts and plays were brought into the factories, while the financial and social barriers inhibiting worker use of concert halls and theatres were relaxed, together with dress codes and tiered ticket pricing. Plush thresholds no longer intimidated *hoi polloi*. While Carl Böhm, Eugen Jochum and Wilhelm Furtwängler played to a new class of concert goer, 'Strength through Joy' began its assault on the ultimate citadel of bourgeois high culture by block purchase of tickets to Bayreuth. Inevitably, snobbery – like water – rediscovered its level, as signs began to proliferate indicating that businesses did not cater to 'Strength through Joy' patrons.[100]

Given the secular drift from a class to a mass consumer society – in which the contours of class are constantly evolving according to employment patterns and social attitudes – it is notoriously difficult to isolate the impact of any single factor on this process, whether twelve years of peace and wartime dictatorship, or the maelstrom of devastation and dispossession visited upon Germany from 1945.[101] Whatever the Nazis' egalitarian rhetoric, working-class people persisted in a 'them and us' mentality, even though the exiled Social Democrats detected an appreciable rise in 'petit bourgeois' thinking, a common derogatory term whenever workers failed to conform with ideal stereotypes. Their bosses remained exploitative 'capitalists', while the Social Democrat and union bossocracy of the Weimar period was replaced by a sybaritic army of 'Brown' placemen, who were regarded with universal loathing. Economic recovery was regionally and sectorally patchy, with unemployment in consumer industries and mining lingering for several years. Wages in emergency employment schemes were indistinguishable from welfare, while average real earnings did not recover their 1929 level until 1941.[102] Hours of grinding work increased, while the range of consumption goods diminished. However, there were enough compensations, including Nazi foreign policy, for working-class resistance – as distinct from the enormous bravery of individual workers and others – to remain sufficiently chimerical.

THE BROWN CULT AND THE CHRISTIANS

The Nazis borrowed the term 'co-ordination' from electrical engineering, to describe their transformation of society in conformity with their own ideas, resentments and sentiments. Whether or not one calls this a coherent ideology is almost irrelevant, but the mélange should certainly be taken seriously, however repellent we may regard it. By coincidence, one of their anonymous opponents reporting to the SPD also turned to civil engineering to describe what was taking place before his eyes. It was a remarkable analysis, antedating academic attempts to describe Nazism as a political religion, notably Eric Voegelin's short essay which was published the following year. It is worth considering what the reporter had to say.

Dated 4 April 1937, and concerning the 'Church struggle', the report likened Nazism to a religion, in the sense of demanding of its adherents total submission of their consciences and surrender of their souls. The notion that Nazism was a secular 'worldview' was simply a fog. This political religion had little to do with neo-paganism, which was a distraction from the pseudo-religious properties of Nazism itself. It was unconditional in its claims, inspired fanaticism and practised extreme intolerance of those who thought otherwise. A 'Church-state' had emerged, with cults, dogmas and rites, whose beliefs consisted of a form of millenarianism, in which the demons to be confronted before the end state were Bolsheviks and Jews. You were blindly for it, or you were opposed to it; all intermediary positions were ruled out. But this was only part of what the writer had to say. The conclusion was equally striking. What was occurring reminded the anonymous reporter, as already noted, of the renewal of a railway bridge. Bridges could not be demolished since this would make rail travel impossible. Rather, day by day, each girder or rail was replaced, until the passengers, who had either not paid much attention, or imagined bits and pieces were being refurbished, realised that they were crossing an entirely new structure. It was a slow process, but it was thorough.[103]

It is important, at the outset, to grasp that both neo-paganism and efforts to nazify Christianity itself were second-order considerations, at least for Hitler himself. He had little time for the barmier beliefs of some of his intimates, regarding the ideologue Rosenberg as an obscurantist and Himmler as a loyal crank. In early September 1938, Hitler addressed a convention on German culture within the week-long Party rally. It was an abstruse speech, ostensibly about architecture, but including the cosmos, with a coded warning for Rosenberg and Himmler:

> the cultural evolution of a *Volk* resembles that of the Milky Way. Amongst countless pale stars a few suns radiate. However, all suns and planets are made of the same one material, and all of them observe the same laws. The entire cultural work of a *Volk* must not only be geared toward fulfillment of one mission, but this mission must be pursued in one spirit.
>
> *National Socialism is a cool and highly reasoned approach to reality based upon the greatest of scientific knowledge and its spiritual expression* [my italics]. As we have opened the *Volk*'s heart to these teachings, and as we continue to do so at present, we have no desire of instilling in the *Volk* a mysticism that transcends the purpose and goals of our teachings.
>
> Above all, National Socialism is a *Volk* Movement in essence and under no circumstances a cult movement! Insofar as the enlightenment and registration of our *Volk* demands the use of certain methods, which by now have become part of its traditions, these methods are rooted in experience and realizations that were arrived at by exclusively pragmatic considerations. Hence it will be useful to make these methods part of our heritage at a later date. They have nothing to do with other borrowed methods or expressions derived from other viewpoints which have to this date constituted the essence of cults. For the National Socialist Movement is not a cult movement; rather, it is a *völkisch* and political philosophy which grew out of considerations of an exclusively racist nature. This philosophy does not advocate mystic cults, but rather aims to cultivate and lead a *Volk* determined by its blood.[104]

At first sight, this would appear to negate attempts to construe Nazism as a political religion, but this would be wrong. While Nazism claimed scientific authority for its ideological mélange, it is essential to grasp that the allegedly scientific facts of blood, race and the reharmonisation of mankind with nature were literally sanctified. The view that the 'supreme fundamental value was Life, the perception of the Divine in the unceasing creative movement of Life', had many consequences. First, Nazism was not merely aberrant or straight science run riot, for biological science was invested with religious properties. Nature and Blood usurped God in eternity. Hence, the modern over-emphasis upon Nazi biologistic politics is misleading, for it takes the scientists' self-estimation at face value, and reveals little about the ways in which scientific 'truths' were venerated as objects of mystic wonderment. Learnedly ticking off Hitler for his failure to understand the serology of blood is beside the point; simply ignoring such revealing concepts as 'the racial soul' is actively misleading. Clarity proved compatible with mystery, and religion with science, just as an emphasis upon life-affirmation accompanied an adolescent morbidity. Science was useful to bash Christianity over the head, but the science was heavily invested with religious properties. The laws of nature were a series of bleak, ineluctable tidings, handed down by a remote God, whose demi-divine instrument was literally rubbed out of the picture. Christ was an inconvenience, except when crucified by the Jews. In brief, scientific certitude, so useful to assail the Church, fused with a gnostic apodicticism derived from Pelagian heresies within Christianity itself.

Moreover, a new religion implied adjustments in fundamental values. Some things were cast in stone: 'Everything that serves the preservation of the nation is morally good; everything that in the slightest degree threatens its vitality is wrong and abominable.' But there was dangerous relativism abroad amid the turgid Teutonic mumbo-jumbo:

> A morality based on the demands of life is unable to set up an unchangeable moral code, because the eternal flux of life necessitates a progressive internal readjustment. The ethics of the Life-philosophy cannot and will not provide anything but an orientation, an attitude towards these problems. It is of little avail to educate a man according to rigid, preconceived rules; the one important thing is to open his mind and to penetrate every fibre of his being with the current of life. Increase of vitality, that is the supreme demand of the Life-philosophy.[105]

Just as Nazi biological science consisted of a plurality of emphases and tendencies, so its attitudes towards matters of faith were myriad, with Hitler subscribing to the only essential cult, that of himself. He saw himself as the last chance for mankind before the onset of cosmic desolation, should the race war he envisaged have the wrong outcome.

For unlike the Communists, whose conceit entertained no room for defeat, Nazism was always shadowed by dire imaginings and apocalyptic scenarios. Unlike the Communists, the Nazis were prepared to take the whole of mankind down with them. Indeed, this ideology was posited upon a final confrontation or reckoning with the Jews.[106]

The Nazis hardly had a monopoly over the sacralisation of politics, for since the French Revolution the quest for utopias based on reason, class or nation has been construed as a holy task.[107] Many regimes more or less consciously usurped religious forms, much of it as harmless as the common transference of religious sentiment on to art, foxhunting or a football club. In a secular age, religious emotion has been diffused into various compartments, one of which is organised religion itself, which becomes a private matter on a par with lifestyle options such as vegetarianism or knitting. But Nazism did not merely hijack a few liturgical externals, all the better to win over a largely Christian country. It sank a drillhead into a deep-seated reservoir of existential anxiety, offering salvation from an ontological crisis.

Before seeing how the Hitler cult functioned, we need to say a little about attempts to marginalise or subvert the faith of most Germans. Or to put the matter more subversively, how to pitch politics to a still religious audience. For as religion had progressively accommodated itself to the secular world and politics, so politics not only plundered the property box, but tapped into the anthropological substrata. While Nazism numbered devotees of astrology, the occult and neo-paganism among its followers, these were peripheral to more sinister attempts to divorce Christianity radically from Judaism, and to refashion the content of the Christian message.[108] The largest neo-pagan association, Jakob Hauer's German Faith Movement, with its blend of racial science and Nordic and Eastern mysticism, had forty thousand adherents, drawn from a plethora of sects. Its chief utility was to undermine the content of Christianity, while making even nazified German Christians adopt a defensive posture vis-à-vis these radicals. The ground on which debate occurred perceptibly shifted, with sensible people having to dissipate their energy and learning controverting absurd issues, the least of which was whether Jesus was a Jew.

The Nazis despised Christianity for its Judaic roots, effeminacy, otherworldliness and universality. It appeared life-denying to the life-affirming, mobilising entirely unwanted sentiments and values. Forgiveness was not for resentful haters, nor compassion of much use to people who wanted to stamp the weak into the ground. In a word,

Christianity was a 'soul malady'. Many Nazis were also viscerally anti-clerical, up to and including resisting the emergence of a quasi-clerical caste in their own ranks. One would have to visit the Reformation or the extremes of liberal anti-clericalism in the modern era to find anything analogous to their vicious and vulgar attacks on priests. But it was the substantive values of Christianity which stood in their way, disputing their own total claims, and blocking the moral disinhibition indispensable to their racial rampage. Paying Christianity a back-handed compliment, they realised that only something remarkably similar would obliterate it, namely what has been best described as 'a kind of destructive mimesis'. The fundamental tenets were stripped out, but the remaining diffuse religious emotionality had its uses.[109]

Whatever Christianity's ambivalences and antagonisms towards the Jews, its core concerns with compassion and humility were anathema to a politics of racial egotism, and worship of brutality and strength. These 'aspects' of Christianity would have to be expunged. In Nazi eyes, Christianity was 'foreign' and 'unnatural', or what has been described as the Jews' 'posthumous poison', a notion the Nazis picked up from Nietzsche. Viewed pseudo-historically, it was an eastern Mediterranean 'servant ethic' imposed upon the credulous ancient Germans by force and subterfuge. Christianity had obliterated their values and traditions, sapping their 'racial' vitality.[110] It was concerned with questions beyond human time, situating human beings uncomfortably between the timeless immensity of God and the lower natural world, whereas Nazism wished thoroughly to reintegrate mankind into the latter, even though Nazism was not without pretentions to time-lessness. Man would become a sort of unblinking superior predator, tearing his foes to pieces with the unconcern and unrelenting single-mindedness of a tiger or shark. A remote God would survey the carnage with sublime indifference.

Christianity regarded all earthly existence as transient, while the Nazis thought in terms of rendering life eternal through a sort of biological Great Chain of Being. The individual was nothing, but the racial collective would endure through the aeons. That is what Hitler presumably meant when he said: 'To the Christian doctrine of the infinite significance of the individual human soul . . . I oppose with icy clarity the saving doctrine of the nothingness and insignificance of the individual human being, and of his continued existence in the visible immortality of the nation.'[111] Men otherwise so obsessed with death and destruction sought a thousand years of life through the superior racial properties of their *Volk*. Looked at in these terms, Nazism did not become hubristic at this or that moment in time; hubris characterised the entire enterprise from its inception. What else was a 'thousand-year Reich'?

There was considerable common ground between the Nazis and many churchmen, of both confessions, on anti-Bolshevism, anti-Judaism and the feeling that the country had gone to the dogs. If antisemitism was unforgivable, it was harder to find a distinct position on Communism, given the Jacobin bloodlust abroad in contemporary Spain, or the atheistic intolerance of the Soviet Union, albeit an atheism ironically swathed in quasi-religious trappings often derived from Orthodoxy. Of course, being opposed to Communism did not automatically entail being antisemitic. Since prejudice is often portable, some Catholics and Protestants used the charge of 'Jewishness' to attack *each other*, and, of course, the Jews too.

This is not the place to rehearse the vicissitudes of the so-called 'Church struggle', which was as much a struggle for control of mundane institutions as a conflict over fundamental principles, such as the radical otherness and unknowability of God. It belongs to a deferred discussion of resistance, a subject so important that it warrants extended rather than spasmodic treatment. It suffices to say that Nazi attacks on Christianity hardly encountered a resilient citadel, and were facilitated by Trojan horses constructed, rather than dispatched, within.

The German Christians were a movement within Protestantism, designed to revive religion through intense engagement with *völkisch* politics, creating a people's Church as a community of race and blood. Since Nazism conceived of the German race as an elect with a mission, the bridge German Christians had to negotiate was modest. German Christians, of whom there were about six hundred thousand in the mid-1930s, came in different degrees of radicality and pragmatism, matters which need not detain us here. They sought to counteract the Church's flagging popularity by hitching themselves on to a dynamic quasi-religious political movement. After all, if some Christians can reconcile themselves with Marxist atheism, a movement which invoked the Almighty and promised moral restoration was a second order obstacle. For, in the eyes of many Christians, National Socialism was a quasi-religious movement, in which huge numbers of Protestants and Roman Catholics were involved. Therefore, churchmen should forsake the Churches, effectively following their flock. Many believed that the

German nation was a latterday Israel, in the sense that God was speaking to mankind through its story of persecution and redemption. The Nazis would not have relished the analogy. The German nation and its Church became a manifestation of divine revelation instead of part of a universal fellowship. Its salvation lay with a political party, an idea not entirely alien to such Christian Socialists as Paul Tillich. Some seem to have deluded themselves that they were going to supply the ethical and spiritual content for the allegedly laudable emotions National Socialism had mobilised. The ways in which the German Christians benefited Nazism seem obscure. After all, the notion of a nazified Christianity implied a spiritual deficit within Nazism.[112]

The 'redeemer in the history of the Germans', as Hitler was now styled, seems to have regarded this politically welcome development with characteristic cynicism, remarking: 'The parsons will be made to dig their own graves. They will betray their God to us. They will betray anything for the sake of their miserable little jobs and incomes.'[113] Thinking that a quick German Christian *coup d'état* would resolve things, Hitler threw the weight of the Nazi propaganda apparatus behind them in the July 1933 Church elections, which resulted in their capturing two-thirds of ecclesiastical offices. However, the triumphalist excesses of German Christian radicals, who during a Berlin rally in November 1933 let loose against the Old Testament 'morality of cattle dealers and pimps', resulted in their being dropped by the new 'Reich Bishop' Ludwig Müller, and the disintegration of Protestantism into warring factions and a patchwork of German Christian, neutral and Confessing provincial Churches. A rather conventionally anti-clerical Hitler washed his hands of these troublesome priests, leaving others to make the running in a desultory and disparate series of assaults on Christianity itself.

Christians who could accommodate themselves to a regime so inimical to core as distinct from secondary Christian values had few difficulties in finding theological rationalisations for doing so. In this case, the treason of the clerks was not metaphorical. Some of the finest theological minds in the country, such as those of Paul Althaus or Emanuel Hirsch, found reasons why God had alighted upon the Germans or in support of totalitarian communitarianism and the Führer principle. Others found theological grounds for the 'guest' status conferred upon the Jews.[114] Ironically, theologians who opposed Nazism could often come up with nothing better than the claim that

Nazi emphasis on salvation through racial election indicated that 'Their thinking is completely Jewish,' or 'The racial idea is Judaism.'[115]

Some desparate logic was involved in reconciling Nazism with Christianity. Just as overseas missionaries had sometimes adapted Christianity to the customs and beliefs of heathen peoples, so the German Christians sought to 'set forth into a completely new land of Germanness with a completely new message of Christ'.[116] Paradoxically, while the German Christians espoused the view that 'what God has put asunder, let no man join together', vis-à-vis what they uncharmingly called 'non-Aryan' Christians, the primacy they accorded race resulted in spasmodic efforts to subsume Roman Catholics as well as the historically distinct Protestant territorial Churches within one national supraconfessional Church. However, this was one area where a regime constantly espousing national unity sought nothing of the kind.

The exclusion of Christians of Jewish origins from both congregations and the ministry was accompanied by attempts to purge Christianity of Jewish elements, a process whose consequences were analogous to removing all vital organs in the interests of saving the patient. Few German Christians grasped that this was preparatory, once the Jews had gone, to eradicating Christianity itself. The Old Testament was decanonised, while the Gospels were rewritten to establish that Jesus was not a Jew, the crassest example being that no Jews worked as carpenters. His ethnicity was rearranged, either by describing him as an Aryan or by positing that 'Galileans' were not Jews. His troubles with Pharisees and actions against usurers were viewed through an antisemitic lens. Broadly speaking, a compassionate, suffering Christ was replaced by an angry purger of usurers, or a universal soldier, as the German Christians 'redeemed the Redeemer'. This was the next best thing to following Hitler in obliterating Christ altogether. The Führer talked a lot about God, rarely about the Saviour. If Christ was not immune to reinterpretation, nor were core Christian concepts. Sin was found to be an inconvenience. As the SS journal *Schwarze Korps* explained: 'The abstruse doctrine of Original Sin, whence the need of salvation is said to arise; the Fall – and indeed the whole notion of sin as set forth by the Church, involving reward or punishment in a world beyond – is something intolerable to Nordic man, since it is incompatible with the "heroic" ideology of our blood.'[117] This was part of a wider 'purification of our Volksoul . . . from the diseases caused by Jewish contamination . . . one of which is the self-alienation of the German from his Germanic history. . . . Only by regaining our self-identity shall we emerge as victors out of the struggle for survival.'[118]

Hallelujah was replaced with Heil, and orphans sang a version of 'Silent night' which went:

> Silent night! Holy night! All is calm, all is bright,
> Only the Chancellor steadfast in fight,
> Watches o'er Germany by day and by night,
> Always caring for us.

Attempts to reconfigure the Magi as Slagfid, Egil and Wieland, and Christmas as 'Modraneght' or 'Yule', were not a success, even though SS members were doubtless pleased with Himmler's gifts of 'Yule-lights' more befitting Halloween.

One of the subsidiary objectives, from a German Christian point of view, was to counter the increasing feminisation of religion, with its alleged emphasis upon mawkish sentimentality, by attracting the 'brown men' through a more muscular faith. This side issue need not divert us. Past equivocations about allowing uniformed, flag-waving fellows into the churches went by the board, and the no-nonsense tones of military chaplains ruled the roost. As Provost Grell told the synod of Brandenburg in August 1933: 'revolutionary times are not for weaklings'. Many German Christian pastors took him at his word. Some thought services would be improved by being held in pubs, adopting a commensurately uncouth tone for delivering the new tidings, while others donned uniforms and boots for brawls with their Confessing Church rivals. Few went so far as the 'Revolver Bishop', who used firearms to eject rival clergy from Church offices, but the boarding up of church doors with heavy timbers to prevent the Confessing clergy from holding services was more common.

Hitler dropped the German Christians as a vehicle for assimilating Protestants into the Nazi state, preferring neutrality in the internecine wars of the clergy, but this fiasco merely increased the determination of anti-clerical and anti-Christian Nazis to confine the influence of both Churches to ever narrower ranges of German life. We have seen how the Churches were excluded from collecting for charity, a policy designed to weaken their grip on welfare activities which were progressively usurped by Party formations. Further restrictions occurred in the fields of confessional schools and youth work. The Vatican had made the fatal error when it concluded the Concordat of not agreeing a list of organisations whose immunity was sought, or a working definition of what constituted political activity. By construing everything as political, the Nazis could set to work eradicating diversity in educational provision or in the broader field of youth work. Parental votes relating to the education of their children were influenced by massive propaganda campaigns, house calls, employer threats and withdrawal of Winter Aid from the disadvantaged. The names of dissenting parents were noted. Most flagrantly, those who walked out of polling sessions on registration day in protest were counted as present and affirmative. Tactics used to rig the Reichstag were carried over to humble parents' meetings. Catholic teachers were transferred to Protestant areas and vice versa to promote a sense of isolation. By 1939, all denominational schools had been abolished, along with ecclesiastical private and boarding schools. Having wrecked a rich institutional tapestry, the Nazis set to work obliterating religious instruction as part of the 'community school' curriculum, preventing clergy from entering schools, or encouraging teachers to treat religion as a private matter. Simultaneous scheduling of compulsory Hitler Youth activities was designed to ensure that rival Church events were ill attended.[119]

Nazi assaults on the clergy and Christianity were so crude – up to and including smearing excrement on altars and church doors or desecrating wayside shrines – that they inevitably engendered a popular backlash in areas of entrenched piety. Churches were plastered with anti-clerical posters or others depicting lightly clad BDM members. Pious images were vandalised, to the annoyance of farmers who regarded them as guarantors of good harvests. St Anthony lost his head, St Bernadette ended up in the pond, Christ was heaved on to a dung heap.[120] Hitler Youth members were conspicuous in anti-religious vandalism, like the Wuppertal-Barmen boys who removed a mission cross to use as a target for their rifles, nailing the metal INRI plaque on to a Jewish business to cries of 'Down with the Jews and the Christians'. Where synagogues were not to hand, violence sometimes spilled over on to Christian churches.

Localised Nazi outrages against the most powerful symbol known to mankind did not occur with impunity. Attempts to remove crucifixes from schoolroom walls in Oldenburg and rural Bavaria encountered considerable popular opposition, although it is important to gauge both its extent and its limits.

North German Oldenburg was a sparsely populated agricultural region, whose farming population evinced exceptionally high levels of church attendance and support for the Catholic Centre Party during the Weimar Republic. Living cheek by jowl with Protestants enhanced their siege mentality. The diocesan bishop, Galen of Münster, was a Jesuit-educated aristocratic reactionary whose opposition to Nazi neo-paganism was implacable, beginning with his early hostility to Rosenberg and ending with his principled denunciations of wartime euthanasia, stances not incompatible with rabid anti-Bolshevism or support for his country at war.

In 1936, local Nazi zealots in the Oldenburg state administration decreed that both portraits of Luther and crucifixes were to vanish from school walls. The Protestants in the north obliged, but Catholics in the south demurred. These people may have been plain and unsophisticated, but the cross was the essence of their religious faith. Angry motorists hooted their horns outside the regional government offices, which were deluged with letters of protest. Church bells tolled at odd hours, and two churches sprouted highly visible electrically lit crosses on their towers as symbols of defiance. With even committed Nazis objecting to these policies, few risked assault by removing crucifixes from school walls. For a moment, the Party seemed to disintegrate, in a region where it was a tender plant in the first place, with farmers refusing to join the battle for grain, SA men relinquishing their membership, and people declining to contribute to Winter Aid. The regional Gauleiter decided it was time to revoke the crucifix decree, but rashly decided to hold a public meeting to signal that this was not a case of bowing to pressure. Rehearsing his time as a businessman in Africa in order to illustrate the theme of racial purity, the Gauleiter was interrupted with calls of 'You should have stayed there. What do we want with Africa? We are in Cloppenburg. Get to the point, the crucifix.' He rescinded the decree, to much applause, an event reported in the local press as 'an impressive demonstration of confidence in the Gauleiter by the people of the Münsterland'. A recording of the speech, with heckling edited out, was used to suggest that the official version of these events was true. The crucifixes stayed, but the denominational schools disappeared after a decent delay. Moreover, these protests did not extend to Hitler himself, but were focused on lower-level zealots, for as peasants were reported to have said: 'We have been born Catholics and wish for our own sakes and those of our children to stay Catholics while being followers of the Führer Adolf Hitler.'[121]

Feast days, pilgrimages and religious processions were another flashpoint between the faithful and the Nazis, especially in Catholic regions, where such events were integral to religious faith and an opportunity for a day off. This soon changed, with All Saints Day ceasing to be a public holiday in Silesia or Epiphany in Bavaria. Civil servants were required to work, on the ground that allowing Catholics time off would be divisive, while it was forbidden to display ecclesiastical flags and banners. The reports to the exiled Social Democratic Party leadership, all the more convincing because of their grudging acknowledgement of religious dissent, contain several examples of very impressive numbers of people making it clear that attempts to divide them from their Church were futile. In Aachen, the Nazi authorities did their best to ensure that the annual procession of holy relics became a washout. Permissions to re-route traffic were denied. Prohibitions were imposed on flying yellow and blue papal flags. *Agents provocateurs* were sown among the vast crowd outside the cathedral, shouting 'Heil Moscow', 'Heil Rosenberg' or 'hang the bishops off the lampposts' to precipitate police intervention. The crowd assembled from seven in the morning to fête a number of bishops as though they were pop stars. At each major church this was repeated, with shouts of 'we want to see our bishop' or singing of 'Christ is the new age'. Boys scaled street lanterns to call for three cheers for the hierarchy. When sections of the crowd cried out 'we want our Catholic schools back', the police moved in with considerable violence. On the last day, a huge procession six rows wide marched for an hour through the streets of Aachen.[122] In Catholic Upper Silesia, the Nazis combined attempts to remove holy images from schools with a ban on use of Polish in religious services in this ethnically mixed frontier region. The Nazis set to work impeding the traditional pilgrimage to the St Annaberg, by building a Hitler Youth 'Thing Place' in 1936, and closing the Catholic Pilgrim's Hostel in 1939. Participation was also frustrated, by mine employers offering workers free beer and sausages, roads blocked off, rail passengers filtered singly from stations, and the cancellation of return train services. However, SA and SS men who tried to cordon off the site were inundated by over one hundred and fifty thousand of the faithful. Since Communists, Social Democrats, Jehovah's Witnesses and Jews took part, this amounted to a mass demonstration of solidarity with persecuted Christians. They did not reciprocate when synagogues went up in flames.[123]

Possessed of the authority, technologies and resources of the state, the Nazis sought to intrude their own cult and rites into the lives of ordinary Germans. Some of these efforts proved a miserable failure, with people bored witless by the new theatre or declamatory choruses, and eschewing nazified rites of passage. SS men may have married in bizarre ceremonies under the gaze of their Führer, and have been buried pointing northwards, but these 'customs' did not catch on more generally. However, the revealed aspiration matters as much as whether or not these things were popular.

Greater success was achieved with the Nazi alternative to the traditional calendar, although it never managed to displace Christmas and Easter. The year commenced with the Day of the Seizure of Power (30 January) and progressed through the Promulgation of the Party Programme (24 February), Heroes Memorial Day (16 March), the solemn reception of the Hitler Youth (last Sunday in March), the Führer's birthday (20 April), the National Festival of the German People (1 May), Mother's Day (May), Summer Solstice (21 June), the Reich Party Day (early September), Harvest Thanksgiving (early October), Commemoration of the Movement's Fallen (9 November), which replaced Remembrance Sunday, and the Winter Solstice (21 December and Christmas). These festivals either assimilated existing practices, such as Christmas or May Day, suffusing them with Nazi meanings, or in the case of such innovations as the Commemoration of the Movement's Fallen saturated the proceedings with quasi-religious emotion consisting of a portentous plangency. This must have been a tear-jerker, prompting nausea in any fastidious rationalist or person of genuine religious faith.

Each November, a nazified Passion Play was enacted on the streets of central Munich, commemorating the sacrifice of those who in 1923 had anticipated the victory of 1933. A political fiasco which had put the Leader himself in jail became a portent of the triumphs to come. The fact that Hitler had consciously turned from putschism to the legal route was one of many historical facts which were conveniently overlooked. A dismal group of ne'er-do-wells were reborn as heroes and martyrs to the Movement, for, as the ceremonies indicated, the dead were virtually present. This was less a functional and instrumental usurpation of religious forms than something requiring the folklorist Sir James Frazer, or indeed that antisemitic master of the mythic, the Romanian anthropologist Mircea Eliade.[124]

In the developed idiom, realised by about 1935, Hitler spoke to his veteran comrades in the Bürgerbräukeller on the evening of 8 November. The influence of the Last Supper was just below the beery surface.

Afterwards, he went through the dark streets, lit with flames flickering from urns on top of pylons, to the Feldherrnhalle, where the coffins of the Movement's sixteen martyrs had been conveyed on gun carriages. He ascended the steps of what was soon described as an 'altar', to commune with the coffins draped in swastika flags. The bloodstained original banners of the Movement were present as relics. Veteran Nazis, some bearing new 'Blood Medals', joined him to strains of 'Ich hatt' einem Kameraden', for the object was to assimilate dead and living Nazis to the millions of wartime dead. The surviving 'old fighters' became an improbable band of apostles.

The next day, Hitler laid a wreath at the Feldherrnhalle, before a procession which had marched from the Bürgerbräukeller escorted the coffins to Ludwig Troost's newly built temples on the Königplatz. If Munich was to be the Rome or Mecca of National Socialism, then this was its inner sanctum.[125] Hitler marched alongside rather than at the head of his comrades, in a brief reversion to the role of unknown soldier. As the procession passed each of the 240 pylons bearing the names of other fallen comrades, it stopped while the name rang out, to the sound of drums and trumpets. Cannon shots reverberated as the procession reached its object. The sixteen names were invoked again, with the Hitler Youth responding 'Present', before the band struck up the Badenweiler March and the Deutschlandlied. The high priest strode up the temple steps to lay a wreath. Since the sarcophagi were sunk into the temple floors, these architectural arrangements emphasised the martyrs' living intermediary rather than the dead. The ideological legatees were eternally present in the form of SS guards. Later that night, Hitler presided over the swearing-in oaths of SS recruits in front of the Feldherrnhalle.[126]

These major occasions were essential to the only cult that really mattered in Nazi Germany, that of the Führer himself. They were meticulously choreographed performances, in which the lone star could dramatise himself to the hilt, as the only moving actor amid static and silent crowds. Politics became horrifically personalised, although that is not the same as saying that one man controlled all. How he revelled in it all! With what immune contemporaries called the pasty face of a shopfloor walker or a waiter, alternating manly sincerity, flashes of rage and that simpering smile which passed for contentment, like a tubby matron after devouring a plate of pastries. On Sunday mornings at the September Party rallies, Hitler advanced through one hundred thousand or so SA and SS men, accompanied at a discreet distance by the SA-Chief of Staff and the Reichsführer-SS to commune again with the martyrs' memorial in the Luitpoldarena. All flags dipped to the sound of 'Ich hatt' einem Kameraden', before the Führer walked backwards from the memorial, accompanied by the 'blood banner', which he used to consecrate new Party formation standards.

These exercises in mass bathos were the most visible aspect of the developed Führer cult, in which a man assumed mythic dimensions. The faith which Hitler's earliest and most committed followers invested in their Führer became a mass phenomenon, an unsurprising reaction in a divided country with weak democratic traditions, where many felt so existentially threatened by a succession of crises that they preferred a leap of faith to rational understanding of their predicament. The Führer cult was as much in the eye of the beholder as in the tricks of Goebbels' propaganda apparatus, in so far as people invested Hitler with properties he manifestly lacked. It was not simply a matter of aural, emotional or visual manipulation. The essentials of this cult can be quickly rehearsed. Contrary to any rational understanding of how a dictatorial party works, people believed in a Führer 'without sin', presiding over an army of little Hitlers of whom they were fully prepared to think the worst. Thus the murders of late June 1934 were widely approved of, or tolerated, on the ground that the Führer had purged Röhm's sybaritic homosexuals, a convenient moral rationalisation of murders whose motives were wholly political. In line with the saintly king/bad courtiers syndrome, Hitler became the avenging agent of popular indignation and justice – except that he was not a monarch, but a self-consciously ordinary man, who could articulate the anxieties and desires of his ordinary countrymen in words which made them laugh and cry, switching from coarse diatribes to the most flighty rhetoric. This dissociative process continued throughout the Third Reich, with the ascetic Führer apparently blissfully ignorant of subordinates living the high life, a state of affairs he would rectify if only he knew about it. Imaginary scenarios were invented, by those 'in the know', in which an outraged Führer stumbled into various dens of Nazi iniquity, sweeping the corrupt off to jail. Similarly, and contrary to all evidence, Hitler was regarded as a relatively moderate figure, restraining the excesses of rabid Party radicals, a mistake sometimes made by Western statesmen. But there was more going on than this suggests.

If many people saw their own life's dramas and tragedies, or the daring they could never quite manage, mirrored in Hitler himself, they also received the utmost flattery in return. Their unremarkable existences were invested with heroic proportions within the cosmic drama of race. For Hitler was no latterday Coriolanus, although like Mussolini he occasionally spoke of the mass as malleable clay. Instead, he positively exalted the mass of farmers, mothers, workers and so forth, investing them with the heroic characteristics politicians usually reserve for the armed forces. The broader populace may have created the Hitler myth, but Hitler himself managed the supreme feat of mythologising the myth-makers themselves in a cycle of mutual adoration. They invested in him, and he invested in them.[127] As he said in May 1936:

> We are so fortunate to be able to live among these people, and I am proud to be your Führer. So proud that I cannot imagine anything in this world capable of convincing me to trade it for something else. I would sooner, a thousand times sooner, be the last national comrade among you than a king anywhere else.[128]

AGGRESSION AND VICTIMHOOD

New values were not simply confined to German domestic politics and society, but were projected on to the international stage. Since the road from the 1934 non-aggression pact with Poland, via Munich, to German troops posing beside abandoned Polish frontier posts has been exhaustively recounted, only a few salient features of Nazism as foreign policy will be discussed here.[129]

The notion that Nazi and fascist foreign policies were based on aggression is hardly a remarkable insight. More precisely, they were products of an acute sense of national victimhood, that morally exculpatory excuse for intolerance, persecution and violence in the modern world. Speaking in Gera in June 1934, Hitler expressed this with a crudity befitting his Party Congress audience: 'We do not have the feeling that we are an inferior race, some worthless pack which can and may be kicked around by anyone and everyone; rather, we have the feeling that we are a great *Volk* which only once forgot itself, a *Volk* which, led astray by insane fools, robbed itself of its own power, and has now once more awakened from this insane dream.'[130] It was especially heinous for the European powers to inflict on Germany what they routinely did overseas, the crime of crimes being to introduce colonial troops into the Rhineland, treating it as if it were Algeria or Senegal.

Victimhood engendered extreme self-righteousness, at the top and below. Sir Evelyn Wrench was the 'Europhile' editor and owner of the British conservative *Spectator*, who had visited Germany regularly since 1895. Persecution of the Jews by the Nazis acted as an existential shock, for he subscribed to the common view that high culture and racism were incompatible, whatever his own minor snobberies about Jews. Judging from his book, Wrench was a decent man, hopelessly out of his depth in a country he claimed to know well. The best he could muster as an analogy for 'Hitlerism' was the infallibility of the Pope. Six weeks before the outbreak of war, Wrench returned to the

Reich. In between high-level meetings, he endeavoured to fathom some young SS men, whom he otherwise rather liked:

> It was hopeless. I was confronted by 'shut minds'. We went laboriously through the post-war years and I acknowledged readily the mistakes made at Versailles and afterwards, but when I demanded an equal readiness to see the faults of the Nazi government, I came up against a blank wall. I was dealing with Hitlerian infallibility. I realised there was an unbridgeable chasm between the British and German points of view.[131]

In the perception of most Germans, Versailles was an international attempt to reduce Germany to helotry, although what a regime of military inspection or reparations, imposed on an otherwise sovereign government which was lent money by its former adversaries, who wanted to put Germany back on its feet, had in common with slavery was left undeveloped. Germany had become an Allied colony, the most demeaning fate to impose on civilised Europeans at a time when they unselfconsciously imposed these arrangements on the rest of mankind. Similar resentments were shared by six million Austrian Germans, living in the beached wreck of a once mighty empire, but consisting now of a capital and attached alpine valleys, apparently lacking both economic coherence and *raison d'être*.

International law and institutions were regarded with scepticism and hostility, since they did not seem to cater for ethnic German exclaves scattered across central and eastern Europe. The Nazis took these sentimental self-delusions a stage further by interpreting them as symptomatic of a larger ontological threat, with malign forces allegedly conspiring to subvert the 'Aryan-German race' by rendering asunder what allegedly belonged together. Each Allied concession to Germany, from the Dawes Plan to the Hoover Moratorium suspending reparations payments, was assimilated into this improbable exegesis. This enabled Hitler to behave as if the concessions won peacefully from the Allies by Stresemann and Brüning had never happened, or were not terribly important anyway. He ostentatiously walked out of the League of Nations, and found any number of academics and intellectuals ready to pronounce the obsequies on international jurisprudence, in favour of the rampant egoism of races and states. As in the domestic arena, Hitler regarded international law as an obstacle to higher ends; the League of Nations was an Allied plot.

Hitler was not seeking to reset the balance of European power, in the interests of justice for Germany, but to destroy it, preparatory to creating a racialist empire beyond the most advanced fantasies of his imperial or Weimar revisionist predecessors. Eliding the three periods into an immutable monolith, without regard to context, tenor or time, blurs what was uniquely horrible about Nazism. Elements of this vision overlapped with the recent past, but the racist and revolutionary goals which Hitler gradually revealed shocked many of those who occupied traditional conservative centres of power. If they had simply shared Hitler's mindset, then there would have been no tensions, no opposition and no need for him to replace them with more compliant figures prior to his more risky ventures.[132] Hitler was not interested in tinkering with borders, but in acquiring living space, as if geographical scale were any serious guarantee of national well-being. The simultaneous obsession with demographic increase was only one of several glaring contradictions. This aim was virtually bound to engender another world war, with Hitler being the only European leader prepared to contemplate this dreadful scenario with near equanimity.[133] Neither the full-blown vision nor the lengths Hitler was prepared to go to realise it were on display to the German people, for whom, along with foreign statesmen, there was an alternative rhetoric of rights denied and justice sought. For while Hitler was privately outlining plans and timetables for aggression, gradually initiating his commanders into the process, the public talk was of treatment of Germany as if she were a colony, denial of human rights and, in at least one instance, indignation over maltreatment of socialist workers and refusal to hold democratic elections. It is important not to ignore this insistent self-righteousness just because it does not conform with a rather one-dimensional, and otherwise entirely accurate, view of Hitler as naked aggressor.[134]

The insidious tone, bullying and opportunism which accompanied Hitler's public triumphs can be seen to best advantage in his greatest and penultimate pre-war diplomatic achievement, namely the March 1938 Anschluss with Austria. Austria's problems after the Treaty of Saint-Germain in 1919 were worse than those of post-war Germany, which had been temporarily rather than permanently displaced as a great power. Austria had no way back, except as a client of Italy or by being absorbed into Nazi Germany. The new republic was roughly a quarter of the size and population of the Austrian lands of the Habsburg empire, with a huge and mostly redundant civil service, and a depleted agricultural, industrial and raw-materials base. The former subjects-become-new-neighbours protected their fledgling economies by pulling up the protective drawbridges, further increasing Austrian dependency on foreign loans and Germany. Like Weimar Germany, Austria was ravaged by inflation at the beginning of the decade. Foreign loans in 1923 were made contingent upon more resolute renunciation of Anschluss with Germany, a strategy repeated in 1931 when the French thwarted the Austro-German customs union with a run on Austrian banks. The Austrian slump from 1929 onwards was both more acute and of longer duration than anywhere else in Europe, with a third of the workforce unemployed in 1936, the nadir of the Austrian depression. This enhanced the economic attractions of closer ties with a northern Nazi neighbour by then experiencing labour shortages.

As in Weimar Germany, Austrian post-war politics consisted of radically polarised ideological camps. The main protagonists were the conservative Christian Socials, a rhetorically strident Social Democratic Party and smaller Pan-German and Peasant parties. Austrian Communism never quite got off the ground in a country with its own Austro-Marxist traditions. With the exception of the Pan-Germans, enthusiasm for Anschluss with Germany waxed and waned according to who ruled north of the border, until the diplomatic constellation enabled a brief experiment in 'Austro-fascism' heavily overlain with Catholic corporatist elements.[135] Like Weimar Germany, post-war Austria was blighted by border skirmishing and paramilitary violence, the largest formations being the leftist Schutzbund and the rightist 'home guard' or Heimwehr. Chronic divisiveness also characterised Austrian National Socialism, whose antecedents lay in Czech–German nationality conflicts in the pre-war empire. The Austrian Nazis had no figure remotely analogous to Hitler, whose rise to power in Germany generated splits between older 'workerist' and younger Hitlerian factions, regarding such issues as whether leaders should be elected or imposed from above. They also had difficulties establishing a separate identity in a political landscape where antisemitism was rampant and other parties advocated union with Germany. Although the Austrian Nazi vote increased to over 16 per cent by early 1932, the pool of uncommitted voters was limited in a polity where 90 per cent of the electorate voted, including 80 per cent for the two major parties.[136] Finally, the Austrian Nazis also faced more resolute opponents than those in Germany, with authoritarian pre-emption of fascism paradoxically encouraged by the original Fascist dictator.

Rather than simply spectating while the Nazis replicated their northern march to power and subversion of democratic institutions, the new Christian Social leader Engelbert Dollfuss converted a technical dissolution of parliament into authoritarian rule by emergency decree. Following Spanish and Polish precedents, Dollfuss retroactively created a mass party called the Fatherland Front, absorbing non-Nazi elements in the Heimwehr and the Christian Socials.[137] Encouraged by Mussolini, Dollfuss proscribed both the Social Democrats and the Nazis, the former having incurred the Duce's wrath for exposing the reconditioning and transhipment to Hungary of Italian weaponry. Of course, this experiment in 'Austro-fascism' had internal as well as external causes. Dollfuss's decision to use howitzers to break socialist resistance in 'Red' Viennese housing estates resulted in Hitler assuming the moral highground in a February 1934 interview with Ward Price of the *Daily Mail*. Thanks to Dollfuss, he claimed, sixteen hundred people had been killed and five thousand wounded. By contrast, only twenty-seven people had been killed and 150 wounded in his 'seizure of power'. Without irony, Hitler suggested that Dollfuss try persuasion, for had not the residual eleven million former opponents of Nazism since been 'converted'?[138]

The Austrian Nazis responded to curbs on their activities and closure of their institutional apparatus with terrorist bombings, sometimes using adolescent boys to place explosives in tourist centres. Soon there were up to forty explosions a day. Instead of losing his nerve, Dollfuss purged Nazi sympathisers from the civil service, teaching and the corporate sector, flouting the jurisdictional autonomy of the major universities to weed out the most ardent supporters of Nazism. The leading lights of Nazism were deported to Germany or interned alongside the socialists. Accounts differ as to whether these were concentration camps manqués or convalescent homes for recuperating toughs.

Hitler decided to use the power of the German holidaymaker and an enhanced propaganda campaign to destroy Dollfuss, who at a mere four feet eleven inches tall was an almost ridiculous opponent for a leader about to take on extremely tall British patricians. Tourist visa fees for Austria were increased to one thousand Reichsmarks, which meant that eight thousand Germans holidayed in Austria in July 1933, in contrast to ninety-eight thousand the year before. Tourism fell tenfold. German aircraft dropped leaflets urging Austrians to withhold taxes and withdraw deposit from the banks. Radio Munich broadcast a stream of propaganda, while loudspeakers boomed more over the land borders. Candle-lit swastikas floated down the Danube. The minimal effects of these measures on the Dollfuss regime led the Austrian Nazi leadership to seek to negotiate their way into positions of power. When their outrageous demands were rebuffed, they turned to the more desperate stratagem of putschism. Hitler seems to have been misled into thinking that the Austrian army was about to launch a coup, which he opportunistically welcomed, only to discover when it was in progress that the putsch involved a small group of SS men egged on by Landesleiter Theo Habicht as a means of dominating Austrian Nazism's warring factions.[139] This force shot and fatally wounded Dollfuss. Denied support by the Austrian SA, and opposed by both the army and the Heimwehr, the putsch rapidly collapsed. Mussolini moved four further divisions to support the fifty thousand Italian troops already stationed on the Brenner, in full awareness of the probable instigator of the assassination of his client. As he said, 'It would mean the end of Europe if this country of murderers and pederasts were to overrun Europe.'

Following Dollfuss's lead, his successor Kurt von Schuschnigg rather desperately invested his authoritarian regime with the external trappings of fascism. This was a case of fascism from above, rather than fascism from below. The Fatherland Front adopted a version of the swastika, and spawned a unitary trade union, a leisure arm called 'New Life', a Mother's Aid Society, youth organisation and a blue-uniformed Sturmkorps resembling the SS. There was one key difference, in part determined by the need to do nothing which would jeopardise American loans, and a desire to distinguish themselves from the Nazis. Although the regime imposed employment quotas on Jews in the professions, the Jews lent Dollfuss and Schuschnigg their whole-hearted support, distinguishing creeping 'rubber-soled antisemitism' from the heavy-booted Nazi variety.[140] These two men were Austrian conservative Catholic patriots in fascist garb, rather than radical fanatics bent on external aggression and the birth of a new man. Much the same could be said about Hungary.[141]

The Austrian experiment was primarily undone by the exigencies of Italian diplomacy. Mussolini's Abyssinian and Iberian involvements increased his dependency upon Germany. The *quid pro quo* for German support was that he throw Austria to the wolves. Schuschnigg dissolved the Heimwehr, dismissing its leader Starhemberg from the leadership of the Fatherland Front. Denied Mussolini's protecting hand, he had little alternative but to appease Nazi Germany. In July 1936, he concluded an agreement with Germany, whereby the Germans renounced interference in Austrian affairs in return for acknowledgement by Austria that it was a 'German state' and would not enter into anti-German combinations. The unpublished sections of the agreement were more ominous. Normalisation of economic and cultural relations meant that the Nazis could flood Austria with propaganda. Political detainees, that is Nazi terrorists, were to be released, and their soulmates from the National Opposition admitted to the government. Schuschnigg thought he had a deal, Hitler and Göring – who was making most of the running on the Austrian issue – regarded it as a lever to extract more. Intelligence from the British ambassador Halifax that his government would not oppose evolutionary and peaceful 'alterations' to the status quo in Austria, Czechoslovakia and the contested port of Danzig merely encouraged Hitler in the view that the British were 'worms'. Göring solicited a similar 'green light' from Mussolini.[142] Mounting Nazi interest in Austria was reflected in the dispatch of State Secretary Wilhelm Keppler to liaise between German and Austrian Nazis, and the keen interest taken in the Catholic lawyer Arthur Seyss-Inquart, as the face most likely to slip unopposed into Schuschnigg's cabinet. Indeed Schuschnigg himself proposed this last solution, as the trade-off for Hitler disowning Austrian Nazi radicals, prior to his meeting with the German Führer on 12 February 1938.

The meeting between the reserved Austrian Chancellor and Hitler is notorious in the annals of diplomacy. Schuschnigg's small talk about the room was brushed aside with: 'Yes, my ideas mature here. But we haven't met to talk about the beautiful view and the weather.' Hitler continued: 'I have a historic mission and I am going to fulfil it because Providence has appointed me to do so. . . . You certainly aren't going to believe that you can delay me by so much as half an hour? Who knows – perhaps I'll turn up in Vienna overnight, like a spring storm. Then you'll see something.'[143] Hitler spent much of the time screaming at his interlocutor, or recapitulating his personal odyssey from obscurity to greatness. At lunch, Schuschnigg found himself sandwiched between some of Hitler's more glacial generals, with Keitel dramatically summoned during the afternoon session. In this manner, Schuschnigg was browbeaten into accepting foreign dictation of membership of his cabinet and domestic security policy. Appointing Seyss-Inquart to the Ministry of the Interior was akin to appointing a wolf to guard a sheep pen.[144] Schuschnigg had three days to secure his government's approval or German troops would roll. Speaking to the Reichstag on 20 February 1938, Hitler found kind words for the Austrian Chancellor 'and the warm-hearted readiness with which he accepted my invitation and endeavoured, with me, to find a solution doing equal justice to the interests of both countries and the interests of the German race as a whole, that German race whose sons we all are, no matter where the cradle of our homeland stood'.[145]

Schuschnigg's decision in early March to hold a plebiscite framed to endorse the status quo provoked Hitler into ordering partial mobilisation. Intelligence of the plebiscite reached Hitler from Odilo Globocnik, one of his most trusted Austrian admirers. A vote for the Austrian government would have been a considerable embarrassment to Hitler's tactical espousal of self-determination. The question put – for a 'free, independent, Christian Austria and Fatherland' – was hardly likely to be rejected, but, just in case, the voting age was raised, only 'yes' ballot papers were issued, leaving opponents to supply their own, and the plebiscite was highly public, with opportunities for multiple voting.[146] Confronted with Hitler's willingness to use armed force, Schuschnigg cancelled the plebiscite and resigned in favour of Seyss-Inquart. Austrian Nazis took over in the major cities, unaware that the German troops crossing the borders spelled the end of any autonomist solutions they may have entertained.

It is worth following Hitler along his triumphal path as he reported the reincorporation of his former homeland 'into History'. He delivered a succession of speeches, honing the equivocations and opportunism of the preceding years into a well-rehearsed story. Talk of rights was to the fore in a proclamation read by Göring on 12 March 1938. Schuschnigg and his colleagues had sought 'to procure for themselves an alibi for the unremitting violations of the equal rights of Austrian Germans, a petition was devised with the purpose of completely depriving the majority of this country of its rights!' Hitler became an improbable champion of democratic proprieties: 'There are no lists of voters, no voter cards. There is no such thing as checking a voter's eligibility; there is no obligation as to the confidentiality of the ballot; there is no guarantee for the impartial conduct of the election; there is no supervision when the ballots are counted.'[147]

In interviews and speeches, Hitler stressed his personal 'betrayal' by Chancellor Schuschnigg. He emphasised the alleged hypocrisy of the Allied victors: 'Rights which were self-evidently accorded to the most primitive colonial tribes were withheld from one of this world's old civilised nations for reasons as unacceptable as they were insulting.' The sufferings of Austrian Nazi martyrs grew incrementally: 'They did not even grant them the consideration of a bullet. No, they were hanged! In Vienna alone there are thirteen graves of victims hanged by the noose. More than 400 murdered, and 2,500 shot are the regrettable victims of this most despicable and foul oppression against our *Volk* in modern times.' A week later in Stuttgart he added for good measure ten thousand who had been injured, a tactic he would repeat in occupied Poland.[148] It is almost superfluous to add that the 'victims' were terrorists bent on overthrowing the Austrian government. There was an apparent magnanimity towards defeated Austrian opponents: 'On our part, we are prepared to ship those criminals to these countries on luxury steamers, for all I care. The joy that has overwhelmed us during these few days has made us forget any desire for revenge.' Not quite, because SD death squads were concurrently scurrying around Vienna, doing to death conservatives who had escaped his clutches in 1934. Jews were subjected to a paroxysm of violence as yet without precedent in Germany. Schuschnigg disappeared into a concentration camp.

It was ominous that the suffering ethnic Germans of a vaguely defined central Europe now numbered 'ten millions', indicating that, beyond six million Austrians, Hitler had further acts of liberation in mind. In an interview with the *Daily Mail*, Hitler averred that he had intervened in Austria to spare his native land the ravages of civil war afflicting Spain, where his Condor Legion had spread concord from their bomb bays.[149] Pseudo-religious elements suffused his every public utterance. Regardless of Göring's prominent role in the Anschluss, Hitler swooped down to claim full credit for this 'miracle':

> What has happened in these past weeks is the result of a triumph of an idea, a triumph of will, and even a triumph of persistence and tenacity, and above all it is the result of a miracle of faith, for only faith could have moved these mountains.[150]

Speaking in Frankfurt on 31 March, his life story became a 'pilgrimage throughout Germany'. In a speech delivered in Salzburg a week later he announced: 'In the beginning stood the *Volk*, was the *Volk*, and only then came the Reich.' The blasphemies became boundless:

> I believe that it was also God's will that from here a boy was to be sent into the Reich, allowed to mature, and elevated to become the

nation's Führer, thus enabling him to reintegrate his homeland into the Reich. There is a divine will, and we are its instruments.[151]

These were not simply rhetorical flights, but revealing of the messianic conviction with which Hitler approached the ensuing self-generated crises over Czechoslovakia, whose demise he was actively plotting, and the 'little worms' who temporarily frustrated his designs at Munich. Thereafter, the 'worms' turned, belatedly recognising who and what they were dealing with, and altogether more resolute individuals than Chamberlain took up the gauntlet. But, before tracking Hitler's armies into Poland and across most of Europe, we must chronicle the domestic persecution of Jewish Austrians and Germans, and then the escalation of eugenic policies into cold-blooded murder. Only then will it be possible to get a comprehensive view of the messianic racial war Hitler unleashed on Europe, Eurasia and the world as a whole. The apocalyptic undertones which shadowed Nazism from the beginning were breaking through to the surface.

4

LIVING IN A LAND WITH NO FUTURE: GERMAN JEWS AND THEIR NEIGHBOURS, 1933–1939

In March 1938 the German Reich annexed
the Austrian Republic. This event triggered
innumerable antisemitic outrages, especially in
Vienna. Here a boy is being forced to deface
his father's own business premises.

CONFLICTING SIGNS

Following the 'seizure of power', triumphant National Socialists immediately settled old scores with political opponents and Jews. A movement characterised by activist violence could not be turned off like a tap. SA and SS men hauled their victims to *ad hoc* places of torture and murder set up in barracks, breweries, factories, water towers, ships, pubs and restaurants, of which there were a hundred in Berlin alone. They were subjected to horrific sustained assault.[1] Individual Jews were subject to random intimidation and violence by marauding posses of SA thugs, while Jewish doctors and lawyers were prevented from going about their lawful business.[2] Since the forces of law and order now included SA and SS men bearing armbands marked 'auxiliary police', they were as likely to participate in as to prevent these outrages.

The foreign press commented adversely on locally organised boycotts of Jewish businesses.[3] Hitler and Goebbels decided to use this negative foreign reaction as a pretext for a nationwide boycott to be held on 1 April 1933. Julius Streicher – the *Heldentenor* of Nazi antisemitism – became king for that day. Noting that Hitler was the lodestar, Goebbels hurried off to make the propaganda preparations.[4] Presented as 'a form of self-defence' against the Jews, this semi-official demonstration would also steer semi-spontaneous local actions into more controlled and directed channels.[5] Protestant Church leaders denounced foreign press coverage of events in Germany as being exaggerated horror stories.[6] The widely read Protestant Sunday press published numerous commentaries on the over-representation of Jews in cultural life, the economy, law and medicine, and the need to do something about it, within the bounds of what was sanctioned by the Bible. That left some scope.[7]

Goebbels claimed that the public was solidly behind the boycott, but the picture on the streets was mixed. Despite its brief duration, for many Jewish people the boycott came as a terrible shock. The war veteran Edwin Landau could not grasp how such things could happen in the twentieth century, 'because such things only occurred in the Middle Ages'. He felt hatred for the uniformed 'barbarians' and the smirking faces of passers-by. Everything suddenly seemed strange, like being in a hostile foreign country. Landau found no answers talking to the graves of his parents in the cemetery, nor in the synagogue, where, feeling 'crucified on a swastika', he asked, 'My God, why have you forsaken me?'[8] The Dresden philologist Viktor Klemperer wrote in his diaries: 'I am burdened with greater pressure than during the war, and for the first time in my life I have a deadly political hatred towards a group collectivity (never during the war).'[9] Foreign observers of the boycott, such as Sir Evelyn Wrench, the European-minded owner of the conservative *Spectator*, who knew Germany well, were profoundly shocked. Wrench commented:

> I had come across antisemitism in Eastern Europe before, but I thought racial persecution belonged to another age. Half-civilised peoples might still indulge in it but surely not the Germany I had known. It seemed a horrifying nightmare from which I must wake up. . . . It was as though we were back in the Middle Ages, with their racial intolerance and persecution. This was not mob violence, such as I had witnessed in the tense days of emotion at the outbreak of war in Paris in 1914; when the crowds, surging along the Grands Boulevards, wrecked several German-owned establishments. This was Government-directed and Government-inspired hate.[10]

Despite loitering uniformed thugs, armed with cameras as well as truncheons, arguments sometimes flared among frustrated shoppers, including generals who donned their medals for defiant visits to Jewish-owned stores.[11] These policies pricked consciences and stimulated debate. There were doubtless many conversations such as Viktor Klemperer overheard between a soldier and his girl during the advertisements in a Dresden cinema, which included one for a Jewish-owned business:

> He: 'one really shouldn't go to a Jew to shop'. She, reflective, quite matter of fact, without the least pathos: 'No, really, it's just as good and lasts just as long, really just like in Christian shops – and so much cheaper'. He falls silent. When Hitler, Hindenburg etc. appeared, he clapped enthusiastically. Later, during the utterly American jazzband film, clearly yiddeling at points, he clapped even more enthusiastically.[12]

In Wesel on the Lower Rhine, Erich Leyens, a Jewish war veteran, donned his field grey and medals to distribute leaflets protesting against the boycott outside his family's department store. The leaflets read:

> Our Reich Chancellor Hitler, the Reich Ministers Frick and Göring have repeatedly made the following declaration: 'Anyone who insults a combat veteran in the Third Reich will be punished with imprisonment.'
>
> All three Leyens brothers served as volunteers on the front. They were wounded and were decorated for courageous action. Their father [Hermann] Leyens had been a volunteer in the fight against the Spartacists. His grandfather was wounded at Katzbach during the War of Liberation. With such a record of past national service, do we now have to be subjected to public humiliation? Is this how the fatherland today expresses its gratitude, by placing huge pickets in front of our door with the demand not to buy from our house? We regard this action, which goes hand in hand with the dissemination of slanderous accusations all over town, as an attack on our national and civic honour as well as a desecration of the memory of 12,000 German front soldiers of the Jewish faith who gave their lives in action. Furthermore, we regard this provocation as an affront against every decent citizen. We have no doubt that, even today, there are citizens in Wesel who have the courage of their convictions, which Bismarck once called for, and exemplify German integrity which, especially now, stands steadfastly by our side.

It is worth adding that according to Leyens: 'Voices were raised, loud and clear, in support of the statement in the leaflet. Men gave vent to their indignation. Women, crying, came up and hugged me.'[13]

Judging from recent studies, it is impossible to say whether the boycott met with predominantly positive or negative responses.[14] Although the boycott was called off after one day, it illustrated a dialectic between 'spontaneous' grassroots actions and 'follow-up' state-sponsored measures, while reactivating the general issue of reducing alleged Jewish influence within German life, a theme that struck an obvious chord particularly among professionals and the commercial middle classes, or those who aspired to the security and status of those occupations. While many Germans disapproved of open street violence, this was only part of a test of moral stamina whose more taxing elements included their response to more insidious but legalised forms of discrimination.

Within a week of the boycott, the new government introduced the

Law for the Restoration of the Professional Civil Service, following protracted deliberations with the civil service, who feared its wider repercussions. Although nominally designed to purge the Weimar civil service of actual or alleged political appointees, the law included a clause compulsorily retiring Jews – defined as persons with one Jewish grandparent – from the civil service in so far as they were not front veterans or relatives of men fallen in the Great War. This was a concession to the proprieties of President Hindenburg, who it should be noted, along with Hitler's conservative coalition partners, connived with the Nazis in passing this law. In May, the purely tactical concession to certain categories of Jewish civil servant was partly undone by the simple device of prohibiting the further promotion of men protected by veteran status. The number of Jewish war veterans seems to have surprised the Nazis. Some one hundred thousand Jews had served in the armed forces, seventy-eight thousand at the front. Thirty thousand Jews had been decorated for bravery, and some twelve thousand had died for Kaiser and Fatherland.[15] Recovering from this shocking news, the Nazis set matters to rights by forbidding the inclusion of names of Jewish dead on new war memorials.

If the number of Jewish civil servants was below five thousand in 1933, revealing striking under-representation, civil service practice was paradigmatic for other professions. A separate law concerning admission to the legal profession resulted in the disbarment of fourteen hundred Jewish lawyers and 381 Jewish judges and state prosecutors. The fact that 70 per cent of Jewish lawyers could still technically practise law (although who would want to be represented by pariahs?) probably encouraged Jewish people to clutch at straws, in the sense of identifying a gap between Nazi propaganda and governmental practice.[16] Expelled from medical organisations, Jewish doctors were also gradually prevented from working in public hospitals, in schools or for welfare agencies. By early 1934, twenty-six hundred Jewish physicians had been dismissed.[17] In Munich, Mayor Karl Fiehler restricted Jewish pathologists to the examination of corpses of Jews.[18] Non-Jewish doctors had no inhibitions about destroying professional competitors through such stratagems as using the presence of Jewish judges at beauty contests as an argument for preventing Jews from working as gynaecologists. Measures against doctors soon applied to dentists, who were subjected to *Stürmer* smear tactics, involving photographs of dirty equipment and squalid surgeries, and excluded from working for insurance panels.[19] One of them, Professor Heinz Moral of Rostock, author of Germany's most outstanding dental diagnostic textbook, committed suicide after being dismissed from his university post. In a letter to the dean of faculty he wrote:

> I am a Jew and have never made a secret of it, but my entire outlook is German, and I have always been proud to be a German, whose religion is Jewish. I refuse to change my religion for external reasons. But, simply because I am a Jew, I am being driven from my post. I cannot bear this, because I have always put my heart into my work and have done nothing that transgresses either my oath or my duty. Therefore I am going voluntarily, not to resume my work elsewhere, but rather where there is peace and quiet, the quiet which certain elements have not permitted me, since they believe that a Jew is a less valuable being.[20]

Of an estimated eight hundred Jewish academics in Germany – including men and women of major international reputation – two hundred left the country in 1933 alone.[21] Twenty of these people were Nobel laureates; the eleven physicists included Albert Einstein. Since any artistic activity depended upon membership of the new Chambers of Culture, which was withheld from 'non-Aryans', this haemorrhaging of talent – and of mediocrity – was soon also evident in cinema, journalism, literature, music, painting and theatre. The banned and defamed included the conservative monarchist Arnold Schönberg and his Marxist pupil Hanns Eisler.[22] In marked contrast to reactions to the boycott, these artistic and scientific purges elicited no professional or public protests. This was partly because 'aryanisation' created jobs which could be filled by ambitious non-Jewish Germans. As Max Planck explained to Otto Hahn when the latter suggested a mass academic protest: 'If today thirty professors get up and protest against the government's actions, by tomorrow there will be 150 individuals declaring their solidarity with Hitler, simply because they're after the jobs.'[23] Opportunists within and outside academia and the creative arts had long since convinced themselves that Jews were over-represented in these walks of life.

Not all German Jews were judges, movie directors or professors, although the literature on exiles often conveys this impression, as if it is more shocking that a state persecutes a physicist rather than a butcher or piano tuner. Unfortunately, we know very little about what went on at the level of the people whose equivalents populate the masterly novels of Saul Bellow or Philip Roth – people leading humdrum lives revolving around work and the family, or marooned in loneliness and sadness, who did not emigrate to Hollywood or chairs at Oxford or Princeton, but rather became seamstresses or skivvies and tutors in middle-class British households. Many Jewish people worked in artisan workshops, commerce or industry. The Nazi Factory Cells saw to the sacking of Jewish workers at Leiser, Osram or Orenstein & Koppel. Jewish business people were discriminated against in the awarding of contracts put out to public tender, while recipients of marriage or welfare vouchers were expressly enjoined not to redeem them in Jewish stores. If businesses employing armies of personnel – such as department stores – were less vulnerable at a time of mass unemployment, this temporary protection did not apply to the small retailer, shockingly vulnerable to the malevolence of children or thuggish violence even in well-policed democracies.

Jewish responses to this assault were mixed. They reflected age, gender, marital status, wealth and, indeed, whether an individual was temperamentally disposed to see a glass half empty or half full. Given the difficulties people in liberal democracies had in comprehending that one could single out and persecute a group of people simply by virtue of membership of that group, it is unsurprising that Jewish people could not grasp the enormity of what was happening. Many Jews no doubt felt that they had seen this all before. Jewish pertinacity was sometimes vulgarly expressed as 'We passed through the Red Sea, and we shall pass through the brown shit', for not all Jews used the diction of Goethe or Schiller. Antisemitism was like a freak wave – highly destructive but soon replaced by relatively calm seas, as the emotions which drove it dissipated like frothy seawater ebbing from the sands. In Vienna, the Klaar family, whose patriarch had a sneaking admiration for Hitler, sought and found excuses for Nazi excesses:

> Having used antisemitism to help him achieve power, like so many demagogues before him, did Hitler have any choice but to allow his storm troopers their field day? Had we not been there before? What about Lueger's antisemitic speeches? They had sounded just like Hitler's. And when at last he was Burgomaster of Vienna had he not wined and dined with his wealthy Jewish friends? When reproached for this inconsistency, he replied: I am no enemy of our Viennese Jews; they are not so bad, and we cannot do without them. My Viennese always want to have a good rest, the Jews are the ones who always want to be active.[24]

Others followed their gut instincts. In 1933, forty thousand Jewish people left Germany, in the biggest exodus before 1938, including many young, single people, as well as the politically imperilled or wealthy. This step into the unknown was much more difficult for the elderly, people with aged relatives or infants, or businesses and clienteles built up over generations, or who for cultural reasons could not contemplate living anywhere other than Germany. Who in their right mind would exchange a comfortable life in Berlin or Vienna for the gloomy terraces of 1930s suburban London? This immobility was doubly true for country Jews, whose skills were not in demand elsewhere, who spoke no foreign languages and for whom a trip to the nearest town was an adventure.[25] Optimists felt that matters would stabilise, with Hitler destined for the dustbin of history. These sentiments were shared by Hitler's own Vice-Chancellor Papen, other conservatives and many left-wingers for whom 'fascism' represented the final meltdown of bourgeois capitalism. One could also delude oneself that constitutional norms still prevailed, that one was still living in the *Rechtsstaat* that Jews had once helped to create, or that Nazi violence was the product of malign individuals. There was also a natural human tendency to believe in a disparity between rhetoric and policy, or as the saying went: '*Es wird nicht alles so heiss gegessen, wie es gekocht wird* [The bark was worse than the bite].'[26] Hence, the many letters from Jews to local or national agencies, arguing individual grievances and the writer's record of sterling patriotism. It was not just persecution but the collapse of identity which led some ten thousand German Jews to attempt, or commit, suicide during the years of Nazi rule.[27]

Something more than individual responses was called for. Each representative section of this highly fissiparous community responded after its own fashion. German Zionists noted that Nazi policies struck at Jews as members of a 'race', regardless of whether they were areligious or baptised Christians. Liberal anti-Zionists rediscovered the virtues of community, while enjoining Jews not to emigrate: 'Do your duty here!' The Orthodox wrote to Hitler, underlining their record of patriotism, and requesting 'living space within the living space of the German nation'. Excepting the Orthodox, liberals and Zionists eventually formed a Central Committee for Help and Reconstruction, and in September 1933 the Reich Central Representation of German Jews. Together these organisations helped the increasing numbers of the needy while reskilling people to enhance their prospects for emigration.

They also endeavoured to maintain some semblance of cultural and religious continuity under desperate conditions.[28]

After a lull following the boycott, grassroots antisemitic agitation flared up again in 1935, although we should be cautious in seeing spontaneity where frequency suggests instigation from a central source. Historians have variously detected the handiwork of Goebbels' regional propaganda agents; an SA determined to assert its revolutionary voice after the purges of 1934; and regional Nazi bosses who sought a drastic solution to the 'Jewish Question', rather than what they perceived as drift and vacillation at the top.[29] From July 1935, the exiled Social Democratic Party 'Reports from Germany' chronicled nationwide outrages in some detail. Whatever their deficiencies as sources, namely that they are highly impressionistic, these reports give an immediate sense of the times, like snapshots from across the nation. They can also be supplemented by the memoirs and reminiscences of individuals, which are especially useful in capturing the more personal aspects of discrimination and informal social ostracism.

Across the country, offensive slogans were daubed on walls and shop windows, with arrows painted on the pavement indicating Jewish business premises. Signs reading 'Jews not wanted here' were strung across streets or displayed in the windows of bars, cafés and shops. Wits put up road signs next to hazardous bends which said: 'Fatal bend! Jews permitted to do 120kph'. Effigies of Jews were kicked to pieces or burned in the streets. Pornographically offensive copies of Der Stürmer appeared on the proliferating display pillars, some situated provocatively outside synagogues. At night the windows of houses and shops were smeared with excrement, pitch and paint. Daring gangs of SA men or Hitler Youth stole into Jewish cemeteries to desecrate tombstones. Public places bearing 'Jewish names', such as the Herschel baths in Mannheim (named after its philanthropist founder) were renamed; statues of famous German Jews – such as Mendelssohn in Leipzig – disappeared from public view, much to the annoyance of the conservative lord mayor Carl Goerdeler.[30]

The summer months brought trouble to swimming baths. Near-naked Jews embodied the dual threat of licentiousness and pollution of the water. In Nuremberg, Jews were banned from swimming in the river or public baths in 1933. By 1938 this had been extended to municipal washhouses, for as Mayor Liebel put it: 'One cannot expect any German to climb into a bathtub which was previously used by a Jew.' Such bans were often enforced with mob violence. On 27 June

1935, bathers peacefully disporting themselves at the Rheinbad Herweck baths were rudely interrupted by sixty to eighty Nazis under an SS officer. Semi-clad bathers fled panicstricken into the grounds of Mannheim castle. A Jewish bather had his teeth smashed while another was arrested for trying to prevent the mob throwing his sister into deep water. In Kassel, ten SA men rampaged through a swimming baths, managing in their eagerness to pummel a holidaying Berlin Gestapo officer before he could retrieve his identity card from his clothes.[31] Another magnet for disorder was livestock markets. In Fulda, about a hundred SA men fell upon the cattlemarket, resulting in injured traders and farmers, with stray cattle running amok through the town. Public passivity towards gangs of bullies is, of course, hardly an exclusively German phenomenon. But in Germany during the 1930s gangs of swaggering toughs came hundreds strong, with matters facilitated by a police force which sometimes stood idly by, or intervened to arrest the victims.

Campaigns against named individuals were frequent and especially pernicious. In Wuppertal a kosher butcher was accused of selling sheep's heads and using rotten mincemeat in sausages. His accountant was slandered as a homosexual with a penchant for Jewish boys, whom the butcher paid with free 'kosher meat and poultry'. Regular customers of this 'plague stall' were named and hence socially stigmatised. The 'right place' for the butcher was a concentration camp.[32] A Crimmitschau doctor called Boas was the object of charges of lubriciousness, charges which his professional rivals exploited against him. Unhelpful medical colleagues, and rivals, made his Jewishness public. Shortly afterwards, the windows of Boas' practice were smashed, his surgery ransacked and he himself arrested. In between these two events an article headlined 'Jewish Doctor as Defiler of the Race' had appeared in a local Nazi newspaper whose purpose was to get Boas struck off insurance panel lists. Its scurrilous contents are worth noting. The piece began with the observation that 'many national comrades are of the opinion that the baptised Jew is better and that upon baptism they abandon their shameful practices'. The 'case' of this popular Jewish dermatologist and gynaecologist would prove otherwise. An 'Aryan' girl had frequented his surgery. Boas allegedly seduced her. Failing to 'spit in his face' (there were a lot of questions going begging here), the girl eventually ended the relationship. But there was more shocking news to come. Boas employed a twenty-two-year-old serving girl, the daughter of a Protestant pastor, who as a refugee from Bolshevik Russia should have known better than to leave a girl in the hands of this '*Mädchenschänder*'. The doctor was an alleged morphine addict, even though this libel had not been proven.[33]

Public reactions to incidents such as these were complex and the evidence does not warrant generalisations about the German people as a whole.[34] While in Lübeck a group of League of German Maidens spat at an elderly Jew with a placard around his neck, in Seligenstadt am Main an elderly Catholic man was assaulted for shouting 'one can easily rough up widows and orphans' when he objected to a Jewish widow being similarly treated. Just because premises such as cafés and restaurants bore signs saying 'Jews unwelcome', it does not follow that the owners observed them, especially since – unlike American 'Coloureds' – Jews were not physically distinguishable. Jewish patrons were frequently informed that the sign had to be there, but that they should ignore it. Sometimes the sign was then turned to the wall. When SA men demonstrated against municipally licensed ice-cream vendors, a crowd formed and uttered such remarks as 'The yobs have nothing better to do than riot' or 'They're too lazy to work so they kick up a stink with ice-cream sellers.'[35] In a Hessian village, peasants publicly vilified for selling cattle to Jews – who paid more, and paid promptly – protested until the authorities removed the offensive lists. Many people ostentatiously shopped in Jewish-owned stores, ignoring the ubiquitous Nazi photographers recording them. Of course, the act of shopping in a Jewish store and dealings between peasants and Jewish livestock traders prove very little. In rural Lippe for example there were no 'Aryan' cattle dealers, so farmers had no alternatives.[36] It is erroneous to claim that they were always exercising some sort of choice. Elsewhere, continued patronage of Jews had more to do with a fair price and credit opportunities than philosemitism. Like friendship, limited commercial dealings with individual Jews did not preclude prejudices against an abstraction.[37] Some farmers, of course, enjoyed good relations with Jewish traders, and as a matter of human decency would not break off contact, until denunciation and the attentions of the Gestapo forced their hand.

A handful of reports describing large gatherings of people are of some interest. Photographs of public meetings bedecked with antisemitic slogans are suggestive, but tell us nothing about how antisemitism was actually received by the crowd, any more than glossy posters give us the views of an audience at a cinema or theatre. In late August 1935, the Hamburg Nazis began stirring things up for a major meeting to be addressed by the Franconian antisemite Julius Streicher. About two hundred display columns appeared in the outer suburbs. Hordes of SA men rode through areas inhabited by Jews, tossing flaming torches down on to the street to cries of '*Judah verrecke.*' Posters advertising the meeting covered every wall, with concessionary admission charges for the unemployed. Attendance for Party members was compulsory. As many as twenty thousand people eventually crammed into the stadium. It was a warm August night. Ten minutes into the speech, Streicher noticed that some people were falling asleep. It was time for both jackets, and metaphorical gloves, to come off. First, the speaker turned on 'the educated' upper classes; next he assailed the foreign press, eliciting polite applause from the pockets of Party activists stationed around the hall. Disowning the epithet 'the Franconian Butcher of Jews', Streicher got into his stride. Bellowing against the Churches, he offered his condensed version of Christianity. Jesus could not have been a Jew since he drove the money changers from the Temple. Jesus was like Hitler, sent by God to redeem mankind. A small sect had burgeoned into a mass movement, engendering the hatred of the Pharisees/Reactionaries/Stahlhelm 'of the time'.

Somehow Streicher got on to rape, for logic was not his forte. Jewish blood in the body of Aryan woman would take ten generations to work itself out. He told the story of a professor's daughter who married a Jew. As he edged towards the punchline, with pauses and winks, married couples blushed, the young grinned in prurient anticipation. 'And what lay in the crib, national comrades? A little ape.' This was met with an embarrassed, icy silence. But Streicher was not finished. The woman left her husband, subsequently marrying an SS man. Again, she bore him an ape. His explanation of this phenomenon was accompanied with knee bends and arm gestures depicting the tooing and flowing of Aryan and Jewish blood until he concluded, 'I warn you, German women.' People left the meeting before it was over, and the slight applause came from Streicher's strategically situated claque. Clearly, the audience did not care for this salivating display of one man's obscure sexual fantasies. Antisemitism did not encounter a value-free world; it collided with views about decency, decorum and what one could talk about in public.[38] This was the 1930s, when public displays of tastelessness and vulgarity were less commonplace than they became later in the century.

Let us move on a year to August 1936. The conductor of the Silesian Philharmonic Orchestra, Hesslin, had been told to choose between his Jewish wife and his post. He chose his wife, resigned and accepted a job in Vienna. His valedictory concert was sold out. It was also frequently interrupted by bursts of applause. Attempts to stop this after the concert by downing the lights were to no avail. Drawn by the noise, a party of Nazis came from another part of the building. They saw what was happening and shouted antisemitic abuse at the conductor. The audience booed and whistled at the Nazis, calling them 'obscene louts'. Hesslin did not grasp what was happening until he was told that the audience resented his being insulted. He made a gracious speech of thanks. The audience carried him back to his hotel, where there were further ovations. Such actions on the part of a large number of people deserve to be noticed.[39] Middle-class concert-goers had social solidarities that apparently excluded the Jew-baiting rabble, for there was no such entity as 'the Germans', but myriad individuals whose identities included confession or social class as well as nationality. In 1935 the Gestapo issued instructions for the immediate arrest of Jewish performers whose critical stance had won them ovations when the police intervened against them. These things need to be remarked on. They matter in Europe.[40]

These Reports counsel caution in making categorical statements about popular responses to Nazi antisemitism. When the Reports themselves generalise, the impression is mixed. In Bavaria, where there was no 'active response' to the persecution of the Jews, nonetheless racist propaganda was beginning to have an effect, in the sense that people began to believe that the Nazis had a legitimate case, only spoiled by their own excess.[41] In Saxony, there was sympathy for the poorly connected 'little' Jews, together with the feeling that 'many Jews' deserved to be messed around for having tried to capitalise on past political instability. 'Even' Social Democrats agreed that there was a 'Jewish Question' begging resolution, although like most people they deplored Streicher's vulgarity and SA rowdiness. Disapproval of excess was not incompatible with diffuse antisemitism. Most people accepted that Jews were 'another race'. People who earlier would not have known what a Jew was, now blamed them for every misfortune. There were also differences between the social classes and according to educational attainment.

Although this fact is not often remarked on in an historical literature fashionably prone to idealising the lower classes, these socialists reported that ostentatious sympathy for Jewish people was most evident in 'bourgeois circles', with prominent families overtly socialising with Jews.[42] Since most Jews were from this class, this is hardly surprising. In November 1937 it was reported that 'Antisemitism has many opponents among the bourgeoisie.' By contrast, it had made inroads among the broad mass of politically indifferent workers.[43] Higher social class also created a temporary protective shield around well-off Jews, for deference was still operative, reducing harassment to snide remarks when they were out of sight. Their poorer fellows bore the brunt of verbal and physical assault, especially if they lived in the countryside, where there were no hiding places, and much hinged on the protection of local notables. Peasants may have had resort to Jews to buy cattle, hops, timber and so forth (especially since Jews were allegedly generous with credit and payment by instalments), but the informal bonds of social intercourse were rapidly severed, with the political culture providing a pretext for the dishonouring of past debts.[44] Again, however, one should beware generalisation, since studies of Protestant Central Franconia, a hotbed of antisemitism, show rural Jews still going about their business and celebrating their observances down to 1938.[45] In sum, the evidence suggests that relatively small numbers of individuals overtly criticised these outrages against Jews, on a case-by-case basis; that a larger group were active in carrying them out; but that most Germans did not care for public disturbances, even if many of them agreed that there was a 'Jewish Question' requiring *legal* resolution. Disturbingly, this belief transcended whatever experience people actually had of Jews as individuals.[46]

The legal exclusion of Jewish people from the fabric of German society continued. *Ostjuden* and many political and 'racial' refugees living abroad were summarily denaturalised. In August 1934, the German Evangelical Church, whose national synod was dominated by German Christians, introduced an 'Aryan paragraph', affecting a handful of pastors of 'non-Aryan' descent.[47] In May 1935 a new Military Service Law, introducing conscription, made 'Aryan descent' mandatory for service in the armed forces, a blow to a people whose pride in patriotic service is commemorated on the gravestones of the main Jewish cemeteries, such as Weissensee in East Berlin, where one can see that someone's son had been a corporal or medical orderly in some snobby Prussian grenadier guards regiment.[48] Calls to alter fundamentally the legal status of Jews in Germany, reversing the achievements of emancipation, proliferated from early 1935, and were certainly monitored by Jews both in Germany and abroad.[49]

The idea that the Nazi government could go through bouts of inertia and indecision may be at odds with the external appearance of a purposeful, dynamic, self-styled movement, but one should bear in mind the conflicting forces which beset it. As we have seen, antisemitic agitation noticeably flared up in 1935. It was partly the product of intensified propaganda, partly something latent in some people that propaganda brought to the surface. Nazi activists, including some very close to Hitler, wanted clauses observed and promises fulfilled by a government that seemed to be drifting, and whose governing cadres presented a confused, corrupt and unedifying spectacle. By contrast, the population at large disliked the radical activism and hoped clear policies would deny the need for it. Hooliganism was also affecting Germany's foreign image and external trading interests. Either way, there was pressure on the government, temporarily distracted by other concerns, such as a massive inherited economic crisis, to do something on the 'Jewish Question'.

The opportunity to resolve these issues was seized, whether or not because of careful planning is the subject of continuing debate, at the September 1935 Party Rally in Nuremberg. On 18 August in Königsberg, Hitler spoke of the need to implement clauses 4 and 5 of the Party programme with a law regulating the status of Jews. Such a law, he said, was in preparation. A meeting at the Economics Ministry on 20 August attended by several ministers, Adolf Wagner and representatives of the Gestapo and SD was devoted to the domestic and foreign political ramifications of the 'Jewish Question', the resulting consensus being that a law should consign Jews to a lesser status, in which they would also allegedly be protected from terroristic violence.[50] Although the ensuing Citizenship Law and the Law for the Protection of German Blood and Honour (known as the Nuremberg Laws) failed to introduce much conceptual clarity, they did satisfy a conservative desire for legality and stability, while at the same time assuaging the radical Nazi thirst for revolutionary gestures. Hitler himself had his own agenda, namely to use the rally to 'bounce' a foot-dragging bureaucracy into line with his fundamental thinking. Moreover, having leant towards his conservative partners and the military in 1934, he compensated now by leaning towards the activists in his own party.[51] Under the first law, Jews forfeited German citizenship, becoming 'state subjects'. The second law prohibited marriage and sexual intercourse between 'Aryans' and Jews; the employment of female 'Aryan' servants under forty-five years of age in Jewish households; and finally the hoisting by Jews of either German flag. There were no longer exceptions for Jewish war veterans. The slightly quirky content of the second law reflected not only Hitler's bizarre obsessions but also the fact that flags had been in the news a lot (New York dockers had recently burned a swastika on the steamer *Bremen*), and a desire to impute sexual impropriety to Jews.

The variant draft texts of the laws were cobbled together by civil servants flown from Berlin at short notice, who then went back and forth through the crowded streets of Nuremberg soliciting the Führer's approval. We should not mistake the *ad hoc* way in which the laws were fabricated for an absence of will to legislate. Apparently a more hardline package was avoided because civil servants opposed extensive definitions of who was a Jew, and because the representative of the extreme Gerhard Wagner, the Reich Doctors' Leader, spent his time offsetting boredom by playing with a toy tank. Although Hitler eventually opted for a relatively moderate final text, option D, of the Protection law, he omitted the crucial line: 'This law applies only to full-blooded Jews', thus leaving unresolved the matter of whom these laws affected. Daily conclaves of ministerial and racial experts dragged on for weeks to resolve the question of who was a Jew, without which the law would still lack precision. The crux of the matter was whether these measures applied to 'half-Jews'. The Party wanted them categorised as Jews; the civil servants argued that this would give the Jews 200,000 new allies whose 'genetic substance' was 50 per cent 'Aryan'. Eventually, the first of thirteen supplementary decrees, published on 14 November 1935, declared that persons with three or four Jewish grandparents were full Jews; those with two 'Aryan' and two Jewish grandparents were 'half-Jews', considered Jewish only if they practised the Jewish faith, married a Jew or were the legitimate or illegitimate children of Jewish and 'Aryan' parents. The latter were designated *Geltungsjuden*, or those counted as Jews, to distinguish them from people with two Jewish grandparents but who did not meet any of these other four criteria and who were henceforth called *Mischlinge*. Only about 11 per cent of the latter category belonged to the Jewish religious community. Although rather a lot has been made of these people in modern scholarship, we should remember that only the mad categories of Nazi racism made them 'half-Jews', a designation they would most probably have rejected. Since blood was a treacherous guide in these questions, the legislators had to fall back inconsistently on religious criteria. Since state registry offices only covered the period since 1875, the regime relied upon ecclesiastical records to trace ancestry or conversions from Judaism to Christianity, essential to the identification of racial Jews living as 'non-Aryan' Christians. A large question mark hangs over all those clerics who supplied such information from their parish records.[52]

While the legislators determined who was a Jew, the German Supreme Court wrestled with the weighty problem of whether sexual intercourse meant coition, or included 'all forms of natural and unnatural sexual manipulations – that is, coition as well as all those sexual activities with a person of the opposite sex which are designed, in the manner in which they are performed, to serve in place of coition to satisfy the sex drive of at least one of the partners'. This meant that a Jewish man was jailed for two years by a Hamburg court for kissing someone, since in the course of his defence he allowed that, while his sex drive had been weakened by his war experiences, he sometimes ejaculated when embraced. Another Jewish man received two years after a routine visit to a masseuse was converted into a sexual encounter by the Gestapo who interrogated him. In 1939, a Jewish man was jailed for a month by a court in Frankfurt, the 'assault' consisting of having looked at a fifteen-year-old girl while walking at eleven o'clock in the morning in the street. The judgement read:

> The behaviour displayed by the accused had a clearly erotic basis and could only have had the purpose of effecting an approach to the girl who interested him. This approach failed to occur only because the witness refused to cooperate and summonsed the police to her aid. The behaviour of the Jewish defendant toward a German girl expressed disrespect and contempt for the witness, since the accused clearly assumed that he could succeed in his attempt to approach her through his conspicuous behaviour.... Even if the defendant pursued no further intentions with regard to the witness, his outward behaviour at least could not be interpreted otherwise.[53]

Popular reactions to the Nuremberg Laws varied. Hardline antisemites rejoiced that the state had responded concretely to their activism, retroactively legalising months of illegal violence. The laws proved that 'the state is still revolutionary', and that all they had to do was push the problem vigorously enough for the state to follow on with a solution. However, most people thought that the laws would stabilise the situation, confining the Jews to a second-class, semi-autonomous sphere, and that this would lance the boil of street violence. The abrogation of fundamental human rights does not seem to have been generally bothersome. Reports of hostility towards the laws were confined to the liberal bourgeoisie, a few Catholic enclaves, such as Aachen or Allenstein, and businessmen worried about foreign repercussions. Hitler appeared to couple these issues when he said to Party leaders 'that in accordance with these laws the Jews in Germany were being offered opportunities of living their own national life in all areas, as they had never been able to do in any other country. With a view to this the Führer reiterated his order to the Party to avoid all individual actions against Jews.'[54] These appreciably abated in most areas, although in a few cases antisemitic violence continued regardless. Reporting on this 'healing and useful deed', the German News Agency blithely claimed that the laws were simply acknowledging the recent declaration of the International Zionist Congress that 'the Jews are a separate people', blithely overlooking the fact that the majority of Jewish Germans were not Zionists.[55] Reacting manfully to this 'heavy blow', the Reichsvertretung, the Reich Representation of German Jews, hoped that the laws would 'create a basis on which a tolerable relationship becomes possible between the German and Jewish nations', a form of words indicative of the wedge the Nazis had driven between the concepts German and Jewish. Reflecting this, the Reichsvertretung itself was soon renamed Central Representation of Jews in Germany, rather than German Jews.[56] It is important to note that in Hitler's mind the Nuremberg Laws were conditional. In his speech at Nuremberg on 15 September, he construed the laws as a response to domestic and foreign Jewish agitation. The passive–aggressive words barely concealed a threat: 'The German Reich Government is guided by the hope of possibly being able to bring about, by means of a single secular measure, a framework within which the German *Volk* would be in a position to establish tolerable relations with the Jewish people. However, should this hope prove false and intra-German and Jewish agitation proceed on its course, a new evaluation of the situation would have to take place.'[57]

Successive decrees banned Jews from both public office and the legal profession. They also forfeited the uncertain protection of the law. In early 1936, a Jewish businessman contested the compulsory auctioning of his business, a penalty imposed by the tax authorities in Hessen for taxes owing from the years 1931–5. He claimed that the laws of the Third Reich had affected his income and hence his ability to pay. Rejecting his appeal, the court conceded that the plaintiff's income had declined because of laws designed 'to reduce the part played by racially alien members of the Reich in Germany's public life to an acceptable level. The decline in the debtor's income is therefore not a side-effect of a general trend, of which the debtor is an innocent victim and against which he should be protected, but rather a necessary manifestation of that process of healing sick elements.' In the same year, the highest court in Germany revived the medieval notion of civil death to annul retrospectively a contract between a film company and a Jewish director.[58] The rule of law, the barrier between civilised society and barbarism, no longer applied to this group of people, for whom the courts themselves became a Kafkaesque nightmare.

Stipulations against mixed relationships deeply hurt all concerned.[59] About one in ten Jews was married to a non-Jew, or, to put it another way, there were about thirty thousand intermarried couples in 1939. Before the Nuremberg Laws, marriage registrars were instructed to persuade such couples of the error of their ways, with rowdy demonstrations taking place during the ceremony itself to intimidate those who persisted to the registry office. Although the Nazis did not amend the marriage laws until June 1938, with the German partner's belated awareness of the 'Jewish Question' now becoming adequate grounds for divorce, manifold pressures were exerted on German–Jewish partnerships. Most obviously, laws disqualifying Jews from the civil service or the professions could result in financial pressures or fears about loss of status. Families in turn often split when a member decided to stick to his or her beloved, thus stigmatising the non-Jewish partner's relatives. Apart from the snideness of neighbours and strangers, people in such relationships also had to suffer interviews with the Gestapo, who combined threats with inducements to make the non-Jewish partner seek a divorce. It is worth noting that only 7 per cent of people in mixed marriages actually sought a divorce, and that the institution of marriage proved more resilient than Nazi attempts to subvert it.[60] Some of the 7 per cent who ditched their partners for career reasons will be discussed below.

Relations of a less intimate kind were also eroded by the general political climate, as the skeins that make up civilised society were brushed aside. Parallel with antisemitic legislation or dramatic episodes such as the boycott went the slow, steady process of informal ostracism to which Jewish people were subjected and which was personally deeply wounding. In 1933, Erich Leyens received a visit from his old friend Hermann van den Brück, whose brother had died next to Leyens at Verdun. They reminisced about old times, until Brück told Leyens that he felt compelled to join the Nazi Party for professional reasons, and 'could no longer see me; he could not even greet me in the street'.[61] Human spontaneity gave way to calculation. Imagine having friends who could only call at night. This was exactly what Victor Klemperer experienced when a former servant, who had to go because of the effects on her family of her employment in a Jewish household, wished to visit his wife on her birthday: 'She came late in the evening, all worked up. She had wanted to wait for complete darkness and slip in unnoticed, but there had still been someone or other on the street and she had been afraid. She did not realise how terribly it depressed us; her fear was undoubtedly the fear of all "national comrades".'[62]

Something as innocuous as a handshake between two acquaintances on the street became a matter for rapid calculation and moral choice.[63] A Jewish person might suddenly spot a Party lapel badge; the wearer would catch this slight hesitation and walk off. In a society where receiving people at home was not taken for granted, Jewish hosts found their guest lists depleted. A friend of Max Reiner's explained why he could no longer call: 'Look, if we visit you, we won't know who else we might meet there. It only takes one of your other guests to remark innocently that he was with us at your place, and then I'll lose my job. Whoever comes to our house knows from the outset that he must exercise due discretion.'[64] But it is also important to remember the acquaintances who became firm friends in adversity, such as the architect who visited Leyens to cheer him up and to get drunk, despite the risk of social ostracism for consorting with Jews.[65]

Situations deserving a minimum of civility, from servants and waiters in hotels or restaurants, became fraught with potential embarrassment. Having reserved a bed in a Stuttgart hotel, Leo Grünebaum was told on arrival that it had been taken by a customer who had decided to extend his stay. And, of course there were two big conferences in town. The hotelier nonetheless found Grünebaum a room elsewhere. Arriving at the second hotel at eleven at night, Grünebaum filled in the register, including the section on racial provenance. The desk clerk loudly announced to the entire lobby: 'Non-Aryans cannot stay here' and showed a red-faced Grünebaum the door.[66] Sometimes the unreflective, supposedly kind remark, such as 'If only they were all like you!' hurt as much as an open insult, since who in their right mind could wish to be seen as an exception to people generically stigmatised as criminals, Communists and swindlers? A sympathiser might denounce the Nazis as 'riffraff and crooks', but he took the precaution of closing the door to the outer office lest his secretary heard it. Imagine too the subjects that were passed over in silence when Jewish people met friends in public.[67]

Innocent occasions were permeated with hateful sentiments. In Singen, near Konstanz, the 1934 carnival included a float in the form of a railway carriage emblazoned with 'From Berlin to Palestine', from which leered members of the publicans' and small-bore rifle associations. In 1938 the carnival procession included children and their teachers wearing papier-mâché masks with big 'Jewish' noses and the slogan 'The last Lebanese Tyroleans clear out'. A year later, a float took the form of a giant crocodile, marked 'Der Judenfresser' (the Jew-gobbler), from whose jaws sweets were thrown to the crowds to cries of 'Grousers and whiners under the rolling mill'.[68] Everywhere they turned, Jews heard propaganda banging on about Jews. Max Reiner recalled, 'I couldn't pick up German newspapers any more. Jews. . . . Jews. . . . It seemed as if there were no other subjects. They exceeded themselves in insults, threats, ridicule. It wasn't just the news content of these articles which got on my nerves, for example reports that the Reich Minister of Post had removed all postal privileges from blind Jewish war veterans or that Jews in Magdeburg were no longer allowed to use the trams.'[69] Incivility came with a double government imprimatur: racist hatred of the Jews commingled with a gruff revolutionist contempt for the careful courtesies of the bourgeoisie, so that the bad manners of schoolchildren were interpreted as zeal.

Licensed discrimination and economic exclusion also impacted upon the most private sphere: the family. Children became non-persons at school, forced to sit through insulting antisemitic diatribes from their teachers, or publicly stigmatised as Jews. A child who was allowed to attend, but being 'non-Aryan' not permitted to sing, at an annual school festival, and who protested that she wished to sing for her mother, was told: 'I know that you have a mother too, but she is only a Jewish mother.'[70] As many refugees report, children could no longer afford to be children, effectively missing out on adolescence. As one refugee to Britain succinctly recalled: 'One thing is certain – you grow up overnight.'[71] Men whose role was defined by work and who were used to supporting their wives found themselves in the unaccustomed role of house-husbands: 'men without power and women without support'.[72] Women were ostracised from associations or the informal intercourse of cornershops, streets and neighbourhoods.

Those with young children saw child-care arrangements evaporate.[73] Down their husbands went, with former professionals or businessmen having to eke out a living as hawkers or pedlars. Large apartments with fashionable addresses were exchanged for more modest dwellings in poorer neighbourhoods; children used to sleeping alone were now huddled together; the familiar world their parents used to bestride with ease now seemed alien and implacable. Downwardly mobile people with financial worries they had never known before became tense and fractious as power and status within the family became confused. As husbands despaired and psychologically collapsed, women had to put on a brave face, and represent them to authority. What sort of inner calm did these people enjoy, glancing nervously at their pre-packed suitcases, or after a fruitless day spent waiting in line for a visa? The richness of human life was stripped down to basic survival as Jewish people groped for meaning in a world made senseless.

The political situation also affected relationships in the sense that some people made hard choices between their careers and relationships. This was especially the case with people whose personal lives were the subject of gossip or public speculation, notably actors and other famous personalities. This probably makes the following cases rather untypical. The actor Gustav Fröhlich and his Jewish wife Gitta Alpar were invited to a reception given by Goebbels. They sat at a table with Willy Fritsch and Hans Albers, the latter the highest-paid male movie star in Germany. Alpar ostentatiously remained seated, chatting to two other ladies, while everyone else rose to sing the Horst Wessel Lied. An officer and a lady came to the table saying 'Please come with us, Herr Goebbels would like to meet you,' adding 'Herr Fröhlich please,' and 'Not you!' to his wife. Fröhlich simply left her alone in the throng. She returned to Hungary shortly afterwards, where she bore Fröhlich a daughter and divorced him.

Albers himself faced the same problem, although he sought to resolve it in a less unpleasant way. Blond and blue-eyed with a long thin nose and jutting chin, Albers' face fitted Nazi physical ideals rather well, even if ubiquitous hats and a toupé were used to conceal increasing baldness. One problem had to be resolved if Albers was to continue as Germany's answer to Clark Gable. Since the 1920s he had been living with the actress Hansi Burg, daughter of the actor Eugen Burg, who had changed his name from Hirschburg. The precise nature of this relationship taxed several Nazi bureaucrats, all the way up to Hitler's private Chancellery, until in 1935 Albers wrote to

Goebbels: 'I have dissolved my personal relations with Frau Hansi Burg, in fulfilment of my duty to the National Socialist state and in acknowledgement of it. May I, esteemed Herr Reich Minister, moreover request that in view of the changed situation of the National Socialist state, you will extend to me the protection which it affords to its artists.' 'Naturally' Goebbels met him halfway. In reality, although Burg soon married the Norwegian actor Erich Blydt, she and Albers continued to meet in secret, for example in London in 1936. Pressure to terminate the relationship came in the form of being followed by the SD, while film companies were instructed not to negotiate further contracts with him. The relationship was duly terminated, since Albers had a lot to lose with fees of over seventy thousand Reichsmarks per motion picture. He went from strength to strength; Hansi Burg remained in England for the duration; Eugen Burg was murdered in Theresienstadt.[74] In 1945, Hansi Burg returned to Albers, ejecting his then girlfriend from their home, and providing the star with an unimpeachable alibi for the career he had made in the Third Reich.

The word 'indifference' crops up frequently in discussions of German popular responses to the persecution of the Jews. Although its German equivalent may not have the same apathetically neutral connotations, it does have the limited virtue of reminding us that ordinary Germans thought about subjects other than Jews, such as earning a living, educating or enjoying themselves, the diplomatic state of play and so forth. It may well have been the case that many people wearied of hearing the same splenetic slogans and simply filtered them out of their consciousness. However, the term hardly includes those Germans who actively involved themselves in persecuting other people. We must turn to the undergrowth where little folk made use of the Nazi regime to exercise illegal or legal power over others, activating mean-minded resentments in ways which did their fellow man or woman serious harm.

This was most pernicious where the law was being infringed by consenting adults in private or where obscure professional animosities were at work. In an August 1936 SPD report dealing with cases of 'racial miscegenation', mostly concerning couples who had lived together long before the Nuremberg Laws, the subject of blackmail reared its ugly head. In this case females were the blackmailers, since only Jewish men could be prosecuted for this offence. In Mannheim a woman was jailed for six months for trying to wring 500 Marks from her Jewish lover. In Aachen, a woman and two male accomplices were jailed for blackmail and entrapment. She had lured a Jew to her apartment, who was told to hand over 500 Marks to her two menacing associates. The Jewish man was subsequently jailed for five months for 'race defilement'.[75] Young serving girls compulsorily dismissed from Jewish households were quizzed suggestively by the Gestapo, even if their former employer happened to be an octogenarian. The scope for malice in this climate was immense if the servant had departed on bad terms, or if she happened to have a Nazi on the make as a lover.

After the war, the view that the Gestapo had been omnipotent was a convenient alibi for many Germans of various political persuasions. Although the Gestapo deliberately affected an air of sinister omniscience, like most police forces, it was reliant upon co-operation from individual members of the public, whether as volunteer part-time agents or as *ad hoc* informers. Recent detailed studies of Düsseldorf, Lippe, Saarbrücken and Würzburg have greatly enriched understanding of this social aspect of policing, although the fact that the Gestapo had many civilian helpers does not automatically undermine the received view that this was a police state so much as redefine it. What should not be entirely overlooked is that the combination of a police force liberated from all legal restraints and licensed denunciation meant a climate of fear. Victor Klemperer caught this well in his diaries when he wrote:

> But everyone, literally everyone cringes with fear. No letter, no telephone conversation, no word on the street is safe any more. Everyone fears the next person may be an informer. Frau Krappmann warns against the all too National Socialist Frau Lehmann – and Frau Lehmann tells us with great bitterness that her brother has been sentenced to one year in prison because he lent a 'real Communist' a copy of the Red Flag, but the 'real Communist' had been an informer.[76]

Those who experienced this fear were not troubled by academic concerns with how many men sat in any Gestapo regional office. It has been estimated that there was approximately one Gestapo officer per ten thousand people, officers charged with a bewildering array of tasks. For example, in 1937, the Düsseldorf district Gestapo headquarters had a staff of 291 persons, policing a population of four million. Forty-nine of these people were administrators.[77] These figures seem even less impressive, when distributed across sub-stations, juxtaposed against their aggregate populations. One hundred and twenty-eight officers covered Düsseldorf itself (population half a million);

forty-three covered Essen (population 650,000); forty-three Wuppertal, and twenty-eight Duisburg (each with over 400,000 people). In the Würzburg office, twenty-eight men were responsible for all Lower Franconia. Saarbrücken was more generously provided for, but even here many of the 113 employees were office workers, with massive fields of activity dumped on an individual's desk. Of course, while these facts are interesting, none of this was either known or relevant to those contemporaries who believed that there was a secret police-man lurking behind every corner. Perception was all.

But the Gestapo are not our main concern. Often they were desk-bound conduits for information supplied by the public at large rather than a proactive, investigative force. Again, that reality was wholly concealed from the population. In Würzburg, for example, 57 per cent of cases of 'race pollution' were initiated by ordinary citizens, with only one case resulting from Gestapo investigations. No law obliged anyone to denounce fellow citizens to the authorities; indeed in May 1933 the regime made the penalties for malicious denunciation more stringent. In that month, Hitler himself admitted to Minister of Justice Gürtner that 'we are living in a sea of denunciations and human evil ... so that someone denounces another and simultaneously puts himself forward as his successor'.[78] The Nazis undoubtedly encouraged denunciation, but paradoxically they did not care much for the denouncers themselves, and indeed were periodically exercised that they might unleash an uncontrollable flood.[79]

Who denounced whom, and why did they do it? Denunciations mainly emanated from the lower end of the social scale, settling horizontal scores and vertical resentments.[80] The typical culprit was a servant, worker, artisan or salaried employee, with both sexes evenly distributed. Gentlefolk and the nobility had other ways of expressing social power, moved in a world of common values and trust among equals, tended to be regarded deferentially by a lower-class police force, and could activate batteries of professionals and social contacts in their own defence. These are and were observable social facts. The motives of denouncers were myriad, although certain patterns emerge. Most of them were ordinary citizens, not Nazi enthusiasts. A certain self-important type, who liked gossip, snooping and flitting around authority figured frequently, tarting up malice in the guise of bounden duty to the national collective. So did individuals with deep-seated personal grudges and resentments, who were impervious to stigmas still adhering to such ungentlemanly conduct. Merely contemptible in normal democratic conditions, such individuals become lethal in totalitarian dictatorships such as Nazi Germany and the Soviet Union.[81]

Denunciation was also contagious, as the Gestapo itself noted in August 1935 when it described a 'race defilement psychosis'. Parties of schoolgirls scoured the quarters of *Ostjuden* seeking cases of open 'miscegenation', while Nazi Women's Organisation members patrolled the streets armed with cameras to record the evidence.[82] A farmer who would not give his men time off to hear a Hitler speech, and who disciplined a labourer who went, was denounced by this individual for selling cattle to Jews.[83] A hairdresser hotfooted it to the Gestapo on learning from an SA man that the latter had once caught a Jewish cattle trader and a younger 'Aryan' girl *in flagrante delicto* behind the locked door of a room in an inn. The man was sentenced to fifteen months' imprisonment after the girl was persuaded to swop the consensual version of the story for one based on harassment. In July 1938, 'a national comrade' wrote to Austrian Gauleiter Bürckel reporting that a Jewish cognac merchant was secretly trading under an 'Aryan' flag of convenience in the sense that he had leased out his own store to a non-Jewish Viennese. The latter even had the temerity to display the 'Hackenkreuz' (*sic*). The writer was sure that the Gauleiter would soon rectify this outrageous act of deception.[84]

The pernicious consequences of state-sponsored antisemitism, bureaucratic chicanery and the severing of informal social ties can be glimpsed in the diaries of individuals. To call them 'victims' is to practise a well-intentioned form of dehumanisation. Actually, most of these people were considerably more interesting than the 'perpetrators' upon whose characters and psychology so much attention is lavished. One would want to know them. The following details come from a German septuagenarian's account of the years 1935-9.[85]

Albert Herzfeld (1865-1941) was the son of a major textile manufacturer in Düsseldorf, whose factory complex next to the Rhine employed over five hundred people. Albert's uncle Gustav was a noted local philanthropist, who left 100,000 Marks to the city to provide holiday camps for indigent local children. A baptised Protestant, Albert attended the Hohenzollerngymnasium, volunteering for military service in 1886. After a year as an intern in Manchester, he decided that business was not for him, opting instead for the life of a gentleman painter. He studied under Fritz Reusing and Lovis Corinth, specialising in landscapes and portraits of an unremarkable kind. In 1914, he volunteered for active service eight times – notwithstanding that he was forty-eight with a wife and two children. From 1915 he served as a lieutenant, winning the Iron Cross Second Class. After the war, Herzfeld returned to the civilised, comfortable life of the upper-middle class in the delightful family townhouse on the corner of Feldstrasse, with servants, four thousand books, paintings by Liebermann, Rosenthal china and racks of pipes. An attractive, gregarious and intellectually curious man, Herzfeld belonged to a guards regiment veterans' association; historical, philatelic and scientific societies; and an artists' club. He turned out dressed as Napoleon at costume balls. In other words this was a haut-bourgeois life, based on good manners, an appreciation of the finer things in life, intellectual curiosity, ritual and social responsibility towards the less advantaged – a life considerably more substantial than that of an Eichmann or a Heydrich.

The diaries are measured, unhysterical descriptions of the major and minor slights experienced by this astute conservative patriot at the hands of what he variously called 'barbarians', the 'commonest mob' or 'the rabble'. A schoolmaster tenant quit his house, because as a civil servant he could not lodge with 'non-Aryans'.[86] Domestic servants were a perennial problem. Hedwig the maid had to go, because 'non-Aryans' could not employ female servants under forty-five. She left tearfully for a post Herzfeld arranged with a family friend, for he believed in looking after the little people. One of Hedwig's many replacements, a Frau Peck, lied about her age – although she looked fifty, she was in fact forty-four – and hence could not work for a Jew. Ironies and slights multiplied, with what affected him directly reflected in the public space he inhabited. Herzfeld received an honorary medal as a former front veteran in the same week that the Nuremberg Laws rescinded his civic rights. A plaque commemorating his uncle's gift to the city of a pretty statue of a girl throwing a ball was removed from its plinth.[87] Mendelssohnstrasse became Hans-Schlemmstrasse at about the same time.[88] His artists' club sent him seventieth-birthday congratulations and then expelled him eight weeks later. The department store Tietz became the Kaufhaus des Westens; offensive antisemitic placards appeared in display boxes situated outside the synagogue. The swimming pool in the Kaiser-Wilhelm Park bore a sign saying 'Jews are not permitted entry'. A plaque marking Heinrich Heine's house vanished, along with a statue of Mendelssohn. For thirty-five years Herzfeld had patronised the Muschelhaus Reusch for a lunchtime bowl of mussels; now it bore the sign 'Jews unwelcome'. Soon, the same sign stood over the Rheinterrassenrestaurant too. While every 'Lump und Zuchthausler' ('prole and convict') could frequent the spas of Wiesbaden, evidently respectable Jewish people could not. This really rankled, as well it might.[89]

These measures did not exhaust the degradation, or better 'dishonouring', to use a term that retains the tones of an old soldier, which Herzfeld experienced. The subject of Jews appeared again and again in the newspapers or speeches. Apparently the art market was controlled by Jews. Russian Bolsheviks and Spanish Republicans were all Jews. German Communists were all Jews, even though this did not apply to Liebknecht or Thälmann. 'The Jews' failed to stop German football fans enjoying themselves when England played Germany at Tottenham in December 1935, although the enjoyment was short lived since England won 3–0. Herzfeld sometimes read something now publicly called 'the Jewish Manchester Guardian'. When the Mayor of New York, La Guardia, attacked German policy – Herzfeld considered the attack 'tactless and stupid' – *Der Angriff* immediately ran a piece claiming that Benjamin Franklin was an antisemite. As Herzfeld remarked: 'Maintain something boldly enough and some mud will stick' ('Kuhn behaupten, es haftet immer etwas').[90] Not without humour, Herzfeld wrote that if Jews were prohibited from contributing to 'German culture', 'does this mean that I must paint expressionistically?' No, for in 1938 he was banned from painting altogether, even though he had not bothered with it for some years. Were the twelve thousand dead Jewish servicemen going to be expelled from 'Valhalla'? Impossible, but one could get at the dead by banning death notices of Jews from the newspapers, in breach of the ancient maxim 'De mortuis nihil nisi bene' (never speak ill of the dead).[91]

An old man, with a sick wife, his insomnia alternated with terrible nightmares and increasing feelings of metaphysical doom. He had to take sugarlumps laced with droplets of nitroglycerine just to walk or attempt stairs without straining his weak heart. He predicted that those Jews who could not flee would 'be driven into ghettos' or 'struck down dead' or forced to wear yellow hats and badges.[92] A lifelong friend threw himself out of a third-floor window because he could not bear the dismissal of his daughter from a teaching post. Suicides in Austria were especially frequent. Having already been dismissed from a career in the judicial civil service, Herzfeld's daughter was now compulsorily fired by a second employer, with tearful scenes as she bade farewell to her colleagues and an employer who had frequently entertained her at his home.

The Nazi bureaucracy finally got at Herzfeld in earnest at precisely 2.50 p.m. on 29 November 1937 when, as he was returning from a convalescent trip to Italy, a frontier guard confiscated his passport on the train, promising that it would be returned in Düsseldorf. By mid-January 1938 it had not arrived. After repeated letters, in February he was informed by the Düsseldorf police that 'inquiries were still being made' and that 'therefore further requests are pointless'. Someone crossed out the rider 'and will no longer be answered'. In May he was summoned to Room 150 in the police headquarters where an official quizzed him about why he wanted to travel. Giving 'doctor's orders' as the reason, he was told he could apply for his passport four to six weeks before his journey provided he supplied medical evidence that it was necessary. Of course, one needed a passport four months before travelling since otherwise one could not obtain foreign currency.[93]

By now, Herzfeld was anticipating the return of 'medieval torments and slights which we must bear such as a yellow cap or a yellow mark on our clothes with us all being forced to live in a closed ghetto'. In October 1938 somebody daubed 'the Jew remains a Jew' on his portals. He did not dare to post a letter of complaint to the police. On the night of 9/10 November 1938, a mob stormed the house of a neighbour, stabbing the man nine times. Elsewhere, mobs broke into his cousin Robert's house, smashing a Sèvres mirror and using chair-legs to puncture and rip paintings, for such people hated high culture and resented those who possess its products. Jewish doctors watched impotently as their instruments were destroyed, while furniture and pianos were hurled from upper-storey windows. Herzfeld was convinced that the culprits were former Communists whose resentment towards the well-to-do was a sort of transferable skill they took with them into the stormtroopers, for there is nothing like the zeal of the recent convert.[94] A different ideological rhetoric may have been involved, but the pathologies were the same.

There were some consolations in this extended litany of inhumanity. Herzfeld felt that 'the broad public is absolutely not antisemitic' and repeatedly noted that his friends stayed loyal. A Protestant pastor in Brunswick was jailed for six months for urging his flock not to join in the clamour against the Jews. Even such tenuous acquaintances as General Zedlitz-Lippe went out of their way to call, demonstrating solidarity. Nor did Herzfeld allow Nazi politics to spoil a friendship, sending a rather arch poem to a friend who had also reached seventy:

> In den Kreis der Gratulanten
> Der Freunde, Nichten, Vettern, Tanten,
> Die heut' den Weg nach Erckrat wahlen
> Möcht der Nichtarier auch nicht fehlen!
> . . .
> Im Streit der eine mit den andern,
> Doch nur in den polit'schen Fragen,
> ansonsten wir uns gut vertragen.
> Drum Sie's wohl auch nicht sehr geniert,
> Wenn der alte Freund heut' gratuliert
> Und Ihnen wünscht das Allerbeste
> Zu Ihrem siebzigsten Wiegenfeste.
> Als, Nichtarisch' ich den Deutschen Gruss
> Bei Ihnen mir verkneifen muss.
> Doch, jüdischschlau' vermeid ich' Dilemma
> Und rufe: Heil Dir, Tante Emma![95]

After the pogrom, Herzfeld wrote that four-fifths of Party members he knew disapproved of what had happened and that the majority of the German population regarded the events with disgust. But the slights kept coming. In December all Jews were required to surrender weapons. He had to hand over his officer's sabre. In January 1939 he had to sign himself Albert Israel, while his wife became Else Sara. In the same month he was voted out of the philatelic club he had belonged to for twenty years.[96] The couple were ordered to register all precious metals and stones, but no officials could tell them quite how this should be done. The diaries break off on 24 February 1939. Herzfeld's daughter was deported to Minsk on 8 January 1941, where she was killed. Herzfeld and his wife were sent to Theresienstadt in January 1942, where he died a year later. His wife died in Auschwitz-Birkenau some time after her transfer there in August 1944. The contents of their home disappeared.

We have advanced into the era of total expropriation and nation-wide murderous violence, although it should be stressed that both had been taking place for years on a local, individual scale. Expropriation, including the more or less coercive liquidation or sale of Jewish businesses, began in 1933 and was virtually complete by 1937–8.[97] In contrast to the exclusion of Jewish civil servants, until 1938 Entjudung (dejudaisation) had no legal basis, although this did not prove unduly troublesome to either businessmen or the legal authorities. In 1933 there were about one hundred thousand Jewish concerns in Germany, the majority being middling or small enterprises, with another fifty thousand one-man businesses, and a further ten thousand artisan workshops.[98] By April 1938, some 60 per cent had passed into other hands, leaving about forty thousand firms still in existence. Broadly speaking, department stores, major industrial concerns and merchant banks enjoyed a greater respite than smaller businesses, even though in the case of department stores we are dealing with a special hate-object of small business supporters of the Nazi movement. Hitler himself approved a consolidation loan to the Jewish brothers Tietz, owners of the stores soon to become Hertie AG. This paradoxical disparity between the treatment of large and small enterprises was because the unemployment consequences were especially grave when a big firm closed, but also because the anti-capitalism of SA hooligans focused more easily on small shops than on boardrooms. Thus M. M. War-burg, the Hamburg-based merchant bank, was not 'aryanised' until 1938, long after many small Jewish businessmen had been ruined or had emigrated.

The methods used to close a business or to effect a change of ownership included SA boycotts; the withdrawal of credit facilities, official contracts or a place at a trade fair; worrisome indirect pressure from fiscal and foreign currency offices, health, hygiene and labour agencies or indeed the Gestapo; as well as attempts to suborn the workforce, or hints to customers and suppliers that they should take their business elsewhere. In Singen, recipients of marriage loan vouchers for consumer durables were told not to redeem them in Jewish-owned stores.[99] In Parchim in Mecklenburg, the mayor specifically instructed those in receipt of public welfare or pensions that they were forbidden to patronise Jewish shops, unless they wished to lose this support.[100] Antisemitic businessmen formed 'Aryan' sectoral associations, such as the Working Party of Aryan-German Clothing Manufacturers, whose objective was to short-circuit Jewish manufacturers, suppliers and outlets in the garment industry. Jewish businessmen were expelled from commercial associations, forfeiting all the corresponding connections. Thus the Jewish tugboat owner Sylvius Schalscha was forced at gunpoint to resign as chairman of the Oder Shippers Association, while being simultaneously excluded from the Breslau Chamber of Commerce.[101] Firms dependent upon public contracts, such as the construction business Johannes Jeserich AG in Berlin, were 'cleansed' of Jewish directors, and through pressure from the State Commissar for Building in Berlin, who refused to award Jeserich AG road-building contracts unless the Jews were expelled.[102] Both the Nazi Factory Cell Organisation and the German Labour Front used their politico-industrial muscle to force out Jewish managers and directors, finally doling out stickers proclaiming 'German Business' when the firms were 'Jewish' no longer. The Nazi retailers association, NS-Hago, could obviously exert enormous pressure on, for example, a Jewish porcelain manufacturer which was dependent upon them for retail outlets. District Economic advisers (*Gauwirtschaftsführer*) monitored Jewish businesses and established a creeping control over those taking them over. Spotting a gap in the market, a parasitic stratum of advisers, liquidators, middlemen and trustees developed, specialising in identifying, closing, taking over or asset-stripping Jewish businesses. Obviously, German businessmen were to the fore in taking over Jewish competitors, often at knockdown prices. In Nuremberg the presence of Streicher ensured that 'aryanisation' was especially vicious, with Jews disappearing from the bicycle, hops and toy trades. Jews were offered 10 per cent of the value of their businesses or property on the ground that they had allegedly taken advantage of the period of inflation to purchase at artificially low values. Individuals were sometimes beaten until they signed the documentation surrendering their hard-earned assets and possessions. In Nuremberg these included luxury motorcars, which Party members bought at bargain-basement prices, with a Daimler-Benz worth 9,600 Reichsmarks going for 100 Reichsmarks.[103] This was the grubby, greedy reality behind the rhetoric of returning 'ill-gotten' gains to the national community.

This bald description does not do justice to the Machiavellian unscrupulousness deployed against Jewish businessmen. Every Party extortioner or jobsworth saw his chance to profit from someone's misfortune. Writing to SD chief Heydrich in July 1933, a senior Nazi registered his keen distaste for what was going on:

One method is apparently to approach Jewish firms with an offer to help them as party members by joining their board of directors, administrative board, executive board or in some other 'advisory' capacity, naturally in return for a fee. It is suggested that any difficulties arising could then easily be cleared up as a result of existing close ties and cooperation with the party and government administration. Once the ties to the Jewish firm have been firmly established and people have managed in some way to 'get inside', then difficulties of a personal or political nature are soon created for the Jewish owner. One wishes to help as a friend of the firm, but the situation, it is alleged, appears very serious, since it is known that the matter is already being looked into at a high level. During the next phase, the Jewish owner or owners are arrested by senior-level officials, but one goes to great lengths to aid them after their arrest. In the meantime, the agent for sale or transfer of the properties makes his appearance. After release – generally the person is not held in custody longer than three days – the Jewish proprietor or proprietors are informed what great efforts were made to help get them released. Without the personal assistance, without the aid of the office of Gauleiter, where one has excellent connections, the Jew(s) in question would undoubtedly have been placed in a concentration camp. Thus, it is wise for the Jew to show his gratitude to his helper or to the district office in a concrete manner – i.e. to pay. This formula can be played out in a great many different variations based on the same principle.[104]

Major banks were involved in 'aryanisation' in many ways: as victims in the sense that their Jewish directors and employees were dismissed on racial grounds too; as a preferred port of call for Jewish bankers and businessmen who had to choose between liquidation by reputable or disreputable partners, a choice which meant leaving Germany either with something or with nothing; and as culpably involved parties, in the sense of affording would-be 'aryanisers' the credit lines needed to buy out Jewish businesses or as predators in their own right.

One example of a major 'aryanisation' deserves detailed discussion, because it demonstrates how unscrupulous businessmen could deploy the Nazi judicial and police apparatus for commercial ends, and the fluid boundaries between the boardroom and the SA or Gestapo thugs. The Engelhardt Brewery in Berlin (whose product is called 'Schultheiss' today) was the second largest brewing concern in Germany, with regional affiliates such as Hofbrau in Bavaria, Dormunder Ritterbrauerei in the Ruhr, and Winterhuder in Hamburg. Its general director and majority shareholder was the sixty-four-year-old Ignatz Nacher, a Jewish entrepreneur and pioneer of non-alcoholic malt beer favoured by pregnant women, as well as pasteurised beer and refundable bottles. Nacher seems to have been a generous man. His philanthropic activities included 150,000 Reichsmarks for a fund to support widows and orphans of his employees; 300,000 Reichsmarks for the Olga and Ignatz Old People's Home in Gleiwitz; and 50,000 Reichsmarks for a student hostel in Charlottenburg. In 1929, Nacher did something he would live to regret. He authorised his then managing director, Richard Köster, to sell off an office block on Alexanderplatz to a municipal property company for nearly nine million Marks. The site was needed to reduce traffic congestion and for an underground station. The chairman of the property firm then requested, and received, from Nacher 120,000 Marks, as a donation to unspecified political party funds. Köster authorised this last dubious transaction. Exercised by the thought of 'Jewish' beer going down Nazi gullets, in May 1933 the Nazi journalist and newly appointed city commissar Julius Lippert summoned Nacher for an interview, one of several he had with prominent Jewish businessmen, with a revolver lying menacingly on his desk. The shady 1929 political payment was dredged up, with a little help from Köster, whom Nacher had downgraded to a post in Halle, as evidence of an attempt to ramp the selling price of the office block artificially. Nacher was persuaded to 'compensate' Lippert, representing Berlin, with two and a half million Marks in Engelhardt shares. He was told that the firm had to pass into 'Aryan' hands, and was duly edged aside on an illegally reconstituted company board. Köster was brought back, and two representatives of the Dresdner Bank (who held 23 per cent of the shares) were installed on the new board. One of the gentlemen from the Dresdner Bank vowed that Nacher 'would leave the country with a beggar's staff', instigating legal proceedings against him for financial irregularities.[105]

Charged with fraud, Nacher was arrested, although the court actually found that the price he had received for the offices was too low rather than extortionate. Proceedings were postponed to allow the five agencies investigating Nacher to get their stories right. The annual shareholders' meeting in February took place in an atmosphere of intimidation, with SA toughs handing out free beer and acting as stewards. Nacher, who had had a nervous breakdown, allowed a friend and academic economist at the Technical University, Waldemar Koch, to act as his plenipotentiary and speak on his behalf. Koch was assaulted, narrowly avoiding defenestration, when he spoke warmly of Nacher. The men from the Dresdner Bank next demanded restitution of the two and a half million Marks Nacher had given Lippert, abrogating Nacher's pension contract on the grounds of mismanagement of company affairs. Koch was also made to pay for his moment of civil courage and decency. The Dresdner Bank duo consulted the Criminal Police, who then wrote to the Rector of the Technische

Hochschule, indicating that Koch should not have an academic post, and that his wife was Jewish. He was sacked and placed in protective custody. Nacher, who had been sentenced in the interim to a fine and four months' imprisonment for irregularities, took himself off to Munich pending his appeal. He was not a well man.

There he was visited by a merchant banker called Georg Eiden-schink, who expressed a desire to buy the entire Engelhardt breweries, and who parted with heavy hints about his cordial relations with Himmler and Hitler. He helped the ensuing negotiations along by having Nacher arrested and shipped from Munich to Gestapo head-quarters on the Alexanderplatz, near the office block Nacher probably wished he had never clapped eyes on. His defence lawyer next appeared, with a notary. Nacher's release was conditional upon turn-ing over his residual share in the brewery to the lawyer, who sold them on to the Dresdner Bank, for they too were not going to pass on an opportunity to kick a man when he was down. A timely story leaked to the press helped the share price become a bargain.

Although Nacher had been ousted, his troubles were not over. In his cell he was visited by Hans Rattenhüber, a Munich SS officer (who as one of Hitler's bodyguards would eventually tip petrol over his Führer's corpse) and a cousin of Eidenschink. Although Eidenschink was too cash-weak to take on the Dresdner Bank, he was man enough to bully an ageing diabetic locked up in a Gestapo cell. Nacher sold Eidenschink the Bavarian affiliates, and paid him substantial sums for the inconvenience the latter had allegedly suffered in his abortive takeover bid for the whole firm. Rattenhüber tossed Nacher a phial of insulin as he left the cell. Eidenschink tried it on with the Dresdner Bank over the main Engelhardt Brewery, but the sums the bank was prepared to pay into court were astronomic, and a summons to the Gestapo it arranged put the wind up him.[106] Lippert sold the bank his two and a half million shares in return for a stretch of parkland they had been given by a debtor, HRH Prince Friedrich Leopold Prince of Prussia, which they 'presented' to the city. Lippert converted a hunting lodge there into a fine house. The men from the Dresdner Bank moved up the hierarchy, notwithstanding in Hilar Giebel's case the fact that he was married to a Jewish woman. Ignatz Nacher was eventually allowed to emigrate in November 1938, but not before paying a total of 1,796,906 Marks in atonement and exit 'taxes' to the Reich for the privilege of doing so. He died, as predicted, 'with a beggar's staff', in Switzerland on 15 September 1939.[107]

Legalised discrimination, mob violence and the 'dejudaisation' of the German economy were all ultimately designed to force Jewish people to emigrate – thus, it was felt, exporting antisemitism. Hitler did not care how or where they went, keeping his counsel on more radical options, including homicidal possibilities, latent in his personal fantasy world.[108] In 1933, about half a million Jews lived in Germany, with nearly two hundred thousand more in Austria, which in March 1938 became part of the German Reich. The crucial concern, however, was how to eject the Jews at no cost to the nation's finances – that is, how to strip these people of their capital before they left, while knowing full well that foreign countries would not look kindly upon impoverished would-be immigrants. To square this difficult circle, one needed people of intelligence, people who could sit down with foreign dignitaries, and indeed – overcoming their distaste – with Jews, not semi-literate bruisers.

To answer the 'who' question, we must make a brief foray into the corridors marked by bureaucratic acronyms, where persecution was carried out to the sound of clacking typewriters and shuffling index cards, rather than with the thud of boots into groin or faces – although these could be arranged quite easily.

Apart from the Jewish experts in the Gestapo department II 1 B 2, one agency combined dissimulation, efficiency and fertility with unflinching ideological conviction. We saw in an earlier chapter how the SS Sicherheitsdienst (SD) began as an internal security service before branching out into the monitoring of domestic (Amt II) and foreign (Amt III) ideological opponents. From 1935, Department II-112 was dedicated to monitoring Jewish activities. The Department had three sub-sections, for assimilated, Orthodox and Zionist organisations, the last being the speciality of the young Adolf Eichmann, a recruit from the Viennese Vacuum Oil Company. In 1937, Amt II-1 received a new chief, Professor Albert Six, while II-112 was put under the equally keen Dieter Wisliceny, the unemployed son of a penniless Silesian landowner. Theo Dannecker, who at seventeen had tried and failed to run the family laundry business, took over the field of assimilated Jewry. Virtually all of these men were born between 1905 and 1913, and shared backgrounds scarred by the Depression, or careers blighted by their own inadequacy or by the stridency of their politics.[109]

Their mission, there was even a 'statement', changed from monitoring membership of Jewish organisations to an activist role in ousting

Jews from the economy and promoting emigration. To that end, Wisliceny recommended 'smashing assimilationist organisations', while 'cleverly promoting Zionism', partly to divide the Jewish community against itself. They started to think on an international scale, collecting data on Jewish organisations around the world, and ordering summer kit for trips to their antisemitic friend the Grand Mufti of Jerusalem. Co-operation with the policemen of the Gestapo, who had powers of arrest and search, was running smoothly before they were fused in the Reich Main Security Office in September 1939.[110]

These young ideologues were not like the rheumy-eyed vandals of the SA, although one would not care to overrate their civility. They were encouraged to attend evening classes and to pick up a smattering of Hebrew. Instead of daubing slogans on windows, these young men wrote essays entitled 'How I envisage the solution of the Jewish Question' or 'A report on Jews in the cattle trade, with your own suggestions on how to rectify this evil'. They were encouraged to show the maximum initiative in identifying and solving problems, an approach not easily reconciled with the idea of them robotically carrying out orders. As we shall see, many of the problems they solved were of their own making, an almost ineluctable by-product of the requirement to report on their own activities every fourteen days. In 1934, Heydrich himself spelled out the ways in which his men were to approach the 'Jewish Question', employing a striking analogy, and discounting world opinion long before this is conventionally said to have been the case:

> The Jews' possibilities for living are to be curtailed, and not simply in an economic sense. Germany must be for them a country without a future, in which the residual older generation can certainly die, but in which the young cannot live, so that the stimulus to emigrate remains acute. The methods of 'rowdy antisemitism' are to be rejected. One does not fight rats with a revolver, but rather with poison and gas. Foreign political damage has no relationship to local success.[111]

It was not quite true that the SD renounced antisemitic hooliganism, of the sort which occurred in Berlin's main shopping thoroughfare in 1935. In a lengthy memorandum on the 'Jewish Question', probably written by Eichmann in 1937, the usefulness of such riots in spreading existential insecurity among the Jews was explicitly recognised. Interestingly, its author included the comment 'despite this method being illegal'.[112]

One of the main tasks of these young men was to identify a suitable overseas destination for Germany's Jews. It is worth noting that they thought Nazi antisemitic propaganda had failed, and that important sections of the German population, notably the former left, rural Catholics and landowners and army officers, were either explicitly sympathetic to Jews or continued business dealings with them.[113] Their minds turned to suitable destinations. They encouraged Jewish emigration to Palestine, until the Foreign Ministry, and the British government, took fright at the prospect of alienating the Arab world. Other destinations were either closing off (Brazil and South Africa in 1937, Italy in 1938) or, like the USA, had strict quotas for emigrants, which German Jews quickly exceeded. After surveying various options, the SD experts decided that Colombia, Ecuador and Venezuela were suitably impoverished and unlikely to cause political trouble.

SD schemes for Jewish emigration ran parallel with more high-level efforts to deal with what was becoming an international refugee problem. In July 1938, on the initiative of President Roosevelt, representatives of thirty-two nations met in the Hôtel Royal in Evian-les-Bains to find a solution to these problems. Nervous of the Germans, the Swiss had insisted that the conference meet on the French side of Lake Geneva. The delegates spent their time chronicling domestic woes in order to prove that there was no room at the inn. The Americans ruled out emigration quotas, and the British Palestine, as legitimate subjects for discussion. Only a blunt-speaking Australian delegate dropped talk of 'refugees' and spoke explicitly of a different 'race'. Only a representative of Rafael Trujillo in the Dominican Republic offered to take Jews, as part of a corrupt scam to settle government land cheaply. Nobody condemned the government responsible for the 'refugee' problem. The one minor achievement of the conference was the creation of an Intergovernmental Committee under George Rublee, whose brief was to find a way for half a million people to leave Germany while not exceeding immigrant quotas in the host states.

In December 1938, Hjalmar Schacht was sent by Hitler to negotiate with Rublee in London, armed with a scheme to allow an advance guard of one hundred and fifty thousand able-bodied Jews to depart over three years, who would then subsidise the emigration of a further quarter of a million Jewish poor. The Evian states should foot the bill, since Germany regarded the estimated six billion Marks assets owned by the Jews as her own. Twenty-five per cent of this figure would merely be held in trust, to be paid out as and when boycotts on

German exports were lifted. Jews abroad – forced to act in the Nazi image of 'world Jewry' – had to come up with a parallel sum, to pay for travel and settlement, a loan which was to be repaid in the form of purchases of German goods from the trust held in Germany. The remaining 75 per cent of Jewish capital would accrue to the German Reich, in so far as it was not needed to support the residual Jewish population there. Given the breathtaking cynicism of these proposals, and the evident indisposition of the Evian states either to offend the German government or to take Jewish refugees, talks not surprisingly petered out.[114] Increasingly desperate people undertook dangerous journeys across Siberia to war-torn Shanghai or over the oceans in rusting ships to an uncertain refuge in Cuba, Mexico or Palestine. The British permitted children and female domestic servants to enter to cover a shortfall in middle-class households, while conniving with the Arabs to prevent the establishment of a Jewish national homeland in Palestine.

As the young SD men realised, emigration had other predetermined limits. Although the wealthy, children and young able-bodied men were leaving in large numbers, elderly people, women and the poor were simply migrating internally, from vulnerable exclaves in the country and small towns to the relative anonymity of the major cities. This problem, of the Nazis' making, was compounded in March 1938 when the Anschluss with Austria brought a further 195,000 Jews into the Greater Reich, of whom 170,000 lived in Vienna, the world's sixth largest urban Jewish population.

It would be difficult to overrate the Anschluss in terms of its radicalising effect on Nazi antisemitic policy, for, like returned expatriates, the ferocity of the Austrian Germans often outdid the genuine northern article. Most obviously, the Anschluss meant that the Nazis were back to square one in the sense of gaining more Jews than they had managed to force to emigrate from Germany between 1933 and March 1938.[115] With unemployment running at 35 per cent in 1937, or 670,000 people, the former Austrian Republic was still in the depths of a depression, just when Germany had recently recovered from one. Any structural fusion of the two economies would have to stabilise Austria's without damaging Germany's.[116] There was also a long history of antisemitism in Austria, occasionally manifest in political parties, and frequently fanned by the Roman Catholic Church.[117] These things came together.

The erstwhile illegal Austrian Nazis were so appetent, and Viennese antisemitism so frenzied, that both public order and the smooth transfer to official hands of the loot were threatened. Touring Austria in 1934, the president of the British Board of Deputies Neville Laski concluded that:

> The Austrian people are poor. The Austrian professional classes are very depressed. The young people of the lower middle classes who seek professional appointments are like the young Nazis – disappointed in their expectations. I asked . . . what Austrian Nazis stood for apart from the question of pan-Germanism. I was told . . . that things could not be worse than they were and that as so many Austrians anticipated some sort of eventual union with Germany, to be an Austrian Nazi was to be a contingent holder of a job. To be a Nazi was to be an optimist.[118]

Their day had come.

To the sound of pealing church bells and cries of 'Juda verrecke!' ('Judah perish!') the Viennese fell upon the Jews, even before the motorised spearhead of the Wehrmacht had got there. Columns of Jewish people were organised to scrub the streets with nail- or tooth-brushes for the amusement of their Gentile neighbours, themselves busily defacing walls with words like 'Saujud', 'Zionstern' or 'Juden-sau'. Distinguished Jewish actresses were sent to clean the lavatories in SA barracks.[119] In Lower Austria cleaning soon developed into heavy canal and road work. Cars were confiscated, businesses plundered, and homes stripped of valuables in an orgy of theft.[120] By late 1938, an estimated forty thousand homes had been 'aryanised', with the Jews crammed into insalubrious circumstances which conveniently confirmed Nazi propaganda about Jews and hygiene. An estimated twenty-five thousand 'commissary administrators' instantly latched themselves on to Jewish businesses either at the behest of the local Party or on their own initiative.

It is instructive to see what happened when, as in the following case, thieves fell out. Josef Bien was a forty-six-year-old Jewish furrier with a thriving business in the Mariahilferstrasse near the West station which was patronised by many tourists. An army veteran, he had been wounded in the neck and shoulder while serving in the Carpathians.[121] In July 1938, Karl Kolarik, a fellow furrier, announced that he was the new 'commissary administrator' of the business. This entailed a brief daily visit, and the removal of 50 Marks from the till each Saturday, after Kolarik had paid Bien 'his' 75 Marks weekly 'wages'.[122] Kolarik wrote reports on Bien's conduct of the business, which notwithstanding his own dips into the till he conceded was well managed. Another fellow furrier, one Anton Giulio, then appeared, inquiring whether Bien would sell the business. Not taking no for an answer, Giulio tried to force Bien to sign the business away. In the event Giulio did not get the firm, an interest in which was assigned to a fourth furrier called Eduard Witeschnik.[123]

The Bien premises were pillaged by the local Nazis on 10 November 1938. They took 3,400 Reichsmarks in cash and 20,000 Reichsmarks' worth of stock. An indignant Commissar Kolarik, who arrived on the scene, temporarily took up Bien's case. He even interceded on behalf of Bien's workforce, who were owed their wages. One of the Nazis who robbed the store was an ex-employee of Witeschnik, who himself seems to have known where the stolen goods were. Witeschnik was then awarded the shop. Rather tactlessly, the latter then began selling clothing in it which obviously belonged to the stolen stock. It transpired that he purchased it as a job lot for 2,300 Reichsmarks.[124] His own valuations included 140 Reichsmarks for a coat which he then sold for 750 Reichsmarks. Although Witeschnik was formally disqualified from taking over the furrier's, this does not seem to have stopped him doing so. Bien was banned from entering his former shop.

Even Austrian 'old fighters' were appalled by these ugly depredations. Writing to Gauleiter Bürckel on 27 April 1938, a former illegal National Socialist deplored the way in which Jews, including an elderly rabbi, were being made to stand outside shops with placards saying 'Aryans do not buy from the Jews'. This filled the writer with shame, as did Jews being forced to clean the streets or to carry out humiliating physical exercises. He asked, 'Is this National Socialism?' He considered such things anathema to National Socialism, and doubted whether it would enhance recruitment to the cause.[125] By mid-March, both Berlin and the Austrian Nazi leaders were seriously concerned that matters had got out of hand, although they publicly preferred to blame Communists allegedly masquerading in Nazi uniforms for the excesses of their own rank and file. The *Völkischer Beobachter* insisted that 'the rule of law prevails in Germany. That means nothing occurs without a legal basis . . . no one may instigate pogroms, not even Mrs Hinterhuber against Sara Kohn in the third courtyard, mezzanine floor, by the water tap.'[126]

The apocryphal Mrs Hinterhuber aside, the Nazi authorities in both Berlin and Vienna were aware that the system of commissary administrators was a licence to rob, a temporary gesture to their own following, which would have to be superseded by a long, cold look at the overall structure of the Austrian economy, much of which could be shut down entirely. A central control mechanism was established in May 1938 under the direction of two Austrian Nazis, Walter Rafelsberger and Hans Fischbock, as well as German economists such as Rudolf Gater, author of a thesis on the conjunctural prognostications of the Harvard Institute, or Walter Emmerich from Hamburg, whose interest was in Vienna as the 'gateway to south-eastern Europe'. Beginning with the Viennese shoe industry, these men systematically liquidated large sections of Jewish-owned artisanal, manufacturing and service sectors, presiding over the modernisation and reassignment of the remainder. Other players, under the aegis of Wilhelm Keppler, set about the rationalisation of major banks and large-scale industry. The results of their collective labours are there to see in countless charts, graphs and graphics showing the 'dejudaisation' of the Austrian economy.[127] These people could show the Reich Germans a thing or two when it came to dealing brutally and expeditiously with Jews.

Given the sustained ferocity of Austrian antisemitism, vast numbers of Viennese Jews were desperate to leave the country. However, legal emigration involved dozens of formalities in separate government departments, with the resulting queues attracting extortioners like flies to a dung heap and each jobsworth requiring a bribe for that precious stamp or signature. In other words, the procedures were both corrupt and slow, even before one adds the complications which arose in dealings with foreign consulates and embassies of the sort undergone by George Clare's family. Having been sent to Vienna to get a handle on Jewish organisations, Eichmann saw an opportunity to solve a problem in such a way as to maximise his own power and chances for promotion.

Jewish community leaders, hopelessly overrun with would-be emigrants, turned to Eichmann to simplify procedures and for permission to approach the Joint Distribution Committee for financial assistance. Eichmann, who was not so proud as to ignore a good idea even when it originated with his victims, saw a chance here for a 'Central Office for the Emigration of Austrian Jewry', and grasped it with both hands. Soon he had moved his office into the former Rothschild home on the Prinz-Eugen Strasse. He acquired a larger staff, consisting entirely of twenty-five- to thirty-year-old ex-manual workers with records of unemployment and membership of the Austrian Nazi Party. Moving upwards from the dole queues to strutting about in black uniforms in a former Rothschild residence, they abused and systematically robbed the Jewish people who processed before them as if they were desk-bound bandits. Periodically they broke the monotony of completing forms with random interrogations. If questions such as 'What are you?' were answered 'I am a Jewish swindler, a crook,' the applicant would receive only a sardonic 'Very good,' rather than a punch in the face. In a progress report dated 21 November 1938, Eichmann boasted that 350 Jews a day were leaving Austria via his office, with total figures massively inflated to impress his Berlin superiors. Eichmann's office was the last port of call for Jewish people, but it was by no means the only official agency engaged in pauperising them. One unresolved problem was that emigration inevitably resulted in an increasingly proletarianised residue of impoverished Jews. Again, Austria was becoming paradigmatic, although events would have to take a further malign turn for this to be acted upon.

POGROM

As Eichmann and others worked assiduously in Vienna, the hooligan and terroristic elements in the Party in Germany and Austria were about to exceed their own earlier excesses, with the collusion and explicit encouragement of the nation's leaders. In a sense, Reichskristallnacht in November 1938 was the end, rather than a beginning, of a cycle and style of street violence, although it paradoxically paved the way for something more systematic and hence far worse. Hot violence, being driven by passion, was liable to peter out as moods changed; cold bureaucratic violence was a full-time career option.

The pretext, as opposed to cause, was the protest shooting of Ernst vom Rath, a Legation secretary in the German embassy on the rue de Lille in Paris, by Herschel Grynszpan, a seventeen-year-old Polish Jew. By all accounts the victim was the cultivated scion of an aristocratic family who was lukewarm about Nazism. His murderer was an 'eastern Jew', a category of being occupying a special place in the paranoid and phobic Nazi mentality, as we have seen. *Ostjuden* were not only 'Jews' but 'eastern', that is from a backward, uncivilised and threatening unknown, associated with inundations of Mongols, Poles, Russians and Jewish immigrants.

This shooting, deplored by most German Jews, was provoked by a chain of events beginning in March 1938 when the Polish government rendered stateless thousands of Poles living abroad, including fifty thousand Polish Jews living in Germany, in a drastic attempt to stem the tide of Jewish refugees fleeing Austria in the wake of the Anschluss. For it should not go unremarked that partly in order to outflank the rabidly antisemitic National Democratic (or Endek) Party, with their calls to ghettoise and expel the Jews, the post-Pilsudski governments of Poland tolerated Endek boycotts and pogroms, while themselves seeking to exclude Jews from business, medicine, the law and the universities, while seeking diplomatic ways of resettling the Jews in Palestine or Madagascar, options toyed with by the Nazis.[128] The position of Poland's indigenous Jews was extremely bleak, that of Jews caught between two antisemitic regimes the bleakest of all. In October, the German authorities rounded up seventeen thousand of these people and with considerable violence bundled them across the border, or rather, since the Poles refused to admit them, pushed them into a desolate no-man's land between the two countries.[129] The deportees included the parents and two sisters of Herschel Grynszpan, who was living alone, illegally and stateless, in Paris. Anguished news from his sister, fused with what he read of events in Germany, produced a state of mind which French investigators later recorded:

> I acted . . . because of love for my parents and for my people who were subjected unjustly to outrageous treatment. . . . It is not, after all, a crime to be Jewish. I am not a dog. I have the right to live. My people have a right to exist on this earth.[130]

On 7 November, Grynszpan sought an audience with the German ambassador, but was referred to the more lowly Ernst vom Rath, whom Grynszpan shot five times. Rath was not a Nazi. While he lay critically ill, the Nazi propaganda machine went to work, construing the assassination as the product of an international Jewish conspiracy, and artificially linking it with the 1936 slaying in Davos of Wilhelm Gustloff, a leading Swiss Nazi, by David Frankfurter, a Yugoslav Jewish student. Hitler's oration at Gustloff's funeral in February 1936 may have been 'moderate', but it is worth noting how he detected a Jewish conspiracy behind the murder:

> a guiding hand organised these crimes and will continue to do so. Now, for the first time, the party responsible for these deeds has become visible. . . . Thus our Party Comrade was struck down by the power which is waging a fanatical battle not only against our German *Volk*, but against every free, autonomous, and independent people. We understand the declaration of war, and we will respond! My dear Party Comrade, your death was not in vain![131]

Schemes floated by Hitler then, such as a retaliatory tax on German Jews, which economic and foreign policy considerations, including the imminence of the Winter Olympics in Garmisch Partenkirchen, had tempered, were revived with a vengeance.[132] Minds that subscribed to conspiracy theories had no trouble in reconciling a Yugoslav or a Pole with Germans or Austrians, provided perpetrators and victims all shared the common denominator of being Jewish. With the newspapers devoting front-page coverage to Rath's decline, and explicitly connecting his shooting with that of Gustloff two years earlier, the atmosphere resembled the sultriness before a thunderstorm.[133] In parts of Hessen and Magdeburg-Anhalt, ugly antisemitic demonstrations occurred on 7 and 8 November. In Rothenburg and Bad Hersfeld, the synagogues were looted or destroyed.[134] Receiving a report from the Gestapo in Kassel on the activities of a thousand-strong mob which ran amok in the city, Heydrich passed it to Hans Lammers in the Reich Chancellery without additional comment. On 9 November, outside activists made their appearance alongside local Nazis, whipping up emotions with inflammatory speeches.[135] Here were manifestations of spontaneous combustion below, which by a few dexterous moves and carefully chosen words, could be fanned into a nationwide conflagration.

Ernst vom Rath conveniently expired of his wounds at about 4 p.m. on 9 November. His death coincided with a date redolent with symbolism in the Nazi calendar, namely the solemn commemoration of those who had died on 9 November 1923 in Munich during the abortive Hitler putsch. On that date, as already noted, the Nazi 'old fighters' gathered together with their Führer for a *Kameradschafts-abend*. One can imagine the atmosphere, oscillating between self-righteous indignation at the event in Paris and shared memories of a recent past largely characterised by employment of boots, fists, bottles and knives against opponents. The key players were Hitler and Goebbels, whose diary account of these events has recently surfaced in Moscow. Hitler had urgent whisperings with Goebbels, sanctioning the continuation of the demonstrations, preventing the police from interfering, and ordering the detention of twenty to thirty thousand Jews by way of reprisal. He then left the Alte Rathaussaal, presumably to put distance between himself and what he had just authorised.

That constitutes the bare minimum, albeit a considerable minimum since it rendered a group of people fair game, of what passed between them. One's imagination can supply the intensity of emotion involved, the feeling that now in the wake of the Anschluss and the Munich Agreement they could unleash ferocious violence with relative impunity. Aggressive and vengeful by nature, these men literally talked up a pogrom. Goebbels' zeal may be partly explained in that for weeks beforehand he had been in bad odour with Hitler because of his messy liaison with the Czech filmstar Lida Baarova, an affair whose termination Hitler linked with Goebbels' future political career.[136] At ten that evening, Goebbels duly delivered an antisemitic tirade ending with a

call for vengeance against the Jews. The assembled Party and SA
leaders made a flurry of telephone calls – 'Alles saust gleich an die
Telephone' – to the regions from the Rheinischer Hof hotel, relaying
their impressions of the meeting, suggestions and, in some cases,
explicit instructions to commit murder. Each subsequent telephone call
down the chain of command no doubt involved further brutalisation
of expression, so that as a result of a call from SA-Standarte 411
Wesermünde, three Jews were killed in Lesum.[137]

To argue that 'lack of co-ordination' is the most salient feature of
these events may be literally true, in the sense that implementation
varied from place to place, but this underplays the emotionally charged
atmosphere, and implies the incompatibility of improvisation and
ideological conviction.[138] By the time Goebbels went back to his hotel,
the sky was 'blood red' with flames.[139] Although Goebbels was the
immediate instigator, when Popitz, the Prussian Minister of Finance,
told Göring that the perpetrators should be punished, Göring replied:
'My dear Popitz, do you wish to punish the Führer?'[140] As Goebbels
debriefed Hitler on 10 November in the Osteria restaurant, he noted
that 'His [Hitler's] views are very radical and aggressive.' He wanted
the Jews to cover the costs of the damage and gradually to expropriate
their businesses.[141] Hitler was obviously not only in charge, but already
racing many steps ahead. The pogrom seems to have taken the SS
leadership by surprise, although Himmler and Heydrich rapidly recovered. From the bar of the Hotel Vier Jahreszeiten, Heydrich hastened
to Hitler's flat on the Aussere Prinzregenten Strasse, where a cautious
Himmler indicated that Goebbels was in charge. In follow-up wire
transmissions, Heydrich instructed the Gestapo and SD on their role,
on who was and who was not to be harmed, together with instructions
to detain as many adult male Jews, preferably the rich, as the cells
would hold once the 'events' had run their course.[142] There is some
evidence to suggest that the SS had been preparing such a move
beforehand, and that the pogrom gave them a welcome pretext to
pursue their own agenda. Many preparations have to be made to arrest
and confine twenty to thirty thousand people.

As a few examples from different parts of Germany and Austria
demonstrate, the local implementation of the pogrom varied from
tragedy to farce. One of the senior Nazis gathered in Munich was the
Tyrolese Gauleiter Franz Hofer, who telephoned his subordinates in
Innsbruck with the news that 'it would not matter that much whether
one or the other Jew was killed'. He met senior police, SA and SS

chiefs when he reached Innsbruck at 1 a.m. on 9/10 November, it being noteworthy that all of these men were available for a meeting at such an improbable hour, more befitting gangsters than policemen or politicians. Another felicitous coincidence was that at midnight the SS had held an oath-swearing ceremony on the Innsbruck Adolf-Hitler Platz. The SS company leaders met with SS-Oberführer Hanns von Feil, himself fresh from the conclave with Hofer. SS veterans were ordered to change into civilian clothes, and to await lists of Jews supplied by the local Plenipotentiary for Aryanisation. Those selected to take part in the pogrom were ideological fanatics, all of whom had served long prison sentences for Nazi activities during the time of Dollfuss and Schussnigg. Some of them were members of the notorious 'T Group' which specialised in assassinating political opponents before the Anschluss. Socially speaking, they were a motley bunch of butchers' boys, boxers and ski instructors, and the leader of the Innsbruck student fraternity Suevia. These men regarded their selection as a 'special honour', even if what they did that night made a few of them physically sick. Feil then dispatched these squads to a particular street where they were 'to kill with as little noise as possible' the named male members of three Jewish families whom none of the killers knew personally. The first victim was knifed three times in the head, and beaten with a coal shovel. The second was stabbed in the back with an SS dagger, while the third was stabbed and battered to death with pistols. These horrible crimes were committed in the victims' own homes, in front of their wives and children. Another murder squad abducted its victim from his home in Kranebitten, killing him with rocks before throwing his corpse into the Inn.[143]

In sedate Wiesbaden, three SA men sat in the waiting room of the main station, notionally awaiting the return home of their standard from Munich. Like the Innsbruck SS men, they just happened to be there at a time when most people were asleep in bed. At two in the morning they received a telephone call from a Brigadeführer Kraft ordering them to don civilian clothes in order to destroy local synagogues.[144] Duly dressed, they drove to Rüdesheim, parking their vehicle away from the target, and telling the synagogue caretaker whom they disturbed to return to bed. Having broken into the building, they tipped five litres of petrol over the furnishings they had not looted, which they lit with paper, almost managing to kill themselves as the petrol ignited with a blast they had not anticipated. The local police did nothing, despite finding a clue that even a dullard could not miss, namely a piece of paper with the heading 'Higher SA Leadership Munich'. Since local people managed to put out the ineptly laid fire, another gang returned the next day to do the job properly.

Known by the epithet 'Reichskristallnacht', the pogrom was not only murderous, but an opportunity for mindless and resentful mobs to loot and vandalise the homes of their social superiors, a fact broadly congruent with the broad socio-economic profile of the German Jewish community. They destroyed anything not easily removed – slashing paintings, breaking furniture and pianos, or shattering marble and porcelain with sledgehammers – while stealing cash, cameras, jewellery and so forth.[145] Others were simply thieves, posting guards outside shops while their colleagues went out the rear exits laden with booty. One SA man, convicted of robbing a clothing store in Usingen, was found to have stolen four pullovers, two bedside rugs, three suits, one overcoat, one roll of cloth, four damask bedspreads and material for twelve pillows, five pairs of braces, five suspender belts, three casual jackets, one blue woollen blanket and a bicycle.[146] Every petty criminal saw his chance. A Cologne-based fraudster and thief holidaying in the bars and whorehouses of Düsseldorf decided to recoup the cash he had squandered by attaching himself to an SA unit raiding a flat inhabited by a Jewish family, demanding 50 Marks with menaces.[147] It was also an opportunity for fit young men to chase, punch and kick often elderly victims, including women, while children were terrorised with guns. In some places, Jews were publicly humiliated by being forced to walk over their prayer shawls; to read *Mein Kampf* aloud; or to sing the Nazi Horst Wessel Lied.[148] In Beuthen in Upper Silesia, parties of Jews were made to stand for hours in front of the burning synagogue.[149] Jews who ventured out on to the streets in the wake of the pogrom were sometimes pursued by gangs of malevolent, spitting children who hit them about the legs with sticks.[150]

An estimated 7,500 business premises were damaged or destroyed. A Jewish community worker in Berlin described scenes on the Kurfürstendamm which reminded him of a war zone. The mob had levered open iron shutters with crowbars. In an office-equipment shop, they had smashed heavy calculators and typewriters, meticulously prising out each key, and festooning the shop with red and black typewriter ribbons. In a gentlemen's outfitters, each overcoat and suit had the arms cut off or was slashed with a knife. This was dedicated vandalism. Cakes and tarts slid down the walls of a patisserie, while alcohol-sodden glass covered the floor.[151] Cars had to take alternative routes lest the glass shards shred their tyres, pedestrians walked down the centre of streets to avoid the debris on the pavements. In 1938–9 the Anglo-Irish writer Hubert Butler was working for the Quaker 'Friends Centre' in Vienna, helping Jews complete emigration forms and touring the Bolivian, Mexican or Peruvian embassies on their behalf to secure visas. One day he walked along the Prater Strasse to the large Prater Park. He wrote: 'The street must have had a great many Jewish shopkeepers in it, because all the way down there were broken windows in front of looted shops with "VERHOLUNG NACH DACHAU" scrawled over the surviving panes, and the air was full of mindless hatred that war, which fosters all our basest passions, would inevitably make murderous.'[152]

The perpetrators were under orders to destroy every synagogue in the country. Sporadic attacks on synagogues had occurred during the Weimar Republic, and in the early years of the Nazi government, particularly if the architectural style was conspicuously oriental, a style sometimes imposed upon the Jewish community by earlier rulers. The object of old folk fears, synagogues drew trouble like iron filings to a magnet. Religious services were interrupted with teargas projectiles, windows were broken, and in a few cases gallows were erected opposite the entrances, whose meaning was unambiguous. In 1938, the Nazi authorities discovered that traffic congestion was a useful pretext for demolishing these fine old buildings. The main Munich synagogue on Herzog-Max Strasse was torn down in the summer of 1938 to improve the city's traffic flow. The old synagogue on Hans-Sachs Platz in Nuremberg was demolished that August, on the grounds that it was 'an unGerman, oriental structure' which spoiled the demi-timbered medieval character of the town. The events of 9/10 November 1938 had nothing in common with leisurely demolition.

In Vienna, the local edition of the *Völkischer Beobachter* published the location of the city's synagogues and prayer houses a few days before they were destroyed. Dedicated bands, armed with axes, crow-bars, sledgehammers and cans of petrol, broke in, smashing furniture and lighting fires. Objects of immense communal value, including the written word of God, were torn up or burned. In so far as the fire brigade were not active participants, they were under orders to play their hoses on the roofs and walls of neighbouring structures, to contain rather than extinguish the conflagration. Nameless 'experts' put in an appearance to advise on the comparabilities of blowing up or setting fire to synagogues where the risk of fire spreading was great and small charges could collapse the building neatly. For some perpetrators, the pogrom was an exciting experience they would have liked to repeat, a carnival of bestial passions. Reporting to their superiors in Breslau on 11 November 1938, the Oppeln section of the SS chronicled how they had wreaked havoc upon the Jews of Upper Silesia, burning synagogues in Oppeln, Karlsrühe, Landsberg, Rosenberg, Strehlitz, Tost, Peiskretscham, Gleiwitz, Hindenburg, Beuthen, Langendorf, Ratibor, Troppau, Jagerndorf, Leobschutz, Neustadt, Zulz and Cosel. Keen for credit where credit was due, the report said: 'The perpetrators of all these actions were the SS. The SA made no noteworthy contribution.' Commenting on morale, the report added: 'All troops and leaders took great delight in the action. Such orders should be given more often.'[153]

The SS were also institutionally involved in the pogrom, in the sense that thirty thousand Jews were imprisoned for brief periods in its concentration camps, arrests intended to terrorise them into hasty emigration. The detention, transportation and incarceration of such numbers of people was a massive logistical undertaking. It was also an utterly terrifying experience for the people concerned, who were thrown into a world circumscribed by barbed wire, watchtowers and machine guns, where extremely brutal guards were encouraged to do what they liked. Siegmund Weltlinger returned from taking his daughter to piano classes to find a Gestapo officer ensconced in his home. He was arrested and taken by train through suburban north Berlin to Sachsenhausen concentration camp. Unloaded in total darkness, the Jews were insulted, kicked and hit with rifle butts. The camp commandant introduced them to a stark set of rules:

> You are here to atone for the cowardly assassination committed by your Polish racial comrade Grunspan. You must remain here as hostages so that world Jewry carries out no more murders. You are not in a sanatorium but in a crematorium. Every SS order is to be obeyed. If they wish, the SS has the right to shoot you. Our boys are damned good shots. There is therefore no point in trying to escape. The barbed wire around the camp is electrified. Whoever touches it will die instantly. Shots will be fired at all escapees. You must work for your upkeep. We'll make sure you work off your fat bellies.

After a night spent standing on the parade ground, the Jews were stripped of their clothes and valuables, shorn, and dressed in dehumanising blue and white striped uniforms. Reassembled on the parade ground, 'we no longer recognised one another in these outfits'. Those standing near the front were insulted or attacked by the SS. Anyone who struck back, and some did, was beaten senseless.[154] Max Moses Polke was sent to Buchenwald near Weimar. After they had spent hours facing the wall in the station tunnel, lorries took him and his fellow detainees to the camp. Again the prisoners were forced to run the gauntlet of SS men before being forced to stand for hours on the parade ground. At night, two thousand men were crammed into five-storey bunks in a wooden barracks measuring fifty metres by ten metres. Individuals were beaten up, with deaths being attributed to suicide. Trips to the latrines were perilous, with some unfortunates simply falling into these three-metre-deep pits and drowning in excrement. People who went mad or had epileptic fits were shot for 'resistance', while those with special dietary requirements, such as diabetics, perished.[155]

The pogrom and the wave of arrests, *of its victims*, happened the length and breadth of Germany and Austria before finally petering out in some places as late as 13 November. The shocking impact of these events on the Jews can be gauged from the fact that in Vienna alone some 680 Jews committed suicide during these days and nights.[156] These events compelled people to have an opinion on the persecution of the Jews, even if many of them spent the night of 9/10 November asleep. Reactions were informed by a variety of factors including pre-existing moral values based on common decency, humanitarianism, Christianity, law and order, the inviolability of private property or indeed the brutal example being given to the young.[157]

Among the middle and upper classes, there were feelings of shame and embarrassment that a civilised country could witness such scenes, as well as contempt for the hooligan mobs responsible for them. Former ambassador to Rome Ulrich von Hassell discussed the pogrom at some length in successive entries in his diary. Writing under the burden of 'crushing emotions', Hassell noted both the hostile foreign reaction and what the 'vile persecution' based on 'the lowest instincts' revealed about the present system of government which was ultimately responsible for it.[158] Almost a month later, Hassell still experienced 'a deep sense of shame which has weighed heavily on all decent and thoughtful people since the hideous events of the November [pogrom]. There is talk of little else.' Even many leading Nazis, including those responsible, 'secretly condemn the pogrom'.[159] Hassell noted that foreign commentators distinguished between 'the people and the group responsible for acts such as these', with no one being taken in by the public talk of spontaneous popular indignation over Rath's assassination. Shame that such barbarities could occur in a civilised nation was a common response. After all, history showed that such things only happened in Tsarist Russia. Allied to this were fears that the pogrom would seriously impair Germany's image abroad.

Evidence from outside and within Nazi circles shows that significant swathes of German opinion, especially, according to SD Reports, in the Roman Catholic south and west, regarded the pogrom with disgust. This was partly because Nazi attacks on the Roman Catholic Church were implicitly elided with the assault on people of a cognate faith, and because traditions of 'love thy neighbour' proved stronger than incitement to kill him or her.[160] Nazi racial antisemitism seemed of a piece with Nazi anti-clericalism and neo-paganism. Among Roman Catholic Germans, there was a real fear that they might be next on the list of Nazi victims, a not entirely unjustified fear since the mobs sometimes ransacked church property when no synagogue was to hand, determined to commit outrages against any manifestation of the sacred.[161] Although according to the SD's own Reports criticism was minimal in rural Protestant areas, individual Protestant clergy did protest, albeit in questionable terms. In December 1938, a Protestant pastor put his signature to the following letter to Hitler, Göring and Goebbels:

> The events that occurred amongst our people on and after November 9th of this year force me to take a clear stand. Far be it from me to disregard the sins that many members of the Jewish people have committed against our Fatherland, especially during the last decades; and, far be it from me to deny the right of orderly and moderate proceedings against the Jewish race. But not only will I on no account justify the numerous excesses against Jewry that took place on or after Nov. 9 of this year (it is unnecessary to go into details) but I reject them, deeply ashamed, as they are a blot on the good name of the Germans.
>
> First of all, I, as a Protestant Christian, have no doubt that carrying out and tolerance of such reprisals will evoke the wrath of God against our people and Fatherland, as sure as there is a God in heaven. Just as Israel is cursed and on trial because they were the first who rejected Christ, so surely that same curse will fall upon each and every nation that, by similar deeds, denies Christ in the same way.

I have spoken out of the ardent concern of a Christian who prays to his God every day for his people and their rulers. May God hearken to my voice, hopefully not the only one of this kind. With due respect to the authorities.

Erich Klapproth

Pastor.[162]

The liberal middle classes also voiced distaste for the pogrom. In Stuttgart, the liberal industrialist Robert Bosch and his managing director Hans Walz, both formerly active in the Association for Defence against Antisemitism, funded the illegal emigration of Jews and transferred half a million Reichsmarks to a Dutch bank designed to tide emigrants over the difficult transitional period.[163] More generally, middle-class people did not care for arson, theft or gratuitous violence. A few were genuinely concerned about the example being set younger people, often the most enthusiastic peripheral participants in the outrages.[164] Some actively afforded Jews succour during their days and nights of tribulation. In early 1939, a middle-class Saxon reporter for the exiled Social Democrats noted that all of his acquaintances, without exception, were disgusted by the pogrom. Some of them, including senior civil servants, had done their best to protect Jewish people by hiding them at home or facilitating their emigration abroad. They distanced themselves from the Nazis by not inviting them to social events, where they would often be acerbic about these absentees, and about Goebbels as the pogrom's apparent major mover. An altogether subsidiary concern in these circles was the wanton destruction of property, and the ensuing insurance claims, or the fact that the destruction ludicrously coincided with public exhortations to save and recycle such things as sardine cans or toothpaste tubes.[165] The SD also noted that 'many believed they had openly to stand up for the Jews. . . . People stood up for the poor oppressed Jews'.[166] Some regional SD Reports noted that neither the farmers nor the working classes voiced any support for the Jews, with support being confined to 'the so-called better circles'.[167]

In a climate of denunciation, it took courage to speak on behalf of or actively help Jewish people. That people did so rather militates against the notion that Germany was monomanically antisemitic. Sometimes, like the Beuthen bank director denounced by a waiter for publicly condemning the pogrom, such courageous people faced imprisonment. A middle-class mother and son, apprehended while helping a Jewish shop owner clear up her devastated Bonn store, were publicly vilified in a regional newspaper for their 'feeble sentimentality' and misplaced 'humanity': 'in this question there is only one true humanity: the eradication of this world plague'.[168]

If the events of the pogrom necessarily bulk large, subsequent legal measures were of greater general significance in the sense that the Jews were systematically pauperised and delivered into the sinister bureaucratic embrace of the SS. For, as Goebbels noted, so far from defusing anti-Jewish animosities, 'the whole question has now been moved on a great deal further'.[169] Having temporarily assuaged the bloodlust of their more loutish followers, discovering in the process through their own sociological reports that the majority of Germans did not care for open violence, the Nazi leadership reverted to legalised forms of persecution.

As the embers of burned-out buildings still smoked, Göring, acting in his capacity as Supremo for the Four Year Plan, and under explicit instructions from Hitler, chaired a meeting with about one hundred participants on 12 November 1938. Minutes of parts of this marathon four-hour session, whose antisemitic badinage is as noteworthy as its substantive conclusions, have survived.[170] Göring was fed up with street demonstrations, although he fully understood popular frustration regarding promises of action on the economic front, which were allegedly not being honoured. Here he conveniently overlooked 'aryanisation' plans presented by Minister of the Interior Frick that summer, or indeed a meeting he chaired on 14 October where the talk was of ghettos and work columns, and not just of how the state should reassert its grip on 'wild' 'aryanisations'.[171] After the pogrom, Nazi minds were especially exercised by questions of glass and insurance. Plate glass came from Belgium, indeed Germany would need to purchase half of Belgium's annual production to repair the damage incurred a few days before, at an estimated cost in foreign currency of three thousand million Reichsmarks. Then there was the tricky business of German insurance companies, which had either insured Jewish businesses or had underwritten themselves again abroad. Insurance claims relating to the pogrom were estimated at 225 million Reichsmarks. The solution to these difficulties was a cynically titled Decree for the Restitution of the Street Scene, designed to make the victims liable for the damage caused by the mobs, which also meant that the insurance payments went straight to the government's coffers. This was followed by a one-off capital levy, called 'atonement' for the 'Jewish' assassination of Rath, consisting of one thousand million

Reichsmarks, levied at the rate of 20–25 per cent on all capital holdings over 5,000 Reichsmarks.[172] A Decree on the Exclusion of Jews from German Economic Life banned Jews from all independent business activity, from cornershops to wholesale trade.[173] A Law on the Use of Jewish Assets meant that securities went into closed accounts and that Jews could no longer buy or sell jewels, precious metals or works of art freely.[174]

A bald recitation of these measures does not convey the political dynamics of the discussion, the antisemitic humour, nor the future possibilities which were aired during its interminable course. For these people as often revealed that they thought far ahead, as they appeared to react to unforeseen circumstances. The bluff chairman did most of the talking. Bored by the complexity of the financial and insurance issues arising from the pogrom, Göring ventured the thought that it would have been better had two hundred Jews been killed than that such material damage had been incurred. Actually, that number had been killed, but he appeared not to have noticed. Surveying the measures agreed upon, he commented, 'the swine won't commit a second murder so quickly. I must confess, I would not like to be a Jew in Germany.'[175] Contemplating the prospect of a war in the near future, he went on, 'it is obvious that we in Germany will first of all make sure of settling accounts with the Jews'. Goebbels' interventions were both frivolous and malicious. He wanted Jews banned from baths, beaches, cinemas, circuses, theatres and 'German' forests. Göring suggested confining them to certain parts of forests which could then be populated with animals 'which look damned similar to Jews – yes, the elk has a curved nose'. There was a bizarre digression about whether or not to create segregated compartments for Jews in trains. What if only one Jew wanted to catch a certain train? Should he be given a carriage to himself? Of course not, for laws had their limits: 'We will kick him out and he will have to sit all alone in the lavatory all the way.'[176]

But, beneath the snide surface, power was visibly shifting elsewhere. Hans Fischbock from Vienna had much to say for himself, like a brainy visiting undergraduate keen to shine at the top of the class. There was no evidence of self-awareness here. Fischbock volunteered, with eager obsequiousness: 'In Austria, we already have a precise plan, Herr Generalfeldmarschall.' According to his plans, based on study of each sector of the economy, only three to three and a half thousand firms would remain in business out of the total of seventeen thousand to be 'aryanised': 'In this manner we will have eradicated all publicly visible Jewish businesses.' Göring: 'Outstanding!'[177] Heydrich was especially exercised by what would happen to the Jews after they had been excluded from the economy, specifically how they were to be physically removed from Germany. It was easy enough to force rich Jews to leave; the problem was the residual 'Jewish mob'. This resonated with the conservative Schwerin von Krosigk, who commented: 'The decisive point is that we don't retain the whole societal proletariat. Dealing with them will always be a terrible burden.' Frick: 'And a danger too.' Smoothly extolling the achievements of Eichmann's Central Office in Vienna, Heydrich casually suggested creating a similar agency in the old Reich.[178] The fate of the Jews thereby moved further into the hands of the SS. Emigration spread over eight to ten years would inevitably mean having to support Jewish 'proletarians' in the interim. It might be an idea to identify the Jews with some sort of uniform or badge. He saw no need for ghettos since they 'would be a permanent hideout for criminals and first of all a source of epidemics and the like'. This was a revealing train of thought. Far better to let things continue as they were, with 'Jews controlled by the watchful eyes of the entire population'.[179]

While the Jews underwent the only social mobility afforded by the Nazi regime, that is universally downwards, control of their collective destiny passed into the hands of policemen on the ground that Jews and the poor (two increasingly indistinct categories) were inherently criminal. The mood in the SS was becoming apocalyptic. On 9 November 1938, Himmler delivered his annual address to SS-Gruppenführern, a meandering speech with idiosyncratic exhortations that 'the SS will be everywhere a model of punctiliousness and courtesy and human consideration for all other national comrades'. He was optimistic that antisemitism was being successfully exported: 'Furthermore the Czechei [the derogatory term for Czechoslovakia] is becoming antisemitic, the whole Balkans are becoming antisemitic, the whole of Palestine is in a quandary towards the Jews, so that soon the world will have no room for the Jews.' Projecting his own deepest wishes on to the 'enemy', Himmler argued that the latter would try to 'burn out and annihilate' what he called 'the country of origin of antisemitism'. Jews were being transformed from victims into aggressors. He enjoined his audience to be clear that 'if we are the loser in the struggle which will decide this, not even a reservation of Germans will remain, but rather everyone will be starved out and slaughtered. This will affect everyone, whether or not he is now a very enthusiastic supporter of the Third Reich, it will suffice that he speaks German and that he has a German mother.'[180] Murder was on his mind, although the potential murderers were the Jews. These patterns of thought stuck, and we will encounter them again.

Two weeks after Reichskristallnacht, on 24 November 1938, the SS journal *Das Schwarze Korps* took stock of the new situation created by the pogrom under the headline 'Jews, what now?' It boasted of a growing immunity to world opinion, nearly a year before the chauvinistic cacophony of war drowned it out altogether. It is important to stress this point, since the war is often held to have disinhibited the Nazis, whereas this article shows that they were disinhibiting themselves a year before it started. In other words, what are unreflectively described as 'war crimes' had a genealogy which owed nothing to war at all. Experience had shown that the civilised world was indifferent to the Jews, with the humanitarian rhetoric contradicted by restrictive immigration requirements:

> Neither Mr Roosevelt, nor an English Archbishop, nor any other prominent diploma-democrat would put his dear daughter in the bed of a greasy Eastern European Jew; only, when it is a question of Germany, they suddenly know nothing of any Jewish Question, only of the 'persecution of innocents because of their religion', as though we had ever been interested in anything a Jew believes or doesn't believe.

The message was no longer being received:

> Today we react to their screeching as to a continuous noise that is not capable of becoming any louder. It is known that the human ear can hear sounds only up to a certain level of vibration. Sounds and noises of still higher frequencies are not heard. We have become immune to any increase in the great screaming of world Jewry.

Having built such armed might that 'no power in the world can stop us' (for hubris was intrinsic to this mentality), it was time for a 'total solution' of the 'Jewish Question'. Economic separation was not enough: 'It means much more!' Jews, or rather 'murderers and criminals', should be segregated in special streets or housing blocks, with as little contact with Germans as possible. Since Jews were allegedly incapable of working for a living, they would consume their own mysteriously undepleted resources, with rich Jews forced to subsidise the poor. 'They will all sink down into a criminal existence, in accordance with their deepest blood-conditioned nature.' Of course, the SS, standing in here for the German people, were not going to watch this last scenario with equanimity, especially since the Jews would seek 'revenge'. They would not tolerate 'a breeding ground for Bolshevism and an umbrella organisation for the political and criminal sub-humans'; the 'Jewish underworld' would have to be eliminated 'with fire and sword'.[181] What is so striking here is the conflation of Jews, criminality, Bolshevism and sub-humanity, a conflation which apparently legitimised messianic violence, ostensibly to force the departure of people who because of the regime's policies, and restrictive foreign immigration laws, were poorly placed to go anywhere. Again, as in Himmler's speech, the chosen imagery was apocalyptic and violent, the analogue of the slaughter which Himmler imagined the Jews would commit against Germany if she were not victorious in the coming struggle.

The contrast between the realities of life for Jews in Greater Germany and these dire imaginings could not have been starker. Isolated in their homes, or hurrying along hostile streets – not resting on the yellow-painted segregated benches reserved for them in public parks – the remaining Jews in Germany and Austria would be desperately vulnerable should Hitler, Himmler, Heydrich, Eichmann and their kind decide that emigration was no longer a desirable or viable option. Murderous violence was still at this stage a means to another end, enforced emigration, but in some circles the very fine balance was appreciably tilting, making murder – not as yet conceived as a continent-wide bureaucratic mission – an end in itself.

The extreme vulnerability of the Jews was also apparent in other respects. Since increasing numbers of Jews were destitute, the feeling grew that they should be compelled to work for their upkeep. Starting in Austria in October 1938, and imitated in the major cities of the Reich from December, labour offices directed separate columns of Jews to work in isolation on rubbish dumps, road building and street cleaning, a form of compulsory labour hitherto used only against the recalcitrant unemployed. The following April, a new Law Concerning Rental Situations of Jews enabled a landlord to evict Jewish tenants if he could prove accommodation was available for them elsewhere. This enabled municipal and regional housing authorities effectively to resettle Jews in specific Jewish areas, or in overcrowded houses uncharmingly designated the Judenhaus.[182]

In early January 1939, the philologist Victor Klemperer took a break from typing and mailing copies of his curriculum vitae to Lima, Jerusalem or Sydney: 'SOS calls', as he called them, which remained unacknowledged across the oceans of indifference with which most societies regularly greet the desperate. Living increasingly on his nerves, the days of enforced unemployment dragged with a terrible emptiness, as he half-heartedly tried to learn English. In his understated way, Klemperer remarked that he now had to sign himself Victor 'Israel' Klemperer when he went to the bank, while even the titles of books were now being adjusted by the publishers, so that Howard Spring's *O Absalom* became *Beloved Sons* or Frederick Wright's *The Chronicle of Aaron Kane*, retitled *The Chronicle of Captain Kane*, came with a disclaimer explaining that Old Testament Christian names were frequent in the age of puritanism. On 10 January Klemperer reflected at length on the artificiality of the 'German or west European Jewish question'. It is worth seeing how he tried to make sense of events:

> Until 1933 and for at least a good century before that, the German Jews were entirely German and nothing else. Proof: the thousands and thousands of half- and quarter-Jews etc. Jews and 'persons of Jewish descent', proof that Jews and Germans lived and worked together without friction in all spheres of German life. The antisemitism which was always present is not at all proof to the contrary, because the friction between Jews and 'Aryans' was not half so great as, for example, that between Protestants and Catholics, or between employers and employees, or between East Prussians, for example, and Southern Bavarians, or Rhinelanders and Berliners. The German Jews were a part of the German nation, as the French Jews were part of the French nation etc. They played their part within the life of Germany, by no means as a burden on the whole. Their role was rarely that of the worker, still less of the agricultural labourer. They were, and remain (even though now they no longer wish to remain so), Germans, in the main intellectuals and educated people. If the intention is now to expatriate them *en masse*, transplanting them into agricultural professions, then that will inevitably fail and cause unrest everywhere. Because everywhere they will remain Germans and intellectuals. There is only one solution to the German or west European Jewish question: the defeat of its inventors. What must be treated separately is the matter of eastern Jews, which again I do not regard as a specifically Jewish question, because for a long while those who are too poor or hungry for civilisation, or both, have been pouring into Western countries and forming an underclass there, out of which vital forces crowd upwards. Which does no harm to any nation, because race, in

the sense of purity of blood, is a zoological notion, a concept which long ago ceased to correspond with any reality, is at any rate even less a reality than the old, strict distinction between the spheres of man and wife. The pure or religious Zionist cause is something for sectarians, without significance to the majority, something very private and backward, like all sectarian matters, a kind of open-air museum, like the Old Dutch village near Amsterdam. It seems complete madness to me if specifically Jewish states are now to be set up in Rhodesia or somewhere. That would be letting the Nazis throw us back thousands of years. The Jews concerned are committing a crime – admittedly one must allow them extenuating circumstances – if they agree to this game. It is both absurd and a crime against nature and civilisation if west European emigrants are now to be completely transformed into agricultural labourers. The movement back to nature has proven itself contrary to nature a thousand times over, because development is part of nature and regression is against nature. The solutions of the Jewish question can only be found in deliverance from those who discovered it. And the world – because now this really does concern the world – will be forced to act accordingly.[183]

A few weeks later, Klemperer noted Hitler's recent address to the Reichstag: 'In his Reichstag speech on 30 January Hitler again turned all his opponents into Jews and threatened the "annihilation" of the Jews of Europe if they conspired to bring about war against Germany.'[184] Judging from this diary entry, Klemperer did not attach any special importance to this extraordinary outburst from the leader of a civilised country. A few historians also persist in regarding the speech as a 'metaphor'.

The Reichstag met every 30 January to celebrate Hitler's accession to power. On this sixth anniversary Hitler fulminated for over two hours, blaming the Jews for Germany's deteriorating diplomatic situation, and mocking the democracies for being ungrateful for presenting them with so many of these 'magnificent people'. There is film of the occasion, showing Hitler shedding the veneer of statesmanship he had briefly tried out, like a morning coat on a bookmaker, and reverting to the low, gangster-like mode that was his essence. At one key point he interjected the threat which Klemperer noted without any comment:

In my life I have often been a prophet, and I have mostly been laughed at. At the time of my struggle for power, it was mostly the Jewish people who laughed at the prophecy that one day I would attain in Germany the leadership of the state and therewith of the entire nation, and that among other problems I would also solve the Jewish one. I think that the uproarious laughter of that time has in the meantime remained stuck in German Jewry's throat. Today I want to be a prophet again: If international finance Jewry inside and outside Europe again succeeds in precipitating the nations into a world war, the result will not be the Bolshevisation of the earth, and with it the victory of Jewry, but the annihilation of the Jewish race in Europe.

On one level, this threatening tirade – delivered with passion to frenzied applause – was directed at Jews abroad, whom Hitler held responsible for criticism of his regime in America and mounting hostility towards appeasement evident in Great Britain, a hostility partly engendered by the shocking scenes of November. After all, 'the Jew' – as maleficent cosmic conspirator – lurked behind everything that stood in the way of an ascendant Germany. The threat may also have been designed to blackmail Western governments into bank-rolling the emigration of German Jews, through a loan of one and half billion Reichsmarks, to be repaid in ten years' time through German exports.[185]

But on a profounder level Hitler was outlining a potential scenario, should his bid for power be thwarted by a general war and a rerun of 1918, that hour of total national abasement. He was shaping the contours of what he might do, with the prophetic mode he adopted subtracting his personal responsibility from what might happen. What he would undoubtedly commission was being divorced from human agency. It was a prophecy; things would just happen. Nothing directly connects this speech with the murderous assault against European Jewry which commenced two years later with the invasion of Russia. But as Philippe Burrin has said: 'By verbalizing his innermost purpose, he also exalted, and empowered, himself' – without, it should be said, directly associating himself with any atrocities. Events had to snake and turn before mass murder became possible. Other options would have to shut down; internal thresholds grow lower; feelings become dulled by wartime brutality; the fog lift to reveal radiant futures or descend in anticipation of an apocalypse; casuistries be spun to reconcile decency with murder; the stakes rise to the prospect of stupendous triumphs or the depths of ignominy. All this had not happened in January 1939. And yet, when that assault *was* happening, this speech was frequently referred to by Hitler, twice in 1942 and three times in 1943, as the prior notice that it *would* – not could – happen, like some sort of anchor or reference point in a tempest.

For Klemperer, dulled by six years of publicly expressed antisemitism, the speech was not remarkable, deserving less space than his nuanced ratiocinations about the assimilated character of Jews in western Europe, his dismissal of the Zionists and snobbery towards the *Ostjuden*. In the final analysis, these distinctions and nuances would not matter. By contrast, for some of Hitler's audience, the speech was further licence to go a stage further in their search for a solution to the 'Jewish Question', with the ratchet of what was possible moving further up the scale of radicality. Once these men were let loose, in circumstances where there was no law, and their own sense of superiority was inherent, something Nietzsche described fairly presciently would happen. In 1887 he wrote:

> the same people who are so strongly held in check by custom, respect, habit, gratitude and even more through spying on one another and through peer group jealousy, who, on the other hand, behave towards one another by showing such resourcefulness in consideration, self-control, delicacy, loyalty, pride and friendship – they are not much better than uncaged beasts of prey in the world outside where the strange, the foreign, begin. There they enjoy freedom from every social constraint, in the wilderness they compensate for the tension which is caused by being closed in and fenced in by the peace of the community for so long, they return to the innocent conscience of the wild beast, as exultant monsters, who perhaps go away having committed a hideous succession of murder, arson, rape and torture, in a mood of bravado and spiritual equilibrium as though they had simply played a student's prank, convinced that poets will now have something to sing and celebrate for quite some time now. At the centre of these noble races we cannot fail to see the blond beast of prey, the magnificent blond beast avidly prowling round for spoil and victory, this hidden centre needs release from time to time, the beast must out again, must return to the wild.[186]

Here was a thought to capture and stir imaginations, bored with, and resentful of, the idyll of bourgeois contentment, although ironically the grim, squalid reality of bureaucrats, drunks, fanatics and weeping executioners would have taxed Nietzsche's imagination by their ordinariness and lack of nobility of spirit. As we began by saying, the signs were still ambiguous, although a combination of intention and circumstances would introduce a terrible clarity.[187]

5

'EXTINGUISHING THE IDEAS OF YESTERDAY': EUGENICS AND 'EUTHANASIA'

Totalitarian regimes are sometimes described as 'gardening states', which sought to transform society by eradicating those they regarded as 'alien' or 'unfit', so that the 'fit' might flourish. The Third Reich's supreme gardener, Heinrich Himmler, is shown here admiring a prize tulip at a market garden in the late 1930s.

BREEDING THE BEST?

Decades before the 1930s, doctors, psychiatrists, scientists and pundits in many countries thought that industrial, urban society was engendering biological degeneration. Nations were being undermined by ever increasing cohorts of unfit individuals, whose alcoholism, anti-social behaviour, criminality or mental deficiency were multiplied by inheritance. Their defective 'germ plasm', the term the cell biologist August Weissmann used for what we call genes, rather than the environment or poverty, was held to be at fault. Modern medicine and welfare were counter-selectively perpetuating these problems, with each beneficial scientific advance representing a Pyrrhic victory.[1] These concerns were not restricted to predominantly industrial societies. In mainly rural societies, such as Iceland or Sweden, interest in plant- and stock-breeding fused with concern about such conditions as deaf-mutism stemming from consanguinity, or the allegedly anti-social activities of the Tattars, whose appearance or lifestyle deviated from Nordic aesthetic ideals and social conformity.[2]

Externally, societies seemed to be threatened by more prolific peoples, as if national potency was seriously a matter of mere population numbers. The French feared the prolific birthrate of their martial eastern neighbours, and Germans trembled at the thought of the 'Slavic hordes'. Migration represented a source of eugenic anxiety in several societies. Eugenicists worried they were either losing the right, or gaining the wrong, sort of people. In North America, dominant Anglo-Saxons were perturbed both by the influx of penniless eastern and southern Europeans into urban slums and by the fecundity of indigenous 'poor white trash', who were undermining the vitality of the white race vis-à-vis Afro-American Blacks. Apparently, northern reformers introduced these 'progressive' notions to ill-educated Southerners.[3] Scandinavians lamented the loss of Nordic types to North America. Since it would be misleading to imply that this was an exclusively European concern, one should mention that in China

eugenicists blamed miscegenation for that country's ills and called for
the elimination of 'unfit elements', and that eugenics was a going
concern in Brazil and India.[4]

Scattered eugenic pioneers acquired institutional bases, and a 'gene
race', rather like the later Space or AIDs-cure races, commenced
between eugenicists in various countries. The world's first professorial
chair in eugenics was established in 1909, at University College London, that bastion of educational progressivism and religious non-
conformity; the first dedicated Institute for Racial Biology at Uppsala
in Sweden in 1922. It tantalised a wide range of progressive figures,
such as Keynes and the Webbs in Britain, the latter founders of the
London School of Economics, another cutting-edge sort of place.
However, the British pioneers of eugenics were rapidly overtaken by
the Americans and Germans, although both the *New Statesman* and
Manchester Guardian continued to express a sympathetic interest into
the 1930s.[5] Commencing with Indiana in 1899, thirty-five North
American states eventually permitted the eugenic sterilisation of mentally handicapped people. California sterilised more people than any
other state. Wealthy philanthropists bore the costs of the eugenics
laboratory at Cold Spring Harbor, and indeed of the Department for
Genealogy and Demography at the Kaiser-Wilhelm Institute in Munich
when funds were tight in the Weimar Republic. German eugenicists in
turn enthused over American sterilisation laws and the 1924 Immigration Restriction Act, suggesting that similar legislation would keep
eastern Jews and southern Europeans out of Germany. American
studies of 'poor white trash' families, such as the Jukes, or of the
genetically good and bad descendants of the Kallikaks, were effortlessly
absorbed into the visual repertory of the National Socialists. Both
American eugenicists and their admirers in Germany stressed the
enormous costs to taxpayers ensuing from anti-social families such as
the Jukes, and of public asylums.[6]

As well as being an international scientific trend, eugenics spanned
conventional political divides, and attracted enthusiasts from both
sexes. Although eugenicists included extreme antisemitic fringes, routinely bent on producing blond, blue-eyed Nordic people, they also
numbered socialists, including socialist Jews. In Britain, where in 1931
a Labour MP endeavoured to introduce legislation permitting voluntary sterilisation, the Fabian socialist Sidney Webb gave the game away
about this enthusiasm, when he announced, 'no consistent eugenicist
can be a "laissez-faire" individualist unless he throws up the game in

despair. He must interfere, interfere, interfere!' Apart from a doctrinaire credulousness towards the prophylactic powers of modern science, some illiberal socialists wished to police and reform the lifestyles of those 'Lumpenproletarians' who did not conform to their ideals of what working-class people should be. To which authoritarian left-wingers would presumably respond that advocates of laissez-aller do not have to live next to the wilfully anti-social.

But it is important to remember that politics did not consist solely of a left–right divide. Eugenics was multifaceted, alternately presenting hard and soft faces according to the public climate of the times, or tailored to national circumstances. If Christians did not like the sound of progressive new moralities, or the idea of reducing the cost of institutional care through sterilisation, especially when they had impressive networks of charitable homes and asylums as an alternative to sterilisation, they could hardly find much to disagree with in the eugenicists' emphasis on careful thought about marriage partners, the preservation of the family and the virtues of a temperate lifestyle. There was room for co-operation here.[7]

Right- and left-wing eugenicists were at one in seeing opportunities for experts and professionals such as themselves to plan and direct the future of biological collectivities through positive or negative eugenic measures built into burgeoning health and welfare systems.[8] In the British case, the power and status of civil servants vis-à-vis academics and scientists, and a disdain for 'clever' eggheads, may partly explain why eugenics met with greater scepticism than in Germany, where the professoriate basked in uncritical acclaim.[9] In the land of Burke and Hare, the notorious body-snatchers, there was a cultural indisposition to people being 'cut up', while the likes of G. K. Chesterton were effective in expressing the objections of two million British Roman Catholics. The position of traditional conservatives was complicated, and should not be conflated with that of the extreme right or, in this case, the 'progressive' left. Critical of the mounting costs of welfare, conservatives also spoke of its inherent tendency towards anonymity and bureaucratisation, and the morally corrupting effects on the dependent poor, emphasising instead responsibilities rather than rights, including the duty of individuals and communities to assist one another.[10] Both their critique of the moral deleteriousness of welfare dependency and the stress upon the obligations of individuals – whether rich or poor – separated traditional conservatism from Nazism's obsessions with the future collective health of the Aryan-

Germanic race. Eugenics sat better with the big state since it virtually depended on the existence of armies of professional do-gooders.

A final point might be made regarding the relationships between eugenics, Nazi racism and science in general, since a rather unthinking anti-science mood is abroad among arty moralists. As has been repeatedly stressed, Nazism invested natural laws with religious authority, so it is simple-minded to blame something so nebulously Hegelian as the 'spirit of science', or indeed the technocratic character of modern medicine, for the inhuman policies of Nazi Germany. Science, after all, cannot be reduced to hereditarian biology, so to criticise its 'spirit' seems sweeping.[11] Nazism effortlessly accommodated homeopathic and holistic medicine, as symbolised by the herb plantations in Dachau and the SS monopolisation of mineral-water production, and was not without faddish, life-reforming elements, whether concerning the harmful effects of smoking or the need to eat organic bread. This was a reflection not just of a more general, and far less benign, concern with authenticity and purity, but also of a mindset hostile to the capitalist food industry.[12]

The 'science' supporting eugenic policies was mostly a matter of faith, as was evident when ethically aware and responsible scientists used conventional scientific reasoning to question the eugenicists' zealously held pseudo-scientific assumptions. The fact that psychiatrists abused shell-shocked soldiers is more remarked upon than that scientists deduced from shell-shock that mental illness could result from external trauma and was curable.[13] There was also nothing specifically scientific in the enthusiasm some eugenicists, and for that matter Hitler, evinced for the alleged practices of ancient or primitive societies such as the Spartans, but this does not lead to wholesale condemnation of classics.[14] 'Modern' humanitarianism was routinely castigated for the problems of the present, and for the long-term ruin allegedly facing the racial collective if it ignored the primordial dictates of nature. The links between this strange mix and modern science are by no means self-evident.

Neither the internationality of eugenics nor American or Scandinavian enthusiasm for sterilisation adequately accounts for the scale or systematic viciousness of Nazi racial-hygienic policies, which resulted not only in the sterilisation of about four hundred thousand people in a decade, but also – from a rather different starting point – in the deliberate murder of about two hundred thousand people in the wartime 'euthanasia' programme. These policies had a hinterland, part of which was what some contemporaries perceived as a change in the moral climate.

In Germany, the First World War contributed a brutalisation of feeling, an acute sense of national grievance and resentments about economic cost and human loss. The latter were compounded by the economic crises of the Weimar Republic, so that the balance gradually tilted away from positive welfare measures towards the cheaper preventive option of sterilisation. A similar response to the Depression occurred among eugenicists in several countries. Fitful pre-war concern about counter-selectively conserving people who were both economically burdensome and biologically deleterious to the health of the collective racial organism was heightened by the losses of the First World War – notwithstanding the fact that in Germany the casualties included approximately seventy thousand asylum inmates, who died through neglect and undernourishment during the latter part of the war. Perceptive observers realised that the war itself had altered things for the worse. Shifts in conduct on the battlefield, where machine guns and poison gas made chivalry redundant, had their analogues on the home front.[15] Addressing the plenary conference of the German Psychiatric Association in May 1920, its chairman Karl Bonhoeffer, father of the theologian Dietrich, said:

> It could almost seem as if we have witnessed a change in the concept of humanity. I simply mean that we were forced by the terrible exigencies of war to ascribe a different value to the life of the individual than was the case before, and that in the years of starvation during the war we had to get used to watching our patients die of malnutrition in vast numbers, almost approving of this, in the knowledge that perhaps the healthy could be kept alive through these sacrifices. But in emphasising the right of the healthy to stay alive, which is an inevitable result of periods of necessity, there is also a danger of going too far: a danger that the self-sacrificing subordination of the strong to the needs of the helpless and ill, which lies at the heart of any true concern for the sick, will give ground to the demand of the healthy to live.[16]

Discussions of euthanasia commenced before 1914, and initially revolved around issues of individual autonomy. They quickly developed into discussions of reducing costs. Thus in 1910 Dr Heinz Potthoff, a member of the progressive liberal association Freisinnige Vereinigung, aired the thought that the nation's welfare capital would be better expended on the healthy than on unproductive 'cripples and idiots'. Little separated the progressive rhetoric of such liberals from that used later by the National Socialists.

After the First World War, these ideas were given considerable salience by the tract *Permission for the Destruction of Life Unworthy of Life* by Karl Binding and Alfred Hoche, published in 1920. Binding was a distinguished academic lawyer who died before the tract was published. Hoche was a psychiatrist, whose claims to fame included rather plangent poetry, and macabre experiments on the spinal cords of victims of the guillotine. In their tract, Binding and Hoche stressed the historical and spatial relativity of Judaeo-Christian respect for the sanctity of human life by reference to ancient or primitive societies. Twentieth-century Germans were enjoined to emulate Spartans and Inuit, who killed respectively their sickly infants and their aged parents. At roughly the same time, a distinguished American psychiatrist Dr Alfred Blumer was extolling the 'barbaric Scots' who killed defective babies *and their mothers*. Progress apparently lay in regression to the mores of earlier times, a sure sign of men who found the contemporary world perplexing. Simple pity was expended in vain, since 'where there is no suffering, there can also be no pity'. Having identified 'lives unworth living' in correspondingly emotive and lurid language, the authors argued that 'incurable idiots' should be killed, along with the terminally ill or critically injured, whose wishes could be either ascertained or anticipated.[17]

High concerns about moral systems or the emotional burden to relatives of the sick were soon displaced by questions of material cost, as Hoche calculated the direct and indirect burden occasioned by twenty or thirty 'idiots' living to the age of fifty. Much of the indignation Hoche evinced when he contrasted fit people struck down on battlefields or in disasters in mines with the allegedly meaningless lives of 'ballast existences' in the asylums may be attributable to the grief he experienced through losing his only son at Langemarck rather than the mindset that presumably goes with someone whose scientific work involved loitering behind guillotines. Both authors were cavalier in their discussion of how consent should be ascertained or how these measures would be implemented without error. A taboo had been broken: doctors were being encouraged to take life.[18] The ensuing debate occupied an ever widening number of professionals, many of whom unequivocally rejected these arguments, invariably because of the scope for abuse, despite the apparent concern of the authors with legal safeguards. Opponents included several radical eugenicists, who argued that a concern with fine breeding had nothing to do with the separate issue of fine dying, for the aim was to prevent the birth of 'life unworthy of life' rather than to kill such people once they existed.[19] Again, these elementary complications are often overlooked by those seeking to damn abortion, genetics, euthanasia and so forth with the 'lessons' of Nazi Germany.

The long-term fate of the vulnerable was not helped by Ewald Meltzer, an advocate of sterilisation *and* a staunch critic of Binding and Hoche, whose straw poll of parents of 'idiotic' children in his charge indicated that many of them would not have been unsympathetic to the state covertly killing them. In their reported comments, some parents outlined ways in which this might be done which anticipated Nazi practice over a decade later. Writing in 1936, Meltzer did not entirely rule out 'euthanasia' killings either, albeit in the specific case of wartime triage, which his generation had already experienced. The poll of parental opinion which Meltzer conducted in the mid-1920s was destined to be used in Nazi 'euthanasia' propaganda. The fact that his poll was misused in this way does not alter the reality of the opinions expressed in it, opinions which are sometimes heard nowadays from the parents of such children.[20]

Beyond debates about euthanasia between academics, doctors and lawyers, other developments militated in favour of radical solutions, while further marginalising already isolated people. First, criticism of psychiatry from both left and right as an expensive and repressive waste of time, and Weimar governmental concern to cut costs, combined to galvanise a few psychiatric reformers such as Gustav Kolb and Hermann Simon, both depressed by the therapeutic dereliction of the large provincial asylums. After some years of crying in the wilderness, these two men found a more congenial political and professional response to their local ventures in community care and occupational therapy, chiefly because the reforms would save money and medicalise psychiatry. These reforms included outpatient provision and paid family fostering, or the introduction of occupational therapy (or unpaid work) to the asylums. The economic benefits were plain for all to see. While it cost 1,277 Reichsmarks to keep one person in Munich's Eglfing-Haar asylum, the annual overheads of one outpatient clinic in Munich servicing the needs of thousands was 2,000 Reichsmarks.[21] Similarly, substantial economies ensued from asylums where up to 80 per cent of the patients worked, whether in agricultural or light industrial facilities such as cigar rolling, or running errands and

answering the telephone, often for minimal wages. These facts made a
nonsense of Nazi claims that asylums housed 'burdens' and 'ballast
existences' who were dead weights on hard-working 'national comrades'. The professional psychiatric journals soon exuded optimism
about these busy institutions, with countless individuals such as Valentin Faltlhauser of Erlangen adopting similar outpatient strategies in
Erfurt or Nuremberg. This was not surprising since these reforms
served to medicalise psychiatric care, making asylums more like hospitals and less like warehouses, and promised an enhanced rate of success
in acute cases.

Inevitably, these reforms had their demerits, although this did not
automatically invalidate them. Following their discharged patients out
into the wider world, many psychiatrists realised that the patients were
the tip of an iceberg, whose submerged bulk consisted of ramified
family abnormalities. Being of an increasingly hereditarian cast of
mind, psychiatrists (and their scientific colleagues) began mapping this
information in primitive databanks. Rendered pessimistic by the scale
of the problem, a growing number began to think of sterilisation as
the solution. Again, this was an international tendency. In Britain, the
1929 Woods Committee on Mental Deficiency reported that a quarter
of a million mental defectives were living outside asylums, a fact which
led the Eugenics Society to found the Committee for Legalising Eugenic
Sterilisation and to support Major Church's 1931 private member's
bill licensing voluntary sterilisation. It is worth emphasising too that
the 1930 papal encyclical *Casti connubi* was primarily condemnatory
of the thirty or so US states which had introduced sterilisation of
mental incompetents.[22]

The introduction of occupational therapy in asylums indirectly
drew attention to the therapy-resistant remainder of chronic patients,
whose existence in the back wards constituted a permanent reminder
of the inherent limitations of the psychiatric project. In other words,
psychiatric reform highlighted sub-marginal members of an already
isolated constituency.[23] Long before the Nazis came to power, some
psychiatrists advocated sterilising the unfit, although few thought
killing the incurably mentally or physically handicapped was a desirable or feasible option. Enthusiasts such as Heinrich Boeters in
Zwickau tested the existing legal parameters by carrying out, and
then publicising, illegal operations. Enthusiasts also included Christian
welfare functionaries, such as Hans Harmsen of the Protestant
Inner Mission, for whom sterilisation was 'a moral duty, which can be

explained as love of one's neighbour and responsibility towards future generations'.[24] A nebulous future was prepared with the rhetoric of love, sacrifice and duty rather than the language of hate.

A few psychiatrists protested against these trends. In 1923 the respected Berlin *Ordinarius* Karl Bonhoeffer wrote a highly critical report for the Prussian provincial health council's Committee on Population Policy and Racial Hygiene on Boeters' draft law for the compulsory sterilisation of those born blind or deaf, idiots, epileptics, mental patients, criminals, sex offenders and parents of more than two illegitimate children. He challenged the right of the state to interfere in the personal sphere, and questioned Boeters' claims that there had been a marked increase in mental illness or that the conditions targeted by his draft law were hereditary.[25] In 1932, when the Prussian provincial health council debated a draft law on voluntary sterilisation, Bonhoeffer raised a number of technical objections. Another eminent psychiatrist, Oswald Bumke of Munich, went further when he cautioned that:

> if one were to drag the discussion of sterilisation into today's arena of political struggle, then one would probably pretty soon hear less talk about the mentally ill, but more regarding Aryans and non-Aryans, and of the blond Germanic race and the less valuable round-skulls. It is certainly unlikely that anything positive would arise from this; on the contrary, both science in general, and genealogy and eugenics in particular, would be damaged in ways from which they would not easily recover.

Bumke also warned that making a fetish of cost would result in the view that 'we must not merely kill all of the mentally ill and psychopaths, but every cripple, including wounded war veterans, all the old maids who are no longer working, all the widows who no longer have children to raise, and all the invalids and old age pensioners'. Debates about eugenic sterilisation and euthanasia sprang from different sources, with not all advocates of the former being in favour of the latter, but some contemporaries were beginning to discuss them in the same breath.[26]

Attempts to introduce eugenic voluntary sterilisation antedated a National Socialist government, with regional initiatives enjoying cross-party support in 1924, 1928 and 1932. According to the latest studies, eugenicists (that is, a coalition of doctors and women) in the Social Democratic Party made most of the running in seeking to introduce such measures. In late July 1933 the Nazis introduced the Law for the Prevention of Hereditarily Diseased Progeny, with effect from 1 January 1934. If in many respects the law mirrored earlier draft legislation, the crucial difference was that sterilisation could now be compulsory. This law specified eight allegedly hereditary illnesses: congenital feeblemindedness; schizophrenia; manic–depressive illness; epilepsy; Huntington's Chorea; hereditary blindness and deafness; and severe physical malformation, whose hereditary character had been 'sufficiently established by research'. This was worryingly open-ended.

Of course this last point was patently untrue in the 1930s, the clue being the absence of the prefix 'hereditary' from schizophrenia or manic–depressive illness, a sleight of hand designed to cover cases where the cause was exogenous. Clearly construed as a modest start, the law also made it possible to sterilise chronic alcoholics, again an elastic category of persons.[27] Successive amendments sanctioned the sterilisation of children over ten, although the direct use of force applied only to the over-fourteens; compulsion to appear before public medical examiners; the withdrawal of the right to legal representation from persons brought before the new Hereditary Health Courts; and in 1935 the sanctioning of eugenic abortion up to and including women in the sixth month of pregnancy. In 1936, the law was amended to include X-ray sterilisation of women over thirty-eight.[28]

Sterilisation was usually instigated by public health doctors operating from within the thousand or so State Health Offices created by the 3 July 1934 Law for the unification of the public health system, or by the directors of asylums and homes in the case of people living in institutions. Enhanced state control was the indispensable preliminary to the implementation of the eugenic utopia. For one often unremarked aspect of these issues is that whereas in the United States psychiatrists moved from asylums to private practice, thus severing their ties with the state, in Germany the opposite seems to have happened, as they literally became 'sentinels guarding the hereditary stream of the nation'.[29] More generally, all those involved with the sick were now obliged to report (the soft term for denounce) what they knew about a person to the public health authorities, who would then trawl through his or her life-history including family background, school records, dealings with welfare agencies, employment history and the lay opinion of neighbours and policemen. An interview with a public health doctor usually preceded a sterilisation application to the Hereditary Health Courts. In Frankfurt am Main, separate agencies concerned with looking after the lame, alcoholics, ex-prisoners, tramps and vagrants were physically moved to the new City Health Office to enhance inter-agency co-operation against the new unified constituency of the biologically damaged. By 1938, this one agency disposed of 280,000 index cards and a quarter of a million files in its Heredity Archive.[30] Similar databanks were compiled in other parts of Germany, often by rabid professorial enthusiasts such as Karl Astel, Rainer Fetscher and Heinrich Wilhelm Kranz. By 1938, Astel and his team had compiled data on a quarter of the population of Thuringia, 'so that henceforth the less valuable, the asocial, and criminals could more easily be excluded than before'.[31] Kranz, a veteran of a Marburg student corps which had supported the Kapp putsch, ran a hereditary-biology research office from within the University of Giessen, whose rector he became in 1940. Together with his large number of assistants, Kranz built up vast hereditary databanks on the population of Hessen, while promoting the new role of doctors as 'political soldiers' of the Führer through lectures, speeches and a stream of articles.[32]

Invasiveness was not confined to patients in institutions, who constituted 30 to 40 per cent of those sterilised, because their opportunities to reproduce were so limited. The strict segregation of the sexes rather militated against the idea put about in eugenic propaganda that they were producing further generations of damaged people within asylums. But then propaganda which smoothly conflated blind ten-year-olds with rapists and murderers was not strong on logic. Ranging beyond the asylums, sterilisation based upon *hereditary* illnesses necessarily entailed both a search for former patients and investigation of even quite remote family relations. Old patient records were scoured for information on entire families, in breach of all customary proprieties regarding medical confidentiality. A man treated for psychopathic disorder in 1921, who in the interim had become a successful small businessman, was the subject of a sterilisation application fourteen years later, despite the fact that 'psychopathy' was not mentioned in the legislation. Others were put through a similar ordeal on the basis of family connections with people they hardly knew, as when Hermann Pfannmüller took the opportunity afforded by the examination of a young woman to discover a further twenty-one 'degenerates' in the family, recommending the sterilisation of ten of these people. In some areas, psychiatrists encouraged teachers to make children devise family trees, in an attempt to co-opt them in the sterilisation of their own families.[33]

Since the deranged and seriously mentally ill tended to be institutionalised, the reporting agencies concentrated upon the 'feebleminded'
in the wider community, a category of persons which made up 60 per
cent of those sterilised. But what was congenital 'feeblemindedness'?
The German Psychiatric Association thought in terms of idiocy (an IQ
of 0–19) or imbecility (an IQ of 20–49). However, the men whose
task it was to outline the precise scope of the sterilisation law wished
to include 'mild feeblemindedness', or debility, that is people with an
IQ of 50–70. This was no academic matter, for while one hundred
thousand people were liable to sterilisation under the first rubric,
nearly a million would be affected by the second, including about 10
per cent of recruits to the armed forces.[34] There was also the matter of
the not inconsiderable number of intellectually challenged members of
the Nazi Party, including brawny brown-shirted farmboys, who were
thick as two short planks. Party officials hastened to blame the
educational system rather than hereditary factors. In 1936 the deputy
Reich Doctors' Leader Bartels evinced an atypical environmentalist
scepticism:

> When a peasant boy from Masuria who has hardly had any experience
> of schooling because he always had to work in the fields, comes to
> Berlin and joins some Party formation or other, and then commits
> some stupidity while drunk, this is soon followed by an application to
> have him examined with a view to his eventual sterilisation. Then there
> is the famous questionnaire, e.g. 'When was Columbus born?' and the
> boy answers 'no' to everything saying 'I don't know anything about
> that', because it is quite possible that he has never had the chance to
> learn these things. A doctor who has examined him only once certainly
> cannot, on this basis, come to a final verdict that the boy is of lesser
> value, because perhaps his abilities have never been able to come to
> fruition.[35]

This was only one minor irony in Nazi enthusiasm for eugenic
fitness and racial purity. The major irony was captured by the writer
Samuel Beckett, who stayed in Germany during the 1930s. The latest
definition of an Aryan, he wrote, was 'He must be blond like Hitler,
thin like Göring, handsome like Goebbels, virile like Röhm – and be
called Rosenberg.'[36] Rarely can such an unprepossessing group of
people have had so much to say about fitness and purity.

Contemporaries knew that intelligence tests were of limited use
since studies of normal and backward students at schools in Samland,

East Prussia, revealed identical levels of ignorance regarding Bismarck or Christopher Columbus. Only 7 per cent of normal children could spot the difference between a state prosecutor and a lawyer, as could two of the backward cohort. However, in the first of many Catch-22 situations, when individuals could make short work of intelligence tests, notions like 'moral insanity' were to hand to sterilise them on the basis of their lifestyle, notions which revealed a worrying degree of diagnostic subjectivity. Questions about who was Luther or where the sun rises and sets were superseded by why do people pray or tell the truth, as if an ability to answer these questions correctly was proof of moral probity. On a less rarefied level, sterilisation could ensue if existing children were unkempt, if beds were not made or the washing up left undone. And then there was the matter of people who had recovered from mental illness or who had been successfully treated for alcoholism or impaired sight. Since the legislators were interested in the long term, people who had recovered, become abstinent or been successfully operated on for cataracts were still sterilised since the aim was to eradicate a putative underlying pathology. Eugenic and medical journals (by now often indistinct entities) brimmed with articles about whether severe physical malformation included congenital dislocated hips, a woman who was 140 centimetres tall, people with hare-lips and cleft palates, or whether autistic savants could be feebleminded. Although this literature is too tedious to consider in any detail, its most striking feature is the remorseless pedantry with which even rare abnormalities were investigated. Careers were helped along with mind-less discussions about whether to sterilise midgets or whether parapleg-ics could have sexual intercourse.

The decision to sterilise a person was taken by the new Hereditary Health Courts, of which there were 220, with a further tier of eighteen Higher Courts to hear appeals. Consisting of a judge, a public health doctor and one other medical 'expert' (whose expertise often lay in fields unconnected with the illnesses the law specified), these courts could call for further testimony or documentation, or act solely on the base of the original application for sterilisation. It frequently happened that the doctor or psychiatrist who instigated the proceedings also sat on the Hereditary Health Court, as was the case with the Kaufbeuren psychiatrist Valentin Faltlhauser, who sat as a judge on the Hereditary Health Court at Kempten.[37] This in itself violated civilised legal customs, even before one considers the prevailing precept: 'The judge must always bear in mind Hitler's words that "the right to personal freedom always gives way to the duty of preserving the race".'[38] Many of these judges were of the same mind as one of the doctor–judges in Bremen, who enjoined all his medical colleagues 'to extinguish the ideas of yesterday' by zealously soliciting the sterilisation of their patients.[39] In other words, they were often eugenic zealots, whose most salient characteristic was not impartiality on these very issues. Their messianic fervour for this pseudo-science was often articulated in pseudo-religious language, with the victims 'sacrificing' themselves for the good of the collective. Once opposed to sterilisation *on scientific grounds*, Carl Schneider now described sterilisation as 'a responsible attempt before God to provide a new time with new people'. This sounded portentous enough, but its vacuous highmindedness was depressing.

Proceedings in the Hereditary Health Courts were often extremely heated, not only for the individual whose health or way of life was on trial, but also for their families, in view of the allegedly hereditary character of the illnesses. Hearings were also extremely brief. In Frankfurt the Hereditary Health Court convened once a week to consider between fifteen and twenty cases. Each received ten to fifteen minutes' deliberation. This was extended to half an hour when it was deemed necessary to include the objects of these deliberations for a face-to-face evaluation.[40] Appeals to the Higher Courts had to take place within one month. If they were overruled, the operation had to be carried out within a fortnight, with the use of force if necessary. Operations were carried out by about 140 designated doctors working on a *pro rata* basis. They involved ligation of the fallopian tubes for women, and vasectomy for men. Some five thousand people died through surgical complications; the majority of them women because of the more complicated nature of the surgery. Instances of gross medical negligence, for example use of the wrong anaesthetic, were simply covered up. Apart from those who committed suicide in the wake of the operation, many of those sterilised suffered enduring traumatisation, and do so today whenever they are reminded of the fact that they have no children or grandchildren. Sterilisation was not only a gross violation of human dignity, or of fundamental beliefs if the person was Catholic, it also meant becoming a second-class citizen. That this was especially onerous can be seen from the number of people who indignantly insisted on the contribution they made to the community, often with the aid of testimonials from their employers. Their relatives felt obliged to stress the impeccable health of their families, or the exogenous circumstances affecting a particular individual. Like other totalitarian societies, this one played upon human guilt, putting the psychological onus on the individual to prove his or her value to the collective, as if people have to justify why they are alive or why they should have children.

Many issues surrounding the introduction of compulsory sterilisation deserve further comment. These policies had to be presented to the wider population. That many people were anxious about these measures can be seen from an exchange of correspondence between the Oberpräsident in Wiesbaden and the Frankfurt City Health Office. The former was appalled that hereditarily ill individuals or their relatives were boycotting 'Aryan' doctors in favour of Jewish doctors who would be loath to instigate sterilisations. Jewish doctors were to be reminded of their duty. So too were 'Aryan' doctors in Frankfurt, with the aid of monthly displays of who was, or was not, completing the required number of applications for sterilisation.

Since eugenic practice potentially touched so many Germans, considerable efforts were made to persuade the public of the necessity for these policies. After decades of keeping gates locked and walls high, asylums became transparent, as thousands of visitors trooped through them on guided tours, which were replete with lectures, films and especially shocking human exhibits. Between 1933 and 1939, over twenty-one thousand people, including six thousand SS men from Bad Tolz, visited Munich's Eglfing-Haar asylum alone. Although sometimes visitors were moved to pity, or disgust, at the brutal treatment of the 'exhibits' by medical staff, the reaction of one SS officer who came out suggesting setting up machine guns at the entrances was presumably not untypical of members of that formation.[41] Racial-political propaganda flourished, in the sense that up to 1938 the Racial Political Office in Berlin trained 3,600 people to disseminate it. Since the collaboration of doctors was crucial, special courses were organised for them; while in the universities chairs of racial hygiene were established, with attendance at lectures and an examination in this field becoming obligatory for medical students. Karl Bonhoeffer seems to have used such courses held under the aegis of the Berlin Society for Neurology and Psychiatry to remind these audiences that such illnesses as schizophrenia were amorphous and labile. In 1936 the authorities banned these courses and the publication of Bonhoeffer's lectures to them.[42]

Building on earlier eugenicist propaganda, Nazi agencies subjected the German people to a comprehensive barrage of graphics, slides and documentary films which put the case for compulsory sterilisation. The nation was threatened by rapidly proliferating hordes of congenital idiots. Graphics in journals such as *Neues Volk* or *Volk und Rasse* contrasted the deviant offspring of alcoholics and prostitutes with the norms expected of decent 'national comrades'. The latter were shown literally burdened by simian 'creatures', for the agenda here involved disputing the human personality of the people concerned. Sacks of money were depicted to quantify the amounts being spent on different categories of the handicapped. Indeed, no occasion was missed to contrast the enormous sums allegedly squandered on the mentally and physically handicapped, or the commodious conditions enjoyed by people in asylums or prisons, with the modest, post-Depression living standards of many German workers. Why should healthy youngsters have to play in dankly insalubrious urban courtyards while mental patients enjoyed luxury, light and fresh air in converted baroque castles? Why should healthy little boys and girls have to run around barefoot in the snow, when 'millions' were being expended on cripples and idiots?

Films such as *Erbkrank*, made in 1936, persistently elided the sick with the criminal, in the latter case invariably sex offenders or murderers, while emphasising the number of family houses that could be built for the sums spent on asylums and prisons. *Victim of the Past*, shown in all five thousand German cinemas, utilised interviews with mad people, while an urgent commentary noted that: 'The Jewish race is particularly heavily represented among the insane, and provision is made for their care too. Healthy German national comrades have to work to feed and clean up after them. Anyone who visits one of the larger asylums can establish this fact.'[43] In a society well versed in spotting Jews, few watching the accompanying interviews with patients would have missed the verbal and visual clues given off by a 'facetious' Jewish patient to a doctor speaking to her from behind her shoulder, in a manner almost guaranteed to distress and irritate anyone.

While stoking mass resentment against vulnerable individuals, these films sought to subvert traditional moral values which might inhibit smooth implementation of these policies. Every visual trick in the filmmaker's book was used, and every possible angle was covered by progressively slick scriptwriters. Scientists and doctors were frequently used to lend eugenic claims an element of irrefutable authority, in a society where academics and professionals still basked in uncritical public esteem towards the 'Herr Doktor' or 'Herr Professor', rather than being identified with Hollywood or Pinewood's barmy scientists. Since no one can be nasty to nurses, these films contrasted the 'waste' of their youthful energies and 'idealism' (many of them had just drifted into the job in the wake of the Depression) with the allegedly inert or insensate objects of their dedication. Platitudinous observations about nature – 'Everything that is weak for life will ineluctably be destroyed' – were designed to make these policies seem like the fulfilment of the inevitable, or indeed analogous to the fate of weeds in a garden. Modern welfarism was denigrated as counter-selective, or rather as a 'sin' – for there were many unattributed borrowings from Christianity – against the 'law of natural selection'. Appropriating and inverting the moral language of their opponents, words like duty, deliverance, mercy and sacrifice tripped off the tongues of people for whom compassion, humanity or pity were anathema, part of a liberal or Christian moral order they consciously sought to replace.[44]

Propaganda is sometimes dismissed as a matter of preaching to the converted. Actually, propaganda also has the function of sowing moral confusion, or opening up undreamed of vistas, rather as modern advertising tempts people to buy sickly drinks by associating them with yachts and sultry girls in the Seychelles. In this case, propaganda encouraged and incited people to doubt venerable religious precepts, or to entertain thoughts which under normal circumstances they might have remained blissfully ignorant of. For there was a commitment to open minds here to transgressive possibilities. The fact that these films shocked or inspired pity in some people was their only (minor) drawback. In order to mobilise the masses behind their agenda, the Nazis had to undermine those who espoused competing values, sometimes just by practising them. The two major Churches were touched by these policies in many ways: not least by the fact that they ran extensive networks of charitable foundations, often specialising in the low-cost maintenance of incurables or backward children, which meant that they would have to choose whether to co-operate in sterilising their own charges, or at the very least seek advice from their respective hierarchies.

Neither Church was entirely impervious to compromise with the new scientific thought of the time, especially when it conformed with traditional family values and spoke of moral improvement. Both were concerned with institutional survival, and partially shared a common language with the Nazis of antisemitism, nationalism and anti-Bolshevism, although the accents were often different.[45] The Protestant Inner Mission disposed of hundreds of institutions for the physically disabled, the mentally ill, epileptics, geriatric patients and difficult juveniles. Its Standing Conference on Eugenics convened for the first time in Treysa in May 1931 under the chairmanship of Hans Harmsen. The invitation stated: 'The exaggerated protective measures for the anti-social and less valuable stemming from a misdirected humanitarianism have led to an ever stronger increase in the anti-social groups in the population.' The ensuing Treysaer Resolution advocated differential welfare provision and the decriminalisation of eugenic sterilisation. Although the conference rejected the arguments of Binding and Hoche regarding the depersonalisation of full idiots, and stressed the Fifth Commandment, it also noted that the artificial prolongation of life was as much an interference in God's handiwork as shortening it by some form of 'mercy killing'.[46]

Some Protestant theologians legitimised the abandonment of universal welfare by arguing that God had created such supra-individual entities as the family, nations or races whose future well-being overrode the rights of individuals, which in recent times had come to be regarded as absolute. Having supported the terms of the Prussian draft law on voluntary sterilisation, the Protestant Church accepted the compulsory measures of the National Socialists, merely arguing that force should not be employed in their own establishments and that the sterilisation of the deaf or blind should remain voluntary. Sterilisations of 2,399 inmates of Protestant asylums were carried out in 1934; and 3,140 in the first half of 1935.

It would be misleading to depict all asylums as reluctant participants, given that their staff often welcomed the advent of authoritarian national government. Annual reports of asylums such as Schwäbisch Hall or Stetten were positively self-congratulatory about how staff persuaded patients to 'volunteer' for eugenic sterilisation, or how they had coped manfully with the extra workload involved. A few Protestant asylum doctors were prepared to countenance even more radical remedies for the burden represented by the sick. Addressing his local Nazi Party group in 1937, Adolf Boeckh, chief doctor of the Lutheran Neuendettelsau asylum in central Franconia, managed to confuse eugenic euthanasia with God's handiwork:

> Although the Creator had certainly inflicted illness upon the destiny of mankind, the most severe forms of idiocy and the totally grotesque

disintegration of the personality had nothing to do with God's countenance . . . the Creator had set a warning in our hearts in the form of our
life affirming feeling, that we should not maintain these travesties of
human beings through an exaggerated, and therefore false, type of
compassion, but rather that we should return them to the Creator.[47]

The Roman Catholic Church, with its parallel network, the Caritas
Association, was also not entirely immune to eugenic fashions. Nazi
eugenics struck at the heart of Catholic teaching on the sanctity of
human life, in ways which Nazi antisemitism regrettably did not. The
Church's ultramontane hierarchical structure and hostility to Darwinism had some rather specific saving graces, although no liberal would
wish to labour them. Among the few Roman Catholics who advocated
eugenic measures was the former Jesuit Hermann Muckermann, who
led the section for eugenic studies at the Kaiser-Wilhelm Institute until
his dismissal, notionally for having referred to Hitler as 'an idiot'.[48]
Commencing as a eugenic pro-natalist, Muckermann gradually came
to accept the necessity for eugenic sterilisation. He proselytised these
views, both in influential Catholic circles, and through his more
popular publications.

There were also individual academic theologians, notably Joseph
Mayer of Paderborn, who by asserting that the well-being of the
community was more important than the physical integrity of individuals were prepared to countenance both abortion and eugenic sterilisation, in contravention of canon law on the procreative function of
marriage, as recently elaborated in Pius XI's 1930 encyclical *Casti
connubi*.[49] But this was very much a maverick view, of importance
only because the Nazis sought to make use of it. Most Catholic
theologians were critical of the Nazi view of race as the paramount
good, while stressing that mankind had no business in interfering in
God's handiwork, including His less than perfect creations.[50] However,
theological writing was only part of the Church's response.

The May 1933 Catholic Bishops' Conference at Fulda discussed
and opposed the draft sterilisation law, whose promulgation was
postponed until late July that year so as not to upset concurrent
negotiations for the Concordat with the Vatican. But when they
reconvened in August their opposition had become muted. More
precisely, in subsequent dealings with the Minister of the Interior the
bishops confined their expressions of disquiet to the questions of
conscience which sterilisation *might* pose for Roman Catholic asylum

staff, doctors, judges and nurses. The Minister of the Interior met them halfway by exempting Catholics from the duty of applying (or actively soliciting) sterilisations, *as distinct from reporting* the names of people whose illnesses came within the ambit of eugenic legislation. Catholic casuistry found a useful distinction between morally neutral 'reporting' and 'formal co-operation' or active solicitation. Subsequent pastoral letters were disapproving of sterilisation, in a non-specific fashion. No uniform instructions were issued as to how confessors should handle civil servants, doctors or nurses whose consciences were perturbed by participation in Nazi racial policy.[51]

Some of the latter were not content with the ensuing silence. In 1934 a care worker wrote to the Bishop of Limburg outlining how her duties enmeshed her in the Law for the Prevention of Hereditarily Diseased Progeny. She could not collaborate with what she described as 'such violent interference in God's right as creator and the personal rights of the individual, not to speak of the consequences for them, especially psychological, which can be anticipated'. The idea of doing anything against the will of God literally terrified her 'innermost soul'. The Bishop replied on 19 August, agreeing that her stance was certainly correct. But her job was at stake. Apart from concurring that she should not influence clients to volunteer for sterilisation, the Bishop suggested that she should carry out the rest of the duties connected with sterilisation, that is reporting such cases or researching their family background, 'so that in this fashion it will be possible for you to continue further with the important office of a carer within the municipal social services'.[52]

Opposing or subverting Nazi eugenic policies was not akin to exposing some institutional abuse within, for example, the educational or healthcare systems of modern democratic societies, where coercive sanctions for 'whistle-blowing' are real enough. Since dismissal was the least of one's problems, extreme circumspection was advisable. Being part of the residual Establishment, both ecclesiastical hierarchies preferred to emphasise common interests in preserving the moral order, or appeals to the better natures of those Nazi leaders with whom some sort of dialogue was still possible. They tried to distinguish between individuals in a government of mixed social and political composition, and to probe whether there was a gap between rhetoric and practice. This promised more dividends than outraged confrontation, however compelling this stance might be to Professor Hindsight.

Assuming that they did not agree with eugenic sterilisation, the directors and staff of religious institutions for the sick or deviant had a more limited range of available stratagems. One should bear in mind that people who worked in such institutions often did so precisely because they found the bigger world an uncongenial place, and were therefore inherently ill equipped to deal with government by gangsters. Even frustrating Nazi policy took real courage, since the Nazis had no scruples about altering the tax exempt status of charitable or private foundations to ruin them, or bringing false accusations of child abuse (a distribution of chocolate expedited things) against the staff to discredit and harass them. The perception that informers and spies were everywhere was also something of a disincentive to organised protest. Nonetheless, institutions such as the home for the blind at Pfaffenhausen in Swabia endeavoured to protect their charges from the sterilisation law by segregating the sexes or curtailing outside contacts, thus pre-empting the need for such drastic measures.[53] In other parts of Germany, Catholic nursing staff instructed their charges in how to answer the standardised intelligence tests – the answer to 'who was Luther?' presumably not 'a heretic' – which played such an important part in deciding cases for sterilisation.[54]

The Churches were not the only organisations avowedly concerned with the poor and disadvantaged. Just as traditional Christian ambivalence towards the Jews led to a mealy-mouthed response to Nazi antisemitism, so socialist enthusiasm for science and authoritarian collectivism led to some strange reactions to Nazi eugenic policies. The Social Democratic Party 'Reports from Germany' regularly chronicled cases of compulsory sterilisation, especially if they resulted in fatalities or had a transparently political motive.[55] However, socialist doctors writing in the *International Medical Bulletin* were more equivocal on this issue, and indeed on euthanasia. In 1934, the socialist *Bulletin* published a ringing endorsement of the ideas of Binding and Hoche, which concluded: 'Study of this brochure by Professor Dr. jur. Binding and Dr. A. Hoche is strongly recommended to those, especially doctors and lawyers, who wish to familiarise themselves with questions which have become highly topical today, assuming that the edition has not been destroyed by those in power in the Third Reich.'[56]

Socialist criticism of the inhumanity of compulsory sterilisation was tempered by belief in the absolute necessity for state-directed eugenic measures, and indeed criticism that Nazi legislation did not go far enough. A Swedish doctor writing in 1934 remarked: 'The idea of reducing the number of carriers of bad genes is entirely reasonable. It will naturally be considered within the preventative health measures in socialist community life.'[57] Similarly, another socialist doctor opined, 'the scientific and social preconditions of real eugenics will only be created by a social revolution'. The Nazi legislation, 'which in many respects corresponds to the initiatives which socialist thinking doctors and cultural politicians put forward earlier against reactionary opposition', would make little impact on the problem of recessive genes: 'the law is partly too ambitious, because it encompasses things which hereditarian biology and psychiatry have not yet clarified, partly too narrow in relation to the hidden objective, since it only encompasses dominant genes'.[58]

The men and women affected by these policies generally came from poorer backgrounds, although this was by no means always the case, since no social class was immune to mental illness or physical handicaps. In other words, eugenics cannot simply be apostrophised as the solution to a putative 'social question'. Nor were those affected solely from the urban poor, since even a remote East Friesian village such as Moorsdorf was touched by these policies, largely one suspects because 60 per cent of its 'anti-social' inhabitants had voted for the Communists.[59] Regardless of who these people were, it is incorrect to depict them as passive objects of these policies, since the disadvantaged found surprising reserves of resourcefulness, while the better-off mobilised batteries of professionals. Some of them found ways of delaying, if not evading, the surgeon's scalpel. As the Hereditary Health Courts became less cavalier in their decision making, so the objects of their deliberations found ways of spinning out the proceedings, by calling witnesses or second opinions. Cases lasting minutes could thus be spun out for months.

Flight was a further alternative. One Frankfurt woman apparently fled the country, saying that she would return after her forty-fifth birthday when sterilisation would be superfluous. Another volunteered to enter an asylum at her own expense. All went well for four years as her small pension of 58.20 Reichsmarks per month covered the charges of the Valentinus asylum. However, in 1940 she was transferred to Eichberg, which cost a further 2.50 Reichsmarks per month. An application to sterilise her was not long coming, since the Frankfurt Welfare Office would be paying the difference. In 1943, proceedings were dropped since, after seven years in an asylum, the woman had reached an age when sterilisation would be otiose.[60] Others faced with involuntary sterilisation simply missed appointments or escaped from hospital waiting rooms, until the police finally caught up with them. One wily Bremerhaven merchant seaman managed to jump ships abroad throughout the Third Reich.

Less dramatically, people mobilised lawyers or sympathetic doctors to intercede on their behalf, or themselves pointed out that 'research on heredity is still in its infancy' ('wenn ich annehmen darf steckt der Erbforschung noch in Kinderschuhen'). Lawyers acting as legal guardians sometimes raised awkward questions. When the director of Hadamar tried to sterilise an eighteen-year-old girl with gonorrhoea on the grounds that she was 'hereditarily damaged, intellectually debilitated, sexually unrestrained, workshy, without a sense of family, led an anti-social way of life and would most probably have offspring with the same damaged genetic properties', her lawyer pointed out that none of these things actually figured among the illnesses which occasioned sterilisation. Undeterred, the director of Hadamar replied that cases of 'superficial feeblemindedness' 'must' be covered by the law, since such people tended to have children with similar partners, 'thus' causing 'grave hereditary damage'. She was sterilised in 1936.[61]

Sterilisation was prescriptive in the sense of curtailing eugenically undesirable lineages, for Nazi propaganda spoke of armies, clans and hordes rather than individuals. It did nothing to correct the behaviour of existing 'anti-social' families. What evidence we have again suggests a harsher climate, in which beyond the sort of sanctions used against wayward individuals in democratic societies loomed the watchtowers of the concentration camps. Alcoholics in Augsburg came within the ambit of Dr Hermann Pfannmüller, who subsequently became director of Eglfing-Haar and a euthanasia killer. Involved with a Catholic sanatorium for problem drinkers, Pfannmüller apparently favoured psychotherapy, and was not unsympathetic to environmental explanations of alcoholism. His less indulgent attitude towards the incurable or refractory was apparent in three cases which crossed his path in 1937.

A man called Flick (not his real name) lived together with his wife Franziska and three children in one room in Augsburg. It was small but clean, and the children were well turned out. He was a poorly paid auxiliary worker on the *Autobahn*. Earning 38 Reichsmarks per week, Flick fitfully gave his wife between 15 and 25 Reichsmarks, despite the fact that their monthly rent alone was 22 Reichsmarks. Much of the time Franziska received nothing at all, for on pay day Flick would hurtle into the nearest pub, arriving home early next morning, hitting and spitting at his wife, before falling into bed dressed in his wet shoes and clothes. The initiative in this case came from Franziska, who wanted something done about her drunken husband. We cannot simply ignore her 'input', nor Flick's boorish conduct. Pfannmüller painstakingly recorded the couple's life histories. Flick had a string of petty convictions, mostly for begging or disturbing the peace. The doctor then interviewed them, coming to the view that Flick was 'shameless, totally unreasonable, cold and rough. Character defects: weak-willed, unrestrained, alcohol intolerant, sexually active despite his moral–ethical defects and despite the existence of tertiary syphilis.' He recommended sterilisation, exclusion from all welfare support on the ground that they were 'an anti-social large family', and, 'despite his organic heart defect, compulsory training in a concentration camp recommends itself in the event that Flick continues to burden public welfare any further'.[62]

Another drunk to cross Pfannmüller's sights was Schmidt, again a fictitious name. Schmidt's domestic arrangements were rather fractious. He claimed that his wife and stepson regularly attacked him with boiling water, knives and a poker. Compelled to defend himself, Schmidt conceded that an axe or knife somehow always found their way into his own hands. Unconvinced by this, Pfannmüller made Schmidt sign the following undertaking:

> I swear that in future I will remain sober and will never threaten my relatives. If anyone finds me in an intoxicated state, I agree to immediate police involvement. I have also been informed that in the event of intoxication having been established as well as actions or threats against my relatives, there will be an application to send me to the concentration camp at Dachau. I also agree to police co-supervision. I agree to outpatient treatment, which I will attend every Wednesday evening.[63]

This declaration did not have the requisite deterrent effect. A few weeks later, Schmidt arrived home blind drunk, screaming at his wife: 'I don't want to see you again, get out, or I'll take that knife and cut your throat.' Pfannmüller had him sent to a concentration camp.

A final case concerns Oegg, again an invented name. Oegg was a drunk who over many years had been supported by the Red Cross, the Salvation Army and public assistance. He beat his wife, and his children seemed neglected and undernourished. In 1933, although the family had been given a new home, both now drank to excess, with the wife careering from one side of the street to the other in a state of extreme intoxication. By Christmas 1936, even the children were drunk, presumably to take their minds off having no food or shoes. Oegg used his sickness benefit to purchase liquor; his wife was convicted for assaulting a welfare inspector. Aided by a number of telephone calls from the juvenile and welfare authorities Pfannmüller recommended: 'Treatment is impossible and completely pointless. Oegg is an anti-social, feebleminded drinker, an unrestrained, defective character, who belongs in the concentration camp at Dachau with a view to focused training and correction. Sterilisation seems to be in motion. It will be necessary to remove their rights as guardians of the children . . . we make application that he be dispatched there [to Dachau] as soon as possible.'[64]

It is in the nature of things that we tend to have to view such people through the documentation of their persecutors, or suitably recycled by historians who see these people as victims, which they undoubtedly were. Rarely do we have autonomous personal accounts of people deemed to have been anti-social. Elvira Hempel, a retired Hamburg taxi driver, has written a startlingly unsentimental autobiographical account of life in an anti-social family in Magdeburg in the 1930s. Classified as being 'feebleminded', she was also one of the lucky few to have avoided being killed in the course of the 'euthanasia' programme.

Elvira Hempel's father was a burglar and confidence trickster for whom the needs of his children came last. Children were born every year (Elvira herself in 1931), with six surviving after nine had died prematurely. The children did not attend school; instead they picked over a local rubbish heap in search of scrap to sell and clothing to put on. They were permanently hungry, and lacked shoes even in winter. Visiting churchmen brought food parcels. By regularly converting and reconverting from Protestantism to Roman Catholicism, the Hempel children were eventually able to extort a change of clothing and a bicycle. The police were frequent callers: either for the father or for one of her brothers who had also taken up burglary. Unable to pay the rent, the Hempels were turfed out on to the streets. Having eventually found a one-room basement flat to sleep in, her mother approached the juvenile services for help. Three brothers were soon taken into care. Elvira's mother then deposited her with her grandparents.

In the summer of 1936 Elvira fell ill and was hospitalised. Using the pretext that the grandfather had tuberculosis, the juvenile services committed Elvira to a children's home. As a persistent bed-wetter, she was punished after mealtimes by being stripped and showered with buckets of cold water. In 1938, she was declared feebleminded, and transferred along with her three-year-old sister Lisa to the paediatric section of the asylum at Uchtspringe: 'Here I was surrounded by people who were not proper people, and whose like I had never seen before. One child had only one eye, another had a very small head, as if the head had not grown. Another had half its face contorted, many had epileptic fits. And there were also idiots, real idiots.' This choice of words is in itself noteworthy. She maintained her own sanity in this dismal institution by doing things and helping the nursing staff. By 1939 she knew that handicapped infants were being starved or killed in the asylum by a personage she called the 'Totenmann'.

On 28 August 1940, for there is independent documentation to corroborate Elvira's story, her sister – whom she had looked after as if she were an animated doll – was taken away. The nurses next came for her too. She was interviewed by an unknown woman who was obviously trying to test her intelligence with questions such as 'Can you name the four seasons?' or 'How many months are there in a year?' She then messed up an exercise involving putting together cards depicting a vase and a bunch of flowers. Elvira was then taken by bus to what turned out to be the T-4 extermination centre in the prison at Brandenburg. She was told to undress – this took a long time since fortuitously her dress had many buttons – as a preliminary to joining other children who had been sent through a heavy door. Eventually a man who had been studying a file told her to dress again. She was sent to join the two other children who had survived her transport. After a few weeks she was moved to Brandenburg-Gorden, from where she was transferred in March 1941 to Altscherbitz.[65]

There were also many local and regional initiatives against the 'anti-social' as a group. Although it is well known that the Nazis introduced measures which encouraged and rewarded prolific mothers, such as medals, loans for having four children and concessionary entertainment or travel, it should be borne in mind that they distinguished between racially desirable families 'rich in children' and eugenically undesirable 'large families'. Since quality counted more than quantity, it was never a question of children at any price. Keen to encourage a healthy birthrate among professionals or the respectable working classes, the Nazis were also determined – as we have seen – to curb the fertility of the eugenically undesirable. Since, as hereditarians, racial scientists taught that such people created or gravitated to certain insalubrious environments, the solution was either literally to erase that environment or to remove families from it. In Hamburg, a group of temporarily unemployed academics developed a geography of anti-sociality in the city, with the highest incidences happily located in one of the areas where Communist voters were thick on the ground. These dockside slums were subsequently demolished to disperse inhabitants designated as being 'biological Bolsheviks'. Apart from reducing benefits to make the anti-social change their behaviour in the desired direction, some places established dedicated colonies to get a grip on problem families.[66]

The mayor of Heidelberg, Otto Wetzel, was a firm advocate of such colonies, which would represent an advance – in terms of biologistic control – over the existing practice of dumping such people in shabby temporary housing on the outskirts of the university city. In Heidelberg, the authorities created a colony for the anti-social on a site near the town gasworks. It soon acquired the neutral name 'Wichern settlement'. Free to come and go, the 'anti-social' settlers were given allotments to tend and rabbits to feed themselves with. The welfare authorities then went to work vetting the families, removing the redeemable or refractory to other institutions.

A more thoroughgoing attempt at social engineering was essayed by the welfare authorities in Bremen. The Senator for Employment, Technology and Welfare pioneered a colony at Hashude that was a halfway house between a sink housing estate and a concentration camp. Copying a 'controlled housing estate' built in The Hague in 1923, for again we should note the internationality of these developments, the Bremen authorities spent 600,000 Reichsmarks on their own project. This consisted of eighty-four houses in an L-shaped format, designed to enhance control from a central observation point located in the angle. The houses had no back doors and the surrounding double hedge concealed a barbed-wire fence. There was only one way in or out, via a guardhouse manned day and night. Stone and iron were used extensively, since this made it difficult for the inhabitants to burn or destroy their surroundings. Families were sent to Hashude for a year, during which they had to evince signs of improved behaviour. Many of them were rent-defaulters and layabouts, with chronic family difficulties. At Hashude, the men worked to pay the rent, while the women did housework under the eagle-eyes of female social workers who monitored their cleanliness and orderliness. There was a kindergarten for small children. Petty rules abounded, with collective sanctions and cells for those who refused to work or were disruptive. Serious offences were punished by a spell at Teufelsmoor or relocation to a concentration camp. Since anti-social recidivism among ex-inmates proved high, this expensive experiment in controlled housing was closed in 1940 and not repeated elsewhere in Germany.[67]

Local coercive initiatives were also much in evidence in the case of Sinti and Roma, or Gypsies, who were uniquely caught in the cross-fire of the Nazis' criminal, eugenic and racial concerns. Although the sterilisation law, the November 1933 law concerning habitual offenders and the 1935 Nuremberg Laws did not address them directly, as 'born' criminals prone to 'social feeblemindedness' they frequently came within the ambit of the first two laws. Similarly, commentaries on the Nuremberg Laws extended the concept of racial aliens to include Gypsies and the descendants of Arab or African French troops who had once occupied parts of western Germany. Both groups were henceforth excluded from marriages with 'Aryans'. The knotty problem represented by the fact that the Gypsies originally came from northern India, and hence were unimpeachably 'Aryan', was solved by racial scientists such as Robert Ritter, who posited that during their migration to Europe they had interbred with 'Asiatics' and criminals, giving rise to a population which was 90 per cent anti-social and deviant. Ritter's research would help isolate the minority of 'pure' Gypsies from the bastardised majority.[68] Heinrich Wilhelm Kranz vehemently advocated sterilising Sinti and Roma. In an article entitled 'Gypsies, as they really are', he described them as 'Nomads . . . of another race, who because of their vermin, filth and stench remain foreign to us to this day'.[69]

While Ritter and his team of young assistants quietly got on with the business of assessing and registering Sinti and Roma according to these criteria, the public and local authorities availed themselves of the new climate to disburden themselves of this perceived social nuisance. This is a tricky subject, which does not deserve to be studied by the fiery light of contemporary political correctness. To put this at its blandest, cultural differences sometimes generated real problems, which are not exhausted by talk of folkloric prejudices or race. Thus in 1930 the neighbours of several adjacent streets in Frankfurt am Main complained about 'Gypsies' in their midst. They were fouling the place with human waste and disturbing people with nighttime fights and alarums. Their children had odd habits. Property values were depreciating and tenants seeking rent rebates. When the city authorities let the issue drift, the Nazi Party took up the residents' case.[70] In Berlin, the Olympic Games provided the pretext to corral six hundred Sinti and Roma on an insalubrious and out-of-the-way site at Marzahn, a site which gradually took on the hallmarks of a closed camp. Indeed, it was the local authorities who persistently badgered the SS to reclassify Marzahn as a concentration camp in order not to have to pay for it. Two lavatories and three standpipes soon contributed to the spread of rampant infections. In Berleburg in the Rhineland, the local mayor regarded such hermetically sealed camps as a means of promoting incest among the Gypsies, with incest likely to occasion the sort of hereditary diseases covered by the sterilisation law.

In Düsseldorf, the authorities fretted about a large squatters' settlement called Heinefeld housing over twelve hundred people, of whom only seventy or so were Sinti and Roma, which had mushroomed upon a former firing range used by the French military. While the local painter Otto Pankok painted its picturesque denizens, the authorities were agitated by a typhus epidemic in 1932, and an assault by three Gypsies on a municipal housing officer three years later. The prefabs and tin huts at Heinefeld were soon torn down. All Gypsies in the city were then concentrated in a purpose-built camp at Hoherweg, replete with an armed guard patrolling the place at night with a torch, dog and whip. Instead of drawing upon welfare support, the inhabitants of the camp had to pay the municipality 6 Reichsmarks' monthly rent. With their right to ply an independent existence as craftsmen or musicians, the Gypsies were dragooned into compulsory labour schemes, laying railway track, or factory work in the glassworks at Gerresheim.[71] Similar camps were established in Cologne, Frankfurt am Main and Salzburg. These camps were often a response to complaints about Gypsies from ordinary residents, a response which also undoubtedly suited the desire of local authorities to shed the unanticipated educational, health, utilities and welfare costs of people who tended to pop up in unexpected places.[72]

Inheriting patchy regional legislation whose effect was often just to move Sinti and Roma elsewhere, the Nazis centralised the apparatus of persecution in the Reich Central Office for the Fight against the Gypsy Nuisance which was established in 1936. The materials assembled by the police in Munich and by the racial scientist Robert Ritter, a child psychologist by avocation, were then made available to this agency, which from 1938 was a department of the Reich Criminal

Police Office in Berlin. The thrust of Ritter's state-sponsored research was to distinguish between a handful of pure Gypsies, Gypsy 'half-castes' and persons living a 'Gypsy-like' way of life. Genealogical interviews and research into Romany carried out by Ritter's team of assistants resulted in databanks on Germany's Gypsy population. Part of the costs of this effort were defrayed by the Reich Main Security Office. The intention was to reverse existing policy, in the sense that pure Gypsies were to be allowed to travel within controlled limits – as a sort of anthropological curiosity – while the settled 'half-castes' were to be prevented from assimilating into the German Lumpenproletariat by sterilisation or isolation in camps. Gradually, the municipal camps were transformed into SS-patrolled collection points: the exit point for deportation to the concentration-camp empire.

As we have seen in various contexts, the Nazi government created a harsher political climate in which local or regional initiatives were encouraged against various undesirable constituencies. Anywhere between two and five hundred thousand Germans had no fixed abode in 1933, many of them desperately seeking work in more economically favoured parts of the country. The Nazis issued homeless people with Vagrants' Registration Books recording their stays in approved shelters strung along designated routes. Those without these books were classified as 'disorderly wanderers' and could be imprisoned.[73] Since money given to beggars was money denied to Winter Aid or other Nazi charities, and since they were a nuisance and a blot on the image of a nation joyously returning to work, the Nazis essayed a radical solution. Following a press campaign which emphasised criminal gangs of the sort colourfully depicted by Bert Brecht and Fritz Lang in the Weimar Republic, the police and SA rounded up a hundred thousand vagrants between 18 and 23 September 1933. Since no provision had been made to detain these people, they were mostly released. In several places, the new tougher climate enabled city authorities to send unemployed men to camps with more or less coercive regimes such as Rickling in the case of Hamburg or Teufelsmoor in that of Bremen, where the workshy spent ten hours a day cutting turf and were kept under armed guard.[74]

Although individual Sinti and Roma or 'anti-social' people were undeniably sent to concentration camps before 1938, in that year Himmler's police apparatus launched a series of massive nationwide raids against the 'anti-social', resulting in their 'preventive detention' in concentration camps, a form of detention hitherto restricted to political opponents or career criminals. These arrests also reflected the self-aggrandising tendencies at work within the police, as well as Himmler's own view of policing as a form of preventive epidemiology. More personal reasons may have been at work. In December 1937, a female beggar who had lost both legs in an accident on a farm tried to tap the Reichsführer-SS for money near Munich's Marienplatz. Low on the milk of human kindness, he ordered the arrest of all Munich's beggars and their incarceration in Dachau, although the police failed to find this particular woman. A year later, labour exchanges were told to report to the Gestapo all able-bodied men who either declined to work or left their job without good reason. The local and criminal police made their own inquiries into stray individuals, often with the aid of Party or state welfare agencies. Precisely who was to be picked up and consigned to Buchenwald was left to the Gestapo men on the ground. They were advised that they should focus on the young and fit, rather than hopeless drunks, the old and sick. 'Anti-social' members of the Nazi Party or its formations were expressly excluded. Since the Gestapo did not dispose of detailed data on the 'anti-social', they availed themselves of information provided by welfare agencies in violation of all notions of client confidentiality. The agencies saw an opportunity to cut welfare costs, including the fees for keeping anti-social people in institutions, while even a few arrests in a town such as Münster seemed to deter a remarkable number of people from claiming public assistance.

Between 21 and 30 April 1938, the Gestapo detained about two thousand 'workshy' men across the country. Since technically the job of detaining run-of-the-mill criminals in protective custody was that of the criminal police, that summer Heydrich instructed them to round up the 'anti-social', a significant terminological difference squared by the first sentence of his instructions: 'Since criminality has its roots in the anti-social . . .'. Each criminal police office was told to detain at least two hundred people, including tramps, beggars, Gypsies, convicted or active pimps, violent criminals and all male Jews sentenced to more than one month's imprisonment. The game was given away by the repeated references to the labour requirements of the Four Year Plan, and the instructions to arrest only able-bodied men. The arrests began at dawn on 13 June 1938. The police combed railway station halls, dosshouses, hostels and overnight shelters. Lists of those arrested reveal a cast of drifters and drunks, with bronchitis, rickets and stomach ailments. The pimps included a high proportion of violent, drunken slobs who whiled away their time in louche pubs surrounded by prostitutes. In many areas, the police significantly exceeded their quotas of arrests. Instead of arresting three thousand people (two hundred by each of fourteen criminal police head offices) the SS reported that they had detained ten thousand. It should be emphasised that no courts were involved in these preventive arrests. The police had taken over a field hitherto controlled by local authorities with the aid of due process of law. Indeed, the latter were rudely informed at a conference in August 1938 that there was no need for them to advocate a law enhancing their own powers to detain people in workhouses, since 'now and in the future, the German police . . . will take care of the cleansing of the anti-social from the national community'.[75]

The ten thousand 'anti-social' men detained under 'Aktion Workshy in the Reich' were incarcerated in the new generation of concentration camps, Flossenbürg, Mauthausen and Neuengamme, which were located near stone quarries, or in Buchenwald and Sachsenhausen, which had their own brick-making facilities. That seems to be why they were arrested, since the SS German Earth and Stone Company needed labour to generate the raw materials necessary for Hitler's and Speer's massive public construction projects. A dose of discipline, hard work and fresh air was all these individuals needed; judging from the debilitated, wheezy condition of many of those arrested, this combination probably proved fatal. A no less important reason for the arrests was the deterrent effect they would have on all 'national comrades'. The fate of the 'anti-social', an elastic term which could be redefined at will, warned that 'parasites on the community cannot be tolerated in the National Socialist state'.

The mass arrests of the 'anti-social' radically altered the composition of the concentration-camp population. In Sachsenhausen, seventeen hundred political detainees were swamped by over six thousand new arrivals from the ranks of the 'workshy'. Often constitutionally challenged and poorly clothed, these 'black triangle' prisoners also lacked the group solidarity of the often mutually antithetical criminal 'greens' and political 'reds'. Not much united a beggar with a pimp, or a Gypsy with a drunk. Accounts of their existence in the camps by surviving prisoners suggest the extreme atomisation and group anonymity of the 'anti-social', who seemed to lack the will to resist in the event that they were not camp informers.[76] They were located only a little higher than Jews and homosexuals in the camp hierarchies. In Mauthausen in Lower Austria, they expired in the stone quarries, crushed beneath loads of stone. In Buchenwald in central Germany, they slid around in the cold and wet of a clay mine at nearby Berlstedt, or choked on the sulphurous fumes of the brick-kilns.[77] Political prisoners who controlled labour allocation in Buchenwald admitted to sending the 'anti-social' out on external work details on the grounds that they were expendable.[78]

So far we have been considering the fate of people who mostly lived at large, albeit on the margins of German society. Eugenic policies struck with most force against people confined within institutions for the backward, delinquent, handicapped or mad, people for whom evasion or flight were not feasible options. It is time to turn to the fate of these marginalised, vulnerable individuals. Broadly speaking, the advent of a Nazi government brought with it significant changes in the officials responsible for running asylums, and in the doctors and nursing staff employed within them. At a regional and national level overall policy became the preserve of the radically unsympathetic. Wilhelm Hinsen, director of the Eichberg asylum, recalled that at a conference attended by colleagues from other establishments the official responsible for asylums in his area, Fritz Bernotat, remarked, 'If I was a doctor, I would do away with these patients,' to which Hinsen replied, 'German medicine can congratulate itself that you are not a doctor.'[79] In Upper Bavaria, control over the asylums was exercised by Professor Walter 'Bubi' Schultze, who in 1933 publicly objected to 'beefing up the physically and mentally hopeless and valueless', while extolling the exterminatory virtues of concentration camps in the battle against the unfit and deviant. Both Bernotat and Schultze are known to have discussed the idea of killing incurable psychiatric patients and 'idiotic' children during the mid-1930s. The asylum inspector Professor Kleist, of Frankfurt University, deplored the managerialist brutalisation of language apparent in such phrases as 'an unproductive burden on the national community' and the all-consuming obsession with cost.

Further changes of personnel were apparent in the asylums themselves. Again, Hinsen at Eichberg was informed that 'in future you will get only SS doctors; they know how to handle a needle'.[80] In 1938, Hinsen was himself edged out of his directorship by one such recruit: the thuggish Dr Friedrich Mennecke. In Hamburg, the new officials responsible for the health and welfare system sent out questionnaires to the asylums requesting information on the political affiliations of everyone from the vegetable peelers upwards. Doubtful cases, that is anyone who belonged to the SPD, were referred back to the asylums for detailed investigation. Administrators in the Langenhorn asylum then spent much time trying to retain the services of, for example, a fifty-eight-year-old laundry worker who had been an SPD member since 1906. One explained that the man was too old and stupid to be a threat to the present state; another that he had moaned every time he had paid his Party dues, and was a nationalist at heart, who had been under unspecified pressure to support the socialists. Gossip and tittle-tattle ran riot through the asylum.[81]

Exiled socialist doctors writing in the *International Medical Bulletin* noted the effects of these personnel changes with extreme concern. Remarking upon the influx of unemployed SA members into the caring professions, the *Bulletin* commented:

> Methods of care are used which resemble those employed in the concentration camps. The SA people who are currently serving do not carry out their duties in accordance with the principles of humanity. They lack any psychological understanding for the sick. Instead of attention to individuals, there is the voice of command. Occupational therapy has been supplanted by community work which is not geared to the needs of the individual, but to the priorities of the works leadership. The fantastic work which has been done in this field during the last decade has been nullified with one blow. The mad houses – which today again deserve this designation – have reverted to the standards reached fifty years ago.[82]

We might bear this in mind when we hear talk of 'modernisation' from doctors and psychiatrists who maltreated and murdered their own patients.

Life in the asylums was rapidly militarised and politicised, often by the asylums themselves. Staff were encouraged to join Nazi formations, to participate in meetings and evening education courses, and to listen to speeches from the Führer broadcast over loudspeaker systems. The patients were militarised too, often to their own obvious pleasure, since it is patronising to imagine that the backward, blind or handicapped were somehow cut off from wider political currents. This process enveloped all types of institution. At Roman Catholic Mariaberg in Württemberg, handicapped children marched 'in neat order through the asylum courtyard and out into the grounds. From there one Hitler song after another rang out until the onset of night put an end to the singing.' Visitors to classrooms were met with a loud 'Heil

Hitler!', for the children 'wanted to be real Hitler Youths too'. In the Protestant Hephata asylum for epileptics and the feebleminded, prayers were said for the Führer, and his birthday was celebrated by decorating his portrait. In Baden, Direktor Möckel at Wiesloch even tried to enter his asylum in competitions for the status of National Socialist 'model concern', although a psychiatric asylum was not especially suited to the competition criteria. In Berlin, blind children in the Steglitz District Home for the Blind read *Mein Kampf* in braille, learned racial science by touching mannequin heads of 'Aryans' and 'non-Aryans', and gave the Hitler salute in their Hitler Youth uniforms. While we should be careful in assuming that all such outward signs of conformity were genuine, the evidence is so overwhelming that it is unlikely that much of it was not heartfelt.[83]

Although compulsory sterilisation tends to dominate discussions of conditions in asylums, all patients were no less affected by expenditure cuts and rationalisation. They had been affected by cuts for some time, since during the economic crises of the Weimar Republic psychiatrists had been busy economising on food, heat, light and soap, even calculating how much cubic air space an individual might need to breathe. These depressing trends were aggravated in the 1930s, despite the overall recovery of the German economy. Many specialist facilities were closed; 'outmoded' notions of optimum asylum capacity were abandoned; while the daily sums expended per patient were revised downwards. At huge cost, eighteen hundred mental patients were transferred from the attractive park asylum of Friedrichsberg in Hamburg, and replaced by deserving elderly or orphaned 'national comrades', who would better appreciate these resplendent surroundings. One result of rationalisation and the closure of specialist facilities was chronic overcrowding. At Weilmünster in 1938, over fifteen hundred patients occupied facilities which had housed 650 people four years earlier. In many asylums, doctor–patient ratios declined from a 1:150 to 1:300. At Eichberg, the official inspector Professor Kleist was appalled to discover that each doctor was tending 446 patients. Since asylum doctors were frequently seconded to Hereditary Health Courts this further adversely affected doctor–patient ratios, as did compiling eugenic data or completing sterilisation applications, each of which occupied up to three hours of their time. According to the psychiatrist responsible, it took twelve hundred working hours to referee eugenically 366 trainees in one Hamburg orphanage.[84] Form-filling reduced the amount of time doctors could devote to patients.

Directors of asylums also competed with one another to make the most drastic economies. Apart from cutting expenditure on food or clothing, they substituted herbs such as mullein, peppermint or camomile for costly sedatives, using graphs to display the resulting savings.[85] Patients recalled an extremely monotonous diet: 'In the morning there was turnip on bread. We usually smeared that on the bread the night before so that it had time to sink in. There was also coffee in a tin mug, with no milk or sugar. Lunch was at noon. Turnips or swedes once more, cooked without any fat. Always the same thing. There were usually three potatoes, boiled in their skins. Once a week we had beetroot. At three o'clock we had coffee again, and bread with syrup.'[86] It is difficult to judge whether there was an increase in the brutalisation of inmates of institutions. There was a very fine line between isolating or restraining difficult individuals and using such techniques to punish people one did not like. Forms of therapy such as wrapping people in wet sheets or immersing them in cold baths could also be employed as a form of punishment. Some asylums, such as Hephata, permitted what to us seem savage forms of corporal punishment; others such as Eichberg had grim isolation cells. Anyone even vaguely familiar with conditions in British county asylums at this time will not hurry to point to the exceptionality of daily brutality and inhumanity in the asylums of Germany.

As elsewhere during the 1930s, occupational therapy was augmented by new somatic shock treatments. Psychiatric journals extolled the wonder-working effects of new therapies, including insulin coma therapy, cardiozol and electro-shock treatment. In the eyes of many psychiatrists, these had the important merits of being both comparatively cheap and demonstrably scientific, significant criteria when psychiatry's many critics tended to point to exorbitant costs and a dismal curative record. As Hans Roemer of Illenau put it: 'According to the most recent statistics, on 31 December 1935 there were about 160,000 patients in approximately 256 public and private psychiatric asylums; according to this writer's very cautious calculations, the general and purposeful adoption of this form of treatment would save about 10%, i.e. 16,000 psychiatric beds, which at a daily rate of 2RMs per patient would result in a saving of ten to twelve million Reichsmarks.'[87] Professional journals overflowed with articles describing semi-miraculous cures, often from the viewpoint of the patient. Whatever the therapeutic merits of these new treatments, one adverse consequence was once again to turn the spotlight upon those patient groups upon whom such treatments made no impact. Selective intensive treatment of acute cases, often involving many nursing personnel, was accompanied by the neglect of the chronic and incurable languishing in back wards. Some psychiatrists were clearly contemplating killing these human reminders of the limits of their own discipline. In 1935, Karl Knab published an article arguing: 'We have before us in these asylums in addition to idiots on the lowest level, spiritual ruins whose number is not insignificant, notwithstanding all our therapeutic endeavours, patient material which, as mere cost-occasioning ballast, should be eradicated by being killed in a painless fashion, which is justifiable in terms of the self-preservatory finance policy of a nation fighting for its very existence, without shaking the cultural foundations of its cultural values.'[88] Apart from the use of terms such as 'patient material', the stress upon the compatibility of killing and cultural values is worth noting. Four years later, Hermann Pfannmüller noted that such ideas were moving from academic contemplation to active consideration: 'Almost all of these patients are kept in asylums at public cost. The problem of whether to maintain this patient material under the most primitive conditions or to eradicate it has now become a subject for serious discussion once more.'[89] This was ominous.

MEDICALISED MASS MURDER

Although questions of cost and eugenic fitness have figured prominently in this discussion, we should not lose sight of the rather separate discourse concerning euthanasia, understood in the sense of persons requesting ultimate relief from unendurable suffering. The undeniable existence of such people – in Nazi Germany as in other societies – provided an opportunity for policies which were only tangentially to do with either mercy-killing or concern with suffering individuals.

As we saw earlier, in the mid-1920s, Ewald Meltzer had documented the desire of some parents to be disburdened of their mentally defective children, in most cases because they could not cope with them either emotionally or financially. In Nazi Germany, one of the ways in which plain folk could seek the review of some legal problem or turn for relief from their individual misery was to write to the Chancellery of the Führer. This was where a woman dying of cancer and the parents of a malformed infant called Knauer turned to seek sanction for 'mercy killing', although we should not imagine correspondence raining down from Germans wishing to die.[90]

Hitler had touched on the subject of eugenic infanticide in a speech to the 1929 Nuremberg Party rally:

> If Germany was to get a million children a year and was to remove 700–800,000 of the weakest people then the final result might even be an increase in strength. The most dangerous thing is for us to cut off the natural process of selection and thereby rob ourselves of the possibility of acquiring able people. The first born are not always the most talented or strongest people. Sparta, the clearest case of a racial state in history, implemented these racial laws in a systematic way. We implement the exact opposite in an equally systematic way. As a result of our modern sentimental humanitarianism we are trying to maintain the weak at the expense of the healthy.[91]

Shortly after coming to power, the Prussian Interior Minister Hanns Kerrl floated plans to license 'euthanasia' in a commission designed to reform the criminal law. The Catholic Justice Minister Gürtner was among those who rejected what he termed 'the realisation of Nietzschean ideas'. So too did the Reich Doctors' Leader Gerhard Wagner and the man who succeeded him, Leonardo Conti. Virtually all Nazi commentators drew a distinction between preventing the future creation of 'life unworthy of life' through sterilisation and the deliberate destruction of existing lives through 'euthanasia'.[92] The latter was simply too controversial to be attempted in peacetime. This apparent consensus tends to highlight the singular contribution of Hitler. Hitler made the connection between war and 'euthanasia' at least four years before he invaded Poland, informing Gustav Wagner that 'if war should break out, he would take up the euthanasia question and implement it'.[93] In the summer of 1939 he allegedly told Leonardo Conti, Martin Bormann and Hans Lammers that:

> He regarded it as right that the worthless lives of seriously ill mental patients should be eradicated. He took as examples the severe mental illnesses in which the patients could only be kept lying on sand or sawdust, because they perpetually dirtied themselves, cases in which these patients put their own excrement in their mouths as if it were food, and things similar. Continuing on from that, he said that he thought it right that the worthless lives of such creatures should be ended, and that this would result in certain savings in terms of hospitals, doctors and nursing staff.[94]

Hitler authorised the head of the Chancellery of the Führer, Philipp Bouhler, and the accident surgeon attached to his retinue, Professor Karl Brandt, to authorise designated doctors to carry out 'mercy killings'.[95] This authorisation was presumably engineered by medical members of the killing programme, anxious about any legal repercussions, although it is important to underline the fact that this document had no force in law, and that the 'euthanasia' programme never enjoyed legal sanction. It was murder even in terms of the laws of the Third Reich.

With suspicious alacrity, the Chancellery of the Führer elaborated bureaucratic and medical structures to run a 'euthanasia' campaign for 'malformed infants', the pretext being the sort of pleas coming from anxious parents such as the Knauer family. In August 1939, doctors and midwives were obliged to notify a Reich committee for the scientific registering of serious hereditary and congenital illnesses of cases of Down's Syndrome, micro- and hydrocephaly, the absence of a limb or spastic paralysis. Two laymen, Hans Hefelmann and Richard von Hegener, then made a preliminary selection of cases for 'euthanasia' which were then reviewed by three medical referees, Professors Werner Catel, Hans Heinze and Ernst Wentzler, who then marked the forms with symbols advising the appropriate course of action. In '+' cases slated for 'euthanasia', the child was then transferred to one of around thirty special paediatric clinics, often on the pretext that these could afford them expert treatment.

Since nothing is simple, we should note that in some cases the initiative to have the child killed came from his or her parents, most of whom were unable to cope with a handicapped child.[96] The parents of Jutta M., a three-year-old with severe developmental problems stemming from premature birth, twice refused to take the child home from the Langenhorn asylum. Her father explained: 'Since I am employed as an electrical engineer in an armaments factory, with commensurately onerous duties, I am entitled to expect to be looked after by a healthy wife. It is our wish to have another healthy child soon. This expectation will be crushed, to our great distress, if we are forced to take the incurable child again.' The doctor who subsequently killed Jutta noted that: 'She [the mother] has ceased visiting the child again so as not to be distressed by the sight of it. The father is in agreement with a successful treatment.'[97] In other words, the Nazis commenced their 'euthanasia' campaign at the point where they were likely to encounter the least line of resistance, as they knew from discussion of this issue in the 1920s.

Once in these special clinics, the children were subjected to intensive tests, some involving painful experiments. Daily doses of barbiturates such as Luminal mixed into food and drink served to suppress their breathing, so that they succumbed to pulmonary illnesses, or else they were killed with overdoses of morphium-scopolamin. Parents who were concerned to monitor the progress of their children were placated with lies or prevented from visiting until the child was already dead. Up to six thousand infants, and children up to sixteen years of age, for the age range was quietly raised from three, to eight, to twelve and finally sixteen years of age, were subsequently killed in this children's 'euthanasia' programme. An expanded pool of medical and psychiatric expertise was created for the vaster project of decimating the adult asylum population, an operation known by its codename 'Aktion T-4' after the gloomy villa at Tiergartenstrasse 4 in Berlin which served as headquarters. Gathered together in Berlin in late July 1939, these men were informed by Bouhler that it was necessary to kill a proportion of psychiatric patients to create bedspace for anticipated military casualties. There would be no public legal sanction, but they were reassured that their activities would not result in prosecution under paragraph 211 of the existing Criminal Code.

Premeditating murderers have to pose the questions: how, who and where? After deciding against mass coach or train 'accidents', the problem was handed over to forensic chemists in Arthur Nebe's Reich Criminal Police Office. One of them, Dr Albert Widmann, recalled a case of death by fume inhalation and resolved upon the use of carbon monoxide gas. Bouhler apparently alighted upon the idea of using showerheads to introduce it. The gas was manufactured by the IG Farben plant at Ludwigshafen, and then supplied to 'Jennerwein and Brenner' (the *noms de guerre* of Viktor Brack of the Chancellery of the Führer and his chief associate Werner Blankenberg) as if this was a firm rather than T-4. The question 'who' involved both victims and perpetrators. At a meeting on 9 October 1939, Herbert Linden, the official in the Ministry of the Interior responsible for asylums, reported that forms had been sent to the asylums which would serve to identify possible victims. Brack said that the overall target figure had been reached with the aid of a mathematical ratio:

> The number is arrived at through a calculation on the basis of a ratio of 1000:10:5:1. That means that out of 1,000 people 10 require psychiatric treatment; of these 5 in residential form. And of these, one patient will come under the programme. If one applies this to the population of the Greater German Reich, then one must reckon with 65,000–75,000 cases. With this statement the question of 'who?' can be regarded as settled.[98]

Not quite however, because there was still the matter of who was to kill the patients. Broadly speaking, those who organised the 'euthanasia' programme were convinced of its eugenic or philosophical necessity, notably Professors Karl Brandt, Werner Catel, Werner Heyde, Max de Crinis, Paul Nitsche and Carl Schneider. This does not preclude other motives, such as a desire to flit about in the corridors of power, by men clearly tantalised by what Heyde called 'the power' radiating from the proximity of the Führer.[99] De Crinis and Heyde had histories of involvement with respectively the SD and SS. De Crinis seems to have been drawn to playacting as a spy (with a bit part in the entrapment of British secret service agents at Venlo); Heyde was a

clandestine homosexual whose research involved him in work with the
SS in concentration camps.[100] If ambition and ideological conviction
explain the motives of the main conspirators, we need look no further
than Heyde and Herbert Linden, occasionally assisted by the Reicharzt-
SS Robert Grawitz, to discover how junior doctors were selected to
kill people. A minority demurred. One of Grawitz's would-be recruits,
Werner Kirchert, proved immune to the offers of double pay, extra
alcohol, books and a radio, thus also illustrating that those who did
get involved chose to do so. He found Hefelmann's idea of mass
accidents methodologically unpersuasive. Another doctor who said no
was Dr Friedrich Hölzel of Eglfing-Haar, whom Hermann Pfannmüller
attempted to appoint as head of the children's 'euthanasia' programme
in that asylum. Mulling over these questions during a vacation ruined
by constant rain, Hölzel rejected Pfannmüller's offer. In a long letter
dated 28 August 1940, Hölzel said:

> The new measures are so convincing that I thought I could let personal
> considerations go by the board. But it is one thing to approve of
> measures of the State with full conviction, and another to carry them
> out oneself in their final consequences. I am reminded of the difference
> which exists between a judge and an executioner. Therefore, despite all
> intellectual insight and goodwill on my part, I cannot escape the
> realisation that according to my personal nature I am not suitable for
> this task. Lively as my desire is in many cases to improve upon the
> natural course of things, it is equally repugnant to me to carry this out
> as a systematic policy after cold-blooded deliberation and according to
> objective scientific principles, and without any feeling towards the
> patient.[101]

However, there were enough doctors who said yes. Herbert Linden
approached the regional health administrators Walter Schultze and
Ludwig Sprauer, who in turn recommended doctors Pfannmüller
and Schreck, neither of whom had any qualms about killing people.
Schreck took refereeing 'euthanasia' forms to new Stakhanovite heights,
sometimes processing fifteen thousand forms a month, on occasion in
a tavern over a glass or two of wine.[102] Heyde came up with the names
of former Würzburg students, such as Dr Klaus Endruweit or Dr
Aquilin Ulrich. The Nazi Student Leader at Würzburg University
apparently told Ulrich that Heyde wished to see him. They met in
Heyde's office, where the professor outlined the nature of the 'euthanasia' programme and asked whether Ulrich was ready to participate.

After a few days to mull the matter over, Ulrich assented, and was immediately exempted from military service in Poland. The induction process was incremental. He was summoned to the Chancellery of the Führer in Berlin to be told his duties, and that same afternoon driven to Brandenburg to inspect the facilities and procedures. He returned two weeks later, by now using the pseudonym 'Dr Schmitt', to begin his duties gassing five thousand people in the period March to August 1940. Although Ulrich admitted leaving the Roman Catholic Church for political reasons in the summer of 1939, at his first trial in 1965 he claimed that the intelligence from his T-4 recruiter that the Protestants had already agreed to 'euthanasia', and that the Roman Catholics were only negotiating over such details as the provision of the last sacraments to the victims, had been crucial in overcoming his own alleged reservations about participating. Although this claim emanated from men who were obviously ideologically hostile to religion (as he evidently was), he did not bother to check its veracity with his brother, who was a Catholic priest.[103]

We can also follow the induction and vetting procedures in the case of the thirty-two-year-old Bodo Gorgass, whom Fritz Bernotat in Wiesbaden dispatched to Berlin, where Brack told him that he was one of the 'particularly trusted' doctors chosen to kill mental patients. Being in 'one of the most important buildings in the Reich' had a certain effect on him, as well it might. He was sent to Hartheim in Austria, where a colleague told him that these killings had the imprimatur of some of the big names in his field – there was talk of Heyde, Nitsche and Schneider, the second of whom soon arrived in person to underline the scrupulousness of killing procedures. Gorgass's Hartheim colleague, the flute-playing Dr Georg Renno, similarly admitted: 'The notion that a state could pass a law that was illegal was beyond my conception, particularly since people of station and name accepted the euthanasia programme.' Big names and grand places went a long way with a certain type of academic professional, as their petit bourgeois insecurity fused with a scientific culture based on endorsement by 'authorities'. Young and ambitious, they often found themselves in comparatively senior positions long before this would have happened under normal circumstances or by virtue of their talents. Soon, all that was left of Bodo Gorgass as a moral actor was his momentary bridling on one occasion at the prospect of having to gas a pregnant woman: he arranged for her to be killed by lethal injection instead.[104]

Because these men were doctors, ostensibly dedicated to healing people, an egregious assumption seems to be that some equally lofty considerations must have resulted in them turning on manometers of gas cylinders, an activity that could have been performed by a trained monkey rather than people with academic degrees. Building on these false premises, and with the usual academic delight in paradox, it is assumed that ambition and opportunism alone do not explain why doctors killed. Actually, people go into medicine for all sorts of reasons utterly unconnected with a vocation to do good. They are no more or less 'idealistic' than people who become businessmen, chemists, engineers, historians, journalists or lawyers. If these men and women had hoped for socio-economic advancement, then the Depression and changes in the health system under Weimar led many of them to radical politics and a visceral hatred of the Republic. Roughly 45 per cent of doctors were members of the Nazi Party, and many more doctors belonged to the SS than comparable professionals, with the sole exception of law-yers.[105] Their medical education tended to treat ethics as an obligatory sideline, somehow unconnected with the more important scientific side of their training. This was what Brandt meant when at his trial he said: 'One may hang a copy of the Oath of Hippocrates in one's office but nobody pays any attention to it.' In any case, even the Hippocratic Oath was subject to creeping reinterpretation, with medical historians redefin-ing ethics away from concern with the individual in favour of the health of the biological collective. One could still subscribe to Hippocrates, after a fashion.[106] Finally, successive waves of psychiatric reform had continued to leave behind a hard core of the chronically ill that constituted a permanent challenge to the curative strike-rate of the psychiatric profession. Any combination of these factors could result in doctors killing people, before one adds the fact that many of these men thought that the mentally and physically handicapped were a burden to themselves and others, or indeed – as in the cases of Faltlhauser or Gorgass – had experienced these same issues in their own families.

Doctors were not solely responsible for mass murder. The nurses and orderlies selected to work in T-4 asylums were either the so-called 'Berliners', that is men and women centrally chosen for deployment to these six asylums, the residue of original staff members who remained after the rest had been transferred elsewhere, or people brought in from other asylums in the vicinity. Among the first group was Pauline K., whose bluff charm was accompanied by a frighteningly matter-of-fact attitude to murder. Born in the Ukraine in 1900, she had migrated with her family to Westphalia. A psychiatric nurse for fifteen years,

Pauline K. was summoned to Berlin in December 1939 to be informed that she was being considered for the 'euthanasia' programme. After a few moments' reflection, she chose to participate, for 'none of us had moral reservations'. As she later said: 'It was absolutely voluntary for those at this gathering to agree to participate.' And participate she did, systematically murdering people for four years in Grafeneck, Hadamar, Bernburg and Kaufbeuren-Irsee, with the mortality charts dipping whenever she took her annual holidays.[107]

The second group, of what might be termed residuals, are more complicated. Irmgard Huber was born in 1901, one of a family of ten children. After elementary school, she worked as a domestic servant, before moving into psychiatric nursing. She joined the staff at Hadamar in 1932. A few years later she began a sad, unreciprocated love affair with Alfons Klein, an asylum administrator. In 1940, she was one of the Hadamar personnel retained to implement 'euthanasia' killings. The presence of the 'Berliners' enabled Huber to perpetuate the psychological fiction that she was somehow removed from the killings. She merely attended morning conferences where, as chief nurse, she received and relayed instructions to kill patients. Neither her belief that killing was wrong, her resulting psychological suffering, nor her recorded acts of kindness to individual patients prevented her from participating in these killings.[108] The third category included Paul Reuter, a rather simple Hessian peasant. An early recruit to the Nazi Party, Reuter regularly attended its rallies at Nuremberg, a fact which was presumably on file. An unemployed farm worker, his SA membership secured him work in the Weilmünster asylum. After brief military service in Poland, he was chosen to join the T-4 staff at Hadamar. There he was told that the patients were 'life unworthy of life', and that the money spent looking after them could be better spent on housing for families 'rich in children'.[109]

The men and women who staffed the T-4 bureaucracy in Berlin and the Community Patients Transport Service, and who ran the asylums where patients were killed, were recruited by word of mouth, often on the basis of personal connections. Thus Hermann Schweninger, T-4's leading propaganda filmmaker, had known Brack since he was sixteen; Dietrich Allers knew Werner Blankenberg; Adolf Kaufmann joined his brother Robert; a telephonist was recruited because her sister was Reinhard Tillmann, the T-4 administrator's, secretary and so on. As Dietrich Allers said: 'I was always of the opinion that most people got in through connections.' At Hartheim, many of the secretaries posted there seem to have been acquainted with the Gau inspector Stefan Schachermayr. They were bored in their existing jobs, hungry for more pay or improved status, or were attracted by the prospect of doing 'secret' work. The central and asylum offices generated the usual office politics and romances, as if they were running a shipping agency rather than extermination centres. Although some of the asylum office staff tried to maintain a compartmentalised perspective, isolating their own immediate duties from their ultimate consequences, this was by no means always the case, since macabre curiosity sometimes propelled office workers down to the cellars to gawp through glass apertures and spy-holes at people in their final extremities.

At the grim physical end, those who had to handle the dead were recruited, like Paul Reuter, because their Party records suggested ideological reliability or because they knew someone. Vinzenz Nohel, who became something of an expert in hauling corpses and burning them at Hartheim, moved from being a low-paid mechanic to earning about double his salary down in the castle basement. The connection with T-4 was made by his brother, an SA-Brigadeführer. SS men, such as Kurt Franz or Josef 'Seppl' Oberhauser, were also seconded from the concentration camps to oversee the grim business of burning corpses. Involvement in the 'euthanasia' programme was the halfway house in their giddy social ascent from being butchers, cooks, policemen or tram conductors to arbiters of life and death over poor Polish Jews and the Jewish bourgeoisie of Amsterdam, Paris or Salonika in the extermination camps. Brutal, drunk and insensitive to all but their own misery, these individuals used a barrackroom black humour, helped along with a daily ration of a quarter litre of schnapps, to obliterate their occasional nightmares, muttering among themselves in their rheumy-eyed way about the 'shit work' they were responsible for.

Having solved 'how' and 'who', the only remaining question was 'where'. Herbert Linden met with Egon Stahle in Stuttgart. Stahle recommended the Samaritan home for cripples at Grafeneck, a Renaissance castle high up in the Swabian Alb. Linden and Stahle paid it a flying visit, to ascertain its useful combination of accessibility and remoteness. They were shortly followed by visitors travelling incognito, including Brack (alias 'Jennerwein'), Werner Heyde and Reinhard Vorberg (alias 'Hintertal'). Coachloads of SS men in civvies arrived later, and together with local craftsmen began fitting the castle out as an extermination centre. The gas chamber was installed where sheds now house chickens and farm machinery. Bernotat presumably alighted upon Hadamar near Limburg. His personal involvement was reflected not only in the choice of Bodo Gorgass as a 'euthanasia' doctor, but in the fact that his brother-in-law was the fitter who installed the piping which fed gas into the fake shower room. There were six such extermination centres: Bernburg, Brandenburg, Grafeneck, Hadamar, Hartheim and Sonnenstein.[110]

The arrival of Registration Form 1, requesting detailed information on patients, was the first formal contact between T-4 in Berlin and hundreds of public, private and religious asylums throughout the land. The form – ostensibly to facilitate 'economic planning' – sought information on patients suffering from designated physical and mental illnesses who performed merely mechanical tasks; patients who had been in asylums for more than five years; and information on the criminally insane, foreign nationals and 'racial aliens'. The arrival of these forms presented the cautious with a dilemma. Many asylum administrators no doubt saw nothing untoward, believing that the forms were a means of separating chronic and acute patients, with the former being hived off to lower-cost facilities where they were cared for without their condition being treated, in line with the general drift of psychiatric thinking in the late 1920s and early 1930s. Others thought the forms were a type of wartime labour conscription. In order to retain valuable workers for the asylum economy, they then made the fateful decision to underestimate deliberately the patients' labour capacity. The suspicious minority included the asylum administrator Dr George Andreae and his superior Dr Ludwig Gessner in the Hanover region, and, more ambivalently, Professor Walter Creutz and Heinz Haake in the Rhineland, who severally and in tandem sought to deflect the 'euthanasia' programme from their respective areas, co-operating nonetheless once their objections had been countered.[111]

Asylum directors had between three and ten weeks to complete the registration forms. This left a little scope for delay, deliberate incompetence or extreme pedantry. As rumours spread that persons being transferred were being killed, a few asylum directors went to considerable lengths to protect their charges. They deserve to be commemorated. Thus Dr John of the private Christophsbad asylum at Göppingen found work for some of his patients with local firms, making it difficult for T-4 to retrieve them. Religious institutions such as Attl, Schonbrunn or Ursberg tried reclassifying state-funded patients as private payers. Some asylums endeavoured to release patients into the custody of their relatives, although they not infrequently met a blank indisposition to do so. Since political persuasion is sometimes a poor guide to an individual's behaviour, it should not surprise that the Nazi 'old fighter' Karsten Jaspersen of Bethel distinguished himself by deliberately falsifying patient records in such a way as to exclude them from T-4's initial criteria. He altered schizophrenia to reactive psychosis and manic–depressive illness to cyclothemia.

Delay or non-compliance in completing these forms brought no relief, since T-4 would simply dispatch roving teams of assessors to do the work *in situ* in a crassly perfunctory fashion.[112] Anticipating the likelihood of unpleasant scenes in the asylums, T-4 built a degree of plea-bargaining into their calculations. This left a small aperture for the asylum administrators and doctors to save a certain number of patients, even as it opened them to the charge of complicity in the process of selection. Many asylum staff sought to replace T-4's crude selection criteria with precision based on knowledge of individuals. Invariably this entailed retaining people with whom one had some sort of emotional bond, or who had proved their economic utility to the asylum in line with reform psychiatric thinking since the 1920s. Thus the asylum administrator at Markgröningen stressed that one patient 'saves the asylum the cost of having to employ someone as a gardener', while another 'works the whole year as an assiduous and punctual agricultural labourer'. These attempts to save individuals took on an air of desperation by the time the leader of a T-4 Community Patient Transport Service convoy parked in the asylum forecourt had become the only negotiating partner. As knowledge spread among the patients – for the T-4 transport personnel let slip remarks like soon there will be seventy-five fewer 'silly clots' in the world – the arrival of these transport buses occasioned scenes of distress and panic.

Others contemplated their fate in a surprisingly calm and reflective manner. In October 1940, an epileptic woman wrote the following to her retired doctor father, whom she had earlier alerted to what was happening. The father had been to the health authorities in Stuttgart, where he was reassured that *if* such policies were being implemented epileptics were being excluded. The asylum advised him to contact T-4 to have his daughter's name struck off the transport list. What proved to be her last letter read:

> Dearest beloved Father!
>   Unfortunately it cannot be otherwise. Today I must write these words of farewell as I leave this earthly life for an eternal home. This

will cause you and yours much, much heartache. But think that I must die as a martyr, and that this is not happening without the will of my heavenly redeemer, for whom I have longed for many years. Father, good Father, I do not want to part from you without asking you and all my dear brothers and sisters once more for forgiveness, for all that I have failed you in throughout my entire life. May the dear Lord God accept my illness and this sacrifice as a penance for this.

Best of fathers, don't hold anything against your child, who loved you so very profoundly; always think that I am going to heaven, where we will all be reunited together with God and our deceased dear ones. Dear Father, I am going with firm resolve and trust in God, never doubting in his good deeds, which he tests us with, but which unfortunately we do not comprehend when we are here. We will reap our reward on judgement day. Decreed by God! Please, tell this to my dear brothers and sisters. I won't lament, but shall be happy. I send you this little picture by way of a memento, your child will be meeting the saints in this way too.

I embrace you with undying love and with the firm promise I made when we last said our goodbyes, that I will persevere with fortitude.

Your child Helene.

On 2 October 1940. Please pray a lot for the peace of my soul. See you again, good Father, in heaven.

Her father did manage to get Helene struck off the lists, but it was too late. He received notification of her omission shortly after a letter informing him of her death in Brandenburg from 'breathing problems'.[113]

Following pathetic farewells from staff and friends whom they had known for years, the people selected for destruction now found themselves in the hands of uncaring strangers whose sole function was to expedite their murder. Buses and trains took them either directly to one of the extermination centres, or to a network of holding institutions used to stagger the flow of sick humanity to the crematoria. There they were disembarked, and shepherded through carefully rehearsed procedures, culminating in their being locked into hermetically sealed gas chambers disguised as showers. Some victims walked in equipped with face flannels, soap and scrubbing brushes. Doctors stationed in adjacent alcoves turned on the manometers of gas cylinders, duties determined by the need to maintain the medical façade masking mass murder. Death came in the dark, as the terrified victims rolled off benches or collapsed on the floor, or beat their hands against the doors when they realised what was happening to them. Ventilators extracted remaining fumes, enabling 'burners' or 'disinfectors' to move in to disentangle the corpses, which after the removal of gold teeth or research-driven autopsy were trundled along miniature railtracks, or slid across wet floors to the ovens. Their ashes were dumped in rivers or arbitrarily distributed in urns.

Every time this procedure was conducted, thick palls of black smoke furled skywards from the asylums, often polluting the surrounding area with noxious smells. A man living near Hartheim in Upper Austria recalled: 'This stench was so disgusting that sometimes when we returned home from work in the fields we couldn't hold down a single bite.' People were unable to leave windows open, and had to seal them at night to prevent the smells invading their bedrooms. Clutches of human hair swirled in the breeze. Although businesses and pubs which served the T-4 teams from the asylums seem to have welcomed these grim customers, occasionally a resident of places near the extermination centres was arrested for expressing disquiet about what was being done in their immediate vicinity. In Hartheim, the spread of rumours led to a meeting in the Trauner tavern addressed by the T-4 chief in the Castle, the ox-like ex-detective Christian Wirth. Wirth first claimed that shoes, images of saints and vestments were being burned there. Since this lacked credibility, he added that oil and oil-based products were being resynthesised as a clear fluid used in submarines. He finished by threatening his audience that anyone who spread rumours about burning humans would be executed or sent to a concentration camp.[114]

Since no one disappears in advanced societies without an accompanying trail of paper, T-4 registry offices then set to work systematically faking the cause and place of death. Death certificates were completed with the aid of a checklist of over sixty causes of death, each accompanied with a paragraph outlining its suitability for different ages and sexes:

> Pneumonia is an ideal cause of death for our action, because the population at large always regard it as a critical illness which means that its life-threatening character will be plausible.
>
> Strokes. This cause of death is especially suitable in the case of older people, of at least forty or more years of age; in the case of young people it is so rare that one should not choose it.[115]

In so far as the administrators did not seek to continue drawing maintenance payments for people who were already dead, they sent out standardised letters of condolence to relatives. The more inventive administrators introduced the odd customised reference, while announcing that the person had been cremated to prevent contagious diseases. Maps and coloured pins enabled them to stagger what would otherwise seem like a suspicious volume of deaths if victims happened to come from small places, with people who died in Hadamar being regularly registered as having died in Bernburg or Sonnenstein. A special registry office, using the fictitious address Chelm Mental Asylum PO Box 882 Lublin, was used to register the deaths of Jewish psychiatric patients who had been gassed in Brandenburg or shot in German-occupied Poland.[116]

Although this conspiracy to commit mass murder prided itself on having taken care of the last detail, inevitably questions were asked by a concerned public. Sometimes this concern was expressed in highly ambiguous ways. In late 1941 a man wrote to the army authorities on 'Elimination of the Mentally Ill'. He said: 'Whatever possessed our government to adopt this course – no one knows. Some say the institutions had to be cleared because of the many air force officers with nervous illnesses, others talk about economic measures with a view to feeding our population. But that misses the point. One counters these arguments simply by pointing to the many millions of Jews who are still in the country. Why do these dregs of society still live while our sick are simply being murdered?'

We can follow the mounting disquiet of ordinary people in a remarkable series of letters found during the restoration of the Protestant Diakoniewerk at Gallneukirchen, letters which had not been touched since 1941. In January of that year at least sixty-four handicapped people, aged between two and seventy-seven, were taken on the forty-kilometre journey to Hartheim to be killed. Relatives of patients were first informed of the transfers, allegedly to Sonnenstein, over a hundred kilometres away, some time after this had already taken place. This unorthodox procedure set alarms ringing. On 20 January 1941, a pharmacist in Wels wrote to one of the nursing staff at Gallneukirchen, a Sister Anna:

> Today I was informed that V. had been relocated to the asylum at Sonnenstein near Pirna, but otherwise nothing else. No one even asked us. Where is Sonnenstein? Why have they taken V. there? Is Gallneukirchen going to be fully or partly closed? Why didn't you write, Sister? What is going on there? Is the Sonnenstein asylum any good? Dear Sister, I am deeply unhappy and sad and would like to know for

certain about V.'s circumstances. The poor boy causes us so much heartache!

The authorities at Gallneukirchen replied with details of railway connections from Wels to Pirna. A week later, the boy's mother wrote that she had been informed that V. had died of 'blood-poisoning from warts on his lips' in Sonnenstein. The boy's death had 'driven a needle into her heart . . . I could cry to heaven how terrible I feel!' As soon as she had heard of the transfer, she had been unable to sleep, constantly imagining V. in his asylum clothing: 'a mother senses everything'. It is worth quoting what she wrote next to convey the existential doubt and suffering that these policies caused ordinary people:

> Destiny, dear Sister, is so hard and has completely broken me, because I always hoped that God alone would be merciful. The little bug never did anyone any harm but despite this was not allowed to live. My husband is also away. We wanted to visit you on Tuesday, and on Wednesday he is dead. God give me strength that I should not doubt his greatness and power, because the light of the world has become dark, and God has not heard our prayers . . . Please pardon this typed letter, dear Sister, but my hands are shaking so much that I cannot write . . . My pain is so great and profound that I can only find consolation in tears.[117]

Relatives drew attention to striking coincidences. One woman wrote to the authorities at Gallneukirchen on 28 January 1941, thanking them for the news that 'our Hansi' had died five days earlier, 'and indeed in the same asylum in which his father also died not quite three weeks after his transfer there. In Hansi's case things happened even more quickly, since he did not even last ten days there.'[118]

Others denounced this monumental deception in forthright terms. Having buried the ashes of her daughter Trudi, Rosa N. wrote to the nursing staff at Gallneukirchen informing them that she would be visiting them:

> Perhaps then you can explain in more detail about the terrible things that have been going on. I can't even imagine how the whole thing occurred, whether Gertrud was taken away on her own, who organised everything, in what fashion the child was transported elsewhere. What the asylum Sonnenstein wrote is all lies, which I am not inclined to believe. They sent on a list of Trudi's clothes and laundry which I have received. I find it risible that they are attempting to be so punctilious with these irrelevant matters.[119]

Other people placed insinuating death notices in local newspapers, making it clear through their use of phrases such as 'sudden and unexpected death' that they did not believe the official version.[120] A brave few made the difficult journey to the asylums to register their scepticism in person.

Articulate middle-class professionals or the well connected were naturally in a better position to kick up a fuss than more lowly members of society. Even the former were not immune to retaliation. During the war, a retired philologist made repeated inquiries to Dr Walter Schmidt of the Eichberg asylum regarding the condition of his son Hans, a schizophrenic patient. The father was then suddenly informed that Hans had died of 'his incurable illness'. This phrase raised suspicions since the asylum had never informed the family of the 'incurability' of their son. The philologist wrote, raising a number of awkward questions. The replies to his increasingly accusatory letters progressed from the evasively accommodating to veiled and then overt threats. The penultimate communication read:

> In the course of the year we repeatedly detect the ingratitude of relatives of *hereditarily ill* mental patients ... We categorically reject your slur that the thing seems 'really shady' to you. However, in view of the *hereditary* character of your son's illness, we will refrain from holding this against you. However, we must urgently counsel you to be more circumspect in future in your attitude towards the authorities.

When this failed to stop the philologist's letters, the threat became explicit:

> The nature and tone of your letter gives me cause to view you in a psychiatric light. I cannot refrain from notifying you that in the event you do not cease burdening us with letters, I will be compelled to have you examined by the public health doctor. At the end of the day, you are dealing with a public authority, which you cannot assail when you feel like it.[121]

This was the societal essence of totalitarianism, with cowardly minor bureaucratic bullies invoking bigger bullies to grind the critical and non-compliant into submission.

Inevitably, distressed relatives turned to clerics and lawyers. The latter were often professionally concerned with people immured in asylums and secure hospitals. Lawyers had to field complaints regarding deaths in suspicious circumstances, and dealt with questions of inheritance and wardship, detention for psychiatric evaluation, and indeed prosecutions for the crime of spreading malicious gossip. In July 1940, a provincial judge in Brandenburg, Lothar Kreyssig, made it his business to protest to Minister of Justice Franz Gürtner that persons whom he had responsibility for as wards of court had been illegally transferred from Brandenburg-Gorden to be murdered. This was part of a trend to remove entire groups of people from the protection normally afforded by the rule of law, with the asylums following the concentration camps into an extra-legal limbo.

Since Kreyssig was one of the few people to come out of this business with credit, it is worth dwelling on his character and possible motives. Kreyssig, who had corresponded with Gregor Strasser about strategies to combat unemployment, and who had voted for the NSDAP, was a Confessing Christian, who had repeatedly come to the attention of the Nazis for his 'reactionary' stances and manifest hostility to the totalitarian claims of their government. As he once put it: 'States come and go, but the Word in the Bible endures.' Remarks like that were assiduously reported by colleagues and informers. His personal circumstances undoubtedly facilitated a principled stand. He had requested a transfer from Chemnitz to Brandenburg in order to be near a farm he had purchased from former economic supremo Hjalmar Schacht, with a view to bringing up his young children close to the soil. Moving to this backwater indicates that he was not concerned with his career, a significant advantage if one was going to take on the authorities. And take them on he did. Kreyssig refused to be fobbed off with evasive explanations from either the Nazi People's Court prosecutor Roland Freisler or Franz Gürtner about what was happening in the asylums. This independent-minded individual threatened to instigate charges of murder against all and sundry, personally warning the asylum directors within his jurisdiction that he would prosecute them if they transferred any further patients subject to his authority. He also tried to instigate charges of murder against the officials responsible for the 'euthanasia' programme. Even when Gürtner personally showed him a facsimile of Hitler's letter of authorisation to Bouhler and Brandt, Kreyssig queried its legality, a line which resulted in Hitler's approving his compulsory premature retirement from the judiciary.[122]

Clerics learned about the 'euthanasia' programme either from relatives of victims or because they were connected with ecclesiastical welfare institutions or with the provision of spiritual solace in other types of asylum. They could not avoid knowing about it if terrified patients sometimes ran amok in the middle of services in asylum chapels. Some clergy asked awkward questions. For example, the pastor of the Protestant community in Rottmann wrote on 27 January 1941 to the rector of Gallneukirchen:

> The parents of Johann L. who was in the refuge at Gallneukirchen received the entirely unexpected news from the asylum of Sonnenstein at Pirna that their son had died of blood-poisoning from erysipelas. He had been cremated immediately because of the risk of contagion. The ashes could be buried in his home town. May I permit myself the following questions: Why were the parents not asked for their consent to the transfer of their son from Gallneukirchen? If the parents, or the mother, had known about this, then they would certainly have taken the child home with them. He could have been supported by his brother, who earns a lot, and could have worked for his daily bread. Was Johann L. already injured in some way in Gallneukirchen in order for him to have died of blood-poisoning as a result of erysipelas? Or, remarkably enough, did he only suffer this injury after he arrived in Pirna? Does this rare occurrence happen often, that patients are taken away, and then suddenly die the moment they leave Gallneukirchen, and then are immediately cremated on account of the risk of contagion?[123]

The reply noted that many such letters had been received by the asylum authorities, who had been instructed not to give any further details.

Having been directly confronted by these policies at Lobetal, Pastor Gerhard Braune addressed an extraordinary memorandum to Hitler detailing the extent of the 'euthanasia' programme, and systematically refuting the economic and logistic rationale for it. Using the numbers embossed on the urns of ashes sent to relatives, Braune came up with the damning fact that at Grafeneck 2,019 people had died in a forty-three-day period in an asylum with only one hundred beds available. A fortnight later Braune was informed that Hitler had seen his memorandum, but could do nothing to stop matters, beyond ensuring that they were carried out less haphazardly. Braune was shortly arrested and detained in 'protective custody' for three months.[124]

Being part of the residual Establishment, an Establishment that the Nazis both closely monitored and publicly scorned, senior clergy tended to err on the side of caution, a posture that their age, backgrounds and responsibilities would in any case favour. Sometimes their appeals to the moral sensibilities of selected Nazi leaders were embarrassing. Writing to Frick on 19 July 1940, Bishop Theophil Wurm of Württemberg lauded the recent victory over France, and expressed understanding – having once ministered in an asylum – for how people could arrive at the view that it would be better to put an end to 'such existences', while still protesting against the scope of the recent killings. This sort of appeal tends to look worse with hindsight than it probably did at the time.

Exchanging theological niceties with mass murderers was even less edifying. One senior cleric, Bishop Heinrich Wienken of Berlin, was deputed by the Fulda episcopal synod to represent the views of the Roman Catholic Church to the authorities, which in this case meant Herbert Linden and Hans Hefelmann of T-4, both primed with a memorandum by the renegade Catholic theologian Mayer which appears to have sanctioned 'mercy killing'. Although we only have Hefelmann's various post-war accounts of what was said in these meetings, it seems that Wienken went native to the extent of being sharply disowned by Cardinal Michael Faulhaber. Specifically, Wienken was ready to 'tolerate' such policies within revised parameters. They would apply only to 'complete idiots', who would be given the sacraments, while mentally ill Catholic priests would be excluded from their ambit. Hitler refused to give these guarantees in writing. Negotiations collapsed when on 2 December 1940 Pope Pius XII unequivocally condemned the killing of 'life unworthy of life'. Wienken would subsequently crop up negotiating with Eichmann on behalf of so-called 'non-Aryan' Christians.[125]

One senior cleric ventured down the road of public confrontation. As in the case of Lothar Kreyssig, the fusion of the personal and the principled was striking. The bishop of Münster, Clemens August Graf von Galen, was the scion of an old aristocratic Catholic family from Dinklage in Westphalia. A Jesuit-trained, snobbish ultra-conservative, with attitudes that would make modern liberals cringe, Galen had been close to the circle around Papen. He regarded the Nazis as foreigners and upstarts, needing no lessons on being a German patriot from people who hailed from 'Riga, Reval, or Cairo or even Chile', by which he meant Rosenberg, Hess and Darré. Like Kreyssig, this was truly a man secure in himself. Galen had a record of dissent, opposing visits to Münster from the neo-pagan in chief, Rosenberg, and objecting to the dissolution of Catholic lay organisations.[126] We can follow his mounting exasperation through a series of Gestapo, police and SD reports on his see of Münster. Heavy bombing raids against Aachen and Münster from 11 July 1941 resulted in the expropriation of several religious houses, which were used as shelters for the homeless.

There were popular demonstrations as the Gestapo instructed the religious to pack a suitcase and leave. Those affected included Jesuit foundations in Münster.

Galen's sermons in the Lamberti church soon developed into tumultuous occasions. With tears running down his face, Galen asked: 'Which of you can say that the Jesuits or missionary sisters have committed some wrong?' The faithful shouted 'No one!' Calling for prayers on behalf of priests incarcerated in concentration camps, Galen heightened the emotional atmosphere by saying: 'One can do nothing against the measures of the Gestapo, so I have to anticipate that one day I will be arrested too.' Although Karsten Jaspersen had relayed to him intelligence about the 'euthanasia' programme about a year earlier, it seems likely that only when these measures touched the Marienthal asylum in his diocese did he decide to go public. On 3 August he combined protests against these expropriations with grave accusations regarding the 'euthanasia' programme. In a remarkable sermon, combining fact, passion and an Old Testament deity rumbling in the heavens, Galen chronicled what he knew of T-4's *modus operandi*. He then revealed that under the requirements of Paragraph 139 of the Penal Code, obliging people to report the intention to commit a major crime, he had instigated charges of murder under Paragraph 211. This was to throw the gauntlet down with a vengeance. He outlined the utilitarian rationale for the 'euthanasia' programme, denouncing the pseudo-scientific commodification and objectification of humanity it embodied:

> We are not dealing with machines, horses and cows whose only function is to serve mankind, to produce goods for man. One may smash them, one may slaughter them as soon as they no longer fulfil this function. No, we are dealing with human beings, our fellow human beings, our brothers and sisters. With poor people, sick people, if you like unproductive people. But have they forfeited the right to life? Have you, have I the right to live only so long as we are productive, so long as we are recognised by others as productive?

Following the logic of this argument, Galen warned that these policies would result in the murder by the state of any 'unproductive' lives, be it the incapacitated, geriatrics or even seriously wounded soldiers. This last point, which was prescient, broke a massive taboo among his auditors. The law would offer no protection, and people would shun their own doctors. The Gestapo and police reports give an indication of the ferocity with which Galen delivered this sermon. Sometimes he shouted the words, terrifying the mothers of men who were serving in the field in Russia. Party members left the church 'snorting with rage' (*wutschnäubend*), scurrying off to report their impotent fury. A woman who had attended the sermon hurried home to guard her elderly mother lest the Gestapo take her away to be murdered. Other people were refusing to undergo x-rays, lest it have some untoward connection with the subject of Galen's sermon. Word of the sermon went a very long way. The BBC made broadcasts concerning it, the RAF dropped copies of it over Germany. It made the front page of the *Daily Express*. From a lonely outpost in northern Lapland, a Nazi official serving as an army captain, who thought 'euthanasia' was the logical corollary of sterilisation, wrote home: 'the sermons of our querulous bishop have even penetrated here. A few of my soldiers have been sent copies of them from home. In this way, despite the war, the Churches have occasioned a certain disquiet among the soldiers.' Ordinary Germans who were caught with hectographed copies of the sermon, or who discussed it with colleagues, were arrested and sent to concentration camps.[127] Although Nazi leaders contemplated taking drastic action against Galen, the prevailing view was that a reckoning with him should be deferred for the duration, after which, to cite Hitler himself: 'he may rest assured that in the balancing of our accounts no "t" will remain uncrossed, no "i" left undotted'.[128] This turned out to be an idle threat since Galen survived all of them.

Having reached their projected target of seventy thousand victims, the T-4 perpetrators were told by Hitler to halt the mass gassing of mental patients. Thenceforth, patients would be killed by starvation and lethal medication in a larger number of extermination centres located within several asylums. This would be easier to conceal than the sudden removal and simultaneous disappearance of big groups of people. Popular disquiet also played a part in this decision, with considerable resources being deployed in an immensely cunning 1941 feature film – *Ich klage an* – explicitly designed to confuse questions of individual autonomy with the very separate issue of the state eugenically culling the mentally and physically disabled.[129] Millions of people saw this very smoothly executed attempt to insinuate these issues through a triangular love story cum courtroom drama involving some of the best-known character actors and stars of the day. Director Wolfgang Libeneiner's film itself triggered widespread debate about the issues involved, with many people erroneously identifying it as a direct response to Galen's charges, rather than a device for ushering in laws sanctioning euthanasia. But there was a further reason why this phase of the 'euthanasia' programme was suspended, and then redirected rather than abandoned.

In early 1941, Himmler approached Bouhler to use the gassing facilities of T-4 to murder 'ballast existences' in the concentration camps, which lacked facilities for mass, as opposed to individual, murder. Under the terms of an arrangement known by the code 'Aktion 14f13' (the abbreviation used by the Inspectorate of Concentration Camps combined with the code for the death of a 'sick' inmate), ailing prisoners were selected by SS camp doctors, no doubt with much scope for likes and dislikes, perfunctorily 'examined' by visiting T-4 doctors, and then dispatched to 'rest homes' at Bernburg, Hartheim and Sonnenstein, where they were murdered.[130] We know a lot about this process because of the testimony of former inmates, who observed these crimes at close quarters, and from the letters which Dr Friedrich Mennecke wrote each day to his wife Eva from his hotel lodgings near Dachau or Buchenwald. Ensconced behind tables, the doctors glanced at the 'portions' or 'pats' being paraded past them. A mindless competitive concern with statistics achieved during each session took over. Prisoners who had artificial limbs, wore spectacles or who had life histories the doctors did not care for were speedily chosen for extermination. 'Diagnoses' were scribbled on their files, including such medical novelties as 'Felizia Sara N. Homeless Jewish whore who hangs around combat troops' or 'Emilie Sara H. Regular miscegenation. In the camp: unbelievably insolent'.[131] Between fifteen and twenty thousand people were murdered in this way in the three T-4 asylums which assumed this burden on behalf of the SS, rather as a firm obliges another temporarily overstretched with a major order. Staff in the T-4 extermination centres do not even seem to have noticed that they were killing prisoners dressed in striped blue uniforms rather than psychiatric patients.

Having entered the orbit of the camp empire, with a specific expertise in mass murder, it was only logical that Himmler should turn to the same address when the enormous project of murdering the Jews of Poland was being mooted and similar questions arose about the most effective methods. According to Brack, at some time in the autumn of 1941 Himmler 'told me that Hitler had some time ago given him the order for the extermination of the Jews. He said that preparations had already been made, and I think that he used the expression that for reasons of camouflage one would have to work as quickly as possible.'[132] Bouhler instructed Brack to make nearly a hundred T-4 personnel available to Odilo Globocnik, the SS- and Police Leader in Lublin. By late November 1941, the first T-4 teams arrived at Belzec.[133] Pseudo-medical killing finally became an integral aspect of racial mass murder, with doctors in SS uniforms on the selection ramps of Auschwitz, or in the case of Irmfried Eberl briefly commanding Treblinka, while the killers of the SS donned white coats and stethoscopes as they busied around Kulmhof. In an infernal parody, people were enjoined to breathe deeply when they entered 'delousing' or 'inhalation' rooms which killed them in minutes. Smoke, flames and noxious fumes would soon engulf other parts of Europe, as if some ugly heavy industry were disfiguring an undeveloped country, albeit one in the business of commodifying and destroying people – although one should not over-industrialise or over-medicalise the Holocaust, which included direct violence of a primitive kind.

The projected gains of the 'euthanasia' programme have survived, even if we no longer know what happened to the personal effects and valuables of those killed, slim pickings given that such people probably had little in the first place. But of course their gold teeth or wedding rings were not the primary issue. They represented a 'ballast' or 'burden' upon the national economy, a 'burden' on the collective future. Killing became a form of cost saving. In 1941, T-4 statisticians elaborated the monthly kill-rates at four asylums designated B, C, D and E and calculated global totals. Graphs showed how the deaths of the 70,273 people achieved so far would save a projected 885,439,800 Reichsmarks by 1951, with separate graphs detailing how much butter, eggs, marmalade, meat and potatoes would no longer be consumed, together with their monetary equivalents.[134] A copy of these accounts can be seen in the United States Holocaust Memorial Museum in Washington, its fading pages and cold precision being hard to connect with so much human suffering. But before finally relating 'euthanasia' to the 'Final Solution', we must follow the Nazis into occupied Poland, where both the mentally ill and that nation's socio-economic and intellectual elites were butchered, and then to the killing fields of the former Soviet Union.

6

'THE DANE IS NOT A POLE, BUT RATHER A TEUTON': OCCUPATION AND COLLABORATION IN EUROPE, 1939–1943

The first Vichy government. Pétain is in the centre, with
Laval on his right and Weygand on his left.

INVISIBLE MEN?

Hitler had employed bluff, diplomacy and subversion against Austria and Czechoslovakia, which were wholly or partially absorbed into the German Reich, but after September 1939 he resorted to massive military force against Poland. The Molotov–Ribbentrop Non-Aggression Pact of August 1939 convinced him that Britain and France, which on past evidence he regarded as ineffectual and weak, could not fight a general war to save Poland, and this suggested that the effects of Nazi aggression against her could be localised. Convinced by Western efforts to bring the Poles to the negotiating table that he was dealing with British and French leaders 'who are below average. No personalities. No masters, men of action', in fact 'little worms', Hitler failed to understand that Poland was not primarily what was at issue. The British and French had drawn a line in the sand with their guarantees to Poland in the spring, signalling that they would not countenance further unilateral German challenges to their rights and status as great European powers. Hitler decided to risk crossing that line, although the ensuing war was general rather than local. It apparently came as a shock to him when it was declared.[1]

German agents had already commenced destabilising Poland, with such terroristic outrages as the bombing of the Tarnow railway station in late August 1939.[2] The night before the invasion, SS units sporting Polish-style moustaches and sideburns dissembled three attacks, including one against the German radio station at Gleiwitz, just behind the frontier with Poland. An SS team interrupted the evening programme being relayed from Radio Breslau, connecting a microphone to enable an interpreter to broadcast patriotic slogans in Polish, against a background of shouts and gunfire. A local Polish nationalist, Franz Honiok, who had been arrested by the SS on 30 August, was brought along in a drugged state, and left shot dead at the entrance. His body was then propped up in the transmission room for the benefit of the police photographer. Since one corpse did not possess the intended dramatic effect, another was added to the same room, probably from the stock of 'tin cans', the SS code for prisoners brought from concentration camps for precisely this purpose. Although these semi-farcical 'attacks' did not incline the British and French to abandon their obligations to Poland, they did signify, if anyone needed further proof, that the Nazis were prepared to extend their domestic criminality into the conduct of international relations.[3]

On 1 September, fifty German divisions broke into Poland from three sides. The tenacious resistance of the Polish armed forces against overwhelming odds was nullified by the inertia of their British and French allies, and the stab in the back delivered by the Soviet Union, which invaded eastern Poland on 17 September. Sixty-six thousand Polish soldiers died in the conflict, and seven hundred thousand were captured by the Germans, three hundred thousand by the Soviets.[4] Apart from the Soviet-occupied east, large parts of Poland were incorporated into West and East Prussia, Silesia and the newly created 'Warthegau' around Posen, leaving a rump German-administered remnant called the General Government. In early November 1940, Hitler quipped to his associates, 'They could all offload their rubbish into the General Government. Jews, the sick, slackers etc.'[5]

Following the German invasion of Poland, months of 'phoney war' with the British and French ensued. Since the British and French were unable to influence the course of events in eastern Europe, they resorted to economic blockade, while planning to cut off Germany's supplies of iron ore from Sweden, and oil from the Caucasus and Romania, if necessary by bombing the latter and stirring up Moslem discontent in the southern Soviet Union. Initially, the war had an unreal note of restraint about it. Suggestions for floating fluvial mines up the Rhine, shelling the Saar from France, setting the Black Forest ablaze, or bombing the Krupps works at Essen were rejected by the Western Allies, in the last case because the munitions factories were 'private property'. Both sides also took care to use airpower in a discriminatory way. A shooting war commenced in early April 1940, when Hitler turned northwards against Norway. The invasion of Denmark and Norway was followed by a devastating attack on France through Belgium, the Netherlands and Luxemburg.[6] France's imposing and respected armed forces were swept aside, by an enemy which dared the militarily impossible and had a superior command of the operational arts and the combined tactical use of aircraft and armour. These conquests made Hitler, and his Italian confederate, the masters of Europe, and it was a near-run thing whether the British could withstand him in their island fastness. Despite forty-three thousand people being killed, and a further eighty-six thousand injured by German bombing, the majority of them being Londoners, whose city was attacked on seventy-six consecutive nights, they did survive, thanks to the British, Dominion, Free Czech, French and Polish fighter pilots of the RAF in the ensuing Battle of Britain.

Political arrangements in Nazi-occupied Europe were various. All but 8 per cent of the most industrially important parts of Czechoslovakia were converted into a Protectorate of Bohemia-Moravia or directly absorbed by Germany. Ethnic Germans became citizens of the Reich, while the Czechs were confined to citizenship of what amounted to a German colony, whose 'autonomous' government was totally controlled by successive Reich Protectors. Slovakia seceded under the clerical regime of Monsignor Jozef Tiso, and seems to have been written off by the Germans as a more benighted version of Catholic Bavaria.[7] A Danish coalition government functioned under German military occupation until 1943, subject to the control of plenipotentiaries from Berlin's Foreign Ministry working from the Copenhagen embassy. Direct military rule continued in strategically crucial Belgium, while both the Netherlands and Norway were subjected to civilian Reich Commissars, respectively Arthur Seyss-Inquart and Josef Terboven. Northern and western France, together with the entire Atlantic littoral, were placed under military rule, leaving the poorer and less populous centre and south to the newly established regime at Vichy, arrangements which spared Germany the financial and manpower burdens of total occupation.[8] A demarcation line restricted contact and traffic between the two zones. The industrial Nord and Pas de Calais were ruled from Belgium, a further 'forbidden zone' was designated for German settlement, and Alsace-Lorraine, lost after 1870, was reincorporated into the Reich. In early 1941, Italian military difficulties led to the extension of German rule to Yugoslavia and Greece, a complication which delayed the commencement of the invasion of the Soviet Union. In Serbia, the Germans sanctioned a collaborationist Government of National Salvation under General Milan Nedić, while in Croatia Mussolini and Hitler recognised Ante Pavelić's Ustasha Independent State of Croatia.[9] The Nazi empire reached its zenith after 22 June 1941, the same day on which Napoleon had ventured into

Russia 129 years earlier. Because that titanic struggle, involving genocide against Jews and Gypsies, did most to bring about Nazism's
nemesis, it will be treated separately.

German occupation was a rude intrusion into the lives of the
peoples affected, exposing all of them to alien rule, and some to
deportation, terror and mass murder. Very, very few people wanted
the Germans there, regardless of how they conducted themselves under
occupation. This distorted national economies, lowered standards of
living and imposed restrictions on the liberties of individuals. That was
why the faint voices of freedom and hope issuing from exiled 'free'
government radio transmitters in Britain assumed such importance,
and why people who lived through those times are still stirred by the
snatches of music which signalled these broadcasts or memories of
urgent voices announcing 'Ici Londres.' Of course, not all memories of
the war are so noble. In some countries, occupation was accompanied
by the intimate barbarities of civil war, accounting in Yugoslavia for
all but 10 to 15 per cent of the enormous wartime death toll. Memory
of this still grievously informs continuing conflicts, as if the events of
more than half a century ago occurred but yesterday. By contrast,
many former German soldiers have rose-tinted memories of their own
war experiences, characterised by the quest for black market sausages
in 'Krakau', the German name for Cracow, or the tedium of guarding
rocks and waves, sentiments well captured by Heinrich Böll in his
1947 novella *The Legacy* (*Das Vermächtnis*) about service on the
Normandy coast:

> The futility was appalling. There stood the men every morning with
> their machine guns or mortars, drilling, drilling, in the sand dunes,
> practising the movements they had ceased to master because they had
> been practising them for too long. They were personally acquainted
> with almost every grain of sand. And every morning the same, every
> night the same, and always only the one enemy, the sea; all around
> them, minefields, empty buildings.[10]

Those Germans propitiously situated in the Channel Islands, France
or Greece enjoyed conditions similar to an extended holiday, with
beaches and sunbathing for those who liked that sort of thing; with
Parisian salons or tours of the Acropolis for the more cerebral. 'Up to
now, it's just been a Strength through Joy trip,' wrote one participant
in the invasion of France.[11] Their opponents noted this too. Gustave
Folcher, a Languedoc peasant, was wounded and captured on the

Marne on 15 June 1940. Trudging along in a line of prisoners, Folcher watched long columns of motorised German troops pass by:

> We had been deluged with German soldiers taking photographs, for nearly all of them had a camera and wanted to take endless views of the interminable column of prisoners. . . . The German army had a truly proud bearing and the soldiers, those close to us anyway, didn't seem tired. Comfortably seated in deep armchairs, they made war almost as tourists, while we, on foot all the time, had wandered for thousands of kilometres over all the roads of the north and east.[12]

Among the Germans in Paris a no less relaxed atmosphere prevailed. Walter Bargatzky recalled the gathering of 'colourful birds' seconded to the German military administration in the luxurious Hôtel Majestic in Paris, where a spirit analogous to a gentlemen's club prevailed, while the less gentlemanly SS opened shop at 72, avenue Foch. Young men from the German provinces moved around the Majestic, recently vacated by the international rich, absorbing the 'splendour, wealth and worldliness' of its ambience. One might even encounter a casually dressed General Carl Heinrich von Stülpnagel, browsing in the English language bookshop on the rue de Rivoli.[13] Captain Ernst Jünger seems to have slid effortlessly into the more vacuous Parisian literary salons, dining at Maxim's or Prunier's, and exploring cemeteries and churches, on his own.[14] An encounter with the novelist–physician Louis Ferdinand (Céline) on 7 December 1941 evidently shook Jünger:

> he [Céline] says how surprised and stupefied he is that we soldiers do not shoot, hang, exterminate the Jews – he is stupefied that someone availed of a bayonet should not make unrestricted use of it. 'If the Bolsheviks were in Paris; they'd show you how to go about it; they'd show you how one purifies a population; neighbourhood by neighbourhood, house by house. If I carried a bayonet, I'd know what I had to do'.[15]

Another diarist, Ulrich von Hassell, visited Paris during the winter of 1941, noting the medley of Frenchmen and uniformed soldiers on the subways, and the 'pathetically eager faces' of young soldiers – many of them 'students thrust into uniform' – at a Rodin and Manet exhibition in the Orangerie.[16] There they are in countless photographs, watching the races at Longchamps or L'Auteuil, boating on the lake in the Bois, or eyeing lissom dancers at the Moulin Rouge or in *Scheherazade*.[17]

German troops stationed in the Channel Islands appreciated their staider charms, replete with flowers, palm trees and deferential British bobbies, and 'felt like holiday-makers'.[18] The Gulf Stream made unseasonable bathing possible. Other felicitous postings included the Protectorate of Bohemia and Moravia, which with its relative abundance of consumer goods, tasty beer and fine crystal was known to the Germans as 'the land of smiles'. German troops in Poland also made tourist-like observations in their personal diaries. Wolfgang Rieschock was an eighteen-year-old from Neukölln in Berlin, conscripted following completion of Reich Labour Service in early 1939. Moving into Poland at 6 a.m. on 2 September, his diary entries included: 'Talked a lot with the village inhabitants. It was very interesting,' or 'First of all we went shopping, everything was very cheap: a massive white loaf (weighing about five pounds) for 60 Grozy=30Pf! A half pound of Jagdwurst 50 Grozy (=25Pf) a grilled chop 25 Pfennig, 1 litre of milk 5 Pfennig!!!. . . . Naturally I talk a lot with people. I am finding everything very interesting.'[19] Even in Russia, scene of the most appalling savagery, historians have uncovered pockets of normality, where German soldiers effectively retired from the war raging around them, striking deals with local partisan chiefs and putting their feet up in remote blockhouses. But of course these various German perspectives on the war are merely one angle of vision.

For these were not simply (armed) tourists, and nor were they perceived as such by the vast majority of the occupied populations of Europe, for whom their presence was a moral challenge and an unwelcome event in their lives. An initial curiosity, sometimes involving admiration for the Germans' nice manners and fine physiques or the desire to see these fearsome living legends of men close up, gave way to accommodation and sullen antipathy. Although reactions to individual German soldiers varied, according to whether they were lost or billeted in one's home, or how they behaved, the response to the Germans *in toto* was often a glacial indifference, as if they were simply not there, a response so subtle that it probably passed many of the occupiers by. Jean-Paul Sartre caught the French mood well when he recalled that 'they seemed to us more like furniture than human beings'.[20] Even when physical proximity was inevitable, people avoided eye contact and recognition:

When you enter the Metro, we squeeze together to make room for you. You are an untouchable. I bow my head so that you cannot see where my eyes are directed and to deny you the joy of the flash of an exchanged look. There you are in the midst of us, like an object, surrounded by silence and ice.[21]

A cartoon in an underground newspaper reversed the polarities, by depicting a rotund German soldier standing at a bus stop, surrounded by the featureless outlines of civilians, as if they were invisible to him.[22]

Regardless of how winning individual Germans were, people were enjoined to remember that these were little cogs in a larger, pernicious machine. Being beastly to the Germans became a patriotic duty, a mood difficult to recreate at a time when Europeans are constantly enjoined to be nice to each other and not to perpetuate national stereotypes. Everywhere, Germans were given derogatory nicknames: 'Szwab' in Poland, 'Moffen' in the Netherlands, 'Pinseliky' in Czechoslovakia, or 'les Boches' or 'les doryphores' (potato beetles) in France and francophone Belgium.[23] Perceived generically as earnest and humourless, the Nazi occupiers became the butt of endless jokes. In Warsaw, signs reading 'For Germans only' proliferated on cemetery gates and lampposts, while fake advertisements read, 'Frost – the best method against pests', in thinly veiled allusion to the climatic perils of the Eastern Front.[24] One can only imagine what silkily ambiguous knives were jabbed into their backs in the course of conversations, in dozens of languages which they could not really understand. Passive resistance began with blank incomprehension, with the inhabitants of Prague answering 'Nerozumim,' 'I don't understand,' to every utterance in German.[25] But how did one respond if a German soldier held open a door, helped carry a suitcase at a station or stuttered some eirenic platitude such as 'Krieg kaputt, gut. Krieg nicht gut' in a desperate attempt to distance himself from what he represented? Did one say thank you or nod in approbation?

As if to underline the acute moral dilemmas raised by Nazi occupation, across Europe resistance forces produced moral injunctions, with universal sentiments displaced by narrower patriotic imperatives. The earliest pamphlets, such as the French socialist Jean Texcier's *Conseils à l'Occupé*, which appeared in July 1940, concentrated upon the need to maintain dignified distance towards the occupier, suggesting that some needed to be reminded of how to behave in a situation fraught with potential moral ambiguities. The French were advised to meet questions in German with incomprehension, and to avoid such things as public concerts by military bands, in favour of the purer melodies of birdsong.[26] Such tracts proliferated across Europe. In May 1940, two Polish underground bulletins published ten commandments, including the injunctions:

> Polish is your mother tongue. You shall not learn the language of the enemy under the knout. Even if you speak his language, you should not use it. Do not make the aggressor's unwanted stay in your Fatherland any easier. Answer all questions in Polish: 'I don't understand'. You should not give the enemy an address nor show him the way (unless it is wrong). Restrain your inborn Polish courtesy and hospitality. For you, the occupying soldier, the enemy official and the occupier's celebrations should not exist. Maintain reserve and seriousness on the streets and in public places, do not laugh or talk loudly: you might end up in one of the enemy's perfidious propaganda films. . . . You are expected neither to deal with nor to provoke the invader. You should be calm and collected. No laughing. You should never forget for a moment who has destroyed your country; who has robbed and murdered your compatriots, who has kicked and abused your brothers and sisters.[27]

These injunctions, and the assassination likely to visit any Pole who transgressed, seem to have worked, since students of collaboration in Poland have concluded that, with the possible exception of the 'Blue Police' and an infinitesimal fascist fringe, it was conspicuous by its absence.[28] The virtual absence of Polish collaboration, which may reflect the fact that the Nazis did not regard Poles as fit partners for a dialogue, did not preclude areas of partial common interest between occupiers and occupied, as reflected in the belief that Nazi policy towards the Jews was 'an unpleasant but necessary solution to an intractable problem', although one should resist the invidious tendency to treat Poles as co-perpetrators of the Holocaust.[29] As the occupations wore on, moral tracts progressed from advocating dignified distance to more detailed instructions designed to isolate the Germans and local collaborators, and calls for sabotage and subversion. Thus, in August 1941, the French *Libération* recommended boycotts of German propaganda films and magazines such as *Signal* or *Gringoire* and of cafés, hotels and restaurants which showed 'complaisancy' towards the invader; called for the daubing of swastikas on businesses which worked for or traded with Germany; and stressed the need for employees working in war-related industries to inform the resistance on how to commit sabotage.[30]

The privileged position enjoyed by Germans in all occupied

countries meant that morally based distance was reinforced by envy and resentment as they took over the best apartments or hotel rooms and went to the front of every queue. The conquest of women touched a neuralgic point, namely that it reflected poorly on their native male protectors, the price being savage shearings of their heads after the liberation. Lonely young women, whose husbands were in captivity or who had fled compulsory labour service, or who worked for the Germans as cooks, laundresses, maids and secretaries, paid the price of enduring shame, which was often eluded by senior French public servants. Between 1940 and 1943, German soldiers fathered between fifty and seventy thousand illegitimate children with French women. While prostitution could be forgiven as business as usual, 'horizontal collaboration' between 'respectable' women and Germans – based on physical attraction, material need or the absence of two million Frenchmen in prison camps – was excoriated, since in the most flagrant fashion it subverted attempts to isolate the occupier emotionally and physically.[31] This dilemma, if it was one, affected women ranging from Coco Chanel to chambermaids. Parisian homosexuals apparently had a field day with their uniformed German counterparts, engaging in activities which would have put them in a concentration camp had they been living in Germany.[32] But beyond sexual relations, even when people resumed relations with German friends and colleagues, these were often strained and uncomfortable in the new circumstances. Did one invite them to one's home? Should one insist they wore civilian clothes? Should one meet them in a public place such as a café or restaurant? Which conversational gambits should be avoided? In the rarefied international physics community, the Dane Niels Bohr was angered by insensitive remarks about the war made by his old friend Werner Heisenberg, and the latter's apparent belief that it was amity as usual, even in scientific fields whose military application was obvious. Nevertheless, Bohr overruled his wife by deciding to receive Heisenberg at home.[33]

Choices made by individuals under German occupation left a question mark over their reputations for years to come. To take a frivolous example, after 1944 popular entertainers such as Maurice Chevalier, Edith Piaf or Charles Trenet had to justify their recent conduct. Having been attacked by Vichy censors for lyrics sentimentalising urban loucheness, Chevalier reformed his repertoire with songs like 'Our hope': 'If you want to know / What's in my heart tonight / Sing along with me / Tra la la la la / And let's have hope ... Let's hope for blue skies again / And sing of our dear old France'. Although anyone responsible for this execrable rubbish deserved to be punished, it was more a matter of where the songs had been performed that interested post-war interrogators:

> I, the undersigned, Chevalier, Maurice certify, that I quickly realized that when the Government asked me to sing for French prisoners in Germany, in December 1941, that they were seeking to compromise me. For this performance, instead of a fee, I demanded that ten prisoners be freed and this was promised. . . . For four years I have refused to make a film. During the entire German occupation I sang only twelve weeks in Paris, and from the end of 1942 never reappeared on the Paris stage. In April 1943 I completely retired from the stage and remained on my property above Cannes.[34]

About nine thousand French people did not get the chance to exculpate themselves since they were summarily executed in the 'épuration', a process repeated across occupied Europe.[35] In Tito's Yugoslavia, post-war purges were used as a cover for the annihilation of anti-Communists as well as fascist collaborators, including eighteen thousand anti-Titoist forces repatriated by the British.[36] This in turn left a sour taste in the mouths of British officers responsible for these measures, a mood reflected in Evelyn Waugh's *Unconditional Surrender*. Nazism forced a bewildering range of choices, not just upon occupied populations, but also on neutrals such as Sweden or Switzerland, and, as this British example shows, on their opponents.[37] Since this could be the subject of several books in itself, the emphasis in this highly selective tour of occupied Europe is on the complex interaction of Germans and others, albeit at the expense of the role of neutrals and opponents.

Countries such as Belgium, Czechoslovakia, France, Denmark, the Netherlands and Norway were initially spared the lethal policies pursued in occupied Poland, where on average three thousand Poles died each day during the occupation, half of them Christian Poles, half of them Jews.[38] Nonetheless, it is worth remembering that in the case of Czechoslovakia a quarter of a million people were killed during the war. Nazism represented a challenge to the European and global balance of power and to civilised values everywhere, blighting the lives of tens of millions of people throughout Europe. There were gross restrictions on individual freedom, and such shared tribulations as conscription for forced labour and chronic hunger, with an estimated three hundred thousand Greeks dying of starvation during the occupation as German looting of food and the disruption of normal market mechanisms took effect.[39] In Paris, up to 270,000 people were dependent on subsidised communal restaurants for a square meal. Ersatz foodstuffs, the conversion of flowerbeds and window boxes to grow vegetables, trips to the countryside and the moral perils of the black market became the norm for those not part of charmed German–collaborator circles. In most countries, the quality of life deteriorated, with curfews, blackouts, raids, longer working hours, fuel shortages or restricted and inadequate transport systems. The price of food soared, sixfold in occupied Paris between 1940 and 1943; seventyfold in occupied Warsaw between 1939 and 1944. In Brussels, the German commander in chief noted the poor people rifling through dustbins for scraps before dawn each day. Cats and dogs disappeared, and recipes abounded with inventive ways of preparing horsemeat, potatoes, swedes or turnips. Smokers combed the pavements for cigarette butts: ruining their health, but suppressing hunger more effectively than non-smokers.

In his characteristically restrained way, the painter Georges Braque caught the austerity and drabness of domestic existence in wartime Paris in such pictures as *The Stove* (1942), with the coal bucket both prominent and empty. Fuel shortages made the long winter of 1940/1 especially severe, with many people staying in bed for long periods, with rising being akin to plunging into a freezing swimming pool.[40] Illnesses such as tuberculosis, dysentery and hepatitis were common because of poor diet, as were such stress-related phenomena as breakdowns, heart attacks, skin disease, stomach ulcers and irregular menstruation, unsurprising in societies where people could be shot for not carrying an identity card or for sheltering an unregistered person.[41] One consequence of poor diet was that in France the average height of boys and girls growing up between 1935 and 1944 declined by respectively seven and eleven centimetres.[42] Paradoxically, many of Germany's wartime allies, such as Croatia, Italy, Romania and Slovakia, experienced lower bread rations than many occupied countries.

Regardless of the comparative degree of general terror in each occupied country, everywhere people suspected of resistance found themselves dragged into Gestapo torture chambers, with the only exit routes being summary execution or dispatch to a concentration camp. Each of these places of terror had its own distinctive rituals of violence, but all reeked of frightened humans, whose pathetic remnants consist of cryptic messages etched on the walls of former cells in Paris, Prague or Trieste. In many countries, resistance and occupier became locked in an escalating spiral of terror and counter-terror, with many innocent people killed in the crossfire. With the remarkable exception of Denmark, where it was not for want of trying, Jewish people were identified, corralled, removed and murdered.

In all occupied societies, people grudgingly accommodated themselves to the fact of German conquest, with only small minorities from various ends of the political spectrum, or confessional persuasion, initially engaging in collaboration or resistance. Everywhere, people in the public and private sectors had to maintain civil administration, the food supply, law and order, production or public transport, activities which were undoubtedly in the interests of the occupier, but without which civilised life for the occupied would have collapsed. The dilemmas individuals faced, and their choices, were not easy, with *ex post facto* outrage from armchair moralists, especially in countries which were not occupied, being regarded as a bore nowadays.

Collaboration describes a spectrum of behaviour ranging from neutral co-operation, opportunism and ideological affinity to treasonable conduct as defined by the laws of the lands concerned, of which the Norwegian Vidkun Quisling was the most egregious example.[43] The borders between the myriad shades of collaboration were vague. Even within the darkest hues of political collaboration, there were as many shades of black or brown as in a Rembrandt self-portrait. In many countries, politically marginal minorities took advantage of the conditions created by German occupation to try to implement long-harboured or opportunistically adopted ideological agendas, which in most cases had been rejected by the vast majority of their fellow countrymen, conservative, liberal and socialist alike. Some historians of France have used the awkward term 'collaborationism' to distinguish the ideological fervour of impotent French fascists from the 'collaboration' practised by the highly potent elite groups, who used the limited independence afforded by German occupation to avenge themselves upon domestic enemies and to implement an authoritarian 'National Revolution'.[44]

There were certainly substantial differences between the angry sectarian misfits and polished social elites, who made a choice to collaborate with the Germans rather than going into exile. Most of the former had long histories of marginalisation behind them, which may explain how they coped with the intensified social ostracism that now befell them. Regardless of the indigenous origins of their ideologies and resentments, the various fascist parties had long since looked and sounded like foreigners, with their black or brown shirts, leaders called *Fører* or *Leider* and paramilitary *Specialardelingen* in Norway (even the acronym was SA) or *Weerafdeelingen* in the Netherlands.[45] In France, a significant number of these people were former Communists, for example the mayors of working-class districts such as Montreuil, Pierrefitte or Saint-Denis, who joined the erstwhile Communist Party functionary Jacques Doriot's Parti Populaire Français. One totalitarian organisation was much like another, and the utopian racial egalitarianism of National Socialism eased the switch from one party of the envious and resentfully radical to the other. Wartime collaboration compounded the fascists' acute isolation. In November 1941, the Norwegian Nasjonal Samling fascist party had to open the Viktoria, a special restaurant in Oslo, 'as a place where they could feel at home', in a close-knit society akin to an extended family which rejected them. Such different figures as the taciturn Lutheran ex-Defence Minister Quisling and the young Catholic Rexist Léon Degrelle shared a common trajectory of rejection, self-exclusion and the adoption of unsound views expressed in commensurately intemperate language, resulting in the first case in treason, and in the second service on the Eastern Front.[46] A similar path was followed by the British Union of Fascists leader, Sir Oswald Mosley, who, ill at ease with both the Conservative and Labour parties, gradually stepped outside the circle of what was deemed respectable opinion, even if he continued to enjoy the company of respectable people alongside misfits and thugs.

Wherever they came from, these fascist leaders were overwhelmingly at one in the belief that their own societies were so morally degenerate – Degrelle's pre-war banner depicted a broom – and liberalism so atrophied and senescent that they sought salvation in an amoral, foreign, totalitarian dictatorship, whose strength they admired. Much of the extreme left throughout Europe had suffered from the same peculiar complex, with regard to the other source of strength in the Kremlin. On these issues the fascists were in agreement with much broader swathes of opinion which had become hostile to both liberal economics and parliamentary democracy, not to speak of being viscerally anti-Bolshevik.[47] In so far as Vichy had a coherent or stable programme, this was an attempt to cleanse the decadent France of the Third Republic under Nazi auspices, although some of the old-style Maurassians, and for that matter Xavier Vallat, the first enforcer of Vichy's antisemitic laws, were often implacably anti-German.

The Netherlands reveals yet further layers of complexity, which make it more like Vichy France and less like Scandinavia than it would care to seem. Dutch authorities, such as the police, began close co-operation with the Gestapo in the mid-1930s, notably in monitoring German left-wing exiles. German Nazis were prominently represented at the 1937 wedding of Princess Juliana and Prince Bernhard zur Lippe-Biesterfeld, himself an honorary member of an SS cavalry unit, and the Dutch government found unrespectable reasons for not admitting German Jewish refugees.[48] After the occupation, many con-servative bourgeois joined former Prime Minister Hendrik Colijn's Nederlandse Unie (Netherlands Union), because they were weary of fissiparous inter-war Dutch democratic politics, and were convinced that the future lay with a triumphal Nazi Germany, a huge neighbour they could never ignore. But membership of the Union was also an affirmation of the House of Orange and a rejection of the 'unDutch' fascist Nationaal Socialistische Beweging (NSB) of Anton Mussert.[49] There were wheels within wheels in the fascist camp too. Mussert was not in favour of German absorption of the Netherlands, so the SS backed a 'Germanic' faction within the NSB led by the still more radical Rost van Tonningen. The German authorities in Norway similarly tried to supplant the bumptious Quisling with the more compliant police chief Jonas Lie.[50] Not only did collaboration consist of degrees, but the German authorities often subscribed to radically different versions of how best to secure perpetual German dominance, with their own rivalries translated into competing clienteles among the local fascists.

In eastern Europe, the question of collaboration was immensely complicated by the fact that their peoples had been persecuted by the governments which the Germans replaced, and that the potential forces of 'liberation' included a totalitarian dictatorship whose brutish record in these parts eclipsed that of the Nazis. In May 1940, even Heinrich Himmler initially rejected the Bolshevik method of exterminating entire populations as being 'unGerman'. Were Ukrainians supposed to be enthusiastic about restoring the rule of Poles who treated them as second-class citizens, or of the Soviets who had murdered seven million Ukrainians during the terror famine of the 1930s?[51] Collaboration also raises the delicate matter of the deliberate rewriting of the historical record in the interests of contemporary state mythologies in such countries as Serbia. In their version of the occupation, heroic Serb partisans resisted massive Axis forces, while 'all' Croats became adherents of the fanatically anti-Serb and antisemitic Ustasha, and the Bosnian Moslems members of the Handschar SS Division, a simple story used by the Serbs to delegitimise the Croats and Moslems in the West and to deter NATO using force against them. In reality, both royalist Chetniks and Tito's Communist partisans fought a complex internecine war for dominance of Yugoslavia, sometimes against the severely depleted divisions of inexperienced or burned-out troops whom Hitler rested there.[52] That the Ustasha struck with terrifying ferocity against Orthodox Serbs, Jews and Gypsies, killing 325,000 Serbs alone, did – and does – not make every present-day Croat nationalist a fascist, nor afford the Serbs an historical licence to drive out and slaughter these people, for the experience of past vicitimhood is not a mandate to persecute others.[53] Tito's multi-ethnic partisans, among whose ranks was numbered Franjo Tudjmann, were neither above deals with the Germans nor willing to be diverted from the struggle for post-war dominance. In March 1943 Tito instructed his forces *en route* to Montenegro, 'do not fight the Germans', adding: 'Your most important task . . . is to annihilate the Chetniks of Draža Mihailović and to destroy their command apparatus which represents the greatest danger to the development of the National Liberation Struggle.'[54] About nine hundred thousand people died in wartime Yugoslavia, killed by immiscible nationalist fanatics, both Croat and Serb, rather than by German or Italian occupation forces.

Most wartime collaborators banked on German victory and Allied defeat. As the Dutch politician Colijn wrote: 'Europe and Germany: Germany and Europe, this will be the relationship to be reckoned with from now until any humanly foreseeable future. One must forget any preference one may have for one thing or another: normally one's influence on the course of things is next to nothing, but in this particular case it is literally nothing.'[55] They were therefore exceptionally preoccupied with what Germany had to offer by way of a post-war settlement. Intermediary German officials often palmed these individuals off with talk of a reorganised fascist Europe. By contrast, Hitler, who regarded all such talk as presumptuous irrelevance, dealt with collaborator elites either by keeping local fascists at arm's length or by using them to frighten the local elites into line. European fascists were so many pawns on his big game-board. Writing to Mussolini on 25 May 1940, he confused the Walloon Léon Degrelle with the Flemish fascist Joris van Severen, whom the French had recently shot, and mistook the non-fascist Colonel J. A. Mussert for his brother Anton, the *Leider* of the Dutch NSB, whom he had met in 1936.[56] According to Otto Abetz, the German ambassador to Paris, Hitler stumbled whenever he tried to pronounce the imported and germanised term 'Kollaboration', as if he could not get used to a concept coined by, and invested with excess meaning by, foreigners.[57] It took interminable negotiations for a Mussert or a Quisling to see the new master of Europe, a right of access enjoyed by every Nazi regional Gauleiter. The fascist collaborators' names are not even mentioned in standard biographies of Hitler.[58] The Führer sometimes explained to his intimates what was obvious to everyone except European fascists. On 26 April 1942, Goebbels reported him as saying:

Talk of collaboration is only designed for the moment. Incidentally, he'd rather first see deeds and not hear words. He said, should the war turn out as he wished, then France must pay dearly, because it caused and inaugurated it. It would be thrown back to its borders in 1500; that means that Burgundy will become part of the territory of the Reich once again. We will thereby recover a country with which scarcely any German province is comparable in terms of wealth and beauty.[59]

For perhaps the insurmountable stumbling block for collaborators and collaborationists alike was that Hitler was not offering a pan-European fascistic federation, along the lines of the Fascist International essayed by the Italians in the 1930s, nor was he prepared to moderate crushing demands for goods or labour, to ease the lot of local familiars whose names he could not remember.[60] There were no 'visible results' for those such as the former socialist politician Pierre Laval, stalking the lonely path of collaboration. The inequalities of this dialogue and the naivety of the collaborator supplicants can be sampled from Laval's conversations with Hitler in the wake of the 1942 Allied landings in North Africa:

> Whereas in the past wars had been fought between village and village, and later between country and country, an entire continent must now be organized for peace. But this was not possible if each country insisted on putting forward certain demands for the satisfaction of its natural greed. . . . He did not want certain egoisms to hinder the construction of the structure desired by the peoples of Europe [he was talking about the Italians]. . . . This conversation showed . . . that he wanted to do everything to facilitate Germany's victory. But in order to carry out this aim, he required certain moral and political preconditions, i.e. the victors must help him by creating a suitable atmosphere.[61]

Many French people regarded collaboration as 'a one-way street'; Laval needed 'some gesture or declaration which would render his task in France more easy'. A few hours after this conversation Hitler, who was not given to obliging people, ordered the occupation of the rest of France. German intransigence made a nonsense of the claim put forward by collaborators that their actions had deflected the Nazi application of the Polish worst-case scenario to their respective countries, even supposing that such people were privy to German intentions, which was not the case. Apart from the fact that the Germans regarded the inhabitants of the Low Countries, France and Scandinavia in a different light from Slavs, there was scant evidence that the existence of the Vichy regime ameliorated the lives of the French more than the lives experienced by nations under direct German civilian or military occupation. In what respects was life in Vichy France better than that in occupied Denmark, the Netherlands or Norway?[62] The notion that Vichy was a 'shield' was self-deceptive and self-serving. The airy speculations of intellectuals were even more preposterous, some of whom, according to Ninetta Jucker, who lived through the occupation, believed that the French were destined to play Greeks to German Romans, a conceit Harold Macmillan subsequently entertained vis-à-vis Eisenhower and Kennedy and Anglo-American relations in general.[63]

Ideas for a post-liberal economic order were popular in many circles during the troubled 1920s and early 1930s. Hence during 1940–1 there was much talk about something called a New Order in Europe, with plans for abolishing passports, for a Reichsmark currency bloc and for a common European postage stamp, the cauchemars of modern 'Eurosceptics'.[64] Actually, what was being actively considered more closely resembled the Japanese Co-Prosperity Sphere in East Asia and the Pacific than arrangements freely entered into since 1945 by demo-cratically elected European governments. To compare present arrange-ments with the past is an outrageous oversimplification, which ignores the antecedents of the EU in the idealism of wartime resistance movements, and the not inconsiderable difference between dissolving Germany in a Europe of regions and outright German dominance. What was afoot was an old-fashioned economic imperialism, with an industrially developed core surrounded by a periphery producing food and raw materials, along the lines of the relationship Britain was said to have with her empire. Indeed, in 1937 a garrulous Göring had told his English friend Group Captain Christie: 'We want an empire.'

Paradoxically, talk of economic integration, with Germany as the manufacturing heartland of a tariff-free zone detached from the inter-national economy, was most intense in 1940–1, when German interest in developing rather than pillaging the occupied economies was low-est.[65] But it was not entirely a matter of hot air, since concrete steps were taken by Germany to usurp the role of the City of London by denominating all international transactions in Reichsmarks. This meant that trade and capital transfers or transfers of patent rights, pensions and production rights increasingly passed through Berlin. German influence was also fostered through capital penetration, with both the Reichswerke Hermann Göring and private sector banks and corporations acquiring controlling stock in banks and businesses in occupied countries.[66] German insurance firms swiftly supplanted the once dominant British, in auto, fire and theft sectors, and also in large-risk underwriting, with the new Association for Coverage of Major Risks intended to usurp the functions of Lloyd's of London. As one leading historian has observed: 'The New Order economy did not remain on the drawing board; the foundations and much of the scaffolding were set up during the war.' When military reverses in the East led Germany to substitute limited economic co-ordination and a degree of inward investment for crude exploitation, there was less talk of economic integration, but correspondingly more concerning the putative defence of 'Western' civilisation against Bolshevik armies or Afro-American airmen.[67]

But German domination of what was a dialogue should not be over-emphasised, a dialogue moreover involving many partners who were weary of the economic dislocation of the 1930s, and resentful of the position of Britain or the United States of America. Europe was both a political and economic issue, however much the bankers and insurers thought otherwise. Much of the European rhetoric emanated from European collaborators, keen to assert the importance of small countries with proud historical traditions within the emergent National Socialist 'New Order'. Accepting overall German hegemony, the Rexist Degrelle stressed Belgium's role as both a 'jetty' to North American markets and a 'turntable' for Europe as a whole, chucking in for good measure the rich north–south cultural dialogue evident in early modern Antwerp.[68] By October 1940, his Norwegian colleague Quisling had abandoned earlier schemes for a Greater Nordic Union, mediating between Britain and Germany, in favour of a 'Pan-Germanic federation', with a federal flag and the Führer as federal president.[69] Mussert preferred a 'Germanic Reich', consisting of a confederation of states, with the Waffen-SS as its common defence force, and the Dutch having access to *Lebensraum* in the East, where they could bring to bear their experiences in Java or Sumatra, while retaining control of their colonial empire.[70] All of these individuals conceded Germany the right to organise Europe. However, their subscription to a profusion of fascist nation states collided with Hitler's racially exclusive obsession with Germandom. They wanted to retain a slice of a cake Hitler was not prepared to cut up.

Hitler was not interested in conceding collaborators even a bit-part role, since Germany, rather than Europe, figured most prominently in his thinking. It is evident from his periodic remarks about Europe that entire areas simply did not interest him culturally or emotionally, beyond what he could lever out of them by way of coal, labour, iron ore and tungsten. He loathed the early European movement, dismissing its leading exponent, Coudenhove-Kalergi, as 'everybody's bastard'. Pan-Europeanism smacked of pacifism and mechanical economism, and reminded him of the pre-unification German Confederation or the Hapsburg empire, whose internal conflicts vitiated their capacity to project power externally in a significant way.[71] Hitler was interested in German dominance of the continent, with a view to exploiting its resources for his great schemes in the East, not in some sort of amicable partnership.[72] Germany did not need 'European' assistance to conquer the British. When Laval indicated to Field Marshal Brauchitsch that France would join the war, he was rebuffed with: 'We don't need your help, which wouldn't signify very much anyway.'[73]

Rather than needing allies, at the height of their power the Nazi leaders were contemplating the disappearance of some of Europe's smaller states and the drastic attenuation of France herself, which they regarded as the hereditary foe, lynchpin of Versailles, and source of democratic ideals which they had just comprehensively vanquished. Those at the top dealt in very broad brushstrokes, resulting in the dissolution of existing nation states. For example, a discussion at Göring's headquarters on 19 July 1940 envisaged the elimination of Dutch economic independence, the incorporation of Alsace-Lorraine, Luxemburg and Norway into the Reich, and the creation of an independent state in Brittany. Ominously, the participants concluded: 'Ideas are also in the air concerning Belgium, special treatment of the Flemings there, creation of a Burgundian state.'[74] The difference between German and foreign blood was the paramount concern, but there were ancillary saloon-bar prejudices too. Belgium could be divided between 'Germanic' Flemings and 'non-Germanic' Walloons, the former belonged to the Reich, the latter were to be excluded. Half of France was 'Nordic', but there was the 'clerical masonic South', or 'a blood that will always be foreign to us'. Half of Italy (the northern half) was to Hitler's liking, especially Florence, Rome and Venice, and of course the Italian Fascists. But the Italian south seemed to be populated by desiccated aristocrats, whom Mussolini should have let the 'Reds' exterminate.[75] As for benighted Catholic and peripheral Spain, where Franco had recently made a saint an honorary field marshal for a military miracle performed during the Civil War, Hitler demonstratively said this was a country he never planned to visit. He regarded Franco as an obtuse, wily peasant.[76]

When Hitler envisaged the Greater Reich, he thought of central, northern and north-western Europe, with the 'East' as a surrogate British India, whose inhabitants would be cowed and fobbed off with glass beads. When he spoke of future European unification, the analogy was with the forging of the Bismarckian empire from the states of Germany, a process which divided the German nation by excluding Austria. He did not even mention southern Europe: 'The immense labour involved in the welding of northern, western, central and eastern Europe into one entity will be quickly forgotten.'[77] In other words, Europe meant nothing to Hitler, whose views were an amalgam of brutal imperialism, chauvinistic prejudice and blood-based racism. He was solely interested in absolute, permanent German dominance over the north and east of the continent, with the rest being left to his Italian ally. Compared with the obsessive, visceral hatred he directed against Jews and Bolsheviks, his talk of a 'New Order' in Europe seems fleeting, cynical and pallid, for constructive thinking was evidently beyond him. His hostility to Europe was particularly evident when some collaborator regimes imagined that the German assault on Soviet Russia could be transformed into a pan-European crusade. In July 1941, he rejected 'the assertion in an impudent Vichy newspaper that the war against the Soviet Union was Europe's war and that therefore it had to be conducted for Europe as a whole'. This line changed only when Germany began losing the war, and another rhetoric was called for to mobilise more manpower.

Hitler's emphatic views did not preclude the schemes of others. As we have seen, Nazi propagandists, businessmen, historians and international relations experts (sometimes the same entity) generated plans for Europe's future in great profusion. It is worth emphasising that these schemes were subordinate to racial-political criteria in the circles that most mattered, and that prospective 'partners' did not have a choice in the matter. It is also noteworthy that planning for western Europe was both more conventional and much less systematic than for the eastern half of the continent, where the SS enjoyed *de facto* supremacy. There was no western European equivalent of the 'Generalplan Ost', the masterplans for reorganising the whole of European Russia, let alone balsa-wood models of town squares and peasant farmsteads. The West did not stimulate Nazi imaginations in the same way as the East. Whereas there the Nazis imagined they had a *tabula rasa*, which they could draw upon at will, sometimes on the basis of having been there in mists of times disturbingly actual in their consciousness, in the West they had to tread gingerly because of collaborationist regimes and ethnic affinities, or because the West, with its advanced bureaucracies and developed skills base, could be exploited more thoroughly by leaving things relatively alone. Moreover, planning to integrate the Franco-German coal industry was not the same as planning to move the Poles to Brazil or Siberia. Nazi plans for Europe included realistic schemes for the efficient economic exploitation of the continent; turgid jurisprudential tracts outlining a European 'Monroe Doctrine'; works of pseudo-history extolling ahistorical versions of the medieval Holy Roman Empire; and quasi-ethnographic attempts to destroy existing nation states in favour of a patchwork quilt of sub-atomic regional particles.[78]

Europe was not simply a form of economic organisation, but also a charged cultural concept with potential propaganda value. The 'European idea', that is a congeries of evocation, myth and perception, was initially employed negatively, to alienate 'Europeans' from the 'extra-European' powers, Britain, the Soviet Union and the United States of America, or as the deferred pay-off for nations the Nazis had attacked, and whose occupation regimes were manifestly oppressive and predatory.[79] The Nazis claimed they were bringing peace and harmony to a continent menaced by Bolshevism from the East, dollar imperialism and cultural 'Americanisation', and, last but not least, divisive mischief-making by a peripheral Britain, the arch practitioner of balance-of-power politics.[80] This found a ready response in France, where hostility to America was already intense in some quarters in the 1930s, and where the British were perceived as arrogant and perfidious.[81] The Dutch elites were also anti-Bolshevik, not least because they had lost a total of one billion guilders when the Bolsheviks reneged on foreign debt which was owed to individuals rather than major banks.

This idea of a Europe reliant on itself alone was given theoretical expression in Carl Schmitt's version of a German 'Monroe Doctrine', whereby key hegemonial powers, in this case Germany, were entitled to exclude other powers from their continental spheres of influence, where they could do what they liked, including determining which peoples were fit for existence as individual nation states. Only the Reich, with its slippery historical frontiers, remained truly sovereign, with a depleted number of lesser nations in planetary orbit around its sun. This idea was employed by Hitler in an appeal to American non-interventionists, and then, once the United States had become a belligerent, as a form of anti-American propaganda. The slogan was 'Europe for the Europeans!'[82]

As the Blitzkrieg against the Soviet Union became a war of attrition, revealing the inadequacies of Germany's own economic and human resources, European rhetoric was used to drum up cannon-fodder and to mobilise the economies of the entire continent. Here at least Nazi propaganda resonated among both European fascists and broad swathes of opinion, including conservatives in the European resistance movements, who realised that the defeat of Nazism might entail extending the power of the Soviet Union. In a narrower sense, anti-Bolshevism removed a few charismatic pests such as Degrelle or Doriot to eastern battlefields, and edged cautious collaborators to go beyond general expressions of goodwill to active military commitment.[83] Fighting Bolshevism in Russia not only became an acid test of loyalty to the Nazis, but gave collaboration an added dimension, almost a moral purpose, beyond acquiescence in German conquests. The reality of anti-Bolshevism can be gauged from the fact that fifty thousand west Europeans fought in national formations on the Eastern Front, together with enormous expeditionary forces from Finland, Italy, Spain or Romania, which dwarfed the International Brigades that had fought in Spain during the 1930s. Those who fought were effectively acknowledging that only Nazi Germany had the political will to lead Europe, converting treason to their own nations into patriotism towards a greater 'Europe' menaced by Bolshevism. The regimes which encouraged them to go to Russia cynically regarded them as levers to extract territorial bargains and concessions from the Germans.[84] The claim to be defending European civilisation against Stalin's armies was a weak one, since the former included Auschwitz and countless other sites of Nazi depravity.

Nazi European rhetoric was also designed to counteract the pronouncements of Churchill and Roosevelt regarding the post-war era, in a belated attempt to match the Allies' greater reserves of moral capital.[85] In March 1943, a rather desperate Goebbels told foreign journalists that 'New Europe would not be held together by compulsion but achieved on a voluntary basis. No dictatorship over individual European countries. . . . No European country would be compelled to adopt a particular regime. If countries wish to preserve traditional democracy that is their own affair.'[86] In the same month, Foreign Minister Ribbentrop's foreign policy experts delivered a draft foundation document for a European Confederation, which began: 'In order to give tangible expression to the common destiny of European peoples and to ensure that wars never break out again among them, the States here represented have for all time established a European Confederation.'[87] Commenting on this document, the diplomat Cecil Renthe-Fink remarked: 'the assumption of common tasks and France's own future interest would entitle us to make additional demands which the French government would be obliged solemnly to accept. Among other things France would have to provide larger contingents for the European war of liberation, thus saving valuable German blood.'[88] Gottlob Berger, the Waffen-SS's leading exponent of Europeanism, expressed this more starkly when he wrote to Himmler: 'No German mother weeps for every foreigner who falls in battle.' In other words, commonality of European aims masked enhanced unilateral German exploitation.

But there was yet another, odder European future on offer, which proved distressingly appealing to romantically inclined young men across the continent. Race, and a desacralised 'Reich' based on 'Germanic' blood, figured prominently among the concerns of the Reichsführer-SS, with historical mythologies employed to give resonance to Waffen-SS divisions named 'Charlemagne' or 'Hohenstaufen', regal names which imperially blurred the borders of nation-state Germany. Beyond the historical window-dressing was a pervasive concern with 'blood', a substance to be harvested and husbanded by this strange little man. Himmler sought to pool 'Germanic' blood, an aim reflected in the creation in 1935 of an SS-Standarte called 'Germania', which admitted 'Germanic' foreigners, and his patronage of the wilder 'Germanic' fringes of the European fascist parties which like all political parties encompassed a spectrum of views. Just as the SS was most implacable in its persecution of the racially unwanted, so it single-mindedly pursued the goal of integrating all Germans on the basis of racial equality.[89] Himmler sincerely meant it when he warned his German SS men to behave respectfully towards their foreign racial comrades. The SS were to be the racially selected elite within a racially conceived Greater Germanic Reich, based on an enlarged Germany.

Beyond the call of blood to blood, for a substance had a voice in these circles, was the more pragmatic consideration that the military had a stranglehold on recruitment, and that the only way to bypass this was for the SS to resort to ethnic Germans and Germanic foreigners. In 1940, the SS required an annual addition of eighteen thousand men. Since the army only allowed them 2 per cent of German draftees, or twelve thousand men that year, this meant a shortfall of six thousand recruits.[90] Berger, chief of SS recruitment, began with men from Hungary, Romania and Yugoslavia, moving on to Belgium, Denmark, the Netherlands and Norway. Dutchmen and Norwegians would develop an enhanced 'Germanic' consciousness, while the Germans would become aware of a greater 'Germanic' identity.[91] In order to make the SS an attractive option for these recruits, Berger emphasised racial and cultural commonalities, and, following the attack on the Soviet Union, the crusade against Bolshevism. Because of the course of the war in Russia, stringent racial criteria were reluctantly abandoned in favour of quantitative imperatives, so that peoples such as the Bosnian Moslems or Ukrainians soon had their own SS formations, called 'Scimitar' or 'Galicia'.

SS subscription to a Greater Germanic Reich was not simply a means of acquiring soldiers, but also a way of asserting that organisation's influence within the occupied countries of Europe, and in the competition for power and influence within the Nazi leadership. Accusing the Nazi Party rulers of occupied Norway of semi-separatist tendencies, virtually of having gone 'native', the SS promoted itself as the force which would bind together the 'Germanic' elites of Germany and the occupied countries. The Reich Commissars were not only challenged by over-mighty Higher SS- and Police Leaders, but found themselves sidelined by Himmler in their dealings with 'Germanic–*völkisch* groups' in the countries they were ostensibly responsible for.[92] But even within the SS there was no unity of opinion, for beyond Himmler's racial Germanocentrism was a more general ethnocentric approach encompassing the non-Germanic peoples of Europe, in whom Himmler had scant interest.

EAST, WEST, AND THE BALKANS

If the Nazis' talk of Europe was essentially cynical, what considerations determined their treatment of the countries which they occupied? Issues that mattered most were the position a people occupied in the Nazi racial hierarchy; whether a country was seen as backward or developed; the degree to which economic or strategic objectives could be achieved with a minimum of coercion and interference; and, finally, the institutional provenance of the regime the Nazis imposed upon them. This resulted, particularly in northern Europe, in competition between variant model occupations, themselves enmeshed in the internecine struggles for power in Berlin. The tough approach of Party men such as Terboven in Oslo was compared with the softly-softly line of the Foreign Ministry in Copenhagen. Success was measured in terms of the economic rakeoff, the passivity of the population (as reflected in the size of the German apparatus needed to control them) or the general attitude they evinced towards Nazi Germany.[93] Social class also sometimes played a part, with the nationally conscious middle and upper classes of Bohemia-Moravia and Poland being treated considerably worse under Nazi occupation, which meant that they were murdered, than the mass of ordinary workers. In the Protectorate, Heydrich favoured the industrial working class with extra rations, and, in eerie anticipation of post-war Communist arrangements, threw open to them the hotels of Kalovy Vary and had them celebrated in novels entitled *The Boys in Blue Overalls* written by his stooges. In Poland, both the Nazis and the Soviets abducted or murdered the clergy, intelligentsia and upper classes to nullify Polish statehood.

Cultural factors played as great a role as social class in determining the general tenor of Nazi occupation. Whereas in occupied France many Germans displayed an inferiority complex, particularly if they were provincials who had never experienced a world metropolis such as Paris, in the occupied East many Germans came primed with prejudice and a sense of cultural superiority amounting to a colonial mission. This was part of a more general release from civilised bour-geois restraints, in what were perceived as backward countries, popu-lated by allegedly inferior races with a bewildering propensity for armed resistance. As some German generals noted, boorish thuggery spread very quickly, in marked contrast to how German soldiers behaved in western or northern Europe. No Pole could have imagined conditions in the Channel Islands, where NCOs lined German troops up in front of flower beds, barking at them: 'You can look at the flowers, you can smell the flowers, but in no circumstances are you to pick the flowers.'[94] However, this apparently compelling anecdote requires instant qualification, for the island of Alderney included slave labour camps of the sort described by Georgi Ivanovich Kondakov.[95] There were pockets of terror (and normality) everywhere in the empire.

Moreover, the Balkan experiences of war suggest that barbarism was not confined to Poland or the occupied areas of the Soviet Union, although these figure much more prominently in the literature. Wher-ever the Germans encountered armed resistance, there were reprisals, sometimes because the resisters wanted them to happen in order to spread discontentment. There were complex moral calculations on all sides. Whatever interest individual Germans showed in the splendours of ancient Greece was not reflected in their savage handling of the 'bandits' who assailed them, and was simply not present at all in Yugoslavia, where the German army thought little of shooting twenty thousand Serbs between September 1941 and February 1942 by way of reprisals. The people and terrain were ideal for guerrilla warfare, and Hitler knew what should be done with them: 'What should you do: the swine have barricaded themselves in a house in which there are also women and children. Should the soldier set fire to the house or not? If he sets fire to it, the innocent are burned. There shouldn't be any doubt about this! He must burn it down!'[96]

In occupied France, the issue of reprisals apparently discomfited some of the senior army officers. The decision to carry out large-scale shootings of hostages resulted in the alienation of the German military administration and the resignation of the Paris Commander Otto von Stülpnagel, who wrote: 'I can no longer reconcile mass shootings with my conscience, nor answer to history for them.' In a private letter to Keitel, Stülpnagel undid himself by recommending the mass deporta-tion of Communists and Jews to the East as a more efficacious alternative deterrent.[97] Although conventional standards of decency towards non-Jews initially prevailed in western and northern Europe, which were not plagued by irregular warfare, convergence gradually occurred – as demonstrated by such outrages as the massacre at Oradour-sur-Glane – as Nazism descended into a paroxysm of violence. Scenes hitherto confined to eastern Europe, that is people hanging from balconies or telegraph poles, edged their way westwards. By contrast, from the beginning, a separate moral sphere existed in the East, as literally reflected in the decision to extend the German customs border to the outer edge of occupied Poland, maintaining the police frontier along the former German–Polish border, so that people needed special permits to enter a lawless zone. Massive brutalities were perpetrated there on a daily basis. Complex cultural attitudes towards the East, a high-level toleration of lawless conduct, and collapse of civilised bourgeois restraints under the influence of alcohol or a psychopathic bloodlust were at work in places where little men could play God.[98] Finally, Greece and the Balkans represented an intermediary zone, where the latitudinarian rules of conduct being elaborated in the spring of 1941 for the invasion of Russia were already in evidence, and which in turn interacted with guerrilla warfare and/or inter-ethnic animosities to create conditions of extreme savagery.[99] Let us turn first to the occupied East, beginning with the regime of unrestrained terror established in Poland, the nightmare scenario among the occupied nations of Europe.

Hitler decided to reject the idea of creating a satellite state in Poland to use as a bargaining chip during the 'phoney war', and opted for annexation, exploitation and germanisation, once it was clear that no terms from the West were on offer.[100] Vast tracts of Poland, with a predominantly Polish population, were simply incorporated into the Reich. Poland forfeited about ten million people, together with her most fertile agricultural lands and much of her industrial economy, although the Poles soon discovered that the Germans were keener to acquire industry than people. Some eleven million people were left in what was initially called the General Government of the Occupied Polish Areas, consisting of the Polish province of Lublin and parts of Cracow and Warsaw. The seat of government was relocated from Warsaw to Cracow, to erase Polish statehood further, with Hans Frank, the Munich Nazi Party lawyer, installing himself in the former royal residence. The Axis war correspondent Curzio Malaparte left vivid descriptions of the amorality and vulgarity which characterised Frank's court, with its interminable post-prandial discussions about Jews or German and Polish national character:

Before me sat Frank, on his high stiff-backed chair in the old Polish royal palace of the Wawel in Cracow, as if he were sitting on the throne of the Jagiellons and Sobieskis. He appeared to be fully persuaded that the great Polish traditions of royalty and chivalry were being revived in him. There was a light of innocent pride on his face, with its pale, swollen cheeks and the hooked nose suggesting a will both vainglorious and uncertain. His black glossy hair was brushed back revealing a high ivory-white forehead. There was something at once childish and senile in him: in his full pouting lips of an angry child, in his prominent eyes with their thick, heavy eyelids that seemed to be too large for his eyes, and in his habit of keeping his eyelids lowered – thus cutting two deep, straight furrows across his temples. A slight film of sweat covered his face, and by the light of the large Dutch lamps and the silver candlesticks that ranged along the table and were reflected in the Bohemian glass and Saxon china, his face shone as if it were wrapped in a cellophane mask. 'My one ambition', said Frank thrusting himself back against his chair by propping his hands against the edge of the table, 'is to elevate the Polish people to the honour of European civilisation.'[101]

In fact, this lord of life and death – people joked that the General Government should be called 'Frank-Reich' – was an imitation bully, oscillating uneasily between conciliation and attempts to outdo the SS with displays of hardness, but never totally in charge of what was technically described as a 'secondary country of the Reich'.[102] Eastern Poland also experienced terror. Although the half of Poland occupied by Soviet forces does not directly concern us, its thirteen million inhabitants were rendered amenable to life in the workers' paradise by the murder of their elites, mass arrests and the deportation eastwards of one and a half million people, of whom 30 per cent had perished by 1941.[103] After the invasion of the Soviet Union that summer, the General Government assumed its final dimensions, consisting of five districts: Cracow, Warsaw, Lublin, Radom and Galicia. So much for the administrative contours of German rule, what of changing policy and daily practice?

German army administration in Poland was abolished within a month in favour of civilian rule. Hitler subsequently informed Keitel that 'The armed forces should welcome the opportunity of dispensing with administrative questions in Poland.'[104] This remark indicated that Hitler was not going to achieve his ethnic–political goals in Poland with the army, whose initial proclamation to the Poles unhelpfully read: 'The armed forces do not regard the population as their enemy.

All international legal stipulations will be respected.'[105] Hardline Nazis, such as Arthur Greiser and Albert Forster, were appointed to the leadership of the incorporated and annexed territories. The spirit of things to come was further evident when on 7 October Heinrich Himmler acquired the title Reich Commissioner for the Strengthening of Ethnic Germandom, with responsibility for the ethnic reordering of Poland through expulsion and repatriation. His local reach was represented by Higher SS- and Police Leaders who were appointed to each incorporated or occupied territory, a practice soon extended to the rest of occupied Europe. Together with the Central Offices for Immigration and the labour, concentration and extermination camps, this amounted to an enormous quasi-territorial power-base for this most fanatical of Nazi agencies.

The perception that the army was not a reliable tool for the grisly activities Hitler envisaged was strengthened by the protests some of its leaders registered after being confronted by the excesses perpetrated by the five SS task forces which shadowed their troops, a practice developed from the Anschluss with Austria and the occupation of Czechoslovakia.[106] The task forces' initial orders were to neutralise resistance behind German lines and Polish chauvinistic organisations, such as the Western Marches Association, lists of whose membership had been circulated beforehand. The names of thirty thousand Poles were included in special pursuit lists. The general atmosphere deteriorated as Poles turned on ethnic Germans regarded as fifth columnists, while ethnic Germans retaliated with vigilante groups called the Selbstschutz.[107] The most notorious incident occurred at Bromberg, where on 3 September 1939 – 'Bloody Sunday' – retreating Polish troops were fired upon, perhaps by snipers deployed among the ethnic German population, hundreds of whom were summarily executed by way of reprisal. Einsatzgruppe IV, one of the five units mentioned earlier, proceeded to murder hundreds of Poles in the town. Conflating non-existent pre-war atrocities against ethnic Germans with incidents which happened during the fighting, Hitler worked himself into a rage against the Poles. Speaking on 6 October 1939, he said:

> It is my duty to speak of the fate of the hundreds of thousands of Germans . . . who since March have been subjected to really appalling terror. Even today, it cannot be established how many of them have been deported and where they are. In places which were inhabited by hundreds of Germans there are no longer any men left. They have all

been exterminated. In other places women have been raped and murdered, girls and children have been defiled and killed.[108]

By early 1940, the German authorities had registered the deaths of 5,500 ethnic Germans. In February, Hitler ordered the withdrawal of these figures, and the use of fifty-eight thousand for official purposes, of whom thirteen thousand were 'identifiable murders' and forty-five thousand persons reported missing. This order of magnitude would legitimise German atrocities. Nazi publicists such as Edwin Dwinger or the historian Kurt Lück wrote lurid accounts of the September massacres, accounts explicitly designed to justify German reprisals: 'If a nation treats defenceless people in this way, there is nothing it does not deserve, everything will be legal, whatever happens.'[109]

In the weeks following the invasion, the Nazis clarified their long- and short-term goals. Intellectuals were to be 'rendered harmless', the lower classes resettled for use as migrant labour, and Jews concentrated in ghettos to facilitate their expulsion to destinations as yet undecided.[110] The messy realities created by these decisions appalled a number of the army officers. Murderous SS actions lacked elementary logic and threatened to destabilise areas in which German control was tenuous. In Bromberg, the Second SS-Totenkopfstandarte 'Brandenburg' arrested all male Jews in response to the burning down of two houses, after the Germans had set fire to two synagogues. When an army officer objected that the prisons lacked the capacity to hold ten thousand people, an SS officer replied that they would shoot those that could not be imprisoned.[111] Some army officers registered with extreme distaste incidents in which Jews were forced to sing while crawling across the floors of synagogues, or to smear excrement on the faces of their fellows. Since this conveys the general climate, there is no need to multiply instances of cruelty and murder for the sake of it. In a letter to his wife dated 21 November 1939, the pint-sized Colonel Hellmuth Stieff described conditions in occupied Warsaw so terrible that 'one moves about there not as a victor but like the guilty party'. The most fantastical horror propaganda could not match what was happening, ostensibly in the name of 'righteous outrage regarding the crimes perpetrated against ethnic Germans'. He continued:

The extermination of entire races including women and children is only possible by a sub-humanity that no longer deserves the name German. I am ashamed to be a German! This minority, which besmirches the name of Germany through arson, murder and plunder, will be the undoing of the whole German nation, unless we can soon put a stop to their game. For such things, as they have been described and verified for me by the most informed parties, must summon forth avenging nemesis. Or else this riff-raff will one day do the same thing to us decent people, terrorising their own nation with their pathological passions.[112]

German army animosity towards the SS reflected both ethical distaste and professional concern that the SS was becoming a 'state within a state' rather than a subordinate police agency.[113] General Küchler ordered the disarming, recall and court-martialling of SS units responsible for anti-Jewish atrocities in his jurisdiction, referring to the units concerned as 'blots upon the army'.[114] Hitler's response to cases involving formal charges was to declare an amnesty for all offences committed before 4 October 1939 in alleged reaction to 'Bloody Sunday' in Bromberg. When this failed to stem complaints from the army, on 17 October Hitler simply removed the SS and police from military jurisdiction.

However, a few generals continued to protest and they deserve not to be forgotten. Colonel-General Blaskowitz, the senior commander in Poland, was an East Prussian career soldier and devout Christian. Both factors created distance between himself and the regime, although his belief in the supra-political role of the military meant that he subsequently remained aloof from the military resistance.[115] He sent two memoranda to Field Marshal Brauchitsch, in which he said that the forces of 'law and order' were creating terror among the civilian population, and were regarded as executioners by the army. He did not know how the SS hierarchy regarded men given over to the 'intoxication of blood', but the fact that they wore field grey was 'an intolerable burden' upon the army. With subsequent lists of SS atrocities in Poland circulating among the officers on the Western Front, in his second memorandum, dated 6 February 1940, Blaskowitz wrote that it was misguided and pointless to shoot 'tens of thousands of Jews and Poles'. Such actions presented Allied propagandists with a heaven-sent opportunity, and had engendered not only 'deep disgust, but also great pity for the Jewish population' among antisemitic Poles, for not all antisemites, whether Polish or German, seem to have been 'eliminationist'.[116] Worse, however, was 'the brutalization and moral debasement which, in a very short time, will spread like a plague among valuable German manpower'. Blaskowitz continued: 'in a very short time we shall be faced with the rule of the thug. Like-minded people and those with warped characters will very soon come together so that, as is now the case in Poland, they can give full expression to their animal and pathological instincts. It is hardly possible to keep them in check any longer, since they can well believe themselves to be officially authorised and justified in committing any act of cruelty.'[117]

One did not have to be a conservative general to be concerned about the slide into brutality. We have already encountered the eighteen-year-old conscript Wolfgang Rieschock. Rieschock, who hailed from a pacifist Social Democrat background, noted in his diary the 'master race' mentality evinced towards the Poles by the Pomeranian peasants in his unit, and the brutality of officers and NCOs. Their preferred method of interrogation was a blow to the face or shooting out the victims' silhouettes as they stood against a tree. Of one sergeant Rieschock wrote: 'He used his power as an NCO in a sadistic fashion. That is often the case with little men like Unteroffizier Wagner, when they have power in their hands, they use it to the utmost and enjoy it to the full.'[118] Adrenaline flowed when a man stood behind or over another quaking person, with a gun in his steady or trembling hand; a moment of absolute power that many recorded in photographs. Such things spread, like a contagion, with each act leading to further moral deadening, reinforced by copious quantities of alcohol, an ubiquitous liquid participant in many of these atrocities. Still devoted to self-contained, regulated military violence, Blaskowitz wrote that every soldier felt 'repelled and revolted' by activities which were effectively taking place under their protective mantel. He demanded the court martialling of those responsible, adding that 'The idea that one can intimidate the Polish population by terrorism and rub their noses in the dirt will certainly prove false.' His colleague General Ulex called for the recall of all senior and junior security police personnel from Poland.

Blaskowitz's first memorandum made its way to Hitler's desk. The Führer read it with mounting anger, commenting that 'one can't fight a war with Salvation Army methods', and that he had never liked Blaskowitz anyway. The affair was settled with a compromise that boded ill for the army. Colonel-General Bock wrote to all commanders of army groups and individual armies, regretting unfortunate 'misinterventions' on the part of the security forces, but acknowledging that 'otherwise uncommonly harsh measures towards the Polish population of the occupied areas' were justified by the need to 'secure German *Lebensraum* and the solutions to ethnic political problems ordered by the Führer'. Himmler was then invited to address an audience of senior commanders, thus 'affording them the opportunity of having things illuminated from his perspective on things'. Reassured that the army did not object to 'hardness', but merely to 'the danger of brutalisation', Himmler addressed a gathering of generals at Koblenz on 13 March 1940. Deploying his own moral probity as a sort of blanket guarantee, he remarked that he had never seen any excesses himself, before sharing a confidence designed to dissipate all dissent: 'I never do anything that the Führer does not know about.'[119] The generals made no public protest.

As for Blaskowitz, in early May he was transferred to the Western Front, and then humiliatingly relieved of his command on 3 June in the midst of the offensive. The only colonel-general to be denied a field-marshal's baton, his subsequent career consisted of endless repostings and recalls, as if he was deemed unreliable, and ended with unjustified charges of war crimes, and his throwing himself down a stairwell in the Allied prison at Nuremberg. His replacement in Poland issued an order which included the comment: 'The achievement of a final solution of this ethnic struggle, which has been raging for centuries along our eastern frontier, requires particularly tough measures.' As we shall see, the polarity between the military and the SS was not quite as wide as enthusiasts for Blaskowitz and his ilk imagine, since the SS was not alone in having radical plans for Poland.

The broad brushstrokes of Nazi policy in Poland were sketched by Hitler for Keitel in mid-October 1939. Having begun without much of the baggage surrounding traditional Prussian policy towards Poland, a fact reflected in his 1934 non-aggression pact, Hitler seems to have rapidly internalised the anti-Polish prejudices common among many in Prussia-Germany after two centuries of suppressing Polish nationalism. In a rare instance of self-criticism, Hitler said: 'My Polish policy in the past was at variance with the views of the nation.'[120] His remarks to Keitel reflected some of the core elements of Prussian polonophobia. Some of this was encapsulated by the term 'Polish mismanagement', a venerable pejorative phrase, which conjured up anarchic aristocrats and ramshackle rustic hovels. Many Germans believed they were culturally superior to the Poles, with a historic mission to civilise them. Indeed, a few argued that since Teutonic tribes were the aboriginal inhabitants of an ill-defined 'East', the Slavs were history's squatters. Culturally determined arrogance, on which the Germans hardly had a monopoly, was accompanied by fear regarding demographic inundation or the inclusion of the Poles in a more menacing Slavic racial totality stretching into deepest Russia.[121] Many of these themes were reflected in Hitler's initial dispositions. The Germans were to resist the temptation of bringing order to chaos: 'the standard of living in the country is to remain low; it is of use to us only as a reservoir of labour'. The establishment of an administration independent of the ministries in Berlin would free the powers in Poland from the need to observe legal niceties. There was to be no attempt to stabilise the situation in Poland; 'Polish mismanagement' should prevail. This arrangement would also enable him to cleanse the Reich itself of 'Jews and Polacks'.[122]

The aims of Nazi policy towards Poland – which changed according to external constraints over time – were to destroy her social and intellectual elites and her integrity as a nation; to effect large-scale ethnic cleansing, involving the deportation of Poles and Jews, policies eventuating in the depletion of the former and the mass murder of the latter; and, finally, to barbarise Polish cultural life, with a view to converting the Poles into semi-educated helots labouring for Germany. Reviewing this earlier period from the vantage point of August 1943, Frank remarked that many had said that Poland was nothing more than a 'shit heap' (*Misthaufen*) which would supply bread, grain and 'workers and workers and workers'.[123] Moreover, the thought of deporting or killing the entire Polish population also certainly crossed the minds of several Nazi officials, some of whom countenanced the bizarre thought of relocating the Poles to Brazil or western Siberia. Some of these Nazi policies were not exclusive to Poland, since ethnic cleansing also occurred in Alsace-Lorraine, and the regional separatist card was played in Brittany, while secondary schools and universities were temporarily or permanently closed in several other occupied countries. Although there were some superficially common features with the most extreme periods of Prussian or imperial hegemony in Poland, Nazi policy was so radically racist and violent as to constitute a different phenomenon, where contrasts are as evident as continuities.

Large sections of Poland's elites – civil servants, priests, professors and noblemen, who were perceived on both sides of the Nazi–Soviet demarcation line as bearers of unwanted national consciousness – were either summarily shot or dispatched to concentration camps. The entire faculty of the ancient Jagiellonian University in Cracow was summoned to a meeting with the Gestapo in November 1939 and then deported to Sachsenhausen; some seventeen hundred Polish priests were sent to Dachau, of whom half died in miserable circumstances.[124]

In the summer of 1940, while the 'searchlight' of world opinion was focused on France, three and a half thousand Polish intellectuals (and three thousand professional criminals) were rounded up under an Extraordinary Pacification Programme (AB action) organised by Frank, police chief Wilhelm Krüger and Bruno Streckenbach on Hitler's direct order, and shot in a forest outside Warsaw – for, as Frank put it, deporting them to German concentration camps would be more bother than it was worth. Remarking 'we are not murderers', Frank was most concerned about the psychological burden upon the SS men involved, who were reassured with a special decree designed to mask the arbitrariness of what they were doing. Clearly it was terrible work, since Streckenbach wept when he discussed it, commenting that his men had to drink heavily in order to carry out their orders.[125] Of 280,000 individuals statistically defined in 1938 as pursuing intellectual professions, forty-eight thousand perished during the war, including 57 per cent of judges and lawyers, and 29 per cent of clergy.[126] Melitta Maschmann, a League of German Maidens official in the Warthegau, recalled: 'The fact that one never encountered Poles from the better classes, led me to the false conclusion that the Polish nation consisted of proletarians, peasants and the poor. No wonder, I said to myself, that throughout its history it has always had to suffer prolonged periods of foreign rule. Obviously, it was unable to form an enduringly capable ruling class.'[127]

This was precisely the effect the murder of Poland's social and intellectual elites was designed to achieve. As Hitler said on 2 October 1940: 'There can only be one master for the Poles, and that should be the German; there cannot, and should not, be two masters side by side, and therefore all representatives of the Polish intelligentsia are to be killed. That sounds harsh, but it is only the law of life.' Speaking in Metz, a month earlier, Himmler recalled that in Poland 'we had to be hard enough – you shall hear this and at the same time forget it again – to shoot thousands of prominent Poles'.[128] But it was not simply the Polish elites who were vulnerable to Nazi brutality. People already regarded as expendable, 'ballast existences', in Germany itself, namely psychiatric patients, were cold-bloodedly murdered by SS units to create emergency barracks space for the German military.[129]

The murder of Poland's elites was one deliberate strategy employed to nullify her statehood; another was to exploit her lack of ethnic homogeneity, to highlight the fact that this creation of Versailles was artificial and meaningless. Throughout the Weimar Republic, German academic experts on Poland had been insistent that Poland was a sort of prison for oppressed minorities, views which these scholars were not slow in bringing to the attention of their political masters.[130] In his discursive 'Thoughts on the Treatment of the Alien Population in the East' dated 15 May 1940, Himmler began by saying that:

> In our treatment of the foreign ethnic groups in the east we must endeavour to recognize and foster as many such individual groups as possible, i.e. apart from the Poles and Jews, the Ukrainians, White Ruthenians, Gorales, Lemkes, and Kashubians. If there are any more ethnic splinter groups to be found then these too.

As the case of the Bretons shows, attempts to fan regionalism into separatism were not confined to Poland, although these policies were most consequentially pursued in that country.

One group that attracted German interest in Poland were the Goral shepherds in the Tatra Mountains around Zakopane, who before the war had developed a slight cultural and linguistic regional identity. Hans Frank and Himmler began to take an interest in the Gorals, claiming that the latter were not ethnically Polish. Himmler and his Boswell, the truly awful scribbler Hanns Johst, visited Zakopane and its environs in a horse and trap during the winter of 1939. Zakopane was a mountain spa resort, a Polish Upper Bavaria or Switzerland. In the first of many eccentric diversions, Johst lamented the way in which tourism was turning 'chubby' girls into chambermaids and 'solid' lads into waiters 'thirsting for tips'. Sleighs sped Himmler and Johst to the Gorals, like a malevolent witch and her familiar racing across the ice and snow in a cartoon fairytale. Ethnographical lectures punctuated Johst's account of the trip, for these men could bore on endlessly about such subjects:

> The Gorals . . . Gora is a Slavic word meaning mountain in German. Therefore, a mountain folk. Germanic in origin, this race has maintained its purity in the valley folds of the Tatra mountains, remaining completely isolated, with the swastika carved into the timbers of their gables, speaking their own language and hating everything which is Polish or Jewish.[131]

The itinerant duo dropped in on the Gorals at home, receiving round flat loaves and sheep's cheese, and admiring the carvings and fixtures, such as a lock 'so ancient and primitive like those described by Homer in the Odyssey' that it caught the Reichsführer-SS's attention.

They watched a Goral folk dance, an opportunity for Johst to extemporise on the thought that 'the history of dance is the history of physical movement, of bodily consciousness', before going shopping in an ethnic crafts centre. The fruits of their ethnographic enthusiasm for the Gorals were slight. A Goralian Committee was created, which distributed identity cards marked with a 'G' rather than a 'P', designed to make people opt for a separate identity, and some effort was put into the promotion of dialect, folk dancing and costume, the universal vernacular of bogus nationalisms. Since only twenty-seven thousand people opted for the 'G' card, and the Tatra Mountains became a major source of resistance, it is to be assumed that it took more than a few stooges and peasants in folk costume being photographed with Frank or Himmler to shake the Gorals' identity with Poland.

The Ukrainians seemed to have more promise. Throughout the 1930s, the Polish government discriminated against the sizeable Ukrainian minority, while the armed wing of the Organisation of Ukrainian Nationalists (OUN) responded with a campaign of political assassinations.[132] Most of the West Ukraine came under Soviet rule in 1939–41, but some half a million Ukrainians were included in the German-occupied zone. In studied contrast to his treatment of the Poles, Hans Frank sanctioned the Cracow-based Ukrainian Central Committee social-welfare agency, a Ukrainian police and schools and freedom for the Orthodox and Uniate Churches. Ukrainians were intruded into lower official positions in overwhelmingly Polish areas in a clear policy of divide and rule. However, German relations with Ukrainian nationalists were complicated when OUN fragmented into moderate and revolutionary factions under Andrii Melnyk and Stepan Bandera, with German policy-makers themselves split between those who wished to use these people and those who were contemptuous of them. These different agendas culminated in Bandera's proclamation of an independent Ukraine in Lviv on 30 June 1941, a *fait accompli* which resulted in Bandera's arrest and incarceration in Sachsenhausen. In other words, while the Nazis were prepared to privilege the Ukrainians in order to nullify Poland, they were not going to permit the creation of an independent Ukraine encompassing the areas newly liberated from the Soviet Union.[133] Throughout 1941, the SS and Gestapo arrested and executed members of both OUN factions. To underline the maxim that 'Ukraine does not exist . . . it is merely a geographical concept,' Galicia was incorporated into the General Government, 'Transnistria' handed over to the Romanians, and the

rump Ukraine placed under a particularly brutal German administration. These matters will be developed in successive chapters.

Murdering Poland's elites and exploiting her ethnic faultlines were
accompanied by expulsions of hundreds of thousands of people on
the basis of their race, a fact not always coincident with the actual
reason for their expulsion. Responsibility for ethnically cleansing and
(re)germanising the incorporated territories was assumed by Himmler,
with the Reich Main Security Office and willing academic experts as
the brains behind the operation, while ethnic Germans, the army and
the regular and security police acted as his local executants. Hack
academics, including some of the finest (historical) minds in the
business, such as Hermann Aubin, Werner Conze, Walter Kuhn or
Theodor Schieder, volunteered their expertise in this hour of the
experts. A sort of erudite mindlessness fused with total insensitivity to
other people. First, the requisite space had to be created in a country
widely perceived by Nazi Germany's voodoo economists as being both
overpopulated and overdue for rationalisation, although there were
few direct links between policy and the cogitations of economists.[134]
Following a period of spontaneous expulsions, tens of thousands of
Poles were systematically herded from West Prussia and the Warthegau
to the General Government. The people concerned were surprised in
the night, and given a few minutes to pack a few belongings, before
being herded to railway stations. Goods trains carrying up to a
thousand people took the long way around in freezing conditions to
the General Government, where the stunned human 'freight' was
unloaded, together with the bodies of those who had died during the
journey. Those who survived literally had nowhere to go, since the
authorities in the General Government had made no arrangements for
their reception. To minimise the confusion, intermediary camps were
established which also enabled the SS to sieve out potential labour for
Germany. Those especially subject to deportation included people who
had migrated westwards as part of the effort to 'polonise' these areas
after Versailles, political activists, landowners or the urban well-to-do,
intellectuals, professors and professionals.[135] Ethnic Germans also
sometimes settled old scores by including Poles they did not like or
whose property they coveted on the lists of deportees.

Despite the fact that Hans Frank was manifestly unable to cope
with the 340,000 people dumped into the General Government during
1939–40, in Berlin Heydrich and his planners were arranging to expel
a further 563,000 people in 1941, a figure which did not include the

237,000 people the army were independently seeking to deport from areas they wished to monopolise as training grounds and potential settlements for military veterans. For, while some senior army officers were protesting about SS excesses in Poland, others were working with Himmler, agreeing to deploy two and a half million Jews in eastern Poland to dig a gigantic anti-tank ditch along the frontier with Russia.[136] As for the vast numbers of deportations contemplated by Heydrich for 1941, the logistical demands of Operation Barbarossa ensured that a mere thirty-six thousand people were deported to the General Government. This did not prevent the forced concentration of Poles *within* the incorporated territories. Hundreds of thousands of Poles were expelled from the inner cities to remote suburbs, from sunny apartments to dark basements, or into special 'reservations' in Kalisz or Miksztat where the soil was poor. Nor were the Poles safe within the General Government. They were forced out of the huge areas taken over by the army, while in November 1941 the SS- and Police Leader in Lublin, Odilo Globocnik, began a trial expulsion of eight villages in the Zamość region, a sort of local feasibility study for the massive deportations being mooted as part of the developing General Plan East.[137]

Having denuded the space of its inhabitants, the Nazis set about resettling and rationalising the Polish countryside. It is worth probing a little deeper into the mindset responsible for this vast attempt at ethnic cleansing, a peculiar amalgam of bad history, racism and a sense of mission, combined in Himmler's case with bizarre, pedantic details and plangent sentimentality. Words like probe, deep or mindset automatically suggest profound psychological mystery, but we are treading in the autodidactic shallows, with men unremarkable when left tending a farm or running a hardware shop in some provincial backwater, but noteworthy when in possession of terrible powers encompassing a continent. Himmler addressed SS leaders on the evening of 24 October 1939 in the officers' mess in Posen on the subject of resettlement in Poland. His speech skipped gaily across continents and millennia. Beginning with the claim that the Germans had inhabited these territories three thousand years ago, for like all vulgar minds Himmler's was obsessed with origins, he reached the contemporary world via the Boers trekking across South Africa. He was much taken with warrior–settlers. They would be an outpost against 'Slavdom'. It would be an arduous life, in which 'only the strongest would survive', but the result would be 'a strong, child-rich nation'.

Having established that 'the Germans must be the leading men in all things, the Poles their helpers', Himmler depicted an ersatz medieval paradise, with quasi-manorial domains and dues rendered in natural produce. In each village, a core of Germans from the Old Reich – Bavarians, Swabians, East Friesians and so forth – would be surrounded by ethnic German repatriates from further afield, who would learn the agricultural techniques of the twentieth century from the former. Not content with describing villages, Himmler spent considerable time on the bathrooms and showers to which the sweaty farmers would return from the fields; his preference for brick over concrete; and his aversion towards 'kitsch and urban clutter' in domestic furnishings. After five years each settlement would give the appearance of being German thanks to 'the blonde girls and lads' scampering in its environs. After fifty to eighty years had elapsed, there would be twenty million German settlers, with each of the ten million peasants having eight to ten children. Having reached stasis, the demand for more land would necessitate further war, or as Himmler had it: 'more land would have to be won by the sword'.[138] That winter, Himmler and his amanuensis Johst drove up and down Poland in the Reichsführer's BMW. The car was progressively wrecked by potholes, in literal illustration of 'Polish mismanagement', a trope not entirely without verisimilitude. Scribbling away, Johst captured the sense of superiority and mission all too faithfully:

> The Poles are not a state-building nation. They lack even the most elementary preconditions for it. I drove alongside the Reichsführer-SS up and down that country. A country which has so little feeling for systematic settlement, that is not even up to dealing with the style of a village, has no claim to any sort of independent political status within the European area. It is a colonial country!

Periodically the two alighted, vaulted ditches and strode across fields pockmarked with grenade craters. Himmler would pick up soil, inhale its damp organic odour, crumble the earth between his fingers and then glance 'across the wide, wide space, which was full, abundantly full with this good, fertile earth. And so we stood there like prehistoric farmers and laughed to one another with twinkling eyes. . . . All of this was now once more German soil! Here the German plough will soon change the picture. Here trees and bushes will soon be planted. Hedges will grow, and weasel and hedgehog, buzzard and hawk will prevent the destruction of half the harvest by mice and other vermin.' Even the heavens were not safe from the Reichsführer's ambition: as he imagined orchards of fruit trees and tidy villages, so he thought that hedges and woods would shift the rainclouds eastwards, slaking this dry land.[139] Soon academics would be investigating how indeed to transform the flat landscape to make it more attractive to German settlers, artificially engineering a different climate.

It proved difficult to induce Germans to forsake the Reich for these inclement eastern regions, notwithstanding instant housing from which the occupants had been rudely ejected and special supplementary payments. Under the programme 'Home to the Reich', hundreds of thousands of ethnic Germans from the Baltic, Bessarabia, Bukovina and Volhynia were repatriated for resettlement in the incorporated territories. Teams of Nazi negotiators travelled to the countries concerned to haggle with the Estonian and Latvian governments, or with the NKVD in the case of the Soviets, about relinquishing skilled artisans or arrangements for the payment of debts, taxes and the liquidation of assets.[140] The repatriation of half a million ethnic Germans during 1939–41 was accompanied by propaganda about the peaceful rationalisation of ethnic anomalies; the mindless statistical celebration of the logistics involved; and sentimental guff regarding people whose connections with twentieth-century Germany were tenuous, as blood rejoined blood and heart spoke to heart. Himmler and Johst met one such party of homecomers as their wagons clattered over the iron railway bridge at Przemyśl over the San one cold January morning. 'Now we are here,' said the horny-handed peasants from Volhynia, as tears welled in their eyes. Johst took the opportunity to list the virtues of his friend, the organiser of this latterday tribal migration or 'Völkerwanderung': 'One must have the faith of a Heinrich Himmler, one must be close to the heart of the Führer and have forgotten the word "impossible" a long time ago not to become fainthearted in the face of this task.'[141] In Radymno, the Reichsführer received a delegation of four Soviet commissars, come to thank him for the 'comradeship' evinced while trading humans on their common frontier, as the 'two peoples (marched arm in arm, so to speak) on the road to socialism'.

Reality for the repatriates rarely measured up to the folksy scenes described by Hanns Johst. They were often shunted back and forth between about fifteen hundred holding camps, and subjected to a bewildering range of checks by the myriad Nazi agencies involved in their resettlement. Complex, subjective racial assessments, with identification of eye and hair colour and craniological measurement, meant that three hundred thousand repatriates were deemed to be unsuitable for resettlement, with the individuals concerned left languishing in what amounted to refugee camps.[142] Those who were settled in the Polish countryside sometimes found it difficult to make the transition from the extensive farming they had practised in Russia, tipping animal manure into streams on the ground that they had no use for it, or scything down asparagus because they had never seen it and did not appreciate its prime commercial value.[143] Even when these half a million repatriates were added to the six hundred thousand ethnic Germans residing in pre-war Poland, it was obvious that 'former' Poland was not going to be germanised by resettlements alone, even assuming that wartime logistics would permit further massive transfers of population when roads and railways were needed to shift armies.

Hence the Nazis resorted to a different tack, recategorising about two million Poles as ethnically German. Like the exploitation of ethnic or regional divisions, the creation of privileged ethnic groups was another way of turning people against each other, with each group being issued with different-coloured identity cards. It was also a way of raising cannon-fodder, since some two hundred thousand of these newly discovered Germans were liable for military conscription. It is crucial to bear in mind when considering quite technical issues that, like the 1935 Nuremberg Laws, the various categories involved represented the difference between having some rights and having no rights at all in a society based on racial segregation.

The idea of an Ethnic German Register began in the Warthegau as an attempt to ring-fence the privileged ethnic German minority. Obsessed with 'fishing out the racially valuable people from this [Polish] mishmash', Himmler devised extended categories, permitting the reclassification of Poles as Germans. The first two groups enjoyed Reich citizenship, although only the higher category could join the Nazi Party. The third group were so-called 'state members', consisting of ethnic Germans who had gone 'native', or ethnic Poles who had been 'germanised' through marriage. This category also included people of intermediary nationality, such as the Kashubians, Masurians, Silesians and 'Water Poles'. Although these people enjoyed the same employment rights and rations as the higher categories, they were disbarred from public employment, and needed permission to marry. The fourth category encompassed 'renegades', that is Poles who had not woken up to the fact that their physical appearance or way of life made them racially German. Since this category included many people who were demonstrative in their existing Polish identity, police powers of deportation could be used to encourage them to be German. Their 'state membership' was also dependent upon a ten-year probationary period. Like the higher categories, persons in Group Four were exempt from the 15 per cent special tax imposed on Poles, and received German wages, but were disbarred from official positions.[144] All of these categories would merge over a long period of time, especially since all those in Groups Three and Four were to be 'intensively re-educated' in the Old Reich. Some two million Poles were entered as ethnic Germans on these lists (the degree of coercion or consent has yet to be determined by Polish historians).[145]

The thoroughness with which the lists were created varied between the different incorporated territories, since Himmler's insistence on stringent racial tests did not suit all of Hitler's eastern satraps – notably Gauleiter Albert Forster – who took a competitive approach to germanising 'their' fiefdoms or who regarded the whole process as a destabilising nuisance. Those not included in this charmed circle – six million Poles in the case of the incorporated territories – were merely 'protected members of the German Reich', with restricted rights and subject to discriminatory practices. Perhaps this is best described by the observation that the position of the Poles was beginning to approximate to that of the Jews. Following a decree dated 17 September 1940, the property of Poles and Jews in the incorporated territories was liable to sequestration, often simply because 'the property is required for the public welfare ... or the strengthening of ethnic Germandom'. From 4 December 1941, Poles and Jews were subject to the same draconian legal code. Juveniles and adults could be executed for such offences as making derogatory remarks about Germans or tearing down official notices, while both groups were denied elementary legal rights in German courts.[146]

These formal arrangements underpinned both the incipient racial hierarchy and the discrimination and segregation which the Poles endured under Nazi occupation. The hierarchy took the form of Reich Germans, ethnic Germans, privileged minorities such as the Ukrainians, followed by Poles, Gypsies and Jews. Poles were not allowed to use their own language in dealings with an officialdom which spoke German. Poles who could not manage this were advised to bring along an interpreter.[147] They received significantly lower wages and had to pay supplementary taxes ranging from 20 to 30 per cent of their gross income, plus membership dues for the German Labour Front, which they were not entitled to belong to. From 1942/3 Poles were not entitled to holidays.[148] They were debarred from cinemas, concerts, exhibitions, libraries, museums and theatres. Subject to curfew restrictions, Poles also needed special permission to travel by bus, tram or train. They were prohibited from owning bicycles, cameras, radios, boots, leather briefcases, musical instruments, gramophones and telephones. An intensely Catholic people, the Poles saw their wayside shrines torn down and the number of churches severely depleted, with the remaining priests entirely dependent upon the charity of their congregations.[149] In Posen, seat of Greiser's grim anti-clerical regime, thirty churches had been reduced to four by October 1941, with thirteen closed, ten used for storage and the rest converted into music or riding schools, a book depository and a scene-painting workshop. Four priests ministered to two hundred thousand Catholics.[150] Poles had to display due modesty in their encounters with the 'master race': stepping off the pavement and removing their caps, saluting both men and symbols. Thus, on 15 September 1941, the Landrat of Turek, Fritz Klemm, let it be known that:

> I decree that Poles of both sexes must salute all military vehicles and vehicles bearing pennants. This decree is necessary for two reasons:
>
> 1. Because the Poles have become cheeky and presumptuous,
> 2. Because the reputation and standing of the German Reich, whose representatives we are, demands that through his salute the Pole freshly acknowledges day in day out the German form of rule in this land.[151]

In so far as Poles were allowed into shops – many now emblazoned with the words 'German business' – they had to suffer in silence as Germans walked to the front to be served. Like the Jews, Poles forfeited the right to elementary courtesy, with any boorish German jobsworth referring to them in the familiar 'Du', a matter which rankled in a society with a developed sense of courtesy and social propriety. Guidelines issued by Hitler's satraps reminded the Germans not to fraternise with Poles, with protective custody awaiting any who infringed these regulations.[152] The complete inversion of reality – the idea that Poland was really Germany with Poles as unwanted 'foreigners' – was cosmetically promoted by the eradication of Polish place and street names, with Łódź becoming Litzmannstadt or Cracow's Rynek Glownie now Adolf-Hitler Platz.

Not all Reich Germans elected to play the role of 'little lord Gods' that the regime expected of those serving in the East. In other words, decency was at least an option even within this grim context, a barely audible counterpoint to the major theme of massive brutality. Alexander Hohenstein was a middle-aged local government official, punitively transferred from a small town in Lower Lusatia following years of confrontation with the local NSDAP to be district mayor of Poniatowec in the Warthegau.[153] Hohenstein's diaries for the years 1941–2 reveal a German nationalist, whose membership of the Nazi Party seems to have been nominal, struggling to maintain human decency against those who sought to subvert it. In a sense, it is the atypicality of Hohenstein's diaries which makes them so revealing, as behaviour we take for granted became utterly exceptional in this nightmare context. From the start, Hohenstein made it clear that he did not want Poles or Jews, of whom three thousand resided in the Poniatowec ghetto, to vacate the pavement as he went about his business, a practice he regarded as a 'risible exaggeration of the oft propagated thesis of German racial superiority':

> No, gentlemen, I am not going along with that. You may do it if you wish, but you can't expect me to violate so grossly my conception of human dignity. That goes against my good upbringing. If someone shows me respect, then I owe him that too. It is self-evident that I acknowledge people when they greet me. There is no authority which is going to forbid me observing the most elementary manners.

He extended the same consideration towards the Jews, for 'in the first instance I am a human being and I will defend my ethical principles against whoever it may be'.[154]

A low-key antisemite rather than an 'eliminationist', Hohenstein nonetheless went out of his way to ease the arduous journey of a thousand Jews who were transferred from Herrensitz to 'his' ghetto, and repeatedly arranging deliveries of extra potatoes and firewood.[155] He paid Jews who brought bathwater to his home, and used public funds to care for the Jewish cemetery, actions which Nazi officials disapproved of:[156] he shocked the new Jewish ghetto doctor by asking him to sit down, calling him 'Herr Doktor Korte', rather than the obligatory, demeaning 'handler of the sick'.[157] He continued to discuss German and Polish literature, and exchange gifts, with the dentist wife of the Jewish elder Goldeborn, for whom Hohenstein was the last link with the civilised world: 'Yes indeed, she is a pure racial Jewess. But she has a heart of gold – What do differences of race, blood, skin colour matter in relation to the soul! The worth of a human being is determined by the heart alone.'[158] These tensions between unreflective racism and instinctual human decency probably jostled in the minds of many Germans at the time. The fate of both Poles and Jews troubled Hohenstein's conscience. Saturday 19 April 1941 was a cold, cloudy day with heavy rain turning the streets into running streams. Another fifty Jewish families were *en route* from Herrensitz to the ghetto in Poniatowec. Hohenstein reflected:

> It burdens me like a debt. It is not personal, but rather part of the greater debt which we Germans here in the East are burdened with, particularly towards the Jews. Nothing good will come of it! In my spirit I am with that sad column. I can envisage what it looks like. The images from 18 February will remain in my soul for the rest of my life.[159]

Direct confrontation with organised criminality came in March 1942. The SS informed Hohenstein that they were going to hang five Jewish 'criminals', all from Poniatowec, in the market place, and that he had to choose a sixth victim from the ghetto. Hohenstein experienced a choking sensation, as the SS men droned on about the technical details of the gallows in their matter-of-fact way. When he objected that he could not think of any capital offenders among the Jews of Poniatowec, the SS men replied:

> What are you always talking about criminals for? What sort of views have you acquired living in this dump? ... All Jews are criminals, without exception, the scum of humanity. They all deserve to vanish from the face of the earth.[160]

The following week, five Jews were hanged (with their own relatives putting the rope around their necks) in a farrago of a public execution. That there were not six resulted in a public confrontation between the Kreisleiter (the district leader) and Hohenstein, who remained adamant that he could find no suitable victim.[161]

Hohenstein went on leave in the Reich in April 1942. Returning to Poniatowec in May, he discovered that the Jewish population had been confined in the church for ten days and then deported to Chelmno. On 12 May he learned what had happened from a young SS officer who had returned to collect the Jews' clothing: 'All the Jews have gone the same way, and will continue to go the same way. First we have liberated the countryside and the small towns from these parasites, and now we are letting the major ghettos run down. The day on which Europe can be considered to be free of Jews can be calculated according to the capacity of the gassing installations.' The grim details of how these functioned were described by this young, lean SS officer, 'as if he were describing the workings of a sugar factory'.[162] Even within the lawless world the Nazis created in Poland there were men like Hohenstein, determined to cling on to what they regarded as civilised conduct, but impotent and isolated in the face of ideological fanatics and psychopaths.

The latter were also a growing menace to Hans Frank himself. Himmler's wide-ranging competences in occupied Poland made clashes between Wilhelm Krüger, his police chief on the spot, and Frank almost a weekly occurrence. The notorious corruption and inefficiency of Frank's regime enabled Himmler to form an anti-Frank coalition with Bormann and Lammers. On 5 March 1942, Frank was summoned to Lammers' train to meet his accusers. Himmler acted as prosecutor, censoriously enumerating the ten fur coats Frau Frank had acquired at bargain-basement prices; the gold bracelets, pens and rings the Franks had purloined from Jews; and the convoys of food – two hundred thousand eggs; 150 pounds of beef, twenty geese, 25 pounds of salami and dried fruit – and the sheets, angels and icons which Frank had shipped to his estate at Schobernhof. For high and low, the Nazis practised the injunction 'enrichez-vous'. Corruption charges were compounded by Frank's belated public subscription to the rule of law in a series of lectures at German universities. His local difficulties with the SS in Poland led him to say: 'I shall continue to assert, with all the force at my command, that it would be bad if the Police State were to be presented as the ideal of National Socialism. Nowadays many people say that humanity is an out-of-date notion, something incompatible with the severity of the period. That is not my opinion.'[163]

Hitler stripped Frank of all his Party offices. Frank's difficulties with the SS intersected with a wider reappraisal of human and material resources which hitherto had been profligately squandered. In February 1943, Goebbels signalled that it was time to draw a line under talk about colonies and resettlements, and indeed demeaning descriptions of Slavs as 'beasts, barbarians etc.'. This enabled Hans Frank to contemplate limited cultural and educational concessions to the Poles, designed to foster collaboration. Word of this untoward change reached Hitler, who instructed Lammers to write a crushing rebuke, ordering Frank to rescind any measures already taken.[164] Lammers probably savoured the task since he was plotting with Bormann and Himmler to oust Frank, and several of his appointees, replacing him with the hardliner Greiser.[165]

Frank retaliated with two memoranda to Hitler, the first of which questioned whether it was advisable for Himmler to pursue grandiose resettlement plans in the middle of 'a struggle for existence'. Here Frank had a ready example to hand. Noting the failure of Globocnik to consult him about the Zamość resettlements, he detailed the chaos this had caused. Globocnik's men had driven peasants from their homes at ten minutes' notice, touching off waves of panic and mass defection to the partisans. The Order Police were shooting women and children, ranging from two to over eighty years of age, in reprisal for attacks on German villages. No arrangements had been made to feed or help ten thousand ethnic German settlers get started in their new settlements. Moving from the local to the general, Frank wondered whether Himmler's representatives considered themselves 'emancipated' from the existing administration, since they seemed to confiscate anything – farms, monasteries, sanatoria, the property of Jews – that took their fancy.[166] A tiny Polish fascist organisation called Miecz i Plug (Sword and Plough) enabled Frank to strengthen his defence. These people had written to Hitler offering to participate in the war against Bolshevism, an offer Hitler relayed to Frank for his opinion. Citing Goebbels' 'really revolutionary statement' by way of reinforcement, Frank wrote to Hitler rejecting the proposal while managing the novel feat of indicting his own regime in Poland by blaming everyone else for it. This set the scene for a major shift in policy. The discovery in April 1943 of the mass graves at Katyn, where the Soviets had slain fifteen thousand Poles in the interests of building socialism in other people's countries, provided the immediate pretext. Arguing from 'rational calculation' rather than 'emotional sympathy' with the Poles, Frank wrote:

> The struggle against Bolshevism will appear all the more justified and necessary to every alien nation the more strongly and the more strikingly the German leadership and the prospects for the individuals living under it differ from the Bolshevik rule of force and from Bolshevik economic forms and ways of life. Thus the exploitation of the Katyn atrocities will depend on the precondition that such massacres do not occur under German rule. The alien people must

gradually come to feel that the Germans are introducing a brighter and
better principle for Europe in place of the Bolshevik world.[167]

Frank concluded, with an eye to Hitler's prejudices, that he was
merely trying to unravel the present confusion between short-term
needs, which he regarded as the immediate priority, and long-term
goals, over which, he implied, there was no disagreement. Just to
ensure that he was not regarded as a bourgeois softy, he added: 'Please
be reassured, however, that I do not wish to carry out the measures I
have proposed with a fanfare or in a way which could be interpreted
by Polandom in terms of the weakness of the German leadership.'
Stripped of its European flimflammery, Frank was saying that, at this
moment of crisis, the efficient economic exploitation of Poland should
have priority over the longer-term goal of germanisation, whose
accompaniment was indiscriminate terror. It took no great intelligence
to read Himmler's name between the lines of Frank's memos and of
Goebbels' earlier instructions to his propagandists. Frank's wish to
change course faced the major obstacle that he was a discredited figure,
and that Himmler was not going to be diverted from his mission.
Himmler simply sacrificed Globocnik, who was recalled and then
dispatched to Trieste to murder putative partisans, while Krüger was
replaced in November 1943 by the more diplomatic Wilhelm Koppe,
while still palming Frank off by paying lip-service to future co-
operation.

There is a record of their agreement, each of whose points confirmed that Himmler was the winner. Promising not to disrupt the
peace of the land or the local economy, Himmler poked fun at Frank
by remarking that 'we' should not be 'over-anxious' about the consequences of resettlement. Elaborating a detailed programme for germanising Lublin, Himmler concluded: 'As discussed by us, the precondition
for all of these measures is complete co-operation between the administration on the one hand and the SS and Police on the other, and an
absolutely unbureaucratic approach in the realisation of all our common intentions.'[168] Offering his resignation some fourteen times before
the matter was resolved for him, Frank continued to advocate the
scarcely credible line based on present pragmatism followed by terror
later. Speaking to an audience of Party political leaders on 14 January
1944, he opined that after the war 'we can make mincemeat out of the
Poles and the Ukrainians and all the other people hanging around
here', but that for the time being 'Politics is more than force. Force is

a ridiculously simple matter like the ABC. Statesmanship begins where force ends. . . . If I give the Poles something to eat, if I leave them their churches and give them schools, I do it not as a friend of the Poles but as the politician responsible for this area, and I strongly resent anyone poking their snout in. People who do not bear the responsibility can easily shoot their mouths off.'[169] In July 1944 Frank was still writing to Kaltenbrunner recommending such vacuities as reopening Polish high schools, universities and theological colleges in the hope that this would 'facilitate and accelerate German victory'.[170] By this time, Frank was bobbing ineffectually beside spiralling terrorism and counter-terrorism, with the Red Army discernible on the horizon.

In contrast to the lawless conditions in eastern Europe, bourgeois restraints were observed in western Europe and Scandinavia, where cultural and ethnic affinity and similar levels of socio-economic development prevailed. In Denmark, General Falkenhorst warned his troops to say nothing that would offend the Danes' national honour, with more to be gained by a friendly, humorous tone than by a Prussian gruffness liable to remind the anglophile Danes of the cession of Schleswig-Holstein in 1864.[171] A Luftwaffe general put the matter succinctly when he remarked to a colleague: 'The Dane is not a Pole, but rather a Teuton.'[172] Although Denmark was occupied, the existing four-party coalition government and Folketing parliament continued to function, with only the marginal Communists and Danish Nazis excluded. This government dealt with a German plenipotentiary – successively the diplomat Cecil Renthe-Fink and from November 1942 Werner Best – representing the Foreign Ministry, although Best had other masters. Denmark was thus the one occupied country subordinate to the German Foreign Ministry, and a parliamentary democracy under a totalitarian dictatorship. It was a democracy, however, with significant constraints upon its foreign policy and military forces, the latter reduced by 50 per cent, and one in which the occupying power could dictate the resignations of government ministers. The Conservative Party leader and Minister of Trade, John Christmas Müller, was forced out because of his strident anglophilia; the Minister of Justice, Harald Petersen, had to resign for not acting with sufficient resolution after a football match between Danes and Admiral-Wien turned into an ugly brawl between Danish fans and German soldiers.[173]

These unique occupation arrangements made a large military presence unnecessary, while minimising disruption to marine engineering yards and the flow of vital dairy products and cement from Denmark to Germany. While in 1939 some 23 per cent of Danish agricultural exports went to Germany, by 1941 this had risen to 75 per cent, with Denmark covering between 10 and 15 per cent of Germany's food-stuffs. About thirty thousand Danes also worked each year in northern Germany. Apart from acting as a pseudo-democratic showcase, this subtle form of occupation reflected a cool appreciation of the limited potentialities of Frits Claussen's Danish Nazi Party (DNSAP) in this anglophile, democratic-minded and tolerant nation. Although the con-duct of the Danish government was not immune from criticism, much of it directed at the Social Democrats and the trades unions, its object was to secure the continuity of democracy in Denmark rather than the radical restructuring of Danish society along the lines of Vichy.[174] The German defeat of France in 1940 led to the abandonment of a neutralist attentism in favour of Foreign Minister Erik Scavenius' attempts to link Denmark to a German currency bloc, and Denmark's adherence to the Anti-Comintern Pact in November 1941, a step which increased domestic unrest and pressure in Germany to abandon the existing course of showing-off Denmark as a 'parade horse' among occupied nations.

The event which precipitated a change in German policy in Den-mark may seem trivial, but was emblematic for the failure to win over the Danish elites and masses to a positive view of Germany. In September 1942, King Christian X responded with a peremptory telegram to Hitler's best wishes for his seventy-second birthday. Not used to being snubbed, Hitler recalled the commander in chief Ludtke, replacing him with General Hannecken, a deskbound warrior straining to demonstrate his hidden martial qualities towards subject popula-tions. Renthe-Fink was simultaneously replaced by SS-Gruppenführer Werner Best, in the erroneous belief that this SS ideologue would also pursue hardline policies. The Social Democrat Prime Minister, Buhl, stepped down in favour of Erik Scavenius, who formed a coalition government notionally reflecting a more pro-German orientation but which still rested on the democratic political parties. Claussen's Nazis were lost in the wash. These modified arrangements spared Denmark the worst tribulations of war, although they courted the risk that the Allies would regard Denmark as an appendage of Germany. They enabled the Germans to exploit economically four million Danes with just two hundred German personnel, whereas five thousand Germans were needed to hold down two million Norwegians. The Germans were so sure of the viability of these arrangements that in March 1943 they permitted parliamentary elections, the result being a vote of 92 per cent for the existing coalition parties, and a dismal 2 per cent for Claussen's Danish Nazis, with most of their vote from the ethnic German minority. A dejected Claussen joined the Waffen-SS as a field doctor. Himmler had him confined to an asylum in Würzburg, after Claussen had drunkenly assaulted nursing staff in a Minsk field hospital.

However, stability in Denmark proved illusory. Worried that Denmark might set a bad example to other occupied nations, the British dispatched Special Operations Executive teams to Denmark to co-ordinate sabotage. They did the same in the case of Czechoslovakia, with the assassination of Heydrich causing appalling reprisals. Such incidents were interpreted by the German army as harbingers of a British landing. Acts of sabotage occurred at the rate of twenty per week, and were gradually compounded by spontaneous strikes in Odense and North Jutland. Hannecken relayed news of these disturbances to Hitler, who in any case had put himself in the picture through a chance briefing from a German military photographer. Best was summoned to the Wolf's Lair, Hitler's East Prussian HQ at Rastenburg, and informed that existing governmental arrangements were finished. The Germans delivered an ultimatum to the Danish government requiring it to suppress civil disturbances, which the Danes rejected on 29 August 1943. A state of military emergency ensued. Under Operation Safari, Hannecken disarmed and interned the Danish armed forces – with the Danish navy putting up a fierce fight. A nighttime curfew was introduced, and strikes or meetings of more than five persons were banned.

Since Hannecken had not thought about what sort of regime would ensue, Best partially restored his own authority, although it is noteworthy that the new Higher SS- and Police Leader Günther Pancke was not subject to his control. A government of senior civil servants replaced elected politicians. Saboteurs were dealt with in special police courts. But it was too late to stabilise the situation. Continued sabotage, including the assassination of informers, prompted Himmler and Hitler to explore the option of extra-judicial counter-terror, a policy Hitler personally instructed Best to pursue in Denmark.[175] Unlike court martials, this left no martyrs. The SS counter-terrorism expert Otto Schwerdt and various assassins loaned by Otto Skorzeny joined Alfred Naujocks, the hero of the 1939 attack on the undefended Gleiwitz transmitter, in Copenhagen. Operating as 'Group Peter' these men then proceeded to plant bombs in cinemas and hotels, shooting opposition journalists, lawyers and professors after each resistance attack. Although Best was theoretically supposed to vet their targets, he soon noted that the SS assassins had managed to turn 'Copenhagen into a European Chicago'.

Against a background of strikes, Best was again summoned to Hitler where he valiantly protested against the counter-terror campaign. Hitler brushed him off and, when Best tried to speak, dismissed him, saying: 'I won't listen to this!'[176] By the time he returned to Denmark, Best realised that not only shadowy SS units, but also the chiefs of the SS apparatus in Denmark, were operating independently of him. The Security Police commander Bovensiepen had eleven saboteurs executed at Roskilde without any reference to Best. Pancke incited strikes, and then in September 1944 disarmed the Danish police force, dispatching over two thousand of them to Buchenwald. Best was out of town when this happened, returning to find his own residence cordoned off by the Security Police and the telephone disconnected. These men were literally out of control. But by this time the alternative Best himself represented consisted of nothing more than rough justice in a police court. The 'model occupation' had simplified itself into whether people were murdered by SS men in or out of uniform. Even in this most exceptional occupied country, Nazi rule had followed its own logic to its brutal conclusion.

Between 1920 and 1934 Norway had suffered a protracted depression, with high rates of unemployment and bouts of labour militancy. Although the Labour Party dropped its rhetorical revolutionism, some middle-class circles continued to perceive Labour as a threat, calling for a national government based on the spirit of Norway's historic 1905 break with Sweden. A few people stepped outside the circle of democratic politics altogether. Having tried out various left-wing identities, the reserve army officer Vidkun Quisling augmented his Nordic racialism with a hatred of Russian Bolshevism formed by his sojourns in that country, and emerged in the 1930s as an extreme right-wing Minister of Defence in an Agrarian Party government. A taciturn isolate given to gestures which revealed a fundamental lack of sound judgement, Quisling was forced to resign in 1933, founding his own party: the Nasjonal Samling (NS) or National Union. This attracted students and voteless schoolboys, businessmen, farmers, lawyers and soldiers. The Nazi influence was reflected in the abbreviation of 'Partifører' to the more evocative 'Fører'. Quisling began to envisage a role for himself and his country in reconciling Britain – against which he had no special animus – with Nazi Germany. In the event, in December 1939 he met Admiral Raeder in Berlin, who was interested in Norway's extensive coastline, suggesting a simultaneous coup and German invasion. In subsequent meetings with Hitler, Quisling sounded the right note, in the sense of conjuring up imaginary connections between the Norwegian Conservative Party leader, Carl Hambro, and the British Secretary for War, Leslie Hore-Belisha, based on the otherwise irrelevant fact that both men were Jews, to prompt Hitler into doing something in Norway.

In April, the military reservist Quisling met German intelligence officers in Copenhagen to betray details of his country's airfields, coastal defences and state of military preparedness.[177] The man whose name has become universally synonymous with treason literally committed it, although we should bear in mind that collaboration was not always coextensive with the crime of treason. In the event, Operation Weserübung on 9 April 1940 only briefly enabled Quisling to barge his way to power, for neither King Haakon VII, who was still at large, nor Hitler would recognise his hastily formed government, which manifestly lacked all legitimacy, a fact more troublesome to the former than to the latter. The Norwegian Establishment, orchestrated by the Chief Justice of the Supreme Court, vehemently rejected Quisling's coup regime, and won German backing for the formation of an Administrative Council in the German-occupied areas. Continued British and Norwegian military activity led Hitler to lance the festering political situation in Norway by appointing the Essen Gauleiter Josef Terboven as Reich Commissioner. Terboven exercised power through a Commissarial Council, banning all political parties except the Nasjonal Samling. Although Terboven detested Quisling, and actively tried to replace him as party leader, he reluctantly recognised that the Nasjonal Samling was the only available vehicle to 'nazify' Norwegian society.

Quisling tried to outflank Terboven by appealing to patrons in Berlin, including Raeder, Rosenberg and even Hitler, while expanding the Party outwards in an attempt to make it appear a viable future government. Hence the NS spawned a number of sectoral organisations for labour, sport, youth, welfare and women, while trying to infiltrate and subvert existing farmers' associations, trades unions and the university. Formal ascendancy frequently proved no substitute for moral authority. There were also sinister attempts by the NS to control appointments and promotions within the civil service, judiciary and police force. This attempted nazification of Norwegian society was not

especially successful, since less than 2 per cent of Norwegians joined
the Party, or about sixty thousand people during the entire occupation.[178] Outbreaks of resistance – such as the Oslo 'milk strike' in
September 1941 – led to the proclamation of a state of emergency, and
the execution of two union leaders and the imprisonment of several
others. Since Terboven had been sent to Norway to convert the
Norwegians into the Führer's friends, this major setback inclined Hitler
to allow Quisling into government.

On 1 February the ministers of the Commissarial Council duly
resigned, while in the Akerhus Castle the fifty-four-year-old Quisling
was proclaimed head of a Norwegian national government. A grim
Terboven tried to minimise the significance of the occasion, while
Quisling talked the moment up, gabbling on about 'a new, a free
and great nationally conscious Norway', albeit initially speaking in
German. In a country which valued personal austerity, Quisling stood
out in terms of conspicuous consumption. He lived in a villa called
Gimle in an exclusive Oslo suburb, with mock Viking furniture, eight
thousand bottles of wine, and various artefacts looted from the royal
family or the Freemasons, but with their monograms filed off. State
monies were diverted to pay for this establishment, and for a country
'cabin', optimistically called the Eagle's Nest. In power, Quisling
pressed on with his attempts to nazify Norwegian society, managing
to alienate successive swathes of opinion rather than isolating each in
turn. For example, he picked on the teachers, and attempted to
dragoon them into the Norway Teachers' Corporation. Not only did
the teachers refuse to render a declaration of loyalty to this NS
organisation, but militancy spread to parents' organisations, and then
to the Lutheran Church, which objected to the monopolistic pretensions of the NS Youth Organisation and to NS attempts to hold
fascistic memorial services in the National Cathedral at Trondheim.
Quisling tried to tough this conflict out, which resulted in the bishops
breaking off relations with the state and the expulsion of all Norway's
bishops from their offices. Virtually all of Norway's pastors then
resigned their civil functions, losing their salaries but gaining the
enhanced support of their parishioners. The appointment of surrogate
NS lay pastors merely resulted in parallel churches: one full, the other
empty. Not all Christians behaved badly in this period.

Terboven meanwhile struck at the teachers. Thirteen hundred of
them were arrested in March 1942, and sent to concentration camps,
where they were subjected to various humiliations designed to make

them join the Teachers' Corporation. Five hundred were dispatched to Arctic Norway on a small steamer called the *Skjerstad*. Both the Education Minister and Quisling himself descended on schools to conduct interrogations designed to establish the loyalty of individual teachers. The resistance Quisling provoked led to the German decision to rein him in. As if to signify this, Quisling was informed that all communications with Hitler would henceforth have to pass via Terboven, against whom he had frequently conspired with his patrons in Berlin. The only exit route from this unenviable position seemed to lie in even closer collaboration with Germany. Quisling threw himself into recruiting men for a Norwegian Legion, promising the Germans thirty thousand men, but delivering one-thirtieth of this figure. Another six thousand Norwegians served in a variety of SS formations such as the Regiment Nordland, the Germanic SS 'Norway' and police and ski battalions. Quisling was also prominent in the National Work Effort, a German scheme designed to mobilise and redirect labour to war-related enterprises. The more expansive Quisling's rhetoric about Norway's place in a nazified Europe, the less his control of Norwegian society had any reality to it. An emboldened resistance movement blew up the office containing the registration cards for Work Effort, while in the following year it sabotaged attempts to make the issuance of ration cards dependent upon registration for labour conscription, by hijacking in broad daylight a lorry containing seventy-five thousand ration cards.

Germany retained direct control of the industrialised and most populous regions of northern France, leaving Vichy with the fruit and wine of the south. In a calculated gesture designed to mollify, or paralyse, his erstwhile opponent through moderation, Hitler sanctioned a small army and a deactivated fleet, and refrained from interfering in France's colonial arrangements. Germany retained about a million French prisoners of war as labour and leverage on Vichy, imposing a crippling regime of occupation costs, calculated according to an outrageous exchange rate. Although, the Jews apart, the Germans did not pursue racial politics with the dedication they demonstrated in Poland, they did seriously investigate various manifestations of regionalism in France, as they initially toyed with the idea of fracturing France into various pieces.

The most systematic exponent of these ideas was Werner Best, who before his sojourn in Denmark was transferred to Paris from the Reich Main Security Office to churn out eccentric ethnographic memoranda, to the bemusement of the military elite in the Hôtel Majestic.[179] Best argued that nation states were superstructural overlays on the ethnographic fundaments of Europe. In contrast to Carl Schmitt, whose 'Monroe Doctrine' was not only self-evidently stuck in the rut of nineteenth-century thought, but seemed to inhibit external intervention in, say, Russia's 'greater space', Best and his circle were genuinely bent upon a 'New Order' – based on releasing individual peoples from the 'artificial' confines of the nation state, to cement overall German dominance. For while everywhere else would dissolve into regional fragments, there was no corresponding talk of recognising the ethnological parts of Germany, along the lines of freedom for the Friesians or Swabians. In a wide-ranging maximalist programme drawn up in November 1941, Best proposed the incorporation of the Netherlands, Flanders and northern France into the Reich, and a protectorate over Brittany; the fusion of Northern Ireland with the Republic; the creation of a federal Britain, with autonomy for Scotland, Wales and Cornwall; and independence for the Basques, Catalans and Galicians. After all, how could one deny these advanced regional fragments what had been granted to the Croats or Slovaks?[180]

As a result of short-term economic and political priorities, these vistas came to nothing. This was not for want of collaborators among the regional fragments themselves, keen to circumvent their own immediate metropolis by toadying to remoter centres of power. In the case of France, regionalism represented a vital force, based upon cultural and linguistic identities and royalist or religious hostility towards the Revolution and the aggressively secular Third Republic. While Burgundian or Occitanian 'identities' were largely the product of febrile academics and poets, in Alsace-Lorraine and Brittany they were rooted in widespread feelings of cultural or linguistic difference, compounded in the latter case by resentment at Brittany's backwardness. Heavy-handed French policies after 1918 had led to the formation of an Alsatian autonomist movement, which in turn spawned the more extreme Elsass-Löthringer Partei, little more than an Alsatian version of the Nazi Party.[181] Alsatian refugees had a hard time in the places they were evacuated to during the 'phoney war', while French soldiers vandalised their homes in their absence.[182]

A similar trajectory from moderate regionalism to extreme autonomism was followed by some Bretons during the 1930s, with the terrorists of 'Gwenn ha du' (Black and White) making contact with German intelligence, which supplied them with arms courtesy of a tuna boat called the *Abadenn Casement*, operated by their colleagues in the Irish Republican Army (IRA).[183] All parties involved communicated through a crazed vernacular based on race, with the 'Celts' preening themselves as the west European counterparts of their 'Nordic' Nazi allies: 'La race bretonne est une race supérieure.' The expectations of the 'Celts' from Nazi Germany meant a surprising attitude towards other small countries, as is evident from a 1938 Parti National Breton poster which read: 'Pas une goutte de sang breton pour les Tchèques!' ('Not a drop of Breton blood for the Czechs!')[184] These people were parochial in every negative sense of the word, the fascistic, resentful face of petty nationalism everywhere, and blind to the fact that their Nazi sponsors could not have cared less about them.

However much the Germans flirted with Rennes, they were loath to offend their regular girl at Vichy. The Celtic potentialities (involving Cornwall, Wales, Scotland and Ireland) were a mixed blessing, since the pull of 'race' was as likely to draw the Bretons into the British camp as towards Germany. Himmler was interested in Germans rather than Celts, and the Foreign Ministry thought in traditional categories of inter-state relations. The immediate goal of mollifying Vichy, to maximise the exploitation of France's economic resources, nullified any schemes to fracture the French state. Vichy fobbed Brittany off with a few cultural gestures. The newspaper *L'Heure Breton* proclaimed its solidarity with the Reich in its fight against 'Anglo-Saxon capitalism ... and Jewish Marxism', but the Bretons' hour never struck.[185]

French territorial integrity was more seriously affected by the annexation of Alsace-Lorraine to the neighbouring Saar-Palatinate and Baden. Twenty-two thousand indigenous Jews were deported to France, together with six and a half thousand German Jews, whom Gauleiter Bürckel and Wagner ejected from the core parts of their extended fiefdoms. Bürckel also expelled one hundred thousand French-speaking peasants from Lorraine, while Wagner either deported, or prevented the return from France of, one hundred and five thousand Alsatians, the majority from the francophile bourgeoisie, although the expulsions were portrayed, in the totalitarian manner of Fidel Castro, as a clearout of alcoholics, criminals, pimps and homosexuals. The SS railed against the application of superficial linguistic or political criteria in these deportations, on the ground that such a transfusion of German blood would strengthen its decadent French recipients.[186]

As in occupied Poland, where the Nazis were busily restoring a forgotten German presence, so in Alsace-Lorraine they began stripping off what they called the 'welschen Tünsche' or 'Frenchified veneer'. Schemes were soon afoot to demolish the allegedly shoddy structures put up by the French, leaving German timber-frame buildings in lonely splendour. Trams became *Strassenbahnen*, the *trottoir* the *Bürgersteig*; and the *Coiffeur* the *Friseur*. Dead veterans ceased to be 'Morts pendant la grand guerre' and became 'Gefallen für Deutschland'. Statues of Jeanne d'Arc, Kléber and Rapp vanished from their plinths in the ubiquitous Adolf-Hitler-Plätze; disapproving eyes noted taps marked 'chaud' and 'froid', or cruets with 'sel' and 'poivre'. As they tried to turn René into Rainer, the Nazis created absurd dichotomies, in which descendants of the many Huguenots in the Reich retained their French names, while Alsatians had to germanise theirs. Patriotic kitsch – mugs, plates, certificates and posters – was removed from houses; the *tricolore* was torn into rags and floorcloths. From 1 June 1941, possession of the French flag could result in a year in a concentration camp. Unable to use Himmler's camp at Natzweiler, the francophobe Wagner opened his own camp near Schirmeck for Alsatian 'thick-heads'.[187] An extraordinary *official* campaign was launched to rid Alsatian heads of the beret, that stereotypically (Basque) manifestation of Frenchness. Onion sellers were apparently spared these attentions. French was no longer taught, not even as a foreign language. Whereas elsewhere in the Reich, French was the preferred foreign tongue, in Alsace children learned English, Italian or Spanish. That three-quarters of Alsatians were Catholics presented a special challenge to the Nazis. The bishops of Strasbourg and Metz were either expelled or not allowed to return, all church lay activities – such as scouting – were banned, and people were deterred from attending church by prohibitive church taxes and such simple expedients as the distribution of ration cards at the same time as church services.[188] Although many Alsatians were not keen on the 'Schwöwe', as they called the Germans, 'Schwöwe' they now were: 'It is entirely irrelevant whether you want it, whether you know it or whether you believe it. Any more than whether a Chinese believes or doesn't believe that he is Chinese.'[189]

If German ambitions in France concerned how to maximise exploitation of the French economy in Germany's interest, Vichy used the opportunity provided by German conquest to carry out a thoroughgoing purge of French society, and a refashioning of France in its own image. The leading historian of Vichy France, Robert Paxton, began his account with the simple assertion: 'To an extent unique among the occupied nations of Western Europe, France went beyond mere administration during the occupation to carry out a domestic revolution in institutions and values.'[190] Only the latter need concern us here, although the revolution in values obviously assumed institutional contours. The sudden emotional shock of defeat, while intellectually explicable in terms of a poorly executed defensive strategic posture, and armed forces overstretched between metropolitan France, Corsica, Algeria and Indo-China, sparked off a search for its ultimate causes in a country already widely dissatisfied with the Third Republic. Clerics talked much of sin to a population which rediscovered visceral religiosity like a person suffering acute stomach pains. The causes alighted upon by the men of Vichy were intimately bound up with the composition of that regime. Since the latter was more faction-ridden and unstable (there were seven ministerial reshuffles between July 1940 and April 1942) than what preceded it, all generalisations about its composition or direction should be treated with circumspection. Hitler identified the general problem when he said: 'In the Vichy Government alone a whole heap of tendencies is apparent – antisemitic nationalism, clerical pro-semitism, royalism, the spirit of revolution and so on,' even if the second tendency he mentioned was underrepresented.[191]

Vichy represented the triumph of notable elites, technocrats and lapsarian leftists over what they perceived to be the provincial political fixers and loquacious southern lawyers who ran the Third Republic. At the summit was Philippe Pétain, the architect of the armistice with Germany. At eighty-four a rather improbable man of destiny, Pétain was popularly associated with the lenient treatment of mutineers and the patient, but deadly, defence of Verdun during the 1914–18 war. He was on the right of the political spectrum, but wise enough not to advertise this, leading many on the left to dissociate him from anti-democratic or royalist generals. His natural taciturnity helped promote an image of sphinx-like cunning, and was perceived as a relief from the chattering tongues of professional politicians.[192] Taciturnity was a virtue in a nation of elegant talkers. Although Pétain's civil marriage to a divorcee in 1920, his record as a roué and his off-the-cuff remarks such as 'Un bonne messe n'a jamais fait de mal à personne' suggest a casual attitude to religion, the Pétain cult was bolstered by clerics prepared blasphemously to parody the Lord's Prayer in his honour: 'Notre Père, qui êtes / A notre tête / Que votre nom soit glorifié / . . . Et délivrez-nous du Mal / O Maréchal'.[193] Hitler regarded him as a man who was past it, not up to the dictates of the moment: 'To make a comparison, I would say it would be like giving the principal part in an opera to some famous old singer covered with glory, and then, when faced with a deplorable result, consoling oneself by saying that twenty or thirty years ago, anyway, he had a throat of gold.'[194]

While the existing chamber voted Pétain full powers and annulled the 1875 constitution, the influence of professional politicians was displaced by a broader group of notables representing the various elites of French society. The apparent exception to this rule, the ex-socialist political fixer Pierre Laval, proved it, since he owed his prominence at Vichy to the fact that he simultaneously manipulated parliamentary politicians while being openly contemptuous of them.[195] This contrary posture evidently failed to impress Hitler, who once described Laval to Mussolini and Ciano as 'a dirty democratic cheap-jack politician who doesn't believe what he says', and elsewhere as 'nothing but a parliamentary hack'.[196] Although the Vichy leadership liked to use the term honourable to describe their arrangements with the Germans, the realities of their situation were clear from the fact that Fernand de Brinon was appointed Vichy's ambassador to the German authorities in occupied Paris.

Although militant fascists gradually populated those Vichy agencies concerned with antisemitism, security and propaganda, their presence was minimal in such fields as education, finance, foreign affairs and religion, where the traditional elites predominated. Clerics, military men, senior civil servants and technocratic experts from the Grandes Ecoles comprised the nucleus of the Vichy regime, reflecting the extent to which anti-democratic authoritarianism had permeated these rarefied circles already. Given a chance, they took not an inch but a mile.[197] At the centre, senior civil servants usurped the functions of elected politicians, while in the provinces and municipalities government appointees replaced democratically elected mayors and councillors. The powers of the prefecture were consolidated and extended. The Légion des Anciens Combattants became the favoured instrument for anchoring the regime in the wider population, with veterans of the Great War outnumbering those from the current conflict. This was part claque, part welfare organisation, a transmission belt rather than a political party. Senior clergy became conspicuous fixtures at patriotic gatherings, ready with a patriotic homily for every occasion.

Vichy's 'National Revolution' was an attempt to reform what its leaders perceived as a corrupt and flawed society, whose decadence had resulted in the disaster of the summer of 1940, a catastrophe that was viewed in some quarters as a Biblical plague upon those who had led the children of France astray. Here Vichy drew upon deep wells of antisemitism, anti-socialism and Catholic moralism, rather than upon the social radicalism of febrile French fascists, the latter often contemptuous of the bourgeois gerontocracy of the Hôtel du Parc, the centre of Vichy government. Moral discourse obviated talk of military failure, a happy circumstance for a government that included so many defeated generals.

The general thrust of the 'National Revolution' was that collective duties overrode individual rights, and that Work, Family and Country should usurp Liberty, Equality and Fraternity. It was perhaps unfortunate that the acronym for 'Travail, Famille, Patrie' – TFP – mirrored 'Travaux Forcés en perpetuité' or 'forced labour for life'.[198] Compared with the vengeance Vichy visited upon its real or imaginary enemies, the 'National Revolution' seems a half-hearted affair, without the messianic fervour evident in Germany, whose martial virility these people often admired, even when they harboured germanophobic prejudices. There was a conservative moralism in its narrow sense, replete with attacks on abortion, divorce, jazz, prostitution, short skirts and the 'France de l'apéro', even though alcoholic aperitifs constituted a mere 1.8 per cent of French alcohol consumption. Blaming military defeat on hard liquor was nothing new in France, since seventy years earlier both right- and left-wing abstentionists had blamed the defeat at Sedan on absinthe addicts. The Vichy anti-alcohol-cum-health lobby lauded organic beverages – such as beer, cider, cognac, rum and wine – while attempting to restrict consumption of industrially synthesised aniseed substitutes, such as Berger, Pernod, Ricard or Suze, even though it is not difficult to detect the hand of the viticulturalists ruining the competition.[199]

Vichy moralism was apparent too in the books weeded out from libraries, with such steamy exotica as *Cléopâtre voluptueuse* or *La Danseuse de Singapore* vanishing together with the drear certainties of Lenin, Blum and Kautsky. Moralism was evident in the public service sector too. People were not employed, or were dismissed, because of drink problems or the loose behaviour of their wives, as well as for their suspect politics.[200] Predictably, moral puritanism was undermined by the fact that Abel Bonnard, one of Vichy's many Ministers of Education, was an agnostic homosexual, and was called 'Gestapette', an elision of Gestapo and *tapette* or faggot, by his many detractors in what still is a notoriously homophobic culture. In so far as Vichy managed to detect the source of decadence, it alighted upon France's declining birthrate, an identification first systematically explored in the nineteenth century by the conservative sociologist Frédéric Le Play and picked up by the Catholic family movement.

The answer to the interconnected demographic crisis and urban decadence seemed to lie in the promotion of large, stable, rural families.[201] This discourse was most aggressively converted into policy by the government of Edouard Daladier with its Family Code of July 1939. This envisaged ten-year jail sentences for convicted abortionists, cash incentives for couples who had a child within the first two years of marriage, the abandonment of partible inheritance, and the adoption of marriage loans for young farmers to reverse migration from the countryside. Vichy perpetuated these policies, with endless rhetoric about the family as 'la cellule essentielle'. Divorce laws were tightened, with divorce prohibited during the first three years of marriage under a law of April 1941. In keeping with the emphasis on fatherhood in French pro-natalist tradition, prolific paternity was rewarded with automatic representation on various committees, while childless bachelors were discriminated against. Women were expelled from certain professions and given an educational diet of cooking and housekeeping. Motherhood was not only regarded as a duty to the state and hence fêted, if not rewarded, but was interpreted as essential to the psychological health of women, 'for if there is something sadder than a garden without flowers . . . it is a woman without children'.[202]

A concern with physical and psychological health also partly informed the regime's peasant-worshipping ruralism, while in sport the ex-Wimbledon champion and Davis Cup winner Jean Borotra promoted Olympic-style amateurism over money-driven professionalism.[203] Since not much could be done with the old reprobate France, considerable attention was devoted to the youthful future. Left-wing, pacifist schoolteachers were blamed for their allegedly unique contribution to the defeat, and were purged or subjected to enhanced monitoring. They were not entirely blameless, since in the 1930s they had been in the vanguard of expurgating and revising chauvinistic accounts of German history, and pushing internationalism and pacifism, a posture which led many to find excuses for Nazi Germany, just as so many *Lumpenintellektueller* the world over would exculpate Stalin.[204] Although Vichy never created a monopolistic youth organisation, youth was mobilised in the Chantiers de la Jeunesse, with all twenty-year-olds undergoing an ersatz national service, consisting of manual labour, Catholic moralism and a slanted version of the national story. There was also a narrowing definition of ethnicity, at a time when France seemed to be awash with refugees from her eastern and southern neighbours. The 'true France' would first have to rid herself of 'anti-France', the *métèques* (from the Greek for 'alien'), who, since Protestantism was no longer considered a threat, primarily consisted of Freemasons and Jews, particularly radicalised eastern European immigrants. Vichy set about discriminating against these groups without prior German prompting.

Freemasons were feared by right-wing, clerical France as an occultic force with sinister international English and Jewish connections – the name Rothschild served multiple functions here – and as a corrupt nexus for radical businessmen, doctors, lawyers, teachers and twenty-five of the thirty-five members of Léon Blum's Popular Front government. In reality, the Freemasons were a more modest lot: liberal anti-clericalism and a dose of rationalist mumbo-jumbo went hand in hand with conviviality, philanthropy, and an old pals' network. The director of the Bibliothèque nationale, Bernard Fay, was appointed 'delegate of the French government to liquidate masonic lodges', with a separate registry of France's fifty thousand Freemasons and a dedicated unit to police them. In October 1940, an exhibition on Freemasonry – the Exposition Maçonnique – was opened at the Petit Palais, attracting over a million visitors in Paris and when it toured the provinces, come to gawp at aprons and triangles and the revealed names of those who *really* ran things.[205]

Having emerged from the Great War anxious that it had too few citizens, post-war France encouraged immigration, only to decide in the austere economic climate of the 1930s that while she did not mind immigrants, she did not much care for refugees from Nazi Germany and Poland. An existing French antisemitic discourse, hitherto overwhelmingly focused upon the supposed power of wealthy indigenous Jews, which did not fail to resonate on the left, metamorphosed into attacks against impoverished proletarianised refugees from antisemitism in Germany and Poland. There was no question of blaming the source of the problem, namely the policies of these governments, for France, like the Netherlands, was frightened of Hitler's Germany, and did not wish to undermine her Polish ally. Indeed, in 1937, the socialist deputy and Minister for the Colonies Marius Moutet gave an ill-judged interview in which he suggested that France might open some of her colonies, including Guiyana, New Caledonia and Madagascar, to Jewish settlers from eastern Europe.

The idea of segregating the Jews on Madagascar was an *idée fixe* in international antisemitic circles. It was first floated by Paul de Lagarde in 1885, but in the 1930s its most vociferous proponents were the British fascists Henry Hamilton Beamish and Arnold Leese, together with their admirers in Nazi Germany. Beamish spoke on a Munich platform next to Hitler in 1923, and articles by him began to appear from 1926 in the *Völkischer Beobachter* outlining three solutions to the 'Jewish Question': extermination, assimilation or compulsory segregation. The Polish government, which sought overseas colonies to reinforce its country's great-power pretensions, and as somewhere to ship a large unassimilable Jewish minority, leaped at this suggestion. Although a Polish Jewish investigatory commission visited the island, both hostility towards Jewish immigration from the existing settler population and French concerns that the Poles might use Jewish settlers to assert claims on the colony, in the manner of Nazi exploitation of Sudeten Germans, ensured that these projects came to nothing for the moment.[206]

Against a constant background noise from an intellectually gifted extreme right, the French civil service, and its political masters, adopted an increasingly hard-hearted attitude to the desperate refugees in their midst. They represented competition for scarce jobs, and as British Prime Minister Neville Chamberlain agreed in conversation with Daladier and Bonnet, regarding his own country's position on Jewish refugees, might trigger antisemitism against the assimilated Jewish populations. The 1938 assassination of the German diplomat Rath in Paris by a refugee Polish Jew raised concerns that 'the Jews' might drag France into a war with Germany. This was as true of the pacifist left as of the radical right, with the magazine *Redressement* asking in early 1939: 'surely we are not going to war over 100,000 Polish Jews?' Jewish refugees in France were subjected to every conceivable form of discrimination, culminating in many being interned after September 1939, in what were called *camps de concentration*, recently vacated by exiled Spanish republicans who had fled Franco's Spain. People whose misfortune was to have comparative experience of such camps as Dachau noted that Gurs, Les Milles or Rivesaltes left nothing to be desired in terms of neglect and poor diet. The artist Felix Nussbaum left especially haunting pictures of daily life in them. This is another way of saying that the antisemitic measures which Vichy adopted in the autumn of 1940 were a continuation of policies already in train during the later 1930s.[207]

At a time when the Germans were concentrating on the war with Britain, and then with the invasion of Russia, the French authorities took the opportunity to solve what they regarded as 'their' Jewish problem. In August 1940, the Vichy government repealed the Law Marchandeau, which had suppressed explicit antisemitism in the French press. This meant that France's not inconsiderable number of otherwise highly gifted intellectual antisemites could publish what they liked. In early October, the Statute on the Jews defined who was a Jew and sanctioned exclusion of Jews from the upper echelons of the civil service, the armed forces, the professions, and the worlds of entertainment, arts and media. A law which had granted French citizenship to Jews in Algeria in 1870 was rescinded, at the insistence of Algerian colonists and despite objections from many Algerian Moslems, who sensed that they might be next in line for this form of discrimination. Indeed, these issues were connected, since the French colonists detected the hand of metropolitan Jewry behind attempts to grant citizenship to limited numbers of Arabs.

It is worth stressing that these were purely home-grown measures rather than responses to alleged German pressures, with their legal aspects enforced by French courts and policemen, and their informal side – such as disbarring Jewish academics, lawyers or medical doctors – undertaken by French institutions and professional bodies. Similarly, whatever tactical games were being played to reassert the administrative unity of a country the Germans had divided, French officials directed the new Commissariat-General for Jewish Affairs, and played a co-equal role with the Germans in creating a national Jewish Council, the Union Générale des Israélites de France, whose subtle wording mirrored that of the Reich Association of Jews *in* Germany. As the one-eyed, and one-legged, germanophobic war veteran Xavier Vallat indignantly explained to the impertinent young SD Jewish expert Theodor Dannecker: 'I have been an antisemite far longer than you! What's more, I am old enough to be your father!' – an outburst which had a resonance beyond this contretemps between these individuals. Yet we should be careful not to align too closely the rather distinctive registers of French and German antisemites. Vichy antisemitism was designed to force foreign Jews out of France, and indigenous Jews to assimilate to vanishing point, with no distinctive identity or socio-economic profile. That did not correspond entirely with what the Nazis

did between 1933 and 1941, that is, to force all Jews out of German
territory, most especially those who were highly assimilated and hence
most dangerous. We shall see in a later chapter what transpired when
this French policy was confronted by quite other Nazi aims.

The moral ambiguities of occupation can be sampled with the aid
of two prominent social groups, businessmen and the Roman Catholic
Church. Businessmen, that unsatisfactory generic term for a bewildering variety of humanity, were roundly condemned by the ascendant
left after the liberation, from the vantage point of never having to meet
wage costs or register a profit to shareholders on the basis of their own
talents. In reality, to anyone not dogmatically inimical to capitalism,
there is no evidence that businessmen were more or less prone to
collaboration than any other occupational grouping, certainly not
academics, intellectuals and journalists, whose antics take up a disproportionately large share of the literature on collaboration. By contrast,
only recently has any attention been devoted to the fact that, say,
railway workers almost never delayed or sabotaged trains, in contrast
to military traffic.

Businessmen had been shaken by the pro-trades unionist culture of
the Popular Front, but, since this had already been reversed by the
governments of Daladier and Reynaud, Vichy represented no added
value. Business reacted in a variety of ways to the rather different
challenge represented by German occupation. Some captains of industry such as Louis Renault or André Dubonnet attended tri-weekly
lunches in the Ritz with Lavalists and German industrialists, although
whether this tells us much more than that big businessmen were
catholic in their choice of lunch partners remains an open question.

A brief glance at the Michelin tyre dynasty illustrates the other side
of the coin. Marcel, the second son of the family patriarch André
Michelin, organised the Maquis in the Puy-de-Dôme and Cantal, dying
in the camp at Ohrdruf in January 1945; André's grandson Jean-Luc
Michelin was caught attempting to smuggle confidential BMW blue-
prints from Munich to London and was interned in Dachau; Marcel's
son Jean-Pierre died in combat as one of the first Free French troops in
Corsica; his illegitimate brother Philippe was an Allied airman, who
according to rumour participated in the RAF's attack on the Michelin
plant in March 1944; while Mme Jean Michelin was deported to
Germany for hiding resistance fugitives.[208]

The Hispano-Suiza luxury fast car manufacturer was run by the
Swiss inventor Marc Birkigt, with Spanish and Swiss majority share-

holders. During the Great War, Hispano-Suiza diversified into aero-engines, and guns which could fire through the propellers, re-employing aircraft styling in its post-war luxury car output. In the 1930s, Hispano-Suiza refashioned itself as a French company dedicated to military aero-engine production. Following France's defeat, Birkigt sent copies of his latest designs to the British and retired to Barcelona. Rather than produce engines for the Germans, the Tarbes factory turned to electric motors and aluminium cooking utensils. In contrast to Gnome & Rhône or Schneider-Creusot, the directors of Hispano-Suiza refused to collaborate with Daimler-Benz, a stance which resulted in its French chief executive being briefly imprisoned by the Germans. In 1943, the Germans lost patience with the company, dismantled the Tarbes factory, and shipped nineteen trainloads including its 2,215 machine tools to the Reich.[209]

The other collaborationist side of the coin involved varying degrees of involvement with the Germans. Proponents of economic modernisation and rationalisation occasionally came to the fore in the *comités d'organisation* formed after August 1940 to deal with exigencies of the moment. The general idea was to group together industries by sector, organising, for example, the allocation of raw materials. This led to contacts between these committees and the Germans, the latter interested in instructing the French in efficiency gains in economies of scarcity, and in the standardisation of ideas and methods. Expert talked to expert, a dialogue whose limitations were evident from Albert Speer's descriptions of his September 1943 meeting with the French Minister of Production Jean Bichelonne, a professor at the Sorbonne:

> We were both young, we believed the future was on our side, and both of us therefore promised ourselves that someday we would avoid the mistakes of the First World War generation that was presently governing. . . . Such were the utopian thoughts in which Bichelonne and I lost ourselves for a while at that time – a token of the world of illusions and dreams in which we were moving.[210]

Another area of co-operation arose when Göring began farming out non-essential civilian production to the occupied countries, enabling German industry to concentrate on military hardware. This allowed manufacturers in optics and precision engineering to retrieve machinery recently looted by the Germans. Some French businessmen entered into sectoral arrangements with German firms: with market pooling in return for raw materials. The acceptance of German contracts involved an increasing number of French firms, seven thousand in 1941 rose to fourteen thousand by 1944. The most obviously compromised were in industries such as reinforced concrete, notably firms which participated in the construction of Germany's gigantic Atlantic fortifications. Simple distinctions between actively soliciting a German contract and passively accepting one are of limited use. Was there a meaningful difference between taking on an order to retain a workforce that might otherwise have been relocated to Germany, and placing an advertisement in the German *Pariser Zeitung* drawing attention to their eagerness to collaborate?[211] Although some businessmen collusively extended their plant to enhance profits, ruthlessly discarding existing French clients, or entered into long-term arrangements with German partners which reflected confidence in German victory, many exhibited the *Bridge on the River Kwai* syndrome, a narrowing of vision to essentially professional or technical concerns, at the expense of the wider picture. Other businesses continued to service a purely local economy, although the latter has received far less scholarly attention than sectors most obviously sucked into dealings with the various branches of the occupying power.

Similar grey ambiguities characterised the Catholic Church. Although France had significant Protestant enclaves, 80 per cent of the French were baptised Catholics, of whom perhaps a third actively practised their religion. The Catholic Church had slight purchase on the urban lower classes, and was losing its hold on the countryside through rural depopulation. Despite a powerful social Catholic movement, and such aberrations as 'red' priests and democratic Dominicans, the Church leant towards the right, identifying the Communists with the anti-clerical atrocities of the Spanish Republicans or the tyranny in the Kremlin, and the Popular Front government with Freemasonry and materialism. As Eugen Weber has it, 'Catholicism was the Right at prayer.'[212] However, many leading Catholic intellectuals, including d'Harcourt and Maritain, were opposed to antisemitism and racism. The Catholic Church was simultaneously hostile to Nazism, which it regarded as a form of neo-paganism, but compromised by the benefits it hoped to accrue from Vichy, which only ruled by dint of the Nazis' protective hand. For Vichy offered the prospect of reChristianising France by re-establishing Christian values, blunting the challenge of militant Republican secularism. The elderly hierarchy, many of them war veterans themselves, were generally loyal to the person of Pétain, but at no point did they collectively embrace collaboration as a body.

The official Church strategy was 'loyalty without enthralment'.[213] There were areas of consensus between Church and Vichy, notably regarding the purge of Freemasons, and indeed occasional points of interest with Nazi Germany, especially concerning the invasion of the Soviet Union, although few went as far as the aged Cardinal Baudrillart: 'As a priest and a Frenchman . . . should I refuse to approve this noble common enterprise, in which Germany is taking the lead?' Vichy favoured the Catholic Church by reintroducing God to the state school system, allowing members of religious orders to teach in state schools, while subsidising Church schools and the construction and restoration of churches. Prominent Catholic laymen who served the regime included Bernard Fay, Raphael Alibert and Xavier Vallat, all prominent in the persecution of Freemasons and Jews. Vallat, according to Cardinal Gerlier, was 'an excellent Christian'. In line with the trend already apparent in Italy and Germany, the French hierarchy tacitly accepted an authoritarian regime. They were fixated on the battles of the past rather than on the challenges of the present.[214] The net effect was that lack of principled leadership from the very top left Catholics without guidance in complex circumstances, an effect not corrected even when the hierarchy began to adjust their position to take into account probable German defeat. Of course, silence regarding discrimination against the Jews prior to the era of deportations was not something over which the Churches had a monopoly; neither the socialists nor the Communists had anything to say about this subject either. The other side of this coin was the Christians who were actively involved in resistance, the majority being from the traditional right, the bourgeoisie and the middle classes. Both French Protestants, who were often regarded as being part of 'anti-France', and left-wing Catholics were involved in rescue efforts on behalf of the Jews. Some of the most impressive resistance networks were organised by Christians, notably Combat Resistance centred on Limoges, Liberté, Libération, Franc-Tireur and so forth.[215]

Apart from their manifest lack of support in the occupied societies of Europe, most national collaborationist projects failed because Hitler had not conquered the continent in order to make bargains, which would one day restore the independence of individual countries within his 'New Order'. This would have restricted his room for manoeuvre and undercut his bid for permanent German dominance.[216] The rhetoric employed by middle-echelon representatives of the German regime, such as Otto Abetz, was dismissed by its leading lights with

characteristic bluntness. Thus in August 1942 Göring observed: 'Only
Herr Abetz goes in for collaboration. I don't collaborate. I view the
French gentlemen's collaboration only in one light: if they deliver
whatever they can, until they can deliver no more, and if they do so
voluntarily, then I'll say I am collaborating. But if they devour everything themselves, then they aren't collaborating.' All local political
arrangements were subordinated to the aim of exploiting occupied
Europe in the interests of Germany's war machine.

Each occupied country was subjected to crippling occupation costs,
which in the case of France were fixed at 20 million Reichsmarks per
day, at the devalued exchange rate of 20 francs to the Mark. Just how
exorbitant these levies were has been illustrated by the estimate that if
it cost 22 francs per day to keep one French soldier in the field in
1940, then the occupation costs levied by the Germans would have
maintained an occupation army in France numbering eighteen million
men.[217] In fact, France was paying fifty times the real cost of a German
garrison of three hundred thousand. These burdens were further
multiplied by the subtraction from the French economy of prisoners of
war and forced labour; rigged trading agreements which encompassed
French trade with other countries as well as Germany; food, raw
materials or plant simply diverted eastwards; and business interests
abroad – such as the Les Mines des Bors copper mines in Yugoslavia –
usurped by the Germans with the aid of their surplus francs. Although
much had been expected of the occupied economies of the East, in
reality France alone was responsible for at least 42 per cent of the total
foreign contribution to the German wartime economy, while the
Germans pondered the tangled wreckage of factories destroyed by
the retreating Soviets.[218]

The position of local collaborators was further undermined by the
Nazi decision to rectify acute labour shortages by conscripting foreigners, many of them young and female, rather than fully mobilising
German women. Some of these people were volunteers, attracted by
the prospect of higher wages, but these were atypical. In eastern Europe
the Nazis had no hesitation in resorting to coercion, raiding cinemas
and schools to round up an unwilling workforce. The SS Reich Main
Security Office, ever alert to biological implications, immediately elaborated a series of demeaning regulations designed to isolate these racial
undesirables from the general German population. The conquests in
the West generated about 1.2 million French prisoners of war, the
majority deployed in agriculture or construction, 120,000 Belgian

civilians and 110,000 Yugoslavs, in addition to 270,000 workers from allied Italy. Belgian, Dutch and Norwegian prisoners of war were repatriated. Flushed with victory, advocates and opponents of foreign labour in Germany agreed that the three million foreigners there by the end of 1940 represented a tolerable figure, provided they were categorised and treated along racial lines, and dispersed throughout different sectors of the economy. Debates occurred about whether Germany should operate a regime of skills apartheid. Should Germans occupy the skilled jobs, above a class of racially categorised labouring helots, or was it in the interests of racial vitality for Germans to sweat and get their hands dirty, or to tend trees, fish and so forth? Initially expecting a rapid result in Russia, German authorities evinced no interest in employing Russian prisoners of war, a stance which indirectly contributed to the deaths in captivity of over three million of them. Chronic labour shortages led Hitler and Göring to revise their earlier opposition to deploying eastern labour. Göring thought that, while Germans belonged in the arms industry, 'the Russian' could hump rocks and live off cats and horses. Since only four hundred thousand of the available pool of just over one million Soviet prisoners of war was fit for work, it was inevitable that the Nazis looked towards the Soviet civilian population to bridge the gap between supply and demand.

A centralised labour procurement agency was established under the ex-merchant seaman Fritz Sauckel in March 1942, which combed western and eastern Europe in search of a workforce.[219] The ruthless tactics used in Poland were repeated in the occupied parts of the Soviet Union, with the added incentive that villages were burned if their mayors failed to present candidates for work in Germany, a form of words which conceals the reality of locking people in cellars until the Germans were ready to deport them. Between April and December 1942, about forty thousand people were deported to Germany each week, the average age being twenty, but including people as young as fifteen. By the end of 1942, there were 1.7 million Soviet civilians or prisoners of war at work in Germany. Western Europe was not spared Sauckel's attentions, but there was some pretence at negotiation with collaborationist regimes, vainly seeking some concessions to brandish in front of their populations. In the spring of 1942, Laval responded to Sauckel's demand for three hundred and fifty thousand additional workers, including one hundred and fifty thousand skilled men, with the idea of sending volunteer workers to Germany in return for the relief of French prisoners of war. Laval sought a straightforward one-to-one exchange; Sauckel settled on three workers per prisoner. Announcing this shoddy deal on 22 June 1942, Laval made the mistake of saying: 'I desire the victory of Germany, because, without it, bolshevism would tomorrow establish itself everywhere. France cannot remain passive or indifferent before the immensity of the sacrifices Germany is willing to make in order to construct a Europe in which we must take our place,' a remark which did more than anything else to put him in front of a firing squad after the war.

Since conditions for foreign workers were hardly alluring, there was a massive shortfall in the anticipated targets of volunteer workers. By September 1942, only seventeen thousand of the projected one hundred and fifty thousand skilled workers had been recruited. The deficiency was rectified by round-ups and factory closures in the northern zone. Faced with further German demands, Laval responded with the Service du Travail Obligatoire introduced on 16 February 1943 and designed to conscript the 1920–2 age cohorts. It should be noted that this measure made no mention of exchanging workers for prisoners, although a quarter of a million were granted civilian status, to free up the German troops guarding them. Labour conscription was one of the main reasons why young men fled to the *maquis*, with the French police failing to bestir themselves to prevent them.

Laval attempted to rationalise his indulgence of Sauckel's demands by specious distinctions between an expendable and 'national' work-force, while his colleague Bichelonne explored the tactic of playing off one Nazi leader against another. One result of his conversations with Speer mentioned above was the creation of decentralised S- or Speer-Betriebe, which ring-fenced workers in conscription-proof factories in the occupied territories in return for 80 per cent of their output going to Germany.[220] But there was no triumph of rationality over plunder. The nature of the Nazi regime, involving stalemate between irreconcilable positions, both of which were then pursued simultaneously, meant that the S-Betriebe brought only marginal relief from Sauckel's importunity.[221] It was in the nature of the Nazi empire that even those people most ideologically disposed to them were treated as instruments to be played with, or discarded, at will. There was no 'New Order' involving some sort of remodelling of relations between fascist states; the term was a euphemism for German imperial dominance, two talismanic words strung together to conceal a reversion to conditions of utter lawlessness in which depravity flourished. Whether this was sometimes dressed up in the forms of modern technocracy may be academically interesting, but it is also incidental. Any concessions, or rather tactical amelioration of Nazi demands conceded to local collaborators or on behalf of specific populations, were based on a calculation of how best to prevent defeat by the Allies.

How might this most transient of modern empires be viewed in the longer perspective which separates us from other empires, both ancient and modern? The Nazi empire was created by violence, lived by violence and was destroyed by violence. In contrast to other empires created by armed might, which bequeathed art and literature that are still widely admired, or administrations, customs, languages and legal codes that Europeans and non-Europeans still adhere to, from Ireland to India, the tawdry Nazi anti-civilisation left nothing of any worth behind, except perhaps its contemporary function as a secular synonym for human evil. Nazism's material remains number a few third-rate buildings, for Albert Speer was hardly Bernini, Wren or Lutyens, concrete coastal fortifications too dense to destroy, and the wooden huts, wind-swept parade grounds, watchtowers and barbed wire of the concentration camps, which are paradoxically restored, rather than left to rot and rust. Nazism was literally 'from nothing to nothing': with its powerful imaginative afterlife curiously disembodied from its pitiful achievements. Rarely can an empire have existed about which nothing positive could be said, notwithstanding the happy memories of wartime tourism with which we began. Even in the limited terms of its own aesthetic politics, the Nazi 'New Order' was merely the universalisation of ugliness.

7

A BLITZKRIEG TOO FAR?
THE GERMAN INVASION AND
OCCUPATION OF THE SOVIET UNION,
1941–1943

The multinational invasion of the Soviet empire commenced in the searing heat of the summer of 1941. Hitler and most of his generals imagined the campaign could be won within weeks. It concluded, four vicious winter campaigns later, with the Red Army triumphant in Berlin.

'SEE YOU AGAIN IN SIBERIA'

The greatest military conflict of modern times erupted amid scenes of utmost normality. On Saturday 21 June 1941, the German panzer commander Heinz Guderian visited forward positions overlooking the Tsarist Russian fortress at Brest-Litovsk on the confluence of the Bug and Muchawiec rivers. Through fieldglasses he observed that Soviet defences were unattended. Within the fortress, Red Army soldiers, many of them Chechens, drilled to the tunes of a military band. The town was usually garrisoned by eight thousand soldiers, but this weekend the force stood at three and a half thousand because of leave or assignments elsewhere. At midnight, the Berlin–Moscow express train crossed the Bug in the direction of Brest, with a Soviet grain train rumbling over the frontier in the opposite direction somewhat later.[1]

Warnings that something untoward was afoot had been flowing in to the Soviet regime for months. Since February, Dekanozov, the Soviet ambassador in Berlin, had reported what seemed to be German preparations for war to Foreign Minister Molotov. Molotov downplayed the threat because of his role in making the 1939 Non-Aggression Pact, whose secret appendices had licensed Nazi and Soviet aggression against Poland and the Baltic States. Careerism, hierarchy and the caution endemic among the Soviet Establishment meant that Dekanazov did not express his fears directly to Stalin.[2] Soviet foreign intelligence services supplied crucial information which was ignored. In Tokyo, the Soviet agent Richard Sorge had managed to build a highly effective intelligence network during the 1930s. Sorge's cover of a boozy but well-informed German journalist, together with his war record as a five-times wounded veteran, smoothed his contacts with the German embassy and all who visited it from Berlin. Many lonely visiting military men benefited from Sorge's in-depth knowledge of Tokyo's loucher attractions and his drunk's eagerness to turn every night into a carnival. Sorge also had excellent intelligence on foreign policy debates within the Japanese cabinet and armed forces. Ironically, this dedicated Communist spy suspected that, had he returned to Moscow in the late 1930s, he would have been shot, as were most of his Fourth Department superiors. In late May 1941, Sorge learned that an invasion was scheduled for around 20 June, and relayed this information to Moscow. There the message was marked 'Suspicious. To be listed with telegrams intended as provocation'. The lack of reaction sent Sorge further down a self-destructive spiral of drunken binges and motorbike accidents.[3]

Meanwhile, in Moscow the NKVD resorted to such stratagems as simultaneously locking German diplomatic couriers in the elevator and a bathroom of the Hotel Metropol to photograph the contents of an attaché case in their bedroom. The information gained was mixed. A letter from the russophile conservative German ambassador Schulenburg to his Foreign Minister, Ribbentrop, confidently anticipated resolving any conflicts, while also reporting that his embassy staff was being reduced to a minimum as German diplomats prepared to evacuate the Moscow embassy. A Soviet agent who attended a German embassy cocktail party to scout locations for listening devices noted that packers had removed many of the decorations and paintings.[4] According to his most recent Russian biographer, Stalin set great store on the relative prices of mutton and fleeces in Germany, since he calculated that without sheepskin coats for the winter the Germans could not possibly attack.[5] Information from British intelligence sources, as well as from Soviet spies operating within it, bore the taint of attempts to inveigle Stalin into an intra-imperialist war.[6] After all, when the British had predicted a German invasion of the Soviet Union for May, the Germans had instead attacked the British on the island of Crete.

When in May 1941 Schulenburg told Dekanozov of Hitler's plans to attack the Soviet Union, Dekanozov relayed the news to Molotov, who informed Stalin. The latter commented: 'We shall consider that disinformation has now reached the level of ambassadors.' In mid-June, a Soviet agent in the Luftwaffe reported that final preparations for an invasion had been made. Stalin scribbled the response: 'Comrade Merkulov, you can send your "source" from the staff of the German airforce to his fucking mother. This is not a "source", but disinformation.'[7] Two days before the invasion, Commissar of Foreign Trade Mikoyan received information from the chief of the port of Riga that all twenty-five German merchant ships in the harbour were preparing to sail on 21 June, regardless of whether they had loaded or unloaded cargoes. He told Stalin that this highly unusual action could only be preparation for war. Stalin replied that, since Hitler would regard detaining the ships as an act of provocation, they should be allowed to put to sea.[8] Massive troop concentrations and ominously regular Luftwaffe overflights were discounted as attempts by Hitler to bluff Stalin into yet further concessions to his German allies. Sometimes German deserters from the 170 divisions arrayed over the frontier were not only disbelieved but shot.

On 21 June Dekanozov sought out Lavrenti Beria, head of the NKVD, to inform him that an attack would commence the next day. Beria told Stalin that the ambassador would be called to account for 'bombarding' them with disinformation. On the same day, Beria dismissed an accurate report from the head of military intelligence on the force Germany had massed on the frontier, with the marginal comment: 'My people and I, Iosif Vissarionovich, firmly remember your wise prediction: Hitler will not attack us in 1941.'[9] By two in the morning, attempts to forward information from further deserters proved impossible, since German special forces had already cut the telephone lines. From three o'clock onwards, the tocsin sounded and the bleary-eyed denizens of Moscow ministries, many nursing hangovers from Saturday night, scurried back to their desks. Shortly after retiring following a long Politburo session, Stalin was woken by a telephone call from Marshal Zhukov, the Soviet Chief of Staff, informing him of the German attack. Stalin at first believed it was the work of a few maverick German generals. This was criminal negligence rather than mere idiocy. Oddly enough, those quick to criminalise, say, Field Marshal Haig, seem loath to apply the same logic to Stalin.

Operation Barbarossa, the greatest land invasion in modern warfare, commenced at that hour with a barrage from thousands of guns and waves of dive-bombers whining through the dawn sky. By late morning, the Luftwaffe had destroyed 890 Soviet aircraft, most of them caught unawares on the ground. By 12 July, some 6,857 Russian aircraft had been put out of commission, with the loss of 550 German aeroplanes.[10] The NKVD had decided to relocate and reconstruct the airbases in line with Stalin's post-1939 territorial gains, which meant that fighter aircraft were conveniently concentrated on relatively few functioning airfields. The Luftwaffe roved above the roadways, bombing and machine-gunning fleeing soldiers and civilians on the ground. Although Luftwaffe historians tend to highlight the daring annihilation of stationary aircraft, it is worth noting what they did to towns. A Russian historian who survived a raid on Minsk recalls:

On the morning of 24 June 1941, a Tuesday, I saw it myself, a squadron of ninety-six aircraft flying over Minsk. They bombed the town all day long. The entire centre was destroyed. Only a couple of large buildings were left standing. Everything else in the centre was in ruins. When this bombing began that morning I was in the Pedagogical Institute. We were at work. During the bombardment we crept into the cellar. And then, when we came out, what did we see there! Burning houses, ashes, ruins. And corpses everywhere in the streets. People wanted to get out of the town during the bombing. But they could not flee quickly enough since the streets were jam packed. And those that were outside were mown down by low-flying German aircraft.[11]

It was what Americans call a 'turkey shoot'. A few hours after Guderian had watched Soviet troops drilling in Brest, submersible tanks from his 18th Panzer left their jumping-off positions to negotiate thirteen feet of water in the River Bug, with the aid of waterproofing developed earlier for the invasion of England. Brest was suddenly bombarded with five thousand shells and bombs each minute. Attacking the fortress from three directions, German forces anticipated capturing it within eight hours. In the event, the garrison, which included large numbers of Chechen troops, held out for a month as Army Group Centre bypassed this local difficulty *en route* for Smolensk. Seventeen of Brest's three and a half thousand defenders survived.[12] The German army made rapid progress elsewhere, partly because Stalin had decided to move his fortifications westwards from the old 1939 borders. The new fortifications were not complete, for the NKVD failed to supply sufficient camp labour, while the old fortifications had been demolished.[13]

Modern post-Soviet Russian biographers of Stalin disagree on whether Stalin went into a blue funk or remained completely in control as befitted the self-styled 'Man of Steel'. Dmitri Volkogonov claims that 'Stalin had never had so great a shock in his life,' while Edvard Radzinsky details a constant round of meetings, many of them devoted to identifying scapegoats to blame. Having initially ordered his generals not to respond offensively to what he persisted in regarding as provocation by wayward German generals, for each flash of reality required some commensurately implausible explanation, Stalin retired to his dacha at Kuntsevo, remarking, 'All that Lenin created, we have lost,' or, in its more vulgar form, 'Lenin left us a great inheritance and we, his heirs, have fucked it all up.'[14] When the Politburo sought him out, Stalin thought it was to make him resign. The thought passed when the creepy Molotov, who had organised this pilgrimage, requested that Stalin return to work.[15]

The Axis invasion force, organised in three Army Groups, was both vast and multinational. Seventy-five per cent of the German field army, or over three million men, together with six hundred thousand Croats, Finns, Romanians, Hungarians, Italians, Slovaks and Spaniards, teemed across the frontier in the direction of Leningrad, Moscow and the Ukraine. Each of Hitler's allies had their own, partially interrelated, expansionary or revanchist motives for attacking the Soviet Union. The Finns sought to continue the Winter War in order to regain territory lost under the Peace of Moscow of 12 March 1940.[16] It was a separate war within a war, fought according to conventional rules, and including the possibility of a separate peace. With a keen eye on Hitler's promises to Finland, Antonescu's Romania sought the restoration of Bessarabia and North Bukovina, and territory reaching towards Soviet Moldavia.[17]

Hungarian participation was in turn the product of fear that Hitler would reward his loyal Romanian ally by rescinding control of Transylvania, ceded to Hungary in 1940, as well as being an attempt to neutralise the fascist Arrow Cross, advocates of total conformity with German policy. The Germans helped along the Budapest government's slow decision-making by bombing Kassa and claiming that this was the work of the Red Air Force.[18] Hitler regarded the presence of sixty-two thousand Italian troops in the Corpo di Spedizione Italiano in Russia as a mixed blessing. Hitler had no illusions about why these troops, sent by Mussolini with much accompanying fanfare about an anti-Bolshevik crusade, were in Russia, namely as 'harvest hands' in the forthcoming division and spoliation of conquered territory.

Less tangible support came from the German Churches, whose prayers accompanied the advancing armies and whose view of the enemy was distinctly unChristian.[19] Roman Catholic clerics, including such notable opponents of the Nazi regime as Bornewasser of Trier or Galen of Münster, spoke colourfully of a 'hotbed of people who through their enmity to God and their hatred of Christ have almost degenerated into beasts', or of the 'Bolshevik colossus, this murdering, soul-destroying, nation-destroying monster', or of 'the liberation of the deeply religiously inclined Russian people from the twenty-four years of Bolshevik pollution and partial destruction'.

In the months before Barbarossa, maps were scoured and memories probed in order to construct a working view of the enemy. From the deep past, Coulaincourt, Ségur and Clausewitz were trawled for historical precedents. From the recent past, former Free Corps fighters such as Erwin Dwinger, or Reichswehr officers who had studied air, gas and tank warfare with the Soviets in the 1920s, were questioned about their experiences.[20] As was the case before the invasion of Poland, a host of academic 'experts' on the East (*Ostforscher*) – economists, geographers, historians, linguists and racial scientists – came out of the academic woodwork to proffer their detailed knowledge of Russia or the Soviet Union. This was the hour of the experts.[21]

Inevitably, all of this information both reflected, or was combined with, longer-term perceptions and deeply entrenched stereotypes of the East in general and the Russians in particular. Nineteenth-century liberal and socialist Germans lived in dread of the knouts and sabres of the Tsars' semi-barbaric Cossack armies. Twentieth-century German conservatives remembered a particularly brutal Russian occupation of their East Prussian rural heartland during the First World War, when 'The Russian army resembled migrating rats who, in times of great destruction, forsake their hiding places in the Siberian tundra in order to eat bare the settled lands. Ever fresh hordes come forth in a brown milling mass from the seething steppe.'[22] They also deeply, and justifiably, feared the 'Asiatic' terror of Lenin and his accomplices, conveniently confusing it with the febrile sectarian revolutionism they had brutally crushed in Berlin or Munich. They were not alone in this since even the sectarian revolutionist Rosa Luxemburg had complained about the 'Tatar-Mongolian savagery' of Lenin's Bolsheviks. In sum, regardless of admiration for the stoic peasants as mediated by Tolstoy, or the psychological sophistication of Dostoevsky, something at once inferior and threatening lurked out in the East.

Hubris and derogatory metaphors first coined by Baltic German russophobes before the First World War were apparent during the planning stage at the very highest levels. Jodl remarked to Warlimont, 'the Russian colossus will be proved to be a pig's bladder; prick it and it will burst', while Hitler was reported as saying, 'the Russian Armed Forces are like a headless colossus with feet of clay'. Goebbels believed that 'Bolshevism would collapse like a house of cards.' Most German generals were fixated with a rapid and devastating campaign of eight to ten weeks' duration against an opponent whose commanders allegedly thought in rigidly schematic terms and whose men were demoralised, dull-witted helots.[23] The disastrous Soviet record in Finland and

Poland seemed to confirm this view. Much less attention was paid to the Far Eastern campaign, where the Soviets had beaten the Japanese Kwantung army at Nomanahon, or such factors as climate, distance and logistics. It is important to bear this in mind, in view of the number of memoirs by German generals which seek to shift the reasons for progressive failure on to Hitler alone. The minority of German commanders whose prognostications were pessimistic confined themselves to ambiguously ironic remarks, notably when Rundstedt bade farewell to Ritter von Leeb on 4 May 1941 with the ominous words: 'Well then, see you again in Siberia.'[24]

Confidence that the Red Army could be smashed quickly went together with the knowledge that the Soviet Union disposed of enormous human and material capital which the Russians were in the process of mobilising. This lent urgency to the timing of the German attack. A German army study of the Red Army dated 15 January 1941 warned that the Soviet armaments industry was both modern and capable of producing up-to-date weaponry; that the Soviets had been relocating their armaments industry east of the Urals since the late 1920s; and that, despite the purges of the officer corps, the Red Army consisted of millions of willing soldiers. Studies like these contributed to the belief that 1941 might represent an unrepeatable window of opportunity.[25] The military view combined with the pressing need for the raw materials of the Soviet empire, and the desire to deny the British a further ally before the United States entered the war, to produce the attack on Russia. From Hitler's point of view, there was too much to gain against an apparently weak opponent, and too much to lose if this opponent recovered as rapidly as he seemed to be doing. Just before the invasion, Hitler remarked that he was standing before a closed door, behind which lay the unknown. If this campaign went wrong, then everything would be over. In other words, the war was preconceived in apocalyptic terms.

The initial success of the invasion seemed to confirm the dominant army view. The Axis advance was so rapid that as early as 3 July Franz Halder, the Chief of General Staff, noted in his diary that 'the Russian campaign has been won in the space of two weeks'. His mind was already racing ahead to denying the Soviets the economic resources for future recovery; the continuing irritant of Britain; and a possible thrust through the Caucasus to Iran. This overconfidence was reflected in Hitler's decision of 14 July to switch armaments priorities from the army to the navy and Luftwaffe.[26] Having reached maximum output in July 1941, by December production of weapons for the army had fallen by 29 per cent. Instead, the number of warships being produced was doubled, while a record five million men were recorded as having been excused military service. By that time, the Germans were being repulsed from Moscow, and warships were not what they most needed. Huge turbine engines in shipbuilding yards were monuments to Hitler's folly.

Optimistic initial assessments were gradually belied by conditions on the ground. On paper everything looked impressive. In four vast battles of encirclement before September, the Germans captured 3,800 tanks, 6,000 artillery weapons and 872,000 prisoners. However, before the end of August, German losses amounted to 409,998 killed or wounded, with only 232,000 men in reserve to replace them.[27] Conditions on the ground were deteriorating. Heavily laden infantrymen slogged along poor roads and tracks, covered in sweat and dust and plagued by stinging insects, towards destinations that only served to underline how gigantic this country was. Mental horizons formed by the regions of Germany had to stretch to infinitude. The rigours of forced marches in the summer heat were duly superseded by the mud from the autumn rains, miring men, vehicles and horses alike. The mud was so viscous that sometimes a boot remained behind when a soldier tried to extract his foot. Something of the sinister enormity of a fitfully beguiling landscape was caught by Manstein, the German commander on the southernmost front:

> I now found myself in the vast expanses of the steppes, which were almost entirely devoid of natural obstacles, even if they did not offer any cover either. . . . The only variety was offered by the small rivers, the beds of which had dried up in summer-time to form deep, steep-banked fissures known as balkas. Nevertheless, the very monotony of the steppes gave them a strange and unique fascination. Everyone was captivated at one time or other by the endlessness of the landscape, through which it was possible to drive for hours on end – often guided by the compass – without encountering the least rise in the ground or setting eyes on a single human being or habitation. The distant horizon seemed like some mountain ridge behind which a paradise might beckon, but it only stretched on and on. The poles of the Anglo-Iranian telegraph line, built some years before by Siemens, alone served to break the eternal sameness of it all. Yet at sunset these steppes were transformed into a dazzling blaze of colour.[28]

By 6 October, the problems of mud were compounded by the first light falls of snow. Wheeled vehicles could advance only by being shunted or towed by tracked craft, and even chains and tow-ropes had to be dropped from the air in the first indication that the German army was ill equipped for the ordeal ahead. With temperatures down to minus 8 degrees and falling in early November, machine guns jammed, telescopic sights proved useless, engines had to be de-iced with fires underneath, tanks without spiked tracks slid around, while the intense cold penetrated thin denim uniforms and worn leather boots. Each soldier had to think about how to stay warm and dry, preventing rain or snow from trickling down collars, inside boots or up their sleeves when one upturned arm held a rifle strap. Sartorial confusion reigned, with many German soldiers dressed in captured Russian fur hats, overcoats and felt boots, with insulation provided by newspaper, to protect themselves from what by early December had become temperatures of minus 32 degrees. They began to take on the unnatural bulk of well-padded tramps. Such shelter as existed, assuming it had not been booby-trapped by the retreating Russians, was equally lethal since the foul air encouraged respiratory illnesses and lice. Of course, these harsh weather conditions also applied to the Russians, who, it seemed to ordinary German soldiers, were being collected from nowhere, given vodka and a weapon, and then thrown, wave-like, into virtually suicidal attacks. As they advanced deeper into the desolation of the Russian winter, the German army shed any vestigial human curiosity or sympathy for the Russian population, whose material civilisation was analogous to that of a backward country, replacing this with a dull, uncomprehending hatred for this alien people. Imaginations quick to sentimentalise hearth and home had no apparent feeling for the hearths and homes immediately around them.[29]

Strategic errors and failure to anticipate appalling climatic conditions were now compounded by co-ordinated Soviet resistance, and a desperate effort on the Soviet home front, although in this war home and fighting fronts were inextricably confused. Having already dissipated his armour between three armies stretched along a front whose width reached fifteen hundred miles, with a depth of a thousand miles at maximum extent, Hitler diverted much of the flanking armour from the central Moscow front either southwards, to take the Donets Basin and Crimea, or north to put pressure on Leningrad. Remonstrations from commanders who wished to concentrate on the Soviet capital were met with the remark: 'My generals know nothing about the economic aspects of the war.' Major victories were achieved in the south, including the taking of half a million Soviet prisoners at Kiev, and Leningrad was subjected to close investment. But ill-equipped and exhausted German troops were then thrown into the long-range haul against Moscow precisely when conditions were least propitious and the number of combat-ready tanks had shrunk by 50 per cent. This was to be an exercise of sheer willpower over mere matter.

Stalin reasserted his grip on the shambles his own policies had largely created. He wheeled out Molotov in the first radio appeal to the Soviet people, thus distancing himself from the Non-Aggression Pact. On 3 July Stalin himself came on the wireless, his low, toneless voice accompanied by deep and weary breathing and frequent sips of water. The contrast between the even delivery and the tragedy that was unfolding apparently moved many people and, via clear instructions regarding scorched-earth policies and partisan warfare, left them with the impression that there was ultimately someone in charge. The opening form of address struck an unfamiliar personal and indeed religious note: 'Comrades, citizens, brothers and sisters, fighters of our Army and Navy! I am speaking to you, my friends!' Acknowledging that 'a serious threat hangs over our country', he proceeded to justify the Nazi–Soviet Pact:

> A non-aggression pact is a peace pact between two states, and that was the Pact that Germany proposed to us in 1939. No peace-loving state could have rejected such a pact with another country, even if scoundrels like Hitler and Ribbentrop stood at its head. All the more so, as this Pact did not in any way violate the territorial integrity, independence or honour of our country.[30]

The violations of Baltic, Finnish or Polish integrity, independence and honour by Soviet forces were lost in the ether. Amid all the references to heroic resistance to imminent enslavement by 'German princes and barons', for Marxist–Leninist ideology did not comfortably accommodate invading armies consisting of enthusiastic Bavarian farmboys or butchers and carpenters from Darmstadt or Düsseldorf, Stalin characteristically warmed to the subject of the fight against the enemy within, still mysteriously omnipresent despite the murderous purges of the 1930s:

> A merciless struggle must be undertaken against all deserters and panic-mongers. . . . We must destroy spies, diversionists and enemy paratroopers . . . Military tribunals should immediately try anyone who, through panic or cowardice, is interfering with our defence, regardless of position or rank.

In subsequent weeks and months, the resort to state terror was as instinctual as it was real. Generals such as Korobkov and Pavlov whom Stalin blamed for his own mistakes were shot for criminal negligence. Other able commanders, such as Meretskov, named by Pavlov under torture as part of a putative anti-Soviet conspiracy, were temporarily arrested and then three months later sent to command armies. This was not a unique experience. One of the most able commanders, the Russo-Pole Rokossovsky, who had been imprisoned and tortured in August 1937, was only released in March 1940 following the débâcle of the Soviet–Finnish war, which proved that talent was in short supply. He went to his command via a spell in a sanatorium.[31] Grotesquely, General Kachalov was tried *in absentia* for desertion in October 1941, notwithstanding his having been killed by a German direct hit in August, a mistake not rectified until 1956, his family being meanwhile tainted by this 'traitor to the Fatherland'.[32] Twenty other generals committed suicide following the failures of that summer. They never included Stalin's own military stooges.

Taking advantage of emergency wartime conditions, Stalin also executed those suspected opponents who had somehow survived the purges of the late 1930s. As they fell back from the advancing Germans, the NKVD systematically executed political prisoners and all those serving ten or more years in jail. In the Ukraine, NKVD tribunals slaughtered 1,000–2,000 political prisoners in Lutsk, 837 in Sambir, 500 in Dubno, 3,000–4,000 in Lviv, 850 in Drogobych, 1,500 in Stanyslav and so on. Order No. 270 of 16 August 1941 criminalised the families of officers and Communists taken prisoner, and deprived the families of lesser ranks who met the same fate of access to rations and welfare.[33] Those who entered captivity wounded and unconscious like General Ponedelin would disappear into the gulag system, after years of German captivity, to be shot long after the war. Men who had escaped encirclement or imprisonment were sent to mine-laying units or NKVD screening camps. NKVD 'Special Sections' were used to weed out 'unreliable elements' and to keep Red Army troops at gunpoint on the front line. On 25 July the NKVD rounded up and shot a thousand 'deserters'; in another notorious incident, they disarmed a large number of Red Army soldiers who had evaded encirclement, and who were then massacred by the Germans while *en route* to an NKVD screening centre. They had no guns.[34]

The NKVD was also active in shooting all Germans in its North Russian and Siberian concentration camps, and in uprooting

650,000–700,000 ethnic Germans, who were deported to Kazakhstan and Siberia. In so far as they survived journeys in cattle trucks lasting three months – and on one train alone four hundred children died – the male deportees were sent down the mines while their families lived in fenced-in camps ringed with NKVD watchtowers. Community dignitaries were simply shot. In order to rationalise their own murderousness, in August 1941 the Soviets dropped parachutists masquerading as German troops on Volga German settlements, who then asked villagers to hide them as the putative vanguard of the invading Wehrmacht. Anyone falling for this ploy was subsequently shot, as were villagers caught with swastika flags in the house, flags which the Communists had helpfully distributed to these people in 1939 to celebrate the Nazi–Soviet Pact.[35]

With the advance on Moscow slowed by the weather and by dogged Russian resistance, Hitler, whose mind thought in feet and inches of captured ground, simply rejected advice in favour of strategic retreat. Isolated far from the front in his Wolf's Lair at Rastenburg, and surrounded by cronies with no responsibilities beyond concurring even with the way he mispronounced foreign names such as 'Tschemberlein' or 'Eisenh-o-wer', Hitler received his senior commanders like 'a magistrate in a police court'.[36] Generals who advocated tactical withdrawal were sarcastically rebuffed: 'Sir, where in God's name do you propose to go back to, how far do you want to go back?. . . . Do you want to go back 50 kilometres; do you think it is less cold there?'[37] On 20 December 1941, Guderian flew to Rastenburg to remonstrate along the same lines. The ensuing conversation was a typical example of Hitler's autodidactic, self-validating, pseudo-populist reference to his own worm's eye experience of earlier conflicts. As Manstein noted, 'although Hitler was always harping on his "soldierly" outlook and loved to recall that he had acquired his military experience as a frontline soldier, his character had as little in common with the thoughts and emotions of soldiers as had his party with the Prussian virtues which it was so fond of invoking'.[38] Almost before Guderian had even spoken, he sensed an unfriendly atmosphere in the dim light of the conference room:

> *Hitler:* 'If that is the case [withdrawal] they must dig into the ground where they are and hold every square yard of land.'
> *Guderian:* 'Digging into the ground is no longer feasible in most places, since it is frozen to a depth of five feet and our wretched entrenching tools won't go through it. . . .'

> *Hitler:* 'In that case they must blast craters with heavy howitzers. We
> had to do that in the First World War in Flanders.'[39]

It was no use pointing out that conditions in Flanders were otherwise;
that shells were limited; and that such a strategy would lead in Russian
conditions to a few tub-sized craters in the frozen ground. The
discussion moved on to whether the objectives were worth the human
sacrifice. When Guderian suggested that they were not and spelled out
the casualties and inadequate equipment, Hitler responded:

> I know that you have not spared yourself and that you have spent a
> great deal of time with the troops. I grant you that. But you are seeing
> events at too close a range. You have been too deeply impressed by the
> suffering of the soldiers. You feel too much pity for them. You should
> stand back more. Believe me, things appear clearer when examined at
> longer range.[40]

Manstein also provides astute insights on Hitler as a would-be
warlord:

> He was a man who saw fighting only in terms of the utmost brutality.
> His way of thinking conformed more to a mental picture of masses of
> the enemy bleeding to death before our lines than to the conception of
> a subtle fencer who knows how to make an occasional step backwards
> in order to lunge for the decisive thrust. For the art of war he
> substituted a brutal force which, as he saw it, was guaranteed maxi-
> mum effectiveness by the will-power behind it. . . . Despite the pains
> Hitler took to stress his own former status as a front-line soldier, I still
> never had the feeling that his heart belonged to the fighting troops.
> Losses, as far as he was concerned, were merely figures which reduced
> fighting power. They are unlikely to have seriously disturbed him as a
> human being.[41]

While Hitler was pondering the 'longer range' from the vantage
point of Rastenburg, Stalin lived up to his grim reputation as the
bureaucrat's bureaucrat by centralising ultimate civilian control of
the war in the State Defence Committee (the only soldier present was
Voroshilov) and military power in the Supreme Command or Stavka,
which he also chaired.[42] He could match Hitler not only in brutality
and personal rudeness, but also in holding forth with irrelevant details
from his capacious memory, albeit displaying his mastery of the
nomenklatura rather than Hitler's well-known *rage des nombres*.
Like Hitler, he made catastrophic interventions in military dispositions, usually by ordering ill-prepared counter-offensives. Ultimately,

however, Stalin listened to the advice of professionals, increasingly adjudicating between various alternative proposals, which his generals then wisely attributed to his strategic genius, while his opposite in Berlin followed the dictates of destiny and Providence.[43] One can all too clearly imagine Hitler's wild monologues and tirades, in contrast to Stalin's menacingly taciturn presence, with that impassive pock-marked face silently puffing on a pipe or sipping lemon tea. Whatever their temperamental dissimilarities, the two dictators shared an indisposition to visit the fighting fronts, and a total indifference to casualties or other losses, including in Stalin's case the capture and death of his son Yakov, an event shrugged off and never recalled in conversation. Truly a man of steel.

It would be wrong to over-personalise the Soviet war effort. A political culture of all-powerful Party bosses used to rhetorical battles, campaigns and Stakhanovite-style shock work quickly adapted to the exigencies of total war. But we should be careful not to echo Soviet propaganda by imagining that the war was an advertisement for state socialism. Paradoxically, the Soviet Union may have had to *demobilise*, to allow the enterprise, initiative and improvisation necessary for the war effort. An Evacuation Council supervised the relocation eastwards of strategically vital plant and twenty-five million workers. This was a massive undertaking, balancing civilian and military rail transport requirements, or assessing when to move power-generating equipment which was needed by hospitals and factories in the west, but also in the new industrial centres springing up in the east which lacked their own utilities.[44]

It was also urgent since the area conquered by the Germans contained 40 per cent of the Soviet population, 60 per cent of its arms industry, 38 per cent of its cattle, 60 per cent of its swine, 63 per cent of its coal, 71 per cent of its iron ore, 57 per cent of rolled steel production and so forth. Factories responsible for producing two-thirds of Soviet ammunition were either destroyed or fell into German hands.[45] Evacuation was not an unrelieved success story. Only seventeen out of sixty-four steel works were removed from the Donets Basin, while at one depot in the Ukraine alone the Germans found two hundred thousand tons of processed metals. But there were enough successes. For example, in late December 1941 the Zaporozhstal steel works in the Ukraine was removed to near Chelyabinsk in the Urals, with the job being completed in six weeks despite the need to heat the ground to lay foundations and despite the fact that cement froze. Some fifteen hundred major enterprises were evacuated by the end of 1941, using a million or so railway wagons as transport. This mass evacuation of plant and labour was accompanied by the conversion of consumer manufacturing industries. Bicycle factories turned out flamethrowers, and typewriter makers switched to producing automatic firearms. Gigantic plants, such as Tankograd at Chelyabinsk, used mass production techniques to manufacture vast numbers of mechanically uncomplicated T-34 tanks, the standardised weapon which would play such a part in rolling back Hitler's more sophisticated, yet fatally variegated, armoured spearheads. In 1941, a fifth of Soviet weapons had been produced in the east; a year later the fraction had increased to three-quarters.[46]

But winning a war is never simply a matter of superior economic performance. Hitler's attack on the Soviet Union managed to bestow upon the Communist regime a popular legitimacy that was at best notional at its inception, and which it had forfeited even among many old believers during the terroristic depredations of the 1930s. Although many citizens of the Soviet empire undoubtedly welcomed the Germans as liberators, with, as we shall see, some groups better represented in the Wehrmacht than in the Red Army, German policy equally rapidly disabused people of residual illusions. German atrocities against civilians and prisoners of war left the Soviet population with no alternative to rallying to Stalin's calculating appeals to simple patriotism, a strategy already heavily prefigured in the doctrine of 'Socialism in One Country'. The latter was now invested with historical grandeur through reference to great composers, writers and Tsarist generals.

For security reasons, the twenty-fourth anniversary celebrations of the October Revolution were held in the depths of Moscow's Mayakovsky underground station on the night of 6 November rather than in the Bolshoi Theatre, although the interior of the latter was recreated in the station for the benefit of newsreel cameras. Sandwiches and soft drinks were distributed from a stationary train while Stalin and the Politburo arrived on another.[47] In his address, to an audience of NKVD men, Stalin said:

> It is these people without honour or conscience, these people with the morality of animals, who have the effrontery to call for the extermination of the great Russian nation – the nation of Plekhanov and Lenin, of Belinsky and Chernyshevsky, of Pushkin and Tolstoy, of Gorki and Chekhov, of Glinka and Tchaikovsky, of Sechenov and Pavlov, of Suvorov and Kutuzov![48]

The following morning Stalin spoke at a march-past on Red Square, with heavy snow grounding German bombers while German troops stood only thirty miles away. With NKVD radio operators atop Lenin's tomb maintaining contact with their brigade defending Moscow, and a field hospital set up in the GUM store, Stalin invoked the heroes of the Russian past for a soldiery standing massed in the snow:

> The war you are waging is a war of liberation, a just war. May you be inspired in this war by the heroic figures of our great ancestors, Alexander Nevsky, Dimitri Donskoi, Minin and Pozharsky, Alexander Suvorov, Michael Kutuzov!

A regime that had ostentatiously installed Museums of Atheism in cathedrals, and which only restored Sunday as a day of universal rest in 1940, suddenly had no qualms about reopening churches, with monks collecting money to fund tank regiments. A few years later, the re-established Orthodox Patriarch offered prayers for the tyrant in the Kremlin.[49] The author of the 'Godless Five-Year Plan' was soon authorising a tour of the miracle-working icon of Our Lady of Kazan through besieged Soviet cities. In September 1941, Stalin again restored another aspect of the past he and his colleagues had obliterated, when he authorised the creation of Guards divisions in which crack troops were paid double the usual soldier's salary, and restored the insignia of rank to Soviet officers. They may have looked like over-decorated Christmas trees ever since, but they were preferable to some pseudo-egalitarian rabble. Although Stalin's diplomatic miscalculations and refusal to pre-empt the German attack had played a major role in the catastrophe, henceforth he was personally associated with each victory in the 'patriotic war', lending his own name to a 'doctrine' of military strategy, and fêted abroad by people such as British press barons who should have known better. Defeats were ascribed to others, or reconstrued as not defeats at all.

We should resist the temptation of projecting back on to wartime what has since been learned about the imperial corruption of the former Soviet Union. Most citizens of the Soviet Union fought and worked for the elementary reason that their homeland was under dire threat from a murderous enemy, rather than for the survival of its political system. In a society with no possibilities for free discussion, they knew nothing of the wilful incompetence which had allowed German armies to sweep into their midst. Beyond this basic human instinct, the Soviet system itself could draw on the naive enthusiasm of many ordinary people, who despite all the evidence to the contrary were convinced they were making the world a better place. How else does one account for the epic labours of 'accelerators', 'three hundreders' and 'thousanders' who increased their own productivity by herculean percentages? There is also probably much in the novelist Vasily Grossman's view that many Russians saw the war as a chance to correct the abuses and horrors of the Communist system, even though most were generic:

> Nearly everyone believed that good would triumph, that honest men, who hadn't hesitated to sacrifice their lives, would be able to build a good and just life. This faith was all the more touching in that these men thought that they themselves would be unlikely to survive until the end of the war; indeed, they felt astonished each evening to have survived one more day.[50]

Soviet propaganda encouraged this delusion regarding the possible relaxation of controls after the war. In other words, they were fighting for what might be rather than for what was. A Marxist–Leninist dictatorship could also rely upon naked terror and the miserable ghosts of human beings consigned to its depths. Beria's NKVD took a leading role in the evacuation of plant and in munitions production. As a defence industry official put it: 'Everyone in the plants and offices and institutions directly or indirectly connected with armaments and munitions was gripped by dread fear. Beria was no engineer. He was placed in control for the precise purpose of inspiring deadly fear.'[51] The gulags also provided a captive workforce: thirty-nine thousand prisoners for weapons and ammunition production, forty thousand to build aircraft and tanks; over 448,000 to construct railways. Even here, Solzhenitsyn reports that prisoners were infected by a sense of patriotism – 'Coal for Leningrad', 'Mortar shells for the troops' being the slogans. This is less remarkable than it seems, since many of the prisoners were Russian nationalists. Hundreds of thousands of others were conscripted into penal battalions, to be expended clearing minefields and other obstacles. Whether they felt the pull of patriotism remains unrecorded.[52] We should also remember that *matériel* equivalent to about a tenth of Soviet production was sent to Russia, at great human cost, by convoy from Britain and the United States of America, since Hitler's faltering legions had failed to take Murmansk. These Lend–Lease supplies, which will be discussed in greater detail in the final chapter, enabled the Soviet Union to free enormous numbers of men for the armed forces, and to devote an otherwise impossible level of industrial production exclusively to military purposes. It enabled the Soviet Union dangerously to skew her entire economy.

Slowed down by Soviet resistance and the atrocious road system, the final German assault on Moscow began in mid-November. Advance parties of German troops penetrated to the outskirts of the city, within sight of the Kremlin's spires. The NKVD was used to stop mass panic and flight. Aided by citizen militias, often consisting of what Stalin contemptuously regarded as the 'four-eyed intelligentsia', Zhukov's defending armies suffered twenty times the German level of casualties. But the Wehrmacht could advance no further. Stalin ordered a counter-attack to prevent the Germans digging in for the winter, as they had done at Leningrad. The fifty-eight fresh divisions available to Zhukov included troops transferred from the East.

This was largely made possible by Richard Sorge in Tokyo, who established that to resupply the Kwantung army bogged down in northern China the oil-deficient Japanese were going to invade French Indo-China and the Dutch East Indies rather than eastern Siberia. Apart from agents relating discussions in the Japanese cabinet and armed forces, Sorge's team included men and women monitoring the type of kit being issued to Japanese troops, with fur-lined coats ominous for the Russians, and tropical uniforms bad for the inhabitants of 'orphaned' European South-East Asian colonies. Despite the German embassy's efforts to talk the Japanese into war, Sorge grew certain that Japan would wait for the Germans to finish off the Russians before risking an invasion of eastern Siberia. They would then harvest the persimmons at minimal cost.[53] Well-equipped Soviet troops, including men accustomed to foul Siberian conditions, fell upon the German armies stalled before Moscow. The fighting was hard and lasted for over a month. The Germans retreated, but it was not a rout. For any advantage accruing from this victory was thrown away when Stalin ordered a series of poorly prepared offensives designed to propel German troops from Russia: the tragic consequence was nearly half a million further losses, at the expense of only eighty thousand Germans.[54]

There was a tragic individual footnote. In late October, Sorge's network was uncovered. Since he anticipated being shot if he fled to Russia, he and his colleagues were banking on setting up shop in Nazi Germany, without touching base in Moscow. Over the next three years, both he and his Japanese captors imagined that Stalin would trade him for a Japanese agent. Meanwhile, Sorge's Russian wife died in the gulag. The Japanese underestimated Stalin's desire to bury any inconvenient witnesses to his wilful misreading of events before the June 1941 invasion. Sorge was not released, but hanged in 1944 in Sugamo prison, although Russian streets were apparently named in his honour.

The failure of Operation Typhoon before Moscow was followed by several fractious scenes at Hitler's headquarters during the planning and execution of the 1942 summer campaign. When Halder responded sharply to what was tantamount to a charge of cowardice, Hitler exploded: 'Colonel-General Halder, how dare you use language like that to me! Do you think you can teach me what the man at the front is thinking? What do you know about what goes on at the front? Where were you in the First World War? And you try to pretend that I don't understand what it's like at the front. I won't stand that! It's outrageous!'[55] Circumstances forced a number of changes among senior German commanders. Field Marshal Rundstedt was dismissed, while Reichenau, one of Hitler's most ideological generals, suffered a heart attack shortly after assuming command of Sixth Army, and then was killed in an aircrash as he was being flown back to Germany.

Having parried the over-ambitious Soviet winter counter-offensives, Hitler scaled down his plans for the 1942 summer campaign. This was indicative of how things had changed since the vast three-pronged thrusts of mid-1941. He opted for a major push southwards towards the oilfields of the Caucasus, with a simultaneous punch eastwards to encircle Soviet forces on the Don. He could then either dispatch this army south to Astrakhan or direct it northwards towards the rear of Moscow.[56] The latter was what Stalin imagined the Germans were up to, even after a freak aircrash delivered German plans into Russian hands. He refused to believe they were genuine.

At first, Operation Blue, which commenced in late June 1942, proceeded as planned. But within a month Hitler decided to rewrite its scope to include the capture of Stalingrad as well as the eastern Black Sea coast and the whole of the Caucasus rather than just its oilfields. Hitler connived with Stalin in transforming the struggle for the city which bore the latter's name, and which was bound up with his early history, into a real and talismanic battle of wills. Having already vowed to raze Leningrad and Moscow to the ground, Hitler proclaimed his intention of murdering all Stalingrad's male citizens and deporting women and children, on the ground that its 'thoroughly communistic inhabitants were especially dangerous'.[57] This was to be no ordinary battle.

While Hitler entrusted command of Reichenau's Sixth Army to Friedrich Paulus, a colourless middle-class military bureaucrat with scant combat experience, Stalin summoned Marshal Georgi Zhukov, whose military career stretched back to the First World War and included the Russian and Spanish Civil Wars, the Battle of Khalkin-Gol in Mongolia, and latterly the defence of Leningrad and the repulse of the Wehrmacht before Moscow. It was not an even match.[58] With a keen eye for enemy weaknesses, Zhukov devised a plan which involved holding Stalingrad while launching a massive pincer movement to isolate Paulus' Sixth Army from potential relief.[59] It was the first of what were to be a succession of Soviet operations planned with enormous care and thoroughness, conceived on an ever vaster scale.[60] Responsibility for retaining Stalingrad itself fell on General Vasiliy Chuikov, a thick-set jolly Russian with a mouthful of gold teeth, who had moved rapidly up the Red Army ladder during the 'command vacuum' of the 1930s. His disastrous role in the campaign against Finland seemed to check his progress, and he was sent to China as a military attaché. Conscious of black marks in his copybook in a culture which frequently punished failure by firing squad, Chuikov rose to the occasion, with the wider strategic dispositions in the hands of the brighter Zhukov.[61]

With a record acquired the previous year of brutal depredations against Ukrainian civilians (entire cities were starved and so-called partisans hanged) as well as complicity in the murder of Ukrainian Jews, the Sixth Army set off to dislodge the Red Army from Stalingrad into the Volga.[62] Whereas a year before they had enjoyed the bountiful produce of the Ukraine, deliberately denied to the starving inhabitants of Kiev and Kharkov, next to whom they settled like uniformed locusts, they now crossed the barren and inhospitable steppe, fitfully followed by herds of cattle, and with instructions to live off a land that bore nothing. The railway links were repeatedly cut by Russian saboteurs.

At the end of the line stood one of those bleak and windswept Soviet cities, with its back to Asia. The city was comprehensively bombed on 23 August by six hundred German aeroplanes, with forty thousand civilians killed.[63] The military consequences of this were distinctly mixed, since it created an untraversable killing ground amid the ruins. Tanks proved to be of limited use in a town whose elongated shape and huge factories, grain elevators and railway stations made a decisive blow difficult, while providing ample cover for its defenders even when gutted or in ruins. Tank crews spent hours pounding shells into buildings, prevented by limited gun elevation from bringing down the upper floors, while unable to make much impact on the enemy scurrying around in the cellars and sewers. Around every corner lurked a Russian tank or artillery piece, while from above came grenades and the Luftwaffe's own bombs, which did not distinguish friend from foe. Supplied from the opposite river bank, the Soviets stayed within hailing distance of their German opponents, to minimise the value of German airpower, while maximising their own skills at close-quarter combat with grenades, tommy guns and knives. Their sharpshooters were so adept that the Germans felt obliged to call upon the services of the super-sniper Heinz Thorwald, head of the sniper training school at Zossen; after a few days and nights during which Thorwald shot several Russians, he momentarily revealed his position under a sheet of metal in no-man's land, and was duly killed by his Soviet counterparts.[64] The Soviets fired shells and salvoes of Katyusha rockets from the east bank of the Volga, over the heads of the pockets of Russian soldiers in the city and on to the Germans in the city centre. At night they ferried over reinforcements, including fit young guardsmen: 'All of them young and tall, and healthy, many of them in paratroop uniform, with knives and daggers tucked into their belts. They went in for bayonet charges, and would throw a dead Nazi over their shoulder like a sack of straw. For house to house fighting, there was nothing quite like them. They would attack in small groups, and, breaking into houses and cellars, they would use knives and daggers.'[65] The intense heat of the summer gave way to the first chill of autumn air.

Sixth Army exhausted itself in countless major and minor offensives in the ruins of the city, never apparently latching on to the strategy of working its way along the river bank from both north and south to cut the Russians off from the 'ant heap' of activity across the Volga. Back in Moscow, Sixth Army's fate was being sealed. In the Kremlin on the morning of 13 November, Zhukov outlined to Stalin the finely tuned plans he had been developing for a massive counter-offensive. According to Zhukov, the meeting went well, with Stalin silently puffing on his pipe and stroking his moustache to signal his approval.[66] Stalin concluded the meeting with the words: 'Return to Stalingrad tomorrow morning and make a check that troops and commands are ready to start the operation.' Enormous care was taken to deceive the Germans about Soviet intentions, while documents and interrogations of prisoners revealed the poor morale of German and Romanian forces. At 6 a.m. on 19/20 November, the Russian defenders of Stalingrad heard the muffled thud of gunfire through the foggy dawn. Zhukov had launched a vast pincer offensive, codenamed Uranus, whose effect was to encircle Paulus' forces, cutting them off from outside relief at a depth that facilitated the manoeuvring of Russian reinforcements against any approaching hostile force. Stalin had quietly abandoned the mindless offensives of the earlier part of the war in favour of the hitherto heretical notion of deep operations.

Instead of encouraging Paulus in his initial desire to evacuate the city as quickly as possible, Hitler ordered him to stay put. The three hundred thousand troops in Stalingrad were to be supplied from the air, even though the Luftwaffe was in no position to airlift the minimum daily requirement of five hundred tons of fuel, food, medicines and munitions. Göring airily and irresponsibly talked up what the air force could deliver. Manstein was brought in as commander of the new Army Group Don. He also insisted that Paulus remain in Stalingrad until relief came in the shape of Operation Winter Tempest, consisting of the bulk of Fourth Panzer Army under Hermann Hoth. With Hitler refusing and Paulus reluctant to countenance a simultaneous breakout, Hoth's armoured thrust petered out against a Soviet pre-emptive strike codenamed Operation Little Saturn.[67]

The effect of these operations was to leave a quarter of a million men cut off from all hope of relief, without adequate supplies, and encircled by superior forces, under a dysentery-ridden commander whose strongpoint was not initiative in a crisis. As weather conditions deteriorated, and the Soviets took the airfields, the supplies landed inside the 'Cauldron' dwindled to a hundred tons a day, with a corresponding reduction in the numbers of wounded making the return journey. With the capture of Gumrak airfield, supplies had to be dropped in canisters, with soldiers lying down in cross-shaped formations in a pitiful attempt to give these measures some semblance of accuracy. Although the pre-Stalingrad record of Sixth Army suggests they were far from being blameless victims expended by a callous and incompetent leadership, the ordinary soldiers obviously underwent a protracted and terrible ordeal which it would be churlish to disparage. Men with complicated stomach wounds were simply set aside to die by overworked field surgeons, since lengthy operations were a luxury and their stretchers would take up too much space in relief flights. Fingers, toes and ears damaged by frostbite were amputated with minimal anaesthetic and no aftercare.[68] With their clothing infested by fleas and lice, and mice running over their faces at night, sometimes eating frozen toes, the soldiers of the Sixth Army had also to deal with hunger. Letters home spoke of how, having adjusted to a diet of horsemeat, they were next reduced to cooking cats: 'The day before yesterday we slaughtered a cat. I can tell you, although I would never have thought it possible, it tasted wonderful.' Men made lame jokes about being so thin that they could dress and undress behind a broom handle as their thoughts focused on a small piece of bread.[69] Food became an obsession. In a letter to his mother dated 8 December 1942, a soldier wrote:

> Because of supply problems, our rations have been halved. Some days there is only fifty grams of bread, which means a bite in the morning and a mouthful in the evening. Since yesterday, the daily bread ration has been raised to two hundred and fifty grams. Everything depends on the weather, since when it is foggy our transport planes cannot fly because of the danger of freezing up. Lunch isn't what it should be for this time of year. Thin as water. One sits at meals, already thinking about the next meal. . . . Every crumb of bread, which before one would have swept off the table, has become precious. I've never learned the value of bread as I have during recent weeks. Potatoes, yes, potatoes, seem to me like images in a dream! The soil here yields nothing edible: only steppe.[70]

On 15 January 1943, a young soldier called Hermann wrote:

> Cold and hunger wear down even the best soldiers. Just like last year, the number of cases of frostbite on feet and hands has risen. The Russians are dropping a lot of propaganda leaflets, and each day call upon us to surrender since our position is hopeless. But we're not entirely without hope, even if we can see that we have no meat to eat. We've still got our two horses, but then that's that. We've even cooked lungs ourselves, simply to have something in our stomachs. I eat only once a day – at midday. After I've spooned down my watery soup, I quickly swallow my bit of bread with sausage or butter, then I eagerly await tomorrow's lunch.[71]

Christmas and New Year were evocatively burdensome when spent in a dimly lit bunker or a frozen hole in the ground, listening to the Christmas carols which the Russians malevolently broadcast through loudspeakers. Writing on 30 December 1942, a soldier described the homesickness and loneliness they were all experiencing:

> This year we had a sad Christmas without mail or a tree, no candles, indeed nothing that signified Christmas at all. I don't know how often I heard the words Germany or home spoken on Christmas Eve, but it was very frequent. I am lying in a bunker with a twenty-two-year-old. The lad cried on Christmas Eve like a child, I tell you we all had tears in our eyes when we heard there was no mail. Although I am only just twenty-one myself, I gritted my teeth and said: 'perhaps the mail will come tomorrow', even though I didn't believe this myself.[72]

While the National Socialist leadership purveyed the myth of Sixth Army heroically expiring in battle like the Spartans at Thermopylae, the reality was an immense number of men starving to death in miserable makeshift shelters. The erstwhile spearhead had degenerated into an atomised mass of hungry beggars. Remonstrating with a Luftwaffe officer on 19 January 1943, Paulus said: 'As commander of an army what should I say when a man comes to me and begs: Herr Colonel-General, a piece of bread? It's already the fourth day on which the men have had nothing to eat. . . . We can't retake a position any more, because the men are collapsing with exhaustion. . . . The last horses have been eaten. . . . Can you even imagine that soldiers are falling upon the old corpse of a horse, cutting off the head and eating the brains raw?'[73] On 31 January, the Russians closed in on Paulus' headquarters in the Univermag store. A German officer hailed a young Russian lieutenant with the words: 'Our big chief wants to talk to your big chief.' After protracted exchanges, Lieutenant Yelchenko was admitted to the building, where he came across Paulus, lying sick and unshaven on an iron bed. Yelchenko said: 'Well, that finishes it.' The forlorn Field Marshal Paulus nodded in agreement. Ninety thousand German soldiers and their Romanian confederates emerged blinking from their bunkers to face the whim of their captors. Those not killed on the spot began the long march into captivity, from which six thousand would return alive a decade later from confinement in Soviet labour camps.

Wider Soviet offensives that winter, and the successful German counter-thrust at Kharkov in mid-March, resulted in mutual exhaustion and a ragged front line, whose most anomalous feature was the Soviet salient around Kursk. This salient preoccupied military planners on both sides during the lull in fighting brought on by the spring thaw.[74] Opinion on the German side was split between advocates of back- and forehand strategies. In the former scenario, the German army would await an inevitable Soviet breakout from the salient, for the reconquest of the Donets and Ukraine was surely too tempting a target, wearing them down with countless defensive battles before launching their own limited offensive. The forehand strategy, which enjoyed Hitler's support, involved concentrating Germany's rather diminished resources for a limited offensive while the Russians were still refitting after the winter. Similar debates took place on the Soviet side. While Stalin advocated a full-scale offensive, many of his commanders pressed for an attritionist, defensive posture prior to a massive counter-offensive. In the end, these commanders prevailed.

Hitler's constant postponement of what was codenamed Operation Citadel was prompted by his worries about an imminent Allied landing in the Mediterranean, and the conflicting counsels of his generals. Having studied reconnaissance photographs of the Soviet defensive positions, General Model requested more tanks. Heinz Guderian, the new Inspector-General of Armoured Troops, who could see no point in an offensive in the East that year, muddied the waters further by arguing that the new tanks coming on stream, such as the Panther and Tiger, needed further evaluation before being committed in such a crucial battle. These protracted debates and the ensuing instructions were closely monitored by the British codebreakers at Bletchley Park, so that Hitler's final decision to authorise Citadel reached Stalin rather more quickly than it did his own generals.

These delays enabled the Soviets to develop their response very carefully. The Red Air Force, which specialised in the artillery-style air offensive, disposed of nearly three thousand aircraft at Kursk, including the formidable Ilyushin Il-2m3 equipped with anti-tank bombs and cannon which could rip through most armour. Over forty dummy airfields, replete with fake aircraft and control towers, confused the Luftwaffe as to where the real Red Air Force strength lay. On the ground, the Kursk salient was turned into a fortress. The Soviets laid over a million mines, at a density of about one per foot, and set up five hundred miles of barbed-wire entanglements, some of it electrified. Complex networks of trenches, gun emplacements and wide anti-tank ditches, built with the help of three hundred thousand civilians, completed the conversion of the salient into a formidable series of obstacles, whose defensive echelons stretched back over a hundred miles. At the points where they anticipated German attacks, the

Russians had as many as 150 heavy guns per mile. Much of the build-up of over a million troops took place at night, under strict blackout and with disembarkation away from obvious targets such as stations. Communications were limited to ten-second bursts of radio traffic impossible to intercept. Partisans were let loose on the German railways, with each attack causing bottlenecks and hence tempting targets for Soviet bombers. The equivalent of one thousand linear kilometres of railway were disabled, drastically reducing the one hundred thousand tons of supplies the Germans needed every day.[75]

After much prevarication, Hitler finally set 4 July as the date for Citadel, on a battlefield the size of Wales. Various attempts were made to disguise the timing, including ostentatiously dispatching Manstein to decorate Antonescu in Bucharest, and then quietly flying him straight back to the Kursk front. Both British intelligence and German deserters gave the Russians the exact day and time of the attack, enabling Zhukov to launch a massive artillery barrage at 2.20 a.m., ten minutes before the German artillery strike. The German advance when it came reflected the mistake of waiting months for the latest types of armour. Many of the new Panther tanks belched flames from their exhausts before grinding to a halt with burned-out engines. Clusters of heavily armed Tigers could blast the lighter T-34s at long distance, but were easily outmanoeuvred or surrounded, or were susceptible to a shell (or ramming) at point-blank range. Perhaps equally worryingly, German radio interceptors noted that, in contrast to what they had experienced in 1941, Russian commanders were not signalling their superiors with the panicky refrain: 'Am under attack, what should I do?'[76]

The most decisive engagement during this vast battle took place on the southern bend of the Kursk salient in the orchards and wheatfields of the small town of Prokhorovka. German armour under General Hoth, including such fearsome formations as 'Totenkopf', 'Das Reich' and the 'Leibstandarte Adolf Hitler', penetrated the Soviet front before exhaustion and Russian resistance forced them to a halt. Both sides paused, with the Russians committing a fresh tank army from their reserves to meet Hoth's attack. The two armies collided hull to hull on the morning of 12 July oblivious to the thunderstorms overhead. The battlefield was so tight (about three square miles) and the concentration of armour so dense that both commanders rapidly lost control of their formations, as tanks careered around in the wheatfields, churning up clouds of dust to add to the exhaust fumes and explosions.

Any advantages of weight and firepower enjoyed by German armour were lost in point-blank combat against an enemy that never gave up, and whose tank drivers (including women) steered according to the directions indicated by the tank commander's feet resting on their shoulders. Over three hundred German tanks were destroyed alone that day. Russian veterans admit to taking few prisoners in a fight where neither side gave or expected any quarter. By nine o'clock that night the battle was over. Any lingering doubts about where the strategic initiative now lay were over too, as Soviet offensives became bolder, and largely dictated the pace of events.

CRIMES WITHOUT WAR

The military history of the German invasion of the Soviet Union barely conveys the prolonged nightmare which enveloped that empire; nor does it explain the hatred which added a special viciousness to the conflict on both sides. Many wars include instances of brutality and inhumanity, especially when they involve irregulars, but this is rarely either premeditated or systemic. The German campaign in the Soviet Union was both. As a final reckoning between two antagonistic dictatorships, and a biologistic campaign against Bolsheviks, Jews, Gypsies and Slavic 'Untermenschen', the war in the East had a fundamentally different register from that in the West. The line between conventional and ideological warfare was erased long before the fighting commenced, and then compounded by conditions on the ground. This applied to the treatment of captured enemy combatants or enemy civilians. These themes will be discussed in turn below.

A few bleak facts and comparisons may illustrate the fate of Soviet prisoners of war. During the First World War, some 1,434,500 Russians were captured by the German army; 5.4 per cent of them died in captivity. Between the 1941 invasion and 1945 some 5,700,000 Red Army soldiers were captured by the Germans and their allies; 930,000 of these men and women were recovered alive from German prisoner-of-war camps in January 1945. As many as one million further prisoners had been released during the war, many of them more or less voluntarily serving the Wehrmacht in either combat or auxiliary capacities. Another half a million had managed to escape or had been liberated by the Red Army. The remainder, consisting of about 3,300,000 prisoners (or 57.5 per cent of the original total), had died in captivity. The record of German prisoners of war in Soviet hands was equally bleak, although not statistically commensurate. Of the 3,155,000 men captured, 1,185,000 (or 37.5 per cent of the total) died while in captivity. By contrast, of the 232,000 British or American soldiers in German hands, 8,348 (or 3.5 per cent of the total captured) had died by 1945.[77]

The juridical relationship between Germany and the Soviet Union was unclear, which probably 'legitimised' German atrocities at a level so academically rarefied that it is irrelevant. Since law in general was a bourgeois anachronism, the Soviet Union had not ratified the 1929 Geneva Convention on prisoners of war, nor had it expressly acknowledged the 1895/1907 Hague Laws of Land Warfare. Stalin also declined the offices of the Red Cross. Although this meant that the German government considered itself bound by no international obligations towards Russia, this was not strictly juridically true, since both sides were bound by well-established conventions of warfare as they had evolved since the early modern period. These stipulated that prisoners of war were entitled to humane treatment; with clothing, food and shelter roughly on a par with that enjoyed by one's own reserve army troops. Matters were therefore not quite as ill defined as the Germans maintained. The Soviet Union had also ratified the 1929 Geneva Convention on treatment of captured enemy wounded. One should also note that Soviet attempts to subscribe formally to the Hague Convention in July 1941 via Swedish intermediacy were deliberately frustrated by the Nazi leadership.[78]

Those involved have advanced more or less cogent reasons why such an immense proportion of Soviet prisoners of war died. The system was suddenly overloaded by vast numbers of prisoners. Soviet soldiers had low levels of resistance because the Red Army had been operating in areas where Stalin had ordered the destruction of all plant and foodstuffs. Atrocious weather and epidemic diseases devastated the prisoner population. All of these things were partially true, but they fall well short of the whole truth.[79] What is missing is human agency and intentionality within this exculpatory fog of contingent circumstances.

In a war which was meant to be won in weeks, the treatment of prisoners was accorded low priority. Military planners knew that massive battles of encirclement would yield commensurately large numbers of captives. The huge number of prisoner fatalities was therefore firstly a product of decisions to keep the majority of prisoners in Russia, in areas which were being systematically stripped of resources to feed the German army, and where in order not to impair German military effectiveness provision of food, shelter or transport would be minimal. This was compounded by another salient feature of

National Socialist thinking, namely that entire peoples were ascribed different racial values. This view of things was carried over into its treatment of prisoners of war as well as of the burgeoning foreign labour force. British and American prisoners were treated relatively well, not least because their governments would have carried out reprisals against German prisoners, Flemings were treated better than Walloons, Frenchmen better than Poles and so on. Russians occupied almost the lowest rung in this hierarchy, being regarded as expendable. Instructions on the treatment of Russian prisoners of war, issued on 16 June 1941, were saturated with National Socialist ideology, and were designed to prohibit even minimal human relations between prisoners and their guards or German civilians. Any signs of 'resistance' were to be 'ruthlessly eradicated'. This was a world away from the relatively decent conditions experienced by British or American prisoners of war in Germany. In the case of the Russians, there was no reciprocity.

Since the ruthless exploitation of Russia's resources was intrinsic to Hitler's war aims and to the maintenance of both military and domestic morale, the deliberate starvation of the enemy population, including prisoners of war, was built into the planning of the invasion and occupation. If German civilian planners such as Herbert Backe could countenance the deaths of 'x-million people through starvation' with all too evident equanimity, so their military equivalents had resolved that Red Army prisoners would receive rations well below the minimum necessary to sustain life. Red Army prisoners received 20 grams of millet or bread per day as they trudged forlornly back through Belarus. In August 1941 these *ad hoc* arrangements were replaced by consolidated rations equivalent to 2,100 calories per day for prisoners who worked and 2,040 for those who did not. These levels were rarely attained except in the paper world of military bureaucrats. In September, a committee chaired by Göring decided that in order to stabilise or improve the wartime rations of the German civilian population it would be necessary to reduce the rations of 'Bolshevik prisoners'. Unembarrassed by his own pinguidity, he also made a few off-the-cuff suggestions about eating cats and horses.[80] Soon after, the Quarter-Master General Eduard Wagner reduced the rations of non-working prisoners to 1,500 calories per day, that is two-thirds of the minimum necessary to stay alive. The effects of this were catastrophic. Even the commandants of concentration camps complained that 5 to 10 per cent of the Russians they were sent were actually half dead or dead on arrival, thus presumably denying them the task of murdering them. In a prisoner-of-war camp in Silesia, men were eating grass, flowers, raw potatoes or each other. Columns of hungry and exhausted men were lucky if their route passed crops such as sugar beets, rotting because the refineries had been blown up during the Soviet retreat. A German industrialist visiting the Ukraine to organise the takeover of a steel plant recorded:

> Endless columns of prisoners passed by. In one case, there were 12,500 men guarded by only thirty German soldiers. Those who were unable to walk were shot. We spent the night in a small village because we were stuck in the mud. There we found a transit camp, where we witnessed how at night the prisoners cooked and ate their comrades who had been shot by our sentries for indiscipline. The prisoners' food consisted of potatoes from the villagers. Each man received at most two potatoes a day.[81]

Russian prisoners walked to captivity partly because the Soviet railway network was widely cast, but also because those in charge of returning empty trucks and wagons steadfastly refused to have them occupied by dirty, lice-ridden prisoners. This meant that prisoners had to march distances of over five hundred kilometres, driven on by guards who shot them by the wayside when they could go no further. This was sometimes done in full public view, as for example in Smolensk in October 1941, where 120 Soviet prisoners were mown down in the town centre. It made a very poor impression on the civilian population, with word of beatings and shootings spreading like wildfire. The Axis war correspondent Curzio Malaparte, who wrote much of his book *Kaputt* while in the Ukraine, has left us a haunting description of the fate of a group of Soviet prisoners. On one occasion he was present at what were cynically dubbed 'lessons in the open' in a collective farm, or *kolkhoz*, attached to a village near Nemirovskoye. A group of Soviet captives were lined up in the farmyard, soaked through by the incessant rain. Some were big, crop-haired farmboys; others lean, stern-looking artisans and engineers. A short, corpulent German corporal, employing the benign tones of a schoolmaster, began to set them a reading test. Those who passed would work as clerks; those who failed would work in the docks or on the land. Old copies of *Izvestia* and *Pravda* were distributed to groups of five men, who then read from the sodden newsprint. The majority who failed to read fluently were sent to the left; the literate minority passed to the right. All of which was accompanied by much jocularity on the part of the prisoners, with calls of 'Clerks!' or 'Stones on the back!' from the respective groups, and arch asides by their captors. And so it went on for about an hour until eighty-seven men were on the left and thirty-one on the right. The latter group were then marched off to a wall where they were shot by the waiting SS. The colonel in charge explained: 'Russia must be cleared of all this learned rabble. The peasants and workers who can read and write too well are dangerous. They are all Communists.'[82]

Some German commanders, such as General Tettau, ordered a stop to these practices; others, such as Reichenau, positively encouraged them. When the winter made marches impossible, the prisoners were shipped in open railway goods wagons. This brought no relief since their trains had low priority, and moved at a snail's pace as civilian and military bureaucrats in the occupied territories exchanged cables, letters, memoranda and telephone calls regarding the appropriate forms and permissions. If their trains halted in towns and villages, they might also be fortunate enough to fight one another over potatoes and bread thrown in by sympathetic civilians. Many simply froze to death. In one case, one thousand men died on a train somewhere along the two-hundred-kilometre journey from Bobrujsk to Minsk. The use of covered cars made little difference since these were unheated. In early December 1941, it was reported that 'between 25 and 70 per cent' of prisoners were dying in transit.[83]

The prisoner-of-war camp system was multi-layered. In front-line areas, prisoners were confined in Army POW Collection Points; in rear areas in POW transit camps (Dulags); and in civilian- or Wehrmacht-administered territories in Stalags and Oflags for respectively men and officers. Conditions in these camps were atrocious. In so far as preparations had been made, these involved fencing off open-air sites. Penned in, prisoners were handed a few implements (including cooking pots) with which to dig holes in the ground which they then covered with whatever materials were available. Huddled together in the summer heat or freezing cold they were prey to lice, pneumonia, typhus and other diseases. Hitler expressly declined a Red Cross offer of vaccination materials. The SS volunteered the simpler solution of shooting the sick prisoners. Maltreatment of prisoners was condoned and encouraged by the army leadership. In a summary of regulations governing treatment of prisoners, General Reinecke began with the bald statement 'Bolshevism is the deadly enemy of National Socialist Germany.' Every soldier was to maintain his distance from and display a 'correct' coolness towards these prisoners. Any dissent was to be dealt with instantly with the bayonet, riflestock or a bullet. There was a shoot-to-kill policy in the case of escapees, with no shouted warnings or warning shots. Order within POW camps was to be preserved by a selected group of Russian prisoners armed with clubs and whips. In a bizarre endeavour to distinguish between military violence and brutality, Reinecke stipulated that German troops were not allowed to use either.[84]

These directives were a relatively late addition to an earlier complex of criminal orders designed to transform the invasion of Russia into an ideological war against 'Jewish Bolshevism' rather than a conventional military conflict. They are important since the general removal of legal restraints meant that the only source of decency was human conscience. We must go back some months to uncover the lines of responsibility. While the war's moral parameters were determined by Hitler, they were given authority, detail and legality by senior Wehrmacht officers, notably Halder. Of course, the politicisation of the German army was an ongoing affair rather than something that suddenly occurred in the context of the invasion of Russia. Senior German soldiers had aided and abetted the murder by the SS of Röhm and his associates in 1934, and senior officers had ordered the 'eradication' by the military police of Communists in the Sudetenland in 1938 or the summary shooting of Czech and German political exiles by the regular army in France in 1940. Some of them also tacitly approved the depredations of the Einsatzgruppen in Poland, or like Jodl, Keitel or Reinecke were actively involved in disseminating National Socialist ideology for military consumption. The expansion of the officer corps from 3,800 in 1935 to 35,000 professionals (and equivalent numbers of reservists) by 1941 may well have diluted and subverted their core values, in the twofold sense that the new recruits were merely functional professionals bereft of external moral reference points, while simultaneously sheer numbers and social dilution made the enforcement of informal codes of behaviour through close contact between social equals more difficult.[85] The Wehrmacht did not arrive in Russia either 'unpoliticised' or with an unblemished record.

Although planning for Barbarossa had commenced in June 1940, directives on the conduct of the war began to flow only after March 1941, as if Hitler wished to see how the initial decision was received before revealing just how far he was about to go in realising his ideological objectives. Dealing with a traditionalist body of men who had to be handled carefully, he preferred to introduce his own values, by stages, a few at a time. Sketchy preliminary directives passed back and forth between Hitler and his senior generals from December 1940 to March 1941, with Jodl raising the question of collaboration with the SS in the 'rendering harmless' of Bolshevik cadres and commissars, and hence the exclusion of these people from military jurisdiction. At two conferences attended by military leaders on 17 and 30 March 1941, Hitler's stark views on the conduct of this war were recorded, and internalised, by Halder:

> The intelligentsia appointed by Stalin must be exterminated. The leadership apparatus of the Russian empire must be destroyed. The use of the most brutal violence is necessary in the Greater Russian region. Ideological ties do not really hold the Russian people tightly together. It will collapse if one gets rid of the functionaries.[86]

Speaking to 250 senior officers in the Reich Chancellery on 30 March, and tactically confining his remarks to political rather than racial issues, Hitler gradually revealed the cards from the deck on his table, pitching his remarks in a way that would appeal to his thoroughly anti-Communist audience:

> Communism is a tremendous danger for the future. We must get away from the standpoint of soldierly comradeship. The Communist is from first to last no comrade. It is a war of extermination. If we do not regard it as such, we may defeat the enemy, but in thirty years' time we will again be confronted by the Communist enemy. We are not fighting a war in order to conserve the enemy. . . . Fight against Russia: destruction of the Bolshevik commissars and the Communist intelligentsia. . . . It is not a question of courts martial. The leaders of the troops must know what is involved. They must take the lead in the struggle. The troops must defend themselves with the methods with which they are attacked. Commissars and the GPU people are criminals and must be treated as such. That does not mean that the troops need get out of hand. The leader must draw up orders in accordance with the sentiments of his troops. The struggle will be very different from that in the West. In the East toughness now means mildness in the future. The leaders must make the sacrifice of overcoming their scruples.[87]

Although some of those present later claimed to have been outraged by aspects of this two-and-a-half-hour talk (waiting for Hitler to leave the room before murmuring their responses), the reality was that they hurried away to turn his words into legal forms, in so far as they had not independently initiated similar measures already. In contrast to the campaign in Poland, Barbarossa witnessed early and harmonious co-operation between the military and the security forces. On 26 March – that is four days before the conference at which Hitler spoke – the Quarter-Master General Wagner came to an agreement with the Chief of the Security Police and SD, Reinhard Heydrich, which was endorsed and issued as an order by Field Marshal Brauchitsch a month later, regarding the operational space to be allotted to the four SS Einsatz-gruppen which were assembling at their base in the Police School at Pretzsch. Under the terms of this agreement, 'On Co-operation with the Security Police and SD in the Eastern War Which Is Envisaged', the latter were empowered to carry out 'executive measures' against enemy civilians involved in 'anti-German and anti-state activities' in army group areas, and a rather more restricted range of functions in army rear and operational areas.[88] In other words, activities which had appalled some German officers in Poland, including ironically Wagner himself, were to be tolerated on a much vaster scale, against a deliberately loosely defined group of victims, provided this did not interfere with military operations. This may have been a way of keeping the Wehrmacht's uniform clean, but its effect nonetheless was to leave it looking very shabby. This was not the only instance of formal military and SS co-operation.

With the role of the SS carefully defined, so as to preclude any disputes about respective competences, army commanders next turned to the question of military jurisdiction. The latter applied only to disciplinary matters within the German army. In other words, hostile civilians, including those who distributed leaflets or refused to obey a German order, were denied any rights, and indeed could be killed with impunity by German soldiers without resort to legal process and merely subject to the approval of an officer. As the drafts of this directive did the rounds, Halder insisted on including collective repri-sals against places where it was impossible to establish quickly the identity of an individual sharpshooter or saboteur. This reflected a long Prussian tradition of extreme measures against suspected enemy irregulars which has so far not been properly investigated. Clearly aware of the dark forces that these orders could unleash, the High Command tried to re-establish some vestiges of control by prohibiting arbitrary individual outrages lest they lead to anarchy and the moral brutalisation of all and sundry. This was a case of having one's cake and eating it. A revised final version of this directive was authorised by Keitel on 13 May 1941.[89]

The final element in this complex of criminal orders was the so-called Commissar Order of 6 June 1941. Modern German research has demonstrated that senior generals, including once again Halder, formulated this infamous directive, by which civilian and military Communist Party functionaries were to be identified (by their starred, hammer-and-sickle lapel badges) and murdered by the army either on the spot or in rear areas. Effectively, the army was assuming the functions hitherto performed by the Einsatzgruppen: the killing of an entire group of people solely by virtue of their membership of that group and without formal process. The general intention, essayed earlier by both the Nazis and the Soviets in occupied Poland, was to destroy the ruling elite of the country concerned on the assumption that they were the bearers of national consciousness. Inevitably, there were weasel attempts to justify this in terms of the 'asiatic-barbarian' manner in which such cadres would treat German prisoners, or by arguing that the Red Army would swiftly disintegrate without these political fanatics. Ironically, Stalin had virtually phased out the commissars as an unnecessary hangover from the Civil War. The supposed cruelty of the enemy – which was real enough in some instances – justified the Wehrmacht's indiscriminate, systematic and wholesale resort to carnage. These measures were also quietly extended to so-called 'politruks', that is more lowly Party functionaries attached to individual companies.[90]

Since it was not unknown for lower-level officers to ignore the Commissar Order, and hence for 'commissars' to filter back into the POW camp system, in mid-July 1941 a conference was convened to deal with this problem, whose participants included General Reinecke and SS-Gruppenführer Müller of the Reich Security Main Office. Although the Abwehr representative Lieutenant-Colonel Lahousen mentioned both the ill-effects on military morale of the shooting of commissars (and the resultant effect upon Soviet readiness to capitulate), Reinecke argued that the officer corps had to abandon the ethics of the 'ice age' in favour of National Socialist values.[91] Sensing an opportunity, Müller volunteered the services of the SD both to identify potential victims and to kill them at one remove from the military. According to directives issued on 8 September, POW camp commandants and their intelligence officers were to co-operate with the SS security agencies. Suspects were to be weeded out from the camps, with the aid of informers, and shot at some suitable remove. The foreign branch of the Abwehr raised objections. These methods contravened international law; and would affect military discipline and morale. They would give the Russians a propaganda victory on a plate; and would mean that the Wehrmacht would be formally responsible for people another agency was killing. Approving and covering these measures, Keitel explicitly rejected the Abwehr's hankering for outmoded 'chivalrous warfare'. These agreements and directives necessarily involved, and indeed stipulated, smooth co-operation between the POW camps and the SD. However, matters were not always so smooth in practice.

The general drift towards officially licensed, and potentially inflationary, criminality was rounded off by the broad brushwork of the 'Guidelines for the Conduct of the Troops in Russia' issued in May 1941, part of which read:

> This struggle requires ruthless and energetic action against Bolshevik agitators, guerrillas, saboteurs and Jews, and the total elimination of all active or passive resistance. The members of the Red Army – including prisoners – must be treated with extreme reserve and the greatest caution since one must reckon with devious methods of combat. The asiatic soldiers of the Red Army in particular are devious, cunning and without feeling.[92]

These orders were fed down the chain by senior commanding officers, several of whom unreflectingly elided Jews with Bolshevism. Thus, on 2 May 1941, General Erich Hoepner, who would end his days in 1944 swaying from a length of piano wire following his involvement in the Bomb Plot, wrote:

> The war against Russia is an important chapter in the struggle for existence of the German nation. It is the old battle of the Germanic against the Slav peoples, of the defence of European culture against Moscovite–asiatic inundation, and the repulse of Jewish Bolshevism. The objective of this battle must be the destruction of present-day Russia and it must therefore be conducted with unprecedented severity. Every military action must be guided in planning and execution by an iron will to exterminate the enemy mercilessly and totally. In particular, no adherents of the present Russian–Bolshevik system are to be spared.[93]

Field Marshal von Reichenau gave his directives a more explicitly hardline antisemitic edge on 10 October 1941:

The main aim of the campaign against the Jewish–Bolshevist system is the complete destruction of its forces and the extermination of the asiatic influence in the sphere of European culture. As a result, the troops have to take on tasks which go beyond the conventional purely military ones. In the eastern sphere the soldier is not simply a fighter according to the rules of war, but the supporter of a ruthless racial ideology and the avenger of all the bestialities which have been inflicted on the German nation and those ethnic groups related to it. For this reason, the soldiers must show full understanding of the need for the severe but just atonement being required of the Jewish subhumans.[94]

And so did Field Marshal Manstein, who relayed Reichenau's orders to other armies in his group, and General Hoth, whom we have already encountered, who in November 1941 instructed his troops:

Every sign of active or passive resistance or any sort of machinations on the part of Jewish–Bolshevik agitators are to be immediately and pitilessly exterminated. . . . These circles are the intellectual supports of Bolshevism, the bearers of its murderous organisation, the helpmates of the partisans. It is the same Jewish class of beings who have done so much damage to our own Fatherland by virtue of their activities against the nation and civilisation, and who promote anti-German tendencies throughout the world, and who will be the harbingers of revenge. Their extermination is a dictate of our own survival.[95]

Estimates of how many commissars were killed range between 140,000 and 580,000.[96] That the Commissar Order was widely implemented is not doubted, even by those who draw attention to low-level exceptions within larger military formations. The one alleged large-scale exception to this rule, namely General Hans-Jürgen von Arnim's 17th Panzer Division, is apparently contradicted by the evidence of his divisional record. Sometimes, moral indignation was combined with overt antisemitism – the two were not mutually exclusive – as reflected in the remarks of another panzer officer, General Lemensen, regarding the shooting of prisoners of war, deserters and criminals:

This is murder! The German Wehrmacht is waging this war against Bolshevism, but not against the united Russian peoples. We want to bring back peace, calm, and order to this land which has suffered terribly for many years from the oppression of a Jewish and criminal group. . . . A Russian soldier who has been taken prisoner while wearing a uniform and after he put up a brave fight, has the right to decent treatment. . . . This instruction does not change anything regarding the Führer's order on the ruthless action to be taken against partisans and Bolshevik commissars.[97]

On a lower level, there is evidence that individual officers disapproved of the ways in which the SS went about selecting political and racial 'undesirables' among prisoners of war. In November 1941, the commandant of Dulag 185 at Mogilev, Major Wittmer, refused to hand Jewish prisoners of war over to an Einsatzkommando, which resulted in a formal complaint from its commander to SS-Obergruppenführer Erich von dem Bach-Zelewski. The Major said that he had no orders to hand over Jews, and as far as he was concerned that ended the matter. He also disapproved of another of this SS officer's local initiatives, the instant liquidation of all young males who could not explain what they were doing on the roads, on the ground that they were *a priori* 'asocial' or 'partisans'. The SS officer conceded in his report that Wittmer had no hesitation in having mutinying Soviet prisoners summarily shot, but he needed to evince more ideological resolution on the 'Jewish Question'. Nothing appears to have come of his refusal to co-operate with the Einsatzkommando or of the complaint to Bach-Zelewski.[98] A further example of obvious Wehrmacht discomfiture with the activities of the SS comes from Bavaria. Captain Wilhelm H. was an Abwehr officer in the POW camp Stalag VIIA at Moosburg between 1939 and March 1944. In September 1941 he was instructed to co-operate with a team of Gestapo men from Munich who would be arriving to select victims from among the camp's fifteen hundred to two thousand Russian prisoners. Asked by Wilhelm H. how he proposed to do this, given that he knew neither Russian nor anything about its political system, the Gestapo leader said that this was none of the Captain's business. What actually counted was numbers, the fulfilling of quotas, percentages and targets. Soon, two hundred Russians were *en route* to Dachau. The Gestapo leader later complained to another army officer Major Meinel that his men were psychologically finished by the shootings they had carried out, thus giving the game away as to the fate of the Russian prisoners in Dachau.[99]

We know relatively precisely what happened to Russian prisoners of war once they reached the concentration camps Buchenwald, Dachau, Flossenbürg, Gross-Rosen, Mauthausen, Neuengamme, Sachsenhausen and Auschwitz. At Sachsenhausen, the Inspector of Concentration Camps Theodor Eicke explained to camp staff that Hitler had decreed that eighteen thousand Soviet commissars were to be shot in retaliation for shootings of German prisoners in Russia. They met their end in circumstances which reek of deviousness and moral squalor. A shower room in one of the barracks was equipped with a height-measuring device whose sliding head-level concealed a slot through which prisoners were shot in the back of the neck by men concealed in a box behind the wall.[100] In Buchenwald, Russian captives were taken to a converted riding stables, undressed and led individually into a medical examination room. Blaring music from a gramophone drowned out the sound of what followed from the next group of victims. Members of 'Kommando 99', dressed in medical white, man-oeuvred the victim to a measuring device through which concealed shooters killed them with a 7.65mm pistol. Non-Russian prisoners then had precisely three minutes to remove the corpse and to hose down the walls and gutters. Each shooter killed eight people in succession (thus emptying their magazines), and the action only paused to allow for the clearing of the mortuary after every thirty-five to forty victims.[101] In Mauthausen, the Russians were issued with soap and towels and then gassed in pseudo-shower chambers; in Auschwitz or Gross-Rosen they were killed by an injection of phenol or hydrocyanic acid administered to the heart by doctors or medical orderlies. Other uses for Soviet prisoners included an incident at Zhitomir in August 1941 when a group of them were shot with captured Red Army dum-dum bullets so that German military doctors could accurately observe, and write up, the effects of these munitions on the human body.[102]

While no serious scholar contests the premeditated and systemic criminality of the war in Russia, it would obviously be misleading and unfair to argue that it was all-pervasive. Nine or ten million German men fought on the Eastern Front for more or less longer periods of time. Their experiences were myriad: changing tank tracks and servicing engines; more or less passive and prosaic occupation duties; the nerve-wracking pursuit of partisans in forests and swamps; intense firefights bringing and giving death or serious injury; captivity or desertion; as well as politically or racially motivated mass murder on a scale that is incomprehensible. A modern account by the eminent scholar Omer Bartov emphasises such factors as the general demodern-ization of warfare on this front; the ways in which massive casualties destroyed the loyalties of micro, primary groups, leaving soldiers with nothing to identify with other than the macro group of race and nation; the interplay between extremely harsh military discipline and the sanctioning of atrocities against civilians and enemy prisoners; and, finally, the fact that 'Hitler's Army' had massively internalised the dictator's racist perspectives.[103] Other accounts, which seek to correct an over-schematic translation of ideological fanaticism into action, themselves run the risk of distortion, by highlighting essentially anecdotal instances of 'slipper soldiers', who having lost all vestiges of martial bearing or purpose sat by the stove drinking vodka with the local partisan commanders.[104] The reality of the Eastern Front may not be best captured simply by splitting the difference between these positions.

Accounts which stress ideological fanaticism emphasise the degeneration of a modern mobile war into one of demodernised attrition in conditions that often resembled the Western Front in 1914–18. Casualty rates were enormous. During the first six months of fighting, the army in the East lost three-quarters of a million men, rising to a million casualties by March 1942, of whom a quarter were killed or missing. The crack Gross Deutschland Regiment began the campaign six thousand strong; by the end of 1941 it had sustained 4,070 casualties; by February 1942 it consisted of three officers and thirty other ranks. By December 1941, 6th and 7th Panzer Divisions comprised respectively 180 and 200 men, while 18th Panzer Division numbered four infantry battalions.[105] Such massive casualty rates meant that formations increasingly consisted of hurriedly assembled strangers, lacking the close regional or social bonds which normally knitted soldiers together. In the face of obvious enemy superiority in generalship, materials and manpower, the German troops were held together by ferocious military discipline that punished even minor infractions, let alone desertion, panic or self-mutilation, by firing squad. Some fifteen thousand men were executed by courts martial on the Eastern Front, with hundreds of thousands more sentenced to penal battalions or terms of imprisonment. This should be contrasted with the forty and one hundred British and French soldiers respectively executed during the Second World War.[106] The problem with relating these general factors to racial atrocities is that the latter were pre-planned, and commenced once German troops and policemen crossed the frontiers, and hence cannot be ascribed to the subsequent deterioration or demodernisation of the German army.

Compensation for draconian combat discipline consisted of virtual licence to do with others what one liked. German troops practised self-help by simply stealing food, livestock, draught animals, wagons, clothing and felt boots, regardless of the hardships this entailed for the civilian population. Even the pack animals were fed with the straw from the roofs of peasant houses. Soldiers also indiscriminately looted the contents of houses, as is evident from a report in November 1941 from Rear Area 582: 'The items stolen include, for example, scarves, cushion covers, tablecloths, handtowels, men's trousers, curtain material, men's jackets, all types of cloth, men's coats, bedspreads, samovars, wristwatches, children's underwear and clothing, mourning-dress, women's and children's shoes, women's clothing, ladies' under-wear, etc.'[107] In some places, the scale of what vanished suggests a form of organised criminality. Thus during late 1941 in Witebsk, 188 cows were stolen, as well as 15 tonnes of salt, and a million sheets of plywood. In other places the military vandalised plant and machinery, or destroyed such resources as fishstocks by fishing with handgrenades, in what were forms of delinquency. The slightest resistance was dealt with by extreme violence.

Military brutality was also influenced by the conditioning these soldiers had undergone both while growing up in Nazi Germany and in the form of ideological instruction during their time in the army. Although one should exercise due caution when discussing such an enormous number of men, from different backgrounds, generations and political or religious persuasions, it would be surprising if many of them did not ardently believe in *Volk*, Reich and Führer, in Germany's superior right of conquest and dominance, or in the cultural and racial inferiority of other peoples. Such sentiments were common to many peoples at the time, and it is both anachronistic and a form of inverse racism to imagine that Germans were somehow immune to them. Nor did the Germans have a monopoly of hatred of the enemy. In a 1942 article entitled 'The Justification of Hatred', the Soviet war correspondent Ilya Ehrenburg proved adept at the dehumanising stereotyping of the enemy:

> This war is unlike former wars. For the first time our people face not men but cruel and vile monsters, savages equipped with every techni-cally perfected weapon, scum acting according to rule and quoting science, who have turned the massacre of babies into the last word of state wisdom. Hatred has not come easily to us. . . . We hate the Nazis because we love our country, the people, humanity. In this lies the strength of our hatred and also its justification. When we encounter the Fascists we realize how blind hatred has laid waste the soul of Germany. That kind of hatred is alien to us. We hate every Nazi for

being the representative of a man-hating principle, we hate him for the widows' tears, for the crippled childhood of the orphans, for the pitiable hordes of refugees, for the trampled fields, for the annihilation of millions of lives. We are fighting not men but automata in human likeness. Our hatred of them is the stronger because outwardly they appear to be men, because they can laugh and pat a dog or a horse, because in their diaries they indulge in self-analysis, because they are disguised as human beings, as civilised Europeans.[108]

It is not hard to find evidence of the 'master race' mentality among the ordinary German soldiery, especially if one looks in quasi-official Nazi compilations of opinion. However, such propaganda works were designed to show that the army was solidly behind the worldview of their Führer. Hence collections of letters from soldiers, if that is what they really were, recycled for propaganda purposes, are unsurprisingly suffused with racism, as when a private wrote home in August 1941:

What would have happened to cultural Europe, had these sons of the Steppe, poisoned and drunk with a destructive poison, these incited sub-humans, invaded our beautiful Germany? Endlessly we thank our Führer, with love and loyalty, the saviour and historical figure.

A lance-corporal wrote:

Only a Jew can be a Bolshevik, for this blood-sucker there can be nothing nicer than to be a Bolshevik. . . . Wherever one spits one finds a Jew. . . . As far as I know. . . . not a single Jew has worked in the workers' paradise, everyone, even the smallest blood-sucker, has a post where he naturally enjoys great privileges.[109]

The suffusion of these letters with crude Nazi racial hatreds and their relentless uniformity of outlook should give us pause for thought, or at least prompt us to go through the archives of the publishers to see whether these letters were real or undoctored. Letters recently discovered in Moscow, which came from captured German military post offices, prisoners of war or the dead, spoke a rather different, more personal language, as these men thought about their families or the prospect of violent death in the weak light of candle-lit bunkers.

The overwhelming majority of these letters, many of them painstakingly written by men for whom grammar, spelling and the articulation of emotion were an unaccustomed effort, were concerned with what was happening at home. These men did not write about Jews or any Russian civilians; they wanted news from their parents, wives, girlfriends, siblings and children, or they imaginatively recreated what they were themselves missing. When they discussed the war, this largely took the form of describing physical exertions and privations such as forced marches, lack of food and shelter, or problems of personal hygiene. Their world had literally shrunk to what was making their legs itch or their stomachs rumble. The enemy did not figure especially large in these descriptions, except as an unwelcome element of danger that periodically intruded into the permanent quest for food and warmth. In a letter to a friend dated 18 November 1942, a soldier called Ernst gave a vivid account of life in a hut in the suburbs of Stalingrad:

> Dear Ludwig!
> The spectre of the Russian winter has not yet appeared – perhaps it is still on the way from the far kirghiz steppe? We can still take − 16 degrees. The day before yesterday it snowed for the first time, while tonight the wind turned a downpour into ice. I ventured out today – it was classic – like going skating. Nothing much was missing, and a vehicle had crashed into a ditch.
> Thank God, the onset of cold weather means we've seen the back of swarms of flies. It still hums with them, however these 'flies' are not affected by the seasons, and the Bolsheviks certainly not.
> We've taken up quarters in a hotly contested suburb of Stalingrad. Hopefully, we'll spend the winter in solid huts we are doing up. First, we've given the hovels a thorough clean, since dirt is considered a social virtue in this paradise. We've hammered and sawed away, swinging the paint brush too, so that the interior now seems pleasant. The stove gives out a cosy warmth. We sit here in our corner in the evening, which makes being here bearable. As soon as we moved into the hut, the guerrilla war against lice and fleas commenced in earnest. How it itches and pinches, creeps and crawls, burning your skin when the enemy attacks. Each morning begins with a battle of extermination, and then all through the day a tearing one's shirt away from the body to hunt them more freely. Despite washing it's impossible to get rid of these brutes.[110]

Having covered the weather and fleas, Ernst turned to the Russians. His comments on 'der Russe' were not without grudging admiration:

> Stalingrad still has not fallen. You may well have been wondering about that. We don't since we are hard by the edge of events. The Russian fights ferociously over every metre. Naturally, Stalin has deployed his elite troops here, i.e. almost exclusively political commis-

sars and officers. They each have to be done to death. And also the Russians have a masterly grasp of how to camouflage and defend themselves in the ruins of the city. The battle has already cost much blood. Still, by the end of this year, the west bank will have been cleaned out.

As the war progressed, the predominant sentiment was to return home alive. As Herbert, another soldier, wrote to his parents in January 1943:

> I will be pleased if I don't see this thrice-damned Russia ever again since in time it is enough to finish off anyone. Like almost all of my comrades I only have one wish: to get out of this workers' paradise and never to hear of it or see it again. We all have only one desire: peace and quiet and enough to eat, and then they can all kiss our arses.[111]

Others reflected on life, death and salvation in what amounted to pre-combat final testaments. In January 1942 a soldier called Sim wrote to his sister about matters he did not wish to share with his pregnant wife Lottel lest it adversely affect her health. Recently transferred to combat duties, this deeply religious man wrote:

> There is a reason why I am writing this letter to you, in the eventuality that God does not pass me by with the bitter chalice of death, for then, as soon as you receive the news, you can relay this letter as my farewell greeting above all to Lotte, but also to all the others . . .
>
> Believe in Jesus Christ – there is no one else who can remove the sting of dying. God knows how very close I am to Lotte and Klaus. It feels like a sword piercing my heart when I think about you all, and that I may not see you again, and what distress Lotte and you will feel, what bitterness and grief!. . . . But I know that if we do not see each other on Earth again, we will see each other when Jesus Christ summons us to the last judgement. I need to say all this to you, both to remind and warn you not to dismiss this message out of hand, never betraying our Lord, and living according to how the Lord of life and death revealed in the Scriptures. If this is not the case, then we will never see each other again, then death will really be a hideous visage, and then one's entire life will have been a pointless egotistical struggle.[112]

OTHER PEOPLE'S WARS

Warfare is not simply a matter of battles and weapons, but the pursuit of politics by other means. The supra-military aim of the war in the Soviet Union was to realise a vision of territorial expansion, bringing long-term economic security and perpetual racial renewal in its wake. It was not fought simply to isolate the British or to secure oil. Within the vision there were many different emphases, and indeed variant visions, which were more pragmatically sensitive to circumstances in the Soviet Union. The political influence exerted by their proponents, and such variable factors as the course of the war itself, also affected German debates about the future of the occupied eastern territories. Although some historians have concentrated on the 'modernising' destructive fantasies of sundry middle echelon technocratic planners, it is important to remember that other Germans, not least in the army, had a relatively subtle grasp of the political realities of the Soviet empire, and advocated other policies.

Hitler's views on Russia were characteristically unsubtle. Judging from his *Table Talk*, the record of his nightly ruminations on prehistoric dogs or an Aryan Jesus and such random *obiter dicta* as 'tarts adore poachers', delivered to a largely captive audience, he was simultaneously drawn to, and repelled by, 'the East', that shorthand term for that undifferentiated vastness that lay beyond Germany's eastern border before 'it' metamorphosed into the Orient. His constructive fantasies included huge roads raised on ridges so that the icy winds would clear the snow, while the traffic passed Kreis' tenebrous monuments to the (German) dead; or double-decker trains speeding gay German Labour Front holidaymakers to the beach resorts of the Black Sea. The 'space' would be settled and shaped by veteran soldier–farmers from Germany, together with Danish, Dutch, Norwegian and Swedish settlers in the north 'by special arrangement'. The settlers were to enjoy large farms; officialdom handsome headquarters; with 'palaces' for the regional governors. German colonial society would be a literal and metaphorical 'fortress', closed to outsiders, since 'the least of our stable-lads must be superior to any native'. The negative features of this vision predominated, with crassness commingled with callousness. Although Hitler repeatedly and explicitly took British rule in India as his exemplar – 'Our role in Russia will be analogous to that of England in India.... The Russian space is our India. Like the English, we shall rule this empire with a handful of men' – his notion of colonial rule was like something he had read in a lurid book about the more squalid British (or German) African colonies than about centuries of complex British involvement in the sub-continent, which left its imprimatur on everything from cuisine to cricket.[113] The Russians were 'a mass of born slaves, who feel the need of a master'. Outsiders (that is, the Germans) had introduced the principle of organised society to peoples accustomed to behaving in the anti-social manner of 'rabbits'.[114] Uncivilisation was to be encouraged: 'no vaccination for the Russians, and no soap to get the dirt off them. . . . But let them have all the spirits and tobacco they want.'[115]

Callousness and crude exploitation characterise virtually everything Hitler said about Russia. On 17 October 1941 he remarked:

> We're not going to play at children's nurses: we're absolutely without obligations as far as these people are concerned. To struggle against the hovels, chase away the fleas, provide German teachers, bring out newspapers – very little of that for us! . . . For the rest, let them know just enough to understand our highway signs, so that they won't get themselves run over by our vehicles![116]

Economic intercourse would be of the most rudimentary kind, a matter of scarves and glass beads for the natives:

> At harvest time we will set up markets at all the centres of any importance. There we will buy up all the cereals and fruit, and sell the more trashy products of our own manufacture. . . . Our agricultural machinery factories, our transport companies, our manufacturers of household goods and so forth will find there an enormous market for their goods. It will also be a splendid market for cheap cotton goods – the more brightly coloured the better. Why should we thwart the longing of these people for bright colours?[117]

Future rebellions would be suppressed by dropping 'a few bombs on their cities'; while, *mutatis mutandis*, every year a 'troop of Kirghizes' would be paraded through Berlin 'to strike their imaginations with the size of our monuments'.[118] Although there was nothing here except a desire to destroy, exploit and overawe, this dystopian vision would set the parameters for policy in occupied Russia.

A crucial meeting held on 16 July 1941 between Hitler, Bormann, Göring, Lammers, Keitel and Rosenberg illustrated the deciding voice of Hitler in questions of major policy. The meeting ran from three in the afternoon until eight at night, with one break for coffee. Hitler began by expressing his annoyance with a Vichy newspaper which had had the temerity to suggest that the invasion was a 'European war', the implication being that there would also be European dividends for the clients of the victors. He insisted that there was no need to make German goals explicit, 'the important thing is that we ourselves know what it is we want'. There were to be no self-limiting public declarations of policy; 'all the necessary measures – shootings, resettlement etc. – we will and can do despite this'. There was to be no 'seesaw policy' (*Schaukelpolitik*), but rather the remorseless pursuit of a single goal, permanent German hegemony and the eradication of any other military power west of the Urals. He had learned this singlemindedness from the English, who in India also showed how they never staked all on any given indigenous ruler. No Slav, Chechen, Cossack or Ukrainian was to be allowed to carry a gun. In this 'Garden of Eden' bombers would suppress revolts, and any Slav who even looked askance at a German could be shot dead. Keitel and Göring joined in the tough talk. Göring brushed aside Rosenberg's interjections about culture and universities of Kiev as fripperies which got in the way of the primordial quest for food; Keitel spoke of individual and collective reprisals for sloppiness or failure to prevent acts of sabotage. Control visibly slipped away from Rosenberg as more forceful players messed up his personnel plans for the dominion he notionally ruled as Minister for the Occupied Eastern Territories. Thanks to Göring, and Hitler who made the final dispositions, the lapsarian Marxist Erich 'the Red' Koch rather than Sauckel was dispatched to the Ukraine.[119]

Since a number of Russian historians, including those with Soviet sympathies, have conceded that the Germans missed 'a fortuitous opportunity to separate Stalin from the Soviet people', alternative options are not simply an exercise in right-wing wishful thinking, even if they largely remained unrealised because of the political weight against them.[120] Some Germans displayed an informed understanding of the unpopularity of Soviet rule, and of the profound ethnic and religious fissures in many parts of that vast empire. There were also diplomatic considerations, such as Finnish fellow feeling for the Estonians or Turkish concern for the (Moslem) peoples of the Caucasus, which exercised an ameliorating influence around the margins of German policy.[121] Some German policy-makers thought in terms of driving a wedge between the Kremlin and the Russian population along the lines of the slogan 'Liberation, not Conquest'. Others shared Hitler's rampant russophobia, but combined this with an appreciation of the ethnic heterogeneity of the Soviet Union. Rosenberg envisaged a protectorate over Lithuania, Latvia, Estonia and Belarus; an enlarged and notionally independent Ukraine; some sort of Caucasian federation; and, corralled by this *cordon sanitaire*, a revived but reduced 'Muscovy', whose expansionary dynamic would be redirected towards Asia and which would serve as a dumping ground for 'undesirables'.[122]

The Ukraine has had a bad press in Western circles for whom it is virtually synonymous with concentration-camp guards or the SS 'Galicia' Division, whose formation in 1943 many Ukrainian nationalists actually opposed. Others calculated that in the coming chaos it was essential to have a Ukrainian army of some sort. The former Soviet Union sedulously criminalised the entire Ukrainian diaspora, many of whom fought in American or Canadian armed forces, largely because until 1953 it had to contend with Ukrainian guerrilla fighters. Two million Ukrainians also fought in the Red Army. These elementary facts need to be borne in mind. They are easy to establish, if one is vaguely curious about other people, rather than keen to relay pernicious stereotypes.

The overall fate of the Ukraine during the Second World War was appalling, since it was a primary battleground. Some seven hundred cities and towns and twenty-eight thousand villages were destroyed, and nearly seven million people were killed, including virtually all Jews. There were obvious practical reasons why Ukrainians collaborated with the Germans, beyond bread and salt receptions laid on by antisemites for the Nazi invaders. In 1931–3, between five and seven million people had starved to death in a terror famine, after the Communists seized the 1932 harvest and then denied aid to the Ukraine. People attempting to reach regions where food was abundant were prevented from doing so. They ate bark and rats and eventually each other instead. The journalist Walter Duranty and the playwright George Bernard Shaw were among the leading Western deniers that this had even happened.

As the Soviets pulled out in 1941, often with fleeing Communist Party officials in the van, their security agencies liquidated thousands of nationalist leaders, and wrecked the country's infrastructure through a policy of scorched earth. The Dnieper hydro-electric plants, blast furnaces and mines were largely ruined. Since the Ukrainian Soviet government was relocated to Ufa in the Ural Bashkir republic, there was an immediate leadership vacuum. Various German agencies had longstanding contacts with Ukrainian émigrés who were grouped in moderate Andrei Melnyk and intransigent Stepan Bandera factions of OUN, the Organisation of Ukrainian Nationalists. These factions were known as OUN-M and OUN-B. When Bandera's supporters declared a Ukrainian state, centred on Lviv, on the back of the German invasion, this lasted all of a week, with Bandera himself being arrested and deported to Germany. Galicia did not become the nucleus of a Ukrainian state, but rather a province added to the German-ruled Polish Government General. Neither Poland nor the Ukraine was to enjoy statehood under Nazi auspices. In order to nullify Polish statehood through the promotion of ethnic antagonism, Ukrainian cultural autonomy was encouraged in Galicia by the Germans, while paradoxically it was ruthlessly repressed in rump Ukraine itself. Parts of the southern Ukraine were handed over to Romania which it ruled as 'Transnistria', while Erich Koch set up shop in the small town of Rivne, rather than Kiev, to underline the nullity of Ukrainian statehood, just as his colleague Hans Frank's Polish capital was Cracow rather than Warsaw.

In the autumn of 1941, the SS violently suppressed both OUN factions, executing the mayor of Kiev and a leading poetess. The nationalists went underground as the Ukrainian Insurgent Army (UPA), which fought a complex triangular war against the Germans and against Soviet and Polish partisans, a war which was still going on eight years after liberation happened in western Europe. Despite having no external source of support akin to the French resistance or the Soviet partisans, between thirty and forty thousand Ukrainians waged their own war against both the Germans and the Soviet partisans. In the western Ukraine, the UPA fought a vicious war against the Polish underground Home Army, in which thousands of civilians were slaughtered. Now that Ukraine and countless other states have their freedom, their particular experiences of the Second World War may cease being subsumed within that of the Soviet Union.[123]

The non-politically active Ukrainian majority had to survive as best they could. Collaboration was not as straightforward a case of treason as in western Europe, since most Ukrainians had little or no loyalty to earlier Polish or Soviet governments. Collaboration represented a chance to restore a statehood they had only briefly experienced before under German auspices during the First World War. The urban population had no choice other than to work for the Germans, for the alternative was starvation, since the Germans controlled access to food. As for the peasantry, in so far as they could produce food at all, with partisans destroying dairies, grain storage depots, machinery and herds, they faced constant German demands for foodstuffs. The consequences of refusal were a warning, then a whipping, and then having their homes burned down while they and their families were shot. The Ukraine also bore the brunt of ruthless labour procurement policies. It may have been politically convenient for the Soviet Union to regard all collaborators as 'alien' nationalists who had slipped back from exile, but this was certainly not how the returning Communist Party initially saw things, when in November 1944 it registered that Ukrainian collaborators had included over fifty-seven thousand of their own members.[124]

In the Baltic States of Estonia, Latvia and Lithuania, the Germans similarly encountered peoples with historic grievances against Russia and the Soviet Union, beginning with Tsarist suppression of their languages and ending with NKVD death squads. During their occupation of the Baltic States in 1940–1, the Soviets killed or deported an estimated 34,250 Latvians, nearly 60,000 Estonians and 75,000 Lithuanians in the interests of 'sovietising' these subtly distinctive societies.[125] Harking back to an ahistorical version of the Hansa and the Teutonic Knights, the Nazis thought of 'germanising' the 'racially suitable' members of the indigenous population coupled with extensive German colonisation and the deportation of 'undesirables'. Those nationalists who thought the Germans had come as liberators were quickly disappointed. On 24 June 1941, after German tanks had arrived in the night, Lithuanian nationalists in Vilnius established a Citizens Committee in anticipation of independence. A rather irritated German official reported to Lieutenant-General Wilhelm Schubert that the nationalists were acting as if they were 'absolutely equal partners in the territory liberated from the Russians' and 'as if the Germans had only gone to war with the Russians in order to liberate Lithuania and to grant it independence'. The official had rapidly disabused a certain Professor Jurgutis, the Foreign Minister of former Lithuania, of any dreams of independence, sharply reminding him who was boss.[126] As German casualties in the East mounted, the issue of enhanced Baltic autonomy and future independence became intertwined with the establishment of Baltic SS units, with the Latvians and Estonians offering to co-operate in return for political concessions. The latter came to naught.

German rule in occupied Soviet territory consisted of giant areas of military and civilian control. Behind the front lines, with a depth of fifteeen to twenty-five kilometres, lay the 'Army Rear Areas' of another fifty or so kilometres, and then a hundred kilometres more of the 'Army Group Rear Areas'. Military occupation policy depended on the officers in charge, the attitude and composition of the population, and whether German interests were short or long range, extensive or limited. Thus in Army Group Centre's Rear Area officers such as Schlabrenndorff, Gersdorff and Tresckow actually rebuilt primary and specialised schools, while in the Caucasus, where Hitler's interest was limited to oil, officers slipped into place by Stauffenberg at OKH (Army High Command) restored religious freedom to Buddhists, Moslems and Orthodox Christians, while accelerating the conversion of the *kolkhozy* into co-operatives.[127] Lest one purveys too roseate an impression of military rule, it is important to remember that the concessions to minorities were not extended to Gypsies, Jews or the mentally ill, who were systematically slaughtered, or to the surrounding majority populations, who along with the non-Russian minorities were subjected to the full depredations of an army that lived off what they produced.

Behind these necessarily labile layers of military administration lay two enormous civilian-controlled Reich Commissariats, notionally subordinated to Rosenberg's Berlin-based Ostministerium (OMi), whose sobriquet 'Cha-ostministerium', or 'chaos ministry', reflected its improvised incoherence. Rosenberg was only notionally in control of either Koch in Rivne (or rather in Königsberg, where he preferred to reside) or Hinrich Lohse in Riga, since these unreconstructed Party bullies enjoyed direct access to Hitler. Screaming sessions, and the construction of coalitions to outdo one another at the highest level, characterised the relationship between Koch and Rosenberg, a relationship mirrored in the Baltic in the simultaneous feud between Lohse and his nominal subordinate in Tallinn, Generalkommissar Litzmann. Further inroads into Rosenberg's fictive empire were made by Göring's multinational economic agency; Sauckel's forced labour procurement agency; Speer's munitions apparatus; and Himmler's grim racial warriors, the Higher SS- and Police Leaders, whose orders came directly from Berlin.

The quality of the German administration in the field was not high, with a huge influx of abrasive bullies and losers from the more populist branches of the NSDAP, who were accurately described by the term 'Ostnieten' or 'eastern nobodies'. Guidelines telling them how to behave are instructive. Germany lacked England's long imperial tradition of transforming young people into 'Führernaturen'. The Germans were to be 'comradely among themselves, responsible to their superiors, and authoritarian towards their subordinates'. One must not explain oneself to a Russian for 'he can talk better than you since he is a born dialectician and has inherited a philosophical disposition', and Germans should conceal their own mistakes. The Russians were effeminate and sentimental, which was why they had pleaded with every foreign conqueror, 'Come and rule over us!' The Germans were to show no weakness, in the form either of tears or of convivial over-indulgence, and were to be totally impervious to either 'charm' or 'corruption, denunciation and byzantinism'. The Russian could stand just about anything: 'since his stomach is flexible, no false pity'. It was no use whining to superiors: 'Help yourself, then God will help you!'[128]

The reality of occupation officialdom was far removed from these injunctions to personal austerity. Modestly endowed German bureaucrats could strut about, whip in hand, among the 'natives', or 'niggers' as Koch called them. Secretaries in the bloated administrative capitals enjoyed salaries that were three times those of an army lieutenant. Corruption was rife, with the Ukraine becoming the 'junk market of the Reich'. German officials and their families acted as conduits for commodities such as salt, cheap jewellery, unfashionable shoes and garish dresses sent by their relatives in the Reich, which were then exchanged with the Ukrainians for eggs, oil, bacon and ham, which they dispatched, illegally, via rail or post back to the Reich.[129] In the sticks, fourteen thousand agricultural leaders – as these upwardly mobile former farmers were called – braved the partisans in order to be mistranslated by their interpreters, or misled by Soviet collective farm functionaries and resentful Russian or Ukrainian peasants.[130]

Germany had gone to war with one of the most ethnically and confessionally diverse societies in the world. This fact was potentially encouraging. Although half the Soviet population were ethnic Russians, and three-quarters Slavs, the remaining quarter of the Soviet

Union's population consisted of over a hundred different nationalities. It was here that national collaboration became a live possibility. Many of these peoples had substantive grievances against the Soviet regime, regarding Lenin's guarantees of national autonomy as worthless. A few examples must suffice. In the south, the Crimean Tatar Moslem clergy and intelligentsia were murdered in the 1920s and 1930s in an anti-intellectual and anti-clerical campaign, between thirty and forty thousand peasants were deported in the interests of collectivisation, and thousands died in the course of the 1931–3 man-made famine. By the time the Nazis arrived, half the Tatar population had been deported or destroyed, with the residual local intelligentsia and leadership liquidated during the purges.[131]

The ethnically Russian, yet distinctive, Cossacks were closely identified by the Bolsheviks with the Tsarist and White regimes, and hence were subjected to policies whose effect was to destroy their traditional way of life. Similarly repressive policies were pursued by the Bolsheviks towards the nomadic Mongolian Kalmyk herdsmen. The regime compelled the Kalmyks to settle, substituting clay huts for tents, while reducing individual ownership of livestock, a mark of social prestige, from treble to single figures. Five thousand Kalmyk intellectuals were liquidated, including the poet Amur-Sanan, and their Buddhist monasteries and temples were closed and pillaged. In the summer of 1942, the NKVD helped themselves to two million cattle, and Kalmyk guerrilla groups were formed shortly afterwards to prevent this.[132] Surely there was a legacy of hatred here which any invader could build on?

Initially, Hitler was adamantine in his opposition to using indigenous forces, other than as 'Hiwis' or auxiliary volunteers, who were deployed as non-combatant supply troops. The steady depletion of the German army in Russia gradually brought about a change in policy regarding indigenous combat troops, promoted by more enlightened officers in Foreign Armies East of the Wehrmacht High Command such as Reinhard Gehlen, Alexis von Roenne, Wilfried Strik-Strikfeldt and Schenk von Stauffenberg, who realised that the war in Russia also had to have a political dimension. Local commanders also improvised contingents of 'eastern troops'. Beginning with a directive dated 17 December 1941, six national legions were formed, of Armenians, Azeris, Georgians, North Caucasians, Turkestanis and Volga Tatars, consisting of fifteen battalions in late 1942 and another twenty-one battalions in early 1943.[133] There was also a three-thousand-strong

Kalmyk cavalry corps. This came about largely through the commitment of individual German officers, such as the forty-four-year-old former architect Dr Doll, whose swastika armband apparently reminded his Kalmyk troops of a Buddhist health symbol and who encouraged the Kalmyk rich in Elitsa to feed their poorer compatriots. Mayoral elections were held in Kalmyk settlements, collectivisation was immediately terminated, and individuals were allowed to own as much livestock as they wished. Their military effectiveness was limited to intelligence gathering and detecting acts of sabotage. Judging from reports on their daily activities, the Kalmyks' forte was checking railway lines for loosened or missing ties and concealed explosive charges which they then notified to the nearest German authorities, thus averting massive German military casualties.

Following Doll's death in July 1944, the Kalmyks were absorbed into a Caucasian formation of the Waffen-SS.[134] The Waffen-SS became the leading, if reluctant, supporter of indigenous forces, with its depleted ranks being more than replenished with Latvians, Estonians and, from 1943 onwards, Ukrainians. The SS also assumed control of indigenous auxiliary police and anti-partisan forces in the two Reichkommissariats, while Balts and Ukrainians released from prisoner-of-war camps received ideological instruction and SS training in the notorious Trawniki base established in October 1941, whence they would go on to operate death camps for Jews.[135]

Cossack troops were sporadically deployed on the Eastern Front by the Germans from the summer of 1941 onwards. The German 14th Panzer Corps was perplexed to discover that the Soviet Ninth Army they were attacking was being simultaneously assaulted by a mysterious force situated in their rear. This turned out to be Nicholas Nazarenko's Don Cossacks. A survivor of Soviet labour camps, Nazarenko indignantly told the Germans who wished to disarm his troops that he had been fighting the Bolsheviks since 1918. Another Cossack, Major Ivan Kononov, persuaded the entire Soviet 436th Regiment to desert to the Germans, largely it seems because the Bolsheviks had hanged his father and shot his mother during the last stages of the First World War. Keeping Cossack émigré leaders at arm's length, lest they seek substantive political changes, the Germans appointed one of their own as overall commander of Cossack forces. Helmuth von Pannwitz had grown up within sight of Tsarist Cossack troops on the Russo-German Polish border. A professional cavalry officer and Free Corps veteran, Pannwitz served with enormous distinction on the Eastern

Front and was rewarded with the task of organising the disparate
Cossack hosts. Apart from the support of Kleist and Zeitzler, Pannwitz
found an unlikely ally in the shape of the SS, whose race 'experts' now
decided that the Cossacks were not Slavs but misplaced 'Aryan' Goths.
Based at Mielau in East Prussia, Pannwitz organised a Cossack Division, replete with such exotic Atamans as Nicholas Kulakov, who
having lost both legs during the Civil War in 1920 spent the next
twenty years (carving wooden legs) hiding under his own house until
his liberation by German forces. The Cossack Division was then
entrained for Yugoslavia to fight the Balkan manifestation of the
Bolshevik menace.[136]

But collaboration was far from being the exclusive preserve of
either non-Russian or marginalised Slav ethnic groups such as the
Cossacks. Russian historians have only begun to explore the realities
of occupation that lurked behind the self-serving ideology of the Great
Patriotic War, whose bemedalled heroes would grimly preside over the
Soviet empire until 1990. An untold number of Communist officials
simply switched allegiances in a predictable demonstration of how an
amoral predeliction for control, power and terror outweighed any
nominal ideological antipathy.[137] About one million Russians also had
varying degrees of involvement with the German armed forces, the
majority being unarmed auxiliaries or 'Hiwis', but also up to a quarter
of a million combat troops, some of which we have already encountered. The various SS and police formations scouring the occupied
territories for Jews, Gypsies and 'partisans' would not have been so
effective had it not been for the agents and village mayors who helped
them. The most notorious instance of collaboration with the Germans
is associated with General Vlasov and the Committee for the Liberation of the Peoples of Russia.

Andrei Andreyevich Vlasov was born in 1900, into a peasant family
with thirteen children. As he wrote in his 'Open Letter' of March
1943, Vlasov was a typical product of the Soviet system, who had not
been personally 'harmed' by it in any way. He served in the Red Army
during the Civil War, rising quickly through the ranks to the post of
company commander. He joined the Communist Party in 1930, and in
1938 was sent to China to promote the Soviet dual strategy of support
for Chiang Kai-shek against the Japanese and for the Communists
against their own ally Chiang. He bravely commanded Soviet forces
during the breakout from Kiev and then in the defence of Moscow.
On 24 January 1942 he was promoted to lieutenant-general and

awarded the Order of the Red Banner. In the spring he was dispatched to the Volkhov Front, to command the Second Shock Army, which was intended to relieve the pressure on Leningrad. High-level disagreements about precisely who was in charge of the Front resulted in the encirclement of Vlasov's troops, who were then poorly supplied and forbidden to withdraw. Ordering his troops to disperse and survive as best as they could, Vlasov himself spent weeks wandering around in a forest.

Before his capture by the Germans in a hut on 12 July 1942, Vlasov probably turned over in his mind the factors which made him collaborate. According to the 'Open Letter':

> I realised that none of those things for which the Russian people had fought during the Civil War had been achieved by Bolshevik victory. I saw what a difficult life a Russian worker led and how the peasant was forcibly driven to join the collective farms. Millions of Russian people disappeared, having been arrested and shot without trial. I saw everything Russian was being destroyed, that time-servers were being given positions of command in the Red Army, people to whom the interests of the Russian nation were of no importance.[138]

He also had accumulated many negative impressions of Stalin's Russia, not least the deportation of people as kulaks for owning a cow; the lies one was supposed to live for the sake of personal advancement; the faces missing from the officer corps when he returned from China; and, finally, the lives expended on the Volkhov Front, and the fate awaiting any commander who had lost an army. Far from being an unreconstructed reactionary (antisemitism was after all something he shared with Stalin), Vlasov wrote that he wanted to 'complete the national revolution'.

Detained in a VIP camp at Vinnitsa in the Ukraine, Vlasov had a series of meetings with high-level German officials who were drawn to his suggestion of a Russian National Army to liberate the country from Stalinism. Paradoxically, many of these prisoners thought that they had more freedom in a Nazi prison camp than they had had as free men in the Soviet Union. Although German military propagandists were mainly interested in using Vlasov's name to encourage desertion from the Red Army, sympathetic German 'minders', notably Strik-Strikfeldt, indulged Vlasov's growing political ambitions by organising the distribution of his Smolensk Declaration and speaking tours of the occupied areas. The Smolensk Declaration was a curious combination of anti-Stalinism, liberal reform proposals and misrepresentation of Nazi policy. The guiding thoughts were eternal friendship and peace with honour with Germany, and happiness for the Russian people. Bolshevism and Stalinism were not only held responsible for the recent military disasters, but, in an eccentric inversion of Marxist theories that fascists were 'agents' of big business, were represented as being the instruments of Anglo-American capitalists bent on the economic spoliation of Russia. The description of Nazi goals in Russia was partial in the extreme:

> Germany, meanwhile, is not waging war against the Russian people and their Motherland, but only against Bolshevism. Germany does not wish to encroach on the living space of the Russian people or on their national and political liberties. Adolf Hitler's National Socialist Germany aims to organise a 'New Europe' without Bolsheviks and Capitalists, in which every nation is guaranteed an honourable place.[139]

The 'New Russia' would involve the abolition of the *kolkhozy*; restoration of private commerce and ownership; freedom of thought; social justice and workers' rights, including rights to employment, education, leisure and an untroubled old age. Attempts to convert these heady goals into reality through a Russian Liberation Army were stymied by the hostility of Hitler and Himmler to the idea of arming Slavs, a view apparently confirmed by high desertion rates among existing 'Eastern Troops'. Himmler seems also to have been incensed by a remark from Vlasov, whom he called 'a Bolshevik butcher's apprentice', to the effect that he would soon be playing host to the Germans in Russia. Vlasov was put on ice, in slightly sordid union with his second (bigamous) wife, the widow of an SS officer. As far as Hitler was concerned, the only legitimate function for Vlasov or the Red Army officers in the camp at Dabendorf was to encourage desertions from the enemy – quite literally in the run-up to Citadel, when for weeks the latter were deployed in Operation Silver Lining broadcasting to their compatriots through loudspeakers so powerful that they could be heard miles away. Hitler clearly saw that, if he allowed Vlasov an army, the General would use this to lever political concessions which totally contradicted Nazi war aims in Russia.

The worsening situation on the Eastern Front at least changed Himmler's mind. He met Vlasov in September 1944 and, favourably impressed by this tall and rather unworldly figure, authorised him to form a division of Russian troops and to publish a manifesto. This was made public in Prague, the last Slav city in German hands, although no prominent Nazi leaders turned up for the ceremony. In January 1945, Vlasov was given command of two severely depleted divisions which he wished to preserve for a future Anglo-American war on Soviet Communism, but which the Nazis regarded as cannon-fodder. Vlasov was detained by the Red Army while trying to reach American lines, and after torture and a perfunctory trial was hanged as a traitor in post-war Moscow. Broadly speaking, while the Nazis were willing to exploit 'native' forces opportunistically to make up for their own loss of manpower, this never translated into a change of policy towards the occupied Soviet Union. This does not lessen the personal tragedy of Vlasov and his supporters, who through choice and force of circumstances had to operate in the unforgiving zone between two murderous dictatorships.

Economic and military necessity, as well as ideological rigidity, also stalled attempts to reform the Bolshevik socio-economic order in ways which might have appealed to the mass of the indigenous population. As we have seen, Hitler's conception of future German–Russian economic relations was based upon colonial exploitation. Practical concerns ensured that there was no more than cosmetic tinkering with the institution of the collective farm or *kolkhoz*, while the state farms (*sovkhozy*) and tractor depots were simply taken over by the Germans. Crudely executed Russian-language propaganda posters depicted happy peasants liberated by German arms from the burden of collectivisation, entering with outstretched arms into a fabular world of 'the free farmer on his own land'.[140] In reality, decollectivisation, with all of the decentralisation and dislocation that entailed, would have massively complicated access to food, one of the reasons why the Bolsheviks had introduced collectivisation in the first place. As State Secretary Backe, one of the most vocal opponents of reform, remarked, if the Soviets had not established collective farms, the Germans would have had to do it for them.

Not everyone shared this view. A loose and heterogeneous group of pragmatists, consisting of diplomats, economists and intelligence officers, recognised the danger of alienating the rural population and pressed for reforms. These were eventually implemented on paper. The Agrarian Decree issued in February 1942 was an unsatisfactory compromise between these opposed views. It simply renamed the *kolkhozy* as *obshchinnoe khoziaistvo* (communal economies), which in an uncanny echo of Marxist deferred gratification were to be a 'transitional form' (*Übergangsform*) before the nirvana of wholesale reprivatisation.[141] The slogan was 'Have patience'. Minor concessions to the peasantry included granting their small household plots private and tax-free status, in usufruct rather than ownership, and unlimited livestock. These reforms were stymied by Hitler's hardline satraps in the East. Speaking in Rowno in late August 1942, Erich Koch said:

> There is no liberated Ukraine. Our aim must be that every Ukrainian labours for Germany, not that we benefit the people here. The Ukraine has to deliver what is lacking in Germany. If this people works ten hours a day, then eight of those hours have to be work for us. All sentimental reservations have to be set aside. This nation must be ruled with an iron fist so that it assists us in winning the war. We haven't liberated it in order to benefit the Ukraine, but rather to secure the living space and food base needed by Germany.[142]

Pre-invasion Nazi industrial strategy for occupied Russia envisaged the elimination through closure or transfer to Germany of all Soviet industry, with the exception of extractive industries such as coalmining and oil. The most primitive forms of colonial exploitation predicated on the exchange of Soviet raw materials for German manufactured goods ensued. The failure to achieve rapid victory meant that these simple ideas were superseded by a more nuanced approach, involving the reactivation of a growing proportion of Soviet industrial capacity. Both large and small Soviet enterprises were reopened or rebuilt in order to satisfy the demands of the German war machine. This was a slow process. Whereas in pre-war Minsk there had been 332 factories with a workforce of about forty thousand people, by October 1941 only 39 factories and 3,378 workers had been reactivated. Forms of multi-national control already evident in other parts of Nazi-occupied Europe were translated to the occupied Soviet Union. Overall economic control was exercised by Göring and his State Secretary Paul Korner through the Wirtschaftsführungsstab Ost, including also Backe, Thomas from the Armed Forces High Command, and Syrup from the Ministry of Economics. The fundamental goals of economic policy were set out in a memorandum dated 8 November 1941:

> The highest possible productive surpluses to supply the Reich and the remaining countries of Europe are to be achieved through cheap production and the maintenance of the low standard of living of the indigenous population. In this manner it will be possible not only broadly to satisfy the European demand for food and raw materials,

but also at the same time to provide the Reich with a source of income which will enable it to cover in a few decades a significant proportion of the debts it has contracted to finance the war while largely sparing the German taxpayer.[143]

Various mechanisms were used to harness the industrial economy of occupied Russia to German interests, including direct state ownership; mixed state and private-sector continent-wide monopolies for essential commodities; state and private trusteeships where the firms concerned operated a given plant on behalf of the state with the question of ownership indefinitely deferred; and, finally, direct private-sector control. Equally characteristic of the Nazi economy in general was the presence of major players from the German private sector in what were nominally state-controlled agencies and concerns. The latter were invited to become 'foster-parents' of Soviet firms, so that for example in August 1942 the IG Farben industrialist Paul Pleiger confirmed that the Krupp concern would assume control of the Asov Steel Works in Mariupol and an engineering works in Kramatorsk. A list of German 'foster-parents' reflecting the position reached in the coal and iron and steel industries by March 1943 included such firms as Bischoff in Recklinghausen, Dortmund-Horder, Krupp, Mannesmann, Siemens-Schuckert and Hoesch AG.[144] The standard business abbreviation 'GmbH' (company with limited liability) was soon cynically referred to as 'Greift mit beiden Handen' or 'grab with both hands'.[145]

By and large, levels of production were disappointing. Whereas pre-war annual Soviet coal production in the Donets Basin was 90 million tonnes, only 4.1 million tonnes were mined throughout the entire German occupation. Similarly, the iron ore mines of Kriwoi Rog produced about 12 per cent of what had been achieved under Soviet administration. Occupied Russia supplied the Reich with about one-seventh of what it gleaned from France. Ironically, whereas in 1940 Germany had imported 700,000 tons of barley under regular commercial agreements, in 1942 requisition yielded a mere 120,468 tons.[146] The Germans received far more raw materials from Stalin in peacetime than they did from the territory they occupied. According to informed observers such as Minister of Finance Schwerin von Krosigk, the restoration of production was hampered by massive over-bureaucratisation, as 'organisations, societies and constructions of every sort shoot out from the ground like mushrooms', and by the influx to the East of a small army of talentless German white-collar workers who then paid themselves vastly inflated salaries while their 'native' subordinates did the work. Instead of yielding surpluses to alleviate the Reich's mounting debt, the occupied Soviet Union was actually having to be subsidised.[147] Further reasons for low Soviet productivity were not explored in this memorandum. Whereas the German occupiers at least had to consider a coherent policy towards the peasantry, industrial labour warranted no such consideration, beyond whether or not to export it forcibly to Germany. That a Russian miner worked at 50 to 60 per cent of the capacity of his German counterpart was not attributed to his receiving an eighth of the latter's wages.

Although, as we have seen, some marginal elements in the German regime and the military advocated more pragmatic policies in the Soviet Union, the dominant plans and practice were based on murder and gross exploitation. As in the case of the occupation of Poland, a small army of academic 'experts' volunteered their thoughts on the ultimate fate of the former Soviet Union. Puffed up with self-importance, these people flitted in and out of the corridors of power, in a simultaneously ludicrous and terrifying illustration of the maxim that a little learning is a dangerous thing, especially when that learning consisted of a denatured, functional pursuit of 'relevance' on the part of an intermediary class of experts whose ambition was power for themselves. A dangerous example of this phenomenon was SS-Oberführer Professor Konrad Meyer, a young agronomist whose gift was to convert Himmler's eccentric concerns into coldly technocratic schemes for ethnic cleansing, although we should never mistake the surface rationality for the underlying madness in the case of either individual.[148] Apparently Himmler found talking to such people about the thickness of farmhouse walls or the shape of colonial villages a form of relaxation after days spent running a continental police empire.[149]

Having made a name for himself in the context of the expulsion of Poles and Jews from the incorporated territories, Meyer was commissioned to produce a plan which encompassed the vastly augmented area created by Barbarossa. Even within the SS, planning was a congested field. In an inaugural address in October 1941 to senior members of the occupation regime in Prague, the new Reichsprotektor, Reinhard Heydrich, outlined his conception of settlement in the East. There were to be two moral universes consisting of peoples cognate with the Germans who would receive relatively decent treatment; while beyond, in the East, a German military elite would rule Slav 'helots'. A form of human polderisation would ensue, with an outer wall of soldier–farmers keeping out the human 'storm flood of Asia', and protecting the ever expanding rings of German settlement behind it.[150]

The Reich Main Security Office of the SS also drew up a global plan for the East in late 1941, whose contents can be reconstructed from a critical commentary by Dr Erhard Wetzel, the desk officer for racial policy in Rosenberg's OMi. This plan would have taken thirty years to implement after the end of the war. It covered Poland, the Baltic, White Russia, parts of the Ukraine, 'Ingermanland' (the Leningrad area) and 'Gothengau' (the Crimean peninsula). On their days off from slaughtering people, members of Einsatzgruppe D apparently spent their time searching caves for ancient Gothic artefacts. The SS planners envisaged ten million German settlers moving east, with thirty-one million of the forty-five million indigenous inhabitants being relocated to western Siberia. Here Wetzel punctiliously corrected SS arithmetic, since their figure of forty-five million appeared both to be too low and to include five or six million Jews who would have been 'got rid of' before the resettlement. The actual population would have been sixty to sixty-five million, of whom forty-six to fifty-one million would be moved. Deportations were to be percentual according to nationality. Thus 80–85 per cent of Poles (or twenty to twenty-four million people) were to go. Pondering their destination, Wetzel discounted Siberia (which would be weakened as a bulwark against rump Russia), allowed that 'one cannot liquidate the Poles like the Jews', and then opted for sending the Polish intelligentsia to Brazil in exchange for ethnic German repatriates while the lower orders would go to Siberia, where, together with other peoples who would be 'pumped in', they would constitute a denatured, 'Americanised' hodge-podge distinct from the Russians. Censuring the SS for their reticence on this last grouping, Wetzel proffered much detailed advice on how to curb Russian fecundity. Apart from mass-produced prophylactics, he suggested the retraining of midwives as abortionists and deliberate undertraining of paediatricians; voluntary sterilisation; and the cessation of all public health measures designed to diminish infant mortality.[151]

The obvious statistical errors and logistical improbabilities in the RSHA plan led Himmler to turn to the more practised Meyer. In May 1942, Meyer delivered the memorandum 'Generalplan Ost: Legal, Economic and Spatial Foundations for Development in the East'. The plan, which now exists only in summary form, envisaged the creation of three vast 'marcher settlements' (Ingermanland, Memel-Narew and Gothengau) whose population would be 50 per cent German, and which would be linked to the Reich at hundred-kilometre intervals by thirty-six 'settlement strongpoints', whose population would be a quarter German. This plan would take twenty-five years to implement, would involve five million German settlers, and would cost 66 billion Reichsmarks.[152] Himmler liked the deliberate exclusion of OMi from the 'marches', but wanted the timescale shortened by five years, the integration of Alsace-Lorraine and Bohemia-Moravia into the plan, and the accelerated 'germanisation' of the General Government and parts of the Baltic. Meyer was commissioned to produce a general settlement plan incorporating these revisions.

If these long-range plans reveal the essential inhumanity of Nazi intentions in the East, day-to-day treatment of the civilian population virtually guaranteed sullen non-cooperation and virulent hatred. Three areas deserve closer attention: the deliberate starvation of large numbers of people; the forced procurement of labour; and the indiscriminate brutality employed in the course of anti-partisan warfare.

The conquest of Soviet Russia was not solely an ideological showdown with 'Jewish Bolshevism', nor a gigantic form of ethnic cleansing, but also a quest for a secure long-term economic base from which to mount the bid for world power.[153] Since the fields shimmering with wheat of Hitler's imagining proved chimerical, German economic experts, notably State Secretary Herbert Backe, developed the simple expedient of starving millions of Russians by diverting food to the military and the German home front. This was presented as the only way out of a developing crisis whose first symptoms were a cut in the domestic German meat ration, but whose consequences were precisely the same as those elaborated in the 'Generalplan Ost'. In other words, one could arrive at the same desired 'solution' through any number of formulae. The underlying pathology was fundamentally murderous whatever the rationalising gloss put upon it.

Beginning with the fact that Tsarist Russia had exported agricultural surpluses, Backe attributed the recent decline to both Bolshevik incompetence and the demand represented by a growing and increasingly urbanised population. Surpluses could be engineered for German use only by curtailing consumption, a policy rendered easier by the fact that the main areas of demand in the 'wooded zones' in the north (the industrial cities of Leningrad and Moscow) were far from the Black Earth region in the south which generated the surpluses. 'Absolute clarity must reign' in respect of the certainty that these urban populations would starve: 'As a result, x million people will doubtless starve, if we extract what we need from the land.'[154]

These plans dovetailed with Hitler's more primitive destructive fantasies towards the populations of cities he identified with Bolshevism, or which he regarded as 'objects' of prestige. On 8 July 1941, Halder recorded in his diary that 'it is the Führer's firm decision that Moscow and Leningrad will be razed to the ground, in order to prevent people remaining there whom we will have to feed during the winter. The towns must be destroyed by the Luftwaffe. Tanks must not be deployed for this purpose. A national catastrophe which will rob not only Bolshevism but also Moscowdom of its centre.'[155] By early September 1941, Leningrad was isolated from the rest of Russia except for a precarious route across Lake Lagoda. Three million people were trapped inside the city and its suburban environs in what would become a siege lasting nine hundred days. Intensely suspicious of Leningrad particularism with its shades of the murdered Party boss Kirov, Stalin disbanded the three-man Defence Council, on the spurious ground that its functions overlapped with that of the Leningrad Front Command. By prioritising the hasty improvisation of trenches and gun emplacements to check the German advance, the Soviet authorities neglected both the possibility of mass evacuation of non-essential civilians, notably children, and the laying in of food in the event of a siege. Food was actually being removed from the city to supply other unoccupied areas. Rationing was belatedly and incompetently introduced, as well as ghastly substitute foods such as flour adulterated with cellulose or a jelly made from a massive load of sheep guts, whose odour was neutralised with cloves. By the onset of winter, with eighteen hours of darkness and temperatures plummeting to −40 degrees, electricity and central heating ceased, with people reduced to stripping wallpaper in order to cook the glue as a soup or drinking the contents of their medicine cupboards. Some people killed and ate their own cats and dogs, with mustard and vinegar failing to mask the taste, and using the fur to make gloves.

The German army cut the main railway line running into Leningrad, while the Luftwaffe harassed what sea traffic there was across the lake. The hasty improvisation of a two-hundred-mile road circling north of German forces proved futile since it was so narrow, and the snow so deep, that traffic frequently ground to a halt. With Hitler insisting that capitulation would be refused, German generals pondered what to do with the besieged city. The possibilities, discussed in late September 1941, included occupation (rejected because with it would go responsibility for feeding two million people); a gigantic electrified fence and machine guns to seal the city off (rejected because the ensuing epidemics might spread to German troops and because the latter were unlikely to shoot escaping women and children routinely); exit routes through which women and children could be sent eastwards or distributed across the countryside, while the rest of the population starved to death (deemed possible); and, finally, demolition of the city and the handing over of the ruins to the Finnish ally. It was decided to press on with the siege and bombardment. Bombs and shells rained down on the city, bringing random death to a queue or passers-by. An eyewitness reported:

> I was in the Nevsky once when a shell landed close by. And ten yards away from me was a man whose head was cut clean off by a shell splinter. It was horrible. I saw him make his last two steps with his head off – and a bloody mess all round before he collapsed. I vomited right there and then, and was quite ill for the rest of the day – though I had already seen many terrible things before. I shall never forget the night when a children's hospital was hit by an oil bomb; many children were killed, and the whole house was blazing, and some perished in the flames. It's bad for one's nerves to see such things happen; our ambulance services have instructions to wash away blood on the pavement as quickly as possible after a shell has landed.[156]

In November, eleven thousand people died, in December fifty-two thousand, in January 1942 between three and a half and four thousand people a day. The first worrying signs of people going to pieces were when men stopped shaving and women became indifferent to their appearance or ceased menstruating. Ages became confused, with children looking prematurely old, while the bodies of the middle-aged became childlike. Even the most routine movement, such as climbing stairs or getting into bed, became a major effort, with the dying simply rocking or slumbering. Corpses were collected and dumped in mass graves excavated from the frozen ground with explosives. Funerals were characterised by an absence of emotion. Apathetic dullness replaced tears. None of this affected the Party leaders in the warm and well-lit Smolny Institute, who had their own bakers and confectioners producing cakes and rum chocolates for their exclusive delectation, photographs of which were until the fall of Communism filed in the archives under the entry 'precision engineering'.

Pressure on the population was eventually relieved by the evacuation of women, children and the elderly and the construction of a route across the frozen lake along which supplies were brought. Fuel lines and electric power were restored in the spring by laying pipelines and cables along the bottom of the lake. Over six hundred thousand people died in the course of the siege of Leningrad, as a result of starvation strategies which were applied to other cities such as Kharkov or Kiev. Through such intangible media as Shostakovich's Seventh 'Leningrad' Symphony, the heroism and tragedy of Leningrad were communicated to a much wider Soviet public.

As was the case in other parts of German-occupied Europe, the forced requisition of labour was also a source of fear and resentment. Russian civilians and prisoners of war were compelled to work for the occupation authorities, the former as a result of a general edict on labour service issued by Rosenberg on 19 December 1941. Although Hitler was initially indisposed to exposing German or other foreign labourers to Soviet workers 'polluted by Bolshevism', he changed his mind because of the enormous calls on domestic manpower made by the war in Russia and a reluctance to conscript German women. Göring established the ground rules for the mass employment of Russians, now ironically lauded for the 'amazing development of Russian industry' under the Bolsheviks. In operational areas, Germans were no longer to be involved in heavy labour on roads or railways: 'German skilled workers belong in the arms industry; shovelling and breaking rocks is not their job, that's why the Russian is there.'[157] The deployment of Russians in the Reich would enable the regime to repatriate other foreign workers who ate more and produced less, while relying less on German female labour. The Russian prisoners of war (and as we have seen many of them were already dead) were destined for the railways, arms factories, construction, agriculture and the mines. They were to be housed in camps and worked in groups, with no disciplinary sanctions other than reduction of rations or execution. Shoes should be wooden, but underwear was superfluous 'since the Russian is scarcely used to it'.

There was little difference in the treatment of Russian civilians, except that they were to be given 'a little pocket money' in lieu of wages. Having belatedly discovered that immense numbers of Russian prisoners of war were dead, labour experts redirected their attention to civilian sources. Together with Albert Speer, the Plenipotentiary for Labour Procurement Fritz Sauckel turned towards Russia and the Ukraine. The voluntarist approach soon failed to produce significant results. Of course, in the case of many industrial workers, there was nothing 'voluntary' about their decision to go to Germany, since the occupiers both shut down plant that the Soviets had not disabled and pursued policies expressly designed to starve the urban population.[158] Stories also rapidly filtered back – via letters, or the oral testimony of pregnant women and the sick who were simply repatriated to save the cost of caring for them – of the appalling conditions eastern workers could expect inside the Reich. Compulsion gained ground.[159] A young Ukrainian woman described the *modus operandi*:

> It commenced with the arrival of a German called Graf Spreti in February 1942 who came to requisition labour. The Germans held a large meeting in a cinema. A crowd of people went along to see what was going on. Spreti said: 'I would like you citizens of Uman to go voluntarily to Germany to assist the German armed forces.' He promised us paradise. But we already knew what to make of such promises, and asked: 'What will happen if we don't want to go?' Graf Spreti replied: 'In that case we will politely demand despite this that you go.' That was on 10 February. Two days later they went from house to house and took away all of the young people. They took us to a big school and at five o'clock in the morning to the station. There they shoved us into railway wagons, which were then bolted. The journey became a nightmare lasting several weeks.[160]

German agencies responsible for intercepting and interpreting correspondence between Russian or Ukrainian civilians registered 'a sharp worsening of mood' tantamount to 'a terrified panic' resulting from the coercive requisitioning of labour. One of the letter-writers described what happened in a village on 1 October 1942. It is worth noting not just the violence used, but also the role of the village elder and the complete indifference whether the people taken were physically capable of working:

> You can't imagine what depredations occurred. You can doubtless well recall what we were told about the Soviets during the time of Polish rule: it is as unbelievable now as it was then, but then we didn't believe it. There was an order to muster twenty-five workers, the people designated by the Labour Office received registration cards, but none

of them turned up, all of them had fled. The German police appeared and began setting fire to the houses of those who had fled. The fire was intense since it hadn't rained for two months, and the bales of hay were stacked in the yards. You can imagine what happened. They would not permit the people who hurried out to extinguish the fire, hitting and arresting them, so that six farmsteads burned down. The police set fire to other houses, people fell to their knees and kissed their hands, but the police hit them with rubber truncheons and threatened to burn the whole village down. I don't know how things would have ended had I. Sapurkany not gone out into the middle of it all. He promised that workers would be there by morning. While the fire raged, the militia went through the nearby villages, detaining workers in custody. Where they couldn't find workers, they locked up the parents until their children reappeared. . . . They are snatching people like the knackers used to catch stray dogs. They have been hunting for a week, and still don't have enough. The workers they caught have been locked in a school, and are not allowed out even to go to the lavatory, but have to do it in the same room like pigs. Many people from the villages went on the same day on a pilgrimage to the monastery at Potschaew. They were all arrested, locked up, and will be sent to work. Among them were cripples, the blind and old men and women. At our annual market, Romanow was there. The village elder came up to him and said that he should come along, but he wouldn't. They bound his hands behind his back, and led him naked to the police. When he was told to get out of the cart, he refused, saying that they should free his hands first. Two guards beat him so much that his skin was broken in three places. His mother and sister screamed, and they were beaten too.[161]

On 12 August 1942, Sauckel attended a conference in Kiev to encourage inter-agency collaboration and to underline the urgency of his procurement activities. In return, he had to listen to a series of discouraging oral reports from district officials. They had too few men to be able to enter areas in which partisans were active. Ever bolder, the latter were assassinating German officials and those who served them, while abducting entire families. People were afraid to sleep in their own homes. Furthermore, no sooner had one managed to round up a group of workers than they ran away. Of 2,600 men loaded on to one train, one thousand had jumped out during the journey. Indeed, 25 per cent of every transport managed to flee during the journey. One could not rely on the Ukrainian guards to preside over the shipment to Germany of their own people. Other officials were perplexed as to how they were supposed to keep the military supplied with grain or timber when at the same time they were being required to deplete the labour force. What exactly were the priorities?[162]

Even when the diligent SS were brought in to do the job, the results were disappointing. According to a report by the SD and Security Police Chief in Kiev dated 20 July 1942, in the early hours of a Sunday morning they combed houses, rounding up a total of 1,645 people whose papers were not in order. Although this yielded three wanted (political) criminals, the raid failed to meet its intended objective. Only 255 of those detained could be shipped to the Reich. The rest were able to produce the correct documentation, were too sick to work or were hurriedly retrieved from the SS by their German employers.[163] In one noteworthy case, even the SS complained that the Labour Offices were requisitioning totally unsuitable people. On 9 December 1942, an SS-Obersturmbannführer reported to his superior that a train had recently arrived in Kiev from Przemśyl laden with 319 Ukrainian workers. They were all seriously ill. Eighty-one had the infectious eye disease trachoma, fifty-four were suffering from tuberculosis, and five were blind. What angered the SS officer was that someone had managed to declare these people fit for work, wasting administrative time and scarce transport in order to ship them to the Reich, whence they were immediately returned.[164] Reporting again a few days later, the same SS officer answered his own question by noting that labour recruitment officials were simply assembling entire villages, selecting every third man or woman.[165] Apart from the treatment 'eastern workers' received in Germany, the manner in which they had been brought there was one of the main reasons for the mass alienation of the Russian and Ukrainian civilian population.

German occupation policy was one factor contributing to the growth of partisan activity. From the mid-1920s, the Soviet Union had made limited preparations for partisan warfare, training special cadres, burying arms caches and creating camouflaged bases. Ironically, detailed studies of partisan warfare, notably by Marshal Tukhachev-sky, were primarily designed to suppress 'banditry' of the sort the Red Army encountered after the Civil War in Belorussia and Turkestan. Tukhachevsky's own solution had favoured concentration camps and inducements designed to break ties between the 'bandits' and their peasant supporters. All preparations for partisan warfare were abruptly terminated in the late 1930s. The bases were destroyed and training schools closed. Tukhachevsky was shot in the course of the purges of the armed forces. Stalin's antipathy to partisan warfare stemmed from his belief that an offensive Red Army could defend the Soviet state alone, and his fear that large numbers of armed units from non-Russian nationalities might turn on their Soviet masters. In this last respect he was right.[166]

These fateful decisions were hastily revoked on 3 July 1941, although it was many months before Moscow asserted its control over the NKVD, Communist Party, Komsomol or Red Army partisan units which sprang into existence, or were cut off, in German-occupied territories. The first units, consisting of perhaps a total of thirty thousand people spread over a vast area, were not a major success. They lacked food and equipment, notably radios, and their political composition, heavily laden with Communists, did not endear them to the inhabitants of the Baltic, Crimea and Ukraine. The extremely harsh winter of 1941/2 affected the partisans and Germans alike. Food was not easy to find and, if it was seized from the peasants, militated against a sympathetic environment. The absence of foliage and deep snow made the partisans vulnerable to aerial spotting and follow-up search-and-destroy missions.

German policy was co-responsible for the revival of the partisan movement in the spring of 1942. German treatment of Soviet prisoners of war diminished the advantages of surrender, while German occupation policy alienated populations which had sometimes greeted the Wehrmacht as potential liberators. As we have seen, the arbitrariness of labour procurement also resulted in large-scale flight to the partisans. Complaining to Sauckel in a letter dated 21 December 1942, Rosenberg wrote:

> Reports I have received enable me to perceive that the increase in the number of bands in the occupied eastern territories is largely attributable to the fact that, in the areas concerned, labour procurement measures are regarded as a form of mass deportation, to the extent that those who feel threatened by these measures prefer to take their chances by flight to the woods or by going over directly to the bandits.[167]

Finally, the winter campaign had shattered the myth of German invincibility, and hence brought the prospect of a return of Soviet rule. No doubt many people who became, or aided and abetted, partisans made complex calculations about present oppression by an invader whose impetus had stalled, and the return of a regime with a proven capacity for vindictiveness and terror, which was using the partisans to demonstrate its long reach even while its fortunes were at their nadir. This dilemma was summed up neatly by one Russian who was reported as saying: 'If I stay with the Germans, I shall be shot when the Bolsheviks come; if the Bolsheviks don't come, I shall be shot sooner or later by the Germans. Thus, if I stay with the Germans, it means certain death; if I join the partisans, I shall probably save myself.' Soviet propaganda leaflets warned collaborators: 'if you fight against us in future as you have up to now, then a merciless judgement awaits you, if not today, and if not tomorrow, then the day after tomorrow'.[168]

In May 1942, regional Party direction of the partisans was replaced by the Red Army's Central Staff for Partisan Warfare under Lieutenant-General Panteleymon Ponomarenko, the First Secretary of the Belorussian Communist Party and a close associate of Stalin. This arrangement gave the appearance of popular Red Army control, while actually centralising unpopular Communist Party direction of the partisan movement. Contact between the partisans in the occupied 'Little Land' and their controllers in the 'Great Land' were increased by the increased provision of radios as well as by means of commissars and NKVD sections. The reformed partisan bands had a strength of between three hundred and fifty and two thousand men and women, with a military command structure and specialist personnel including doctors and explosives and counter-intelligence experts. The NKVD Administration for Special Tasks provided training in sabotage and the services of professional assassins. One named N. I. Kuznetsov was a confident and handsome Russian, who had grown up among exiled Germans in Siberia, and whom the NKVD infiltrated into diplomatic circles in Moscow. In 1942 he was parachuted into western Ukraine where, disguised as a wounded German supply corps officer, he specialised in the point-blank assassination of German officials. Captured by Bandera's Ukrainian partisans, Kuznetsov blew himself up with a grenade before the Gestapo managed to interrogate him.[169]

Geography largely dictated the partisans' zone of operations. The steppe afforded almost no cover. The principal mountainous regions in the Caucasus and Crimea were inhabited by peoples who were at best neutral towards the Germans and deeply hostile to the Soviets. Partisans there could also be dealt with by experienced alpine troops. This left the areas of dense forest and swamps around the tributaries of the Pripyat, and further north, the woodlands between Minsk and

Smolensk, and the forests of the Valdai Hills south-east of Leningrad. In other words, the partisans were effectively confined to an area equal to a third of the German-occupied territories.[170] Within these areas, partisan units specialised in disrupting communications and supply routes, blowing up rail and telegraph links or bridges. Before the Battle of Kursk, they destroyed the equivalent of one thousand linear kilometres of railway line, severely impeding the flow of the one hundred thousand tons of *matériel* which the German army needed every day. The larger groups ambushed German columns, using the cover of woods to mow them down with oblique and cross-fire, or even to make two German columns fire on each other, by inserting themselves between them at night and firing in both directions. Other partisan tasks included killing key Nazi personnel, with Erich Koch blown to pieces by a mine in his bed, which left his wife unharmed, or abducting German troops, who were flown to Moscow for interrogation about enemy dispositions.[171]

The initial German response to partisan activities was piecemeal and incoherent, in the sense that there was no single authority responsible for security across the entire occupied zone, a situation which reflected the overlapping, and sometimes mutually antithetical, competences of civilian administrations, the army and SS, as well as different definitions of 'security'. The scale of the problem was immense. Occupying an area about one million square miles at maximum extent, the Germans opted to protect lines of communication, major towns, supply depots and essential economic resources. A town such as Orel was ringed with barbed wire at a distance of twenty kilometres from the centre, with intensive security checks on people entering or leaving it. The army deployed nine Security Divisions, accompanied by seven battalions of motorised police, consisting of older cohorts led by ageing reserve or retired officers. The SS deployed the four mobile Einsatzgruppen, whose principal activity was murdering civilians for racial reasons, as well as regiments of Order Police, various Waffen-SS units, and formations such as the Sonderkommando Dirlewanger or the Kaminski Brigade.[172] Even had they all been exclusively dedicated to one task, and many of these units were mainly involved in racial-biological warfare, these forces, consisting of perhaps 110,000 men, faced an uphill task in securing upwards of nearly a million square miles of hostile territory. Post-war German trial documents concerning the Einsatzgruppen are littered with hundreds of appalling accounts of drunken rape and torture sessions in

Godforsaken cellars in Krasnodar, or the burying alive in wells of hundreds of innocent men, women and children in sleepy villages.

Like strategic bombing, the military effectiveness of partisan warfare is disputed and difficult to assess. Those who claim that the Soviet partisan war had little impact on German military operations are surely missing the point that it caused widespread economic disruption, tied down manpower which could have been deployed elsewhere, and, by instilling fear and provoking extreme counter-measures, drove a wedge between occupiers and occupied. Reports from German economic agencies spoke of constant disruption which German security forces were unable to prevent. One lengthy report concerning the month of July 1942 recorded a campaign of assassination against low-level collaborators such as village mayors, and noted that 236 milking depots, dairies and mills as well as 17 per cent of sawmills had been disabled. Milk was being poisoned, explosive devices were slipped into grain about to be milled, and even a visit to the theatre brought the risk that the actors were plotting to blow up the audience. Main roads had been mined while minor routes were totally interdicted. Any sort of work in the forests and woods was out of the question. People who might once have collaborated with the Germans were now unsure of themselves. In what was regarded by the Germans as a revealing, if unamusing, anecdote, these officials reported:

> On 7.7 the forester Malaschtschenko appeared at the Economic Command Post to return his service rifle since this only seemed to him to be a permanent danger to his life. He also requested the issuance of a stamped receipt which he could then show to the partisans during their next attack as proof that he had really surrendered his weapon. This permit was issued in order to protect the forester. The fact that a German agency is forced to issue permits on behalf of the partisans illustrates better than any other example what the situation is at present.[173]

These activities had virtually brought economic activity to a standstill, interrupting vital supplies to the front-line troops. The dominant German response to partisan warfare was redolent of that of other regular armies frustrated by an invisible opponent and surprised by popular resistance. First, they endeavoured to use language itself to depoliticise the enemy, referred to now as 'bands', 'bandits' or occasionally 'Franktireur', in revealing acknowledgement of the fact that this sort of warfare had a long Prussian history. Secondly, they enhanced security by guarding railways and main roads, while endeavouring to restrict unauthorised civilian movement. Houses had to display lists of occupants, and anyone caught without a travel permit at night could be shot. A deadly competition ensued to guard or disable railways and telecommunications. The partisans began by simply bending or loosening rails (preferably on a decline), graduating via magnetic or pressure mines and serial explosives to charges encased in wood or tiny amounts of trinitrotoluene which were difficult to use and detect. As a matter of policy they destroyed derailed locomotives and killed all guards and engine crews. The Germans responded by raising the stakes. Apart from sniffer and tracker dogs, they cleared the undergrowth from beside the tracks; dug ditches filled with barbed wire; built lines of guardhouses to ensure a rapid response; used trains laden with rocks to trigger explosives in advance; and above all deployed repair crews and assiduous rescheduling to minimise any disruption.

Thirdly, there were fitful attempts to rationalise the overall direction of anti-partisan warfare, attempts which fell well short of co-ordinating SS and army activities under a unified command system. SS anti-partisan operations were directed from July 1942 by SS-Gruppenführer Knoblauch of the Reichsführer's Command Staff and from spring 1943 by Generalmajor der Waffen-SS Ernst Rode. Liaison with the military and overall policy was supplied by SS-Obergruppenführer Erich von dem Bach-Zelewski first as Plenipotentiary and from early 1943 as Chief of Anti-Bandit Formations, a title which stopped well short of any control of army operations in this area. Himmler continued to intervene with platitudinous analyses of the enemy, as well as such suggestions as 'it is self-evident that interrogations, when necessary, are to be conducted with the utmost brutality', or 'Death alone does not mean much to the pig-headed Slav; he reckons on it from the word go. By contrast he is afraid of blows; and above all he fears retaliatory measures against his clan.'[174]

The German occupiers practised the taking of hostages and random reprisals against civilians who had the misfortune to inhabit areas where partisans were active. An order issued by Göring on 16 October 1942 regarding the securing of railways illustrates the way in which the sort of security measures discussed above easily tipped over into the murder of civilians. Any unauthorised Russian found within a thousand metres of a railway track was to be shot. Any Russian caught committing acts of sabotage 'was to be hanged from the nearest

telegraph pole – in the event that he is captured alive'. Villages closest
to where lines were destroyed were to be burned down, while 'the
male population is to be shot, and the women and children sent to
camps'.[175] Ten days later Göring also ordered the removal of all food
and livestock from areas where partisans were active, and the deportation for labour of all able-bodied adults in these areas. No heed was
to be paid either to such factors as agricultural production, while
children were to be sent to rear-area camps. The air force often
bombed partisan bases or the adjacent villages.[176]

Active anti-partisan combat, that is the business of taking the war
to the enemy, also swiftly degenerated into the indiscriminate and
mindless terrorisation of civilians. On 7 December 1941, the High
Command of Sixth Army announced rather prematurely that partisan
activity had to all intents and purposes been 'eradicated' in their sector.
The report continued:

> In the course of this action several thousand have been publicly hanged
> or shot in the army's area. Experience shows that death by hanging is
> particularly terrifying. In Charkow, several hundred partisans and
> suspect elements were hanged in the town. Acts of sabotage have since
> ceased. Experience reveals: only those measures succeed which frighten
> the population more than the terrorism of the partisans.[177]

A constant stream of directives, orders and operational instructions
prove beyond any doubt that the terrorisation of civilians was licensed
and ordered by the Nazi leadership and senior generals alike. Instructions issued by Eleventh Army on 15 December 1941 clearly stated:
'The population must be more frightened of our reprisals than of the
partisans.'[178] The message relayed from Hitler by Keitel was 'whatever
succeeds is correct' and that: 'The troops must have the right and duty
to use, in this fight, any means, even against women and children,
provided they are conducive to success. Scruples, of any sort whatsoever, are a crime against the German people and against the front-line
soldier. . . . No German participating in action against bands or their
associates is to be held responsible for acts of violence either from a
disciplinary or a judicial point of view.'[179] Instructions to the troops
on how to conduct interrogations of suspects began with the premise
that 'people here expect to be interrogated according to the methods
of the NKVD, i.e. they reckon on being beaten up from the start'. This
involved up to seventy-five blows with an oxtail whip for men, or a

rubber tube for women, with the victim being shot in the back of the neck after he or she had given the required information.[180]

Operating in often intractable terrain, against an enemy who was himself (or herself) frequently barbaric, devious and indistinguishable from the civilian population, soldiers and policemen with no external disciplinary constraints slipped into routinised brutality, a sure indication that they were losing. Civilians were hanged, raped, shot and tortured and their homes destroyed by men who were often drunk. Evidence for this is not simply oral or written, since cheap cameras made this an amateur cameraman's war, despite a general prohibition on photography, especially by members of the Einsatzgruppen. Thousands of photographs, taken from dead or captured German soldiers by the Russians, or discovered among the possessions of veterans, record mass executions by hanging or shooting of putative partisans. The latter hang, sack-like, from urban balconies or wayside telegraph poles, or were laid out as dead game in front of the men who had killed them. The latter stare gormlessly at the camera. Why anyone should want to photograph such scenes remains unclear.[181] Judging from the way in which the majority of these pictures were composed, few of the photographers seem to have been registering revulsion or shock at what they were witnessing, albeit through the remove of a lens. That would have required less physical distance from the faces of their subjects, as is customary in modern war photo-reportage. Rather, the photographs reflect a prurient desire to record something that was initially not an everyday sight, while also capturing those moments of absolute power over other human beings that the war in the East afforded. The photographs would tell the tale and capture the frisson more effectively than stories. They could be embellished; a photograph was a window into reality. They were really there, they had transgressed the taboos. Soviet veterans of the war in Afghanistan in the 1980s, in which a million Afghans died, who speak openly on camera about their conduct without fear of legal retribution, are more eloquent than fifty-year-old German legal depositions about the related experience of burning Pathan women and children, or trying out high-powered weapons on the human body in what amounted to amateur clinical exercises. The analogy is relevant in a further sense.

As in subsequent (lost) irregular wars, 'success' was registered in statistical 'body counts' which did not withstand close scrutiny. Soldiers achieved meaningless kill rates, against an elusive enemy. In other words, they wanted to flee the forests and swamps as expeditiously as possible, notching up impressive tallies of civilian victims rather than taking on the partisans in firefights within the sepulchral gloom of the forests or amid the reeds of the marshes. In July 1943 an SS officer, Herf, wrote to the Head of the SS Personnel Main Office drawing his attention to the cooking of the books and the '6000/480' problem, that is how only 480 rifles had been recovered from six thousand dead 'partisans' in the course of the recent Operation Kottbus. The commander of the operation, SS-Obergruppenführer Curt von Gottberg, had also 'liquidated' 3,709 others, and killed two thousand local people by ordering them into a minefield. Told that the 'bandits' regularly destroyed their own weapons to affect innocence, Herf commented, 'How easy it must be to suppress these guerrillas – when they destroy their own weapons.'[182] All attempts to integrate anti-partisan warfare with more conciliatory policies towards the civilian population came to naught. The war became one of illusions, which made less and less of an impact on the enemy, as the security forces blundered around while the partisans eluded them.

The anti-partisan war was also a convenient cover, and useful pretext, for racial-biological extermination. Reporting to his superior on 23 June 1942, Major-General Bruno Scultetus of the 281 Security Division none too dexterously rationalised the shooting of 128 Gypsies by the Secret Field Police. Partisans had been active in his region in the second half of May, although the only incident he mentioned was an attack on a lorry in which a lieutenant had been wounded. 'At the same time' Gypsies had been seen in the area. They had no fixed abode, begged rather than worked, 'and represented a burden in every respect'. Lest this seemed like an injunction to shoot the homeless, Scultetus switched his ground. 'General experience', confirmed again in Russia, taught that Gypsies often operated as spies. Moving from general to local experience, Scultetus gave a few circumstantial details: the (dead) Gypsies included many men of military age; one of those interrogated said that older Gypsies discussed the activities of partisans; Gypsies had camped near where the one attack had taken place. Moving back to the general, Scultetus remarked that 'during their interrogation, all of the Gypsies made a very unfavourable and shifty impression, and frequently contradicted themselves'. Of course there was no 'absolute proof' that Gypsies had aided and abetted partisans; nonetheless, the suspicion was so high, and the potential danger to the military so great, that 'their eradication seemed necessary'. Scultetus was then very careful to cover his men by detailing the precise origin of the order to kill the Gypsies, concluding with the point that since these shootings there had been no further partisan attacks in this area. One hundred and twenty-eight people had been killed because their 'race' was slated for destruction, because they fitted an approximate enemy profile, and because a few old men had talked about the war at night.[183]

Confirmation that the anti-partisan war was used to carry out ethnic murder comes from a variety of sources. As Hitler said to his intimates on 16 July 1941, 'it gives us the chance of exterminating anything that opposes us'. Reflecting on these activities at Nuremberg, Bach-Zelewski confirmed that this was so, and that there was such a phenomenon as intentional chaos:

> leaders at the top who are conscious of their responsibilities cannot abandon the execution of reprisals to the caprice of individual commanders. This lack of direction in responsible quarters is a cowardly devolution of responsibility on to lower echelons. But if it is obvious to everyone that lack of direction leads to a chaos of reprisals and nevertheless no clear orders are given, then the only possible conclusion is that this chaos is intended by the leaders at the top. There is no question but that reprisals both by the Wehrmacht and by SS and Police units overshot the mark by a long way. This fact was repeatedly established at conferences with generals held by Schenckendorff. Moreover the fight against partisans was gradually used as an excuse to carry out other measures, such as the extermination of Jews and Gypsies, the systematic reduction of the Slavic peoples by some 30,000,000 souls (in order to secure the supremacy of the German people), and the terrorisation of civilians by shooting and looting. The Commanders-in-Chief with whom I came in contact and with whom I collaborated (for instance Field Marshals Weichs, Küchler, Bock, and Kluge, Colonel-General Reinhardt and General Kitzinger) were as well aware as I of the purposes and methods of anti-partisan warfare.[184]

Bach-Zelewski was well placed to know about the convenient conflation of Jews and partisans. On 30 July 1941 he met with Himmler and Standartenführer Hermann Fegelein of the SS-Cavalry Regiment in Baranowicze, where it was agreed that 'all Jews must be shot. Drive the Jewish females into the swamps.' Fegelein relayed this order to SS-Sturmbannführer Herthes, who on 2 or 3 August told Sturmbannführer Franz Magill of the SS-Cavalry Regiment: 'The Jews are the reservoir of the partisans; they support the latter.'[185] Magill then gave orders to this effect to cavalry squadrons 1 and 2, radioing 3 and 4 who were operating at some distance.

Magill was born in 1900, the son of a day labourer in Kleist, Köslin. After service during the tailend of the 1914–18 war, he joined a regiment of hussars stationed at Stolp in Pomerania. He left the Reichswehr in 1930 as a sergeant and horse-riding instructor. After three years teaching at a riding academy in Berlin-Zehlendorf, he became an instructor at the SS riding school in Braunschweig. In 1939 he was transferred to Berlin to form an SS cavalry squadron as part of the SS-Totenkopf Reiterstandarte. He was then sent to Lublin to organise the 2 SS-Cavalry Regiment and put at the disposal of Bach-Zelewski. Deemed unready for front-line combat, the Regiment was initially deployed mopping up the remnants of a Russian cavalry formation left behind in the swamps near Slutsk. Within a week of arriving in Russia in late July, their orders had changed to broader 'political pacification', including shooting commissars, functionaries and all who aided the partisans.

Some time between 30 July and 1 August Herthes was told by Himmler or Bach-Zelewski to kill the Jews. Herthes made much of the fact that his troop commanders were to evince 'unbending hardness' and that 'all the petty personal, human weaknesses and the different characters of individuals must be balanced out by the overall attitude of the leadership corps'.[186] Allegedly shocked by orders to kill all male Jews over fourteen and to drive the rest into the swamps, Magill sought confirmation from regimental headquarters, thus resolving his brief crisis of conscience. Between August and November, brigade orders shifted from 'Partisan bands operate with the support of the Jewish population' (13 August) to 'In the event that a unit remains in a place for a long period of time, Jewish quarters or ghettos are to be set up, in the event that they cannot be exterminated immediately. Naturally, one should note that the craftsmen are to be retained' (28 November). Magill and his men headed for Pinsk, where the SD and local militias supervised the gathering together of the Jewish population. Two thousand men were then marched for an hour through potato fields to a collective farm where local people had dug trenches. They stood in line for hours, crying, praying and screaming while those at the front were shot in the back of the neck. One hundred men were kept back to fill in the trenches, before being shot themselves. Another one thousand Jews were shot a few days later.

Since Fegelein was in Warsaw, Bach-Zelewski took it upon himself to visit the troops, arriving in his Fieseler Storch, shooting at Russian stragglers from the cockpit window with his sub-machine gun along the route. Medals were dispensed to the Jew-shooting 'heroes'.[187] It was here that he used the crisp formula: 'Where there is a partisan, there is also a Jew, and where there is a Jew, there is also a partisan.' One partisan attack on a militiaman had resulted in the deaths of over four and a half thousand Jews. The grim reality of 'anti-partisan' warfare was recorded in matter-of-fact and minute detail in the war diaries of the SS units concerned. For example, in a report covering operations between noon on 3 August and noon on 6 August 1941, the 1st SS Motorised Infantry Brigade gave the 'result' as being:

Jews shot	*Ostrog*	*Hrycow*	*Kuniow-Radohoszcz*
Men	732	268	109
Women	225	–	50
Former Russian soldiers (partisans)	–	–	1

Total: 1385 persons[188]

With chilling regularity the detailed reports, such as one dated 8/9 August 1941, record the execution of Jews: '232 Jews who afforded the bandits assistance'; '9 Bolshevik Jews in Mal-Goroschki'; '59 Jews shot, 8 Russians captured, search for weapons unsuccessful'; '36 Bolshevik Jews were shot in the villages' and so on.[189] A report on a putative anti-partisan sweep in the Pripyat swamps between 27 July and 11 August 1941 begins with the damning admission, 'impressions of combat: none'. The author of the report, Magill, gave a glowing account of the mainly Ukrainian rural population, who had greeted his SS-Cavalry Regiment with milk, eggs and tables covered with white cloths and laid out with the traditional bread and salt. In one place they were met by the strains of a village choir. Like an anthropologist among strange tribes, Magill noted that 'in racial terms' the stocky inhabitants made a good impression, with their fecundity reflected in the large numbers of children. They dwelt in wooden huts with thatched roofs, and possessed good school buildings. The terrain consisted of swamp interspersed with sandy stretches. Canals and channels crisscrossed the area, with occasional clumps of birch and pine. Collectivisation had been in the process of being introduced in the countryside; Magill returned some cows to poverty-stricken farmers.

The urban artisans had been grouped in co-operatives. Jews seemed to be preferred as doctors.

And so the Regiment rode on. The journey was free of incident; the equipment lagged behind because the tracks were a morass; a few horses were lamed, others had to be rested for long intervals; some wagons broke down; and a handful of weapons were lost. Gradually Magill's report slipped into a different register as the tourist part of the journey was superseded by the business end of the mission. 'Pacification' involved questioning village mayors about partisan activities. Some mayors rushed to assist; others were questioned in the manner usual on the Eastern Front. Partisans, or rather suspected partisans, were identified, interrogated and shot. Magill casually remarked that 'Jewish plunderers' were also shot. What he and his regiment were actually doing was indicated by a paragraph which reads:

> Driving women and children into the swamps was not as successful as it should have been, since the swamps were not deep enough for them to sink. Because of a depth of one metre, most cases reached solid ground [probably sand] so that drowning was not possible.[190]

None of this involved partisans. They encountered no Communists, merely persons suspected of Communist activity. Most of the reports on the 'bands' turned out to be exaggerated. Weapon searches proved otiose. One Polish priest had been shot for propagandising a Polish national revival, in what was a predominantly Ukrainian area. Again circling around what he and his men had done, Magill noted that the Ukrainians spoke quite well of the Jews, but had nonetheless helped him herd them together. The total number of 'plunderers etc.' shot by this one unit came to 6,526 people, presumably including the women and children they had failed to drown in a shallow swamp. Post-war trial records include interrogations of the men who did this. One man who shot men and women but baulked at shooting children recalled: 'The Jews behaved themselves in an exemplary fashion. No one tried to flee for his life, I could only marvel at them.' He and his comrades thought what they were doing 'a horrible madness': 'I was taught to observe the fifth and seventh commandments and suddenly I had to commit murder. I only pulled the trigger because in the event of refusing I would have been bumped off myself.'[191] The operation was deemed 'a success'.

It is time to relate these episodes, albeit involving the existential terrorising and murder of thousands of people, to the vaster criminal enterprise which was taking shape across the length and breadth of Axis and occupied Europe, for which the racial war in the Soviet empire represented a crucial catalyst, a final lowering of the threshold of what was thought humanly possible. Developments we have viewed separately in the context of eugenics and euthanasia, the deportations and settlement of Poland and the racial war in Russia were to combine into the evil project of the 'Final Solution'. This emerged from the chrysalis of earlier atrocities, whose scope it superseded.

8

'IRON TIMES, IRON BROOMS': RACIAL WAR AGAINST THE JEWS

The German-Jewish artist Felix Nussbaum lived underground in
Belgium following a harrowing period incarcerated in concentration
camps in southern France. In *Death Triumphant* he depicts himself as the
organist on the centre right of the painting, with significant artefacts from
his life shown in a frieze along the bottom. Shortly after this picture was
completed Nussbaum and his wife were arrested and deported to
Auschwitz where they perished in August 1944.

Nazi warfare had a dual character and purpose, which Hermann Göring expressed with uncommon clarity: 'This war is not the Second World War. This is the great racial war. In the final analysis it is about whether the German and Aryan prevails here, or whether the Jew rules the world, and that is what we are fighting for out there.'[1] Beyond conventional engagements such as the battles of Britain, Stalingrad or Kursk, a diabolic project was afoot, whose local, slippery manifestations included Magill's SS cavalrymen seeking to drown women and children in Ukrainian swamps. The Nazis' refashioned warfare was a means of achieving the racial 'purification' of Europe, and involved both relocating entire populations and killing every Jewish man, woman and child that they could round up or capture. The comprehensiveness of the 'Final Solution' differentiated it from Nazi violence towards such categories of people as Communists, conservative Catholic Poles or homosexuals, persecution of whom did not routinely extend to killing every family member. The Nazi onslaught against the Jews was both the central element of a broader biologistic framework and *sui generis*, in terms of how the Nazis perceived Jews as an existential threat, and the implacable ferocity of the campaign's implementation. *Mutatis mutandis*, such horrors as the Nazi 'euthanasia' programme, which led to the deaths of over a hundred thousand people, drew on discourses other than antisemitism.[2] But this was not a competition, least of all for the victims, that is principally six million Jews, so we will leave the not very enlightening discussion of uniqueness in favour of other matters.

Violent ethnic reorganisation commenced in Poland, after the brief high-intensity war had abated. To call these policies 'war crimes' is misleading; murder is perfectly serviceable. Polish elites were systematically slain and the masses (whether Christian or Jew) expelled from territories then annexed to Germany. These policies were mirrored across the demarcation line with the Soviet Union, which occupied eastern Poland.[3] Racial warfare achieved a still higher level of ferocity during Germany's invasion of the Soviet empire (including countries the Soviets themselves had only recently invaded) before being generalised into a gigantic programme of extermination that stretched across the entire sphere of German influence, including the territories of Axis allies – a programme that prospectively menaced Jews who lived in neutral or enemy nations such as Ireland, Sweden, Switzerland and England.

The mass murder of the Jews evolved, not in a simple, linear way, but as a result of blockages and stoppages, options denied and opportunities seized upon, rather as a deadly virus bypasses the human immune system, until the whole continent bore witness to its malignant presence. The enterprise was so vast and detailed in execution, its victims ranging from complete urban communities to infants hidden in remote haylofts, that it is difficult to convey its terrible scope in any account aspiring to depth let alone geographical comprehensiveness. Since a full account would exceed the bounds of this book, nothing more is offered here than a few carefully selected routes into this continent-wide catastrophe, although a broader explanation of when and why decisions were made accompanies the detailed discussions of examples drawn from various countries.

Given the enormities visited upon Jewish people, it is sometimes difficult to grasp that between September 1939 and mid-1941 they were not always an immediate priority for the Nazis, or that between those dates the dominant German policy was to expel them from Europe, albeit with death fully calculated as part of the equation. The expulsion of the Jews from Greater Germany was part of a larger strategy of reordering ethnic relations that involved Poles and ethnic Germans too, but there was no equivalence in how these three groups were treated. Once Poland had been 'denationalised' through the decapitation of her elites, the Polish masses were destined for helotry rather than death. Only Jews were to disappear from Europe through emigration to the German empire's periphery or overseas, or into execution pits and gas chambers.

That we have suddenly ceased talking of Poland and have spoken of Europe, rather militates against attempts to align the Holocaust with the phenomenon of 'ethnic cleansing' in the present. The Nazis did not simply seek to expel Jews from territories they claimed were aboriginally German, with murder as a welcome by-product of achieving that end. The Holocaust was more than the sum total of wickedness generated by antagonistic *ethnoi*. The relationship of Europe's Jews to the Nazis was not that of the Albanians or Croats to the Serbs. The Nazis actively sought out Jews in countries with which they had no connection, and which Germans had neither settled nor had any desire to settle, transporting them hundreds or thousands of miles to their deaths in extermination camps in Poland. What may be locally true of parts of occupied Poland cannot be generalised as an explanation of why the Nazis killed Jews from Amsterdam, Paris or Corfu. The Holocaust was not simply 'ethnic cleansing' *avant la lettre* or writ large, nor just a big dip in the graph of generalised twentieth-century barbarity.[4]

But, while the Nazis' murderousness towards the Jews was *sui generis*, it had a hinterland in their treatment of others. The first two groups to be killed after the war began were Austrian, German and Polish psychiatric patients, together with Polish intellectual and social elites. This makes it hard to construe Nazi violence simply as the outgrowth of a unique strain of German antisemitism, since the psychiatric victims were Austrian or German, while the Poles killed included antisemites.[5] The psychiatric patients occupied space and consumed resources; the Poles personified a nationhood which the Nazis, and their Soviet accomplices, wished to extinguish. These policies were then extended into the Soviet Union, or rather into the territories the Russians had conquered and which the Germans then invaded, with the difference that the term 'intelligentsia' was used by the Germans as a synonym for Bolsheviks and Jews, concepts inextricably meshed in the minds of many National Socialists, who ignored the fact that many Jews were conservatives, liberals, social democrats or apolitical. The first task, then, is to establish the broader context of Nazi racial policy, and to see how murderousness towards many others was redirected so implacably and massively towards the Jews.

EXPULSION AND REPATRIATION

The Nazis' conquest of Poland in September 1939 marked the transition from the semi-coerced emigration of German and Austrian Jews to foreign states to their mass deportation to the peripheries of Nazi power. In May 1939, Germany's residual Jewish population numbered 330,892, struggling to survive against deliberately induced indigence. Two-thirds of these people had no gainful employment and many were elderly; half were concentrated in Berlin or Vienna.[6] Indigent Jewish people confirmed Nazi notions of Jewish 'parasitism'. Bureaucrats armed with slide rules were already calculating how many German or Austrian psychiatric patients should be killed to diminish costs, liberate hospital bedspace and purify the race, goals that coalesced around so-called incurable patients.[7]

In September 1939, slightly under two million Polish Jews were abruptly added to the number of Jews subject to German power. In the summer of 1941 the conquest of the Baltic, Belorussia, Galicia, the Ukraine and the Crimea further multiplied these figures. The war closed down many options for legal flight, unless one was prepared to hazard life in Stalin's empire, as about three hundred thousand people did. Sheer numbers influenced Nazi policy, since the Jewish population of Warsaw equalled in size the Jewish population remaining in Greater Germany. Moreover, these were 'eastern Jews' or *Ostjuden*, the German (and German-Jewish) stereotypes for Eastern Jewry, wherein antisemitism fused with anti-Slavism.[8] These abstractions yielded a visceral dislike of the clothing, hairstyles, humble living conditions, exotic names, yiddish language, gestures, exotic smells and slaughtering customs of what were considered the unreconstructed 'oriental' poor.[9] Poor many of them were, since pre-war Endek Party influence on Polish government policy, which discriminated against Jews, had already reduced a third of them to abject poverty.[10] Nazi propaganda demonised eastern Jews as the originators of both Bolshevism and rapacious capitalism, and then dehumanised them by making them live under appalling conditions or deliberately starving them. Gradually they forfeited their individuality, becoming the anonymous destitute; glassy eyes staring from paper-thin faces at men devoid of both charity and humanity. Images that evoke pity, or indeed indifference, elicited from the Nazis only greater hatred, for in the East they thought they had found the source of the 'world Jewish problem'. They say that travel, even in wartime, broadens the mind. But here was a case where it failed to do so. In going eastwards the Nazi leaders reconfirmed their darkest imaginings. After visiting the Łódź ghetto Goebbels wrote: 'It is indescribable. These aren't human beings any more, these are animals. This is therefore not a humanitarian, but rather a surgical task. One must make cuts here, moreover really radical ones.'[11] Images of religious slaughter were duly used to fuel self-righteous indignation on the part of the animal-loving vegetarian Jew-hating Hitler.[12]

Apart from the countless numbers of Polish Jews who were sadistically humiliated by all sections of the invading forces, and sometimes by Christian Poles, an estimated seven thousand of them were murdered before 1939 was out.[13] Although the conditions of German occupation in Poland made for a higher degree of public violence than had been visited on the Jews of Germany and Austria in November 1938 – for the Nazis did not care about Polish sensibilities, or they egregiously presumed Poles to be antisemitic – the mocking, vicious treatment of Polish Jews bears more than a passing resemblance to the earlier torments. On 10 November 1939 – the anniversary of Kristallnacht – the four main synagogues in Łódź were burned down by way of celebration.[14] German policemen and soldiers, many of them drunk, enjoyed humiliating and hurting others, sometimes receiving the censure and disapproval of their superiors.[15] Even dead Jews were treated with monumental indignity. In March 1940, the ruling mayor of Posen tried to deposit two corpses of Jews from his camp at Główno in the Jewish cemetery at nearby Schwaningen. They were left unburied and the accompanying written request was directed to Schwaningen's Jewish community. Schwaningen's mayor indignantly pointed out to his counterpart in Posen that his town was 'judenfrei' and the Jewish cemetery defunct. He had a mind to build on it: 'If Mr Ruling Mayor is of the view that the corpses of Jews who have died in his town cannot be accommodated in his district, for a long time now the town of Schwaningen has ceased to be available as a substitute.'[16]

Heydrich set out SS policy towards Polish Jews in guidelines to the Einsatzgruppen issued on 21 September 1939. Distinguishing between a secret 'final aim' and the stages towards it, he ordered that Jews be concentrated in the larger cities, which in the parts of Poland not destined for incorporation into Germany were chosen because of proximity to railway lines and junctions. The intended destination for all Jews was a 'reservation' south-east of Cracow, an area which Heydrich specifically exempted from these measures.

To get a grip on the Jewish masses with minimal manpower, Heydrich ordered the formation of Councils of Jewish Elders (Judenräte), 'fully responsible, in the literal sense of the word, for the exact and prompt implementation of directives already issued or to be issued in the future'.[17] In his view, the Councils were a device to maximise Nazi control of the Jews. They combined the functions of the pre-war kehillas, or Jewish communal authorities, and many of the tasks of local or central government. These included assigning apartments, allocating labour, collecting taxes, organising courts and policing, the provision of hospitals, orphanages, prisons and schools and overseeing basic utilities such as power or sewage disposal. These were massive tasks in themselves, quite apart from the nerve-wracking business of dealing with Nazi officialdom. The Councils were surrogate governments, but all the substantive attributes of sovereignty lay with their persecutors. Their power may have been tangible enough to the inhabitants of the ghettos, who often bitterly resented their arrogance, authoritarianism and corruption, but they were ultimately corks bobbing along on the eddying currents of Nazi policy. Since they were the only indirect point of contact between the Jewish population and their oppressors, they, rather than the Jews as such, will be the focus of attention in our discussion of the victims.

Relations between Council members and the Nazis were absolutely unequal, in the sense that the latter brooked no argument, and could finish any contrariness by resorting to their fists or revolvers. The relationship was inherently asymmetrical. The Nazis commanded; the Jewish Councils pleaded, reasoned, supplicated. Anyone would in these circumstances. The first encounter on 11 November 1939 between the Gestapo and the thirty men Chaim Rumkowski initially selected for the Łódź Council resulted in all but three being shot next day, with Rumkowski being beaten when he vainly interceded on their behalf.[18] These drastic sanctions were omnipresent, a fact in all dealings between Nazis and Jews. More routine intercourse was characterised by hostility and malice on the part of Nazi officialdom. On 6 January 1943, two Kovno ghetto council members were summoned to see Keiffler, the deputy city governor. He was seeking ways of taking over the ghetto's internal transportation system, which seemed to be working too efficiently. He wanted Jews, rather than horses, to draw carts. Small talk prefaced the bad news. The Lithuanian Pittsburgh-educated lawyer Avraham Tory left a detailed account of existence in this ghetto, including his version of this meeting:

> A stranger, eavesdropping on this conversation, would think that we were faced with a well-mannered man showing great interest in friends whom he had not seen for a long time. In fact, Keiffler's questions are correct and to the point. But if the aforementioned imaginary stranger were to peer through the keyhole at the partners in this conversation, he would behold a weird scene: Keiffler stretching himself on his armchair, puffing smoke from his cigar, from time to time looking at Garfunkel and me with eyes full of disgust and contempt. At the same time, he would see both of us standing on our feet throughout the meeting, anxiously following not only the drift of his questions but the tone of his voice, his facial expression, and his gaze penetrating the depths of one's soul. The stranger would realise that this was not exactly a conversation between friends – that we stood in front of a beast of prey in human disguise, an aggressive biting animal eager to inflict pain. We are trying to defend ourselves as best as we can, to give the right answer to every question, to avert danger. This cat and mouse game occurs because all the statements of the person who asks the questions are false. That is what our conversation with Keiffler and his ilk are like. They are always on the offensive, whether openly or by means of apparently innocent questions, whereas we must find a proper and logical reply to questions whose drift is clear. At long last, Keiffler gets to his main purpose in this conversation: cleanliness in the stables is not observed, and several horses have been taken sick. The transportation department will therefore be taken over by the city governor. . . . Keiffler said all this quietly, composedly, and serenely, as if we were not affected by his decision at all. He did not ask, nor did he want to know, how the new arrangement would work in the ghetto or what its impact would be on the lives of the ghetto inmates.[19]

Wilfully blind to the consequences of their own decisions, the Nazis also deliberately operated an uncertainty principle. Again, Avraham Tory caught this very well:

> We must understand that, from their point of view, our situation must always remain unclear, we are not allowed to understand anything, even if our lives are at stake. Anything that happens to us must occur

like a bolt from the blue. We are to remain always in a state of anticipation, without understanding what is going on around us.[20]

Since many existing Jewish leaders fled the German advance, the Nazis made do with whoever was to hand. In some places, the Councils were chosen by lot, drawn by rabbis. Some Council members were from the traditional Jewish elites, but this option was not available in places conquered by the Soviets, for the Jewish elites were alongside the Gentile elites in concentration camps in Siberia. Chaim Rumkowski, the controversial Elder of the Łódź Ghetto Council, was apparently chosen because his distinguished mane of white hair made him look the part. In Warsaw, the Polish mayor designated the assimilated engineer Adam Czerniakow head of the Jewish religious community, a post the Nazis then transformed into the chairmanship of the Jewish Council. Community leaders were also sometimes permitted to hold elections. In Kovno, Dr Elkes, the most outstanding candidate as elder, demurred on the grounds of inadequate experience in public administration. A rabbi changed his mind:

> Dr Elkes, you may be our Oberjude for whoever wants to regard you as such, but for us you will be our community leader. We all know that your path will be fraught with hardship and danger, but we will go with you all the way, and may God come to our aid.[21]

The Jews of Poland had to work with the hand they were dealt. They sometimes discovered that their cards were not good. As Czerniakow wrote after a visit from Rumkowski: 'That one is self-important. Arrogant and stupid. Dangerous too, because he convinces the authorities that things are going well with him.'[22] Whatever their failings, these men were under constant stress, the least of which were Czerniakow's headaches and insomnia. They could not reveal this when they met the Nazis, for there would be throngs of people scanning their faces for signs of how things went, with endless possibilities for misinterpretation, rumour and panic. Regardless of how they felt, these men had to be endlessly resourceful every single day. Incidents over which they had no control became pretexts for collective extortion or reprisals. Impromptu demands for levies and exactions came with every 'offence'. If the money was not found, people died. In June 1941, Czerniakow wrote in his diary: 'It is raining. Fortunately that does not involve charges on the community.'[23]

While the Jews were gradually subjected to these controls, Himmler, acting after October 1939 as Reich Commissar for the Strengthening of Ethnic Germandom, was simultaneously negotiating with the Soviet authorities for the repatriation of the Baltic, Galician and Volhynian Germans. This was notionally in exchange for Ruthenian and Ukrainian minorities marooned in German-occupied Poland, although the latter tended to prefer remaining in Poland than to chance things with a fully qualified rather than apprentice mass murderer. To Hitler, resolution of the 'Jewish Question' was one element within the larger project of resolving ethnic anomalies across the board, notably the consolidation of ethnic Germans – this last category was liberally interpreted for the connections were often tenuous among the scattered German fragments living in towns or rural ethnic exclaves across eastern Europe. For Stalin, these transfers rid him of a foreign urban bourgeoisie and enterprising peasantry at a stroke.[24]

The Nazi leadership not only seriously underrated the logistic problems such transfers involved, but also took decisions that had economic rather than ethnic logic, for cupidity vied with race consciousness. Thus Poland's second city, the textile centre of Łódź, was aggregated to the Warthegau, the German designation for that part of incorporated Poland, even though this added two hundred thousand more Jews to those Heydrich was planning to deport to the General Government. This decision clearly perplexed the racial purist Goebbels, who wrote: 'Why must this rubbish tip now become a German town! Wanting to germanise Łódź is a labour of Sisyphus.'[25] Worse, at least from this perspective, followed. Göring's rapacious interest in industrial centres added three more towns with substantial Jewish populations to Upper Silesia, making a total of 550,000 unanticipated Jews in territories ostensibly to be rendered free of them. Matters were further complicated by the decision to eject Poles too from these newly incorporated territories, and by Himmler's sudden decision to deposit Tyrolean Germans, rather than Jews, in the area near Cracow. In other words, regardless of the simplicity of Heydrich's guidelines, the Jewish issue was rapidly compounded by interrelated ethnic German and Polish problems, while the proposed destination for the Jews had simply vanished.

There were other obstacles to the smooth settlement of ethnic Germans. There were more people steaming in ships towards Gdingen or rolling in trains across the eastern plains than could be rapidly absorbed either in towns, where an influx of Reich German officials beat them to it, or as farmers – for the interests of existing, or putative, ethnic Germans in Poland had also to be considered, and property rights were complicated. Himmler's own ramified resettlement apparatus could employ only a fraction of incoming white-collar workers, and not all young males met Waffen-SS admission criteria. Nor was it solely a question of straightforward exchange of ethnic Germans for Polish or Jewish deportees. Since it was decided to match or improve the former's standard of living, the number of deportees had to be double the number of repatriates, another instance of self-imposed constraints. Resettlements affected Jews and Poles in another respect. Theoretically, the Reich Ministry of Finance would redisburse money from Soviet oil and grain deliveries to the ethnic Germans, in place of their abandoned assets. In practice, since these funds were diverted to pay for the costs of war, ethnic Germans were compensated by the expropriation of Jewish and Polish assets, which were finite; this meant that sooner or later the ethnic Germans might themselves become an economic burden, a fate that was a certainty for the Jews and Poles, whose assets they were consuming. Poles capable of labour would be shipped to the Reich, with the unproductive residue left to their own devices in the General Government. But for how long would the Nazis tolerate the existence of impoverished Jews, whose dependency was a result of their own racist policies?

A further, self-engendered complication was that these events in Poland were not isolated from developments elsewhere. The emergence of Frank's General Government as a peripheral dumping ground for Jewish and Polish deportees acted as a stimulus to any Nazi potentate, keen to excel in the competitive stakes of making his fiefdom free of Jews.[26] The enthusiasm for this enterprise came from below as well as above. Far down the feeding chain, local Nazi Party comrades wondered why Viennese Jews were consuming rations, living in large apartments and not performing forced labour when informed opinion believed they were responsible for the war. Why not send them east of the Vistula river, or lodge them in the upper storeys of buildings where they would bear the brunt of Allied air raids?[27] Across the Greater Reich, the expulsion of the Jews was seen as the miracle solution to a housing shortage, although Jews constituted less than 1 per cent of the population, and hence were statistically irrelevant in this context. Any demands to expel such Jews presupposed the willingness of someone else to take them. But what if the General Government resisted accepting the burden of absorbing everyone else's racial outcasts? What if its own civil and military rulers exacerbated the general confusion by trying to relocate ethnic Germans and Poles from areas designed for the Jews, or to remove the latter from places near German military bases? Deportation to the General Government was accompanied by resettlement from and deportation within it. Vast transfers of people had been set in motion, without any sober appreciation of what was involved, and with the probability that the resulting conflicts over short-term aims rather than end goals would generate ever bolder radical solutions. The structural circumstances surrounding the 'Final Solution' were a deliberate product of individual human agency, not a species of *deus ex machina*. Each complication which the Nazis sought to correct arose only because of their own earlier decisions.

Moreover, the human objects of these policies did not constitute an argument for the status quo. Of the half-million ethnic Germans repatriated in 1939–41, some 436,000 languished in various types of reception or observation camps, pending a resettlement that never came.[28] They began to vent their frustration, while the official initial enthusiasm towards them degenerated into mere refugee management. The situation of the Jews was much more parlous. Any resources Jews possessed were depleted by daily acts of state-sanctioned robbery and by their deliberate exclusion from entire sectors of the economy under a process of instantaneous 'aryanisation'. Graphs and graphics, worthy of a management seminar, illustrated the audacity with which this was done. Other burdens on the Jews were immense numbers of deportees arriving in what were already crowded *de facto* ghettos, and support had to be found for indigent families of Jews shipped off to slave-labour camps in the Lublin district.[29] This was bound to raise the question of what would happen in the event of total dependency, for Jews were disqualified from obtaining welfare. This dependency reinforced Nazi stereotypes of Jews as unproductive 'parasites', just as the developing dirt and squalor enabled them to elide Jews with vermin, as notoriously exemplified by the film *The Eternal Jew*. These problems were entirely created by the Nazi regime, with no concern whatsoever for entirely predictable human consequences of any given policy. To call them structural problems is rather misleading, since 'structures' such as these were the product of choice and intention as well as circumstance. People chose blindness to the human misery ensuing from their actions.

Another area of absolute dependency was simultaneously being resolved by murder. Organisationally related only tangentially to the continuing T-4 'euthanasia' programme in Germany and Austria, the Nazis' killing of sick patients quickly stole into the eastern provinces of Germany and incorporated Poland. Psychiatric patients in West Prussian and Pomeranian asylums were systematically murdered to create space for new Waffen-SS battalions which moved into the emptied asylum buildings. Space ancillary to SS requirements was used to house temporarily some ethnic Germans, although this was not the primary motivation for these killings.[30] Close-range shootings of asylum patients were carried out by a special SS unit called the SS-Wachsturmbann Eimann, by local Selbstschutz units, or by SS Einsatzkommandos. The victims often thought they were going on an outing, chatting away to men who then blew their brains out.[31] The men responsible for these killings had an apparently simple understanding of how they came to be doing such a thing: on joining the SS they were 'in for a penny, in for a pound'.

These policies were extended to the Wartheland, as the Warthegau was initially called. Patients were murdered in a static gassing installation at Fort VII in Posen during November and December 1939, and in vans converted to deliver bottled carbon-monoxide gas operated by a special detachment, called the Sonderkommando Lange, named after its leader SS-Haupsturmführer Herbert Lange. In May 1940, Lange's team killed more than fifteen hundred patients at Soldau, batches of whom were driven off at three-hourly intervals in a van marked 'Kaiser's Coffee', never to be seen again.[32] As is apparent in a correspondence between Lange's superior, Wilhelm Koppe, and the East Prussian Higher SS- and Police Chief Wilhelm Rediess, Lange's skills were hired out, at a price, to kill people in other administrative jurisdictions, their disappearance being described euphemistically as 'evacuation'. Incidental at this time to the fate of the Jewish masses, this element of Nazi murderousness was nonetheless edging to their proximity, with the men on the ground – and those giving them orders – becoming steadily inured to and fluent in surreptitiously killing large numbers of people, a process that was acquiring its own specialist euphemistic vocabulary.

While the murder of psychiatric patients was extended into Poland, where the SS (and NKVD) were also systematically murdering the nation's intellectual and social elites, eager minds were at work on how best to convert into reality the Nazis' general intentions to deport Jews. On 10 September 1939, the young emigration expert Adolf Eichmann and Franz Walter Stahlecker discussed plans to deport to eastern Poland Polish Jews living in Moravska-Ostrava (in the Czech Protectorate where Stahlecker commanded the Security Police in

Prague) and Vienna, where Eichmann had cut his teeth on the 'Jewish Question'. The plan went to Heydrich and then back as an order to Eichmann from the head of the Gestapo, Heinrich Müller, although the latter mentioned Moravska-Ostrava and Kattowitz rather than Vienna.[33] Eichmann nonetheless told the leader of the Viennese Jewish community to choose poor, able-bodied men for resettlement. Talk of this opening door spread, with the head of the Reich Criminal Police Office inquiring whether Eichmann could include Berlin's Gypsies in his calculations.[34] He suggested appending a few cars of Gypsies to the trains deporting Viennese Jews. He alighted upon Nisko on the San, south of the Lublin district, in eastern Poland, which he, Stahlecker and a Soviet commissar toured on 12–15 October. The first shipments of Jews equipped with joinery tools departed from Moravka-Ostrava, Kattowitz and Vienna on 18 and 20 October 1939. The SS guards converted the Jews' Reichsmarks into złoty well below the official exchange rate during the journey in a typical display of punctilious corruption. However, once disembarked in Nisko, only a small number of Jews were set to work building a camp; the rest were robbed and bundled over the demarcation line with Russia to the accompaniment of gunfire. This disorderly shambles displeased local administrators, the army and of course the Russians.

Why was the Nisko scheme so abruptly abandoned? First, it required transport which the army needed or which Göring required to ship potatoes and sugar beet to Germany. Secondly, Eichmann seemed to be taking liberties with his superiors' authority, pushing ahead a messy, piecemeal operation when they wanted a tidy over-all solution. Thirdly, deporting urbanised Jews from Kattowitz, Moravska-Ostrava or Vienna did not solve the problem of where to deposit ethnic German peasants from Galicia or Volhynia arriving in the incorporated parts of Poland. Although the technical feasibility of mass deportations had been demonstrated, the geographical and occu-pational origins of the Nisko deportees were tangential to the problem at hand. Bürckel in Vienna and Wagner in Lower Silesia would have to wait while Himmler and Heydrich created space for ethnic Germans in incorporated Poland and Frank was persuaded to take their Poles and Jews.[35]

Although Nisko dropped out of the frame, with the surviving Jews being repatriated, interest in a Jewish reservation in the Lublin district grew. Some features of the district, which had been traded with the Soviet Union for Lithuania, are worth emphasis. First, when Frank's deputy, Arthur Seyss-Inquart, visited this waterlogged region in November 1939, he pronounced its suitability for the depletion of the numbers of Jews to be sent there.[36] Minds that still baulked at mass extermination as something only Bolsheviks did were comfortable with less than total murder through brutality and processes of attrition. Secondly, Lublin's frontier location meant an exceptional amount of construction activity was going on, with army, air force, civil and SS interest in large-scale forced labour to build airfields, anti-tank ditches and major drainage projects. Maybe these two things could be combined?[37]

Deportations to Lublin were a grim business. An anonymous report forwarded to Himmler in March 1940 described the evacuation of 160 German Jews from Schneidemühl to Lublin that winter. They were allowed to take nothing with them. No bedding, food, handbags, money or utensils, and they were stripped of the extra underwear and coats they donned for the journey. They were dispersed among three villages thirty kilometres from Lublin, with children and eighty-year-olds trudging fourteen hours a day through deep snow in temperatures of −22 degrees. The route was strewn with corpses from an earlier transport from Stettin. The frostbitten toes and fingers of survivors had to be amputated.[38] By the summer of 1940, fifty to seventy thousand Jews were lodged in seventy-six separate camps in the Lublin district, working in atrocious conditions on various projects. The Polish doctor Zygmunt Klukowski described these camps:

> The conditions at the labor camps are terrifying. . . . The work there is digging deep trenches. The trenches are part of a system to dry out existing swamps and prepare the land for future cultivation. The workers are standing in water the whole day. They are very poorly fed and live in filthy barracks. The barracks are located several kilometers from the job sites, so besides the long hours of work the camp inmates must walk another two hours a day to and from the camp. During the walk the Germans beat the prisoners with their fists and sticks.[39]

After 1 November 1939, Himmler's SS-1 and Police Leader in Lublin was the part-Slovene Austrian policeman Odilo Globocnik, a man whose energy and ruthlessness distinguished him from the run of his SS associates.[40] In Lublin, Globocnik recruited his own private army called the Selbstschutz, or self-defence unit, consisting of about a thousand ethnic German men, the majority farmhands and artisans in their twenties and thirties. He also presided over singular examples of

Nazi inhumanity, including an eighty-strong brigade of conditionally discharged poachers led by the convicted pervert Dr Oskar Dirlewanger, who acted as guards at the Dzikow camp for Jews near the Bug. In other circumstances they might have been fêted as primitive rebels.

A series of orders posted by Dirlewanger to impose order on these crooks *in their own quarters* gives an indirect view of the mayhem they visited upon Jews unfortunate enough to be in their vicinity. Drunken troops smashed doors and windows, carousing and dancing into the early hours, strewing rubbish across the courtyard and garden. The lightbulbs had to be removed at ten every night for these were favoured targets for random gunfire. Known to his men as 'our Gandhi' because of his gaunt appearance, Dirlewanger tried to draw a halt to what he called their 'Gypsy misrule' or 'Zigeunerunleben'.[41] Dirlewanger himself was under investigation by Globocnik. The charges included having employed an SS physician to poison fifty-seven Jews, a practice he rationalised by saying that this meant a better chance of preserving their clothing and teeth than shooting. He found the moral order in Lublin confusing: 'Lublin is a funny place; on the one hand I have relations with a Jewess, and drink schnapps with Jews; on the other I'm so heartless and poison males and females.'[42] These forces backed up Globocnik's bid to monopolise control of the Jews in the Lublin district, effectively removing them and their labour from the civilian authorities. He began by establishing a series of workshops, making the Jewish Council defray the cost of guarding them, and then contracted out Jewish labour to army or civilian construction projects. A series of primitive camps, including Belzec, sprang up along the frontier with the Soviet Union. Although both of Globocnik's ambitions, namely to train a non-Reich German private army and to gain exclusive SS control of Jews engaged on harebrained construction projects, eventually collapsed like a house of cards, experience was acquired which was generalised under more propitious conditions.[43]

The dismal fate of the Jews sent to the Lublin district was still secondary, as it would be in this perverse set of priorities, to the major problem represented by the ethnic German repatriates. Gossip had it that Himmler had overreached himself, with Goebbels noting in his diaries: 'At present, Himmler is displacing nations. Not always successfully.' The ethnic Germans may have been prospective settlers, but their reality was that of camp inmates, in itself a startling admission of failure. They became objects of charity, lectures and neglect. A refugee camp psychosis developed. Apart from the unsolved problem of their ultimate destiny, racial scientific punctiliousness and a security fear that the NKVD might have smuggled the odd suspect apple into the barrel meant further delays. The ethnic Germans were subject to debriefing sessions designed to ascertain their political commitments, and to elaborate racial checks during which their physical data were recorded on cards. Yet further resettlement experts and their academic entourage fussed about matching people and skills to locations. Equally time-consuming procedures were adopted to vet the Polish population, looking for submerged ethnic Germans, that is Poles who looked like Germans, or for Poles whose membership of chauvinistic organisations such as Catholic Action or the West Marches Association made their deportation from the General Government a priority.[44] Simply laying hands on Poles who could be deported as forced labour or to the General Government was difficult, since they fled at the first sight of German officials. To resolve these problems created by the Nazis' own policies, Himmler ordered the total deportation of Jews and various categories of Poles from the incorporated territories by February 1940, or altogether about one million people. His own subordinates scaled this down to the more modest task of deporting over eighty thousand Poles and Jews from the Warthegau to make space for ethnic Germans from the Baltic. This débâcle was dressed up as the 'first short-range plan'. It was as if these men belatedly realised that a cake has to be cut up in order to eat it.

The Frank regime in Cracow resisted its designated role as a general human rubbish dump. It had support from Göring, who objected to the disruption of food transports caused by trains filled with people rather than fuel and food. Frank intended to make his fiefdom productive; his plans militated against taking in other colleagues' allegedly workshy racial undesirables, or, worse, the non-productive residue left after Polish labour had been subtracted. Furthermore, the army was reducing the space available for deportees in the General Government through its insistence that only ethnic Germans should reside within a fifty-kilometre radius of their burgeoning facilities in eastern Poland. For example, in the summer of 1940 it decided to create a huge artillery range in southern Konin county. The Armed Forces High Command liaised with SS-Gruppenführer Koppe: eighty thousand Poles and four thousand Jews had to be relocated. First, nearly two thousand ethnic Germans were moved to the north of the county, taking over two or three Polish farms per family. This duly stymied plans to settle incoming Volhynian Germans in the same spot. Ten thousand Poles expelled from the north then joined sixty thousand in the south, making a total of seventy thousand to be deported to the General Government in order to create the artillery range. The detailed accounts did not mention Poles who refused to move or ethnic Germans in the north who claimed that they had 'loaned' the Poles inventory now being usurped by incoming ethnic Germans from the south: such complications were frequent.[45] Moving people was not a simple business.

But what was happening to the Jews of Poland while the Nazi leaders were grappling, inefficiently, with impossible numbers of deportees and migrants? Initial Nazi policy towards the Jews involved concentrating, controlling and exploiting them, with greater or lesser degrees of arbitrariness and terror, with a view to expelling them elsewhere. Crammed into insalubrious districts, and subjected to daily sequestrations not just of cash and valuables, but of birdcages, door handles and hot-water bottles, the Jews had no other resource than their depleted physical strength to earn the minimum needed for survival.[46] They were used as forced labour, with the stewards of the Jewish Councils ensuring order and compliance; stigmatised with identificatory armbands; subjected to curfews; their movements restricted, with deportees from the smaller towns confined to existing Jewish quarters in big cities. Long before Jews were officially confined in ghettos, senior Nazi leaders hoped that overcrowding would fatally deplete the Jews through disease and malnourishment. As Frank put it on 25 November, 'The more that die, the better,' or Himmler: 'It's high time that this rabble is driven together in ghettos, and then plague will creep in and they'll croak.' These were not metaphors, and there seems no convincing reason why we should not assume that words reflected intentions.[47]

Although local authorities established ghettos for reasons that are difficult to generalise about, they were all severely reduced versions of existing Jewish quarters, or deliberately placed because in insalubrious quarters. Jews from surrounding areas were then added to the urban Jewish population, in the case of Piotrków, the first ghetto to be established, eight thousand 'refugees' – or internal deportees – joined a similar number already present. In Warsaw, 30 per cent of the city's population was crammed into 2.4 per cent of its urban space based on sections of seventy-three of its eighteen hundred streets.[48] This was an unnatural level of congestion, but in addition yet more people were later scooped up from the towns and villages of the entire Warsaw district, bringing the total ghetto population to more than four hundred thousand people in a district where 280,000 people had once lived tolerably. This resulted not only in lamentable domestic overcrowding, with an average of just over nine people to each room, but in conditions on narrow streets more akin to the milling hordes on a major metropolitan business or shopping thoroughfare.[49]

Apart from the desire to control the Jews, what factors went into this ghettoisation? Financially ghettos were a cheaper option than costly concentration camps. There was no need to construct barracks, guardhouses or watchtowers, or to lay on electric or gas power and sanitation facilities. Instead, Jews were crammed into scaled-down residential districts. While concentration camps tended, by the laws of logic, to become everburgeoning fixed facilities, the logic behind the use of ghettos was to make them diminish to vanishing point. This also reflected the Nazis' relative indifference towards utilising Jews as productive labour; as distinct from brutalising and humiliating them on massive projects as meaningless as Stalin's construction projects.[50] Even when sections of the Łódź ghetto administration tried to make productive use of Jewish labour, they showed no concern for the workforce *per se*. Production was totally divorced from concern for the producer.

Other motives were at work too. First, ghettoisation facilitated extortion. As Greiser informed a gathering of Party officials in January 1940: 'The Jews will remain there until what they have amassed to exchange for food is returned and then they will be shoved over the border. Then the empty ghetto will be razed to the ground by fire.'[51] Greed was not the only motive; in major towns ghettoisation created more living space for Germans and Poles and brutally clarified the ethnic geography, for these were peoples destined to live apart. There was also a colonialist improvement mission that was integral to the Nazi sense of being 'bearers of culture' in the undeveloped East. Cities such as Łódź or Warsaw were an affront to their aesthetic sense and desire for orderliness. Architects and town planners tried to impose a German countenance on ancient cities, for as a newspaper had it: 'Litzmannstadt [as Łódź was soon renamed] must become more beautiful!' Technical drawings, entitled 'Warsaw – The new German City', dated February 1940, were emblazoned with the slogan: 'The Deconstruction of the Polish City. The Construction of the German City. The Resettlement of the Jews'.[52] In Łódź, 160,000 Jews were ejected from their homes in January 1940 and concentrated in the Baluty, Stare

Miasto (Old Town) and Marysin districts, near the Jewish cemetery, to make room for German bureaucrats, fifteen thousand Baltic Germans and bulldozers come to improve the place.[53] They were crammed into about thirty-two thousand mainly one-room apartments in wooden buildings, of which 725 had running water, 95 per cent lacked lavatories or sewage connections, and the majority had no electricity.[54]

The more protracted evolution of the Warsaw ghetto illustrates that ghettoisation was also a fall-back position after major deportation schemes came to nothing. Having tried to establish a ghetto in Warsaw in November 1939, only to see their plans wrecked by a tactical alliance between the Jewish Council and the German military commander, the Nazi civil authorities in Warsaw returned to the project in early 1940. The Madagascar Plan, which we will discuss shortly, rendered these plans otiose, and then in October the Jews were abruptly relocated to a ghetto, which was sealed off a month later. Waldemar Schön's retrospective 1941 account of the genesis of the ghetto largely explains these tergiversations. On the one hand, there was not much point in establishing sealed ghettos as long as resettlement to Lublin, or elsewhere, was being mooted. On the other hand, German medical experts in Warsaw insisted upon the urgent isolation of the alleged carriers of typhus, lest an alleged epidemic spread to German bureaucrats and soldiers.

Unless they were uniquely incompetent, and Germany was in the vanguard of typhus studies, these doctors must have known that the disease was not ethnically idiosyncratic, and that improved diet, living conditions and sanitation were the surest way to combat it. This was clear to the scientist Professor Ludwik Hirszfeld, himself confined in the ghetto: 'This is the way the authorities hoped to isolate the carriers of the deadly germs. People calling themselves doctors supported this theory. [But] science long ago abolished medieval quarantines, not only because they were inhumane but because they were inefficient.' Since the incidence of typhus was already declining before the ghetto was established, removing grounds for fearing an epidemic, and since brick walls do not inhibit the communication of such a disease to surrounding populations, one can only conclude that this self-serving rationalisation was designed to promote the identity soon displayed on warning signs: 'Jew–Louse–Typhus'.[55] In other words, the alleged identity of Jews and typhus was an ideological construct designed to rationalise a policy adopted only after another plan for the Jews had been ruled out. The spuriousness of the doctors' line of argument can be easily gauged from the fact that coach parties of German soldiers toured the ghetto 'as if it was a zoo'.[56] Expert opinion was simultaneously advocating the subtraction of the Jews from economic life in the interests of rationalising Poland's ramshackle economy. Contraction of the 'Jewish sector' would create space for the expansion of the Polish sectors. All lines of thought conveniently converged on the Jews, whose removal was becoming a universal panacea for architectural, economic, medical, settlement and security problems, rationalising ulterior prejudice.[57]

While town planners, doctors and economists endeavoured to isolate the Jews, at the highest level a fantastic project was doing the rounds as to where to deposit them. The idea of deporting Jews to the French colony of Madagascar had been a stock in trade among European antisemites since the 1880s.[58] The Polish government approached both the French and British in 1937 with a view to sending a million Jews either there or to British southern Africa. Although the British proved unsympathetic, in May Prime Minister Léon Blum and Colonial Minister Montet permitted a Polish mission to visit Madagascar to ascertain its suitability for Polish Jews.[59] The two Jewish members of the mission pronounced the island unsuitable for more than five hundred families; their Polish colleague recommended five to seven thousand.[60] In 1938 Foreign Minister Bonnet suggested to Ribbentrop shipping ten thousand Jewish refugees to the island; in 1939 Chamberlain and Roosevelt inquired whether Mussolini could accommodate Jews in Ethiopia. However outlandish the idea of sending Jews to British Guiana, Ethiopia or Madagascar seems from our perspective, at the time it was debated by serious international statesmen. The Nazis interpreted this as evidence of an antisemitic consensus. In March 1938 Heydrich seems to have told Eichmann to investigate a diplomatic resolution of the 'Jewish Question' 'as has already been discussed between France and Poland'.

Under the circumstances of mid-1940 the Madagascar solution displaced, or rather complemented, the Lublin reservation as a long-term solution. Himmler alluded to something of the sort in thoughts on the treatment of alien populations in the East when he wrote on 15 May: 'I hope to see the term "Jew" completely eliminated through the possibility of a large-scale emigration of all Jews to Africa or to some colony.'[61] The idea, which presupposed the neutralisation of the Royal Navy, and whose broader context was the prospect of a German empire across central Africa, was dusted down for discussion by Franz

Rademacher, head of the Jewish desk in Foreign Ministry Department Germany III. Sitting in his formerly Jewish-owned apartment, with a hastily assembled library on the 'Jewish Question', Rademacher thought he had the solution to the problem.[62] Like his political masters, he knew that the war had two purposes: 'The present war has a double face: one is imperialistic – the securing of political, military and economic space necessary for Germany as a world power, one supra-national – liberation of the world from the chains of Jewry and Freemasonry.'

While Palestine was ruled out as a destination ('danger of a second Rome!'), mass deportation elsewhere seemed to be the answer. One could retain the Lublin solution for the biologically 'regenerative' and politically militant eastern Jews, who could be used as hostages against the imagined actions of their American coreligionists, while shipping off the more passive western European Jews to Madagascar. According to Rademacher's 3 July 1940 memorandum, the island was to be transferred to Germany as a mandate, with areas not needed for airfields or naval bases subject to an SS police governor. The existing forty thousand European settlers were to be transferred elsewhere, while the fate of the indigenous population was left unresolved. Jews would be stripped of their respective citizenships, but allowed limited self-administration within the mandate, which demonstrated German generosity towards them. An intra-European bank would receive the Jews' liquidated assets, and release funds to the SS to cover the costs of transportation and resettlement. Viktor Brack, of the T-4 'euthanasia' programme, was to be in charge of transportation. This was potentially sinister. So was Rademacher's description of the island as a 'great ghetto', where the SS would expertly control the Jews on the basis of their extensive experience, and so was the explicit threat to use these captive Jews as a brake on American Jewry.

That summer Rademacher called for data on the Jewish population of Europe and information on Madagascar. The statistician Friedrich Burgdörfer, calculating the population density on the island, was disingenuous when he stated that it would be lower than in the Reich, since large parts of Madagascar were arid, diseased and hot, hence unfit for comfortable habitation. The earlier Polish mission had pronounced it suitable for five hundred to seven thousand families. An academic geologist reported that with no precious mineral deposits or fossil fuels, but only graphite, the place was not too well favoured for the Jews of Europe. It does not take much imagination to see that many people were going to perish either *en route* to or as a result of conditions on the island. Hitler said as much when in May 1942, recalling the abandoned project, he enthused over the debilitating biological effects of tropical climates.[63]

Rademacher's plan also represented a Foreign Ministry bid for control of the 'Final Solution'. Heydrich duly reminded the interloping Rademacher that he had been in charge of Jewish emigration since January 1939, and not without a little success. In August 1940 he produced counter-proposals for 'dear comrade Rademacher', elaborated by Theodor Dannecker, the ambitious SD officer, who had been lobbying for such a solution since 1938. The counter-proposals virtually cut out the Foreign Ministry, and involved dispatching fifteen hundred Jews from Europe every day for four years.[64] Talk of this bold solution circulated at many levels. Hitler mentioned it to Mussolini; Greiser discussed it with Frank. Eichmann called in the representatives of the Jews of Berlin, Prague and Vienna to ascertain their opinion. On 1 July 1940 Gerhard Mende, head of the Jewish desk in the Warsaw Gestapo, informed Council chairman Adam Czerniakow that 'the war would be over in a month and that the Jews would depart for Madagascar'.[65] The Gauleiters of Baden and the Saar Palatinate clearly thought this was going to be sooner rather than later since with Hitler's approval they deported over six thousand German Jews to Vichy France via Alsace-Lorraine. These otherwise inexplicable deportations suggest that the Madagascar plan was entertained quite seriously.

So too does another, often unremarked, aspect of Nazi antisemitism. As Germany's military successes multiplied during 1940, so belief in the cunning and power of the Jews briefly diminished, displaced by the thought that they might actually be 'stupid', a notion that flew in the face of the stereotypes of 'smart' or 'satanic' Jews. Even Hitler showed a faint empathy, as he numbered the Jews among the races exploited by the perfidious British, as race hatred was briefly upstaged by resentment towards a real imperial power.[66] Did the desire to gloat over the Jews' misfortune – for what emotional and psychological emptiness would there have been without them, what jokes and slurs would have been meaningless in their absence – accompany the desire to decimate or destroy them? It reminds one that a few pure Gypsies were to be kept on a reservation as a living ethnic curiosity. For Jews were a preferred object for jokes. Frank spoke about Madagascar to a Party gathering in Cracow:

As soon as sea communications permit the shipment of the Jews (laughter in the audience), they shall be shipped, piece by piece, man by man, woman by woman, girl by girl. I hope, gentlemen, you will not complain on that account (merriment in the hall). I believe, therefore, that we are already, as they say, out of the morass.[67]

Antisemitic cartoons depicted bewildered eastern Jews arriving by boat amid palm trees and Gauguinesque natives. But the moment for gloating passed, and the self-induced and licensed chaos worsened.

The Madagascar plan was predicated on the defeat of Great Britain. The failure to neutralise Britain and the concomitant risk to sea traffic in the Atlantic denied the plan practicality. In early February 1941, Hitler touched on this subject during a meeting. When Bormann inquired how the Jews were to be moved overseas, Hitler suggested Ley's 'Strength through Joy' cruise liner fleet, but then worried about the fate of their German crews in seas infested with British submarines. The unconcern about the liner's passengers was characteristic. The reorientation eastwards of the main war effort led to a corresponding reorientation of thoughts on a territorial solution of the 'Jewish Question'. By February 1942, the fertile Rademacher had to acknowledge that the project was dead, since alternative possibilities had opened up in the East. Hitler broached the 'Madagascar solution' in subsequent conversations with foreign leaders, but by then it had become a cover for more radical measures.[68]

While the Madagascar solution evaporated, there was still the problem of Jews left languishing in Poland's ghettos. Sheer survival, and ambiguities in Nazi policy, fostered belief that if the Jews could demonstrate self-sufficiency, or indeed productive value, to the Nazis, then the latter would have a material stake in not killing them. It was a reasonable calculation to make, provided the Nazis were interested in economic rationality. In September 1940, the Łódź Jewish Council received a German loan (from confiscated Jewish funds) which began the productivisation of the ghetto. By 1943, the Łódź Jewish Council had succeeded in organising some 117 factories, warehouses and sorting offices, with 85 per cent of the adult population working. Similar workshops, laundering clothes, repairing shoes, making bandages, brushes, candles, soap or toys opened in Kovno, where Jews also built a German airfield.[69]

Situated in Poland's equivalent of Manchester, the Łódź ghetto exemplified the 'rescue through work' strategy. It became a sweatshop writ large, with starving people producing an enormous range of goods and services in *ad hoc* factories and workshops, where the power frequently gave out and conditions were grim.[70] German firms were keen to contract work there, not least because Łódź was remote from Allied bombing, and labour costs were unusually competitive. The products and services included cattle-bone combs, corsets and bras for the Berlin market, cartridge casings, cigarette boxes, fur coats, rubber wear for motorcyclists, paper bags, alterations and cleaning, and the embroidering of swastikas and insignia on uniforms. Former skilled artisans now did rudimentary production-line work in factories numbering hundreds or thousands. Work was a demoralising affair, for wages only covered inadequate rations. While the Nazi authorities in the Warthegau, where Łódź was situated, were the main beneficiaries of ghetto labour, the Jews came last in the pecking order for fuel and food, as the authorities diverted wage payments by German firms into their own coffers. The wider backdrop to productive ghettos was a process of attrition which killed about half a million people through disease and deliberate starvation.

This 'rescue through work' strategy recommended itself for other reasons. It made psychological sense to employ people, rather than leaving them to contemplate their dire misfortune in enforced idleness. Since one of the most egregious antisemitic stereotypes was of Jewish economic 'parasitism', the Jews decided to counter this by demonstrating their belief in hard work. As Jakob Gens of Vilna had it: 'Both in the maintenance of industry, and in our work in individual units, we must prove that, contrary to the accepted assumption that we are not fit for any kind of work, we have been very useful.'[71] Above all, Council leaders calculated that economic rationality would prevail, and that they were dealing with forces which could be reasoned with rather than with ideological fanatics who were oblivious to any rational assumptions. Since the local Nazi ghetto administrators were themselves of many minds, and awaiting definitive decisions from their respective political masters, this was not an unreasonable view to take. The Council leaders tried to find method in the enveloping insanity, and in the process sometimes lost their own way in this moral maze.[72]

Productivity became an end in itself, an unsurprising development in the isolation of the ghetto. For what dark thoughts might be engendered by the exercise of imagination? Council leaders made a fetish of work, exhorting tired and demotivated people to greater labours through slogans such as 'Work is our guide' displayed on the walls.[73] Cinemagoers will be familiar with the *Bridge on the River Kwai* syndrome, where obtuse certainty that one man can save all led to the obliteration of all other perspectives. The young Dawid Sierakowski caught this when he wrote of the Łódź ghetto Elder Rumkowski: 'all he cares about is increasing productivity, while starvation remains the same'.[74] Whether this reflected juvenile insight or the judgemental arrogance of adolescence is hard to determine. Massive disparities between various ghetto elites and the ghetto poor heightened these social tensions.

But the obsession with production was not simply a question of internalising some of the goals and values of their own persecutors. In the logic of things, an obsession with work meant a corresponding impatience with the unproductive, who became a drag on limited resources. The Łódź ghetto chronicle noted: 'The ghetto has not only become a labour camp, where there is no place for people who are not working, but also some sort of Nietzschean experimental laboratory from which only the "very strong" emerge in one piece.'[75] This would take on even more terrible forms during the era of deportations, as the Jewish Councils adopted a form of social triage to meet Nazi demands with the least damage to their communities.

The Madagascar plan was the nebulous background to a foreground of self-generated problems induced by the Nazis' own decisions. In August 1940, Germany agreed to take back tens of thousands of ethnic Germans from Transylvanian territory Romania had ceded to Hungary, while in September Germany and the Soviet Union agreed the repatriation of a further 137,077 ethnic Germans from Bessarabia and North Bukovina, occupied since June by the Soviet Union. These new arrivals would swell the numbers of ethnic Germans already languishing in holding camps, awaiting somewhere to go. This catastrophe led Heydrich to envisage the deportation of over seven hundred thousand Poles from the incorporated territories during 1941. Nor was there any abatement in the desire of Nazi leaders to cleanse their own territories of Jews. Not only Greiser, but now Schirach in Vienna, Forster in Danzig and Koch in Königsberg were actively hustling Frank to take 'their' Jews, with Hitler scaling down their expectations to reconcile them with Frank's passionate reluctance to accommodate them. Once again Hitler created concord among his subordinates, who, according to Goebbels, 'may all offload their rubbish on the General Government. Jews, the sick, idlers etc. And Frank strives against this. Not entirely without reason. He wants to make Poland into a model country. That's going too far. He cannot and should not do that.'[76] Although some Jews were deported from West Prussia, Hitler accorded priority to removing sixty thousand Viennese Jews to resolve an 'Aryan' housing shortage.

Within the General Government, Frank's own officials were pressing him to do something about the Jews whom they themselves had concentrated in circumstances that were logically bound, once the Jews had been systematically robbed to pay for their food and fuel, to burden the German authorities. In turn, the army, instructed since 18 December to complete preparations for Operation Barbarossa by 15 May 1941, and with its artillery ranges, marshalling yards and training areas proliferating as three million men assembled to invade Russia, pushed for the relocation of half a million Poles within both the incorporated territories and the General Government. About one million people were to be deported during 1941, without any evident concern for how they were to be supported, and without having regard to such details as military competition for the same transport facilities. By 15 March, when a quarter of a million people should have been deported, only a tenth of them had been expelled; bearing in mind the formula for replacing Poles with ethnic Germans, only five thousand spaces had been created for over a quarter of a million expectant people.[77] The priority given to the build-up for Barbarossa meant further displacements of populations.

THE VISION UNFOLDS AGAINST SOVIET JEWS

The vistas opened up by Operation Barbarossa enabled the Nazi leaders to wish away all the problems they had created, postponing them for a brief duration, and mentally relocating a 'final territorial solution' to beyond where German armies were fighting. Communism also intensified the Nazis' demonisation of the Jews, to whom were ascribed the all too apparent evils of the Bolshevik tyranny. Since the Nazis regarded Jews as the chief supports of the Soviet regime, if they were to be killed, then that regime would collapse like a house of cards. The combination of frustration at the course of military events and ideological fanaticism effectively sealed the fate of the Jews, although we are not quite amid the European-wide 'Final Solution'. The Jews slipped towards an indeterminate and militarily uncontested 'East', but with information as to how the Nazis conceived this, equivalent to what is known about Lublin or Madagascar, not available. Hitler still mentioned Madagascar to Mussolini three weeks before the invasion of Russia, but this had become 'Siberia or Madagascar' in remarks to the Croatian General Kvaternik a month after the campaign started.[78] There may be a missing link here, for odd references were made to western Siberia, the Soviet Arctic gulags or the Pripyat marshes as possible, impossible, locations for the Jews, even as policy gradually took another turn.

Plans have survived, but they were not primarily concerned with Jews. From the summer of 1941 and early 1942, competing teams of SS planners – in Himmler's Reich Commissariat and Heydrich's Reich Main Security Office – turned their minds to the resettlement eastwards of tens of millions of Slavs from Poland and former regions of the Soviet Union slated now for future germanisation. These planners continued to factor Jews into the equation long after their colleagues had begun murdering them.[79] Either they were recycling plans which have vanished, or their authors were peculiarly underprivileged regarding information about what was happening to the Jews. Some idea of

what might have been discussed may be concealed within evidence
dating from long after the time when the fate of the Jews had been
decided. At the 20 January 1942 Wannsee Conference, Heydrich
announced that the Jews of Europe would be worked to death in the
East, with any survivors being killed by more direct means. Yet two
weeks later, on 4 February, in a secret address in Prague, he spoke of
the deportation of eleven million Jews to Arctic concentration camps
in the Soviet Union, to be erected by an advanced guard of Czechs
deemed unsuitable for germanisation.[80] Soviet camp capacity was then
estimated at between fifteen and twenty millions. It may be that Siberia
was indeed an option, but one Hitler ruled out, on the ground that its
notorious climatic rigours would inadvertently produce super-tough
Jews, although the evidence of the Soviet gulags did not support this
theory.[81] Futuristic intentions, involving the deaths of tens of millions
of Slavs, for whose realisation plans continued to be made, became a
way of disguising what 'deportation', 'evacuation' or 'resettlement' of
the Jews had come to mean, and may have incorporated a link in the
planning process between the abandoned Madagascar solution and the
'Final Solution'. But this is the world of 'may', 'might' and 'maybe'; in
reality, other policies were being pursued. What really matters is that
the Nazi leadership invaded Russia to realise an ideological mission;
their subordinates were liberated from any of the circumstantial constraints on their activities in western or northern Europe. The Nietzschean 'beast of prey' was on the rampage, although Nietzsche could
not have imagined his ordinary ignobility. What had to be done
furtively in the night in western Europe could be done 'out there'
without regard to local sensibilities, and often in full view of the
German administration and army.

Specific orders paved the way for Operation Barbarossa to become
a war of racial extermination. In an earlier chapter we saw how SS–
army jurisdictions were clarified, with the army brought into the
business of summary murder along a series of unequivocal ideological
guidelines. Soldiers also sometimes helped the SS in their non-military
tasks. The preparations included the formation of four Einsatzgruppen
or mobile task forces, A, B, C and D, which operated as a series of
smaller Einsatzkommandos and Sonderkommandos to maximise territorial coverage, like multiplying cancer cells spreading through the
body. Although their primary function was to kill or to incite others
to kill people, their tasks also included securing enemy archives, anti-
partisan operations and such idiosyncratic commissions as scouring

caves for the archaeological remnants of Goths in the Crimea. It was as if the Reich Main Security Office had acquired wheels, literally so for each Group replicated the RSHA division of functions. These mobile units were assembled from May 1941 onwards at the frontier police school at Pretzsch and two other towns in Saxony, which together with the radio school at Fulda and the Security Police leadership school in Charlottenburg were controlled by the Personnel Department of Main Office I of the Reich Main Security Office (RSHA) in Berlin headed by Bruno Streckenbach. The nucleus was already at Pretzsch, preparing for Operation Sealion against England, in which they would have arrested or killed thousands of named individuals.[82] English speakers were replaced with men who knew some Russian. Additional recruits included three to four thousand men from the Criminal Police, Gestapo, SD and Waffen-SS, as well as Reserve Police Battalion 9, whose ranks were distributed among the four main units. Nothing seems to have distinguished their behaviour from their more ideologically saturated colleagues. Also present were men either chosen for, or acting as instructors to, a fast-stream Security Police cadre called the Leitende Dienst, that is men already selected for their political reliability and future promise for a five-term training course, including three at Berlin University. Many of the commanders of the Einsatzkommandos were desk officers in Main Office I of the Reich Main Security Office.[83] Historians have routinely made much of the fact that many of them were lawyers or economists, two-thirds of whom had higher education, and a third doctorates; less is predictably made of the truth that a doctorate sometimes merely betokens an assiduous mindlessness, signifying nothing about the wider personality.[84] For, ironically enough, the universities were precisely the places in Germany which fostered an elite form of antisemitism, whose radicality was ill disguised within a carapace of 'scientific objectivity' towards the 'Jewish Question'. Now these former student radicals had the chance to implement what they had so often talked of in their exclusive circles.[85]

More might also be made of the fact that these policemen were keen to see combat, with the prospect of decorations and rapid promotions. There was a war on, and these able-bodied men wished to be in the thick of it, even when their age or rank militated against this. Better still if there were intimations of hidden secrets within the secret of the invasion, for those involved could consider themselves not only the regime's praetorian guard, but its gnostic elect. It might be consoling to imagine that men who murdered women and children were personally cowardly, and thus to marginalise them from conventional notions of soldiering, but was this the case? Eagerness for combat was evident at the very highest levels. Heydrich flew fighter combat missions in Russia, on one occasion surprising the members of Einsatzkommando 10a as they realised the identity of the downed pilot tugging off his flight overalls as he strode towards them.[86] Arthur Nebe, head of the Criminal Police, was keen to acquire decorations and the SS rank of general, using that title as soon as he took command of Einsatzgruppe B in the field. The ranks were quick to spot a medal-seeker, such as Dr Kurt Christmann, who joined Group D in the field in August 1942. His 'chest pains' (*Brustschmerzen*) gave rise to doggerel verse:

> Christ bore a wooden cross,
> Christmann an iron one,
> Christ bore it undeserved,
> like Christmann his one.[87]

Officer appointments involved careful scrutiny of individuals, with Heydrich and Streckenbach making regular changes to their lists of names; the ranks were filled by quotas imposed on agencies deemed overstaffed.[88] We know next to nothing about the content of the officers' non-military instruction at Pretzsch, or of what was discussed when their leaders visited the RHSA, or when specialists on Bolshevism delivered talks. Our information on the Einsatzgruppen stems largely from their own reports. The various sub-units traversing an area reported back to their Kommando staff, which in turn reported either by courier or radio to the relatively stationary Group Staff headquarters. Strict guidelines instructed couriers to burn everything in the event of capture. There was to be no photography.[89] Weekly or biweekly edited highlights were then relayed by courier, radio or teletype to Group IV A1 of Office IV of the Reich Main Security Office in Berlin, where they were edited by Heinrich Müller, discussed in conference and condensed into Operational Situation Reports, which were seen by Hitler and Himmler. The scholar who knows these reports best, ironically enough, concludes that beyond their informational content they seem to have had no obvious function whatsoever.[90] Local units in the field sometimes produced maps, with coffins symbolising their kill rates, and Jewish populations marked as 'still present'.[91] In other words, apart from relatively sparse contemporary documentation and the extrapolated digests of their own reports, we must largely rely on a massive quantity of post-war trial materials to see what part these formations played in the genesis of the 'Final Solution'. Finally, four groups rapidly became five. In early June 1941 Heydrich allowed Eberhard Schöngarth, the Security Police and SD commander in the General Government, to form a fifth unit 'for special tasks' which from July operated behind Group B in the Ukraine and Belorussia.[92]

The first major study of these killing squads followed the line taken by Otto Ohlendorf, the only group commander who was tried at Nuremberg, to the effect that, a few days prior to their departure from Pretzsch, Bruno Streckenbach – whom Ohlendorf presumed dead in 1945 – communicated Hitler's order to kill the Jews they encountered in Russia.[93] This view was adopted by most of Ohlendorf's co-defendants, upon whom he still exerted influence. One dissenter insisted that his own group leader had communicated such an order only in August 1941, several weeks after the campaign had commenced, but little was made of this anomaly. But when in 1955 the still living Streckenbach was amnestied from a sentence of twenty-five years' hard labour in Russia, he strongly disputed having given such an order. Further trials were held, previous testimonies were revised and new versions were added. An increasing number testified to having received orders to kill Jews when operations were under way, while those who stuck to a prior order now highlighted Heydrich rather than Streckenbach.[94]

Attention refocused on two farewell gatherings at which Heydrich addressed respectively the officers and men: the first held on 17 June 1941 in the Reich Main Security Office in Berlin, the second at Pretzsch a few days later. Some former officers claimed in their post-war trials that Heydrich had issued an order to kill the Jews; others denied that this had been the case, and said that these gatherings had been taken up with farewells and routinised injunctions to hardness unexceptional in these circles and circumstances. As for the Pretzsch assembly, Heydrich spoke without a microphone to a large body of men, some of whom testified that his words were inaudible – incidentally an almost classic illustration of the lies, limitations and pitfalls which characterise this evidence. Although we should not discount the possibility that other instructions were communicated to the officers during the regular briefing sessions they had with senior figures in the Reich Main Security Office,[95] their operational functions, as described in a communication from Heydrich to Himmler's four Higher SS- and Police Leaders in Russia, did not include a generalised injunction to kill the Jews:

> All of the following are to be executed:
>
> Officials of the Comintern . . . top and medium-level officials and radical lower-level officials of the Party, Central Committee and district and sub-district committees
> People's Commissars
> Jews in Party and state employment, and other radical elements (saboteurs, propagandists, snipers, assassins, inciters, etc.)[96]

In other words, this was a more radical and ethnically specific version of what had been done in Poland, whose primary purpose was to destroy what the Nazis regarded as the supports of the Soviet state. Killing these people would hasten the military collapse of the Soviet Union and secure German hegemony.[97] Inevitably, such orders were open-ended. How exactly were the Einsatzgruppen going to establish who was who? It was unlikely that Communists, Jewish or otherwise, were going to oblige by walking about with Party cards and insignias in their lapels. Local accomplices could identify victims, but the general presumption was that any 'intellectual' was a Communist and that all males of military age – did one qualify to be shot at fifteen, sixteen, forty or fifty? – were saboteurs and subversives. And how did they identify Jews? Not easily, for in October 1941 Sipo and SD units touring POW camps were learnedly informed that because Soviet Jews since 1920–1 had ceased circumcision in order to disguise their ethnic origins, this was not a reliable guide to whom to shoot.[98] In other words the order had an enormous degree of elasticity built in, for there was as much precision here as in the Communist Khmer Rouge identification of 'intellectuals' by their smooth palms or spectacles.[99] And that was before these units were under pressure of time, which itself militated against scrupulosity.

In contrast to the non-precision of this instruction, with its close, but not exact, emulation of the Commissar Order, the instruction not to put any obstacles in the way of the 'self-cleansing' measures of indigenous anti-Communist and antisemitic forces was looser. This was not going to be a problem, since on 17 and 29 June Heydrich had instructed his more politically intelligent commanders to incite, or intensify, local pogroms against Communists and Jewish men, without leaving their own fingerprints on the touchpaper – a written circumspection that may have been intended for a military audience. There were other reasons why these shootings may have been restricted to males, in contrast to subsequent killings. The killing squads shadowed the army, using unstable circumstances as both a cover and pretext for what they were doing. They could exploit the ambiguities of war zones to the maximum, claiming that they were enforcing security. With their own forces too few to kill upwards of 2.75–2.9 million Jews stranded in German-occupied territory, they could return for the women and children, whom they herded into makeshift ghettos – or so it would seem, if one posits a general order issued prior to the invasion to kill Jews for being Jewish.[100] In other words the order was to kill as many Jews as they deemed feasible under the circumstances.[101] If one does not make that assumption, it is barely conceivable that they killed in line with Heydrich's instructions, to warn remaining Jews of what would happen if they resisted eventual deportation further eastwards, and to terrify their as yet unconquered opponents into fleeing before them.[102] There was also a need gradually to desensitise the killers themselves, before they embarked on a higher order of slaughter, which, judging from many accounts, disturbed even their sensibilities. Given the care with which these men were chosen, it is unlikely that no consideration was paid to their responses to exceptionally 'harsh' orders, which needed to be justified and rationalised.

Some men had refused to serve, others dropped out once they had experienced what they might have been able to contemplate in the abstract, which suggests that racial stereotyping may not bear the weight customarily put upon it. As with other formations, there were illnesses, attempts to transfer to group headquarters, or requests to be transferred to other duties. Not only were there no capital disciplinary consequences, but there could not be, since no SS officer was entitled summarily to execute his subordinates; Himmler reserved to himself even cases involving SS men caught speeding, and the right to confirm all capital sentences imposed on his subordinates.[103] It was probably inevitable that the renegade Catholic priest Albert Hartl and the former medical doctor Thomas should have taken to reflecting on the types of men that killed with such apparent facility, for doctors and priests sometimes think about such matters. Some of the men were subject to sadistic impulses, enjoying each execution and photographing it to relive their strange pleasures later, although few of them were clinically sadists, in the sense of deriving sexual pleasure from harming people.

Others broke down in tears, drank excessively or had nervous break-downs; one man went berserk in a barracks and shot dead several of his colleagues. Many regularly experienced temporary impotence.[104] By November 1941 at least one psychiatric hospital specialised in treating SS men 'who have broken down while executing women and children'.[105]

Apart from the minority who were psychopathically or sadistically inclined, most of these men had to be convinced of the necessity of what they were doing, for antisemitism alone does not seem to have been the sole motivating factor, although only a fool would seek to discount it. But they killed Latvian lunatics, Gypsies, Polish professors and Soviet prisoners of war with the same grim determination as they killed Jews. Such differences as emerged included the level of antici-pated resistance. Thus on Christmas Day 1942 a small party of SS men endeavoured to shoot two lorry-loads of Soviet prisoners who had lost either legs or arms. The legless were not a challenge, but the ambulant wounded overpowered their murderers, whose heavy coats restricted their dexterity with guns and prevented them from releasing the safety catches quickly enough. Two SS men were shot and the prisoners escaped. One SS man had enjoined his colleague to keep his gun cocked 'since we were not dealing with Jews here'.[106] Leaving aside those officers who claimed they were not especially antisemitic, those who were distinguished between 'acceptable' policies of economic and political exclusion of Jews and the horrors of mass extermination. This disparity was resolved by the conviction, which propaganda reinforced, that 'Jewry was the bearer of Bolshevism, in so far as the entire Bolshevik leadership was occupied by Jews'.[107] Together with constant stress on the need to execute looters, saboteurs and partisans, this would square things with the army, where even generals opposed to Hitler, such as Carl-Heinrich Stülpnagel, worked harmoniously with the Einsatzgruppen 'against Bolshevism . . . and above all against . . . Jewry, which works for its objectives'.[108]

This erroneous conviction was reinforced not only by Nazi propa-ganda but by what seemed to be evidence all around them. The Nazis had a very keen interest in exaggerating the pervasiveness of antisemit-ism in eastern Europe and the Soviet empire, since this made their own depredations seem unexceptional. That is precisely why the Einsatz-gruppen allowed the photographing and filming of selective incidents involving non-Germans. The subject deserves nuanced treatment. A generation of German historians whose achievement was to break with the denials and evasions of many of their predecessors is automatically wary of talk of other guilty parties, lest this relativise primary German culpability. This can seem to outsiders an almost proprietorial attitude to guilt, for like the Jews and martyrdom this is a no-win situation, in which one man's honest confrontation is another's self-flagellation, and insistent remembrance is another's excuse for collective narcissism.[109]

In countries whose fragile independence had been brutally extinguished by Soviet occupation, some people made direct connections, however absurd and tenuous, between Jewry and Communism. The reality was otherwise. In Lithuania, Jews had supported the movement for national independence and had fought to defend Lithuania against the Poles and the Soviet Union. Yet during the late 1930s laws that guaranteed minority rights were rescinded and Jewish–Lithuanian relations deteriorated. The Soviet occupation of Lithuania in June 1940 affected Jews disproportionately, while paradoxically intensifying the feeling among Lithuanian nationalists that Jews were uniquely responsible for it. Jews owned 57 per cent of plant and 83 per cent of businesses nationalised by the Soviet socialists. Traditional Jewish community life was assaulted: 'bourgeois' Hebrew was outlawed in favour of 'proletarian' Yiddish, and the Sabbath was made a compulsory day of work. Of the sixty thousand people deported from Lithuania to Siberia, twelve thousand of them were Jews, that is about twice their representation in the general population. Yet local nationalist fanatics were more interested in the fact that some of those carrying out deportations were Jewish, and that 15.2 per cent of the Lithuanian Communist Party was too. The fact that Jews were no longer discriminated against in higher education, or that a few moved into management positions in nationalised industries, convinced them that the Jews were to blame for the evils of the Soviet period.[110]

During the Nazi invasion, assorted volunteers, including released criminals, sometimes outdid the Einsatzgruppen in murdering Jews. In Kovno, a German colonel drawn to a petrol station by applause and shouts of 'bravo' forced his way through a crowd including women holding their children high for a more advantageous view. On the forecourt, a powerfully built Lithuanian was bludgeoning people to death. A German photographer witnessed the scene, noting that the young man briefly laid down his crowbar to mount a pile of corpses, playing the Lithuanian national anthem on a harmonica to general glee. The colonel was subsequently told by his superiors that this was purely an internal matter, in which the Germans had no business.[111]

Not quite, because Einsatzgruppe A was hovering in the shadows, channelling pogroms into systematic operations and organising heterogeneous Lithuanian forces into effective auxiliary formations.[112] According to its own reports, it had most success in Lithuania, less in Latvia, where the Soviets had murdered most of the nationalist leaders, and none in Estonia, where the tiny Jewish population did not excite the animosity of local nationalists.[113] The Lithuanians were most forthcoming about their motivation in killing Jews. When a German soldier asked a Lithuanian colleague how he could shoot his fellow countrymen he was told: 'After what we suffered under the rule of Russian Jewish commissars, after the Russian invasion of Lithuania, it is not so difficult.' Such men were impervious to reason, conveniently ignoring the fact that the Soviets had stolen (or nationalised) Jewish businesses, or that Jewish reactionary 'bourgeois', democratic socialists and Zionists disappeared to Siberia.[114] Ninety-five per cent of Lithuania's Jews were murdered, or about 140,000 people, between one-half and two-thirds of them by indigenous Lithuanian forces.[115]

In Latvia, the 1922 constitution guaranteed minority rights; left-wing Jews supported the post-independence Social Democratic government, and conservative Jews applauded the authoritarian regime of Karlis Ulmanis, which came to power in a putsch in 1934. Modelling himself on Mussolini, Ulmanis prohibited antisemitic publications and organisations, including the anti-German but violently antisemitic *Perkonkrusts* ('Thundercross'), while continuing to admit Jewish refugees from Nazism long after many democratic countries had ceased to do so. When the Soviets occupied Latvia in the summer of 1940, they deported fifteen thousand people, including five thousand Jews, to Siberia.[116] Contrary to the view that Jews were especially prominent in Latvian or Russian Communist circles, it is more likely that the incoming Russians deliberately stoked up animosity between Jews and Latvians in the interests of a divide-and-rule policy.[117] The political and socio-economic casualties of this brief Soviet occupation turned expectantly to the Nazis, egregiously misidentifying Jews with the terrors of the recent past, notwithstanding the fact that most Chekists or NKVD were ethnic Russians. Viktor Arajs, a former duelling fraternity student and part-time policeman, who opportunistically switched from Communism to anti-Soviet partisan, quickly made contact with Group A after the Nazi invasion. Radicals sought out other radicals. Stahlecker commissioned him to form a unit to 'cleanse the country from harmful elements'. Arajs set up shop in a building on Valdemarstrasse in Riga, advertising in the newspaper *Tevija* for men to assist in 'cleansing the country of harmful elements'. A hundred men responded, including large numbers of fraternity students and athletes drawn to their masculine camaraderie. In early July 1941, Arajs' team helped the Nazis massacre imprisoned Jews. They toured Latvia in a blue bus, shooting Jews wherever they found them, returning drunk and in song. In Riga, they spent their time raping and terrorising Jews, when not drinking themselves under the table in extension of the practices of their student or police days, and boasting of their daily kill-rates. On 8 December 1941, they helped shoot Jews from the Riga ghetto in Rumbala forest. By 1942 the battalion strength Sonderkommando 'Arajs' was redeployed in anti-partisan operations, before being dissolved into the Latvian Legion of the Waffen-SS.[118]

To the south, terrible recent experiences overshadowed the Ukraine, where starving people had been reduced to cannibalism within living memory. Conditions after 1939 in Soviet-occupied western Ukraine, or eastern Galicia, were so bad that Jews who had fled there from the General Government implored Nazi officials concerned with the repatriation of ethnic Germans to take them too, for 'they would rather perform forced labour in Germany or live in a concentration camp than remain where they are'.[119] A paucity of information about Nazi antisemitism, as distinct from German 'fascism', together with the regimes the Soviets imposed on the Baltic States or Ukraine may explain why relatively few Jews fled eastwards during the Nazi invasion. An influx of east Ukrainian Communists, led by Nikita Khrushchev, systematically robbed the inhabitants and shipped socially or politically undesirable citizens – whether Poles, Jews or Ukrainian nationalists – to Soviet concentration camps. Traditional pluralistic Jewish community life was suppressed in favour of an atheistic, 'proletarian'–yiddish conformity. Affluent Jews were pauperised, intellectuals deported, while doctors and teachers found the career obstacles of the Polish period removed, and some of the radicalised young appeared to welcome and collaborate with the Communists. The war simplified these distinctions; we need to re-establish them. Yesterday's victims became today's tyrants, and like found like, as returning Organisation of Ukrainian Nationalist (OUN) exiles accompanied the Nazis into the Soviet empire. If they were not antisemitic, then they soon became so in the interests of currying favour with their Nazi patrons and sponsors.[120] Memories and evidence of Soviet barbarity helped to ratchet up the atmosphere of hatred.

Following the outbreak of war, NKVD killing squads had massacred thousands of prisoners in Dubno, Lutsk, Lviv, Rivne, Sambir, Stanyslav and Tarnopol.[121] They included Ukrainian nationalists, Poles, Jews and downed German pilots, whose bodies were mutilated and burned with petrol. Even children were nailed to the walls. Discovery of these murders touched off a vengeful fury among Ukrainian nationalists, many of whom automatically misidentified Jews and Bolsheviks. This was outrageous since a number of the victims of the NKVD were Jews. In a letter sent to police headquarters in Lviv by OUN activists, the refrain was 'Long live greater independent Ukraine without Jews, Poles and Germans. Poles behind the San, Germans to Berlin, Jews to the gallows.'[122] Former Soviet policemen, at the disposal of the putative Ukrainian nationalist government, and mobs of ordinary people turned on the Jews. The German army sometimes joined in. Goebbels dispatched up to twenty journalists and radio broadcasters to reveal 'Moscow without the Mask' and to 'forge the iron while it still glows'.[123] Men from Einsatzkommandos 5 and 6 commenced operations amid this charnel house. One of them, Hauptscharführer Felix Landau, had volunteered to forget a complicated tryst with a twenty-year-old typist. In his diary, thoughts of Gertrude alternated with images of German pilots with their ears cut off and eyes poked out and of Jews left strewn around the streets by their Ukrainian killers; and descriptions of such tasks as shooting thirty-two Polish intellectuals at five in the morning, and three hundred Poles and Jews during the afternoon.[124] His colleagues took charge of a thousand Jews whom the Ukrainians had corralled on a sports ground, and shot a hundred men by way of 'reprisals'. Since this did not assuage Hitler, who thought the newsreel footage of NKVD crimes in Lviv the best he had seen, he ordered more substantial measures, which resulted in virtually all Jews in the sports ground being shot.[125] About four thousand Jews were murdered in Lviv.

Neither mob violence nor the depredations of Ukrainian policemen, who constituted 1 per cent of the population, should be assumed to typify the attitude of Ukrainians in general. Apart from saturating the Ukraine with antisemitic propaganda, the Germans warned the population that: 'Should anyone give shelter to a Jew or let him stay overnight he, as well as the members of his household, will be shot by a firing squad immediately.' Any initial enthusiasm for German occupation quickly disappeared. Many Ukrainians woke up to the prospect best expressed in a popular saying: 'The German may have come – good; for the Jews – kaput; for the Gypsies – as well; for the Ukrainians – later.' More subtly, even those whose attitude towards Jews was equivocal, such as the Uniate archbishop Andrei Sheptyts'kyi, began to deplore the brutalising impact of Nazi occupation on younger members of the Ukrainian population. The archbishop wrote in these terms to both Himmler and Pope Pius XII, while denouncing 'murder addiction' in his pastoral letters. He also personally gave asylum to one hundred and fifty Jewish children and fifteen rabbis, an act of bravery emulated by other Ukrainian clergy, or by such individuals as the director of the Lviv library of the Academy of Sciences, who hid eight people in his own home, and two hundred in the library itself.[126]

If Bolshevik crimes were not available to the Nazis as a pretext, then any explosion, fire or assassination that set nerves on edge and pulses quickening would do to justify indiscriminate 'reprisals' against the Jewish population. If there was no pretext, the Jews were shot anyway. A report from the politically astute Stahlecker of Einsatzgruppe A reveals that he was aware that the identification of Jews with Communists was overly simplistic. Admitting that they had taken on tasks which taxed their ingenuity, on 17 September Group C reported that, even if every Jew was killed, this would not eradicate the Bolshevik threat. It continued: 'Bolshevik activity relies upon Jews, Russians, Georgians, Armenians, Poles, Latvians, Ukrainians; the Bolshevik apparatus is in no way identical with the Jewish population.' In other words, these men knew that their primary rationalisation was a lie. Moreover, killing Jewish artisans, traders and workers would paralyse the local economy. The only solution was to use the Jews as forced labour, which would in any case bring about their eventual liquidation.[127] A similar line was taken in December by the antisemitic academic Peter-Heinz Seraphim, a logistics expert in the Ukraine. He contrasted the anxious, sullen compliance of the Jewish population with the dubious claim that they were deeply engaged in partisan activity or sabotage. The Jews had reason to be anxious, since by that time the Nazis had murdered between one hundred and fifty and two hundred thousand of them.[128]

South of the Ukraine, impoverished Romania had an autochtonous tradition of ferocious antisemitism, heightened by the nation's sudden ingestion and disgorging of ethnically complex territories five times

greater than the *regat*, or Old Kingdom, of Romania, in which ethnic
Romanians were only 70 per cent of the population. The extreme right
was represented by the League of the Archangel Michael, which in
1930 had spawned a youth wing called the Iron Guard, which is why
Romanian fascists were sometimes called guardists or legionaries.[129]
The loss of Bukovina, Bessarabia and northern Transylvania during
1940 to the Soviet Union was regarded as a national humiliation, with
grown men weeping on the streets of Bucharest and returning soldiers
lashing out at Jews they encountered when evacuating these territories.[130] Following the abdication of King Carol II, the general and
former Defence Minister Ion Antonescu proclaimed himself 'Conducator' (or 'Leader'), and brought Horia Sima, leader of the radically
antisemitic Iron Guard, into his government. Relations between the
military strongman Antonescu and Sima's collection of renegade Communist workers and messianic Christian fanatics were strained. However, both confederates blamed radicalised Jews for the loss of massive
tracts of 'Romania Mare' or 'Greater Romania'. As Antonescu put it:
'Even before the appearance of the Soviet troops, the Jews of Bessarabia and Bukovina spat upon our officers, they tore their uniforms, and
when they had the chance, the cowards beat our soldiers to death with
cudgels.'[131] Together with the Ukrainian minority, the Jews were going
to be expelled eastwards – in the Ukrainians' case providing a textbook
example of how oppressors in one context become victims in another.
Germany effectively took over the Romanian economy, creating about
seven hundred corporations in which Germans were the leading shareholders. Some 330,000 German troops entered Romania as 'advisers'
come to guard the oilfields.

Relations between Antonescu and Sima, backed respectively by
Hitler and Himmler, deteriorated.[132] Since Sima reminded Hitler of the
permanent revolutionaries around Röhm whom he had slaughtered in
1934, on 14 January 1941 he gave Antonescu his blessing for a
commensurate strike should the opportunity arise. He told him: 'You
have to get rid of them. In every movement there are fanatic militants
who think that in destroying they are doing their duty. These people
must not be allowed to act.'[133] The opportunity came a few days later
with an attempted Legionary coup – an odd coup, because Antonescu
allowed his opponents to carry out a three-day pogrom in the Jewish
districts of Bucharest before the army crushed them. Two points are
worth stressing. First, Antonescu and Sima agreed on the fiction that
the Jews had caused this power struggle between them: Sima called

Antonescu an agent of 'Judaeo-masonry', while Antonescu accused his erstwhile 'children' of being Communists. Second, the number of victims – 120 Jews killed on the streets or literally butchered in a Bucharest abattoir – exceeded those killed in Germany during the November 1938 Reichskristallnacht.[134] The SD slipped some Legionaries away to Germany, but two thousand were imprisoned, and then released to join the ranks of the Romanian army.[135] This vengeful force lined up alongside the Germans for the attack on Russia.

Elsewhere, mid-ranking members of the SS turned their attention to the alleged economic burden and health hazard represented by ghettoised Jews in Poland. It may be that their experience with millions of unwanted Jews in Poland influenced the decision simply to shoot the yet further millions in the Soviet Union, and that procedure then affected events in occupied Poland, in the sense that a search began for a less public or psychologically burdensome method of murdering people.[136] On 16 July 1941, SS-Sturmbannführer Rolf Heinz Höppner in Posen wrote to his superior Eichmann concerning discussions in the Warthegau about the Jews there. One option was to create a camp for three hundred thousand Jews near the coal basin. This would isolate the Jews from the surrounding population, minimising the risks of epidemics. He added: 'There is a danger of not being able to feed all the Jews this winter. Serious consideration is required on the question of whether the most humanitarian solution would not be to finish off those Jews who are unfit for work by some expedient means. In any case that would be less unpleasant than allowing them to die from hunger.'

Sterilisation of Jewish women of child-bearing age would also effectively solve the Jewish problem 'with this generation'. As yet, Gauleiter Greiser had not expressed a preference for killing Jews, and the Łódź Government President Uebelhör was making too much profit from the labour of Jews to wish to kill them. In a personal note to Eichmann, Höppner added: 'These things do sound somewhat fantastic but, in my opinion, they are entirely feasible'[137] – feasible, but still in competition with other strategies, as the projected massive camp or the productivist lobby in the Łódź ghetto administration suggests.[138]

If we assume that policy was forged at the centre in Berlin, rather than that the centre passively endorsed a series of local initiatives, then when did an initial campaign of murder against Communists and restricted categories of Jews in Russia escalate to killing all Jews in the Soviet Union? Those who say that this occurred in the summer of

1941 cite Hitler's expansive mood at a high-level meeting held on 16 July at his Rastenburg headquarters. The 'Garden of Eden' was at hand, with Soviet resort to partisan warfare giving 'us the opportunity to exterminate anyone who is hostile to us', he said.[139] Hitler sensed imminent victory. In that euphoric moment it was possible to kill 'anyone who even looks askance at us'.[140] The problem with the notes of this meeting is that they do not mention Jews, and hence should not be used to imply that the 16 July meeting was the starting point for killing them.[141] They convey a prevailing mood: nothing more. Relatively few scholars now attach much importance to this meeting, shifting the ultimate decisions to later that autumn or winter.

These explanations sometimes posit the onset of a vengeful moroseness when the Russian campaign, which was intended to be won in weeks, turned into a war of attrition. A global coalition began massing against Germany. Hitler had already coupled this scenario with dire prophecies regarding the Jews. He began to repeat them.[142] The invasion was an enormous gamble for very high stakes. The resources to wage war against Britain and, if necessary, America depended upon its outcome. Initial over-optimistic expectations of rapid victory had to be scaled down. The Soviets seemed to conjure troops from nowhere, drawing upon deeper resources than had been anticipated by intelligence agencies whose inquiries had stopped short of Magnitogorsk and Omsk. The Russians fought with a gritty determination and ferocity; they were Nazi Germany's 'first serious adversary'. By mid-August, when a drained Hitler conferred at length with Goebbels, he was not so certain of victory: fantasising aloud about the possible fall of either Churchill or Stalin. He was worried about staunching the increasing flow of German blood, for he mentioned this on two occasions. He repeated his 'prophecy' of 30 January 1939, warning that: 'In the East, the Jews are being forced to foot the bill for the damage; in Germany they have already paid in part and will have to pay even more in future.'[143]

While Hitler's mood turned apocalyptic and vengeful, Himmler embarked on a heightened level of activity. It seems unlikely that the two things were unconnected, or that actions were unrelated to intentions. He met Odilo Globocnik in Lublin, before returning east to see two of the Higher SS- and Police Leaders – Prützmann and Bach-Zelewski.[144] Heydrich and Eichmann worked on the parallel problem of deporting the entirety of central European Jewry.[145] For the murder of Soviet Jews had created a space into which the Jews of Europe could be driven, as indeed they initially were, pending decisions to kill them in camps in eastern Poland, decisions which may have depended on the international strategic picture, for here we are making informed guesses. Behind the Eastern Front, Himmler quadrupled forces dedicated to killing Jews. Since May 1941 what amounted to a personal army of various SS forces operated under the direction of Kurt Knoblauch, the leader of the Command Staff Reichsführer-SS. These forces consisted of twenty-five thousand SS men, organised in infantry and motorised brigades, as well as cavalry formations such as those of Franz Magill. These men were placed at the disposal of the Higher SS- and Police Leaders Bach-Zelewski, Jeckeln and Prützmann, and were unleashed against the Jews either directly or under the camouflage of a campaign against partisans. This is how Magill's horsemen came to be drowning women and children in a swamp. It has been estimated that Himmler's private army killed about one hundred thousand Jews.[146] But the build-up of forces engaged in exterminating Soviet Jews went further. Large numbers of Order Police battalions, that is uniformed career policemen under the overall command of Kurt Daluege, were attached to the Higher SS-1 and Police Leaders in Russia, while indigenous Jew-killers were expanded into auxiliary defence forces numbering tens of thousands.[147] This order of manpower could, and would, annihilate the mass of 'Soviet' Jewry. A new urgency was also apparent in the operations of the Einsatzgruppen. Whereas they murdered approximately sixty-three thousand Jews down to mid-August 1941, in the ensuing four months they killed half a million people.[148]

The increase in, and diversification of, forces deployed in these extended operations was accompanied by further twists in the rationalisation of their activities. For the alleged threat was no longer adult male Jews – many of whom were already dead – but rather women and children, who might produce avengers or mature to take their own revenge. This was taking the very long-term view. During September, Himmler still peddled the reprisal line, but with this significant modification:

On 1 September, six SS officers were found in the Weniza forest in the following condition: they had been stripped of their clothing and hanged with their legs up. Their entrails had been taken out. Such an act demands revenge, and since the Jews did it, we will utterly extirpate them. *Even the brood in the cradle must be crushed like a puffed-up toad. We are living in an iron time and have to sweep with iron brooms.* Everyone has therefore to do his duty without asking his conscience first.[149]

Since this was as implausible as the deed was monstrous, rationalisations shifted from justifying the choice of victim to the perpetrators' rigours of self-overcoming. They duly became victims themselves, the real emotional casualties of their own actions. Moral relativism reached its nadir. A few SS killers seem to have subscribed to a pseudo-philosophical view of what they were doing, as when a member of an Einsatzgruppe recalled:

> We believed in those times that we had achieved new higher values. It was a matter of struggling against, or rather repressing, the materialism and egoism of the individual. That this brought about an inversion of values, that one retreated even further from humanism, was by no means clear to me at the time.[150]

But this was too articulate and knowing to be a majority view. Reality was just as likely to be personified by Hans Krüger, who in October 1941 oversaw the murder of ten thousand Jews in a cemetery outside Stanislau, striding up and down a mass grave firing his gun furiously, while snatching a sausage and a bottle of vodka from a table which had been provided. He then charged the Jewish Council two thousand złoty for the spent ammunition. Krüger's conduct a few days earlier had been more like that typical of Europe in about AD 700 than of the mid-twentieth century. He had killed the Jews of Nadorna in a dry run for the Stanislau massacre, taunting his Orthodox victims with shouts of 'Where is your God? Where is your Jehovah?'[151] But these are extremes, which tell us little about the run of killers.

One apparent concern of those who ordered men to kill people was that they should not stray too far from the path of human decency, let alone become chronic alcoholics or psychopaths permanently lost to human society. They were not to walk on the wild side. The object was to engineer selective moral disengagement, rather than to unleash demi-human predators, although that was often the consequence of the former policy. Expected to do abnormal things, these men were nonetheless required to remain normal. Hence Himmler's repeated attempts to couple hardness with decency and his insistence that killings should be followed by abstemious 'comradely get-togethers' over dinner to discuss the 'sublimities of German intellectual and emotional life'.[152] Hence too the search for a less direct method of killing, which led, via experiments blowing up Russian psychiatric patients with high explosives, to the introduction of mobile and static gassing technologies, an innovation primarily designed to minimise the psychological distress of the murderers rather than the existential terror of their victims.[153] Direct killing was also streamlined and systematised, with diagrams indicating how to do it.[154]

Inevitably, the human reality of the killers failed to correspond with Himmler's ideal 'new man'. Here an immediate word of caution is appropriate, in terms both of the nature of the available evidence, much of it stemming from post-war legal depositions, and of the range of killers who have been studied, most notably some of the many Order Police units. These were not ideologically driven killers of the kind that staffed the Einsatzgruppen or other SS formations, but middle-aged policemen whose formative years often lay before the advent of a Nazi government, or whose socio-economic background was in classes often said to be relatively cool towards National Socialism, although that may reflect the insufficiency of that sort of explanation. For, while structuralist historians have told us much about the involvement of Germany's elites in bringing Hitler to power in 1933, they also tended to marginalise as 'hangman's assistants' (*Schergen*) the men who implemented Nazi policy during the war, either for reasons of fastidiousness regarding their gruesome actions or because such inquiries might upset an implicit desire to see non-elite groups as less culpable, an approach whose other aspect was a keen interest in the relative immunity of non-elite classes to National Socialism.[155]

Since the precise course of events affecting one of these police battalions may not typify others, it seems difficult to use such a unit as evidence for the collective 'psyche' of the German people, or for potentialities within human beings in general. But we will work with what we have before us, for Christopher Browning's study of Reserve Police Battalion 101 affords unusual insights into the characters of mass murderers. Battalion 101 seems highly unusual for any military formation, in the sense that its commander, Major Wilhelm Trapp, offered his men the 'extraordinary' choice of participating in, or opting out of, their first major massacre. Trapp may have been tortured by what he ordered, but he nonetheless explained to his men that Jews in America had instigated the 1933 boycott of German goods (it was now July 1942 and the scene was a small Polish village), that bombs were raining down on German cities, and that some Jews in the village were involved with the partisans. All of which apparently justified killing men, women and children.[156] Members of other Order Police battalions, such as 309 and 322, which have also been studied, were not offered a choice, although some of them occasionally reported sick. They were given, and were expected, to obey orders.[157]

Thanks to Major Trapp, his men had to wrestle openly with dilemmas which men in other units may have resolved in private. In response to Trapp's offer, a few men, to be precise a dozen out of nearly five hundred, promptly seized the chance not to participate. Moreover, some of those who decided to shoot soon made their excuses and left, or found ways of what, in this context, seems grotesque to describe as 'shirking'. Other participants began to misaim deliberately, or ceased firing, because the man standing next to them had no aim at all. For this was killing of the closest kind, with the unit doctor's clinical explanation of how to use a fixed bayonet to line up a fatal bullet bearing scant resemblance to the gory reality.[158] The men who carried out the shooting of fifteen hundred Jews in Józefów, rationalised the deed in varous ways. If they had not done it, someone else would. Others spoke of not wishing to lose face with their comrades, or, more honestly, that they were too cowardly to opt out. One man claimed he only shot children, since his neighbour had shot their mothers: 'I reasoned with myself that after all without its mother the child could not live any longer.' Afterwards, the men got drunk, with 'a sense of shame and horror' pervading their barracks. Of the minority who opted out at the start of the massacre, two argued that their age, financial independence and lack of ambition within the police force made it easier for them to say no than was the case with their careerist colleagues.

In other words, a variety of motives were apparent among the participants, although admission of antisemitism was conspicuously absent, since it would have constituted a 'base motive' under post-war German law, which was the context of the documents Christopher Browning was the first to study. Since these men were equally capable of turning their hands to killing Christian Poles, it seems improbable that antisemitism quite bears the weight that has subsequently been put upon it.[159] These men's responses to their actions were sufficiently negative for their superiors to rely on surrogates to handle the business of killing, that is drunken Soviet POW auxiliaries, towards whom the Germans could affect moral superiority, or by deploying the German policemen to supervise round-ups and deportations to dedicated extermination centres. Barbarity could be ascribed to Ukrainians, or whoever, with the Germans priding themselves on their clinical professionalism. What happened in the camps was someone else's business. Month after month of this, interspersed with 'Jew-hunts' for Jews who had eluded major sweeps, progressively deadened many of these men to what they were doing. They had become practised killers.

Since this unit was put in the untypical position of being presented with a choice, it is unsurprising that questions of choice figure so prominently in discussions of it. Do the specific dynamics of this group of five hundred men sufficiently explain why men in general commit mass murder? Do these middle-aged, and apparently reluctant, murderers from one atypical unit within a police formation not only numbering tens of thousands, but regarded by the SS as the scrapings of the manpower barrel, tell us much about the motivation behind the Holocaust? Surely the wider climate in which group dynamics operate is as, or more, important? And what if the Milgram experiments, uncritically cited in so much of the historical literature on our alleged capacity to commit torture, were not a value-free scientific exercise, whose behaviourist conclusions we should uncritically accept, but rather merely reflected Stanley Milgram's own prejudices that working-class American Blacks and Italian Catholics were likely to obey orders to torture people, while nice white middle-class Protestant North Europeans were disinclined to do so, although that was clearly not the case in Nazi Germany?[160]

These dreadful deeds were committed amid other German formations. One incident, from the thousands of incidents, is instructive since it brought together in one small place army codes of honour, residual humanitarianism, ideological fanaticism and the moral cowardice characteristic of most bureaucracies. This was how killing children was rationalised on the ground, by men in control of themselves, and with vestigial moral anchorings, rather than by antisemitic automata, dyspeptic human wrecks, or missionary zealots who needed no rationalisation at all. The rôle of military chaplains deserves notice.

In mid-August 1941, men from Sonderkommando 4a and a Waffen-SS company murdered between six hundred and eight hundred adult Jews in the Ukrainian town of Bjelaja-Zerkow near Kiev.[161] Although most of the Jewish children were shot soon after, about ninety orphans aged between a few months and five or six were confined on the upper floors of a building near a German army billet. They had been there for twenty-four hours. It was extremely hot – a German officer remarked on the saturated brownness of his suntan – and these children, without water, covered with flies, and reduced to eating mortar prised from the brickwork, cried and screamed throughout the night. Disturbed in their sleep, and in some cases by the children's plight, soldiers called in their two Catholic and Protestant military chaplains, who inspected the building and voiced their disquiet, about the children rather than the adults who had been shot, to their division-level equivalents.[162] The latter then approached the General Staff Officer of the 295th Infantry Division, a forty-two-year-old professional soldier called Helmuth Groscurth, who was the son of a Lutheran minister, asking him to take up the children's cause.[163]

Groscurth visited the orphans. During the visit, he encountered an SD Oberscharführer Jager, who announced that these children 'were to be got rid of too'. Groscurth called upon the local army Commandant, who referred him to the regional Field Commandant. The latter, a Lieutenant-Colonel Riedl, informed him that he was aware of these orders, could do nothing about them, and in any case regarded them as legitimate. Groscurth took steps to stop his men visiting the building, requesting that the Sonderkommando delay removing the children during the evening until he had obtained clarification from Army Group South headquarters. Army Group headquarters relayed this request up to Sixth Army. Field Marshal Reichenau postponed the action, after which the Field Commandant sent the children food and water.

On 21 August a meeting eventually took place between Groscurth, Captain Luley from military counter-intelligence, Standartenführer Paul Blöbel, Obersturmführer August Hafner and Field Commandant Riedl. Moral questions were swiftly supplanted by proprieties, reproaches, and a retreat into technicalities. Outnumbered and threatened, Groscurth explained that his objections merely concerned the sloppy way in which the crying children had been left amid his soldiers. Luley and Riedl were dismissive of the meddling by the two military chaplains: 'it would be better if the priests concerned themselves with the spiritual solace of the soldiers'. The two SD men left the soldiers to argue over the troublesome priests, satisfied that, since 'technical deficiencies' had been resolved, it was a matter of 'finding a form of rapid resolution'. This narrowing of a moral problem to a mere technicality typified their approach. Riedl blamed Groscurth for the twenty-four-hour hiatus, remarking that 'he regarded the extermination of Jewish women and children as an urgent necessity, regardless of the form it took'. Maliciously, Hafner suggested that snooping soldiers should carry out the shooting, under the leadership of officers responsible for the delay. Groscurth quickly deflected this suggestion. Blöbel added that the killing of children had been sanctioned by Reichenau, a point already confirmed to Groscurth by a staff officer from Army Group headquarters. Groscurth left as the rest settled down to discussing the technicalities of shooting ninety small children.

Groscurth noted in his account of the meeting that violence and brutality against defenceless civilians ran counter to the military code. Nothing appeared to distinguish measures already taken by the Germans against women and children from the much bruited atrocities of the Soviet NKVD in 'liberated' towns such as Lviv. Troops expected their officers to do something. In future, such killings should occur somewhere far from the army. Had no one anticipated a problem with children, and especially infants, if the parents were shot? He added: 'This should have happened immediately after the getting rid of the parents, in order to prevent inhuman suffering.'[164] In his comments on Groscurth's report, Reichenau deplored the implied analogy between the SS and NKVD, and the fact that the report was doing the rounds, closing with the remark, 'It would be generally better if this report had not been written.'[165] These were not quite the final tergiversations regarding the shooting of ninety orphans. Hafner disliked using young Waffen-SS men to kill children, since they probably had children of a similar age. Blöbel suggested Hafner's own Sonderkommando, but Hafner protested that these men too had small children. After ten minutes they agreed to use the Ukrainian militia, who that afternoon shot the children in a wood, trembling as they did so. No one cared whether they had children or not, and Groscurth's men dug the grave.[166] All participants had crossed the threshold of killing children as well as adults: some felt uneasy, including Groscurth, Hafner and the Ukrainian militiamen, but cross the threshold they did all the same.

Another troubling aspect of these events, troubling if one wishes to ascribe responsibility for the murder of the Jews to a uniquely aberrant German form of antisemitism, was that these Austrians, ethnic Germans or Reich Germans (the ethnic Germans being products of Baltic, Hungarian, Romanian and Soviet cultures) were not acting alone. As Solzhenitsyn wrote of his own experiences: 'Gradually it was disclosed to me that the line separating good and evil passes not through states, nor between classes, nor between political parties either – but right through every human heart – and through all human hearts.'[167] Inter-ethnic hatred ran like a loose live cable through vast tracts of east

central Europe, snaking down from the Baltic to the Balkans, passing
through the hearts of individuals from a bewildering variety of national
backgrounds. Lack of manpower and the need for consensus meant
that everywhere German formations were padded out with indigenous
murder squads and so-called defence units or Schutzmannschaften,
some of which consisted of discharged Soviet prisoners of war. They
also had more autonomous confederates.[168]

Since existing scholarship focuses mainly on the Baltic, let us
venture southwards, following the destructive swathe of the smallest
formation, Otto Ohlendorf's Einsatzgruppe D, seeing where it takes
us, while picking up the Romanians along the way – a journey driven
by curiosity about these places rather than the desire to disperse
responsibility, or to blame any particular nation. Group D was originally allocated a killing ground covering Bessarabia, the southern
Ukraine, the Crimea and Caucasus. Its six hundred men were appended
to Schobert's Eleventh Army of Army Group South, fighting alongside
the Romanian Third and Fourth armies. As they rapidly discovered,
Group D arrived amid a genocide already well under way.

At an 8 July 1941 cabinet meeting, the Romanian 'Conducator'
cast aside 'sugary and vapid humanitarianism'; like the German Führer, he felt the hour of national destiny had struck:

> You must be merciless. . . . I do not know when, after how many
> centuries, the Romanian nation will again enjoy this total freedom of
> action, with the possibility for ethnic purification and national revision.
> This is the hour when we are masters on our territory. Let it be used!
> I do not mind if history judges us barbarians. The Roman empire
> performed a series of barbarous acts against its contemporaries, and
> yet it was the greatest political establishment. There are no other
> favourable moments in our history. If need be, shoot with machine
> guns, and I say that there is no law.[169]

The forces unleashed by these words struck first in the Moldavian
frontier town of Iaşi, a university town of one hundred thousand souls
and hotbed of antisemitism. Iaşi was home to A. C. Cuza, the patriarch
of Romanian antisemitism, and adoptive home of Corneliu Codreanu,
the martyred former 'Captain' of the Legion, murdered by King Carol.
It was known as 'Legionary City'. Half the population were Jews.
Units of the Intelligence Service (or SSI) Esalon Operativ – the Romanian version of the Einsatzgruppen – moved into this unstable frontier
town, putting up posters blaming the Jews for the war, while purport-

ing to discover lights which flashed signals to Soviet planes concealed in the chimneys of their houses. Christians marked their doors with a cross to avert any errors. Between 23 and 30 June these units, together with Romanian regular troops, local citizens and the SS, fell upon the Jews of Iaşi, killing ten thousand people. This was not a wild pogrom, but mass slaughter conducted by organs of the state, including the police and army in an environment where the state declared there to be 'no law'. As Antonescu remarked: 'I let the mob loose to massacre them. I withdrew to my citadel, and after the massacre I restored order.' The SSI instigated the 'pogrom', with Antonescu himself ensuring that it was prolonged. A 30 June military telegram read: 'General Antonescu ordered that all the Jewish Communists from Iaşi and those found with red flags and firearms were to be executed tonight.'

Here we can also get the feel of things, not from the dehumanised number-crunching of the Einsatzgruppen, or the anguished accounts of survivors, but from a third party. The Axis war correspondent Curzio Malaparte was in Iaşi, reporting for the *Corriere della Sera*, whiling away the days before Operation Barbarossa reading Harold Nicolson's *Helen's Tower*. The pogrom was palpable:

> A strange anguish weighed upon the city. A huge, massive and monstrous disaster, oiled, polished, tuned up like a steel machine was going to catch and grind into pulp the houses, the trees, the streets and the inhabitants of Iaşi, *fara copii* [except the children].'

Mysterious gunfire – the Romanian special forces fired a few blanks – and talk of Soviet parachutists touched off what had been discussed so openly that a delegation of Jews, including the former director of a prison Malaparte had once been incarcerated in, implored him to prevent it. But it was too late, as he said, 'I have lost the ability to act. . . . I am an Italian.' And then it was off:

> Hordes of Jews pursued by soldiers and maddened civilians armed with knives and crowbars fled along the steets; groups of policemen smashed in house doors with their rifle butts; windows opened suddenly and screaming dishevelled women in nightgowns appeared with their arms raised in the air; some threw themselves from windows and their faces hit the asphalt with a dull thud. Squads of soldiers hurled hand grenades through the little windows level with the street into the cellars where many people had vainly sought safety; some soldiers dropped to their knees to look at the results of the explosions within the cellars and turned laughing faces to their companions. Where the slaughter

had been heaviest the feet slipped in blood; everywhere the hysterical and ferocious toil of the pogrom filled the houses and streets with shot, with weeping, with terrible screams and cruel laughter.[170]

A few days later, Malaparte drove with the Fascist journalist Lino Pellegrini and the Italian consul in Iaşi to trace Pellegrini's landlord, a Jewish lawyer whom the Romanians had dragged from the consulate building in violation of all diplomatic proprieties. Finding a corpse in Romania was 'like looking for a needle in a haystack'. They were received obtusely by Chirilovici, the Iaşi Chief of Police, whose pogrom had coincidentally spoiled Pellegrini's honeymoon. Eventually, they were directed to a concentration camp established by the Chief about twenty miles out of town. Iaşi's surviving Jews were supposed to be *en route* to it in a boarded-up train. The Italians encountered this train, which had moved twenty miles in three days under sweltering summer skies. Ordering the driver to open one of ten freight cars, the Italian consul was buried under tumbling corpses. By afternoon they had identified the lawyer among the bodies laid out beside the railway, as local Gypsies tugged off the Jews' clothes and valuables, like carrion swooping from a distance.[171] This was one of two death trains to leave Iaşi on 30 June. About fifteen hundred people died on the first; over one thousand on the second.

After he had ejected the Soviets from Bessarabia and Bukovina, Antonescu took the domestically controversial decision to cross the River Dniester. By supporting Germany's ambitions further east, he calculated that Hitler would reward him with northern Transylvania, to be prised from allied Hungarian hands. Although Russia's defeat would be necessary to secure Bessarabia and Bukovina, the Romanian army would rather have fought the Hungarians than the Russians. Hence, illiterate Romanian peasant soldiers, who had rarely seen a tractor, let alone a tank, were hurled against the keenly defended Black Sea port of Odessa.[172] Using all the advantages of interior lines, the Soviets could also reinforce themselves from the Crimea and Caucasus, landing marines and Katyusha rockets, while shelling the Romanians from the cruiser *Komintern* in the harbour. Tellingly, more mortars were being manufactured in Odessa than were available to the entire Romanian army. This was a grim siege, even by the standards of this war, with starving Romanian soldiers foraging the countryside for food, and officers screaming and swearing at their men to stop mass panic.[173] When Antonescu was on the verge of throwing in the towel,

Hitler relocated German troops freed up by the capture of Kiev. The Red Army finally vacated Odessa in mid-October to reinforce the Crimea. They slipped out without the Romanians noticing. The victors had suffered 17,729 dead and over seventy-four thousand wounded or missing in action. Stalin declared Odessa a 'Hero City'. During the victory parade in Bucharest, some of the German guests were perturbed to see Romanian tanks emblazoned with 'Now on to Budapest!' The Romanian army entered Odessa in a foul frame of mind. The place had been flooded, horses shot and war *matériel* left in the streets or dumped in the harbour.

It is time to reintroduce Einsatzgruppe D into a picture that can be reduced to flags, lines and statistical insets on a map, but which probably resembled scenes from hell. With the longest route to their operational area, sub-units of Group D, numbering about one hundred men, crossed Austria and Hungary into northern Romania. From a few photographs of similar units, one can see them with their neat uniforms, suitcases, trucks, typewriters, rifles and machine guns, like colonial policemen on a hunting trip. In Iaşi, Sonderkommando 10a discovered that the Romanians had done their work for them. Similar scenes awaited them as they entered Belzi, where they killed fifteen Jews whom the Romanians had left for dead, and destroyed the two remaining synagogues which the Romanians had not already levelled. At Petschanka, a sub-unit split off for the town of Kodyma. There they helped the German army raid the Jewish quarter, detaining and interrogating four to five hundred male Jews, of whom ninety-seven were shot by firing squads consisting of Sonderkommando 10a and regular German soldiers.

Meanwhile, Sonderkommando 10b reached Czernowitz in North Bukovina. They were disappointed to discover a Romanian jail contained only indigent rather than intellectual Jews. Since the Romanians seemed more interested in neutralising local Ukrainian nationalists, whom the Germans wished to cultivate, the latter thought it would be desirable to portray meetings of Jews as 'conspiracies' to activate the Romanians against the Jewish intelligentsia.[174] In other words, they thought the Romanians were killing the wrong Jews. Together, Germans and Romanians killed two thousand of the city's fifty thousand Jews. Dividing into two smaller formations, the Sonderkommando reached Hotin and Kamenets-Podolsk. In Hotin they used Ukrainian informants to identify Jewish Party officials, lawyers and rabbis, whom they shot, exempting only Jewish medical doctors.

SS-Sturmbannführer Paul Zapp's Sonderkommando 11a arrived in Kishinev on 17 July 1941. They established a ghetto as well as investigating arson, an attack on an ambulance and signals flashing up to the Red Air Force. Five hundred and fifty-one Jews were shot in 'reprisal' for these occurrences.[175] In August, Zapp's men killed 230 Jews in Nikolayev; in September about four to five thousand Jews in the ghetto. These numbers were established only after prosecutors calculated the work rate of four teams of ten men, each firing every ten minutes for six hours – with a two-hour interval for lunch – over a three-day period.[176] Much to Ohlendorf's irritation, the German army insisted upon deploying his men to guard peasants (and Jews) bringing in the harvest, lest the Romanian soldiery consume it. Not for nothing did the local Ukrainians and Russians refer contemptuously to the Romanians as 'Gypsies'. They were also employed preventing the Romanian expulsion of the Jews over the bridges of the Dniester into the territory known as Transnistria, a belt of land between the Dniester and the Bug, which the Romanians administered, but did not annex, from August 1941 onwards. Men from units 10b, 11a and 12 forced six thousand Jews over the crossing at Mogilev-Podolsk, before the Romanians disabled the bridges to stop the re-entry of a further eleven thousand. These Jews were then marched to a more southerly crossing at Jampol, with 'hundreds' of exhausted stragglers being shot along the way. The Romanians propelled approximately thirty-five thousand Jews over the Dniester; Group D managed to drive back 27,500. About twelve hundred Jews were shot. Elsewhere, Jews were driven across rivers until the Romanians grew tired of the game, and shot those who had not already drowned. In Cherson, where Group D scurried about under a massive Soviet artillery barrage, they created a ghetto and slave labour gangs, killing four hundred male Jews and eleven women, together with such rare prizes as the GPU boss in the city – rare because many reports noted that Soviet functionaries had fled. Seventeen Jews were shot for not wearing mandatory Stars of David.[177] The goods of Jews being shot were handed over to local widows and orphans; a fund was created from Jewish monies to cover the salaries of teachers, for these men combined charity with murder, a calculated hearts and minds campaign, based on largesse at the Jews' expense.

During the autumn, the proliferating sub-units of Group D shadowed the German army as it invaded the Crimea, while Sonderkommando 11b tarried until the Romanian Fourth Army took Odessa. According to their own statistics, down to 16 September 1941 Group

D had killed 13,315 people. In the next fifteen days they killed a further 22,467.[178] In October, they alighted upon several isolated ethnic German villages, with evocative names such as Worms or Speyer, where the people were so poor – in the wake of collectivisation – that they lacked beds or cots. These items were therefore appropriated from Jews who had ceased to need either. During the first fortnight of October 1941, Group D shot a further 4,891 Jews.[179]

Some 150,000–160,000 Jews were killed in Bessarabia and North Bukovina, the vast majority by the Romanian Fourth army and Esalon Operativ. Occasionally Group D complained about the Romanians' lack of method or failure to bury the dead. In August 1941, Heydrich recalled his Jewish expert in the Bucharest embassy, allegedly in protest at the friendliness Romanian troops sometimes demonstrated towards Jews. The Romanian ambassador to Berlin indignantly rebutted this charge, pointing to 'an old and elemental hatred of the Jews' among his fellow countrymen.[180] Those Jews who survived these initial onslaughts were gathered together in camps and ghettos, and then driven across the Dniester into Transnistria. At every stage of the process, they were subjected to the extortionate demands of the Romanian army and civil authorities, so that by the time they reached their destination they had nothing. On 11 October 1941, Wilhelm Filderman, the President of the Federation of Jewish Congregations in Romania, wrote to Antonescu interceding on behalf of these deportees, for whom Transnistria signified the 'death, death, death of innocent people with no other guilt than that of being Jews'.[181] In Romania, contacts between Jewish elites and the regime were never severed entirely. In his 19 October reply, Antonescu brushed aside Filderman's pleas with the thought:

Did you give any thought last year to what was in our hearts during the evacuation of Bessarabia and what is happening to us daily and hourly when we are paying with our blood . . . with very much blood for the hatred of your co-religionists in Bessarabia, to the manner in which we were treated during our withdrawal from Bessarabia, and upon our return, how they received us, during our passage from the Dniester to Odessa and in the regions of the Sea of Azov? . . . During the Bolshevik occupation, those whom you now bewail, informed on good Romanians, thus surrendering them to the orgies of the Russians and bringing grief and mourning into numerous Romanian homes. . . . Do not pity, if you really have a soul, those who do not deserve it; pity those who merit it![182]

There was a bizarre postscript:

> PS – A wounded soldier of Piatra Neamt was buried alive upon the
> order and before the eyes of Jewish Commissars in spite of his pleas
> not to be buried as he had four children.

This sense of betrayal, grievance and national reassertion – a
travesty of the realities of Romanian treatment of the Jews – was
compounded by an incident within days of the arrival of Romanian
troops in Odessa, which had the largest Jewish population of any
Soviet city. Odessa has about two hundred kilometres of underground
catacombs carved out of the spongy rock used to construct the city.
At about six on the evening of 22 October delayed-action mines
planted by Soviet commandos were detonated under an NKVD building on Marazli Street used as Romanian Fourth Army headquarters.
The forty-one dead included General Glogojeanu and five German
naval officers, and there were thirty-nine wounded.[183] Preliminary
reprisals set in motion by General Trestioreanu commenced an hour
and thirty minutes later, and involved hanging about five thousand
Jews and Communists from lampposts and telegraph and tram poles
in every square, with deterrent placards around the victims' necks.[184]
A survivor described Odessa as 'the city of the hanged'.[185] This began
rather than exhausted 'reprisals'. According to German intelligence
reports, next morning nineteen thousand Jews were herded into the
docks, where they were shot and incinerated with petrol. By midday,
Antonescu formally ordered the execution of two hundred Communists per dead Romanian or German officer and one hundred more for
the dead of other ranks. A victim was to be drawn from every Jewish
family. These killings coincided with the funerals of the bomb attack
victims. A handwritten note, subsequently referred to as Order No.
563, survives in the Romanian military archives, despite instructions
to destroy it:

> For General Macici. As reprisals, Marshal Antonescu orders: 1. The
> execution of all the Jews of Bessarabia who fled Odessa. 2. All
> individuals covered by the provisions of Order No. 302858/3161 of 23
> October 1941 who were not yet executed, and others that can be
> added, will be crammed into a previously mined building that will be
> blown up. This is to take place on the day our victims are buried. 3.
> This order is to be destroyed after it is read. Colonel Davidescu, Chief
> of the Military Cabinet. No. 563 of 24 October 1941, 302858.[186]

The Romanians marched thousands of Jews to the *kolkhoz* at Dalnik. Those not shot *en route* were mown down and cast into trenches. Since this was too slow, the Romanians packed the survivors into warehouses, gunning them down or throwing grenades through embrasures in the walls. Forty thousand Jews died at Dalnik.[187] The twenty thousand surviving Jews of Odessa were killed the following spring after their deportation to Transnistria.[188] And the Nazis? Bereft of anyone to kill, Einsatzkommando IIb eventually found five hundred Jews in a jail and shot them behind the former NKVD sanatorium.[189]

Ohlendorf's mobile headquarters moved in November from Niko-layev to Simferopol on the Crimea, where two commandos commenced operations, while two other units crossed into the northern Cauca-sus.[190] Their spring report was worthy of the academic Ohlendorf had once been. The Crimean peninsula was relatively prosperous in com-parison to the rest of the Soviet Union, with a large number of sanatoria and hotels in the coastal south, where Party bigwigs basked in the sun or moderated their alcoholism. The population was ethnic-ally diverse, well educated and used to tourists. Wages and prices were compared. There were tensions between Moslem Tatars and Russians, and between Turkic Karaimen, with their heretical form of Judaism, and Tatar Krimshaks, who were deemed racial Jews. The former rejected the Talmud and had supported the Whites in the Civil War; the latter practised Judaism and had been passive towards the Bolshe-viks. This proved crucial, since while the Karaimen were left alone, six thousand Krimshaks were shot. In the Yaila Mountains of southern Crimea, Group D worked with the army in tracking down and killing substantial partisan groups: real combat operations which took up much space in their reports. Satisfied that the Germans were not going to kill them too, the local Tatar population dragged along Jews for murder, or requested permission to shoot them themselves.[191] The poor weather conditions were used as an excuse for the relatively slow progress made during late December, although from 16 November to 15 December Group D had killed a further 17,645 Jews and 824 Gypsies.[192] Over Christmas and the New Year they concentrated on Jews in small places, registering 3,176 deaths. A further four thousand Jews had been killed by the end of January. By mid-February 1942 they were scraping an empty barrel, in the sense that they were having to hunt down Jews who had survived by using false identity papers. In early March, the number of victims described as 'anti-socials, Gypsies and mentally ill' exceeded the numbers of dead Jews.

Nothing differentiated the brutality deployed against any of these groups of victims, as the following incident proves.

That month Group D acquired three gassing vans: six-ton trucks complete with fake windows and painted curtains, and emblazoned with the Ten of Hearts.[193] The local Russians called them 'the soul killers'. During 1942, they reached the northern shores of the Sea of Azov, searching out people to kill in the northern Caucasus. Einsatzkommando 10a arrived in Yeisk that June. They alighted upon a home for 270 mentally and physically handicapped children aged between four and seventeen. The unit commander Kurt Trimborn ordered up the van, telling the staff of the home that their charges were going on 'an outing'. He regarded these children as 'useless mouths'. The ambulant inmates were hurled into the van by their feet. After repeat trips, the unit returned in the evening for the bedridden.[194] These killings made an impression on men who had been murdering people daily for twelve months. Soviet offensives in early 1943 signalled the moment to retreat, with Group D being redeployed to anti-partisan warfare in the Pripyat swamps. The Soviets disinterred the children of Yeisk from a grave in a garden south of town.

According to the men themselves, many of these killings were accompanied by such diversions as making a victim climb into and out of a grave to see whether it was wide enough to accommodate him or her. A Jew who called an SD man 'German swine, murderer' was clubbed to death with a machine-pistol which broke under the impact.[195] Nothing much is added by simply aggregating instances of individual barbarity. Post-war testimony recalls vivid incidents, blond or pregnant victims, babies, the odd futile plea, moments with sharp, human contours, within the great blur of destroyed humanity. A few survivors convey something of the infinitely repeated existential terror of the victims. Anna Gutkina was a young Jewish woman living in Mariupol. On about 18 October 1941, men from Group D ordered all Jews to report to a courtyard, bringing food for a day, their valuables and the keys to their homes. Gutkina went with her immediate family, including her parents and three sisters, their two infant children and twelve other relatives. Transferred to a deserted Soviet barracks, columns of five hundred male Jews and lorry-loads of the elderly, women and children, including Anna Gutkina, were transferred to a depot attached to the *kolkhoz* Maxim-Gorky. She heard gunfire in the distance. Her column halted at a stream, where, meeting her father and sister Fanny, she realised they were going to be shot. Groups of one hundred people were marched to an anti-tank ditch, ordered to undress and told to sit on the edge of the ditch. Her father and sister Fanny sat beside her. A bullet hit the right side of her head, causing her to tumble on to the chest of her father, who had fallen backwards beside the ditch. Boots pushed Gutkina into it. Anna Gutkina regained conciousness during the night, and crawled out from under the corpses. Her family did not.[196] Another survivor, Ivan Kotov, was a skilled turner with chronic health problems who on 22 August 1942 visited the municipal hospital in Krasnodar to collect a medical certificate. He called just at the time the SS were loading patients into a gassing van. Caught observing this, Kotov was thrown into the van too, where he found himself amid distressed people. As the van moved off, he began to choke. Having once had air-raid training, he tore off his shirt, wet it with urine and wrapped it around his face. After losing consciousness he awoke in a hole in the ground.[197] By the time it withdrew from Russia, Einsatzgruppe D had killed over ninety thousand people, the lowest total registered by these four formations (Group D was the smallest), who were one element among many deployed to wipe out between 2.6 and 2.9 million Soviet Jews who came under Nazi occupation. There were few survivors.[198]

THE VISION COMPLETED: THE CONTINENT-WIDE HOLOCAUST

The months it took for murder in the former Soviet Union to achieve its full momentum and scope were probably mirrored in the months that elapsed between decisions to kill the Jews of Europe, which began with the transportation of Jews into existing killing grounds in the East, and ended with industrialised extermination camps in Poland with a continental catchment area. If the decision to kill all Jews living within the occupied Soviet Union was the result of escalation between mid-July and October 1941, then Heydrich's solicitation of Göring's imprimatur on 31 July to prepare 'an overall plan of the preliminary organisational, practical and financial measures for the intended final solution [*Endlösung*] of the Jewish Question' marked the commencement of the vaster, and politically more sensitive, process of evacuating the Jews of Europe.[199] Many historians view this document as a 'smoking gun', in their search for firm ground amid so many terminological ambiguities and unrecorded conversations.[200] Major events such as the Holocaust must be reflected in key documentation. But this auto-authorisation document can also be read as a continuation of the existing policy combining deportation and decimation, rather than the beginning of a qualitatively different undertaking.[201] Comprehension was not aided by the Nazis' deliberate carrying over of the same terms – Final Solution, evacuation, resettlement – as euphemisms for mass murder.

However, one common-sense point must be stressed. Only Hitler had the panoramic view. He alone operated at the Antonescu, Horthy, Laval, Mussolini, Pétain, Quisling level. Given the extreme political sensitivity of extracting Jews who were citizens of other countries, it seems highly improbable that the authorisation to commence the 'Final Solution' would not have come from him in person. Adverse reactions to the 'euthanasia' programme may have made him very cautious about committing any equivalent authorisation to paper in a case much more freighted with political complexities. Although the current emphasis on the role of local initiatives has many merits, it is important to remember that Eichmann and Globocnik did not operate at the high diplomatic level, nor for that matter did Greiser, Himmler or Heydrich. Grand policy was not their business. With the broad brushstrokes in place, the details could be left to the underlings, whose fervour and fanaticism resulted in a counterflow of solutions to entirely self-engendered problems.

Self-created local 'problems' in Poland were not unconnected with self-created outside pressures. During deliberations with Goebbels in mid-August 1941, Hitler allowed his Minister to introduce the wearing of the Star of David to isolate the Jews of Berlin further, assuring him that, as soon as the campaign in the East was over, the Jews would be pushed eastwards, making Berlin 'free of Jews'. It was a 'scandal' that seventy-eight thousand Jews, 'mostly parasites', continued to disfigure the city, undermining public morale: 'We must approach the problem without any sentimentality. One only has to imagine what the Jews would do to us if they had the power, to know what one must do given that we have the power.'[202] Conversations like these were the ultimate source of the 'pressures' afflicting local authorities in Poland and the Baltic.

The human consequences were that from mid-October 1941 German Jews began to receive summonses to appear at designated collection points for 'evacuation' to an unspecified destination. They were informed that their property had been confiscated, including any that they had given or sold to a third party, transactions which were retroactively nullified. Care was taken to ensure that, under Nazi law, evacuation 'to the East' did not constitute 'abroad', for emigration by Jews had been prohibited that autumn. Every aspect of 'evacuation' was carefully specified: the amount of luggage and food rations, the rent and utility bills to be settled, and the keys to be handed to the Gestapo. Apartments were to be left 'clean and tidy'. Every official document concerning deportees, together with details of their residual assets, was left inside a Gestapo file, stamped 'evacuated'. The people concerned had lost their civic identity; now they could be deported and murdered.[203] Their property could be sold off at bargain-basement prices, while even their suits and fur coats would wend their way back to new owners in Greater Germany.

These policies took place within an increasingly strapped economic and military context. It occasionally struck some Nazi officials as being absurd that Jewish skilled workers were being murdered, or their labour squandered on meaningless projects, at a time when Germany was experiencing acute labour shortages in vital sectors of the war economy. By September 1941, there were 2.6 million unfilled vacancies. This gap was filled by the abandonment of the earlier profligate attitude towards Soviet POWs, and the decision to take civilian workers from the occupied eastern territories. These decisions were interpreted by sections of the SS in two ways, both devastating for the Jews of Europe. The Reich Main Security Office could argue that most Jews were immediately expendable, and pursued their annihilation with utter implacability. By contrast, Oswald Pohl's SS Main Office for Economy and Administration (WVHA), which in March 1942 had absorbed the Inspectorate of Concentration Camps, was more attuned to the economic requirements of the war economy, and hence began to develop a strategy of extermination through labour. Since the RSHA was not going to allow the deployment of Jews in contexts it could not control, this opened the way for the siting of camps near factories or the introduction of factories to the camps themselves.[204] A small proportion of Jews would be retained and worked to death in a spreading network of satellite camps attached to the principal concentration camps. An economy of killing had been established.

The temporary retention of Jewish labour did not substantially affect the fate of the vast majority of Jewish people. During the autumn of 1941, various murderous options were explored, some of which came to nothing. Those that amounted to something ran parallel with, rather than mutually exclusive of, mass shootings and industrialised killing centres. One suggestion, from an SS officer in the German embassy in Paris, in August 1941 – which combined slave labour and decimation in the service of the armed forces – involved using Jewish slave labour to reconstruct Transit Route IV, from Przemyśl via Lviv and Tarnopol towards the south-east, to take heavy military vehicles. The road surface would be laid on rubble made from the pulverised remnants of Jewish gravestones and synagogues.[205] Some twenty thousand Jews subsequently died, either in fifteen slave-labour camps dotted along this route, or by shooting once they could work no longer, in precise prefigurement of the *modus operandi* Heydrich would outline at the Wannsee Conference. Another option, investigated during October, involved using the inland waterways of the Dnieper and Bug to ship Jews to a camp at Mogilev, for which massive crematoria were ordered, which subsequently found their way to Auschwitz.[206] While this would have circumvented the problems arising from overloading strategic railroads, it failed to take account of the inadequacies of the Soviet waterway system. One could also issue a decree making it legal to shoot any Jew found at large or outside a designated area. Such a decree was promulgated on 15 October 1941 in the General Government. At first there was a notional trial before a Special Court. Soon, any Jew – or Pole who sheltered Jews – found outside a ghetto was simply gunned down.[207] And finally one could unleash the security forces against existing ghettos, as was done in the towns and villages of Galicia.

Several regions, which we have already encountered, assumed particular salience amid a general hardening of policy towards the Jews. As Hitler insisted on the step-by-step removal of the Jews from the Reich, beginning with the major cities of Berlin, Prague and Vienna, attention focused on the Łódź ghetto within German Litzmannstadt. It is probable that the advanced thinking of men such as Greiser or Höppner regarding killing non-productive Jews emboldened Eichmann to jog their elbows with a *fait accompli* involving deporting sixty thousand western Jews and five thousand Austrian Gypsies. Each deliberate application of pressure would have a knock-on effect, like a stone causing ripples of water. The Gestapo within the ghetto had already met them halfway, in the sense of splitting the ghetto into two parts for working and for merely 'maintained' Jews. The former would be fed, the latter decimated with minimal rations. This strategy echoed the differential provisioning of acute and chronic patients advocated before and during the 'euthanasia' programme. Further deportations into the ghetto would create 'impossible circumstances', and predictably bestirred the Łódź ghetto administration to fire off protests against Eichmann's 'Gypsy horse-trading'. On 4 October 1941, Government President Uebelhör in Łódź wrote to Himmler highlighting the acute economic dislocation that would result from this policy and the likelihood that Gypsies would set fire to raw materials being processed for the army, while archly observing of the inevitable overcrowding that during the Weimar Republic 'we thought' a density of three thousand people per square kilometre represented a sure 'breeding ground for Communism'. In his reply, Himmler systematically demolished each of these arguments, suggesting that if Gypsies committed arson, Uebelhör should immediately hang ten of them, regardless of whether they were guilty or not: 'This way you will have the best fire brigade in the ghetto in the Gypsies, who will evince a zeal that you have never seen before.'[208] In subsequent correspondence with his soulmate Greiser about the difficult Uebelhör, Himmler suggested the latter take a vacation now that he had 'recognised that the edifice of the Reich is higher than the church tower of Łódź'.

Having aimed high, Eichmann went to Łódź to secure a compromise, namely twenty rather than sixty thousand deportees, plus the five thousand Gypsies. During these negotiations, Rademacher of the Foreign Ministry relayed another 'problem': the diplomatic and military authorities in Serbia urgently wished to ship eight thousand Jews from Belgrade down the Danube to Romania, or to relocate them to the General Government or Russia. Exasperated by Rademacher, and with other matters in mind, Eichmann 'said roughly, that the military was responsible for order in Serbia and had to shoot insurgent Jews. To my inquiry he simply repeated "Shoot" and hung up.' Eichmann was not just in charge of trains, compartmentalising his mind from the eventuating horrors, but a lord of life and death on the telephone. Rademacher and two of Eichmann's team went to Belgrade, only to learn that most of these male Jews had already been shot by the army under Keitel's dispositions regarding reprisals.[209] Eichmann could not fit a trip to Belgrade into his schedule because he was finessing a deal between Greiser and Himmler, to resolve the problem of how to accommodate German Jews and Austrian Gypsies in the overcrowded Łódź ghetto. Whereas Uebelhör sought to pre-empt these deportations, Greiser cunningly solicited help from Himmler in resolving 'their' problem. He agreed to take these deportees if Himmler would oblige by disposing of anyone deemed surplus to requirements. Someone else decided that the process of selecting the victims should be delegated to the Elder of the Łódź Jewish Council, in a manner paradigmatic for other deportations from ghettos.

German and Czech Jews, and the Gypsies, arrived in the Łódź ghetto during October and early November. The Jews came from Emden, Duisburg, Krefeld, Mönchengladbach, Oberhausen, Rheydt and Trier. Apparently, during these months the police and Gestapo experimented at two separate locations in shooting and gassing large numbers of people.[210] On 20 December, the German authorities in Łódź demanded the resettlement of twenty thousand people, with a six-man commission established by Rumkowski and including the police and prison chiefs, selecting 'undesirable elements from the point of view of the ghetto's public interest'.[211] In other words, they had to implement a form of extreme social triage, or sorting of people according to their alleged value. The first to depart were prisoners, prostitutes, 'undesirable elements' and the families of those doing forced labour.[212] In February 1942 other 'socially harmful' individuals disappeared, including three hundred sewermen, this job being a punishment for strikers, thieves and those who resisted the Jewish Council. By March, it was the turn of welfare recipients, and anyone with a conviction registered by the courts.[213] In four successive waves, between 16 January and 12 September 1942, a total of 70,849 people were spirited away in the dead of night in trains, consisting of twenty passenger cars each containing over fifty people. On 9 July 1942, the Łódź Gestapo announced that there was room once more for 'circa 55,000 Jews'.

The Nazis went to great lengths to deceive the victims. Reassurance abounded, while inquiries were shuttled back and forth between agencies. Jewish Council leaders thought they had relationships with Nazi officials whom they met on a regular basis. In Warsaw, Adam Czerniakow was told that rumours of deportations were 'stuff and nonsense'; his interlocutor, the ghetto administrator Heinz Auerswald, even released Jewish children imprisoned for smuggling, a gesture hard to reconcile with annihilation. Two days later, Czerniakow was told to assemble six thousand people each day for deportation. If he failed to meet these quotas, his wife would be shot. On 23 July 1942, Czerniakow closed his office door and took a lethal overdose.[214] For these were not matters of academic contemplation, akin to philosophy students debating which person to eject from a lifeboat. With hindsight one can draw up hierarchies of preferable conduct, but hindsight knows what happened, free from the messy competing emotions and pressures of the moment. In these circumstances, many Councils turned for advice and justification to the wise, with rabbis sitting through the night, seeking guidance in their holy books; but the wisest had no greater wisdom than they.[215] For example, suicide might seem the heroic option, but then there would be no possibility of negotiating individual exemptions; no negative selection of doctors over criminals; and no guarantee that one's successor – and there would be one – would have greater competence or integrity. Flight was an option for those in ghettos such as Vilna near forests infested with partisans, but as Avraham Tory wrote: 'Not everyone can brave such conditions. Not everyone has a strong fist to defend himself. Not everyone can be a hero.'[216] The Nazis' *modus operandi* left a small space where Council leaders could delude themselves that they were making a difference, concealing the fact that their demands were inflationary and ultimately insatiable. Even ostensibly compliant Council leaders, such as Gens or

Rumkowski, spent hours agonising over what they were doing, desperately bargaining and pleading with men who felt no pity, and for whom the Council leaders were at best an irrelevance. Since the latter did not know the fate of deportees, they operated in a fog of not knowing whether to send the sick and elderly, or the young and fit who might survive the rigours of forced labour. The Nazis did not see a moral dilemma; even the most unscrupulous Council leader would have embraced any alternative. Here is Rumkowski on 4 September 1942, making these mental tribulations public knowledge:

> Yesterday. . . . I was given the order to send away more than 20,000 Jews from the ghetto, and if I did not – 'we will do it ourselves'. The question arose: 'Should we have accepted this and carried it out ourselves, or left it to others?' But as we were guided not by the thought: 'how many will be lost?' but 'how many can be saved?' we arrived at the conclusion – those closest to me at work, that is, and myself – that however difficult it was going to be, we must take upon ourselves the carrying out of this decree. I must carry out this difficult and bloody operation, I must cut off limbs in order to save the body! Common sense requires us to know that those must be saved who can be saved and who have a chance of being saved and not those whom there is not a chance to save in any case.[217]

The Łódź deportees were taken to a gas-van garage sixty kilometres west of the city at Kulmhof (or Chelmno) in the Warthbrücken (or Kolo) district. This was a village of 250 people on the Ner tributary of the Warthe. Awaiting them was the Sonderkommando 'Lange', augmented by about a hundred men from the regular police, who had occupied a dilapidated mansion, together with a camp located in a pine forest about four kilometres away. The Jews were escorted into the mansion, given an emollient talk in the courtyard about their useful skills, undressed and herded into the cellars, from which the only exit was via a ramp into zinc-lined gassing vans. Men flitting about with white coats and stethoscopes, stolen from the luggage of Jewish doctors, lent the operation a reassuringly medicalised aspect; bars of soap and face flannels gave the victims the illusion they were *en route* to a bath.[218] The van doors closed shut, the engines revved and, after the ten minutes needed to kill the occupants, the vans set off for the forest camp with their 'cargo'.[219] Between December 1941 and March 1943, a total of 145,000 people were killed at Kulmhof in this manner.

We know about the *modus operandi* because one man survived

this first stage of Kulmhof's operations. There was also post-war trial testimony of key German personnel. Very soon the walls of the cellar bore graffiti in Yiddish reading: 'Whoever comes here will not leave here alive.' Minatory notes filtered back to the ghetto in the empty trains. Out in the woods, teams of Jews, Poles and Ukrainians subjected corpses to a search for gold teeth, rings and concealed valuables. Michal Podchlebnik, a saddler from Kolo, worked in the woods, and discovered that among the bodies pulled from the third van to arrive on a Tuesday morning were his wife, seven-year-old son and five-year-old daughter.[220] He lay down next to his wife and asked to be shot, but was beaten to his feet to shouts of 'The fellow can still work well.' Despite the appalling nature of what they were doing, the Kulmhof team of former bakers, butchers, chauffeurs, tool makers and taxi drivers got through each day. The identity of victims was apparent from the provenance of the cigarettes the guards traded with local villagers.[221] Killing became a form of routinised work, a struggle with machines which malfunctioned and with an often refractory 'product'. A heavy off-duty sociability compensated for the awfulness of each day, with vestigial sensibilities obliterated over time. Some of them regarded this nightmare as a good posting: 'he [Haefele] felt fine in an extermination camp, he received good money and vacations. Whether it was male or female it was all the same; in the end it was exactly like treading on a beetle on the ground.'[222] Speaking in 1962, Haefele then scuffed his shoe on the ground.[223] In February 1944, Greiser reactivated Kulmhof, where between 23 June and 14 July a further seven thousand Jews were gassed. That August the remaining sixty thousand Jews in Łódź were shipped to Auschwitz. They included Rumkowski, who, punctilious to the last, ordered that all the ghetto's lights be switched off so as not to attract Allied bombers. Two thousand Łódź Jews were registered into the camp. The rest immediately perished. Throughout the deportations, the Gestapo informed the Jews of Łódź that the deportees were housed in a camp vacated by Volhynian Germans at Warthbrücken in Kolo county, where they were farming or repairing roads.[224]

Since the Łódź authorities were reluctant to take the forty thousand Jews excluded from Eichmann's compromise, Eichmann turned to his old acquaintance Stahlecker in Riga, and his colleague Arthur Nebe in Minsk. The latter were to receive the Jews in concentration camps, which like Salaspils in Latvia were not yet built. The self-generated problem of where to put these German Jews, which created difficulties with the civil administration and the military, was resolved by murdering twelve thousand Jews in the Minsk ghetto on 7 November 1941. Several thousand German Jews were then deposited in a 'German ghetto' in Minsk, to the discomfort of the Reich Commissar for White Ruthenia, Wilhelm Kube, who was amazed to see 'people from our own cultural milieu, who are somewhat different from the indigenous brutish horde'. These included decorated war veterans, skilled craftsmen, and half- or quarter-Jews. Although Kube wanted the Jews of Russia killed as quickly as possible, he drew the line at German Jews. A long list of his failings was sent to Heydrich. He and his wife had a Jewish barber and household flunkeys, whom they rewarded with fruit and vegetables. Kube had given sweets to children, and he had thanked a Jewish man who had rescued his expensive car from a blazing garage. He regularly upbraided German officials for abusing Jews, and had indicated that the German Jews would enjoy his protection.[225] Kube's superior Hinrich Lohse was more exercised by the obvious economic irrationality of killing people working on behalf of the German war effort. His critics, notably Stahlecker, complained that Lohse was living in the past of the General Government where ghettos and labour had been the solution. Lohse's Berlin superiors agreed, reminding him that: 'In principle, economic considerations are not to be taken into account in the settlement of the problem.'

Himmler made a few deft changes of personnel to bring killings in the Baltic up to speed with operations further south. Since he had 'only' killed half of Latvia's sixty-six thousand Jews by October, Stahlecker was moved eastwards, and the lacklustre Higher SS- and Police Leader Hans Prützmann was replaced by Friedrich Jeckeln, brought northwards from the Ukraine. This was a mass murderer on a par with Globocnik: a brisk, hard man with a mission, in his late forties, who in April 1941 had written to a friend: 'I myself will, as I have learned secretly, be used in connection with great events, which are to be expected.' Jeckeln met Himmler in Berlin where he was told to counter any squeamishness from Lohse with the line: 'Tell Lohse that it is my order, and that it is also the express wish of the Führer.'

Jeckeln reached Riga in November and, wasting no time, toured the environs of the city in search of a suitable killing ground. Since murder was his business, technical details that any normal mind could not countenance absolutely mattered. The Rumbala forest included elevated ground, admittedly visible, but offsetting the problem of waterlogged trenches in this sandy soil. The dead had to stay put, not rise with the water-table. Three terraced pits were dug, resembling inverted pyramids. Since there were seven daylight hours, everything would have to be done with extreme alacrity, another excuse for shutting out the awfulness of the task at hand by treating it as a technical one. On 27 November the ghetto was split into working and non-working parts, with 4,500–5,000 people conserved in the latter. On 29 November, Jeckeln shot German Jews brought by train prior to his clearing of the ghetto. On the 30th search parties scoured the non-working ghetto, knocking up Jewish households. There was a light fall of snow and it was already − 7 degrees. About 600–1,000 people, including the sick and immobile, were shot in their homes or on the streets. Columns of one thousand Jews were marched out of Riga, beginning at 4 a.m., each taking three hours to reach the forest. The last left Riga at noon. Those not killed *en route* were funnelled through seventeen hundred German and Latvian policemen; undressed on a meadow; and then shot packed like sardines, by a man armed with a Russian sub-machine gun set to fire shots singly from a fifty-bullet clip. This determined when the next shooter took over. By nightfall, twelve thousand people had been killed. After a week's break, the exercise was repeated with a further twelve thousand people. Jeckeln's men, who had murdered a further two thousand Jews from the train or in the ghetto, had expended twenty-six thousand rounds of ammunition. Twenty-six thousand people had been murdered.[226]

The French filmmaker Claude Lanzmann once absurdly claimed that extermination camps were situated in Poland because of the alleged pervasiveness of antisemitism there. Actually, there is plenty of evidence that sites in the Soviet empire were mooted, such as Mogilev, Salaspils and so forth. An installation resembling Kulmhof was to be created in Lviv in order systematically to murder Galician Jews. In November, a district doctor in Lemberg contacted Herbert Linden in the Interior Ministry – the bureaucratic *éminence gris* of the 'euthanasia' programme – inquiring about the loan of T-4 personnel to kill twelve hundred patients in the Lviv–Kulparkow psychiatric hospital. Three sites were probably under consideration since Eichmann visited Lublin, Minsk and Lviv in rapid succession.[227] The Lviv district doctor inquired about costs and technical details. In his reply, Linden remarked that he could not spell this out on paper – costs would be no obstacle – but he would explain the technical details face to face. Because the Soviet railway system could hardly cope with military traffic, no extermination centres were built in Lviv, Mogilev or Salaspils.

Instead, the decision was taken to concentrate the largest killing operations within the Lublin area. Galician Jews continued to die on Transit Route IV, in a strange echo of the half-truth built into the minutes of the Wannsee Conference, but the Lublin District was designated as the epicentre of the 'Final Solution'. Himmler turned to Globocnik, who had experience of setting up camps and training the men to staff them, not to speak of a bottomless malevolence towards Jews. Himmler met Globocnik with alarming frequency – five times alone in October 1941. In that month he ordered the opening of a training camp at Trawniki, south of Lublin, where Ukrainian prisoners of war who preferred collaboration to starving to death alongside three million Russians were schooled in SS brutality. After all, Globocnik had already demonstrated with his self-defence unit that he could take a thousand ethnic German farmhands, most of whom had never been near Germany, and convert them into brutal torturers and killers.[228] It seems probable, and in line with the gradualism we have seen throughout, that Globocnik received a relatively restricted initial assignment, involving killing a proportion of the Jews of the General Government in the initial facility at Belzec.[229] His roving camp constructor, Richard Thomalla, built a small camp on the site of the defunct labour camp used in 1939–40, which consisted of a handful of buildings ringed by double fences, next to a disused railway branch line. While Ukrainians provided the guards, Philip Bouhler, of the Chancellery of the Führer, made available to Globocnik around ninety of the four hundred or so T-4 personnel, under the ghoulish Christian Wirth – a highly decorated First World War infantryman with the sobriquet 'Savage Christian'. Each of what became three camps – Belzec, Sobibor and Treblinka – had a nucleus of about twenty to thirty experienced killers. T-4 personnel had recently obliged the SS camp empire, at a time when it had no mass extermination facilities, by gassing 'sick' prisoners within 'euthanasia' facilities. Having by autumn 1941 completed its primary mission, the 'euthanasia' organisation found another, larger task awaiting it. Men who had killed the crazed or halt – not to speak of the sane disadvantaged – for nearly two years, came to eastern Poland to kill Jewish men, women and children in far greater numbers.[230] Whether news of this fresh assignment was broken to them by Bouhler in Berlin or by Globocnik in Lublin is unknown, since the only account we have, from an imprisoned Franz Stangl, seems utterly implausible to anyone acquainted with the facts.[231] These men were not reluctant murderers. Globocnik welcomed 'so much new work' and wished to bury iron tablets recording his achievements, before fear of retribution led him to rediscover whatever vestiges of humanity were left in him.[232]

It took few personnel to make trainloads of people disappear within a few hours. Men redeployed from the 'euthanasia' programme experimented with different methods of gassing Jews who were brought solely for that purpose. At Belzec they opted for a dismounted tank engine, not requiring the time-consuming shipment eastwards of bottled carbon monoxide gas from German factories. The Reich Security Main Office simultaneously liaised with the Transport Ministry and the railways directorate in Cracow. Questions about where so many Jewish people were going were answered with the intelligence that they would be dispersed throughout the countryside. No one seems to have wondered why there were not substantial towns in the tiny places to which so many millions of people were being deported.

Logically, since Belzec straddled Lublin and Galicia, these were the first populations to go. Jews working for the authorities were separated from the rest and received identity papers; the Jewish police in the ghettos was enhanced. Search parties consisting of various types of German policemen and Trawnikis, named after their training base, descended on the ghettos, gathering the Jews at assembly points, and loading them on to goods wagons for the journey to Belzec. Many of these hunters were intoxicated, gunning down anyone who sought to flee or who offered resistance.[233] Separate units combed the ghetto's cellars and hiding places, lobbing grenades to finish off or flush out stragglers. The very young or the immobilised aged in orphanages or hospitals were shot on the spot. The post-war trials of Gestapo officers in Łódź included charges that they had in mid-air shot children thrown out of hospital windows; gunned down a woman presumptuous enough to address them in broken German; seized small children to brain them against walls; dragged older children from hiding places to shouts of: 'We have no bread in Germany for this filth.'[234] Given the relationship between not working and deportation, by the second wave of deportations to hit the Łódź ghetto, some Jews were walking around with their cheeks rouged or with their emaciated bodies artificially upholstered to give the appearance of health.[235]

Every stage in the journey to Belzec was nightmarish, beginning with the round-ups and forced marches to holding pens before transportation. We can follow the horrors of these trains from detailed reports made by the police officers in charge of them. On 10 September

1942 Josef Jacklein reported on the deportation to Belzec of 8,200
Jews from Kolomea in Galicia. Five guards at the front and rear of a
fifty-one-car train proved useless in preventing many people from
escaping through windows or via the flooring. Five stops from
Stanislau, Jacklein telephoned ahead for nails and planks to block the
escape routes (and air holes). Since the Jews had taken tools for
their resettlement, this process had to be repeated at every station.
In Lemberg (Lviv) about a thousand Jews in cars marked 'L' were
diverted to a labour camp, while a thousand local Jews were put
aboard. The replacement engine was so old that the train crawled up
inclines, allowing Jews to jump to freedom. Having expended all their
ammunition, and two hundred rounds donated by the army, the guards
were reduced to using pistols or rocks to kill escaping Jews. Conditions
inside the train were hellish. Some cars had 220 occupants. It was
extremely hot, and the stench of dead bodies was overpowering. When
the train was unloaded in Belzec at ten o'clock the next night, two
thousand Jews were found dead.[236] Although this transport was exceptionally sloppy, one wonders what proportion of deportees died on
each journey.

Jews not dead on arrival at Belzec were enjoined to enter a 'bath
and inhalation chamber' as a preliminary to further 'resettlement'.
Everything was geared up literally to paralyse the victims' reactions:
instantaneous brutality combined with speed and such deceptive reas-
surances as announcements for skilled craftsmen. The SS competed to
discover the most passifying stratagems, which were solely designed to
expedite killings and to maximise numbers of victims. At Treblinka,
victims were sometimes told they were about to be shipped to Madagascar, a faint echo of long-abandoned Nazi policies. Their deaths
were far from being a clean process. As the Waffen-SS sanitation
expert Kurt Gerstein witnessed, things could go horribly awry with the
gassing procedure, as when people were kept locked in a gas chamber
for several hours when the diesel engines malfunctioned.[237] Any resistance was ruthlessly repressed. A rabbi who arrived at Sobibor refused
to believe the emollient talk and, picking up a handful of sand,
declaimed: 'You see how I'm scattering this sand slowly, grain by
grain, and it's carried away by the breeze? That's what will happen to
you: this whole great Reich of yours will vanish like flying dust and
passing smoke.' He struck a guard for good measure. The Austrian
commandant Franz Reichleitner prevented the guard beating the rabbi
to a pulp. Waiting a while, he took the rabbi aside and shot him.[238]

The naked victims were herded from the reception camp down a 'tube', with branches of fir concealing barbed wire fences, and gassed in a converted barracks. Sobibor became operational in April 1942; experiences gleaned at Belzec and Sobibor in turn informed the construction of Treblinka, which, activated from mid-June, was dedicated to the killing of the Jews of Warsaw. A keenly competitive spirit prevailed among the personnel of these three camps, which was of the essence of the 'Final Solution'. Erich Bauer, known to Sobibor inmates as 'the master of gas', recalled: 'In the canteen at Sobibor I once overheard a conversation between Frenzel, Stangl, and Wagner. They were talking about the number of victims in the extermination camps at Belzec, Treblinka as well as Sobibor, and for reasons of competitiveness expressed their regret that Sobibor occupied last position.' Much the same mentality was evident among the Einsatzgruppen commanders. These men were literally suffering from a *rage des nombres*.[239]

Belzec and Sobibor were reconstructed to enhance their competitiveness. Belzec's three gas chambers became six during the summer of 1942. They were solid structures, embellished with potted plants outside the doors, a Star of David on the roof, and signs reading, 'The Hackenholt Foundation', a macabre joke based on the surname of the man, Lorenz Hackenholt, operating the diesel engines. The three gas chambers at Treblinka continued to function while a further ten were added, which could accommodate four thousand people at a time. A fake railway station was built, with a painted clock whose hands never moved. Stangl recalled of the place: 'It is difficult to describe it adequately now, but it became really beautiful,' by which he meant the make-believe world he constructed for his men inside the camp, which included flowerbeds, a mess and a zoo with rare birds.[240] In the interim, probably in May 1942, between the construction of Belzec and the activation of Treblinka, killing operations were extended to all the Jews of the General Government and the rest of occupied Europe. The three 'Aktion Reinhard' camps would murder the Jews of the General Government, while Auschwitz, a camp within a former Austro-Hungarian army barracks in Silesia, would have a vaster continental catchment area.

Auschwitz was an SS–industrial joint enterprise, with tax concessions for firms investing in the region, as well as being a prisoner-of-war camp and political prison for Soviets and Poles. The first mass murders at Auschwitz, involving use of 'Zyklon B' gas, were in September 1941, when 850 Soviet POWs and 'sick' prisoners were killed in the crematorium of the base camp. The method was chosen because stocks of this odourless commercial fumigant were already to hand, having been used to minimise the spread of disease. Modern scholarship has shown that accounts by Rudolf Hoess, the commandant of Auschwitz, of his role within the 'Final Solution' reflected his erratic attitude towards dates, and his desire to construct a certain picture of himself for posterity, namely that he was a misunderstood piece of humanity. He claimed that in the summer of 1941 Himmler commissioned him with the implementation of the 'Final Solution'. His dating of the meeting has been shown to be incorrect; and so are attempts to connect this alleged meeting with the 16 July 1941 Rastenburg conference, where, as we have seen, Hitler did not mention the Jews.[241]

Eichmann arrived at Auschwitz in the spring of 1942, to explain the modalities of transport, which must have involved victims from outside the Soviet Union and General Government, since Eichmann had no jurisdiction over either area. The Reich Main Security Office apparently supplied Hoess with graphic survivor accounts of how entire nations were liquidated in Soviet gulags or through slave labour projects such as the White Sea canal.[242] Throughout early to mid-1942, larger gas chambers were installed in a former farmhouse at Birkenau, a few miles from the base camp, which from July onwards began consuming Jews, directed there by SS doctors who perfunctorily screened deportees on the unloading ramp. Up to 90 per cent of each transport were deemed expendable, disappearing within hours of being arbitrarily separated from their families, who soon discovered from fellow inmates the significance of the permanent smell of burning and the columns of smoke ascending from the crematoria. More and more gas chambers were added, so that by mid-1943 the Auschwitz-Birkenau killing operation was so enormous that it was the equivalent of industrial overcapacity, a situation rectified as more Jews were killed there in the ensuing eight months than in the previous two years.[243] In sum, an estimated 1.1 million people died at Auschwitz, all but 122,000 of them Jews.

In July 1942, Himmler acceded to Globocnik's wish to kill every Jew in the General Government by New Year's Eve, in so far as they were not indispensable to the SS's own economic operations. Globocnik's notoriety had filtered through to Goebbels:

The Jews are now being forced eastwards from the General Government, commencing with Lublin. A pretty barbaric method, not to be described in detail, is being used here, and not much of the Jews themselves remains afterwards. . . . The former Gauleiter of Vienna [Globocnik] is in charge of this operation, and is doing it with considerable circumspection and with methods which do not attract much attention. A judicial sentence is being carried out against the Jews which is certainly barbaric, but which they have fully deserved. What the Führer prophesied in the eventuality of the Jews bringing about a new world war has begun to be realised in the most terrible fashion. In these matters, one cannot let sentimentality prevail. If we did not defend ourselves against them, the Jews would exterminate us. It is a life and death struggle between the Aryan race and the Jewish bacillus. No other government and no other regime could muster the strength for a general solution of this question. Here too, the Führer is the untiring advocate and champion of a radical solution, which the situation demands, and which therefore appears inevitable. Thank God the war affords us a series of opportunities which were denied us in peacetime. We must make use of them. The ghettos in the towns of the General Government which have been made vacant can now be filled with the Jews expelled from the Reich, and then the process can be repeated after a certain time.[244]

What explains the decision to extend killing to the whole of European Jewry? Warning bells began to sound in the autumn of 1941, when notice was dramatically served on the Jews of western Europe too. It is important to grasp before this discussion even commences that what follows had nothing whatsoever to do with rationalising economies or settlement plans, but involved antisemitism fused with security issues. From the summer of 1941, there was a marked increase in French resistance attacks against members of the German armed forces. Communists were blamed. Hostages were taken, from among whose number people were tried and executed. Hitler thought that this was an insufficient response, and ordered the summary shooting of a hundred hostages for each German soldier killed. Whereas the German army administration in Paris wished to retain some flexibility and room for escalation, Hitler saw the attacks on German troops as part of a Europe-wide Communist conspiracy. The army warned against importing 'Polish methods' to France, and of the dangers of playing into the hands of a resistance which actively sought German reprisals. There had to be another solution.[245]

The army administration was not the sole player in occupied France. On 2 October 1941, mysterious explosions rocked seven Parisian synagogues. Heydrich's chief of security police, Helmut

Knochen, blamed Eugène Deloncle's French antisemites, although owing to a drunken SD officer talking in his cups it soon became known that Knochen himself had supplied them with 30 grams of explosives, dispatched from the Reich Main Security Office in Berlin. When the military commander Otto von Stülpnagel wrote to Berlin demanding Knochen's recall, Heydrich in turn wrote to the army High Command explaining that he had authorised the Paris bombing by way of reprisal for earlier resistance woundings of Laval and Vichy minister Marcel Déat. He added that he had acted 'only from the moment when, at the highest level, Jewry had been forcefully designated as the culpable incendiary in Europe, one which must definitively disappear from Europe'.[246] The terrorist bombings in Paris were designed to bounce the military government in Paris into accepting retaliatory arrests and deportations of French Jews, as an alternative to reprisal shootings of French hostages. Actually, this was precisely the solution Stülpnagel had independently arrived at, to avenge the deaths of German soldiers, without upsetting the French with random reprisals. Hostages would still be executed, but every time a German was killed, five hundred Communists and Jews would be deported eastwards. The SS and French police would do the German army's dirty work for it. Deporting foreign Jews and Communists would satisfy Hitler, without disturbing either the sensibilities of the army or the policy of collaboration. Since soldiers went back and forth from the East to the West, with Paris being a favoured place to spend their leave, it is inconceivable that the denizens of the Hôtel Majestic did not know exactly what fate awaited Jews deported to eastern Europe. These policies were about to be centrally co-ordinated.[247]

On 29 November 1941, Heydrich invited twelve leading civil servants and SS figures to a conference to be convened at midday on 9 December. Its ostensible purpose was to achieve definitive resolution of the question of who was to be regarded as a Jew, for among the German Jews being deported to the East were Great War veterans, 'half-Jews' and Jewish spouses of 'Aryan' partners. Lack of precision was causing problems at both ends. Anonymous letters protested these policies at the German end, and a few courageous men such as Count Helmuth James von Moltke took up the cudgels on behalf of individuals. As we have seen, in the East some Nazi functionaries baulked at killing assimilated German Jews without unequivocal higher authorisation. A messy situation ensued, whereby some of the deportees were being murdered on arrival, others were starving to death, while still others were consigned to ghettos whose original inmates had been killed to make room for them.[248] This reflected the broader picture we have been describing, whereby Jews were being killed with different regional intensities all over eastern Europe and the Baltic, that being the burden of much contemporary German scholarship, while everywhere else within the Nazi empire there was a desire to make individual territories 'Judenrein'. These were not people attuned to contradiction, inconsistency or piecemeal solutions. They thought big and needed clear lines. They wanted someone to assume overall responsibility for taking the Jews off their hands. That person was to hand.

In the invitations, Eichmann confused the Interpol headquarters at Kleinen Wannsee 16 with an imposing lakeside villa Am Grossen Wannsee 56/58. Heydrich's Nordhav Foundation had purchased this villa from a right-wing businessman called Friedrich Minoux, who had been imprisoned for fraud. It was notionally part of a network of rest and recreation homes for SS personnel, including the island of Fehmarn, where Heydrich also purchased a house, but it was probably intended as a suburban mansion befitting the future status Heydrich envisaged.[249] An SS guesthouse with low rates and a pick-up service from the S-Bahn station, the villa's amenities included a billiard room for SS men who wished to relax when on business in the capital. It was a suitable conference centre, away from the hustle and bustle of the centre, with the icy waters of the lake lapping at the jetty. While it was briefly fashionable to minimise the import of the conference as a mere co-ordinating instance, more recent scholarship has highlighted its importance for pinning down when these policies were finally decided upon.

The German declaration of war on the United States on 11 December meant the conference was postponed until 20 January 1942. It lasted between one and two hours, and was probably held in the dining room. Eichmann, whose modest rank belied his status, watched over the stenotypist, ensuring that the minutes did not convey the spirit of the meeting, where the actual talk was of 'killing and elimination and destruction'. By the time it was convened, the purpose of the Wannsee Conference was not to resolve who were Jews to facilitate their deportation from Germany. American entry into the war had brought about the situation Hitler had 'prophesied' on 30 January

1939, a 'prophecy' coupled with dire consequences for the Jews, whose hand he detected behind Roosevelt's decision. The conference's purpose changed accordingly.

Hitler addressed fifty Reich- and Gauleiter on 12 December 1941 in his private apartment at the Reich Chancellery. The gist of what he said was recorded. It was time to 'clear the decks' on the 'Jewish Question', without 'sentimentality' or 'pity'. Those who had caused a conflict costing Germany so many dead were to pay for it with their own lives. This was incitement to general murder. Although this does not tell us when Hitler had decided *in his own mind* to murder the Jews of Europe, for that may have been latent all along, it probably does represent the hardest evidence we have for when he decided to share this decision with his most tried and trusted followers. They certainly took away this message, since they now spoke of clarity having been achieved, or emulated Hitler's very words and tone in their own speeches on the subject.[250] On 18 December 1941, Himmler noted in his appointment book after an afternoon session with Hitler: 'Jewish question / exterminate as partisans'. Although that probably does not bear quite the weight that has been put upon it, it does show very clearly that at this level murder was more than in the air, and that the preferred camouflage used in Russia was to be generalised, as Heydrich's Parisian bombers had already demonstrated.

The vistas opened up by Hitler's speech probably explain why the Wannsee Conference was postponed for six weeks, and why it now included agendas beyond the matter of who was to be designated a Jew. The Wannsee Conference did not inaugurate the 'Final Solution', since most of the participants represented the third tier in their agencies and ministries, rather than the most senior decision makers. Like most meetings, several agendas and interests were represented, with games being played at different levels. The original subject matter of determining who was a Jew in Germany was now subsidiary to plans being feverishly adumbrated to kill every Jew in Europe. It had become a formal sit-down between mass murderers and senior civil servants. One participant, Gauleiter Meyer of North Westphalia, had attended the 12 December 1941 meeting in Hitler's apartment. At least one conferee, Dr Rudolf Lange, had assisted both Stahlecker and Jeckeln in murdering the Jews of Latvia. Eichmann had organised everybody's deportation. Other SS participants included Lange's 'Ostland' colleague Eberhard Schöngarth, 'Gestapo' Müller, and Otto Hofmann from the Race and Resettlement Office, while the occupied East was represented by State Secretary Josef Bühler and Reichsamtsleiter Dr Leibbrandt. This group therefore consisted of men already inextricably involved with the murder of Jews, or representing territories where this had already taken place, or would do so in the future. The intention was to iron out, and pre-empt, the sort of conflicts between civil and security agencies which had sometimes arisen in the Baltic.

The other participants included representatives of the Foreign, Interior and Justice Ministries, the Four Year Plan apparatus and the Party and Reich Chancelleries. All of them knew about aspects of policies already in motion, for some of them – such as Luther from the Foreign Ministry – came armed with their own agendas. Representatives from the Finance and Transport Ministries were superfluous, since questions concerning the possessions of deported Jews had already been managed, while the Reich Main Security Office dealt directly with the railway authorities. After all, these were just technicalities. The temporary exemption of Jews working in arms factories and the talk of exploiting the labour value of the able-bodied was presumably intended to placate Erich Neumann representing the Four Year Plan agency. The conference was designed to test the reactions of a ministerial bureaucracy which would inevitably have to be initiated into the massive operations which were projected. In the event, although Stuckart of the Interior Ministry tried to maintain his ministry's interest in determining who was a Jew, he surprised Eichmann by the robustness of his language.

Heydrich, who assumed the burden of solving everybody's 'Jewish problem', unveiled absolutely unequivocal intelligence that the Jews were going to be killed, with the biologically resilient survivors of slave labour being polished off by some more radical method. The assembled bureaucrats did not demur. Finally, Heydrich restated his personal control of the 'Final Solution', both at the sharp end and wherever Jews were to be deported from, 'without regard to geographic boundaries', although no one present had much of an interest in disputing either issue. No one would have to bother any longer with grubby regional killing centres, randomly established to resolve each local 'Jewish Question', and which were unsuited to killing Jews from elsewhere. Best of all, the regional advocates of making territories 'free of Jews' would not have to take any responsibility themselves. Heydrich and the SS had assumed everybody's problem, and had outlined how they planned to proceed. Relieved by the absence of resistance to this monstrous undertaking, and excited by the powers he had accrued,

Heydrich conferred briefly with Eichmann and Müller in a side room, drinking a celebratory cognac, dispelling the tension of problems they had anticipated but never encountered, in the course of agreeing how to implement the murder of eleven million people.[251] That afternoon he authorised the award of decorations to several veterans of mass shootings and gassing operations on the Eastern Front. The full project stood revealed, based on Hitler's decision to sanction an SS-led global solution to everyone else's local 'Jewish problem'.

Each of the paths we have already followed flowed into the 'Final Solution', tributaries of human suffering flowing into a dead sea. Auschwitz has become its synonym, but Auschwitz was simply the largest killing centre among many. It tells both all and part of the story. Some half a million people perished in the ghettos of occupied Poland, expiring paper-thin in doorways and dumped unceremoniously into mass graves. Up to two million people were shot or gassed in the former Soviet Union, by the various mobile forces at Himmler's disposal and sundry indigenous collaborators. Having wiped out the major Jewish population centres, the shooting squads returned to do the fine-tuning, killing rural Jewish populations in small and great operations. As we have seen, about 145,000 people were murdered at Kulmhof. There were two survivors. Down to 1943, the three 'Aktion Reinhard' death camps consumed the lives of nearly two million people, nine hundred thousand alone at Treblinka. The minimum estimate of the numbers of people who perished at Auschwitz, where extermination through labour complemented a death camp, in a specific combination only emulated at Majdanek, is one million one hundred thousand people. As many as two hundred thousand people were killed at Majdanek.[252]

The implementation of these policies on a continental scale required more than the routinised activism of countless German officials. Across occupied Europe, Nazi Germany lacked the manpower to conduct raids, to guard those detained in camps or dispatched to their deaths on deportation trains, and so relied heavily on the co-operation of indigenous authorities. France was an especially interesting case, in political terms a halfway house between countries such as Belgium or the Netherlands, which were under direct German control, and Hungary or Romania, which were Hitler's allies with their own authoritarian governments. While France, a quarter of whose Jewish population perished in the Holocaust, stands favourable comparison with the Netherlands, three-quarters of whose Jews died, it does not emerge too well from comparisons with the regimes of Horthy or Antonescu, at least in terms of policy towards native Hungarian or Romanian Jews, for, as we have seen, Antonescu was responsible for massive killings outside Romania itself. In mid-1942 there were some 2,500–3,500 German policemen in occupied France, who lacked the local knowledge or strength to do more than round up relatively small numbers of Jews. After November, this force was spread even more thinly, as German forces entered the unoccupied zone. Vichy's assent to the deportation of foreign Jews was given by Laval's second administration. This decision was of a piece with the earlier view that stateless and foreign Jews were expendable, with the difference that assent to deportation was bound up with attempts to incline Hitler to regularise Vichy's status, in order to win Vichy greater domestic credibility. The Nazis had no intention of delimiting which Jews they wished to kill, but they allowed Laval and his colleagues this illusion, by starting with the thin edge of the wedge, that is with foreign Jews.

There were also some key changes of personnel that summer. Himmler dispatched Carl Oberg from Radom to Paris as Higher SS- and Police Leader, almost symbolising the westward extension of policies already well in hand in Poland. The conservative nationalist antisemite Vallat was replaced as Commissioner-General for Jewish Affairs by Louis Darquier de Pellepoix, a career antisemite of the most ideological kind, who had been in Nazi pay since the late 1930s. The esteem with which the SS regarded him can be gauged from their insistence that he and his staff provide proof of their own 'Aryan' ancestry. They would not have done that with Vallat. On 4 March 1942, the SD Jewish specialist in France, Theodor Dannecker, was recalled to a conference with Eichmann in Berlin, where he and colleagues from Belgium and the Netherlands were instructed to initiate local preparations for the deportation of the Jews to the East. This included one hundred thousand Jews from France. If Dannecker did not learn their fate then, he certainly did a little later, for at the end of the month he personally supervised a trial deportation, accompanying one thousand Jews in a passenger train to Auschwitz. From this experience he learned that cattle cars required fewer guards. In early May, Heydrich paid a week-long visit to Paris, a creative reconnaissance trip, whose ulterior motive may have been a plot for him to replace the military government, from which vantage point he could keep a watchful eye on Vichy. Heydrich met Oberg, Helmut Knochen and René Bousquet, the civil servant in charge of French police in Vichy's Interior Ministry. Heydrich dangled the prospect of restoring French control over the police in the occupied zone, a sufficient *quid pro quo* to ensure Bousquet's participation in rounding up foreign Jews. It is worth noting his involvement in plotting actions which his own government had not yet authorised.[253]

Following cabinet decisions taken in early July 1942, nine thousand French policemen went into action rounding up Jews in the Paris area. Operation Spring Wind netted nearly thirteen thousand people, or half of the target figure, for some French policemen tipped off potential victims, who then managed to elude capture. Those Jews who were apprehended were held in an indoor bicycling stadium, the Vélodrome d'Hiver, until they were removed to a half-built housing estate about eight miles outside the city centre at Drancy, or to other locations. Conditions in the 'Vél d'Hiv' and at Drancy were atrocious, whether under the French or, after June 1943, under Alois Brunner, a leading Austrian light of Eichmann's deportation team. These measures were next extended to foreign Jews in the Vichy zone, with French police-men conducting the round-ups and guarding freight wagons which took the Jews to Drancy, and then to the Franco-German border at Noveant, from which it was a further three days to Auschwitz. Forty-two thousand Jews made this journey by the close of 1942. They left on trains which departed with a thousand people each Sunday, Tues-day and Thursday, with more inmates arriving to take their places every Monday, Wednesday and Saturday.

The highly public transshipment and deportation of men, women and children bestirred the Catholic hierarchy to voice its misgivings both in private and in public. The fact that many of these elderly clerics were Vichy loyalists who had not opposed earlier discriminatory measures against the Jews may have given their words added force: 'The Jews are real men and women. They cannot be abused without limit. . . . They are part of the human species. They are our brothers like so many others.' Further protests were stilled, by the clerics themselves, who took fright as resistance groups and the Allies ran with their own earlier utterances, and in the wake of large-scale state subsidies for Catholic and Protestant schools and theological faculties. Further deportations occurred in 1943 and 1944, resulting in a total of about seventy-five thousand French Jews who were delivered by the French to their murderers. But the tide of war was turning against Germany, and measures against assimilated French Jews were unpopu-lar, especially in a wider climate of indiscriminate Nazi violence towards Frenchmen suspected of resistance activities. Laval resisted pressure to denaturalise French Jews, while Nazi agencies became progressively reliant on militant French antisemites and fascists for the implementation of their policies.[254]

These policies were implemented the length and breadth of Europe. Salonika in northern Greece was once known as the Jerusalem of the Balkans. A chilly blast from the north swept away something complex and venerable, as if a sledgehammer had been brought down on a delicate figurine. Although Jews had been present in Salonika since pre-Christian times, the community's character was stamped by an influx of Spanish-speaking Sephardim who had fled the most Catholic monarchs Ferdinand and Isabella. The older generation spoke Ladino, a form of old-Castilian with borrowings from six other languages, reflecting their protracted travels to Greece. Hellenisation campaigns under the dictator Iannis Metaxas (1936–41) meant that many younger people communicated with the surrounding Christian population in the majority vernacular. Like other Jewish communities in Greece, the Jews of Salonika kept themselves to themselves, opting for close ties with the royal family and Metaxas to protect their autonomy in a society where antisemitism in any case had little purchase, beyond young and unemployed Anatolian Greek refugees.[255] Four thousand Jewish men from Salonika fought with the Greek army resisting the initial Italian invasion.[256]

Although the Italians seized the lion's share of occupied Greece, including Athens, the Nazis took Macedonia and eastern Thrace, and thus the majority of Greek Jews, while Bulgaria occupied the northeastern parts of the country. Fifty-six thousand Jews lived in Salonika at the time of the German occupation on 9 April, or about a quarter of the city's population, and four-fifths of Greek Jewry. It was a community with a rich past, in gradual decline.[257] A fire had ravaged the city in 1917, and relations between Jews and Anatolian Greek refugees were tense. Many Jews worked in commerce, dyeing, printing and textiles or as stevedores in the docks, Salonika being the only port in Europe to shut down for the Sabbath. Apart from the systematic theft of their famed libraries by professorial pilferers dispatched by Rosenberg, the Jews of Salonika suffered no worse fate than their Christian compatriots before July 1942. Like the Greek population in general, the Jews had a bad time during the first winter of occupation, which was rigorously cold. They may have been reassured by Prime Minister Tsolacoglou's announcement that he valued the loyalty of the

Jews during the recent war, and that they would continue to enjoy the rights they had had hitherto.

On 11 July 1942, German army authorities imposed forced labour on the male Jewish population. This led to the creation of a committee to mediate between Germans and Jews. A total of eighteen thousand Jews performed forced labour. Since this was deleterious for those concerned, in October the Jewish community offered to deflect it by paying two billion drachmas. When they failed to produce a small fraction of this sum, the old Jewish cemetery was opened as a source of quarried marble to any Greeks who wished to help themselves.

Eichmann's associate Rolf Günther arrived in Athens in January 1943 to negotiate the deportation of the Jews from the German-occupied regions of Greece. Presumably they had been hoping to take the Jews of the Italian zones too, but they found that this was diplomatically impracticable.[258] Cognisant of the fate of the Jews of Serbia – by this date there were none – the army leadership acquiesced in the deportation of Salonika's Jews, whom they regarded as a potential security threat in the event of an Allied landing. In early February 1943, an enhanced SD team arrived in Salonika, including Alois Brunner and Dieter Wisliceny. A Polish-born rabbi, Dr Koretz, was made president of the Jewish Council. The Nazis organised the ghettoisation of the Jewish population in a district called Aghia Paraskevi, and set about registering and stealing the Jews' assets and possessions, so that their headquarters on Velisaros Street came to resemble Ali Baba's cave. Jews slated for deportation were moved to a smaller ghetto called Baron de Hirsch, after the Jewish philanthropist of that name, in the poorer district near the railway station. In mid-March these Jews were told that they were being resettled in Cracow, and heads of families were issued with cheques to be redeemed in złoty. Jews stockpiled knapsacks, tools and warm clothing. Three-quarters of the first train carrying 2,400 Jews were gassed within hours of entering Auschwitz-Birkenau. Some 45,324 Jews left Salonika for Auschwitz, of whom about eleven thousand briefly survived selections on the ramp. Since someone had forgotten that the Reichsbahn took only Reichsmarks and not drachmas, for once the Reichsbahn gener-ously waived its fees. Koretz, who had vainly tried, with the help of the Orthodox Metropolitan, to get the Prime Minister to intercede with the Nazis, died of typhus in Bergen-Belsen. About nine thousand Greek Jews were deported the following year, with small insular communities from Corfu, Crete or Rhodes being taken by ship to a concentration camp at Chaidari near Athens, and then on to Auschwitz by train. The contrast between these sunny, fragrant islands and the muddy cesspool of Auschwitz in the March cold must have been uniquely soul-destroying. Despite Germany's deteriorating military position, essential transport was tied up moving handfuls of Jews sixteen hundred kilometres across Europe. Totally ill-suited to the rigours of an eastern European climate, and largely unable to communicate with fellow prisoners, only 358 Greek Jews survived the camp. Those who did not included twelve thousand children.[259] There was one ray of light in Greece. In contrast to the compliant Koretz, the Athenian rabbi Eliyahu Barzilai refused Wisliceny's requests for lists of Athens' Jews, mislaid the archives and sought the help of the Orthodox Metropolitan. The latter offered hiding places in churches and monasteries. The Greek resistance also sheltered Jews in its mountain fastnesses, in return for the community's money. Athenian Jewry survived.

Industrialised death camps were the most tangible manifestations of a process extending across thousands of other camps, where people were worked to death or otherwise brutalised, and of mass shootings across the countryside of eastern Europe, as the killing squads crisscrossed the hamlets and small towns to root out every Jew who had somehow survived the first onslaughts. Shootings were both small or mind-bogglingly vast. In central Europe, mass deportations to extermination camps came in waves, subject to the competing demands for personnel and transport for the harvest, or the latest offensive on the Russian front, and such variables as railways needing repair, or gas chambers rebuilding to enhance their capacity. People in closed ghettos were most vulnerable to these deportations. Those living in small places, where deportation by rail was not an option, or who had fled into the woods, were tracked down by killing squads including the Order Police battalions. Flying squadrons of policemen sped into isolated farmsteads to kill their Jewish workers.[260] Others followed Polish trackers into the woods, looking for chimneys revealing underground bunkers, into which they threw grenades to kill the occupants. The only Jews given a temporary reprieve were those who were selected to work as slaves, including the forty-five thousand who by June 1943 remained in Globocnik's Lublin district labour camps.

The Warsaw ghetto uprising in April 1943 lent added urgency to the extermination of the Jews, with Hitler urging on Himmler, and the latter transmitting this to his subordinates. The Jews were once again depicted as a 'security threat', which countervailed against residual arguments about their temporary economic utility. In May, Himmler decreed that the employment of Jews in the armament industry in the General Government should cease.[261] As large tracts of eastern Europe slipped into the semi-anarchy of partisan bands, so anti-partisan warfare subsumed the quest for Jews who had evaded destruction. The existence of Jewish partisans became an excuse for stepping up the tempo of liquidating captive Jewish populations. Thus, on 8 September 1942, the General Commissar of White Ruthenia in Minsk advocated accelerated cleansing of the Jews and the reduction of the residual Jewish skilled labour force to the essential minimum.[262] In the Baltic, the SS began collecting separate data on Jewish partisan activity to support their tenuous identification of partisans with the remaining Jewish population. On 29 December Himmler reported to Hitler, using the large typewriter with a special face designed for the Führer's failing eyesight, that in the Ukraine between 1 September and 1 December 1942 around ten thousand partisans had been killed (a thousand or so in combat), along with fourteen thousand partisan collaborators and suspects, before casually noting the 'execution' of 363,211 Jews during this period.[263]

When even the security of the extermination camps seemed to be challenged, as prisoner revolts erupted in Sobibor and Treblinka, Globocnik's successor as SS- and Police Leader in Lublin, Jakob Sporrenberg, received orders to liquidate all residual labour camps in Lublin. Operation Harvest Festival (Erntefest) in early November 1943 resulted in the shooting of forty-five thousand Jews into zig-zag air-raid trenches. Loud music was broadcast to drown out the gunfire, as Sporrenberg circled overhead in his Fieseler Storch. Jewish inmates of the Majdanek, Trawniki and Poniatowa camps were also massacred. Lublin had become 'Judenfrei'.[264] Harvest Festival was exceeded only by the enormous massacre carried out by the Romanians in Odessa. Long after the extermination camps had been demolished, shootings of Jews continued, not least those being brought back from the contracting fronts to camps in the Reich on the death marches, which, together with the 1944 extermination of Hungarian Jewry, will be discussed in the final chapter.

The Nazis were not the only Axis power to operate murderous camp regimes. Entire Jewish populations were killed through a combination of brutality and neglect, in places where there were no gas chambers, and where the Germans were present but not in charge. Under the 30 August 1941 Tighina agreement, Transnistria was administered by the Romanians under Governor Gheorghe Alexianu, with a series of prefects and praetors imposed on thirteen Romanian *judets* sub-divided into sixty-four Soviet *rayons*. The Romanian regime was unsure whether it actually wanted Transnistria as anything other than a bargaining counter to use against Hungary, although some 'Greater Romanian' fanatics aggressively pursued policies of 'Romanianisation', while others saw it as a 'dumping ground' for ethnic undesirables.

There were approximately 210,000 Jews indigenous to the region, including the 35,000–40,000 who survived the massacre in Odessa. Eighty per cent of these people were murdered by the Romanian gendarmerie and Esalon-Operativ, Einsatzgruppe D or Ukrainian militiamen during the first six months of occupation. These Moldavian and Ukrainian Jews were collected into concentration camps aA cmecetka, Bogdanovca and Dumanovca or handed over to Ohlendorf's Group DA t Bogdanovca on 21 December 1941, the Romanian mass murderers Modest Isopescu, Aristide Padure and Vasile Manescu organised the killing of forty-eight thousand people by fire and grenades. In Dumanovca they murdered eighteen thousand people, at Acmecetka they starved four thousand to death.[265] In total, the Romanians killed about ninety thousand Jews in Transnistria, with the Nazis murdering about forty thousand more.

About sixty-four thousand survivors of the initial slaughter in Bessarabia and North Bukovina were detained in holding camps, such as Edineti, Rautel and Vertujeni, and deported to Transnistria between October 1941 and January 1942, together with about the same number of people from South Bukovina and Dorohoi province in central Romania. This was followed during mid-1942 by further deportations, including some Jews from the Regat, or Romania proper, which brought the total number of Jews sent to Transnistria to about one hundred and sixty thousand people.[266] Every stage of the move to Transnistria was punctuated by extortionate demands from the Romanian authorities, through whom they were processed, until they entered this nightmarish place, sometimes without the clothes they had been wearing. The Bank of Romania imposed punitive compulsory exchange rates on deportees; their guards sometimes collected a small fee from local peasants for shooting Jews, so that the peasants could make off with their boots and clothing.

Transnistria had been ravaged and ruined by warfare. The deportees were initially dispersed throughout towns and villages, dwelling in

caves, clay hovels, ruins and stables without sanitation and infested
with fleas and lice. In former Jewish quarters, the houses sometimes
bore graffiti reading: 'Here was murdered [a name] with all his
family.'²⁶⁷ During the winter of 1941/2, about 30 to 50 per cent of the
deportees perished during a typhus epidemic. Although the Jews were
not initially confined in ghettos, they were subjected to forced labour,
with the authorities embezzling the pittance that the Jews were supposed to receive. Starting in June 1942, some 117 ghettos and camps
were established in Transnistria, with conditions varying according to
the character and zeal of the Romanian authorities, the proximity of
Einsatzgruppe D and the extent to which the Jewish community could
pay off venal Romanian officials or organise some semblance of
civilised existence under these desperate conditions. The Jewish communities of Mogilev and Sargorod were notable in this regard. When
the International Red Cross delegate Charles Kolb toured the region in
December 1943, he found just over fifty-four thousand people alive,
and wondered what had happened to the missing 241,000 other
deportees. He saw through the Potemkin façade of contented Jews
and fires lit for his visit, to the reality of disease, hunger and inadequate bedding and clothing afflicting the remnants of extinguished
communities.²⁶⁸

But what of the three hundred thousand Jewish people still within
the Regat? Paradoxically, the country which ran Germany a close
second in massacring Jews was also the country in which more Jews
survived than anywhere else in occupied Europe. Subjected to discrimination, crippling financial exactions and compulsory labour, the Jews
were nonetheless spared ghettoisation and identification. From the
Nazi point of view, the rot began when the Romanian government
picked its own national Jewish Council, called the Centre of the Jews,
rather than accepting Nazi nominees. This meant that the Jews were
represented vis-à-vis the authorities by men who included friends and
business associates of senior Romanian politicians. Dr Nador Ghingold
was a friend of the widow of the antisemite Octavian Goga; M.
Strohminger was a schoolfriend of Prime Minister Mihai Antonescu.²⁶⁹
German officials began to pressurise the Romanian regime to make the
Jews available for deportation. A representative of Eichmann arrived
in Bucharest in July 1942, to begin planning the removal of Romania's
Jews to Belzec. In August, the Foreign Ministry reported to the Reich
Main Security Office that Ion and Mihai Antonescu had consented to
the deportation of Jews from Arad, Timişoara and Turda provinces.

The head of the Romanian Jewish Commissariat, the ex-journalist Radu Lecca, would be arriving in Berlin to sort out the details. This visit went badly wrong, in the sense that Lecca was brusquely treated by Foreign Ministry officials, who thought they were discussing details with an oily rag rather than making decisions with a ship's officer. Both offended and opportunistic, Antonescu banned deportations from the Regat, and ordered improved treatment and then the partial repatriation to Romania of Jews who had survived the Transnistrian camps. High-level Romanian discussions of Transnistria's Jews blithely ignored how the Jews had come to be there in the first place, with Antonescu disclaiming all responsibility while warning that these survivors should not be killed by the Germans.

Apart from German highhandedness towards Lecca, why did these mass murderers experience a change of heart? First, Antonescu was subject to high-powered lobbying from the Apostolic Nuncio and the Queen Mother Elena, as well as the Swiss ambassador to Romania, René de Veck. The Jews of the Banat and Transylvania, who were first in line for deportation, 'donated' one hundred million lei towards a magnificent hospital being built by Antonescu's physician. Secondly, Antonescu was open to appeals from Romania's Jewish establishment, notably Filderman and Rabbi Safran, for, as we have seen, a dialogue of sorts endured between regime and Jews that was unimaginable in Germany. Finally, Antonescu was keenly aware of how the war was developing.[270] Studied independence gradually shifted to outright defiance, as Romania prepared to desert the Axis and the Nazis moved in to defend Transnistria from the Soviets. Discussions about the fate of Transnistria's surviving Jews, who were eventually repatriated or allowed to leave for Palestine, took on the character of preparing postwar alibis as the Soviets swept towards Romania.

At the same time as the Romanians were opportunistically reversing their policies towards the Jews, alibis – or rather self-justifications – of a different kind were being given their most systematic exposition. Many of history's murderers have staked out the moral high ground, killing for love of confession or country, or in the name of social equality. Himmler did the same in a speech to senior SS officers, among others, delivered in Posen in October 1943. Much of the speech was taken up with the military achievements of the Waffen-SS, with Himmler's duties as praetorian of the nation, or the enumeration of SS secondary virtues. Himmler spoke for over three hours – judging from the recording he had made of the speech, in the monotone of a man with no need for oratory. In this company, he could call a spade a spade:

> Whether other nations live in prosperity or perish through hunger only interests me in so far as we can use them as slaves for our civilisation, otherwise this is of no interest to me. Whether or not ten thousand Russian females drop down with exhaustion while digging an anti-tank ditch only interests me in so far as the anti-tank ditch is completed for Germany. We will never be brutal and heartless where it is unnecessary to be so; that is clear. We Germans, who are the only people on earth to have a decent attitude towards animals, will adopt a decent attitude towards these human animals, but it is a crime against our own blood to be concerned about them or to give them ideals, whereby things will be made still more difficult for our sons and grandsons. If someone comes to me and says: 'I can't build an anti-tank ditch with women or children. That is inhuman because they'll die doing it' – then I have to reply: 'You are a murderer of your own blood, for if that anti-tank ditch is not built, then German soldiers will die, and these are sons of German mothers. That is our blood.'

He had successfully 'inoculated' the SS with the mindset that 'our concern, our duty, is to our people and our blood'; everything else was 'lather' (*Seifenschaum*). About two hours into the speech, Himmler touched on 'a really grave chapter' that was not for general consumption: 'I am referring here to the evacuation of the Jews, the extermination of the Jewish people.' Having formally acknowledged the euphemism involved, Himmler derided those Germans who talked about mass extermination without the benefit of personal experience. Each had his 'first-rate Jew' who should be exempted from these policies. However, this special audience was made of sterner stuff:

> Most of you men know what it is like to see 100 corpses side by side, or 500 or 1,000. To have stood fast through this and – except for cases of human weakness – to have stayed decent that has made us hard. This is an unwritten and never-to-be written page of glory in our history, for we know how difficult it would be for us if today – under bombing raids and the hardships and deprivations of war – we were still to have the Jews in every city as secret saboteurs, agitators and inciters. If the Jews were still lodged in the body of the German nation, we would probably have reached by now the stage of 1916–17.

In his sole display of emotion, Himmler angrily rejected hypothetical charges of pecuniary gain: 'The wealth they possessed we took from them. . . . We have taken none of it for ourselves.' Anyone who acted to the contrary 'is a dead man', even if he stole a cigarette. Mercifully he did not censure the victims for smoking. Having excluded a cupidity that was omnipresent throughout the 'Final Solution', whether individuals rifling through pockets, bank accounts plundered by the banks themselves, or trainloads of inventorised goods and suitcases of money in hundreds of currencies shipped to the Reich, this most banal of moralists concluded:

> We had the moral right, we had the duty towards our people, to destroy this people that wanted to destroy us. But we do not have the right to enrich ourselves by so much as a fur, as a watch, by one Mark or a cigarette or anything else. We have exterminated a bacterium because we do not want in the end to be infected by the bacterium and die of it. I will not see so much as a small area of sepsis appear here or gain a hold. Wherever it may form, we will cauterise it. All in all, however, we can say that we have carried out this most difficult of tasks in a spirit of love for our people. And we have suffered no harm in our inner being, our soul, our character.[271]

Justifications for killing defenceless people had reached their apogee with killing described as a by-product of love, in none too subtle perversion of theological sophistries once used to legitimise crusader slaughter of Moslems, Jews and pagans, but blended with the exclusionary nationalism and blood-based racism of the nineteenth and early twentieth centuries. This exclusive, sentimental love for one's own kind was more worrying than Himmler's Pooterish fastidiousness about rifling the pockets of the dead, or the lack of self-awareness regarding the harm that had been done to the souls of so many, including his own. The words themselves being a witches' whirly-gig of grotesque moral involution.

A few months before this speech, the Kovno ghetto survivor Avraham Tory made the following entry in his diary:

> Despite the seven chambers of hell that the Jews – as individuals and as a community – have gone through, our spirit has not been crushed. Our eyes are wide open and we are attuned to what is going on around us. We do not forget for one moment the hallowed purpose of our people. Everything that we do, all the things we go through, seem to us as a necessary evil, a temporary hardship, so that we may reach our goal and fulfill our duty to keep on going, and to keep spinning the golden thread of the eternal glory of Israel, in order to prove to the

world the will of our people to live under any conditions and situations. These goals supply us with the moral strength to preserve our lives and to ensure the future of our people.[272]

Moral strength confronted moral 'right'; life was affirmed as others so cruelly denied it. There was a human poetry about Tory's 'golden thread' and 'eternal glory' entirely absent from Himmler's grim talk of corpses, bacteria and sepsis, for beyond his sententious references to love lay nothing but death and destruction, the abregation of all it is to be fully human.

9

'WHEN GOD WILLS IT, EVEN A BROOM CAN SHOOT': RESISTANCE IN GERMANY, 1933–1945

The distinguished diplomat and former
ambassador to Rome, Ulrich von Hassell,
was highly critical of the Nazi regime and
was executed for his part in the 20 July
1944 bomb plot.

THE LEFT RECOVERS AND MAKES NEW FRIENDS

The earliest organised resistance to National Socialism came from the left. Thousands of Communists were incarcerated by the Nazis on account of their political affiliations or as old scores were settled. United resistance by the left was rendered impossible by police repression, a dogmatic sectarianism compounded by class and historical animosities, and the atomisation of employed and unemployed, skilled and unskilled, young and old, intensified by the Depression and secular trends towards a more individualistic consumer society. In this sense, Nazi Germany was a crossroads between the tribalism of the past, and the more atomised arrangements of the present.[1] The left was also inherently fissiparous, with several schismatic entities, either situated between the two mass parties of Communists and Social Democrats or operating covertly within them.[2] Some of these self-consciously elite groups, whose ideology occasionally blended left and right in maverick confusion, proved better adapted to covert activities, and less prone to spies and informers, than the former mass labour parties. The trades unions were affiliated to four umbrella organisations: the Social Democrat ADGB and Communist RGO, as well as the Roman Catholic DGB and Hirsch-Dunker unions.

The major faultline running through the left wing of the working class, for by no means all workers came under that rubric, was hostility between the Communists and Social Democrats. Between 1928 and 1934 the Communist Party (KPD) adhered to an inflationary use of the term 'fascism' to describe not only the Nazis, but also the previous chancellors and the 'social fascists' of the SPD. Again and again KPD and Comintern resolutions in the early 1930s stressed that 'our strategy directs its main thrust against Social Democracy', with Nazism downgraded as a second-order threat with which one could occasionally collaborate.[3] All that can be said for this ultra-leftist line was that its clarity appealed to younger, more marginalised and radically resentful sections of the unemployed working class who comprised the Party rank and file during the Weimar Republic.[4] In practice, it meant that, when the Nazis removed a bust of former Social Democrat Reich President Ebert from Frankfurt's Paulskirche, the Communist *Arbeiterzeitung* commented:

> Without Ebert, Noske, Severing etc. it would have been impossible for the SA and SS to be running around today. We Communists have a suggestion to make to the Nazis: put the statue of Ebert back in its former place, and put the highest Nazi medal around his neck for his undying services to the reaction.[5]

Much of the historical literature on the KPD – and not only that which legitimised the dictatorship in the German Democratic Republic – tends to celebrate the heroism of ordinary comrades and functionaries, without discussing the society they wished to bring about, their values or their relationship to events within the international Communist movement or to the regime of Stalin. The sceptical scrutiny of motives accorded other forms of resistance is routinely withheld from Marxists, either because their ordinariness and tenacity are regarded as their own justification, or because of the phenomenon of there being 'no enemies to the left', as epitomised by the Sartrean sophism of silence about Soviet camps 'pour ne pas désespérer Billancourt' – that is, the Communist voters of this Parisian suburb. However, unsentimental observers are invariably stuck when enjoined to admire self-sacrificing fanaticism, for this is neither especially admirable – many Nazis vainly expended their lives too – nor separable from the aims, ideology and mentality informing it. After all, many Communists who emerged from the appalling conditions of Nazi concentration camps nonetheless had no qualms about inflicting similar experiences on other people after their rule had been imposed throughout eastern Europe by Soviet tanks.[6]

The German Communist Party, like its 1930s British or French equivalents, consisted of grimly authoritarian Stalinists rather than chi-chi 'Euro-Communists' of a later vintage. Many were emotionally in thrall to the dictatorial dystopia in the East, a leap of faith by people dedicated to an ostensibly scientific doctrine. As it happened, seven members of the exiled German Politburo, and forty-one of the sixty-eight KPD leaders who fled to Moscow, were murdered there, as Stalin's purges reached into foreign Communist parties and the Comintern apparatus.[7] These realities notwithstanding, most members of the sect believed in this mythical land, allegedly populated by cheery harvesters and muscular steel workers, presided over by their 'Great Leader'. Of course, this utopia existed only in the pages of *Rote Fahne* or in the reports of fellow travellers who knew only the edited highlights. A tactical insistence on such rights as free speech camouflaged the desire for a dictatorship of the proletariat, in which dissenting views would have been eradicated and the 'class enemy' extirpated. As the Czech Communist Klement Gottwald openly announced in the National Assembly: 'We go to Moscow to learn from the Russian Bolsheviks how to wring your necks. And you know that the Russian Bolsheviks are masters at it!'

Compensating for their objective circumstances, the Communists viewed themselves as an avant-garde, with values such as fanaticism, hardness and self-sacrifice derived from cheap pamphlets about the Russian Bolsheviks. They inhabited a paranoid sectarian sub-culture, menaced by Social Democrats, Trotskyite deviationists and international capitalists, and spoke a slogan-laden jargon heavy with 'hirelings' or 'lackeys'.[8] Wedded to the notion that Nazism was a bosses' plot, to an economistic view of how societies function, and to a deterministic, predictive view of history, the Communists never quite grasped the irrational potency of Nazism in the here and now, and indeed deliberately blotted out earlier rather subtle analyses of Italian Fascism. Moral self-righteousness concealed a ruthless amorality, rationalised by bizarrely disjunctive thought processes beyond the ken of ordinary mortals, namely an inexhaustible capacity to excuse Stalinism in the belief of deferred human betterment or to rationalise its tortuous strategies. 'It's good that Stalin has such people shot,' commented a young Rhine bargeman docking in Rotterdam when asked about the Moscow show trials, although more sophisticated versions of the same grossness continued to be peddled in western Europe and America for decades afterwards.[9]

Beyond these generic characteristics of the sect, above and beyond any localised, second-order idiosyncrasies, the Communists' determinist analysis of the 'situation' in Germany consisted of wishful thinking, while their tactics guaranteed self-immolation. Imagining that 'fascism' was evanescent and revolution imminent, they endeavoured to maintain the organisational sinews of their Party, for organisation was everything, while reminding the world of their continued presence. Nazism would inevitably spiral into chaos, as the capitalist 'wire pullers' parted company with the Party's 'petit bourgeois' following, leaving the Communists triumphant in the revolutionary dawn. They were horribly wrong. Authoritarian bureaucratic centralisation, known as 'democratic centralism', translated to a submerged Party, proved catastrophic; as did attempts to combine agitation and clandestinity. The maintenance of membership lists and regular collection of Party dues, the distribution of leaflets or slogans daubed on walls, made it relatively easy for the Gestapo to track down individuals.[10] The Gestapo's discovery of the Communists' own surveillance records on Trotskyist sects proved unhelpful to the latter. Thousands of leaflets and newspapers were printed and distributed, but these did not bring in new supporters to replace those being arrested. The Nazis, now aided by a police force often consisting of former Social Democrats, took the battle into the Communist camp with an unprecedented ferocity. Working-class citadels of Communism were surrounded and searched for subversive literature and weapons. Communists detained by the SA or Gestapo in *ad hoc* concentration camps were roughed up or tortured until they revealed the names of other comrades. Working-class Nazis reported irregular comings and goings. In other words, the Party effectively sacrificed the freedom, and in some cases lives, of the rank and file to no appreciable purpose other than maintaining the morale of its diminishing basis.

From 1934 the dictates of Soviet foreign policy brought a tactical revision of the ultra-leftist course, in favour of grudging co-operation with 'bourgeois' forces and Social Democrats. Implementation of this shift was uneven, since some cadres had limited contact with the exiled leadership and doggedly adhered to the 'social fascist' line, rejecting tactical 'opportunism'. Terms such as 'democracy' or 'nation' filtered into Communist literature in a reprise of their tactics during the French occupation of the Ruhr. This was accompanied by 'entryist' tactics, whereby Communists were to infiltrate such Nazi organisations as the German Labour Front, in order to politicise the workers' economistic grievances.

Both tactics proved unsuccessful. Communists were too well known to agitate freely, while membership of the Labour Front marked them as collaborators, and brought the danger of reverse infiltration by Gestapo informers. Moreover, disgruntled workers, including Nazis, tended to decouple local grievances about hours, prices, wages or the availability of consumer goods from Nazism's egalitarian accoutrements or foreign policy triumphs, just as they decoupled resentment at nest-feathering Party bosses from the incorruptible Führer.[11] The Communists were well represented among the former unemployed labouring on work-creation projects such as bridges, dams or roads, where poor conditions engendered disproportional militancy, but these isolated workers were easy prey for the Gestapo. Meanwhile, the Communists made few inroads into the heavy industrial workforce, where in any case solidarities were collapsing under the dual impact of performance-oriented competition and rates of pay set by skill shortages. The Communists' political message was simply filtered out as an unwanted interference. Attempts to build bridges to other opponents of the regime may have had some local successes, but Communist rationalisations of GPU atrocities during the Spanish Civil War or Stalin's purges hardly endeared them to potential allies.[12]

Having undermined the 'popular front' strategy by its own conduct, the Soviet leadership was confirmed in its view of relying on itself alone. This was signalled by the August 1939 Molotov–Ribbentrop Pact, and was fraternally cemented when Stalin deported about five hundred Communist exiles back to Nazi Germany.[13] Stalinist stooges, such as the odious Palme Dutt in Britain, ensured that this line was adopted by national Communist parties. By now living in a ghetto-like fantasy world, many German Communists imagined that Hitler would release imprisoned activists, or allow the KPD to operate semi-legally. In conservative opposition circles, the Pact confirmed the view that Nazism was a form of 'brown Bolshevism'. In working-class and Social Democratic circles, the Pact was seen as a great betrayal, reminiscent of Nazi–Communist collusion against Otto Braun and Severing.[14] After six years of illegal activity, the remnants of the Party consisted of informal localised networks of activists too fearful to do anything, loosely linked to a Party executive being depleted in Moscow. The Communists had reached the starting point of the Social Democrats. They were so inconsequential that the Gestapo reallocated desk officers to other more pressing targets such as homosexuals, Jews and Freemasons. Arrests of Communists declined vertiginously from five hundred in January 1939 to seventy in April 1940.[15]

Localised clandestine groups gradually re-formed in both Berlin and the regions, including the Uhrig–Römer and Saefkow–Jacob Groups, which co-ordinated the printing and dissemination of propaganda and sabotage in arms factories. The Uhrig group, named after the Berlin toolmaker Robert Uhrig, had networks in several cities, with eighty activists in one Berlin arms factory alone. In 1940–1 Uhrig developed close relations with another resistance network led by Josef 'Beppo' Römer. The latter's route to resistance and the guillotine was circuitous, reminding us that people's political affiliations were not set in stone, and that individuals traded allegiances, either because they changed or because the parties they once disliked gradually inclined towards them.

A survivor of both the Western and Eastern Fronts in the Great War, Römer was the former chieftain of the Free Corps 'Oberland', which had crushed the left-wing regime in post-war Munich and liberated the Annaberg in Upper Silesia from Polish nationalist insurgents. The French sentenced him to death *in absentia* for his involvement in terroristic activities in the occupied Ruhr, during which the KPD made its first tactical approach to the nationalist right, via the so-called Schlageter line, when the Party adopted this dead Nazi as a martyrological mascot. Anti-bourgeois, nationalistic and sympathetic to Russia in equal measures, Römer drifted via 'National Bolshevism' to the Nazi Party, until the KPD's espousal of national and social liberation enabled him to defect to that camp. The catalyst seems to have been the case of the Reichswehr officer Richard Scheringer, who, imprisoned for Nazi affiliations, made a very public conversion to Communism in 1931.[16] Römer edited the anti-fascist journal *Aufbruch*, recanting his former Free Corps involvements: they were guard dogs acting on behalf of business interests. Shortly after the Nazi 'seizure of power', the renegade Römer was arrested and, after long imprisonment, placed in 'protective custody' in Dachau. Appeals on his behalf were personally vetoed by Hitler.

After five years' detention, Römer was released in July 1939. He immediately began organising small left-wing resistance cells in Munich and Berlin, forging contacts with opposition circles in the civil service and military. The members included actors, electricians, furniture makers, stage carpenters and painters. During this period Römer produced pamphlets highlighting the scarcity of resources – notably certain metals and oil – underlying Germany's prosecution of the war. By September 1941 his groups were collaborating with the resisters organised by Robert Uhrig, with 'Red Orchestra' and representatives of Wilhelm Knöchen's organisation in the Rhine–Ruhr. Römer advocated training armed cadres and sabotage in the factories. Together with Uhrig, he published a bimonthly *Information Service* analysing the current political situation, setting out goals and advising on appropriate targets for sabotage: 'The supply of petrol is Hitler's Achilles heel. Every action which destroys petrol weakens his war-making potential.' Partly as a consequence of his involvement with the

Uhrig group, Römer was arrested in February 1942, tried over two years later, and guillotined in Brandenburg-Gorden in September 1944. Roland Freisler's judgement against him posited two people. The 'model' soldier and Free Corps hero had become somebody else, 'losing himself in Communism'. He was 'no longer the man of the years 1914 to 1932'.[17]

Another resistance network, dubbed 'Red Orchestra' by the Gestapo, was erroneously identified with Soviet military intelligence activities in Germany and beyond, but in reality consisted of several discrete groups of around 150 men and women, which coalesced in the period between the Non-Aggression Pact and the invasion of the Soviet Union. The minority which opted for espionage had little success. Harro Schulze-Boysen and Arvid Harnack passed on information about the invasion to contacts in the Soviet embassy, information which Stalin discounted; attempts to establish radio contact with Moscow after 1941 were an unmitigated disaster, since the equipment supplied by the Soviets was defective. The groups had more luck with leaflet campaigns which drew attention to Nazi atrocities in occupied Europe.[18] The only Central Committee functionary active in Germany, Wilhelm Knöchen, briefly succeeded in organising a resistance network in the Rhine–Ruhr area, with a monthly underground newspaper, before his betrayal and arrest in early 1943. Again, the statistics of Gestapo arrests militate against any overestimation of Communist resistance activities in the closing years of the war. The majority of those arrested for disrupting or sabotaging production were foreign forced workers rather than Germans, Communist or otherwise. Those detained in Dortmund or Düsseldorf who figured under the Gestapo rubric 'reactionary opposition' now exceeded those registered under 'Communism/Marxism'.[19] Communist resistance had been smashed. Other resistance circles rash enough to put out feelers to them soon regretted it, for the remnants of the KPD were riddled with informers.

The Social Democrat leadership joined Communists and Conservatives in an initial underestimation of the exceptionality of the Nazi 'seizure of power'. The ageing leadership imagined a reversion to the conditions of triumph in adversity endured under Bismarck's Socialist Law. The leadership fractured between those favouring tactical compromise at home and those preferring intransigence directed from abroad, although Julius Leber and Carlo Mierendorff recommended underground activity in Germany. The leadership of the new, Prague-based SOPADE maintained links with activists in Germany through sixteen border secretariats. Agents stationed across the borders crossed into Germany, bringing literature hidden in bicycles, prams and rucksacks. A stream of reliable information on conditions in Nazi Germany flowed out, notably the impressive series of 'Green' reports based on anecdotal and hard information collated by agents. Although some Social Democrats formed resistance groups, the majority of former members and supporters withdrew from political activity, concentrating on maintaining loose contacts by disguising themselves as innocuous social and sporting associations. In contrast to futile and gestural Communist heroics they quietly maintained their morale and values, doing little to attract or merit the attention of the Gestapo, a stance which it is difficult to describe as resistance, except in a highly passive sense, and as applicable to many members of both Churches.[20] They were like mammals hibernating during winter, discussing the current situation over a beer in a pub or with family and friends in their homes, activities whose subversive nature was difficult to determine.

The capacity of Social Democrats to maintain group solidarities in the workplace varied from case to case. Dockers employed at Bremen's AG Weser worked in small gangs distributed across a massive site, and were so hard to monitor that exasperated Gestapo officers suggested putting barbed wire around the entire operation. It was a rash employee who dared to give the 'Hitler salute' or wear Nazi insignia in this solidly Social Democratic context. By contrast, workers reskilled to work in the Nazi 'model concern' of Focke-Wulff responded to the firm's cultural and leisure offerings, while increasingly identifying with the pioneering problem-solving aspects of its aeronautical products, as worker solidarities reformed around essentially technical questions.[21]

In some respects, the trades unions represented the most realistic strategists of the left, although not all unionists were socialists. The main non-Communist umbrella union organisations, to which some two hundred unions were affiliated, had begun to coalesce before the Nazi 'seizure of power'. However, in April 1933 they offered Hitler an historic compromise, based on the abandonment of class struggle, internationalism and links with political parties, in return for a unitary trades union movement. Rejecting this offer of collaboration, Hitler struck at the union leadership and its assets, attempting to console the working class with the German Labour Front, which lacked the most substantive attributes of trades unions. The results of elections to works councils suggest that this strategy failed to win the workers over, for no further elections were held after 1935. According to Willy Brandt, the future Berlin mayor and West German Chancellor, in many factories lip-service was paid to the functionaries of the Labour Front, while actual relations may have been regulated by tried and trusted union representatives.[22]

The trades union movement gradually reconstituted itself abroad, wisely opting to serve the interests of activists in Germany rather than seeking to give them orders. Within Germany, workers in certain sectors, such as metal and wood workers, railwaymen and seafarers, maintained impressive illegal networks, which would have played a key role in a general strike attendant upon a military coup. Two former union leaders – the Social Democrat Wilhelm Leuschner and the Catholic Jakob Kaiser – forged connections with the conservative and military resistance, under cover, in the first case, of his ownership of a factory with the patent to manufacture chrome beer pumps and non-corrosive screws, a role which enabled him to travel legitimately.[23] Reactivating contacts between union leaders and the military which stemmed from the era of General Schleicher, Leuschner made it clear to his interlocutors from the circle around Beck and Goerdeler that any action by the working class would follow rather than precede a military coup, thus forestalling any repetition of the unfortunate events of 1918 from which the left had acquired the odium of treason.[24] Regardless of whatever popular resistance potentialities would have been unleashed by a coup, and which were briefly manifested in the 'anti-fascist' committees immediately after the war, the direct challenge to the Nazi dictatorship would have to come from those much nearer to the centres of power, from men whose relationship with National Socialism was initially ambiguous. Since several leading socialists were drawn to these circles, partly in an effort to transcend the tribal, they will be discussed in this new, altered context, where unexpected alliances flourished.

THE THRILL OF 'ENERGETIC PRIMITIVENESS' AND THE RIGHT

Established elites connived at putting Hitler in power, but this is only part of the complex story of conservative relations with National Socialism. Like the left, whose divisions fatally weakened their response to Nazism, German conservatism was split between irreconcilable traditions, nullifying any united conservative response to the challenge of Nazism. While right-wingers universally welcomed an end to the Weimar Republic, some were satisfied with the post-1930 authoritarian chancellorships, regarding governmental collaboration between conservatives and Nazis with extreme trepidation.[25] The pietist Pomeranian Junker and 'revolutionary conservative' Ewald von Kleist-Schmenzin (1890–1944) regarded 'nazified' workers on his estate in the early 1930s as just as much of a problem as the radicalised labourers he and his landowning colleagues had broken a decade before, and he was notably sceptical of the strategy of 'taming' Hitler:

> Do not think that when you board an express train, the driver of which is deranged, you can somehow take over the controls. You may well travel very fast, but when the train reaches the points it will suddenly be derailed. The fundamental mistake is the pretension to total power; that is the devil's work. Only God can claim total power. If a human being does so then the perversion of power must follow.[26]

Having decided that Hitler was a dangerous 'clown' as long ago as the Munich putsch, Kleist articulated what he regarded as the key differences between Nazism and conservatism in a pamphlet called *National Socialism: A Threat*. It is important to cite this since it demonstrates very clearly that men such as Kleist were motivated not solely by their putative class interests, but rather by concerns which are ineluctably marginalised by an increasingly secular-minded historical literature:

> It is the attitude to religion which separates and must always separate Conservative thinking from National Socialism. The basis of Conser-

vative politics is that obedience to God and faith in him must also determine the whole of public life. Hitler and National Socialism adopt a fundamentally different position. . . . It is a fact that Hitler . . . only acknowledges race and its demands as the highest law governing state activity. That is a materialism irreconcilable with faith and Christianity. According to Hitler, it is the task of the state not to develop talents, but only to nurture racial characteristics![27]

Such inflexible convictions resulted in a series of run-ins with the Nazi authorities, and would subsequently involve Kleist in visits to England to stiffen the response of Chamberlain's government to Nazi aggression, to the betrayal of military intelligence to the Swedes, and finally to his sanctioning of his eldest son's bid to kill Hitler on the ground that whoever failed to take up that particular poisoned chalice would forfeit the right to happiness. But this is to anticipate.

Having approved or engineered Hitler's coming to power, some members of the conservative elites were soon keen to eject him, belatedly realising the bankruptcy of their strategy of 'taming' Hitler within 'their' cabinet. A few felt: 'We are partly responsible for "this chap" coming to power: we must get rid of him.'[28] Vice-Chancellor Papen tried to construct a conservative counterweight to Nazism by packing his office with young conservative and mainly Catholic aristocrats, including Herbert von Bose, Count Hans Reinhard von Kageneck, Baron Wilhelm von Ketteler, Friedrich-Karl von Savigny and Fritz-Günther von Tschirschky. This became a clearing house for complaints about the illegalities and oppressions of the Nazis in power. Its moving spirit was the Calvinist and Young Conservative lawyer Edgar Julius Jung. Since both Jung's ideas and his attempts to mobilise wider anti-Nazi constituencies anticipate the ideas and political constellations of the resistance a decade later, it is worth considering him in greater detail.

Jung was responsible for attempts to invest successively the nationalist press baron Hugenberg and Papen with a coherent conservative political philosophy, the main intellectual influences on him being the Catholic corporatist Othmar Spann, Vilfredo Pareto and a Nietzschean philosopher of religion called Leonard Ziegler. Jung had played a minor part in the assassination in 1924 of the Rhenish separatist Franz-Josef Heinz-Orbis, and had links to industrial and paramilitary right-wing circles. Having welcomed the contribution of the 'energetic primitiveness' of the Nazi movement to the destruction of the Weimar Republic, whose demerits were expressed in the title of his book *Rule by Mediocrity*, Jung thought that Nazism's anti-intellectual and un-stable mass should be rapidly deactivated, leaving the way clear for the 'revolutionary conservative' ideas of men such as himself. This was extreme hubris on the part of a bright young man at home in the world of elite clubs and think-tanks, but was ill suited to the dema-gogic, messianic and plebiscitary realities Hitler represented. However, it was redeemed by the fact that Jung's Christian beliefs led him to reject the Nazis' attempts 'totally' to politicise every corner of life, and to argue that since Europe shared a common Christian heritage and an external threat from emerging global economies it should reject the extreme ethnocentric nationalism of the Nazis in favour of co-operation and federalism.[29] This made him unusual in German conservative circles, with many of his ideas anticipating those of the wartime Kreisau Circle. He seems to have envisaged some sort of supra-national elective monarchy along the lines of the medieval Holy Roman Empire. Calvinism and past practice suggest that he had no religious qualms about assassination as a political weapon.

THE GENERALS WHO DITHERED

Strained relations between Hitler and the SA, between the latter and the army, and finally between Hitler and Catholic lay organisations, such as Erich Klausener's Catholic Action, disappointed by the fruits of the Concordat, probably led Jung and Bose to pick this moment for a conservative fronde against Hitler. Persuaded that assassinating Hitler would disqualify him from any future political role in Germany, Jung fell back on the idea of a major speech by Papen, which would act as a catalyst for the army, and sundry Catholic and conservative forces, to act against SA anarchy and Nazism. Jung wrote the speech which Papen delivered to rapturous applause at the University of Marburg on 17 June 1934, Marburg being a stronghold of the former conservative DNVP.[30] Jung took the precaution of publishing the speech before he delivered it to Papen so tardily that the latter could not amend it. Although Papen was careful to praise the 'positive' achievements of Hitler and the Nazi movement in overcoming the endemic divisiveness of the Weimar Republic, he was critical of a highly unPrussian personality cult, while careful to avoid naming the prime culprit, and implied that one-party rule was a transitory stage. Large sections of the speech were taken up with the problems of intellectual life under this government, a subject on which Jung clearly felt very strongly. Papen criticised attempts to replace the press with government information and propaganda services, for 'only weaklings cannot tolerate criticism'. If the Nazis' exploitation of democracy had proved to be tactically superior to the revolution from above advocated by 'revolutionary conservatives', this was no reason to lambast the latter with the quasi-Marxist term 'reactionaries'. If the Nazi activists' anti-intellectualism had some justification, this was no excuse for continued attacks on mind or spirit in general, still less for the displacement of scientists of world renown by mediocrities possessed of a Party membership book.

Papen's more general criticisms were directed at the totalitarian claims of a single class or party, and at the dangers of permanent revolution. Acknowledging the 'direct democracy' represented by the Nazi Party, he said it was time to replace its monopolistic position with an organic society based on estates. A society divided between Spartans and helots would merely result in the former having nothing to do but repress the latter, a process which weakened Sparta's external power. Defending 'freedom' as an aboriginal German value, he argued for the unassailability of the 'security and freedom of private areas of life'. Finally, Papen warned those advocating a second revolution that a third would surely follow, with the guillotine consuming those responsible for it. He reminded Hitler that the sole concern of a 'statesman' was 'nation and state' – the state being the ultimate guarantor of the citizen's claim to 'iron justice' – and not the perpetuation of the dualism of 'state' and 'Party'.[31]

In the event, the army failed to act, and Papen proved an empty vessel, twice offering Hitler his resignation to atone for his errors. Publicity for his speech was suppressed by the Gestapo. But some sixty thousand Catholics attended a rally in Berlin's Hoppegarten at which Klausener delivered a speech, an event which increased Hitler's animus against these circles. Jung was arrested the following day, on the pretext of treasonable dealings with the Austrian government. He was taken to a suburban wood and shot in the course of the 'Night of the Long Knives' a few days later. Meanwhile, Herbert von Bose's attempts to involve Hindenburg and General Fritsch in a putsch unfortunately came to the attention of the Hitler loyalist Blomberg. SS assassins gunned down Bose in the Vice-Chancellery, and Erich Klausener of Catholic Action in his offices at the Transport Ministry.

Other members of Papen's staff managed to flee, subsequently joining Papen as advisers in his new capacity as special plenipotentiary to Austria. There they forged links with clerical–fascist circles associated with Othmar Spann. Baron Wilhelm von Ketteler's unblemished corpse was fished out of the Danube on 25 April 1938. He had gone missing on 13 March, the day after German forces entered Austria. During the interim Himmler, Heydrich and Kaltenbrunner were ostentatiously supportive in their dealings with the distressed Papen, although they counselled against his offer of a large reward for information about the missing attaché lest he had fled abroad. Himmler ordered the police to make strenuous efforts to trace the Baron. Ketteler's friends used the old-boy network to make inquiries among contacts in the Nazi security police in Austria. They were eventually told, 'Hands off Ketteler, he's since gone bathing,' and that 'one can also drown in a bathtub'. This was indeed what had happened to Ketteler, at the hands of Heydrich's SD agents – the forerunners of the Einsatzgruppen – come to short-circuit any links between exiled German conservatives and their Austrian equivalents, and it was they who dumped his body in the Danube. Papen became ambassador to Turkey.[32]

If the bloodbath of 30 June 1934 terminated one source of conservative opposition, it also sowed the dragon's teeth of others, although we should be careful not to exaggerate its significance. After all, General Walther von Reichenau apparently conferred with Himmler and Göring prior to the events, nodding or shaking his head while going through their lists of people to be murdered. As both beneficiaries and facilitators of Hitler's purge of the SA, the army leadership acquiesced in the murder of two generals, digesting the claim that Schleicher had been in touch with foreign powers or shot while resisting arrest, a view which did not easily accommodate why the SS had shot Schleicher's wife too when they burst into their Neubabelsberg home. Calls for an investigation were not pursued with any vigour. However, a few soldiers were disturbed by Hitler's resort to the methods of a 'band of robbers'. Captain Henning von Tresckow, whose battalion of the 9th Infantry Regiment was put on alert during these events, was profoundly shocked by the murderousness of a leader he otherwise supported. In military intelligence – the Abwehr – Hans Oster (1887–1945) was kept informed of the bloody details of the purge by Hans Bernd Gisevius in the Gestapo. Stunned by the killing of two generals, Oster could also see the wood for the trees, namely the political advantage over the army which the purge had given the SS, which thenceforth began to develop armed formations.[33] Kleist-Schmenzin and Schulenburg were also highly alarmed by the purge, with good reason, for had either of them been at home at the time they would have been victims of it.

Disgust at the methods of the regime was compounded by anxiety over creeping unilateral changes to the terms of the original bargain affording Hitler's misrule military underpinning. Virtually all of the soldiers who figured in the resistance to Hitler were fervent in their hatred of the Weimar Republic, with its divisive parties and internationalist–pacifistic tendencies, and actively welcomed Hitler's dictatorship. They thought that Hitler's mass support would integrate the nation behind the economic efforts necessary for enhanced rearmament, while his foreign policy would afford the military the optimum conditions to deploy to greatest advantage. More guns overcame moral scruples. In return for passing up the role of king-makers, the army received conscripts and more and better armaments. Within the army leadership there were variant readings of the relation-ship between the one-party state and the armed forces. The High Command, under Werner von Fritsch and Ludwig Beck, wished to preserve traditional Prussian military values, even if it meant doing without 'all those damnable innovations, cars, tanks etc.', drawing the nation towards the standards of the army. The Armed Forces High Command, notably Blomberg and his political adviser Reichenau, were more disposed to dissolve the old in the new, manoeuvring the army closer to the Nazis. Moreover, Reichenau had ambitions to lead a consolidated General Staff of the Armed Forces.[34] Rancorous disagree-ments and personality conflicts at the top were accompanied by a massive influx of new faces into the officer corps, which at nearly ninety thousand men at the outbreak of war was almost as large as the entire Weimar Reichswehr. When these young men took their oaths to 'Führer and Reich Chancellor' rather than to '*Volk* and Fatherland', the generals had to assume that they meant it.[35] Since the number of generals underwent a commensurate expansion – from 261 in 1938 to over a thousand by 1943 – differences of outlook within the caste itself multiplied.[36]

By 1938 Hitler felt emboldened to break his bargain with the conservative elites. He was no longer willing to defer; their caution no longer met his needs of the hour. There had been 'very sharp exchanges' involving Foreign Minister Neurath and Generals Fritsch and Blomberg when on 5 November 1937 Hitler had outlined his future foreign policy moves to an audience of senior figures. The manner of the two generals' departure caused widespread fury in military circles, not least because a political coup was executed under the camouflage of moral outrage regarding the generals' private affairs.[37] On 12 January 1938, Blomberg married Luise Margarethe Gruhn, a typist with the Reich Egg Marketing Board, with Göring and Hitler acting as witnesses. Göring had encouraged Blomberg to marry this 'simple girl from the people', having already been apprised by the Gestapo of her part-time career as a pornographic model. Blomberg's resignation duly followed. A few weeks later, Hitler gave his military adjutant Colonel Hossbach the shocking tidings that Freiherr Werner von Fritsch was a practising homosexual. The 'evidence' stemmed from a criminal blackmailer, Otto Schmidt, who in 1936 falsely identified 'a' General Fritsch as a party to a homosexualist tryst he had witnessed near Wannsee station, and who had bought Schmidt's silence. At the time, Hitler had seen the relevant Gestapo files and ordered 'this muck' to be destroyed. Nevertheless, both the files and Schmidt, by now basking in his role as star witness, were on hand when two years later Hitler confronted Fritsch in the Reich Chancellery library. Schmidt positively identified the general. Fritsch resigned, and did not do his defence much good by volunteering himself for Gestapo investigation.[38]

Details of the squalid background to the ousting of Blomberg and Fritsch reached Oster from his contacts Gisevius and Arthur Nebe, the head of the SS Reich Criminal Police Office, a figure so morally challenging that he is virtually airbrushed out of many accounts of the resistance. Nebe may have indicated that it was a case of mistaken identity, involving a Captain von *Frisch*, which Himmler and Heydrich were busily covering up. Oster tried to persuade the twelve generals commanding troops to resign in protest. In this he was helped by Carl Goerdeler (1884–1945), the former Lord Mayor of Leipzig.

Goerdeler, a liberal conservative monarchist, had worked amicably with the Nazi Party in Leipzig, an arrangement which enabled him to play a national role in reforming local government and economic policy. He became Reich Price Commissioner in 1934. As he wrote in an August 1934 memorandum to Hitler: 'It would be truly deplorable if the most sober judgements, best experiences, and finest characters to be found in the German people were not enlisted in making use to the greatest national advantage of the conditions that have thus been created.'[39] However his advocacy of international economic co-operation and market self-regulation clashed with Hitler's belief in autarchy, mounting state controls and the primacy of accelerated rearmament. Göring declared a report Goerdeler produced in 1936 'unusable' and its publication was suppressed.[40] Although in 1934 Goerdeler did not mind the marginalisation of Mendelssohn's music, provided this was not done for reasons of official 'racial policy', when the Leipzig Nazis removed a statue of the composer from outside the Gewandhaus in his absence he decided it was time to go abroad for a while. The oppositional industrialist Robert Bosch generously covered his expenses, with Göring authorising these visits as a private source of insight into the perspectives of foreign governments.[41]

The Fritsch affair also acted as a catalyst for the rising bureaucrat and vice-president of the Berlin police Fritz-Dietlof Graf von der

Schulenburg (1902–44), a man whose role in the resistance was punctuated with periods of backsliding. Schulenburg was deeply hostile to the Weimar Republic, and had joined the Nazi Party in February 1932. He welcomed the 'seizure of power' as a defeat for 'the powers of Jewry, capital and the Catholic Church'. He initially followed other conservatives in imagining that they could remould the amorphous and coalitional Nazi regime in the manner of their choosing, in his case as a modernised version of seventeenth- and eighteenth-century Prussia, with the state resting on the trinity of army, civil service and popular 'will' as embodied by the Nazi Party. His belief that an authoritarian state was the only way to protect the lower classes from plutocratic exploitation earned him the sobriquet of the 'Red Count', which reflected his sympathy with the working man rather than their political representatives. Schulenburg's first opportunity to put his lofty 'Prussian Socialist' ideals into practice came as personal adviser to Erich Koch, whose appointment as Oberpräsident in East Prussia he played a part in. He was soon disabused. Plans to effect the structural reform of the backward East Prussian economy degenerated into kickbacks for Koch and his circle, while qualified civil servants were passed over in favour of Nazi boobies. This replicated what Schulenburg took to be Weimar politicisation of the civil service. If he thought that Röhm received his just deserts, he was shaken by the slaying of Gregor Strasser. Retiring to run a rural backwater in Samland, Schulenburg's administrative competence and reforming radicalism resulted in his appointment in Berlin, where contrary to expectations he got on well with his superior Wolf von Helldorf. He also deepened his acquaintance with Peter Graf Yorck von Wartenburg and Nikolaus Graf von Üxküll-Gyllenband. At the height of the Fritsch affair, which challenged his conception of the fundamental role of the army, Schulenburg informed General Witzleben, the commander of the Berlin military district, that if the soldiers were to move against the Gestapo the Berlin police would be spectators.[42]

Fritsch's friends sought in vain to move the generals to protest his treatment. The ultimate stumbling block proved to be the Chief of General Staff Ludwig Beck, who despite all evidence to the contrary persisted in the fiction that the Gestapo rather than Hitler had machinated against his colleague.[43] Moreover, when even General Franz von Halder suggested a raid against Gestapo headquarters, Beck cut him off angrily: 'Mutiny, revolution. Such words do not exist in the dictionary of a German officer!' His subscription to old-fashioned values can be seen from his encouragement of Fritsch in his bizarre quest to settle things through a duel with Himmler. In the event, Fritsch was tried and exonerated by a military court. Having made himself actual rather than nominal supreme commander of the armed forces, Hitler could afford a small gesture of magnanimity to the disgraced Fritsch – appointing him honorary commander of the 12th Artillery Regiment. The gesture was not appreciated, with Fritsch throwing his life away during the invasion of Poland.[44] Himmler had his star witness Otto Schmidt shot. And the generals? When advised that Wilhelm Keitel was 'an officer manager', Hitler replied, 'That is just the kind of man I need,' making him chief of the new-fangled High Command of the Armed Forces. The army was entrusted to Walther von Brauchitsch, whose marital arrangements were not dissimilar to those of the disgraced Blomberg. Financial difficulties meant that he was unable to divorce his wife, to marry the divorcee with whom he had been involved for several years. Hitler paid off his wife as part of the divorce settlement.[45] Oster, Goerdeler and Schulenburg became key players in virtually every subsequent conspiracy against Hitler, even though the Abwehr officer made a better conspirator than the former Price Commissioner. They were shortly joined by Ludwig Beck.

Beyond the Fritsch affair lay a tendency for supporters of Hitler to become loyal critics, a stance hard to sustain with a leader with pretensions to omniscience. They tried to criticise the system from within; when this failed, some drew the obvious conclusion. Senior members of the elites gradually realised that they were no longer privileged advisers-by-right on major issues of policy, but functional professionals there to do Hitler's bidding, an insufferable position for men who identified themselves with the nation's higher interests. This was most obviously so in the case of Beck, whose loyalty broke in the course of the foreign policy crises over the Sudetenland during April to September 1938 – specifically, over whether military force was appropriate when anticipated British and French intervention might prematurely halt any chances of regaining great-power status. Whereas Hitler was prepared to gamble, Beck needed to be convinced that any ensuing general war could be won. There were also proprieties at stake, namely that the generals' had a co-determinative function concerning major issues of state, including the decision to go to war, and, less narrowly, that beyond any professional concerns they were believed to be co-responsible for the ultimate destinies of their country. Since Hitler refused to see Beck after March 1938, the Chief of General Staff was reduced to conveying his doubts via Brauchitsch. On 16 July that year Beck told him:

> The most senior commanders in the Wehrmacht are called upon and qualified above all others for this task, because the Wehrmacht is the executive instrument of the leadership of the state in the conduct of the war. At stake here are ultimate decisions concerning the continued existence of the nation; history will indict these commanders of blood guilt if they do not act according to their professional and political knowledge and conscience. Their soldierly obedience has a limit beyond which their knowledge and their responsibility forbid them to carry out an order. If their advice and warnings in such a situation are not heard, they have the right and duty before the nation and before history to resign from their posts. If they all act thus with a united will, the execution of an act of war is impossible. Thereby they will have saved their Fatherland from the worst, from ruin. It is a lack of greatness in a soldier in the highest position, and a lack of understanding of his duty, if at such times he sees his duties and tasks only in the restricted confines of his military assignments, without becoming conscious of his supreme responsibility before the entire nation.[46]

In a rather inchoate series of slogans designed to accompany any collective démarche by the generals, Beck still endeavoured to square the circle by accommodating Hitler himself:

> For the Führer – against war – against the tyranny of the Party bosses – peace with the church – freedom of expression – away with Cheka methods – back to the rule of law in the Reich – reduction of all levies by half – no more building of palaces – housing for the people – Prussian honesty and simplicity.[47]

Put slightly differently, the conflict may be construed narrowly in terms of deference, proprieties and tactics, or mechanistically in terms of the relations of a powerful elite group to the Nazis, but it cannot be reduced to either without doing some violence to the facts. A fundamental problem with Hitler's leadership attracted a more diffuse set of criticisms of the nature of the regime. These included Nazi persecution of the Christian Churches, interference in the press and the life of the mind, and what Beck called 'the nightmare of the Gestapo'.[48] None of these men shared Hitler's twisted view of war as biologically beneficent, and their views on foreign policy objectives were far from homogeneous. Both Kleist-Schmenzin and Weizsäcker, for example, were implacably opposed to the Anschluss on the grounds that it would increase the number of Roman Catholics and that Austrians and Germans were divided by a common language. Stymied by the irresolution of Brauchitsch and other senior colleagues in the face of Hitler's determination, Beck was forced out in August, becoming a central figure in subsequent conspiracies against the Führer.

Opposition to Hitler's reckless rush towards war in the autumn of 1938 took two related forms, whose interdependence partly explains their failure: first, informal visits to Paris and London – such as those undertaken by Kleist-Schmenzin and Goerdeler – designed to stiffen the resolve of Western politicians to Hitler's aggression, and secondly, planning for a coup, with Beck's successor Franz Halder licensing the spadework of Hans Oster. Together with Gisevius and Hjalmar Schacht, who was to assume a leading role, Oster sounded out several generals, and secured the benevolent neutrality of the Berlin police through Helldorf and Schulenburg. Since the coup was to be represented in terms of military restoration of order after a putative SS putsch, Arthur Nebe was co-opted to reveal the locations of all SS units in Germany.[49] The question of what to do with Hitler led to the development of a plot within a plot. Beck and others favoured taking him alive and putting him on trial; Oster wanted a panel of psychiatrists under Karl Bonhoeffer which would declare him insane; Halder recommended a fatal accident. The ex-Free Corps commander Major Wilhelm Heinz, member of a circle that included the trade unionist Wilhelm Leuschner, who was to lead a raid on the Reich Chancellery, had decided to shoot Hitler in the ensuing mêlée. But the conspiracy hinged on an external dimension.

Opposition feelers extended to the British during 1938 were frustrated by the indeterminate status of their envoys, and their interlocutors' belief that their foreign policy goals sometimes appeared to exceed those of the Nazis, notably Kleist's robust claims to parts of Poland. Focused as they were on putative 'moderates' and 'extremists' within Hitler's government, the British were sceptical of bold talk of coups from circles hitherto characterised by inertia, even when they were more personally inclined to these men than Prime Minister Chamberlain, who said they reminded him of 'Jacobites at the Court of France in King William's time'.[50] Moreover, the plotters presumed that the British would risk going to the brink of war with the same recklessness they themselves had discerned in Hitler, and would issue prior assurances to people with no ascertainable record of rebellion against the

Nazis and whose goals resembled a past the British leadership vividly remembered – all this at a time when Hitler might still respond to reason. In other words, it seemed a case of pursuing Hitler's aims, but without Hitler.[51] Too many imponderables were at work here. The coup depended upon British guarantees of a non-punitive response, lest Hitler's demise be construed as another 'stab in the back'. The lower-level conspirators depended upon the constancy of Halder, while he in turn worried about Nazis among the junior officers. Moreover, Hitler was a wild card, enjoying massive acclaim for having achieved his ends while avoiding war. As Halder said: 'What shall we do now? He succeeds at everything.'[52]

The military leadership reverted to its professional role during the invasion of Poland, a country for which they felt no sympathy. The Nazi–Soviet Pact appeared to have cut down the odds against a swift strike at Poland, leaving Britain and France raging on the sidelines. However, the atrocities committed in Poland, which – as we saw in an earlier chapter – appalled a number of generals, notably Blaskowitz, and Hitler's decision to extend the war westwards, regalvanised the conspirators who thought that a purely defensive posture in the West might put the war to sleep before it had started. A reduction in the interval between ordering an attack and troop movements designed to maximise surprise made a co-ordinated military coup more difficult, as did repeated postponements of the invasion. But this was an excuse for irresolution at the top, induced by fear as Hitler fulminated knowingly about the 'spirit of Zossen'. Although Halder regularly took a gun to his meetings with 'Emil', as he called Hitler, he did not believe that generals were natural assassins, and hence failed to use it. Attempts to delegate the task to Admiral Wilhelm Canaris and the Abwehr were resented on the grounds that they were not assassins either, and because Canaris thought that a military coup was the essential pre-requisite for action against Hitler. In other words, buck-passing led to a certain paralysed circularity. In fact, there was a willing assassin, the diplomat Erich Kordt, with access to Hitler, but, as Oster established, Kordt would first have to undergo an Abwehr explosives course, and the bomb would then have to be independently procured so as not to arouse suspicion. This last desideratum proved virtually impossible following Georg Elser's lone attempt to bomb Hitler on 9 November 1939 in Munich's Löwenbrau restaurant.[53] Ironically, Arthur Nebe headed the minute forensic examination of the debris, which led to those who had constructed the bomb. Meanwhile, the plotting generals had resigned themselves to the extension of the war, with Halder convinced that it was intolerable for the Germans to be 'a nation of helots' for the English.[54]

If the coup came to nothing, individual officers sought to frustrate Hitler's objectives by betraying military intelligence to the enemy. The 'Nazi' general Reichenau vainly tried to reason with Hitler, and then tipped off Belgian and Dutch intelligence contacts about the timing of an attack, to whose objectives he did not demur. It may also be the case that this deeply unattractive individual felt disgruntled when he emerged from the Blomberg–Fritsch affair empty-handed.[55] Oster betrayed the details of the imminent German invasion to friends in Belgian and Dutch intelligence. He had formed a friendship with the Dutch attaché Gijsbertus Sas during the 1936 Berlin Olympic Games. In October 1939, he told Sas that planning concerned an invasion of Belgium, but that he would hand over information as soon as the Netherlands came into the frame. Sas passed this intelligence to his Belgian opposite numbers. In the spring of 1940, Oster informed Sas about the timing of Operation Weserübung against Denmark and Norway, information which found its way to Britain, and on the night of 9 May 1940 told him that an attack in the West was scheduled for the following morning. It was not Oster's fault that Dutch intelligence took a sceptical view of the reliability of their own military attaché.[56]

Oster's rather gentle countenance, and reputation as a lady's man, belied his cold calculation that his actions would result in such a prohibitive casualty rate as to stall further development of the invasion. He was also risking a demeaning death by hanging for offences which had gone beyond treason against the head of state to the betrayal of his country's military secrets. As Oster explained to Sas: 'One might say that I am a traitor, but in reality I am not; I consider myself a better German than all those who run after Hitler. It is my plan and my duty to free Germany, and at the same time the world, of this plague.' Since the Nazis had corrupted nationalism beyond recognition, Oster could legitimately claim to have transformed treason into a patriotic imperative.[57]

CLASS AND HISTORY

Oster was midway between an older group of 'notable' resisters such as Beck, Goerdeler, Hassell and Popitz and an up-and-coming generation, including a large number of younger aristocrats, whose formative years lay in republican rather than imperial Germany. Between the distinct age groups there were similarities and subtle differences. The commonalities included an elite's disdain for an upstart political movement whose leaders were corrupt, hypocritical, murderous, unpleasant and vulgar. Hitler and his associates may have enjoyed a brief vogue in society salons due to their uncouth, radical chic, but this was soon replaced by distaste for the socially confused and kitschy quality of life at the various Nazi courts. Several of the men we have encountered remarked on this. In September 1940, Ulrich von Hassell attended a lunch for foreign dignitaries given by Hitler Youth leader Baldur von Schirach in Vienna's Hofburg:

> At the reception for the guests he showed himself adroit and amiable. Every now and then, however, the bombastic Party ruffian would come to the surface. As, for instance, at lunch, when he sat between Ricci [the Italian Minister of Corporations] and the Turkish ambassador, he carelessly glanced over all kinds of papers which were brought to him – a needless but intentional showing off. We were served on imperial porcelain and silver by servants in the imperial livery – a demonstration of bad taste which caused good General Bardolff resignedly to shake his head. . . . At the reception in the Rathaus, following a performance of the lovely Magic Flute, Schirach behaved like a sovereign with the daughter of the 'Reich-Drunkard' Hoffman; he was accompanied by an adjutant, heavy with gold braid, who whispered the names of the guests. But later on he took his place, like a petit bourgeois, beside his august wife.[58]

The fastidious Fritz-Dietlof von der Schulenburg caught the shameless hypocrisy of these erstwhile revolutionaries, exchanging their leather jackets for braid and uniforms, and the shallow, Hollywood quality of life at a Nazi court in a letter to his wife about a summer evening in 1941 hosted by Erich Koch:

> Everything beautiful and fun, but a mite too elegantly attired, and too refined and dignified in expression. The servants shuffle gingerly, and with great dignity, albeit a bit too quietly and gravely through the vast rooms, serving coffee and cake. The atmosphere of a distinguished country house doesn't prevail here; this is like the world of film, with everything larger than life as in a film. What a contrast to the period 1932/33 when the same persons entered the scene as revolutionary fighters for Prussian socialism, not disguising this even in their external appearance. Nowadays, the same men are saturated and outwardly civilised, enjoying wealth and power to the utmost.[59]

Members of illustrious families which had served their country in one capacity or another for generations were especially indignant about being told what it was to be German by politicians whose personal links with Germany were tenuous. For example, in 1937, as already noted, the aristocratic Catholic bishop of Münster Clemens August Graf von Galen, whose family had ruled part of Westphalia for generations, spoke scathingly about lectures on quintessential German characteristics from people who came from 'Riga, Reval, or Cairo or even Chile', a reference to Rosenberg, Hess and Darré.[60] It was especially galling that the Nazis' all too apparent enjoyment of the fruits and trappings of power, and petit-bourgeois fawning over people with titles, was accompanied by resentful attacks on the upper classes and intelligentsia.[61] On 17 September 1938 Ulrich von Hassell noted:

> Hitler's speeches are all demagogic and spiced with sharp attacks on the entire upper class. The closing speech at the Party conference was of the same sort, delivered in wild, boisterous tones. The mounting hatred against the upper class has been inflamed by the warnings of the generals, with the exception of Keitel, against war. At the same time there is a growing aversion to all independent people. Whoever does not crawl in the dust is regarded as stuck up.[62]

Although many upper-class conservatives had hoped to exploit the mass dynamism of Nazism, others had a Nietzschean dread of 'mass man' as personified by Hitler. Friedrich Reck-Malleczewen (1884–1945) was born on an East Prussian estate bordering Russia. He abandoned a military career to study medicine, before opting for the life of a theatre critic and writer in southern Germany. In 1933 he converted to Catholicism, and, disgusted by the political landscape, retreated into bucolic isolation on a small estate in the Bavarian Chiemgau. Reck had conceived a deep loathing for Hitler, whom he none too subtly compared with the sixteenth-century messianic fanatic Jan Böckelson in a novel he published in 1937, as we saw in the Introduction.[63] In Reck's remarkable diary, Hitler becomes the 'Moloch', 'Great Manitou', 'that forelocked gypsy' or 'our vegetarian Tamerlane'. He lived to regret not having shot Hitler when he sat near by in Munich's Osteria restaurant, watching the 'raw-vegetable Genghis Khan, teetotalling Alexander, [and] womanless Napoleon, an effigy of Bismarck', polishing off his pulses and potatoes, 'but I took him for a character out of a comic strip, and did not shoot'.[64] In the event, Reck's minor acts of non-conformity led to his incarceration and death in Dachau in the closing stages of the war.

With an outlook on mankind not dissimilar to a conflation of Ferdinand Céline, Evelyn Waugh and Wyndham Lewis, Reck-Malleczewen thought that 'the mass type is now to be found much more frequently in the boardrooms of the large corporations and among the sons and daughters of rich industrialists than among the workers', a view which seems to have chimed with Hannah Arendt when she wrote *The Origins of Totalitarianism*, analysing phenomena which cost Reck his life, for Arendt, like Reck, was not afraid of giving offence to the demotic hordes – independent of their social class – when they deserved it.[65]

Since significant numbers of noblemen had responded to Himmler's offers of honorary SS membership, or his attempts to woo the horsey set through the purchase of stud farms and creation of SS cavalry regiments, the aim being to fuse their 'damn good blood' with SS meritocrats, Reck-Malleczewen was not sparing of criticism of his own kind.[66] In April 1939 he watched the antics of a group of SS noblemen in a basement nightclub in Berlin. There was nothing so revealingly depressing as watching people enjoying themselves. His thoughts closely echoed Nietzsche's ruminations on the 'innocence of the beast of prey conscience, like jubilant monsters, who perhaps come from a ghostly bout of murder, arson, rape, and torture, with bravado and a moral equanimity, as though merely some wild student's prank had been played . . . the magnificent blond brute, avidly rampant for spoil and victory', but there was disgust here rather than celebration:

From my table I examined their faces. They were bearers of old blood-bespattered names. . . . At first sight they look like a group of dragonslayers or like archangels who have checked in their wings in the cloakroom. . . . Until a second harder look . . . until the sound of this whorehouse jargon and the coarseness of their expressions bring quite a different analogy to mind.

The first thing is the frightening emptiness of their faces. Then one observes, in the eyes, a kind of flicker from time to time, a sudden lighting-up. This has nothing to do with youth. It is the typical look of this generation, the immediate reflection of a basic and completely hysterical savagery. . . .

. . . woe to Europe if this hysteria that confronts us now gets free rein. These young men would turn the paintings of Leonardo into an ash-heap if their Führer stamped them degenerate. They would not hesitate to send cathedrals tumbling into the air, using the hellish arts of IG Farben, if this were part of a given situation. Or they will perpetrate still worse things and worst, most dreadful of all, they will be totally incapable of even sensing the deep degradation of their existence.[67]

Upper-class distaste for the Nazis was not merely a matter of the latter's confusions with the cutlery or solely about mechanical shifts of power blocs and the displacement of an established elite by uncouth upstarts. Many resisters, including clerics and socialists, saw Nazism as symptomatic of a broader cultural and spiritual crisis, namely the alienation and atomisation attendant upon the 'massification' of modern society, with totalitarianism giving meaning to and ordering anomically drifting rootless people. Reck-Malleczewen's vitriolic musings on his contemporaries were not far removed from the socialist Theodor Haubach, who saw in Brueghel's paintings: 'a premonition of the consequences of the mass age', whereby 'the masses, having escaped the control and discipline of religion, and alone and alienated from their gods . . . degenerate into grotesques, monstrosities and ghosts'.[68] The conservative Goerdeler feared 'a welling up of brutish men, of the rag tag and bobtail of the inexperienced and ignorant'.[69] The Jesuit Lothar König wrote of the Soviet Union, where: 'Moral norms and ethos, science and technology, education and art are all employed to depersonalise, to drive into the mass and breed collective men. . . . There are to be no more individual personalities, only soulless machines who grow together in the involution and multiplication of mechanical external functions and abilities into the united force and activity of the collective without any will of their own.'[70] The political consequences of mass irreligion figured prominently in the concerns of

Helmuth James von Moltke (1907–45), whose Kreisau Circle became one of the foci of resistance to Hitler. In 1939 Moltke wrote that: 'An unbelieving mass will sell itself to any politician, but a class of believers will not.' Key co-ordinates had been abandoned, leaving modern man bobbing adrift on perilous seas. In a letter to his wife Freya, dated 25 August 1940, Moltke commented on a passage in Goethe concerning the need to inculcate children with three kinds of reverence, revealing much about the importance he attached to both religion and the relationship between freedom and order:

> National Socialism has once more taught us reverence for what is below us, i.e, material things, blood, ancestry, our bodies. To that extent it is right, and we should not forget the lesson. But it has killed reverence for what is above us, that is, God or whatever you may wish to call it, and has tried to lower this under us by the deification of things of this world which fall under the rubric of the reverence due to that which is below us. Similarly NS has destroyed reverence for what is equal to us by trying to put at least some of those who are equal to us beneath us. . . . A human being can be free only in the framework of the natural order and an order is natural only if it leaves man free. We won't be able to describe at what point this balance is achieved, but we will see and feel it; nobody can say how it is to be achieved, we have to try it. It is a process of trial and error.[71]

Before discussing their hopes and plans for Germany's future, let's try to view a few of these men in the round, for their historical stature only emerges clearly in this way. A supporter of the Weimar Republic, Moltke had been active since the late 1920s in bringing together young people from various backgrounds to co-operate with each other, discussing contemporary problems in *ad hoc* work camps. Since his political views subsequently closed off a career as a judge, Moltke became an international jurist, qualifying at the English bar, but preferring to return to Germany, where he worked as a lawyer in the Foreign Countries Division of the Abwehr. Shortly before the November 1938 pogrom, he was active helping Jews to leave the country since a close reading of Nazi organs which spoke of 'ghettos and confiscation of property' led him to fear the worst before it happened.[72] His wartime duties became a daily struggle to retain some vestiges of decency in the conduct of hostilities. He occasionally congratulated himself on his successes: 'when I survey these four months, I find that I've never before prevented so much evil and achieved so much good. It astounds me. And the agreeable part of it is that nobody will ever find out about it, or take note of it, so that nobody will see ways to oppose it'.[73]

Ulrich von Hassell was an old-school conservative diplomat, who having taken a bullet in the chest at the Battle of the Marne served his country in Copenhagen and Belgrade and from November 1932 as ambassador to Rome. It is worth stressing that, although as a conservative he would have preferred something other than the Weimar Republic, there was never any suggestion that he was disloyal to its interests. Tall and urbane, Hassell spoke several languages, and had a keen interest in such historical personalities as Bismarck and Andrássy, Castlereagh and Canning. His alienation from Nazism stemmed from frictions with its representatives in his embassy, and from the Nazis' rejection of his desire to pursue revisionism through reconciliation with Britain as well as Italy, in favour of exclusive links with Italy through the Anti-Comintern Pact. He was incandescent with rage when his opposite number Ribbentrop was brought in from London for the signing ceremony in November 1937. In February 1938 Hassell was recalled and put on the diplomatic reserve list, a position which still enabled him to move on the fringes of power and to travel abroad. He gravitated towards Beck, Goerdeler and Popitz and during the winter of 1939–40 had his first contacts as a representative of the 'opposition' with what turned out to be a freelance 'representative' of the British government. Increasingly convinced that it was necessary to extirpate Prussian militarism, the British were hardly likely to pay much attention to a man they identified with the 'old' rather than 'another' Germany, the marital connection with Alfred Tirpitz being unfortunate.[74]

Ulrich von Hassell's diaries, written up at his country home at Ebershausen and hidden in a grotto, were punctuated with disgust and shame at Nazi persecution of the Jews, atrocities in Poland and the murder of the handicapped and mentally ill. In late 1938 Hassell wrote 'under crushing emotions evoked by the vile persecution of the Jews', of 'the devilish barbarity with which the SS treated the unfortunate Jews' and of the 'deep sense of shame which has weighed heavily upon all decent and thoughtful people since the hideous events of November [the pogrom]'.[75] On 19 October he noted: 'the brutal use of air power and the shocking bestialities of the SS, especially towards the Jews. . . . When people use their revolvers to shoot down a group of Jews herded into a synagogue one is filled with shame.'[76] A lawyer friend informed him of events in Poland: 'The hungry workers are gradually getting weaker, the Jews are systematically being exterminated, and a devilish campaign is being launched against the Polish intelligentsia with the express purpose of annihilating it'.[77] Goerdeler and Popitz told him 'horrible things about moral laxity in the occupied areas as well as here at home', including 'the systematic and uncontrolled killing of the so-called "incurably insane". . . . At home we are steering an increasingly obvious course. The most revolting aspect at the moment is the unrestrained mass slaughter of the so-called incurably insane.'[78] In August 1941 he wrote: 'The whole war in the east is terrible – a return to savagery,' and described how a young officer had been ordered to kill 350 civilians confined in a barn.[79] From Hans von Dohnanyi and others he learned of 'the continuance of repulsive cruelties, particularly against the Jews, who were shamelessly shot down in batches', and of horrible 'experiments' on Jews with explosive munitions.[80] In November he wrote: 'There is revulsion on the part of all decent people toward the shameless measures taken against the Jews and prisoners in the east, and against harmless and often distinguished Jews in Berlin and other large cities.'[81]

Nazi barbarism in Russia deeply preoccupied Moltke both privately and professionally. He opposed the legal sophistries used to legitimise maltreatment of Russian prisoners and civilians. He pointed to eighteenth century precedents governing the handling of prisoners, and to recent Soviet decrees, which by conforming to international law confounded Nazi claims that the Soviets took no prisoners. When letters from German prisoners were deliberately withheld to foster this false impression, members of the Abwehr purloined a batch and delivered them in person.[82] The onset in 1941 of the deportation and murder of the Jews prompted the question: 'May I know this and yet sit at my table in my heated flat and have tea? Don't I thereby become guilty too? What shall I say when I am asked: and what did you do during that time?' He was highly self-critical, capturing precisely the ambiguity, and deficiencies, in his own responses to these events:

How can anyone know these things and still walk around free? With what right? Is it not inevitable that his turn will come too one day, and that he too will be rolled into the gutter? – All this is only summer-lightning, for the storm is still ahead – If only I could get rid of the terrible feeling that I have let myself be corrupted, that I do not react keenly enough to such things, that they torment me without producing a spontaneous reaction. I have mistrained myself, for in such things, too, I react with my head. I think about a possible reaction instead of acting.[83]

Yet Moltke was no Hamlet, paralysed by his own doubts and reasonableness. On 7 November 1941 he had his only official dealings with the ramified bureaucracy of the 'Final Solution', at a conference in the Foreign Ministry convened to discuss the eleventh decree under the Reich Citizenship Law, rendering German Jews abroad stateless, including those already deported. He stood his ground against all of the other twenty-four participants in the meeting, the result being that the decree was held up. The others reminded him of chameleons, 'in a healthy society they look healthy, in a sick one, like ours, they look sick. And really they are neither one nor the other. They are mere filler.'[84] So many committee men, individually bland, empty and non-descript, collectively doing other people harm. Over the coming nights he lay awake into the early hours thinking about Jews and Russians. He persuaded three generals to write to a fourth rescinding Wehrmacht approval of these measures. This 'proves the general rule that as soon as one man takes a stand, a surprising number of others will stand too. But there always has to be one to go first; otherwise it does not work.'[85] The eleventh decree was published on 25 November 1941. During the war Moltke maintained contacts with the Norwegian oppositional bishop Berggrav, and with resistance circles in Denmark and the Netherlands. In October 1943 he tipped off a Danish contact about the imminence of deportations of the Jews. Apart from these activities, he also endeavoured to support those army commanders in Belgium and France who sought to deflect Hitler's orders regarding reprisal shooting of hostages.[86]

Few of the conservative resisters seem to have subscribed to Hitler's vicious eugenic and racial theories, with their beastly rhetoric of 'ballast existences', Slavic helots and Jewish sub-humanity. Hassell, for example, repeatedly poured scorn on this nonsense in his diaries, being especially disappointed when Mussolini dropped his sceptical view of Nazi racism and espoused a similar line. But while most members of conservative resistance circles were appalled by racially motivated violence, not least because of its mob excesses and negative diplomatic repercussions, they were also men of their class and time in believing that there was a 'Jewish Question' requiring resolution. This was partly a matter of the social snobbery of insiders towards outsiders; partly a reflection of the widespread belief that Jews were over-represented in certain areas of cultural, economic and political life. Hence many resisters advocated discriminatory measures against their Jewish fellow citizens. Goerdeler, Hassell and Popitz all sought to reduce Jewish 'influence', trying to square an impossible circle, in the sense of keeping discrimination within the bounds of legality. Goerdeler wrote to Hitler in 1934 urging that antisemitic policies be kept within legal channels, adding: 'What the law has provided will hardly be questioned by reasonable people abroad as a means of self-protection, as long as everything is now carried out with iron discipline and the avoidance of excesses and petty persecutions.'[87]

Something of the ambivalent attitude of these men towards the Jews can be gleaned from documents which advocated the rescinding of persecutory measures. Writing shortly before the onset of deportations and mass murder, Goerdeler recommended the revocation of most of the discriminatory measures against the Jews of Germany, compensation for those who had suffered, and the alleviation of the inhuman conditions prevailing in the ghettos of occupied eastern Europe. His long-term strategy involved an international agreement to create a Jewish state in Canada or South America, to which Jews should emigrate, in so far as their desire to assimilate had not been evidenced by service during the First World War, citizenship held since 1871, baptism or descent from a mixed marriage concluded before 1933. In practice, eastern Jews were to leave, albeit enjoying the restricted range of civic rights available to aliens, be they English or French, to trade or pursue commerce but not to stand for public office or vote, should they choose to live in Germany, while assimilated German Jews would be unaffected.[88] This may seem terribly lame with hindsight, and evidence of the pervasiveness of racism in German society, in the twofold sense that social antisemitism endured and that the resisters knew the Germans well enough not to be strident on behalf of Jews, but it may be amenable to other forms of explanation.[89]

Whatever criticisms may be made of how the various resistance circles construed the future, and it is important to remember that their ideas were tailored to an emergency, with any possibilities for further adaptation cut short by their judicial murder, it is crucial to emphasise that they overwhelmingly shared a belief in the need to restore the rule of law and judicial independence, and to end arbitrary policing and denunciation, in other words, all those things which Beck summed up as 'Cheka methods', using the most vividly shocking analogy available to him in the late 1930s.[90] Instead of criticising resistance plans ahistorically in terms of the Basic Law of the Federal Republic, it is fairer to view them as products of specific historical experiences; of compromises and tactical accommodations; or in terms of the wider constituencies they were hoping to rally, in the event of success in removing Hitler. It seems invidious to censure retrospectively a man such as Hassell for not espousing views congruent with post-war democracy, since his formative experiences predated even the Weimar Republic. There may be respectable political reasons for doing this, but they do not make good history. Ideas which are easy to parody as 'reactionary' made sense both in terms of German experience under the Nazis and when compared with subsequent transitions from authoritarianism to democracy elsewhere. For example, restricting the universal franchise to people of mature years, and eligibility for the Reichstag to the over-thirty-fives, seems eccentric if one overlooks the marked tendency for young people in the Weimar Republic to support the two totalitarian parties or leftist splinter groups.[91] What can be dismissed as an arrogant belief that their fellow citizens needed to be educated up for democracy was also shared by most forms of liberalism, and indeed by the democratically elected Allied governments, as they demonstrated during the occupation of post-war Germany. Finally, Goerdeler's musings on the restoration of a Hohenzollern (constitutional) monarchy may seem ridiculous, by the lights of either that dynasty's past or a confident and prosperous West German democratic republic, but it did not seem so when Spain emerged from the era of Franco.[92]

The most developed plans for Germany's post-Nazi future stemmed from the prolific pen of Carl Goerdeler, and from the meetings which Moltke convened at Kreisau or such locations as Ernst von Borsig's estate at Gross-Behnitz near Berlin, although it is important to emphasise that the Kreisau Circle was more than an agreeable series of smart weekends in country houses.[93] In a letter smuggled to his friend Lionel Curtis in March 1943, Moltke spoke of the universal tribulations of wartime, and of the specific burdens of conspiracy. Apart from not being able to use the post or telephone, one had constantly to practise self-censorship in conversation, lest one's interlocutor succumb to police interrogation.[94] The Kreisau Circle encompassed an impressive range of individuals from diverse backgrounds, whose key common attribute was a capacity to transcend the tribal allegiances of the past. Many had experience in the youth movement or in alleviating poverty in distressed areas. A significant number had family ties and friends in

Britain and the United States, notably Moltke and Adam von Trott zu Solz, or had studied and travelled abroad, in some cases becoming interested in Confucianism or Indian mysticism. Some had served with great distinction during the First World War, notably the Jesuit Augustin Rosch and the socialist Carlo Mierendorff, both of whom held the Iron Cross first class. Others were leading administrators, economists and theologians with a developed sense of social responsibility. So far from being armchair radicals, the Kreisau Circle included people whose careers had been ruined by Nazism; Jesuit priests who had had up to one hundred interviews with the Gestapo; or heterodox socialists such as the friends Theo Haubach and Carlo Mierendorff, freed after years in concentration camps.[95]

Mierendorff is worth a closer look. He grew up in Darmstadt, volunteering for military service as a seventeen-year-old in August 1914. Invalided home in 1915, he returned to the Western Front in the summer of 1917 where he later won the Iron Cross for bravery. In Darmstadt, he belonged to a circle of small-town intellectuals called the Garret. He abandoned his burgeoning career as an expressionist writer, on the ground that the arts were a self-indulgent luxury, in favour of radical journalism. He studied political economy, becoming active in student politics, and was almost sent down because of his role in the Lenard affair at Heidelberg. Philipp Lenard, a Nobel laureate physicist and ferocious antisemite, ostentatiously refused to close down the physics institute or lower the republican flag on a day of national mourning commemorating the assassinated Foreign Minister Walter Rathenau. Lenard had actually called for Rathenau's elimination. When students stormed the institute, Mierendorff tried to protect Lenard, a fact noted by the university disciplinary committee, which refused to take Lenard's part.[96] Thereafter, Mierendorff embarked on a political career, as secretary to the transport workers union and to the SPD's Reichstag secretariat, before becoming Wilhelm Leuschner's government press officer in Hessen, and a Reichstag deputy from 1930. There were inevitable tensions between the 'bosses' of the unions and SPD and young socialist intellectuals such as Mierendorff. The former were at the limits of their capacities; live wires such as Mierendorff were on the up and up, treating jobs as mere staging posts in their careers. A leader of the 'young right' within the SPD, Mierendorff was dismissive of its obsessions with internal discipline and the professorial approach to politics of its leaders, men who could 'grow a beard down to their knees' in the course of a speech about youth.

Deeply critical of the response of a desiccated 'scientific' Marxism to Hitler's challenge, Mierendorff became one of the most perceptive analysts of the heterogeneous psychological and social forces from which the Nazis drew their strength. He combed the job-seekers' section of Nazi papers, identifying their typical supporters as males between eighteen and twenty-seven years old, drawn to its thuggish forms of heroism.[97] An admirer of the Belgian socialist intellectual (and wartime fascist collaborator) Hendrik de Man and of Ernst Bloch, Mierendorff realised the psychological potency of symbols, helping a Russian constructivist friend to design counter-iconography to the Nazi swastika: three parallel 'freedom arrows', which could be daubed across the former, neutralising its jagged potency, or shown 'chasing' a 'fleeing' swastika, tipped on its side and equipped with 'feet'. He was an active supporter of the militant Reichsbanner and of uniformed, extra-parliamentary paramilitary response to the Nazis' attempts to control the streets.[98]

Mierendorff's political activities and emotionally charged rhetoric gradually made him a marked man. He spoke passionately – he was known as Mr Big Noise – and went down well with students and the Jewish organisations whom he often addressed. In his journalistic incarnation he took a leading role in exposing the 'Boxheimer documents' allegedly detailing Nazi plans for a coup.[99] In his only speech to the Reichstag on 6 February 1931, he taunted the Nazi deputies for imagining that their 'hocus-pocus' and cries of 'Heil Hitler' or 'Judah perish' were likely to solve Germany's economic crisis. He took on Goebbels personally. How dare the latter claim to speak for former veterans, when he had spent the war studying literature in Heidelberg while Mierendorff was in the trenches? At that point he fished his medal from his trouser pocket and brandished it at Goebbels, shouting to the Speaker: 'Ask Herr Goebbels again where is his Iron Cross, first class!' Mierendorff was picked up by the Gestapo in June 1933. He was detained in a succession of camps, a disused paper factory at Osthofen near Worms, the grim fortress of Lichtenburg near Torgau, where the SS specialised in breaking intellectuals, and finally the newly completed Buchenwald near Weimar. Something of an international *cause célèbre*, Mierendorff also had old acquaintances in the higher reaches of the SS, a fact which may explain his release in February

1938. In order to join the Reich Writers' Chamber – the *sine qua non* for earning a meagre living as a writer – Mierendorff had to submit a written recantation of his previous views. In this he rather lamely said that his rejection of liberalism was due to a reading of Nietzsche during his imprisonment (in fact he had read Shakespeare), which drew the marginal Gestapo comment, 'Hadn't he heard of Nietzsche during his time as a student?' Thenceforth, 'Willmer', as the Gestapo insisted Mierendorff call himself to destroy the potency of his name, was engaged as the editor of the works newsletter in the Lignite Petroleum Company, whose hub was the 'valley of stinking blockhouses', as the metropolitan Mierendorff had it, at Böhlen near Leipzig. After Gestapo surveillance was relaxed, Mierendorff travelled more widely and developed contacts with resistance circles. Carl Zuckmayer had introduced him to Moltke in 1927; now in 1941 he became part of the Kreisau Circle, where his pseudonym was 'Dr Friedrich'. A few months after drawing up one of the great documents connected with the Kreisau Circle, Mierendorff was killed during a huge British night raid on Leipzig, buried alive in the cellar in which he had taken refuge.[100]

The Kreisau discussions commenced in the autumn of 1941, as two separate groups linked to Moltke and his friend Peter Graf Yorck von Wartenburg gradually coalesced. For security reasons, small thematic working parties were formed which operated independently, and then fed ideas into larger gatherings disguised as weekend house parties. Correspondence relied heavily on euphemism and codenames, as we have seen in the case of Mierendorff cum 'Dr Friedrich'. Contacts were simultaneously established with both the military resistance and senior clergy, notably the Roman Catholic bishop of Berlin Konrad Graf von Preysing and the Lutheran bishop Theophil Wurm of Württemberg. One result of this was that Moltke was able to influence the content of their pastoral letters. Having been drawn into these circles, the participants – who included many difficult or large personalities – seem to have discussed their differences for hours on end until there was an elemental breakthrough to trust and co-operation. Sticking points included whether or not Hitler should be assassinated, with Gerstenmaier, Haeften and Trott in favour, and Gablentz, Rosch and Moltke against. 'Why are we opposed to the Third Reich, why are we opposed to National Socialism?' Moltke asked. 'Isn't it precisely because it is a lawless system? We cannot set about creating something new, initiating a renewal, by committing a lawless act ourselves. And murder is always unlawful.'[101]

Relations with the 'notable' resisters around Goerdeler were disappointing. Goerdeler was too impulsive and garrulous to be a natural conspirator – Yorck used to joke that 'the latest news going round Berlin opposition groups today is . . .' – and seemed too wedded to the past for men trying to break the mould of political thinking. This was not simply a matter of Goerdeler's monarchism, but of his attempts to salvage as much of Germany from the jaws of defeat as possible, a stance which Moltke rejected in favour of a fresh start from a totally new basis.[102] The key meeting between the main figures from both camps on 8 January 1943 in Yorck's Berlin house was acrimonious and, in terms of results, a damp squib. The older men evidently thought patronisingly in terms of 'seniors' and 'juniors', lamenting the latter's lack of political experience; Moltke regarded Beck, Goerdeler and Hassell as 'their Excellencies', and skewered them with a reference to Kerensky, the ineffectual figure Lenin had brushed aside.[103]

Before making some of the common criticisms of resistance plans for a post-Nazi Germany, it is important to stress that all these men believed passionately in the need to restore the rule of law and the basic freedoms of the individual, neither automatically incompatible with an authoritarian polity, as had been demonstrated by Imperial Germany. The Kreisau Circle may have debated the future relationship between individual, community and state, but they were at one in seeking to reverse the totalitarian atomisation of society and resulting control of the individual. A chaotic, self-aggrandising and perpetually intrusive totalitarian state with a monopoly on the energies and loyalties of the de-individualised subject was to be countered by a revival of small communities and voluntary associations – rather like what we call 'civil society' – which would act as buffers to the state's ambitions, thus conveniently overlooking the highly repressive potentialities of small communities. The future polity was to be rebuilt from the bottom upwards, with political rights dependent upon active citizenship within the local community. The latter would inculcate the sense of responsibility equipping people for indirect election to higher office, again running the risk of perpetuating some village or small-town self-regarding moralising oligarchy. Although these communities were supposed to spring to life spontaneously, macro socio-economic policy would give them a helping hand, in the first of many instances where the organic was corrected by artistry.

Germany and Austria were to be remodelled along federalist decentralised lines, with greater powers conferred on an enhanced (perhaps

nineteen) number of Länder, or regional states, an approach redolent
of Catholic notions of 'subsidiarity'. These were to be designed according to optimal norms rather than reflecting existing historical patterns,
for there was nothing historical to fall back on in the case of the largest
state, Prussia. There was no mention of political parties, which along
with social class were tainted terms in these circles, while the apex of
the ensuing political system, which it would be tedious to describe,
reflected further democratic deficits. Neither Goerdeler nor the Kreisau
Circle entertained the notion of ministerial responsibility to parliament,
while placing untoward trust in the democratic instincts of the heads
of professional associations, union leaders and principals of universities
who were to figure in a corporatist second chamber. Rather similar
ideas were alive and well in Britain at the turn of the millennium as it
sought to reform the House of Lords.[104]

The secular flight from the land and the spiritual impoverishment
of life in big cities were to be reversed by subsidising rural wages and
prices, resettlement and housing programmes, and the prohibition of
further industrialisation in medium-sized towns, to which tranches
of the central administration were to be relocated. While these
ideas undoubtedly reflected the widespread view that big-city life was
biologically and morally deleterious, they were not merely a cunning
scheme to preserve larger landed property. Goerdeler and Trott wanted
to break up large estates, while Moltke and Stauffenberg believed in,
and practised, a policy of voluntary renunciation of parts of their own
inheritances. Rather, it was a forlorn and rather romantic attempt to
preserve the one intact organic niche remaining in modern society.
Workers were to participate in management decision-making and share
in the profits. Since national trade unions could signify a return to
class conflict, unions were to operate only at the individual plant level.
Here the small-is-beautiful approach of Kreisau parted company with
Goerdeler, who wished to restore national unions because they were
inherently conservative.[105] On the whole, Goerdeler was resistant to
state interference in the economy. While Moltke and his associates
believed in the advantages of a mixed economy, they thought the state
should guarantee full employment and nationalise certain key industries such as coal, iron and steel and petro-chemicals.

There was a further parting of the ways over the issue of Germany's
future role, with Goerdeler wedded to traditional notions of German
(benevolent) hegemony, and only belatedly espousing the virtues of
Europe, airily claiming that it 'would not be difficult to agree as to

details' of a European army or European ministries of economics and foreign affairs, matters still controverted half a century later.[106] In this respect, Moltke was more consistently flighty or idealistic, depending on one's view of an issue this author has no strong opinions on. A common classical, Christian and social democratic heritage was to form the basis for a supra-national federal state, with the existing nations of France, Germany and Italy divided so that a series of roughly equal 'historically conditioned self-governing bodies' would eventuate. There was to be a European parliament, two cabinets (one executive, the other consultative), a secretariat, a conference of ambassadors and bodies to direct Europe's macro economy. Moltke could not quite make up his mind whether Britain would be in, or join Russia outside, a federation which would reach into the Baltic and include Poland. Rather loftily he thought Britain should have close economic links with Europe, but retain her empire and close ties with the United States, even perhaps recovering the leading role in the relationship. Venturing beyond Europe, Moltke wished Britain to retain her colonies, while 'Europe' took over those of France and Italy, and he thought it vital to create a post-war international organisation and to beef up the International Court at The Hague. So far from being anachronistically irrelevant, these concerns seem prescient in a Europe that is still wrestling with the relationship of national centres to regions; the position of Britain; the problems of the power and size of some of its continental members; and the elaboration of international jurisdictions to protect human rights. Sixties criticisms of this agenda seem rather old-fashioned.

HOUR OF DESTINY FOR THE COLONELS

Planning by the Kreisau Circle still presupposed a coup, which was increasingly becoming the concern of the colonels rather than the generals.[107] The invasion of the former Soviet Union in June 1941 contributed to a shift in the resistance's centre of gravity towards younger officers serving on the Eastern Front. Whereas most generals were products of the empire, either regarding Hitler as an ersatz Kaiser or paralysed by his daring boorishness, the colonels, captains and lieutenants had mostly reached maturity in the Weimar Republic. Age differences obviously resulted in a renewed militancy and vigour. Having responded positively to the temptations of Nazism, rather than just having to accommodate it to views formed by another age, the disillusionment when confronted by criminality and incompetence may have been all the greater.[108] Unlike the generals, middle-rank and junior officers witnessed Nazi atrocities and the human cost of strategic miscalculations at first hand.[109] Some experienced what amounted to an existential shock, akin to some horribly intimate betrayal; others had a more ambivalent relationship to atrocities.

The staff headquarters of Army Group Centre on the Russian front became the source of a series of attempts on Hitler's life, one of which almost succeeded, the accent being on almost, since every attempt was beset by unforeseen circumstances – not least, stemming from the enhanced security measures taken by a neurotic and suspicious dictator.[110] Armchair assassins, who imagine that killing Hitler was easy, might recall the faces of Iraqi generals in Saddam Hussein's entourage. The leading conspirator was Lieutenant-Colonel Henning von Tresckow (1901–44), who in 1939–40 had tried to move the generals to act during the hiatus before the western offensive. Tresckow used his position as senior operations officer, and the cover provided by his uncle Field Marshal Fedor von Bock, to appoint opponents of Hitler to Group Centre headquarters, with Fabian von Schlabrendorff joining as an ordnance officer and Rudolf Freiherr von Gersdorff having responsibility for intelligence and radio interception. In his efforts to work on his superiors, and to cement civilian–military resistance contacts, Tresckow smuggled Goerdeler to a meeting with Hans Kluge, the commander in chief of this army group.[111]

The technical details of the assassination attempts emanating from Army Group Centre are so well known as to warrant only a brief reprise, for this is not a manual on bomb-making. On 13 March 1943, they successfully smuggled a bomb into the cargo bay of Hitler's plane for the return flight from their headquarters at Krassnyi Bor to his headquarters at Vinnitsa in the Ukraine. The bomb failed to explode. A few weeks later, Gersdorff equipped himself as a suicide bomber, and vainly tried to keep pace with Hitler as he scurried through an exhibition of captured Soviet weaponry in Berlin's Zeughaus. Finally, Tresckow and his associates were behind the efforts in late 1943 and early 1944 by Captain Axel Freiherr von dem Bussche and Ewald-Heinrich Kleist-Schmenzin to kill Hitler by suicide bombing as he inspected new army uniforms, and by Eberhard von Breitenbach to shoot him in conference at the Berghof. What drove these officers to attempt to assassinate Hitler, an immense step for men for whom loyalty and obedience were the watchwords of their profession?

First, we need to say something of their professional and social background, for 'Hitler's army' had many discrete niches, where traditional values lingered despite attempts to convert the military into political soldiers. In 1926 Tresckow abandoned stockbroking to join the 9th Infantry Regiment, having already won the Iron Cross as a junior officer in 1918. The Reichswehr successor to the imperial 1st Foot Guards, the regiment was known as the 'Graf Neun' or 'I.R. von 9' because of the many Prussian aristocrats in its officer corps. Based at Potsdam, the barracks were within earshot of the Garnisonkirche whose bells intoned 'Üb immer Treu und Redlichkeit'. Elderly veterans still toasted the Kaiser in faraway Doorn during regimental dinners. Relations between officers and men were relaxed but patriarchal; the officers' mess tolerant of heterodox views expressed beside the fire-side.[112] Nineteen active or reserve members of the 9th Infantry figured in the rollcall of resisters.[113] Another aristocratic regiment, the 17th Cavalry, which absorbed the royal Bavarian Heavy Horse, provided a certain south German pendant, including Stauffenberg, whose uncle had commanded the old regiment, Ludwig Freiherr von Leonrod, and Albrecht Mertz von Quirnheim.[114] Apart from being friends and contemporaries, many of the aristocratic resisters were interrelated, which facilitated conspiracy and made penetration by spies almost impossible.

So-called 'critical historians' sometimes have the unappealing habit of dismissing the 20 July plotters as 'a typical aristocratic Hussars' charge', while earnestly extolling the self-sacrifices of the under-privileged Communists.[115] These conservative, easily cultured, good-humoured, intelligent, patriotic, physically prepossessing and stylish men would have been ill suited to the modern academy. For them, aristocracy entailed obligations, a virtually incomprehensible notion in cultures which only recognise rights. As was said of Moltke and Yorck: 'They were convinced that as aristocrats they had to grapple with the guilt that lay upon the nation that their ancestors had led.'[116] Beyond the 'comic strip' dictators of the present they could draw independence of mind from such mythic family figures as Gneisenau, Moltke or Yorck, historical connections which also afforded them a degree of protection, making the fist of the Gestapo hesitate a while before it landed in their faces.[117] They were fortunate too in being married to self-possessed women, with whom they discussed their dilemmas or conducted intense correspondence (most notably Moltke's letters to Freya), women who shouldered duties uncommon to their class and time. They ran wartime households, which in this case often meant supervising considerable agrarian enterprises, sometimes taking part in clandestine meetings or helping the conspiracies along. The risks they were running became evident only later when they and other members of their families were incarcerated in prisons and camps.[118] Above all, many resisters discovered an intense religious faith; as Moltke wrote to Freya on 17 March 1940:

Today is a long and quiet day; or so at least I hope, for it is still morning. Your husband got up slowly, washed a little, had a delicious breakfast, and then listened to the Suite in B minor. I've already got very fond of it. Then I read the Bible a little more, an activity I pursue with more enjoyment now than ever before. It used to be all stories to me, at least the Old Testament, but now it is all contemporary to me. I find it much more gripping than ever before.[119]

Questions of conscience, culpability, guilt and the resistance are complex, and deserve to be treated without hysteria or partiality. However, it is immediately clear that memories of the dead do not always conform with the historical record of their actions, and that individual reactions to atrocities cannot be generalised to the entire military resistance, still less across the civilian–military resistance divide. While still based at Posen prior to Barbarossa, Tresckow allegedly protested vehemently against 'criminal orders' issued before the invasion. He told Gersdorff that guilt would weigh upon the Germans for a hundred years 'and not just on Hitler alone, but on you and me, your wife and mine, your children and my children, the woman crossing the road now, and the boy playing with a ball over there'.[120] He tried in vain to move 'Onkel Fedi' Bock to join Leeb and Rundstedt in a démarche by the field marshals against these orders.[121] If this is true, then what follows is rather hard to reconcile with it.

Following the invasion, Army Group Centre's headquarters moved to Borisov on the Beresina. There, Tresckow and his intelligence officer Gersdorff were directly confronted by Nazi criminality, as Einsatzgruppe B scurried about in Group Centre's wake, under the command, until the end of October 1941, of SS-Brigadeführer Arthur Nebe, who as we saw earlier had been involved in anti-Hitler conspiracies since 1938. Before his recall to Berlin at the end of October, Nebe's command was responsible for murdering 45,467 people. Reports from Einsatzgruppe B went routinely to Gersdorff, who was their military liaison officer, and were sometimes passed on to Tresckow, Bock and Kluge.[122] Of course, knowledge is not the same as approbation.

Since Nebe represents an embarrassment for the military resistance, his story has to be marginalised or misrepresented. Some surviving resisters claimed that his Abwehr contacts pressed him to take this command in order to stay at the centre of the SS; that Nebe circumvented orders and exaggerated Group B's reports of killings; and that mysterious Latvian formations were imposed on his designated territory because of some alleged SS dissatisfaction with his performance.[123] This tendency spread to the second edition of *SS-Staat*, by the Austrian conservative concentration camp survivor Eugen Kogon, who felt moved to correct his initial assessment of Nebe as 'one of the least well known, but merciless functionaries of the SS apparatus' to a 'figure not without certain tragic aspects'.[124] There is no indication that a reluctant Nebe would have ceased being at the centre of the SS if he had turned down this posting. He volunteered for this assignment, the most charitable explanation being that he thought it would bring decorations and promotion – important to a man who relished being called 'Herr General' before he became one. Nor did he massage the statistics by adding noughts; rather he exhorted his men to exceed the numbers of people murdered by rival units, and refined the method of killing by trial gassings of lunatics in a Minsk asylum. Film of this squalid business was found in his Berlin apartment. Finally, there is no evidence of any Latvians being imposed on him, an unlikely way of treating a senior SS officer.[125] Nebe indeed drank copious quantities of Veuve Cliquot, and had himself recalled because of illness. He was also promoted to the SS equivalent rank to a general and awarded the Kriegsverdienst Kreuz. Whether this qualifies him as a 'tragic' figure seems doubtful.

The epiphet seems more deserved by the tortured figure of Kurt Gerstein, paradoxically a clearer case of the 'ambiguity of good' and of the pitfalls of opposing a totalitarian regime from the inside. The son of a pious and emotionally unbending judge, Gerstein had studied mining engineering. Active in the Evangelical Youth Movement, he joined the Nazi Party in May and the SA in October 1933, hoping to reconcile his intense religious feeling with his no less intense extreme nationalistic politics. An adherent of the Confessing Church, Gerstein was opposed to the German Christians and to attempts by the Hitler Youth to take over Protestant youth groups. In early 1935, he was grievously assaulted after he made a solo protest during a performance of a Nazi irreligious play. A year later he was arrested for attempting to mail thousands of Confessing Church leaflets to hundreds of Reich judges and officials. He was excluded from the NSDAP, losing the right to work in state-owned mines, a plight he sought to resolve by studying medicine. A private income enabled him to produce more religious tracts, which when detected by the Gestapo resulted in a six-week spell in Welzheim concentration camp.

The following years were blighted by poor employment prospects and attempts to have his case heard by higher Party courts. In early 1941 his sister-in-law was killed during the 'euthanasia' programme; in March he volunteered for the Waffen-SS. Whether the two things were connected remains an open question; but what is not in doubt is that Gerstein had resolved to 'see things from the inside'. Because of his background in engineering and medicine, he was assigned to the Waffen-SS Hygiene department, with responsibility for disinfection equipment and water filtration systems in camps. In June 1942, by which time he was head of the Waffen-SS disinfection services, Gertein was ordered to move a large consignment of prussic acid from a factory near Prague to Lublin in Poland. There, Odilo Globocnik informed him that his future work would include disinfecting large quantities of clothing and replacing the diesel-engine gassing technology used in the three 'Aktion Reinhard' camps with quicker-acting prussic acid. At Belzec, Gerstein watched as Wirth and his staff managed to take nearly four hours gassing part of a transport of six thousand Jews from Lviv, for the engines malfunctioned. Using his stopwatch to record the delay precisely, for he did not cease to function as an engineer, Gerstein recalled: 'I prayed with them. I pressed myself into a corner and cried out to my God and theirs. How glad I should have been to go into the gas chambers with them! How gladly I should have died the same death as theirs! . . . But I could not do this yet. I felt I must not succumb to the temptation to die with these people.'

Thereafter, Gerstein took it upon himself to tell all and sundry about what he had seen. He buttonholed the Swedish diplomat Baron von Otter on an overnight train; the Swiss press attaché Hochstrasser; the Berlin Protestant bishop Dibelius; a Dutch engineer; and the coadjutor of the Catholic archbishop of Berlin Konrad von Preysing, since the Apostolic Nuncio had turned him away from the door. He was a desperate man, permanently on the verge of a nervous breakdown; talking too much to complete strangers, and with illegal BBC broadcasts blaring out in his apartment home. Responsible for ordering Zyklon B gas for the SS, Gerstein seems to have sabotaged two consignments by insisting that the deliveries were dangerously unstable, and hence had to be used immediately as fumigants. A denazification court convened five years after Gerstein's suicide in a French prison came to a mixed verdict. He had undoubtedly risked much in informing people about mass murder, and hence had committed acts of resistance. But after what he saw in Belzec he should have found a way to opt out, instead of his sabotage of 'trifling' quantities of toxic chemicals. Put slightly differently, that was to say that he was guilty of a double failure, not only in the sense of making no impression on the machinery of destruction, but in failing to stand aside ostentatiously while the Jews were murdered.[126]

Arthur Nebe was not the only murderer abroad behind Army Group Centre. Hours before the invasion, Tresckow met SS-Brigade-führer Kurt Knoblauch to arrange relations between Army Group Centre and SS cavalry and motorised formations from the Kommandostab Reichsführer-SS, including Magill's horsemen, whom we have repeatedly encountered in the Pripyat marshes. These forces killed fourteen thousand Jews there in about two weeks. They reported excellent relations with Army Group Centre. Three members of the military resistance, including Gersdorff, were also invited to a practical seminar on anti-partisan warfare at Mogilev in September 1941, addressed by Bach-Zelewski, Nebe and Hermann Fegelein, the commander of these SS cavalrymen. The seminar culminated in two dawn raids on villages, during which the inhabitants were interrogated about partisans, and thirty-two 'suspect, non-local Jews' shot.[127] Yet Gersdorff wrote in Group Centre's official war diary that officers disapproved of the shooting of Jews, prisoners and commissars. The killing of prisoners, which they especially deplored, had a self-interested aspect, since 'it especially stiffened the enemy's resistance'. Together, these crimes were construed as a stain on the honour of the German army.[128]

This is difficult to reconcile with their relations with Nebe and the Kommandostab Reichsführer-SS, or with the killing of enormous numbers of Russian civilians. Gersdorff himself was formally responsible for the Secret Field Police (Geheime Feldpolizei) which during October 1942 killed one thousand people, including 133 Jews, in Army Group Centre's area. Moreover, in the Group's rear area combined large-scale anti-partisan operations resulted in the deaths of a quarter of a million Russian civilians, as a given area was encircled and then 'combed out', a euphemism for lining up the inhabitants of villages and shooting them. In June 1944, Tresckow personally signed an order whereby orphaned boys and girls of ten to thirteen years old netted in anti-partisan operations were to be deported for forced labour in Germany, a fate which befell 4,500 children.

Members of the military resistance reacted variously to atrocities on the Eastern Front, and to the see-saw of German military fortunes. Some came out badly, others well. They were implacably hostile to the Bolshevik dictatorship, but divided in how best to neutralise it. Thus Colonel-General Erich Hoepner, an opponent of Hitler since 1938, issued battle instructions to his 4th Panzer Group in May 1941 which spoke of 'the Germans' ancient struggle against Slavdom, the defence of European civilisation from Muscovite-Asiatic inundation, defence against Jewish-Bolshevism' and the need for 'unprecedented harshness' and the 'merciless, total extermination of the enemy' especially in the case of 'bearers of the present Russian-Bolshevik system'.[129]

Fritz-Dietlof von der Schulenburg volunteered for the army in the summer of 1940, joining the illustrious 9th Infantry Regiment. Schulenburg's critical faculties seem to have been dulled by an almost sacral view of battle – 'I was filled by God' – and adolescent awe in the midst of the 'most perfect war machine seen for centuries, or even thousands of years'. In Russia, he took exception to the unsystematic shooting of prisoners, because it would lead to the disinhibition of the common soldier and the unleashing of 'drives' which would be hard to rein in. Since he thought that the Bolshevik enemy deserved 'no pardon', Schulenburg thought it best if they died in battle or on the orders of officers such as himself, who presumably had no 'drives' to set free.[130] Murder of prisoners was a disciplinary problem that assumed ethical aspects only for the rank and file of the German army. Although in his diaries Schulenburg noted SS atrocities against Jews, these were a symptom, rather than a symbol, of Nazi departure from the basis of legality, requiring no extra comment or action. Whatever prompted him to resist, it does not appear to have been massacres of Jews or non-Jews in Russia. Nor, one must probably conclude, was it as determinative for Gersdorff or Treskow as it has been made to seem.

But this is not the whole story. Another member of the 9th Infantry Regiment, the much decorated Captain Axel Freiherr von dem Bussche, was posted to the Ukraine in the summer of 1942, where in October he witnessed SS killing of over a thousand Jews at Dubno airbase. At first, Bussche thought of invoking the common law concerning defence against unlawful attack. On later reflection, he decided that the only response for a Christian was to strip off, lie down and wait to be shot, in a demonstration of common humanity.[131] Shortly before his death in 1992, Bussche said: 'Some traditional harmony had been destroyed here. We had seen it, but we were not able to put it in words. Something was shattered there. It is my responsibility and guilt that I am still alive.'[132]

If moral outrage at the conduct of this war seems to have been retrospectively generalised from individuals such as Bussche to men with a more equivocal stance, what else may have prompted them to try to kill Hitler? Could it be that retrospective emphasis on their alleged, and reported, reactions to atrocities has drawn attention away from issues that may have seemed just as pressing to soldiers engaged in a desperate conflict which they meant to win without Hitler? We need to grasp imaginatively what might have really mattered to them, rather than casting around for signs of their alertness to what matters half a century later. Humanitarian concerns were probably mixed with much more pragmatic considerations, for even the best have morally confused motives.

It is striking that many of these military resisters believed that the war in Russia was lost when it started, a view uncommon in the higher reaches of the German army, where hubris reigned. In this respect they were similar to Dietrich Bonhoeffer, who also knew how important it was to look beyond superficial success. In September 1941 he amazed Willem Visser 't Hooft by saying, 'It's all over now, isn't it?', adding, 'I mean, we are at the beginning of the end. Hitler will never get out of this.'[133] Erich Hoepner, whom we have just encountered, called the invasion 'hara-kiri'. Schlabrendorff thought that the invasion of Russia was akin to an elephant trampling an antheap. It would obliterate thousands and thousands of ants, but in the end they would strip the elephant to the bone.[134] Tresckow anticipated defeat 'as certain as the Amen in church'; Lieutenant-General Olbricht said that 'our army is a mere puff of wind on the vast Russian steppes'.[135] Problems with the disciplinary and human consequences of the 'criminal orders' were compounded by amazement at the strategies adopted. This applied to the original dissipation of the attacking force along vast fronts and against three objectives, instead of an all-out lunge against Moscow, and to the bouts of high-level bickering and resignations which thenceforth accompanied strategic decisions, and which were symbolised from the end of 1942 by the distance separating Führer headquarters at the Bavarian Berghof from the General Staff at Mauerwald in East Prussia. In his regular lecture on command structure to the War Academy from 1941 onwards, Stauffenberg would hatch crisscrossed lines linked to an alphabet soup of organisational boxes on the blackboard, asking the audience whether they thought the war winnable with such a 'structure'.[136]

Finally, these officers realised that the key to victory in Russia lay through a realist approach, which might win over a population oppressed by Communism. In his diary, Fritz-Dietlof von der Schulenburg lauded the powers of endurance of the Russian peasantry, which after twenty-five years of enforced egalitarianism and irreligion still kept icons in the corner. Pondering Russia's future administration, he wrote: 'Moreover, one can only rule a country recently liberated from Bolshevism with principles diametrically opposed to Bolshevism. Property, freedom of the person, of expression, of religion, are indispensable elements of this policy.'[137] Tresckow advocated land reform, religious tolerance and a measure of self-government, and the creation of a Russian 'army of liberation', making do with experimental units led by Georgii Zhilenkov, the former first Party secretary of a district of Moscow. Stauffenberg wanted indigenous volunteer formations, and a benevolent occupation administration in the North Caucasus.[138]

Instead of exploiting the simmering hatred many Soviet citizens and soldiers had for their own regime, the Nazi leadership persisted in refusing to exploit this asset because of racial-ideological dogmatism. In Stauffenberg's case these views went hand in hand with the realisation that anti-Jewish atrocities were not localised aberrations but part of an organised rampage.[139] From the summer of 1942 he began openly to advocate the killing of Hitler.

Claus Schenk von Stauffenberg's disenchantment with Hitler set in later than that of many of his fellow military resisters, but it was intense. A tall, physically impressive Catholic from Bamberg in south Germany, Stauffenberg provided the élan missing since Oster's arrest in mid-1943. He was an accomplished cellist and horseman, and, together with his brother Berthold, a member of the esoteric circle around the symbolist poet Stefan George called Secret Germany.[140] This was an elite society, rather like an ancient academy, whence would come future leaders of Germany. A big man in every sense of the word, Stauffenberg's politics did not admit of facile classification, like a number of the men we have already encountered, for it may be that resistance was intimately connected to an ability to ignore conventional party or tribal allegiances, or to strike political postures to test others or just for the sake of it. As his widow recalled in an interview:

> My husband was not one who could be packaged in a box, on which is then written: This is so and so, and he reacts in such and such a fashion. He let things come to him, and then made up his mind. All of us undergo transformations. Moreover, one of his characteristics was that he really enjoyed playing the devil's advocate. Conservatives were convinced that he was a ferocious Nazi, and ferocious Nazis were convinced he was an unreconstructed conservative. He was neither.[141]

Having tried in vain to move the generals to action, Stauffenberg decided that the colonels would have to act unilaterally. His first direct contact with Hitler occurred on 7 June 1944 at a briefing session attended by Göring, Himmler, Keitel and Speer. Göring appeared to be wearing cosmetics, Speer to be the only sane person present among psychopaths. Hitler's eyes were hooded, his hands palpitated. It was hard to breathe since the atmosphere was rank and rotten. Stauffenberg's alienation was complete.

The events of 20 July 1944 have been recounted so well and so often by Peter Hoffmann as to require no detailed recapitulation here. Under 'Valkyrie Level II' devised by Stauffenberg and Tresckow, assassination was combined with the mobilisation of the Home Army against the SS and Party, which were to be blamed for Hitler's death. The role of assassin devolved on Stauffenberg, who had returned grievously wounded from service with 10th Panzer Division in North Africa to become Chief of Staff to the Home Army. Stauffenberg was also expected to return to Berlin after the assassination to trigger the coup. However, he would need the co-operation of more senior officers, especially General Fromm, in the Bendlerstrasse army head-quarters, for suspicious or wavering troop commanders would inevit-ably seek verbal confirmation of strange orders accompanied by even stranger proclamations coming off the teleprinter. After the coup had started, Fromm refused to co-operate and suggested Stauffenberg kill himself. Although the latter tried to keep the momentum going, by midnight the game was up. Resistance forces in Paris, Prague and Vienna had greater success in corralling the SS than the army had with its own troops in the capital, where units loyal to Hitler isolated army headquarters. Inside that building, Fromm gradually regained control, having Stauffenberg and three other conspirators shot in the courtyard by the light of headlamps to occlude his own shady role in the conspiracy. General Ludwig Beck was forced to commit suicide. In Paris, General Stülpnagel had to release Oberg and Knöchen of the SS, whom he had earlier arrested, desperately trying to save himself and his staff by hosting a macabre drinks party for these two in the Hôtel Raphaël. Next morning, *en route* to Berlin, he halted his car by a canal near Verdun, where he had served in the Great War, and unsuccessfully tried to shoot himself. He was later tried and led blind to the gallows. In eastern Poland, Major-General Henning von Tres-ckow killed himself with a grenade.[142]

Some two hundred people were tried in batches by a 'People's Court' and executed by slow strangulation, including virtually all of those discussed so far in this account. Despite torture, intimidation and various petty humiliations designed to maximise the indignity of the occasion, their essential decency shone through. Dazed, depressed and resigned to their fate, they treated Hitler's 'Vyshin-sky', Roland Freisler, who indeed had been a Soviet Commissar after the October Revolution, with contempt, as if he were a bothersome glove-puppet.[143] Moltke had been in custody since January 1944, and had no ascertainable connections with the assassination attempt. Indeed, he thought that Nazism should be allowed to destroy itself, allowing a fresh start on a new basis. The case against him concerned his associations with the Jesuits, the crime being independent thought. Moltke remarked on how his Christian Scientist parents would have reacted: 'That I should die as a martyr for St Ignatius Loyola . . . really is comical, and I already tremble at the thought of Papi's paternal indignation, since he was always so anti-Catholic. The rest he will approve, but that! Even Mami won't be wholly in agreement.'[144] A verbal spat developed between Moltke and Freisler, who said: 'Only in one respect are we and Christianity alike; we demand the whole man! . . . Who do you take your orders from? From the Other World or from Adolf Hitler? Who commands your loyalty and your faith?' Moltke was judicially murdered for thinking the wrong thoughts. Ewald von Kleist-Schmenzin, with whom we began this account, was tried for conspiring with the English in 1938 and because his name figured on a list of future regional administrators. He stopped Freisler in his tracks when he said: 'Yes, I have pursued high treason since 30 January 1933, always and with every means. I made no secret of my struggle against Hitler and National Socialism. I regard this struggle as a commandment from God. God alone will be my judge.' At that point proceedings were halted by air-raid sirens. American bombs flattened the courthouse walls, and Freisler was killed by falling masonry.[145] Kleist's trial resumed in February 1945; he was executed in early April. There was a bizarre footnote to the conspiracy. Imagining in his enveloping paranoia that the game was up, Arthur Nebe faked his own suicide, before going on the run, pursued by detectives from his own criminal police office. He hid on a farm outside Berlin, regaling his hosts with tales of Scotland Yard, until his whereabouts were betrayed by a jealous former lady friend. Former associates such as Heinrich Müller suddenly insisted on the formal *per Sie*, rather than the more intimate *Du*, address. Nebe was interrogated by his former colleagues in the Prinz-Albrecht Strasse, imprisoned in Buchenwald, and executed in early March 1945.[146]

Two final observations might be made about the plot that failed, since it is sometimes seen as a case of acting at ten to twelve, or as doomed to failure. In the nine months following the 20 July plot, nearly five million German civilians and soldiers lost their lives, not to speak of Allied and Soviet fatalities, or entire Jewish communities murdered in the final frenzy. Moderating or preventing this by prematurely collapsing the Western Front, as many of the conspirators wished to do, would surely have been a desirable outcome. Most of the conspirators realised that their chances of success were slight.

Living by simple codes of honour and sacrifice, they effectively elected to die by them, realising that, as Stauffenberg put it: 'Even worse than failure is to yield to shame and coercion without a struggle.' For whatever motives, the conspirators set aside their doubts, and took a huge leap in the dark. Tresckow put the matter succinctly when he told Stauffenberg: 'The assassination must be attempted, coute que coute. Even if it fails, we must take action in Berlin. For the practical purpose no longer matters; what matters now is that the German resistance movement must take the plunge before the eyes of the world and of history. Compared to that, nothing else matters.'[147]

MEN OF GOD

National Socialism, like other totalitarian dictatorships, parodied many of the eschatological and liturgical attributes of redemptive religions, while being fundamentally antagonistic towards the Churches: rivals, as the Nazis saw it, in the subtle, totalising control of minds.[148] However, the overwhelmingly Christian character of the German people meant that Hitler dissembled his personal views behind preachy invocations of the Almighty, and distanced himself from the radically irreligious within his own Party, even though his own views were probably more extreme. During the Weimar period, he periodically traduced the Roman Catholic Centre Party for engaging in coalitions with 'atheist internationalists' in the SPD. In reality, his views were a mixture of materialist biology, a faux-Nietzschean contempt for core, as distinct from secondary, Christian values, and a visceral anti-clericalism. Even though he disdained a confrontation with wearers of 'petticoats and cassocks', in the long term a showdown would come:

> The war will be over one day. I shall then consider that my life's final task will be to solve the religious problem. Only then will the German nation be entirely secure once and for all. I don't interfere in matters of belief. Therefore I can't allow churchmen to interfere with temporal affairs. The organised lie must be smashed. The State must remain the absolute master. When I was younger, I thought that it was necessary to set about matters with dynamite. I've since realised that there's room for a little subtlety. The rotten branch falls of itself. The final state must be: in St Peter's chair, a senile officiant; facing him, a few sinister old women, as gaga and as poor in spirit as anyone could wish. The young and healthy are on our side.

Rude though they were, these views were roughly congruent with the heated rhetoric of nineteenth-century Church–State conflicts. But, in what followed, Hitler forsook this terrain for things Emil Combes would have found horrible: 'Christ was an Aryan' rather than a Jew; St Paul was responsible for mobilising the 'criminal underworld' on behalf of 'proto-Bolshevism'. Christianity signified nothing but 'wholehearted Bolshevism under a tinsel of metaphysics'. 'What is this God who takes pleasure only in seeing men grovel before him?' What was the Christian heaven compared to that of Islam? Christianity was 'an invention of sick brains', 'a negro with his tabus is crushingly superior to the human being who seriously believes in Transubstantiation'. He continued:

> By what would you have me replace the Christians' picture of the Beyond? . . . The soul and the mind migrate, just as the body returns to nature. Thus life is eternally reborn from life. As for the "why?" of all that, I feel no need to rack my brains on the subject. The soul is unplumbable. . . . Man judges everything in relation to himself. What is bigger than himself is big, what is smaller is small. Only one thing is certain, that one is part of the spectacle. Everyone finds his own role. Joy exists for everybody. I dream of a state of affairs in which every man would know that he lives and dies for the preservation of the species.[149]

This was probably where things tended, with Greiser's Godless Warthegau functioning as the laboratory for future policy. For policies inhibited for reasons of state in Germany or Austria, not to speak of France or Norway, could be implemented with radical impunity in occupied Poland, particularly since Roman Catholicism was so integral to a Polish nationhood the Nazis sought to extirpate. A densely rich spiritual scene was rapidly reduced to a desert. By 1941, almost all of the churches and chapels in the diocese of Posen-Gnesen were closed, and 11 per cent of the Catholic clergy had been murdered. Virtually all the remainder had been deported or imprisoned.[150] Many of them suffered martyrdom in Nazi concentration camps.

This is not the place to rehearse the history of the 'Church Struggle' with National Socialism, for its underlying impulses often had little to do with resistance. The 'Church Struggle' involved manning the ramparts of the Church, in defence of a way of life and a worldview free from the contaminants abroad in Germany during the 1930s. For the effect, as opposed to intent, was sometimes exclusionary, there being scant protest regarding people persecuted for political or racial reasons. While the Churches were undoubtedly beleaguered, and faced extinction in the long term, they bolted the gates of the innermost sanctum, leaving others to the mercies of the neo-barbarian hordes rampaging outside. Even the notion that they resisted 'reluctantly' probably puts things too strongly, for spasmodic protests over issues directly touching the Church and core Christian teachings were accompanied by silence about terrible crimes against their fellow man and sincere professions of loyalty during times of national crisis.[151]

One major problem arose when the Churches dealt with National Socialism: the ambiguity of its ideology and the extremely slippery relationship between ideology and political strategy.[152] In his opening policy statement in the Reichstag, Hitler announced that 'the national government sees in both Christian denominations the most important factor for the maintenance of our society'.[153] Protestant anxieties about a third Roman Catholic chancellor in succession were allayed by the rumour that, although nominally Catholic, Hitler 'thought like' a Protestant. Duly deceived, many senior clerics publicly endorsed Hitler's chancellorship, choosing to see this as the advent of a new ethical–spiritual age beyond the materialism and turmoil of the Weimar Republic.[154] However, many senior clerics were simultaneously exercised by the anti-Christian views of Alfred Rosenberg's *Mythos des 20. Jahrhunderts*, with Bishop Galen of Münster stating, 'if this is National Socialist ideology, then we reject National Socialist ideology', and organising a major religious procession when Rosenberg sought to speak in his diocese.[155] However, the bishops backed off as Hitler informally deprecated Rosenberg's book and blamed them for giving it free publicity by making a fuss over it.[156] His slipperiness regarding dogmatic inessentials and the clerics' longing for order and stability – and hostility to liberalism and the left – meant that a precarious *modus vivendi* was achieved.

Hitler's initial strategy towards the Churches was twofold. The dominant faith, with about forty million nominal adherents, would be controlled through the self-coordination of the autochthonous state Churches, to be realised through state patronage of a sect called the German Christians and the imposition of a Protestant 'Reich Bishop'. As for the Catholics, Pius XI himself believed that diplomacy was the way to secure the Church's apostolic mission to a godless society, and to that end concluded some forty concordats with, among others, Poland in 1925, Italy in 1929 and Germany on 20 July 1933. From Hitler's view, this restricted the Roman Catholic minority Church to cultic and caritative functions, thereby neutralising the Catholic Centre Party, while conferring the highest form of international recognition on his regime. From the Church's viewpoint, it protected Catholic apostolic organisations, and drew a clear line in the sand, infractions of which could be legally contested.[157] This conformed with Pius XI's belief that movements such as Catholic Action, with their campaigns for family life or against pornography – if you will, for the 'rechristian-isation' of modern society – advanced the cause better than confessional parties, with their inherent tendency to fragment along class lines over economic issues, and their pursuit of compromise and secular agendas. The Church had sold the pass for reasons of institutional self-preservation, however it sought to justify this.[158]

Paradoxically, the first enterprise was frustrated by the zealotry of the German Christians, the self-styled 'SA of Jesus Christ', and the manifest inadequacy of the government-backed Reich Bishop Ludwig Müller. The German Christians' statement of principles included:

> We stand on the ground of positive Christianity. We profess an affirmative faith in Christ, fitting our race and being in accordance with the German Lutheran mind and heroic piety.
>
> Mere compassion is 'charity' and leads to presumption, paired with bad conscience, and effeminates a nation. We know something about Christian obligation and charity toward the helpless, but we also demand the protection of the nation from the unfit and inferior.
>
> We see a great danger to our nationality in the Jewish Mission. It promises to allow foreign blood into our nation. . . . Marriages between Jews and Germans particularly must be prohibited.[159]

When the German Christians sought to introduce the 'Aryan para-graph' into Church governance, compulsorily retiring ministers of 'non-Aryan' racial origin, for some this was a step too far. It resulted in the formation of a Pastors' Emergency League, even though its moving spirit, Martin Niemöller, himself had old-fashioned views about Jews. The ranks of the Emergency League swelled when German Christians called for the eradication of the Old Testament with its 'Jewish morality of rewards, and its stories of cattle-dealers and concubines'. Apart from expunging the 'Rabbi Paul' from the Gospels, converted Jews were to worship in a segregated Jewish Christian Church.[160] By January 1934, seven thousand of the eighteen thousand Protestant pastors in Germany belonged to the Emergency League, the rest to the majoritarian German Evangelical Church. The League became the Confessing Church, which held its first national synod at Barmen in late May 1934. Its identifying attribute was that 'the Church must remain the Church' and that the Gospels, stripped of secularised accretions, were normative. This bore the imprint of Karl Barth, the influential Swiss reformed theologian then working in Bonn.

Resistance by Protestant churchmen was handicapped by a four-hundred-year-old tradition of 'throne and altar' based on Romans chapter 13, with its functional separation of temporal and spiritual powers, and by the political homelessness of German Protestants during the Weimar Republic, a problem many resolved by supporting the Nazi Party. It was largely overlooked that Luther had also sanctioned disobedience when the secular power degenerated into the 'beast from the bottomless pit', or that Scottish or Swiss Calvinism – as Barth pointed out – made resistance to tyranny an imperative, a view which came to be influential in reformed circles within the Old Prussian Confessing Church.[161]

However, ambiguities characterised the Confessing Church too. The Barmen Declaration acknowledged the doctrine of separation of powers, while simultaneously rejecting the current claims of the state as the sole and total arbiter of human existence. It wished to remain loyal, but its defence of Church autonomy had a tendency to make it disloyal, at least in terms of the ecclesiastical policy of a government with totalitarian aspirations. Just once, in 1936, the 'fraternal' wing of the Confessing Church raised its voice on behalf of the 'voiceless in the land', in a secret memorandum to Hitler protesting 'deconfessionalisation', the propagation of hatred of the Jews, concentration camps, the Gestapo, and the ubiquity of eavesdropping and espionage. There was no acknowledgement or reply, and the exercise was never repeated along such a broad range of issues.[162] The head of the agency identified with this document – a watered-down version of which was read from the pulpits – was murdered a year later in Sachsenhausen concentration camp.

There was no nazified trojan horse within the Roman Catholic priesthood, nor any sect resembling the heretical German Christians, although individual priests sometimes had strange views about Jews. The hierarchical and international character of the Catholic Church, focused on an institution which had seen off despots, tyrants and murderous revolutionists, lent German Catholics external support largely lacking in the case of German Protestants. Periodic papal encyclicals and letters, such as *Casti connubi* (1930), *Non Abbiamo Bisogno* (1931) and *Mit brennender Sorge* (1937), laid down a line not subject to democratic discussion in a highly authoritarian institution.

So far, so propitious. However, in the 1930s, both Pius XI and many Catholic intellectuals gave their support to authoritarian regimes in Austria, Poland, Portugal and Spain, partly because of the threat from atheistic and anti-clerical parties or regimes, such as the Spanish Republicans, partly in idealistic pursuit of a Catholic-corporatist 'third way' between liberal individualism and totalitarian fascism and Marxism, a way briefly realised in Dolfuss' Austria and in the timewarps of Salazar's Portugal or De Valera's Ireland.

These trends were evident in Germany too, but were complicated there by what was specific to National Socialism rather than to various brands of authoritarianism or fascism elsewhere. If many German Roman Catholics had authoritarian sympathies, and identified Jews with Bolshevism or liberal-capitalistic modernity, they deplored attempts to 'aryanise' Christianity, the materialist or neo-pagan aspects of Nazi race ideology, and the totalitarianism reflected in the regime's aspirations, if not always in its quotidian structural realities. These things explain many of the frictions between Catholics and Nazism. However, the desire of these erstwhile 'enemies' of the Bismarckian Reich, and their establishment leadership, to be loyal to the state, and Hitler's tactical distancing of himself from his madder followers, produced a *modus vivendi* between the Church and government. The Concordat with the Vatican mirrored these ambiguities. State Secretary Pacelli, the future Pius XII, was careful to point out that a diplomatic treaty did not identify the Vatican with a political ideology. It was a treaty both *with* a totalitarian state and *against* a totalitarian ideology. But, beyond these niceties, 'Te Deums' celebrating the Concordat or telegrams congratulating Hitler on his birthdays conspired to create a different impression, while differences in temperament and approach rendered the corporate response of the Catholic episcopate less than impressive.

Neither Church was left to its own devices. Attempts by the new Church Affairs Minister Hanns Kerrl to establish good relations between Church and state were doomed to failure, because Kerrl lacked political weight, while more powerful figures such as Heydrich and Himmler regarded the Churches as pertaining to their sphere of 'combating opponents'. Assaults on Catholic lay organisations and the confessional press were followed by crude campaigns against religious orders, with denunciations of monks and nuns as crooks, libertines, paedophiles and pederasts. Charitable tax exemption was removed from Church property not directly used for worship, and innumerable specialist Church welfare facilities for the blind, deaf, epileptic or handicapped rationalised out of existence, a blow which affected the Caritas and Inner Mission caritative networks. Although, as we have seen, the latter was not immune to modern eugenic fashions, both the hereditary health laws and the wartime 'euthanasia' programme struck at fundamental Christian identification with the weak and teachings on procreation, eventually resulting in behind-the-scenes lobbying or, more rarely, public protest, notably by the bishop of Münster Clemens Graf von Galen.[163]

However, even Galen's coruscating verbal assault was not free from ambiguities and had no functional effects. Galen had known about 'euthanasia' killings for over a year before he spoke out, and it may be significant that he only did so when in the summer of 1941 the Gestapo closed Jesuit and Sisters of the Immaculate Conception houses in Münster as part of a wider campaign of expropriation of Church property. Although his sermon, which enjoyed national and international notoriety, undoubtedly moved some Nazi leaders to contemplate murdering him, its effects on the 'euthanasia' programme were minimal. The medical killing of children continued unimpeded; gassing facilities were used to murder concentration-camp inmates; while the 'euthanasia' killing of adult psychiatric patients went on by other means down to the final days of the war. It is debatable whether Galen's sermon, or the isolated popular protests which preceded it, stopped anything much at all.[164]

Taken in isolation, such clerical protests might be viewed as 'resistance', were it not for simultaneous rejection of subversive activities and ringing endorsements of the regime's foreign policy and military triumphs. In other words, protest over single issues did not automatically result in fundamental rejection of a system of government, any more than people prepared to break the law opposing abortion reject the prevailing system of government in democracies.[165] In August 1935, the Fulda Bishops' Conference assured the government that Catholic associations 'reject all subversive attitudes and conduct, refrain from any political activity and especially will resolutely repel all attempted approaches of Communism'.[166] Far from desiring Hitler's death, cardinals Bertram and Faulhaber congratulated him for surviving Georg Elser's lone assassination bid on 8 November 1939, with a 'Te Deum' being sung in Munich's cathedral 'to thank the Divine Providence in the name of the archdiocese for the Führer's fortunate escape from the criminal attempt made on his life'.

Catholic bishops celebrated the victory of German arms in Catholic Poland, notwithstanding the fact that Vatican radio and the *Osservatore Romano* publicised intelligence from Cardinal Hlond about atrocities against the Polish Catholic clergy. This fact makes their silence about the Jews less than surprising. Church bells were rung to celebrate that victory, as they were rung after the fall of France. Catholic clergy also helped the regime camouflage a war of racial-ideological murder in Russia by presenting it as a 'crusade' against atheistic Bolshevism, a formula which barely covered murdering Jews in Catholic Poland.[167] Nor did the Church protest the confinement of multifarious victims in concentration camps, beyond half-hearted attempts to bring spiritual solace to Catholics detained within them. And with the exception of a few brave men such as Provost Bernhard Lichtenberg of Berlin, who died in Dachau because he insisted on praying each day for deported Jews, protests regarding antisemitic measures were largely confined to the fate of 'non-Aryan' Christians rather than Jews *qua* Jews. Even when in late 1941 the Catholic bishops protested proposals compulsorily to divorce partners in mixed marriages, Cardinal Bertram felt moved to insist that his words were not motivated by 'lack of love for the German nation, or of feeling for national dignity, or of underestimation of the harmful Jewish influences upon German culture and national interests'.[168] This bleak story is not materially altered by the fact that the Catholic 'Raphaelsverein' or the Protestant 'Büro Grüber' managed to smuggle a few Jewish people out of the country. Even when forthrightly denouncing Nazi murder of the handicapped and mentally ill, Bishop Galen was careful to add the rider that 'We Christians make no revolution. We will continue to do our duty in obedience to God, out of love for people and Fatherland. . . . We will continue to fight against the external enemy; against the enemy in our midst who tortures and beats us, we cannot fight with arms and there remains only one weapon: strong tenacious, obstinate perseverance.' This was the deeply ambivalent background to the more exclusive affair of resistance by a very few churchmen to National Socialism.

Active resistance by churchmen involved a minority, supported by a larger penumbra who simply admired these individuals without necessarily knowing what they were doing. For example, the Benedictine monks of Ettal probably had little inkling of what the Protestant theologian Bonhoeffer was doing in their midst at the turn of 1940–1, but he derived great solace and intellectual stimulation from being there, imbibing Catholic views on abortion, contraception and sterilisation, for his projected book on ethics. He alternated his stays at Ettal with visits to the Kleist clan in Pomerania, with whom he had a long-standing friendship since his experimental Confessing Church seminary at Finkenwalde, which was supported by, among others, the Pietist Ewald von Kleist-Schmenzin, whom we have already encountered.

The son of the distinguished psychiatrist Karl Bonhoeffer, Dietrich grew up in a privileged upper-middle-class household in Berlin's Grü-newald, making his mark as a theologian at a remarkably young age. He travelled widely in America, where he acquired his love of Harlem and African-American spirituals – recordings of 'Swing Low Sweet Chariot' subsequently resounded around Finkenwalde. It was there too in 1931 that he first encountered racial discrimination, and the problem of how Christians should respond to it, when an international campaign was launched on behalf of nine young black men sentenced to death for allegedly raping a white female. Albert Einstein was quick to offer his support; the Lutheran clergyman Otto Dibelius refused it.[169]

This experience was subsequently incorporated into his understanding of the wider responsibilities to God and society of people in the professions. As vicar to the German church at Sydenham in south London, Bonhoeffer formed enduring friendships with English clerics, notably George Bell of Chichester. Adamantine in his defence of the Church against National Socialism, and active in building up an institutional framework parallel to a Church which had gone native, Bonhoeffer was acutely conscious of the persecution of the Jews, not least since this affected both his brother-in-law Gerhard Leibholz and his best friend and fellow theologian Franz Hildebrandt, both of Jewish origin. Through his father, who was a judge in a higher hereditary health court, Bonhoeffer was also intimately acquainted with Nazi eugenic policies. Partly on the basis of his own experiences of handicapped people at Bethel, he strongly believed in their special proximity to God, both in terms of their acuter awareness of human frailty and mortality and as a reminder of Christ's central earthly activity of healing. He modified civil rights concerns he encountered in the States to claim a basic human right to propagate, thereby keenly contesting the Nazi fetishisation of health and the hubristic enterprise of manufacturing 'perfect' people on the basis of reason and science.[170] In other words, Bonhoeffer believed in defending the Church but then extended that defence to all who were vulnerable to persecution. In April 1933 he wrote: 'The Church has an unconditional obligation towards the victims of any social order, even where those victims do not belong to the Christian community.' It was the Church's task 'not only to bind up the victims beneath the wheel, but also to put a spoke in that wheel'.[171]

He himself was gradually marginalised by the regime, being forbidden to teach, publish or visit certain locations in Berlin except the family home. Bonhoeffer gradually crossed a line between theological opposition to active resistance. It is important to stress that in 1939 he could have remained in America, but, like Moltke, consciously chose to return to Germany: 'I must live through this difficult period of our national history with the Christian people of Germany.' He learned about the Nazi 'euthanasia' programme from his father, whose Berlin successor Maximinian de Crinis and former assistant Hermann Nitsche were its leading culprits. Bonhoeffer *père* joined Bodelschwingh of Bethel in briefing Pastor Gerhard Braune with information he used in his famous memorandum to Hitler.

Having decided that the 'ultimate' necessitated the 'penultimate', Dietrich Bonhoeffer signalled to his brother-in-law Hans von Dohnanyi his willingness to work as an Abwehr special agent, no small step for a former pacifist.[172] His ostensible brief was to monitor his ecumenical friends, with whom in reality he was forging contacts on behalf of resisters within the Abwehr. To this end, Bonhoeffer undertook missions abroad, notably to Switzerland and Sweden. In Switzerland he alerted Willem Visser 't Hooft to the existence of the 'euthanasia' programme, which duly found its way into a BBC broadcast by Bishop Bell. During this meeting, Visser 't Hooft asked Bonhoeffer what he prayed for, and received the answer: 'If you want to know, I pray for the defeat of my country, for I think that is the only possibility of paying for all the suffering my country has caused in the world.'[173] In Sweden, Bonhoeffer secretly met Bishop Bell, in order to relay to His Majesty's Government the earnestness of the conspiracy against Hitler by revealing some of the names involved, and to secure a new German government from Allied attack, essential to neutralise any renewed talk of a 'stab in the back', should the resistance manage to kill Hitler.[174] Despite Bell's efforts, a British indisposition to distinguish Germans from Nazis, and the terms of Britain's alliance with the Soviet Union prohibiting separate negotiations with the enemy, meant that the ecumenical route to the British government proved fruitless.

Bonhoeffer's role in conspiracies against Hitler was not central, but his moral presence and legacy were substantial. He never mistook gestures for more substantive actions, enjoining a friend to follow patrons of a café saluting the fall of France: 'We shall have to run risks for very different things now, but not for that salute.'[175] He had strikingly uncomplicated views on political assassination, at least for a Lutheran theologian of a conservative political disposition. Although Bell's story about Bonhoeffer calling Hitler 'the Antichrist' is probably apocryphal, he did remark, 'No, he is not the Antichrist; Hitler is not big enough for that; the Antichrist uses him, but he is not as stupid as that man,' a formulation from which the Devil came out favourably.[176] Bonhoeffer exuded optimism when it was hard to see beyond the regime's successes, and gave moral support to a number of resisters – although Moltke found the combination of bookishness and radicalism as unappealing as Bonhoeffer found the count's equivocations about assassination – before and during his detention.

And finally there was the extraordinary strength of faith Bonhoeffer manifested during his long imprisonment – in Tegel military prison, Gestapo cells and Buchenwald. Arrested on 5 April 1943 in the course of investigations into the Abwehr, Bonhoeffer was sufficiently self-possessed gradually to persuade his interrogators to drop the most serious charges, for it was difficult to distinguish among his illicit and licit Abwehr activities, until he was fatally compromised by documentary evidence which surfaced in the wake of the 20 July conspiracy. Having discovered the dragging of prison time, Bonhoeffer developed a physical and intellectual regimen that soon left no time to spare. His parents, fiancée, and friends provided him with books unobtainable in the library of Tegel prison, books he used to make major departures in a new 'non-religious' theology, in which Christianity was reconciled with a contemporary, secular humanity 'become of age'. He won over many of his guards, while offering spiritual consolation to his various fellow prisoners, except when he found their views abhorrent. After more rigorous confinement in Prinz-Albrecht Strasse and Buchenwald, Bonhoeffer was hanged in early April 1945 at Flossenbürg concentration camp. Shortly before his death he told an Italian fellow prisoner 'that as a pastor he considered his duty not only to console or to take care of the victims of exalted men who drove madly a motor-car in a crowded street, but also to try to stop them'.

Bonhoeffer's Roman Catholic counterpart was the Jesuit priest Alfred Delp (1907–45). Whereas Bonhoeffer was a scion of the academic haute bourgeoisie, Delp came from modest circumstances in Hessian Lampertheim, a dormitory market town for factory workers in industrial Mannheim. The son of confessionally mixed parentage,

Delp was baptised a Catholic, but educated as a Protestant, until in 1921 he chose confirmation in the Catholic Church. Active in the Neudeutschland youth movement, he decided to join the Jesuit Order. Apart from the occasional indication that he was a demanding character, it was a life almost devoid of personality, lived out in a succession of seminaries. He underwent the noviciate at Feldkirch in the Vorarlberg, and then studied scholastic philosophy for three years at Pullach near Munich, before returning to Feldkirch as a schoolmaster in the Jesuit Stella Matutina. From 1934 he studied theology in the Jesuit house at Valkenburg in Holland and Sankt Georgen/Frankfurt, before being ordained in 1937, returning to Munich first as a preacher and then as editor of the Jesuit monthly *Stimmen der Zeit*. Influenced by Catholic Action, Delp was interested in the 'third idea' beyond liberal individualism and Marxist collectivism, and in Catholic solutions to social questions. In October 1941, the Jesuit provincial Augustin Rosch, who had recently formed a Committee for the Affairs of Religious Orders of the Fulda Bishops' Conference to combat Nazi attacks on religious orders, had a clandestine meeting with Helmuth von Moltke. Rosch subsequently introduced Alfred Delp and Lothar König to what became the Kreisau Circle. From Moltke's point of view, the Jesuits were a useful conduit to the Catholic episcopate and to south German resisters, such as the Bavarian monarchist circle around Franz Sperr. Delp's involvement had another unanticipated advantage. His keen interest in the social question – about which he produced position papers – helped socialists such as Mierendorff co-operate more enthusiastically with Prussian aristocrats.[177] Delp was arrested on 28 July 1944 while celebrating mass. He was tortured. A travesty of a trial took place between 9 and 11 January 1945. A Jesuit defendant enabled Freisler to discern an international 'Black' conspiracy, and to give vent to anti-clerical fury: 'No German would touch a Jesuit with a barge-pole!. . . . If I know there is a Jesuit Provincial in a town, it is almost a reason for me not to go to that town.'[178] Delp was sentenced to death and hanged on 2 February 1945. His last thoughts were, 'This was not a trial: it was simply a functioning of the will to annihilate.' By that date, 'the will to annihilate' had become general, as Nazism lashed out in a race to realise its destructive mission, while Allied bombs detonated across German cities, bringing indiscriminate death and destruction to the guilty and the innocent, and indeed to the 'solitary witnesses' of the resistance.[179]

10

'PLAYING A PART IN A FILM':
WAR AND PEACE, 1943–1948

Allied airpower, with aircrew drawn from 'Free Europe' as well as the UK and USA, played a vital role in disrupting the German economy and forcing Germany to divert enormous resources for home defence, which might have been deployed on the Eastern Front. Here, American aircrew return from a mission prior to the Allied invasion of Normandy in June 1944.

THE AMERICAN CENTURY

Hitler's decision to declare war on the United States of America in December 1941, as the invasion of the Soviet Union lost momentum, probably signified the moment when hubris solicited nemesis. The fight was hard and the prospects of an Allied victory far from certain, but from that point onwards the odds did not favour Nazi Germany. There seems no compelling reason to revise this widely held view, although hubris might be said to have characterised Hitler's whole political enterprise.[1] The declaration of war against America clarified the ambiguities of President Roosevelt's 'short of war' policy of openly assisting Britain, and then Russia, while transforming America into the 'arsenal of democracy'. Hitler miscalculated that the United States would focus upon the Pacific, or spread her efforts and resources too thinly between the European and Pacific theatres. In fact, the United States adopted a strategy of waging war on 'Germany first'. War resolved contradictions in Hitler's personal view of America. These included respect for America's economic dynamism, eugenic policies and stringent immigration laws, and indeed for the New Deal, together with European snobbery towards America's allegedly brittle and materialist culture. Hitler was an autodidact from a provincial central European backwater, hence he was ignorant of America's artistic achievements and liberal philosophical traditions, but then so were many central European intellectuals, who preferred the convolutions of Heidegger to American pragmatism.[2]

As relations with America gradually deteriorated, Hitler revised his view that America was an advertisement for the virtues of the displaced 'Aryan' race, in favour of the notion that America's Anglo-Saxon ruling elites were tools of 'international Jewry'.[3] His mind stuck in this groove, his universal explanatory key to all human history. He claimed that America was 'a decayed country', riven with racial tensions and social inequalities, it's society 'half Judaised and the other half negrified'.[4] Göring agreed, in assuming that America was a *quantité négligeable*: 'What does the USA amount to anyway?' In April 1942, Ciano accompanied Mussolini to meet Hitler at Salzburg. He caught the arrogant wishful thinking in circles which by then were dimly cognisant that the Soviet Union was not tottering on feet of clay, and whose geo-political and racial theories had withered under the blast of reality. There was a touch of fear apparent in a one-way conversation, itself symptomatic of the deficiencies of the Axis, in comparison with the developing Anglo-American dialogue:

> America is a big bluff. This slogan is repeated by everyone, big and little, in the conference rooms and in the antechambers. In my opinion, the thought of what the Americans can and will do disturbs them all, and the Germans shut their eyes to it. But this does not keep the more intelligent and the more honest from thinking about what America can do, and they feel shivers down their spines. Hitler talks, talks, talks, talks. Mussolini suffers – he who is in the habit of talking himself, and who, instead, has to remain practically silent. On the second day, after lunch, when everything had been said, Hitler talked uninterruptedly for an hour and forty minutes. He omitted absolutely no argument: war and peace, religion and philosophy, art and history. Mussolini automatically looked at his watch.[5]

Hitler gradually awoke to the creative, economic, intellectual and military potentialities he had stirred against himself, like a man surprised at the effects of poking a stick into a large beehive. In early February 1942, he commented on the American economy, in terms partially endorsed by modern historians of comparative wartime economies:

> The great success of the Americans consists essentially in the fact that they produce quantitatively as much as we do with two-thirds less labour. We've always been hypnotised by the slogan: 'the craftsmanship of the German worker'. We tried to persuade ourselves that we could thus achieve an unsurpassable result. That's merely a bluff of which we ourselves are the victims. A gigantic modern press works with a precision that necessarily outclasses manual labour. . . . In America everything is machine-made, so that they can employ the most utter cretins in their factories. Their workers have no need of specialised training, and are therefore interchangeable. We must encourage and develop the manufacture of machine-tools.[6]

There was more to the mobilisation of the United States than reconfiguring machinery to enable unskilled 'cretins' to operate them.

The extent of the ground to be made up was awesome. The American army, with 188,000 men under arms, ranked between those of Bulgaria and Portugal. Eight thousand men carried new Garand rifles; the rest had Springfields dating from the First World War. There were twenty medium tanks and only nineteen new B-17 bombers. When manoeuvres were held in Kentucky in 1940, rented trucks were painted with the word 'tank', and pie plates marked '.50 caliber' were glued on to rifles to represent machine guns. Discipline was poor and the men unfit. Promotion within the officer corps was by seniority, so that talented men had to wait decades to replace incompetent time-servers.

Some of the ablest minds in the country, from corporate business, the law and organised labour, were identified as having the skills to mobilise the economy for whatever war America or her allies had to fight. They staffed improvised super-agencies, for, although nowadays it is insufficiently remarked on, the Nazis had no monopoly in using charismatic personalities and *ad hoc* structures to bypass sclerotic bureaucracy. Long before Pearl Harbor, businessmen who were reluctant to risk conversion of capacity to arms production, or to be traduced from the left as 'merchants of death', were persuaded to do so under a formula sometimes described as 'involuntary voluntarism'. The process was assisted by contracts under which government assumed part of the risks of sudden reversion to peacetime. Hard-won union rights were guaranteed, and union leaders sometimes heard in high counsels, although strikes remained a problem which occasionally had to be resolved with force.

Some nine hundred thousand men were drafted from September 1940 for one year's service under the Selective Training and Service Act. Renewal of the act passed Congress in August 1941 by one vote, indicating the strength of anti-militarist and neutralist sentiment in America. The morale of these conscripts was successfully maintained, even though war seemed remote. Gigantic manoeuvres were held in Louisiana, Tennessee and the Carolinas. These helped identify hopeless commanders who were then retired. As General McNair put it, 'We're going to start at the top and work down. We've got some bum Generals, and maybe I'm one of them, but we're going to weed them out.' This cleared the way for the ascent of Bradley, Devers, Eisenhower and Patton, all names recorded in Chief of Staff George C. Marshall's 'little black book' of talent.[7]

Patton boosted morale through his imposing omnipresence, and such vivid *obiter dicta* as 'Misses do not kill, but a bullet in the heart or a bayonet in the guts do.' He sometimes included verse in his addresses to his troops:

> Ere yet we loose the legions –
> Ere yet we draw the blade,
> Jehovah of the Thunder,
> Lord God of Battles, aid!

In March 1942, Patton assumed command of a vast training camp in the California desert, designed to simulate combat conditions in North Africa. It was known as 'Little Libya'. As Patton put it: 'If you can work successfully here, in this country, it will be no difficulty at all to kill the assorted sons of bitches you meet in any other country.'[8] This was a warrior of the type that win wars. Economic mobilisation was achieved at a time of great changes in the nature of warfare, which engendered enormous uncertainties as to the kind of forces and inventory which needed to be assembled. By demonstrating the superiority of combined air and armoured spearheads, blasting a way forward for massed infantry, Nazi Blitzkrieg tactics exposed huge potential deficits in the equipment of America's existing armed forces. Not only did those responsible have to think about redesigning everything from helmets and rifles to bombers, fighters, field guns and tanks, but research and development had to be balanced against mass production, the economies of scale and efficiency of big business versus the social benefits of small firms, and so on.[9]

The simple statistics of economic mobilisation were remarkable. Factories worked an average of ninety rather than forty hours a week, with an estimated 25 per cent average increase in productivity. Government aid created massive new concerns to make up for deficits in aluminium or synthetic rubber.[10] All these things involved complex arguments about the advantages of concentration versus the dangers of monopolies, and trade-offs between such birthrights as driving cars at speed against the need to conserve scarce rubber. Assembly lines and prefabrication techniques were adapted to producing aircraft, ships and munitions, to a total value of $181 billion. The record for constructing a welded Liberty ship, 'built by the mile and chopped off by the yard', was fourteen days. A bomber emerged from Ford's sixty-seven-acre Willow Run plant near Detroit approximately every 108 minutes. By the close of 1942, American arms production equalled the combined total of Germany, Italy and Japan; by 1944 it had doubled it. In that year, America produced 40 per cent of the weaponry available to all combatants, bringing enhanced American suasion in Allied counsels. For many of these products were destined for America's principal allies: a declining empire centred on the world's oldest parliamentary democracy, a totalitarian dictatorship of unfathomable barbarity, and a corrupt China convulsed by Japanese invasion and Communist revolution.[11]

American aid to Britain commenced before Pearl Harbor with fifty superannuated destroyers exchanged for naval bases, and half of America's current aircraft production. It shifted gear in March 1941, when the exhaustion of Britain's dollar reserves resulted in the replacement of 'cash and carry' by Lend–Lease arrangements. Homespun metaphors abounded on both sides of the American interventionist and isolationist fence. Roosevelt spoke of not charging a neighbour for a garden hose required to extinguish a fire; Senator Robert Taft compared Lend–Lease to loaning chewing gum: 'Once it's been used, you didn't want it back.'[12] One of those to testify in Congress against the Lend–Lease Bill was Joe Kennedy, the less than helpful Irish-American former US ambassador to the Court of St James's, whose anglophobic influence was counterbalanced by Ed Murrow's powerful CBS broadcasts on the nightly ordeal of the British people.[13] American troops next replaced the British in Iceland, enabling American ships to protect supply convoys aggressively on that stage of the Atlantic crossing. Clashes with German submarines grew more frequent, despite the deciphering of German codes. German consular operations in the United States were closed down as 'subversive'. By September 1941, the US Navy was effectively at war with Nazi Germany in the Atlantic. From November 1941, Lend–Lease facilities were extended to Russia.

Huge volumes of materials, estimated to be worth between $42 and $50 billion, a third of which went to the Soviet Union, were shipped across the Atlantic. Those destined for Russia travelled on via Persia, and from Scapa Flow to Archangel and Murmansk. The air route was only marginally less perilous than maritime convoys. Some 74 per cent of Lend–Lease aircraft were flown from American factories across Canada to Alaska, where Soviet pilots took over for the long, cold flight across the featureless Siberian tundra.[14] This handover, and the Soviets' refusal to give the Americans information or intelligence about their economy and war effort, was qualitatively different from the Anglo-American relationship with its pooled intelligence, shared military facilities, combined commands and joint operations. Some nine thousand British diplomatic and military personnel spent the war on the Potomac. Roosevelt's belated attempt in 1943 to include Soviet observers at deliberations of the Combined Chiefs was stymied by the British Prime Minister, in the knowledge that these men were cyphers of Stalin, and that no reciprocal arrangements would be forthcoming at Stavka in Moscow.

There were certainly tensions between the Americans and British, a relationship best described as based on 'competitive co-operation', tensions occasionally evident at the highest level.[15] Churchill's more mercurial schemes irritated Roosevelt, while Churchill bridled at being marginalised within the emergent bigger picture of American post-war relations with the Soviets, towards whom Roosevelt exhibited an internationalist indulgence. On the American side, there was underlying suspicion that American arms were being used to salvage British imperial interests, or to prop up reactionary regimes, and scant appreciation of Britain's desire to practise traditional European balance-of-power politics instead of aggressive democratic internationalism. The two leaders also differed in their estimation of their lesser confederates. Roosevelt had little time for the exiled Poles, whose representative authority he doubted, or for General Charles de Gaulle, whom he regarded as a nobody and a nuisance. Having gone to war over Poland, and convinced that a strong France was in their long-term interest, the British had a European perspective on these issues. Britain's influence significantly waned by the end of the war, as was evident from the refusal of both Roosevelt and Truman to gang up beforehand with Churchill when they met Stalin, notably at Teheran and Yalta.

The alliance with the Soviet Union raised awkward issues. Curiosity about America's most exotic ally, whom Roosevelt met for the first time at Teheran, crumbling his Lucky Strikes into Dunhill pipes, soon entailed the sanitisation and sentimentalisation of a mass murderer. At the time this was not confined to the usual left-wing apologists for and worshippers of naked power, as the example of Britain's conservative press baron Beaverbrook independently demonstrated, with his toasts to 'the gentlemen of the Red Army'. Joseph Davies, former US ambassador to Moscow, and one of Roosevelt's chief intermediaries with the Soviets, brushed aside purges of 'measly anti-Stalinists' in his bestselling *Mission to Moscow* (1941), while Roosevelt sought to pin the blame for the Katyn massacres of Polish allies on Goebbels' Ministry of Propaganda rather than on 'U.J' (Uncle Joe). No attempts were made to use aid as a means of restraining use of the Red Army as an instrument to further otherwise highly unpopular Communist take-overs of eastern European countries, even if by that stage Stalin ostentatiously declined it. There was no conditionality or reciprocity. The consequences of this, namely the imposition of totalitarianism, were borne by the peoples of Russia's outer empire for half a century.[16]

Although the former Soviet Union minimised the contribution of Lend–Lease to the Soviet war effort, claiming that it was equal to 4 per cent of Soviet military production, a post-ideological generation of Russian scholars has begun to acknowledge its crucial importance. Without American deliveries of high-octane aviation fuel, totalling one and a half times Soviet production, the Russians could not have sustained significant air warfare, not to mention that by late 1943 about 80 per cent of the Luftwaffe were engaged in fighting the British and Americans, with huge numbers of dual-purpose guns subtracted from the Eastern Front to defend German cities. This argument works in reverse, for in the winter of 1941 events in Russia prevented Germany from maximising the number of aircraft deployed in Sicily to protect supply lines to North Africa, with most of the aircraft stationed in Sicily transferred to the Balkans, to replace those dispatched to Russia for the 1942 summer offensive. When the Allies invaded North Africa in November 1942, German aircraft and troops, which might have relieved those trapped at Stalingrad, had to be diverted to contain them. These interconnections between theatres mattered, and should not be lost from view through enthusiasm for Russia's undoubtedly remarkable war effort.

Nor might there have been so many Soviet aircraft, or T-34 tank engines, without the 328,100 tons of aluminium delivered by the Western Allies. For it remains otherwise hard to explain how, with half the aluminium at their disposal that the Germans had, the Russians managed to produce one and a half times more aircraft, unless there is something missing from Soviet official statistics, namely the Lend–Lease contribution. But beyond the mountains of spam and leather boots, there was another vital Western contribution to Russia's war. The operational mobility of Soviet ground forces in the latter part of the war was inconceivable without over four hundred thousand US vehicles to replace Russia's worn-out vehicle park, not to speak of rails and station platforms, nearly two thousand locomotives and over eleven thousand freight wagons. Without Lend–Lease, Russia's domestic economy would have consisted of disconnected pools of activity, while the Red Army would have had to march rather than ride, without its aircraft and tanks being in radio communication with one another. Without Lend–Lease, the Soviet Union's diminished post-invasion economic base would not have been able to concentrate on producing weaponry rather than consumer goods, food and machine tools.[17]

Apart from the contribution of Western capitalism, a further necessarily underplayed aspect of the Soviet war effort was the selective, and temporary, dismantling of Stalinist socialism. Militarily incompetent political fanatics and Party hacks, who bullied and intimidated professional commanders, were restrained, while traditional military hierarchies and elite forces were restored. A country whose leaders wished to hurl her into the future at any human cost rediscovered a temporary respect for tradition – whether in restoring military supply systems, dating from Tsarist times, or exploiting the power of prayer in soliciting victory.[18] More subtly, a heavily centralised and mobilised peacetime economy, with no room for expansion when disaster struck, was put into reverse gear, with greater tolerance of managerial autonomy and market mechanisms. A system which stifled individual initiative, with army commanders too terrified of being shot to sign orders to retreat, underwent a brief period of liberalisation under the pressure of necessity. Whatever else Russia's war may have been, it was no advertisement for Stalinist socialism. The prospect that a reformed socialism might ensue was not a compelling argument for the existing system, which reverted to type as soon as its elite leadership was in the clear. No reformed red dawn broke, bitterly disappointing those who expected relief for so much sacrifice.[19]

American aid was also crucial in maintaining Britain's maritime lifelines, it being in America's national interest to sustain peoples with whom it had bonds of language, kinship and political culture. More mundanely, the greatest concentration of industrial power outside the US itself could not be allowed to fall into Hitler's hands. Although the emphasis on Anglo-Saxon identity and destiny had rather sinister origins, as an elite's defence mechanism against non-Anglo-Saxon immigrants to the United States, nonetheless the two countries' elites were closely entwined, through business, education and marriage, with even the Prince of Wales passing up the throne for an American woman, and a series of 'Atlanticist' institutions, such as Chatham House, the Council of Foreign Relations and the Pilgrims and Rhodes Trusts which kept these sympathies alive.[20] Sympathy was far from automatic, and had to be advocated against those who had no special liking for the British, as exemplified by (Cambridge-educated) Quincy Howe's 1937 bestseller *England Expects Every American to Do his Duty*. Across the pond, there were also 'little Englanders' who would have endorsed Neville Chamberlain's view: 'Heaven knows I don't want the Americans to fight for us; we would have to pay too dearly for that if they had any right to be in on the peace.' Fortunately, these last views did not prevail.

The initial Anglo-American war effort concerned the battle for supremacy in the Atlantic. This was largely a war of technologies and tonnages. German submarines may have enjoyed much initial success in sinking Allied ships, but American shipyards increased their production from 1.16 million tons in 1941 to 13.5 million tons in 1943, while various technical innovations such as long-range aircraft, centimetric radar and convoy systems began to take the edge off German U-boat warfare. In late 1942, German submarines sank over seven hundred thousand tons of shipping, but following the summer of 1943, this fell to under one hundred thousand tons, with the maximum of seventy-three thousand tons achieved in the month before Germany's capitulation. Germany's own surface fleet was progressively confined to coastal duties or to the Norwegian fjords.[21]

The fortunes of war turned against Hitler, not just in Russia, where Stalingrad was an unmitigated disaster, impacting badly on domestic morale, but in North Africa, where Montgomery's victory at El Alamein broke Eighth Army's poor record against Rommel's Afrika Korps. The Allies read encrypted Axis radio traffic, enabling the British to anticipate Rommel's dispositions, and to sink supply ships according to what they were carrying. The British benefited from American supplies of tanks equalling those already available to them, and twice the number of their existing motor vehicles. Far from his fuel supplies, and without air cover, Rommel was ordered to stand and fight an enemy which then propelled him fifteen hundred miles across the desert. This was not the first or last instance in which Hitler insisted that commanders adopt tactics which flew in the face of their own style of warfare.

In November 1942, combined Anglo-American forces landed in French Morocco and Algeria. In keeping with an implicit Allied dual-track policy towards France, the Americans preferred to deal with renegade Vichy generals, excluding de Gaulle's Free French forces from the invasion. This was due to Roosevelt's keen animus towards the general, and the belief that a Free French presence would inflame Vichy

French resistance. The embarrassment of dealing with Admiral Darlan, Vicky's representative in North Africa, was resolved when he was assassinated on Christmas Eve 1942. Eisenhower described it as an 'an act of Providence'.[22] German resources which were desperately needed in Russia had to be diverted to North Africa, while they also moved into the non-occupied Vichy zone in metropolitan France. Although German reinforcements poured into a bridgehead in Tunisia, lack of co-ordination on the Italo-German side, and animosity between Rommel and his fellow panzer commander Arnim, resulted in Axis forces being penned in a pocket around Tunis, with their supplies cut off by Allied aircraft and naval blockade. German soldiers began to send farewell letters and personal effects to their families, which affected morale on the home front. Rommel was evacuated for reasons of ill-health, while 275,000 Axis troops entered captivity, the largest force to be captured to date. Germans dubbed this second disaster 'Tunisgrad'.[23]

Operation Torch in North Africa was the result of a series of complicated Allied trade-offs. It demonstrated the viability of combined command, and the feasibility of large-scale seaborne invasion. By contrast, although the German Commander-in-Chief South, Kesselring, enjoyed excellent relations with his Italian counterpart Cavallero, Rommel could circumvent both by appealing directly to Hitler. Intense battles, for example at the Kasserine Pass, provided American soldiers with a steeper learning curve than the bitter three-year induction of their British allies, while commanders of genius, such as Bradley and Patton, distinguished themselves further from the pack. The campaign in North Africa was significant in further respects. Anglo-American dealings with Darlan and General Giraud indirectly contributed to the promulgation at Casablanca in January 1943 of the doctrine of unconditional surrender, reassuring the domestic public, and Stalin, that there would be no separate peace with the Axis governments, or any section of the German elites, including those whose enthusiasm for Hitler had cooled in the interim. Roosevelt sprang the notion on Churchill shortly before the final press conference at Casablanca. The term was borrowed from the nickname of Ulysses Grant, 'Old Unconditional Surrender'. Churchill recalled that since Victory was not in sight, 'Defiance was the note'. He added of the doctrine: 'It is false to suggest that it prolonged the war. Negotiation with Hitler was impossible. He was a maniac with supreme power to play his hand out to the end, which he did; and so did we.'[24] Ironically, at about this time,

Stalin was undertaking soundings in Sweden with representatives of the German government, while forming a possible future government of Germany from among captured German officers. Whether these initiatives were designed to pressure the Anglo-Americans into launching a second European front or a low-cost means of inducing Hitler to pull back to the borders of 1941 (or 1914) remains unclear.[25]

The protracted North African campaign meant that there would be no invasion of northern Europe in 1943. Suspicious that the British had imperialistic agendas, the Americans extracted a commitment to invade France in May 1944, insisting on the return to Britain of forces from the Mediterranean, and refusing to squander troops in ill-conceived British adventures east of Italy. Churchill's schemes began to irritate Roosevelt. However much in line with traditional Britain's policy of flexing her naval muscles around the peripheries of a continental opponent, or influenced by fear of a repeat of the Great War bloodbath, if a landing became a stalemate, Roosevelt could see little sense in speculative diversions into the Dodecanese or the Balkans, when the crow-fly route to Berlin lay across France and western Germany. There was no point in 'wasting men and material in the Balkan mountains', where Greek and Yugoslav partisans seemed more intent on killing each other than killing German soldiers. The Chief of Staff General Marshall was loath to see a single American soldier 'die for Rhodes'. Neither Roosevelt nor Churchill was motivated at this juncture by any idea of forestalling the Red Army's conquest of eastern Europe, since their main concern was to keep the Russians fighting Hitler's Germany, rather than checking the advance of Communism.[26]

In July 1943, American and British troops landed in Sicily under Operation Husky. Their more temperamental commanders bickered their way across the island. Mussolini was forced to resign, with Badoglio's government announcing the cessation of hostilities that autumn, the prelude to a vicious civil war in the north of the peninsula and Italian intervention on the Allied side in the south. In line with long-laid plans, German troops were reassigned to Italy, where they disarmed their former confederates, who in any case had long demonstrated their 'unsoundness' in dealing with the Jews.[27] Pent-up German animosities were unleashed against these 'traitors'. About ten thousand Italian soldiers were summarily executed for allegedly passing their weapons to insurgents and partisans. Vengeful German soldiers also took the opportunity to loot Florentine jewellery stores or to rob people on Rome's streets of their wallets and watches. In some jointly occupied territories, or places which the Germans had to reconquer, their former allies were massacred. The worst incidents occurred on the island of Cephalonia, where an estimated five thousand Italian soldiers were murdered by German troops after they had surrendered.[28] Since Hitler could not tolerate humiliation of a fellow millennial man, German glider troops delivered Mussolini from confinement, to be installed as head of the puppet Repubblica Sociale Italiana at Salo on Lake Garda. Enormous quantities of idle munitions, including tanks and aircraft, were hauled north of the Alps, as were machine tools and entire armaments factories. A German war economy hungry for labour turned its covetous eyes southwards. That autumn, half a million Italian troops were locked into railway cars and shipped northwards, not as prisoners of war, but as 'military internees', who would later be used as forced labour. We will re-encounter them shortly.

Despite coming from a Luftwaffe background, Field Marshal 'Smiling Albert' Kesselring successfully organised both the extraction of up to eighty thousand German troops from Sicily, a sort of German Dunkirk, and a fighting withdrawal, based on the Gustav and Gothic lines, which ensured that the Allies had to fight for twenty months to gain control of Italy below the Po.[29] The ferocious fighting at Salerno, Anzio and Monte Cassino spoke for the stolid talents of this most unflashy of German generals, although his record was tarnished by the extremely harsh measures employed against Italian partisans, who were as hard to distinguish from civilians here as elsewhere.

The Allies' invasion of Italy brought their air forces within striking distance of hitherto inaccessible targets in southern Germany and eastern Europe. Specifically, Allied bombers, 85 per cent from the USAAF Fifteenth Air Force, carried out raids on the cities of Bucharest, Budapest and Sofia, designed to make Romania, Hungary and Bulgaria rethink their political allegiances. One unintended consequence was to make the inhabitants of these countries more amenable to Communist claims that at least the Soviets did not bomb women and children.[30] Finally, whereas the German army in Italy became reliant on significant numbers of unreliable 'eastern troops' for logistical support, or had to redeploy men from France or Russia, the Allies were able to subtract forces for the D-Day landings. The Italian campaign also forced Hitler to retain divisions in the Balkans, lest the Allies pursue Churchill's 'Vienna Alternative' of striking through the Ljubljana Gap into Austria, Greece and Yugoslavia, a strategy by now governed by the idea of inducing the Russians to keep their 'hands off Greece and Yugoslavia'.[31]

British-inspired prudence throughout 1942–3 regarding the timing of a landing in northern Europe required an emollient for Stalin, who suspected his allies were deliberately trying to bleed his armies to death. This was a product of his belief in a wider intra-imperialist anti-Bolshevik plot, in which the Anglo-American war with Hitler was a temporary form of false consciousness on the part of his 'real' opponents. For their part, the British took time to get over who had invaded Poland and the Baltic States, and who had been supplying Hitler's war economy until the eve of Operation Barbarossa. Placating Stalin was not the sole reason for the RAF and US Army Air Force strategic bombing campaign, but Churchill endeavoured to curdle Stalin's blood with the thought of the bombs raining down on German cities, fuelling Stalin's imagination with regular copies of Air Marshal Arthur Harris' infamous Blue Books containing photographic records of the devastation.[32] When the two leaders met in Moscow in August 1942, Stalin's froideur towards Churchill thawed when news of Operation Torch was followed by promises of a sustained strategic bombing campaign. Stalin suggested devastating houses as well as factories, although the British needed little encouragement. The two men then discussed likely targets, until, in Averell Harriman's words: 'Between the two of them, they soon destroyed most of the important industrial cities of Germany.'[33]

Faith in the ability of strategic bombing to deliver a knock-out blow to the enemy's industrial heartland had complex roots. Bombing would avoid the carnage of the First World War trenches; its cost-effectiveness had been established in aerial policing of desert tribesmen. Whether human or material, cost counted in democracies, whose citizens dreaded huge military casualties. Bombing was a demotic way of warfare, assuaging popular demands for vengeance against what seemed an undifferentiated pattern of German aerial aggression from Guernica, through Warsaw and Rotterdam, to London and Coventry. This was dubbed the 'Jupiter Complex' by one sceptical British government scientist, that is the desire to visit retaliatory thunderbolts upon the enemy. Furthermore, bombing reflected a democratic perspective on warfare. Its advocates assumed that civilian morale functioned much the same way in every political system, overlooking the fact that morale might operate quite differently in democracies from totalitarian dictatorships. One of the few to question this, realising that in a police state 'the concentration camp [was] around the corner', was Air Marshal Arthur Harris, who inherited, rather than initiated, the decision to pursue area bombing against Germany.[34] Yet in some respects Harris was also a prisoner of the Nazis' own perspectives, since it was they who attached critical importance to the collapse of *civilian* morale in losing Germany an earlier conflict.[35]

Harris was almost typecast for the role of villain that he has been made to assume. He bombed Germany with all the bloodymindedness of a man who once disabused a young constable, concerned that Harris' off-duty speeding might prove fatal, with the observation: 'Young man, I kill thousands of people every night.' In so far as he was troubled by ethical considerations, rather than the survival of his young aircrews, Harris convinced himself that bombing was 'a comparatively humane method', or at least no worse than naval blockade, with its slow and silent starvation of the elderly, the young or the mad during and after the Great War. One form of killing was direct and highly visible; the other indirect and invisible. Distinctions between the two were so much hypocritical squeamishness.[36]

Partly with an eye on America, both sides began the Second World War with attempts to avoid charges of having initiated all-out aerial warfare. However, the inaccuracy of bombing technology and the decision to attack at night to minimise heavy daylight losses meant that both sides shifted from precise military and industrial targets to indiscriminate attacks on cities. Coventry and Southampton were bombed by the Luftwaffe; Mannheim by the Royal Air Force.[37] Historical hindsight regarding the tactical employment and legality of earlier German bombing campaigns in Spain, Warsaw or Holland is beside the point. Few British people knew or cared about the niceties of German airpower after about forty-five thousand people had been killed in the Blitz against London and various provincial cities.[38] American and British cinema audiences were appalled by scenes of flames licking the walls of St Paul's, scenes which Roosevelt transposed to the urban canyons of Manhattan, should Germany dispose to transatlantic bombers. One of those watching London burning from the roof of the Air Ministry was Arthur Harris, who claimed that 'this was the one occasion and the only one when I did feel vengeful, and then it was only for the moment'.[39]

Following the Casablanca conference in January 1943, the British and Americans were committed to Operation Pointblank, the strategic bombing campaign against German cities. The Americans favoured precision daylight attacks by heavily armed bombers which could neutralise German fighters. This enabled them to claim the moral highground, always important when the Republic makes war, even as their bombs rained down indiscriminately through dense cloud from a vast height. The British clung to night area bombing as a way of destroying civilian morale through 'de-housing', but also as their uniquely independent contribution to an Allied war effort which was increasingly dominated by America and Russia. The RAF secured huge resources.[40]

Area bombing was a response to studies such as the Butt and Singleton reports in the 1930s which had established the technical impossibility of accurately bombing enemy factories. This led Bomber Command to refocus on the general 'de-housing' of entire cities, with bombers using a central mark (sometimes ironically docks or a factory) as an aiming point for carpets of bombs 'creeping back' on residential districts. Churchill's scientific adviser Professor Lindemann played a key part in winning this argument. When combined with devices which confused German radar, these tactics were used to terrible effect against Hamburg in July 1943, where according to a leading British expert 'there were no sizeable industrial establishments anywhere in the area that it was hoped to bomb. No part of the attack was planned to fall south of the river where the U-boat yards and other major war industries were located. It was pure Area Bombing.' Approximately forty thousand people died in a man-made inferno, with a further million rendered homeless.[41] The British press crowed with plebeian wit that 'Hamburg has been Hamburgered', needlessly echoing earlier German talk of towns being 'Coventryed'.

Bombing was and remains a highly controversial form of warfare, with endless possibilities for what is uncharmingly called 'collateral damage', despite the use of supposedly highly accurate smart munitions. It is uniquely dependent upon weather, which in north-western Europe permitted flying operations for an average of eight days a month. Since the Second World War, bombing has routinely fallen short of high strategic expectations, although its advocates claimed at the time that target priorities kept changing and expanding, so that its fullest possibilities were never explored. Bombing continues to raise ethical questions. At the time, it occasioned moral anxieties not just among the awkward or highminded, but even at the Buckinghamshire headquarters of Bomber Command. Stung by a moralising homily on the theme 'God is my co-pilot', delivered by the sententious socialist Stafford Cripps, which earned Cripps a rebuke from Churchill, Harris organised a riposte entitled 'The Ethics of Bombing'. The headquarters chaplain stood up at the lecture's conclusion and observed that the talk should have been called 'The Bombing of Ethics', a scene which would be hard to envisage at the headquarters of the Luftwaffe, let alone among those who conceived of Auschwitz. But as the Marquis of Salisbury observed to the Air Minister in 1943: 'we do not take the devil as our example'.[42]

Defenders of bombing, rendered uneasy by the grim reality of indiscriminately killing women and children, often stress the military risks involved. That chuntering slowly towards Germany in a freezing aircraft, to be harried by fighters and flak, was an unnerving experience can be gleaned from stories of aircrew resorting to lucky charms or the Bible, to counteract the psychological effects of the statistical probability of being killed, before thirty missions were over.[43] Whatever else it may have been, bombing was not the war of preference for the cowardly. About 140,000 Allied aircrew were killed, in circumstances which engendered compartmentalised thinking, and left little room for moral inhibitions. To follow moral relativists in equating it with the entirely risk-free enterprise of Nazi genocide is outrageous.[44]

Bombing's defenders follow the post-war Allied bombing surveys in highlighting the indirect effects of the strategic bombing campaign. The German war economy was driven underground or dispersed away from the cities. The economy gradually fragmented into regionally discrete units, which in turn made extended transportation routes highly vulnerable to aerial interdiction. In March 1944, it was estimated that two million people were needed to restore severed transport links, but there were only 180,000 railwaymen and 100,000 prisoners of war available. Those in charge of Germany's war economy concurred, by highlighting the disruption of freight transport as being most responsible for hampering Germany's ability to wage war: 'The development of the effects of air raids on production shows clearly that the effects of direct bombing, although still increasing (in spite of the very heavy raids in the first months of 1944), progressively declined in significance and in its proportional share in causing the decline in production *when compared with the extensive effects caused by transport difficulties* [my italics].'[45]

Significant volumes of enemy equipment and raw materials were diverted from the fighting fronts to home defence. Materials such as aluminium, which might have gone into producing forty-four thousand extra fighter aircraft, went into shell fuses for anti-aircraft guns. Moreover, without bombing, the German army would otherwise have disposed of double the quantity of field artillery that it possessed. Eight hundred thousand people had to operate air defence systems. Moreover, heavily armed Allied bombers, escorted by long-range Mustang fighters equipped with auxiliary fuel tanks, wiped out the Luftwaffe's own fewest of the few, seriously distorting the production of aircraft in favour of fighters rather than bombers.

Bombing also had indirect political effects on the enemy. It exposed the Nazi leadership to ridicule once it had failed the minimal test of any government, to protect its subjects from aggression. Malicious comments about Göring began to leach towards Hitler. Popular demands for retaliation against the British encouraged Hitler to squander resources equivalent to twenty-four thousand new fighters (or a functioning ground-to-air missile system) on the V1 flying bomb and V2 ballistic missiles, which never amounted to more than a vengeance-driven tokenism. Randomly destroying the odd London suburban street, however terrible for the unfortunate inhabitants, was not comparable with the Allies' destruction of entire urban districts.[46]

WHEN THE RUSSIANS CAME

If bombing represented a low-cost Western way of warfare, tailored to populations with recent memories of massive land-war casualties, no such inhibitions prevailed in the East. A relentless series of Soviet offensives throughout late 1943 and early 1944 forced the Wehrmacht backwards, a broad trend interspersed with localised German victories. By the end of this period, the Germans and their Axis allies had been ejected from the Crimea, the Caucasus and much of the Ukraine. Both the Hungarians and the Romanians, whose armies were destroyed in the Crimea, looked for exit routes from the war.

The reappearance of the Red Army and its NKVD appendages in the newly 'liberated' parts of the Soviet imperium was a very mixed blessing for their inhabitants. Liberation became a pretext for deportations and murder. NKVD units ran amok among the Crimean Tatars, raping women and murdering their menfolk, on the pretext that the Tatars had collaborated with the Nazis. In fact, the Nazis had routinely used Tatar prisoners of war to illustrate 'Mongol sub-humanity' in their disgusting publications. In May 1944, the First Deputy Minister for State Security, Ivan Serov, who in 1939 had deported Baltic opponents of Communist imperialism, began the round-up of all Crimean Tatars, regardless of whether they were former collaborators or bearers of the title 'Hero of the Soviet Union'. Up to 46 per cent of the Tatars perished on long train journeys to exile in Tashkent in Uzbekistan or to concentration camps in the Sverdlovsk region of the Urals, where they were joined by Tatars demobilised from the Red Army and returned from German captivity. Every trace of Crimean Tatar culture was obliterated, whether ancestral gravestones, place names or Marxist–Leninist tracts in their own language. Ukrainian settlers were bribed to take their place.[47]

Turkic Karachais, Buddhist Kalmyks, Balkars, Meskhetian Turks, Pontic Greeks, Kurds, Chechens and Ingush met a similar fate. Some of these peoples have disappeared leaving little trace, others, unsurprisingly, have major grievances against the Russians, which in the 1990s erupted into war. In late February 1944, nineteen thousand NKVD, NKGB and SMERSH officers descended on Grozny, the capital of Chechnya, under the supervision of Beria and Serov. They were accompanied by one hundred thousand NKVD troops. They swept through Chechen villages, using Lend-Lease-Lease Studebaker trucks to remove the inhabitants to waiting cattle wagons in Grozny station. Those deemed untransportable by virtue of age or infirmity were sometimes herded into barns and burned, or machine-gunned. With that symmetry Stalin savoured, Chechen Communists who aided the deportations were themselves deported. Within two weeks, Beria could report to Stalin the successful deportation to Kazakhstan of nearly half a million people. Crammed forty-five to a car for a rail journey which lasted a month, many perished, including large numbers of children.[48] Within five years, a quarter of the Chechen population had succumbed to maltreatment and starvation. Their culture was obliterated, with even the gravestones being used to repair roads.[49] Since these deportations included Chechens who had defended Brest-Litovsk in 1941 against the Germans or Crimean Tatar partisans and Red Army veterans, the motive for their deportation was unlikely to have been collaboration with the Nazis, but the desire to purge Moslems from the borderlands with Turkey.

Hitler's refusal to countenance controlled retreats was partly determined by the vital importance of the Ukraine to the German war economy. Retreat to purchase space and time was no longer an option. It also reflected his psychological disposition towards holding designated fortress strongpoints, until his favourite Nazi 'firefighting' generals, such as Model or Schörner, could relieve them, a policy which led to disaster during the Red Army's next summer offensive. By contrast, the Russians carefully analysed and learned from their earlier mistakes, although these sources have only recently been declassified.[50] In consequence, during 1943–4 they had rolled back the Germans up to six hundred miles in some sectors. The human effort involved in traversing these huge distances was best conveyed by a long sequence of unedited newsreel footage of Russian soldiers dragging themselves across the knee-deep saltwater inlet of Lake Sivash, which Andrey Tarkovsky included in his autobiographical film *Mirror*. The newsreel cameraman was killed on the day he shot these scenes. Thanks to myriad efforts such as these, the Red Army stood poised in early 1944 to strike into Finland in the north and Hungary and Romania in the south, with only Army Group Centre clinging on to a protruding salient in Belorussia.[51]

In the summer of 1944, as German forces were belatedly rushed to contain the Allied landings in Normandy, the Soviets launched Operation Bagration, a series of multi-front strategic offensives designed to knock out entire German army groups. Army Group Centre were expertly deceived into imagining that the blow would fall either to the south or north of them by fake radio traffic or aircraft patrolling non-existent concentrations of Russian forces. Artillery units fired salvoes before being replaced by mock weapons; loudspeakers broadcast the juddering noise from massed tractor engines. Entire Russian armies redeployed silently at night or when inclement weather made aerial reconnaissance impossible. German military intelligence digested what the Russians fed them: 'the Soviet main effort would continue in the South towards the Balkans, where it would take advantage of the clearly shaky state of Germany's allies and finally establish the long-coveted Soviet hegemony in southeastern Europe. North of the Pripyat Marshes, the Eastern Intelligence Branch predicted the front would stay quiet.'[52]

Prior to the offensive, which coincided with the third anniversary of Barbarossa, partisans disrupted German communications and rail traffic. The Red Army had also internalised many of the Wehrmacht's own doctrines, combining mobility with massive air strikes, for which the forty serviceable aircraft which the Luftwaffe had in place were no match. A Soviet force of one and a quarter million men punched a two-hundred-mile hole in the German front between Ostrov and Kovel. Since many of Army Group Centre's forces were located in cities such as Minsk, the Russians swept past them, ironically having mastered enveloping tactics once used by the Germans themselves. Three hundred and fifty thousand German troops were captured, an even greater loss than the numbers forced to surrender at Stalingrad or Tunis. This indisposition to die fighting was indicative of demoralisation at the level of the ordinary *Landser*, and of officers too junior to warrant the massive bribes Hitler used to maintain the fighting spirit of his senior commanders. Worryingly, Hitler's satraps in what remained of the 'German East' noted that the fleeing soldiery seemed utterly bereft of fighting spirit, sometimes failing to destroy equipment they had abandoned, or throwing away their own light weapons. Troops had to be corralled on army training bases so 'they would again resume the orderly form that the German people expect of their armed forces'.[53]

Hitler refused permission for Army Group North to link up with the remnants of Model's Army Group Centre, leaving an entire army marooned in the Baltic. The Germans succeeded in checking the momentum of the Soviet advance towards Warsaw and into East Prussia, but in the south the Red Army entered Romania. King Michael I accepted Antonescu's departure and declared a ceasefire. Hitler bombed Bucharest in an attempt to replace the government of General Constantin Sanatescu with the Iron Guard leader Horia Sima, hitherto held in a German concentration camp. Romania declared war on both Hungary and Germany. The Red Army captured the Ploesti oilfields and in September linked up with Tito's forces in Yugoslavia. A few days after Romania's change of heart, the Finnish leader Mannerheim sued for a truce with the Russians, with Hitler having to accept the withdrawal of German forces from Finland. Since he simultaneously tried to retain control of the Petsamo nickel mines and the island of sur Sari, Finland was forced to declare war on Germany to forestall Russian occupation. She succeeded.

Bulgaria was the next to attempt to change sides, after the Soviet Union had declared war and occupied it anyway. German forces began the long retreat from Greece, back to their Croatian ally, leaving remnants cut off on the Greek islands. Although German forces checked Russian and Romanian incursions into Hungary, the Regent Horthy had had enough, unilaterally announcing a ceasefire. Hitler's one-man miracle weapon, Otto Skorzeny, the saviour of Mussolini, was deputed to arrest Horthy. A new government under the Arrow Cross leader Ferenc Szálasi continued to fight on the side of Germany. Two Russian armies converged on Budapest. If an isolated Army Group North managed to cling on to greatly reduced territories in the Baltic, while a Soviet thrust into East Prussia was repulsed at Gumbinnen, the Red Army's next major offensive would be into the Reich itself.

Two final aspects of the Bagration offensive may be highlighted, since they successively illustrate both the criminal degeneracy of the Nazi regime and Stalin's roving eye for the main political chance. First, as the Russians crossed Belorussia, they encountered a 'desert zone', with a million houses burned, crops deliberately ploughed under, and no evidence of livestock. Men had either defected to the partisans, or had been abducted for forced labour in Germany. In so far as the cities and towns had not been destroyed, Russian sappers had to deactivate, as in Minsk, up to four thousand delayed-action bombs, mines and booby-traps. There was no trace of the Jews, either alive or dead, although this was not a major concern to Soviet forces.

Since mid-1942, a secret unit called Einsatzkommando 1005, under Paul Blöbel, the former commander of Einsatzgruppe C's Sonderkommando 4a, had been disinterring shallow mass graves, whose locations Blöbel and his SS colleagues were well placed to know, since they had carried out many of these atrocities themselves. Initially, this ghoulish operation was conceived as a response to environmental problems, contaminating air and water, but it became a race to destroy physical evidence before it was uncovered by the Russians. Corpses were stacked and burned on pyres made of railway sleepers doused with oil or petrol. A bone pulveriser obliterated the very last physical traces, not excepting the Russian and Jewish prisoners who were forced to perform these tasks before being murdered. Incredibly, as we will see below, as this unit endeavoured to obliterate evidence of past crimes, the SS and their indigenous confederates were simultaneously engaged in murdering Jewish populations which had hitherto survived.[54]

In July 1943, Soviet troops in the Lublin area entered the Majdanek extermination camp, whose material by-product, clothing, pens, shoes and toys, was piled high in a warehouse on Lublin's Chopin Street. Russian troops reflected upon the emptiness of eight hundred thousand pairs of empty shoes. Requests from Hitler Youth units for bed-linen or crockery, or from a local woman for a pram and complete layette, did not improve the tempers of the Soviet soldiers who were escorted through the camp.[55] At no point did Soviet military newspapers mention the fact that the victims were mainly Jews; instead they spoke of 'Soviet citizens'. Soviet troops overran the former sites of Belzec, Sobibor and Treblinka the following summer. They were sites, because all of these camp installations had been carefully dismantled, and replaced with farmhouses made from the bricks of the gas chambers, and planted with lupin and pine. The farmhouses were occupied by former camp guards and their families, their primary purpose being to prevent local peasants from disturbing the camouflaged sites by searching for valuables glinting amid the ashes, sand and splinters of bone.[56]

Soviet liberation of Nazi extermination camps – most of whose ambulant survivors were already on death marches into the interior of the Reich – should not lead us to overlook the role of the Red Army as a political instrument facilitating Communist usurpations. These things happened simultaneously, so they deserve to be discussed in parallel, without forcing causal connections or using one to mitigate the other, as some seek to do. Accounts which pass over these things in silence are lopsided, and open to charges that human misery is ethically divisible and subject to something akin to sole proprietorship.

In Warsaw, General Tadeusz Bor-Komorowski took the momentous decision in early August 1944 to trigger Operation Tempest, a rising by the underground Home Army. His intention was to liberate the Polish capital, so that Stalin would have to treat with the exiled Polish government rather than impose his own Communist regime on Poland. Had they done nothing, the Poles would probably have been accused of collusion with the Nazis by a Soviet leader whose antipathy towards them was deep-seated. Curiously, they seem not to have learned from the suppression of the rising in the Jewish ghetto a year earlier, notably the need to lay in effective stockpiles of arms and supplies.

Stalin's pre-primed instrument was not the pre-war Polish Communist Party, whose exiled Trotskyite leaders he had murdered in the late 1930s, but a so-called Polish Committee of National Liberation, a group of stooges under the close supervision of Soviet security agencies. The Polish Workers Party, established in 1941, has been described by a leading British expert as 'hardly having enough native Polish communists to run a factory, let alone a country of some thirty million people'.[57] Curiously, the Warsaw Poles also believed the sincerity of calls from the Moscow-based Radio Kosziusko for an uprising, and mistook the appearance of one Soviet tank in the suburb of Praga as evidence of a larger Soviet force. Their own arms were also dispersed throughout the Polish countryside.[58]

The alacrity with which Field Marshal Walter Model, Hitler's 'firefighter', rushed forces to check the Russians' progress towards the Vistula city indirectly doomed the rising. So did Stalin's refusal to allow American aircraft to land on the hundred or so Russian airbases within an hour of Warsaw, following long-haul supply drops originating from bases in Bari. Churchill and Roosevelt contemplated ordering aircraft to land without permission.[59] It was indicative of Stalin's hatred of what he dubbed 'adventurers and criminals' that when he authorised a belated supply drop as a sop to Churchill and Roosevelt, the canisters lacked parachutes.[60]

One of the major atrocities of the Second World War was perpetrated against Warsaw's population. Himmler relished the opportunity to 'extinguish' the Polish problem definitively. His commander of anti-partisan operations, Erich vom dem Bach-Zelewski, received the men and tools for the job. As well as SS and police units, Azeris, the renegade Kaminsky brigade and Ukrainians, too intoxicated to be of much use, the infamous Dirlewanger Battalion descended on Poland's capital. Fresh from a tour of duty incinerating Belorussian villagers in barns or herding old women and children into minefields, followed by combat against the Red Army's assault on Army Group Centre, this dastardly crew were unleashed on Warsaw.

The Battalion's nucleus of poachers had been augmented by recruits from the SS detention centre at Danzig-Matzkau and from military jails at Anklam, Bruchsal, Glatz and Torgau. Convicted SS homosexuals, paedophiles, rapists, sadists, thieves and murderers, who had chosen their German victims badly in a formation where these activities were standard operating practice against lesser races, were joined by larger numbers of criminals and some political prisoners from Auschwitz, Buchenwald, Dachau, Neuengamme and Sachsenhausen. One Afro-German, eight sterilisees and a few Gypsies were subsequently sent back lest they compromise the racial tone. Some of the political prisoners immediately defected to the Russians, although Dirlewanger's public execution of a deserter on the first day, and random beatings, hangings and shootings thereafter, fostered group solidarities.

Hardened SS troops, who themselves used women and children to shield advancing armour or routinely massacred prisoners, watched as Dirlewanger's men stormed heavily defended apartment buildings, simply throwing the captured occupants out of fourth- or fifth-storey windows. Civilians lying in underground hospitals were machine-gunned, along with their doctors and nurses. Anyone who moved was shot – in the case of women, routinely after having been raped and robbed, by men whose arms and fingers were covered with looted jewellery. The casualty rate in Dirlewanger's Battalion was startling, with 860 men reinforced by 2,500, but only 648 emerging alive from the fighting. Some shot each other in alcohol-induced fury. Apart from gas, flamethrowers, flooding and remote-controlled tracked robots called 'Goliath', used to carry explosives into buildings, titanically proportioned siege mortars were deployed, like the 150-ton 'Karl'. These could lob a heavy projectile up to four miles, which, crashing to the foundations of buildings, collapsed them under the force of the explosion.[61]

Forty thousand civilians were executed in the first five days, with a quarter of a million dying during the retaking of the city. After the insurgent remnants surrendered, the remaining civilian population was expelled or evacuated. German sappers then demolished over 80 per cent of Warsaw, blowing it apart on a street-by-street basis. An entire city was erased from the map, as if it were a latterday Carthage or Persepolis.[62] Perhaps nowhere else was the moral turpitude of the Nazi regime brought into sharper focus, with the bureaucrats and lawyers who operated the murderous executive state, whose horrors were uncovered at Majdanek, dependent on the dregs of its own camps and prisons to commit mass murder, with distinguished Wehrmacht generals then congratulating them on the felicitous outcome.

Beyond Warsaw, Home Army forces which co-operated with the Russians in liberating Lviv and Vilno were offered the choice of joining Berling's Communist army or being sent to the gulag. Their officers were shot by the NKVD. Their offence was to have sought the liberation of territories which Moscow had already decided no longer belonged to Poland. Although exiled Poles contributed over two hundred thousand men to the Allied war effort, comprising 20 per cent of RAF fighter pilots, not to speak of infantry or airborne troops who fought desperately at Monte Cassino and Arnhem, Home Army leaders and democratic politicians were invited to a meeting with General Ivanov, abducted and subsequently convicted of collaboration with the Nazis at show trials in Moscow. Some received ten-year prison sentences. This despicable treatment of people who, from a British perspective, had been fighting Nazi Germany since September 1939 led to a chill in relations between Stalin and Churchill, whose consequences were tempered by Roosevelt's continued faith in the former as his co-architect of the post-war 'world order'.[63]

As the Red Army sledgehammered its way into eastern Germany, the Western Allies landed in Normandy, with a sophisticated campaign of deception indulging German expectations that invasions were planned for Norway or across the Pas de Calais. Moreover, the Germans anticipated an assault on a major port from which to disembark supplies and reinforcements, failing to consider that the Allies might bring *ad hoc* harbour installations, or pump fuel through a cross-Channel pipeline. Huge reinforced-concrete gun emplacements, built by the Organisation Todt, along the French coast indicate the difficulty of predicting where the blow would fall. German commanders were hopelessly at loggerheads about whether to repulse an invading force on the beaches, ranging their forces along a lengthy coastline, or to concentrate them inland as a mobile reserve wherever they would be most effective. While the uncertain location of the attack recommended this last strategy, it also made movement of these forces highly vulnerable to Allied aircraft. The latter included ten thousand combat planes, against an initial Luftwaffe complement of three hundred. These forces interdicted bridges, marshalling yards and railway lines not already destroyed by the French resistance, critically delaying the ability of German forces to prevent ever growing numbers of Allied men and *matériel* from coming ashore. When weather permitted, waves of tactical aircraft with cannon and rockets or dropping high explosives and napalm annihilated once formidable, but already depleted, armoured formations.[64]

Weather was crucial in another respect: the Allies had the far-flung meteorological stations to predict breaks in a temporary depression, while the Germans, having lost their weather stations, were reduced to drawing the wrong conclusions from the Channel's billowing waves and grey skies. After agonising delays and the turbulent Channel crossing, the Allies came and they conquered[65] – five thousand ships, carrying 175,000 men from twelve nations, protected by six thousand aircraft. Localised German resistance kept Allied forces fighting among the hedgerows for several weeks, until cut down by massive air attacks, but, by late August, French and American troops had entered Paris. The Vichy leaders and sundry fascist collaborators slithered away to Sigmaringen in southern Germany.

In the three months from June to September 1944, the German army had lost one and a quarter million men killed or missing to either the Western Allies or on the Eastern Front. There was one embarrassing issue linking both theatres. In the weeks following the D-Day landings, British and American units took increasing numbers of Russian-speaking captives, dressed in the field grey of Europe's quondam racial elite. These were former prisoners of war who had been pressed into German service, the alternative being to fall into the clutches of a Soviet dictator who regarded captivity as a form of ideological contamination and hence as a passport via filtration centres to the gulag. There was no equivalence between them and British prisoners of war liberated by the Russians, for, whereas the latter were keen to return home, this could not be said of many of the former, who began to threaten suicide when confronted with this prospect. Having first denied the existence of such people, at a dinner in Moscow, Stalin told Eden that 'he would be extremely grateful if any arrangements could be made to get them back here'. Since Eden's own view was that 'we cannot afford to be sentimental about this', repatriation was not difficult to arrange. Soviet liaison officers toured British camps, reassuring the inmates about their future treatment. Since some of those put aboard ships bound for Odessa had cut their own throats in their eagerness to return to the workers' paradise, these visits could not be deemed successful. According to British witnesses, ironically aboard the ship *Empire Pride*, some repatriated prisoners were machine-gunned within earshot of them on the quayside, while the rest were sent to the gulags. But this is to anticipate some of the less than glorious aspects of the alliance between Western democracies and a totalitarian dictatorship.[66]

In mid-December 1944, Hitler essayed his final major offensive amid the fog and snow of the Ardennes forest. The objective was to cross the Meuse, and then to converge on Antwerp, encircling American forces and denying the Allies a major port from which to resupply their armies. The example of Frederick the Great seems to have informed the political strategy: to shatter the morale of the Western Allies so that they would settle for something less than total victory, enabling Hitler to concentrate his remaining forces against the Soviets in the East. Of course, as some of his commanders appreciated, as they discussed these operations in an underground conference chamber, with an SS guard glowering from behind each chair, there was little prospect of success, not least because the terrain, with its hills, woods, canals and villages, was inherently unsuited to mobile warfare. Initial German advantages in terms of deceiving the Allies as to their intentions, or the poor flying conditions, were neutralised as the American army doubled its motorised infantry forces in four days and trebled its armour. Heavy German tanks were immobilised by lack of fuel, since they had no reserves and were dependent upon capturing the fuel drums of their enemies.[67]

BENEATH THE BOMBS

The Nazi leadership's bizarre and self-conscious terminus with destiny had ramifications for millions of ordinary people, including ordinary Germans, that rather unsatisfactory way of describing people without significant political power. If Hitler was no longer in control of events, these people were utterly at their mercy. To omit those Germans who languished in camps or prisons, or silently prayed for the end of a regime they had never supported, not to speak of those blasted or incinerated by bombing, adolescent boys thrown into an unwinnable war, or women raped by invading soldiers is to caricature the human tragedy of this conflict. While it may have been psychologically necessary, at the time, to filter these people from the consciousness of those waging war against Nazi aggressors, there seems scant reason to do so from the perspective of more than half a century, whence a certain magnanimity, rather than undying vengeance, may be in order. Of course, it is also unsatisfactory to depict all German civilians simply as 'victims', for, as we shall see, they sometimes created victims of their own, complexities which may lead some to wonder whether the trinity of victims, perpetrators and bystanders may require future refinement.

What follows is a story of the progressive isolation of a leadership determined to go down in flames from an increasingly atomised civilian and military mass increasingly bent on personal survival. The latter literally lost faith, and had to confront a terrible inner emptiness. This development of separate paths between rulers and ruled was a gradual process.

America's entry into the war disturbed many Germans, who realised that her enormous untapped resources contrasted unfavourably with their own war economy, which rationalisation was squeezing to the limits.[68] The unanticipated defeat at Stalingrad, and the prolongation of the war through a third gruelling winter, began to sap Hitler's personal prestige. Having deftly exchanged the unpopular brown Party uniform, with its odour of graft and corruption, for the Wehrmacht's field grey, Hitler committed the demagogue's cardinal error of secreting himself in remote command centres. He rarely addressed the nation, or sought to improve morale in devastated cities, which led even his closest supporters to make adverse comparisons with Churchill, who was often seen grimly picking his way through rubble.[69] Dictators are never a laughing matter, least of all to themselves. By the spring of 1943 Hitler had become the butt of popular jokes, none of which seem funny, but of which retirement to write a book called 'My Mistake' at least borders on the amusing.[70] Moreover, Hitler's over-identification with military strategy became a personal liability. When disaster struck, the blame attached to him. Victory at Stalingrad was trumpeted by an over-eager propaganda apparatus, with nothing to smooth the way for the dismal reality of ninety thousand men tramping off into Soviet captivity under a newly appointed field marshal. Ulrich von Hassell noted the consequences of Hitler's close involvement in the campaign:

> For the first time Hitler was not able to get out from under the responsibility; for the first time the critical rumours are aimed straight at him. There has been exposed for all eyes to see the lack of military ability of 'the most brilliant strategist of all time', that is, our megalomaniac corporal. This was concealed up to now by a few intuitive master strokes, the lucky results of risks that were in themselves unjustified, and the short-comings of our enemies. It is clear to all that precious blood has been shed foolishly or even criminally for purposes of prestige alone. Since strictly military affairs are involved this time, the eyes of the generals were opened, too . . . It is significant that Hitler did not dare to speak on January 30! Who would have believed this a short time ago?[71]

SD reports on opinion were more circumlocutory, but much may be read between the lines. People had grown weary of the repetitive use of terms such as heroism or sacrifice in broadcasts and the press. The exceptional was reduced to the quotidian, and hence lost its emotional purchase.[72] They questioned the inevitability of such sacrifices, and began to argue the strategic toss, aided and abetted by gossipy telephonists or army paymasters who became global strategists while on leave. Military demoralisation began to spread to civilians, as it had done in 1918.[73] Why had aerial reconnaissance not detected such a build-up of encircling Russian forces? Who had so grievously underestimated the resilience of the Red Army? Would the army in the

Caucasus meet the same fate? Some saw this as the turning point of the war; others the beginning of the end. It was no longer a matter of victory, but of bringing the war to a more or less satisfactory conclusion.[74] There was evidence that the regime's anti-Bolshevik horror propaganda, and the abuse heaped upon the Western 'Luftgangsters' was not having the desired impact. Workers emboldened to vent Marxist sympathies expressed the view that conditions under the Russians could not be worse than what they were experiencing, since, at most, the Soviets would 'liquidate' a few capitalists, testimony of a sort to the survival of *Ressentiment*. Other workers felt that things would not be so bad were the Americans to 'dictate' the peace, 'for they will only try to do business, and their capitalists will need the Germans'. In western and southern Germany, Catholics and monarchists began to look forward to being part of an imminent 'Anglo-American sphere' of influence.[75] People ceased using the salutation 'Heil Hitler', reverting to 'Grüss Gott' or 'Guten Tag', and distanced themselves from both leadership and Party.[76]

Monitoring of reactions to Hitler's speech on Heroes Memorial Day, delivered a week late on 21 March, indicate that his oratorical skills had become rusty. Listeners were relieved that Hitler was not injured or unwell – SD code for rumours that he had gone mad – but disappointed that he gabbled through the speech in a flat monotone. Some maliciously attributed his alacrity to an Allied air raid. There was no explicit reference to Stalingrad. Hitler's claim that only 542,000 German troops had died in the war to date, encountered considerable scepticism, as did his view that the Eastern Front had stabilised.[77]

If the Eastern and Southern fronts brought nothing but gloom, the impact of the Allied strategic bombing campaign upon German morale and production was more ambiguous. Although as the Marquis of Salisbury noted at the time, one should not cite Hitler as an excuse for anything, it is important to bear in mind that in September 1940 the Führer publicly promised that: 'If the British air force drops two, three, or four thousand kilograms of bombs, we will drop a hundred and fifty thousand, a million kilograms in one night. If they announce that they will attack our cities on a large scale – we shall wipe out their cities! We shall put these night pirates out of business, so help us God! The hour will come when one of us will crack, and it will not be National Socialist Germany.' Speer attended a supper that year at which Hitler spoke of the Great Fire of London:

Have you ever looked at a map of London? It is so closely built up that one source of fire alone would suffice to destroy the whole city, as happened once before, two hundred years ago. Göring wants to use innumerable incendiary bombs of an altogether new type to create sources of fire in all parts of London. Fires everywhere. Thousands of them. Then they'll unite in one gigantic area conflagration. Göring has the right idea. Explosive bombs don't work, but it can be done with incendiary bombs – total destruction of London. What use will their fire department be once that really starts![78]

Beginning with the raid on Lübeck in March 1942, Allied bombers operated around the clock when weather permitted, against targets in north and north-western Germany, with occasional forays against more southerly locations such as Augsburg, Munich and Nuremberg. The gross statistical effects of these raids included 305,000 people killed and nearly eight hundred thousand injured. One million eight hundred thousand homes were destroyed, and twenty million people deprived of basic utilities, and nearly five million people evacuated.[79] Emergency housing programmes proved inadequate, with people crammed together in increasingly insalubrious circumstances in cellars or bare Nissen huts.[80] The sustained intensity of Allied bombing raids on Germany militates against simple comparisons between the effects on civilian morale in Britain and Germany. In the baldest terms, ten times more German civilians were killed than the number who perished in London and British provincial cities. Bombing may have sometimes intensified local solidarities, inducing a business-as-usual mentality among the tradespeople of Lübeck, while leading to a collective desire for revenge, but the former was not much in evidence in cities such as Hamburg, where the Allies caused a major catastrophe in July–August 1943, nor was there compensatory retaliation with 'miracle weapons'.

For this was what the victims wanted – as they put it – meeting 'like with like' ('Gleiches mit Gleichem'). What did they mean when they argued, as security police reports make plain, that Germany should abandon her hitherto allegedly 'humane' conduct of the war?[81] Fortunately for their enemies, talk of compressed-air and rocket-propelled super-guns, nerve and respiratory gases or atomic bombs devastating British cities remained in the realm of wishful thinking, not to mention rumours of a thousand Japanese kamikaze pilots being brought by U-boat to attack England.[82] The Nazi regime talked up retaliation in response to popular demand, and then talked down when neither a 'baby Blitz' on London between January and March 1944, nor the use of V1 flying bombs and V2 ballistic missiles achieved the anticipated dividends.[83] Other propagandistic appeals fell flat. When Allied bombing generated unexpected solidarities, with intellectuals and Roman Catholics appalled by the destruction of Cologne cathedral, an over-emphasis upon destruction of the German cultural heritage provoked anger among workers more concerned with the deaths of women and children: 'Germany can live without Cologne cathedral, but not without its people.'[84]

Constant Allied air raids exposed not only the inability of Hitler to retaliate in kind, but also the porosity of Germany's air defences. Blame increasingly adhered to Hermann Göring, the butt of many jokes, although it should have included Hitler too, who by this time was increasingly dictating air-war strategy. Instead of producing large volumes of standardised fighters, Hitler believed that air defence was best left to flak crews on the ground, while the air force should conduct a retaliatory bombing offensive against Britain, in which quality of machine would defeat mere quantity. The bombing offensive by ill-trained Luftwaffe pilots in medium-range or mechanically unsound heavy bombers disintegrated against British air defences. On Hitler's instructions, new fighter aircraft, including Me 262 jets, were squandered in repulsing the Allied invasion of Normandy, leaving Germany virtually defenceless in the air for the rest of the war. The consequences for the civilian population were terrible.[85]

The major raids were devastating, leaving survivors dazed by concussion, coughing and spluttering, and the dead so reduced by heat that their corpses could be carried in suitcases. The four nights of Operation Gomorrah against Hamburg accounted for the equivalent of two-thirds of the bombing fatalities caused in Britain throughout the entire war. Subject to over a hundred minor raids, Hamburg had hitherto evaded the fate of Cologne. Literally so, for in May 1942 severe storms over northern Germany led the RAF to redirect the first thousand-bomber raid from the Hanseatic port to the Rhineland city.[86] In late July 1943 Harris ordered nearly eight hundred aircraft into a sustained assault on Hamburg, with the RAF alone dropping 8,344 tons of high-explosive and incendiary bombs on its northern residential districts. Since considerable efforts had been made to lessen the impact of fire-bombing on Hamburg, with sand stored or spread to extinguish incendiary devices which penetrated housing, the impact of these raids was especially demoralising.[87]

Summer temperatures of 30 degrees centigrade combined with low humidity meant that the bombs started a fire in a sawmill and timber yard which then combusted with fires elsewhere. According to RAF airmen, it was 'like putting another shovelful of coal into a furnace'. Freak air currents spread a storm of fire across a four-square-mile area. People on the streets flashed into flames, while those huddled in shelters died asleep as the fresh air was replaced by lethal gases and smoke. Others were transformed into fine ash. By the time the raids ceased, forty-five thousand people had been killed, and a further thirty-seven thousand injured. Nine hundred thousand people had also lost their homes.[88] Expectations that raids such as this would force a collapse of civilian morale or rioting in the streets proved unfounded, but up to two-thirds of the population of Hamburg fled the city between the raids, spreading despondency and panic into the countryside. About a quarter of the population of Berlin left the city between March 1943 and March 1944, while the population of Würzburg halved during the war.[89]

Opinion is divided on the impact of bombing on industrial production and morale. This is largely because the Allies' post-war bombing surveys worked with dubious information and notions of how the German war economy had functioned, partly derived from self-serving sources such as Albert Speer, but also because they sometimes sought to confirm their own presuppositions. If the direct impact of bombing on war production was as low as is often claimed, then why were so many men and munitions redeployed from the land war to defending German cities? At a minimum, area bombing placed a ceiling on many of the key features of Speer's rationalisation of war production, namely preventing the concentration of production in fewer large-scale enterprises, which lay at the heart of his intentions. Dispersal of production ensued, which made transportation links vulnerable to further bombing.[90]

The effects of bombing on popular morale are harder to determine. The British Bombing Survey Unit concluded that 'there is no indication that his morale reached breaking-point as a result of air attacks. . . . Even the mounting toll of casualties failed to break the hold which the Nazi Party had over the German population. As Speer has said: "the outlook of the people was often poor, but their behaviour was almost excellent".'[91] They had no means of assessing the impact of homelessness, sleeplessness and frayed nerves on efficiency at work; indeed they were not looking for this, but rather signs of contagious mass panic and its political consequences. The American bombing surveys studied popular opinion in a more systematic way, and discovered that one in three Germans claimed that the factor most affecting their morale had been Allied bombing. But they too were primarily focused on how this failed to translate into political trouble, thereby failing to understand the reality of life under a police dictatorship.[92]

The evidence from contemporary German sources is more ambiguous. Civil servants and local government officers were slow to return to work in devastated cities, with only seventy-eight of two thousand municipal employees reporting for work in Krefeld four days after the raids.[93] On the other hand, in December 1943 thirteen large employers in Berlin reported that very high percentages (85–99 per cent) of their workforce had reported for work shortly after major bombing raids, including contingents of foreign workers.[94] After the war Karl-Otto Saur testified that 'the workers and their families, German and foreign alike, tried with almost incredible perseverance to get to their places of work as usual in spite of all the difficulties'.[95] There was a different picture at Ford's in Cologne or BMW in Munich, where respectively a quarter and a fifth of the workforces absented themselves from work.[96] But no firm conclusions can be drawn from such patchy evidence.

One inadvertent result of the collapse of local government was a partial revival in the fortunes of the Nazi Party and its formations. The Party may have been widely synonymous with graft and privilege, but in this context formations such as the Hitler Youth or People's Welfare distinguished themselves putting out fires, organising the clearing of rubble, identifying and burying the dead, and helping those affected by bombing to reconstruct their lives.[97] By late 1942, all forty-two Party Gauleiter had become Reich Defence Commissioners, with responsibility for civil defence, a role which some, such as Hamburg's Karl Kaufmann, in other respects an obnoxious individual, performed with distinction in the wake of the summer 1943 raids on the city. Typically, the Reichsführer-SS added a quotient of insanity. In February 1944, Himmler informed a gathering of German civic leaders that bombing should be regarded as a time of opportunity, enabling them to impress their names on the history of their cities, by replacing the ruined architecture of a discredited 'liberal era' with true National Socialist buildings.[98]

Whatever local solidarities were fostered by bombing, it created unbridgeable realms of experience, which contradicted rhetoric about the 'national community' united in adversity. In a country with strong regional affinities, disproportionate concentration of bombing on the north and west led to complaints that the victims had been 'written off' by the remote Berlin authorities.[99] Among miners living in Düsseldorf the refrain was 'Dear Tommy, please fly further on your way; spare us poor miners for today. Fly instead against those people in Berlin; they're the ones who voted Hitler in.'[100] Solidarity between cities fragmented; for example, the inhabitants of Würzburg refused to countenance the relocation of industries from Schweinfurt lest the factories act as magnets for the bombers. People huddled together in communal air-raid shelters resented being bossed about by wardens and, their nerves tested to breaking point, bickered and fought with each other.[101] Unsurprisingly, not a few people went completely mad. Rumours suggested that Party bosses and other prominent people enjoyed customised air-raid shelters.[102]

The adverse effects of war on the family – not least wives looking elsewhere for sexual satisfaction which their soldier husbands received in military brothels, and a generation of wild fatherless children – were compounded. Families hitherto spared conscription were separated as the father went to work in a relocated factory, school-age children to one rural district and mothers and infants to another. This atomisation of the population into ever smaller 'communities of fate' continued beyond the end of the war, as did the progressive redefinition of roles within the family, with neither wives nor adolescent children prepared to subordinate themselves to the returning father.[103]

Bombing had repercussions beyond those immediately affected. Victims of bombing regarded themselves as a species apart, requiring special consideration from those hitherto spared their ordeal. There were the bombed and the unbombed. Nobody seemed to grasp what the former had suffered. After a major raid, public transport was inoperative, factories and workshops were covered with dust and rubble, there was no water to wash or shave with, or electricity or gas for cooking, heat or light, and something as commonplace as a plate or spoon became a cherished possession. If they ventured out, there were no cinemas or theatres, newspaper kiosks or shops, but the considerable risk of delayed-action bombs and falling masonry.[104] Evacuees and refugees from the major cities spread word of exaggerated casualty rates, and told lurid stories to their shocked rural hosts of women drowning their infants or human torches being shot by the SS in the streets.[105]

Survivors of urban raids, whose evacuation was sometimes insensitively handled, also sought to assert a total moral claim on hitherto unaffected country folk, with whom they often had little in common. Complaints ranged from having to rise too early, to being fed 'pig food', by which they meant such regional delicacies as *Kirschknödel* in the Alpine regions or *Bratkartoffel mit Quark* in Pomerania. Some evacuees were grossly exploited as cheap labour, although a number of them acquired the peasant trick of extorting valuables in return for food from fresh waves of urban refugees.[106] Peasant households in turn resented the owners of hundred-bedroom mansions who successfully resisted housing evacuees,[107] and, in regions where their own taciturnity was proverbial, the constant inane chatter of garrulous urban refugees.[108] More subtly, as evacuees from Hamburg to southern Germany discovered, the Nazis' bureaucratisation of charity and welfare meant that individuals no longer felt any sense of social obligation to people they sometimes referred to as 'Gypsies'.[109]

Of course, the impact of bombing was not confined to the home front, but began to affect military morale. For if troops on leave from the Eastern Front sowed despondency about the fighting qualities of the Red Army, so they themselves wondered what they were fighting for when they found their homes in ruins.[110] Ugly confrontations occurred when soldiers who had spent weeks searching for lost relatives demanded that broadcasters make announcements seeking their whereabouts. For the German military was not immune to collapsing morale. It began, as in the First World War, among troops in occupied and rear areas, or in reserve barracks on the home front, where the devil made work for idle hands. There were regular complaints about the *dolce vita* conditions prevailing in France, where 'there is no unity, no common will, no readiness to sacrifice, only whoring, boozing, self-indulgence and feasting, no will any more to win at any cost'. Overmanned rear-area bases and headquarters were rife with petty corruption, while the mood of those in German barracks was bleak. Officers had to be reminded that their cynicism and weariness might adversely affect morale, while thoughts turned to creating a class of Nazi political commissar.[111] Soldiers on leave tried to wise up their relatives to the realities of war *à outrance*, but frequently seem to have encountered blank incomprehension.

The task of maintaining morale on the domestic 'fighting front' devolved on Goebbels, aided by a judicial and police state which acted ruthlessly against dissenters. Exemplary death sentences were handed down by the People's Courts to those who impugned the leadership's conduct of the war. On 18 February 1943, Goebbels played upon fear of Bolshevism to prepare and rouse the nation for further exertions, obliquely seeking to bounce Hitler into sanctioning more drastic mobilisation of the economy and society than he had been prepared to countenance by dint of Germany's alleged experiences in 1918. European civilisation was menaced; only intensified mobilisation of the German population without regard to social position would save the day. War was declared on those in starched collars and on 'fine ladies' with permanent waves in their dyed hair. In other words, purely tactical Europeanism was allied with Jacobinism in a combined appeal to fear and resentment.[112]

Goebbels spoke to a hand-picked but allegedly 'representative' audience gathered in Berlin's Sportspalast. The first rows consisted of the blind, halt and lame, including fifty holders of the Oak Leaf Cluster of the Knight's Cross with their Red Cross nurses. There were also token workers, intellectuals and scientists, and a scattering of women. It was indicative of Goebbels' flight from reality that he mistook this audience for a 'cross-section' of the German people.[113] Countering the Panglossian view that life under the Soviets would not be too bad, he claimed that 'Behind the onrushing Soviet divisions we can see the Jewish liquidation squads – behind which looms terror, the spectre of mass starvation and unbridled anarchy in Europe.' This was said with an eye on the Western Allies and neutrals, in the vain expectation that they might be co-opted into checking the advance of the Soviets. In a lengthy digression on the Jews, Goebbels almost let slip the unspeakable when he remarked: 'Germany in any case has no intention of bowing to this threat, but means to counter it in time and if necessary with the most complete and radical exter— [*corrects himself*] elimination of Jewry'. For the speech, interspersed with cries of 'Out with the Jews', was being broadcast live to the nation just after eight in the evening. This was followed by calls for the German people to shoulder some of the burden weighing down their lonely leader, whose miscalculations had brought catastrophe upon them. Goebbels reverted to type by pandering to demotic resentment, conjuring up rich *bons vivants* in clubs and restaurants, or riding in the Tiergarten.[114]

He reached the rhetorical crescendo, a series of challenges and responses. 'Do you want total war? (*Loud cries of 'Yes!' Loud applause.*) 'Do you want it, if necessary, more total and more radical than we can ever imagine it today?' (*Loud cries of 'Yes!' Applause.*)[115] The shouting and stamping continued twenty minutes after the speech had ended. According to SD reports the speech was well received, although some people wondered why full mobilisation had not been adopted earlier.[116] Even these expressions of doubt were too much for Goebbels, whose diaries record his criticisms of the SD monitoring service as being too attuned to disheartened Berlin civil servants.[117] But the restored mood proved evanescent against both the steady stream of military disasters and the persistence of manifest wartime inequalities.[118] As Speer discovered, later that evening at Goebbels' residence, the passion he had heard was an actor's playing on the psychology of a carefully selected and rehearsed audience, it being worrying that the actor was confusing this atypical audience with the mood of a country.[119] In fact, these exhortations to heroic death and sacrifice bore scant resemblance to the mood abroad in Germany. As the population shrank from anything tainted with 'ideology', it sought solace in the Churches, for so much grief and loss required greater consolation than the Nazi leadership's hate-filled tirades could afford them.[120]

KILLING THE JEWS AT ALL COSTS

At a time when some Germans began citing the fate of the Jews to counteract their own government's use of horror propaganda regarding bombing or the conduct of the Russians, the Nazi leadership sought relief from events it could not control by pushing to completion the core mission of exterminating the Jews. The two things were psychologically interconnected, in so far as the Jews were used as scapegoats for the otherwise inexplicable. If they were eliminated, then all would allegedly be well, for surely they held the ultimate key to Allied invincibility and Axis malperformance? Axis reverses on the battlefields of Europe acted as a spur to the destruction of those Jewish populations which had so far eluded the 'Final Solution of the Jewish Question'. The largest surviving European Jewish population was in Hungary, consisting of some eight hundred thousand souls. About four hundred thousand lived in Trianon Hungary (the reduced Hungarian state that emerged from the Habsburg Empire), over three hundred thousand in territories Hungary acquired by aligning herself with Hitler. There were also thirty-five thousand refugees from Austria, Germany and Czechoslovakia. For all of these people, Hungary was an unstable raft amid a raging sea of barbarity, but from the Nazi view this community reminded them of unfinished business before the Reich succumbed to an apocalypse of its own making.[121] How had Hungarian Jews, about one hundred thousand of whom were converts to Christianity, come to this pass?

After the First World War, Hungary suffered from what might be called the 'Trianon complex', with latent resentments towards the Jews amplified by the country's diminished economic and territorial base. It had entered that war as a privileged part of an empire; it left it as a small nation of no great consequence. Under the authoritarian–conservative Regent (for life) Miklós Horthy, an admiral in a land with no navy, successive Hungarian revisionist governments sought to regain territory on the back of the diplomatic upheavals wrought by

Nazi Germany and Fascist Italy, while reducing the alleged predominance of Jews in commerce and the liberal professions through four 'Jewish Laws' introduced between 1938 and 1941. As in Fascist Italy, these measures partly reflected the radicalising influence of Germany, but also in this case indigenous antisemitism.[122] However, unlike Italy, these measures were also a strategy whereby radical right populist prime ministers sought to appease and contain the extreme fascist right, increasingly dominated by the Arrow Cross movement of Ferenc Szálasi. For the latter's social-revolutionary goals and pronounced working-class support were a threat to the continued dominance of aristocratic conservatives. The desire to lay hands on the property of Jews might spiral out of control, affecting the property of conservative magnates who had hitherto encouraged and tolerated the Jews as a surrogate native bourgeoisie.[123] Where such measures would ultimately have led is a moot point, but it is debatable whether without Nazi pressure interacting with the indigenous fascist right a Hungarian Holocaust would have happened.[124]

Hungarian complicity in Nazi anti-Jewish measures quickened with the invasion of Russia. In August 1941, over eighteen thousand 'stateless' Jews were deported to Kamenets-Podolsk in the Ukraine, where they were murdered by the Einsatzgruppen. In January 1942, Hungarian troops themselves carried out massacres of Serbs, Jews and others in Novi Sad in northern Serbia. Popular outrage felled Bardossy's government, and resulted in a Hungarian war crimes trial in 1943, although four of the accused fled to a ready refuge in Hitler's Germany.[125] Jews were also press-ganged into penal labour battalions attached to Hungarian forces on the Eastern Front, where they witnessed massacres of Jews, before their own remnants struggled back from Voronezh with the defeated Hungarian Second Army.[126] Those Hungarian Jewish forced labourers who worked in German-controlled territories gradually drew Nazi attention to the one major anomaly in a Europe otherwise 'Judenrein'.

Hitler's personal involvement in the destruction of Hungarian Jewry was very, very close. In April 1943, he lectured Horthy at Klessheim Castle on the 'parasitic' character of the Jews. He stated baldly that in Poland:

> if the Jews did not work, they were shot. If they could not work, they had to succumb. They had to be treated like a tuberculosis bacillus, with which a healthy body may become infected. This was not cruel, if

one remembers that even innocent creatures of nature, such as hares and deer, have to be killed, so that no harm is caused by them. Why should the beasts who wanted to bring us Bolshevism be spared more? Nations that did not rid themselves of the Jews perished.[127]

In subsequent talks with the Hungarian ambassador Döme Sztojay, Ribbentrop indicated that he knew of Hungarian approaches to the Americans and British, in which protection of Hungarian Jewry was a bargaining gambit, coupling this intelligence with criticism of the 'stagnation' of antisemitic legislation. This attempt to exert crude diplomatic pressure on the Hungarian government was rebuffed by the Prime Minister Miklós Kallay, who in a speech declined to 'resettle' the Jews, so long as no destination had materialised, an extremely deft way of embarrassing the Nazis.[128] Faced with mounting evidence that the Hungarians were about to emulate the Italians in making peace, in February 1944 Hitler ordered preparations for Operation Margarethe, the occupation of Hungary. Unusually, Hitler included in the Wehrmacht's marching orders the intelligence that Hungary's imminent defection from Axis ranks was the result of treason on the part of reactionary aristocrats 'related to Jews'.[129] While two mechanised divisions moved into Hungary, Hitler met Horthy at Klessheim Castle, forcing him to reconstruct his government. Döme Sztojay became prime minister. Hitler also remarked that 'Finland had only six thousand Jews and what a subversive activity even these performed against Finland's standing her ground further.' Horthy agreed to supply one hundred thousand Jews as forced labour for Speer's underground aircraft factories. He saw this as an opportunity to get rid of unassimilated Jews, whom he hated.[130]

A large SS and police contingent followed on the heels of the invading army, including a two-hundred-man Special Task Force led by Eichmann which had already planned its operations while based at Mauthausen. It was an experienced team, including Franz Abromeit, Theodor Dannecker, Hermann Krumey, Franz Novak and Dieter Wisliceny. They moved into offices in the Budapest Hotel Majestic, conveniently located next door to the headquarters of the Hungarian police force. The morning after the occupation, a central Jewish Council was organised, in order to get a collective purchase on the Jewish population.[131] Eichmann's team used the occasion to furnish their quarters with canvases by Watteau and a grand piano, donated by terrified Jews.[132] Wisliceny simultaneously established close working relations with three figures newly appointed to the Hungarian Interior Ministry, namely Laszlo Endre, the Minister, Laszlo Baky, the civil servant in charge of the police, and Laszlo Ferenczy, the head of the gendarmerie. All three were dedicated antisemites.

As long as they had direct control over the Jewish population through the Council, the SS could relinquish the socio-economic exclusion of the Jews to the Hungarians themselves. Sztojay's government passed a long day drafting and passing further antisemitic legislation. Businesses designated Jewish were closed, farms expropriated, and Jews excluded from the professions still open to them. Their books, cars, radios and telephones were confiscated. Identification followed, with the Catholic Cardinal Seredi fighting a rearguard action to exclude the not inconsiderable number of converted Jews from wearing the Star of David. While Dannecker led arrests of over eight thousand named Jewish individuals, many simply doctors and lawyers culled from the telephone directory, Eichmann fine-tuned the imminent deportations with his Hungarian interlocutors. The country was divided into six zones. Hungarian gendarmes would collect Jews from rural areas and concentrate them in urban ghettos, prior to their removal to zonal camps. The decision to commence deportations in the two most easterly zones was a result of the proximity of the Soviets, and a way of fostering the illusion that Jews in the Magyar heartlands would be safe, while those in more exiguous territories were sacrificed. In each zone Jews were expelled from villages, after which their houses were ransacked, and they were then robbed blind by the gendarmes at local and regional collection points. Several people expired while being tortured to reveal the location of hidden valuables. Each zone was systematically combed, until the Hungarian police snatch squads reached the suburbs of the capital. In Budapest itself, where two hundred thousand Jews lived, Jews were forced into apartment buildings near factories and stations where their presence was supposed to deter Allied warplanes. The number of apartments allocated to them was subject to constant contraction. Since the planned deportation of Budapest's Jewry was not likely to pass unnoticed, it was intended to organise a series of explosions and attacks on policemen, which together with evidence of alleged Jewish currency speculation would legitimise arrests and deportations. This technique had been employed in Paris.[133]

The first trial deportation trains left Hungary in late April 1944, with the deportees compelled to send reassuring postcards from a place called 'Waldsee', which the recipients on the Budapest Jewish Council could not locate on any map. Someone looked more closely at the pencil-written addresses, noticing the letters '-itz', still visible after Auschwitz had been erased and corrected to 'Waldsee'.[134] Following interventions by Eichmann with Himmler, locomotives and goods wagons sufficient for four forty-five-car trains per day were made available, while a Reichsbahn conference in Vienna in early May, which Hungarian gendarmes attended, planned the least logistically and politically troublesome route. Each train containing three thousand people, that is twelve thousand deportees per day, was escorted by Hungarian gendarmes as far as Kassa, where German authorities took over for the rest of the three-day journey to Auschwitz. By this stage, these Jewish people had no luggage or personal possessions, only the clothes they were wearing. Given the enormous scale of the task, a number of practised mass murderers were seconded to Auschwitz, including the former commandant Rudolf Hoess. The latter, promoted to deputy chief of the Inspectorate of Concentration Camps in November 1943, requested temporary secondment to his former post to preside over what was immodestly called 'Aktion Hoess'. Crematoria were refurbished, chimneys reinforced, new railtrack laid, and forty- to fifty-metre incineration pits dug for the anticipated difficulties in disposing of the bodies. Human fats were recycled from there to boost the intensity of the crematoria. The Auschwitz inmate Sonderkommando was increased to 860 men, together with a further two thousand to sort the loot in the 'Canada' warehouse. Of 438,000 Hungarian Jews sent to Auschwitz, about 10 per cent were selected for extermination through labour, the rest being reduced to smoke and fine dust.[135]

There was one unanticipated delay in the destruction of Hungarian Jews. On 6 July 1944, Horthy announced that he would no longer tolerate the deportations. Ten days later he asked Hitler to remove all SS and Gestapo personnel, and declared his lack of confidence in Sztojay's government. Endre and Baky were arrested. Hitler expressed his extreme displeasure, demanding immediate measures against the Jews of Budapest, a demand backed up by the dispatch of two additional armoured units to Hungary. Eichmann carried on regardless of Horthy, consigning to Auschwitz seventeen hundred Jews from a camp thirty kilometres outside the capital. When Horthy learned of this, from the Jewish Council, he halted the train at the border and the Jews were brought back. Eichmann determined to hoodwink Horthy, whom he privately referred to as 'the old fool' ('der alte Trottel'). A few days later, Eichmann detained the entire Jewish Council in his offices, where they sat until late in the evening, fretting at the imminent curfew, while trucks took the Jews Horthy had just reprieved to Rakocsaba, where they were entrained to their deaths. It was this devious implacability which makes some baulk at the triteness of the term 'banality of evil' to describe such people, for it does not quite convey the willlingness of those concerned to circumvent or surmount each and every obstacle.

Furious at this chicanery, and aware of how the strategic wind was blowing, Horthy announced in August that Budapest's Jews would be dispersed to camps in the interior. Eichmann appeared to be recalled to Berlin, where the dissolution of his team was announced. They went to the Plattensee to recuperate. If Horthy was planning to switch sides, this was frustrated by the arrival of Erich von dem Bach-Zelewski and the Nazi 'Übermensch' Skorzeny, who kidnapped the Regent's deputy and son and flew him packed in a crate to Mauthausen. The Geza Lakatos government was duly replaced by that of the Arrow Cross leader Szálasi, with his bizarre blend of Christian messianism and Hungarian chauvinism. Eichmann returned to Budapest. Since the Auschwitz operation had closed down, Eichmann demanded that the Hungarians march fifty thousand Jews to the border with Austria, while the remaining Jews of Budapest were to be confined in a ghetto. Three columns of Jews set off on the 150-kilometre odyssey. Those who arrived were detained in Mauthausen. Despite Soviet encirclement of the Hungarian capital, Eichmann and Dannecker persisted in organising transports of Jews to the Reich, until they left with the last German troops to flee the city. Culpable beyond redemption, and developing a martyr complex of their own, these men performed their tasks with the punctiliousness of bureaucrats switching the lights out before leaving the office.[136]

Those Jews who survived these death marches to Germany were often destined for SS underground armaments factories. As the borders of the Nazi 'New Order' contracted, so the SS inner industrialised camp empire expanded in those areas not constantly blighted by Allied bombing. This sometimes entailed moving plant underground. One notorious hell-hole was the subterranean complex hewn under the rocks of Kaunstein in northern Thuringia. Former anhydrite and gypsum mines were used in the 1930s to store chemicals and fuel in a series of side bays. In late August 1943, an advance party of inmates from Buchenwald were moved to Kaunstein to convert the mines into a vast underground factory for the serial production of V2 rockets. This initial group was used to blast and drill assembly halls, being forced to sleep in unventilated side shafts, where they were disturbed by periodic explosions, the noise of cement mixers and pneumatic drills, and clouds of dust. The walls were dripping wet. Movement was only possible in whatever light came from carbide lamps penetrating the swirling dust, with prisoners tripping over cables in the dark to the accompaniment of incomprehensible shouts and savage blows. Each working shift was twelve hours long, and consisted of shifting heavy rocks by hand. Any signs of weariness, such as not moving at double time, resulted in lethal assault by the SS guards. There was no water; sawn-off petrol cans provided primitive sanitation. Nearly three thousand prisoners died between October 1943 and March 1944 in this preparatory stage of the operation. A further one thousand sick inmates perished on the long slow route to Bergen-Belsen and Lublin once their labour power had been used up. Albert Speer congratulated the camp commander on the alacrity with which he had the factory up and running, being characteristically impervious as to how this feat had been achieved.[137]

Thereafter, as many as twelve thousand camp inmates were transferred to what became a separate camp complex known as Dora-Mittelbau I, with its own ring of up to forty satellite camps, Mittelbau II, III and so forth, housing nearly twenty thousand people. By March 1945, this scattered complex contained about forty thousand prisoners. Under the indifferent gaze of German engineers and foremen, notably the chief rocket scientist Professor Wernher von Braun, prisoners worked on subterranean assembly lines, producing up to six hundred rockets per month, as well as other munitions. Prisoners suspected of sabotage were incarcerated in a special set of cells where they were tortured by the SD or hanged from steel girders suspended over the factory floor by a crane. Others were horribly beaten by the SS on the initiative of civilian foremen and managers. By the end of each working day, a heap of corpses had accumulated next to the first-aid station – prisoners who had collapsed or been done to death by their guards. According to survivors, these heaps of human beings were as remarked upon as worn brushes or broken tools.[138]

In March 1944, a thousand mainly tubercular slave labourers were transferred from Dora-Mittelbau to a 'recuperation camp' at Bergen-Belsen on the Lüneburg Heath. They joined a few thousand so-called 'privileged' Jews, with foreign papers, whom the SS wished to use as bargaining counters. From the autumn onwards, camp capacity swelled as prisoners were brought from camps threatened by Soviet advances in the East. Even those who had survived Auschwitz found conditions in Bergen-Belsen dreadful, with people eating grass or licking food spilled on the ground. Neither wired into the SS economic empire nor a dedicated extermination centre, and with a remit which for the SS was a contradiction in terms, Bergen-Belsen was a fetid shambles. Yet more and more inmates were somehow crammed in, with disease and starvation killing fifty thousand of them before they were liberated by the British.[139]

These miserable human beings were at the extreme range of a gigantic army of voluntary, forced and slave 'foreign labour' inside Germany during the closing stages of the war. The highest recorded figure of nearly eight million foreign civilians and POWs was reached in August 1944. Deployed to release non-essential German men for military duties, while making it superfluous to utilise the labour power of German women, lest this demoralise the German war effort, 'foreign workers' were subject to conflicting lines of Nazi policy, of which a constant was racism, modified only by military circumstances or the exigencies of the war economy. Simply speaking, the SS security police sought to isolate foreign workers from the German civilian population through a host of degrading and discriminatory measures, ranging from the demeaning identificatory symbols attached to their clothing through to beatings for under-performance, or public execution of certain categories of foreigners for consorting with German women. The SS sought to impose this racial-ideological way of seeing things, regardless of the consequences for the productive capacity of foreign labour, or whether their ever more complex racial hierarchies did not conform exactly with the inherited prejudices or empirical experience of the German population. Since the very notion of introducing more 'foreign blood' was anathema in these circles, draconian policies towards foreign slave labour were a form of compensation for a blatant ideological compromise.

By contrast, those responsible for managing the war economy sought to alleviate the dire conditions of many foreign workers, not for 'sentimental' reasons, never at a premium in Nazi circles except concerning the Germans themselves, but because this would enhance their productivity. The inhumanity of these 'pragmatists' can be gleaned from a policy statement by Fritz Sauckel, as the chief procurer of foreign labour, situated midway between the Speers of this world and the implacable racial dogmatists. 'It must be remembered', he averred, 'that the output even of a machine is conditioned by the amount of fuel, skill and care given to it. In the case of men, even of a low type and race, how many more factors must be considered than in the case of a machine!'[140] These distinctions were temporary and tactical rather than absolute, for there was scant evidence of any concern from the 'pragmatic' camp, when German arms were conquering Russia and labour was relatively abundant, regarding the deaths of three million Soviet prisoners of war or, to put it at its minimum, the mysterious exodus of Jews who might have been used as labour. Had German military fortunes revived, it is doubtful whether more would have been heard from advocates of liberalisation, vis-à-vis those whose plans encompassed the crushing of the eastern occupied territories.[141]

These high-level policy issues took place in a society which was becoming habituated to the existence of an immense underclass, performing tasks which German *Herrenmenchen* were not going to perform in future. Contemporary compensation disputes necessarily focus attention on the management and shareholders of huge corporations, who conform to a myopic left-wing demonology. But complicity was never restricted to the denizens of the boardrooms, who were not generally those responsible for hitting recalcitrant foreign workers on the head with a shovel, however much guilt they bear for engineering the framework where this happened.

If some Nazi ideologues fretted that foreign labour would result in a nation of spoilt idlers, not to speak of the disappearance of such folk skills as forestry or mining, this was often a small price to pay when viewed from the perspective of the ordinary German housewife, peasant or worker. Foreign forced labour was the most tangible dividend of victory. Modest German households could revert to the domestic arrangements of the previous century, with a quiescent Polish or Ukrainian skivvy, rather than a German peasant girl, cleaning or minding the children. Lowly rustics could lord it over French or Polish prisoners of war transformed into agricultural labourers. German coalminers – probably the most secure civilian job in wartime, because miners were almost immune to conscription – could rest while Russians delivered their production quotas, and were denied bread or given a bash with a shovel whenever they slackened. There was little evidence of international solidarities in the mines.[142]

In contrast to the Jews, who were taken elsewhere to be murdered, the maltreatment of foreign workers happened under the noses of the civilian population. One could hardly avoid seeing them, although many doubtless succeeded, tramping disconsolately through the streets. SS camps came to the factories, and the foreign workers toiled under German supervision, with some workers transferred to in-house factory guard details. Moreover, police coercion came into play only after German workers – followed by their foremen and bosses – had decided that this was required by making an issue of it. Then, the Gestapo either detained 'slackers' in their own facilities, or sent them to a Labour Education Camp, where during a space of weeks offenders would be 'taught' the meaning of work, often alongside German 'slackers' sent there for the same reasons.

The Nazis also discovered that their official 'scientific' racism, with its schematic hierarchies of 'western' and 'eastern' workers, did not automatically correlate with the informal 'unscientific' prejudices of their own population. Prejudice was unamenable to social engineering. Contrary to the official position, the cognate Dutch and the allied Italians were heartily disliked by the general population. The former did little to conceal their hostility to the Germans, while the latter were snobbish about liver sausage and sauerkraut, lackadaisical at work, and liable to ambush strolling women with protestations of undying affection. Resentment towards hitherto privileged Italians became outright hostility towards the six hundred thousand Italian 'Military Internees' who were detained in Germany.

The Italians were kept in deplorable conditions, in camps whose conditions approximated those of the surviving Russians. Some of their most senior officers were cold-bloodedly murdered. In addition to being robbed of every personal possession, including blankets and shoes, the Italians were so undernourished that they sometimes resembled 'living skeletons'.[143] Moreover, once deployed within the German economy, internees were exposed to the 'icy rejection and contempt' of the civilian population, and sometimes the violence of workers who regarded them as 'traitors'. Being spat at was the least of their tribulations. The Italians sought in vain the solidarity of other foreign workers and prisoners, who rejected them as former confederates of the Nazis. The 'Badoglios' had not fallen honourably into German captivity, and hence did not deserve the rights accorded other prisoners of war under the Geneva Convention. Some Germans, whose opinions were recorded by the SD, felt that the Italians deserved the unique status reserved for the Jews as the 'refuse of humanity'; others that work should be a form of retribution. Once the Italians were deployed within the economy, many German civilians cast aspersions on their attitude to work. A group of young Italian sailors in Frankfurt an der Oder, detailed to move bricks twenty metres, did so nonchalantly with one hand in their pockets, the other clasping a single brick, at the tempo of 'a funeral procession'. Some Italians failed to grasp that the Germans were now the 'foremen of Europe', and loitered around with coat collars up and hands in their pockets, as their German foreman worked up a sweat mending the roads. Everywhere, groups of Italians had the temerity to assail passing German women with songs and wolf-whistles.[144]

In contrast to universal hostility towards the Italians, relations between Germans and other groups of foreign workers did not always conform to Nazi expectations. Rigid schematisation broke down in the face of complex human realities. In regions accustomed to seasonal labour, it was difficult to impress upon German peasants the differences between pre-war migrant workers and wartime helots. The former may have been exploited as cheap labour, and discussed in derogatory terms as 'shit Polacks', but they were still human beings, with whom Germans could dance, drink, sleep and worship.[145] None of this elementary human contact was permissible from a Nazi biologistic perspective, but matters looked otherwise to devout Bavarians and Silesians, with religious commonalities with the Catholic Poles, or to women whose husbands were at war while they toiled alone on remote farms. In that context, ideology counted for little or nothing, the elementary human need for comfort and intimate consolation being everything.

Both sides risked a heavy price for intimacies, which we only know through denunciations which other Germans made to the Gestapo. Any Polish or 'Eastern' man discovered having sexual congress with a German woman was liable to execution, it having been conceded that Polish women were more vulnerable to exploitation by German men in dominant positions.[146] Justice was extremely rough and devoid of legal procedure, with the Polish men being hanged and the German women, some of whom may have been raped by the Poles, exposed to public humiliation. Both the ritual humiliation, including shaven heads and pillorying, and a number of the executions were public, leading some to remark that: 'Thumb-screw and torture chambers are all that is needed; then we shall be fully back in the Middle Ages.' Others appeared in large numbers to gawp at the barbaric spectacle.[147]

BIRTH OF THE MYTH

As Anglo-American and Russian forces converged on the Reich, Allied aircraft ranged with impunity overhead, in silvery streams leaving white vapour trails across the skies, or as a monotonous rolling drone of engines through the night. More bombs were dropped in the last quarter of 1944 than in the whole of 1943. In the first quarter of 1945, the British and Americans dropped the equivalent of a fifth of the tonnage of bombs dropped in the entire war. The most enduringly controversial raid was carried out by Anglo-American aircraft against the Saxon capital Dresden on the night of 13/14 February 1945. One of the most detailed accounts of what it was like to be in a city which burned so bright that night became day was left by Victor Klemperer in his diaries. At one point his wife Eva paused to light a cigarette, and realising she had no matches, turned to something burning on the ground. It was a corpse.[148] Over thirty-five thousand people died, although the exact number may have been higher, since more importance was attached to burning their corpses than counting them. The involvement of the SS, and the methods used – stacking bodies on latticed railway sleepers soaked in fuel – beg a number of questions.[149]

Like the conventional and nuclear attacks on Japan, the Dresden raid was partly motivated by fear that Allied armies would sustain enormous casualties in a conquest of Germany which might be protracted. Allied commanders had no reason to disbelieve Nazi propaganda, whereby fortress cities would be defended to the last bullet, with guerrilla-type resistance thereafter. Orders had indeed been issued to form 'Werewolf' units for the post-war period. Arguments from the former German Democratic Republic, to the effect that the bombing of Dresden was designed, like the atom bombs, to deter Stalin, lack all credibility. Having persuaded Stalin to commence his westward offensive earlier than he wanted, Churchill offered assistance in preventing the eastward redeployment of German forces by destroying major communications junctions in eastern Germany. Three targets recommended themselves: Leipzig, Chemnitz and Dresden. On 8 February 1945 the Americans informed the Soviets that raids on Dresden were scheduled for five days' time. The Russians declined to veto it.[150] The RAF Bomber Command briefing notes for the raid read:

> In the midst of winter with refugees pouring westwards and troops to be rested, roofs are at a premium, not only to give shelter to workers, refugees and troops alike, but to house the administrative services displaced from other areas. At one time well known for its china, Dresden has developed into an industrial city of first-class importance, and like any large city with its multiplicity of telephone and rail facilities, is of major value for controlling the defence of that part of the front now threatened by Marshal Koniev's breakthrough.[151]

Much of this was pretty thin stuff, concealing an enterprise whose dubiety has been discussed ever since. Whatever else it was, Dresden was not 'an industrial city of first-class importance'. Controversy began at the time, with a revealing briefing by an RAF officer at SHAEF (Supreme Headquarters Allied Expeditionary Force) prompting an Associated Press dispatch which claimed that there had been a shift in policy towards 'deliberate terror bombing of German population centres'. Actually, that policy had been pursued for the previous two years. Churchill began to paddle away from Harris, albeit toning down a memorandum which criticised 'mere acts of terror and wanton destruction' in favour of a more anodyne formulation regarding the jeopardising of Britain's post-war access to German housing materials. 'Bert' Harris would have none of this. He despised what he mistook for sentimentality, writing: 'The feeling, such as there is, over Dresden could easily be explained by any psychiatrist. It is connected with German bands and Dresden shepherdesses.' Harris insisted that Dresden was a legitimate target, whose destruction had shortened the war. Still using brutal tones which his political masters now deemed inexpedient, and echoing Bismarck's well-known *obiter dictum* on the Balkans, Harris maliciously added: 'I do not personally regard the whole of the remaining cities of Germany as worth the bones of one British Grenadier.'[152]

The ground war came to a conclusion. During the winter of 1944/5, the Soviets launched successive offensives across the eastern borders of Germany and Austria, capturing the industrial regions of Silesia at the end of January. Between January and March 1945, Hitler transferred 'Sepp' Dietrich's refitted Sixth SS Panzer Army from the

Ardennes to spearhead a final localised offensive – 'Operation Spring Awakening' – in Hungary, intended to secure Germany's last remaining oil supplies. The Russians crushed it.[153] The defence of Germany's eastern regions, that is East Prussia, Pomerania and Silesia, was entrusted to his more fanatical generals, together with the Party Gauleiter Koch and Hanke. Himmler was placed in command of a new Army Group Vistula, realising his ambition of commanding a field rather than Replacement Army. His opening exhortation to his officers was an irrelevant rant, in which the lineal descendants of the 'Alte Fritz' were warned that they would be summarily shot if they did not repel the oncoming 'Bolshevik hordes . . . beasts and destroyers of every humane order'.[154] *Pour encourager les autres*, a senior SS officer was executed for failings in the defence of Bromberg. Himmler was an unmitigated disaster as a field commander, as Hitler ruefully acknowledged. Goebbels remarked, accurately enough, that the Reichsführer-SS 'is certainly a fusspot, but not a warlord'.[155] Each eastern redoubt, including Breslau and Königsberg, was reduced after ferocious fighting, with civilians being evacuated far too late in the proceedings.

In the West, Anglo-American armies crossed the Rhine, the strategic intention being to divide and destroy enemy forces in northern and southern Germany. Over three hundred thousand German troops were encircled within the Ruhr cauldron, where their commander Model committed suicide rather than surrender. Germany had lost her one remaining industrial conurbation. Within the Ruhr cities, further atrocities were committed, with the Gestapo murdering both German detainees and thousands of Soviet foreign-labourer prisoners, the majority detained for looting, in Bochum, Dortmund, Essen and Gelsenkirchen.[156] After destroying a further pocket of resistance in the forests of the Harz, Bradley and Patton advanced to the Elbe, where in late April American troops met the Red Army at Torgau, with badges and caps being exchanged amid general jubilation. British and Canadian armies conquered north-western Germany. In a campaign intended to bolster claims to an independent zone of occupation, French forces under de Lattre fought their way into south-west Germany, while the US Seventh Army entered Austria and linked up at the Brenner with Allied forces advancing through northern Italy. These offensives allowed the German army no time to consolidate, and denied Hitler a Thuringian or Alpine fastness from which to organise a miraculous recovery of Nazi fortunes. This last development had bearings on his subsequent suicide.

Nazi Germany's defeat was experienced in many modes, as the paths of leaders and led diverged. Many soldiers and most civilians wanted the end to come as quickly as possible. Since there is no reason to doubt that many of these people had once espoused Nazi sympathies, what they experienced must have been akin to a loss of faith. For some the psychological confusions of the time were too much to bear. 'He died in the year '45 from grief, from inside, because he had been so mistaken. He also said, "That scoundrel [*Lump*] Hitler. How could he? . . . He did not think it right what happened then. He died at the end of the year '45. One saw . . . from day to day he shrank more and more internally. He did not overcome it. He simply slowly withered,' recalled one woman of her father-in-law, a Nazi-supporting railway official.[157]

Others, whether in the military, in the Gestapo or civilians, lashed out at anyone to hand – which meant deserters, juvenile delinquents and foreign workers displaced from their camps – whom they held responsible for defeat and a breakdown of public order. For in the last months of the war burglary, looting, rape and robbery became endemic in some areas, the organised form involving hybrid 'gangs' of German criminals and their foreign-worker accomplices. The latter had little alternative, since once they had fled their camps, or the camps had been bombed, they had no other means of survival. When caught, members of these gangs were sometimes hanged in public, as in Cologne in October 1944, or subjected to lynch justice by irate German civilians.

The organs of repression continued to function with lethal efficiency, whether in the camps, with their last-minute revenge killings, on the death marches, where those who could not walk were shot by the wayside, or in the bomb craters of the major cities, which filled with executed German delinquents and foreign workers. Death marches involved transferring huge numbers of the three-quarters of a million remaining concentration-camp inmates into the interior of the Reich. A low estimate of those who died *en route* is a quarter of a million, of whom half were Jews, making it difficult to see antisemitism as the exclusive motive for this barbarous conduct. The marchers, many barefoot in deep snow, were herded about by guards who no longer received orders, and who shot the exhausted. They also machine-gunned people into the sea, or burned thousands of people in barns, while sometimes taking the most arduous routes so that their captives would die. Some of the male and female guards were driven

by a vengeful desire to kill as many prisoners as possible while they
still had time, others clung to what they knew best, which in their case
was killing.[158]

At the rotten core of this regime, defeat was being transformed into
a world-historical spectacle. At the highest level, the principal actors
opted for a tawdry apocalyptic drama, enacted with an eye to posterity, in which other people – including above all the German people –
were so many expendable extras. Past sentimentality towards the
German race and nation was superseded by utter contempt for a
people which had failed the test of greatness.[159] It is important not to
invest these shabby scenes with an unwarrantable grandiosity, for the
theatrical time was bought with human lives.

At the close of 1944, the German armed forces still numbered some
ten million men, or double the figure with which Germany had entered
the war in September 1939. Despite the degraded composition of these
forces, Hitler refused to redeploy two million troops from the remaining outposts of empire, in Austria, Hungary, Italy, Norway, the
Balkans and the Baltic to defend Germany. These troops might prove
useful bargaining counters should the Western Allies fall out with the
Soviets, which was the only grand strategy Hitler possessed. History's
most notorious gambler had exhausted his stock of tricks. Fixated on
collapsing enemy coalitions, Hitler also lacked a credible strategy for
the defence of the Reich itself, beyond a nihilistic desire to leave
nothing standing after him should the worst come to the worst.

Those who had ideas on how best to postpone defeat found
themselves frustrated by lack of resources. For example, in March
1944 the tank supremo Guderian recommended the formation of an
offensive armoured reserve, but this came to nothing, since the
machines, if not the men, were no longer available in the requisite
quantities. In May that year, eleven hundred new tanks and mobile
guns were supposed to be available in line with production forecasts;
the number eventually delivered to widely dispersed forces was one
hundred.[160] An army whose mobility had once been legendary was
increasingly moving on foot or bicycle, in so far as it could move at all
under random strafing from low-flying fighter-bombers. Within a year,
Hitler was reduced to directing the movements of individual tanks.
Instead of acknowledging the absolute superiority of Allied firepower,
Hitler's regime instinctively fell back on domestic subversion as the
key to Germany's misfortunes. The reflexive solution was enhanced
coercion. Regular army morale was increasingly held together by

roving courts martial, which left deserters and the disillusioned shot dead or hanging by the waysides. Signs attached to their corpses read 'I am a deserter'. Sights long familiar in the Balkans, Ukraine and Russia, and which had latterly seeped into Italy or France, began to appear on the streets of Germany.[161] Emulating Stalin, from March 1945, Hitler excluded from state financial support the families of those who had been captured without being critically wounded. These measures did nothing to improve military morale. According to a report by General Ritter von Hengl, while combat veterans and the young fought bravely, many soldiers were tired and apathetic, or cowards and deserters who allowed themselves to be captured.[162] The tide of those surrendering to the Western Allies rose from slightly over half a million men in the first quarter of 1945 to 4,600,000 a month later. These men calculated that they had less to fear in American or British captivity than from the random violence being meted out by their own side. Even the Wehrmacht's draconian discipline had lost its deterrent function. With characteristic cynicism, Goebbels regretted that Germany had not seceded from the Geneva Convention.[163]

While the regular army drifted into Allied captivity, the onus of defence fell upon the civilian population, to cover gaps not filled by *ad hoc* forces mustered from the otherwise redundant air force and navy. Hitler Youth were cobbled together in formations with resonant names – 'Clausewitz', 'Scharnhorst' and so forth – but little to recommend them in engagements with battle-hardened Allied troops equipped with massive firepower. Women were drafted into operating searchlights or non-combatant duties, since only the Bolsheviks used *Flintenweiber* as soldiers. Even this ideological taboo was subsequently set aside. From September 1944 onwards, German civilians were conscripted to reinforce frontier fortifications. At first this provided a successful form of 'occupational therapy', but any positive benefits were soon vitiated by the sight of Party officials bawling orders from the warmth of their official cars to people knee deep in freezing mud.[164]

These defences were then manned by the Volkssturm, a Party-controlled citizen militia, consisting of able-bodied men aged between sixteen and sixty. Those too decrepit to fight were assigned passive guard duties. These units lacked uniforms, and were often armed with shotguns and hunting rifles, with as little as ten rounds apiece. The sole exception was relatively generous supplies of the new 'people-friendly' *Panzerfaust*, an anti-tank bazooka which some militias used to deadly effect. Announcement of the Volkssturm's existence was delayed until 18 October 1944, the anniversary of the Battle of Leipzig, for the intention – as with the film *Kolberg* – was to invoke the spirit of the Wars of Liberation against Napoleon. The Volkssturm was partly an attempt to bind any potential sources of sedition closely to the regime, and tartly a reflection of an inhuman philosophy, which regarded the death of civilians as preferable to whatever tribulations they might face under Allied occupation. These units performed well on the eastern borders, but in the west they often jettisoned their arms and dissolved into the chaos which replaced civil society. Some participated in murdering foreign workers accused of sundry crimes.

Attempts were made to enthuse the civilian fighting man through propaganda which highlighted the murder, rape and plunder which characterised the Red Army's presence in eastern Germany. Ironically, what was undoubtedly happening was frequently dismissed as a Nazi propaganda trick, especially by those ideologically disposed to think well of the Soviets. Nor did this technique always have the desired effect, since some people were aware of crimes which had been committed in Germany's name, and which they claimed excused Russian atrocities: 'Have we not murdered thousands of Jews? Don't soldiers again and again report that Jews in Poland have had to dig their own graves? And how did we treat the Jews in the concentration camp in Alsace? Jews are human beings too. By doing all this we have shown the enemy what they can do with us if they win.'[165]

People living in Romania, Hungary, northern Serbia and the eastern parts of Germany liberated by the Red Army already had bitter experience of Soviet liberation. Red Army soldiers burned villages and raped women who fell into their hands, especially if they were from non-Slavic nationalities. Their leaders turned a blind eye to these actions, when they were not positively encouraging them, for Stalin was keen not to deny his legions the perks of the job. Wanton destruction was partly motivated by livid resentment at the higher standard of living these men encountered in wartime Germany: 'They lived well, the parasites. Great big farms in East Prussia, and pretty posh houses in the towns that hadn't been burned out or bombed to hell. And look at these dachas here! Why did these people who were living so well have to invade us?' Unsurprisingly, special barbarity was reserved for owners of large landed estates in the East, whom Marxist ideology stereotyped as the *fons et origo* of Nazism.[166] A class recently decimated by Hitler was subjected to renewed persecution. A feeling of inferiority towards the Germans – which Nazi propaganda about

'Mongol' *Untermenschen* had helped to foster – required some compensatory humiliation of German manhood through deliberate despoliation of their womenfolk. It was the final demonstration that the men had no power. Matters were not helped by the mindsets ingrained by both Nazi and Soviet propaganda, which created an anxious and suspicious atmosphere that ratcheted up tension between occupied and occupier. One errant word or gesture, and nemesis followed. If the stillness following ferocious battles was sometimes reward enough, for the waves of replacement troops who followed into Germany, drunken rapine and a nervy resort to violence replicated the combat experience. They kept replicating it into the late 1940s.

The relatively restrained behaviour of American troops, who were not entirely innocent of these crimes of violence, encouraged civilians to surrender. The Nazis endeavoured to stop this with the only methods they knew. Harsh measures were adopted to counteract the spread of 'defeatism'. The army, Party and police agreed a policy of shooting the male inhabitants of houses which displayed white flags, while in Hessian Ingolheim the 'defeatist' mayor was hanged at the instigation of Gauleiter Sprenger. Special courts, staffed by judges from the Party, army or Waffen-SS, handed out up to five hundred death sentences per month, for now the German people had themselves become the regime's enemy, whatever its earlier commitments and enthusiasms.[167]

If most Germans were keen to survive as best they could, the Nazi leadership and fanaticised remnants of the Party and its formations succumbed to their darkest thoughts. Here, Will was supposed to triumph. There was no such thing as defeat, only sacrifice and suicide before the onset of 'grandiose doom'. Generals long since degraded into one functional elite among many sought to redeem their caste from the contempt and suspicion which Hitler openly expressed towards them, with mindless avocations of a readiness for ultimate sacrifice. Rhetoric replaced clear thinking. Four days after the assassination attempt against Hitler, Jodl told his staff: 'I am convinced that we can overcome this situation, but even if fortune does not smile upon us, then we must be determined to be the last who gather with our weapons around the Führer, thereby justifying ourselves to posterity.'[168] The circle of generals in whom Hitler had any confidence shrank to fanatics like Model or Schörner, and eventually to the dedicated few who defended him in Berlin – 'him' rather than Berlin or the Berliners being the paramount consideration.

Concern with posterity was apparent among the Nazi leadership, whose final weeks were akin to rehearsals for a drama, designed to perpetuate their malignant presence into indefinite posterity, an endeavour in which they have been notably successful, judging from their all-pervasive presence at the start of the new millennium. Addressing his Propaganda Ministry staff on 17 April 1945, Goebbels made analogies between *Kolberg*, the enormously expensive Agfacolor costume drama about ordinary Pomeranian folk resisting Napoleon's armies in 1807, which used 187,000 extras withdrawn from the battlefront, and a film he thought he would star in:

> Gentlemen, in a hundred years' time they will be showing another fine colour film describing the terrible days we are living through. Don't you want to play a part in this film, to be brought back to life in a hundred years' time? Everybody now has a chance to choose the part which he will play in the film a hundred years hence. I can assure you that it will be a fine and elevating picture. And for the sake of this prospect it is worth standing fast. Hold out now, so that a hundred years hence the audience does not hoot and whistle when you appear on the screen.[169]

For history's most enduring B-movie villains were self-consciously assigning themselves parts within an A-movie which runs and runs, increasingly in the debased form of documentaries, made-for-TV soaps and lurid magazines and books which have scraped the barrel of sensation until it has almost worn away. The Nazis cynically manipulated posterity as they had manipulated their contemporaries; by way of continuity, they are cynically manipulated in their turn by a 'Hitler industry' for which there seems to be an insatiable market. A regime which had lived by image perished by it, in a final triumph of style over substance, as the greatest stage villains of all departed what they called the stage of history, leaving a lingering trail of evil beyond the curtains.[170]

By the last stage of the war, leading Nazis were unable to distinguish their own drama from the wishful thinking and period dress ideology of *Kolberg*. Tellingly, on 28 March 1945, Hitler contrasted the defeatism of the Wehrmacht with Gauleiter Karl Hanke's role in the defence of Breslau, calling him 'the Nettelbeck of this war', and thereby directly alluding to Heinrich George's doughty mayor in Veit Harlan's film, whose courage contrasted favourably with the Clausewitzian realism of Prussian generals. All participants in the final shabby drama were acting out roles within the century's most powerful medium, beginning the process whereby the Nazis would become a fixture of the media scene for the next several decades.[171] What happened to Kolberg itself – on 19 March 1945, Goebbels decided it best to suppress mention of the fact that the city had just fallen to the Russians – was as nothing compared with the insidious posthumous infiltration of the Nazis into the modern consciousness through the most modern medium available. It was doubly insidious since most of the surviving footage was made at their behest, and not surprisingly depicts them at what they regarded as their best.[172]

In early March, belated attempts were made to create three defensive lines blocking the Red Army's advance towards Berlin from the Oder. On 16 April 1945 Hitler issued a general proclamation which read:

> For the last time the Jewish-Bolshevik deadly foe has come forth with his masses to attack. He is seeking to destroy Germany and to exterminate our people. Many of you soldiers from the East already know yourselves what fate threatens above all German women and children. While the elderly, menfolk and children will be murdered, women and girls will be degraded into barrack-room whores. The rest will be marched off to Siberia.

If this dire vision was especially lurid, that was because Hitler was projecting on to his enemies what he had authorised in their countries. Now he sought to bring about an apocalyptic catastrophe within a Germany whose people had proved themselves 'weaker' than the nations of the East, for there could only be a biologistic explanation for this catastrophe. In his final weeks, Hitler's lightly worn aestheticism fell away to reveal a vulgar creature, memorably described as 'a cake-gobbling human wreck', otherwise filled with morbid adolescent fantasies of doom and destruction.[173] Reverting to his earlier 'revolutionist' self, Goebbels encouraged Hitler in this mood, bent as he was on burying under rubble 'the last so-called achievements of the bourgeois nineteenth century'.[174] Under the 'Nero' order, everything was to be destroyed. Mines were to be blown, canals blocked with scuppered barges, telephone exchanges and lines ruined, together with the nation's cultural heritage.

When not trying to stimulate his own jaded appetite with scenes of carnage and infernos, Hitler took refuge from his inner terrors, staving off the prospect of captivity or imminent death with hopes that his enemies' coalitions would dissolve, alternating with stylised imaginings of a heroic last stand, whose paragons were Leonidas' Spartans and the Nibelungs. Goebbels took to reading to Hitler aloud from Carlyle's life of Frederick the Great. The contrasting reality was a blank, broken man, his puffy face simpering inanely, as he stroked the anxious faces and felt the hands of Hitler Youth boys, about whose imminent deaths he cared nothing. The leader who had once elicited faith with apparent facility was now reduced to begging his departing friends to believe in his counter-version of reality: 'If you would believe that the war can still be won, if you could at least have faith in that, all would be well. . . . One must believe that all will turn out well. . . . Do you still hope for a successful continuance of the war, or is your faith shattered?'[175]

Neither history nor the Hitler Youth brought relief from the inexorable prospect of defeat. Hastily reinforced defensive positions, notably on the Seelow Heights east of the capital, were overrun by huge Soviet armies, which by 25 April had encircled Berlin. Hitler hoped that salvation would come from German forces still at large to the west and north of the capital. These forces made no impression on the Russians. Hitler's closest subordinates, Göring, Himmler and Speer, decamped to the few remaining areas not under Allied armies, while the leadership of the army and navy (for there was no longer an air force) followed. Shortly afterwards, Hitler learned that Göring was attempting to supplant him, while Himmler had been taking soundings with the British via Swedish intermediaries. Himmler's liaison officer at Hitler's headquarters was taken above ground and shot in the Reich Chancellery's inner courtyard. Treason provided a temporary stimulant to minds accustoming themselves to the fact that the game was up.

Hitler's final situation conferences were a bizarre mixture of geopolitical reflections and recriminations, interspersed with strategic dispositions of a worryingly localised nature. He hoped that the Allies would fall out at San Francisco, and that America and Britain would belatedly recognise that there was only one man capable of holding back the 'Bolshevik colossus', which was grabbing most of eastern Europe, though the British had once protested about the loss of part of Poland. Hitler repeatedly stressed that he was not going to decamp to the Obersalzberg, nor depart the 'world stage' as an 'infamous refugee': 'Better to end the struggle honourably, than to live a few months or years more in dishonour and infamy.' Goebbels concurred, reminding this drained wreck of his world-historical significance: 'If the Führer were to meet an honourable death in Berlin, with Europe falling to the Bolsheviks, within five years at the latest, the Führer would become a legendary personality and National Socialism mythic, because he would have been sanctified by this greatest and last act, and all the human frailties which today people criticise him for would be wiped away at one stroke.' Hitler agreed: 'That is the decision. To save everything here, and only here, and to deploy the last man, that is our duty.'[176] This heroic rhetoric, for one might ask 'duty to whom?', contrasted with the misanthropic gloating with which Goebbels set a close subordinate to rights about the nature of the German people:

> the German people deserved the fate that awaited them. . . . he remarked cynically that the German people had after all chosen this fate themselves. 'In the referendum on Germany's quitting the League of Nations they chose in a free vote to reject a policy of subordination and in favour of a bold gamble. Well, the gamble hadn't come off. . . . Yes, that may surprise some people, including my colleagues. But have no illusions. I never compelled anybody to work for me, just as we didn't compel the German people. They themselves gave us the job to do. Why did you work with me? Now, you'll have your little throat cut.' Striding towards the door, he turned round once more and shouted: 'but the earth will shake as we leave the scene.'[177]

These references to scenes and stages abounded in the concluding days and hours. With nowhere to flee, and loath to fall alive into enemy captivity, Hitler decided to offer the Russians the most bloody 'defensive defeat' in history, a characteristically apocalyptic and inverted analysis of reality. The price was paid, not by him sixteen metres below the ground in a bunker, but by ordinary Berliners who found themselves amid a raging battle. Having been thwarted in his desire to ruin the entire economy with his 'Nero' order of 19 March, Hitler ordered the destruction of Berlin's remaining bridges, and the flooding of rail tunnels used to shelter wounded German soldiers. For they were completely expendable too. As the Russians fought their way through the streets, defence of the 'inner citadel' in the government district devolved upon forty-five thousand German troops, including French and Latvian Waffen-SS men, forty thousand members of the Volkssturm, and three thousand boys from the Hitler Youth.

At his final situation conference on 27 April, Hitler claimed that he was staying put, to give himself the moral entitlement to proceed against weakness. 'The captain too goes down with his ship.' He reflected that he had come to power prematurely. Had he waited a while, with Hindenburg dying rather earlier, he could have assumed the presidency, which would have spared him costly 'compromises' with the old elites. He had become distracted by the work of economic and military reconstruction; 'otherwise thousands would have been got rid of at that time'. In fact, 'in retrospect one regrets that one is so good'.[178]

On 28 April, Hitler married Eva Braun, in a symbolic bow to convention, and the following afternoon, he poisoned and shot himself in a failsafe desire to elude captivity. His corpse was burned in the grounds of the Reich Chancellery; his remains were removed by the Russians, with the ensuing 'mystery' fuelling a further stream of macabre kitsch for several decades. On 1 May, the newly designated Reich Chancellor, Goebbels, poisoned himself and his family. Power passed to the new Reich President Grand Admiral Dönitz in Schleswig-Holstein.

Shortly before he died by his own hand, Hitler dictated his own script, or 'final political testament' as he grandiosely entitled it. A demented criminal converted himself into a martyred hero. Reviewing the last three decades, he claimed to have been motivated 'solely by love and loyalty to my people in all my thoughts, acts and life'. This had steeled him for 'the most difficult decisions which have ever confronted mortal man'. He repeatedly laid responsibility for the outbreak of war in 1939 at the door of the Jews. In line with his direst 'prophecies', he said: 'I further left no one in doubt that this time millions of children of Europe's Aryan peoples would not die of hunger, millions of grown men would not suffer death, nor would hundreds of thousands of women and children be burned and bombed to death in the towns, without the real criminal having to atone for this guilt, even if by more humane means.'

These apocalyptic horizons inexorably narrowed to the drama in Berlin. He was going 'to share my fate with those millions of others who have taken upon themselves to do the same'. In fact, he was planning to kill himself, and, judging from their actions, the 'millions' were not intent on following him. He spoke in the clichés of his own propaganda, of a 'radiant renaissance of the National Socialist move-ment' and of 'leaders' who 'must march ahead as shining examples, faithfully fulfilling their duty unto death'. In the second part of his testament, Hitler expelled Göring and Himmler from the Party, naming a new government of 'honourable men' including such criminals as

Backe, Bormann, Seyss-Inquart and Thierack. The words 'death' and 'perish' abounded in his description of the future. He concluded on a note of implacability: 'Above all, I adjure the leaders of the nation and those under them to scrupulous observance of the laws of race and to merciless opposition to the universal poisoner of all peoples, International Jewry.'[179] This final call was as hopeless as a cry in deep space.

MAKING PEACE

The Dönitz 'government' operated in Flensburg for a further three weeks, although there was virtually nothing left to govern. One of its few creditable acts was to strip Himmler of his authority. Attempts to maintain governmental continuity and to bargain terms through partial ceasefires in the west came to naught.[180] German forces in Italy, Denmark, Holland and north-west Germany capitulated independently. After a few days' tergiversation, Jodl was authorised to sign a general surrender, with effect from 8 May 1945, at Eisenhower's headquarters in Reims, a ceremony which was repeated at the Red Army headquarters at Karlshorst with Keitel as the principal German signatory. Almost as an afterthought, the Allies arrested the Dönitz 'government', despite Churchill's musings on using it as a future central administration. Two days earlier, and only after his efforts to negotiate separately with the West had come to nothing, Himmler stole away dressed as a private soldier, but, being identified, poisoned himself in British captivity.

When the fighting ceased, large swathes of urban Germany lay in ruins. While the level of destruction of major industries was between 10 and 20 per cent, half of the urban housing stock was devastated. This meant that only eight million homes were available for fourteen million households. Vast numbers of people were grief-stricken and displaced, with relatives lost, missing or in Allied captivity. Children lacked food, and were below their normal height and weight, while even in late 1946 one hundred thousand people in Hamburg exhibited the physical effects of malnutrition. Millions of people, from dozens of different backgrounds, existed in camps for displaced persons, expellees and refugees.

The four Allies assumed formal power in Germany with the Berlin Declaration of 5 June 1945. Military commanders in chief became governors of their respective occupied zones. The latter were roughly congruent with what each Allied army had conquered, but not with the German states, which were subsumed within what evolved into *Länder* in the West, and, after 1952, *Bezirke* in the East. The largest state of Prussia, which now straddled all four occupied zones, was formally abolished in February 1947. The Russian military administration was based at Berlin-Karlshorst, the Americans in the former headquarters of IG Farben in Frankfurt am Main, the French in Baden-Baden, while the British distributed themselves over several locations in north-west Germany. Ultimate power was vested in the four-power Control Council based in a Berlin divided into four sectors, and by subordinate Control Committees.

Germans with unimpeachable political pedigrees, normally involving careers as democratic Weimar politicians followed by exile, imprisonment or quiescence under the Nazis, were installed in administrative positions. These gradually developed into elected offices after the licensing of political parties and the holding of elections. The Weimar democratic parties reconceived themselves as the social democratic SPD, conservative CDU/CSU and liberal FDP; in the East, the SPD was forced into a shotgun wedding with the Communists as the SED (Socialist Unity Party). Intransigent 'Schumacherites', that is Social Democrats who would have no truck with Communism, became the primary target for Soviet and East German secret policemen supported by new networks of spies and informants. The Americans and British created intra-zonal co-ordinating bodies, based in Stuttgart and Hamburg, which became the precursors in miniature of new federal governing agencies. In the East, the Soviet Military Administration created central administrative agencies, for example for agriculture, energy and fuel and post and telecommunications, virtually all of which were controlled by Communists. Whatever the declared intention to deal with Germany as a unity, from the outset two distinct political entities began to coalesce, whose differences would be deepened by the onset of the Cold War. For this we must turn briefly to summit diplomacy.[181]

The Allies had accorded overwhelming priority to destroying Hitler's Germany, partly to defer the inevitable differences of policy between them, which became acute once Hitler had been removed. Radical plans, whether Churchill's Danubian federation, which involved detaching Bavaria and joining it with Austria and Hungary, or the Morgenthau Plan, to repastoralise the German economy, fell victim to pragmatic considerations. Although Roosevelt and Churchill signed up to the plan at their Quebec meeting in September 1944, leaks to the press of its contents strengthened the opposition to

Morgenthau that was being orchestrated by Henry Stimson, the Secretary for War, who favoured magnanimity and reconstruction. According to Stimson, the United States military was less than sanguinary towards the Germans: 'It was very interesting to find that Army officers have a better respect for the law in those matters than civilians who talk about them and who are anxious to go ahead and chop everybody's head off without trial or hearing.'[182]

The Allies agreed that National Socialism had to be utterly extirpated, and that Germany's capacity to wage wars of aggression – of which the short count was two and the long count five – be permanently curtailed. There would have to be war crimes trials and a lengthy military occupation, to impress on the Germans the totality of their defeat and the iniquity of their earlier ways. When joined with the perception that German society had to be restructured to eliminate the alleged socio-economic roots of Nazism, a view as widespread in the West as in the East and enjoying the support of many Germans, there remained four negative consensual goals. These were demilitarisation, denazification, decartelisation and democratisation. A number of these were open to radically different interpretations, notably regarding what the Western Allies and the Soviets understood by the last and most important of these 'four Ds'.[183]

Mistrust between the Western Allies and the Soviets had many causes, perhaps reaching beyond the hiatus of the 1941–5 wartime alliance to the legacy of 1917. Some of these issues have been touched on already. They included the belated launching of a Second Front, and Soviet conduct during the Warsaw Uprising. The Soviets felt excluded from the deal struck between German forces in Italy and Allied commanders; the Allies resented the way in which the Soviets used access to Berlin to lever the Americans out of Mecklenburg, Saxony and Thuringia. Some American commanders never took to the Russians, with Patton telling a group of American correspondents on the morning the war ended: 'They ["tin soldier politicians in Washington"] have allowed us to kick hell out of one bastard and at the same time forced us to help establish a second one as evil or more evil than the first. We have won a series of battles, not a war for peace.' A few days later he described Zhukov as 'comic opera, covered with medals', and the Russians as 'a scurvy race and simply savages', adding, 'We could beat hell out of them.'[184]

For the contradictions between spheres of influence for Stalin and free political self-determination had become glaring in eastern Europe, where Communist regimes were imposed in Bulgaria, Poland and Romania, Stalin's glacis to prevent future German aggression, to put it charitably. The notion of 'open spheres of influence' was like trying to square a circle, because Communists could not come to power in these countries except by massive fraud and chicanery. By May 1945, Churchill was using the term Iron Curtain to describe the screen behind which Stalin was breaking earlier undertakings. While this was true of Iran and Turkey, it was actually Albania and Yugoslavia which were chiefly responsible for backing the Communists in the Greek civil war. In the same month, President Truman abruptly terminated Lend–Lease deliveries to America's allies, on the legitimate ground that these arrangements did not extend to post-war reconstruction. Although this decision was temporarily reversed, to encourage the Soviets into war against Japan, the damage to American–Russian relations was considerable.

Since the previous meetings of the Big Three had been at Stalin's convenience, the latter was prevailed upon to venture to the western periphery of his newly extended imperium for the last great wartime conference. Codenamed Terminal, the conference was held in the Cecilienhof at Potsdam, with the participants housed in a colony of villas at nearby Babelsberg, the poor man's Hollywood. Beria set to work commandeering a fifteen-room mansion for Stalin, and sixty-four further villas, while servants were flown from Russia to run bakeries, kitchens and sequestered farms for replenishments. Seven regiments of NKVD troops and fifteen hundred operational troops provided local security. Loath to fly, Stalin arrived in a special train last used by the Russian tsars, with seventeen thousand NKVD troops lining the route, and eight armoured trains patrolling the track, as he entered recently conquered territory. He wore the newly designed uniform of a 'generalissimo', a title he had awarded himself, to set him apart from Soviet commanders whose fame clearly rankled. The cogs were already turning to downgrade Zhukov to a command in Odessa for allegedly plotting a coup. Other Russian generals were not so fortunate.[185]

The thirteen plenary sessions were held in the afternoons, with the evenings offering an embarrassment of rivalrous junketing, in which genteel string quartets alternated with the Royal Air Force band. Stalin whiled away the time writing the same word – 'reparations' – or doodling packs of wolves against a red background. In the plenary sessions, Churchill and Stalin sniped at one another over the future disposition of the German fleet, or whether the Germany which they agreed neither to enslave nor exterminate meant the Germany of 1937, or the ruins they beheld on their tours of the bombed-out metropolis. Stalin corrected any misapprehensions regarding East Prussia, threatening to 'hunt away' any German administration which dared to venture into a Königsberg rapidly becoming Kaliningrad.

The Polish Question absorbed much energy. At Yalta, there had been general agreement to compensate Poland for losses in the east with German territory in the west, although what was to be taken was left unspecified, notably the precise location of the western Polish border. Matters were complicated by the exiled Poles' refusal to relinquish territories east of the Curzon Line, or to court permanent German revanchism through expansion westwards. They also scented permanent dependency on the Soviet Union. But the exiled Poles were rapidly becoming an irrelevance. In July 1944 Stalin had concluded a secret frontier agreement with his Lublin Communist clients, which afforded the latter Soviet protection for a frontier on the Oder–Neisse rivers. At Yalta, Roosevelt and Churchill tacitly accepted these arrangements, although they deferred the definitive western frontier to a future peace settlement. With Soviet encouragement, in March 1945 the provisional Polish government – which neither London nor Washington recognised as such – began creating new 'Voivodships' in former German eastern provinces. At Potsdam, it was less what the Soviets and Poles had done than their unilateral *modus operandi* which irritated the Western Allies. Truman declined to accept the elevation of Poland into a fifth occupying power without prior Allied consent. Stalin replied that, since eastern Germany was now allegedly bereft of inhabitants, the Poles had little alternative other than to establish administrative arrangements. Truman indicated how regrettable he would find it, if a reparations settlement were to be delayed because parts of Germany were occupied by a power with no entitlement to do so. Churchill reminded Stalin of the burden which the loss of the agrarian east and the westwards flight of the Germans was imposing on the Allied zones.[186]

Almost as if it was a normal occurrence, the three leaders hardly blinked at enormous transfers of population which were happening before their eyes. Vast numbers of ethnic and Reich Germans had belatedly sought to flee the Red Army, trudging through the snows of a ferocious winter or evacuated by ship from East Prussian harbours. For many of these people, this was their second experience of dislocation, for they had been repatriated in 1939–40 from the Baltic or eastern Europe under the slogan 'Heim ins Reich'. An insistence on fighting to the last man meant that orderly evacuation was so delayed that it developed into mass flight. Deliberate and violent expulsions followed, approximating what is nowadays called 'ethnic cleansing'. Expulsions were carried out with terrible brutality, by the Soviets, Czechs and Poles. As the Polish Communist leader Wladyslaw Gomulka put it: 'We must expel all the Germans because countries are built on national lines and not on multinational ones.'[187] Germans were assaulted, and in some cases murdered, without regard to their individual conduct during the past twelve years, for anti-Nazis, Social Democrats and Communists were expelled too. Of the eleven and a half million ethnic Germans moved from the East, some 2,280,000 died during the transfer.

Western governments were aware that the border changes they were agreeing would result in a massive refugee crisis, which their advance estimates put at between six to seven million people. The one slight justification for expulsions was categorically ruled out. Arguments that these transfers were retribution for past German crimes was deemed inexpedient, and we have seen that the Poles and Czechs made no attempt to exclude even Germans of a left-wing persuasion. The British advised the exiled Czechoslovak leader Eduard Beneš to abandon any pretence that expulsions might be linked to how individual ethnic Germans had conducted themselves under the Nazi occupation, since this would limit the extent of the envisaged transfers, while such procedures would slow down what was intended as a radical solution. Both the British and Americans acquiesced in Czechoslovak plans to expel all but eight hundred thousand of over three million ethnic Germans over a two-year period. At the very highest levels, these policies were legitimised with frequent reference to the allegedly smooth ethnic transfers between Greece and Turkey following the 1923 Lausanne Conference, which had in fact involved considerable hardship.[188]

What these transfers entailed for individuals can be illustrated by the case of the manager of the Glatz branch of the Deutsche Bank in Lower Silesia. He was sixty-three years old, married with a son and daughter, who shared their home with a friend and her two grown-up daughters at the end of the war. Having liberated the town on the night of 8 and 9 May 1945, drunken Soviet troops smashed through the door shortly before dawn in search of valuables. They took his son's watch. Four Russians next serially raped his friend's two daughters. More Russians followed in the afternoon to loot his desk and steal tobacco, followed by a further pair who had heard tell of the raped daughters. The two families spent that night sleeping outdoors. Two days later they were evicted, with whatever possessions they could carry. Attempts by Russian troops to lure him into a building were evaded, for it was usual for the person concerned to emerge without clothing or shoes. On 28 May a Polish administration took over. All Germans were required to identify themselves with white armbands, to make discrimination easier. Germans received little to eat, and were required to perform forced labour. In November 1945, the family was expelled from its temporary quarters, for the Poles had driven them from a house which the Russians had effectively wrecked. In March 1946 the family was taken to the station, loaded on to goods wagons and transported to Alvensleben, from whence a passenger train took them to East Friesland. This odyssey was not untypical.[189]

Allied occupation policy within Germany included the inhibition of future war-making potential, and the extraction of reparations from an economy which was to be treated as a unity. In the Western zones, notorious trusts and monopolies were disaggregated, notably the vast chemicals combine IG Farben, which was dissolved into its constituent parts, such as Agfa, BASF, Bayer and Hoechst. The British unravelled mining combines in the Ruhr. A few major industrial installations were stripped of their machinery and dismantled, notably the Hermann-Göring-Werke at Salzgitter. But the intention of doing this to over twelve hundred plants was abandoned when the Americans absorbed the potentially deleterious consequences of this programme, which was extremely unpopular, not least with the Germans whom it threw out of work. Ironically, this was at a time when Germans of all political persuasions were prepared to countenance socialisation of major industries and utilities, on the ground that capitalism had allegedly played a key role in the rise of Nazism. But the Allies knew that their own taxpayers would not stump up to cover the inevitable costs of such an enterprise, and nor were they overly keen to see a new German state equipped with such a concentration of economic power. Moreover, their own experience disproved any automatic connection between capitalism and dictatorship.[190]

In the East, other notions prevailed. Socialisation proved perfectly compatible with grim dictatorship. Calculating that the Nazis had caused $128 billion worth of damage in the Soviet Union, the Russians reckoned that $10 billion in reparations was a small price to extract. The modalities were established at a separate conference of foreign ministers, with the Soviets securing percentages of industrial goods from the Western zones, in return for agricultural produce and raw materials from the East.

Apart from individual looting and plundering by Russian troops, who helped themselves to bedding, boots, jewellery, watches and so on, the Soviets sequestered the property of alleged Nazis – in practice anyone with a bit of money – with Marshal Zhukov leading the way by using such loot to furnish several apartments. Art treasures, archives and libraries followed, sometimes including those which the Nazis had looted in Russia. In this way, the records of the Parisian police or of the German Freemasons ended in a suburb of Moscow, just as the records of Bolshevik Smolensk went via Nazi Germany to America.

The Soviets also systematically dismantled perhaps as much as a third of their zone's industrial productive capacity, a devastating blow to a country already on its knees. German workers were forced to carry out the work unpaid, with beatings for anyone who demurred, regardless of whether or not they were Communists. Moreover, over two hundred mines and factories were turned over for the exclusive benefit of the Russians. These included the 'commanding heights' of the economy, whose owners were disbarred on the ground that 'monopoly capitalists' were identical with Nazis. By a minor irony, the one place where former Nazis were guaranteed employment was in these Soviet Stock Companies, whose anxious Russian managers were more interested in meeting production targets than in the political pasts of those who helped them do so. These Soviet-controlled enterprises creamed off the lion's share of raw materials and spares, further depleting what was left to the zonal economy. Since an undifferentiated class of 'Junkers', many of whom were dead, was also fingered as being uniquely responsible for Nazism, large landed estates were broken up for the benefit of the landless peasant farmers and jobless workers from the bombed-out cities. For many years, the Soviet Union also disposed of the unpaid labour of over three million prisoners of war, as well as of civilians deported from occupied territory as forced labour.[191]

An acute economic crisis in the winter of 1946/7, and the problem of what to do with millions of expellees, refugees and released prisoners of war, meant that the Western Allies had little alternative other than to repair the war-ravaged infrastructure and restore production.

The extraction of reparations, based on the principle of inter-zonal exchanges, and a reluctance to subsidise Germany, militated in favour of stimulating German exports. The alternative was for Germany to become a charge on Allied taxpayers, with the British especially ill-equipped to afford the £200 million they had to put into Germany between 1945 and 1948. Neither the Treasury nor the British public wished to subsidise Germany, especially when in July 1946 bread rationing had to be imposed in the UK for the first time, a step never undertaken even during the war, to keep grain flowing from Britain to Germany.[192] The Control Council's 1946 Level of Industry Plan fixed production ceilings in key industrial sectors. This policy was in turn superseded by the Anglo-American decision to create the Bizone or 'Bizonia', that is to treat their zones as an integral unit, with the drift from the East being accelerated by the inclusion of Western Germany in the Marshall Plan for post-war reconstruction, and the creation the following summer of the Deutsche Mark.

Since the war against Nazism had assumed the form of a moral crusade, post-war Europe saw a process of 'political cleansing' of Nazis and their fascist confederates, which claimed many lives across the continent. Unhysterical counts of victims of summary execution in France speak of ten thousand people; in Croatia the number was in the region of one hundred thousand. 'Cleansing' took both 'wild' and legalised forms, although the latter were often perfunctory. Some collaborators deserved little sympathy; others were victims of personal grudges or the settling of political scores, with 'anti-fascism' being a pretext for imprisoning or killing conservative, liberal and social democrat anti-Communists.[193]

The problem the Allies faced in Germany was of a different order of magnitude to that confronting those dealing with fascist collaborators in many former occupied countries, who had never enjoyed widespread popularity, and who were theoretically easy to quarantine from the general population. Nazism permeated German society like a pervasive cancer, scattered through the body politic as if someone had thrown a handful of fine sand. Before 1945, some six million people belonged to the Nazi Party, with millions more involved with affiliated organisations. Arguably, it was this contrast which made it impossible to carry out a radical purge in Germany, even before the Cold War made it inexpedient.[194]

In broad terms, Allied policy in Germany sought retribution for those guilty of monstrous crimes, and the future exorcism of what nowadays might be called a National Socialist mindset. The quest for justice had to be counterbalanced against the realities of post-war reconstruction, or what their own populations deemed seemly as the interval between offence and retribution lengthened. Allied public attention was diverted by the use of two atomic bombs on Japan, the Palestine emergency and the retreat from India, and the onset of Cold War tensions. For the lofty utopian principles enunciated by Roosevelt and Truman had turned sour on encountering the grim realities of Soviet diplomacy, which when wedded with a reluctance to repeat the mistakes of appeasement, and with a collapse of British power, drew America into the defence of Europe, and a global policy of containing Communism. Against these enormous vistas, the trial of Nazi rulers paled into relative insignificance.

The most urgent Allied task was rapidly to intern anyone likely to offer organised resistance to the occupation, for not unreasonably the Allies anticipated future trouble. War crimes suspects and certain broad categories of person were subject to automatic arrest, in the last case by dint of their organisational affiliations. The Western Allies held 182,000 such persons in former prisoner-of-war camps; the Soviets detained about 122,600 in Special Camps, or *Spetslager*, sometimes set up in former concentration camps, including Buchenwald and Sachsen-hausen as well as the infamous Bautzen. The internees included anti-Communists detained under the all-purpose 'anti-fascist' rubric. Some of these people were discreetly murdered. The low figure for deaths in these camps 'as a result of sickness' is 42,800.[195]

The major Nazi war criminals were tried by an international court at Nuremberg. Following prompting from exiled governments, whose citizens had suffered the most grievously under Nazi occupation, general Allied intentions to hold war crimes trials had been announced after the September 1943 Moscow foreign ministers' conference. The intention was to use national jurisdictions, except in the case of those 'whose offences have no particular geographical localisation'. At Tehe-ran, Stalin had aired a desire to shoot fifty thousand German officers, which prompted Churchill to walk out in disgust. Ironically, at the time Churchill was initiating plans for the summary execution of around a hundred leading Nazis who were to be declared international outlaws. By the time they met at Yalta, Stalin had come round to the idea of trials, which the Soviets had begun conducting since 1943, a policy which the British fell in with at San Francisco in April 1945. American experts in prosecuting stock-exchange fraud played a key role in charging leading Nazis with conspiracy to commit aggression and in pursuing criminal organisations. Both the British and the Americans had considerable reservations about working with the deputy president of the Soviet Supreme Court, Ion Nikitchenko, who had presided over the 1935 Moscow show trials.

Twenty-two leading civilian and military leaders, including representatives of six organisations, were arraigned on four counts, which included conspiracy to wage aggressive war, crimes against peace, war crimes and crimes against humanity. These last charges excluded crimes committed against the German people, of which there had been many. Eleven men were sentenced to death, and were hanged at dawn on 16 October 1946. Their corpses were photographed, to prove that they were really dead. Four were acquitted, including Neurath and Papen, while the remainder received long terms of imprisonment. The presence of Soviet judges and prosecutors was not without ironies, in a context dealing with either mass murder or aggression, considerable efforts having to be made to prevent the defendants from introducing the secret protocols of the Molotov–Ribbentrop Pact, or the matter of responsibility for the Katyn massacres, which the Soviets insisted on including in the proceedings, against the advice of their democratic colleagues. The Nuremberg trials were conducted fairly, and the guilt of those sentenced was incontestable, even in terms of laws extant in Germany itself throughout the entire Nazi period. The trials also represented the first documented insights into the detailed workings of a criminal regime, shortly after it had ceased to function.[196]

Subsequent trials included the twelve American Nuremberg 'successor' trials, which concerned representative cross-sections of Nazi criminality. Both the 'doctors' trial' and the Einsatzgruppen case did something to fathom the most despicable depths of 'euthanasia' killings and medical 'experimentation', or the murderous onslaught against Soviet Jewry. Military tribunals heard cases against former concentration camp personnel or people who had committed atrocities against Allied servicemen. Nazi criminals whose depredations had extended across Europe were handed over to other Allied governments. Some eighteen hundred internees were surrendered to the Poles between 1946 and 1950 for six major war crimes trials. About 6 per cent were acquitted and a further 50 per cent imprisoned for under five years. Eleven per cent were sentenced to death, not all of whom were executed. Rudolf Hoess was hanged in a corner of his former dominion, not far from a gas chamber. Ironically, at the same time as Nazi war criminals were receiving scrupulously fair trials in Poland, some 4,400 Poles were sentenced to death for 'political offences' by Stalinised Polish military courts, of whom 70 per cent were executed. One could be generous and scrupulous with German Nazis, but not with anti-Communists.[197]

From late 1945, German courts were empowered to try Germans accused of crimes against their co-nationals or stateless persons. Allied refusal to allow them to reinvestigate people already tried by the Allies meant that some of those appearing as witnesses were guilty of more heinous offences than those against whom they testified. By 1950, when German courts were authorised to try all Nazi crimes, some 4,419 people had been convicted in what had become the Federal Republic, and over twelve thousand in the East. After the virtual cessation of such trials in the mid-1950s, a central agency to co-ordinate investigations and prosecutions was established in 1958 in Ludwigsburg. Wherever a lack of will to deal with Nazi criminality lay, it was not there, for down to 1992 prosecutors initiated proceedings against 103,823 individuals. However, the legal system included too many former Nazis, and made overly fine distinctions between motives and degrees of culpability. For how else could only 6,487 persons have been convicted over this period? Prosecutions of Nazi war criminals continue to this day in Germany, most recently a case involving a Ukrainian participant in the 'Harvest Festival' massacres, and in countries, such as Australia and Britain, which have introduced retroactive war crimes legislation.[198]

Taken together, it is doubtful whether these trials had a wider didactic effect. Trials conducted by the Allies were open to the charge of 'victors' justice', however unwarranted this was in practice. The German Churches played a conspicuous role in pleading on behalf of the accused, at a time when they said little or nothing about the Nazis' enormous number of victims.[199] Weariness also set in regarding the constant diet of depravity and horror, against which human psychological defence mechanisms rebelled. This mood spread to some of the Allied nations, where public opinion began to turn against trying German generals, who had captured innocent imaginations on the Allied side during the conflict. Even Churchill felt moved to contribute to Manstein's defence fund. It proved difficult to sustain either the quest for justice or outrage in societies concerned with post-war reconstruction, the threat of Communism and, in Britain's case, the Palestine emergency, where Zionist terrorism subverted British sympathies for Jews.[200] The formation of the Federal Republic in 1949, and increasing Cold War tensions over Berlin or in Korea, meant that the Allies needed to reintegrate Germany into the defence of the West, which inclined them to clemency towards convicted war criminals. By 1958, virtually all of them had been released from Landsberg prison.[201]

The other arm of Allied policy was 'denazification', that is a deeper cleansing of German society of people compromised by pronounced Nazi sympathies. This assumed different forms and dimensions in the four occupied zones, not to mention different approaches within the sub-zonal regions. All four zonal governments dispensed with the assistance of *ad hoc* German 'anti-fascist' committees. Denazification was most radically pursued in the Soviet zone, where it was simultaneously used as an instrument of socio-economic restructuring, to consolidate a Marxist–Leninist–Stalinist dictatorship. Nazis were those who had enjoyed power, wealth and influence in the preceding twelve years, a blanket category joined by anyone politically opposed to a Marxist–Leninist society. This group lost their property and positions, except in cases where their skills were indispensable. In total, over half a million people were dismissed from their jobs and disbarred from future non-menial employment. This included virtually the entire judiciary and state prosecutors, who then had to be hurriedly replaced by new recruits ready and willing to practise 'people's justice'. People from humbler backgrounds, who exhibited a willingness to co-operate with the new dispensation, were routinely exempted from punishment by virtue of their proletarian or peasant credentials. In other words, in the Soviet-occupied zone, denazification was in line with the complacent, prejudiced and simplistic assumptions underlying orthodox Marxist analysis of the roots of 'fascism'.

Practice in the zones occupied by the free world varied. Initially, the Americans combined internment of 'dangerous' cases with automatic dismissal from their posts of anyone belonging to the NSDAP or its affiliates before 1937. This was less than just, since it included people who had joined the Party for pragmatic reasons, and it was self-defeating in the sense that it deprived society (and the occupiers) of a wide range of professional talents. The onus gradually shifted from retribution to rehabilitation. Opportunities to reform the civil service were missed. From February 1946, the Americans resorted to issuing detailed questionnaires, with 131 responses demanded, to all twelve million adults in their zone of occupation, which were designed to establish degrees of individual complicity. The results were converted into five categories, ranging from major offenders to those given a clean bill of health. Some three million people were then to be subjected to 545 German-run denazification committees operating under American oversight. Numbers were reduced by excluding those born since 1919, or people grievously maimed in the war. There were inevitably malicious denunciations. A former university rector who had praised the Nazi regime in an inaugural speech had unwisely made a hundred copies, all but two of which he gave to friends. When he dutifully handed one to his American investigating officer, the latter said: 'Thank you, but I have already received forty-seven unsolicited copies.'[202]

Inevitably, many collusive testimonies were rendered on behalf of the guilty by people deemed unimpeachable or as society's ranks closed around them. By some irony, the most compromised individuals were to be dealt with last, which meant that their hearings coincided with a skills shortage in the economy, and the onset of the Cold War, in which even the dirtiest of hands were needed, as the quiet migration of Nazi secret policemen, engineers and 'Sovietologists' into Western and Eastern intelligence agencies and other government services independently established. Already, the men responsible for the incipient East German secret police force, Criminal Police K-5, were developing an admiration for the technical efficiency and the 'exactness and cleanness' of their Gestapo forerunners. A new department, called Intelligence and Information, began to recruit a network of confidential agents and informers. Fresh from his depredations in the Crimea and Chechnya, Lieutenant General Ivan Serov built his own German-based NKVD apparatus to deal with alleged spies and saboteurs with the usual Soviet methods of intimidation and torture.[203]

The Russians took the lead in stopping denazification programmes in April 1948; the Western powers soon followed. It left many former Nazis ensconced in senior civil service positions, not to mention the private sector, where in the Western zones the process was much less thoroughgoing. Despite 'Odessa File'-style mythology of SS veterans controlling the 'commanding heights' of an increasingly prosperous West Germany, as distinct from the reality of their evading justice through self-help networks, such neo-Nazi revivals as have arisen in the last several decades have tended to come from more marginal constituencies, indistinguishable from their crazed counterparts elsewhere.

Denazification programmes were accompanied by a wider process of 're-education' in democratic values. The major structural obstacles had been obliterated by Nazism, war and territorial loss, although we should remember that these structures consisted of people. The once politically powerful Prussian landed aristocracy had lost their estates in the East, and frequently their lives, either under Nazism or during the Russian occupation. Having ceased to play a political role under Hitler, the armed forces emerged discredited and defeated.[204] Hence, the German businessman and manager finally came into his own, partly because the economy was the only national vocation in which anyone could take pride, especially in its subsequent social market incarnation, which removed the hard edges from capitalism. The German elites were structurally reconciled to democracy.

Cultural denazification was guaranteed to make hackles rise in a society which prided itself on its cultural and intellectual achievements, notwithstanding the fact that *Kultur* had not inhibited widespread susceptibility to the politics of faith of the most unsophisticated kind, least of all among the most highly educated, nor the creation of the most finely honed industrial killing machine hitherto known to mankind. Unsurprisingly, many people preferred aspersions against the 'barbaric' Russians, despite an imaginative literature which with Chekhov, Dostoevsky, Pushkin and Tolstoy could not be said to be outclassed by the German literary canon, or against the 'materialistic' Americans, who at the time were producing such modernist giants as Jackson Pollock and Frank Lloyd Wright.

With the exception of the British occupied zone, where the Germans were allowed to make their own arrangements, tension arose over the future educational system, which was up for grabs since all schools were either closed or had been flattened. In the Soviet zone, all distinctive educational provision was abolished, and, since 70 per cent of teachers had belonged to the Nazi Party, thousands of replacements were quickly trained from 'anti-fascist' and working-class constituencies. School books were rewritten to reflect the scientific creed of Marxist–Leninism. The French similarly dismissed thousands of teachers and abolished both single-sex and denominational institutions. Following the 1946 Zook Report, the Americans decided to introduce a system of comprehensive non-denominational education, which ran into ferocious opposition from Catholic traditionalists, especially in Bavaria, and from defenders of the humanistic grammar schools for academically gifted children. Since the Americans were seeking to impose a uniformity unknown to most European countries, and alien to the practice of the American elites themselves, this was perhaps erring on the side of hypocrisy.

Educational reforms, many of which were stymied by confessional or regional interests, were accompanied by an extensive programme of cultural re-education, a term used unselfconsciously despite its Orwellian tone. In the Soviet zone, this involved fabricating long traditions of Russo-German fraternity, statues of Marx, Lenin and Stalin, and affirmations of loyalty on the part of the conquered towards victors who profoundly suspected and despised them. The only local cult permitted was that of the martyred KPD leader Ernst Thälmann.[205] As elsewhere in the Soviet bloc, the specific fate of all the Jews was obliterated from public memory in favour of the new creed of 'anti-fascism'.

Initially, radio and the press were under stringent Allied control, partly because they were the main means of imparting information to the occupied population. As greater freedom was conceded to the Germans, they were encouraged to adopt the Allies' own media arrangements as exemplars, with the British keen on a version of the autonomous public-service BBC, the Soviets on total state control, and the Americans favouring decentralised commercial services. Newspapers edited under Allied auspices were replaced by papers published under Allied licence. Several great newspapers emerged, including the *Frankfurter Allgemeine*, *Die Welt* and the *Süddeutsche Zeitung*, in which information was kept distinct from opinion, together with impressive weeklies such as *Der Spiegel* and *Die Zeit*. Major historians, restored to their professorial chairs, began reflecting on the recent 'catastrophe', in so far as they were not personally embroiled in it, wrestling with such weighty questions as whether Nazism was the offspring of general or local traditions, of the French Revolution or of an illiberal German historical trajectory. The most popular mass medium, before television came on the scene, was the cinema. Foreign imports dominated the post-war years, whether in the East or the West. Domestic products largely consisted of 'rubble films' about the exertions of reconstruction, or films recut from stock shot in the Nazi period, rearranged to send a non-political message. Newsreels continued to be an important part of cinema-going, with the occupying powers using them as thinly veiled advertisements for their respective ways of life. Attempts to make the German population revisit recent horrors through compulsory showing of short monochrome films dedicated to Nazi 'death mills' – such as Hadamar and Ohrdruf – were as resented as compulsory visits to defunct concentration camps.[206]

A diffuse and pallid pseudo-religiosity settled upon the public cult of the resisters of 20 July, or the 'martyred' ethnic German expellees and the returned remnants of those captured at Stalingrad. It was like high voltage suddenly going to ground.

It is time to step back from a world momentarily numbed by the crimes of the Nazis and their allies and sympathisers, and to consider these events from a contemporary perspective. While it is possible to draw positive conclusions, it is important to emphasise that these are intellectually akin to discovering that one's house is built over a mineshaft and is permeated with radon gas, or that some futuristic edifice stands on a former toxic waste dump. In the profoundest sense, this is a story devoid of a happy ending, however much we might try to find one, for that is our nature.

The complex story of West Germany's simultaneous integration into both the European and Atlantic communities and, teething troubles apart, her subsequent absorption of her eastern neighbour, could occupy many more books. The astonishing achievement of the Germans themselves has been to turn their backs on the politics of faith, or on notions that Germany can strike out on a separate path to greatness at the expense of her neighbours, a path which has twice brought disaster in its wake, much of it visited upon the Germans, losers of both world wars. Whatever complexities marked Germany's negotiation of her Nazi past, which is itself the object of intense academic scrutiny, contemporary Germany seems much like her fellow members of the European Union, with common anxieties about globalisation, the appropriate balance between deregulated markets, taxes and welfare provision, or the corrupting effects of one party being in power too long, on either the federal or the regional level. None of these problems is confined to Germany. Nowadays there are conspicuously fewer warning voices regarding the durability of German democracy than there were when New Left violence was at its zenith in the 1970s, or as anti-social or lunatic-fringe elements attacked certain categories of foreigners in the 1980s. Again, as a glance at France or Britain will confirm, these are scarcely localised problems. Internationally, even politicians who in their youth were crassly and vociferously anti-American are now among the most robust advocates of German military participation in NATO interventions wherever human rights are abused, although high motives do not put such enterprises beyond critical scrutiny. Whatever course she chooses to pursue within these parameters, Germany will inevitably encounter criticism both from within and from without, as is the case with any powerful country, but at least this is increasingly likely to concern what she is doing in the present, so that she will cease to be judged by what happened in the past. It is clearly invidious to treat any country along the lines of the maxim 'damned if they do, damned if they don't', not to speak of visiting the sins of the grandfathers on the sons, and Germany is no exception.

Paradoxically, as 'being beastly to the Germans' has become unfashionable among many sophisticated people, not to speak of a younger generation that is far more European-minded than any before it, so the spotlight has shifted to the acrimonious ways in which the Holocaust is being institutionalised and memoralised. This is unfortunate, for it dishonours both the survivors and several generations of able and serious scholars who have reconstructed the whens and wheres, if not always the whys, of what happened, an activity not to be confused with pontificating on television or in the 'op-ed' pages of newspapers. Unease regarding these excrescences extends into the Jewish communities of Europe, Israel and North America too. But these things, which trivialise the Holocaust by reducing it to the cultural climate and personalities of our time, have little to do with the enormity of the original event itself, about which there should be no confusion. That is why the racially motivated criminality of the Nazi regime (and of others both within and beyond Germany) literally permeates this book, for no aspect of that past was untainted by it. Nothing can ultimately be detached from these horrors, neither Nazi economic nor Nazi leisure policy, and certainly not the military history of the war. There is no 'normal' history somehow adjacent to, or detached from, the fact of the Holocaust, which breaks the bounds of whatever intellectual framework we variously impose upon it. This is one of the many ways in which epistemological advances in the study of history have led to greater insights regarding this very subject than has been achieved by an approach based on the mere accumulation of archival 'facts', especially when those 'facts' have been accumulated for narrowly forensic purposes, which explain little about the meta-physical motives behind the Nazi project.

So, setting our sights on the medium-range ground, what generalisable conclusions can we reach about the time evoked in this book? However much the modes of memorialisation and representation are debated in the future, the history of the Third Reich reminds us what can happen when desperate people turn to the politics of faith, purveyed by a mock-messiah resembling Signorelli's great depiction of the Anti-Christ in Orvieto Cathedral but whose imaginative world was some loathsome travesty of the mythic world of Wagner, divested of the latter's syncretist religiosity and dedication to art, and devoted instead to permanent racial struggle. The Nazis' beastly ideology blended modern scientific rationality, the weeding capability of the 'gardening state', with a bowlderised Christianity, a fusion which gave it its potency. The practice involved cruelty towards those who were undermining the 'race', or allegedly conspiring to bring about its destruction. The rest of the population were bathed in narcissistic ethno-sentimentality, enjoying a brief improvement in their standard of living and vistas of national greatness. A full plate, work and a wage packet considerably reduced people's interest in their fellow man. A minority grumbled about this or that aspect of Nazi policy, while not seeing the enormity of the whole, an insight which only very few allowed themselves amid so much incontrovertible evidence. It is the diffusion of such perspectives among relatively large parts of the population which gives grounds for hope. In an actuarial sense, we have become more 'risk-averse'. There are no 'quick-fix' leaps to happiness, even assuming that that is a desirable objective, judging by the devastating human consequences of such enterprises in the twentieth century. The historical balance sheet endorses this judgement. The regimes established by what have been called 'armed bohemians' produced nothing of any lasting moment. Their leaders embodied the negation of everything worthwhile about being human; their followers demeaned and shamed themselves. It is not an edifying story. In this sense, the lower register, the more pragmatic ambitions, the talk of taxes, markets, education, health and welfare, evident in the political cultures of Europe and North America, constitute progress, even though we as yet lack historians with the gift of conveying its many remarkable Jamesian virtues. Our lives may be more boring than those who lived in apocalyptic times, but being bored is greatly preferable to being prematurely dead because of some ideological fantasy.

NOTES

ABBREVIATIONS

ADAP	Akten zur deutschen auswärtigen Politik 1918–45 (Baden Baden 1950)
BA	Bundesarchiv
CEH	*Central European History*
GStA	Geheimes Staatsarchiv, Berlin
GuG	*Geschichte und Gesellschaft*
HGS	*Holocaust and Genocide Studies*
HHStAW	Hessisches Hauptstaatsarchiv Wiesbaden
HMK	D. C. Watt (ed.), *Hitler's Main Kampf* (London 1990)
IAB	*Internationals Ärztliches Bulletin*
IMT	*International Military Tribunal*
JCH	*Journal of Contemporary History*
JMH	*Journal of Modern History*
LIBY	*Leo Baeck Institute Yearbook*
MadR	H. Boberach (ed.), *Meldungen aus dem Reich* (Herrsching 1984)
SK	*Das Schwarze Korps*
StAM	Staatsarchiv München
TLS	*Times Literary Supplement*
USHMM	United States Holocaust Memorial Museum
VfZ	*Vierteljahreshefte für Zeitgeschichte*
ZSL	Zentrale Stelle des Landesjustizverwaltungen

INTRODUCTION – NATIONAL SOCIALISM, POLITICAL RELIGIONS AND TOTALITARIANISM

1. Eric Voegelin, *Hitler and the Germans*, trans. and ed. Detlev Clemens and Brendan Purcell, *The Collected Works of Eric Voegelin*, vol. 31 (Columbia, Mo. 1999), p. 119.
2. John P. Dunlop, *Russia Confronts Chechnya. Roots of a Separatist Conflict* (Cambridge 1998) discusses all but the 1999–2000 war in Chechnya.
3. For reasoned, unhysterical discussions of these questions by contemporary philosophers see Richard Norman, *Ethics, Killing and War* (Cambridge 1995) and Jonathan Glover, *Humanity. A Moral History of the Twentieth Century* (London 1999).
4. Konrad Heiden, *The Fuehrer* (London originally 1944, new edn 1999) p. 113.
5. Alexis de Tocqueville, *De la Démocratie en Amérique. Oeuvres complètes* (Paris 1864) 3, p. 519.
6. The *locus classicus* is Julien Benda, *The Treason of the Intellectuals* (New York 1968), but see also Raymond Aron's *The Opium of the Intellectuals* (New York 1957); the important collection by W. Berger and W. Pehle (eds), *Denken im Zwiespalt. Über den Verrat von Intellektuellen im 20. Jahrhundert* (Frankfurt am Main 1996); and Robert Conquest, *Reflections on a Ravaged Century* (London 1999). Much can also be learned from George Mosse, 'Fascism and the Intellectuals' in his *The Fascist Revolution* (New York 1999) pp. 95–116.
7. Bertrand Russell, *The Practice and Theory of Bolshevism* (London 1920) pp. 15–17.
8. Victor Klemperer, *I Shall Bear Witness. The Diaries of Viktor Klemperer 1933–1941* (London 1998) entry dated 14 July 1934, p. 71.
9. Friedrich Percyval Reck-Malleczewen, *Böckelson. Geschichte eines Massenwahns* (Stuttgart 1968).
10. For examples see E. Schlund, *Neugermanisches Heidentum im heutigen Deutschland* (Munich 1924); R. Karwehl, 'Politisches Messiastum', *Zwischen den Zeiten* (1931) pp. 519ff.; Theodor Heuss, *Hitlers Weg* (Tübingen 1968 edition of 1932 original); Robert Welsch, 'Christentum und Völkische Bewegung', *Jüdische Rundschau* 37, p. 28; and Eric Voegelin, *Die politische Religionen* (Munich 1996 edition of 1938 original).
11. *Deutschland-Berichte der Sozialdemokratischen Partei Deutschlands (SOPADE)* (1937) 4, entry dated 4 April 1937, pp. 497–9.
12. See W. Lienemann, 'Die Zerstörung der Menschlichkeit im Nationalsozialismus und das Ethos der Menschenrechte', in S. Pfürtner *et al.*, *Ethik in der europäischen Geschichte* (Stuttgart 1988) 2, pp. 148–52;

for the Soviet Union see Lynne Atwood and Catriona Kelly, 'Programmes for Identity. The "New Man" and the "New Woman"', in Kelly and D. Shepherd (eds), *Constructing Russian Culture in the Age of Revolution 1881–1940* (Oxford 1998) pp. 256–90.

13. Jakob Talmon, *The Origins of Totalitarian Democracy* (London 1952) p. 148.

14. For revolutionary 'cults' see Mona Ozouf, *Festivals and the French Revolution* (Cambridge, Mass. 1988).

15. Elaine Pagel, *The Origins of Satan* (London 1995).

16. Norman Cohn, *The Pursuit of the Millennium. Revolutionary Millenarians and Mystical Anarchists of the Middle Ages* (London 1957).

17. Emilio Gentile, *The Sacralization of Politics in Fascist Italy* (Cambridge, Mass. 1996) pp. 30–1; Uriel Tal, *Structures of German 'Political Theology' in the Nazi Era* (Tel Aviv 1979) p. 21.

18. See Eric Voegelin, *Autobiographical Reflections* (Baton Rouge 1989); Raymond Aron, 'Les Religions Séculaire', reprinted in *Une Histoire du XXe siècle* (Paris 1996) pp. 139–222; Talmon, *The Origins of Totalitarian Democracy*; *idem, Political Messianism. The Romantic Phase* (London 1960); and *idem, Myth of the Nation and Vision of Revolution. Ideological Polarization in the Twentieth Century* (New Brunswick 1991 reprint of 1981 original).

19. For brilliant explications of Voegelin's life's work, going far beyond his initial reflections on Nazism into his mature political thought and reflections on history and order, see especially Ellis Sandoz, *The Voegelinian Revolution. A Biographical Introduction* (Baton Rouge 1981) pp. 50–70 and Barry Cooper, *Eric Voegelin and the Foundations of Modern Political Science* (Columbia 1999), pp. 1–11.

20. Gentile, *The Sacralization of Politics* p. 149.

21. Cohn, *The Pursuit of the Millennium*; George Mosse, *The Nationalization of the Masses. Political Symbolism and Mass Movements from the Napoleonic Wars through the Third Reich* (New York 1975) and his important essay 'Towards a General Theory of Fascism', in his *The Fascist Revolution* pp. 1–44; James Billington, *Fire in the Minds of Men. Origins of the Revolutionary Faith* (New York 1980); James Rhodes, *The Hitler Movement. A Modern Millenarian Revolution* (Stanford 1980); Hans-Joachim Gamm, *Der braune Kult* (Hamburg 1962); Uriel Tal, *Political Faith of Nazism Prior to the Holocaust* (Tel Aviv 1978); *idem, Structures of German 'Political Theology' in the Nazi Era*; and *idem, 'Aspects of Consecration of Politics in the Nazi Era', in O. D. Kulka and P. R. Mendes-Flohr (eds), *Judaism and Christianity under the Impact of National Socialism 1919–1945* (Jerusalem 1987) pp. 63–95; Klaus Vondung, *Magie und Manipulation. Ideologische Kult und politische Religion des Nationalsozialismus* (Göttingen 1971); *idem, Die*

Apokalypse in Deutschland (Munich 1988); Michael Oakeshott, *The Politics of Faith and the Politics of Scepticism* (New Haven 1996). See also Robert N. Bellah, 'Civil Religion in America' *idem, Beyond Belief. Essays on Religion in a Post-Traditionalist World* (Berkeley 1970) pp. 168–89 for a comparative perspective.

22. Saul Friedländer, *Nazi Germany and the Jews. The Years of Persecution 1933–1939* (London 1997); Philippe Burrin, 'Political Religion. The Relevance of a Concept', *History & Memory* (1997) 9, pp. 321–52; Emilio Gentile, 'Fascism as Political Religion', *JCH* (1990) 25, pp. 229–51 ; *idem, The Sacralization of Politics*; Michael Ley, *Genozid und Heilserwartungen. Zum nationalsozialistischen Mord am europäischen Judentum* (Vienna 1993); Claus-Ekkehard Bärsch, *Die politische Religion des Nationalsozialismus* (Munich 1998); Hans Maier, *Politische Religionen. Die totalitären Regime und das Christentum* (Freiburg 1995); Maier (ed.), *Totalitarismus und politische Religion. Konzepte des Diktaturvergleichs* (Paderborn 1996); Michael Ley and Julius H. Schoeps (eds), *Der Nationalsozialismus als politische Religion* (Bodenheim 1997); Jean-Pierre Sironneau, *Sécularisation et religions politiques* (Paris 1982).

23. David Kertzer, *Rituals, Politics and Power* (New Haven 1988). See also Edouard Conte and Cornelia Essner, *La Quête de la race. Une anthropologie du nazisme* (Paris 1995); on the final point see Saul Friedländer, 'The "Final Solution". On the Unease of Interpretation', in Peter Hayes (ed.), *Lessons and Legacies* (Evanston 1991) pp. 28ff., and Ley, *Genozid und Heilserwartungen* pp. 213ff.

24. Leszek Kolakowski, *Religion* (London 1993) pp. 178ff. On the reordering of the chronology of modern German history see G. Eley, 'Is There a History of the Kaiserreich?', in his *Society, Culture and the State in Germany 1870–1930* (Ann Arbor 1997) pp. 40–1.

25. For outstanding examples see Hugo Ott, *Martin Heidegger. A Political Life* (London 1993); Hans Sluga, *Heidegger's Crisis* (Cambridge, Mass. 1993); Thomas Powers, *Heisenberg's War* (London 1993); Gitta Sereny, *Albert Speer. His Battle with the Truth* (London 1997).

26. For example, John Clark and Aaron Wildavsky, *The Moral Collapse of Communism. Poland as a Cautionary Tale* (San Francisco 1990). I am grateful to Timothy Garton Ash for this reference. The literature on Nazi Germany has so far failed to produce anything even approximating Czesław Miłosz's *The Captive Mind* (London 1953).

27. For examples of calls for faith to move mountains see Gentile, *The Sacralization of Politics* p. 14 and Max Domarus (ed.), *Hitler. Speeches and Proclamations* (London 1990–7) 2, p. 646.

28. Contrary to the view of Mosse, 'Towards a General Theory of Fascism' p. 30.

29. Domarus (ed.), *Hitler. Speeches and Proclamations* 2, p. 1146.

30. See R. Pois, *National Socialism and the Religion of Nature* (Beckenham 1986).

31. See especially Friedländer, *Nazi Germany and the Jews* 1, pp. 87ff. The analogy with Koch and Pasteur is from H. R. Trevor-Roper (ed.), *Hitler's Table Talk 1941–44* (Oxford 1988) entry dated 22 February 1942, p. 332.

32. For this example see Vladimir Bukovsky, 'Totalitarianism in Crisis. Is There a Smooth Transition to Democracy?', in Ellen Frankel Paul (ed.), *Totalitarianism at the Crossroads* (New Brunswick 1990) pp. 9–10.

33. For reliable histories of the concept see Eckhard Jesse (ed.), *Totalitarismus im 20. Jahrhundert* (Baden-Baden 1996); Hans Maier (ed.), *Totalitarismus und politische Religion* (Paderborn 1996) two volumes, and especially his fine survey 'Totalitarismus und "politische Religionen". Konzepte des Diktaturvergleichs', in his *Politische Religionen* (Freiburg im Breisgau 1995) pp. 21–36; and Alfons Söllner (ed.), *Totalitarismus. Eine Ideengeschichte des 20. Jahrhundert* (Berlin 1997). Abbott Gleason, *Totalitarianism. An Inner History of the Cold War* (Oxford 1995) is an extreme liberal American reading of aspects of the subject.

34. Leon Trotsky, *Stalin* (London 1947) p. 421.

35. William Steinhoff, *George Orwell and the Origins of 1984* (Ann Arbor 1975) is the best discussion of Orwell's sources.

36. K.-D. Bracher, 'Die totalitäre Utopie', in his *Die totalitäre Erfahrung* (Munich 1987) p. 54; George Orwell, *Nineteen Eighty-Four* (London 1949 and subsequent editions); see Bernard Crick, *George Orwell. A Life* (London 1980) p. 388 and Robert Conquest, 'Orwell. 1984', in his *Tyrants and Typewriters. Communiqués from the Struggle for Truth* (Lexington, Mass. 1989) pp. 86–96.

37. For the critical view see Walter Laqueur, 'The Arendt Cult. Hannah Arendt as Political Commentator', *JCH* (1998) 33, pp. 483–96.

38. For an excellent discussion see Margaret Canovan, *The Political Thought of Hannah Arendt* (London 1974) pp. 16–50.

39. For example, K.-D. Bracher, 'Totalitarianism as Concept and Reality', in his *Turning Points in Modern Times. Essays on German and European History* (Cambridge, Mass. 1995) p. 145 and Carl J. Friedrich and Zbigniew K. Brzezinski, *Totalitarian Dictatorship and Autocracy* (New York 1963) pp. 13 and 87–8.

40. As argued by Oakeshott, *The Politics of Faith* pp. 45ff.

41. See Irving Kristol's review of Talmon in *Commentary* (1952) vol. 14, p. 287–9.

42. See the important discussion of his work by Yehoshua Arieli, 'Jacob Talmon – An Intellectual Portrait', in The Israel Academy of Sciences

and Humanities (ed.), *International Colloquium in Memory of Jacob L. Talmon* (Jerusalem 1984) pp. 1–34.

43. Friedrich and Brzezinski, *Totalitarian Dictatorship and Autocracy* pp. 57–60.

44. Raymond Aron, 'On Totalitarianism', in his *Democracy and Totalitarianism* (New York 1965) pp. 203–4.

45. Friedrich and Brzezinski, *Totalitarian Dictatorship and Autocracy* p. 7.

46. K.-D. Bracher 'Die Ausbreitung des Totalitarismus', in his *Die totalitäre Erfahrung* p. 25, and Leonard Shapiro, *Totalitarianism* (London 1972) p. 69.

47. On this see Walter Laqueur, 'Is There Now, or Has There Ever Been, Such a Thing as Totalitarianism?', *Commentary* (1985) 80, pp. 20–35, and his brilliant book *The Dream that Failed. Reflections on the Soviet Union* (Oxford 1994).

48. See Yehuda Bauer, 'The Significance of the Final Solution', in D. Cesarani (ed.), *The Final Solution* (London 1994) pp. 300–9.

49. For a recent account by a participant see Waldemar Lotnik, *Nine Lives. Ethnic Conflict in the Polish–Ukrainian Borderlands* (London 1999) and Ann Applebaum, *Beween East and West* (London 1997) for a stylish account of the archaeology of many of these conflicts.

1. THE WEIMAR REPUBLIC, 1918–1933

1. P. Thorne (ed.), *Henry James. A Life in Letters* (London 1999) no. 284, pp. 540–2.

2. Niall Ferguson, 'The German Inter-war Economy. Political Choice versus Economic Determinism', in M. Fulbrook (ed.), *German History since 1800* (London 1997) p. 261; Richard Bessel, *Germany after the First World War* (Oxford 1993) p. 31.

3. Otto Baumgarten, *Geistige und sittliche Wirkungen des Krieges in Deutschland* (Stuttgart 1927) pp. 27ff.

4. G. Feldman, 'Kriegswirtschaft und Zwangswirtschaft', in Wolfgang Michalka (ed.), *Der Erste Weltkrieg. Wirkung, Wahrnehmung, Analyse* (Munich 1994) pp. 472–3.

5. R. Moeller, 'Dimensions of Social Conflict in the Great War. The View from the German Countryside', *CEH* (1981) 14, pp. 142–68.

6. H. Berding, *Moderner Antisemitismus in Deutschland* (Frankfurt am Main 1988) p. 172.

7. E. Zechlin, *Die deutsche Politik und die Juden im Ersten Weltkrieg* (Göttingen 1969); Saul Friedländer, 'Die politischen Veränderungen der Kriegszeit und ihre Auswirkungen auf die Judenfrage', in W. Mosse (ed.), *Deutsches Judentum in Krieg und Revolution 1916–1923*

(Tübingen 1971) pp. 37–9; W. Angress, 'The German Army's "Juden-zahlung" of 1916', *LBIY* (1978) 23, pp. 117ff.

8. Niall Ferguson, *The Pity of War* (London 1998) pp. 181–6.

9. Fritz Stern, *The Politics of Cultural Despair. A Study of the Rise of Germanic Ideology* (Berkeley 1961) pp. 209–11.

10. Amos Perlmutter, *New World Orders* (Chapel Hill 1997).

11. B. Ulrich and B. Ziemann (eds), *Frontalltag im Ersten Weltkrieg. Wahn und Wirklichkeit* (Frankfurt am Main 1994) pp. 199–208 for these examples.

12. William L. Patch Jnr, *Heinrich Brüning and the Dissolution of the Weimar Republic* (Cambridge 1998) p. 22.

13. Modris Eksteins, *Rites of Spring. The Great War and the Birth of the Modern Age* (New York 1989) p. 191. Jay Winter, *Sites of Memory, Sites of Mourning* (Cambridge 1989).

14. For the above see Wilhelm Mommsen, 'The Social Consequences of World War One. The Case of Germany', in A. Marwick (ed.), *Total War and Social Change* (London 1988); Heinrich August Winkler, *Weimar 1918–1933. Die Geschichte der ersten deutschen Demokratie* (Munich 1998).

15. On the relationship between the army and Weimar, see F. L. Carsten, *The Reichswehr and Politics 1918–1933* (Berkeley 1973).

16. For a brilliant sketch of those times see Eberhard Kolb, '1918/19. Die Steckengebliebenen Revolution', in C. Stern and H. A. Winkler (eds), *Wendepunkte deutscher Geschichte 1848–1990* (Frankfurt am Main 1994) pp. 112–13.

17. Fundamental works include G. Feldman, *Army, Industry and Labor in Germany 1914–1918* (Princeton 1966) and his 'The Origins of the Stinnes–Legien Agreement. A Documentation', *Internationale wissenschaftliche Korrespondenz zur Geschichte der deutschen Arbeiterbewegung* 19–20 December 1972, pp. 45ff.

18. See especially Wolfgang Mommsen, 'The German Revolution 1918–1920', in his *Imperial Germany* (London 1995) p. 245. On German organised labour see Heinrich August Winkler, *Von der Revolution zur Stabilisierung. Arbeiter und Arbeiterbewegung in der Weimarer Republik 1918–1924* (Berlin 1985); see also Hans Mommsen, 'Social Democracy on the Defensive', in his *From Weimar to Auschwitz* (Oxford 1991) pp. 39ff., and Horst Moeller, *Weimar. Die unvollendete Demokratie* (Munich 1985).

19. Klaus Schönhoven, *Reformismus und Radikalismus. Gespaltene Arbeiterbewegung im Weimarer Sozialstaat* (Munich 1989) pp. 77ff.

20. Robert Waite, *Vanguard of Nazism. The Free Corps Movement in Postwar Germany 1918–1923* (New York 1969) p. 267.

21. On the Free Corps see Hagen Schultze, *Freikorps und Republik*

1918–1920 (Boppard 1969) and the more lurid Klaus Theleweit, *Male Fantasies* (Oxford 1987). See also the excellent study by Steven Aschheim, *The Nietzsche Legacy in Germany 1890–1990* (Berkeley 1992) pp. 156ff.

22. Waite, *Vanguard of Nazism* p. 56.
23. Richard Pipes, *Russia under the Bolshevik Regime 1919–1924* (London 1994) p. 112.
24. Richard J. Crampton, *Eastern Europe in the Twentieth Century* (London 1994) pp. 81–4.
25. Alan Fisher, *The Crimean Tatars* (Stanford 1978) pp. 132–3.
26. Leonard Schapiro, 'The Role of the Jews in the Russian Revolutionary Movement', in his *Russian Studies*, ed. Ellen Dahrendorf (New York 1987) p. 273.
27. Walter Z. Laqueur, *Russia and Germany* (revised edn New York 1990) pp. 62ff.
28. Uwe Lohalm, *Völkischer Radikalismus. Die Geschichte des Deutsch-völkischen Schutz- und Trutz-Bundes 1919–1923* (Hamburg 1970) p. 53.
29. For the details see Aleksandr M. Nekrich, *Pariahs, Partners, Predators. German–Soviet Relations 1922–1941* (New York 1997).
30. All quotations from the outstanding Uwe-Kai Merz, *Das Schreckbild. Deutschland und der Bolschewismus 1917 bis 1921* (Berlin 1995) pp. 165–93.
31. Vladimir Brovkin (ed.), *Dear Comrades. Menshevik Reports on the Bolshevik Revolution and the Civil War* (Stanford 1991).
32. The best accounts of events in Bavaria are Allan Mitchell, *Revolution in Bavaria 1918–1919. The Eisner Regime and the Soviet Republic* (Princeton 1965) and David Clay Large, *Where Ghosts Walked* (New York 1997).
33. Large, *Where Ghosts Walked* p. 115.
34. Waite, *Vanguard of Nazism* p. 89.
35. Reinhard Rürup, 'Demokratische Revolution und "dritter Weg"', *GuG* (1983) 9, pp. 278–301.
36. Gerald Feldman 'Die Demobilmachung und die Sozialordnung der Zwischenkriegszeit in Europa', *GuG* (1983) 9, pp. 156–77; Fritz Blaich, *Der Schwarze Freitag. Inflation und Wirtschaftskrise* (Munich 1985) pp. 35–51; and Charles Maier, *Recasting Bourgeois Europe* (Princeton 1975).
37. G. Pridham, *Hitler's Rise to Power. The Nazi Movement in Bavaria 1923–33* (London 1973) p. 154.
38. Hans Mommsen, *Aufstieg und Untergang der Republik von Weimar 1918–1933* (Berlin 1997) pp. 35–72 puts the case for missed opportunities; Richard Bessel, 'Why Did the Weimar Republic Collapse?', in

Ian Kershaw (ed.), *Weimar. Why Did German Democracy Fail?* (London 1990) pp. 128–32 argues the opposite case.

39. Moeller, *Weimar. Die unvollendete Demokratie* pp. 191–2.

40. R. Rürup, 'Enstehung und Grundlagen der Weimarer Verfassung', in E. Kolb (ed.), *Vom Kaiserreich zur Weimarer Republik* (Cologne 1972) pp. 218ff.; Karl Dietrich Bracher, *The Age of Ideologies* (London 1984) pp. 44ff. and 64ff. See also the suggestive essay by Richard Bessel, 'The Formation and Dissolution of a German National Electorate from Kaiserreich to Third Reich', in Larry E. Jones and James Rettalack (eds), *Elections, Mass Politics and Social Change in Modern Germany* (Cambridge 1992) pp. 413–14.

41. George L. Mosse, *The Nationalization of the Masses* (Ithaca 1975) pp. 124–5.

42. Kessler, diary entry dated 21 August 1919 cited in Anton Kaes, Martin Jay and Edward Dimendburg (eds), *The Weimar Republic Sourcebook* (Berkeley 1994) p. 52.

43. Hermann Ullstein, *The Rise and Fall of the House of Ullstein* (London 1940) pp. 142–3.

44. James Diehl, *The Thanks of the Fatherland* (Chapel Hill 1993) p. 18.

45. Fritz Stern, 'Adenauer in Weimar', in his *The Failure of Illiberalism* (New York 1992) pp. 164–5.

46. Lohalm, *Völkischer Radikalismus* pp. 183–6.

47. The statistics are from H. A. Jacobsen, 'Militär, Staat und Gesellschaft in der Weimarer Republik', in Karl Dietrich Bracher (ed.), *Die Weimarer Republik 1918–1933* (Bonn 1987) pp. 350–5.

48. Balanced assessments of the peace-making process include Peter Krüger, *Versailles. Deutsche Außenpolitik zwischen Revisionismus und Friedenssicherung* (Munich 1986) and his monumental *Die Außenpolitik der Republik von Weimar* (Darmstadt 1985).

49. See Ulrich Herbert, *Best* (Bonn 1996) esp. pp. 95–100. See also Manfred Boemeke, Gerald D. Feldman and Elisabeth Glaser (eds), *The Treaty of Versailles. A Reassessment after 75 Years* (Cambridge 1998) for the latest research.

50. On German–Polish relations see the excellent study by Volker Kellermann, *Schwarzer Adler, Weisser Adler. Die Polenpolitik der Weimarer Republik* (Cologne 1970) and Martin Broszat's brilliant *Zweihundert Jahre Deutsche Polenpolitik* (Munich 1972) pp. 201ff.

51. See M. Lee and W. Michalka, *German Foreign Policy 1917–1933* (Oxford 1987) pp. 22ff.

52. See Kurt Nowak's outstanding *Geschichte des Christentums in Deutschland. Religion, Politik und Gesellschaft vom Ende der Aufklärung bis zur Mitte des 20. Jahrhunderts* (Munich 1995) esp. pp. 197–204.

53. Mommsen, *Aufstieg und Untergang* p. 146.

54. For the pervasiveness of stereotyping see George Mosse, *Fallen Soldiers* (Oxford 1990) p. 178.

55. P. C. Witt, *Friedrich Ebert* (Bonn 1982).

56. Moeller, *Weimar. Die unvollendete Demokratie* pp. 66ff.

57. G. Paul, *Aufstand der Bilder. Die NS-Propaganda vor 1933* (Bonn 1996) pp. 27–8.

58. Waite, *Vanguard of Nazism* pp. 189ff.

59. O. Flechtheim, *Die KPD in der Weimarer Republik* (Frankfurt am Main 1969) p. 148.

60. Rudy Koshar, *Social Life, Local Politics and Nazism. Marburg 1880–1935* (Chapel Hill 1986) pp. 152–4.

61. Fritz Stern, 'Walther Rathenau and the Vision of Modernity', in his *Einstein's German World* (Cambridge, Mass. 1999) p. 193.

62. Richard Bessel, 'Militarismus im innenpolitischen Leben der Weimarer Republik', in K.-J. Müller and E. Opitz (eds), *Militär und Militarismus in der Weimarer Republik* (Düsseldorf 1978) p. 199.

63. Niall Ferguson, 'Keynes and the German Inflation', *English Historical Review* (1995) 110, pp. 368–91.

64. Flechtheim, *Die KPD* p. 178.

65. Konrad Heiden, *The Fuehrer* (London originally 1944, new edn 1999) p. 106. Of the books on the moral inversions caused by inflation, see most obviously Hans Ostwald, *Sittengeschichte der Inflation. Ein Kulturdokument aus den Jahren des Marktsturzes* (Berlin 1922).

66. Thomas Wehrling, 'Berlin Is Becoming a Whore', in Kaes *et al.* (eds), *The Weimar Republic. Sourcebook* doc. 316, pp. 721–3.

67. For the social and psychological effects of inflation see Gerald D. Feldman, *The Great Disorder. Politics, Economics and Society in the German Inflation 1914–1924* (New York 1993) pp. 513ff.

68. Herbert, *Best* p. 79.

69. Mommsen, *Aufstieg und Untergang* pp. 184ff.

70. G. Mai, 'Thüringen in der Weimarer Republik', in D. Heiden and G. Mai (eds), *Thüringen auf dem Weg ins 'Dritte Reich'* (Erfurt 1997) pp. 18–20.

71. Feldman, *The Great Disorder* pp. 701–3.

72. Communist strategies are well described by Ben Fowkes, *Communism in Germany under the Weimar Republic* (London 1984) pp. 91–110.

73. Carsten, *The Reichswehr and Politics* p. 181.

74. Winkler, *Weimar* p. 259.

75. Stanley Payne, *A History of Fascism 1914–1945* (London 1995) pp. 129–30.

76. D. Petzina, 'The Extent and Causes of Unemployment in the Weimar Republic', in Peter Stachura (ed.), *Unemployment and the Great Depression in Weimar Germany* (London 1986) pp. 44–5.

77. H. James, 'Economic Reasons for the Collapse of the Weimar Republic', in Kershaw (ed.), *Weimar. Why Did German Democracy Fail?* pp. 33ff.

78. Gerhard A. Ritter, 'Kontinuität und Umformung des deutschen Parteiensystems 1918–1920', in Kolb (ed.), *Vom Kaiserreich zur Weimarer Republik* pp. 257ff.

79. D. Walker, 'The German Nationalist People's Party', *JCH* (1979) 12, pp. 628–9.

80. Jeremy Noakes, *The Nazi Party in Lower Saxony 1921–1933* (Oxford 1971) p. 29.

81. Mommsen, *Aufstieg und Untergang* pp. 316–19.

82. Reichstag debate on 25 June 1922, extracts reprinted in W. Michalka and G. Niedhart (eds), *Deutsche Geschichte 1918–1933. Dokumente zur Innen- und Außenpolitik* (Frankfurt am Main 1992) pp. 61–2, and for a vivid evocation of the Reichstag see Jürgen Schmädeke, *Der Deutsche Reichstag* (Munich 1994) pp. 74–94.

83. J. M. Diehl, *Paramilitary Politics in the Weimar Republic* (Bloomington 1977) p. 194.

84. The most comprehensive account of the parties remains E. Matthias and R. Morsey (eds), *Das Ende der Parteien 1933* (Düsseldorf 1960).

85. See Heinrich August Winkler, 'Eduard Bernstein as a Critic of Social Democracy', in R. Fletcher (ed.), *Bernstein to Brandt* (London 1987) pp. 167–75.

86. See the fascinating discussion in Harold James, *The German Slump. Politics and Economics 1924–1936* (Oxford 1986) pp. 85ff.

87. James, 'Economic Reasons for the Collapse of the Weimar Republic' p. 36.

88. William Sheridan Allen, *The Nazi Seizure of Power* (rev. edn New York 1984) p. 34.

89. Hans Mommsen 'Social Democracy on the Defensive', in his *From Weimar to Auschwitz* p. 49 is an insightful account by an eminent historian with strong SPD sympathies.

90. William Brustein, 'Blue-Collar Nazis', in C. Fischer (ed.), *The Rise of National Socialism and the German Working Classes in Weimar Germany* (Providence 1996) pp. 144–6.

91. Schönhoven, *Reformismus und Radikalismus* p. 113.

92. Adelheid von Saldern, 'Sozialmilieus und Aufstieg des Nationalsozialismus in Norddeutschland (1930–1933)', in Frank Bajohr (ed.), *Norddeutschland im Nationalsozialismus* (Hamburg 1993) pp. 26–7.

93. Winkler, 'Eduard Bernstein' p. 177.

94. J. Petzold, *Franz von Papen. Ein deutsches Verhängnis* (Munich 1995) pp. 31ff.

95. Oded Heilbronner, 'The Black Forest', in Fischer (ed.), *The Rise of National Socialism* pp. 218ff.

96. Martin Conway, *Catholic Politics in Europe 1918–1945* (London 1997) pp. 40ff.

97. Pridham, *Hitler's Rise to Power* p. 170.

98. David Blackbourn, 'Catholics, the Centre Party and Antisemitism', in his *Populists and Patricians* (London 1978) pp. 168ff.

99. R. Morsey, 'Die Deutsche Zentrumspartei', in Matthias and Morsey (eds), *Das Ende der Parteien* p. 290.

100. Peter G. Pulzer, *The Rise of Political Antisemitism in Germany and Austria* (New York, London 1964) pp. 88–101.

101. Shelley Baranowski, 'The Sanctity of Rural Life', *German History* (1991) 9, p. 21.

102. D. Niewyk, *The Jews in Weimar Germany* (Manchester 1980) pp. 70–2.

103. M. Brenner, *The Renaissance of Jewish Culture in Weimar Germany* (New Haven 1996).

104. Above all Steven Aschheim, *Brothers and Strangers* (Madison 1982).

105. Pridham, *Hitler's Rise to Power* pp. 66–7.

106. Larry Eugene Jones, 'Generational Conflict and the Problem of Political Mobilisation in the Weimar Republic', in Jones and Rettalack (eds), *Elections, Mass Politics* pp. 351–5, and Jones' monumental *German Liberalism and the Dissolution of the Weimar Party System 1918–1933* (Chapel Hill 1988).

107. Peter Fritzsche, 'Breakdown or Breakthrough? Conservatives and the November Revolution', in Larry E. Jones and James Rettalack (eds), *Between Reform, Reaction and Resistance. Studies in the History of German Conservatism from 1789 to 1945* (Oxford 1993) pp. 299ff.; see also Kim Holmes, 'The Forsaken Past', *JCH* (1982) 17, pp. 671ff.

108. Stern, *The Politics of Cultural Despair* pp. 245ff.

109. Lohalm, *Völkischer Radikalismus* pp. 194–201.

110. Noakes, *The Nazi Party in Lower Saxony* pp. 16–17; Allen, *The Nazi Seizure of Power* p. 58; Peter Fritzsche, *Germans into Nazis* (Cambridge, Mass. 1998) p. 193.

111. Thomas Childers, *The Nazi Voter* (Chapel Hill 1983) p. 99.

112. Thomas Childers, 'Inflation, Stabilization and Political Realignment in Germany 1924 to 1928', in G. Feldman *et al.* (eds), *The German Inflation* (Berlin 1982) p. 425.

113. Geoff Eley, 'Conservatives and Radical Nationalists in Germany. The Production of Fascist Potentials 1912–28', in M. Blinkhorn (ed.), *Fascists and Conservatives* (London 1994) pp. 61–8; see also Attila Channady, 'The Dissolution of the German National People's Party 1924–1930', *JMH* (1967) 39, pp. 65–91.

114. Jane Caplan, 'Speaking the Right Language. The Nazi Party and the Civil Service Vote in the Weimar Republic', in T. Childers (ed.), *The Formation of the Nazi Constituency* (London 1986) p. 189.

115. Childers, *The Nazi Voter* p. 65.

116. Bessel, *Germany after the First World War* p. 201.

117. Noakes, *The Nazi Party in Lower Saxony* p. 110.

118. Gustavo Corni, *Hitler and the Peasants. Agrarian Policy in the Third Reich* (Oxford 1990) pp. 5–10.

119. David Crew, *Germans on Welfare* (New York 1998) pp. 90–1.

120. M. Hughes, 'Economic Interest, Social Attitudes, and Creditor Ideology. Responses to Inflation', in G. Feldman *et al.* (eds), *Die deutsche Inflation* (Berlin 1982) pp. 402–3.

121. Jürgen Falter, 'The Social Bases of Political Cleavages in the Weimar Republic, 1919–1933', in Jones and Rettalack (eds), *Elections, Mass Politics* pp. 377–80.

122. See Larry E. Jones, ' "The Dying Middle". Weimar Germany and the Fragmentation of Bourgeois Politics', *CEH* (1972) 5, pp. 23ff.; *idem*, 'Inflation, Revaluation, and the Crisis of Middle-Class Politics' *CEH* (1979) 12, pp. 143ff.; *idem*, 'The Dissolution of the Bourgeois Party System in the Weimar Republic', in R. Bessel and E. Feuchtwanger (eds), *Social Change and Political Development in Weimar Germany* (London 1981) pp. 268–88; and Childers, 'Inflation, Stabilization and Political Realignment in Germany 1924 to 1928' pp. 409ff.

123. Jones, *German Liberalism* pp. 263–5; T. Childers, 'The Middle Classes and National Socialism', in D. Blackbourn and R. Evans (eds), *The German Bourgeoisie* (London 1991) pp. 329ff.; and *idem*, 'The Social Language of Politics in Germany', *American Historical Review* (1990) 95, pp. 331–58.

124. T. Childers, 'Interest and Ideology. Anti-System Politics in the Era of Stabilization' in G. Feldman (ed.), *Die Nachwirkungen der Inflation auf die deutsche Geschichte 1924–1933* (Munich 1985) p. 9.

125. Holmes, 'The Forsaken Past' p. 680.

126. Corni, *Hitler and the Peasants* p. 11 for these figures.

127. G. Stoltenberg, *Politische Strömungen im schleswig-holsteinischen Landvolk 1918–1933* (Düsseldorf 1962).

128. J. Bergmann and K. Megerle, 'Protest und Aufruhr der Landwirtschaft in der Weimarer Republik (1924–1933)', in J. Bergmann *et al.* (eds), *Regionen im historischen Vergleich* (Düsseldorf 1988) esp. pp. 245ff.

129. Jonathan Osmond, *Rural Protest* (London 1993) pp. 137–8.

130. For the above see Peter Fritzsche, 'Presidential Victory and Popular Festivity in Weimar Germany. Hindenburg's 1925 Election', *CEH* (1990) 23, pp. 205ff., and Jürgen Falter, 'The Two Hindenburg Elections of 1925 and 1932' in the same issue of the *CEH* pp. 225ff.

131. See Günther Mai, ' "Verteidigungskrieg" und "Volksgemeinschaft" ', in W. Michalka (ed.), *Der Erste Weltkrieg* (Munich 1994) pp.583–602.

132. For the above see Birgitte Hamann, *Hitlers Wien* (Munich 1998) esp. pp. 337ff.

133. Most recently Ian Kershaw, *Hitler 1889–1936. Hubris* (London 1998) pp. 87–105. See also A. Bullock, *Hitler. A Study in Tyranny* (London 1964), and Joachim Fest's brilliant literary masterpiece *Hitler* (London 1974).

134. Jeremy Noakes and Geoffrey Pridham (eds), *Nazism 1919–1945. A Documentary Reader* (Exeter 1983–8) p. 33.

135. D. C. Watt (ed.), *Hitler's Mein Kampf* (London 1990) (hereafter cited as *HMK*) 2, ch. 1, p. 375.

136. H. Arendt, *The Origins of Totalitarianism* (New York 1973) pp. 470–1.

137. *HMK* 2, ch. 11, p. 296; Kershaw, *Hitler* p. 243.

138. *HMK* 2, ch. 11, p. 60.

139. *Ibid.* p. 270.

140. *Ibid.* p. 260.

141. Robert Wistrich, *Antisemitism. The Longest Hatred* (London 1991).

142. Several works examine the archaeology of antisemitism; see Norman Cohn, *Warrant for Genocide* (London 1996) for an outstanding example.

143. A point made long ago by Ernst Nolte, *Der Faschismus in seiner Epoche* (5th edn Munich 1979) p. 408.

144. Peter Pulzer, 'Why Was There a Jewish Question in Imperial Germany?', *LBIY* (1980) 25, pp. 137ff.

145. Avraham Barkai, 'Der Kapitalist', in J. Schoeps and J. Schlör (eds), *Antisemitismus. Vorurteile und Mythen* (Munich 1995) pp. 265ff. On Social Democracy and antisemitism see R. Leuchen-Seppel, *Sozialdemokratie und Antisemitismus im Kaiserreich* (Bonn 1978) and D. Niewyck, *Socialist, Antisemite and Jew* (Baton Rouge 1971).

146. Edmund Silberner, 'Two Studies of Modern Antisemitism. The Jew-hatred of Mikhail Bakunin', *Historia Judaica* (1952) 14, pp. 93ff.

147. See the important discussion by Michael Marrus, 'The Theory and Practice of Antisemitism', *Commentary* (1982) 74, pp. 38–42.

148. Sharing no common ground with A. Lindemann, *Esau's Tears. Modern Antisemitism and the Rise of the Jews* (Cambridge 1997).

149. For the exceptions that proved the rule see M. Kaufman, 'The Daily Life of the Village and Country Jews in Hessen', *Yad Vashem Studies* (1992) 22, pp. 151–2.

150. Carl von Ossietsky, 'Antisemites', in Kaes *et al.* (eds), *Weimar Republic Sourcebook* p. 278.

151. Fritz Stern, 'Paul Ehrlich. The Founder of Chemotherapy', in his *Einstein's German World* pp. 32–3.

152. George L. Mosse, 'German Jews and Liberalism in Retrospect', in his

Confronting the Nation. Jewish and Western Nationalism (Hanover 1993) ch. 10.

153. A point well made by Hannah Arendt, *The Origins of Totalitarianism* pp. 14ff.

154. Shulamit Volkov, *Jüdisches Leben und Antisemitismus im 19. und 20. Jahrhundert* (Munich 1990) pp. 27–8.

155. Noakes, *The Nazi Party in Lower Saxony* p. 26.

156. Saul Friedländer, *Nazi Germany and the Jews. The Years of Persecution 1933–1939* (London 1997) 1, pp. 87–90.

157. T. S. Eliot is the only one of these figures whose antisemitic prejudices have attracted much interest. See Christopher Ricks, *T. S. Eliot and Prejudice* (London 1988).

158. P. L. Rose, *Race and Revolution* (London 1992) for the prosecution, and Michael Tanner, *Wagner* (London 1997) for an informed defence.

159. Keith Ansell-Pearson (ed.) *Friedrich Nietzsche. On the Genealogy of Morality* (Cambridge 1994) p. 96; see also Ben Macintyre, *Forgotten Fatherland. The Search for Elizabeth Nietzsche* (London 1992), and Lesley Chamberlain, *Nietzsche in Turin* (London 1996). The definitive study of Nietzsche and Nazism is Aschheim, *The Nietzsche Legacy in Germany.* See also Y. Yovel, 'Nietzsche and the Jews', in J. Golomb (ed.), *Nietzsche and Jewish Culture* (London 1997) pp. 122–4.

160. For a good exposition of these issues see George Mosse, *The Crisis of German Ideology* (New York 1981) pp. 93–8.

161. F. Spotts, *Bayreuth. A History of the Wagner Festival* (New Haven 1994) pp. 136–44.

162. Eberhard Jäckel, *Hitler's World View* (Cambridge, Mass. 1981) remains the best study of these issues.

163. *HMK* 2, ch. 1, p. 391. Of course such attitudes were common among the less sophisticated exponents of empire, who nonetheless had nothing whatsoever to do with the Holocaust of European Jewry.

164. *Ibid.* p. 367.

165. *Ibid.* 2, ch. 15, p. 621; P. Crook, *Darwinism, War and History* (Cambridge 1994).

166. *HMK* 2, ch. 1, p. 370.

167. *Ibid.* p. 373.

168. For example *ibid.* ch. 3, pp. 412–13; 'Here, too, we should learn by example from the Catholic Church . . . it is none the less unwilling to sacrifice so much as one little syllable of its dogmas' (p. 417).

169. Uriel Tal, *Political Faith of Nazism Prior to the Holocaust* (Tel Aviv 1978) p. 30.

170. *HMK* 2, ch. 5, p. 155.

171. *Ibid.* ch. 15, p. 620.

172. Heiden, *The Fuehrer* pp. 90–1.
173. Pridham, *Hitler's Rise to Power* pp. 32–5.
174. Noakes, *The Nazi Party in Lower Saxony* p. 59.
175. Mommsen, *Aufstieg und Untergang* pp. 398–402 stresses affinities with neo-conservatism in order to deny the Strasserite wing the character of a Nazi 'left'.
176. Pridham, *Hitler's Rise to Power* pp. 54–5; histories of the SA include C. Fischer, *Stormtroopers. A Social, Economic and Ideological Analysis* (London 1983) and P. Merkl, *The Making of a Stormtrooper* (Princeton 1980).
177. Richard Bessel, 'Violence as Propaganda. The Role of the Storm Troopers in the Rise of National Socialism', in Childers (ed.), *Formation of the Nazi Constituency* p. 132.
178. Rudy Koshar, 'Contentious Citadel. Bourgeois Crisis and Nazism in Marburg/Lahn 1880–1933', in Childers (ed.), *Formation of the Nazi Constituency* pp. 23–5, and his 'From *Stammtisch* to Party. Nazi Joiners and the Contradictions of Grass Roots Fascism in Weimar Germany', *JMH* (1987) 59, pp. 1–24.
179. Pridham, *Hitler's Rise to Power* pp. 110–13.
180. Allen, *The Nazi Seizure of Power* pp. 32–3, and H. Fogel and D. Rebentisch, 'Organisation und Struktur der NSDAP in südhessischen Arbeiterwohngemeinden', in E. Hennig (ed.), *Hessen unterm Hakenkreuz* (Frankfurt am Main 1983) pp. 332ff.
181. Wolfram Pyra, 'Ländlich-evangelisches Milieu und Nationalsozialismus bis 1933', in H. Moeller, A. Wirsching and W. Ziegler (eds), *National-sozialismus in der Region* (Munich 1996) esp. pp. 204ff.
182. S. Baranowski, 'Convergence on the Right. Agrarian Elite Radicalism and Nazi Populism in Pomerania 1928–33', in Jones and Rettalack (eds), *Reform, Reaction and Resistance* pp. 421–3.
183. Allen, *The Nazi Seizure of Power* pp. 49–57.
184. R. Hamilton, *Who Voted for Hitler?* (Princeton 1982) p. 323.
185. Noakes and Pridham (eds), *Nazism 1919–1945* 1, p. 80.
186. For the details see Herbert, *Best* pp. 64ff.
187. E. Kolb, *The Weimar Republic* (London 1988) p. 101; G. Giles, 'National Socialism and the Educated Elite in the Weimar Republic', in P. Stachura (ed.), *The Nazi Machtergreifung* (London 1983) pp. 58ff., and M. Steinberg, *Sabers and Brown Shirts* (Chicago 1973).
188. Koshar, *Social Life, Local Politics and Nazism. Marburg* pp. 196–7.
189. H. A. Winkler, 'Antisemitism in Weimar Society', in Herbert Strauss (ed.), *Hostages of Modernization* (Berlin 1993) 3/1, pp. 201–2.
190. For indirect confirmation of the above see Eric Voegelin, *Autobiographical Reflections* (Baton Rouge 1989) pp. 28–33.

191. Friedrich Meinecke, *The German Catastrophe* (Boston 1950 edn of 1946 German original) p. 32.

192. Michael Kater, 'Professionalisation and Socialisation of Physicians in Wilhelmine and Weimar Germany', *JCH* (1985) 20, pp. 677–701, and *idem*, 'Hitler's Early Doctors. Nazi Physicians in Predepression Germany', *JMH* (1987) 59, pp. 25–52.

193. G. Mai, 'National Socialist Factory Cell Organisation and the German Labour Front', in Fischer (ed.), *The Rise of National Socialism* pp. 119–23, and *idem*, 'Die Nationalsozialistische Betriebszellen-Organisation', in Heiden and Mai (eds), *Nationalsozialismus in Thüringen* pp. 165–88.

194. Horst Gies, 'NSDAP und landwirtschaftliche Organisationen in der Endphase der Weimarer Republik', *VfZ* (1967) 15, pp. 341–76.

195. Pridham, *Hitler's Rise to Power* pp. 118–23.

196. Corni, *Hitler and the Peasants* pp. 25–31.

197. Hamilton, *Who Voted for Hitler?* p. 246.

198. *HMK*, 2, ch. 1, p. 430.

199. For these examples see Kater, 'Hitler's Early Doctors', pp. 36 and 46; Pridham, *Hitler's Rise to Power* pp. 85–9 and 101.

200. E. Hennig, 'Der Hunger naht', in Hennig (ed.), *Hessen unterm Hakenkreuz* pp. 403–4.

201. Allen, *The Nazi Seizure of Power* p. 81.

202. Ralf Georg Reuth (ed.), *Joseph Goebbels. Tagebücher* (Munich 1992) 1, entry dated 22 May 1928, p. 291.

203. *Ibid.* entry dated 13 June 1928, pp. 297–8.

204. Bessel, 'Violence as Propaganda' p. 132.

205. Richard Bessel, *Political Violence and the Rise of Nazism* (New Haven 1984) pp. 34ff.

206. Fogel and Rebentisch, 'Organisation und Struktur' pp. 337–8.

207. Allen, *The Nazi Seizure of Power* p. 79.

208. Christian Streifler, *Kampf um die Macht. Kommunisten und Nationalsozialisten am Ende der Weimarer Republik* (Berlin 1993) pp. 80–1.

209. *HMK* 2, ch. 1, p. 433.

210. Lohalm, *Völkischer Radikalismus* pp. 264–5.

211. *HMK* 2, ch. 1, p. 432.

212. Pridham, *Hitler's Rise to Power* p. 182.

213. J. P. Stern, *Hitler. The Führer and the People* (London 1975) p. 10.

214. Sabine Behrenbeck, *Der Kult um die toten Helden. Nationalsozialistische Mythen, Riten und Symbole* (Vierow 1996) esp. pp. 95–9.

215. Joachim Fest, *The Face of the Third Reich* (London 1979). Chs 2 and 3 are characteristically brilliant on Hitler as an orator.

216. Noakes and Pridham (eds), *Nazism 1919–1945* 1, doc. 51, p. 74.

217. Hessisches Hauptstaatsarchiv, Wiesbaden 483/2190 81st SA Regiment, Frankfurt am Main, cited by Fischer, *The Rise of National Socialism* as doc. 18, p. 143.

218. Theodore Abel, *Why Hitler Came to Power* (Cambridge, Mass. 1986 reprint of 1938 original) p. 218.

219. Hans-Ulrich Thamer, *Verführung und Gewalt. Deutschland 1933–1945* (Berlin 1986) pp. 141–2.

220. Paul, *Aufstand der Bilder* pp. 127–32.

221. Reuth (ed.), *Joseph Goebbels. Tagebücher* 1, entry dated 17 November 1928, p. 335.

222. *Ibid.* entry dated 24 November 1928, pp. 336–7; see also Helmut Heiber, *Goebbels. A Biography* (London 1972) pp. 65–6.

223. Streifler, *Kampf um die Macht* p. 336.

224. Reuth (ed.), *Joseph Goebbels. Tagebücher* 2, entry dated 19 January 1930, p. 447.

225. *HMK* 2, ch. 7, pp. 448–53.

226. Oded Heilbronner, 'The Role of Antisemitism in the Nazi Party's Activity and Propaganda', *LBIY* (1990) 35, pp. 396ff.

227. Michalka and Niedhart (eds), *Deutsche Geschichte 1918–1933. Dokumente zur Innen- und Außenpolitik* doc. 92, pp. 175–7.

228. Peter Stachura, 'The Development of Unemployment in Modern German History', in Stachura (ed.), *Unemployment and the Great Depression* pp. 11–16.

229. Kolb, *The Weimar Republic* pp. 80–2.

230. Winkler, *Weimar* esp. pp. 472–3.

231. Mommsen, *Aufstieg und Untergang* p. 501.

232. Noakes, *The Nazi Party in Lower Saxony* p. 133.

233. G. Neliba, 'Wilhelm Frick und Thüringen', in Heiden and Mai (eds), *Nationalsozialismus in Thüringen* pp. 75ff.; Noakes, *The Nazi Party in Lower Saxony* pp. 222ff.

234. P. Stachura, 'The Social and Welfare Implications of Youth Unemployment in Weimar Germany', in Stachura (ed.) *Unemployment and the Great Depression* pp. 136–9.

235. Heinrich August Winkler, *Der Weg in der Katastrophe* (Bonn 1990) pp. 19–99; and above all David Crew, *Germans on Welfare. From Weimar to Hitler* (New York 1998).

236. Crew, *Germans on Welfare* pp. 157–65.

237. Blaich, *Der Schwarze Freitag* pp. 74–5.

238. Bessel, *Political Violence and the Rise of Nazism* pp. 49–53.

239. Allen, *The Nazi Seizure of Power* pp. 24–5.

240. Blaich, *Der Schwarze Freitag* pp. 75–6.

241. Streifler, *Kampf um die Macht* pp. 83–90.

242. C. Fischer, 'Unemployment and Left-wing Radicalism in Weimar

Germany', in Stachura (ed.), *Unemployment and the Great Depression* p. 215.

243. Jürgen Falter, *Hitlers Wähler* (Munich 1991) pp. 296ff.

244. Eva Rosenhaft, *Beating the Fascists? The German Communists and Political Violence 1929–1933* (Cambridge 1983) p. 50.

245. *Ibid.* pp. 116–17.

246. K. McDermott and J. Agnew, *The Comintern* (Basingstoke 1996) p. 118.

247. Streifler, *Kampf um die Macht* pp. 222–60 and 282–91.

248. Bessel, *Political Violence and the Rise of Nazism* pp. 87–92.

249. Richard Bessel, 'The Potempa Murder', *CEH* (1977) 10, pp. 241–54.

250. Streifler, *Kampf um die Macht* pp. 77–80 and 113–15.

251. Patrick Leigh Fermor, *A Time of Gifts* (London 1977) p. 130.

252. Michalka and Niedhart (eds), *Deutsche Geschichte 1918–1933. Dokumente zur Innen- und Außenpolitik* doc. 99, p. 187.

253. See especially Jürgen Falter, 'Warum die deutschen Arbeiter während des "Dritten Reiches" zu Hitler standen', *GuG* (1987) 13, pp. 217–31, and his *Hitlers Wähler*; Detlef Muhlberger, *Hitler's Followers* (London 1991); and various essays in U. Backes *et al.* (eds), *Die Schatten der Vergangenheit* (Berlin 1990). English-language contributions to this debate include C. Fischer, 'Workers, the Middle Classes, and the Rise of National Socialism', *German History* (1991) 9, pp. 357–73, and Fischer (ed.), *The Rise of National Socialism*.

254. Falter, *Hitlers Wähler* p. 116.

255. C. Szejnmann, 'The Rise of the Nazi Party in Saxony', in Fischer (ed.), *The Rise of National Socialism* p. 200.

256. Abel, *Why Hitler Came to Power* pp. 236–42.

257. See Avraham Barkai, *Das Wirtschaftssystem des Nationalsozialismus* (Frankfurt am Main 1988) pp. 34ff.

258. See especially the brilliant study by Brustein, 'Blue-Collar Nazis', in Fischer (ed.) *The Rise of National Socialism* pp. 143–58.

259. Hans Mommsen, 'Class War or Co-Determination', in his *From Weimar to Auschwitz* p. 75. See also M. Schneider, *Das Arbeitsbeschaffungsprogramm des ADGB* (Bonn 1975).

260. Childers, *The Nazi Voter* pp. 181–5.

261. The most devastating critique of orthodox Marxist (or Stalinist) 'analyses' of 'fascism' is still Wolfgang Wippermann, *Faschismustheorien* (5th edn Darmstadt 1989) pp. 11ff. See also Martin Kitchen's remarkably similar account in his *Fascism* (London 1976).

262. McDermott and Agnew, *The Comintern* p. 112.

263. See William Patch's brilliant study *Heinrich Brüning* p. 240.

264. *Ibid.* pp. 150ff.

265. Carsten, *The Reichswehr and Politics* pp. 338–50.

266. Petzold, *Franz von Papen* pp. 25–53.

267. *Ibid.* pp. 66–7.

268. Geheimes Staatsarchiv (ed.), *Preussen in der Weimarer Republik* (Berlin 1982) pp. 21–3.

269. Falter, *Hitlers Wähler* p. 37.

270. Winkler, *Weimar* p. 535.

271. Reuth (ed.), *Joseph Goebbels. Tagebücher* 2, entries dated 2 and 4 November 1932, pp. 710–12.

272. The definitive account is Henry Ashby Turner, *German Big Business and the Rise of Hitler* (Oxford 1985).

273. Noakes and Pridham, *Nazism 1919–1945* 1, docs 80–1, pp. 111–14.

274. Reuth (ed.), *Joseph Goebbels. Tagebücher* 2, entry dated 7 December 1932, p. 733 n. 97, and Fest, *Hitler* p. 530, citing Laski's *Daily Herald* article dated 21 November 1932.

2. THE DEMISE OF THE RULE OF LAW

1. *Völkischer Beobachter* 11 August 1932, p. 3, cited by Karen Hartmann, ' "Schutzhaft" 1933 bis 1936', G. Mörsch (ed.), *Konzentrationslager Oranienburg* (Berlin 1994) p. 34.

2. Ralf Georg Reuth (ed.), *Joseph Goebbels. Tagebücher* (Munich 1992) 2, entry dated 9 December 1932, p. 734.

3. J. Noakes and G. Pridham (eds), *Nazism 1919–1945. A Documentary Reader* (Exeter 1983–8) 1, doc. 82, p. 115.

4. For these arrangements and much more see Henry A. Turner's outstanding *Hitler's Thirty Days to Power* (London 1996) pp. 96–7.

5. On the role of large landowners see H.-E. Volkmann, 'Deutsche Agrareliten auf Revisions-und Expansionskurs', in M. Broszat and K. Schwabe (eds), *Die deutschen Eliten und der Weg in den Zweiten Weltkrieg* (Munich 1989) pp. 336ff.

6. Turner, *Hitler's Thirty Days to Power* pp. 148–50.

7. J. Petzold, *Franz von Papen. Ein deutsches Verhängnis* (Berlin 1995) pp. 152–62.

8. Reuth (ed.), *Joseph Goebbels. Tagebücher* 2, entry dated 31 January 1933, p. 757.

9. For the various types of camp see J. Tuchel, 'Herrschaftssicherung und Terror – Zur Funktion und Wirkung nationalsozialistischer Konzentrationslager 1933 und 1934', unpublished lecture (1983) pp. 11ff.

10. Anon. (ed.), *Nazi Persecution of the Catholic Church* (London 1940) p. 236; Ingo Müller, *Hitler's Justice* (Cambridge, Mass. 1991) pp. 47–8.

11. Max Domarus (ed.), *Hitler. Speeches and Proclamations 1932–1945* (London 1990–7) 1, pp. 245–50.

12. Reuth (ed.), *Joseph Goebbels. Tagebücher* 2, entry dated 11 February 1933, p. 763.

13. Noakes and Pridham (eds), *Nazism 1919–1945* 1, doc. 106, p. 159.

14. William Patch, *Heinrich Brüning and the Dissolution of the Weimar Republic* (Cambridge 1998) pp. 298–9.

15. Noakes and Pridham (eds), *Nazism 1919–1945* 1, doc. 107, p. 159.

16. W. Frank, *Zur Geschichte des Nationalsozialismus* (Hamburg 1934) p. 32.

17. Domarus (ed.), *Hitler. Speeches and Proclamations* 1, p. 293.

18. M. Broszat, *The Hitler State* (London 1981) p. 84.

19. J. Schmädeke, *Der Deutsche Reichstag* (Munich 1994) pp. 110ff.

20. See especially Ian Kershaw, *Hitler 1889–1936. Hubris* (London 1998).

21. E. Matthias and R. Morsey (eds), *Das Ende der Parteien 1933* (Düsseldorf 1960).

22. Most new orthodox positions are fairly set forth in Ian Kershaw's *The Nazi Dictatorship* (London 1995). For a sceptical view see Saul Friedländer's *TLS* review of Ian Kershaw's *Hitler* (2 October 1998).

23. Otto Kirchheimer, 'The Legal Order of National Socialism', in F. Burin and K. Shell (eds), *Politics, Law and Social Change. Selected Essays of Otto Kirchheimer* (New York 1969) pp. 88ff. is still fundamental. See also his *Von der Weimarer Republik zum Faschismus. Die Auflösung der demokratischen Rechtsordnung* (Frankfurt am Main 1976). On Nazi denigration of the Weimar legal system see Manfred Krohn, *Die deutsche Justiz im Urteil der Nationalsozialisten 1920–1933* (Frankfurt am Main 1991).

24. R. Bessel, 'Die "Modernisierung" der Polizei im Nationalsozialismus', in F. Bajohr (ed.), *Norddeutschland im Nationalsozialismus* (Hamburg 1993) p. 380.

25. M. Knop, H. Krause and R. Schwarz, 'Die Häftlinge des Konzentrationslagers Oranienburg', in Mörsch (ed.), *Konzentrationslager Oranienburg* p. 51.

26. Bundesminister der Justiz (ed.), *Im Namen des Deutschen Volkes. Justiz und Nationalsozialismus* (Cologne 1989) p. 88.

27. H.-E. Niermann, *Die Durchsetzung politischer und politisierter Strafjustiz im Dritten Reich* (Düsseldorf 1995) p. 309.

28. For a good discussion of this see N. Frei, *National Socialist Rule in Germany. The Führer State 1933–1945* (Oxford 1993) pp. 9–27.

29. On Gürtner see L. Gruchmann's monumental *Justiz im Dritten Reich* (1988) and his 'Franz Gürtner', in R. Smelser, E. Syring and R. Zitelmann (eds), *Die braune Elite II* (Darmstadt 1993) pp. 128–36.

30. Domarus (ed.), *Hitler. Speeches and Proclamations* 1, pp. 498–9.

31. Richard Pipes, *The Russian Revolution 1899–1919* (London 1990)

pp. 796–800; see also the still useful Otto Kirchheimer, *Politische Justiz* (Frankfurt am Main 1981).

32. Diemut Majer, 'Justiz und Polizei im "Dritten Reich"', in R. Dreier and W. Sellert (eds), *Recht und Justiz im 'Dritten Reich'* (Frankfurt am Main 1989) esp. pp. 146–7.

33. For discussion of recent literature on Schmitt, including the second wind his often banal ideas have been enjoying among left- and right-wing extremists, see Mark Lilla, 'The Enemy of Liberalism', *New York Review of Books* (1997) 44, pp. 38ff.

34. M. Stolleis, 'In the Belly of the Beast. Constitutional Legal Theory under National Socialism', in his *The Law under the Swastika* (Chicago 1998) p. 96.

35. Excellent studies of the Soviet judicial system include Harold Berman, *Justice in the USSR* (Cambridge, Mass. 1963) and Peter Solomon, *Soviet Criminal Justice under Stalin* (Cambridge 1996) pp. 31ff. See also Richard Pipes, *Russia under the Bolshevik Regime 1919–1924* (London 1994) pp. 401–3. One searches in vain for any comparative discussion of the demise of the rule of law in Bolshevik Russia or Nazi Germany in Ian Kershaw and Moshe Lewin (eds), *Stalinism and Nazism. Dictatorship in Comparison* (Cambridge 1997), although the demolition of legal security and human rights might be thought rather crucial to what distinguished these totalitarian regimes from democracies.

36. Solomon, *Soviet Criminal Justice* pp. 147–8.

37. H. Ruping, 'Zur Praxis der Strafjustiz im "Dritten Reich"', in Dreier and Sellert (eds), *Recht und Justiz* pp. 183–4.

38. Diemut Majer, 'Zum Verhältnis von Staatsanwaltschaft und Polizei im Nationalsozialismus', in Udo Reifner and B.-R. Sonnen (eds), *Strafjustiz und Polizei im Dritten Reich* (Frankfurt am Main 1984) p. 136.

39. Niermann, *Die Durchsetzung politischer und politisierter Strafjustiz* p. 206.

40. Noakes and Pridham, *Nazism 1919–1945* 2, doc. 355, p. 483.

41. H.-L. Schreiber, 'Die Strafgesetzgebung im "Dritten Reich"', in Dreier and Sellert (eds), *Recht und Justiz* p. 163.

42. R. Evans, *Rituals of Retribution* (Oxford 1996).

43. For numerous examples see P. Hüttenberger, 'Heimtückefälle vor dem Sondergericht München', in M. Broszat *et al.* (eds), *Bayern in der NS-Zeit* (Munich 1981) 4, pp. 435–526.

44. D. Dolling, 'Kriminologie im "Dritten Reich"', in Dreier and Sellert (eds), *Recht und Justiz* pp. 194ff.

45. Himmler speech dated 1939, B. Smith and A. Peterson (eds), *Heinrich Himmler. Geheimreden 1933–1945* (Frankfurt am Main 1974) p. 110.

46. See S. Bloch, 'The Political Misuse of Psychiatry in the Soviet Union', in

Bloch and P. Chodoff (eds), *Psychiatric Ethics* (Oxford 1991) pp. 493–515.

47. See Herbert, *Best* pp. 173–4 for these important insights.

48. H.-G. Stümke and R. Finke, *Rosa Winkel, Rosa Listen* (Hamburg 1981) pp. 217–21 for the text of Himmler's 1937 speech.

49. M. Löffler, *Das Diensttagebuch des Reichsjustizministers Gürtner 1934 bis 1938* (Frankfurt am Main 1997) p. 124.

50. R. Angermund, *Deutsche Richterschaft 1919–1945* (Frankfurt am Main 1990).

51. Löffler, *Das Diensttagebuch* pp. 99–103.

52. Bundesminister der Justiz (ed.), *Im Namen des Deutschen Volkes* pp. 171ff.

53. H. Boberach (ed.), *Richterbriefe. Dokumente zur Beeinflussung der deutschen Rechtssprechung 1942–1944* (Boppard 1975).

54. 'Rechtswahrer oder bezahlter Kuli?', *SK* 5 August 1937, Folge 31, p. 6; and Löffler, *Das Diensttagebuch* pp. 107ff. for the *Stürmer* case.

55. See A. Blumberg-Ebel's excellent *Sondergerichtsbarkeit und 'politischer Katholizismus' im Dritten Reich* (Mainz 1990) p. 42.

56. Niermann, *Die Durchsetzung politischer und politisierter Strafjustiz* pp. 208–12.

57. Angermund, *Deutsche Richterschaft* p. 137.

58. See especially Niermann, *Die Durchsetzung politischer und politisierter Strafjustiz* pp. 241–7.

59. For numerous examples of offences see Hüttenberger, 'Heimtückefälle vor dem Sondergericht München' pp. 435ff.

60. B. Dörner, 'Das Konzentrationslager Oranienburg und die Justiz', in Mörsch (ed.), *Konzentrationslager Oranienburg* pp. 71–2.

61. Blumberg-Ebel, *Sondergerichtsbarkeit* pp. 61–7.

62. H. G. Hockerts, *Die Sittlichkeitsprozesse gegen katholische Ordensangehörige und Priester 1936/37* (Mainz 1971); G. Lewy, *The Catholic Church and Nazi Germany* (London 1964) p. 156; J. Conway, *The Nazi Persecution of the Churches* (London 1968) p. 159.

63. Anon. (ed.), *Nazi Persecution of the Catholic Church* pp. 298–325.

64. Niermann, *Die Durchsetzung politischer und politisierter Strafjustiz* pp. 295ff.

65. *Ibid.* p. 10 n. 252.

66. Löffler, *Das Diensttagebuch* pp. 114–23.

67. Solomon, *Soviet Criminal Justice* p. 100.

68. For the original verdict see Bundesminister der Justiz (ed.), *Im Namen des Deutschen Volkes* pp. 191–2.

69. K. Schilde and J. Tuchel, *Columbia-Haus. Berliner Konzentrationslager 1933–1936* (Berlin 1990) p. 32.

70. Gruchmann, *Justiz im Dritten Reich* p. 570.
71. Ilse Staff (ed.), *Justiz im Dritten Reich* (Frankfurt am Main 1964) p. 147.
72. Schilde and Tuchel, *Columbia-Haus* pp. 52–6.
73. *Ibid.* pp. 636ff. for the above.
74. Gruchmann, *Justiz im Dritten Reich* p. 698.
75. Dörner, 'Das Konzentrationslager Oranienburg und die Justiz' pp. 69–70.
76. Gruchmann, *Justiz im Dritten Reich* pp. 705–10.
77. For a succinct discussion of 'Schutzhaft' see M. Broszat, 'Nationalsozialistische Konzentrationslager', in Broszat *et al.*, *Anatomie des SS-Staates* (Munich 1979) 2, pp. 13–15.
78. Reinhard Rürup (ed.), *Topographie des Terrors* (Berlin 1989) p. 97.
79. On this see W. Ayass, 'Ein Gebot der nationalen Arbeitsdisziplin', in Ayass *et al.* (eds), *Feinderklärung und Prävention, Beiträge zur Geschichte der nationalsozialistischen Gesundheits- und Sozialpolitik* (Berlin 1988) 6, pp. 43ff.
80. Noakes and Pridham, *Nazism 1919–1945* 2, doc. 372, p. 501.
81. For details see R. Gellately, *The Gestapo and German Society* (Oxford 1990) pp. 36ff.
82. See S. Aronson, *Reinhard Heydrich und die frühe Geschichte von Gestapo und SD* (Stuttgart 1971), and G. Browder, *Foundations of the Nazi Police State: The Formation of Sipo and SD* (Lexington 1990).
83. Aronson, *Reinhard Heydrich* pp. 141–4.
84. G. Browder, *Hitler's Enforcers. The Gestapo and the SS Security Service in the Nazi Revolution* (Oxford 1996) pp. 116–19.
85. C. Graf, 'Kontinuitäten und Brüche', in G. Paul and K.-M. Mallmann (eds), *Die Gestapo. Mythos und Realität* (Darmstadt 1996) pp. 79–80.
86. Herbert, *Best* pp. 146–7; Robert L. Koehl, *The Black Corps* (Madison 1983) pp. 135–41 is an excellent guide to these issues.
87. For a clear discussion of the politics of this period see Heinz Höhne, *The Order of the Death's Head* (London 1969) pp. 76–84.
88. K. D. Bracher, *The German Dictatorship* (London 1970) p. 440.
89. Browder, *Hitler's Enforcers* pp. 36, 63, 122, 177 for these figures.
90. Jörg Kammler, 'Nationalsozialistische Machtergreifung und Gestapo- am Beispiel der Staatspolizeistelle für den Regierungsbezirk Kassel', in Eike Hennig (ed.), *Hessen unterm Hakenkreuz* (Frankfurt am Main 1984) pp. 515–17.
91. G. Paul, 'Ganz normale Akademiker', in Paul and Mallmann (eds), *Die Gestapo* pp. 240ff.
92. Andreas Seeger, *'Gestapo-Müller'. Die Karriere eines Schreibtischtäters* (Berlin 1996) pp. 34–5.

93. Browder, *Hitler's Enforcers* p. 70. See also Eric Johnson, *Nazi Terror: The Gestapo, Jews, and Ordinary Germans* (New York 1999)

94. K.-M. Mallmann, 'Die V-Leute der Gestapo', in Paul and Mallmann (eds), *Die Gestapo* pp. 268ff.; see also R. Gellately, 'Surveillance and Disobedience', in F. Nicosia and L. Stokes (eds), *Germans against Nazism* (Oxford 1990) pp. 20ff.

95. Michael Wildt, 'Der Hamburger Gestapochef Bruno Streckenbach', in F. Bajohr and J. Szodrzynski (eds), *Hamburg in der NS-Zeit* (Hamburg 1995) pp. 102–3.

96. Rürup (ed.), *Topographie des Terrors* pp. 82–96.

97. *Deutschland-Berichte der Sozialdemokratischen Partei Deutschlands (SOPADE)* (1936) 3, pp. 49–52.

98. Heinz Boberach (ed.), *Meldungen aus dem Reich. Die geheimen Lageberichte des Sicherheitsdienstes der SS 1938–1945* (Herrsching 1984) 1, p. 13.

99. 'Gemeinsame Anordnung für den Sicherheitsdienst der Reichsführer-SS und die Geheime Staatspolizei', in Michael Wildt (ed.), *Die Judenpolitik des SD 1935 bis 1938. Eine Dokumentation* (Munich 1995) doc. 14, pp. 118–20.

100. Hans Buchheim, 'Die SS. Das Herrschaftsinstrument', in Broszat *et al.* (eds), *Anatomie des SS-Staates* 1, p. 61.

101. Dieter Wisliceny's memorandum on the 'Jewish Question' dated 7 April 1937 and Herbert Hagen's report on co-operation between the SD and Gestapo dated 29 June 1937, in Wildt (ed.), *Die Judenpolitik* docs 12 and 13 pp. 110–18.

102. Himmler speech dated 1934, in B. Smith and A. Peterson (eds), *Heinrich Himmler. Geheimreden 1933–1945* (Frankfurt am Main 1974) p. 109.

103. Aronson, *Reinhard Heydrich* p. 201.

104. Herbert, *Best* pp. 187–8.

105. Lutz Hachmeister, *Der Gegnerforscher. Die Karriere des SS-Führers Franz Alfred Six* (Munich 1998).

106. Memorandum 'On the Jewish Problem', probably written by Eichmann in January 1939, in Wildt (ed.) *Die Judenpolitik* doc. 9, p. 99.

107. R. Heydrich, 'Wandlungen unseres Kampfes', *SK* 8–29 May 1935, Folge 10–13, front page.

108. ' "Weisse Juden" in der Wissenschaft', *SK* 15 July 1937, Folge 28, p. 8.

109. Alan Beyerchen, *Scientists under Hitler. Politics and the Physics Community in the Third Reich* (New Haven 1977) pp. 156ff.

110. 'Ein mutiger Schritt', *SK* 11 March 1937, Folge, p. 18; 'Zum Thema: Grandentod', *SK* 18 March 1937, p. 9; Michael Burleigh, *Death and Deliverance. 'Euthanasia' in Germany c. 1900–1945* (Cambridge 1994) p. 44.

111. Boberach (ed.), *Meldungen aus dem Reich* 2 pp. 8–20.

112. Herbert, *Best* p. 190.

113. See especially W. Wippermann, *Der Ordensstaat als Ideologie* (Berlin 1969).

114. Heinrich Himmler, *Die Schutzstaffel als antibolschewistische Kampforganisation* (Munich 1936) p. 29.

115. J. Ackermann, *Heinrich Himmler als Ideologe* (Göttingen 1970) p. 142.

116. Himmler speech dated 1937, in Smith and Peterson (eds), *Heinrich Himmler. Geheimreden* p. 74; see also Jeremy Noakes, 'Nazism and High Society' in M. Burleigh (ed.), *Confronting the Nazi Past* (London and New York 1996) pp. 57–9.

117. Höhne, *The Order of the Death's Head* pp. 123ff.

118. H. Ziegler, *Nazi Germany's New Aristocracy. The SS Leadership 1925–1939* (New Jersey 1989).

119. Ackermann, *Heinrich Himmler als Ideologe* pp. 106–7.

120. Höhne, *The Order of the Death's Head* pp. 143–4.

121. Buchheim, 'Die SS. Das Herrschaftsinstrument' esp. pp. 235–40.

122. Herbert, *Best* pp. 44–5.

123. 'Flamen und Deutsche', *SK* 30 January 1941, p. 4.

124. Ackermann, *Heinrich Himmler als Ideologe* p. 90.

125. Himmler speech dated 1935, in Smith and Peterson (eds), *Heinrich Himmler. Geheimreden* pp. 85–6.

126. Wolfgang Sofsky, *The Order of Terror* (Princeton 1998) pp. 28–35.

127. *Deutschland-Berichte der SOPADE* (1935) 2, report dated 2 March 1935, p. 370.

128. *Ibid.* report dated 2 July 1935, pp. 820–4 for a detailed report on conditions in Gross-Strelitz.

129. For the duration of their existence see G. Schwarz, *Die nationalsozialistischen Lager* (Frankfurt am Main 1996) pp. 167–71.

130. D. Krause-Vilmar, 'Das Konzentrationslager Breitenau 1933/34', in Hennig (ed.), *Hessen unterm Hakenkreuz* p. 487; see also his *Das Konzentrationslager Breitenau* (Marburg 1998), and G. Richter (ed.), *Breitenau. Zur Geschichte eines nationalsozialistischen Konzentrations- und Arbeitserziehungslager* (Kassel 1993).

131. B. Sösemann and J. Schulz, 'Nationalsozialismus und Propaganda', in Mörsch (ed.), *Konzentrationslager Oranienburg* pp. 89–91.

132. L. Wieland, *Die Konzentrationslager Langlütjen und Ochtumsand* (Bremerhaven 1992).

133. Koehl, *The Black Corps* p. 129.

134. Noakes and Pridham (eds), *Nazism 1919–1945* 2, doc. 373, pp. 502–4.

135. On camps see the early classic Eugen Kogon, *Der SS-Staat* (13th edn Munich 1974); Martin Broszat's quasi-forensic 'Nationalsozialistische Konzentrationslager 1933–1945', in Broszat *et al. Anatomie des*

SS-Staates 2, pp. 13–132; J. Tuchel, *Konzentrationslager* (Boppard 1991); A. Kaminski, *Konzentrationslager 1896 bis heute* (Stuttgart 1982); and the brilliant comparative study by Tzvetan Todorov, *Facing the Extremes. Moral Life in the Concentration Camps* (New York 1997).

136. J. Tuchel, 'Die Systematisierung der Gewalt', in Mörsch (ed.), *Konzentrationslager Oranienburg* p. 124.

137. 'K.Z. und seine Insassen', *SK* 18 February 1936, Folge 7, p. 10.

138. Himmler speech dated 1939, in Smith and Peterson (eds), *Heinrich Himmler. Geheimreden* p. 111.

139. Schilde and Tuchel, *Columbia-Haus* p. 54.

140. *Deutschland-Berichte der SOPADE* (1935) 2, entry dated 2 March 1935, pp. 371–2.

141. Primo Levi, *If This Is A Man* (London 1987) p. 35.

142. Benedikt Kautsky, *Devils and the Damned* (London 1960) pp. 59–60.

143. For examples see Gordon Horowitz, *In the Shadow of Death* (London 1991) p. 17.

144. Heinz Heger, *The Men with the Pink Triangle* (London 1986) p. 51.

145. For examples of sexual sadism or homo- and heterosexual rape see David Hackett (ed.), *The Buchenwald Report* (Boulder 1995) pp. 158–60, and Heger, *The Men with the Pink Triangle* pp. 54–6.

146. M. Hrdlicka, *Alltag im KZ. Das Lager Sachsenhausen bei Berlin* (Opladen 1992) pp. 64–5.

147. P. Grünewald, 'Das KZ Osthofen' in Hennig (ed.), *Hessen unterm Hakenkreuz* p. 501.

148. B. Perz, "müssen zu reiszenden Bestien erzogen werden". Der Einsatz von Hunden zur Bewachung in den Konzentrationslagern', *Dachauer Hefte* (1992) 12, pp. 155–6.

149. See *Deutschland-Berichte der SOPADE* (1936) 3, entry dated 3 December 1936, pp. 1607–35 for accounts of several camps.

150. H. Langbein, *Against All Hope* (London 1996) p. 155.

151. See especially Michael André Bernstein's outstanding *Foregone Conclusions. Against Apocalyptic History* (Berkeley 1994).

152. Noakes and Pridham (eds) *Nazism 1919–1945* doc. 270, pp. 385–6.

153. P. Reichel, *Der schöne Schein des Dritten Reiches* (Munich 1991) p. 164.

154. For the above see mainly A. Diller, *Rundfunkpolitik im Dritten Reich* (Munich 1980); J. Wulf, *Presse und Funk im Dritten Reich* (Gütersloh 1964).

155. For a good survey of the press see Oron Hale, *The Captive Press in the Third Reich* (Princeton 1973).

156. On this see W. Wippermann, *'Machtergreifung' Berlin 1933* (Berlin 1982) p. 205.

157. N. Frei and J. Schmitz, *Journalismus im Dritten Reich* (Munich 1989) pp. 37–8.

158. Herman Ullstein, *The Rise and Fall of the House of Ullstein* (London 1944) pp. 15–41.

159. Frei and Schmitz, *Journalismus* p. 31.

160. Jack Schamash, 'At Home with Hitler', *Evening Standard* 10 November 1998, p. 25, based on the November 1938 edition of *Homes and Gardens*.

161. Ralf Georg Reuth, *Goebbels* (London 1993) p. 174.

162. The fundamental text is Eric Voegelin's 1938 *Die politischen Religionen* (2nd edn Munich 1996).

163. Domarus (ed.), *Hitler. Speeches and Proclamations* 2, 6 September 1937, p. 922.

164. Angela Schwarz, *Die Reise ins Dritte Reich* (Göttingen 1993) p. 225.

165. A. Speer, *Inside the Third Reich* (London 1970) p. 100.

166. On this, J. P. Stern's otherwise rather pretentious *Hitler. The Führer and the People* (London 1975) is convincing.

167. Reichel, *Der schöne Schein* pp. 116ff.

168. Domarus (ed.), *Hitler. Speeches and Proclamations* 2, p. 931.

169. *Ibid.* p. 932.

170. On this see above all Ian Kershaw's *The 'Hitler Myth'. Image and Reality in the Third Reich* (Oxford 1987) esp. pp. 48–82.

171. For the text see Beatrice and Helmut Heiber (eds), *Die Rückseite des Hakenkreuzes* (Munich 1993) doc. 200, pp. 148–9, from which all of the preceding communications to Hitler are also taken.

172. Noakes and Pridham (eds), *Nazism 1919–1945* 2, doc. 297, p. 417.

3. NEW TIMES, NEW MAN

1. For examples see C. Fischer, *Stormtroopers. A Social, Economic and Ideological Analysis* (London 1983).

2. See H. Vorländer, 'Erich Hilgenfeldt. Reichswalter der NSV', in R. Smelser, E. Syring and R. Zitelmann (eds), *Die braune Elite II* (Darmstadt 1993) pp. 166–78.

3. *Ibid.* p. 132.

4. See especially Horst Seithe and Frauke Hagemann, *Das Deutsche Rote Kreuz im Dritten Reich (1933–1939)* (Frankfurt am Main 1993), and on the wider context Caroline Moorhead, *Dunant's Dream* (London 1998). For a general introduction to the relationship between charity and welfare see Paul Weindling, 'The Modernization of Charity in Nineteenth Century Germany and France', in J. Barry and C. Jones

(eds), *Medicine and Charity before the Welfare State* (London 1991) pp. 190–206.

5. See especially Young-Sun Hong, *Welfare, Modernity, and the Weimar State 1919–1933* (Princeton 1998) pp. 231–2.

6. H. Vorländer, *Die NSV. Darstellung und Dokumentation einer national-sozialistischen Organisation* (Boppard am Rhein 1988) pp. 108–12 is fundamental.

7. Seithe and Hagemann, *Das Deutsche Rote Kreuz* pp. 101–12.

8. Leonard Shapiro, *Totalitarianism* (London 1972) pp. 68–9.

9. *Deutschland-Berichte der Sozialdemokratischen Partei Deutschlands* (SOPADE) (1938) 5, entry dated 5 January 1938, p. 78.

10. K. Tennstedt, 'Wohltat und Interesse. Das Winterhilfswerk des Deutschen Volkes', *GuG* (1987) 13, pp. 157–80.

11. Max Domarus (ed.), *Hitler. Speeches and Proclamations 1932–1945* (London 1990–7) 2, speech dated 8 October 1935, p. 717.

12. *Ibid.* p. 955.

13. *Ibid.* pp. 716–17.

14. *Deutschland-Berichte der SOPADE* (1938) 5, entry dated 5 January 1938, p. 86.

15. Domarus (ed.), *Hitler. Speeches and Proclamations* 2, dated 5 October 1937, p. 954, and Vorländer, *Die NSV* illustration facing p. 201.

16. Seithe and Hagemann, *Das Deutsche Rote Kreuz* p. 86.

17. The views of the more *outré* radical fringes can be sampled in the oxymoronic *Living Marxism*; see D. Stoesz and J. Midgley, 'The Radical Right and the Welfare State', in H. Glennerster and Midgley (eds), *The Radical Right and the Welfare State. An International Assessment* (Hemel Hempstead 1991) pp. 31ff.

18. Wolfgang Ayass, ' "Ein Gebot der nationalen Arbeitsdisziplin". Die Aktion "Arbeitsscheu Reich 1938" ', *Beiträge zur Geschichte der national-sozialistischen Gesundheits- und Sozialpolitik* (Berlin 1988) 6, p. 53; see also his *'Asoziale' im Nationalsozialismus* (Stuttgart 1995).

19. See G. Mörsch, *Arbeit und Brot* (Frankfurt am Main 1993) pp. 48–9.

20. Christopher Sachsse and Florian Tennstedt, *Der Wohlfahrtsstaat im Nationalsozialismus* (Stuttgart 1992) p. 119.

21. On this Hong, *Welfare, Modernity* is fundamental.

22. *Deutschland-Berichte der SOPADE* (1936) 3, entry dated 3 October 1936, p. 1282, concerning three hundred workers in an automobile plant.

23. *Ibid.* (1938) 5, entry dated 5 January 1938, p. 83.

24. *Ibid.* (1935) 2, entry dated 2 December 1935, p. 1422.

25. Letter of the NSDAP Gau Franconia, Kreisleitung Weissenburg dated 15 November 1935, in Vorländer, *Die NSV* doc. 48, p. 230.

26. *Deutschland-Berichte der SOPADE* (1935) 2, entry dated 2 February 1935, pp. 200–1.
27. *Ibid.* pp. 197–8.
28. *Ibid.* (1936) 3, entry dated 3 September 1936, pp. 1151–2; see also (1935) 2, entry dated 2 January 1935, pp. 89–91.
29. *Ibid.* (1935) 2, entry dated 2 February 1935, p. 169.
30. *Ibid.* p. 170.
31. *Ibid.* (1935) 2, entry dated 2 July 1935, p. 864.
32. Cornelie Usborne, *The Politics of the Body in Weimar Germany* (Houndsmill 1993) pp. 33–52 is both fascinating and outstanding.
33. M. S. Quine, *Population Politics in Twentieth-Century Europe* (London 1996).
34. Vorländer, *Die NSV* p. 63.
35. For the above see Lisa Pine, *Nazi Family Policy 1933–1945* (Oxford 1997) pp. 24–31.
36. Irmgard Weyrauther's excellent *Muttertag und Mutterkreuz. Der Kult um die 'deutsche Mutter' im Nationalsozialismus* (Frankfurt am Main 1993) pp. 18ff. for the above.
37. See especially Saul Friedländer's brilliant essay *Kitsch und Tod* (Munich 1986) pp. 20ff. and 118ff.
38. Weyrauther, *Muttertag und Mutterkreuz* esp. pp. 162ff.
39. James Rhodes, *The Hitler Movement. A Modern Millenarian Movement* (Stanford 1980) p. 95.
40. For Nazi policy towards homosexuals see G. Grau, *Hidden Holocaust?* (London 1995).
41. F. Kersten, *The Kersten Memoirs 1940–1945* (London 1956) pp. 176–7.
42. G. Lilienthal, *Der 'Lebensborn e.V.' Ein Instrument nationalsozialistischer Rassenpolitik* (Frankfurt am Main 1996).
43. See Josef Meisinger, 'The Combating of Homosexuality and Abortion: A Political Task', in Grau, *Hidden Holocaust?* doc. 38, pp. 110–15.
44. Richard Grunberger, *A Social History of the Third Reich* (London 1974) p. 308.
45. P. Merkl, *Political Violence under the Swastika* (Princeton 1975) pp. 258, 712.
46. Cited by David Welch, *The Third Reich. Politics and Propaganda* (London 1993) p. 63.
47. See Arno Klönne, *Hitlerjugend* (Hanover 1955) and *Jugend im Dritten Reich* (Cologne 1984), and M. Klaus, *Mädchen in der Hitlerjugend* (Cologne 1980) and *Mädchen im Dritten Reich* (Cologne 1983).
48. Detlev Peukert, *Inside Nazi Germany* (London 1987) pp. 145–74, and his *Die Edelweisspiraten* (Cologne 1988) are especially symptomatic.
49. David Welch, *Propaganda and the German Cinema* (Oxford 1983).

50. *Deutschland-Berichte der SOPADE* (1937) 4, entry dated 4 June 1937, p. 852.
51. *Ibid.* (1938) 5, entry dated 5 December 1938, p. 1404.
52. L. Peiffer, *Turnunterricht im Dritten Reich* (Cologne 1987) pp. 40ff.
53. *Deutschland-Berichte der SOPADE*, (1935) 2, entry dated 2 November 1935, p. 1278.
54. *Ibid.* (1939) 6, entry dated 6 March 1939, p. 317.
55. *Ibid.* (1935) 2, entry dated 2 February 1935, p. 215, and (1938) 5, entry dated 5 December 1938, p. 1402.
56. For examples of HJ members being encouraged to denounce their parents see *ibid.* (1937) 4, entry dated 4 June 1937, p. 840; and *ibid.* (1936) 3, entry dated 3 June 1936, p. 769 for parental fear of striking their own children.
57. *Ibid.* (1934) 1, entry dated 1 September 1934, p. 565.
58. *Ibid.* (1938) 5, entry dated 5 December 1938, pp. 1397–8.
59. *Ibid.* (1935) 2, entry dated 2 November 1935, pp. 1287–9.
60. *Ibid.* (1937) 4, entry dated 4 April 1937, p. 494.
61. *Ibid.* (1938) 5, entry dated 5 December 1938, p. 1398.
62. *Ibid.* (1936) 3, entry dated 3 June 1936, p. 769.
63. *Ibid.* (1934) 1, entry dated 1 September 1934, p. 565.
64. *Ibid.* (1935) 2, entry dated 2 June 1935, p. 693, and (1936) 3, entry dated 3 October 1936, p. 1318.
65. Domarus (ed.), *Hitler. Speeches and Proclamations* 1, pp. 360–1.
66. F. Seidler, 'Fritz Todt. From Motorway Builder to Minister of State', in R. Smelser and R. Zitelmann (eds), *The Nazi Elite* (London 1993) pp. 245ff., and his *Fritz Todt* (Munich 1986).
67. For the Weimar prehistory of the Autobahnen see M. Kornrumpf, *HAFRABA e.V Deutsche Autobahn-Planung 1926–1934* (Bonn 1990).
68. J. D. Shand, 'The Reichsautobahnen. Symbol for the Third Reich', *JCH* (1984) 19, p. 193.
69. Hans-Joachim Gamm, *Der braune Kult* (Hamburg 1962) pp. 99–100.
70. Mörsch, *Arbeit und Brot* p. 134.
71. See E. Schulz and E. Gruber, *Mythos Reichsautobahn. Bau und Inszenierung der 'Strassen des Führers' 1933–1941* (Berlin 1996) for the above.
72. On this see the remarkable book by Joan Campbell, *Joy in Work. German Work* (Princeton 1989).
73. See Carola Sachsse, 'Freizeit zwischen Betrieb und Volksgemeinschaft', *Archiv für Sozialgeschichte* (1993) 33, pp. 305–28, and *Siemens, der Nationalsozialismus und die moderne Familie* (Hamburg 1990).
74. Morsch, *Arbeit und Brot* pp. 53–7.
75. Domarus (ed.), *Hitler. Speeches and Proclamations* 2, dated 10 May 1933, p. 320.
76. Rhodes, *The Hitler Movement* pp. 116–20.
77. For this see the important book by E. Heuel, *Der umworbene Stand.*

Die ideologische Integration der Arbeiter im Nationalsozialismus 1933–1935 (Frankfurt am Main 1989) pp. 76–9.

78. Outstanding economic histories include Richard Overy, *The Nazi Economic Recovery 1932–1938* (2nd edn Cambridge 1996), his penetrating biography of Göring, *The Iron Man* (London 1983) and his essay collection *War and the Economy in the Third Reich* (Oxford 1994). There are also excellent histories by Harold James, *The German Slump. Politics and Economics 1924–1936* (Oxford 1986) and Avraham Barkai, *Nazi Economics. Ideology, Theory and Policy* (Oxford 1990).

79. For an excellent discussion of these issues see R. Zitelmann, *Hitler. Selbstverständnis eines Revolutionärs* (Stuttgart 1991) pp. 147ff.

80. Rhodes, *The Hitler Movement* p. 102.

81. Domarus (ed.), *Hitler. Speeches and Proclamations* 2, dated 14 September 1936, p. 839.

82. H. R. Trevor-Roper (ed.), *Hitler's Table Talk 1941–44* (Oxford 1988) entry dated 31 January 1942, p. 268.

83. Jeremy Noakes, 'Nazism and High Society', in M. Burleigh (ed.), *Confronting the Nazi Past* (London 1996) p. 63.

84. Domarus (ed.), *Hitler. Speeches and Proclamations* 2, dated 6 September 1938, p. 1145.

85. *Ibid.* 1, dated 10 May 1933, p. 321.

86. *Ibid.* 2, dated 27 March 1936, p. 798.

87. *Ibid.* 2, dated 25 March 1934, p. 444.

88. *Ibid.* 2, dated 1 May 1937, p. 892.

89. Schwarz, *Die Reise ins Dritte Reich* p. 239.

90. Important studies of the German working class and Nazism include Ulrich Herbert, 'Arbeiterschaft im "Dritten Reich"', *GuG* (1989) 15, pp. 320ff.

91. Heuel, *Der umworbene Stand* pp. 133–6.

92. David Schoenbaum, *Hitler's Social Revolution* (London 1966) pp. 77–8.

93. See Alf Ludtke, 'The "Honor of Labor"', in David Crew (ed.), *Nazism and German Society 1933–1945* (London 1994) pp. 67ff.; on the drawbacks of skilled craftsmanship see Richard J. Overy, *Why the Allies Won* (London 1995) pp. 202–5.

94. For these details see Ronald Smelser, *Robert Ley. Hitler's Labor Front Leader* (Oxford 1988) p. 214.

95. Amt Schönheit der Arbeit (ed.), *Das Taschenbuch Schönheit der Arbeit* (Berlin 1938) and Anson Rabinbach, 'The Aesthetics of Production in the Third Reich', *JCH* (1974) 11, pp. 43–74.

96. Smelser, *Robert Ley* pp. 210–11.

97. J. Rostock and F. Zadnicek, *Paradies Ruinen. Das KdF Seebad der Zwanzigtausend auf Rügen* (Berlin 1995).

98. See G. Mai, 'Warum steht der deutsche Arbeiter zu Hitler?', *GuG* (1986) 12, p. 228.

99. H. Weiss, 'Ideologie der Freizeit im Dritten Reich', *Archiv für Sozialgeschichte* (1993) 33, pp. 289–303.

100. Heuel, *Der umworbene Stand* pp. 426–7.

101. The classic accounts are Schoenbaum, *Hitler's Social Revolution* and R. Dahrendorf, *Society and Democracy in Germany* (London 1968). For the sinister aspects of Nazi social policy see Michael Burleigh and Wolfgang Wippermann, *The Racial State. Germany 1933–1945* (Cambridge 1991).

102. Overy, *The Nazi Economic Recovery* p. 31.

103. *Deutschland-Berichte der SOPADE* (1937) entry dated 4 April 1937, pp. 497–9.

104. Domarus (ed.), *Hitler. Speeches and Proclamations* 2, speech dated 6 September 1938, p. 1146.

105. Anon, (ed.), *Nazi Persecution of the Catholic Church* (London 1940), citing *SK* 1 May 1937, p. 459.

106. On this see especially Philippe Burrin, 'Political Religion', *History & Memory* (1997) 9, pp. 321–49; Klaus Vondung, 'Die Apocalypse des Nationalsozialismus', in M. Ley and J. Schoeps (eds), *Der Nationalsozialismus als politische Religion* (Bodenheim 1997) pp. 33–52; and Claus-Ekkard Bärsch, *Die politische Religion des Nationalsozialismus* (Munich 1998). It is striking that a massive recent literature based on approaches pioneered by Voegelin, Vondung and Rhodes is completely ignored in a largely secularist literature on National Socialism. The same applies to the most sophisticated recent work based on totalitarianism, as distinct from critical engagement with a more limited range of work produced during the Cold War, which allegedly can be marginalised because of its overt political agendas.

107. For the Italian case see E. Gentile, 'Fascism as Political Religion', *JCH* (1990) 25, pp. 229–57.

108. For the barmier aspects of Nazism see N. Goodrick-Clarke, *The Occult Roots of Nazism. Secret Aryan Cults and their Influence on Nazi Ideology* (London 1992).

109. Burrin, 'Political Religion' p. 338.

110. For an excellent discussion of disputes about the conversion of the ancient Germans during the Nazi period see Kurt Meier, *Kreuz und Hakenkreuz. Die evangelische Kirche im Dritten Reich* (Munich 1992) pp. 107–16.

111. Cited by Rhodes, *The Hitler Movement* p. 78.

112. Kurt Nowak, *Geschichte des Christentums in Deutschland* (Munich 1995) p. 252. See also Doris L. Bergen, ' "Germany is our Mission –

Christ is our strength!" The Wehrmacht Chaplaincy and the "German Christian" movement', *Church History* (1997) 66, pp. 522–36.

113. Cited by John Conway, *The Nazi Persecution of the Churches 1933–1945* (London 1968) p. 16.

114. See especially Robert Ericksen, *Theologians under Hitler* (New Haven 1985).

115. Uriel Tal, *Structures of German 'Political Theology' in the Nazi Era* (Tel Aviv 1981) p. 32. See also Doris Bergen, 'Catholics, Protestants, and Antisemitism in Nazi Germany', *CEH* 27, pp. 329–52.

116. Doris Bergen, *Twisted Cross. The German Christian Movement in the Third Reich* (Chapel Hill 1996) p. 29.

117. Anon. (ed.), *Nazi Persecution of the Catholic Church*, citing *SK* 7 January 1937, pp. 440–1.

118. Uriel Tal, *Political Faith of Nazism Prior to the Holocaust* (Tel Aviv 1978) p. 40.

119. Conway, *The Nazi Persecution of the Churches* pp. 175–95.

120. For these and numerous further examples see Anon. (ed.), *Nazi Persecution of the Catholic Church* pp. 544–9; Ian Kershaw, *Popular Opinion and Dissent in the Third Reich. Bavaria 1933–1945* (Oxford 1983) p. 206.

121. See especially Jeremy Noakes, 'The Oldenburg Crucifix Struggle of November 1936. A Case Study of Opposition in the Third Reich', in P. Stachura (ed.), *The Shaping of the Nazi State* (London 1978) pp. 210–33.

122. *Deutschland-Berichte der SOPADE* (1937) 4, entry dated 4 August 1937, pp. 1165–9.

123. *Ibid.* pp. 1176–9.

124. Gamm, *Der braune Kult* pp. 141ff.

125. For the architectural history of the Königsplatz see Sabine Behrenbeck, *Der Kult um die toten Helden. Nationalsozialistische Mythen, Riten und Symbole* (Vierow 1996) pp. 371ff.

126. See Klaus Vondung, *Magie und Manipulation. Ideologischer Kult und politische Religion des Nationalsozialismus* (Göttingen 1971) pp. 83–5.

127. On the Hitler myth see Ian Kershaw's remarkable *The 'Hitler Myth'. Image and Reality in the Third Reich* (Oxford 1987) esp. chs 1–5.

128. Domarus (ed.), *Hitler. Speeches and Proclamations* 2, speech dated 1 May 1936, p. 809.

129. Among the best recent histories are D. C. Watt, *How War Came* (London 1989) and the classics by Jakobsen, Michalka and Weinberg.

130. Domarus (ed.), *Hitler. Speeches and Proclamations* 1, speech dated 16 June 1934, p. 463.

131. Evelyn Wrench, *I Loved Germany* (London 1940) pp. 185–6.

132. For a good discussion of these issues see John Hiden, *Germany and Europe 1919–1939* (London 1977) pp. 158–9.

133. G. Weinberg, *The Foreign Policy of Hitler's Germany. Diplomatic Revolution in Europe 1933–1936* (Chicago 1970) p. x.
134. Kershaw, *The 'Hitler Myth'* p. 122.
135. On this see Klaus-Jörg Siegfried, *Universalismus und Faschismus. Das Gesellschaftsbild Othmar Spanns* (Vienna 1974).
136. Bruce Pauley, *Hitler and the Forgotten Nazis. A History of Austrian National Socialism* (Chapel Hill 1981) p. 79.
137. For this comparison see Stanley Payne's panoramic *A History of Fascism 1914–45* (London 1995) p. 249.
138. Domarus (ed.), *Hitler. Speeches and Proclamations* 1, pp. 433–4.
139. Ian Kershaw, *Hitler 1889–1936. Hubris* (London 1998) p. 523.
140. Bruce Pauley, *From Prejudice to Persecution. A History of Austrian Antisemitism* (Chapel Hill 1992) p. 273. See also now Evan Burr Bukey, *Hitler's Austria. Popular Sentiment in the Nazi Era 1938–1945* (Chapel Hill 2000).
141. Payne, *A History of Fascism* p. 251.
142. For part of text of their discussion see J. Noakes and G. Pridham (eds), *Nazism 1919–1945. A Documentary Reader* (Exeter 1983–8) 3, doc. 505, p. 690.
143. Joachim Fest, *Hitler* (London 1974) p. 809.
144. Domarus (ed.), *Hitler. Speeches and Proclamations* 2, pp. 1013ff.
145. *Ibid.* p. 1032.
146. Pauley, *Hitler and the Forgotten Nazis* p. 206.
147. Domarus (ed.), *Hitler. Speeches and Proclamations* 2, p. 1048.
148. *Ibid.* speeches dated 25 March and 31 March 1938, pp. 1071 and 1079.
149. *Ibid.* interview dated 12 March 1938, p. 1052.
150. *Ibid.* speech dated 25 March 1938, p. 1073.
151. *Ibid.* speech dated 9 April 1938, pp. 1088–9.

4. GERMAN JEWS AND THEIR NEIGHBOURS, 1933–1939

1. Michael Burleigh and Wolfgang Wippermann, *The Racial State. Germany 1933–1945* (Cambridge 1991) p. 76.
2. Avraham Barkai, *From Boycott to Annihilation. The Economic Struggle of German Jews 1933–1943* (Brandeis 1989) pp. 14–15.
3. For an excellent discussion of the boycott see Helmut Genschel, *Die Verdrängung der Juden aus der Wirtschaft im Dritten Reich* (Göttingen 1966) pp. 43ff.
4. Ralf Georg Reuth (ed.), *Joseph Goebbels. Tagebücher* (Munich 1992) 2, p. 787.
5. *Ibid.* pp. 786–7.

6. Kurt Meier, *Kreuz und Hakenkreuz. Die evangelische Kirche im Dritten Reich* (Munich 1992) p. 157.

7. Ino Arndt, 'Machtübernahme und Judenboykott in der Sicht evangelischer Sonntagsblätter', in Wolfgang Benz (ed.), *Miscellanea. Festschrift für Helmut Krausnick zum 75. Geburtstag* (Stuttgart 1980) pp. 15–31.

8. Edwin Landau, 'Für die standen wir in den Schützengruben', in Margarete Limberg and Hubert Rubsaat (eds), *Sie dürften nicht mehr Deutsche sein. Jüdischer Alltag in Selbstzeugnissen 1933–1938* (Frankfurt am Main 1990) pp. 31–3.

9. Victor Klemperer, *Tagebücher 1933–1941* (Berlin 1995) 1, entry dated 7 April 1933, p. 19.

10. Evelyn Wrench, *I Loved Germany* (London 1940) p. 121; Angela Schwarz, *Die Reise ins Dritte Reich* (Göttingen 1993) p. 305.

11. David Bankier, *The Germans and the Final Solution. Public Opinion under Nazism* (Oxford 1992) p. 69.

12. Victor Klemperer, *I Shall Bear Witness* (London 1998) 1, entry dated 31 March 1933, p. 10.

13. For the leaflet's text and reactions to it see Erich Leyens and Lotte Andor, *Years of Estrangement* (Evanston 1996) pp. 11–12.

14. For differing assessments of the popularity of the boycott see Wolfgang Benz, 'Die Deutschen und die Judenverfolgung', and Ursula Büttner, 'Die Deutsche Bevölkerung und die Judenverfolgung 1933–1945', both in Büttner (ed.), *Die Deutschen und die Judenverfolgung im Dritten Reich* (Hamburg 1992) pp. 54–5 and 72–3.

15. On the 'Jew-count' see George Mosse, *Fallen Soldiers. Reshaping the Memory of the World Wars* (Oxford 1990), pp. 175–6.

16. Dirk Blasius, '"Bürgerlicher Tod". Der NS-Unrechtsstaat und die deutschen Juden', *Geschichte im Wissenschaft und Unterricht* (1990) 3, p. 136.

17. Michael H. Kater, *Doctors under Hitler* (Chapel Hill 1989) p. 187.

18. David Clay Large, *Where Ghosts Walked* (New York 1997) p. 247.

19. On Jewish dentists see Michael Kohn, *Zahnärzte 1933–1945* (Berlin 1994) pp. 36ff.

20. Cited by Karl Heinz Jahnke, 'Die Vernichtung der Juden in Mecklenburg', in Arno Herzig and Ina Lorenz (eds), *Verdrängung und Vernichtung der Juden unter dem Nationalsozialismus* (Hamburg 1992) p. 295.

21. Doron Niederland, 'The Emigration of Jewish Academics and Professionals from Germany in the First Years of Nazi Rule', *LBIY* (1988) 33, pp. 285ff.

22. Albrecht Dumling, *Entartete Musik* (London 1995) p. 14.

23. Thomas Powers, *Heisenberg's War. The Secret History of the German Bomb* (London 1993) p. 39.

24. George Clare, *Last Waltz in Vienna* (London 1994) p. 121.

25. Menachem Kaufman, 'The Daily Life of the Village and Country Jews in Hessen from Hitler's Ascent to Power to November 1938', *Yad Vashem Studies* (1992) 22, pp. 189–90.

26. Blasius, ' "Bürgerlicher Tod" ' pp. 132–3.

27. Konrad Kwiet, 'The Ultimate Refuge. Suicide in the Jewish Community under the Nazis', *LBIY* (1988) 32, pp. 146–7.

28. Yehuda Bauer, *A History of the Holocaust* (New York 1982) pp. 113–20.

29. Bankier, *The Germans and the Final Solution*, p. 35; Nathan Stoltzfus, *Resistance of the Heart* (New York 1996), pp. 66–7.

30. *Deutschland-Berichte der SOPADE* (1935) 2, entry dated 2 July 1935, pp. 801ff.

31. *Ibid.* pp. 801–2, 803–4.

32. *Ibid.* pp. 805–6.

33. *Ibid.* pp. 809–10.

34. Daniel Jonah Goldhagen, *Hitler's Willing Executioners. Ordinary Germans and the Holocaust* (London 1996).

35. *Deutschland-Berichte der Sozialdemokratischen Partei Deutschlands (SOPADE)* (1935) 2, entry dated 2 July 1935, p. 812.

36. Gisela Diewald-Kerkmann, *Politische Denunziation im NS-Regime oder die kleine Macht der 'Volksgenossen'* (Bonn 1995) p. 95.

37. Ian Kershaw, *Popular Opinion and Political Dissent in the Third Reich. Bavaria 1933–1945* (Oxford 1983), pp. 243–4 sensibly makes this point.

38. *Deutschland-Berichte der SOPADE* (1935) 2, entry dated August 1935, pp. 933ff.

39. *Ibid.* (1936) 3, entry dated 3 August 1936, p. 986.

40. M. Wildt (ed.), *Die Judenpolitik des SD* (Munich 1995) p. 18.

41. *Deutschland-Berichte der SOPADE* (1935) 2, entry dated 2 August 1935, p. 922.

42. *Ibid.* p. 928.

43. *Ibid.* (1937) 4, entry dated 4 November 1937, p. 1572.

44. Kaufman, 'The Daily Life', pp. 165–6.

45. Steven Lowenstein, 'The Struggle for Survival of Rural Jews in Germany 1933–1938. The Case of Bezirksamt Weissenburg, Mittelfranken', in Arnold Paucker (ed.), *Die Juden im Nationalsozialistischen Deutschland* (Tübingen 1986), pp. 117ff.

46. See above all the careful analysis of Ian Kershaw, 'The Persecution of the Jews and German Popular Opinion in the Third Reich', *LBIY* (1981) 26, pp. 261–89; 'German Popular Opinion and the "Jewish Question" 1939–1943. Some Further Reflections', in Paucker (ed.), *Die Juden im Nationalsozialistischen Deutschland*, pp. 366–86.

47. Meier, *Kreuz und Hakenkreuz* pp. 157ff.; Martin Greschat, 'Die Haltung der deutschen evangelischen Kirchen zur Verfolgung der Juden im Dritten Reich', in Büttner (ed.), *Die Deutschen und die Judenverfolgung* pp. 277–8; Klaus Scholder, *Die Kirchen und das Dritte Reich* (Frankfurt am Main 1977) 1.

48. *Reichsgesetzblatt* (1935) 1, pp. 609–11.

49. Bankier, *The Germans and the Final Solution*, pp. 42ff.

50. See above all the important article by Otto Dov Kulka, 'Die Nürnberger Rassengesetze und die deutsche Bevölkerung im Lichte Geheimer NS-Lage- und Stimmungsberichte', *VfZ* (1984) 32, esp. pp. 615ff.

51. Saul Friedländer, *Nazi Germany and the Jews* (London 1997) 1, p. 149.

52. Jeremy Noakes and Geoffrey Pridham (eds), *Nazism 1919–1945. A Documentary Reader* (Exeter 1983–8) 2, pp. 532–40 is both clear and persuasive.

53. Ingo Müller, *Hitler's Justice. The Courts of the Third Reich* (Cambridge, Mass. 1991) p. 111.

54. Max Domarus (ed.), *Hitler. Reden und Proklamationen 1932–1945* (Neustadt 1962) 1, pp. 538–9.

55. Itzhak Arad, Yisrael Gutman and Abraham Margolis (eds), *Documents on the Holocaust* (Jerusalem 1981) doc. 37, pp. 82–3.

56. *Ibid.* doc. 38, pp. 84–6.

57. Max Domarus (ed.), *Hitler's Speeches and Proclamations 1932–1945* (London 1990–7) 2, speech dated 15 September 1935, p. 706.

58. Blasius, ' "Bürgerlicher Tod" ' pp. 138–9.

59. Walther Höfer, 'Stufen der Judenverfolgung im Dritten Reich 1933–1939', in Herbert Strauss and Norbert Kampe (eds), *Antisemitismus* (Bonn 1984) p. 179.

60. Stoltzfus, *Resistance of the Heart* pp. 43ff.

61. Leyens and Andor, *Years of Estrangement* p. 17.

62. Klemperer, *I Shall Bear Witness* entry dated 10 August 1938, p. 252.

63. Diewald-Kerkmann, *Politische Denunziation im NS-Regime* p. 94.

64. Max Reiner, 'Der Weg zum Paria', in Limberg and Rubsaat (eds) *Sie dürften nicht mehr Deutsche sein* p. 154.

65. Leyens and Andor, *Years of Estrangement* pp. 18–20.

66. Leo Grunebaum, 'Juden unerwünscht in Hotels', in Limberg and Rubsaat (eds), *Sie dürften nicht mehr Deutsche sein* p. 159.

67. Joseph Levy, 'Die guten und die bösen Deutschen', in Limberg and Rubsaat (eds), *Sie dürften nicht mehr Deutsche sein* pp. 179–81.

68. The charming folk practices are illustrated in Reinhard Kappes, '. . . und in Singen gab es keine Juden?', in Alfred Frei and Jens Runge (eds), *Erinnern-Bedenken-Lernen. Das Schicksal von Juden, Zwangsarbeitern*

und Kriegsgefangenen zwischen Hochrhein und Bodensee in den Jahren 1933 bis 1945 (Sigmaringen 1990) pp. 53, 56, 63.

69. Reiner, 'Der Weg zum Paria' p. 155.

70. Julianne Wetzel, 'Ausgrenzung und Verlust des sozialen Umfeldes', Ute and Wolfgang Benz (eds), *Sozialisation und Traumatisierung. Kinder in der Zeit des Nationalsozialismus* (Frankfurt am Main 1992) p. 96.

71. Leonore Davies, in B. Leverton and S. Lowensohn (eds), *I Came Alone. The Stories of the Kindertransports* (Lewes 1990) p. 65.

72. Raul Hilberg, *Perpetrators–Victims–Bystanders. The Jewish Catastrophe 1933–1945* (London 1993) p. 127; on this subject see Lisa Pine, *Nazi Family Policy* (Oxford 1998) pp. 238ff.

73. See M. Kaplan, 'Jewish Women in Nazi Germany', in D. Ofer and L. Weitzmann (eds), *Women in the Holocaust* (New Haven 1998) pp. 40–1.

74. Michaela Krutzen, *Hans Albers. Eine deutsche Karriere* (Weinheim 1995) pp. 149ff.

75. *Deutschland-Berichte der (SOPADE)* (1936) 3, entry dated 3 August 1936, A II, p. 991.

76. Klemperer, *I Shall Bear Witness* 1, entry dated 19 August 1933, p. 29.

77. Klaus-Michael Mallmann and Gerhard Paul, 'Omniscient, Omnipotent, Omnipresent? Gestapo, Society and Resistance', in David Crew (ed.), *Nazism and German Society 1933–1945* (London 1994) p. 174.

78. Cited by Robert Gellately, ' "A Monstrous Uneasiness". Citizen Participation and Persecution of the Jews in Nazi Germany', in Peter Hayes (ed.), *Lessons and Legacies* (Evanston 1991) p. 183.

79. A. Halimi, *La Délation sous l'occupation* (Paris 1983).

80. Robert Gellately, *The Gestapo and German Society. Enforcing Racial Policy 1933–1945* (Oxford 1990) p. 158.

81. The comparative essays in Ian Kershaw and Moshe Lewin (eds), *Stalinism and Nazism. Dictatorships in Comparison* (Cambridge 1996) contain two brief references to this central feature of totalitarian regimes; but see S. Fitzpatrick and R. Gellately (eds), *Accusatory Practices. Denunciation in Modern European History 1789–1989* (Chicago 1997).

82. SPD report.

83. Diewald-Kerkmann, *Politische Denunziation im NS-Regime* p. 96.

84. A national comrade to Gauleiter Bürckel, 14 July 1938, in Hans Safrian and Hans Witek (eds), *Und keiner war dabei. Dokumente des alltäglichen Antisemitismus in Wien 1938* (Vienna 1988) p. 93.

85. Hugo Weidenhaupt (ed.), *Ein nichtarischer Deutscher. Die Tagebücher des Albert Herzfeld 1935–1939* (Düsseldorf 1982).

86. *Ibid.* p. 15.

87. *Ibid.* p. 24.

88. *Ibid.* p. 36.
89. *Ibid.* p. 88.
90. *Ibid.* pp. 77ff.
91. *Ibid.* p. 100.
92. *Ibid.* pp. 30 and 101.
93. *Ibid.* pp. 87ff.
94. *Ibid.* p. 118.
95. *Ibid.* pp. 53–4.
96. *Ibid.* pp. 118–22.
97. Ian Kershaw, *The Nazi Dictatorship* (3rd edn London 1993) p. 94 is incorrect when he writes that, after Reichskristallnacht, 'Jews were now excluded from the economy.' As Avraham Barkai's research makes clear, 1938 was the culmination of a process which had been going on since 1933.
98. Avraham Barkai, 'Die deutschen Unternehmer und die Judenpolitik im "Dritten Reich"', in Büttner (ed.), *Die Deutschen und die Judenverfolgung* p. 209; Barkai, *From Boycott to Annihilation* is detailed and fundamental.
99. Kappes, '. . . und in Singen gab es keine Juden?' pp. 50–1.
100. Jahnke, 'Die Vernichtung der Juden in Mecklenburg' p. 296.
101. Wiener Library, P II b Nr 9, 'Die Stellung der jüdischen Reederei Josef Schalscha in der Oderschiffahrt in der Zeit des Naziregimes'.
102. Lothar Gall, H. James and G. Feldman, *The Deutsche Bank 1870–1945* (London 1995) p. 303.
103. Dirk van Laak, 'Die Mitwirkenden bei der "Arisierung". Dargestellt am Beispiel der rheinisch-westfälischen Industrieregion 1933–1940', in Büttner (ed.), *Die Deutschen und die Judenverfolgung* p. 240; Jörg Wollenberg, 'The Expropriation of "Rapacious" Capital', in Wollenberg (ed.), *The German Public and the Persecution of the Jews 1933–1945* (Princeton 1996) pp. 132–3.
104. Barkai, *From Boycott to Annihilation* pp. 71–2.
105. Johannes Ludwig, *Boykott–Enteignung–Mord. Die 'Entjudung' der deutschen Wirtschaft* (Hamburg 1989) pp. 26ff.
106. *Ibid.* p. 70.
107. Johannes Ludwig, 'Der Revolver lag schon auf dem Tisch', *Die Zeit* (1989) 17, pp. 41–2.
108. Philippe Burrin, *Hitler and the Jews. The Genesis of the Holocaust* (London 1994) pp. 36–7. One of the many merits of Burrin's work is to keep in mind the homicidal undercurrents which shadowed other Nazi policies towards the Jews.
109. Claudia Steur, *Theodore Dannecker. Ein Funktionär der Endlösung* (Essen 1997) pp. 151ff.

110. See above all Hans Safrian, *Eichmann und seine Gehilfen* (Frankfurt 1995) pp. 24–8.

111. Susanne Heim, ' "Deutschland müß ihnen ein Land ohne Zukunft sein". Die Zwangsemigration der Juden 1933 bis 1938', *Beiträge zur Geschichte der nationalsozialistischen Gesundheits- und Sozialpolitik* (Berlin 1993) 10, p. 51.

112. Wildt (ed.), *Die Judenpolitik des SD* doc. 9, p. 99.

113. 'Lagebericht der Abteilung II 112 fur die Zeit vom 1.1–31.3. 1937', in *ibid.* doc. 10, p. 107.

114. Yehuda Bauer, *Jews for Sale? Nazi–Jewish Negotiations 1933–1945* (New Haven 1994) pp. 30ff. is the best recent discussion of the Evian Conference.

115. Yehuda Bauer, 'The Kristallnacht as Turning Point. Jewish Reactions to Nazi Policies', in Michael Marrus (ed.), *The Nazi Holocaust* (Westport 1989) 2, p. 557.

116. For good overviews see Alexander Bankier, '. . . auch nicht von der Frau Hinterhuber. Zu den ökonomischen Aspekten des Novemberpogroms in Wien', in Kurt Schmid and Robert Streibel (eds), *Der Reichspogrom 1938* (Vienna 1989) pp. 70ff., and Gerhard Botz, 'La Persecution des juifs en Autriche. De l'exclusion a l'extermination', in François Berrida (ed.), *La Politique nazie d'extermination* (Paris 1989) pp. 209ff.

117. Karl Stühlpfarrer, 'Judenfeindschaft und Judenverfolgung in Österreich seit dem Ersten Weltkrieg', in Anna Drabek *et al.* (eds), *Das österreichische Judentum* (3rd edn Vienna 1988) pp. 141ff.

118. Cited by William W. Hagen, 'Before the "Final Solution". Towards a Comparative Analysis of Political Antisemitism in Interwar Germany and Poland', *JMH* (1996) 68, pp. 353–4.

119. For these details see the excellent study by Bruce Pauley, *From Prejudice to Persecution. A History of Austrian Antisemitism* (Chapel Hill 1992) pp. 280–9.

120. Elisabeth Klamper, 'Der "Anschlußpogrom" ', in Schmid and Streibel (eds), *Der Reichspogrom 1938* pp. 25–33.

121. Josef Bien to Reichskommissar Bürckel dated 5 January 1939, in Safrian and Witek (eds), *Und keiner war dabei* pp. 125ff. for these details.

122. Josef Bien to the Vermögensverkehrsstelle dated August 1938, in *ibid.* pp. 121–3.

123. Wiener Modeszunft Arisierungsstelle to Eduard Witeschnik dated 12 November 1938, in *ibid.* p. 123.

124. Memorandum and depositions dated 3 and 4 February 1939, in *ibid.* pp. 128ff.

125. Otto Kunz to Gauleiter Bürckel dated 27 April 1938, in *ibid.* pp. 49–50.

126. Safrian, *Eichmann und seine Gehilfen* p. 33.

127. Susanne Heim and Götz Aly, 'Die Ökonomie der Endlösung?', *Beiträge zur Geschichte der nationalsozialistischen Gesundheits- und Sozialpolitik* (Berlin 1987) 5, pp. 20ff.

128. Hagen, 'Before the "Final Solution" '; see also Jerzy Tomaszewski, 'Some Methodological Problems of the Study of Jewish History in Poland between the Two World Wars', *Polin* (1986) 1, pp. 163–75; Antony Polonsky, *Politics in Independent Poland* (Oxford 1972).

129. Trude Maurer, 'The Background for Kristallnacht. The Expulsion of Polish Jews', in Walter H. Pehle (ed.), *November 1938* (Oxford 1991) pp. 44ff.

130. Michael Marrus, 'The Strange Story of Herschel Grynszpan', in Marrus (ed.), *The Nazi Holocaust* (Westport 1989), 2, p. 601; see also Elisabeth Klamper, 'Die "Affaire Herschel Grynszpan" ', *Der Novemberpogrom 1938. Die 'Reichskristallnacht' in Wien* (Vienna 1989) pp. 53ff.

131. Domarus (ed.), *Hitler. Speeches and Proclamations* 2, p. 751.

132. Wolfgang Benz, 'Der November-Pogrom', in Benz (ed.), *Die Juden in Deutschland 1933–1945. Leben unter nationalsozialistischer Herrschaft* (Munich 1988) pp. 499ff.

133. Wolf-Arno Kropat (ed.), *Kristallnacht in Hessen* (Wiesbaden 1988) pp. 19ff. is outstanding.

134. Saskia Rhode, 'Die Zerstörung der Synagogen unter dem Nationalsozialismus', in Herzig and Lorenz (eds), *Verdrängung und Vernichtung* p. 159.

135. Hermann Graml, *Antisemitism in the Third Reich* (Oxford 1992) p. 9.

136. Ralf Georg Reuth, *Goebbels* (London 1993) pp. 236ff.

137. Kropat, *Kristallnacht in Hessen* p. 55.

138. Karl A. Schleunes, *Twisted Road to Auschwitz* (Urbana, Chicago and London 1970) p. 236; Kershaw, *The Nazi Dictatorship* p. 94.

139. This account of events in Munich relies upon the Goebbels diaries found in Moscow; see *Der Spiegel* (1992) 29, pp. 126–8.

140. Ulrich von Hassell, *The von Hassell Diaries* (Boulder 1994) entry dated 17 December 1938, p. 23.

141. *Der Spiegel* (1992) 29, p. 128.

142. Geheimes Blitzfernschreiben des Chefs der Sicherheitspolizei und des Sicherheitsdienstes an alle Staatspolizeileit- und Staatspolizeistellen und an alle SD Oberabschnitte und SD Unterschnitte, 10 November 1938, 1.20 a.m., *International Military Tribunal* (hereafter *IMT*) 31, pp. 516ff.

143. Michael Gehler, 'Murder on Command. The Anti-Jewish Pogrom in Innsbruck 9th–10th November 1938', *LBIY* (1993) 38, pp. 121–34.

144. Benz, 'Der November-Pogrom', pp. 511–12, an account of events in Wiesbaden that flatly contradicts Uwe Dietrich Adam's assertion in his 'How Spontaneous Was the Pogrom?, in Pehle (ed.), *November 1938*

p. 90 that 'nowhere is there evidence of an SA arson unit ready and on call, nowhere have measures been taken to assure a supply of flammable material, nowhere is there a party or SA functionary waiting at his phone for the relaying of the code word'.

145. Benz, 'Der November-Pogrom' p. 520 on Bochum.

146. Kropat, *Kristallnacht in Hessen* pp. 192–5.

147. Anselm Faust, *Die 'Kristallnacht' im Rheinland* (Düsseldorf 1987) pp. 172–3.

148. Peter Loewenberg, 'The Kristallnacht as a Public Degradation Ritual', *LBIY* (1987) 32, p. 313.

149. *Deutschland-Berichte der SOPADE* (1938) 5, entry dated 10 December 1938, p. 1198 (Upper Silesia).

150. *Ibid.* p. 1191 (Saarpfalz).

151. A. Santo, 'Im Dienste der Gemeinde 1923–1939', in Kurt Patzold and Irene Runge (eds), *Kristallnacht. Zum Pogrom 1938* (Cologne 1988) pp. 120–1.

152. Hubert Butler, *Independent Spirit. Essays* (New York 1996) p. 365.

153. Patzold and Runge (eds), *Kristallnacht*, 'Bericht des SS-Abschnitts XXIV, Oppeln, an den SS-Oberabschnitt Südost (Breslau) betr. "Aktion gegen die Juden"', pp. 131–2.

154. Siegmund Weltlinger, *Hast du es schon vergessen?* (Berlin 1954) pp. 9ff.

155. Max Moses Polke, 'Der Hölle entkommen', in Limberg and Rubsaat (eds), *Sie dürften nicht mehr Deutsche sein* pp. 305ff.

156. Pauley, *From Prejudice to Persecution* p. 287.

157. See especially William Sheridan Allen, 'Die deutsche Öffentlichkeit', in Detlev Peukert and Jürgen Reulecke (eds), *Die Reihen fast geschlossen. Beiträge zur Geschichte des Alltags unterm Nationalsozialismus* (Wuppertal 1981) pp. 397–412.

158. Hassell, *Von Hassell Diaries* entry dated 25 November 1938, pp. 14–15.

159. *Ibid.* entry dated 20 December 1938, p. 19.

160. Kershaw, 'The Persecution of the Jews and German Popular Opinion in the Third Reich' pp. 277ff. is both cogent and sane on these issues. His use of the term 'indifference' to characterise German–Jewish relations has not, however, met with universal assent; see Otto Dov Kulka and Aron Rodrigue, 'The German Population and the Jews in the Third Reich', *Yad Vashem Studies* (1984) 16, pp. 421ff.

161. *Deutschland-Berichte der SOPADE* (1938) 5, entry dated 10 December 1938, pp. 1205 and 1209.

162. Otto Dov Kulka, 'Popular Christian Attitudes in the Third Reich to National-Socialist Policies towards the Jews', in Kulka and P. R. Mendes-Flohr (eds), *Judaism and Christianity under the Impact of National Socialism 1919–1945* (Jerusalem 1987) p. 257.

163. Joachim Scholtyseck, 'Die Firma Robert Bosch und ihre Hilfe für Juden', in M. Kiszener (ed.), *Widerstand gegen die Judenverfolgung* (Konstanz 1996) pp. 170ff.

164. *Deutschland-Berichte der SOPADE* (1938) 5, entry dated 10 December 1938, pp. 1210–11.

165. *Ibid.* (1939) 6, entry dated 9 February 1939, pp. 9–10.

166. Heinz Boberach (ed.), *Meldungen aus dem Reich. Die geheimen Lageberichte des Sicherheitsdienstes der SS 1938–1945* (Herrsching 1984) 2, 1938, p. 73.

167. Otto Dov Kulka, 'Public Opinion in Nazi Germany and the Jewish Question', *Jerusalem Quarterly* (1982), 25, p. 135 is persuasive.

168. 'Das ist Verrat am Volke', *Westdeutscher Beobachter* 17 November 1938.

169. Reuth (ed.), *Joseph Goebbels. Tagebücher* 3, entry dated 12 November 1938, p. 1283.

170. *IMT* 28, doc. 1816-PS, pp. 499ff.

171. Genschel, *Die Verdrängung der Juden* pp. 166–72.

172. *Reichsgesetzblatt* (1938) 1, p. 1579.

173. *Ibid.* p. 1580.

174. *Ibid.* pp. 186ff.

175. *Ibid.* p. 538.

176. *Ibid.* pp. 508–9.

177. *Ibid.* pp. 524ff.

178. *Ibid.* p. 533.

179. *Ibid.* p. 534.

180. Bradley Smith and Agnes Petersen (eds), *Heinrich Himmler. Geheimreden 1933 bis 1945* (Berlin 1974), pp. 37–8.

181. 'Juden, was nun?', *SK* 24 November 1938, Folge 47, front page.

182. Wolf Gruner, ' "Am 20. April (Geburtstag des Führers) haben die Juden zu arbeiten . . ." ', in Werner Röhr (ed.), *Faschismus und Rassismus* (Berlin 1992) pp. 148–56; Matthias Schmidt, *Albert Speer. The End of a Myth* (London no date) p. 182.

183. Klemperer, *Tagebücher 1933–1941* 1, entry dated 10 January 1939, pp. 456–7.

184. *Ibid.* entry dated 5 February 1939, p. 461.

185. For this reading of the speech see Hans Mommsen, 'Hitler's Reichstag Speech of 30 January 1939', *History & Memory* (1997) 9, pp. 148–51.

186. Keith Ansell-Pearson (ed.), *Friedrich Nietzsche. On the Genealogy of Morality* (Cambridge 1994) pp. 24–5.

187. Ian Kershaw, *Hitler* (London 1991), pp. 150–1; Burrin, *Hitler and the Jews*, p. 63.

5. EUGENICS AND 'EUTHANASIA'

1. Gisela Bock, 'Sterilization and "Medical" Massacres', in M. Berg and G. Cocks (eds), *Medicine and Modernity* (Cambridge 1997) p. 155; the best account of eugenics in Britain and the USA remains Daniel Kevles, *In the Name of Eugenics* (London 1986).

2. Wolfgang Matl, 'Ein Alptraum vom reinen Schweden', *Die Zeit* 37, 5 September 1997, pp. 13–15; the literature on Scandinavian sterilisation includes Nils Roll-Hansen, 'Eugenic Sterilisation. A Preliminary Comparison of the Scandinavian Experience to That of Germany', *Genome* (1989) 31, pp. 890–5, and Gunnar Broberg and Nils Roll-Hansen (eds), *Eugenics and the Welfare State. Sterilization Policy in Denmark, Sweden, Norway and Finland* (East Lansing 1997).

3. See the important book by Edward Larson, *Sex, Race, and Science. Eugenics in the Deep South* (Baltimore 1998).

4. Paul J. Weindling, *Health, Race and German Politics between National Unification and Nazism* (Cambridge 1988); Frank Dikötter, *The Discourse of Race in Modern China* (London 1992) pp. 164ff.; on the American South see Larson, *Sex, Race, and Science*.

5. Michael Freeden, 'Eugenics and Progressive Thought', *Historical Journal* (1979) 22, p. 667.

6. Stefan Kuhl, *The Nazi Connection* (Oxford 1994).

7. See Michael Schwartz, 'Konfessionelle Milieus und Weimarer Eugenik', *Historische Zeitschrift* (1995) 261, pp. 415–16.

8. On Britain see Freeden, 'Eugenics and Progressive Thought' pp. 645ff., and Matthew Thomson and Paul Weindling, 'Sterilisationspolitik in Grossbritannien und Deutschland', in F.-W. Kersting, K. Teppe and B. Walter (eds), *Nach Hadamar* (Paderborn 1993) pp. 142–7, and on Weimar Germany Michael Schwartz, *Sozialistische Eugenik* (Bonn 1995).

9. E. J. Larson, 'The Rhetoric of Eugenics. Expert Authority and the Mental Deficiency Bill', *British Journal for the History of Science* (1991) 24, pp. 45–60.

10. Christoph Sachsse and Florian Tennstedt, *Der Wohlfahrtsstaat im Nationalsozialismus* (Stuttgart 1992) pp. 46–54.

11. Detlev Peukert, 'The Genesis of the "Final Solution" from the Spirit of Science', in David Crew (ed.), *Nazism and German Society 1933–1945* (London 1994) pp. 274ff.

12. For Nazism's 'progressive' health interventionism see now Robert Proctor, *The Nazi War on Cancer* (Princeton 1999).

13. See Daniel Kevles, 'Grounds for Breeding', *TLS*, 2 January 1998, p. 4.

14. Detlef Bothe, *Neue Deutsche Heilkunde 1933–1945* (Husum 1985).

15. See Omer Bartov, 'Man and the Mass. Reality and the Heroic Image in War' and 'The European Imagination in the Age of Total War' in his *Murder in our Midst* (Oxford 1996) pp. 15–50.

16. For the ways in which asylum directors used statistics on patient mortality during the First World War see Götz Aly, *Reform und Gewissen* (Berlin 1985) p. 50; Karl Bonhoeffer, address, *Allgemeine Zeitschrift für Psychiatrie* (1920/1) 76, p. 600.

17. Karl Binding and Alfred Hoche, *Die Freigabe der Vernichtung lebensunwerten Lebens. Ihr Mass und ihre Form* (Leipzig 1920); studies of this tract include Karl Heinz Häfner and Rolf Winau, 'Die Freigabe der Vernichtung lebensunwerten Lebens. Eine Untersuchung zu der Schrift von Karl Binding und Alfred Hoche', *Medizinhistorisches Journal* (1974) 9, pp. 227–54.

18. Ernst Klee, 'Die Ermordung der Unproduktiven', in Hans-Erich Volkmann (ed.), *Ende des Dritten Reiches – Ende des Zweiten Weltkrieges* (Munich 1995), pp. 343–4.

19. Michael Schwartz, '"Euthanasie" – Debatten in Deutschland (1895–1945)', *VfZ* (1998) 46, p. 629.

20. Ewald Meltzer, *Das Problem der Abkürzung 'lebensunwerten' Lebens* (Halle 1925).

21. Bernhard Richarz, *Heilen, Pflegen, Töten. Zur Alltagsgeschichte einer Heil- und Pflegeanstalt bis zum Ende des Nationalsozialismus* (Göttingen 1987) p. 78.

22. Thomson and Weindling, 'Sterilisationspolitik in Grossbritannien und Deutschland' p. 142.

23. See, above all, Hans-Ludwig Siemen, *Das Grauen is vorprogrammiert* (Giessen 1982).

24. Hans Harmsen, address, *Zeitschrift für psychische Hygiene* (1932) 5, p. 75.

25. Uwe Gerrens, *Medizinisches Ethos und theologische Ethik* (Munich 1996) esp. pp. 80–4.

26. Oswald Bumke, conference paper, *Allgemeine Zeitschrift für Psychiatrie* (1932) 96, pp. 372–3.

27. Arthur Gütt, Ernst Rüdin and Falk Ruttke, *Gesetz zur Verhütung erbkranken Nachwuchses vom 14. Juli 1933* (Berlin 1934) p. 110.

28. Thomas Koch, *Zwangssterilisation im Dritten Reich* (Frankfurt am Main 1994) pp. 12–13; see also Gisela Bock, *Zwangssterilisation im Nationalsozialismus* (Opladen 1986); Christian Ganssmüller, *Die Erbgesundheitspolitik des Dritten Reiches* (Cologne 1987).

29. See Kevles, 'Grounds for Breeding' p. 4.

30. Monika Daum and Hans-Ulrich Deppe, *Zwangssterilisation in Frankfurt am Main 1933–1945* (Frankfurt am Main 1991) p. 44.

31. Berlin Document Centre, Karl Astel personal file, 'Ein Kämpfer für die deutsche Volksgesundheit', *Völkischer Beobachter* 12 March 1938.

32. 'Heinrich Wilhelm Kranz', in Helga Jacobi (ed.), *Aeskulap & Hakenkreuz* (Frankfurt am Main 1989) pp. 131ff.

33. Hans Burkhardt, 'Was kann die psychiatrische offene Fürsorge für Erbforschung und Rassenhygiene leisten?', *Psychiatrisch-Neurologische Wochenschrift* (1934) 36, p. 342.

34. Gerrens, *Medizinisches Ethos* p. 34.

35. Rede des stellvertretenden Reichsärzteführers F. Bartels auf dem 2. Pommersche Ärztetag am 22 August 1936 in Schwinemünde, *Ärzteblatt für Pommern, Mecklenburg und Lübeck* (1936) 18.

36. James Knowlson, *Damned to Fame* (London 1996) p. 297.

37. Valentin Faltlhauser, 'Jahresbericht der Kreis-Heil und Pflegeanstalt Kaufbeuren-Irsee über das Jahr 1934', *Psychiatrisch-Neurologische Wochenschrift* (1935) 37, p. 332.

38. Dr Lang, 'Die Unfruchtbarmachung Erbkranker', *Juristische Wochenschrift* (1933) 37, pp. 2035ff.

39. Stadtarchiv Bremerhaven 560/1/2f. 'Der Präsident der Behörde für das Gesundheitswesen an alle praktizierenden Ärzte Bremens', 20 February 1934.

40. Daum and Deppe, *Zwangssterilisation* p. 88.

41. Gerhard Schmidt, *Selektion in der Heilanstalt 1939–1945* (Frankfurt am Main 1983) p. 26; see also the annual Jahresberichte of the Bezirkskrankenhaus Haar, 1935, p. 23; 1936, pp. 26–8 for details of these tours of the asylum.

42. Gerrens, *Medizinisches Ethos* pp. 89–90.

43. Opfer der Vergangenheit, Bundesarchiv, Filmarchiv Außenstelle Potsdam.

44. Karl Ludwig Rost, *Sterilisation im Film des 'Dritten Reiches'* (Husum 1987).

45. Donald Dietrich, 'Catholic Resistance to Biological and Racist Eugenics in the Third Reich', in F. Nicosia and L. Stokes (eds), *Germans against Nazism* (Oxford 1990) p. 138.

46. Jochen Kaiser, Kurt Nowak and Michael Schwartz (eds), *Eugenik. Sterilisation. 'Euthanasie'. Politische Biologie in Deutschland 1895–1945* (Halle 1992) pp. 106–10 for this resolution.

47. Hans Rössler, 'Die "Euthanasie" Diskussion in Neuendettelsau 1937–1939', *Zeitschrift für bayerischen Kirchengeschichte* (1988) 57, pp. 87–91.

48. Paul Weindling, 'Weimar Eugenics. The Kaiser Wilhelm Institute for Anthropology, Human Heredity and Eugenics in Social Context', *Annals of Science* (1985) 42, p. 316.

49. Donald Dietrich, 'Joseph Mayer and the Missing Memo. A Catholic

Justification for Euthanasia', *Remembering for the Future. Papers Presented at an International Scholars' Conference* (Oxford 1988) 1, pp. 39–40.

50. Dietrich, 'Catholic Resistance to Biological and Racist Eugenics' pp. 140–5.

51. Guenther Lewy, *The Catholic Church and Nazi Germany* (London 1964) pp. 258–63.

52. Cornelia Hoser and Birgit Weber-Diekmann, 'Zwangssterilisation an Hadamarer Anstaltsinsassen', in Dorothee Roer and Dieter Henkel (eds), *Psychiatrie im Faschismus. Die Anstalt Hadamar 1933–1945* (Bonn 1986) p. 134.

53. Gernot Römer, *Die grauen Busse in Schwaben* (Augsburg 1986) pp. 35–7.

54. Bolland and Kowollik, *Heillose Zeiten* p. 63.

55. *Deutschland-Berichte der Sozialdemokratischen Partei Deutschlands (SOPADE)* (1935) 2, pp. 356–7; (1936) 3, pp. 79–80, 1042–3; (1937) 4, pp. 1341, 1353; (1938) 5, pp. 1132–3.

56. F. Limbacher, 'Vernichtung lebensunwerten Lebens', *IAB* (1934) 12, p. 181.

57. Karl Evang, 'Rassenhygiene und Sozialismus', *IAB* (1934) 9, pp. 130–1.

58. Gertrud Lukas, 'Kritische Gedanken zur Sterilisierungfrage', *IAB* (1934) 3–4, pp. 55–62.

59. Andrea Wojak, ' "Ik mut opereert worden, heet' dat. De hemm' nich seggt, worum". NS-Zwangssterilisationen in einem niedersäsischen Dorf', *1999* (1991) pp. 59ff.

60. Daum and Deppe, *Zwangssterilisation* pp. 133–4.

61. *Ibid.* pp. 144–5.

62. Staatsarchiv München (hereafter StAM) Staatsanwaltschaften Nr 17460 II, NSDAP Gauleitung Schwaben to the Städtische Trinkerfürsorgestelle Augsburg, 24 May 1937; Pfannmüller report on F dated 9 June 1937.

63. StAM Nr 17460 II, 'Abschrift der Niederschriften der Beratungsstelle für Nerven- und Gemütskranke Augsburg Medizinalrat Dr. Pfannmüller in Sachen S.', no date.

64. StAM Nr 17460 II, Hermann Pfannmüller to the Politische Polizei in Augsburg, 25 March 1937.

65. Elvira Manthey (née Hempel), *Die Hempelsche* (Lübeck 1994). Frau Manthey was kind enough to relate her experiences in Brandenburg during an interview for my film *Selling Murder*, first shown on Channel 4 TV in 1991 and in over twenty other countries including twice on Germany's Norddeutscher Rundfunk.

66. See Karl-Heinz Roth, 'Städtesanierung und "ausmerzende" Soziologie', in C. Klingemann (ed.), *Rassenmythos und Sozialwissenschaften in Deutschland* (Opladen 1987) pp. 370ff.

67. On Hashude see 'Die letzte Chance', *SK* 20 January 1938, p. 7; W. Voigt, 'Wohnhaft. Die Siedlung als panoptisches Gefängnis', *Arch + 75/76* (August 1984) pp. 82–9; and Lisa Pine, 'The Imprisonment of "Asocial Families" in the Third Reich', *German History* (1995) 13, pp. 182–97.

68. Ute Brücker-Boroujerdi and Wolfgang Wippermann, 'Die Rassenhygienische und Erbbiologische Forschungsstelle im Reichsgesundheitsamt', *Bundesgesundheitsblatt* 33 (1989) pp. 13–19; Joachim S. Hohmann, *Robert Ritter und die Erben der Kriminalbiologie* (Frankfurt am Main 1991).

69. Heinrich Wilhelm Kranz, 'Zigeuner, wie sie wirklich sind', *Neues Volk* (1937) September, pp. 21–7.

70. Eva von Hase-Mihalik and Doris Kreuzkamp, *'du kriegst auch einen schönen Wohnwagen'* (Frankfurt am Main 1990) pp. 34–7.

71. Karola Fings and Frank Sparing, *'z. Zt. Zigeunerlager'. Die Verfolgung der Düsseldorfer Sinti und Roma im Nationalsozialismus* (Cologne 1992) pp. 17–45.

72. Ute Brücker-Boroujerdi and Wolfgang Wippermann, 'Nationalsozialistische Zwangslager in Berlin III', in Wolfgang Ribbe (ed.), *Berliner-Forschungen* (Berlin 1987) 2, pp. 189–201; Michael Zimmermann, 'Die nationalsozialistische Vernichtungspolitik gegen Sinti und Roma', *Aus Politik und Zeitgeschichte* (1987) B 16–17, p. 32; *idem*, 'Von der Diskriminierung zum "Familienlager" Auschwitz', *Dachauer Hefte* (1989) 5, pp. 90–4.

73. Wolfgang Ayass, 'Vagrants and Beggars in Hitler's Reich', in R. J. Evans (ed.), *The German Underworld* (London 1988) pp. 210–37.

74. C. Meyhofer, *Das Wohlfahrtswesen im NS-Staat unter besonderer Berücksichtigung der Situation in Bremen* (Bremen 1988).

75. Wolfgang Ayass, *'Asoziale' im Nationalsozialismus* (Stuttgart 1995) p. 160.

76. For an 'anti-social' informer see David Hackett (ed.), *The Buchenwald Report* (Boulder 1995) p. 269.

77. *Ibid.* p. 191.

78. *Ibid.* pp. 297–8.

79. Hessisches Hauptstaatsarchiv Wiesbaden (hereafter HHStAW), Abt. 461 Nr 32442 (Eichberg Trial) 4, p. 2 (Hinsen testimony).

80. *Ibid.* pp. 101–3 (Hinsen testimony).

81. Peter von Ronn *et al.*, *Wege in den Tod. Hamburgs Anstalt Langenhorn und die Euthanasie in der Zeit des Nationalsozialismus* (Hamburg 1993) pp. 36–7.

82. 'Krankenanstalten im heutigen Deutschland', *IAB* (1934) 3–4, pp. 62–3.

83. See the photographs of the Steglitz Home for the Blind in Hans-Norbert Burkert, Klaus Matuszek and Wolfgang Wippermann (eds), *'Machtergreifung' Berlin 1933* (Berlin 1982) pp. 246–7.

84. Ruth Baumann *et al.*, *Arbeitsfähig oder unbrauchbar? Die Geschichte der Kinder- und Jugendpsychiatrie seit 1933 am Beispiel Hamburgs* (Frankfurt am Main 1994) p. 97.

85. Heinz Faulstich, *Von der Irrenfürsorge zur 'Euthanasie'. Geschichte der badischen Psychiatrie bis 1945* (Freiburg im Breisgau 1993) p. 165.

86. Horst Dickel, 'Alltag in einer Landesheilanstalt im Nationalsozialismus. Das Beispiel Eichberg', in Landeswohlfahrtsverband Hessen (ed.), *Euthanasie in Hadamar* (Kassel 1991) p. 106.

87. Hans Roemer, 'Die Praktische Einführung der Insulin- und Cardiozol-behandlung in den Heil- und Pflegeanstalten', *Allgemeine Zeitschrift für Psychiatrie* (1938) 107, p. 122.

88. Karl Knab, 'Was ist für die Anstaltspsychiatrie wichtiger. Die medikamentöse Behandlung oder die Psychotherapie?', *Psychiatrisch-Neurologische Wochenschrift* (1935) 37, p. 367.

89. Schmidt, *Selektion in den Heilanstalt* p. 21.

90. See Jeremy Noakes, 'Philipp Bouhler und die Kanzlei des Führers der NSDAP', in D. Rebentisch, Karl Teppe (eds), *Verwaltung contra Menschenführung im Staat Hitlers* (Göttingen 1989) pp. 209–36.

91. Adolf Hitler, 'Appell an die deutsche Kraft', *Völkischer Beobachter* (Bayernausgabe) 7 August 1929.

92. Gerrens, *Medizinisches Ethos* pp. 49–53.

93. Imperial War Museum, London, *Medical Trial* Case 1, vol. 6, p. 2397.

94. HHStAW Abt. 631a Nr 79, 'Anklageschrift' against Werner Heyde with Lammers' testimony to the International Military Tribunal at Nuremberg, 7 February 1947.

95. The most important book on the 'euthanasia' programme remains Ernst Klee, *'Euthanasie' im NS-Staat* (Frankfurt am Main 1985).

96. See Michael Burleigh, *Death and Deliverance. 'Euthanasia' in Germany 1900–1945* (Cambridge 1994) pp. 101–2 for details of individual cases.

97. Baumann *et al.*, *Arbeitsfähig oder unbrauchbar?* pp. 126–7.

98. F. Kaul, *Psychiatrie im Strudel der 'Euthanasie'* (Frankfurt am Main 1979) pp. 63ff.

99. Zentrale Stelle des Landesjustizverwaltungen (hereafter ZSL) 'Euthanasie', interrogation of Werner Heyde dated 22 September 1961, p. 168.

100. Hinrich Jasper, *Maximinian de Crinis (1889–1945)* (Husum 1991) pp. 101–2.

101. Imperial War Museum, London, *Medical Trial* Case 1, vol. 4, p. 159.

102. Ernst Klee (ed.), *Dokumente zur 'Euthanasie'* (Frankfurt am Main 1985), no. 32, p. 101.

103. Archive Michael Burleigh, GStA Frankfurt am Main Js 15/61 Anklageschrift gegen Aquilin Ulrich and others, 15 January 1965, pp. 2–5 and 249–51.

104. HHStAW Abt. 461 Nr 32061 (Hadamar Trial) 7, testimony of Bodo Gorgass dated 24 February 1947, p. 17.

105. Michael H. Kater, *Doctors under Hitler* (Chapel Hill 1989) pp. 54–74.

106. Friedrich Kümmel, 'Im Dienst "nationalpolitischer Erziehung"?', in Christoph Meinel and Peter Vosswinkel (eds), *Medizin, Naturwissenschaft, Technik und Nationalsozialismus* (Stuttgart 1994) pp. 295–319.

107. Staatsarchiv Augsburg, Staatsanwaltschaften Ks 1/49 (Trial of Valentin Faltlhauser *et al.*) 2, with graphs of monthly patient mortality and testimony of Sister Gualberta dated 11 May 1948, p. 10.

108. HHStAW Abt. 461 Nr 32061 (Hadamar Trial) 7, testimony of Irmgard Huber dated 25 February 1947.

109. Author's interview with Paul Reuter in 1991 transmitted in the Channel 4 film *Selling Murder*.

110. Hadamar is the most extensively studied; see Christine Vanya (ed.), *Euthanasie in Hadamar* (Kassel 1991).

111. Ralf Seidel and Thorsten Suesse, 'Werkzeuge der Vernichtung. Zum Verhalten von Verwaltungsbeamten und Ärzten bei der "Euthanasie"', in Norbert Frei (ed.), *Medizin und Gesundheitspolitik in der NS-Zeit* (Munich 1991) pp. 253ff.

112. On Jaspersen see J. Thierfelder, 'Karsten Jaspersens Kampf gegen die NS-Krankenmorde', in T. Strohm and Thierfelder (eds), *Diakonie im Dritten Reich* (Heidelberg 1990) pp. 229ff.

113. HHStAW Abt. 631a Nr 359, testimony of Walter M. dated 3 February 1948, with a copy of Helene M.'s final letter.

114. For these details on Hartheim see Gordon J. Horwitz, *In the Shadow of Death* (London 1991) pp. 60–2.

115. HHStAW Abt. 631a Nr 56, undated list of suitable causes of death, pp. 16 and 56.

116. Eugen Kogon, Hermann Langbein and Adalbert Rückerl, *Nazi Mass Murder. A Documentary History of the Use of Poison Gas* (New Haven 1993) p. 32.

117. V. Mladenov to Anna Perner, Martinsstift Gallneukirchen, 20 January 1941; Gallneukirchen authorities to V. Mladenov, 21 January 1941; Magda Mladenov to Anna Perner, 27 January 1941; in Johannes Nuehauser and Michaela Pfaffenwimmer (eds), *Hartheim. Wohin unbekannt* (Freistadt 1992) pp. 35–7 for facsimiles of these letters.

118. *Ibid.* p. 31, Maria B. to Herrn Farnbacher, Gallneukirchen, 28 January 1941.

119. *Ibid.* p. 138, Rosa N. to Schwester Justine, Gallneukirchen, 18 February 1941.

120. For examples see the illustrations in Peter Delius, *Das Ende von Strecknitz* (Kiel 1988).

121. For this exchange of correspondence see Alice Platen-Hallermund's classic 1946 study *Die Tötung Geisteskranker in Deutschland* (reprinted Bonn 1993) pp. 116–21.

122. On Kreyssig see Lothar Gruchmann, 'Ein unbequemer Amtsrichter im Dritten Reich', *VfZ* (1984) 32, pp. 463ff.; *idem, Justiz im Dritten Reich 1933–1940* (Munich 1988) pp. 505ff.

123. Nuehauser and Pfaffenwimmer (eds), *Hartheim* pp. 44–5, Pfarrer Schiefermair to the Rektor Gallneukirchen, 27 January 1941, and the Rektor to Schiefermair, 29 January 1941.

124. For the memorandum dated 9 July 1940 see Klee (ed.), *Dokumente* no. 59 pp. 154ff.

125. ZSL 'Euthanasie', Hefelmann, interrogation of Hans Hefelmann on 30 January 1961, pp. 11–12; Martin Höllen, 'Katholische Kirche und NS-Euthanasie', *Zeitschrift für Kirchengeschichte* (1980), 91, pp. 53ff. is outstanding.

126. On Galen's background see Joachim Kuropka, *Clemens August Graf von Galen* (Cloppenburg 1992).

127. Joachim Kuropka (ed.), *Meldungen aus Münster 1924–1944* (Münster 1992) nos 110, p. 531 (report of the Inspekteur der Sipo und SD, 24 July 1941); 111, p. 533 (report of Inspekteur der Sipo und SD, 31 July 1941); 118, p. 539 (report of NSDAP-Ortsgruppe Appelhülsen, 11 August 1941); 123, p. 542 (report of the Inspekteur der Sipo und SD, 20 August 1941); 135, pp. 551–2 (report of NSDAP-Gauleitung Westfalen Nord, October 1941); 146, p. 558 (Meldungen aus dem Reich, 19 January 1942); 151, p. 561 (Meldungen aus dem Reich, 12 March 1942).

128. Hugh Trevor-Roper (ed.), *Hitler's Table Talk 1941–44* (Oxford 1988) p. 555.

129. Burleigh, *Death and Deliverance* pp. 202–19.

130. See Walter Grode, *Die 'Sonderbehandlung 14f13' in den Konzentrationslagern des Dritten Reiches* (Frankfurt am Main 1987).

131. HHStAW Abt. 631a Nr 1319, containing photographs of these prisoners with Mennecke's 'diagnoses' on the reverse; for Mennecke see Peter Chroust (ed.), *Friedrich Mennecke. Innenansichten eines medizinischen Täters im Nationalsozialismus. Eine Edition seiner Briefe 1935–1947* (Hamburg 1988) two volumes.

132. Imperial War Museum, London, *Medical Trial* Case 1, *US* v. *Karl Brandt et al.*, vol. 116, p. 7508 (May 1947).

133. Dieter Pohl, *Von der 'Judenpolitik' zum Judenmord. Der Distrikt Lublin des Generalgouvernments 1939–1944* (Frankfurt am Main 1993) pp. 105 and 129.

134. National Archives, Washington DC, T1021 Roll 18, Hartheim Statistics, pp. 1–22.

6. OCCUPATION AND COLLABORATION IN EUROPE, 1939–1943

1. Richard Overy, *The Origins of the Second World War* (London 1987) pp. 72–6. The best account of diplomacy in the months before the outbreak of war is D. C. Watt, *How War Came* (London 1989).

2. K. M. Pospieszalski, 'The Bomb Attack at Tarnow and Other Nazi Provocations before and after the Outbreak of the 1939 War', *Polish Western Affairs* (1986) 27, pp. 241ff.

3. Lothar Gruchmann, *Totaler Krieg* (Munich 1991) pp. 11–36.

4. Czesław Madajczyk, *Die Okkupationspolitik Nazideutschlands in Polen 1939–1945* (Cologne 1988) p. 4.

5. Ralf Georg Reuth (ed.), *Joseph Goebbels. Tagebücher* (Munich 1992) 4, entry dated 5 November 1940, p. 1495.

6. For brief descriptions of these campaigns see Ludolf Herbst, *Das national-sozialistische Deutschland 1933–1945* (Frankfurt am Main 1996), pp. 276–9 and 304–11.

7. Alice Teichova, 'The Protectorate of Bohemia and Moravia (1939–1945). The Economic Dimension', in Mikulas Teich (ed.), *Bohemia in History* (Cambridge 1998) pp. 267ff.

8. H. R. Kedward, *Occupied France. Collaboration and Resistance 1940–1944* (Oxford 1985) p. 2.

9. See Philip Cohen, *Serbia's Secret War. Propaganda and the Deceit of History* (College Station 1996) pp. 28ff and 86ff.

10. Heinrich Böll, *A Soldier's Legacy* (London 1985).

11. Klaus Latzel, 'Tourismus und Gewalt', in Hannes Heer and Klaus Naumann (eds), *Vernichtungskrieg. Verbrechen der Wehrmacht 1941–1944* (Hamburg 1995) p. 448.

12. Gustave Folcher, *Marching to Captivity. The War Diaries of a French Peasant 1939–45*, ed. Christopher Hill (London 1996) p. 128. I am grateful to Professor Hill for a copy of the diary.

13. Walter Bargatzky, *Hotel Majestic* (Freiburg im Breisgau 1987) pp. 40–55.

14. Richard Griffiths, 'A Certain Idea of France. Ernst Jünger's Paris Diaries 1941–44', *Journal of European Studies* (1993) 23, pp. 101ff.

15. Frédéric Vitoux, *Céline. A Biography* (New York 1994) p. 378.

16. Ulrich von Hassell, *The von Hassell Diaries* (Oxford 1994) entry dated 3 February 1941, pp. 167–8.

17. David Pryce-Jones, *Paris in the Third Reich* (London 1981) pp. 78–9.

18. Madeleine Bunting, *The Model Occupation. The Channel Islands under German Rule 1940–1945* (London 1995) p. 40.

19. Wolfgang Rieschock, 'Ich war achtzehn', in Christoph Klessmann (ed.), *September 1939* (Frankfurt am Main 1995) p. 162.

20. Jean Paul Sartre, 'Paris unter der Besatzung', *Akzente* (1980) 27, p. 134.
21. Philippe Burrin, *Living with Defeat. France under the German Occupation 1940–1944* (London 1996) p. 196.
22. Harry Stone, *Writing in the Shadow. Resistance Publications in Occupied Europe* (London 1996) illustration on p. 124.
23. Tomasz Szarota, 'Alltag in Warschau und anderen besetzten Hauptstädten', in Klessmann (ed.), *September 1939* pp. 88–9.
24. Tomasz Szarota, *Warschau unter dem Hakenkreuz* (Paderborn 1985), pp. 262–3.
25. Callum MacDonald and Jan Kaplan, *Prague in the Shadow of the Swastika* (London 1995) p. 41.
26. The text is cited in Henri Amouroux, *La Grande Histoire des Français sous l'occupation* (Paris 1994) 4, p. 189.
27. Szarota, *Warschau unter dem Hakenkreuz* p. 284.
28. Czesław Madajczyk, 'Kann man in Polen 1939–1945 von Kollaboration sprechen?', in Werner Rohr (ed.), *Okkupation und Kollaboration 1938–1945* (Berlin 1994) pp. 133ff.
29. Michael Steinlauf, 'Poland', in David Wyman (ed.), *The World Reacts to the Holocaust* (Baltimore 1996) p. 107.
30. Amouroux, *La Grande Histoire des Français* 4, p. 191.
31. Burrin, *Living with Defeat* pp. 206ff.
32. George Mosse, 'On Homosexuality and French Fascism', in his *The Fascist Revolution* (New York 1999) pp. 176–7.
33. Thomas Powers, *Heisenberg's War. The Secret History of the German Bomb* (London 1993) pp. 120–8.
34. Terry Charman, '"*Chansons sous l'occupation*". Maurice Chevalier and Collaboration in occupied France', *Imperial War Museum Review* (1991) 6, pp. 96–110.
35. Henry Rousso, '"L'Épuration". Die politische Säuberung in Frankreich', in K.-D. Henke and H. Wöller (eds), *Politische Säuberung in Europa* (Munich 1991) p. 202.
36. Noel Malcolm, *Bosnia. A Short History* (London 1994) p. 193.
37. For a recent exposure of Swiss relations with the Nazis see Tom Bower, *Nazi Gold* (New York 1997).
38. Richard J. Crampton, *Eastern Europe in the Twentieth Century* (London 1994) p. 197.
39. Mark Mazower, *Inside Hitler's Greece. The Experience of Occupation 1941–1944* (New Haven and London 1993) pp. 23–41.
40. Pryce-Jones, *Paris in the Third Reich* p. 98.
41. MacDonald and Kaplan, *Prague in the Shadow of the Swastika* p. 143.
42. Pryce-Jones, *Paris in the Third Reich* p. 94.
43. Older comparative works on collaboration include Werner Rings, *Living*

with the Enemy (New York 1982); David Littlejohn, *The Patriotic Traitors* (London 1972); Pascal Ory, *Les Collaborateurs 1940–1945* (Paris 1976) and the more recent studies by Czesław Madajczyk, *Faszyzm i okupacje* (Poznan 1983–4) and Yves Durand, *Le Nouvel Ordre européen nazi 1938–1945* (Paris 1990). See also Mark Mazower, 'Hitler's New Order 1939–45', *Diplomacy and Statecraft* (1996) 7, pp. 29–51 for a broad synoptic view.

44. Stanley Hoffmann, 'Collaboration in France during World War II', *JMH* (1968) 40, pp. 375ff. Czesław Madajczyk, 'Zwischen Zusammenarbeit und Kollaboration', in Röhr (ed.), *Okkupation und Kollaboration* p. 55 is sceptical of the value of this auxiliary term.

45. Gerhard Hirschfeld, *Nazi Rule and Dutch Collaboration* (Oxford 1988) p. 262.

46. Martin Conway, *Collaboration in Belgium* (New Haven 1993) pp. 14–15; Oddvar Hoidal, *Vidkun Quisling. A Study in Treason* (Oslo 1989); and Hans Frederik Dahl, *Quisling. A Study in Treachery* (Cambridge 1999).

47. Mazower, 'Hitler's New Order' pp. 29–30.

48. Jan Hermann Brinks, 'The Dutch, the Germans, & the Jews', *History Today* (1999) 49, pp. 17–23.

49. Hirschfeld, *Nazi Rule and Dutch Collaboration* pp. 57ff.

50. Hoidal, *Vidkun Quisling* pp. 491ff.

51. Norman Davies, 'Ethnic Diversity in Twentieth Century Poland', *Polin* (1989) 4, pp. 146–7.

52. Mark Almond, *Europe's Backyard War* (London 1994) p. 140.

53. Marcus Tanner, *Croatia* (New Haven 1997) pp. 190ff.

54. Almond, *Europe's Backyard War* p. 141 is outstanding on the history of former Yugoslavia.

55. Brinks, 'The Dutch, the Germans & the Jews' p. 20.

56. *ADAP* D, IX, no. 317, p. 356.

57. Otto Abetz, *Das offene Problem. Ein Rückblick auf zwei Jahrzehnte deutscher Frankreichpolitik* (Cologne 1951) p. 217.

58. For example Ian Kershaw, *Hitler* (London 1991).

59. Reuth (ed.), *Joseph Goebbels, Tagebücher* 4, entry dated 26 April 1942, p. 1785.

60. On the Fascist International see M. Leeden, *Universal Fascism. The Theory and Practice of the Fascist International 1928–1936* (New York 1972).

61. Geoffrey Warner, *Pierre Laval and the Eclipse of France* (London 1968) pp. 332–3.

62. Robert Paxton, *Vichy France. Old Guard and New Order 1940–1944* (New York 1972) pp. 359ff. is coolly compelling on these comparative speculative possibilities.

63. Ninetta Jucker, *Curfew in Paris. A Record of the German Occupation* (London 1960) p. 58.

64. Karl Megerle, themes for press and propaganda dated 27 September 1941: Michael Salewski, 'Ideas of the National Socialist Government and Party', in Walter Lipgens (ed.) *Documents on the History of European Integration* (Berlin, New York 1985) 1, doc. 14, p. 88. Some of these issues are dealt with in Robert Herzstein's *When Nazi Dreams Came True* (London 1982) and in Ralph Giordano's *Wenn Hitler den Krieg gewonnen hätte* (Hamburg 1991) and less reliably by Hans Werner Neulen, *Europa und das Dritte Reich* (Munich 1987).

65. Alan Milward, *War, Economy and Society 1939–1945* (London 1977) p. 136.

66. Richard Overy, 'German Multi-Nationals and the Nazi State in Occupied Europe', in Overy (ed.), *War and Economy in the Third Reich* (Oxford 1994) pp. 315ff. See also Richard Overy, *Göring. The Iron Man* (London 1984) pp. 109ff.

67. I am grateful to Richard Overy for a copy of his unpublished lecture 'The Economy of the German "New Order"' (1996) for these comments on business and insurance.

68. Léon Degrelle, 'Belgium's Role in the New Europe', *ADAP* D, XI, pp. 288–93.

69. See Hoidal, *Vidkun Quisling* pp. 296ff. and 'Memorandum concerning Settlement of Relations between Norway and Germany' dated 25 October 1940, *ADAP* D, XI, pp. 337–9.

70. Anton Mussert, 'The Dutch state in the new Europe', August 1942: Salewski, 'Ideas of the National Socialist Government and Party' doc. 21, pp. 98–102.

71. *Hitler's Secret Book*, introduced by Telford Taylor (New York 1961) esp. pp. 106–7.

72. For Hitler's views on Europe see Peter Krüger, 'Hitlers Europapolitik', in Wolfgang Benz, Hans Buchheim and Hans Mommsen (eds), *Der Nationalsozialismus* (Frankfurt am Main 1993) esp. pp. 128ff.

73. Paul Kluke, 'Nationalsozialistische Europäideologie', *VfZ* (1955) 3, p. 253.

74. Record of discussion in Göring's headquarters dated 19–20 June 1940, *IMT* 27, pp. 29–31.

75. Hugh Trevor-Roper (ed.), *Hitler's Table Talk 1941–44* (Oxford 1988) entry dated 31 January 1942, pp. 266–9.

76. *Ibid.* entries dated 13 May and 5 June 1942, pp. 479 and 515.

77. *Ibid.* entry dated 29 June 1942, p. 541.

78. See Karl Dreschler, Hans Dress and Gerhart Hass, 'Europapläne des deutschen Imperialismus im zweiten Weltkrieg', in *Zeitschrift für Ges-*

chichtswissenschaft and Lothar Gruchmann, *Nationalsozialistische Grossraumordnung* (Stuttgart 1962).

79. See mainly M. L. Smith and P. M. Stirk (eds), *Making the New Europe* (London 1992).

80. Joachim von Ribbentrop, 'Speech on the Prolongation of the Anti-Comintern Pact' dated 26 November 1941, *Monatshefte für Auswärtige Politik* (1941) 8, pp. 1053ff.; Karl Megerle, 'European Themes' (autumn 1941): Salewski, 'Ideas of the National Socialist Government and Party', doc. 18, p. 95; Werner Daitz, 'Genuine and Spurious Continental Spheres. Laws of Lebensraum' (late 1942): Salewski, 'Ideas of the National Socialist Government and Party' doc. 27, p. 112.

81. Eugen Weber, *The Hollow Years. France in the 1930s* (London 1995) pp. 98ff. for a fascinating account.

82. P. M. Stirk, 'Anti-Americanism in National Socialist Propaganda', in Smith and Stirk (eds), *Making the New Europe* p. 74.

83. M. L. Smith, 'The Anti-Bolshevik Crusade and Europe', in Smith and Stirk (eds), *Making the New Europe* pp. 58ff.

84. Warner, *Pierre Laval and the Eclipse of France* p. 315.

85. On the largely neglected moral aspects of the Second World War, see Richard Overy's outstanding *Why the Allies Won* (London 1995) esp. pp. 298ff.

86. Wipert von Blücher, 'Goebbels's "Principles" for the Reorganisation of Europe' dated 16 March 1943, *ADAP* E, V, pp. 409–10.

87. Joachim von Ribbentrop, 'European Confederation' dated 21 March 1943, *ADAP* E, V, no. 229, pp. 437–41.

88. Cecil Renthe-Fink, 'Note on the Establishment of a European Confederation' dated August 1943: Salewski, 'Ideas of the National Socialist Government and Party' doc. 36, pp. 138–9.

89. Bernd Wegner, *Hitlers politische Soldaten. Die Waffen-SS 1933–1945* (Paderborn 1982) p. 298.

90. Hans-Dieter Loock, 'Zur "Großgermanischen Politik" des Dritten Reiches', *VfZ* (1960) 8, p. 56.

91. Josef Ackermann, *Heinrich Himmler als Ideologe* (Göttingen 1970), p. 183.

92. Loock, 'Zur "Großgermanischen Politik"' pp. 59–60.

93. Ulrich Herbert, *Best* (Bonn 1996) pp. 326–7.

94. Bunting, *The Model Occupation* pp. 40–1.

95. Brian Bonnard (ed.), *Island of Dread* (Stroud 1991).

96. H. Heiber (ed.), *Hitler's Lagebesprechungen* (Stuttgart 1962) pp. 67–8.

97. Eberhard Jäckel, *Frankreich in Hitlers Europa* (Stuttgart 1966) pp. 194–5.

98. See Peter G. Pulzer's powerful and telling critique of Daniel Jonah Goldhagen's *Hitler's Willing Executioners. Ordinary Germans and the Holocaust* (London 1996): 'Psychopaths and Conformists, Adventurers and Moral Cowards', *London Review of Books* (1997) 19, pp. 20–1; on Oradour see Max Hastings, *Das Reich. The March of the 2nd SS Panzer Division through France* (London 1993) esp. pp. 181ff. and 249ff.

99. See the important study by Mark Mazower, 'Military Violence and National Socialist Values. The Wehrmacht in Greece 1941–1944', *Past & Present* (1992) 134, pp. 138ff.

100. Crampton, *Eastern Europe in the Twentieth Century* p. 179.

101. Curzio Malaparte, *Kaputt* (London 1982) pp. 68–9.

102. The most astute portrait of Frank, and indeed of other Nazi leaders, remains Joachim Fest's chapter on him in his excellent collection of biographies *The Face of the Third Reich* (London 1972) esp. p. 325, of which R. Zitelmann, R. Smelser and E. Syring (eds), *Die braune Elite* (Darmstadt, 1990–) is a pale and stylistically indifferent imitation.

103. See Keith Sword (ed.), *The Soviet Takeover of the Polish Eastern Provinces 1939–41* (London 1991); Jan T. Gross, *Revolution from Abroad. The Soviet Conquest of Poland's Western Ukraine and Western Belorussia* (Princeton 1988).

104. Memorandum dated 20 October 1939 recording Hitler's instructions to Keitel on the aims of the occupation in Poland, in Werner Röhr (ed.) *Die faschistische Okkupationspolitik in Polen 1939–1945* (Cologne 1989); Wolfgang Schumann and Ludwig Nestler (eds), *Europa unterm Hakenkreuz. Die faschistische Okkupationspolitik in den zeitweilig besetzten Gebieten der Sowjetunion (1914–1944)* (Berlin 1989) doc. 25, p. 133.

105. Proclamation by Generaloberst Brauchitsch to the people of Poland dated 1 September 1939, in Schumann and Nestler (eds), *Europa unterm Hakenkreuz* doc. 1, p. 110.

106. Herbert, *Best* pp. 234ff.

107. Christian Jansen and Arno Weckbecker, *Der 'Volksdeutsche Selbstschutz' in Polen 1939/40* (Munich 1992).

108. Pospieszalski, 'The Bomb Attack' p. 254 n. 25.

109. The quotation is from Edwin Dwinger, *Der Tod in Polen* (Jena 1940) p. 123. See also Kurt Lück, *Marsch der deutschen in Polen* (Berlin 1940).

110. Aktennotiz von SS-Sturmbannführer Walter Rauff regarding the RSHA conference on 21 September 1939, in Schumann and Nestler (eds), *Europa unterm Hakenkreuz* doc. 12, p. 119; Schnellbrief Heydrichs to the Leaders of the Einsatzgruppen dated 21 September 1939, in *ibid.* doc. 13, pp. 120–2.

111. Report from the commander of Rear Area Army 581 to AOK dated 25 September 1939, in *ibid*. doc. 16, pp. 124–5.

112. Horst Mühleisen (ed.), *Hellmuth Stieff. Briefe* (Berlin 1990) no. 63, pp. 107–8.

113. Report from General Walter Petzel to the Befehlshaber des Ersatzheeres dated 23 November 1939, in Schumann and Nestler (eds), *Europa unterm Hakenkreuz* doc. 33, p. 143.

114. Helmut Krausnick, *Hitlers Einsatzgruppen. Die Truppen des Weltanschauungskrieges 1938–1942* (Frankfurt am Main 1985) pp. 66–7.

115. Christopher Clarke, 'Johannes Blaskowitz', in Ronald Smelser (ed.), *Die Militärelite des Dritten Reiches* (Berlin 1995) pp. 28ff.

116. Goldhagen, *Hitler's Willing Executioners*.

117. J. Noakes and G. Pridham (eds), *Nazism 1919–1945. A Documentary Reader* (Exeter 1983–8) 3, doc. 655, pp. 938ff.

118. Rieschock, 'Ich war achtzehn' p. 165.

119. Krausnick, *Hitlers Einsatzgruppen* p. 87.

120. Jerzy Borejsza, 'Anti-Slavism. Hitler's Vision or the Germans'?', *Polish Perspectives* (1988) 31, pp. 28ff.

121. For these themes see Michael Burleigh, *Germany Turns Eastwards. A Study of 'Ostforschung' in the Third Reich* (Cambridge 1988); see also the chapter 'Germany's Turn to the East' (*sic*) in Robert Jan van Pelt and Deborah Dwork, *Auschwitz. 1270 to the Present* (New Haven 1996) pp. 67–91.

122. Notes dated 20 October 1939 concerning instructions from Hitler to Keitel on 17 October 1939 regarding Poland, in Röhr (ed.), *Die faschistische Okkupationspolitik in Polen* doc. 25, pp. 133–4.

123. Hans Frank speaking to a conference on the economy of the General Government on 3 August 1943, in *ibid*. doc. 156, p. 279.

124. S. Gaweda, *Die Jagiellonische Universität in der Zeit der faschistischen Okkupation 1939–1945* (Jena 1981) pp. 17–18.

125. Frank report to a meeting of police leaders dated 30 May 1940, in Rohr (ed.), *Die faschistische Okkupationspolitik in Polen* doc. 62, pp. 173–4; on the AB-Aktion see Christoph Klessmann, *Die Selbstbehauptung einer Nation* (Düsseldorf 1971) pp. 45–6.

126. Marian Olszewski, 'The Policy of Exterminating Polish Intellectuals', *Polish Western Affairs* (1980) pp. 121–8.

127. Melita Maschmann, *Fazit. Mein Weg in der Hitler-Jugend* (Munich 1983) p. 66.

128. Martin Bormann's notes on Hitler's comments on Poland, *IMT* (Nuremberg 1949) 39, doc. USSR-172, pp. 426ff. Himmler speech to the officers of the Leibstandarte-SS Adolf Hitler on 7 September 1940, doc. PS-1918, p. 7.

129. On this subject see now Völker Riesz, *Die Anfänge der Vernichtung*

'lebensunwerten Lebens' in den Reichsgauen Danzig-Westpreussen und Wartheland 1939/40 (Frankfurt am Main 1995), as well as Michael Burleigh, *Death and Deliverance. 'Euthanasia' in Germany 1900–1945* (Cambridge 1994) pp. 130–3.

130. Burleigh, *Germany Turns Eastwards.*

131. Hanns Johst, *Ruf des Reiches – Echo des Volkes!* (Munich 1940) p. 94.

132. Orest Subtelny, *Ukraine. A History* (Toronto 1994) p. 443.

133. David Marples, *Stalinism in the Ukraine in the 1940s* (London 1992), pp. 47ff.

134. Götz Aly and Susanne Heim, *Vordenker der Vernichtung. Auschwitz und die deutschen Pläne für eine neue europäische Ordnung* (Hamburg 1991) pp. 102ff.

135. Madajcyzk, *Die Okkupationspolitik* p. 412.

136. Rolf-Dieter Müller, *Hitlers Ostkrieg und die deutsche Siedlungspolitik* (Frankfurt am Main 1991) pp. 13–23. Biographical studies of Blaskowitz such as Clarke's (see note 115 above) omit this wider context of military settlement plans in Poland, and hence exaggerate the distance between the SS and the military in Poland.

137. On the 'Generalplan Ost' see M. Rössler and S. Schleiermacher (eds), *Der 'Generalplan Ost'* (Berlin 1993) and Bruno Wasser, *Himmlers Raumplanung im Osten. Der Generalplan Ost in Polen 1940–1944* (Basel 1993).

138. BA Koblenz, NS 2/60, Himmler speech to SS leaders in Posen, p. 119.

139. Johst, *Ruf des Reiches* pp. 91–2.

140. Robert Koehl, *RKFDV. German Resettlement Policy* (Cambridge, Mass. 1957) pp. 90–100.

141. Johst, *Ruf des Reiches* p. 28.

142. See Mathias Hamann, 'Erwünscht und unerwünscht. Die rassenpsychologische Selektion der Ausländer', in Jochen August *et al.* (eds), *Herrenmensch und Arbeitsvölker, Beiträge zur NS-Gesundheits- und Sozialpolitik* (Berlin 1986) 9, pp. 144ff.

143. Alexander Hohenstein, *Wartheländisches Tagebuch aus den Jahren 1941/42* (Stuttgart 1961) entry dated 14 July 1941, pp. 166–9.

144. Himmler, decree dated 12 September 1940 on the 'Überprüfung und Aussonderung der Bevölkerung im annektierten Polen', IMT 31, doc. PS-2916, pp. 290ff.; Madajczyk, *Die Okkupationspolitik* pp. 471–2.

145. Madajczyk, 'Kann man in Polen 1939–1945 von Kollaboration sprechen?' pp. 147–8.

146. 'Sonderstrafrecht für Polen und Juden', *Reichsgesetzblatt* (1941) 1, pp. 759ff.

147. Guidelines issued by Arthur Greiser dated 23 February 1943, in Röhr (ed.), *Die faschistische Okkupationspolitik in Polen* doc. 132, p. 250.

148. Madajczyk, *Die Okkupationspolitik* pp. 263–6.

149. Anon., *The Nazi Kultur in Poland* (London 1945) p. 16.

150. Bernhard Stasiewski, 'Die Kirchenpolitik der Nationalsozialisten im Warthegau 1939–1945', *VfZ* (1959) 1, p. 65.

151. Circular issued by Fritz Klemm on 15 August 1941, in Röhr (ed.), *Die faschistische Okkupationspolitik in Polen* doc. 90, p. 203.

152. Richtlinien von Artur Greiser dated 25 September 1940 für das Verhalten der deutschen Einwohner zur polnischen Bevölkerung, in *ibid.* doc. 77, p. 190.

153. Hohenstein, *Wartheländisches Tagebuch* entry dated 22 September 1941, p. 193.

154. *Ibid.* entries dated 9 January and 18 February 1941, pp. 37–8, 88ff.

155. *Ibid.* diary entries dated 14 April and 21 November 1941, pp. 112, 214.

156. *Ibid.* entries dated 16 and 21 May 1941, pp. 128, 133–4.

157. *Ibid.* entry dated 8 July 1941, pp. 159ff.

158. *Ibid.* entry dated 9 July 1941, pp. 162–3.

159. *Ibid.* entry dated 19 April 1941, p. 118.

160. *Ibid.* entry dated 14 March 1942, pp. 234ff.

161. *Ibid.* entry dated 18 March 1942, pp. 239–43.

162. *Ibid.* entry dated 12 May 1942, pp. 258–62.

163. Heinz Höhne, *The Order of the Death's Head* (London 1969) pp. 294–7.

164. Lammers to Frank dated 25 March 1943, in Röhr (ed.), *Die faschistische Okkupationspolitik in Polen* doc. 137, p. 257.

165. *Ibid.* doc. 141, pp. 260–1.

166. *Ibid.* Hans Frank to Hitler dated 25 May 1943, in *ibid.* doc. 148, pp. 267–70.

167. *Ibid.* doc. 150, p. 271.

168. *Ibid.* Himmler to Frank dated 3 July 1943, in *ibid.* doc. 152, pp. 275–6.

169. *Ibid.* Hans Frank to NSDAP Political Leaders dated 14 January 1944, in *ibid.* doc. 168, p. 292.

170. Memorandum to Ernst Kaltenbrunner dated 5 July 1944, in *ibid.* doc. 182, pp. 302ff.

171. 'Guidelines issued by General Nikolaus von Falkenhorst dated 13 March 1940', in Fritz Petrick (ed.) *Die Okkupationspolitik des deutschen Faschismus in Dänemark und Norwegen 1940–1945*, Bundesarchiv (ed.), *Europa unterm Hakenkreuz* (Berlin 1992) 7, doc. 2, p. 76.

172. General Leonhard Kaupisch to Generalleutnant Karl Bodenschatz dated 20 April 1940, in Petrick (ed.), *Die Okkupationspolitik* doc. 6, p. 80.

173. *Ibid.* pp. 34–40.

174. Hans Kirchhoff, 'Die dänische Staatskollaboration', in Röhr (ed.), *Okkupation und Kollaboration* pp. 107–8.

175. Herbert, *Best* p. 380.

176. Erich Thomsen, *Deutsche Besatzungspolitik* (Düsseldorf 1970) p. 206.

177. Hoidal, *Vidkun Quisling* pp. 338–68.

178. *Ibid.* p. 473.

179. Bargatzky, *Hotel Majestic* p. 50.

180. Herbert, *Best* pp. 290–8.

181. Lothar Kettenacker, *Nationalsozialistische Volkstumspolitik* (Düsseldorf 1986) pp. 100ff.

182. Weber, *The Hollow Years* pp. 267–8.

183. Robert Gildea, *The Past in French History* (New Haven 1994) pp. 199ff.

184. Ory, *Les Collaborateurs* p. 181.

185. Michel Denis, 'Mouvement Breton et Fascisme', in Christian Gras and Georges Livet (eds), *Régions et régionalisme en France du XVIIIe siècle à nos jours* (Paris 1977) p. 495.

186. Kettenacker, *Nationalsozialistische Volkstumspolitik* pp. 250–2.

187. Johnpeter Grill, 'Robert Wagner', in R. Smelser, E. Syring and R. Zitelmann (eds), *Die braune Elite II* (Darmstadt 1993) p. 264.

188. W. D. Halls, *Politics, Society and Christianity in Vichy France* (Oxford 1995) pp. 180–1.

189. Kettenacker, *Nationalsozialistische Volkstumspolitik* p. 175.

190. Paxton, *Vichy France* p. 20.

191. Trevor-Roper (ed.), *Hitler's Table Talk* entry dated 13 May 1942, p. 476.

192. Richard Vinen, *France 1934–1970* (London 1996) pp. 35–8 is excellent on the manifold appeal of Pétain.

193. Halls, *Politics, Society and Christianity in Vichy France* pp. 52–4.

194. Trevor-Roper (ed.), *Hitler's Table Talk* entry dated 13 May 1942, p. 478.

195. Paxton, *Vichy France* p. 259.

196. Warner, *Pierre Laval and the Eclipse of France* p. 238; Trevor-Roper (ed.), *Hitler's Table Talk* entry dated 13 May 1942, p. 478.

197. Burrin, *Living with Defeat* p. 70.

198. John F. Sweets, *Choices in Vichy France. The French under Nazi Occupation* (Oxford 1986) p. 33.

199. Renaud de Rochebrune and Jean-Claude Hazera, *Les Patrons sous l'occupation* (Paris 1995) pp. 437ff.

200. *Ibid.* p. 51.

201. R. Tomlinson, 'The "Disappearance" of France 1896–1940', *Historical Journal* (1985) 28, pp. 405ff.

202. Miranda Pollard, 'Women and the National Revolution', in H. R. Kedward and R. Austin (eds), *Vichy France and the Resistance* (London 1985) p. 43.

203. On Borotra see Jean-Louis Gay-Lescot, *Sport et Education sous Vichy* (Lyon 1991) pp. 31ff.

204. Weber, *The Hollow Years* pp. 20–1 is especially good on the pernicious impact of schoolteachers on the young.

205. Paxton, *Vichy France* pp. 172–3.

206. See now Magnus Brechtken, *'Madagascar für die Juden'* (Munich 1997) pp. 97ff.

207. See the classic account by Michael Marrus and Robert Paxton, *Vichy France and the Jews* (New York 1983) pp. 64–7.

208. De Rochebrune and Hazera, *Les Patrons sous l'occupation* p. 393.

209. *Ibid.* pp. 342ff.

210. Albert Speer, *Inside the Third Reich* (London 1995) p. 423.

211. Burrin, *Living with Defeat* p. 250.

212. Weber, *The Hollow Years* p. 197.

213. Halls, *Politics, Society and Christianity in Vichy France* p. 63.

214. W. Halls, 'Catholicism under Vichy', in Kedward and Austin (eds), *Vichy France and the Resistance* p. 144.

215. *Ibid.* pp. 207ff.

216. Hans Umbreit, 'Die Rolle der Kollaboration in der deutschen Besatzungspolitik', in Rohr (ed.), *Okkupation und Kollaboration* p. 37.

217. Milward, *War, Economy and Society* p. 138.

218. Christoph Buchheim, 'Die besetzten Länder im Dienste der deutschen Kriegswirtschaft', *VfZ* (1984) 32, p. 119.

219. Ulrich Herbert, *Hitler's Foreign Workers. Enforced Foreign Labor in Germany under the Third Reich* (Cambridge 1997) pp. 162–3.

220. Jean-Pierre Azema, *From Munich to the Liberation 1938–1944* (Cambridge 1990) p. 128.

221. *Ibid.* pp. 275–6 for these debates.

7. GERMAN INVASION AND OCCUPATION OF THE SOVIET UNION, 1941–1943

1. Heinz Guderian, *Panzer Leader* (London 1987) p. 153; John Erikson, *The Road to Stalingrad* (London 1993), pp. 106–7.

2. Amy Knight, *Beria. Stalin's First Lieutenant* (Princeton 1993) pp. 107–8.

3. Robert Whymant, *Stalin's Spy. Richard Sorge and the Tokyo Espionage Ring* (London 1996) pp. 164–84.

4. Pavel and Anatoli Sudoplatov, *Special Tasks* (Boston 1995) p. 123.

5. Edvard Radzinsky, *Stalin* (London 1996) pp. 436–7.

6. Gabriel Gorodetsky, 'Stalin und Hitlers Angriff auf die Sowjetunion', in Bernd Wegner (ed.), *Zwei Wege nach Moskau* (Munich 1991) p. 358.

7. Knight, *Beria* pp. 107–8.

8. Stepan A. Mikoyan, 'Barbarossa and the Soviet Leadership', in John Erikson and David Dilks (eds), *Barbarossa, the Axis and the Allies* (Edinburgh 1994) pp. 125–6.

9. Robert Conquest, *Stalin. Breaker of Nations* (London 1991) p. 234.

10. Horst Boog, 'Die Luftwaffe', in Boog *et al.* (eds), *Der Angriff auf die Sowjetunion* (Frankfurt am Main 1991) p. 737.

11. Paul Kohl, *'Ich wundere mich, daß ich noch lebe'. Sowjetische Augenzeugen berichten* (Gütersloh 1990) p. 68.

12. C. Gall and T. de Waal, *Chechnya. A Small Victorious War* (London 1997) pp. 62–3.

13. *Ibid.* p. 31.

14. Conquest, *Stalin* p. 239.

15. Dmitri Volkogonov, *Stalin. Triumph and Tragedy* (London 1991) pp. 406ff.; Radzinsky, *Stalin* pp. 454–5.

16. Manfred Menger, 'Deutschland und der finnische "Sonderkrieg" gegen die Sowjetunion', in Wegner, *Zwei Wege* pp. 547ff.

17. Jürgen Forster, 'Die Gewinnung von Verbündeten in Südosteuropa', in Boog *et al.* (eds), *Der Angriff auf die Sowjetunion* pp. 396ff.

18. *Ibid.* p. 430.

19. Lütz Lemhofer, 'Gegen den gottlosen Bolshewismus. Zur Stellung der Kirchen zum Krieg gegen die Sowjetunion', in Gerd R. Ueberschär and Wolfram Wette (eds), *Der deutsche Überfall auf die Sowjetunion* (Frankfurt am Main 1991) pp. 78–9.

20. Hans-Heinrich Wilhelm, 'Motivation und "Kriegsbild" deutscher Generäle und Offiziere im Krieg gegen die Sowjetunion', in Peter Jahn and Reinhard Rürup (eds), *Erobern und Vernichten. Der Krieg gegen die Sowjetunion 1941–1945* (Berlin 1991) pp. 153–82.

21. See Michael Burleigh, *Germany Turns Eastwards. A Study of 'Ostforschung' in the Third Reich* (Cambridge 1988) and Gabriele Camphausen, *Die wissenschaftliche-historische Russlandforschung im Dritten Reich 1933–1945* (Frankfurt am Main 1990).

22. Peter Jahn, ' "Russenfurcht" und Antibolschewismus'. Zur Entstehung und Wirkung von Feindbildern', in Jahn and Rürup (eds), *Erobern und Vernichten* pp. 52–3.

23. Walter Warlimont, *Inside Hitler's Headquarters 1939–45* (London 1964) p. 140.

24. Andreas Hillgruber, 'Das Russland-Bild der führenden deutschen Militärs vor Beginn des Angriffs auf die Sowjetunion', in Wegner, *Zwei Wege* p. 177.

25. Ludolf Herbst, *Das nationalsozialistische Deutschland 1933–1945* (Frankfurt am Main 1996) pp. 348–9 contains an excellent discussion.

26. B. Kroener, 'Der "erfrorene Blitzkrieg". Strategische Planungen der deutschen Führung gegen die Sowjetunion und die Ursachen ihres Scheiterns', in Wegner, *Zwei Wege* p. 144.

27. Herbst, *Das nationalsozialistische Deutschland* p. 361.

28. Erich von Manstein, *Lost Victories* (Elstree 1987) pp. 208–9.

29. For a vivid and still useful account of conditions, see Alan Clark, *Barbarossa. The Russian–German Conflict* (London 1995).

30. Alexander Werth, *Russia at War 1941–1945* (London 1964) p. 163.

31. See Richard Woff, 'Rokossovsky' and other biographies of these generals in Harold Shukman (ed.), *Stalin's Generals* (London 1993), pp. 177ff.

32. Volkogonov, *Stalin* p. 423.

33. On events in the Ukraine, see Wolodymyr Kosyk, *The Third Reich and the Ukraine* (New York 1993) p. 88; for Order No. 270 see John Barber and Mark Harrison, *The Soviet Home Front 1941–1945* (London 1991) p. 28.

34. Knight, *Beria* p. 114.

35. Ingeborg Fleischhauer, 'Operation Barbarossa and the Deportation', in Fleischhauer and Benjamin Pinkus (eds), *The Soviet Germans. Past and Present* (London 1986) pp. 78ff.

36. Warlimont, *Inside Hitler's Headquarters* pp. 221–5.

37. H.-A. Jacobsen (ed.), *Der Weg zur Teilung der Welt. Politik und Strategie 1939–1945* (Koblenz, Bonn 1977) pp. 138–9.

38. Manstein, *Lost Victories* pp. 280–1.

39. Guderian, *Panzer Leader* p. 265.

40. *Ibid.* p. 266.

41. Manstein, *Lost Victories* p. 281.

42. Seweryn Bialer (ed.), *Stalin and his Generals. Soviet Military Memoirs of World War Two* (New York 1969) pp. 339ff.

43. Geoffrey Hoskins, *A History of the Soviet Union 1917–1991* (London 1992) pp. 274–5 for a crisp description of Stalin as a war leader; see also Alan Bullock, *Hitler and Stalin. Parallel Lives* (London 1991) pp. 699ff.

44. F. Kagan, 'The Evacuation of Soviet Industry in the Wake of "Barbarossa". A Key to the Soviet Victory', *Journal of Slavic Military Studies* (1995) 8, pp. 387–414.

45. Barber and Harrison, *Soviet Home Front* p. 127.

46. Richard J. Overy, *Why the Allies Won* (London 1995) p. 186.

47. Sudoplatov, *Special Tasks* p. 135.

48. Werth, *Russia at War* p. 246.

49. Hosking, *A History of the Soviet Union* p. 236.

50. Vasily Grossmann, *Life and Fate* (London 1995) pp. 231–2.

51. Knight, *Beria* p. 118.

52. Barber and Harrison, *Soviet Home Front* pp. 116ff. and 170 on camp morale.

53. Whymant, *Stalin's Spy* pp. 216ff.

54. On the war in general see the highly informed account by Richard Overy, *Russia's War* (London 1997) pp. 113–22.

55. Warlimont, *Inside Hitler's Headquarters* p. 252.

56. For an excellent analysis of the options, see Bernd Wegner, 'The Road to Defeat. The German Campaigns in Russia 1941–43', *Journal of Strategic Studies* (1990) 13, pp. 114ff.

57. Wolfram Wette and Gerd Ueberschär (eds), *Stalingrad. Mythos und Wirklichkeit einer Schlacht* (Frankfurt am Main 1993) p. 20.

58. Martin Middlebrook, 'Paulus', in Correlli Barnett (ed.), *Hitler's Generals* (London 1989) pp. 361ff.; Viktor Anfilov, 'Zhukov', in Shukman (ed.), *Stalin's Generals* pp. 343ff.

59. Georgi K. Zhukov, *Marshal Zhukov's Greatest Battles* (London 1969) pp. 158ff. for a detailed account of the genesis of Operation Uranus.

60. Volkogonov, *Stalin* pp. 462–3 and 475ff.

61. R. Wolf, 'Vasily Ivanovich Chuikov', in Shukman (ed.), *Stalin's Generals* pp. 67–74.

62. Bernd Boll and Hans Safrian, 'Auf dem Weg nach Stalingrad. Die 6. Armee 1941/42', in Hannes Heer and Klaus Naumann (eds), *Vernichtungskrieg. Verbrechen der Wehrmacht 1941–1944* (Hamburg 1995) pp. 269ff.

63. Werth, *Russia at War* p. 442; see also Anthony Beevor's detailed account *Stalingrad* (London 1998).

64. Clark, *Barbarossa* pp. 243–5.

65. Werth, *Russia at War* p. 462.

66. *Marshal Zhukov's Greatest Battles* p. 169.

67. Gerd Ueberschär, 'Stalingrad – eine Schlacht des Zweiten Weltkrieges', in Wette and Ueberschär (eds), *Stalingrad*, pp. 18ff.

68. Wolfgang U. Eckart, 'Von der Agonie einer mißbrauchten Armee. Anmerkungen zur Verwundeten- und Krankenversorgung im Kessel von Stalingrad', in Wette and Ueberschär (eds), *Stalingrad* pp. 109–12.

69. Landeshauptarchiv Koblenz, Bestand 700, 153 Nr 80 cited in Wolfram Wette, ' "Unsere Stimmung ist auf dem Nullpunkt angekommen" ', in Wette and Ueberschär (eds), *Stalingrad* p. 95; see also Rolf-Dieter Müller, ' "Was wir an Hunger ausstehen müssen, könnt Ihr Euch gar nicht denken', in Wette and Ueberschär (eds), *Stalingrad* pp. 131ff.

70. Anatoly Golovchansky *et al.* (eds), *'Ich will raus aus diesem Wahnsinn'. Deutsche Briefe von der Ostfront 1941–1945 aus sowjetischen Archiven* (Hamburg 1993) p. 150.

71. *Ibid.* pp. 228–9.

72. *Ibid.* pp. 161–2.

73. Müller, 'Was wir an Hunger' p. 143.

74. David M. Glantz, *From the Don to the Dnepr. Soviet Offensive Operations December 1942–August 1943* (London 1991) pp. 215–19.

75. David M. Glantz, *Soviet Military Deception in the Second World War* (London 1989) pp. 152ff.

76. Robin Cross, *Citadel. The Battle of Kursk* (London 1993) pp. 181–2.
77. Wegner, 'The Road to Defeat' p. 109; Christian Streit, *Keine Kameraden. Die Wehrmacht und die sowjetischen Kriegsgefangenen 1941–1945* (Stuttgart 1978) and his 'Die Behandlung und Ermordung sowjetischen Kriegsgefangenen', in Klaus Meyer and Wolfgang Wippermann (eds), *Gegen das Vergessen. Der Vernichtungskrieg gegen die Sowjetunion 1941–1945* (Frankfurt am Main 1992) pp. 91–2; Alfred Streim, *Die Behandlung sowjetischer Kriegsgefangener im 'Fall Barbarossa'. Eine Dokumentation* (Heidelberg 1981).
78. Alfred Streim, *Sowjetische Gefangene in Hitlers Vernichtungskrieg* (Heidelberg 1982) p. 22; see also his 'Das Völkerrecht und die Sowjetischen Kriegsgefangenen', in Wegner (ed.), *Zwei Wege* pp. 291ff.
79. These arguments are rehearsed, and then destroyed, by Streit, *Keine Kameraden* pp. 128–9, whose own contributions are merely modified around the margins by the post-revisionist Theo Schulte, *The German Army and Nazi Policies in Occupied Russia* (Oxford 1989) pp. 180–4.
80. Streit, *Keine Kameraden* p. 145.
81. *Ibid.* p. 152.
82. Curzio Malaparte, *Kaputt* (London 1989) pp. 208–15.
83. Streit, *Keine Kameraden* pp. 162ff.
84. *Ibid.* pp. 181–2 for Reinecke's orders.
85. *Ibid.* pp. 57–8; see also Klaus-Jurgen Müller, 'The Brutalisation of Warfare. Nazi Crimes and the Wehrmacht', in Erickson and Dilks (eds), *Barbarossa* p. 233; and Jürgen Forster, 'The German Army and the Ideological War against the Soviet Union', in Gerhard Hirschfeld (ed.), *The Policies of Genocide. Jews and Soviet Prisoners of War in Nazi Germany* (London 1986) pp. 15–29.
86. Streit, *Keine Kameraden* p. 31.
87. *Ibid.* p. 34.
88. Reprinted in Ueberschär and Wette (eds), *Der deutsche Überfall auf die Sowjetunion* pp. 249–50.
89. Streit, *Keine Kameraden* pp. 33ff.
90. Jürgen Forster, 'Der Kommissar-Befehl', in Boog *et al.* (eds), *Der Angriff auf die Sowjetunion* pp. 520–5; on the subject of Red Army murders of German prisoners see Alfred de Zayas, *The Wehrmacht War Crimes Bureau 1939–1945* (Lincoln, Nebraska 1989) pp. 162ff. On p. 177 de Zayas notes that individual interpretations of generalised injunctions to annihilate the invaders (which primarily meant in battle) were not comparable with orders to kill entire groups of people after they had been captured. The projection of German aggression on to the Red Army is discussed by Omer Bartov, 'Historians on the Eastern Front. Andreas Hillgruber and Germany's Tragedy', in his *Murder in our*

Midst. The Holocaust, Industrial Killing, and Representation (New York, Oxford 1996) pp. 71ff.

91. Streit, *Keine Kameraden* p. 92.

92. 'Richtlinien für das Verhalten der Truppe in Russland', in Ueberschär and Wette (eds), *Der deutsche Überfall auf die Sowjetunion* p. 258.

93. 'Befehl des Befehlshabers der Panzergruppe 4 zur bevorstehenden Kampfführung im Osten', in *ibid.* p. 251.

94. 'Armeebefehl des Oberbefehlhabers der 6. Armee vom 10.10.1941', in *ibid.* p. 285.

95. 'Armeebefehl des Oberbefehlshabers der 17. Armee vom 17.11.1941', in *ibid.* p. 288.

96. Schulte, *The German Army and Nazi Policies* p. 219.

97. Forster, 'The German Army and the Ideological War' pp. 22–3.

98. Streit, *Keine Kameraden* pp. 102–3.

99. Streim, *Sowjetische Gefangene in Hitlers Vernichtungskrieg* pp. 38–45.

100. *Ibid.* pp. 56ff.

101. David Hackett (ed.), *The Buchenwald Report* (Boulder 1995) pp. 238–9.

102. Streim, *Sowjetische Gefangene in Hitlers Vernichtungskrieg* pp. 87–91.

103. Omer Bartov, *Hitler's Army. Soldiers, Nazis and War in the Third Reich* (Oxford 1991); see also his *The Eastern Front 1941–45. German Troops and the Barbarisation of Warfare* (London 1985); 'Von unten betrachtet: Überleben, Zusammenhalt und Brutalität an der Ostfront', in Wegner (ed.), *Zwei Wege* pp. 326ff.; and 'The Myths of the Wehrmacht', *History Today* (1992), 42, pp. 30–6.

104. Schulte, *The German Army and Nazi Policies.*

105. Bartov, *Hitler's Army* pp. 38ff.

106. *Ibid.* pp. 95–6.

107. Schulte, *The German Army and Nazi Policies* p. 112.

108. Ilya Ehrenburg, *The War 1941–45. Men, Years, Life*, trans. by Tatiana Shebunina and Yvonne Kapp (London 1964), pp. 28–9.

109. *Ibid.* pp. 156–60.

110. *'Ich will raus aus diesem Wahnsinn'* pp. 119–20.

111. *Ibid.* pp. 227–8.

112. *Ibid.* pp. 57–8.

113. Hugh Trevor-Roper (ed.), *Hitler's Table Talk 1941–44* (Oxford 1988) pp. 15, 23, 24, 33 etc. for the India analogy.

114. *Ibid.* 17 September 1941, p. 34.

115. *Ibid.* 19–20 February 1942, p. 319.

116. *Ibid.* 17 October 1941, p. 69.

117. *Ibid.* 6 August 1942, p. 617.

118. *Ibid.* 8–9 and 9–10 August 1941, p. 24.

119. Martin Bormann, 'Aktenvermerk', 16 July 1941, in Wolfgang Schumann and Ludwig Nestler (eds), *Europa unterm Hakenkreuz. Die faschistische*

Okkupationspolitik in den zeitweilig besetzten Gebieten der Sowjetunion (1941–1944) (Berlin 1991) pp. 160ff.

120. For example, Leonid Grenkevich, *The Soviet Partisan Movement 1941–1944* (London 1999) p. 111.

121. Timothy P. Mulligan, *The Politics of Illusion and Empire. German Occupation Policy in the Soviet Union 1942–1943* (New York 1988) pp. 37ff.

122. Alexander Dallin, *German Rule in Russia 1941–1945* (2nd edn London 1981) pp. 46ff.

123. On the Ukraine see Bohdan Krawchenko, 'Soviet Ukraine under Nazi Occupation 1941–44', in Yury Boshyk (ed.), *Ukraine during World War II* (Edmonton 1986) pp. 15ff.; David R. Marples, *Stalinism in Ukraine in the 1940s* (London 1992) pp. 42ff.; and Mulligan, *The Politics of Illusion and Empire* pp. 61ff. See now Waldemar Lotnik, *Nine Lives* (London 1999) for the memoirs of a young Polish participant.

124. Oleg Zarubinsky, 'Collaboration of the Population in Occupied Ukrainian Territory. Some Aspects of the Overall Picture', in *Journal of Slavic Military Studies* (1997) 10, pp. 147–50.

125. J. Hiden and P. Salmon, *The Baltic Nations and Europe. Estonia, Latvia and Lithuania in the Twentieth Century* (Harlow 1991) p. 115.

126. Dr Dengel to Generalleutnant Wilhelm Schubert, 3 July 1941, in Schumann and Nestler (eds), *Europa unterm Hakenkreuz* pp. 155–6.

127. Mulligan, *The Politics of Illusion and Empire* pp. 126ff.

128. Herbert Backe, '12 Gebote für das Verhalten der Deutschen im Osten und die Behandlung der Russen', 1 January 1941, in Ueberschär and Wette (eds), *Der deutsche Überfall auf die Sowjetunion* pp. 326–8.

129. Report from the Auslandbriefprüfstelle (no date), in Schumann and Nestler (eds), *Europa unterm Hakenkreuz* pp. 453–4; for a general survey of the German administration see Jonathan Steinberg, 'The Third Reich Reflected. German Civil Administration in the Occupied Soviet Union', *English Historical Review* (1995) 110, pp. 620ff.

130. Bernhard Chiari, 'Deutsche Zivilverwaltung in Weissrussland 1941–1944. Die lokale Perspektive der Besatzungsmacht', *Militärgeschichtliche Mitteilungen* (1993) 52, p. 79.

131. Ann Sheehy and Bohdan Nahaylo, *The Crimean Tatars, Volga Germans and Meskhetians. Soviet Treatment of Some National Minorities*, Minority Rights Group Report No. 6 (London 1980) p. 7.

132. Joachim Hoffmann, *Deutsche und Kalmyken 1942 bis 1945* (4th edn Freiburg im Breisgau 1986).

133. Joachim Hoffmann, *Die Ostlegionen 1941–1943* (3rd edn Freiburg im Breisgau 1986).

134. Hoffmann, *Deutsche und Kalmyken* pp. 50ff.

135. P. B. Black, 'Rehearsal for Reinhard? Odilo Globocnik and the Lublin Selbstschutz', *CEH* (1992) 25, pp. 225–6.

136. Samuel J. Newland, *Cossacks in the German Army* (London 1991) p. 86.

137. See the suggestive piece by Sergei Kudryashov 'The Hidden Dimension. Wartime Collaboration in the Soviet Union', in Erikson and Dilks (eds), *Barbarossa* pp. 238ff.

138. Vlasov, 'Why I Decided to Fight Bolshevism', in Catherine Andreyev, *Vlasov and the Russian Liberation Movement. Soviet Reality and Émigré Theories* (Cambridge 1987) p. 211; see also Joachim Hoffmann, *Die Geschichte der Wlassow-Armee* (Freiburg im Breisgau 1986).

139. 'The Smolensk Declaration', in Andreyev, *Vlasov and the Russian Liberation Movement* p. 207.

140. John Erickson, 'Nazi Posters in Wartime Russia', *History Today* (1994) 44, pp. 14–19.

141. Rosenberg, 'Neue Agrarordnung', in Schumann and Nestler (eds), *Europa unterm Hakenkreuz* pp. 245–8; on these reforms see also Christian Gerlach, 'Die deutsche Agrarreform und die Bevölkerungspolitik in den besetzten sowjetischen Gebieten', *Beiträge zur Geschichte der nationalsozialistischen Gesundheits- und Sozialpolitik* (Berlin 1995) 12, pp. 9ff.

142. 'Aufzeichnungen über die Rede von Erich Koch auf der Tagung in Rowno vom 26. bis 28 August 1942', in Schumann and Nestler (eds), *Europa unterm Hakenkreuz* p. 322.

143. 'Niederschrift einer Beratung unter dem Vorsitz von Reichsmarschall Hermann Göring am 8 November 1941 über Grundsätze bei der wirtschaftlichen Ausbeutung der okkupierten Gebiete der UdSSR', in Schumann and Nestler (eds), *Europa unterm Hakenkreuz* p. 217.

144. *Ibid.* pp. 404–5.

145. Mulligan, *The Politics of Illusion and Empire* p. 108.

146. *Ibid.* p. 100.

147. Lütz Schwerin von Krosigk, 'Denkschrift', 4 September 1942, in Schumann and Nestler (eds), *Europa unterm Hakenkreuz* pp. 324–7.

148. On these plans see above all Rolf-Dieter Müller, *Hitlers Ostkrieg und die deutsche Siedlungspolitik* (Frankfurt am Main 1991); see also Mechtild Rössler, 'Konrad Meyer und der "Generalplan Ost" in der Beurteilung der Nürnberger Prozesse', in M. Rössler and S. Schleiermacher (eds), *Der 'Generalplan Ost'. Hauptlinien der nationalsozialistischen Planungs- und Vernichtungspolitik* (Berlin 1993) pp. 356ff.; my own views on these subjects are to be found in 'A Political Economy of the Final Solution. Reflections on Modernity, Historians and the Holocaust', *Patterns of Prejudice* (1996) 30, pp. 29–41.

149. Gert Gröning and Joachim Wolschke-Bulmahn (eds), *Der Liebe zur*

Landschaft. Teil III: Der Drang nach Osten. Arbeiten zur sozialwissen-schaftlich orientierten Freiraumplanung (Munich 1987) 9, p. 31.

150. Müller, *Hitlers Ostkrieg* pp. 102–3.
151. Helmut Heiber, 'Der Generalplan Ost', *VfZ* (1958) 6, pp. 297ff.
152. Dietrich Eichholtz, 'Der "Generalplan Ost"', *Jahrbuch für Geschichte* (1982) 26, pp. 259ff. for Meyer's memorandum.
153. See above all Rolf-Dieter Müller, 'Das "Unternehmen Barbarossa" als wirtschaftlicher Raubkrieg', in Ueberschär and Wette (eds), *Der deut-sche Überfall auf die Sowjetunion* pp. 125ff.
154. 'Allgemeine wirtschaftspolitische Richtlinien für die Wirtschaftsorgani-sation Ost, Gruppe Landwirtschaft', 23 May 1941, in Ueberschär and Wette (eds), *Der deutsche Überfall auf die Sowjetunion* pp. 323–5; on Backe see also Götz Aly and Susanne Heim, *Vordenker der Vernichtung. Auschwitz und die deutschen Pläne für eine neue europäische Ordnung* (Hamburg 1991) pp. 365ff.
155. Extract from Halder diaries, in Ueberschär and Wette (eds), *Der deut-sche Überfall auf die Sowjetunion* pp. 278–9.
156. Werth, *Russia at War* p. 339; see also the Russian and German accounts in Ales Adamowitsch *et al.* (eds), *Blockade Leningrad 1941–1944* (Hamburg 1992) for what follows.
157. 'Aufzeichnung im Wirtschaftsstab Ost über die von Reichsmarschall Hermann Göring am 7 November 1941 gegebenen Richtlinien für den Arbeitseinsatz von Sowjetbürgern', in Schumann and Nestler (eds), *Europa unterm Hakenkreuz* p. 214.
158. Rolf-Dieter Müller, 'Die Rekrutierung sowjetischer Zwangsarbeiter für die deutsche Kriegswirtschaft', in Ulrich Herbert (ed.), *Europa und der 'Reichseinsatz'* (Essen 1991) pp. 235–7; on Sauckel see Peter W. Becker, 'Fritz Sauckel. Plenipotentiary for the Mobilisation of Labour', in Ron-ald Smelser and Rainer Zitelmann (eds), *The Nazi Elite* (London 1993) pp. 194ff.
159. See the comments reported by the Auslandsbriefprüfstelle Berlin dated 11 November 1942, in Schumann and Nestler (eds), *Europa unterm Hakenkreuz* pp. 358ff.
160. Müller, 'Die Rekrutierung' p. 238.
161. Auslandsprüfstelle Berlin report dated 11 November 1942, 'Anlage 1', in Schumann and Nestler (eds), *Europa unterm Hakenkreuz* pp. 359–60.
162. Notes by SS-Obersturmbannführer Erich Ehrlinger on a conference in the presence of Fritz Sauckel in Kiev on 12 August 1942, in *ibid.* pp. 313–16.
163. Report by SS-Obersturmbannführer Erich Ehrlinger dated 20 July 1942 concerning labour recruitment raids in the Podol district of Kiev, in *ibid.* pp. 302ff.

164. Report by Obersturmbannführer Erich Ehrlinger to SS-Gruppenführer Max Thomas dated 9 December 1942, in *ibid*. p. 366.

165. Report by SS-Sturmbannführer Erich Ehrlinger to SS-Gruppenführer Max Thomas dated 19 December 1942, in *ibid*. pp. 366–8.

166. See A. A. Maslov, 'Concerning the Role of Partisan Warfare in Soviet Military Doctrine in the 1920s and 1930s', *Journal of Slavic Military Studies* (1998) 9, pp. 889–90; Matthew Cooper, *The Phantom War. The German Struggle against Soviet Partisans 1941–1944* (London 1979) p. 12; W. Wilenchik, 'Die Partisanenbewegung in Weissrussland 1941–1944', *Forschungen zur Osteuropäischen Geschichte* (1984) 34, pp. 150–1.

167. Rosenberg to Sauckel, 21 December 1942, in Schumann and Nestler (eds), *Europa unterm Hakenkreuz* p. 147.

168. Grenkevich, *The Soviet Partisan Movement* p. 91.

169. Sudoplatov, *Special Tasks* pp. 130–3.

170. Cooper, *The Phantom War* p. 35; on the operational space left to partisans see Center of Military History, United States Army (ed.), *Combat in Russian Forests and Swamps* (Washington DC 1986) pp. 1–4.

171. For details see Grenkevich, *The Soviet Partisan Movement* pp. 239ff.

172. On Dirlewanger and Kaminsky see Hellmuth Auerbach, 'Die Einheit Dirlewanger', *VfZ* (1962) 10, pp. 250ff.; Alexander Dallin, 'The Kaminsky Brigade. A Case Study of Soviet Disaffection', in A. and J. Rabinowitch (eds), *Revolution and Politics in Russia* (Bloomington 1973) pp. 243–80.

173. Monthly report from Wirtschaftsstabes Ost concerning July 1942, in Schumann and Nestler (eds), *Europa unterm Hakenkreuz* pp. 305ff.

174. Heinrich Himmler, 'Guidelines for the Combating of Bandits', September 1942, in *ibid*. p. 332.

175. Göring order concerning prevention of partisan attacks on railway lines, 16 October 1942, in *ibid*. pp. 339–40.

176. *Ibid*. pp. 340–1.

177. Report from Oberkommando der 6. Armee to Army Group South dated 7 December 1941 regarding mass executions, in *ibid*. p. 237.

178. 'Memorandum on Use of Troops against Partisans' dated 15 December 1941, in Cooper, *The Phantom War*, p. 181; on German strategy see also Bernd Bonwetsch, 'Die Partisanenbekämpfung und ihre Opfer im Rußlandfeldzug 1941–1944', in Meyer and Wippermann (eds), *Gegen das Vergessen* pp. 102ff.

179. Cooper, *The Phantom War* p. 81.

180. 257 Infantry Division directive dated 7 December 1941 regarding identification and interrogation of partisans, in Ernst Klee and Willi Dressen (eds), *'Gott mit uns'. Der deutsche Vernichtungskrieg im Osten 1939–1945* (Frankfurt am Main 1989) pp. 56–9.

181. The subject is not greatly illuminated by either Dieter Reifarth and Viktoria Schmidt-Linsendorf, 'Die Kamera der Täter' or Bernd Huppauf, 'Der entleerte Blick hinter der Kamera', in Heer and Nauman (eds), *Vernichtungskrieg*, pp. 475ff. and 504ff.

182. Cooper, *The Phantom War* pp. 83–4.

183. Report by Generalmajor Bruno Scultetus of the 281 Sicherungsdivision to the Commanding General of Sicherungstruppen and of Army Rear Area North dated 23 June 1942, Schumann and Nestler (eds), *Europa unterm Hakenkreuz* pp. 295–97; on the mass murder of Roma in the former Soviet Union see Wolfgang Wippermann, 'Nur eine Fußnote? Die Verfolgung der sowjetischen Roma. Historiographie, Motive, Verlauf', in Meyer and Wippermann (eds), *Gegen das Vergessen* pp. 75ff.

184. Cooper, *The Phantom War* pp. 56–7.

185. ZSL 204 AR-Z 296/60 Magill u.a. vols 1–7, pp. 1615ff.

186. ZSL 204 AR-Z 296/60 Magill u.a. vols 1–7, p. 62.

187. ZSL, Erich von dem Bach-Zelewski, 'Kriegstagebücher 1941–1945', pp. 6ff.

188. *Unsere Ehre heißt Treue. Kriegstagebuch des Kommandostabes Reichsführer-SS. Tätigkeitsbericht der 1. und 2. SS-Inf. Brigade, der 1. SS-Kav.-Brigade, und von Sonderkommandos der SS* (Vienna 1965) p. 108.

189. 'Tatigkeitsbericht' 1. SS-Inf. Brigade (mot.), 6.8.1941–10.8.1941, in *ibid.* pp. 111–15.

190. 'Bericht über den Verlauf der Pripjet-Aktion', 12 August 1941, in *ibid.* pp. 227–30; see also Ruth-Bettina Birn, 'Zweierlei Wirklichkeit. Fallbeispiele zur Partisanbekämpfung im Osten', in Wegner (ed.), *Zwei Wege* pp. 275ff.

191. ZSL 204 AR-Z 296/60 Magill u.a. vol. 4, Vernehmungsniederschrift Hans Saggau on 11 April 1963, pp. 1210ff.

8. RACIAL WAR AGAINST THE JEWS

1. Cited by Jost Dülffler, *Deutsche Geschichte 1933–1945* (Stuttgart 1992) p. 125.

2. On the biological framework see Michael Burleigh and Wolfgang Wippermann, *The Racial State. Germany 1933–1945* (Cambridge 1991); see also Steven Aschheim, 'On Saul Friedländer', *History & Memory* (1997) 9, p. 37.

3. See Keith Sword (ed.), *The Soviet Takeover of the Polish Eastern Provinces* (London 1991) and Jan Gross, *Revolution from Abroad* (Princeton 1988).

4. Dan Diner, 'On Guilt Discourse and Other Narratives', *History & Memory* (1997) 9, esp. pp. 317–18; for a rare critique of egregious

employment of analogies between the Holocaust and current barbarities arising from ethnic conflicts – the Jews were not waging war on the Nazis – see John Simpson, 'Serbs do not deserve to be branded modern-day Nazis', *Sunday Telegraph* 15 March 1998, p. 27.

5. On the first issue see Raul Hilberg, 'The Goldhagen Phenomenon', *Critical Inquiry* (1997) 23, p. 724.

6. For demographic data on the Jewish population in the Reich see Raul Hilberg, *Die Vernichtung der europäischen Juden* (2nd rev. edn Frankfurt am Main 1990) pp. 164–5; on the pauperisation of the Jews see Avraham Barkai, *From Boycott to Annihilation. The Economic Struggle of German Jews 1933–1945* (Bandeis 1989).

7. See Michael Burleigh, *Death and Deliverance. 'Euthanasia' in Germany 1900–1945* (Cambridge 1994) pp. 111ff.

8. See Steve Aschheim, *Brothers and Strangers* (University of Wisconsin Press 1982) for an excellent discussion of the relationship between German and eastern Jews.

9. The most enlightening discussion of antisemitism and anti-Slavism is Wolfgang Wippermann, 'Probleme und Aufgaben der Beziehungsgeschichte zwischen Deutschen, Polen und Juden', in Stefi Jersch-Wenzel (ed.), *Deutsche–Polen–Juden* (Berlin 1987) esp. pp. 20ff.

10. William Hagen, 'Before the "Final Solution". Towards a Comparative Analysis of Political Antisemitism in Interwar Germany and Poland', *JMH* (1996) 68, p. 375.

11. Ralf Georg Reuth (ed.), *Joseph Goebbels. Tagebücher* (Munich 1992) 3, entry dated 2 November 1939, p. 1340.

12. *Ibid.* entry dated 29 October 1939, p. 1339. These scenes were subsequently incorporated into the final scenes of *Der ewige Jude*.

13. Dieter Pohl, *Von der 'Judenpolitik' zum Judenmord. Der Distrikt Lublin des Generalgouvernements 1939–1944* (Frankfurt am Main 1993) p. 25.

14. Florian Freund *et al.*, 'Das Getto in Litzmannstadt', in Hanno Loewy and Gerhard Schoenberner (eds), *'Unser einziger Weg ist Arbeit'. Das Getto in Łódź 1940–1944* (Vienna 1990), p. 18.

15. Curiously enough, very few accounts of these crimes systematically address the matter of drunkenness, although reference to it is frequent in the sources. Diarists such as Zygmunt Klukowski, *Diary of the Years of Occupation 1939–44* (Urbana 1993) regularly comment on the fact that their occupiers were perpetually drunk. Although alcohol is a notorious disinhibitor, it is also a frequent excuse for delinquent or criminal behaviour.

16. United States Holocaust Memorial Museum (hereafter USHMM) RG-15015M Sipo und SD UWZ, Reel 3, Der Stadtkommissar Schwaningen to the Landrat des Landkreises Posen dated 28 March 1940.

17. Heydrich to Chiefs of all Einsatzgruppen, 21 September 1939, in Yitzhak Arad, Yisrael Gutman and Abraham Margaliot (eds), *Documents on the Holocaust* (Oxford 1987) pp. 173–8.
18. Isaiah Trunk, *Judenrat. The Jewish Councils in Eastern Europe under Nazi Occupation* (New York 1972) p. 23; both Jacob Robinson, *And the Crooked Shall Be Made Straight* (New York 1965) and Leonard Tushnet, *The Pavement of Hell* (London 1972) are also very useful correctives of simplistic and overly judgemental accounts of the enormous variety of Jewish Councils and their manifold responses to Nazi persecution. Other scholarly work on the Jewish Councils includes the published version of a Yivo Colloquium, *Imposed Jewish Governing Bodies under Nazi Rule* (New York 1972); Isaiah Trunk, *Jewish Responses to Nazi Persecution* (New York 1979) and Yisrael Gutman and Cynthia Haft (eds), *Patterns of Jewish Leadership in Nazi Europe 1933–1945* (Jerusalem 1979).
19. Avraham Tory, *The Kovno Ghetto Diary*, ed. with an introduction by Martin Gilbert, historical notes by Dina Porat, trans. by Jerzy Michalowicz (Cambridge, Mass. 1990) entry dated 6 January 1943, pp. 176–7.
20. *Ibid.* entry dated 12 February 1943, p. 209.
21. *Ibid.* entry dated 4 August 1941, p. 28.
22. *Im Warschauer Getto. Das Tagebuch des Adam Czerniakow 1939–1942* (Munich 1986) entry dated 17 May 1942, p. 149.
23. *Ibid.* entries dated 26–27 January 1940, pp. 36–7 for an example of exactions and reprisals; entry dated 11 June 1941, p. 160 for Czerniakow's meteorological comment.
24. Robert Koehl, *RKFDV. German Resettlement Policy* (Cambridge 1957) p. 48 has the merit of considering Stalin's strategies.
25. Reuth (ed.), *Joseph Goebbels. Tagebücher 3*, entry dated 17 November 1939, p. 1351.
26. On the problems of repatriating ethnic Germans see Koehl's still useful *RKFDV* and Christopher R. Browning, 'Nazi Resettlement Policy and the Search for a Solution to the Jewish Question 1939–1941', in his *Paths to Genocide* (Cambridge 1992) pp. 8ff. Both have been elaborated by Götz Aly's outstanding *'Endlösung'. Völkerverschiebung und der Mord an den europäischen Juden* (Frankfurt am Main 1995) esp. pp. 45–6, although this reflects a rather more literal-minded approach to these policies than is adopted here.
27. Hans Safrian, *Eichmann und seiner Gehilfen* (Frankfurt am Main 1995) pp. 68–9.
28. Koehl, *RKFDV* pp. 100–1.
29. Yisrael Gutman, *The Jews of Warsaw 1939–1943* (Bloomington 1982) pp. 18–26.
30. Völker Riess, *Die Anfänge der Vernichtung 'lebensunwerten Lebens' in*

den Reichsgauen Danzig-Westpreussen und Wartheland 1939/40
(Frankfurt am Main 1995) pp. 31–8, 55, 359 repeatedly cautions, on
the basis of a massive trawl of the evidence, against any causal linkage
between these killings and ethnic German resettlements of the sort which
Aly, *'Endlösung'* pp. 114–26 insists upon.

31. ZSL V 203 AR 1101/1962, interrogation of Kurt Eimann dated 20
December 1968, p. 12.
32. For Fort VII Posen see Riess, *Die Anfänge der Vernichtung* pp. 290ff.;
on Lange see Burleigh, *Death and Deliverance* p. 132, and Henry
Friedländer, *The Origins of Nazi Genocide* (Chapel Hill 1995)
pp. 137–40. On gassing vans see Christopher R. Browning, 'The Devel-
opment and Production of the Nazi Gas Van', in his *Fateful Months*
(New York 1985) p. 59.
33. Jonny Moser, 'Nisko. The First Experiment in Deportation', in M.
Marrus (ed.), *The Nazi Holocaust* (Westport 1989) 3, pp. 732–3. See
also Seev Goschen, 'Eichmann und die Nisko-Aktion im Oktober 1939',
VfZ (1981) 27, pp. 82ff., which stresses Eichmann's initiative, and
Miroslav Karny, 'Nisko in der Geschichte der Endlösung', *Judaica
Bohemiae* (1987) 23, pp. 69–84, which emphasises the role of Müller.
On Müller see Andreas Seeger, *'Gestapo-Müller'* (Berlin 1996) p. 117.
34. On this see Michael Zimmermann, *Rassenutopie und Genozid. Die
nationalsozialistische 'Lösung der Zigeunerfrage'* (Hamburg 1996)
p. 168.
35. Moser, 'Nisko' pp. 747–50.
36. *IMT*, 'Bericht über eine Inspektionsreise Seyss-Inquarts in Polen vom 17
bis 22 November 1939', p. 95 (2278-PS).
37. Philip Friedman, 'The Lublin Reservation and the Madagascar Plan', in
Marrus (ed.), *The Nazi Holocaust* 3, p. 709 is probably incorrect when
he writes: 'It is clear that from the very beginning the object was to
exterminate the Jewish refugees and all the talk about "colonization"
was merely a device to keep the Jews calm in order to create the
necessary mood for smooth transportation.'
38. Lammers to Himmler dated 28 March 1940 enclosing 'The Death March
of Lublin' dated 20 March 1940, IMT 'The Ministries Case' 13,
pp. 144–6.
39. Klukowski, *Diary of the Years of Occupation* p. 103.
40. For details on the Lublin district see Pohl, *Von der 'Judenpolitik'* esp.
pp. 79–85.
41. Hans-Peter Klausch, *Antifaschisten in SS-Uniform* (Bremen 1993)
pp. 48–51.
42. USHMM RG-15034M, 'Records of the Kommandeur der Sipo und SD
Lublin', Reel 6, Dirlewanger to a friend called Friedrich dated 20 March
1942.

43. See Peter Black, 'Rehearsal for "Reinhard"? Odilo Globocnik and the Lublin Selbstschutz', *CEH* (1992) 25, pp. 205ff.

44. USHMM RG-15015M, Reel 3, Sipo und SD UWZ Posen, 'Vereine deren Mitglieder für die Abschiebung unbedingt in Frage kommen' dated 16 November 1939.

45. USHMM RG-15015M, Reel 3, Der Chef der Sipo und des SD UWZ Posen Außenstelle Konin to the Chef der Sipo und des SD Posen dated 5 December 1940 and related correspondence.

46. Tory, *The Kovno Ghetto Diary* entry dated 1 April 1942, p. 75 for an order to collect metals.

47. Jewish Historical Commission, Warsaw (ed.), *Faschismus–Getto–Massenmord* (Frankfurt am Main 1960) p. 46; ZSL 'Die Beteiligung der Kreis- und Stadthauptleute an nationalsozialistischen Verbrechen' (Ludwigsburg n.d.) pp. 24–7.

48. Martin Gilbert, *Atlas of the Holocaust* (Oxford 1988) p. 51.

49. Antony Polonsky (ed.), *A Cup of Tears. A Diary of the Warsaw Ghetto* (Oxford 1988) p. 2.

50. Ulrich Herbert, 'Labour and Extermination. Economic Interest and the Primacy of Weltanschauung in National Socialism', *Past & Present* (1993) 138, pp. 158–62.

51. Wolfgang Scheffler, 'Das Getto Łódź in der nationalsozialistischen Judenpolitik', in Loewy and Schoenberner (eds), *'Unser einziger Weg ist Arbeit'* p. 13.

52. See Niels Gutschow, 'Stadtplanung im Warthegau 1939–1944', and Barbara Klain, 'Warschau 1939–1945: Vernichtung durch Planung', both in M. Rössler and S. Schleiermacher (eds), *Der 'Generalplan Ost'* (Berlin 1993) esp. p. 244 (Łódź) and p. 303 (Warsaw).

53. Aly, *'Endlösung'* p. 80.

54. See Lucjan Dobroszycki (ed.), *The Chronicle of the Łódź Ghetto 1941–1944* (New Haven 1984) pp. xxxvii–xxxix; Freund *et al.*, 'Das Getto in Litzmannstadt' p. 19.

55. Lecture by Waldemar Schön on the steps leading to the establishment of the Warsaw Ghetto dated 20 January 1941, in Arad *et al.* (eds), *Documents on the Holocaust* no. 101, pp. 222–6. The material on doctors and typhus can be found in Gutman, *The Jews of Warsaw* pp. 54–5, and Christopher R. Browning, 'Genocide and Public Health', in his *Paths to Genocide* esp. pp. 152–3. See also Charles Roland, *Courage under Siege. Starvation, Disease and Death in the Warsaw Ghetto* (Oxford 1992) esp. pp. 120ff.

56. Tomasz Szarota, *Warschau unter dem Hakenkreuz* (Paderborn 1985) p. 46.

57. See especially Götz Aly and Susanne Heim, *Vordenker der Vernichtung. Auschwitz und die deutschen Pläne für eine neue europäische Ordnung*

(Hamburg 1991) pp. 222ff. For problems in their approach see Christopher Browning, 'German Technocrats, Jewish Labor, and the Final Solution', in his *Paths to Genocide* pp. 59–76; Dan Diner, 'Rationalization and Method' and Ulrich Herbert, 'Racism and Rational Calculation', *Yad Vashem Studies* (1994) 24, respectively pp. 71–108 and 131–45, and Michael Burleigh, 'A Political Economy of the Final Solution?', *Patterns of Prejudice* (1996) 30, pp. 29–41.

58. See Magnus Brechtken, *'Madagaskar für die Juden'. Antisemitische Idee and politische Praxis 1885–1945* (Munich 1997).

59. Michael Marrus and Robert Paxton, *Vichy France and the Jews* (New York 1983) p. 61.

60. Leni Yahil, 'Madagascar. Phantom of a Solution for the Jewish Question', in Marrus (ed.), *The Nazi Holocaust* 3, pp. 685–6.

61. Helmut Krausnick, 'Denkschrift Himmlers über die Behandlung der Fremdvölkischen im Osten', *VfZ* (1957) 2, pp. 194–8.

62. Christopher R. Browning, *The Final Solution and the German Foreign Office* (New York 1978) pp. 35ff.

63. Friedman, 'The Lublin Reservation' p. 725; on Burgdörfer see Götz Aly and Karl Heinz Roth, *Die restlose Erfassung* (Berlin 1984) pp. 86ff.

64. Claudia Steur, *Theodor Dannecker. Ein Funktionär der 'Endlösung'* (Essen 1997) pp. 36–8.

65. *Im Warschauer Getto. Das Tagebuch des Adam Czerniakow* p. 88.

66. Philippe Burrin, *Hitler and the Jews. The Genesis of the Holocaust* (London 1994) p. 80.

67. Friedman, 'The Lublin Reservation' p. 723.

68. Brechtken, *'Madagaskar für die Juden'* pp. 280–3.

69. Yisrael Gutman, 'The Distinctiveness of the Łódź Ghetto', in Michael Unger (ed.), *The Ast Ghetto. Life in the Łódź Ghetto 1940–1944* (Jerusalem 1991) p. 25.

70. Bendet Herschkovitsch, 'Ghetto in Litzmannstadt', in Marrus (ed.), *The Nazi Holocaust* 3, pp. 364ff.

71. Gutman, 'The Concept of Labour' p. 532.

72. Dan Diner, 'Historical Understanding and Counterrationality. The Judenrat as Epistemological Vantage Point', in Saul Friedländer (ed.), *Probing the Limits of Representation* (Cambridge, Mass. 1992) pp. 136ff.

73. Trunk, *Judenrat* p. 401.

74. Alan Adelson (ed.), *The Diary of Dawid Sierakowski* (London 1996) entry dated 29 July 1941, p. 117.

75. Dobroszycki (ed.), *The Chronicle of the Łódź Ghetto* entry dated 28 June 1928, p. 215.

76. Reuth (ed.), *Joseph Goebbels. Tagebücher* 4, entry dated 5 November 1940, p. 1494.

77. Aly, *'Endlösung'* p. 229.

78. *Ibid.* pp. 84, 273–4.

79. Burrin's account of these plans, *Hitler and the Jews* p. 99, is misleading. Wetzel's 1942 critique refers to a version of a missing RSHA Main Office III B plan drawn up after November 1941 and not to Konrad Meyer's July 1941 second version of the 'Generalplan East'. Although the RSHA plan envisaged deporting five to six million Soviet Jews beyond the Urals, Wetzel's commentary contradicts this when he remarks that 'one cannot liquidate [the Poles] like the Jews'. On this see Czesław Madajzyk, 'Vom "Generalplan Ost" zum "Generalsiedlungsplan' and Karl Heinz Roth, ' "Generalplan Ost" – "Gesamtplan Ost" ' both in M. Rössler and S. Schleiermacher (eds), *Der 'Generalplan Ost'. Hauptlinien der national sozialistischen Planungs- und Vernichtungspolitik* (Berlin 1993) pp. 12–17, 26–9 and 38–42.

80. The speech is reprinted in Miroslav Karny (ed.), *Protektoratni politika Reinharda Heydricha* (Prague 1991) pp. 212–24.

81. Friedman, 'The Lublin Reservation' p. 725.

82. Helmut Krausnick, *Hitlers Einsatzgruppen* (Frankfurt am Main 1985) p. 121.

83. ZSL VI 415 AR 1310/63 E32, Anklageschrift gegen Bruno Streckenbach dated 30 June 1973, pp. 9449ff.

84. Benno Müller-Hill, 'The Idea of the Final Solution and the Role of Experts', in D. Cesarani (ed.), *The Final Solution* (London 1994) pp. 62ff. gives the titles of these doctorates.

85. For this important insight see Ulrich Herbert, 'Vernichtungspolitik', in Herbert (ed.), *Nationalsozialistische Vernichtungspolitik 1939–1945* (Frankfurt am Main 1998) pp. 41–4.

86. ZSL II 213 AR 1898/66 ZIII, testimony of Friedrich Niendorf, p. 411.

87. ZSL 213 AR 1898/66, Urteil gegen Kurt Christmann dated 19 December 1980, pp. 18–19.

88. See ZSL VI 415 AR 1310/63 E32, Anklageschrift gegen Bruno Streckenbach dated 30 June 1973, pp. 9504–5.

89. ZSL 213 AR 1898/66 ZIII (Me-Rab), p. 467; ZSL VI 415 AR 1310/63 E32, Anklageschrift gegen Bruno Streckenbach, pp. 9383–9.

90. See Ronald Headland, *Messages of Murder. A Study of the Reports of the Einsatzgruppen of the Security Police and the Security Service 1941–1943* (London 1992) pp. 37ff.

91. For examples see USHMM RG-18002M, Latvian Central State Historical Archive Riga, Reel 18, map marked EK 3/A, no date.

92. Yehoshua Buchler, 'Kommandostab Reichsführer-SS. Himmler's Personal Murder Brigades in 1941', *Holocaust and Genocide Studies* (1986) 1, p. 13.

93. Helmut Krausnick, *Die Truppe des Weltanschauungskrieges* (Stuttgart 1981) and his 'Hitler und die Befehle an die Einsatzgruppen', in

Eberhard Jäckel and Jurgen Rohwer (eds), *Der Mord an den Juden im Zweiten Weltkrieg* (Frankfurt am Main 1987) pp. 89–106.

94. For this see Alfred Streim, 'Zur Eröffnung des allgemeinen Judenvernichtungsbefehls gegenüber den Einsatzgruppen', in Jäckel and Rohwer (eds), *Der Mord an den Juden* pp. 107–19.

95. For this see Ralf Ogorreck, *Die Einsatzgruppen und die 'Genesis der Endlösung'* (Berlin 1996) pp. 107–9.

96. Martin Broszat, Hans-Adolf Jacobsen and Helmut Krausnick, *Anatomie des SS-Staates* (Munich 1979) 2, p. 300 for the text.

97. See especially C. Dieckmann, 'Der Krieg und die Ermordung der litauischen Juden', in Herbert (ed.), *Nationalsozialistische Vernichtungspolitik* pp. 301ff.

98. H. Friedlander and S. Milton (eds), *Archives of the Holocaust* (New York 1993) 22, doc. 90, p. 193, EK 3 copy of Chief of Security Police and SD to Einsatzgruppen dated 10 October 1941.

99. Although agreeing with Alfred Streim's 'The Tasks of the SS Einsatzgruppen', *Simon Wiesenthal Center Annual* (1987) 4, pp. 308ff. regarding the later extension of their orders, the interpretation of this document is perhaps too literal-minded.

100. For this estimate of the Jews vulnerable to direct assault see Yitzhak Arad, 'The Holocaust of Soviet Jewry', *Yad Vashem Studies* (1991) 21, p. 9.

101. Ronald Headland, 'The Einsatzgruppen. The Question of their Initial Operations', *Holocaust and Genocide Studies* (1989) 4, p. 404 is compelling on this point even though his argument that the Einsatzgruppen received orders to kill all Soviet Jews prior to 22 June is not necessarily confirmed by it.

102. Christian Streit, 'Wehrmacht, Soviet POWs, Einsatzgruppen and Anti-Bolshevism in the Emergence of the Final Solution', in Cesarani (ed.), *The Final Solution* pp. 106–7.

103. For these points, see for example ZSL 213 AR 1898/66, Anklageschrift in der Strafsache Kurt Trimborn, pp. 53–4.

104. ZSL II 213 AR 1898/66, 'Ermittlungsverfahren gegen Erich Bock und 3 andere Angehörige des Leitenden Dienstes', p. 986, testimony of Albert Hartl.

105. Michael Balfour and Julian Frisby, *Helmuth von Moltke* (London 1972) p. 175.

106. Statement by SS-Rottenführer Friedrich Hesellbach (December 1942), in Joseph Wulf (ed.), *'Sonderbehandlung' und verwandte Worte in nationalsozialistischen Dokumenten* (Gütersloh 1963) p. 36.

107. ZSL Az 22 Js 202/61 (II 213 AR 1898/66) vol. 6, p. 1350ff., interrogation of Lothar Heimbach dated 9 May 1962.

108. Streit, 'Wehrmacht, Soviet POWs, Einsatzgruppen' p. 110.

109. For an exceptionally intelligent discussion of these issues see Bernd Rusinek, 'Die Kritiker-Falle. Wie man in Verdacht geraten kann', in J. Heil and R. Erb (eds), *Geschichtswissenschaft und Öffentlichkeit* (Frankfurt am Main 1998) pp. 109–30.

110. On pre-war Lithuania see Dov Levin, 'On the Relations between the Baltic Peoples and their Jewish Neighbors before, during and after World War Two', in Yehuda Bauer (ed.), *Remembering for the Future* (Oxford 1989) 1, pp. 171–9, and *idem*, 'Lithuania', in David Wyman (ed.), *The World Reacts to the Holocaust* (Baltimore 1996) pp. 325–35.

111. Ernst Klee, Willi Dressen and Völker Riess (eds), *'Schöne Zeiten'* (Frankfurt am Main 1988) pp. 35–8.

112. See the Stahlecker Report in *IMT* 37, pp. 670–717 and above all Hans-Heinrich Wilhelm, *Die Einsatzgruppe A der Sicherheitspolizei und des SD 1941/42* (Frankfurt am Main 1996) esp. pp. 56ff.

113. Report from Einsatzgruppe A dated 15 October 1941, reprinted in Arad *et al.* (eds) *Documents on the Holocaust* no. 177, pp. 389–93.

114. Peter Lawrence, 'Why Lithuania?', in John Milfull (ed.), *Why Germany? National Socialist Antisemitism and the European Context* (Oxford 1993) pp. 216–17.

115. Dina Porat, 'The Holocaust in Lithuania', in Cesarani (ed.), *The Final Solution* pp. 160 and 163.

116. On what follows see Andrew Ezergailis, *The Holocaust in Latvia* (Riga 1996) pp. 39ff.

117. Andrew Ezergailis, 'Latvia', in Wyman (ed.), *The World Reacts to the Holocaust* pp. 354–68.

118. On Arajs see Martin Knop, 'Viktor Arajs. Kollaboration beim Massenmord', in Barbara Danckwortt, Thorsten Querg and Claudia Schöningh (eds), *Historische Rassismusforschung* (Hamburg 1995) pp. 231–45.

119. Thomas Sandkühler, *'Endlösung' in Galizien* (Bonn 1996) p. 57.

120. See Philip Friedman, 'Ukrainian–Jewish Relations during the Nazi Occupation', in Marrus (ed.), *The Nazi Holocaust* 6, pp. 371ff.

121. Orest Subtelny, *Ukraine. A History* (Toronto 1994) p. 461.

122. Headland, *Messages of Murder* p. 114.

123. Elke Fröhlich (ed.), *Die Tagebücher von Joseph Goebbels. Sämtliche Fragmente* (Munich 1987) 1/4 January 1940–July 1941, pp. 736–9.

124. Klee *et al.* (eds), *'Schöne Zeiten'* pp. 88–91.

125. Ogorreck, *Die Einsatzgruppen* pp. 142–7.

126. M. Koval, 'The Nazi Genocide of the Jews and the Ukrainian Population', and Shimon Redlich, 'Metropolitan Andrii Sheptyts'kyi and the Complexities of Ukrainian–Jewish Relations', both in Zvi Gitelman (ed.), *Bitter Legacy. Confronting the Holocaust in the USSR* (Bloomington 1997) pp. 51ff. and 61–76.

127. Hilberg, *Die Vernichtung der europäischen Juden* 2, p. 358.

128. Report by an armaments inspector in the Ukraine to the Chief of the Wehrwirtschafts- und Rüstungsamtes im OKW, *IMT* 32, pp. 71ff. On Seraphim see Michael Burleigh, *Germany Turns Eastwards. A Study of 'Ostforschung' in the Third Reich* (Cambridge 1988) pp. 143–5 and 220–2; see also Gerhard Volkmer, 'Die Deutsche Forschung zu Osteuropa', in H.-J. Torke (ed.), *Forschungen zur Osteuropäischen Geschichte* (Berlin 1989) 42, pp. 148ff.

129. See Richard J. Crampton, *Eastern Europe in the Twentieth Century* (London 1994) pp. 101–26; Eugen Weber, 'The Men of the Archangel', *JCH* (1966) 1, pp. 101–26; *idem*, 'Rumania', in H. Røgger and E. Weber (eds), *The European Right* (Berkeley 1966); Zev Barbu, 'Rumania', in S. J. Woolf (ed.), *Fascism in Europe* (London 1981) pp. 151ff. See also Paul Shapiro's excellent 'Prelude to Dictatorship in Romania: The National Christian Party in Power', *Canadian–American Slave Studies* (1974) 8, pp. 45–88.

130. I. C. Butnaru, *The Silent Holocaust. Romania and its Jews* (New York 1992) pp. 65–8.

131. Radu Ioanid, *The Sword of the Archangel. Fascist Ideology in Romania* (New York 1990) p. 214.

132. On German–Romanian relations see Julius S. Fischer, *Transnistria. The Forgotten Cemetery* (South Brunswick 1969) pp. 28–9; Andreas Hillgruber, *Hitler, König Carol und Marschall Antonescu* (Wiesbaden 1954).

133. Radu Ioanid, 'The Antonescu Era', in R. Braham (ed.), *The Tragedy of Romanian Jewry* (New York 1994) p. 123.

134. On the coup cum pogrom see Radu Ioanid, 'The Pogrom of Bucharest 21–23 January 1941', *Holocaust and Genocide Studies* (1991) 6, p. 377.

135. Butnaru, *The Silent Holocaust* pp. 81–8.

136. Herbert, 'Labour and Extermination' p. 162 suggests this connection.

137. See Raul Hilberg (ed.), *Documents of Destruction. Germany and Jewry 1933–1945* (Chicago 1971) pp. 87–8.

138. On this see Christopher Browning, 'Nazi Ghettoization Policy in Poland 1939–1941', in his *Paths to Genocide* pp. 28ff.

139. *IMT* 38, pp. 86–94, dated 16 July 1941.

140. Christopher Browning, 'Beyond "Intentionalism" and "Functionalism"', in his *Paths to Genocide* p. 121: 'In July 1941, with the stupendous early victories of the Russian campaign, he accelerated the Einsatzgruppen campaign and solicited the Final Solution . . . It would appear that the euphoria of victory emboldened and tempted an elated Hitler to dare ever more drastic policies.'

141. *Ibid.* pp. 104–5.

142. Burrin, *Hitler and the Jews* suggests this scenario.

143. Reuth (ed.), *Joseph Goebbels. Tagebücher* 4, entry dated 19 August 1941, p. 1658.

144. For Himmler's schedule see Richard Breitman, *The Architect of Genocide. Himmler and the Final Solution* (London, New York 1992) pp. 184–92.

145. Sandkühler, *'Endlösung' in Galizien* p. 128 is the most recent statement of this view.

146. Buchler, 'Kommandostab Reichsführer-SS' pp. 14ff.

147. Browning, 'Beyond "Intentionalism" and "Functionalism"' pp. 105–6; on the Order Police see Richard Breitman, *Official Secrets. What the Nazis Planned, What the British and Americans Knew* (New York 1998) pp. 27ff.

148. Headland, 'The Einsatzgruppen' p. 406.

149. Breitman, *The Architect of Genocide* p. 174.

150. ZSL 22 Js 202/61 (II 213 AR 1898/66), interrogation of Otto Ernst Prast dated 24 April 1962, pp. 1263ff.

151. Sandkühler, *'Endlösung' in Galizien* pp. 150–2.

152. Richard Breitman, 'Himmler and the Terrible Secret', *JCH* (1991) 26, pp. 431–51, Streit, 'Wehrmacht, Soviet POWs, Einsatzgruppen' p. 116 n. 27; and Konrad Kwiet, 'From the Diary of a Killing Unit', in Milfull (ed.) *Why Germany?* p. 88.

153. ZSL 'Euthanasie', Scha-Schq, interrogation of Hans Scheidt dated 6 April 1960, p. 2. On gassing technology see M. Beer. 'Die Entwicklung der Gaswagen beim Mord an den Juden', *VfZ* (1987) 35, pp. 407–9, and C. Gerlach, 'Failure of Plans for an SS Extermination Camp in Mogilev', *Holocaust and Genocide Studies* (1997) 7, pp. 64–5.

154. See John Gordon and Carrol Garrard, *The Bones of Berdichev: the Life and Fate of Vassily Grossman* (New York 1996) p. 18 for the diagram used by Einsatzgruppe C.

155. See the very subtle analysis by Rusinek, 'Die Kritiker-Falle. Wie man in Verdacht geraten kann' esp. pp. 119–24.

156. Christopher Browning, *Ordinary Men. Reserve Police Battalion 101 and the Final Solution in Poland* (New York 1992) p. 2.

157. Breitman, *Official Secrets* p. 51.

158. Browning, *Ordinary Men* p. 60.

159. See especially Christopher Browning, 'Die Debatte über die Täter des Holocaust', in Herbert (ed.), *Nationalsozialistische Vernichtungspolitik* pp. 158–9.

160. See the important unpublished paper by Omer Bartov, 'Reception and Perception: Goldhagen's Holocaust and the World'.

161. Aussage des Offiziersanwärters Liebe dated 14 June 1965, Js 4/65 GStA Frankfurt am Main vol. 7, pp. 1272ff., cited by Klee *et al.* (eds), *'Schöne Zeiten'* pp. 132ff.

162. Meldung Dr Reuss dated 20 August 1941, ZSL Verschiedene, Ord. 301 AAu vol. 121, pp. 490ff.; Meldung Kormann dated 21 August 1941, pp. 495ff., cited by Klee *et al.* (eds), *'Schöne Zeiten'* pp. 135–7.

163. On Groscurth see Raul Hilberg, *Perpetrators, Victims, Bystanders. The Jewish Catastrophe 1933–1945* (London 1995) pp. 58ff. See also Doris Bergen, 'Between God and Hitler. German Military Chaplains and the Crimes of the Third Reich', in Omer Bartov and Phyllis Mack (eds), *In God's Name. Genocide and Religion* (forthcoming).

164. Report dated 21 August 1941, pp. 485ff., cited by Klee *et al.* (eds), *'Schöne Zeiten'* pp. 138–42.

165. Stellungnahme Reichenau dated 26 August 1941, pp. 485ff., 493, cited by Klee *et al.* (eds), *Schöne Zeiten* p. 144.

166. Aussage Hafner dated 31 May 1965, pp. 15ff. der Vernehmung (Js 4/65 GStA Frankfurt am Main, LO-Beschuldigten-Vernehmungen), cited by Klee *et al.* (eds), *Schöne Zeiten* p. 143.

167. Tzvetan Todorov, *Facing the Extremes. Moral Life in the Concentraton Camps* (New York 1997) p. 136.

168. See Richard Breitman, 'Himmler's Police Auxiliaries in the Occupied Soviet Territories', *Simon Wiesenthal Center Annual* (1990) 7, pp. 23ff.; Martin Dean, 'The German Gendarmerie, the Ukrainian Schutzmannschaft and the "Second Wave" of Jewish Killing in Occupied Ukraine', *German History* (1996) 14, pp. 168ff.

169. Jean Ancel, 'The Romanian Way of Solving the Jewish Problem', *Yad Vashem Studies* (1988) 19, p. 190.

170. Curzio Malaparte, *Kaputt* (London 1989) p. 138.

171. *Ibid.* pp. 170ff.

172. On the siege of Odessa see Mark Axworthy, 'Peasant Scapegoat to Industrial Slaughter. The Romanian Soldier at Odessa', in Paul Addison and Angus Calder (eds), *Time to Kill* (London 1997) pp. 221–32.

173. On Romanian operations at Odessa see Mark Axworthy, *Third Axis, Fourth Ally* (London 1995) pp. 49ff.

174. ZSL II 213 AR 1898/66 DI, Ereignismeldungen UdSSR EG D, p. 8220 (hereafter ZSL EG D).

175. *Ibid.* p. 8226.

176. ZSL 213 AR 1900/66, Anklageschrift gegen Paul Zapp dated 25 February 1969.

177. ZSL EG D p. 8248.

178. ZSL EG D p. 8242.

179. ZSL EG D p. 8256.

180. Breitman, *Architect of Genocide* pp. 176–7.

181. Jean Ancel (ed.), *Documents Concerning the Fate of Romanian Jewry during the Holocaust* 1–12, (New York, 1986) 3, pp. 340–1.

182. Fischer, *Transnistria* pp. 72–4.

183. USHMM RG-25.003M, Romanian Ministry of National Defence, Armata A-IV-A, Reel 012, frame 687, Vrancea catre pentru Domnul General Mazarini Nicolae dated 23 October 1941. For background

information on Odessa see Alexander Dallin, *Odessa 1941–1944* US Air Force Project Rand Research Memorandum (Santa Monica 1957).

184. USHMM RG-25.003M, Armata A-IV-A, Reel 012, frame 662, catre Presedentia Consiliuluide Ministri Cabinetal Militar dated 22 October 1941.

185. Ilya Ehrenburg and Vasily Grossman (eds), *The Black Book* (New York 1981) p. 80.

186. USHMM RG-25.003M, Armata A-IV-A, Reel 012, frame 702, telegram no. 563 dated 24 October 1941.

187. Hilberg, *Die Vernichtung der europäischen Juden 2* pp. 320–1; Ioanid, *The Sword of the Archangel*; see also Dora Litani, 'The Destruction of the Jews of Odessa in the Light of Rumanian Documents', in Marrus (ed.), *The Nazi Holocaust 4*, pp. 484ff.

188. On Transnistria see Dalia Ofer, 'The Holocaust in Transnistria', in Lucjan Dobroszycki and Jeffrey S. Gurock (eds) *The Holocaust in the Soviet Union* (New York 1993) pp. 133ff.

189. ZSL II 213 AR 1901/66, Anklageschrift gegen Johannes Schlupper and others dated 19 August 1971, p. 5.

190. USHMM RG-11001 MOI (Osobiy Archive, Moscow) RSHA 'Meldungen aus dem besetzten Ostgebieten' No. 4 dated 11 May 1942, pp. 5–15.

191. ZSL EG D p. 8279.

192. ZSL EG D p. 8286.

193. ZSL 213 AR 1898/66, verdict on Dr Kurt Christmann dated 19 December 1980, p. 13, and ZSL II 213 AR-Z 1898/66, investigation of Erich Bock and others dated 1 September 1961, p. 95.

194. *Ibid.*

195. ZSL II 213 AR 1898/66 Zii (H-Ma), testimony of Alfred Illmer, pp. 300–1.

196. ZSL 213 AR 1896/66, interviews of Russian witnesses, Anna Gutkina dated 7 October 1964, pp. 52ff.

197. ZSL 213 AR 1898/66, Vernehmungsprotokolle russischer Zeugen, testimony of Ivan Kotov, pp. 55ff.

198. Arad, 'The Holocaust of Soviet Jewry' p. 47.

199. Göring to Heydrich dated 31 July 1941, Arad *et al.* (eds), *Documents of the Holocaust* no. 106, p. 233.

200. For example, Browning, 'Beyond "Intentionalism" and "Functionalism"' p. 114.

201. This position is taken by Burrin, *Hitler and the Jews* pp. 115–17; Hans Safrian, *Eichmann und seine Gehilfen* pp. 105–12; Götz Aly, 'Endlösung' pp. 270ff.

202. Reuth (ed.) *Joseph Goebbels, Tagebücher* entry dated 20 August 1941, p. 1661.

203. For this see Wolfgang Benz, *The Holocaust* (New York 1999) pp. 93–6.

204. Herbert, 'Labour and Extermination' esp. pp. 172–4.
205. Sandkühler, *'Endlösung' in Galizien* pp. 132–42.
206. On this see Gerlach, 'Failure of Plans for an SS Extermination Camp in Mogilev' pp. 62ff.
207. Pohl, *Von der 'Judenpolitik'* pp. 93–5.
208. ZSL 203 AR-Z 161/67 Dokumente B p. 0115, Uebelhör to Himmler dated 4 October 1941 and Himmler to Uebelhör dated 10 October 1941, p. 0146.
209. See Browning, *The Final Solution and the German Foreign Office* pp. 56–67.
210. Ian Kershaw, 'Improvised Genocide? The Emergence of the "Final Solution" in the Warthegau,' *Transactions of the Royal Historical Society*, 6th Series (1992) 2, pp. 65–6.
211. For this see Dobroszycki (ed.) *The Chronicle of the Łódź Ghetto* entry dated 20 December 1941, pp. 96–7.
212. *Ibid.* entry dated 10–13 January 1942, p. 120.
213. *Ibid.* entries dated February 1942, p. 131; March 1942, p. 136.
214. *Im Warschauer Getto. Das Tagebuch des Adam Czerniakow* entry dated 20 July 1942, pp. 282–3; Gutman, *The Jews of Warsaw* pp. 201ff.
215. For examples see Robinson, *And the Crooked Shall Be Made Straight* pp. 185–6; Tory, *The Kovno Ghetto Diary* entry dated 28 October 1941, p. 46.
216. Tory, *The Kovno Ghetto Diary* entry dated 19 April 1943, p. 300.
217. Arad *et al.* (eds), *Documents on the Holocaust* no. 129, pp. 283–4.
218. ZSL 203 AR-Z 69/59 Sonderband A testimony of Michal Podchlebnik, pp. 40ff.
219. Eugen Kogon, Hermann Langbein and Adalbert Ruckerl, *Nazi Mass Murder. A Documentary History of the Use of Poison Gas* (New Haven 1993) pp. 73ff.
220. ZSL 203 AR-Z 69/59 Sonderband A, testimony of Michal Podchlebnik, p. 48.
221. ZSL 203 AR-Z 69/59 Sonderband A, testimony of Helena Krol, pp. 321ff.
222. ZSL 203 AR-Z 69/59 Sonderheft, Anklageschrift gegen Gustav Laabs u.a. StA Bonn 8Ks 3/62, p. 129.
223. Fritz Bauer (ed.) *Justiz und NS-Verbrechen. Sammlung Deutscher Straf-urteile wegen NS-Tötungsverbrechen* (Amsterdam 1979) 21, p. 248.
224. Dobroszycki (ed.), *The Chronicle of the Łódź Ghetto* entry dated 10–14 April 1942, p. 145.
225. Helmut Heiber, 'Aus den Akten des Gauleiters Kube', *VfZ* (1956) 4, pp. 86ff. for a litany of SS complaints about Kube.
226. Ezergailis, *The Holocaust in Latvia* pp. 200ff.
227. Sandkühler, *'Endlösung' in Galizien* pp. 159–60.

228. Pohl, *Von der 'Judenpolitik'* pp. 145–6.

229. On Belzec see Michael Tregenza, 'Belzec Death Camp', in Marrus (ed.), *The Nazi Holocaust* 6, pp. 1085ff.

230. See Walter Grode, *Die 'Sonderbehandlung 14f13' in den Konzentrationslagern des Dritten Reiches* (Frankfurt am Main 1987).

231. Gitta Sereny, *Into That Darkness* (London 1974) pp. 102ff.

232. P. Black, 'Odilo Globocnik. Himmlers Vorposten im Osten', in R. Smelser, E. Syring and R. Zitelmann (eds), *Die braune Elite II* (Darmstadt 1993) pp. 111–13.

233. Pohl, *Von der 'Judenpolitik'* p. 114 on drunkenness. Sandkühler, *'Endlösung' in Galizien* pp. 170–3 for a composite description of a ghetto clearance.

234. ZSL 302 AR-Z 161/67, Urteil vom 30 Januar 1985 gegen Helmut Krizon (7Ks 45Js 12/69) p. 93 (defenestration); p. 305 testimony of Simon Feinsilber 3 July 1972 (shooting of woman); ZSL 203 AR-Z 1469/61, Beiheft StA Hannover 2 Js 1023/62, Schwurgerichtsanklage gegen Günther Fuchs und Otto Bradfisch dated 22 October 1962, p. 95 (attempt to converse in German).

235. ZSL 203 AR-Z 161/67, Urteil vom 30 Januar 1985 gegen Helmut Krizon (7Ks 45Js 12/69) p. 272.

236. USHMM RG-11.001M, Osobyi Archive Moscow, Reel 82, frames 61ff., Josef Jacklein report on 'Judenaussiedlung von Kolomea nach Belzec' dated 14 September 1942 and other correspondence relating to this transport.

237. Saul Friedländer, *Counterfeit Nazi. The Ambiguity of Good* (London 1969) pp. 104ff.

238. Yitshak Arad, *Belzec, Sobibor, Treblinka. The Operation Reinhard Death Camps* (Bloomington 1987) pp. 188–9.

239. Benz, *The Holocaust* p. 146.

240. Sereny, *Into That Darkness* p. 166.

241. For the older view see Christopher Browning, 'Beyond "Intentionalism" and "Functionalism"' p. 115. For a detailed study of the misdating of this encounter see Karin Orth, 'Rudolf Hoess und die "Endlösung der Judenfrage"', *Werkstatt Geschichte* (1997) 18, pp. 45–57.

242. Martin Broszat (ed.), *Kommandant in Auschwitz* (Munich 1987) p. 139.

243. On Auschwitz see Raul Hilberg, 'Auschwitz and the Final Solution', in Yisrael Gutman and Michael Berenbaum (eds), *Anatomy of the Auschwitz Death Camp* (Bloomington 1994) pp. 81ff.

244. Reuth (ed.), *Joseph Goebbels. Tagebücher* 4, entry dated 27 March 1942, pp. 1776–7.

245. For the above see Ulrich Herbert, 'Deutsche Militärverwaltung in Paris und die Deportation', in Herbert (ed.), *Nationalsozialistische Vernichtungspolitik* pp. 182–93.

246. Burrin, *Hitler and the Jews* pp. 124–5.

247. Steuer, *Theodor Dannecker* pp. 59–68; Marrus and Paxton, *Vichy France and the Jews* pp. 226–7.

248. Christian Gerlach, 'Die Wannsee-Konferenz, das Schicksal der deutschen Juden und Hitlers politische Grundsatzentscheidung, alle Juden Europas zu ermorden', *Werkstatt Geschichte* (1997) 18, pp. 12ff. is fundamental.

249. Johannes Tuchel, *Am Grossen Wannsee 56/58* (Berlin 1992) pp. 103ff.

250. Gerlach, 'Die Wannsee-Konferenz' esp. pp. 25–31.

251. For an excellent analysis of the Wannsee Conference see Wolfgang Scheffler, 'Die Wannsee-Konferenz und ihre historische Bedeutung', in Gedenkstätte Haus der Wannsee-Konferenz (ed.), *Erinnern für die Zukunft* (Berlin 1993) pp. 17–34.

252. Francisek Piper, 'The Number of Victims', in Gutman and Berenbaum (eds), *Anatomy of the Auschwitz Death Camp* pp. 61ff.

253. Steur, *Theodor Dannecker* p. 76.

254. Marrus and Paxton, *Vichy France and the Jews* pp. 217ff. for the above.

255. Steven Bowman, 'Greek Jews and Christians during World War II', in *Remembering for the Future* 1, pp. 215–21.

256. Ya'acov (Jack) Handeli, *A Greek Jew from Salonika Remembers* (New York 1993) p. 33.

257. See Mark Mazower, 'Homage to Salonika', *Jewish Quarterly* (1997) 166, pp. 36–40.

258. Hilberg, *Die Vernichtung der europäischen Juden* 2, pp. 738–9.

259. Safrian, *Eichmann und seine Gehilfen* pp. 225ff.; Helena Kubica, 'Children', in Gutman and Berenbaum (eds), *Anatomy of the Auschwitz Death Camp* p. 416 on the fate of Greek Jews in Auchwitz. For details on Koretz see Joseph Ben, 'Jewish Leadership in Greece during the Holocaust', in Gutman and Haft (eds), *Patterns of Jewish Leadership* pp. 335ff.

260. Browning, *Ordinary Men* p. 125.

261. Pohl, *Von der 'Judenpolitik'* p. 167.

262. USHMM RG-11001M.05, Osobyi Archive Moscow, Der Generalkommissar für Weissruthenien to the Reichskommissar Ostland and HSSPF Riga dated 8 September 1942.

263. Bundesarchiv-NS 19/2566, Himmler, 'Meldungen an den Führer über Bandenbekämpfung' no. 51 dated 29 December 1942. I am grateful to Martin Dean for a copy of this document.

264. See the excellent discussion of 'Erntefest' in Browning, *Ordinary Men* pp. 133–42.

265. Butnaru, *The Silent Holocaust* pp. 128–9.

266. Dalia Ofer, 'The Holocaust in Transnistria' pp. 133ff.

267. Fischer, *Transnistria* p. 95.

268. USHMM RG-1996.A 580, International Committee of the Red Cross, Reel 9, G44/Sec-186, Charles Kolb, 'Rapport sur le voyage en Transnistrie' dated 14 January 1944, p. 3.
269. Bela Vargo, 'The Ambiguity of Collaborationism. The Center of the Jews in Romania', in Gutman and Haft (eds), *Patterns of Jewish Leadership* pp. 291–3.
270. Ioanid, *The Sword of the Archangel* pp. 231–2.
271. Doc-1919-PS *IMT* 29, pp. 110–73; among many analyses of this speech see Yehuda Bauer, *Jews for Sale? Nazi–Jewish Negotiations 1933–1945* (New Haven 1994) pp. 115ff., and Breitman, *The Architect of Genocide* pp. 242–3.
272. Tory, *The Kovno Ghetto Diary* entry dated 12 February 1943, pp. 209–10.

9. RESISTANCE IN GERMANY, 1933–1945

1. Detlev Peukert, 'Working Class Resistance' in David Clay Large (ed.), *Contending with Hitler* (Cambridge 1991) pp. 42ff.
2. Hanno Dreschler, *Die Sozialistische Arbeiterpartei Deutschlands* (Meisenheim 1965); Werner Link, *Die Geschichte des Internationalen Jugendbundes und des Internationalen Sozialistischen Kampfbundes* (Marburg 1961).
3. K. McDermott and J. Agnew, *The Comintern* (Basingstoke 1996) p. 112.
4. Detlev Peukert, 'Volksfront und Volksbewegungskonzept im kommunistischen Widerstand', in J. Schmädeke and P. Steinbach (eds), *Der Widerstand gegen den Nationalsozialismus* (Munich 1994) pp. 878–9.
5. W. Wippermann, *Das Leben in Frankfurt zur NS-Zeit* 4: *Der Widerstand* (Frankfurt am Main 1986) p. 36.
6. For a critical view of totalitarian heroism see Tzvetan Todorov, *Facing the Extremes. Moral Life in the Concentration Camps* (New York 1996) pp. 187ff.
7. Hermann Weber, 'Die KPD in der Illegalität', in R. Löwenthal and P. von zur Mühlen (eds), *Widerstand und Verweigerung in Deutschland* (Bonn 1984) p. 95; *idem, 'Weisse Flecken' in der Geschichte. Die KPD-Opfer der Stalinischen Säuberungen und ihre Rehabilitierung* (Frankfurt am Main 1989) pp. 19–24; McDermott and Agnew, *The Comintern* pp. 146–7.
8. Detlev Peukert, *Die KPD im Widerstand. Verfolgung und Untergrundsarbeit an Rhein und Ruhr 1933 bis 1945* (Wuppertal 1980) esp. pp. 57–60.
9. Tim Mason, 'Injustice and Resistance. Barrington Moore and the Reaction of German Workers to Nazism', in R. J. Bullen, H. Pogge von

Strandmann and Antony Polonsky (eds), *Ideas into Politics* (Beckenham 1984) pp. 114ff. omits this international context, arguing that 'The fact that murder, arson, and the like did not come easily to them was one of the reasons why they were anti-Nazis in the first place.' This seems hard to reconcile with recent estimates that between 1917 and 1989 world Communism was responsible for the deaths of between 85 and 100 million people. On this see Martin Malia 'The Lesser Evil?' *TLS* 27 March 1998, pp. 3–4.

10. Weber, 'Die KPD in der Illegalität' p. 83.

11. Ulrich Herbert, 'The Real Mystery in Germany. The German Working Class during the Nazi Dictatorship', in M. Burleigh (ed.), *Confronting the Nazi Past* (London 1996) p. 29.

12. Peukert, *Die KPD im Widerstand* pp. 295–7.

13. Benjamin Pinkus, 'Die Deportation der deutschen Minderheit in der Sowjetunion 1941–1945', in Bernd Wegner (ed.), *Zwei Wege nach Moskau* (Munich 1991) p. 467.

14. *Deutschland-Berichte der Sozialdemokratischen Partei Deutschlands (SOPADE) 1934–1940* (Frankfurt am Main 1980) Sechster Jahrgang (1940) pp. 985ff. for these reactions.

15. Peukert, *Die KPD im Widerstand* p. 333 n. 20.

16. On this see Christian Striefler, *Kampf um die Macht* (Berlin 1993) pp. 126ff.

17. Oswald Bindrich and Susanne Römer, *Beppo Romer. Ein Leben zwischen Revolution und Nation* (Berlin 1991).

18. Johannes Tuchel, 'Das Ende der Legenden. Die Rote Kapelle im Widerstand gegen den Nationalsozialismus', in Gerd R. Ueberschär (ed.), *Der 20. Juli 1944* (Frankfurt am Main 1994) pp. 277ff.

19. Peukert, *Die KPD im Widerstand* pp. 385–6.

20. Patrik von zur Mühlen, 'Die SPD zwischen Anpassung und Widerstand', in Schmädeke and Steinbach (eds), *Der Widerstand* pp. 94–6; William Sheridan Allen, 'Die sozialdemokratische Untergrundbewegung', in *ibid.*, pp. 855ff.; Hartmut Mehringer, 'Socialist Resistance', in Wolfgang Benz and Walter H. Pehle (eds), *Encyclopedia of German Resistance* (New York 1997) pp. 25–34.

21. Hans-Josef Steinberg, 'Die Haltung der Arbeiterschaft zum NS-Regime', in Schmädeke and Steinbach (eds), *Der Widerstand* pp. 871–3.

22. Gerhard Beier, 'Die illegale Reichsleitung der Gewerkschaften', in Löwenthal and Mühlen (eds), *Widerstand und Verweigerung* pp. 31–4 is excellent. See also Willy Brandt, 'Opposition Movements in Germany', 25 September 1943, in J. Heideking and C. Mauch (eds), *American Intelligence and the German Resistance to Hitler* (Boulder 1993) p. 108.

23. Manfred Funke, 'Gewerkschaften und Widerstand', in R. Albrecht *et al.*

(eds), *Widerstand und Exil 1933–1945* (Frankfurt am Main 1986) pp. 60ff.; Gerhard Beier, 'Gewerkschaften zwischen Illusion und Aktion', in Schmädeke and Steinbach (eds), *Der Widerstand* pp. 99–111.

24. Hans Mommsen, '20 July and the German Labour Movement', in his *From Weimar to Auschwitz* (Oxford 1991) pp. 189ff.

25. See the important anti-revisionist study by Leonidas E. Hill, 'The National-Conservatives and Opposition to the Third Reich before the Second World War', in Francis Nicosia and Lawrence Stokes (eds), *Germans against Nazism. Essays in Honour of Peter Hoffmann* (Oxford 1990) pp. 221ff.

26. Bodo Scheurig, *Ewald von Kleist-Schmenzin* (Oldenbourg 1968) p. 141; for the preceding comments on German conservatism see Larry Eugene Jones, 'The Limits of Collaboration', in Jones and James Retallack (eds), *Between Reform, Reaction, and Resistance* (Oxford 1993) pp. 468ff., and Larry Jones, 'Nazis, Conservatives, and the Establishment of the Third Reich 1932–34', *Tel Aviver Jahrbuch für deutsche Geschichte* (1994) 23, pp. 41–64.

27. 'Der Nationalsozialismus. Eine Gefahr', in Scheurig, *Ewald von Kleist-Schmenzin* p. 260.

28. For an excellent discussion of the dilemmas of German conservatives see Jeremy Noakes, 'German Conservatives and the Third Reich', in Martin Blinkhorn (ed.), *Fascists and Conservatives* (London 1990) pp. 71–92, and his 'The German Elites and Resistance in the Third Reich', in H. Siefken and H. Vieregg (eds), *Resistance to National Socialism* (Nottingham 1993) pp. 67ff.

29. Edmund Forschbach, *Edgar J. Jung. Ein konservativer Revolutionär. 30 Juni 1934* (Pfullingen 1984) pp. 105–9.

30. Ulrich Schneider, *Marburg 1933–1945* (Frankfurt am Main 1980) pp. 92ff.

31. The speech is reprinted in Forschbach, *Edgar J. Jung* pp. 154–74.

32. On Othmar Spann see Klaus-Jörg Siegfried, *Universalismus und Faschismus. Das Gesellschaftsbild Othmar Spanns* (Vienna 1974); for the fate of Jung's circle see Hermann Graml, 'Vorhut konservativen Widerstands', in Graml (ed.), *Widerstand im Dritten Reich* (Frankfurt am Main 1984) pp. 172–5.

33. Bodo Scheurig, *Henning von Tresckow* (Frankfurt am Main 1987) pp. 54–7; Romedio Galeazzo Graf von Thun-Hohenstein, *Der Verschwörer. General Oster und die Militäropposition* (Berlin 1982) p. 47; Hermann Graml, 'Hans Oster', in Graml (ed.), *Widerstand im Dritten Reich* p. 225.

34. B. Simms, 'Walther von Reichenau', in R. Smelser and E. Syring (eds), *Die Militärelite des Dritten Reiches* (Frankfurt am Main 1995) pp. 429–30.

35. On this see Klaus-Jurgen Müller, *The Army, Politics and Society in Germany 1933–1945* (Manchester 1987) pp. 31–5.

36. Gerd Ueberschär, 'Ansätze und Hindernisse der Militäropposition gegen Hitler in den ersten beiden Kriegsjahren (1939–1941)', in Militärgeschichtlichen Forschungsamt (ed.), *Aufstand des Gewissens. Der militärische Widerstand gegen Hitler und das NS-Regime 1933–1945* (3rd edn Herford 1987) p. 367.

37. Jürgen Schmädeke, 'Die Blomberg–Fritsch-Krise. Vom Widerspruch zum Widerstand', in Schmädeke and Steinbach (eds), *Der Widerstand* p. 377.

38. Thun-Hohenstein, *Der Verschwörer* pp. 59ff.; for SS involvement in the case see Heinz Hohne, *The Order of the Death's Head* (London 1972) pp. 218ff.

39. Theodore S. Hamerow, 'The Conservative Resistance to Hitler and the Fall of the Weimar Republic', in Jones and Retallack (eds) *Between Reform, Reaction, and Resistance* pp. 443–4.

40. Michael Krüger-Charlé, 'Carl Goerdelers Versuche der Durchsetzung einer alternativen Politik 1933 bis 1937', in Schmädeke and Steinbach (eds), *Der Widerstand* esp. pp. 392–7.

41. Gerhard Ritter, *The German Resistance* (London 1958) pp. 82–3; Hamerow, 'The Conservative Resistance to Hitler' p. 457 for Goerdeler's objections to the implementation of Nazi racial policy.

42. Ulrich Heinemann, *Ein konservativer Rebell. Fritz-Dietlof Graf von der Schulenburg* (Berlin 1990) p. 50.

43. For Beck see Klaus-Jurgen Müller, *General Ludwig Beck* (Boppard am Rhein 1980).

44. Joachim Fest, *Plotting Hitler's Death* (London 1996) pp. 64–5.

45. Thun-Hohenstein, *Der Verschwörer* p. 72.

46. Peter Hoffmann, *German Resistance to Hitler* (Cambridge, Mass. 1988) p. 81.

47. Peter Hoffmann, *The History of the German Resistance 1933–1945* (3rd edn Montreal 1996) p. 76.

48. Hill, 'The National-Conservatives and Opposition' pp. 231–3; the trends Hill is criticising can be seen in Klaus-Jürgen Müller, 'Der nationalkonservative Widerstand 1933–1940', in Müller (ed.), *Der deutsche Widerstand 1933–1945* (Paderborn 1986) pp. 40–59 and his 'The Military Opposition to Hitler', in his *The Army, Politics and Society in Germany* pp. 100–22, and 'Deutsche Militär-Elite in der Vorgeschichte des Zweiten Weltkrieges', in Martin Broszat and Klaus Schwabe (eds), *Die deutschen Eliten und der Weg in den Zweiten Weltkrieg* (Munich 1989) pp. 226–90.

49. Hoffmann, *The History of the German Resistance* pp. 88–9.

50. R. A. C. Parker, *Chamberlain and Appeasement. British Policy and the Coming of the Second World War* (London 1993) pp. 153–4.

51. Klemens van Klemperer, *German Resistance to Hitler. The Search for Allies Abroad 1938–1945* (Oxford 1992) pp. 105–10 is a balanced and fair-minded assessment of the positions of all sides in this extraordinary dialogue, which rejects the simplistic view that at Munich 'Chamberlain saved Hitler'.

52. Ueberschär, 'Ansätze und Hindernisse' p. 369.

53. See Lothar Gruchmann, 'Georg Elser', in Graml (ed.), *Widerstand im Dritten Reich* pp. 183ff.

54. 'Das Spiel ist aus – Arthur Nebe', *Der Spiegel* 5 January 1950, pp. 23ff.

55. Hoffmann, *The History of the German Resistance* p. 127; Simms, 'Walther von Reichenau' p. 436 sheds no light on Reichenau's actions.

56. Thun-Hohenstein, *Der Verschwörer* pp. 155, 186–7, 192–3.

57. Klemperer, *German Resistance to Hitler* pp. 192–8 for a sensitive discussion of this remarkable man.

58. Ulrich von Hassell, *The von Hassell Diaries* (Boulder 1994) entry dated 1–3 September 1940, p. 149.

59. Heinemann, *Ein konservativer Rebell* p. 134.

60. Peter Löffler (ed.), *Clemens August Graf von Galen: Akten, Briefe und Predigten 1933–1946* (Mainz 1988) 2, p. 543.

61. Michael Kater, 'Hitler in a Social Context', *CEH* (1981) 14, pp. 243–72.

62. Hassell, *The von Hassell Diaries* entry dated 17 September 1938, p. 1.

63. Friedrich Percyval Reck-Malleczewen, *Böckelson. Geschichte eines Massenwahns* (Stuttgart 1968). On Reck see the memoir in the above by Irmgard Reck-Malleczewen; Klaus Harpprecht, 'Friedrich Reck-Malleczewen', *Der Monat* (1966) 18, pp. 42–5; and Ralf Schnell, *Literarische Innere Emigration 1933–1945* (Stuttgart 1975) pp. 42–6.

64. Friedrich Reck-Malleczewen, *The Diary of a Man in Despair* (London 1995) entry dated 11 August 1936, pp. 27–8.

65. *Ibid.* entry dated January 1942, p. 147.

66. See Jeremy Noakes, 'High Society in the Third Reich', in Burleigh (ed.), *Confronting the Nazi Past* pp. 57–9.

67. Reck-Malleczewen, *The Diary of a Man in Despair* entry dated April 1939, p. 74.

68. Cited by Hans Mommsen, 'Social Views and Constitutional Plans of the Resistance', in Hermann Graml *et al.* (eds), *The German Resistance to Hitler* (London 1970) p. 66.

69. Gerhard Ritter, *The German Resistance. Carl Goerdeler's Struggle against Nazi Tyranny* (London 1958) p. 171.

70. Ger van Roon, *German Resistance to Hitler. Count von Moltke and the Kreisau Circle* (London 1971) pp. 82–83.

71. Beate Ruhm von Oppen (ed.), *Helmuth James von Moltke. Letters to Freya* (London 1991) letter dated 25 August 1940, p. 110.

72. Michael Balfour and Julian Frisby, *Helmuth von Moltke* (London 1972) p. 87; Ger van Roon, 'Graf von Moltke als Völkerrechtler im OKW', *VfZ* (1970) 9, pp. 12–61.

73. Oppen (ed.), *Moltke. Letters to Freya* letter dated 17 December 1939, p. 49.

74. Gregor Schöllgen, *Ulrich von Hassell 1881–1944. Ein Konservativer in der Opposition* (Munich 1990).

75. Hassell, *The von Hassell Diaries* entries dated 25, 27 November and 20 December 1938, pp. 14–15, 19.

76. *Ibid.* entry dated 19 October 1939, p. 79.

77. *Ibid.* entry dated 8 October 1940, p. 152.

78. *Ibid.* entry dated 9 December 1940, p. 161.

79. *Ibid.* entry dated 18 August 1941, p. 207.

80. *Ibid.* entry dated 4 October 1941, p. 218.

81. *Ibid.* entry dated 1 November 1941, p. 221.

82. Balfour and Frisby, *Helmuth von Moltke* pp. 170–1.

83. Oppen (ed.), *Moltke. Letters to Freya* letter dated 21 October 1941, p. 175.

84. *Ibid.* letter dated 8 November 1941, p. 180.

85. *Ibid.* letter dated 13 November 1941, p. 183.

86. Roon, *German Resistance to Hitler* pp. 201–13.

87. Hamerow, 'The Conservative Resistance to Hitler' p. 457.

88. Ritter, *The German Resistance* p. 196 says, 'His [Goerdeler's] solution of the Jewish problem was highly original'; Christoph Dipper, 'Der Widerstand und die Juden', in Schmädeke and Steinbach (eds), *Der Widerstand* pp. 605–8 takes a highly critical stance. For a balanced assessment see Hoffmann, *The History of the German Resistance* pp. 189–90.

89. Anthony Glees, 'The 1944 Plotters and the War of Genocide', *Journal of Holocaust Education* (1995) 4, pp. 51ff. touches on a few of these issues while underrating the involvement of some military resisters in genocidal policies.

90. Ritter, *The German Resistance* p. 174.

91. Mommsen, 'Social Views and Constitutional Plans', p. 115; on 'youth politics' see also Mommsen, 'Generational Conflict and Youth Rebellion in the Weimar Republic', in his *From Weimar to Auschwitz* pp. 34–8.

92. Ritter, *The German Resistance* pp. 190–4; Walther L. Bernecker, 'Monarchy and Democracy. The Political Role of King Juan Carlos in the Spanish Transición', *JCH* (1998) 33, pp. 65–84.

93. On Kreisau see Ger van Roon, *Neuordnung im Widerstand. Der Kreisauer Kreis innerhalb der deutschen Widerstandsbewegung* (Munich 1967); Eugen Gerstenmaier, 'Der Kreisauer Kreis', *VfZ* (1967) 15,

pp. 221–46; Thomas Childers 'The Kreisau Circle and the Twentieth of July', in Large (ed.), *Contending with Hitler* pp. 99–117.

94. Balfour and Frisby, *Helmuth von Moltke* p. 217.

95. Roon, *German Resistance to Hitler* pp. 29–99 for biographical details.

96. For Lenard see Alan Beyerchen, *Scientists under Hitler. Politics and the Physics Community in the Third Reich* (New Haven 1977) pp. 79ff.

97. Heinrich August Winkler, *Der Weg in der Katastrophe. Arbeiter und Arbeiterbewegung in der Weimarer Republik 1930 bis 1933* (Bonn 1990) pp. 194–6.

98. See David Lehman's brilliant *Signs of the Times* (London 1991) pp. 192ff. for de Man.

99. On this see Ulrich Herbert, *Best* (Bonn 1996) pp. 112–27.

100. See mainly Richard Albrecht, *Der militante Sozialdemokrat. Carlo Mierendorff 1897 bis 1943. Eine Biografie* (Bonn 1987) for details of Mierendorff's life and thought.

101. *Ibid.* p. 174.

102. *Ibid.* pp. 158–62.

103. Balfour and Frisby, *Helmuth von Moltke* pp. 206–9; Schöllgen, *Ulrich von Hassell* pp. 102–3.

104. The above is largely based on the reliable account by Roon, *German Resistance to Hitler* pp. 219ff., with marginal critical modifications based on Hans Mommsen, 'Social Views and Constitutional Plans' pp. 55ff.

105. Ritter, *The German Resistance* pp. 186–8.

106. Hermann Graml, 'Resistance Thinking on Foreign Policy', in Graml *et al.* (eds), *The German Resistance to Hitler* p. 42.

107. *Ibid.* pp. 1–54.

108. Fritz Stern, 'National Socialism as Temptation', in his *Dreams and Delusions. The Drama of German History* (New York 1987) pp. 148ff.

109. Wolfgang Schieder, 'Zwei Generationen im militärischen Widerstand gegen Hitler', in Schmädeke and Steinbach (eds), *Der Widerstand* esp. pp. 446ff.

110. Peter Hoffmann, 'Hitler's Personal Security', *JCH* (1973) 8, pp. 25–46; *idem, Die Sicherheit des Diktators* (Munich 1975).

111. Fest, *Plotting Hitler's Death* pp. 189–90.

112. Richard von Weizsäcker, *Vier Zeiten. Erinnerungen* (Berlin 1997) pp. 74ff. for the 'tone' in this illustrious regiment.

113. Scheurig, *Henning von Tresckow* pp. 31ff.; Ekkehard Klausa, 'Preussische Soldatentradition und Widerstand', in Schmädeke and Steinbach (eds), *Der Widerstand* pp. 533–45.

114. Peter Hoffmann, *Stauffenberg. A Family History 1905–1944* (Cambridge 1995) p. 46.

115. Martin Broszat, 'Zur Sozialgeschichte des Deutschen Widerstands' p. 308 for this uncharacteristically ungenerous approach.

116. Roon, *German Resistance to Hitler* p. 145.

117. For a fascinating exploration of these themes see Michael Baigent and Richard Leigh, *Secret Germany* (London 1994); Freya Gräfin von Moltke interview in Dorothee von Meding (ed.), *Mit dem Mut des Herzens* (Berlin 1992) p. 132.

118. For their experiences see Meding (ed.), *Mit dem Mut des Herzens*.

119. Oppen (ed.), *Moltke. Letters to Freya* letter dated 17 March 1940, p. 63.

120. Scheurig, *Henning von Tresckow* p. 115.

121. Hoffmann, *The History of the German Resistance* pp. 267–9.

122. Christian Gerlach, 'Männer des 20. Juli und der Krieg gegen die Sowjetunion', in Hannes Heer and Klaus Naumann (eds), *Vernichtungskrieg. Verbrechen der Wehrmacht* (Hamburg 1995) pp. 428ff.

123. Fabian von Schlabrendorff, *Offiziere gegen Hitler* (Berlin 1984) pp. 50–1. Confidence in this account is not enhanced by the claim on p. 51 that the 'Commissar Order' was issued after rather than before the invasion.

124. Eugen Kogon, *Der SS-Staat* (13th edn Munich 1974) pp. 168–9 n. 1.

125. See 'Das Spiel ist aus – Arthur Nebe', *Der Spiegel* 2 February 1950, esp. pp. 24ff.

126. Saul Friedländer, *Counterfeit Nazi. The Ambiguity of Good* (London 1969) for details of Gerstein's remarkable story.

127. Gerlach, 'Männer des 20. Juli' pp. 432–3.

128. Helmut Krausnick, *Hitlers Einsatzgruppen* (Frankfurt am Main 1985) pp. 156–62 and 197ff.

129. Befehl des Befehlshabers der Panzergruppe 4, Generaloberst Hoepner, dated 2 May 1941, reprinted in Gerd Ueberschär and Wolfram Wette (eds), *Der deutsche Überfall auf die Sowjetunion* (Frankfurt am Main 1991) doc. 5, p. 251.

130. Heinemann, *Ein konservativer Rebell* pp. 69–73.

131. Hoffmann, *The History of the German Resistance* pp. 324–5.

132. Cited by Baigent and Leigh, *Secret Germany* p. 101.

133. Eberhard Bethge, *Dietrich Bonhoeffer* (London 1970) pp. 638–9.

134. Scheurig, *Henning von Tresckow* pp. 112–13.

135. Hoffmann, *Stauffenberg* p. 137.

136. *Ibid.* p. 145.

137. Heinemann, *Ein konservativer Rebell* documentary appendix, Schulenburg's diary entries dated 21 and 27 August 1941 pp. 219–21.

138. These men figure repeatedly in Alexander Dallin's accounts of realist strategies in Russia in his *German Rule in Russia 1941–1945* (2nd edn London 1981) pp. 238ff., 503, 531ff., 548–9, 560–1 etc.; see also more

perfunctory treatments in Scheurig, *Henning von Tresckow* pp. 175ff.; Hoffmann, *Stauffenberg* pp. 149–51.

139. Hoffmann, *Stauffenberg* pp. 151–2.

140. See *Ibid.* pp. 30–41.

141. Nina Grafin von Stauffenberg interviewed in Meding (ed.), *Mit dem Mut des Herzens* p. 291.

142. For details of the assassination attempt see Hoffmann, *The History of the German Resistance* pp. 301ff.

143. On Freisler's background see Fest, *Plotting Hitler's Death* pp. 297–9.

144. Balfour and Frisby, *Helmuth von Moltke* p. 322.

145. Scheurig, *Ewald von Kleist-Schmenzin* pp. 195–6.

146. 'Das Spiel ist aus – Arthur Nebe', *Der Spiegel* 30 March 1950, pp. 20–6; 6 April 1950, pp. 20–5; 13 April 1950, pp. 17–25 for exhaustive details.

147. Fest, *Plotting Hitler's Death* p. 236; these issues of individual witness are sensitively treated by Klemens von Klemperer, ' "What Is the Law that Lies behind These Words?" Antigone's Question and the German Resistance', in M. Geyer and J. Boyer (eds), *Resistance against the Third Reich 1933–1990* (Chicago 1994) pp. 141ff.

148. My thinking has been greatly helped by Hans Maier, ' "Totalitarismus" und "politische Religionen". Konzepte des Diktaturvergleichs', *VfZ* (1995) 45, pp. 387ff.; Philippe Burrin, 'Political Religion. The Relevance of a Concept', *History & Memory* (1997) 9, pp. 321ff.

149. H. R. Trevor-Roper (ed.), *Hitler's Table Talk 1941–44* (Oxford 1988) entry dated 13 December 1941, pp. 142–5.

150. Ian Kershaw, 'Arthur Greiser', in R. Smelser, E. Syring and R. Zitelmann (eds), *Die braune Elite II* (Darmstadt 1993) p. 122; B. Stasiewski, 'Die Kirchenpolitik der Nationalsozialisten im Warthegau 1939–1945', *VfZ* (1959) 7, pp. 46–74.

151. The phrase 'reluctant resistance movement' was coined by Ernst Wolf 'Political and Moral Motives behind the Resistance', in Graml (ed.), *The German Resistance to Hitler* p. 209.

152. Kurt Nowak, *Geschichte des Christentums in Deutschland* (Munich 1995) pp. 239–42 is an excellent recent account.

153. John Conway, *The Nazi Persecution of the Churches 1933–45* (London 1968) p. 20.

154. Guenther Lewy, *The Catholic Church and Nazi Germany* (London 1964) p. 152.

155. See Joachim Kuropka, *Clemens August Graf von Galen* (Cloppenburg 1992) pp. 82ff.

156. Ludwig Volk, 'Die Fuldaer Bischofskonferenz von Hitlers Machtergreifung bis zur Enzyklika "Mit brennender Sorge" ', in Dieter Albrecht (ed.), *Katholische Kirche im Dritten Reich* (Mainz 1976) pp. 46–8.

157. On the Concordat see Heinz Hürten, 'Der katholische Episkopat nach dem Reichskonkordat', in Heydemann and Kettenacker (eds), *Kirchen in der Diktatur* (Göttingen 1992) pp. 109ff.; *idem*, 'Selbstbehauptung und Widerstand der katholischen Kirche,' in Müller (ed.), *Der deutsche Widerstand* pp. 136–9.

158. For the international context see Martin Conway, *Catholic Politics in Europe 1918–1945* (London 1997) esp. pp. 40ff.

159. Conway, *The Nazi Persecution of the Churches* pp. 339–41 for the full text of these June 1932 principles.

160. *Ibid.* pp. 52–3.

161. See Günther van Norden, 'Widerstand im deutschen Protestantismus', in Müller (ed.), *Der deutsche Widerstand* pp. 131ff.

162. Bethge, *Dietrich Bonhoeffer* pp. 440–4.

163. On these themes see Chapter 5 above, and above all Kurt Nowak, *'Euthanasie' und Sterilisation im Dritten Reich* (2nd edn Göttingen 1984).

164. Nathan Stoltzfus, *Resistance of the Heart* (London 1996) pp. 147–9 fails to mention the thirteen months which elapsed between Galen's learning of the 'euthanasia' (July 1940) programme and his 3 August 1941 protest; the impact upon him of Gestapo closure of religious houses in Münster during the summer of 1941; and the continued use of gassing facilities under Aktion 14f13. On these subjects see Michael Burleigh, 'The Churches, Eugenics and the Nazi "Euthanasia" Programme', in his *Ethics and Extermination* (Cambridge 1997) pp. 139–40.

165. See the suggestive essay by Claudia Koonz, 'Ethical Dilemmas and Nazi Eugenics', in Geyer and Boyer (eds), *Resistance against the Third Reich* pp. 15–38.

166. Lewy, *The Catholic Church and Nazi Germany* p. 129.

167. *Ibid.* pp. 226ff.

168. Conway, *The Nazi Persecution of the Churches* pp. 265–6.

169. Uwe Gerrens, *Medizinisches Ethos und theologische Ethik. Karl und Dietrich Bonhoeffer in der Auseinandersetzung um Zwangssterilisation und 'Euthanasie' im Nationalsozialismus* (Munich 1996) p. 135.

170. *Ibid.* p. 156.

171. Bethge, *Dietrich Bonhoeffer* p. 208.

172. Raymond Mengus, 'Dietrich Bonhoeffer and the Decision to Resist', in Geyer and Boyer (eds), *Resistance against the Third Reich* p. 205.

173. Bethge, *Dietrich Bonhoeffer* p. 648.

174. Klemperer, *German Resistance to Hitler* pp. 281ff.

175. Bethge, *Dietrich Bonhoeffer* p. 585.

176. *Ibid.* pp. 626–7.

177. Roman Bleistein, *Alfred Delp* (Frankfurt am Main 1989) pp. 266ff.

178. Oppen (ed.), *Moltke. Letters to Freya* letter dated 10 January 1945, pp. 402–3.

179. Klemens von Klemperer, 'The Solitary Witness', in Large (ed.), *Contending with Hitler* esp. pp. 134–6 for this term.

10. WAR AND PEACE, 1943–1948

1. As was argued in 1991 in Ian Kershaw's *Hitler* (London 1991) p. 163, although in the first volume of his monumental biography *Hitler 1889–1936. Hubris* (London 1998) the onset of hubris has been pushed back to 1936.

2. Eric Voegelin, *Autobiographical Reflections* (Baton Rouge 1989) pp. 28–33 for the 'culture shock' he experienced during a two-year spell in America in the mid-1920s.

3. Despite reticence over Hitler's admiration for US eugenics and immigration laws, there is much of value in D. Junker, 'The Continuity of Ambivalence. German Views of America 1933–1945', in D. Barclay and E. Glaser-Schmidt (eds), *Transatlantic Images and Perceptions. Germany and America since 1776* (Cambridge 1997) pp. 249–54; see also Saul Friedländer, *Auftakt zum Untergang. Hitler und die Vereinigten Staaten* (Stuttgart 1965); G. L. Weinberg, 'Hitler's Image of the United States', in his *World in the Balance* (Hanover 1981) pp. 53–74; R. E. Herzstein, *Roosevelt and Hitler. Prelude to War* (New York 1989); and H. D. Schäfer, 'Amerikanismus im Dritten Reich', in M. Prinz and R. Zitelmann (eds), *Nationalsozialismus und Modernisierung* (Darmstadt 1991) pp. 199–215.

4. H. R. Trevor-Roper (ed.), *Hitler's Table Talk 1941–44* (Oxford 1988) entry dated 7 January 1942, p. 188.

5. Jeremy Noakes and Geoffrey Pridham (eds), *Nazism 1919–1945. A Documentary Reader* (Exeter 1983–8) 3, doc. 600, pp. 838–9.

6. Trevor-Roper (ed.), *Hitler's Table Talk* entry dated 2 February 1942, p. 279.

7. See Richard Ketchum, 'Warming Up on the Sidelines for World War II', *Smithsonian Magazine* (1991) 22, pp. 88–103.

8. Carlo D'Este, *Genius for War* (London 1996) pp. 392ff.

9. See the brilliant account by Keith Eiler, *Mobilizing America. Robert P. Patterson and the War Effort 1940–1945* (Ithaca 1997).

10. For the above see mainly Alan Milward, *War, Economy and Society 1939–1945* (London 1987) pp. 67–70.

11. Ludolf Herbst, *Das nationalsozialistische Deutschland 1933–1945* (Frankfurt am Main 1996) p. 413.

12. Stephen Ambrose, *Rise to Globalism. American Foreign Policy since 1938* (8th rev. edn London 1997) p. 7.

13. For an outstanding account see Robin Edmonds, *The Big Three. Churchill, Roosevelt and Stalin in Peace and at War* (London 1991) pp. 181–2.

14. S. Gribanov, 'The Role of US Lend–Lease Aircraft in Russia in World War II', *Journal of Slavic Military Studies* (1998) 11, pp. 104ff.

15. David Reynolds, *The Creation of the Anglo-American Alliance 1937–1941. A Study in Competitive Cooperation* (London 1981).

16. Amos Perlmutter, *FDR and Stalin. A Not So Grand Alliance* (Columbia 1993) pp. 74–8, 103–4, 121–2 for these important insights.

17. Boris V. Sokolov, 'Lend–Lease in Soviet Military Efforts 1941–1945', *Journal of Slavic Military Studies* (1994) 7, pp. 567–86; for the wider context see Richard J. Overy, *Russia's War* (London 1998) pp. 193–8.

18. Bonwetsch, 'Stalin, the Red Army, and the "Great Patriotic War",' in Ian Kershaw and Moshe Lewin (eds), *Stalinism and Nazism. Dictatorships in Comparison* (Cambridge 1997) pp. 203–7.

19. See especially J. Sapir, 'The Economics of War in the Soviet Union', in Kershaw and Lewin (eds) *Stalinism and Nazism* esp. pp. 233–6.

20. See N. Cull, 'Selling Peace. The Origins, Promotion and Fate of the Anglo-American New Order during the Second World War', *Diplomacy and Statecraft* (1996) 7, pp. 1–28.

21. R. A. C. Parker, *Struggle for Survival. The History of the Second World War* (Oxford 1989) pp. 95–8.

22. Ambrose, *Rise to Globalism* p. 23.

23. H. Boberach (ed.), *Meldungen aus dem Reich* (Herrsching 1984) 13, report no. 380 dated 3 May 1943, p. 5203 (cited hereafter as MadR followed by the volume and report number together with the date).

24. Robert E. Sherwood, *The White House Papers of Harry L. Hopkins* (London 1949) 2, pp. 693–4.

25. Gerhard L. Weinberg, *A World at Arms* (Cambridge 1988) pp. 609–11.

26. Keith Sainsbury, *Churchill and Roosevelt at War* (London 1990) pp. 39ff.

27. See the brilliant study by Jonathan Steinberg, *All or Nothing. The Axis and the Holocaust 1941–43* (London 1990) esp. pp. 206–19.

28. See principally Gerhard Schreiber, *Die italienischen Militärinternierten im deutschen Machtbereich 1943–1945* (Munich 1990) pp. 112 and 157ff.

29. S. Bidwell, 'Kesselring', in Correlli Barnett (ed.), *Hitler's Generals* (London 1989) pp. 279ff.

30. Ronald Schafer, *Wings of Judgement. American Bombing in World War II* (Oxford 1985) pp. 54–9.

31. *Ibid.* pp. 191–2.

32. Gribanov, 'The Role of US Lend–Lease Aircraft in Russia in World War II' pp. 104–5.
33. Richard J. Overy, *Why the Allies Won* (London 1995) p. 102; A. Beaumont, 'The Bomber Offensive as a Second Front', *JCH* (1987) 22, pp. 3–19.
34. A. Harris, *Bomber Offensive* (London 1947, reprinted 1990) p. 79; S. Garrett, *Ethics and Airpower in World War II. The British Bombing of German Cities* (London 1993) p. 72.
35. Harris, *Bomber Offensive* pp. 78 and 176.
36. *Ibid.* pp. 176–7.
37. See R. Pommerin, 'Zur Einsicht bomben?', in Pommerin (ed.), *Dresden unterm Hakenkreuz* (Cologne 1998) pp. 237–8.
38. For a nuanced discussion of German airpower see Horst Boog, 'Harris – A German View', S. Cox (ed.), *Sir Arthur T. Harris. Despatch on War Operations 23rd February 1942 to 8th May 1945* (London 1995) p. xlii, and his 'Der anglo-amerikanischen strategische Luftkrieg über Europa und die deutsche Luftverteidigung', in Boog, (ed.), *Der Globale Krieg* (Stuttgart 1990) pp. 434ff.; and Richard J. Overy, *The Air War 1939–1945* (New York 1980).
39. Harris, *Bomber Offensive* pp. 51–2.
40. The best account of American airpower remains Schafer, *Wings of Judgement*, but see also W. Hays Park, ' "Precision" and "Area" Bombing: Who Did Which, and When?', *Journal of Strategic Studies* (1995) 18, pp. 145–74.
41. Martin Middlebrook, *The Battle of Hamburg. The Firestorm Raid* (London 1980) p. 100.
42. Garrett, *Ethics and Airpower* pp. 83–97.
43. For examples see Max Hastings, *Bomber Command* (London 1993) pp. 69 and 160.
44. See E. Markusen and D. Kopf, *The Holocaust and Strategic Bombing. Genocide and Total War in the 20th Century* (Boulder 1995).
45. Post-war interrogation of Karl-Otto Saur, in Noakes and Pridham (eds), *Nazism 1919–1945* 4, doc. 1074, p. 261.
46. Ian Kershaw, *The 'Hitler Myth'* (Oxford 1987) pp. 206–7.
47. Alan Fisher, *The Crimean Tatars* (Stanford 1978) pp. 162–75.
48. Amy Knight, *Beria. Stalin's First Lieutenant* (Princeton 1993) pp. 126–7.
49. For excellent recent accounts see John B. Dunlop, *Russia Confronts Chechnya. Roots of a Separatist Conflict* (Cambridge 1998) especially pp. 40–84, and C. Gall and T. de Waal, *Chechnya. A Small Victorious War* (London 1997) pp. 56–75, as well as the classics by Robert Conquest, *The Nation Killers* (London 1970) and Alexander Nekrich, *The Punished Peoples* (New York 1978).
50. See K. Larson, 'The Khar'kov Operation, May 1942. From the Archives',

Parts I and II, *Journal of Soviet Military Studies* (1992) 5, pp. 451ff. and 611ff.

51. Andrey Tarkovsky, *Sculpting in Time. Reflections on the Cinema* (London 1986) pp. 130–1.

52. See David Glantz, *Soviet Military Deception in the Second World War* (London 1989) p. 369.

53. Manfred Messerschmidt, 'Die Wehrmacht. Vom Realitätsverlust zum Selbstbetrug', in H. E. Volkmann (ed.), *Ende des Dritten Reiches – Ende des Zweiten Weltkrieges* (Munich 1995) p. 236.

54. S. Spector, 'Aktion 1005 – Effacing the Murder of Millions', *Holocaust and Genocide Studies* (1990) 5, pp. 157–73.

55. Alexander Werth, *Russia at War* (London 1964) pp. 884–99.

56. Yitzhak Arad, *Belzec, Sobibor, Treblinka. The Operation Reinhard Death Camps* (Bloomington 1987) pp. 370–6.

57. Norman Davies, *Heart of Europe* (Oxford 1986) p. 3.

58. For a cool discussion of this contentious subject see Richard J. Crampton, *Eastern Europe in the Twentieth Century* (London 1994) pp. 199–200.

59. Churchill to Roosevelt 25 August 1944, in F. Loewenheim, H. Langley and M. Jonas (eds), *Roosevelt and Churchill. Their Secret Wartime Correspondence* (New York 1990) doc. 424, pp. 567–8.

60. John Erikson, *The Road to Berlin* (London 1983) pp. 270ff.

61. See French MacLean, *The Cruel Hunters. SS-Sonder-Kommando Dirlewanger* (Atglen 1998) and Hans-Peter Klausch, *Antifaschisten in SS-Uniform* (Bremen 1993) pp. 105–20.

62. See J. Ciechanowski, *The Warsaw Rising of 1944* (Cambridge 1974) and J. Hanson, *The Civilian Population and the Warsaw Uprising of 1944* (Cambridge 1982). For the political context see Davies, *Heart of Europe* pp. 90–7.

63. For the details see Stéphane Courtois *et al.*, *Das Schwarzbuch des Kommunismus* (Munich 1998) pp. 408–10.

64. For these details see Overy, *Why the Allies Won* pp. 208–9.

65. The best accounts are Ambrose, *Rise to Globalism*, and Max Hastings, *Overlord* (London, New York 1984).

66. See the brilliant account by Nicholas Bethell, *The Last Secret. Forcible Repatriation to Russia 1944–1947* (rev. edn London 1974) pp. 80ff.

67. C. B. MacDonald, *The Battle of the Bulge* (London 1984).

68. Boberach (ed.), *MadR 10*, report no. 277 dated 20 April 1942, p. 3639.

69. Middlebrook, *The Battle of Hamburg* p. 357.

70. For examples see report from the NSDAP Chancellery for 11–17 April 1943, Noakes and Pridham (eds), *Nazism 1919–1945* 4, doc. 1304, pp. 548–9; and Boberach (ed.), *MadR 14*, report dated 8 July 1943, pp. 5445–6.

71. Ulrich von Hassel.

72. Boberach (ed.), *MadR* 12, report no. 355 dated 1 February 1943, pp. 4734–5.
73. *Ibid.* report no. 360 dated 18 February 1943, p. 4822.
74. *Ibid.* report no. 356 dated 4 February 1943, p. 4751; and report no. 357 dated 8 February 1943, p. 4761.
75. *Ibid.* report no. 359 dated 15 February 1943, p. 4800.
76. *Ibid.* 14, report dated 9 July 1943, p. 5461.
77. *Ibid.* 13, report no. 369 dated 22 March 1943, pp. 4981–2.
78. Albert Speer, *Inside the Third Reich* (London 1995) pp. 388–9.
79. Richard J. Overy, *The Penguin Atlas of the Third Reich* (London 1996) p. 102.
80. See M. Recker, 'Wohnen und Bombardierung im Zweiten Weltkrieg', in L. Nicthammer and P. Lutz (eds), *Wohnen im Wandel* (Wuppertal 1979) pp. 408–28.
81. See Marlis Steinert, *Hitlers Krieg und die Deutschen* (Düsseldorf 1970) p. 363.
82. Boberach (ed.), *MadR* 14, report dated 1 July 1943, p. 5414.
83. See G. Kirwan, 'Allied Bombing and Nazi Domestic Propaganda', *European History Quarterly* (1985) 15, pp. 341–62.
84. Boberach (ed.), *MadR* 14, report dated 8 July 1943, pp. 5448–50, and report dated 22 July 1943, p. 5516, regarding Cologne and Aachen.
85. Richard J. Overy, *Göring. The Iron Man* (London 1984) pp. 194ff.
86. Middlebrook, *The Battle of Hamburg* p. 83.
87. J. Szodrzynski, 'Das Ende der "Volksgemeinschaft"', in Frank Bajohr and Szodrzynski (eds), *Hamburg in der NS-Zeit* (Hamburg 1997) p. 295.
88. Middlebrook, *The Battle of Hamburg* pp. 328–30.
89. C. Klessmann, 'Untergänge-Übergange. Gesellschaftsgeschichtliche Brüche und Kontinuitätslinien vor und nach 1945', in Klesmann (ed.), *Nicht nur Hitlers Krieg. Der Zweite Weltkrieg und die Deutschen* (Düsseldorf 1989) p. 89.
90. See S. Cox, 'The Overall Report in Retrospect', in Cox (ed.), *The Strategic Air War against Germany 1939–1945. The Official Report of the British Bombing Survey Unit* (London 1998) pp. xxvii–xxxix.
91. Cox (ed.), *The Strategic Air War against Germany* p. 77.
92. Kershaw, *The 'Hitler Myth'* p. 207.
93. Boberach (ed.), *MadR* 15, report dated 7 October 1943, pp. 5867–9.
94. *Ibid.* report dated 9 December 1943, pp. 6122–3.
95. Karl-Otto Saur testimony, in Noakes and Pridham (eds), *Nazism. 1919–1945* 4, doc. 1074, p. 261.
96. Overy, *Why the Allies Won* pp. 132–3.
97. For local examples see J. Becker and H. Zabel (eds), *Hagen unterm Hakenkreuz* (2nd edn Hagen 1996) pp. 351–4.

98. R.-D. Müller and G. R. Ueberschär (eds), *Kriegsende 1945* (Frankfurt am Main 1994) p. 36.
99. Boberach (ed.), *MadR* 14, report dated 22 July 1943, p. 5515.
100. Earl R. Beck, *Under the Bombs. The German Home Front 1942–1945* (Lexington 1986) p. 76.
101. Noakes and Pridham (eds), *Nazism 1919–1945* 4, doc. 1320, pp. 566–7.
102. Boberach (ed.), *MadR* 15, report dated 4 October 1943, p. 5834.
103. *Ibid.* 14, report dated 6 September 1943, p. 5721.
104. *Ibid.* report dated 22 July 1943, p. 5515.
105. *Ibid.* report dated 9 July 1943, p. 5463.
106. See the testimony of Frau Ursula Kretzschmar in Alison Owing, *Frauen. German Women Recall the Third Reich* (London 1993) p. 195.
107. Boberach (ed.), *MadR* 14, report dated 15 July 1943, pp. 5478–9.
108. Steinert, *Hitlers Krieg und die Deutschen* p. 468.
109. Boberach (ed.), *MadR* 14, report dated 19 August 1943, p. 5644; David Welch, *The Third Reich. Politics and Propaganda* (London 1993) p. 114.
110. Boberach (ed.), *MadR* 14, report dated 6 September 1943, p. 5716.
111. See Steinert, *Hitlers Krieg und die Deutschen* pp. 341ff.
112. See Ulrich Herbert, *Hitler's Foreign Workers. Enforced Foreign Labor in Germany under the Third Reich* (Cambridge 1997) pp. 258–9.
113. Ralf Georg Reuth (ed.), *Joseph Goebbels. Tagebücher* (Munich 1992) 5, entry dated 19 February 1943, p. 1898.
114. For the text see H. Heiber (ed.), *Goebbels. Reden 1939–1945* (Düsseldorf 1972) 2, no. 17, pp. 172–208.
115. Noakes and Pridham (eds), *Nazism 1919–1945* 4, doc. 1247, pp. 490–4.
116. Boberach (ed.), *MadR* 12, report dated 22 February 1943, pp. 4831–3, and report dated 25 February 1943, pp. 4843–6.
117. Reuth (ed.), *Joseph Goebbels. Tagebücher* 5, entry dated 21 February 1943, p. 1901.
118. Kershaw, *The 'Hitler Myth'* pp. 198–9.
119. Speer, *Inside the Third Reich* p. 354.
120. Steinert, *Hitlers Krieg und die Deutschen* p. 390.
121. Raul Hilberg, *Die Vernichtung der europäischen Juden* (Frankfurt am Main 1982) 2, p. 859; the most comprehensive account of the destruction of Hungarian Jewry is R. Braham, *The Politics of Genocide. The Destruction of Hungarian Jewry* (New York 1982), but see also the recent collection, D. Cesarani (ed.), *Genocide and Rescue. The Holocaust in Hungary 1944* (Oxford 1997).
122. Y. Don 'Economic Implications of the Anti-Jewish Legislation in Hungary' in Cesarani (ed.), *Genocide and Rescue* pp. 47ff.

123. For this important insight see Crampton, *Eastern Europe in the Twentieth Century* p. 189.

124. For the above see István Deák, 'The Peculiarities of Hungarian Fascism', in R. Braham and B. Vago (eds), *The Holocaust in Hungary* (New York 1985) pp. 43–51; M. Szollosi-Janze, *Die Pfeilkreuzlerbewegung in Hungarn* (Munich 1989); Attila Pok, 'Germans, Hungarians and Hungarian Jewry', in Cesarani (ed.), *Genocide and Rescue* pp. 147–53.

125. For the details see R. Braham, 'The Kamenets-Podolsk and Delvidek Massacres. Prelude to the Holocaust in Hungary', *Yad Vashem Studies* (1973) 9, pp. 119–30.

126. R. Braham, *The Hungarian Labor Service System 1939–1945* (New Haven 1977).

127. Braham, *The Politics of Genocide* 1, doc. 103, pp. 218–28.

128. Hilberg, *Die Vernichtung der europäischen Juden* 2, pp. 883–4.

129. Claudia Steur, *Theodor Dannecker. Ein Funktionär der 'Endlösung'* (Tübingen 1997) p. 131.

130. See R. Braham, 'The Rightists, Horthy and the Germans', B. Vago and G. Mosse (eds), *Jews and Non-Jews in Eastern Europe* (Jerusalem 1974) p. 147, and his *Politics of Genocide* (New York 1981) 1, p. 372.

131. R. Braham, 'The Official Jewish Leadership of Wartime Hungary', in Y. Gutman and C. Haft (eds), *Patterns of Jewish Leadership in Nazi Europe 1933–1945* (Jerusalem 1979) pp. 267–85.

132. H. Arendt, *Eichmann in Jerusalem* (London 1977) p. 42ff.

133. Steur, *Theodor Dannecker* pp. 136ff.

134. State of Israel Ministry of Justice (ed.), *The Eichmann Trial. Record of Proceedings in the District Court of Jerusalem* (Jerusalem 1993) 3, Session no. 52, p. 944.

135. For these details see mainly Hans Safrian, *Eichmann und seine Gehilfen* (Frankfurt am Main 1995) pp. 298ff.; and Jean-Claude Pressac and Robert van Pelt, 'The Machinery of Destruction', in Y. Gutman and M. Berenbaum (eds), *Anatomy of the Auschwitz Death Camp* (Bloomington 1994) pp. 237–8.

136. Steur, *Theodore Dannecker* pp. 143–5.

137. On Speer and Dora-Mittelbau see the brief reference in M. Schmidt, *Albert Speer. The End of a Myth* (New York 1984) p. 195.

138. For the above see A. Fiedermann, T. Hess and M. Jaeger, *Das Konzentrationslager Mittelbau Dora* (Berlin 1993), which includes memoirs of former inmates. See also Yves Beon, *Planet Dora* (Boulder 1997); E. Pachaly and K. Pelny, *Konzentrationslager Mittelbau-Dora* (Berlin 1990); T. Hess and T. Seidel, *Vernichtung durch Fortschritt am Beispiel der Raketenproduktion im Konzentrationslager Mittelbau* (Berlin 1995).

139. See C. Lattek, 'Bergen-Belsen. From "Privileged" Camp to Death Camp', *Journal of Holocaust Education* (1996) 5, pp. 37–71.

140. Programmatic statement dated 20 April 1942, in Noakes and Pridham (eds), *Nazism 1919–1945* 4, doc. 1067, p. 242.
141. Herbert, *Hitler's Foreign Workers* p. 397.
142. *Ibid.* p. 243.
143. See especially Schreiber, *Die italienischen Militärinternierten* pp. 444–61.
144. Boberach (ed.), *MadR* 15, report dated 20 December 1943, pp. 6179–86.
145. Germans sleeping with Poles were noted in *ibid. MadR* 3, report no. 24 dated 4 December 1939, p. 528, and report no. 59 dated 28 February 1940, p. 822.
146. For the above see mainly Herbert, *Hitler's Foreign Workers* pp. 100–6; also R. Gellately, *The Gestapo and German Society. Enforcing Racial Policy 1933–1945* (Oxford 1990) p. 226 on peasants and Poles.
147. Gellately, *The Gestapo and German Society* p. 242.
148. Victor Klemperer, *Tagebücher 1942–1945* (Berlin 1996) 2, entry dated 22–24 February 1945, p. 666.
149. Götz Aly, *Macht. Geist. Wahn. Kontinuitäten deutschen Denkens* (Berlin 1997) pp. 55–6.
150. Schafer, *Wings of Judgement* p. 100; see also his 'Sur le bombardement de Dresde', *Revue d'histoire de la Deuxième Guerre Mondiale* (1966) 62, pp. 75–7.
151. Hastings, *Bomber Command* p. 342.
152. Harris to Sir Norman Bottomley, Deputy Chief of Air Staff dated 29 March 1945, in Hastings, *Bomber Command* Appendix C, pp. 368–70.
153. For the details see J. Lucas and M. Cooper, *Hitler's Elite* (London 1990) pp. 171ff.
154. Müller and Ueberschär (eds), *Kriegsende 1945* doc. 3 'Aufruf des Reichsführers-SS' dated 10 February 1945, pp. 156–8.
155. Reuth (ed.), *Joseph Goebbels. Tagebücher 5*, entry dated 31 March 1945, p. 2183.
156. Herbert, *Hitler's Foreign Workers* pp. 370–6.
157. Frau Ursula Kretzschmar, in Owing, *Frauen* p. 195.
158. On these marches see Yehuda Bauer, 'The Death Marches January–May 1945', in M. Marrus (ed.), *The Nazi Holocaust* (Westport 1989) 9, pp. 491–511.
159. For good discussions of these questions see Herbert, *Hitler's Foreign Workers* pp. 372–4, and Ruth Bettina Birn, 'Revising the Holocaust', in N. Finkelstein and Birn, *Nation on Trial* (New York 1998) esp. pp. 126–30.
160. Messerschmidt, 'Die Wehrmacht' pp. 232–3.
161. For Oradour and Tulle see Max Hastings, *Das Reich. The March of the*

2nd SS Panzer Division through France, June 1944 (London 1981) pp. 181ff.

162. Steinert, *Hitlers Krieg und die Deutschen* pp. 552–3.

163. M. Messerschmidt and F. Wüllner, *Die Wehrmachtsjustiz im Dienste des Nationalsozialismus* (Baden-Baden 1987); Reuth (ed.), *Joseph Goebbels. Tagebücher 5*, entry dated 31 March 1945, p. 2181.

164. Steinert, *Hitlers Krieg und die Deutschen* p. 503.

165. Noakes and Pridham (eds), *Nazism 1919–1945* 4, doc. 1380, SD report from Stuttgart dated 6 November 1944, p. 652.

166. For the above see Norman Naimark, *The Russians in Germany. A History of the Soviet Zone of Occupation 1945–1949* (Cambridge, Mass. 1995) pp. 85–6.

167. For these details see mainly Müller and Ueberschär (eds), *Kriegsende 1945* pp. 42–51.

168. Messerschmidt, 'Die Wehrmacht' p. 241.

169. Rudolf Semmler, *Goebbels: The Man Next to Hitler* (London, 1947) entry dated 17 April 1945, p. 194.

170. See Robert Harris, *Selling Hitler* (London 1986).

171. Reuth (ed.), *Joseph Goebbels. Tagebücher 5*, entry dated 28 March 1945, p. 2176; on *Kolberg* see David Welch, *Propaganda and the German Cinema 1933–1945* (Oxford 1983) pp. 221–35.

172. Reuth (ed.), *Joseph Goebbels. Tagebücher 5*, entry dated 19 March 1945, p. 2161.

173. Joachim Fest, *Hitler* (London 1974) pp. 1075ff.

174. H. R. Trevor-Roper, *The Last Days of Hitler* (4th edn, London 1971) p. 51.

175. Speer, *Inside the Third Reich* p. 604.

176. ' ". . . warum dann überhaupt noch leben!" Hitlers Lagebesprechungen am 23, 25 und 27 April 1945', *Der Spiegel* (10 January 1966) 3, 20, pp. 32–46; S. Behrenbeck, *Der Kult um die toten Helden* (Vierow 1996) p. 584.

177. Noakes and Pridham (eds), *Nazism 1919–1945* 4, doc. 1397, p. 667.

178. ' ". . . warum dann überhaupt noch leben!" ' p. 42.

179. For the text see Müller and Ueberschär (eds), *Kriegsende 1945* doc. 17 dated 29 April 1945, pp. 173–6.

180. M. Steinert, *Die 23 Tage des Regierung Dönitz* (Düsseldorf 1967); W. Ludde-Neurath, *Regierung Dönitz. Die letzten Tage des Dritten Reiches* (Leoni 1981).

181. Wolfgang Benz, *Potsdam 1945. Besatzungsherrschaft und Neuaufbau im Vier-Zonen Deutschland* (Munich 1986) pp. 119ff.

182. Arieh Kochavi, *Prelude to Nuremberg. Allied War Crimes Policy and the Quest for Punishment* (Chapel Hill 1998) p. 85.

183. H. Graml, *Die Allierten und die Teilung Deutschlands. Konflikte und*

Entscheidungen 1941–1948 (Frankfurt am Main 1985) and Benz, *Potsdam 1945* are the most comprehensive and expert discussions.

184. D'Este, *Genius for War* pp. 733–8.
185. D. Volkogonov, *Stalin. Triumph and Tragedy* (London 1991) pp. 498–9.
186. On Potsdam see Herbert Feis, *Between War and Peace. The Potsdam Conference* (Princeton 1960) pp. 155ff.
187. Naimark, *The Russians in Germany* p. 146.
188. For the above see mainly K. D. Henke, 'Der Weg nach Potsdam', in W. Benz (ed.), *Die Vertreibung der Deutschen aus dem Osten* (Frankfurt am Main 1985) pp. 49ff.
189. J. Henke, 'Exodus aus Ostpreussen und Schlesien', in Benz (ed.), *Die Vertreibung* pp. 102–4.
190. For these insights see Jürgen Kocka, '1945. Neubeginn oder Restauration?', in C. Stern and H. Winkler (eds), *Wendepunkte deutscher Geschichte 1848–1990* (Frankfurt am Main 1994) pp. 170–1.
191. For the above see mainly Naimark, *The Russians in Germany* pp. 156–93.
192. David Reynolds, 'The Big Three and the Division of Europe 1945–1948', *Diplomacy and Statecraft* (1990) 1, p. 123.
193. For a good comparative account see K.-D. Henke and H. Wöller (eds), *Politische Säuberung in Europa. Die Abrechnung mit Faschismus und Kollaboration nach dem Zweiten Weltkrieg* (Munich 1991).
194. Clemens Vollnhals, 'Entnazifizierung. Politische Säuberung unter alliierter Herrschaft', in Volkmann (ed.), *Ende des Dritten Reiches* p. 378.
195. See R. Knigge-Tesche (ed.), *Internierungspraxis in Ost- und Westdeutschland nach 1945* (Erfurt 1993).
196. See Michael Marrus, *The Nuremberg War Crimes Trial 1945–46. A Documentary History* (New York 1997); Telford Taylor, *Anatomy of the Nuremberg Trials* (Boston 1992); John and Ann Tusa, *The Nuremberg Trial* (London 1983).
197. See Bogdan Musial, 'NS-Kriegsverbrecher vor polnischen Gerichten', *VfZ* (1999) 47, pp. 53–6.
198. See Martin Broszat, 'Siegerjustiz oder Strafrechtliche "Selbstreinigung"', *VfZ* (1981). 29, pp. 540–3 and the series of verdicts contained in *Justiz und NS-Verbrechen. Sammlung deutscher Strafurteile wegen nationalsozialistischer Tötungsverbrechen 1945–1966* (Amsterdam 1978–81).
199. Clemens Vollnhals, 'Die evangelische Kirche', in M. Broszat, K.-D. Henke and H. Wöller (eds), *Von Stalingrad bis zur Währungsreform* (Munich 1988) p. 143.
200. See D. Cesarani, 'Great Britain', in David Wyman (ed.), *The World Reacts to the Holocaust* (Baltimore 1996) pp. 610–14.
201. Kochavi, *Prelude to Nuremberg* pp. 243–5.
202. Fritz Stern, 'Germany Revisited. Berlin 1954', in his *The Failure of Illiberalism* (New York 1992) p. 216.

203. Naimark, *The Russians in Germany* p. 360.
204. See Georg Meyer, 'Soldaten ohne Armee', in Broszat *et al.* (eds), *Vom Stalingrad bis zur Währungsreform* pp. 683ff.
205. Naimark, *The Russians in Germany* p. 440.
206. Brewster Chamberlin, 'Todesmühlen. Ein früher Versuch zur Massen-"Umerziehung" im besetzten Deutschland 1945–1946', *VfZ* (1981) 29, pp. 420–36.

SELECT BIBLIOGRAPHY

A comprehensive bibliography on National Socialism, and related subjects, would fill a few volumes of this length. Such an exercise, valuable in itself, is superfluous in this context. Readers will find Helen Kehr and Janet Langmaid, *The Nazi Era 1919–1945. A Selected Bibliography of Published Works from the Early Roots to 1980* (London 1982) both helpful and undaunting. Here I offer nothing more than a selection of titles with a bearing on a particular approach, together with some books and shorter studies of outstanding merit on specific subjects. More specialist works are cited in the notes to each chapter.

Starting with **general** works, there are many guides to twentieth-century European history and politics. The best is by François Furet, a leading historian of the French Revolution, *The Passing of an Illusion* (Chicago 1999), which underlines the enormous contribution made by French historians to contemporary history. There is also much in Paul Johnson's excellent *A History of Modern Times* (London 1983). For a brilliant account of intellectual climates, see Karl Dietrich Bracher, *The Age of Ideologies. A History of Political Thought in the Twentieth Century* (London 1984). Robert Conquest's *Reflections on a Ravaged Century* (London 1999) is an Anglo-American old master's account of the impact of 'Ideas', of the bigger variety, and of his hopes for the future. Stanley Payne, *A History of Fascism 1914–1945* (London 1995) is an amazingly knowledgeable overview of the pre- and inter-war fascist movements and regimes. Readers prepared to peep occasionally over the borders of Germany will find much of interest in Richard J. Crampton's outstanding *Eastern Europe in the Twentieth Century* (London 1994). Both James Joll, *Europe since 1870* (London 1980) and Mark Mazower, *Dark Continent* (London 1999) are stylish accounts of modern European history in general, from a centre-left point of view. Valuable comparative studies include Martin Blinkhorn (ed.), *Fascists and Conservatives* (London 1990) and Ian Kershaw and Moshe Lewin (eds), *Stalinism and Nazism. Dictatorships in Comparison* (Cambridge 1998).

There is a growing body of work on **political religions**, though some titles are not easy to find. Norman Cohn, *The Pursuit of the Millennium. Revolutionary*

Millenarians and Mystical Anarchists of the Middle Ages (London 1957); Eric Voegelin, *Die politische Religionen* (Munich 1996); Raymond Aron, 'Les Religions séculières', *Une Histoire du XXe siècle* (Paris 1996) pp. 139–222; Jacob Talmon, *The Origins of Totalitarian Democracy* (London 1952); *idem*, *Political Messianism. The Romantic Phase* (London 1960); and *idem*, *Myth of the Nation and Vision of Revolution. Ideological Polarization in the Twentieth Century* (New Brunswick 1991) are all essential starting points. For a fascinating series of essays on Talmon's ideas see Israel Academy of Sciences and Humanities (ed.), *International Colloquium in Memory of Jacob L. Talmon* (Jerusalem 1984). The important studies of the late Uriel Tal can be sampled in his 'Aspects of the Consecration of Politics in the Nazi Era', in O. D. Kulka and P. R. Mendes-Flohr (eds), *Judaism and Christianity under the Impact of National Socialism 1919–1945* (Jerusalem 1987) pp. 63–95. Excellent recent introductions to the general theme of political religions include Jean-Pierre Sironneau, *Sécularisation et religions politiques* (Paris 1982) and Hans Maier, *Politische Religionen. Die totalitären Regime und das Christentum* (Freiburg 1995) and his edited collection, *Totalitarismus und Politische Religionen* (Paderborn 1996). English readers should also consult Philippe Burrin, 'Political Religion. The Relevance of a Concept', *History & Memory* (1997) 9, pp. 321–52, and George L. Mosse, 'Towards a General Theory of Fascism', in his *The Fascist Revolution* (New York 1999) pp. 1–44. Emilio Gentile's *The Sacralisation of Politics in Fascist Italy* (Cambridge, Mass. 1996) brings a similar approach to bear on Italian Fascism in a book of great insight and style, as does Arthur J. Klinghoffer's *Red Apocalypse* (Lanham 1996) for the Soviet Union. Works which apply this approach specifically to National Socialist Germany include Klaus Vondung's *Magie und Manipulation. Ideologischer Kult und politische Religion des National-sozialismus* (Göttingen 1971), Michael Ley and Julius H. Schoeps (eds), *Der Nationalsozialismus als politische Religion* (Bodenheim 1997) and Claus-Ekkehard Bärsch, *Die politische Religion des Nationalsozialismus* (Munich 1998). English readers might consult James Rhodes, *The Hitler Movement. A Modern Millenarian Revolution* (Stanford 1980) and Robert Pois, *National Socialism and the Religion of Nature* (Beckenham 1986).

Books on **totalitarian** ideologies, movements and regimes are abundant, although many are available only in specialist libraries or from on-line secondhand book dealers. An older, but still useful, collection of essays is Carl J. Friedrich (ed.), *Totalitarianism* (Cambridge, Mass. 1954); an equally useful but more recent collection is Ellen Frankel Paul (ed.), *Totalitarianism at the Crossroads* (New Brunswick 1990). Impressive German collections on the history, and uses, of the concept include Eckhard Jesse (ed.), *Totalitarismus im 20. Jahrhundert* (Baden-Baden 1996) and Alfons Söllner (ed.), *Totalitaris-mus. Eine Ideengeschichte des 20. Jahrhundert* (Berlin 1997). Probably the best critical defence of the term is Leonard Shapiro, *Totalitarianism* (London 1972), although there is much of interest too in Hans Buchheim, *Totalitäre Herrschaft. Wesen und Merkmale* (Munich 1962). For the classical texts see Hannah Arendt, *The Origins of Totalitarianism* (London 1958), a difficult book, perhaps best read in conjunction with Margaret Canovan, *The Political Thought of Hannah Arendt* (London 1974); Carl J. Friedrich and Zbigniew K. Brzezinski, *Totalitarian Dictatorship and Autocracy* (New York 1963); and Raymond Aron, *Democracy and Totalitarianism* (New York 1965). Those interested in Aron should consult Tony Judt, *The Burden of Responsibility. Blum, Camus and Aron and the French Twentieth Century* (Chicago 1998) and Brian Anderson, *Raymond Aron* (Lanham 1997). Spirited defences of the concept against its detractors include Walter Z. Laqueur, *The Dream that Failed. Reflections on the Soviet Union* (Oxford 1994) and Karl Dietrich Bracher, *Turning Points in Modern Times* (Cambridge, Mass. 1995) and his *Die totalitäre Erfahrung* (Munich 1987). The detractors' case is ably précised by Abbott Gleason, *Totalitarianism. An Inner History of the Cold War* (Oxford 1995). See also Ian Kershaw, 'Totalitarianism Revisited. Nazism and Stalinism in Comparative Perspective', *Tel Aviver Jahrbuch für deutsche Geschichte* (1994) 23, pp. 23–40 for a less *parti pris* critique, which recognises some merit in the concept.

There are any number of **histories of modern Germany,** many so indebted to hackneyed sociological models that they might have been produced by an inhuman agency. By contrast, the brilliant, individualistic and highly literate account by Gordon C. Craig, *Germany 1866–1945* (Oxford 1978) remains reliable and unrivalled on essentials. Those seeking elegant but thoughtful brevity should seek out Harold James, *A German Identity 1770–1990* (London 1989) and Peter G. Pulzer's *Germany 1870–1945. Politics, State Formation, and War* (Oxford 1997). Essential themes in modern German history, namely the role of illiberal anti-Western ideologies or the various depths of antisemitism are sensitively discussed by Fritz Stern in two important monographs, *The Politics of Cultural Despair. A Study of the Rise of Germanic Ideology* (Berkeley 1961) and *Gold and Iron. Bismarck, Bleichröder and the Building of the German Empire* (New York 1977) and in his important essay collections, *Dreams and Delusions. National Socialism in the Drama of the German Past* (New York 1987) and *Einstein's German World* (Princeton 1999). Wolfgang J. Mommsen, *Imperial Germany 1867–1918. Politics, Culture, and Society in an Authoritarian State* (London 1995) and Geoff Eley (ed.), *Society, Culture, and the State in Germany 1870–1930* (Ann Arbor 1998) both contain work of an exceptionally high standard. Important thematic studies covering several periods include George L. Mosse, *The Nationalization of the Masses* (Ithaca 1975) and *The Crisis of German Ideology. Intellectual Origins of the Third Reich* (New York 1981). The history of Christianity in modern Germany is brilliantly discussed in Kurt Nowak's *Geschichte des Christentums in Deutschland. Religion, Politik und Gesellschaft vom Ende der Aufklärung bis zur Mitte des 20. Jahrhunderts* (Munich 1995). Readers will also find much of value in Peter G. Pulzer, *The Rise of Political Antisemitism in Germany and Austria* (originally New York, London 1964) and Shulamit Volkov, *Jüdisches Leben und Antisemitismus im 19. und 20. Jahrhundert* (Munich 1990). Crucial historical turning points between 1848 and the popular counter-revolution of 1989–90 are discussed in an attractive collection edited by Carola Stern and Heinrich August Winkler, *Wendepunkte deutscher Geschichte 1848–1990* (Frankfurt am Main 1994). Charles S. Maier, *The Unmasterable Past. History, Holocaust, and German National Identity* (Cambridge, Mass. 1988) and Michael André Bernstein, *Foregone Conclusions. Against Apocalyptic History* (Berkeley 1994) are in a class of their own, in terms of their insights and style.

Turning to specific periods and subjects, **the impact of the First World War** on German society is sensitively handled by Günther Mai, *Das Ende des Kaiserreichs. Politik und Kriegsführung im Ersten Weltkrieg* (Munich 1987) and by the contributors to the truly outstanding Wolfgang Michalka (ed.), *Der Erste Weltkrieg. Wirkung, Wahrnehmung, Analyse* (Munich 1994). Richard Bessel, *Germany after the First World War* (Oxford 1993) is a judicious account of the socio-economic aftermath of the war. These grim times can be directly savoured through such excellent source collections as Bernd Ulrich and Benjamin Ziemann (eds), *Frontalltag im Ersten Weltkrieg. Wahn und Wirklichkeit* (Frankfurt am Main 1994) and the same duo's *Krieg im Frieden. Die umkämpfte Erinnerung an den Ersten Weltkrieg* (Frankfurt am Main 1997), and Anton Kees, Martin Jay and Edward Dimendburg (eds), *The Weimar Sourcebook* (Berkeley 1995). Modris Ekstein's *Rites of Spring. The Great War and the Birth of the Modern Age* (New York 1989) provides an international perspective.

Turning to **the Weimar Republic,** the most recent international scholarship on Versailles is represented in Manfred Boemeke, Gerald D. Feldman and Elisabeth Glaser (eds), *The Treaty of Versailles. A Reassessment after 75 Years* (Cambridge 1998), while the inflation is comprehensively described in Gerald D. Feldman, *The Great Disorder. Politics, Economics and Society in the German Inflation 1914–1924* (New York 1993). The best general account of the Weimar Republic is Heinrich August Winkler, *Weimar 1918–1933. Die Geschichte der ersten deutschen Demokratie* (Munich 1998), though there is much in E. Kolb, *The Weimar Republic* (London 1988). The essays in Ian Kershaw (ed.), *Weimar. Why Did German Democracy Fail?* (London 1990) are mostly of exceptionally high quality. The Weimar party political scene is brilliantly discussed in Larry Eugene Jones, *German Liberalism and the*

Dissolution of the Weimar Party System 1918–1933 (Chapel Hill 1988); L. E. Jones and James Rettalack (eds), *Between Reform, Reaction and Resistance. Studies in the History of German Conservatism from 1789 to 1945* (Oxford 1993), and L. E. Jones and J. Rettalack (eds), *Elections, Mass Politics and Social Change in Modern Germany* (Cambridge 1992). The clearest guide to the democratic left is Klaus Schönhoven, *Reformismus und Radikalismus. Gespaltene Arbeiterbewegung im Weimarer Sozialstaat* (Munich 1989). Left-wing totalitarian politics are expertly discussed by Conan Fischer, *The German Communists and the Rise of Nazism* (New York 1991), and in two works of great originality of mind by Kai-Uwe Merz, *Das Schreckbild. Deutschland und der Bolshewismus 1917 bis 1921* (Berlin 1995) and Christian Streifler, *Kampf um die Macht. Kommunisten und Nationalsozialisten am Ende der Weimarer Republik* (Berlin 1993). Donald L. Niewyck, *The Jews in Weimar Germany* (Manchester 1980) is still a useful guide. Compelling biographies of Weimar politicians include William L. Patch Jnr's outstanding *Heinrich Brüning and the Dissolution of the Weimar Republic* (Cambridge 1998). The best account of the last years of the Republic remains Karl Dietrich Bracher, *Die Auflösung der Weimarer Republik. Eine Studie des Machtverfalls in der Demokratie* (Villingen 1971). David Crew, *Germans on Welfare. From Weimar to Hitler* (Oxford 1998) replaces virtually everything else written on the effects of the Depression. Henry Ashby Turner's *Hitler's Thirty Days to Power. January 1933* (London 1996) is a brilliant and gripping reminder that nothing is inevitable.

Books on **National Socialism** are superabundant. The finest collection of sources, and moreover one in which the documents are interwoven with a fascinating analytical narrative, is the four volumes of Jeremy Noakes and Geoffrey Pridham (eds), *Nazism 1919–1945. A Documentary Reader* (Exeter 1983–8). The best one-volume history remains Karl Dietrich Bracher's formidable *The German Dictatorship* (London 1970). Those admirable journals, the *Vierteljahreshefte für Zeitgeschichte* (Stuttgart 1953–), especially the bibliographic supplements, and the *Tel Aviver Jahrbuch für deutsche Geschichte* (1972–) are indispensable for keeping abreast of the avalanche of material. The most authoritative reference work on the entire period is Wolfgang Benz, Hermann Graml and Hermann Wesse (eds), *Enzyklopädie des Nationalsozialismus* (Munich 1998). There are also two decent historical atlases: Michael Freeman, *Atlas of Nazi Germany. A Political, Economic and Social Anatomy of the Third Reich* (2nd edn, London 1995) and Richard J. Overy, *The Penguin Historical Atlas of the Third Reich* (London 1996). Readers a little rusty on the history, or location, of Latvia or Romania should consult Richard and Ben Crampton, *Atlas of Eastern Europe in the Twentieth Century* (London 1996), which is a model of its kind. There are innumerable essay collections on the Nazi period; the best is probably Walter H. Pehle (ed.), *Der historische Ort des Nationalsozialismus. Annäherungen* (Frankfurt am Main 1990). The most reliable guide to some of the key historiographical issues is Ian Kershaw, *The Nazi Dictatorship* (London 1995), although, obviously enough, the present author has a more old-fashioned view on the utility of the term totalitarian.

Theodore Abel, *Why Hitler Came to Power* (originally 1938, Cambridge, Mass. 1986) is a crucial starting point for the self-understanding of the Nazi followers whom he got to write autobiographical accounts. The Nazi Party's electoral fortunes have been most convincingly analysed in Jürgen Falter's *Hitlers Wähler* (Munich 1991) although there is much of value in the less dry account by Thomas Childers, *The Nazi Voter* (Chapel Hill 1983). Virtually every region or major town in Germany has been the subject of detailed researches. The finest of these are Jeremy Noakes, *The Nazi Party in Lower Saxony 1921–1933* (Oxford 1971); Geoffrey Pridham, *Hitler's Rise to Power. The Nazi Movement in Bavaria 1923–33* (London 1973); Martin Broszat and Elke Fröhlich (eds), *Bayern in der NS-Zeit* (Munich 1977–83) six volumes; Frank Bajohr (ed.), *Norddeutschland im Nationalsozialismus* (Hamburg 1993); and Horst Möller, Andrea Wirsching and Walter Ziegler (eds), *Nationalsozialismus in der Region. Beiträge zur regionalen und lokalen Forschungen und zum internationalen Vergleich* (Munich 1996) – all excellent guides to local or regional themes. Bruce Pauley, *Hitler and the Forgotten Nazis. A History of Austrian National Socialism* (Chapel Hill 1981) is a useful reminder of developments beyond Germany's borders. Peter Fritzsche, *Germans into Nazis* (Cambridge, Mass. 1998) is a stylish account of grassroots political culture, with a real breath of life about it. What might be termed the Ken Loach school of wishful thinking about the relationship between capitalism and fascism was comprehensively demolished by Henry Ashby Turner's *German Big Business and the Rise of Hitler* (Oxford 1985). Nazi propaganda has attracted much exceptionally leaden writing; a singular exception is Gerhard Paul's lively *Aufstand der Bilder. Die NS-Propaganda vor 1933* (Bonn 1992), which is a masterpiece of historical writing and the analysis of images.

The best **biographies** include Joachim Fest's literary masterpiece *Hitler* (London 1974) and Ian Kershaw's epic *Hitler 1889–1936. Hubris* (London 1998) and *Hitler 1937–1945. Nemesis* (London 2000). Readers less concerned to be up-to-the-minute will find much of value in Konrad Heiden's recently reissued *Der Führer* (London 2000 reprint of 1944 original). Those unwilling to devote more than an afternoon to Hitler should try Norman Stone, *Hitler* (London 1980), written with his characteristic energy and insight. Eberhard Jäckel's *Hitlers Weltanschauung. Entwurf einer Herrschaft* (Stuttgart 1981) remains the most convincing exposition of Hitler's synthetic ideology. Readers who can overcome a natural abhorrence for the self-righteous original, might dip into Max Domarus (ed.), *Hitler. Speeches and Proclamations 1932–1945* (London 1990–7) three volumes, since many otherwise excellent biographies omit any extended examples of the only 'quality' they routinely ascribe to the dictator, namely his oratory. For the rest of the B-movie cast, the most astute group portrait is Joachim C. Fest's *The Face of the Third Reich* (London 1979). The best biographies include Richard J. Overy's compelling *Göring. The Iron Man* (London 1983) and Joseph Ackermann, *Heinrich Himmler als Ideologe* (Göttingen 1976). Ralf Georg Reuth, *Goebbels* (London 1993) and Reuth (ed.), *Joseph Goebbels. Tagebücher* (Munich 1992) five volumes, the latter excellent guides to the *ressentiment*s of Hitler's Berlin Gauleiter and Progaganda Minister. One has to venture much further down the Nazi feeding chain, to Ulrich Herbert's *Best. Biographische Studien über Radikalismus, Weltanschauung und Vernunft 1903–1989* (Bonn 1996), to find anything of equivalent depth and insight about a lesser Nazi figure. Brief biographical sketches, admittedly often written in the costive style of PhDs, of major and mid-echelon Nazi apparatchiks, are collated in Rainer Zitelmann, Ronald Smelser and Enrico Syring (eds), *Die braune Elite* (Darmstadt 1990–) three volumes.

The great lawyer–scholar Leonard Schapiro's essay 'The Importance of Law in the Study of Politics and History', in Ellen Dahrendorf (ed.), *Leonard Schapiro. Russian Studies* (New York 1987) pp. 29–44 is an excellent reminder that 'legal history' is not just another 'sub-specialism'. The best account of the Nazis' **destruction of the rule of law** is Lothar Gruchmann's monumental *Justiz im Dritten Reich 1930–1940. Anpassung und Unterwerfung in der Ära Gürtner* (Munich 1990). Much can be learned from M. Stolleis, *The Law under the Swastika* (Chicago 1998) and Ralph Angermund, *Deutsche Richterschaft 1919–1945* (Frankfurt am Main 1990) on the judiciary. Readers interested in legal history should also consult F. Burin and K. Shell (eds), *Politics, Law and Social Change. Selected Essays of Otto Kirschheimer* (New York 1969). The Nazi **police state and its social context** are deftly analysed by the contributors to Gerhard Paul and Klaus-Michael Mallmann (eds), *Die Gestapo. Mythos und Realität* (Darmstadt 1996). Delation is ably dealt with in Robert Gellately, *The Gestapo and German Society* (Oxford 1988). The SS Security Service has been brilliantly reconstructed by S. Aronson, *Reinhard Heydrich und die früh Geschichte von Gestapo und SD* (Stuttgart 1971). Lütz Hachmeister, *Der Gegnerforscher. Die Karriere des SS-Führers Franz Alfred Six* (Munich 1998) traces one man's odyssey from resentful student radical to resentful secret policeman. For readers with strong stomachs for other people's misery, the best evocations of **the concentration camps** include K. Schilde and J. Tuchel (eds), *Columbia-Haus. Berliner Konzentrationslager 1933–1936* (Berlin 1990); G. Mörsch (ed.), *Konzentrationslager Oranienburg* (Berlin 1997); and Gordon J. Horwitz, *In the Shadow of Death. Living Outside the Gates of Mauthausen* (London 1991). Direct experience of existence in a Nazi camp is relayed in David Hackett (ed.), *The Buchenwald Report* (Boulder 1996). Tzvetan Todorov, *Facing the Extremes. Moral Life in the Concentration Camps* (New York 1997) is an excellent comparative study of human decencies in the Nazi camps and Soviet gulags.

Interest in **eugenics and 'euthanasia'** in both the German and wider international contexts has grown considerably in recent years. The Australian philosopher John Passmore, provides a longer perspective on this quest in his *The Perfectibility of Man* (London 1970). On eugenics in general, Daniel Kevles, *In the Name of Eugenics. Genetics and the Uses of Human Heredity* (London 1986) is still unrivalled. The classic account of events in Germany, studiously ignored when it appeared in 1948, is Alice Platen-Hallermund, *Die Tötung Geisteskranker in Deutschland* (reprinted Bonn 1993). The complexities of the issues involved are best illustrated by Paul Weindling, *Health, Race and German Politics between National Unification and Nazism 1870–1945* (Cambridge 1989), a book unmarred by an anti-scientific 'spirit' fashionable among some academics and moralists. Eugenicist continuities between Weimar and the Nazi period are traced in Michael Burleigh, *Death and Deliverance. Euthanasia in Germany c. 1900–1945* (Cambridge 1994), with peripheral modification by Michael Schwartz, 'Euthanasie Debatten in Deutschland (1895–1945)', *VfZ* (1998) 46, pp. 617–65. More originally, see Schwartz, *Sozialistische Eugenik* (Bonn 1995). Berhard Richarz, *Heilen, Pflegen, Toten. Zur Alltagsgeschichte einer Heil- und Pflegeanstalt bis zum Ende des Nationalsozialismus* (Göttingen 1987) is a meticulous guide to medicalised atrocities in a Munich asylum, as is Heinz Faulstich, *Von der Irrenfürsorge zur 'Euthanasie'. Geschichte der badischen Psychiatrie bis 1945* (Freiburg im Breisgau 1993), which deserves to be translated for a wider public. Kurt Nowak, *'Euthanasie' und Sterilisation im 'Dritten Reich'. Die Konfrontation der evangelischen und katholischen Kirche mit dem Gesetz zur Verhütung Erbkranken Nachwuchses und der 'Euthanasie'-Aktion* (2nd edn, Göttingen 1984) is authoritative and balanced on the responses of the Churches to eugenic policies, and quite uncontaminated by the GDR historical line. The standard work on 'euthanasia' remains Ernst Klee, *'Euthanasie' in NS-Staat* (Frankfurt am Main 1983). Much Nazi unpleasantness can be ferreted out of the series *Beiträge zur nationalsozialistischen Gesundheits- und Sozialpolitik* (Berlin 1985–) thirteen volumes. For a more subtle approach to these questions see Uwe Gerrens' outstandingly good *Medizinisches Ethos und theologiche Ethik. Karl und Dietrich Bonhoeffer in der Auseinandersetzung um Zwangssterilisation und 'Euthanasie' im Nationalsozialismus* (Munich 1996).

There is a voluminous literature on Nazi **antisemitism** prior to the wartime
Holocaust. References to much of this can be found in the bibliography of
Saul Friedländer's important and monumental *Nazi Germany and the Jews.
The Years of Persecution 1933–1939* (London 1998). The best short account
is Michael Marrus, 'The Theory and Practice of Antisemitism', *Commentary*
(1982) 74, pp. 38–42. Avraham Barkai, *From Boycott to Annihilation. The
Economic Struggle of German Jews 1933–1945* (Brandeis 1989), Hermann
Graml, *Antisemitism in the Third Reich* (Oxford 1992) and Walter H. Pehle
(ed.), *November 1938. From 'Kristallnacht' to Genocide* (Oxford 1991) are
all important too. Ursula Büttner (ed.), *Die Deutschen und die Judenverfolgung im Dritten Reich* (Hamburg 1992) and Arno Herzig and Ina Lorenz
(eds), *Verdrängung und Vernichtung der Juden unter dem Nationalsozialismus*
(Hamburg 1992) contain good detailed studies. Anna Drabek, Wolfgang
Hausler, Kurt Schubert, Karl Stühlpfarrer and Nikolaus Vielmetti, *Das
österreichische Judentum. Voraussetzungen und Geschichte* (Vienna 1988)
and Bruce Pauley, *From Prejudice to Persecution. A History of Austrian Antisemitism* (Chapel Hill 1992) supply a wider context. Victor Klemperer, *I
Shall Bear Witness. The Diaries of Victor Klemperer* (London 1998–9) is an
indispensable contemporary source, as is Michael Wildt (ed.), *Die Judenpolitik
des SD 1935 bis 1938* (Munich 1995) for the mindset of bureaucratic
perpetrators. Readers should also try George Clare, *Last Waltz in Vienna*
(London 1994), both a record and a work of literary genius. The broader
racist context is discussed by Michael Burleigh and Wolfgang Wippermann,
The Racial State. Germany 1933–1945 (Cambridge 1991), while Michael
Zimmermann's *Rassenutopie und Genozid. Die nationalsozialistiche 'Lösung
der Zigeunerfrage'* (Hamburg 1996) is a meticulous account of the persecution
of Sinti and Roma or 'Gypsies'.

Despite its obvious biases, which in this context are no demerit, the most
detailed contemporary observations on **life under the Nazi regime** during the
1930s were collected as the *Deutschland-Berichte der Sozialdemokratischen
Partei Deutschlands (SOPADE) 1934–1940* (reprinted Frankfurt am Main
1980) in seven volumes. Heinz Boberach (ed.), *Meldungen aus dem Reich.
Die geheimen Lageberichte des Sicherheitsdienstes der SS 1938–1945*
(Herrsching 1985) seventeen volumes, is essential for studying the German
population during the war years. Much can be learned about work and
workers from Joan Campbell, *Joy in Work, German Work. The National
Debate 1800–1945* (Princeton 1989) and Günther Mörsch, *Arbeit und Brot.
Studien zu Lage, Stimmung, Einstellung und Verhalten der deutschen Arbeiterschaft 1933–1936/37* (Frankfurt am Main 1993). Heinrich August Winkler's special issue, 'Arbeit und Arbeiter im "Dritten Reich"', *GuG* (1989)
volume 15 is also indispensable. Hitler's pre-war motorway *grand projet* is
brilliantly exposed as a sham by Erhard Schulz and Eckhard Gruber, *Mythos

Reichsautobahn. Bau und Inszenierung der 'Strassen des Führers' 1933–1941 (Berlin 1996). The most succinct introductions to Nazi **economic policies**, about which this author claims not the slightest expertise, are Richard J. Overy, *The Nazi Economic Recovery 1932–1938* (2nd edn Cambridge 1996); Avraham Barkai, *Nazi Economics. Ideology, Theory and Policy* (Oxford 1990); and Harold James, *The German Slump. Politics and Economics 1924–1936* (Oxford 1986). For the strategies of a major industrial corporation see Peter Hayes, *Industry and Ideology. I.G. Farben in the Nazi Era* (Cambridge 1987). Indispensable guides to the rural sector of the economy include J. E. Farquharson, *The Plough and the Swastika. The NSDAP and Agriculture in Germany 1928–1945* (London 1976) and Gustavo Corni, *Hitler and the Peasants. Agrarian Policy in the Third Reich* (Oxford 1990). Nazi racial 'welfarism' is given detailed treatment by Young-Sun Hong, *Welfare, Modernity, and the Weimar State 1919–1933* (Princeton 1998) and by Christoph Sachsse and Florian Tennstedt, *Der Wohlfahrsstaat im Nationalsozialismus. Geschichte der Armenfürsorge in Deutschland* vol. 3 (Stuttgart 1992). The, by turns, bathetic, energetic, pompous and tawdry **surface display** of the Nazi regime is well conveyed in Hans-Joachim Gamm, *Der braune Kult* (Hamburg 1962) and Peter Reichel, *Der Schöne Schein des Dritten Reiches. Faszination und Gewalt des Faschismus* (Munich 1991); Sabine Behrenbeck, *Der Kult um die toten Helden. Nationalsozialistische Mythen, Riten und Symbole* (Vierow 1996) is an excellent account of the adolescent morbidity and plangency which often characterised Nazi public ceremonials, while Ian Kershaw's *The 'Hitler Myth'. Image and Reality in the Third Reich* (Oxford 1987) is the best analysis of the social context of the Führer-cult. Nazi sentimentalisation of motherhood is well treated by Irmgard Weyrauther, *Muttertag und Mutterkreuz. Der Kult um die 'deutsche Mutter' im Nationalsozialismus* (Frankfurt am Main 1993). Attempts to conform Protestantism to Nazism are chronicled in Doris L. Bergen, *Twisted Cross. The German Christian Movement in the Third Reich* (Chapel Hill 1996). Relations between **the army and the Nazi regime** are fluently treated by Gordon Craig, *The Politics of the Prussian Army 1640–1945* (Oxford 1955); Wilhelm Deist, *The Wehrmacht and German Rearmament* (London 1981); and Klaus-Jurgen Müller, *The Army, Politics and Society in Germany 1933–45* (Manchester 1987). Martin Broszat and Klaus Schwabe (eds), *Die deutschen Eliten und der Weg in den Zweiten Weltkrieg* (Munich 1989) is a comprehensive guide to relations between the Nazis and Germany's other major elite groups. J. S. Conway, *The Nazi Persecution of the Churches 1933–45* (London 1968) is still peerless on that subject. Jeremy Noakes, 'Nazism and High Society', in Michael Burleigh (ed.), *Confronting the Nazi Past* (London 1996) pp. 51–65 supplies an important subjective element, namely value judgements about personalities, often missing from academic accounts. Perhaps openly saying that most of these people were disgusting human beings would considerably diminish the point of endlessly raking over them.

By contrast, there seems much point in studying those brave enough to resist such a dread regime, regardless of whether the **resistance** hailed from conservative or socialist, Christian or Jewish groups and individuals. Most of the top chaps who study the subject are represented in Jürgen Schmädeke and Peter Steinbach (eds), *Der Widerstand gegen den Nationalsozialismus* (Munich 1994). Gregor Schöllgen's biography *A Conservative against Hitler. Ulrich von Hassell* (London 1991) is a good companion to *The von Hassell Diaries* (Boulder 1994). Other excellent studies include Klemens von Klemperer, *German Resistance to Hitler. The Search for Allies Abroad 1938–1945* (Oxford 1992) and Peter Hoffmann, *The History of German Resistance to Hitler 1933–1945* (3rd edn Montreal 1996). The English have also made substantial contributions in this area, notably Michael Balfour, *Withstanding Hitler in Germany 1933–45* (London 1988) and (with J. Frisby) *Helmuth von Moltke. A Leader against Hitler* (London 1972). Beate Ruhm von Oppen (ed.), *Helmuth von Moltke. Letters to Freya* (London 1991) is an uplifting intimate source. The best essay collections on this theme include Hedley Bull (ed.), *The Challenge of the Third Reich. The Adam von Trott Memorial Lectures* (Oxford 1986); Richard Löwenthal and Patrik von zur Mühlen (eds), *Widerstand und Verweigerung in Deutschland 1933 bis 1945* (Bonn 1984); Hermann Graml (ed.), *Widerstand im Dritten Reich. Probleme, Ereignisse, Gestalten* (Frankfurt am Main 1984); and David Clay Large (ed.), *Contending with Hitler. Varieties of German Resistance in the Third Reich* (Cambridge 1991). Arnold Paucker, *Jewish Resistance in Germany. The Facts and the Problems* (Berlin 1991) is a very useful pamphlet in a series produced by the German Resistance Memorial Center, Berlin.

The literature on **occupied Europe** mainly focuses on different national experiences. Some significant comparative exceptions include Werner Rings, *Life with the Enemy. Collaboration and Resistance in Hitler's Europe 1939–1945* (New York 1982); Yves Durand, *Le Nouvel Ordre européen nazi 1938–1945* (Paris 1990); Pascal Ory, *Les Collaborateurs 1940–1945* (Paris 1976); and Werner Röhr (ed.), *Okkupation und Kollaboration (1938–1945)* (Berlin 1994). This is part of an eight-volume series now edited by the Bundesarchiv, *Europa unterm Hakenkreuz* (Berlin, Heidelberg 1989–), which is the key source collection for individual German occupations. Important works on resistance include M. R. D. Foot, *Resistance. European Resistance to Nazism 1940–45* (London 1976) and Rab Bennett, *Under the Shadow of the Swastika. The Moral Dilemmas of Resistance and Collaboration in Hitler's Europe* (London 1999). The best studies of occupied countries include Robert Bohn (ed.), *Die deutsche Herrschaft in den 'germanischen' Ländern*

1940–1945 (Wiesbaden 1997); which together with Oddvar Hoidal, *Vidkun Quisling. A Study in Treason* (London 1989) and Hans Frederik Dahl, *Quisling* (Cambridge 1999) are essential reading for the occupation of Norway. Gerhard Hirschfeld's *Nazi Rule and Dutch Collaboration. The Netherlands under German Occupation 1940–1945* (Oxford 1988) is excellent, as is Mark Mazower, *Inside Hitler's Greece. The Experience of Occupation 1941–1944* (New Haven 1993). Martin Conway, *Collaboration in Belgium. Léon Degrelle and the Rexist Movement* (New Haven 1993) is utterly fascinating. The best accounts of Vichy France are Robert Paxton, *Vichy France. Old Guard and New Order 1940–1944* (New York 1972) and Philippe Burrin, *Living with Defeat. France under the German Occupation 1940–1944* (London 1996). An excellent collection of essays is Jean-Pierre Azema and François Bedarida (eds), *Le Régime de Vichy et les français* (Paris 1992). Geoffrey Warner, *Pierre Laval and the Eclipse of France* (London 1968) is a marvellous biography, while Michael Marrus and Robert Paxton, *Vichy France and the Jews* (New York 1983) was seminal on how the Vichy regime anticipated Nazi policy in this area.

Nazi–Soviet collusion at the expense of the Baltic States, Poland and the peace of Europe is dealt with brilliantly by Aleksandr M. Nekrich, *Pariahs, Partners, Predators. German–Soviet Relations 1922–1941* (New York 1997) and Erwin Oberländer (ed.), *Hitler–Stalin-Pakt 1939. Das Ende Ostmitteleuropas?* (Frankfurt am Main 1989). Gustav Herling, *A World Apart* (Oxford 1987) is a moving account of a Pole's imprisonment by the Soviet NKVD. The longer-term perspective on German attitudes towards the East is provided by Wolfgang Wippermann's masterly *Der Deutsche 'Drang nach Osten'. Ideologie und Wirklichkeit eines politischen Schlagwortes* (Darmstadt 1981), Fritz T. Epstein, *Germany and the East. Selected Essays* ed. Robert F. Byrnes (Bloomington 1973); and Walter Laqueur, *Russia and Germany. A Century of Conflict* (New Brunswick 1990). The academic contribution to the destabilisation and dismemberment of Poland is discussed in Michael Burleigh, *Germany Turns Eastwards. A Study of 'Ostforschung' in the Third Reich* (Cambridge 1988), a book which has yet to appear in German. Nazi policy in occupied Poland has been well covered, notably by Martin Broszat, *Nationalsozialistische Polenpolitik 1939–1945* (Stuttgart 1961); Christoph Klessmann, *Die Selbstbehauptung einer Nation. NS-Kulturpolitik und polnische Widerstandsbewegung* (Düsseldorf 1971); Czesław Madajczyk, *Die Okkupationspolitik Nazideutschlands in Polen 1939–1945* (Cologne 1988); and Jan Thomas Gross, *Polish Society under German Occupation* (Princeton 1979). An outstanding survey of foreign forced, or as many prefer to call it slave, labour is Ulrich Herbert, *Hitler's Foreign Workers. Enforced Foreign Labor in Germany under the Third Reich* (Cambridge 1997).

The uniquely barbarous character of **the war against the Soviet Union** has often been rehearsed. Both Alexander Werth, *Russia at War 1941–1945* (London 1964) and Vasily Grossman, *Life and Fate* (London 1985) have the immediacy and insights one would expect from a first-rate journalist and a novelist of genius. Good academic accounts of the war are John Erikson, *The Road to Stalingrad* (London 1975) and *The Road to Berlin. Stalin's War with Germany* (London 1983), though there is a less costive study by Richard J. Overy, *Russia's War* (London 1997), which is informed and fairminded on subjects where hysteria or sentimentality are sometimes rampant. The most recent archival research is contained in the Frank Cass Series on Soviet Military Theory and Practice volumes by Colonel David M. Glantz (ed.), *The Initial Period of War on the Eastern Front. 22 June–August 1941* (London 1993); *From the Don to the Dnepr. Soviet Offensive Operations. December 1942–August 1943* (London 1991); ed. with Harold S. Orenstein, *The Battle for Kursk 1943. The Soviet General Staff Study* (London 1999); *Soviet Military Deception in the Second World War* (London 1989); *Soviet Military Intelligence in War* (London 1990); and *A History of Soviet Airborne Forces* (London 1994). The Cass *Journal of Slavic Military Studies* (1988–) contains the latest American, Russian and Ukrainian research. Good histories of Soviet irregular warfare are Leonid Grenkovich, *The Soviet Partisan Movement 1941–1944* (London 1999) and the older Matthew Cooper, *The Phantom War. The German Struggle against Soviet Partisans* (London 1979). Despite its tone, there is good detailed research in Hannes Heer and Klaus Naumann (eds), *Vernichtungskrieg. Verbrechen der Wehrmacht 1941–1944* (Hamburg 1995), although that chronology begs several questions about events in Poland from 1939 onwards. For less excitable accounts, see Gerd R. Ueberschär and Wolfram Wette (eds), *Der deutsche Überfall auf die Sowjetunion. 'Unternehmung Barbarossa' 1941* (Frankfurt am Main 1991); Horst Boog, Jürgen Forster, Joachim Hoffmann, Ernst Klink, Rolf-Dieter Müller and Gerd R. Ueberschär, *Der Angriff auf die Sowjetunion* (Frankfurt am Main 1991); and above all Bernd Wegner (ed.), *Zwei Wege nach Moskau. Vom Hitler–Stalin Pakt zum 'Unternehmung Barbarossa'* (Munich 1991). For two excellent, but utterly different, accounts of the Battle of Stalingrad, see Wolfram Wette and Gerd R. Ueberschär, *Stalingrad. Mythos und Wirklichkeit einer Schlacht* (Frankfurt am Main 1993) and Anthony Beevor, *Stalingrad* (London 1998), deservedly a bestseller. The terrible fate of (Soviet) captives is dealt with by Christian Streit, *Keine Kameraden. Die Wehrmacht und die sowjetischen Kriegsgefangenen 1941–1945* (Bonn 1991); what happened to them after their 'liberation' or 'repatriation' can be followed in Aleksandr Solzhenitsyn, *The Gulag Archipelago* (London 1986). The Nazi war against the former Soviet Union consisted of occupation as well as major setpiece battles. The best guide to this is Timothy Mulligan, *The Politics of Illusion and Empire. German Occupation Policy in the Soviet Union 1942–43* (New York 1988), although the older Alexander Dallin's *German Rule in Russia 1941–1945* (London 1981) has many hidden insights amid its tortuous prose. Rolf-Dieter Müller, *Hitlers Ostkrieg und die deutsche Siedlungspolitik* (Frankfurt am Main 1991) is excellent on industrial and military thinking about the future of the occupied territories. The Soviet domestic war effort is best approached through John Barber and Mark Harrison, *The Soviet Home Front 1941–1945* (London 1991), not forgetting Edwin Bacon, *The Gulag at War. Stalin's Forced Labour System in the Light of the Archives* (London 1994), a useful reminder that one of the Allied combatants disposed of her own vast network of concentration camps. The hardly explored theme of Soviet collaboration is best approached through Catherine Andreyev, *Vlasov and the Russian Liberation Movement. Soviet Reality and Émigré Theories* (Cambridge 1987) and S. Kudryashov, 'The Hidden Dimension. Wartime Collaboration in the Soviet Union', in J. Erikson and D. Dilks (eds), *Barbarossa. The Axis and the Allies* (Edinburgh 1994). Samuel J. Newland, *Cossacks in the German Army 1941–1945* (London 1991) and Nicholas Bethell, *The Last Secret. Forcible Repatriation to Russia 1944–1947* (rev. edn London 1974) are complementary studies of the Cossack tragedy. On non-ethnic Russian nationalities, see Yuri Boshyk (ed.), *Ukraine during World War II. History and its Aftermath* (Edmonton 1986); David R. Marples, *Stalinism in Ukraine in the 1940s* (London 1992); Alan Fisher, *The Crimean Tatars* (Stanford 1978); John B. Dunlop, *Russia Confronts Chechnya. Roots of a Separatist Conflict* (Cambridge 1998) and C. Gall and T. de Waal, *Chechnya. A Small Victorious War* (London 1997). Nina Tumarkin, *The Living and the Dead. The Rise and Fall of the Cult of World War II in Russia* (New York 1994) is expert on the political instrumentalisation of the 'Great Patriotic War' in the former Soviet Union.

There is a vast literature on **the Holocaust**, the most evil act of the century, a field in which as a non-specialist I have no special insights or expertise. Martin Gilbert, *Atlas of the Holocaust* (Oxford 1988) conveys the sheer scale of this beastly enterprise. Essential source collections include Yitzhak Arad, Shmuel Krakowski and Shmuel Spector (eds), *The Einsatzgruppen Reports* (New York 1989) and Yitzhak Arad, Yisrael Gutman and Abraham Margaliot (eds), *Documents on the Holocaust* (Jerusalem 1981). The excellent journals *Yad Vashem Studies* and *Dachauer Hefte* are the place to turn for the latest research. The Nazis' narrowing down of their own options from expulsions overseas or resettlements of Jewish people to eastern Europe are expertly discussed in two highly original works, Magnus Brechtken, *'Madagaskar für die Juden'. Antisemitische Idee und politische Praxis 1885–1945* (Munich 1997) and Götz Aly, *'Final Solution'. Nazi Population Policy and the Murder of the European Jews* (London 1999), although Christopher Browning, *Paths to Genocide* (Cambridge 1994) had covered much of the latter ground before.

Raul Hilberg's *Die Vernichtung der europäischen Juden* (rev. edn Frankfurt am Main 1990) three volumes, is clearly still without challengers, as a global account closely based on the original sources, whatever rigidities there may be in its structure. Recent German scholarship on the subject is showcased in Ulrich Herbert (ed.), *Nationalsozialistische Vernichtungspolitik 1939–1945. Neue Forschungen und Kontroversen* (Frankfurt am Main 1998), although much of it simply adds an avalanche of local archival detail to what is known already, rather than fundamentally revising our knowledge. The work of Christian Gerlach is a notable exception. The best and briefest English accounts are Michael Marrus, *The Holocaust in History* (London 1989) and Wolfgang Benz, *The Holocaust* (New York 1999). Omer Bartov (ed.), *The Holocaust. Origins, Implementation, Aftermath* (London 2000) contains work by several leading scholars, including a translation of a key article by Gerlach. Philippe Burrin's *Hitler and the Jews. The Genesis of the Holocaust* (London 1989) is an important and original reinterpretation of Hitler's probable thinking from 1939 onwards. The least hysterical, and hence most interesting, works on perpetrators are Hans-Heinrich Wilhelm, *Die Einsatzgruppe A der Sicherheitspolizei und des SD 1941/42* (Frankfurt am Main 1996); Christopher Browning, *Ordinary Men. Reserve Battalion 101 and the Final Solution in Poland* (New York 1993) and Hans Safrian, *Eichmann und seine Gehilfen* (Frankfurt am Main 1995), to which should be added Claudia Steur, *Theodor Dannecker. Ein Funktionär der 'Endlösung'* (Tübingen 1997). Non-German perpetrators are expertly discussed by Radu Ioanid, *The Sword of the Archangel. Fascist Ideology in Romania* (New York 1990) and his *The Holocaust in Romania* (Chicago 2000); Andrew Ezergailis, *The Holocaust in Latvia 1941–1944* (Riga 1996); Zvi Gitelmann (ed.), *Bitter Legacy. Confronting the Holocaust in the USSR* (Bloomington 1997); and Martin Dean, *Collaboration in the Holocaust. Crimes of the Local Police in Belorussia and Ukraine 1941–44* (London 1999). A useful source collection on Romania is Matatias Carp (ed.), *Cartea Neagra* (Bucharest 1996). Randolph Braham, *The Politics of Genocide. The Destruction of Hungarian Jewry* (New York 1982) two volumes, and Michael Marrus and Robert Paxton, *Vichy France and the Jews* (New York 1983) are unrivalled studies of national experiences. Readers interested in Nazi extermination camps should consult Yitzhak Arad, *Belzec, Sobibor, Treblinka. The Operation Reinhard Death Camps* (Bloomington 1987) and Yisrael Gutman and Michael Berenbaum (eds), *Anatomy of the Auschwitz Death Camp* (Bloomington 1994). Jewish responses to the Holocaust are intelligently discussed by Isaiah Trunk, *Judenrat. The Jewish Councils in Eastern Europe under Nazi Occupation* (New York 1972); Yisrael Gutman and Cynthia Haft (eds), *Patterns of Jewish Leadership in Nazi Europe 1933–1945* (Jerusalem 1979); Yisrael Gutman, *The Jews of Warsaw 1939–1943. Ghetto, Underground, Revolt* (Bloomington 1982); and Anna Pawelczynska, *Values and Violence in Auschwitz* (Berkeley 1979). Avraham

Tory, *Surviving the Holocaust. The Kovno Ghetto Diary*, ed. with an introduction by Martin Gilbert, historical notes by Dina Porat (Cambridge, Mass. 1990); and Frank Fox (ed. and trans.) *Calel Perechodnik. Am I a Murderer? Testament of a Jewish Policeman* (Boulder 1996) are moving first-hand accounts by people caught up in this nightmare. Dalia Ofer and Lenore J. Weitzman (eds), *Women in the Holocaust* (New Haven 1998) is an interesting gender-based collection of essays. For insights into the most recent controversy to illumine present-day American society for outsiders, see Johannes Heil and Rainer Erb (eds), *Geschichtswissenschaft und Öffentlichkeit. Der Streit um Daniel J. Goldhagen* (Frankfurt am Main 1998).

There are several excellent histories of **the Second World War**. The latest work is often showcased in the excellent *Journal of Strategic Studies* (1977–). On the immediate diplomatic background see Donald Cameron Watt's masterly *How War Came. The Immediate Origins of the Second World War* (London 1989) and R. A. C. Parker, *Chamberlain and Appeasement. British Policy and the Coming of the Second World War* (London 1993). Three of the best and most succinct surveys of the war are R. A. C. Parker, *Struggle for Survival. The History of the Second World War* (Oxford 1989); Richard J. Overy's outstanding *Why the Allies Won* (London 1995); and Ludolf Herbst, *Das nationalsozialistische Deutschland 1933–1945* (Frankfurt am Main 1996). Gerhard L. Weinberg, *A World at Arms* (Cambridge 1988) is excellent on the full scope of the conflict, even if eastern Europe is not well treated in the interests of maintaining a Manichaean perspective. The multi-volume edition by the Militärgeschichtlichen Forschungsamt, *Das Deutsche Reich und der Zweite Weltkrieg* (Stuttgart 1979–) six volumes, is impressive in detail and tone, and is also slowly appearing in English. The two volumes edited by H. Boog, W. Rahn, R. Stumpf and B. Wegner, *Die Welt im Krieg 1941–1943* (Frankfurt am Main 1992) are especially pertinent. Correlli Barnett (ed.), *Hitler's Generals* (London 1989); Seweryn Bialer (ed.), *Stalin and his Generals* (New York 1969); and Harold Shukman (ed.), *Stalin's Generals* (London 1993) are good guides to the various commanders, while Paul Addison and Angus Calder (eds), *Time to Kill. The Soldier's Experience of War in the West 1939–1945* (London 1997) contains excellent essays on Allied and Axis soldiering. The German experience has been expertly discussed by Omer Bartov, *Hitler's Army* (New York 1991) and more recently by Stephen G. Fritz, *Frontsoldaten. The German Soldier in World War II* (Lexington 1995). Anatoly Golovchansky *et al.* (eds), '*Ich will raus aus diesem Wahnsinn*'. *Deutsche Briefe von der Ostfront 1941–1945 aus sowjetischen Archiven* (Hamburg 1993) is often moving, though this should not occlude the cause for which these men were fighting, any more than massive Red Army losses should lead us to overlook the political functions of Stalin's victorious legions.

The strategic bombing campaign against Germany has attracted excellent scholars. The best British accounts are Max Hastings, *Bomber Command* (London 1979) and Richard J. Overy, *The Air War 1939–1945* (London 1980), while Ronald Schafer, *Wings of Judgement. American Bombing in World War II* (Oxford 1985) is a readable account of the USAAF in the European and Pacific theatres. Stephen A. Garrett, *Ethics and Airpower. The British Bombing of German Cities* (New York 1993) deals with troubled consciences in a sensitive way. Arthur Harris, *Bomber Offensive* (London 1998) is a robust *apologia pro vita sua*. The economic history of the war is clearly set out by Alan S. Milward's *War, Economy and Society 1939–1945* (London 1987) and in a series of path-breaking studies by that scholar of individual wartime economies, such as France, Germany and Norway. J. Barber and M. Harrison, *The Soviet Home Front 1941–1945* (London 1991) and the really outstanding Keith E. Eiler, *Mobilising America. Robert P. Patterson and the War Effort 1940–1945* (Ithaca 1997) are excellent guides to the mobilisation of human and material resources in totalitarian and free societies. David Reynolds, *The Creation of the Anglo-American Alliance 1937–1941* (London 1981); Amos Perlmutter's fascinating *FDR and Stalin. A Not So Grand Alliance 1943–1945* (Columbia 1993); and Keith Sainsbury, *Churchill and Roosevelt at War* (London 1990) are fine accounts of alliance diplomacy. Christoph Klessmann (ed.), *Nicht nur Hitlers Krieg. Der Zweite Weltkrieg und die Deutschen* (Düsseldorf 1989) includes sensitive accounts of the civilian experience in wartime Germany. The advent of peace is discussed in two comprehensive essay collections, R.-D. Müller and G. Ueberschär (eds), *Kriegsende 1945* (Frankfurt am Main 1994) and Hans-Erich Volkmann (ed.), *Ende des Dritten Reiches – Ende des Weltkriegs. Eine perspectivische Rückschau* (Munich 1995). Hermann Graml, *Die Alliierten und die Teilung Deutschlands. Konflikte und Entscheidungen 1941–1948* (Frankfurt am Main 1985) and Wolfgang Benz (ed.), *Potsdam 1945. Besatzungsherrschaft und Neuaufbau im Vier-Zonen Deutschland* (Munich 1986) and *Die Vertreibung der deutschen aus dem Osten* (Frankfurt am Main 1985) are essential to understanding the years immediately after the war. Retribution, legal and illegal, is dealt with by K. D. Henke and H. Wöller (eds), *Politische Säuberung in Europa. Die Abrechnung mit Faschismus und Kollaboration nach dem Zweiten Weltkrieg* (Munich 1991); D. Naimark, *The Russians in Germany. A History of the Soviet Occupation Zone 1945–1949* (Cambridge, Mass. 1995); and an immensely well-researched book by Arieh Kochavi, *Prelude to Nuremberg. Allied War Crimes Policy and the Quest for Punishment* (Chapel Hill 1998). The theme of war and memory is handled intelligently by István Deák, Jan T. Gross and Tony Judt (eds), *The Politics of Retribution in Europe. World War II and its Aftermath* (Princeton 2000).

INDEX